MW00908622

A Dictionary of Confusable Phrases

A Dictionary of Confusable Phrases

More Than 10,000 Idioms and Collocations

YURI DOLGOPOLOV

McFarland & Company, Inc., Publishers
Jefferson, North Carolina, and London

Library of Congress Cataloguing-in-Publication Data

Dolgopolov, Yuri.
A dictionary of confusable phrases : more
than 10,000 idioms and collocations /
Yuri Dolgopolov.
p. cm.
Includes bibliographical references and index.

ISBN 978-0-7864-5855-4
softcover : 50# alkaline paper ∞

1. English language — Idioms — Dictionaries.
2. English language — Usage — Dictionaries. I. Title.
PE1464.D66 2010 423'.13 — dc22 2010026211

British Library cataloguing data are available

© 2010 Yuri Dolgopolov. All rights reserved

No part of this book may be reproduced or transmitted in any form or by any means, electronic or mechanical, including photocopying or recording, or by any information storage and retrieval system, without permission in writing from the publisher.

Cover design by Mark Durr

Manufactured in the United States of America

McFarland & Company, Inc., Publishers
Box 611, Jefferson, North Carolina 28640
www.mcfarlandpub.com

Contents

Preface

To really know English one has to master, along with grammar and words, a reasonably large vocabulary of recurrent collocations, idioms, and metaphorical expressions that reflect the environment, history, and culture of the native speakers and form an essential part of their common language, adding color, dimension and vibrancy to the way they speak and write. Familiarity with idioms and colloquial metaphors and ability to use them appropriately in context are distinguishing markers of a native-like command of English.

Learning a language is challenging enough while learning set expressions (a language-within-a-language) becomes really frustrating at times, not the least owing to the existence in English of a very vast number of what we call phraseological "false friends and enemies"— idiomatic and non-idiomatic expressions that, despite their outward similarity or contrast, have unrelated meanings. Their confusion triggered by false analogy may result in misunderstanding and miscommunication so knowing or not knowing the difference between phraseological "false friends" can mean the difference between understanding or not understanding English.

This dictionary has been specifically designed to "diffuse" potentially confusable expressions. The dictionary pairs more than 10,000 idioms and collocations characterized by similarity or contrast in their wording or metaphorical idea that do not show corresponding similarity or contrast in their meanings. Also included are cases when phraseological units form a semantic mismatch with consonant compound words. This contrastive format enables the language learner to see all potentially confusable units together and so avoid confusing the phrase.

Most dictionary entries are made up of phrases that are in active current use so information about the difference in their meanings and usage is especially essential. Some entries may contain phrases pertaining to professional jargon, slang, expressions that are dated or characteristic of one the principal regional varieties of English. These, though less relevant in terms of their confusion, demonstrate interesting cases of coincidence in imagery through time and space while their contribution to the dictionary allows it to be also used as a regular explanatory dictionary providing definitions to individual idioms, clichés and set expressions.

There are numerous dictionaries of usage covering the difference in the meaning, spelling and pronunciation of *lexical* "false friends"— homographs, homophones and semantically unrelated words characterized by outward similarity. This comprehensive dictionary, however, representing as it does an important cross-section of the language, is unique in that it is the first attempt ever to provide a complete lexicographic inventory of phraseological pseudo-synonyms and -antonyms, both idiomatic and non-idiomatic.

Intended primarily for ESL students at different levels of proficiency, the dictionary can also be used by authors of textbooks and other educational materials who may screen the dictionary data for potentially confusable expressions incorporated in their products so as to caution students against this kind of pitfall and heighten their awareness of phraseological similarities and differences. It can be recommended for use in school and college libraries supporting ESL programs as well as to adults learning English as a second language.

Introduction

FALSE "FRIENDS" AND "ENEMIES" IN ENGLISH PHRASEOLOGY

Even a cursory examination of English phraseology reveals the existence of numerous idiomatic expressions and recurrent word combinations characterized by similarity of wording or imagery without corresponding similarity in their meaning or usage. Phraseological units of this kind usually form pairs and sometimes larger groups of expressions not normally interchangeable in their respective contexts or only interchangeable in some of their meanings so errors can arise whenever one expression is sufficiently close to another to be semantically identified with it, *cf.: bring one's mind to something / bring something to mind* or *at the top of the tree / up a tree.* While positive intralingual transfer may help in the case of perceived linguistic similarities, *cf.: make hay while the sun shines / strike while the iron is hot,* negative intralingual transfer will lead to problems owing to semantic or grammatical differences between units. The probability of their confusion is conditioned by the extent of similarity while their respective linguistic currency determines which unit in the group is likely to be mistaken for another more familiar and seemingly identical expression. Alongside such phraseological "false friends" there exist less numerous cases of "false enemies" or pseudo-antonyms whose form may induce the learner to believe that they are opposite in meaning which in reality they are not,* *cf.: absence of mind / presence of mind* and *come on the carpet / step off the carpet.*

Whereas errors caused by *interlingual* phraseological interference are predetermined by the student's first language and mostly occur when learners pattern phrases in the target language after the models of their own language, errors caused by *intralingual* phraseological interference are generally due to erroneous identification within the framework of the target language of semantically unrelated phraseological units with conceptually related components. Errors of this kind do not depend on the learners' first language and are common to all EFL/ESL students. They may adversely affect comprehension and usage, so learners are in urgent need for practical resource that will systematically address this problem and "defuse" potentially confusable multi-word units. Nonetheless, prior to the present publication there was no dictionary

**The phenomenon of "false friends" is commonly associated with words of different languages relating as formal equivalents for the reason of their material similarity while their meanings are quite different. A similar phenomenon can be observed at the phraseological level when set expressions of one language have formal, semantically dissimilar equivalents in another language (for instance, the following English expressions have their exact formal counterparts in Russian with altogether different meanings:* dirty money, high words, service flat, special school, art film, wind in the head*, etc.).*

specifically devoted to phraseological pitfalls of this kind even though some dictionaries of idioms would provide random cross-references warning of idiomatic expressions whose form may mislead the user into thinking that they are semantically related. At the same time, there exist numerous dictionaries of usage bringing to the attention of the learner the difference in the meaning, spelling, pronunciation, and the range of application of individual words characterized by outward similarity.* The present dictionary, providing systematic contrastive coverage of all kinds of phraseological "false friends" and "enemies," is expected therefore to remedy this imbalance and to fill, at least partially, the existing lexicographical lacuna. Primarily intended for EFL/ESL students as a tool of reference and prophylactics, it presents a complete and orderly catalog of multi-word units that require special consideration because of their interferential potential. Furthermore, the sizeable volume of the dictionary and its user-friendly Phrase Index enable it to be used as a regular phraseological dictionary providing definitions to individual idioms, clichés and set expressions.

In the selection of phrases making up the dictionary I proceeded from the broadest possible concept of phraseology and considered both idiomatic and non-idiomatic recurrent word combinations, prepositional collocations and phrasal verbs. No limits have been set with respect to their structural or pragmatic characteristics, the principal criteria being similarity or contrast in the wording or imagery of multi-word units whose meanings or usage do not show corresponding similarity or contrast. Potentially interferential units were culled from the phraseological pool provided by over a hundred mono- and bilingual dictionaries as well as numerous online databases. Contrastive-differentiating analysis of the totality of phraseological units thus selected made it possible to separate groups of semantically and pragmatically similar phraseological synonyms and variants (*cf.: add fuel to the fire / add fuel to the flames*) from interferentially significant "false friends." This inductive methodology made it possible to concentrate not on the actual interferential interactions of phraseological units (error analysis) but on the hypothetical possibility of their confusion, predicting *all likely cases* of flawed reasoning at phraseological level. As a result, some entries may contain well-known modern phrases whose interferentially relevant oppositions are represented by expressions pertaining to professional or social jargon, slang, as well as by phrases that are regional, dialectal, extinct or rarely heard nowadays. Phraseological oppositions of this sort, though less topical for language learners, demonstrate interesting cases of coincidence in imagery through time and space.

Parallel to potentially confusable phraseological oppositions, there are numerous instances when units longer than the word form similar, semantically contrastive relationships with consonant compound words, *cf.: day-man / man of the day.* In many cases dictionaries differ whether to treat a particular two-word combination as a phrase or a compound and there seems to be no hard and fast rule about which category such an item should be in. The distinction between separate and solid writing of such units becomes relevant, however, when it serves to differentiate between semantically dissimilar entities, *cf.: back drop / backdrop,* or units functioning as different parts of speech, *cf.: common sense / commonsense.* Since their outward similarity may likewise confuse the learner, we deemed it necessary to incorporate all cases involving potentially interferential compounds in the present dictionary.

The dictionary compiled on the above principles is comprehensive in that it encompasses the whole spectrum of phraseological units irrespective of their contemporary status in the language, social currency, or the degree of idiomaticity (that is, semantic interdependence of their components), the units ranging all the way from free word combinations to id-

**See, for example: G. A. Owen,* Dictionary of "Confusibles" *(Somerset: Brodie, 1966); A. Room,* Room's Dictionary of Confusibles *(London: Routledge & Kegan Paul, 1979); L. Urdang,* The Dictionary of Confusable Words *(New York: Facts on File, 1988).*

iomatic expressions. In between these two categories there is a vast layer of the so called set phrases institutionalized as such in the language and originated owing to the ability of words to regularly link up with other words forming their lexical environment. Whereas their global meanings are readily grasped from the meanings of their component parts, relatively independent of each other and used in their literal or metaphorical sense, the meanings of idiomatic expressions proper often appear unmotivated and cannot be deduced from the meanings of their constituents. As regards the degree of their structural mobility, idiomatic expressions are generally more or less invariable in form or order and do not admit of the usual grammatical operations which their literal counterparts will permit. Other types of phrases normally show some degree of variation. Phrases making up the dictionary are just as heterogeneous syntactically: some of them are full sentences (catch phrases, proverbial expressions, rhetorical questions and social formulae) while others function like particular parts of speech (nominal, verbal, adverbial and adjectival phrases).

Phraseological units whose meanings may mistakenly appear similar or opposite can be reduced to the following principal types of interferentially relevant oppositions (in the order of diminishing similarity of their notional components):

- specific cases of phraseological polysemy or homonymy when formally identical units are used differently by British and American speakers, e.g.:

  pavement artist ***(UK)***
  pavement artist ***(US)***

- semantically dissimilar units with identical notional components, relating as pseudo-quantitative variants, when one of the phrases is not really just a shortened form of an extended phrase, e.g.:

  keep one's head
  keep one's head up

- semantically dissimilar units all of whose notional components are identical, e.g.:

  cut loose from something
  cut loose with something

- phrases forming semantic oppositions to analogous solidly spelled compounds, e.g.:

  black eye
  blackeye

- morphologically consonant, though unrelated place names, e.g.:

  Saint John's
  Saint Johns

- semantically dissimilar prepositional phrases with identical notional component preceding the preposition, e.g.:

  absent from something
  absent in something

- semantically dissimilar prepositional phrases with identical notional component following the preposition, e.g.:

  in time
  on time

- semantically distinct phrasal verbs with identical verbal component, e.g.:

  turn on someone
  turn to someone

- semantically dissimilar collocations with identical verbal component taking direct and prepositional object respectively, e.g.:

  advertise for something
  advertise something

- semantically dissimilar units some of whose components are identical while others relate as paronyms, e.g.:

  historic event
  historical event

- semantically dissimilar units with paronymic and identical notional components, which belong to different parts of speech, e.g.:

  curtain raiser
  raise the curtain

- semantically dissimilar units some of whose components are identical while others relate as synonyms, e.g.:

  hold an appointment
  keep an appointment

- semantically dissimilar units some of whose components are identical while others designate contiguous notions, e.g.:
  turn someone's brain
  turn someone's head
- semantically dissimilar units some of whose components are identical while others associate with the same class of things, e.g.:
  lose one's head
  lose one's mind
- phrasal verbs forming structural and semantic oppositions to compound verbs with formally identical component parts represented in reverse order, e.g.:
  do something over
  overdo something
- phraseological units some of whose components are identical while others relate as antonyms, whose imagery may be mistakenly construed as semantically antonymous, e.g.:
  in deep water
  in low water
- semantically dissimilar phrasal verbs with synonymous verbal components and identical prepositions or adverbs, e.g.:
  come off something
  go off something
- semantically unrelated units of similar structure some of whose notional components may match, whose general phraseological idea may appear similar, e.g.:
  when the balloon goes up
  when the eagle flies
- semantically unrelated units that may differ in structure and have no components in common, whose general phraseological idea or imagery may appear similar, e.g.:
  be dead in the water
  sleep with the fishes
- semantically unrelated units that may differ in structure and have no components in common, whose general phraseological idea or imagery may appear antonymous, e.g.:
  carry the torch
  hide one's light under a bushel

Arrangement of the Entries

The arrangement of material in the dictionary is consistently alphabetical. Each entry highlighting the differences of the units it comprises is introduced by the *heading* in bold print that lists alphabetically all units making up the entry. All entries, in turn, are arranged in the dictionary in the alphabetical order of the first phrases of the entry headings. When arranging phraseological units alphabetically the following principles have been observed:

- initial articles are disregarded when determining the alphabetical order;
- simile phrases introducing comparisons are usually given without their optional initial element *as*;
- in the case of hyphenated compounds the hyphen is treated as a space and phrases written as separate words, or hyphenated compound words, precede solidly spelled compounds;
- many phrases include a variable component indicated by the words *his, himself, one, one's, oneself, someone, someone's,* or *something* that are taken into account for alphabetical order.

While listing phrases in their basic or the most usual form, we use the word *someone* to refer to somebody other than the subject, and the word *one* is used where the *one* is the same person as the subject of the sentence. The words *his* and *himself* are used purely conventionally and may refer to both sexes. Each unit treated in the entry is followed by a definition and illustrated by authentic examples of usage in the context providing the correct semantic and pragmatic framework. Potentially confusable phrases represented in sample sentences are underlined, sometimes together with words which are not part of the phrase proper but form its immediate lexical surrounding. Where an item has several meanings the definitions are grouped in numbered sequences of comparative importance. Occasional comments of grammatical nature provided in the dictionary usually signal some grammatical restrictions in the usage of an expression which may refer to certain limitations in tenses and aspects. Such notations and comments may apply to the whole phrase or to some of its meanings. Some entries have cross-references, that is, contain instructions to look up some other entries for the purpose of comparison or caution.

Stylistically colored phrases are normally accompanied by italicized notations which are of special help when the user's knowledge of the language is inadequate as regards recognition of their stylistic value and the ability to use them in specific social contexts. Some of the phrases designated as *dated* show signs of obsolescence though may still be used within limited groups of people, whereas expressions designated as *archaic* are not familiar to the majority of speakers. Other labels may designate various occupational and professional fields with which certain expressions are particularly associated. Phrases contained in the dictionary, both current and obsolete, represent practically all principal stylistical strata: stylistically neutral phrases, colloquial, formal and literary expressions, expressions normally confined to technical use, folksy expressions, dialectal phrases, phrases pertaining to professional or social jargon, slang, as well as expressions peculiar to any of the principal regional varieties of English. Expressions that are not stylistically labeled are considered neutral and may be used in all situations. When stylistic comments apply to all numbered senses of a phrase they are found before the numbered senses, while comments that apply to any one sense are found within the numbered sense before the definition. The mobility of borderlines between various stylistic categories makes it at times difficult to attach unequivocal stylistic tag and stylistic status of many expressions shows considerable fluctuations in different dictionaries. Stylistically marked phrases must be used with particular care because they reflect a special relationship between speakers or a special social occasion or setting. They belong to ironic, jocular, derogatory, euphemistic or other stylistically marked register and are labeled accordingly. Many of them can only be used in informal spoken English and are inadmissible in formal written English. Phrases marked *taboo* or *coarse slang,* included merely for the sake of completeness, warrant special caution in this respect because most of them deal with race, sex, or ethnic origin and may have offensive or insulting implications.

For readers who want to identify a vaguely familiar expression that includes a particular significant word, are not sure of the precise form of an expression as listed in the dictionary, or simply wish to explore the phrase-building potential of individual words, the Phrase Index is compounded by the Key Word Index in which expressions are listed under their second or another semantically dominating component, their first component being given within the general alphabetical arrangement of phrases in the dictionary body and the Phrase Index. We chose to also include as key words units forming the second parts of hyphenated nominal compounds: thus the reader can find "boat-train" under "train," "angel-water" under "water," "copy-cat" under "cat," etc. While certain words can function as different parts of speech or refer to different homonyms, no attempt has been made to reflect such differences in the Key Word Index.

Abbreviations Used in the Dictionary

arch.—archaic
attrib.—attribute
Austral.—Australian
biol.—biological
Canad.—Canadian
coll.—colloquial
cf.—compare
derog.—derogatory
dial.—dialect
euph.—euphemism
exclam.—exclamation
Fr.—French
hist.—historical
imper.—imperative
interj.—interjection
joc.—jocular
liter.—literary
med.—medical
negat.—negative
NZ—New Zealand
pejor.—pejorative
pl.—plural
predic.—predicative
RAF—Royal Air Force
Scot.—Scottish
sl.—slang
smb.—somebody
smth.—something
UK—United Kingdom
U.S.—United States
WWI—World War I
WWII—World War II

DICTIONARY

à la guerre comme à la guerre • c'est la guerre

à la guerre comme à la guerre—(Fr.) is used to tell a person to make do with what one has or do what one has to do: She walked ... with a certain rebellion burning in her heart. It was not the right sort of heart to take to a love-meeting. But à la guerre comme à la guerre!

c'est la guerre—(Fr.) an ironic phrase to provide an excuse for anything that has not gone quite to plan: The long string of projects which were started were never brought to commercial viability.... But, c'est la guerre, eh?

abandon ship • give up the ship

*abandon ship—*1. leave the sinking ship: When the order was given to abandon ship many of the passengers were stunned. They felt that it was safer onboard... 2. *(also: jump ship)* leave a failing organization, etc. before it is too late: For weeks he worked eighteen-hour days, pleading with his staff not to abandon ship.

*give up the ship—*quit trying and surrender; admit defeat: If you are sidetracked by small setbacks don't be discouraged and give up the ship.

abide by something • abide something

*abide by something—*stand firm by smth.; remain true to smth.: The rules were fixed, and I must abide by them.

abide something—(negat.) bear or endure smth.: She could not abide the country, and would not be tempted to leave London.

abide someone • abide with someone

abide someone—(negat.) dislike a person very much: In fact, I can't abide him. Whenever I see him on television, I'm inclined to change the channel.

abide with someone—(liter.) remain or stay with a person: If the American dream is to abide with us, it will, at bottom, depend on the people themselves.

above suspicion • under suspicion

*above suspicion—*too highly respected to be suspected of a crime or wrongdoing: Navy secretary Welles was above suspicion, but he was inexperienced in nautical affairs.

*under suspicion—*considered as possibly guilty of a crime or wrongdoing: He was under suspicion for other crimes, which gave the investigators the legal right to hold him indefinitely.

Note: *The expression is not equivalent in meaning to the phrase* ***on suspicion****—(arrest or detain smb.) on the ground of suspicion:* The police are now free to stop and search anyone merely on suspicion.

absence from something • absence in something

*absence from something—*being temporarily away from a place: I have no one capable of acting for me in my absence from home.

*absence in something—*1. staying temporarily at some place: During my absence in France, I find that new words have been introduced into our parliamentary language. 2. lack or nonexistence in smth.: For Jane, a salient consequence was the absence in her life of a satisfying intimate relationship.

absence of mind • presence of mind

*absence of mind—*the mental state of preoccupation, which causes one to do smth. without realizing it: Through absence of mind he walked out of the shop and left his purchases on the counter.

*presence of mind—*mental alertness which enables one to act quickly in an emergency: With great presence of mind he grabbed the child and pulled it out of the path of the oncoming car.

absorbed by something • absorbed with something

*absorbed by something—*1. *(of liquids)* soaked up by smth.: The solution is absorbed by the brick through its untreated surface. 2. *(of substances)* taken up by chemical action: Whey protein is the best type of protein since it is quickly absorbed by the body. 3. *(of people or things)* incorporated into smth.: Better build the type of home that will be more quickly absorbed by the market.

absorbed with something—(also: absorbed in something) deeply engrossed in smth.: They are often absorbed with their own thoughts and feelings and are fearful of intimacy with others.

abut against something • abut on something

*abut against something—*rest against the end part of smth. firmly: The mountains are volcanic, and sedimentary deposits abut against them at a lower level.

abut on something—(of a plot of land, etc.) border on smth.; lie next to smth.: Our land abuts on the shopping center's parking lot.

academic junk food • junk food

academic junk food—(coll.) college degree courses of no academic value to students: He describes the disintegration of the curriculum into limitless numbers of "interdisciplinary studies" programs that are often academic junk food.

*junk food—*food, as potato chips, hamburgers, and hot dogs, that is high in calories but of little nutritional value: Many schools are selling at break time nothing less than junk foods.

accidents can happen • accidents will happen

*accidents can happen—*is used to say that smth. unforeseen may always occur: Don't commit yourself to completing the book this year — accidents can happen, you know.

accidents will happen— is used to say that some unfortunate events must be accepted as inevitable: Stop going on so about that broken jug. Accidents will happen, you know.

accommodate someone to something • accommodate someone with something

*accommodate someone to something—*adapt or adjust a person to smth.: One of the solutions [of housing] is to accommodate people to the multistory residential building.

*accommodate someone with something—*provide a person with smth., especially as a favor: It was very good of you to accommodate me with the ticket for my journey.

according to Cocker • according to Mrs. Beeton

according to Cocker—(U.S. also: according to Gunter) absolutely correct; exactly as it should be: So you ought to be, according to Cocker, spending all your time in sick rooms.

according to Mrs. Beeton—(UK) an advice of culinary perfection according to Mrs. Beeton's Book of Household Management (1886): According to Mrs. Beeton, the jar has to be shaken once a week until Christmas when delicious drinks can be served.

accurate in something • accurate with something

*accurate in something—*free from mistakes in what one says or does: He was basically careful and accurate in his quotations and references to sources.

*accurate with something—*careful about smth.; treating smth. with responsibility: When writing a composition, be accurate with your quotations.

achieve peace • win the peace

achieve peace—achieve a state in which a nation or community is not at war with another: Neutrality is essential if we are to play a constructive role in achieving peace.

win the peace—carry out successful reconstruction after the war: We may have had enough troops to win the war—but not nearly enough to win the peace.

Achilles of England, the • English Achilles, the

Achilles of England, the—(hist.) 1. the name given to the Duke of Wellington (1769–1852). 2. the name given to John-Talbot, first Earl of Shrewsbury (1373–1453): This great captain, whose merit was acknowledged equally by friends and foes, received the appellation of the Achilles of England.

English Achilles, the— = Achilles of England, the 2: This man was John Talbot, known as the English Achilles, and hero of countless battles.

act as angel • act like an angel

act as angel—act as a sponsor for a firm, organization, etc.: It was agreed that he should act as angel to the enterprise.

act like an angel—be an excellent performer: She sings and acts like an angel and is extremely pleased because Wolfgang has served her extraordinarily well.

act as someone • act for someone

act as someone—perform as an interpreter, guide, etc.: I had a local student who acted as my translator, as my Spanish is extremely rudimentary.

act for someone—represent smb. as a barrister, etc., in a law court: Mr. Bilmes agreed to act for me, attending court as my legal representative.

act foolishly • act the fool

act foolishly—act without reason or good judgment: She acted foolishly in her business dealings, trusting the wrong people or not trusting her employees enough.

act the fool—(also: play the fool) deliberately act so as to appear eccentric or foolish: He was a small, puny lad who acted the fool to stop himself being bullied.

Note: *The expression is not equivalent in meaning to the phrase* ***make a fool of oneself****— act in a way that makes a person appear ridiculous or stupid:* My advice to you is to refrain from making careless comments, for you'll only make a fool of yourself.

act of God • action of God

act of God—1. *(legal)* the action of forces uncontrollable by man, such as hurricane, etc.: In the event of an act of God, the school reserves the right to suspend training. 2. said of the work of God in creation: The doctrine regarded our *a priori* ideas as infused into the intellect by an act of God.

action of God—(also: work of God) = act of God 2: Creation is the origin of the totality of the universe by the action of God.

act one's age • show one's age

act one's age—behave in a manner appropriate to one's age *(often used in asking children to act in a more grown-up fashion):* She doesn't look or act her age, she has no gray hairs, not even crows feet.

show one's age—show signs of being old: Booth is starting to show his age. His face is deeply creased and lined, and his voice has gotten mushy and lispy.

act something out • outact someone

act something out—give expression to thoughts, unconscious fears, etc. in one's actions and behavior: Children often act out their troubled feelings in their games.

Note: *The expression does not correlate in meaning with the intransitive phrasal verb* ***act out****— behave anti-socially or misbehave:* The child with a learning problem may act out to divert attention from, for example, his inability to read.

outact someone—surpass another person in acting or performing: The man can outact just about anybody out there. His prime example is his portrayal of Rollins in *Devil in a Blue Dress.*

action man • man of action

action man—a person who makes a show of being very vigorous and energetic: I had very little in common with the sort of larger-than-life action man I played in film after film.

man of action—smb. who does things and is not content to just meditate or talk: Foscolo was intended for a man of action and strife: ease and fortune unnerved and demoralized him.

actual time • real time

actual time—the time to be compared with the standard or expected time: The actual time of its [Indian summer] occurrence and the character of the weather appear to vary for different regions.

real time—1. the time during which an event occurs: The date displayed by monitors is from the previous day, making it almost impossible to know the real time of air pollution. 2. said of the processing of data which occurs as it is generated: A higher speed in computers means that they can more easily engage in activities in what we call "real time."

Note: *Neither expression is equivalent in meaning to the phrase* ***true time****—the time according to the position of the sun:* True (nonrelative) time can only be measured by using a constant, such as the objective speed of light.

Adam and Eve • Adam-and-Eve

Adam and Eve—1. said of men and women in general: The great dual law which makes Adam and Eve one humanity, the dry land and the seas one globe. 2. *(U.S. diners)* two poached or fried eggs: Diner lingo is one example of a mnemonic device that aids memory. "Adam and Eve" refers to two eggs, usually poached.

Adam-and-Eve—a North American orchid: A woman will carry a piece of Adam-and-Eve root in a little bag round her neck. It's really *Aplectrum hyemale,* useful in bronchial troubles.

Adam and Eve on a log • Adam and Eve on a raft

Adam and Eve on a log—(U.S. diners) two poached eggs with link sausage: Adam and Eve on a log are two poached eggs with link sausage, but there are plenty of other short order cook gems like "Bowl of Red" (chili peppers with meat).

Adam and Eve on a raft—(U.S. diners) two poached eggs on toast: There were Zepps in a Cloud (sausages and mashed) and Adam and Eve on a raft. *Cf.: Adam and Eve on a raft and wreck them—(U.S. diners) two scrambled eggs on toast:* You ask for scrambled eggs on toast, and the waitress says to the chef, "we need an Adam and Eve on a raft and wreck them."

adapted for something • adapted to something

adapted for something—(of things) made suitable for a new use, situation, etc.: The book was adapted for television as a four-part series screened by the BBC.

adapted to something—(of people) accustomed or suitable to smth.: I am not adapted to this business. I was bred a farmer, and ought not to have left that occupation.

add color to something • give color to something

add color to something—(of a story, account, etc.) provide details that would interest and excite readers or listeners: The lecturer told a few jokes to add color to his talk.

give color to something—(also: lend color to something) give plausibility to an account, etc.: His torn clothing gave color to his story that he had been attacked and robbed.

add fuel to the fire • add insult to injury

add fuel to the fire—(also: add fuel to the flames) aggravate discord, etc.; make an already bad situation even worse: Now, to add fuel to the fire, new accusations have emerged over the past several weeks that could cost Ward his position.

add insult to injury—wound a person's self-respect even further; add to the damage already done to smb.'s feelings: He was an hour late and then, to add insult to injury, he spent twenty minutes on the telephone.

add in something • add on something

add in something—1. put or pour smth., especially in recipes: Continue to add in the flour and mix each addition until it is well incorporated. 2. attach or include smth., usually in the middle of a calculation: Before you finish the totals, please add in these new figures.

add on something—attach smth. at the end of a calculation, list, etc.: She wrote me a cold letter, even the inquiry about my health looked as if it had been added on as an afterthought.

add to something • add up to something

add to something—increase or enhance smth.: It's an old building so you get creaky sounds of the old building but I guess it adds to its rustic charm.

add up to something—1. *(of values)* give as a result, when joined: The bombing from B-52 stratofortresses ultimately added up to 800,000 tons of bombs. 2. amount to smth.; signify smth.: All that this adds up to is that you don't want to help, so why not say so at once?

add to taste • add to the taste

add to taste—(in recipes) add in the amount preferred: Tear small pieces from the Hungarian pepper and add to taste; these peppers are very hot.

add to the taste—improve the taste (of a dish): All those spices not only add to the taste but are good for your health.

address oneself to someone • address someone

address oneself to someone—speak or appeal to a person: He came into the room, and addressed himself to me with the best grace in the world.

address someone—1. = *address oneself to someone:* The Education Secretary had to address a hostile crowd of teachers. 2. speak to a person using a nickname or a title: Don't address me as "Colonel"; I'm only a major.

Admiral of the White • White Admiral

Admiral of the White—admiral of the White Squadron (one of the three divisions of the Royal Navy in the 17th century): Admiral of the Red, used to hold the center in an engagement. Admiral of the White, used to hold the van.

White Admiral—any of several butterflies of the genus *Limenitis:* He had seen a white admiral circling higher and higher round an oak tree, but he had never caught it.

admit of something • admit to something

admit of something—leave room for smth.: A careful, detached study of his available statements will admit of no other conclusion.

admit to something—agree, often reluctantly, that smth. is true; confess to smth.: Over a third of the juveniles admitted to owning a firearm.

Note: *The expression does not fully correlate in meaning with the phrase* ***admit something***—1. = *admit to something:* He admitted owning a car which had an index number identical to one Miss Mallalieu had noted. 2. *have room for smth.; allow smth. to enter:* This harbor is dry at low water and admits only small craft even with the tide.

admonish someone for something • admonish someone of something

admonish someone for something—reprove a person on account of smth.: They are frequently admonished for their failure to act quickly.

admonish someone of something—bring smth. to a person's notice as a warning: A gallows erected on an eminence admonished the offenders of the fate that awaited them.

advance of science • advancement of science

advance of science—progress or improvement in science: It is an assumption of our world view that progress consists in the advance of science and technology.

advancement of science—progress in science resulting from the action of an outside agent: The purpose of this legislation was the advancement of science.

advance on something • advance towards something

advance on something—move towards a place (in order to attack, etc.): The enemy advanced on Rome, and at last conquered it.

advance towards something—1. = *advance on something:* The fire has already destroyed about 15 houses in a suburb and is advancing towards the city. 2. be headed for smth.; approach a certain state: The world political system is advancing towards disorder.

advise someone of something • advise someone on something

advise someone of something—give a person information or warning about smth.: The motoring organizations have advised motorists of thick mists on the mountains.

advise someone on something—give a person recommendations or advice about smth.: We are experts in advising people on the best holiday to suit their personal preferences.

Note: *The expression does not correlate in meaning with the phrase* ***advise with someone on something****—consult with a person about smth.:* He advised with them on all matters and followed their directions in all things.

after a time • after time

after a time—when a short time has elapsed: I didn't care for the place at first, but after a time I got to like it.

after time—later than a stipulated time: We cannot wait for anyone who arrives after time.

after all • after all is said and done

after all—1. is used to introduce an additional point which supports the previous statement: They did not expect heavy losses in the air; after all, they had superb aircraft. 2. in spite of what had previously been thought or done: It had to be recognized, after all, that I was still a schoolboy.

after all is said and done—when everything is settled or concluded: After all was said and done, the wedding was a lovely affair.

after the manner of someone • in the manner of someone

after the manner of someone—(of a painting, etc.) executed in conscious imitation of smb.'s manner or style: In those days, I painted human interest subjects, after the manner of Mr. Rockwell. But I still hadn't found myself as an artist.

in the manner of someone—(of a painting, etc.) indicating resemblance to smb.'s style rather than conscious imitation:

They acquired Joan Miro pictures painted in the manner of a 4-year-old struggling to come to terms with the human face.

again and again • every now and again

again and again—(also: time and again) habitually; repeatedly: I was absorbed in "The Cloud on the Sanctuary," reading it again and again.

every now and again—(also: now and again) occasionally; from time to time: Every now and again the ear could catch the sudden splash of pike meeting pike.

agree on something • agree to something • agree with something

agree on something—1. have the same view about smth.: Musicians rarely agree on the way a piece of music should be played. 2. decide on smth.: We've agreed on Spain for our holiday next year.

agree to something—(of a suggestion, statement, etc.) view with favor; accept what has been proposed: Neither the people, nor their representatives, would agree to the plan.

agree with something—1. go along with a person in an opinion or statement: It is great what Martin has done and I agree with his comment. 2. *(of two versions, accounts, etc.)* be similar or fully correspond: This bill doesn't agree with my calculations.

ahead of one's time • before one's time

ahead of one's time—(of people, new ideas, etc.) too advanced to be accepted by one's contemporaries: Men who are ahead of their time can lead the present into the future.

before one's time—1. before a person was born, had arrived, etc.: There was at one time a little cinema, but that was before my time. 2. before the due or expected time: His poverty, and continual harassment by the authorities had made him old before his time. 3. = *ahead of one's time:* Robert Owen, with his enlightened ideas on working conditions in factories, was before his time.

Note: *The expression is not antonymous in meaning to the phrase* ***not before its time****— used of smth. that should have been done long ago:* At last they are installing electric light in the main streets, and not before its time.

ahead of time • before time

ahead of time—(usually showing approval) earlier than expected: The homework was finished ahead of time so he went out to play.

before time—prematurely; before the due or expected time: So far was prepunctuality carried, that Her Majesty was ten minutes before time.

aim at something • aim for something

aim at something—1. point the weapon or object in the direction of smth.: He aimed at the far wall and squeezed the trigger. 2. plan or hope to achieve smth.: We are now aiming at a higher production level.

aim for something— = aim at something 2: For most people, aiming for a higher position at once is the key to job search success.

air boat • inflatable boat

air boat—1. a seaplane with a boatlike fuselage: This class of seaplanes, variously termed "flying-boat" and "air-boat," consists essentially of a long boat-shaped hull, wherein the passengers' seats are contained. 2. a shallow-draft boat driven by an airplane propeller: A Pandora's Box is opening to release a flood of airboats on the long-suffering landscape of crowded Southern Ontario.

inflatable boat—an air-filled rubber boat (for use in an emergency, etc.): The crewmen had to be pulled from the freezing water by colleagues in an inflatable boat.

air gun • air gunner

air gun—a gun in which compressed air is used to propel the charge: Darned if he didn't up with this here air gun and plunk me with a buckshot it carried.

air gunner—an aircrew member whose job is to operate a gun: Too old for piloting he became an air gunner with 235 Squadron Coastal Command.

air lane • airline

air lane—(also: airway) a regular route of travel for aircraft: This will enable controllers to squeeze an extra 20 percent traffic into the crowded air lanes.

airline—1. company that carries passengers and cargo by airplane: The airline has announced it will run daily service to Florida. 2. a tube through which air is passed under pressure: Any big truck lives and dies, steers and brakes, on its air-lines.

air letter • airmail letter

air letter—(also: aerogramme) a sheet of light paper forming a letter for sending by airmail: An air letter is written on a special form supplied by the Post Office.

airmail letter—a letter to be sent by air: Aerogrammes are less expensive than an airmail letter and have the same delivery time.

alien from something • alien to something

alien from something—differing in nature or character from smth.: I am a Christian; therefore, many of the tenets of Buddhism are alien from my faith.

alien to something—contrary or opposed to smth.: I could not consent to the introduction into our national life of a device so alien to all our traditions as the referendum.

alive to something • alive with something

alive to something—aware of smth.; conscious of smth.: He was alive to the danger that pressure might be put on the police, and he might be forced to take ill-advised action.

alive with something—teeming with smth.; full of smth.: The lake was alive with alligators. These could be seen basking along the low banks...

all along • all along the line

all along—all the time: Her employer said he had suspected the girl of pilfering all along.

all along the line—at every point in the course of an activity: These newer family magazines are making the older ones fight for existence all along the line.

all at once • at once

all at once—suddenly and abruptly: There comes over him, all at once, a sort of cold, creepy shudder.

at once—1. immediately: She doesn't know where he is... otherwise she would drive to his address at once. 2. simultaneously; at the same time: Fire service says we cannot be in two places at once.

all but • anything but

all but—almost; nearly: We're all but finished now. We'll be ready in a moment.

anything but—not at all: My father was anything but pleased when he heard my story.

all day and every day • all the days of one's life

all day and every day—during the whole of one day and for a number of days afterwards: We had glorious weather, sunshine all day and every day.

all the days of one's life—for as long as one will live, or has lived: They had known only oppression and bitter poverty all the days of their lives.

all dressed up • dressed up

all dressed up—dressed formally; dressed in one's best clothes: She was glad that she was all dressed up and had done her hair that morning.

dressed up—1. = *all dressed up:* We know little about Mary's appearance (the only description we have is when she is dressed up for her daughter's wedding). 2. wearing fancy clothing; disguised: There was a carnival parade in the city. Annabel was dressed up as a clown and Andy as Zorro.

all eyes • all my eye

all eyes—(predic., coll.) watching eagerly and attentively: She was all eyes as I unwrapped the package.

all my eye—(UK sl.) utter nonsense *(also: all my eye and Betty Martin):* I told him about a secret process, but he knew it was all my eye.

all fur coat and no knickers • all hat and no cattle

all fur coat and no knickers—(UK derog.) said of a person or thing having an impressive appearance with no real substance beneath: Wish I had paid more attention to the bad reviews before I booked. This hotel is all fur coat and no knickers.

all hat and no cattle—(U.S. derog.) said of smb. who tends to talk boastfully without acting on one's words *(also: big hat and no cattle):* Republican leadership promised to support the mission. Unfortunately, however, they've been all hat and no cattle...

all hands and the cook • all the world and his wife

all hands and the cook—1. *(Nautical)* everybody on the ship: Martin threw on the engine, while all hands and the cook sprang to take in sail. 2. everyone from a particular group of people who can possibly contribute: Soon he was rearing his family, and all hands and the cook were busy as bees in caring for the home. *Cf.: all-hands meeting—a mandatory meeting for all employees called by the management:* Bob called an all-hands meeting this afternoon. It's never a good sign...

all the world and his wife—(also: every man and his dog) lots of people; everyone of importance: All the world and his wife were there, so, of course, Dame Margery went also.

all in • all out

all in—(predic., coll.) 1. completely exhausted: I was glad that the laboratory was only a few blocks away, for I was all in by the time I got there. 2. completely or enthusiastically involved in smth.: That was a cruel thing to do and I want to know who was all in on it!

Note: *The expression does not correlate in meaning with the compound* ***all-in****—(attrib.) inclusive of everything:* If you need surgery, go for a fixed price package—an all-in price, irrespective of how long you stay in the hospital.

all out—(coll.) 1. using all one's strength or resources: He made up his mind to go "all out" for his uncle's slum-conversion scheme. 2. entirely; completely: "Were you drunk?" "Not all out, I could keep my feet on the floor." 3. at top speed: The track was ultra-fast all night, with cars running all out the entire evening.

all in all • in all

all in all—1. taking everything into consideration: All in all, they do their best to portray something original. 2. *(of a person or thing)* of supreme importance to smb.: This adventurer made love to the girl that was all in all to me.

in all—in total number: I stayed for three days in all, and throughout those three days I was sitting in their wonderful library.

Note: *The expression does not correlate in meaning with the phrase* ***at all****— under any circumstances:* If that is so, why write at all?

all in one piece • all of a piece

all in one piece—(also: in one piece) without injury; relatively unharmed: I was covered in plaster and my eyes were full of dust, but I was all in one piece and thankful to be alive.

all of a piece—1. of the same kind or quality: It's all of a piece here. The men effeminate, the women unsexed. 2. *(with)* in harmony or consistent with smth.: His rejection of health-care reform is all of a piece with his disregard for the underprivileged.

all kinds of something • all sorts of something

all kinds of something—1. many different kinds of smth.: For many years, Tutt Library has accepted donations of all kinds of books from community supporters. 2. *(coll.)* plenty of smth.; a large amount of smth.: The reality is that the government has all kinds of money. They have more money than they know what to do with.

all sorts of something— = *all kinds of something 1:* Classrooms should be stocked full of all sorts of books and school libraries should be as desirable a destination as the local bookstore.

all mouth and no trousers • all mouth and trousers

all mouth and no trousers—(UK derog.) said of smb. who talks or boasts a lot but doesn't take any action *(also: all talk and no trousers):* How much longer will it take to realize that the leader is all mouth and no trousers?

all mouth and trousers— = *all mouth and no trousers:* Jack is all mouth and trousers, he never does anything he says he will.

all-overs • overalls

all-overs—(coll.) a feeling of great unease or extreme nervousness: We're out of sorts for want of a smoke. We've got the all-overs, haven't us, deary?

overalls—a one-piece garment worn to protect a worker's clothes; loose-fitting work pants with shoulder straps: A man dressed in overalls came out. I caught a glimpse of machinery...

all-red line • thin red line

all-red line—(UK hist., also: all-red route) a telegraph line lying throughout in British territory: Green tells of Fleming's advocacy of a Pacific Cable and the All-Red Line.

thin red line—(UK) 1. *(dated)* the British army *(used with the implication of its supposed invincibility):* Napoleon Bonaparte soon found that in the "thin red line" he had more than met his match. 2. the heroic resistance of few against many: England's thin red line of intellectual royalists is being overrun by "progressive" reformers who sabotage old-fashioned academic virtues.

Note: *The expression does not correlate in meaning with the phrase* ***thin line****— a significantly blurred borderline between two things:* There is often only a thin line between a successful launch and devastating destruction. Rockets are an unforgiving technology.

See also: ragged blue line / thin blue line.

all-red route • red route

all-red route—(UK hist., also: all-red line) a telegraph line lying throughout in British territory: Because all of these locations were part of the British Empire, the cable was also known as the "All Red Route" (as red was the color associated with Britain).

red route—(UK) a proposed expressway marked by a red line along the edge of the road: The idea of the red route as a way of easing traffic congestion was devised by a group of Conservative politicians called the red route group.

all right for you • all right with you

all right for you—usually accompanies a threat of revenge as said by a child angry at a playmate: All right for you, John. See if I ever play with you again.

all right with you—(also: all right by you) suits you; is acceptable to you: Please let me know if that time is all right with you.

all right guy • right guy

all right guy—(coll.) a reliable or trustworthy person: We took a big chance by inviting you and ... you turned out to be an all right guy.

right guy—1. = *all right guy:* I told Gains what the hotel clerk said and how lucky we were he happened to be a right guy. 2. *(coll., also: Mr. Right)* a perfect romantic or marriage partner: When she moved to Madrid she joked that she would never return home if she met the right guy.

all the best • all the better

all the best—is used as a farewell or to close an informal letter: I think your comments are important and will make sure our health writer sees them as well. All the best.

all the better—even more so: He said nothing of this to Miss Celia; but she found it out, and liked him all the better for keeping some of his small worries to himself.

all the time • all the while

all the time—1. through the whole period; continuously: Sue said she knew it all the time. 2. very often; many times: Ruth talks about her trip to Europe all the time. 3. essentially; first and last: You probably are a politician all the time, which is why you never get to behave badly.

Note: *The expression does not correlate in meaning with the phrase* ***all hours****—very late or very early hours:* It is dark: it must be all hours.

all the while— = *all the time 1:* Mary went to college in her home town, and lived at home all the while.

all the way • all the way live

all the way—(U.S. coll., of hamburgers, etc.) with all available extras, such as mustard, relish, etc.: I'd like one double cheeseburger — all the way.

all the way live—(coll.) very exciting; excellent: Man, this place is all the way live.

all together • altogether

all together—perform an action or undergo smth. collectively; assembled in a group: We were herded all together in some detaining room.

altogether—1. entirely; completely: Our results demonstrate an altogether new approach to fabrication of electronic devices. 2. with all included or counted: Invited from abroad were, altogether, about 20 scholars from France, Germany, and other countries. 3. having considered everything; on the whole: Altogether, I am inclined to suspect much less noble ideas motivating Miller's decision.

all washed out • all washed up

all washed out—1. *(of colors)* faded: I think the picture showed a guy in armor kneeling.... No way to tell for sure with colors all washed out. 2. *(coll.)* very tired; quite exhausted: I'm all washed out. I haven't the energy to do anything at all.

all washed up—(coll.) 1. utterly undone: He can perhaps work as a coach, but as a player he is all washed up. 2. = *all washed out 2:* Eventually, I went home feeling all washed up. I just hung around the house.

allied to a nation • allied with a nation

allied to a nation—(of a nation) related to another nation or connected by common origin: This group of nations is closely allied to the Eastern Asiatics.

allied with a nation—(of a nation) having joined forces with another nation: Britain was allied with the United States many times in history.

allow for something • allow of something

allow for something—(also: make allowance for something) take smth. into consideration: It will take thirty minutes to get to the station, allowing for traffic delays.

allow of something—leave room for smth.: There are more than ten other important issues whose settlement allows of no delay.

Note: *Neither expression correlates in meaning with the phrase* ***allow something****—permit smth.:* Do not allow smoking in the car when non-smokers are in it.

ally oneself to someone • ally oneself with someone

ally oneself to someone—unite or affiliate with a person: She sought to ally herself to the older committee members.

ally oneself with someone—unite with a person in opposition to smb. else: The professor allied herself with John against the committee.

along the line • along the lines

along the line—at some point during the course of a situation or activity: Somewhere along the line your strategy has gone badly wrong.

along the lines—(also: on the lines) following a certain pattern or trend: The Communist leadership organized the country along the lines prescribed by the Soviet Union.

amiable person • amicable person

amiable person—smb. of a kind that deserves to be liked: He is an amiable person who willingly obliged and took time carefully to craft his answers to our posed questions.

amicable person—a person exhibiting goodwill or acting as a friend: They ended up shouting at one another. This was somewhat shocking because Steve is such an amicable person.

amoral behavior • immoral behavior

amoral behavior—behavior demonstrating an utter absence of morality: Psychopaths are antisocial persons who can carry out criminal or amoral behavior while perfectly able to distinguish right from wrong.

immoral behavior—behavior demonstrating low or corrupt moral standards: Television heroes whose immoral behavior is often sumptuously rewarded have become role models for many young Americans.

amuse oneself with something • be amused by something

amuse oneself with something—do smth. to pass the time and not become bored: The women amuse themselves with a game something like jack-stones.

be amused by something—think smth. funny and usually laugh because of it: I was highly amused by a comment Bernard Shaw made once.

ancient lights • Old Lights

ancient lights—(UK Law) the legal right of a house owner to receive daylight through windows: England has a doctrine of <u>ancient lights</u> which was firmly rejected here [in the United States].

Old Lights—(hist., also: Old Light men) religious traditionalists who believed the new religious movement (New Lights) threatened established religion: <u>Old Lights</u> won the passage of a law restricting the activities of traveling preachers.

ancient world • old world

ancient world—the region and civilizations (especially of the Greeks and Romans) known during ancient history: Cartagena was recognized as being one of the wealthiest cities of the <u>ancient world</u>.

old world—1. *(Old World, the)* Europe, Asia and Africa: In all the apes of the <u>Old World</u> the same number and kinds of teeth are present as in man. 2. one's previous setting of existence with its customs, traditions, etc.: Kylie found herself back in her <u>old world</u> of Melbourne to spend Christmas with her family.

Note: *The expression does not correlate in meaning with the phrase* ***olde worlde****—(UK attrib.) attractively old-fashioned (but not necessarily authentic):* This <u>olde worlde</u> pub is on the narrow road down to the sea and coast guard station.

and all • and all that

and all—and all other things included: Duncan had stepped backwards over the gunwale of his boat and fallen, camera <u>and all</u> into the Indian Ocean.

Note: *The expression does not correlate in meaning with the phrase* ***any and all****—a redundant expression meaning "any":* A licensed physician should be consulted for diagnosis of <u>any and all</u> medical conditions.

and all that—(coll.) and other similar things considered unnecessary to mention: Ah, but he's known her all his life. Childhood sweethearts <u>and all that</u>.

angel-water • holy water

angel-water—a perfume or cosmetic in which a plant Angelica *(Herba angelica)* is a chief ingredient: <u>Angel-water</u>, an excellent perfume: also a curious wash to beautify the skin.

holy water—water blessed by a priest, used in the Roman and Greek ritual: Before the High Mass on Sundays the celebrant sprinkles the people with <u>holy water</u>.

another kettle of fish • another turn of the screw

another kettle of fish—(also: different kettle of fish, a) a completely different matter or situation: I'd driven an automatic for years but learning to handle a car with gears was <u>another kettle of fish</u> altogether.

another turn of the screw— an action which makes a bad situation worse, especially in order to force a person to do smth.: Each letter from my bank manager was <u>another turn of the screw</u>.

Note: *Neither expression correlates in meaning with the phrase* ***another side on the boat****— an alternative way of doing smth.:* There is <u>another side on the boat</u>; you don't have to do it that way.

See also: other side of the coin, the / other side of the hill, the.

answer for something • answer to something

answer for something—be accountable or responsible for smth.: He has to <u>answer for</u> his indifference to Aboriginal people.

answer to something—1. act in response to smth.: The birds after <u>answering to</u> the call, darted off again. 2. be suitable or satisfactory for smth.: We've been able to find the solution that <u>answers to</u> our needs. 3. match or correspond to smth.: He doesn't <u>answer to</u> the description of the missing man.

answer is a lemon, the • it's a lemon

answer is a lemon, the—(coll.) the answer is unsatisfactory or non-existent: Do all and sundry succeed? Very frankly, "<u>the answer is a lemon</u>." Luck does not support all...

it's a lemon—(U.S. coll.) it is of poor quality and continuously breaks down: What happens if you buy a new car only to find out a month later that <u>it's a lemon</u>?

answer one's calling • answer the call of nature

answer one's calling— fulfill one's destiny in terms of profession by doing what one has a talent for: Makeup artist Elisabeth Fry said in an interview that she "<u>answered her calling</u>" to design jewelry.

answer the call of nature—(euph.) go to the bathroom to relieve oneself: The locals did not have modern toilets. Mong people preferred to dig a hole in their fields to <u>answer the call of nature</u>.

answer someone • answer to someone

answer someone—say smth. to a person in response to a question: I didn't know how to <u>answer her</u>.

answer to someone—be responsible or accountable to a person: The chain of command is such that the Chief of Staff <u>answers to</u> the Defense Minister.

ant's pants • have ants in one's pants

ant's pants—(Austral. sl.) the height of fashion; the ultimate in novelty or style: You always think it's the <u>ant's pants</u>, and then something better comes along.

have ants in one's pants—(coll.) 1. fidget constantly because of extreme nervousness: Why can't you stand still, do you <u>have ants in your pants</u>? 2. be impatient or restless: The boss <u>has ants in his pants</u> and wants us to have it all ready for him on Tuesday morning.

anxious about something • anxious for something

anxious about something—uneasy about smth.; disturbed about what may happen: And then, all the time you were so worried and <u>anxious about</u> the food and the serving.

anxious for something—wishing smth. very much; eager to get or obtain smth.: An incredible silence reigned among the people, <u>anxious for</u> the event, and lost in suspense.

any day • any time

any day—1. on any one day from now: This, too, is something that may happen <u>any day</u> now or that could be a few years off. 2. *(coll.)* is used to express one's willingness or preference: I'd work with Murphy in Canada <u>any day</u> rather than stay in here. 3. *(coll.)* without doubt: You are a good deal better-looking than her, Barbara. You are, <u>any day</u>.

any time—1. at a time which may be very soon: She is going to give birth <u>any time</u> now. 2. at any time one chooses: John is in a private ward, so you can get in <u>any time</u>. 3. no matter when; whenever: <u>Any time</u> you're stuck for a meal come around. 4. is used in response to an expression of gratitude: "Thanks for helping me." "<u>Any time</u>."

any one • anyone

any one—whichever one (person or thing) you choose: Join the Disc of the Month Club, and we will send you <u>any one</u> of these recordings.

anyone—any person; anybody: Is there <u>anyone</u> so wise as to learn by the experience of others?

any place • anyplace

any place—1. anywhere: Most people that travel <u>any place</u> other than the USA can recognize distances in kilometers as well as miles. 2. is used to refer to a specific kind of place: Do you know of <u>any place</u> in Vietnam that would be good for saltwater fly fishing?

anyplace— = *any place* 1: As of June first everyone will need a passport to travel <u>anyplace</u> outside the U.S.

any way • anyway

any way—in any way or manner: The series focuses on three people as they navigate the Hollywood maze, trying to succeed any way they can.

anyway—1. in spite of that; nevertheless: Her mom would know she was telling a white lie, she always knew, but they played the game anyway. 2. = *any way:* During this period of social exploration you may see him trying to get your attention anyway he can. 3. in any case; no matter what: Well I don't know what he said exactly—he didn't like me anyway.

appear as someone • appear for someone

appear as someone—(of an actor) come before the public in any character: The following year he appeared as Hamlet in a controversial production.

appear for someone—represent smb. as a barrister, etc. in a law court: Inspector Sammut prosecuted while Roberto Montalto appeared for the accused.

apply oneself to something • apply to something

apply oneself to something—put all one's energy into smth.: If you apply yourself to the job in hand, you'll soon finish it.

apply to something—1. turn to an organization for help, support, etc.: You must apply to the proper office for permission. 2. *(of rules, laws, etc.)* affect smth.; be relevant to smth.: These policies apply only to very large companies.

approve of something • approve something

approve of something—1. be willing to accept or support smth.: Her father will never approve of her marriage to you. 2. like or admire smth.: The wine was the very same which they had all approved of the day before.

approve something—formally confirm or sanction smth.: The minutes of the meeting were read and approved.

apt at doing something • apt to do something

apt at doing something—able to do smth. efficiently: He is very apt at picking up a new subject.

apt to do something—having a tendency to do smth.: Babies who are small at birth are apt to grow faster.

archaic word • archaistic word

archaic word—a word that is no longer in general use but is still encountered in literature and sometimes used for special effect: Though sparingly ... he weaves some archaic words into his own writing.

archaistic word—a word from an earlier time that is no longer used: The author divided the dialectal vocabulary into the following strata: archaistic words and contemporary words.

arm in arm • hand in hand

arm in arm—with one's arm under or around another person's arm: Sally and Joan were laughing as they walked arm in arm down the street.

hand in hand—1. holding hands: Molly and her stepmother wandered about in the gardens hand in hand, like two babes in the wood. 2. in close association: It provides a unique mix of a professionally educated workforce working hand-in-hand with volunteers.

armchair general • armchair pilot

armchair general—smb. who speaks critically of military matters, etc. but has no real experience: You've never served in the military, which confirms my suspicion that you're just another armchair general.

armchair pilot—a person whose hobby is computer based flight simulation: Authentically modeled after the F-16 control column, this controller is intended for the advanced armchair pilot.

armed forces • armored forces

armed forces—the military forces of a country including the army, navy, air force, etc.: Armenia has followed a policy of developing its armed forces into a professional, well trained military.

armored forces—armored fighting vehicles such as tanks: German armored forces aimed to thrust deep into the enemy rear to sow confusion and disorganization.

around the bend • around the corner

around the bend—(also: round the bend) 1. about to happen very soon: Saint Patrick's day is around the bend and I need a partner for the jig contest. 2. *(coll.)* crazy; insane: Mars is completely around the bend and not the kind of guy you'd want your daughter to go on a date with.

around the corner—(also: round the corner) = around the bend 1: Halloween is just around the corner and candy seems to be everywhere (and at good prices!).

arrive dead on time • be dead on arrival

arrive dead on time—arrive exactly at the expected or prearranged time: We arrived dead on time at Cape Town where we were met by Che in the arrivals hall.

be dead on arrival—be without any chance for success: The idea of legalizing some drugs is a concept that's dead on arrival in many law enforcement circles.

art film • artful film

art film—a film intended to be a serious artistic work, often experimental and not designed for mass appeal: Because it was an "art film," it probably reached the wrong audience.

artful film—a skillful, ingeniously crafted movie: Leni succumbed to every filmmaker's dream—an unlimited budget to make an artful film and not just "a boring newsreel."

***Note:** Neither expression correlates in meaning with the phrase **arty film**—a film characterized by a showy, pretentious display of artistic skill:* As an arty film, it would have been acceptable. As a major, mainstream release, it was a failure.

art work • work of art

art work—(also: art-work) a fine painting, piece of sculpture, etc.: They dreamed of great art-works, lovely compositions, impassioned song.

work of art—1. = *art work 1:* Whether buying stocks or works of art he adopted the same technique. 2. *(hyperbolic)* said of smth. very skillfully made: His own papers were works of art on which he labored with loving care.

as a last resort • in the last resort

as a last resort—as a last means; when everything else has been tried and failed: The imprisonment of a child should be used only as a last resort.

in the last resort—ultimately; in the end: He was worried about his production figures. In the last resort it was the human factor that counted.

as a man • like a man

as a man—1. *(of a group of people) acting* unanimously and at exactly the same time *(also: as one man):* They came forward as a man to welcome their leader. 2. in respect of smb.'s personal character: The stature he acquired both as a man and a leader gave added impetus and credibility to the movement. 3. in the manner appropriate to men, as opposed to women: Mary, still dressed as a man, was soon recruited to Rackham's crew.

like a man—1. in the manner of a brave and honest man: I think, if you haven't the guts to act like a man, you ought to leave this girl alone. 2. in one's normal condition of mind and body: I never had anyone in my life before like this family who make me feel like a man again.

as a matter of fact • fact of the matter is, the

as a matter of fact—as it happens; actually: As a matter of fact, I recently found two small stories that provoked more thought than the other articles I read.

Note: *The expression does not correlate in meaning with the phrase* ***as a matter of course****— as part of a standard procedure; as smth. that one expects automatically to happen:* Medical insurance is provided for students by the Institute as a matter of course.

fact of the matter is, the—the essential or important thing is: The fact of the matter is that she only married me because Zeeman wouldn't get a divorce, and she was punishing him.

as a reward for something • in reward for something

as a reward for something—is used of smth. given to reward a person: I receive as a reward for my services a post with which I am well satisfied.

in reward for something—is used with reference to the reason for the reward: He was presented with a gold watch in reward for his services.

as anything • like anything

as anything— an intensifier used as part of an informal comparison: Natasha was one of these people who's nice as anything until you don't do something she says.

like anything—(coll.) do smth. with great energy or enthusiasm: He waved to us and we waved back like anything.

Note: *The expression is not antonymous in meaning to the phrase* ***like nothing on earth****—(coll.)* 1. *extremely strange; highly unusual:* You may yet meet with a lumbering native bear, like nothing on earth so much as a child's woolly toy. 2. *feeling or looking very ill or miserable:* That dreadful period when you're just coming out of an anesthetic and feeling like nothing on earth is not the time when you want a visitor.

as big as a barn • as big as all outdoors

as big as a barn—very large: The restaurant is as big as a barn — and as plain and welcoming as a farmhouse kitchen.

Note: *The expression is not equivalent in meaning to the phrase* ***as big as they come****— used of a size not likely to be exceeded:* If he did really catch a 20 lb. salmon, he was lucky; that's about as big as they come.

as big as all outdoors—1. very vast and spacious: The store room is as big as all outdoors. 2. huge; great: Bob likes a challenge that's as big as all outdoors.

Note: *Neither expression is related in meaning to the phrase* ***as big as life****—(also: as large as life) used of smb. actually present, especially in a place where a person is not supposed to be:* I thought Tom had gone to Europe. There he is, as big as life.

as far • so far

as far—(also: this far) to a specified point or place: They opened more clinics since people couldn't travel as far for medical care.

so far—1. until now; up to the present time: There has not so far been any book-length study focused on postmodernism. 2. = *as far:* It really makes you think about how amazing it is that you can travel so far in one day.

as far as • so far as

as far as—1. up to a point or place mentioned: We went as far as the Marble Lodge, a keeper's cottage, and came back the same way. 2. to the extent that: As far as I can tell, people reply according to what their experience and knowledge is and to the best of their ability.

so far as— = as far as 2: So far as I can remember, I've always been success-driven and goal-oriented, and all it's gotten me is a mediocre job.

as far as one can see • as far as the eye can see

as far as one can see—in one's opinion: Pete wants nothing serious because as far as he can see we wouldn't get along because we argue all the time.

as far as the eye can see—to the very horizon: A panorama of Lake Michigan and dunes stretching as far as the eye can see unfolds before you.

as good as • as well as

as good as—practically; almost: He as good as promised me the job.

as well as—in addition: We will travel by night as well as by day.

as hell • like hell

as hell—(coll.) extremely; very much *(is used to intensify adjectives):* Nobody believed him of course, and this made him sore as hell.

like hell—1. *(interj.)* not at all; on the contrary *(is used to emphatically contradict a statement):* "I've quite enjoyed it here." "Like hell I have," she added under her breath. 2. *(coll.)* madly; frantically *(is used to intensify verbs):* I fired when something came into my sights and then turned like hell as something fired at me!

as is • as it is

as is—just the way it is *(usually said of goods that may be slightly damaged, without guarantee, etc.):* We bought this samovar as is from an antique dealer.

as it is—1. = *as is:* It was actually a demo but the producers were so impressed with the quality that they took it as it is. 2. in the actual state of affairs; as the situation is: He might have been killed; as it is he was severely injured.

as it was • as it were

as it was—1. just the way it was *(usually said of goods that may be slightly damaged, without guarantee, etc.):* The family bought the estate as it was: ruined, discredited, its buildings in bad condition. 2. in the actual state of affairs; as the situation was: If we had been able to find a taxi, we should have caught the train. As it was we were late.

as it were—in a way; so to speak: He was, as it were, the missing link between the artist and the commercial public.

as much • as much again

as much—1. is used to express equality with the amount specified: The Irish Independent also reports that we've never earned as much. 2. *think or say* virtually the same thing: That a plant will be built is not in doubt: the Government has said as much.

as much again—twice as much: People who sell you goods earn as much again if they sell you this insurance too.

as of now • for now

as of now—from this moment: It's been over a month and a half and still no word. So, as of now I will never order there again.

for now—temporarily; for the time being: The status quo may be good enough for now, but it's not good enough for tomorrow.

as one man • to a man

as one man—(of a group of people) acting unanimously and at exactly the same time *(also: as a man):* As he uttered these words, the members of the convention rose as one man to their feet.

to a man—(also: to the last man) 1. *(of a group of people)* every person without exception: The inhabitants, almost to a man, had left the city. 2. *(of combatants) keep fighting* until none is left alive: The Persian army closed in on them, and the Spartans died fighting to a man.

as security • for security

as security—1. as a pledge against possible financial loss: It is not unusual to require one or more partners to pledge their own property as security for a loan. 2. as a guarantee for the performance of some action: Three of the leading men were seized as security. The Mayor paid the sum and the "bonds" men were released.

for security—in order to ensure safety from possible harm: For security, the door was chained as well as locked.

as thick as peas in a pod • like two peas in a pod

as thick as peas in a pod—(also: as thick as peas in a shell) intimate or very friendly: He and I are as thick as peas in a pod. He comes to me with most of his troubles.

like two peas in a pod—very similar; almost exactly alike: She and Karen are like two peas in a pod — they both sing in clubs, share the same dirty laugh, smoke the same brand of cigarettes.

ask another • ask me another

ask another—is used as an expression of boredom or a protest against a worn-out joke: "I say, Joe, when's a door not a door?" "Oh, ask another."

ask me another—is used to tell that one does not know the answer: "Are you fond of birds, uncle Nic?" "Ask me another, Greta!"

ask for someone's hand • ask someone for a hand

ask for someone's hand—propose to a woman: I've told him I have asked for your hand in marriage and that you've rejected me.

ask someone for a hand—1. ask smb. to help in what one is doing: Sometimes you feel a bit stupid asking someone for a hand. 2. ask the audience, etc. for applause: Asking the audience for a hand for the band he showed his confidence in their abilities.

ask someone in • ask someone out

ask someone in—invite a person into one's home, office, etc.: I sent them my information and they asked me in for an interview.

ask someone out—invite a person out to a disco, restaurant, etc.: I am just not too sure about how to ask her out.

ask someone to leave • ask someone's leave

ask someone to leave—1. ask a person to depart from a place: She said that what she had heard was self-explanatory and asked him to leave. 2. dismiss smb. from employment: The company thought it did not look good, so they asked him to leave. They are very concerned about integrity…

ask someone's leave—(formal) ask smb.'s permission: When he offered her freedom to do as she wished, she asked his leave to join the Order.

ask the question • put the question

ask the question—1. call to a person for an answer to or about smth.: I heard your voice tremble as you asked me the question. 2. *(Horse races)* call upon the horse for a special effort: I asked King Lud the question. He answered in the most generous manner possible and won.

Note: *The expression does not correlate in meaning with the phrase* ***beg the question****—1. take for granted the very point that needs to be proved:* You're simply begging the question in assuming that O'Neill wasn't a racist. 2. *used to indicate that the question really ought to be addressed:* This year's budget deficit is half a trillion dollars. This begs the question: how are we going to balance the budget?

put the question—ask those present at a meeting, etc. to record their votes for or against the proposal: I must put the question to the House, and the House must say "Aye" or "No."

assimilate something into something • assimilate something to something

assimilate something into something—adapt smth. making it part of a larger group: The costs of assimilating a traffic artery into an existing urban area are a massive community burden.

assimilate something to something—make smth. like smth. else: The laws of the defeated country were assimilated to those of the stronger country.

associate with someone • be associated with someone

associate with someone—spend a lot of time in smb.'s company (especially if that person is objectionable): Those extra-moralists refuse to associate with a convict legally pardoned.

be associated with someone—be connected in people's mind with smb. (because of common interests, etc.): He was associated with, although he never joined, the British environmentalists.

at a birth • at birth • at the birth

at a birth—during a single act of reproduction: Cats sometimes have four or five young at a birth.

at birth—at the time when a baby or an animal is born: No animal at birth is mature or perfect in intelligence.

at the birth—1. present or attending during the birth: Josephine did not want her husband at the birth of her own children. 2. during the emergence of smth.: The UN had been the indispensable midwife at the birth of their country.

at a clap • in a clap

at a clap—(dated) with one effort; at once: It was a good occasion to kill all Caesar's Enemies at a clap.

in a clap—(dated) in a moment; immediately *(also: in a clap or two):* Our Master will be on us all now in a clap.

at a distance • in the distance

at a distance—1. not too near: This is where you get truly wonderful views of the Acropolis — seeing it at a distance, the Parthenon grows more impressive. 2. a long way away from smth. in time: Remembering this disaster at a distance, I now feel sure that it was not her fault.

in the distance—far away: A sliver of an island appeared in the distance. The plane made a wide turn and continued its slow descent.

at a draft • on draft

at a draft— drink all of smth. during one continuous action of swallowing: He drank half a pint of beer at a draft.

on draft—(usually of beer) served from a barrel and not sold in bottles: We had no beer on draft and a handful of bottled beers.

at a glance • at first glance

at a glance— notice smth. immediately without having to look carefully: When I warm up for a road race I can usually tell at a glance the newcomers to the sport.

at first glance—(also: at first sight) when first seen or considered: This arrangement pleases at first glance, but soon fatigues the eye by its uniformity.

at a good price • at a goodly price

at a good price—1. *sell* at a fairly high price: It's wise to look far ahead in order to use the market to your advantage and sell at a good price. 2. *buy* at a very low price *(also: at a great price):* He lends people hospital beds, which he happened to get at a good price.

at a goodly price—1. *buy* at a fairly high price: He purchased the fabric at a goodly price, which drove up the cost on the finished product. 2. = *at a good price* 1: The Venus, being a rare and beautiful example of Roman sculpture, might well be sold at a goodly price.

at a heat • in heat

at a heat—*(coll.)* at a single intense effort or action: The new articles having been "thrown off at a heat," stood particularly in want of re-revision.

in heat—*(of animals)* in the state of sexual excitement during the breeding season *(also: on heat)*: "I'm no bitch in heat," she said between tight teeth, "take your paws off me."

See also: at a white heat / in a dead heat.

at a moment • at the moment

at a moment—at one point in time (out of many): He looked up from the desk, caught her at a moment when, against her will, tears had filled her eyes.

Note: *The expression does not fully correlate in meaning with the phrase* ***in a moment***—1. *in a very short time:* The maids are busy preparing your room but they will be done in a moment. 2. = *at a moment:* He forced the responsibility of two lives upon me, and, in a moment of indecision, I failed them.

at the moment—1. at present; just now: There are twenty residents in a converted private house, and at the moment many of them share a room. 2. at a specific point in time: That gentleman was really ruined, and that at the moment when he was about to attain his end.

at a price • at the price

at a price—1. *bought or sold* at a high cost; very expensive: There's fresh asparagus in the shops—at a price! 2. at the cost of much effort and sacrifice: Such is his grip on the market, though it is one obtained at a price.

at the price—1. at the cost indicated: Other wines difficult to beat at the price include three good dry whites from Hungary. 2. at the expense of smth.: The issue will be whether the government will introduce the harsh measures at the price of its own popularity.

at a push • at one push

at a push—*(coll.)* if compelled by need or circumstances: We can sleep seven or eight people in the house at a push.

at one push—with one act of pushing: Do not press the shutter at one push, or otherwise the photograph may be blurred.

at a run • on the run

at a run—*moving* at a running pace: Suddenly, there he was, at a run, hurrying my son to unpack the rifle and climb the mountain with him.

on the run—*(predic.)*—1. running: Although I am perfectly still, I find myself taking quick short breaths, as if I too am on the run. 2. *(also: on the trot)* busy moving from one task to another: It was vacation, and I shouldn't feel bad if I am not on the run every minute of the day. 3. *(also: on the trot)* running away from prison, the police, etc.: He went to meet a *Franc-Tireur* who was on the run after killing several Germans. 4. *(of troops)* retreating; severely defeated: They all believed that this first success should be fully exploited while the enemy was on the run.

at a stretch • on the stretch

at a stretch—1. continuously; without interruption: It was impossible to work for more than an hour or so at a stretch. 2. by making a special effort; by stretching one's resources: We have provided food for fifty people, but we might be able to make it do for sixty at a stretch.

on the stretch—1. tightened and extended: By the inspiratory effort the elastic tissue of the lungs is put on the stretch. 2. = *at a stretch 1:* Though several cars remained stranded for hours on the stretch, the situation was brought under control. 3. *(coll.)* using exaggerated statements: He's always on the stretch.... He never tells the truth except by mistake. 4. *(of nerves)* in the state of tension: The insects whirred and buzzed and the noise kept Harry's nerves on the stretch. 5. *(also: at full stretch)* working as hard as possible: Me and my stoker were on the stretch all the time attending to the engine.

at a stroke • at the stroke

at a stroke—suddenly and with a single action or effort: Some companies were in trouble because Mr. Heath changed strategy at a stroke.

at the stroke—at exactly the time stated or agreed upon: We agreed to meet for lunch, and he arrived at the stroke.

at a time • at one time

at a time—1. simultaneously: We present items, three at a time, and ask informants to pick the one that is most different from the other two. 2. is used of a particular period of time: She grew up in the capital at a time when its artistic life was at its most brilliant.

Note: *The expression does not correlate in meaning with the phrase* ***at times***—*now and then:* Our work is cut out for us, even though it can be heartbreaking at times.

at one time—1. = *at a time* 1: Let's start the dance again, all at one time. 2. at some time in the past: At one time most school teachers were men.

at a walk • in a walk

at a walk—at the ordinary gait: He watched her as she went past at a walk.

in a walk—*(coll.)* 1. quickly and without much thought: If you bother me too much, I'll leave you in a walk! 2. easily and without effort: Sunday is election day, and Viktor Yushenko is expected to win in a walk.

at a white heat • in a dead heat

at a white heat—in a state of intense or extreme emotion: I saw him once while at a white heat of vexation in the library of the White House.

in a dead heat—*(of a race, etc.)* finishing at practically the same time: The horses came to the finish in a dead heat, and, without a photograph, the results were too close to call.

See also: at a heat / in heat.

at a word • in a word

at a word—following the word of command: At a word from the guard they all splashed into the water and washed their faces thoroughly.

in a word—*(introductory or parenthetical)* briefly; in short: Another morning came, but no wife. In a word, she was never heard of more.

at all events • in any event

at all events—anyhow; at any rate: Our landlady may be a bad cook, but at all events she does her best.

in any event—whatever may happen: I hope to go tomorrow; in any event I shall go before Saturday.

Note: *The expression is not equivalent in meaning to the phrase* ***in either event***—*no matter which of two possibilities happens:* You will be notified on the phone or via e-mail. In either event, we will not charge your credit card for a product until it is shipped to you.

at all hours • at any hour

at all hours—continuously, especially at unusual or irregular times: His songs are heard everywhere in the country and at all hours. *Cf.: until all hours—(also: until all hours of the night) until very late at night:* I lived the crazy life of a student—studying until all hours, living in front of my computer, all that.

Note:** The expression does not correlate in meaning with the phrase* ***at all times—*on all occasions; always:* The accessibility of Italy upon this side was at all times a matter of anxiety to her rulers.

at any hour—at any time; whenever one chooses: The knowledge that he might at any hour be called upon stimulated his studies of his duties.

See also: at any one time / at any time.

at an end • at the end

at an end—1. said of smth. used up or exhausted: I must warn you that my patience is almost at an end. 2. be finished; be over: When a checkmate is obtained, the game is at an end.

at the end—1. in the last part of smth.: I think the film's a bit weak at the end. 2. in the farthest part of smth.: The tube is very short and closed at the end.

Note:** The expression is not equivalent in meaning to the phrase* ***in the end—1. *finally; ultimately:* Three months were spent in the drafting of a document which in the end was rejected. 2. *taking one thing with another; as things turn out:* In the end, boys and girls don't communicate the same way.

at any cost • at any price

at any cost—regardless of how much effort or sacrifice is needed: In plain English, it is murder, and it must be stopped at any cost.

at any price—1. = *at any cost:* Peace at any price will not be a long peace. There will be more price to pay, over and over again. 2. *(negat.)* is used to state that under no circumstances will one accept or do smth.: I'm going to leave you. I can't stand my father-in-law at any price.

at any one time • at any time

at any one time—on each separate occasion: These were what were known as "bottle shops," and could not sell less than a bottle of spirits at any one time.

at any time—1. at any given moment: The navigational system enabled our bombers to know exactly where they were at any time en route to Germany. 2. at a time which may be very soon: We may need the trucks at any time. I'll phone if I want you to roll them. 3. at any time one chooses: Anyone is welcome to join in at any time during the day. 4. no matter when; whenever: If at any time you have questions, please feel free to call.

See also: at all hours / at any hour.

at arm's length • close at hand

at arm's length—1. as far away from one as one can reach with the arm: The curtains fell together as the girl and the man stood at arm's length from one another. 2. away from close contact or familiarity: Deep inside she does have a bit of affection for him, but their rivalry has her keeping him at arm's length.

close at hand—1. near enough; in close proximity: The monks were always mindful to establish themselves where there was water close at hand. 2. on close inspection: He was found, close at hand, to be no mean acrid man; but at heart a healthful, strong, sagacious man. 3. *(of an event, etc.)* coming on shortly: This was the moment at which the fortunes of Montague reached the meridian. The decline was close at hand.

at best • at one's best

at best—*(introductory or parenthetical)* even under the most favorable conditions: He can only tie the score, at best.

at one's best—*(predic.)* said of smb. in the best state or condition: Although he was not at his best, he won the match.

at call • within call

at call—*(also: on call)* 1. *(of a doctor, etc.)* available if required: She served as president, then ... twenty years as treasurer, always at call, and handling the money carefully. 2. *(of money, etc.)* available on demand: As a first step, I secured my vast property, so that the income would be certain, and always at call.

within call—near enough to be summoned by calling: Ross was still away on duty, and there was nobody except the native servants within call.

at command • in command • on command

at command—said of smth. at one's disposal (and ready to be used): A constant supply of hot water is at command over the whole house.

in command—1. having the authority to command: Like all those who are seldom in command, the master was proportionally tyrannical and abusive. 2. having control over a situation: He was looking more relaxed and in command than ever before.

on command—at the order given: On command the mother ship would have oriented itself and determined when to launch its subsatellites.

at danger • in danger

at danger—*(of a signal on a railway line, etc.):* in the position giving a warning of danger: A signal is said to be "on," when it is at danger.

in danger—at risk: The euphoria which accompanies altitude sickness robs the pilot of the opportunity of recognizing that he is in danger.

Note:** The expression does not correlate in meaning with the phrase* ***on the danger list—*(of a patient in the hospital) dangerously ill:* Five patients on the danger list were slightly better, the hospital said.

at dusk • in the dusk

at dusk—at the time when the twilight is setting in: The cathedral is closed to the public at dusk each day.

in the dusk—surrounded by the dusk; while it is dusk: One cannot see very far in the dusk.

at first • first of all

at first—in the beginning; originally: At first I disliked spinach, but now I quite love it.

Note:** The expression does not correlate in meaning with the phrase* ***from the first—*from the start:* Although he found English difficult he liked it from the first.

first of all—before anything else: First of all, we need to decide who to invite.

at full length • at great length

at full length—1. with the body stretched out and flat: He never walked again, but was drawn about lying at full length in a sort of bed-carriage. 2. *describing smth.* thoroughly and in detail: The purism of modern times would not allow me to give this story at full length.

at great length— = *at full length 2:* He went on at great length about his favorite hobby.

Note:** The expression does not fully correlate in meaning with the phrase* ***at length—1. = *at great length:* He dwelt at length on the considerable opposition to the entry of Britain into the Common Market. 2. *after a long time or pause:* At length he spoke again, softly, as if he was debating with himself.

at full strength • in full strength

at full strength—1. *working or performing* at maximum capacity: Four refineries that were shut down are now operating at full strength. 2. *(of a group of people)* with all its members present: Although none of our teams were at full strength they all put in spirited performances.

in full strength—(also: in full force) = at full strength 2: The ladies were in full strength ... each of them bringing a dish prepared by themselves.

Note: *Neither expression correlates in meaning with the phrase* ***with all one's strength****— using as much physical effort as one can:* He looped the rope over the branch and pulled with all his strength.

at full time • in the fullness of time

at full time—reaching the normal mass or dimension: At full time the fetus weighs from six and one-half to eight pounds.

Note: *The expression does not correlate in meaning with the phrase* ***full time****—1. the regular number of hours allotted to daily or weekly work:* All the factories we visited were running full time. 2. *(also: high time) time when smth. should be done at once:* The vessel is going to pieces, and it is full time for all who can, to leave her.

in the fullness of time—at the proper or destined time: In the fullness of time, your children and your in-laws become friends.

at hand • in hand

at hand—(also: on hand) within easy reach; close by: Keep a good dictionary at hand as you write. Proofread carefully.

in hand—1. said of smth. being dealt with: If you apply yourself to the job in hand, you'll soon finish it. 2. *(also: on hand)* in one's possession: Sometimes it is a better idea to borrow money than to wait until you have the money in hand.

at hazard • on the hazard

at hazard—1. at random; without plan: The following examples were selected at hazard. 2. at stake; in danger: Their worldly interests were at hazard.

on the hazard— = at hazard 2: Messala's whole fortune was on the hazard.

at high pressure • under high pressure

at high pressure—1. *(of matter)* when strongly pressed: Steam and oxygen at high pressure are introduced at the lower end of the gasifier. 2. *acting* with great energy and speed: As for Robert, he, of course, was living at high pressure all round.

under high pressure—1. *= at high pressure I:* The new material loses its resistance only under high pressure. 2. when strongly persuaded or compelled: Working under high pressure for sustained periods results in stress.

at home • on home ground

at home—(predic.) very competent in smth. *(with the implication that it makes a person feel confident and relaxed):* Melanie is equally at home singing oratorio, jazz or performing in musical theater.

on home ground—1. in the area where one works or lives: It was nice to renew acquaintances of students I've taught and to meet them on "home ground." 2. *= at home:* Godber is on home ground, writing with cold-eyed affection about the Yorkshire mining communities.

at home in something • at home with something

at home in something—very competent in a particular subject *(with the implication that it makes a person feel confident and relaxed):* Richard was at home in mathematics and physics as well as Greek.

at home with something—feeling easy and confident about using smth.: From the day we arrived he was completely at home with the camera.

at home to someone • at home with someone

at home to someone—prepared and willing to receive visitors: Mrs. Hill is not at home to anyone except relatives.

at home with someone—1. on friendly terms with smb.: She described his charm as "magnetic" and said "he was at home with everybody." *2. feeling* comfortable in a person's company: His genial manner made me feel quite at home with him.

at interest • with interest

at interest—(of money) borrowed or lent on the condition that interest is to be paid: The sum was placed in a bank at interest and not to be drawn before a set maturity date.

with interest—1. *(of money) paid* with interest included: The company will return your original investment to you with interest. 2. *return or repay* with increase or addition: The boys make monkey faces at me and I return the compliment with interest.

at it • in it

at it—1. hard at work exerting oneself: He never gives himself any rest; he's always at it. 2. doing smth., especially repeatedly, of which the speaker disapproves: Those children lighting fires in the park. So they are at it again, are they? 3. arguing or quarrelling, especially when this happens repeatedly: There they are at it now, with their caterwauling, squealing, all together. 4. *(euph., sl.)* indulging in sexual intercourse: The couple next door have been at it all night.

in it—taking part in an activity; engaged in smth.: There is no money in boxing. Those of us who started it many years ago are really not in it for the money.

at large • in large

at large—1. not in confinement or captivity: The suspect was not found, and was still at large, police said. 2. unemployed; without an occupation: Are you at large or have you any other occupation? 3. is used of people in general: Did the people at large approve of the government's policy? 4. without definite aim; at random: A single stroke well aimed returns a better result than a score which are delivered at large. 5. at great length; in detail: My mother and I talked at large on the subject.

in large—(also: in the large) as a whole: Are they pledging allegiance to a piece of cloth rather than their family and neighbors: their community in small and in large?

at last • at the last

at last—after much waiting or delay: It is an uplifting thought that truth is to be told at last.

at the last—during the final period: Ah, but you never saw him at the last. He was not at all what he used to be.

Note: *a) The expression does not correlate in meaning with the phrase* ***at the last minute****— at the last possible moment:* The plane took a nose dive. The pilot was able to bring it out at the last minute...

b) The expression does not correlate in meaning with the phrase ***at the latest****—used of smth. that must happen at or before a particular time:* Changes will become necessary by the autumn at the latest.

at need • in need

at need—in time of need: They had the support of older men whose experience could be called upon at need.

in need—requiring help: Many elderly people who are in need fail to apply for a supplementary allowance.

at no time • in no time

at no time—on no occasion; never: This organization has at no time been an official subdivision of the Labor Party.

in no time—very soon: Our lessons by professional instructors will have you phobia-free and swimming in no time.

at noon • in the afternoon

at noon—in the middle of the day; at twelve o'clock: The committee will meet at noon on the third Monday of each month.

in the afternoon—in the period between mid-day and evening: The morning will be set aside for committees to meet and the full group will meet in the afternoon.

at one • in one

at one—in agreement: Here is an inner core of Evangelism in which all true believers are at one.

in one—combined; together: He is President, Chairman and Secretary in one.

at one time and another • at one time or another

at one time and another—from time to time; occasionally: He wanted the robust exchange of love and passion such as he had had with her at one time and another.

at one time or another—1. = *at one time and another:* Most people suffer from headaches at one time or another. 2. one day; sooner or later: God has told the prophets that these events will happen at one time or another.

at one's back • on one's back

at one's back—1. said of smb. pursuing or chasing a person: He hopped on the bike and tore out of the lot, as though the hounds of hell were at his back. 2. said of smb. giving support or protection to a person: He has the head of the Department at his back.

on one's back—1. said of smb. causing trouble to a person: He wants to know who's going to be Sheriff. That's the person who's going to be on his back. 2. said of smb. being a burden to a person (causing expense, etc.): We're the backbone of the country, but you see, Bob, there's too many people on our backs.

Note: *The expression does not correlate in meaning with the phrase* ***on one's shoulders****— being smb.'s responsibility:* I'd like to get the decision made as early as possible because I don't want to have it on my shoulders for the whole season.

at one's command • under one's command

at one's command—1. at smb.'s word or phrase by which an order is given: He presented, at her command, a rose that he gathered. 2. ready to be used; at one's disposal: Never was his inventive force more flexible and more at his command.

under one's command—under smb.'s charge or control: The editorial policy of the Daily Mail was under his total command.

at one's fingertips • to one's fingertips

at one's fingertips—*(of facts, information, etc.)* readily available thanks to thorough knowledge *(also: at one's finger-ends):* Thanks to an excellent filing system, he has all the figures at his fingertips.

to one's fingertips—*(also: to one's finger-ends)* completely; thoroughly: Frank was a gentleman to his fingertips. He was always good to meet and has a word for one and all.

at one's risk • at risk

at one's risk—accepting responsibility; agreeing to make no claims: The consumer shall, at his risk, install and retain control over the equipment.

at risk—exposed to danger; subject to hazard: The initiative aims at developing techniques for identifying individuals at risk for heart attacks.

at one's time of life • in one's lifetime

at one's time of life—at one's age (especially middle age): If I can't bear a bit of pain at my time of life I'm no sportswoman.

in one's lifetime—for the duration of one's life; while a person is alive: In my lifetime, four things have happened to revolutionize farming.

at one's worst • at the worst

at one's worst—said of smb. in the worst or most undesirable state: Glennie was at her worst: still unchanged, wearing her dirty forenoon wrapper.

at the worst—in the worst possible case: If a man played long enough he was sure to win at last, or at the worst, not to come off a loser.

at play • in play

at play—1. playing games: It's a bit like watching children at play, creating an imaginative world that they believe in completely. 2. engaged in gambling (playing cards, etc.): This gentleman has been at play at that there gaming-house over the way.

in play—1. said of smth. done for amusement and not intended to be taken seriously: Don't be offended; I only said it in play. 2. said of factors actively involved or having influence: Mighty forces are in play in the present round of negotiations.

Note: *The expression does not correlate in meaning with the phrase* ***in full play****—in full action or operation; acting with full force:* A desperate fight was going on ... the rebel batteries were in full play.

at present • in the present

at present—right now; at this time *(of a situation that might be temporary):* John lives in London, but at present he is on holiday abroad.

in the present—said of a period of time we are living in: She thinks the world has always been the way it is now, in the present. She probably thinks that George Washington communicated with Thomas Jefferson by email.

Note: *The expression does not correlate in meaning with the phrase* ***for the present****—for the time being; for now:* We have enough butter for the present, though we may have to buy some more next week.

at quiet • on the quiet

at quiet—at peace; in a state of calm or repose: The lives of the poor people arrested were saved, and the country remained at quiet.

on the quiet—said of smth. done privately or in secret: If you are engaged and have got married on the quiet then there is nothing to be ashamed of.

at short hand • in short hand

at short hand— in the short term; quickly: The demo failed because the problem could not be solved at short-hand.

in short hand—using a quick way of writing which utilizes signs instead of words: He had attended all the lectures taking them down in short-hand.

at sight • in sight

at sight—*(also: on sight)* 1. *shoot a person* immediately on seeing him: Had we shot Jodl at sight, that piece of evidence would never have been obtained. 2. *reading music* without previous study: That pianist can read the most difficult music at sight. 3. *(of bank drafts, etc.)* to be paid on presentation: I'll give you a check at sight on the Pennsylvanian Bank.

Note: *The expression does not correlate in meaning with the phrase* ***at first sight****—(also: at first glance) when first seen or considered, often with the implication that one's first impression is* *probably wrong:* At first sight, it would seem they have a point. However, this reasoning is a bit short sighted.

in sight—1. within view: The small jet began to lose height, and soon airport buildings, a runway, and taxi strips were in sight. 2. in one's mental or spiritual vision: His sagacious mind immediately recognized and caught on to the only plan of salvation in sight. 3. said of smth. likely to happen soon: That such a development is not now in sight does not offer conclusive proof of technical infeasibility.

at the back of something • on the back of something

at the back of something—1. behind smth.: At the back of the house there was a large garden. 2. in the part which is farthest from the front: a room at the back of the house; a door at the back of a building. 3. responsible for smth., especially smth. bad: Mr. Tillotson is at the back of the plan to demolish those fine old buildings.

on the back of something—1. on the reverse side of smth.: On the back of the letter was a diagram. 2. in addition to smth.; immediately following smth. *(usually of an unfortunate event):* The child had the measles, and then on the back of that came the scarlet fever.

at the beginning • to begin with

at the beginning—(also: in the beginning) initially; at first: At the begining, he was simply darling to me. Lately, he is distant and not very responsive.

to begin with—(also: to start with) 1. most importantly: There were other considerations that made Dudley unsuitable. To begin with he was already married.... 2. = *at the beginning:* To begin with he was against the Turks, later he suddenly changed policy and joined them for a short period.

at the bottom of something • in the bottom of something

at the bottom of something—1. in the lowest part outside smth.: I stood there at the bottom of the steps. 2. in the part farthest from the front: The poor relations were seated at the bottom of the long table. 3. being the real cause of smth. undesirable: Greed lies at the bottom of our ecological predicament.

in the bottom of something—in the lowest part inside smth.: The fish we had caught were flopping about in the bottom of the boat.

at the bottom of the bag • at the bottom of the barrel

at the bottom of the bag—(also: in the bottom of the bag) remaining as a last resource or possibility: If there's one small favour left at the bottom of the bag, clean-slate my bank account and credit history please.

at the bottom of the barrel—(also: in the bottom of the barrel) among the worst or the least desirable elements of a group: Corporations that don't have time to deal with these issues will find themselves at the bottom of the barrel.

at the conclusion • in conclusion

at the conclusion—at the finish of an event or activity: At the conclusion they remarked that it was a useful exercise and perhaps should happen more often.

in conclusion—1. finally; in the end: He changed sides so often, that in conclusion no side trusted him. 2. to sum up: In conclusion, everybody has his own ways of expressing emotions. In any case we should not let our rage out.

at the conference • in conference

at the conference—1. in the course of the conference: A good deal of discussion at the conference has been about pluralism. 2. attending the conference: The gays at the conference were all people who had "come out"—that is, openly declared themselves to be homosexual.

in conference—busy at a meeting to discuss smth. or exchange views: He went to see the managing editor, but Percy was in conference with the publisher.

at the cutting edge of something • on the knife-edge of something

at the cutting edge of something—(also: on the cutting edge of something) involved in the most advanced developments in a particular field: It is unrealistic to expect to be at the cutting edge of the fashion industry for anything longer than fifteen years.

on the knife-edge of something—(also: on the razor's edge of something) on the brink of smth. bad or dangerous: The expansion of trade hasn't closed the gap between those who live on the cutting edge of the global economy and the billions who live on the knife-edge of survival.

at the depth of something • in the depth of something

at the depth of something—at a specified distance from the top down: At the depth of 180 feet, at what was called the third gallery, the width of ore was, as I have said, 45 feet.

in the depth of something—1. in the deepest or most central part of smth.: In the depth of the valley, there is a lochan (the diminutive of loch) of superlative beauty. 2. in the middle of the winter or night (when the cold or darkness is most intense): In the depth of winter it is quite enough to fire up twice in the twenty-four hours.

at the end of something • in the end of something

at the end of something—1. in the farthest or last part of smth.: The player tries to catch with his teeth a cherry suspended at the end of a string. 2. at the finish of an event or activity: The audience gave him a big hand at the end of the performance. 3. at the conclusion of a period: The fully anglicized spelling *genteel* came in at the end of the 17th century.

in the end of something—1. = *at the end of something 1:* I adjusted the knot in the end of the rope to be as a small as possible and as close to the end of the rope as possible. 2. = *at the end of something 3:* The latter pronunciation appears to have been the only one in common use in the end of the 18th century.

at the end of the day • late in the day

at the end of the day—(coll.) after one has considered all the relevant facts: The question at the end of the day is whether the house is actually worth that amount.

late in the day—1. said of an action taken somewhat late and consequently not fully effective: It's a little late in the day to start talking about policy changes. 2. eventually; at almost the last possible time: It was the pensioners' vote late in the day which influenced the election of Mr. Simmons.

at the feet of someone • at the foot of something

at the feet of someone—on the floor in front of a person, especially to show homage: One of the lay-followers threw her a cloak and ... she prostrated at the feet of the Buddha.

at the foot of something—at the bottom of hills and mountains: The city stretches out at the foot of the mountain, low houses dwarfed by the immensity of the snowcapped peak.

at the front • on the front

at the front—1. *(also: in front)* in the position nearest to the front part of smth.: A loudspeaker system is a box with a grille at the front through which the sound comes. 2. fighting as a member of the armed forces in a war: Women must keep the home industries going for the boys who were fighting at the front.

on the front—1. on the foremost or most important side of smth.: The label on the front of the packet lists the actual net weight. 2. = *at the front* 2. While the Austrian troops were falling back in collapse, German formations on the front retreated with discipline.

at the heart of something • in the heart of something

at the heart of something—at the basis of smth.: The two-stage module is at the heart of the plans to land two men on the moon.

in the heart of something—in the central part of smth.: The Verbas, another Bosnian river, rises in the heart of the country.

at the least • in the least

at the least—(also: at least) 1. at all events; anyway: The process looks rather laborious but at the least it is not dangerous. 2. not less than: At the least a dozen ideas were considered and rejected.

in the least—(negat.) to the smallest degree: So long as the noise is satisfactory the musical quality does not trouble him in the least.

at the market • in the market • on the market

at the market—1. offered for sale: The fact that the wheat from the new crops appeared at the market, allowed to bring down its deficit. 2. *(Stock Exchange)* at the current market price: I never buy at the market. My orders are always a point or two under the market price.

in the market—1. = *at the market 1:* A substance from New York has lately made its appearance in the market under the name of butterine. 2. *(for)* trying to obtain smth. specified: Not everybody watching the advertisement is in the market for our products.

on the market— = *at the market 1:* This vaccine won't be on the market for another six months.

at the maximum • to the maximum

at the maximum—is used of the largest possible quantity: The regiment represents around 500 men at the maximum.

to the maximum—to the greatest degree possible: We must exploit tactical surprise to the maximum.

at the minimum • to the minimum

at the minimum—1. at least the amount or number specified: They could accommodate 100 booths, 50 at the minimum. 2. at the very least: At the minimum we would be under pressure to reveal the names.

to the minimum—to the smallest degree possible: Delay in the hearing of cases should be reduced to the minimum.

at the outside • on the outside

at the outside—as the highest possible figure: This woman is young, I suppose at the outside not thirty.

on the outside—1. on the outer surface: Make sure the contents are clearly labeled on the outside. 2. *(sl.)* out of prison: The funny thing is—on the outside, I was an honest man. I had to come to prison to be a crook.

at the ready • in readiness

at the ready—(of a weapon) in readiness for immediate use: He stalked along, one hand swinging free, the other with his machete held at the ready.

in readiness—1. in a ready or prepared state: Stacks of "no parking" cones were dotted in readiness round the village. 2. ready or prepared to do smth.: The admiral gave orders for the troops to be in readiness to land.

at the rise • on the rise

at the rise—at the start of smth.; at an early stage in smth.: The book portrays American cities at the rise of industrialism.

Note: *The expression does not correlate in meaning with the phrase* ***at rise****—(Theater) when the rising curtain discloses a scene:* At rise we see an interview room with a desk and simple furnishings.

on the rise—1. on the increase: The stealing of intellectual property is on the rise. 2. *(of prices)* going up: Now, with an improving economy, gas prices are on the rise.

at the same time • in the same time

at the same time—1. in addition; as well: The method reduced the cost of processing information and at the same time accelerated the speed of producing data. 2. at the same moment; simultaneously: The same stock may be quoted at the same time in the exchange markets of distant places. 3. nevertheless *(is used to express reservation):* That's all fine and well, but at the same time it seems increasingly unlikely that we will achieve these goals.

in the same time—taking the same amount of time: This explains why a planet travels from point A to point B in the same time that it takes to cover the much shorter span between C and D.

at the side of someone • on the side of someone

at the side of someone—(coll.) compared with another person: She is quite clever at the side of other girls.

on the side of someone—giving support to smb. in a conflict, etc.: Despite Callas' harsh nature, she was always on the side of her students.

at the side of something • on the side of something

at the side of something—situated or placed beside smth.: He fancied he heard the tramp of a troop of horse at the side of the wood.

on the side of something—1. = *at the side of something:* As I was driving I passed the car on the side of the road again. This time the lights were not on. 2. on the side surface of smth.: The Stock Exchange waiter strikes three strokes with a mallet on the side of a rostrum before making formal declaration. 3. supporting smth.; in favor of smth.: Normally, and as a whole, human law is on the side of divine order.

at the sight of someone • in the sight of someone

at the sight of someone—on seeing a person: Does running away at the sight of the police give officers reason enough to stop and search you on the street?

in the sight of someone—1. near enough to be seen by a person: He was brutally killed in the sight of the townspeople. 2. in a person's opinion; as regarded by smb.: In the sight of the world, they were a happily married couple.

at the start • to start with

at the start—(also: at the beginning) initially; at first: At the start he was merely an incompetent abroad, but being a man of intelligence he adapted quickly.

to start with—(also: to begin with) 1. as a first consideration; most importantly: Kurosawa's tale wasn't all that original to start with—it was lifted from Hammet's Red Harvest. 2. = *at the start:* To start with, she was both advising customers and working on the counter but she quickly progressed to concentrate on providing advice.

at the time of something • in the time of something

at the time of something—at the particular point of time: I was in India at the time of my father's death.

in the time of something—(also: in the times of something) during the period associated with smth.: The payment of annates had originated in the time of the crusades.

at the top of the heap • on top of the world

at the top of the heap—(also: at the top of the tree) 1. as high as possible in one's career or profession: Regardless of who is at the top of the heap in our government we are still the most diverse nation. 2. of the highest rank within a group of items: At the top of the heap are private colleges and universities such as Yale, Williams and Harvard which are world renowned.

on top of the world—extremely happy: I was on top of the world and it seemed like just the beginning of a long and glorious career.

at the top of the tree • up a tree

at the top of the tree—(also: at the top of the heap) 1. as high as possible in one's career or profession: You're asking us to believe that a man right at the top of his particular tree, is going to commit forgery. 2. of the highest rank within a group of items: You may be selling products on behalf of another company, or you might be the company at the top of the tree...

up a tree—1. *(coll.)* in trouble or difficulty *(also: up a gum-tree):* The news that no hotel accommodations were obtainable left me rather up a tree. 2. *(sl.)* alcohol intoxicated: Only two glasses of booze and he was up a tree for sure.

***Note:** a) The expression does not correlate in meaning with the phrase **up the pole**—(sl.)* 1. *(UK) confused or muddled:* The Pope told Galileo that he was up the pole for pretending the world was round. 2. *(Irish) pregnant:* "Is she up the pole?" "Better ask Seymour that."

*b) The expression is not antonymous in meaning to the phrase **out of one's tree**—(sl.) crazy; lacking common sense:* I do believe that Bill was out of his tree when he made this decision.

at the trail • on the trail

at the trail—(Military) carrying a rifle in the right hand, the arm at full length, and the gun horizontal: The volunteers are in step, rifles are carried uniformly horizontal at the "trail."

on the trail—1. following a path in a wild or uninhabited region: In discrete valleys were a few cabins, and they stayed in them or *siwashed* (camped on the trail). 2. following traces or tracks in hunting: Jacob's dog leads them into the woods on the trail of a fox, and there they come upon the wreckage of a small plane. 3. following smb.; in pursuit of a person: The police are on the trail of a group of Satanists, believed to have caused a young man's death.

at the utmost • to the utmost

at the utmost—(also: at the most) not more than the number or amount specified: The administration has promised to spend one billion dollars at the utmost on the operation.

to the utmost—to the highest possible degree: The land and the sea were exploited to the utmost for the islanders' subsistence.

at the view of someone • in the view of someone

at the view of someone—at the sight of smb.; on seeing a person: He tried not to laugh out loud at the view of his son dressed like a woman.

in the view of someone—1. near enough to be seen by smb.: She stood in the view of everybody and uttered that strange prediction. 2. in the opinion of a person: In the view of the magistrate, the offence was not a serious one.

at the view of something • with the view of something

at the view of something—at the sight of smth.; on seeing smth.: As you step into the courtyard you are amazed at the view of the trees, grass and flowers.

with the view of something—for the purpose of doing smth.: He commenced a tour of the continent, with the view of acquiring a knowledge of European life.

See also: in view of something / on view of something.

at this minute • this minute

at this minute—(also: at the minute) at present; just now: She's feeding the baby at this minute.

this minute—at once; immediately: You don't have to make a decision this minute.

at this time • this time

at this time—at present; now: A local man is under suspicion but there isn't enough evidence to justify an arrest at this time.

***Note:** The expression is not equivalent in meaning to the phrase **at this time of day**— in present circumstances; when things have reached the stage they now have:* It's no good changing our minds at this time of day; we ought to have done that before.

this time—on this occasion: With the new scroll placed on the bulletin board, all may see who made the honor roll this time.

at work • in work

at work—1. at one's place of employment: He's at work now, but he'll be back at six. 2. engaged in a particular activity: The poor woman was still hard at work at an ironing-table. 3. having a particular influence or effect: The same disastrous processes are at work in the whole of this area.

in work—1. having employment: He has been out of work for a year. He'll be glad to be in regular work again. 2. in process of preparation or completion: The company has three films in work right now. 3. *(of a horse)* in training: I had two horses in work during November and December.

***Note:** a) The expression does not fully correlate in meaning with the phrase **in the works**— = in work 2:* A plan of reorganization is reported to be now in the works.

*b) The expression does not correlate in meaning with the phrase **in labor**—experiencing the pains and efforts of childbirth:* Vane had been in labor for eight hours before her twin daughters were finally born.

attach oneself to someone • attach to someone

attach oneself to someone—associate with a person; become smb.'s constant companion: Fred seems to have attached himself to a much older woman.

attach to someone—(of blame, fault, etc.) become fixed onto a person: A lot of guilt attaches to Henry for his part in the plot.

attached home • semi-detached house

attached home—(U.S.) a house attached to another house on the other side of the shared wall: One son lives in an attached home adjacent to our home.

semi-detached house—(UK) = attached home: What are people's experiences of having a piano in a semi-detached house? Does it depend on how thin the walls are?

attempt at something • attempt on something

attempt at something—an effort to do smth.: This publication is the first attempt at a representation of our knowledge about vitamins and avitaminoses.

attempt on something—1. an act of trying to accomplish smth. difficult: When he makes his next attempt on the world's record, he will be using a "jet-propelled" speed-boat. 2. *(in the phrase "attempt on someone's life")* an act of trying to kill smb. *(usually of an unseccessful attack or assault):* Musharraf survived a second attempt on his life when attackers rammed a car bomb into his motorcade.

attend on someone • attend to someone

attend on someone—1. act as a servant; carry out smb.'s wishes: A king would have as many as one hundred people attending on him. 2. give personal help to smb. (as a nurse, doctor, etc.): Jane has been attending on her sick mother for years.

attend to someone—1. give one's attention to smb.: Attend to me, children, I shan't repeat these instructions. 2. = *attend on someone* 2: She was attending to her sick grandmother when her father came to the door.

attend something • attend to something

attend something—1. go to or be present at an event: Prince Harry attended the ceremony along with other members of the Royal Family. 2. go regularly to an institution such as a school, etc.: As a child, he attended church services with his parents. 3. occur along with smth.: In contrast to the air of celebration which usually attended the sailings of these supertankers, there was an air of gloom.

attend to something—(also: tend to something) take care of smth.; deal with smth.: They ought to attend to the business without unnecessary delay.

attract someone's attention • draw someone's attention

attract someone's attention—get the attention of a person: She spoke loudly to attract everyone's attention.

draw someone's attention—make a person especially aware of smth.: The judge drew the attention of the jury to this detail.

au fait • in fact

au fait—(Fr., UK) familiar with something: We deem it's important that you be au fait with another concept.

in fact—in reality; actually: In fact, it was a wonder anyone survived in the circumstances.

aural signal • oral signal

aural signal—a signal perceived by the ear: Where an aural signal is used in a building security system, a corresponding visual signal must be provided.

oral signal—a signal transmitted by speech: They need to be able to communicate with the minimum of oral signals when the engine is running.

Austral English • Australian English

Austral English—the variety of English spoken by most inhabitants of Australia and New Zealand: The term Austral English is sometimes used to cover the language of the whole of Australasia.

***Note:** The expression does not correlate in meaning with the phrase **Austral language**—the language of the Austral Islands (an archipelago in the South Pacific inhabited by Polynesians):* The origin of the Khasis is still an enigma.... Their language is considered a branch of austral languages.

Australian English—the variety of English spoken by most inhabitants of Australia: There is Australian English, and American English, and Indian English — recognizable ... as a matter of idiom and accent.

autograph book • autographed book

autograph book—a book in which signatures of famous people are collected: As I turn the pages of my autograph book now, each name encapsulates its own little bit of history.

autographed book—a book bearing the author's own signature: In this first edition autographed book, Eugene Cernan describes his personal involvement in mankind's reach for the moon.

autographed copy • autographic copy

autographed copy—a copy of a book, etc. signed by the author: On the day of its publication, Hank had gone jubilantly to Isobel's back door, armed with an autographed copy for her and her husband.

autographic copy—the original copy written by the author: The Library of Congress houses the autographic copy of the Declaration of Independence with corrections by Thomas Jefferson himself.

avenge oneself on someone • avenge someone

avenge oneself on someone—(also: revenge oneself on someone) get even with a person in return for an offence or injury inflicted on oneself: He has avenged himself on those who betrayed him.

avenge someone—(also: revenge someone) get satisfaction for an offence or injury done to another person: If Hamlet wants to avenge his father, what stands in his way?

avoid arrest • evade arrest

avoid arrest—escape being arrested: The government failed to prove that he left Montana with the intent to avoid arrest or prosecution.

evade arrest—escape being arrested, especially for a prolonged period, by cleverness, deceit, etc.: The two men have managed to evade arrest but they have done so in different ways.

B

babe in Christ • child of God

babe in Christ—a newly-made convert to Christianity: Suppose a new Christian man comes from a not so ideal background, and there are elders that are not willing to deal with this babe in Christ.

child of God—1. *(also: God's child)* a human being born of God, that is by God's creation: The meanest peasant felt himself ennobled as a child of God. 2. a member of the untouchable class in Hindu society: She decided he was a Harijan, a child of God, an untouchable.

baby blue-eyes • blue-eyed babies

baby blue-eyes—a delicate California herb *(Nemophila menziesii)* having blue flowers with dark spots: Baby Blue Eyes. This beautiful porcelain blue flower is as delicate as its name.

blue-eyed babies—the plants *Houstonia patens* and *Houstonia caerulea:* The names for the starry *Houstonia* are so charming one scarcely knows which to choose. Blue-eyed Babies, Quaker Ladies, Angel Eyes...

***Note:** The expression does not correlate in meaning with the phrase **blue-eyed boys**—people singled out for special favors by smb. in authority:* During this difficult period, farmers were "blue-eyed boys."

baby-minder • babysitter

baby-minder—a woman who takes small children into her own home and looks after them while their parents are at work: The art of conversation cannot be acquired when eating a solitary television supper with the baby-minder.

babysitter—a woman who goes to smb. else's home to look after small children while their parents are at work: Can't you find a babysitter and come over for dinner.

back bench, the • back seat

back bench, the—1. *(UK Parliament)* members who do not

hold office: Those who sit on the back benches are members of the governing party who are not ministers. These members are known collectively as the back bench. 2. *(U.S. Congress)* new members of Congress considered as a group: Reform often comes from the back bench in Congress. Junior members have the least to lose and the shortest (and usually cleanest) records.

back seat—(in the phrase "take a back seat") a subordinate or less important position: Serious writing took hold of my life when I was in my teens, but with a long work schedule it took a back seat.

back drop • backdrop

back drop—a trampoline stunt in which from a bounce a gymnast lands on his back and then rebounds to an erect position: When doing a back drop it is very easy for the recoil of the bed to bring you back up to your feet.

backdrop—1. a cloth hung across the rear of a stage to serve as scenic background: The vast shuffle area is a stage, with theatrical lighting and backdrops rising as high as 85 feet. 2. the appropriate atmosphere for an event; the setting within which smth. is viewed: Indochina is the backdrop for this tensely written story.

See also: drop back / drop behind.

back-fire • fire back

back-fire—1. *(of an engine)* undergo a mistimed explosion in the cylinder with a loud noise: Some engines have a nasty tendency to back-fire. 2. *(of firearms)* explode: He was held liable for allowing an unqualified teacher to supervise a shooting competition during which a rifle backfired and injured a student. 3. light a fire ahead of an advancing prairie-fire in order to stop it: Man learned to back-fire, so but very few settlers lost their lives from prairie-fires. 4. *(of a plan, etc.)* have the opposite effect to what was intended: One of McGraw's schemes back-fired on him.

fire back—1. return gunfire: Hanson switched the Schmeisser regulator to single-shot and started to fire back. 2. = *back-fire 1:* If engine fires back into carburetor, do a few smooth injections with the primer pump.

back in the saddle • back on track

back in the saddle—back in a position of leadership or authority: After having been out of office for two years, Governor Jones won the election and was back in the saddle.

back on track—back to one's normal activities: A view of the San Francisco skyline, freshly showered and sparkling, unfolded. I was back on track, both literally and figuratively.

back-light • background light

back-light—(Photography) illumination of the subject from behind to produce a highlight along its edge: Halo is the effect obtained in portraiture when a strong back-light is used.

background light—(Photography) illumination of a set or background: One 250-watt bulb is capable of giving enough background light for a whole room.

back off from something • back out of something

back off from something—withdraw from smth. one has promised or agreed to do: Schultz continues to resent Syria's backing off from a peace agreement.

back out of something—1. move out of smth. backwards: He slowly backed out of the room keeping his eye on the angry dog all the time. 2. = *back off from something:* Buying at auction can be risky, in part because buyers can't back out of the sale.

back to basics • back to square one

back to basics—returning to the previously held fundamental principles: In her quest to shape up, Rebekah shunned weight loss clinics and fad diets, instead opting for a back-to-basics approach.

back to square one—returning to the starting-point of an experiment, etc. because of failure or lack of progress: He put forward this analysis of the latest development: "We are back to square one."

back to the drawing-board • back to the salt mines

back to the drawing-board—dealing with the same matter again (because smth. has gone wrong): They make presentations and if the proposal is rejected, it is back to the drawing board.

back to the salt mines—returning to one's work or another duty which might be hard or unpleasant: I'd better get back to the salt mines. I've got a lot of unfinished jobs.

backbite someone • bite something back

backbite someone—slander the reputation of smb. who is absent: People will backbite one another to any extent rather than not be amused.

bite something back—hold back a remark one was about to make: She wanted to tell him her real feelings, but she bit the words back.

backtrack on something • track back to something

backtrack on something—reverse one's position or policy, especially as a result of other people's opposition: He has backtracked on what he told the public during his campaign.

Note: *The expression does not correlate in meaning with the phrase* ***be back on track****— return to one's normal activities:* Within a few months, she was back on track, selling to Canadian shops through a distributor.

track back to something—follow smth. back to its source: We will need to be able to track back to key decisions, and understand why and how they were made.

backwoodsman • woodsman

backwoodsman—1. a settler in the uncleared forest land: It is this which gives that piquancy to the conversation of a backwoodsman. 2. is used of a rough, uneducated person: He sounded like a backwoodsman even in high hat. 3. *(UK)* a member of the House of Lords who rarely attends that body: This speech will encourage the backwoodsmen in the House of Lords to take strong action.

woodsman—(also: woodman) a person who works or hunts in the woods: By nature he was a woodsman and spent most of his time roaming the forests in search of game.

bad apple • bad egg

bad apple—(coll.) a single bad person in a group *(also: rotten apple):* Maybe she was the bad apple of the department, so I made an appointment to meet with another woman.

bad egg—(coll.) a bad or despised individual *(also: rotten egg):* Billy was a bad egg and spent most of his time trying to deceive the villagers. *Cf.: good egg—(coll.) a proper and decent person:* Despite what most people around here think, I think George is a good egg.

bad blood • fresh blood

bad blood—enmity or bitterness among individuals or groups of people: He likewise said that prior to July 14, there was no bad blood between him and the victim.

fresh blood—new members of a group who are likely to have new ideas: It has been nine years since the last Supreme Court vacancy, and the court is in need of fresh blood.

bad boy • bad man

bad boy—(also: Peck's bad boy) 1. an unruly or mischievous child: He was not a bad boy, but he did have one problem: he refused to brush his teeth. 2. an adult person defying the accepted moral or artistic conventions: Michael was the bad boy who stole Tara's heart and eloped with her.

bad man—1. a morally depraved, wicked man: He resented the fact that his mother had to be living with such a bad man as Khun Chang. 2. *(U.S. coll.)* a gunman; a villain: He even appointed a typical "bad man"—that is, manslayer—to office as a proof of his fondness for Arizona.

Badlands, the • badlands

Badlands, the—(U.S.) the barren waste region in South Dakota: Until recently, buffalo had roamed the Badlands.

badlands—barren terrain where soils have been eroded by wind and water: Ground is carved by rain-wash producing an almost impassable surface generally referred to as "badlands."

bad loser • two-time loser

bad loser—a person who loses a game in poor spirit: We could say Rhydian was a bad loser, but then again we could say that Leon was a bad winner.

two-time loser—1. a contestant who loses twice: "Two-time nominee" sounds so much nicer than the alternative—two-time loser—doesn't it? 2. *(sl.)* a twice-convicted criminal: Madill was a two-time loser who did time in prison for burglary. He carried the gun everywhere.

bad money • bad penny, a

bad money—a forged currency: "To ring the changes" in low life means to change bad money for good.

Note: *The expression does not fully correlate in meaning with the phrase* **good money**—1. *money that is genuine, not counterfeit:* They've got some good money, as well as bogus notes. 2. *a fairly large amount of money:* But for his inherent meanness, he would have gladly paid good money to be rid of her.

bad penny, a—an objectionable person or thing that can be counted upon to reappear *(in allusion to the saying "a bad penny always turns up"):* I persevered ... to disuade the dog from darkening my door again but little did I realise at the time, this was a bad penny we were dealing with.

Note: *a) The expression is not antonymous in meaning to the phrase* **pretty penny, a**—*a fairly large amount of money:* You can expect these tape decks to cost a pretty penny, although no price has been set as of yet.

b) The expression is not antonymous in meaning to the phrase **honest penny, an**—*money gained or earned by fair means:* I, then a mere stripling, was trying to make an honest penny by selling homemade candy.

bad money drives out good • bad penny always turns up, a

bad money drives out good—(saying) worthless people or things supplant more valuable: The drain of human resources is one example where "bad money drives out good."

Note: *The expression does not correlate in meaning with the phrase* **throw good money after bad**—*waste more money or supplies in hopes of recouping previous losses:* Creating another failing system to replace the current one is throwing good money after bad.

bad penny always turns up, a—(saying) a worthless person always returns: "What if I never see him again?" "Don't worry. A bad penny always turns up."

bad mouth • foul mouth

bad mouth—1. a curse or spell: I have known of people that have had the record of saying that they could put a bad mouth on you. 2. malicious gossip: Companies don't want people telling their friends about shoddy products. Word of bad-mouth can kill them. 3. a person who speaks ill of people: The world is filled with bad-mouths. We need more caring people.

foul mouth—(also: dirty mouth) a person who uses obscene or abusive language habitually: Terry is turning into a real foul mouth.

bad news • what's the bad news

bad news—(U.S. coll.) said of things, people, or places that are unpleasant or undesirable: Milly these days was plain bad news. Her fascination had evaporated.

what's the bad news—(U.S. joc.) what do I owe: After the clerk had run up all of the clothing Meg had selected, her mother nervously asked what the bad news was.

bad quarter of an hour • good quarter of an hour

bad quarter of an hour—a brief but disagreeable and unnerving period: He had a very bad quarter of an hour. I never knew a man have such hard luck at cards.

good quarter of an hour—not less than a quarter of an hour: He spoke for a good quarter of an hour, walking me through the history of mankind.

bad time • bad times

bad time—1. wrong or unsuitable time: This would be a very bad time to pull our exhaustion on our readers. 2. time when life is difficult: Julia went through a pretty bad time after the accident—seeing psychiatrists and what have you.

bad times—a period of poverty or economic depression: England will not long endure the rulers which these bad times have assigned her.

bag of wind • windbag

bag of wind—(coll.) a talkative, usually pompous person who has little to say: She's nothing but a big bag of wind.

windbag—1. a bag of air as of a bagpipe: The anatomical structure of the sonorous organs of these *Cicadae* did not exactly resemble the wind-bag. 2. = *bag of wind:* He is at best a noisy, pompous wind-bag and braggart. 3. a kind of fish which inflate their bodies when stimulated by fear, etc.: When it [blowfish] is hooked it inflates itself to many times its normal size. Among its aliases are balloon-fish, puffball and wind-bag.

ball is in someone's court, the • have the ball at one's feet

ball is in someone's court, the—is used to say that another person must make the next move: Addison tells him that the ball is in his court. All he has to do is sign the divorce papers and she will too.

have the ball at one's feet—be in a strategically advantageous position: The working class militants have the ball at their feet, as never before.

bang on the door • bang the door

bang on the door—knock on the door violently (with one's fist, etc.): The boys used to bang on the door with sticks.

bang the door—close the door violently so that it makes a loud noise: Mr. Talboys strode out of the room, banging the door after him.

bar girl • bar maid

bar girl—1. a woman who serves drinks at a bar: In her early adulthood, Meili worked as a bargirl in order to pay off debts. 2. *(sl.)* a woman employed by a bar to act as a companion to men customers *(also: B-girl):* The soft purring caresses and total availability of the bar-girls must have seemed irresistible.

bar maid— = *bar girl 1:* A few evenings a week she works as a bar maid in a local pub in Glasgow.

bargain counter • bargaining counter

bargain counter—an area in a store where the goods are sold at cut price: You need to be very careful not to be taken in by the bargain counters in some stores. Very often they're full of shoddy goods.

bargaining counter—a special advantage in negotiations: The de facto occupation of parts of the Russian zone was an important bargaining counter for obtaining satisfaction from the Soviet Government on a number of questions.

bargain on something • bargain over something

bargain on something—count on smth.; depend on smth.: Frankly, I did bargain on Fred's resigning the position.

bargain over something—(also: bargain for something) negotiate about obtaining smth.: We will bargain with the supplier over prices.

barge in on someone • barge into someone

barge in on someone—come rudely into a place and interrupt people in their activities: Albert barged in on Ted without knocking.

barge into someone—1. bump into smb., usually by accident: She just barged into me and nearly knocked me over. 2. meet a person by chance: I barged into him opposite the Old Ship, and I told him about our air-raid.

bark at the moon • cry for the moon

bark at the moon—do smth. which has no effect: If other nations don't adopt similar measures to protect blue sharks, we're just barking at the moon.

cry for the moon—demand smth. impossible: To ask for the matter to be settled by a General Council is to cry for the moon.

base light • basic light

base light—(Photography) diffuse, uniform studio illumination approaching a shadowless condition: In some cases you may want to use a low-level base light.

basic light—(Photography) illumination using the concept of one main light: In addition to the basic light with a simple on/off button, there are also the dimmer switch lights.

Basic English • basic English

Basic English—an essential English vocabulary used for teaching purposes: Basic English is a system in which 850 English words do all the work of over 20,000.

basic English—1. English using few and simple words: I'd picked up a touch of "la tourism" or in basic English, the runs, from the unwashed fruit. 2. *(sl.)* English using vulgar and obscene words: He, Happy, himself no slouch at basic English, was revolted by George's language.

Note: *Neither expression correlates in meaning with the acronym* ***BASIC****—(****B****eginners'* ***A****ll-purpose* ***S****ymbolic* ***I****nstruction* ***C****ode) a computer language using simple English:* When you received your computer a language called BASIC was possibly supplied on a disk.

batman • batsman

batman—a British military officer's personal servant: He told of how his batman mended his clothes; prepared his food; seemed always able to provide him with small comforts.

batsman—a baseball or cricket player who bats: In front of the opposite wicket, there's a player from the opposing team (the "batsman").

be a back seat driver • be in the back seat

be a back seat driver—suggest unwanted advice; tell a person in charge how to do his job: It is always easy to criticize and be a back seat driver.

be in the back seat—(also: take a back seat) take a subordinate position: Dad is now in the back seat. Jonathan is in control of the Rowland Capital family trust.

be a bad life • live a bad life

be a bad life—be not likely to live long enough: Elizabeth all her days was reckoned a "bad life."

live a bad life—lead a life of wickedness or immorality: He is leaving a bad life and should be kept away from the young.

be a bomb • be the bomb

be a bomb—(coll.) be a failure or fiasco: Unfortunately, the film was a bomb and gained a reputation as being the only film on which Mr. Corman lost money.

be the bomb—(U.S. sl., sometimes spelled "be da bomb") be very successful; be received enthusiastically: The show was the "bomb" back in the day when it first aired.

Note: *The expression does not correlate in meaning with the phrase* ***make a bomb****—(sl.) make or earn a great deal of money:* Many of them are too honest to do any [drug] trafficking but the ones that do make a bomb.

be a case in point • be the case

be a case in point—be a particular instance of smth.: People have changed their minds about the Common market, and Mr. Stonchouse is a case in point.

be the case—(often negat.) be a fact; be true: Please contact the rightful owner directly to confirm their interest to sell and if this is the case, to negotiate price.

be a close call • be too close to call

be a close call—(also: be a close shave) said of a dangerous situation that a person just manages to avoid: Though he escaped with his life and his job, it was a close call.

be too close to call—said of the outcome of a competition, etc. that is very hard to judge: The horses came to the finish line in a dead heat, and, without a photograph, the results were too close to call.

Note: *The expression does not correlate in meaning with the phrase* ***be too close to home****—(also: be too close for comfort) dangerously nearby; affecting a person intimately:* A crime that occurred too close to home still has its grip on Chief Inspector Alan Banks.

be a devil • be the very devil

be a devil—1. *(imper.)* is used as a humorous expression of encouragement to persuade a person to do smth.: Be a devil and order us a bottle of wine! 2. be extremely bad or immoral: He was a devil to those of us who thought the war was stupid and pointless. He personified the arbitrary power of the draft...

be the very devil—1. *(also: be the devil incarnate) = be a devil 2:* Though he was a hero to some, he was the very devil to others. 2. *(of a situation)* be very difficult or annoying: My car is super to drive, but it's so big it's the very devil to find a parking place for it.

be a drag on someone • have drag with someone

be a drag on someone—(sl.) be a burden to a person (causing delay or slowing down progress): His wife has been a drag on him all his life.

have drag with someone—(U.S. sl.) have influence over smb.: We had a big drag with the waiter because my old man drank whisky and that meant a good tip.

be a go-getter • have get up and go

be a go-getter—(UK coll.) be an ambitious and hard-working person: As it is a sales position, be sure to come off friendly and energetic like a real go-getter.

have get up and go—(coll.) 1. *(of people)* have vigor and energy: You need to demonstrate, through concrete examples, that you have "get up and go." 2. *(of horses and cars)* have sufficient energy or power, especially if old: The performance is sluggish but the car still has get up and go when you really need it.

be a good hand • have good hands

be a good hand—1. be a diligent, industrious worker: He is a good hand and enjoys his work which he does faithfully and well. 2. possess the necessary skill to do smth. well: He is a good hand at making bows and arrows, and a fine knife would be just the thing for him.

have good hands—(Sport) have the ability to throw a ball well: Chris has good hands, catches the ball well in traffic and is quick enough.

be a good life • live a good life

be a good life—be likely to live long enough: I want to find out if he is a good life to insure. Does he live temperately?

live a good life—lead a morally commendable life: I would like to be remembered as someone who lived a good life.

be a know-all • know it all

be a know-all—said of smb. who thinks he knows everything and annoys people by showing how clever he is: I don't see the point in arguing with someone who plays such a know-all.

know it all—1. be extremely knowledgeable; be fully informed: Did he choose the Pharisees and the Sadducees — the scribes and men who did nothing all day but study the scripture — men who knew it all? 2. is often used with the implication of overconfidence: The older I get, the more I realize that my dad really did know what he was talking about (but I was a young punk who "knew it all"...).

be a law unto oneself • take the law into one's own hands

be a law unto oneself—do what one believes is right and ignore established laws or custom: If the government becomes a law breaker it invites every man to become a law unto himself.

Note: *The expression does not correlate in meaning with the phrase* ***lay down the law****— assert smth. positively; state or declare smth. firmly:* The new basketball coach can recruit, teach and lay down the law, when necessary.

take the law into one's own hands—get justice in one's own way, without involving the police: These men took the law into their own hands. They killed a score of men who, they said, were outlaws of various kinds.

be a little short of something • be little short of something

be a little short of something—just barely fail to have the required amount of smth.: Mr. Rhodes was prevented from sailing for Europe owing to the fact that he was a little short of passage money.

be little short of something—(also: be nothing short of something) be the same as smth.; be nothing less than smth.: A mere look was enough to provoke him to anger that was little short of madness.

be a long day coming • it's going to be a long day

be a long day coming— said of smth. that has taken long to materialize: The team's achieving success by winning the division title has been a long day coming.

it's going to be a long day—1. said of a day perceived as long and boring: With nothing else to be done, and Steve's not arriving before seven, it was going to be a long day. 2. said of a day that is going to be full of troubles: Jack overslept and was stalled in a traffic jam. By the time he arrived at the office, he knew it was going to be a long day.

be a man of character • be quite the character

be a man of character—be a man of good repute: He was a man of character. He performed more acts of charity and kindness than any of us will ever know of.

be quite the character—used as a mild form of reproof or humorous admiration for a person showing independence in thoughts or actions: She is quite the character and always speaks her mind.

be a natural • be natural

be a natural—1. be naturally deficient in intellect; be a half-witted person: She is not quite a natural, that is, not an absolute idiot. 2. have natural talents that make smb. particularly suitable for a task: I'm not a natural. This present play is my last, I've decided.

be natural—demonstrate behavior that is not affected or self-conscious: On the stage he was natural, simple.... 'Twas only that, when he was off, he was acting.

Note: *The expression does not correlate in meaning with the phrase* ***be in one's natural state****—(also: be in a state of nature)* 1. *used of the conditions of people before civilization:* Man in his natural state is the work of God. 2. *(of land or animals) in an uncultivated or undomesticated condition:* The ground was partly cultivated, and partly left in its natural state. 3. *(euph.) completely naked:* How temptingly lovely she was in her natural state! I could not tear my eyes from her. 4. *(of substances) not treated or processed:* a large mass of stone or rock in its natural state; an egg in its natural state in the shell.

be a queer fish • be queer

be a queer fish—(also: be a queer bird) be an eccentric or odd person: He was a queer fish, but they were used to queer fish, and they took him for granted.

be queer—1. = *be a queer fish:* Every woman who steps forward to claim her rights faces the allegation that she is queer. 2. be a homosexual: I always thought he was queer. His roommate was gay and you just couldn't pull them away from each other.

be a sight for sore eyes • be a sight to behold

be a sight for sore eyes—said of a person or thing one is pleased or happy to see: MacLaine is quite a sight for sore eyes when she shows up in the movie.

Note: *The expression is not equivalent in meaning to the phrase* ***be eye candy****—1. be visually attractive:* We waited a little long for our food, and it did help that our waiter was eye candy. 2. *(Internet) used of extra graphics on a Web page that usually makes it look worse:* First I'm told that my site is too simple ... and then I'm told that my site has too much eye candy. *Cf.: be ear candy— said of music with an instant appeal but with little significance:* This is anything but ear-candy, and the music is meant to be listened to and savored many times.

be a sight to behold—1. = *be a sight for sore eyes:* The sunset on the horizon was a sight to behold. The soft glow of orange over the mountains was breath-taking. 2. look untidy, repulsive, or ridiculous: We soon arrived at the local abattoir, which was a sight to behold. Used to the clinical approach of the western world, we were stunned...

Note: *The expression does not fully correlate in meaning with the phrase* ***be a sight****— = be a sight to behold 2:* It was raining and lightning, I was crying, I was cold ... Believe me, I was a sight!

be a standoff • be standoffish

be a standoff—said of a situation in which the two sides in a conflict, etc. are equally matched or equally unyielding: There was a standoff for a few hours, while police spoke to the man urging him to give himself up.

be standoffish—said of a person who is reluctant to show

friendship or enter into conversation: They got on well for a few months, but now they hardly talk to each other, because Lily is so standoffish.

be a steady hand • have a steady hand

be a steady hand—be not given to frivolity, eccentricity, etc.: Thomas is a steady hand, never late for business, never out of temper...

have a steady hand—1. have a firm hand, one not shaky: Mr. Peterson still has a steady hand, shaving himself twice weekly. 2. *(usually of a leader)* be firm and consistent in one's behavior: He has a steady hand and will do an excellent job of guiding the division.

be about to • be not about to

be about to—be on the point of doing smth.: But just as he was about to say something, he forgot what it was he was about to say.

be not about to—1. be not going to do smth. soon: It seems that conventional teaching is not about to be supplanted by virtual universities. 2. *(U.S. coll.)* be unwilling to do smth.: "I'm sorry, I can't lend you the money. I may need it...." "Hey, why don't you just say that you're not about to."

be absent from something • be absent in something

be absent from something—*(of people)* be not present at a place: He is never absent from work without an excuse.

Note: *The expression is not equivalent in meaning to the phrase* ***absent oneself from something****— stay away from an event, etc.; avoid something:* I absented myself from the conversation at the next decent opportunity.

be absent in something—*(of things)* be missing in smth.: The impulsive type of noise (ignition interference and static) is generally absent in radar.

be afraid • be afraid, be very afraid

be afraid—1. be frightened or apprehensive about smth.: Willie recounted his life of drugs and violence in remorseless terms, and said he was not afraid to die. 2. feeling regret about smth.: Mary did not let me send the paper at first, she kept hoping it was a mistake, but I am afraid it is too true.

be afraid, be very afraid—*(imper.)* is used as a humorous cliché to say that smth. unwelcome is imminent: The reservation staff are friendly—but be afraid, be very afraid of the restaurant staff...

be against something • be up against something

be against something—express opposition to smth.: And even though no one in the audience was against the project, there was plenty of skepticism.

be up against something—*(also: come up against something)* encounter a serious obstacle or problem: But now we are up against a different kind of health concern—a potential pandemic. If the bird flu develops the ability to spread easily between humans it will be quite dangerous.

be all wet • be wet

be all wet—*(U.S. coll.)* be completely wrong: If you think I'm going to take that kind of talk from you, you're all wet.

be wet—*(UK coll.)* be unable to make decisions or take firm actions: Don't be so wet! Just tell them that you don't want to go.

Note: *Neither expression correlates in meaning with the phrase* ***be wet behind the ears****—(coll.) be young, naïve, and inexperienced:* For a twenty-five-year-old kid, still wet behind his ears, he got a lot of wisdom from somewhere. *Cf.: be dry behind the ears—be mature or experienced:* The three children, barely dry behind the ears, have taken over running the family dairy.

be ancient history • be history

be ancient history—said of a past event that has lost its original impact or importance: For today's high school students all of that war is ancient history.

be history—1. said of smb. whose career has been brought to an end: We are familiar with that reference: "He is history now," which condemns some poor individual to the rubbish bin of life. 2. = *be ancient history:* After reading the two latest reports, I have to wonder about Bishop Gregory's assertion that this scandal is history.

be assured of something • be sure of something

be assured of something—1. be guaranteed smth.: General Franks is assured of a place in history in a country where former officials are respected even when out of office. 2. have trust in smth.; be positive about smth.: The king was assured of the rectitude of the motives on which he had himself acted. 3. be firmly persuaded of smth.: In 1415, Hus was summoned to defend himself at the Council of Constance, having been assured of a safe conduct.

be sure of something—1. feel confident of smth.: If nothing occurs to stir the rage of this vindictive madman, I am sure of victory. 2. = *be assured of something 2:* The jury are told they cannot convict unless they are "sure" of the man's guilt.

be at each other's throats • cut each other's throats

be at each other's throats—be arguing violently; be very angry with each other: We cannot deal with tomorrow's problems if we are at each other's throats over economic issues.

cut each other's throats—harm each other's interests, especially because of fierce competition: They are cutting each other's throats in their eagerness to finish the work first.

be at loose ends • tie up loose ends

be at loose ends—*(also: be at a loose end)* 1. be without employment or fixed occupation: He was the only stranger in Cyprus who was thus at a loose end, as it were, and not on some professional duty. 2. be in an unsettled or uncertain situation: He's at loose ends. Hates his work, loathes his wife, and the kids bore him to death.

tie up loose ends—deal with some parts of work that have been left over: She spent the afternoon tying up loose ends: editing a feature on California Cuisine, making phone calls, answering memos.

Note: *The expression does not correlate in meaning with the phrase* ***make both ends meet****— live within one's means:* With a family becoming daily more expensive, the little book-keeper had found it hard work to make both ends meet.

be at rest • be resting

be at rest—1. be in a state of physical or mental repose: He sat in his chair, still, but not at rest: expectant evidently. 2. *(of an issue)* be settled or decided: I never can take any office under the present rulers; so that question is at rest. 3. *(euph.)* be dead and buried: He is now at rest after a full and dedicated life. We salute his extraordinary legacy...

be resting—1. *(euph., coll.)* be out of work: I am an interpreter.... At present I am resting. 2. *(of the body of a dead person)* remain at an undertaker's, a chapel, etc. before burial: Remains will be resting at the John Doe Funeral Home.

be at someone's service • be in someone's service

be at someone's service—1. be ready to help or assist a person: I am at your service whenever you should need my advice. 2. *(of things)* be at smb.'s disposal or ready to be used: My car is at your service to take you around Rome and its surroundings.

Note: The expression is not equivalent in meaning to the phrase ***be of service to someone****— be helpful to a person:* On many occasions he was of service to me, always in kindly, unobtrusive ways.

be in someone's service—be working as smb.'s domestic servant: Miss White has been in our service for five years.

be at the back of one's mind • cast one's mind back to something

be at the back of one's mind—(also: be in the back of one's mind) be vaguely aware of smth. that is not present in one's conscious thoughts: There was at the back of his mind an idea, dimly seen at moments, never wholly comprehended.

cast one's mind back to something—think about smth. that happened in the past, which one might not remember well: In order to understand these developments, it is necessary to cast back one's mind to the social attitudes of that period.

be at the crossroads • cross paths

be at the crossroads—be at a critical turning-point at which two or more courses of action are possible: Students are through with their exams and are now at the crossroads of a choice of career.

cross paths—meet or encounter a person: Occasionally they will cross paths, especially to compete in a nationally televised debate arranged by a non-partisan organization.

be aware of something • beware of something

be aware of something—have knowledge of smth.; be conscious of smth.: The government is already aware of an insufficient electricity supply.

beware of something—(imper.) be on guard against smth.: Beware of the rain ... make sure your camera is well-protected if in a side-pocket.

be bad form • be in bad form

be bad form—(of manners or behavior) be improper as judged by accepted social standards: It is considered bad form to arrive too early at a dinner party.

be in bad form—(Sport) be in bad condition of health and training: Even when Henin is in bad form, you need to have real smart strategy to beat her.

be beat • be beaten

be beat—(coll.) 1. *(also: be dead-beat)* be very tired; be utterly exhausted: I am beat from all this packing and moving of stuff. 2. be defeated in a competition: His team was beat because it failed to execute properly during the most critical moments of the game.

be beaten— = *be beat 2:* The moment was really amazing because Brazil, the champion, was beaten badly.

be bent on doing something • have a bent for something

be bent on doing something—be determined to do smth.; have the mind set on smth.: There is always a proportion of the crowd bent on harrying the speaker.

have a bent for something—have a natural interest and ability in a particular area: James, who had a bent for figures, took care of the financial end of the business.

be beside the mark • be off the mark

be beside the mark— be not relevant to the subject under discussion: We were discussing working conditions; his remarks about high rents were beside the mark.

be off the mark—1. *(also: be wide of the mark)* be inaccurate or erroneous in one's judgment: Sometimes he was off the mark. A lot of times he was just misunderstood. 2. starting smth. in response to a situation: The dog-breeder and poultry farmer were quick off the mark in using the new therapy.

Note: Neither expression correlates in meaning with the phrase ***fall short of the mark****—(also: come short of the mark) fail to attain some desired object:* Gilbert's efforts to amuse her often fell short of the mark.

be best at something • be the best at something

be best at something—be more skilled and capable in one particular area relative to others: He excels at most of the subjects taught here, although he is best at chemistry.

be the best at something—be much superior to other people in a particular area: Mrs. Hough is the best at making children feel at home when they are just starting out on their school adventure.

be beyond the law • go beyond the law

be beyond the law—be out of the reach of the law: The sick criminal was arrested at night, but by morning he was beyond the law; he had died in the night.

go beyond the law—be guilty of some criminal offence: To thrash the man yourself is to go beyond the law; he may deserve punishment but you are not allowed to administer it.

be blind to something • turn a blind eye to something

be blind to something—be unable to see or consider what is going on around one: She had been deaf and blind to everything except what had passed between them.

turn a blind eye to something—pretend not to see smth.; overlook smth. deliberately: The police turn a blind eye to this problem because they are only too glad to get lorries from parking there.

be born with a silver spoon in one's mouth • get the wooden spoon

be born with a silver spoon in one's mouth—be born into a rich family: He was born with a silver spoon in his mouth and probably never had to work a day in his life.

get the wooden spoon—be the last in a sporting event or other competition: Previous City Councilor got the wooden spoon — with no votes on the first two counts.

be bothered about someone • bother oneself about someone

be bothered about someone—be concerned about smb.; worry about a person: I am bothered about Freda, she is out so late again.

bother oneself about someone—concern oneself with smb.; preoccupy oneself with a person: Please don't bother yourself about my brother. I'll take care of him.

be canned • be in the can

be canned—(U.S. sl.) be expelled or dismissed from one's employment: When the coach was fired, some said he was canned for siding with John.

be in the can—(sl.) 1. *(of a movie, etc.)* be finished and ready: The scene was "in the can" after twenty-five retakes. 2. *(U.S.)* be in prison: I know that he spent two years in the can for armed robbery.

be carried away by something • be carried off by something

be carried away by something—become eager or enthusiastic about smth.: Roosevelt was carried away by the thought of another large relief project.

be carried off by something—(euph.) be killed (by a disease): Unhappily he never got to the Tradition meeting, he had been carried off by a heart attack.

be clear about something • be in the clear over something

be clear about something—understand smth. completely: Let us be clear about this: the pirates of 1964, like the pirates of old, are simply out after money.

be in the clear over something—be out of a difficulty or trouble caused by smth.: Is the Government in the clear yet over the composition of the committee?

be content with something • content oneself with something

be content with something—be satisfied with smth.; be willing to accept smth.: The questionnaire results showed that 98 percent of students were "content" with their housing situation.

content oneself with something—be satisfied with just one thing and not bother with other things: She hadn't said much but had contented herself with smoking cigarettes and smiling.

be crashed out of something • be crushed out of something

be crashed out of something—fail to perform well enough to stay in a competition: India's hopes of getting a further gold went up in smoke when Gopichand was crashed out of the men's quarter-finals.

be crushed out of something—be ousted of a business, etc.: Rockefeller would approach oil companies with two choices: either sell their company to him, or be crushed out of production.

be crowded out of something • crowd out of something

be crowded out of something—1. be forced out of premises for lack of room: They were crowded out of the room, but sat in the next peering in at the door eagerly. *2.* be ousted from an office, market, etc.: Low-skilled adults are often crowded out of their jobs as better-educated teenagers are drawn into the work force.

crowd out of something—go out of a place in a crowd: The crowd—mostly younger people—complained about the movie fiercely as they crowded out of the theater.

be cut out for the work • one's work is cut out for one

be cut out for the work—be entirely suited for some work or activity: There's no better way to tell if you're cut out for the work than hands-on experience.

one's work is cut out for one—(also: have one's work cut out for one) have a lot of work to do; have a hard task ahead: If you want to shatter the lake trout record, your work is cut out for you.

be dead in the water • sleep with the fishes

be dead in the water—(of a task, project, etc.) be unable to make progress; be a failure: Without an effective leader, our plans for expansion are dead in the water.

sleep with the fishes—(Underworld) be murdered and have the body disposed of *(also: swim with the fishes):* I think I could persuade you to cooperate. That is, unless you'd like to sleep with the fishes.

be dead nuts on something • be dead set on something

be dead nuts on something—1. *(coll.)* placed precisely on the surface of smth.: He caught me dead nuts on the chin, Pepe thought as he lay on the ground. 2. *(coll.)* exactly correspond to smth.: The styling of the new convertible is dead nuts on what a car in this class should be: bold and aristocratic. 3. *(sl.)* be very fond of smth.; be delighted with smth.: Quite frankly, I wasn't dead nuts on meeting with them.

be dead set on something—be fixed in one's purpose; be determined on doing smth.: The administration is dead set on trying to destroy unions. *Cf.: make a dead set at something—make a determined effort to gain smth.:* People can't be allowed to make a dead set at a property like this.

be death on someone • be the death of someone

be death on someone—(coll.) 1. be fatal to a person; be very effective in acting against smb.: The new teacher is death on students who come late to class. 2. be very fond of a person: Fanny hasn't forgotten you ... she was always death on you English chaps.

Note: *The expression does not correlate in meaning with the phrase* ***die on someone****—(also: go dead on someone)* 1. *die while in the charge or care of a person:* "I want to look after her while she's in England." "Suppose she died on you?" 2. *(of an apparatus, appliance, etc. in smb.'s care) break down; cease to function:* My car died on me, and I couldn't get it started.

be the death of someone—(coll.) 1. said of things (especially done repeatedly) which upset or irritate a person: Forty, if she's a day, wears pince-nez and an air of brisk efficiency that will be the death of me. 2. said of smb. who is exceptionally funny or ridiculous: Lili's capering seemed the funniest thing she had ever seen. "Stop, Lili, stop! You'll be the death of me!"

be down for something • be down to something

be down for something— said of a person or thing listed for some activity: Mr. Stansfield's bill was down for second reading on Wednesday.

be down to something—have only a little money or goods left: On the seventh day after the wreck, he was down to his last pint of water.

See also: be up for something / be up to something.

be dressed in rags • have the rags on

be dressed in rags—be dressed in old torn clothes: The work was carried out manually by wretched, scarecrow figures dressed in rags.

have the rags on—(sl.) 1. wear a special kind of clothes: He had the rags on, getting into character, and it just took me aback for a minute. *Cf.: have the glad rags on—wear one's best clothes or formal attire:* Having arrived it was time to get the glad rags on and go to dinner in the town. 2. *(also: have the rag on)* have one's menstrual period: Lana doesn't feel like going out tonight. She's got the rags on.

be empty-handed • have one's hands full

be empty-handed—1. having received or gained nothing: Due to three successive droughts, most farmers are empty-handed. 2. be unarmed: You will learn not only to use weapons, but also to defend against someone who has one while you are empty-handed.

have one's hands full—have much work to do; be very busy: The plumber had his hands full and could not take another job for two weeks.

be evident • be in evidence

be evident—be obvious; be easy to see or understand: It was evident to me that writing must be in God's great plan for my life.

be in evidence—1. be actually present: He was not about, so I looked outside, but he was not in evidence. He had not yet risen. 2. be prominent or conspicuous: He was not in evidence, to any considerable extent, in the voluntary societies of the college.

be eyeball to eyeball • see eye to eye

be eyeball to eyeball—1. sit opposite each other; be face to face: We're eyeball to eyeball and I think the other fellow just blinked. 2. be in the state of defiant confrontation: Once again, it seems, Mr. Rumsfeld and the defense bureaucracy are eyeball to eyeball.

see eye to eye—(often negat.) be of one mind; think alike: Unfortunately he didn't see eye to eye with his parents and there were always arguments at home.

be for sale • be on sale

be for sale—(also: be up for sale) said of a house, car, etc. that an owner wants to sell: I wonder how he heard the house was for sale.

be on sale—1. be available for buying in shops, etc.: Local delicacies, such as cheeses and wines, are on sale here at a very reasonable price. 2. be sold for a special low price: Tomato soup that is usually sold for sixty cents a can is now on sale for fifty cents.

be full of beans • not have a bean

be full of beans—(coll.) 1. be full of energy; be in high spirits: I had a good night's sleep in a hotel and was feeling very full of beans. 2. *(U.S. also: be full of prunes)* exaggerate or talk nonsense: While I often think that you are full of beans I have to say that I agree with much of this.

Note: *The expression is not antonymous in meaning to the phrase* ***not amount to a hill of beans****—(coll.) be of little significance:* What you learn at school doesn't amount to a hill of beans compared with what you can find out for yourself outdoors.

not have a bean—(coll.) have no money whatever: Lady Laura is always staying with people. She hasn't got a bean, I gather.

Note: *The expression does not correlate in meaning with the phrase* ***give someone beans****—(coll.) scold or punish a person severely:* He wanted to give me beans, but Florence wouldn't let him. She said "Father you are not to touch him."

be full of something • have one's fill of something

be full of something—have a large amount of smth.: These brave emigrants were full of hope for a better future.

have one's fill of something—have had enough of smth. such as food: You never know if Charlie has had his fill of liquor. 2. have more of smth. than a person can tolerate: We, like all Americans, have had our fill of senseless crime.

be gone on someone • have a go at someone

be gone on someone—(coll.) be enamored of or in love with a person: He is very gone on girls, is always falling in and out of love.

have a go at someone—(UK coll.) scold or criticize a person: Don't have a go at me — it's your fault we lost the contract.

Note: *The expression does not correlate in meaning with the phrase* ***have a go at something****—(coll.) try doing smth.:* I decided to have a go at the first few assignments and see what happened.

be good form • be in good form

be good form—behave according to custom or etiquette: It is not considered good form to arrive too early at a dinner party.

be in good form—1. *(Sport)* be in good condition of health and training: If a horse is in good form it is likely to win a race. 2. be in good spirits: On Sunday she was in good form and was doing housework. She wasn't in a huff or anything...

be green • be green around the gills

be green—1. be inexperienced: During his speech, Obama praised Bennet while acknowledging he is a bit green in politics.... 2. be environmentally friendly: These are also made with other recycled materials, so yes, they are very green in terms of helping the environment.

be green around the gills—(coll.) 1. look indisposed or unwell: She was green around the gills for several days. I also had a similar experience about five years ago.... 2. look as though one is about to be sick: The poor guy gets motion sickness and is green around the gills as soon as they take off.

be green-eyed • see green in someone's eye

be green-eyed—be jealous or envious: Collectors were green-eyed ... they consoled themselves by saying the collection had cost too much.

see green in someone's eye—think a person to be credulous and inexperienced: Do you see any green in my eye? Do you take me for a fool?

be had • be had up

be had—(coll.) be tricked or deceived: I apologize for being so forceful, but I've been had before; I don't want others to share the experience if I can help.

be had up—(coll.) cause a person to appear in court: I doubt if anybody thought about Chapman as a possible killer much before he was had up.

be hanged • be hung

be hanged—be put to death by hanging: Bentley's appeal against his conviction was dismissed and he was hanged in Wandsworth prison.

Note: *The expression does not correlate in meaning with the phrase* ***be left hanging****—1. (of people) be kept waiting for a decision or answer:* I was left hanging for three weeks before I got a call offering me the job. 2. *(of a decision, answer, etc.) be delayed or not dealt with:* The result is an alienated monologue in which comments are left hanging without response.

be hung—1. *(of paintings)* be exhibited in a gallery, etc.: The members of the Academy were granted the privilege of retouching their pictures after they were hung. 2. *(sl.)* feel annoyed: Fred is hung and looking for somebody to take it out on.

Note: *The expression does not correlate in meaning with the phrase* ***be well-hung****—1. (of meat or game) hung long enough to mature:* The grouse was well hung, and rare.... The meat had a clean taste set off by creamy avocado custard. 2. *(in the phrase "one's tongue is well hung") one is able to speak with ease:* Her tongue was well hung; but she must answer the questions he asked, and say nothing more. 3. *(coarse sl.) used of a man with large genitals:* For a boy of fifteen he was well-hung with a good crop of sandy pubic hair.

See also: be hung over / hang over.

be hardly out of the shell • come out of one's shell

be hardly out of the shell—be too young and inexperienced: You are hardly out of the shell and already you have the temerity to question the authority of the Talmud!

come out of one's shell—(also: crawl out of one's shell) become more sociable and outgoing: Under the soothing influence of coffee and tobacco, he came out of his shell. *Cf.: go into one's shell—(also: retire into one's shell) become shy, quiet, or reserved:* Every time the subject was raised, her son would go into his shell again.

Note: *The expression is not equivalent in meaning to the phrase* ***come out of the closet****—admit openly smth. previously kept secret because one is ashamed or embarrassed about it:* She has decided to come out of the closet today and discuss her life as lesbian.

be headstrong • have a strong head

be headstrong—be self-willed and obstinate: George Eliot's young country hero is headstrong and arrogant, and sees the world in black and white.

have a strong head—(coll.) be not easily intoxicated by liquor: I could drink as much as the best of them and I had, for such a youngster, a tolerable strong head.

Note: *a) Neither expression correlates in meaning with the phrase* ***be strong-minded****— be resolute and determined:* Everyone describes him in a similar way — to say that Clarence was strong minded, had a strong personality, was strong willed.

b) Neither expression is antonymous in meaning to the phrase ***be weak in the head****—(coll.) be mentally retarded (also: be soft in the head):* When he stopped speaking his mouth hung open ... I realized that he was weak in the head.

be heartless • not have the heart

be heartless—be callous, unfeeling, or cruel: He made up his mind that I was heartless and selfish.

not have the heart—(also: have no heart) 1. have no inclination or enthusiasm for smth.: It was the most miserable meal ... and I had not the heart to propose the Loyal Toast at the end. 2. be not cruel or courageous enough to do smth.: I should scold you but I am so glad to see you that I have not the heart.

be high as a kite • fly one's kite high

be high as a kite—(sl.) 1. be very excited or exhilarated: I was as high as a kite and full of the joys of spring. The day was good and getting better.... 2. be very drunk or affected by drugs: When I put you to bed you were high as a kite on vodka.

fly one's kite high—have high ambitions: Those who fly their kite too high may come to grief.

be hooked • go on the hook

be hooked—(sl.) 1. be very dependent or keen on smth.: We're not so hooked on the church, except for those born-again Christians. 2. be addicted to smth.: It's too depressing when you're hooked, besides a girl looks terrible on heroin. 3. be captivated or charmed: Let me tell you, she's really something. Oh, boy, was I hooked.

go on the hook—(U.S. sl.) get into debt: You'll go on the hook for one of those eighty-dollar sports car coats and a ten dollar cap.

Note: *The expression does not correlate in meaning with the phrase* ***get the hook****—(sl.) be removed from a position; be unceremoniously dismissed:* The late Jimmy Snyder got the hook for racially insensitive remarks.

See also: get oneself off the hook / go off the hooks.

be housebroken • break into a house

be housebroken—(of pet animals) be clean in the house (going outside to relieve themselves): This Doberman is housebroken, good on a leash and very intelligent.

Note: *The expression does not correlate in meaning with the phrase* ***be from a broken home****—(of a child) come from a family in which the parents have separated or divorced:* Hailey is from a broken home, and her longing for her father is palpable when she holds up a framed photo of her family.

break into a house—force an entrance into a house with criminal intent: Police are still searching for two men who broke into a house on Parvins Mill Road.

be hung over • hang over

be hung over—(sl.) suffer from a hangover: Do not allow anyone to operate a forklift who is under the influence of alcohol or is hung over.

Note: *The expression does not correlate in meaning with the phrase* ***be hung up****—(sl.)* 1. *be bewildered or mentally confused:* He was more than a little hung up, stupid from lack of sleep, worried about his work. 2. *be delayed or stopped by smth.:* Incidentally, I would have been here much sooner, but I got hung up.

hang over—(of customs, traditions, etc.) remain from the past: There's arrogance that hangs over from the days of Empire, that tells us we don't have to speak a foreign language.

See also: be hanged / be hung.

be hung up on someone • hang up on someone

be hung up on someone—(sl.) be strongly attracted by a person: The girl is really hung up on that musician.

hang up on someone—put a telephone receiver down before one's partner has finished speaking: She hung up on him, and left him feeling like a spanked child.

be in a fix • fix is in, the

be in a fix—(coll.) be in a predicament or difficult situation: So I was in a fix. I didn't want to return until I had contacted them and I couldn't find them.

fix is in, the—(sl.) the case or other matter has already been dishonestly decided: We failed to realize that we were playing by their rules — and the fix was in from the beginning!

be in a flutter • have a flutter

be in a flutter—1. *(also: be all of a flutter)* be in a very nervous, confused, or excited state: The concert is coming soon. I'm in a flutter. 2. *(of a room, etc.)* be in a disordered or untidy state: Let me never see this room in a flutter again.

have a flutter—(coll.) gamble on a small scale: The opportunities of the share market were open.... Men and youths, women and maidens, all could have a "flutter."

be in a war • be in the wars

be in a war—1. *(of a nation)* be in the state of war *(also: be at war):* We are now in a war to the death with the German Empire. 2. participate in a military campaign: They are on the point of putting up a war memorial, though none of the people who were in the war want it.

be in the wars—(Perfect Tense) 1. show signs of rough treatment or injury as a result of fighting, etc.: The boy looks as if he has been in the wars. 2. be in bad shape, having had a lot of misfortunes: Terry's been in the wars a bit since his racing career ended — his wife left him and he became an alcoholic.

be in bad taste • taste bad

be in bad taste—(of a joke, picture, etc.) be slightly indecent or distasteful: I can't for the life of me understand what is in bad taste about it. It is a photo of something that took place.

taste bad—(usually of food)—have an unpleasant taste: That is not to say that instant coffee tastes bad, it's not Starbucks of course, but it also doesn't cost five bucks.

be in deep waters • do a deep dive

be in deep waters—(also: be in deep water) be in trouble or serious financial difficulties: Spence inspected the books and realised the mining company was in deep waters with the falling copper prices.

Note: *The expression does not correlate in meaning with the phrase* ***be too deep for someone****— be too difficult or complicated for a person to understand or deal with successfully:* Perhaps the subject is too deep for me. Or the statements of the ancients too obscure and incoherent...

do a deep dive—explore an issue or subject in-depth: I felt that this book did a deep dive on many topics that other books just briefly introduced.

be in Dutch with someone • go Dutch with someone

be in Dutch with someone—(dated) be in trouble or disfavor with a person: Maybe Barn will fire me when he knows I'm in Dutch with his family.

go Dutch with someone—share the cost of a meal, drink, etc. with a person: Although going Dutch is un-Korean, many young Koreans do go Dutch with their western friends. *Cf.: Dutch treat—one at which each person contributes his or her own share:* They each paid an equal share of the wedding, as it was a Dutch treat.

Note: *The expression does not correlate in meaning with the phrase* ***do the Dutch****—(sl.) commit suicide:* Milan is asked by William Carnine to find out why his daughter, Ellen, committed suicide ("did the Dutch") by jumping off a bridge.

be in heaven • be in the skies

be in heaven—(of dead people) be in the heavenly kingdom and celestial paradise: I know that Angela, who is now in heaven and wonderfully happy, forgives him, and I forgive him too.

Note: *The expression is not antonymous in meaning to the phrase* ***drop from heaven****—(also: drop from the skies) appear unexpectedly as if by magic:* A fulfilling marriage does not drop from heaven. It becomes fulfilling when it's tended like a beautiful garden.

be in the skies—(also: be in the clouds) be given to daydreaming; not act according to the realities of life: You were always in the skies absorbed in your passion for art, and far removed from all base mundane interests.

be in luck • one's luck is in

be in luck—be lucky about smth. on this one occasion: You're in luck — the very car you want has just come in.

one's luck is in—enjoy a period of good luck: I think I'll put some money on the next race, while my luck is in.

be in murky waters • fish in murky waters

be in murky waters—said of a confused situation where people may behave in morally questionable ways: Patton is now trying to continue running the government without the benefit of a budget. This puts him in murky waters.... *Cf.: muddy the waters— make the situation less clear:* Announcements that parts of this or that sector are to be sold, followed by a retraction just a few days later, serve only to muddy the waters.

fish in murky waters—(also: fish in troubled waters) take advantage of a confused or dubious situation: The state has not been careful with its land, which only serves the interest of those who like to fish in murky waters.

be in progress • make progress

be in progress—be done or made; be under way: Discussions were in progress for "an aerobus" to provide cheap travel for large numbers.

make progress—advance or develop towards a better state: As the days went along, I found myself perking up a bit. I seemed to be making progress.

be in someone's blood • run in someone's blood

be in someone's blood—act as an essential factor for smb.'s character and life style: Although my music is not specifically about Tanzania, I feel its influence because it's in my blood.

run in someone's blood—be typical of a person's family or ancestors: Tiger training runs in his blood. His grandfather trained tigers, and his uncles carried on the tradition.

be in someone's shoes • fill someone's shoes

be in someone's shoes—be in smb.'s usually unfortunate situation: I wouldn't like to be in your shoes when he finds out that you have deceived him. *Cf.: walk a mile in someone's shoes — used to imply that one has to experience life from another person's perspective to truly understand him:* "You never really know a man till you walk a mile in his shoes," says Atticus, who is defending an innocent black man.

fill someone's shoes—successfully take over smb.'s responsibilities *(usually with the implication that the person is going to be hard to replace):* She's very capable. I can't think of anyone at this moment who can fill her shoes.

See also: put oneself in someone's shoes / step into someone's shoes.

be in stitches • not have a stitch on

be in stitches—(coll.) be laughing noisily and deeply: We were in stitches! You'll be in stitches too when you see him on the stage!

not have a stitch on—have no clothes on: Little Tommy spent most of the time running around the pool with not a stitch on.

be in the clouds • be on cloud seven

be in the clouds—(also: be in the skies) be given to daydreaming; not act according to the realities of life: I'm so practical, a little too solid perhaps, while you are, and always will be, in the clouds.

Note: *The expression is not antonymous in meaning to the phrase* ***drop from the clouds****—(also: drop from the skies) appear unexpectedly as if by magic:* We were fired upon from behind houses and barns by marksmen, who seemed to "drop from the clouds."

be on cloud seven—(also: be on cloud nine) be extremely happy or euphoric: She was on cloud seven. Gary was the prize catch who could have had any girl he wanted, but he asked her, instead.

be in the club • join the club

be in the club—(coll.) become pregnant *(also: be in the pudding club):* When the doctor told me I was in the club I told him he was daft — that I'd never — well, you know.

join the club—1. *(also: join the crowd)* is used to tell that one has already had a similar, usually unfavorable, experience: You think you'll never be out of debt? Join the club. 2. be one of a number of people sharing smth. in common: Men knew she was available to anyone who cared to take her out for an evening. Peter had avoided joining the club. 3. = *be in the club:* It was not long into my girlfriend's pregnancy that I realized it was not going to be fun. Between the time she "joined the club" and us knowing about it, she went decidedly mad.

be in the race • make the race

be in the race—1. compete for smth. such as public office, etc.: Morris Udall, the "liberal-progressive" spear carrier, will have to win to stay in the race. 2. *(negat.)* not have a chance of winning or obtaining smth.: A few years ago he wouldn't have been in the race to own a car like that.

make the race— = be in the race 1: He might perhaps consider making the Senate race.

be in the running • make the running

be in the running—compete for smth. such as fame, smb.'s affections, etc.: A month before Joyce married Hal, three of Joyce's boy friends seemed to be still in the running. *Cf.: be out of the running—fail to achieve success as a contender:* Halliburton is now out of the running for bids on lucrative construction contracts.

make the running—1. lead over one's competitors in a contest, etc.: The early leaders drop back and allow others to make the running. 2. *(also: do the running)* show initiative; make sure that things get done: He is unsure of himself, half-frightened of the girl, so she has to make the running.

be in the same boat • sail in the same boat

be in the same boat—(also: be in the same box) be in the same, usually unfavorable, position: When John told her how poor he was she said that she was in the same boat.

sail in the same boat—act together; make common cause with a person: If I were you I wouldn't sail in the same boat with someone as corrupt as he is.

be in the swim • swim with the stream

be in the swim—have interest or active role in modern life and social activities: The need to be in the swim — up to date — might not have been the least of our driving forces for general progress.

swim with the stream—(also: float with the stream) act as the majority of people do; behave in a conventional way: Those who prefer to swim with the stream are numerous everywhere.

Note: *The expression does not correlate in meaning with the phrase* ***come on stream****—(also: go on stream) be in active operation:* The second phase of the airport will come on stream in two years.

be in the wind • hang in the wind

be in the wind—1. *(also: be in the air)* be rumored or suspected: Everyone in the industry knew that a change was in the wind. 2. *(sl.)* be alcohol intoxicated: I am not in the wind ... for you see I'm perfectly sober.

Note: *The expression does not correlate in meaning with the phrase* ***in a breeze****—(coll.) easily, without visible effort:* It had been a battle of the sexes and the girls had won in a breeze! No contest really: Girls 4 — Boys nil!

hang in the wind—show signs of uncertainty; hesitate: She waited for what was coming. But he hung in the wind.

be in the wrong • be wrong

be in the wrong—act in a way not morally justifiable: In all questions between a government and an individual, the presumption is that the government is in the wrong.

Note: *The expression does not correlate in meaning with the phrase* ***be in the wrong box****—(UK coll.) be in a wrong position and so in difficulty or trouble:* Mr. O'shea, if you report what a private member says to you then you will be in the wrong box.

be wrong—have the wrong idea or opinion; be incorrect in one's statements, etc.: None of us are so proud as never to confess that we are wrong.

be in trouble • have trouble

be in trouble—1. be in a difficult or dangerous situation: The Youth Board finds the youngsters who are in trouble and begins to work with them. 2. *(euph., of an unmarried woman)* be pregnant: She said she consented to be married to the prisoner as she believed she was in trouble.

Note: *The expression does not correlate in meaning with the phrase* ***be troubled****—1. be put to the inconvenience of doing smth.:* Mineralogists have often been troubled to distinguish with certainty between apatite and nephelin. 2. *be anxious or concerned:* The King was troubled, lest this eloquent man should shake his resolution.

have trouble—experience serious problems: The telegraph lines began to have trouble, and for a while the experts couldn't figure out what was the matter.

be in trouble with someone • have trouble with someone

be in trouble with someone—suffer unhappiness or have problems because of smb.: He has been in trouble with the police arising out of his activities with the British Israelites.

have trouble with someone—1. have problems with smb. because of this person's behavior: The Post Office is having much trouble with people who underpay their letters. 2. = *be in trouble with someone:* This wasn't the first time that my family have had trouble with the police.

be in waiting • lie in wait

be in waiting—1. be in attendance on a person of rank: Esmond's friend, Dick Steele, who was in waiting on the Prince, heard the controversy between the ladies at court. 2. be ready for service: Dr Sinclair, who was in waiting, had the man carefully examined, and it is wonderful to say no bones were broken.

lie in wait—remain hidden while preparing to attack: Police yesterday fired tear gas into a car to immobilize a couple alleged to be lying in wait to rob a cash-filled armoured van.

be in want • be wanting

be in want—be destitute; live in poverty: Many people are now out of work and in want.

be wanting—be deficient or inadequate: Nothing will be wanting to render your stay agreeable.

be in with someone • be with someone

be in with someone—(coll., also: be on the in with someone) be on friendly or familiar terms with a person: We go along for a drink occasionally, but we're not really in with the people staying there. *Cf.: be out with someone—(coll., also: be on the outs with someone) be no longer friendly with a person:* He is out with his former friend and in with his former adversary.

be with someone—(coll.) 1. pay attention to what a person is saying: Are you still with me — or shall I go over it again? 2. support a person; back smb. up: If you do decide to oppose him, then we're with you all the way!

See also: have an in with someone / have it in for someone.

be interested in someone • have an interest in someone

be interested in someone—be keen to know or learn about a person: I do not suppose that George was interested in Stevenson as a writing man.

have an interest in someone—concern oneself about or sympathize with smb.: She happens to be my only sister's child and I have an interest in her.

Note: *Neither expression correlates in meaning with the phrase* ***interest oneself for someone****—seek attention for another person:* I will interest myself for you and try to obtain a promise of the post.

be laid low • lie low

be laid low—1. *(of a disease or injury)* cause a person to take to bed: I've been laid low with this cough most of the winter. 2. be defeated or forced into a humble position: Kidd was laid low by an incredible run of sheer bad luck.

Note: *a) The expression does not correlate in meaning with the phrase* ***be low****—feel weak or depressed; be in low spirits:* I am low today. What is it that makes one day good and another bad?

b) The expression is not antonymous in meaning to the phrase ***be laid up****—1. = be laid low 1:* The test pilot, Robert Turner, was laid up with back injuries for months. 2. *(of a ship) be put in dock, as for repairs:* In 1910 she stranded in Singapore and was laid up with hull damage.

lie low—keep a low profile; try to be inconspicuous: Sarah decided to lie low until the train got underway again.

be left in peace • rest in peace

be left in peace—be free from interference or coercion: These men should be left in peace for they have served their time.

rest in peace—(euph.) said of smb. dead and buried: My grandparents, who now rest in peace, loved Halloween.

be loaded • be loaded for bear

be loaded—(U.S. sl.) 1. be under the influence of drugs or alcohol: I'm not loaded. I'm just a little tipsy. 2. be very rich: Mr. Wilson is loaded, but he is also generous with his money.

be loaded for bear—(U.S. sl.) 1. = *be loaded 1:* Marines are always loaded for bear, and get nicked once in a while. 2. ready for the hardest problems: I'm loaded for bear, and that's good because this is going to be a rough day. 3. very angry: By the time he finished talking, I was loaded for bear.

be loath to do something • loathe doing something

be loath to do something—be unwilling to do smth.: Perhaps you have to ease back on your workload, something most physicians are loath to do.

loathe doing something—have an intense aversion for doing smth.: Thank you for leaving the kitchen so clean and tidy, a job I loath doing after a party.

be milk toast • be toast

be milk toast—(U.S. sl., pejor.) be a timid person who is afraid to assert himself: He will have frequent battles with hospital officials.... A doctor who never gets into scraps with those around him is a milk toast.

be toast—(U.S. sl.) said of a person who will not succeed or will be in deep trouble: They may have gotten him in a position where if he doesn't really shine in those debates, he is toast.

be mixed up • mix it up

be mixed up—(coll.) be confused in one's feelings: No wonder the boy turned criminal, he had been mixed up all through his childhood.

mix it up—(sl.) argue or exchange criticisms; quarrel vigorously: Shaffer was aggressive and didn't mind mixing it up when she had to.

be nettled • be on nettles

be nettled—be vexed or angered: Becker was nettled at the groan from those around the table. "I know it's a lot of money, but this is necessary."

be on nettles—be impatient or anxious: Some of them were on nettles till they learned your name was Dickson.

Note: *Neither expression correlates in meaning with the phrase* ***grasp the nettle****—take decisive or bold action:* It was hoped that, grasping the nettle with resolution, he might suffer no evil results.

be nobody's business • like nobody's business

be nobody's business—said of smth. that does not concern anyone: I look like death warmed up and what I feel is nobody's business.

like nobody's business—(coll.) said of an activity done with great energy or enthusiasm: "He can sing like nobody's business," said Stoker.

be none of someone's business • have no business to do something

be none of someone's business—said of smth. that does not concern a person: She's not his girlfriend, and this matter is none of his business.

have no business to do smth.—have no right to do smth.: This woman had no business to publish his private letters to her.

be of one mind • be single-minded

be of one mind—(of two or more people) be in complete agreement; think alike: Upon sober reflection, I cannot say that I am of one mind with the pastor.

Note: *The expression is not antonymous in meaning to the phrase* ***be in two minds****—(also: be in twenty minds) feel doubtful or hesitate about smth.:* I am still in two minds whether to take the house or not.

be single-minded—have but one purpose; concentrate on accomplishing only one task: Isabella was single-minded in her determination to cause Blanche as much trouble as possible.

be off one's legs • be run off one's legs

be off one's legs—be resting: She didn't know how long she could manage it, but for the time being at least she was off her legs.

Note: *The expression is not antonymous in meaning to the phrase* ***be on one's legs****—(also: be on one's feet)* 1. *be standing up while working:* His sciatica bothers him mainly after being on his legs all day. 2. *get up (to speak, etc.):* "It's a lie!" Foe was on his legs, and he fairly shouted it. 3. *recover after an illness:* Willie is now in the Middlesex Military Hospital.... He is progressing favorably and soon hopes to be on his legs again.

be run off one's legs—(also: be rushed off one's legs) be tired to the point of exhaustion: The servers were run off their legs trying to keep the buffet tables supplied.

be off one's nana • lose one's nana

be off one's nana—(Austral. sl.) be mentally deranged: We've learned to laugh at our predicament. If we hadn't we'd all be off our nanas.

lose one's nana—(Austral. sl.) lose one's temper: Lost my nana with a couple of customers tonight and wish I hadn't.

be off one's nut • get one's nuts off

be off one's nut—(sl.) be out of one's mind; be insane: But is the master off his nut that he has her down here to stay?

get one's nuts off—(coarse sl.) obtain sexual release: Screwin' my white friend's black wife makes me feel even better. Makes me get my nuts off.

be on a high • be on a high horse

be on a high—(coll.) have a feeling of great excitement and happiness: The team are definitely on a high at the moment so we will go to Bahrain feeling very optimistic.

be on a high horse—be very dignified and formal: Every single person I spoke to was on a high horse and treated me like they were doing me a favor.

be on all fours • hit on all four

be on all fours—1. crawl on one's hands and knees: Claud slipped through the hedge on all fours and I followed. 2. *(coll.)* correspond or harmonize with smth.: The railways maintain that conditions in Great Britain and America are not on all fours.

hit on all four—(coll.) work most efficiently *(also: hit on all six):* If we can hit on all four, we can provide incredible value for our members.

be on home ground • play away from home

be on home ground—(also: be on one's own ground) 1. be in the area where one works or lives *(with the implication that it makes a person feel confident and secure):* I was sad to see Argentina lose on penalties. They were doing pretty well considering the Germans were on home ground. 2. be competent in a subject because one is thoroughly familiar with it *(with the implication that it makes a person feel relaxed and comfortable):* Here he is on home ground, spinning webs of excellent dialogues around incidents, holding the spectator spellbound. Here he is at his professional best.

play away from home—(coll.) have an affair on the side: Pink allegedly agreed that Carey could "play away from home" while she is on tour.

be on one's last legs • be the last leg

be on one's last legs—be at the end of one's resources and failing fast: At this point I was on my last legs ... I would have loved nothing more than to have stopped for a rest. *Cf.: need new legs—(also: need fresh legs)* 1. *be in need of rest:* I think I need new legs from all the walking we did. 2. *(Sport) need players who are young:* We need new legs on the team. Veterans are great, but the youth has so much more potential.

be the last leg—be the last part of a trip (separated from other parts by a period of rest, etc.): We were tired but this was the last leg of our journey.

be on one's own ground • stand on one's native soil

be on one's own ground—(also: be on home ground) 1. be in the area where one works or lives *(with the implication that it makes a person feel confident and secure):* Whenever possible he liked to make a point of talking to drug users on their own ground. 2. be competent in a subject because one is thoroughly familiar with it *(with the implication that it makes a person feel relaxed and comfortable):* And where he is on his own ground, as in the chapters dealing with family life, he exercises his well-known mastery of observation.

Note: *The expression does not correlate in meaning with the phrase* ***stand one's own ground****—(also: hold one's ground) maintain one's firm position in an argument, etc:* Perry discovered that he could stand his own ground and still be respected.

stand on one's native soil— be in the land of one's birth: I am looking forward to going back to France and standing once more on my native soil.

be on overtime • be over one's time

be on overtime—work after the usual working hours: The men stayed locked up for two hours until their boss agreed they would repair the faulty central heating immediately—on overtime.

be over one's time—(of a woman) be late in menstruating *(the usual implication being that of unwanted pregnancy):* "A fine father and mentor you are. Don't even realize that she is over her time," he cursed himself...

be on pins and needles • have pins and needles

be on pins and needles—(coll.) be in the state of agitated expectancy: We had been on pins and needles all day long until we received her telegram.

Note: *a) The expression does not correlate in meaning with the phrase* ***be on one's pins****—(coll.) be on one's feet; be in good health:* When I came home after a number of years, I was glad that mother was still on her pins.

b) The expression does not correlate in meaning with the phrase ***be on the needle****—(sl.) be addicted to injectable drugs:* My brother's on the needle, and I want to help him.

have pins and needles—have a pricking tingling sensation in a limb: I have had pins and needles in my left hand for about two weeks now.

be on the fiddle • fiddle about

be on the fiddle—(sl.) be involved in illicit money-making activities: As it was day-time, everyone in the coffee bar was on the dole or on the fiddle.

fiddle about—(coll.) mess about or waste time: I've been fiddling about for ages trying to get the windscreen washers to work properly.

be on the hop • go on the hop

be on the hop—(coll.) 1. be very busy: I'd been on the hop ever since morning, for being in love with Anita was a strenuous calling. 2. play truant; stay away from school, etc.: Remember that day I was on the hop from school? I went down to the city that day...

go on the hop— = be on the hop 2: Ronan used to go "on the hop" (skipping school) when he was a teenager.

Note: *Neither expression correlates in meaning with the phrase* ***catch someone on the hop****—(coll.) catch a person unprepared; take smb. by surprise:* You've caught me on the hop, I'm afraid—give me five minutes to get ready.

be on the look-out for something • look out for something

be on the look-out for something—be watchful wishing to find or acquire smth.: Restaurant manager Jose Padilla is always on the look-out for something new for his customers.

look out for something—(also: watch out for something) 1. be on the alert for smth. harmful or dangerous: There were signs everywhere warning people to look out for falling rocks. 2. = *be on the look-out for something:* I've been looking out for a new job for six months. 3. take care of smth.; protect smth. from harm: When this young man is away from his home, I look out for his property.

See also: outlook for something / outlook on something.

be on the mend • mend one's ways

be on the mend—1. be getting better after illness: He has been on the mend under the excellent care by his wife Phyllis. 2. *(of things)* improve: The economy has been on the mend since the data in the report was gathered.

mend one's ways—improve one's behavior, work, etc.: He is unlikely to mend his ways unless he is forced to do so.

be on the sick • be sick

be on the sick—(coll.) be on sick list; receive sickness benefit: Dad used to be on the sick for a long time and couldn't work.

be sick—1. be unwell; be affected by illness: When she was sick he wanted her to get the best doctor. 2. (have an inclination to) vomit: "Ouch!" said Joss and looked as if she would be sick again.

be on the side of the angels • join the angels

be on the side of the angels—be on the side that is morally right: His motivation to stop whaling is on the side of the angels and I share it.

join the angels—(euph.) die: They were all children once. One day, sooner or later they will all join the angels beyond the garden of death.

be on the top line • sweat on the top line

be on the top line—(coll.) be in the highest state of perfection, readiness, etc.: It cannot be but harmful to the patient to be attended by a doctor who through sheer exhaustion is not on the top line.

sweat on the top-line—(sl.) be close to attaining or obtaining smth.: Here was I sort of sweating on the top line, and I finally got the offer about two days before my time at British Steel expired.

be on the verge of something • verge on something

be on the verge of something—be on the point beyond which smth. bad happens: The country was on the verge of ruin; the revolution was a matter of months.

verge on something—1. border on a particular area: The rear of the park verges on the river. You can see the railroad bridge downstream.... 2. resemble smth.; be similar to smth.: To cling to this idea when it has been shown a thousand times to be erroneous verges on stupidity.

be on the wire • be on wires

be on the wire—(dated) be speaking on the telephone *(also: be over the wire):* He ought to have spoken to Nunez about the broken chain while he was on the wire.

be on wires—(coll.) be in a state of nervous excitement or agitation: "I could not sleep," began the Countess. "I was all, as you say, on wires."

Note: *The expression does not fully correlate in meaning with the phrase* ***be wired****—*1. *be carrying a hidden communications device connecting to other people:* Rodriguez was convicted for receiving bribes from an undercover agent who was wired. 2. *(of premises) be equipped with a microphone, loudspeakers, etc., to transmit sound:* The hall was wired with miles of cables, computer monitors, and loudspeakers to showcase new music. 3. *be programmed like a robot to do smth.:* Remember, he's wired to kill and rape everything in sight — and he knows how to dispose of the body! 4. *(coll.) = be on wires:* Some nights he is so wired until he comes to bed but can't sleep, so he is just watching TV for hours.

be on top of someone • top someone

be on top of someone—1. *(of an approaching vehicle)* suddenly come too close to a person: It was raining and I couldn't see anything until the car was right on top of me and I dove out of the way. 2. said of a small space where people find it difficult to have any privacy: He still lives in Downsea. Near enough for me to babysit but not so close that we're on top of him. 3. said of smth. involving more work than one can cope with: By no stretch of the imagination could our work have been termed exhausting, but it was always on top of you.

top someone—1. exceed a person in height or weight: She was so tall that she topped her father by a head. 2. have the supremacy over smb.: Dance in movies begins with Fred Astaire, and no one has ever really topped him. 3. *(sl.)* kill a person: Tom King wasn't a good enough character to warrant months of interest in who topped him.

be one too many • have one too many

be one too many—*(coll.)* be more than a match for a person: I venture to prophesy that, between us, we shall be one too many for the Colonel.

have one too many—*(coll.)* take more alcohol than one can drink: The man was a little tipsy; it looked like he had had one too many for complete control of his faculties.

be oneself • be oneself again

be oneself—behave in a way that is natural, especially in contrast to the affected manner: I wish you wouldn't act the sophisticated lady. You're far nicer when you are just being yourself.

be oneself again—be in one's normal condition of mind and body after an illness, emotional stress, etc.: After such a long illness, it's good to be myself again.

Note: *Neither expression correlates in meaning with the phrase* ***be full of oneself****— be impressed with one's own work; be too proud of oneself:* Karl is so full of himself. He is a good designer, but I'm so sick of his personality.

be out of one's brain • have brains

be out of one's brain—*(sl.)* be very drunk *(also: be out of one's scull):* By the time I arrived at the party he was out of his brain.

have brains—*(coll.)* be very smart and intelligent: Don't be fooled by her pretty appearance alone, this girl has brains to match!

be out of spirits • lose all spirit

be out of spirits—be dejected or depressed: I was out of spirits at the thought of leaving all my family and friends for so long a time.

lose all spirit—lose courage or confidence: The lad had been so badly treated, that he had lost all spirit.

be out of the ball park • knock it out of the ball park

be out of the ball park—*(coll.)* 1. be not close to the correct amount or number: Their budget "estimates" are out of the ballpark and too high in my opinion. 2. be beyond the boundaries of what is acceptable or possible: The project makes sense only with those recommendations, otherwise, it is out of the ball park.

knock it out of the ball park—*(coll.)* do smth. exceptionally well *(also: hit it out of the ball park):* The film stars Uma Thurman who can take a strong female role and knock it out of the ball park.

be out of the woods • take to the woods

be out of the woods—*(often negat.)* be finally free from trouble or difficulties *(also: be out of the wood):* The Prime Minister is by no means out of the woods, and must fight to defend his leadership.

Note: *The expression does not correlate in meaning with the phrase* ***come out of the woodwork****— appear as though out of nowhere, especially in large numbers:* He won the lottery and has had old "friends" and distant relatives coming out of the woodwork ever since.

take to the woods— run away from one's responsibilities; get away from trouble and hide: When trouble comes, wise men take to their work; weak men take to the woods.

be over someone's head • hang over someone's head

be over someone's head—*(also: be above someone's head)* said of smth. too difficult to understand: I bought a handful of photographic magazines and when I got home to read them, I found they were completely over my head.

Note: *The expression does not correlate in meaning with the phrase* ***be in over one's head****— be involved in a situation too difficult to deal with:* He realized that he was in over his head, and that only his family could help him.

hang over someone's head—*(of an evil, calamity, etc.)* hover over a person; be imminent: Celia Palmer had been acquitted of all the gravest charges hanging over her head this long time.

Note: *Neither expression correlates in meaning with the phrase* ***hold something over someone's head****— remind a person of his mistake or failure:* If I turned up late, my parents would hold it over my head for the rest of my life, but if it's Taylor, well there's always the exception.

be pleased with oneself • please oneself

be pleased with oneself—be much satisfied with what one does: He was very pleased with himself after he had passed his driving test.

please oneself—do whatever one likes, without having to obey others: We don't have to be back by a certain time; we can just please ourselves.

be poorly • be poorly off

be poorly—be feeling unwell: "Kate, your mistress is poorly this morning, and prefers you not go in to her." "Poorly? Oh, but sir, she will want her tea..."

be poorly off—have very little money: Many of the Africans who came here as refugees more than a decade ago are still poorly off.

be put into execution • be put to execution

be put into execution—*(also: be carried into execution)* be carried out: The plan was put into execution and this was the beginning of the manufacture of woolen fabrics.

be put to execution—1. *= be put into execution:* The plan was put to execution, and the group of three moved down, alongside of the rocky wall. 2. suffer the penalty of death: Michael Malik was put to execution in Trinidad. He was accused of murdering a British woman Gale Benson...

be put up against the wall • be up against the wall

be put up against the wall—said of smb. about to be executed by shooting: His appeal was turned down.... The day came round and he was put up against the wall to be shot.

be up against the wall—(also: have one's back against the wall) have run out of options; be pushed to the last extremity: When I was up against the wall and couldn't pay my bills, I knew I had to do something.

Note: *The expression does not correlate in meaning with the phrase* ***come up against a blank wall****—(also: come up against a brick wall) encounter an insurmountable obstacle or difficulty:* We come up against a blank wall. There is a total unwillingness to hear our side of the story.

be quit of someone • be quits with someone

be quit of someone—be free or rid of a person: "On the whole," she continued thoughtfully, "it would be much better if he died. I mean, I'd feel more finally quit of him."

be quits with someone—be even with smb. by repaying a debt or by means of retaliation: He was quits with all the world, and loved others as little as he thought they loved him.

be reflected in something • reflect on something

be reflected in something—be clearly shown in smth.: The low level of interest in the election has been reflected in the unwillingness of the citizens to vote.

reflect on something—bring smth. into question or disfavor: Your behavior reflects on the good name of the school.

be related to someone • relate to someone

be related to someone—be connected by family to smb.: I am distantly related to the Rochesters by the mother's side.

relate to someone—1. concern a person: When it doesn't relate to me I can't find the energy to worry about it. 2. communicate or deal with other people: Children need to learn to relate to other children.

be ringed • be rung

be ringed—1. be encircled or surrounded: The village was ringed by a wall of sharp-thorned acacia branches woven tightly together. 2. *(of birds)* have a numbered ring attached to their legs, so that various aspects of the bird's life can be studied: The first birds to be ringed in southern Africa were Cape Griffons.

be rung—(of a bell, gong, etc.) be caused to sound: The first peal in North America was rung at Christ Church, Philadelphia, in 1850.

be seated • be unseated

be seated—1. *(imper.)* is used as an invitation to sit down: Thank you all for being here today and please be seated. 2. be placed in a chair or other seat: Once they were seated in her office, she started to explain the problem. 3. be established in a position of power or authority: Churchill won and was seated as a Liberal member in the 1906 election.

be unseated—be removed from office: No first-term governor has been unseated in the state since 1918.

be set on doing something • be set to do something

be set on doing something—be determined to do smth.: Roberts was outraged, and thereafter he and Nieuwendyk were set on leaving the team.

be set to do something—be ready and prepared to do smth.: We were set to enjoy the weekend in a deluxe room overlooking Downtown Disney.

be soft in the head • have a hard head

be soft in the head—(coll.) be foolish or mentally retarded *(also: be weak in the head):* One of the curses of being a science-fiction writer is that unsophisticated people assume you to be soft in the head.

Note: *The expression does not correlate in meaning with the phrase* ***be weak-minded****— be not firm or resolute enough:* He was a good guy, but was manipulated.... I guess you could say he was weak minded.

have a hard head—be practical and determined, not influenced by sentiments: He's not the suit and tie you all think he is. He has a hard head but he also has a heart.

be sold on someone • be sold out to someone

be sold on someone—(U.S. coll.) be accepted by a person as worthy: When we first moved in, our neighbors seemed cold and unfriendly, but now we are sold on them. *Cf.: be sold on something— be persuaded to recognize the worth or desirability of smth.:* Parliament, and presumably the citizens, were sold on the idea of creating the Child Support Agency.

be sold out to someone—(coll.) be betrayed deceitfully to smb.: He had little support from the English aristocracy who felt that they had been sold out to Rome.

be someone's right-hand man • stay on the right side of someone

be someone's right-hand man—act as a person's chief assistant: I'm counting on you being my right-hand man.

stay on the right side of someone—(also: keep on the right side of someone) continue to be friendly with smb.: It will pay you to stay on the right side of the boss, as if you annoy him it could cost you your job.

be stiff-necked • have a stiff neck

be stiff-necked—(also: be hard-necked) be stubborn or haughty: She was stiff-necked, but he would make her see reason.

have a stiff neck—suffer from a condition in which the head cannot be moved without pain: By the time the train pulled into the station, he had a stiff neck and an aching back.

Note: *The expression does not correlate in meaning with the phrase* ***have the neck****—(coll.) have the insolence; be presumptuous enough to do smth.:* I asked her how she had the neck to come to the area to open a community center, while she was cutting community jobs.

be stuck for something • be stuck on something

be stuck for something—(coll.) be unable to obtain smth.: An undergraduate is no longer "stuck" for a dinner, a seat at a play, a railroad ticket.

Note: *The expression does not correlate in meaning with the phrase* ***stick up for something****—(coll.) declare oneself in favor of smth.; support a cause:* I shall always like him the better for "sticking up" for old New England.

be stuck on something—(coll.) feel a strong attraction to smth.; be captivated with smth.: I am stuck on the idea that what we are missing most in our culture today is truth.

be stuck on someone • be stuck with someone

be stuck on someone—(sl.) feel a strong attraction to a person: You'd say she was kind of stuck on the fellow at the first meeting although it was a blind date.

be stuck with someone—(coll.) be unable to get rid of an unwanted person: The truly sad thing is that I am stuck with him for the rest of my life.

be stuck up • be stuck-up

be stuck up—1. *(sl.)* said of an armed robbery: It was only the previous night that he had been "stuck up," with a pistol at his head. 2. *(coll.)* be hindered from proceeding on a journey, etc.: Luckily, we got stuck up in a town and not in the middle of nowhere.

be stuck-up—(coll.) be conceited; insolently refusing to be companionable: Most people when they meet me expect me to be mean or "stuck-up" because of the title.

be taken ill • take it ill

be taken ill—come down with a disease: The assigned attorney originally scheduled to try the case was taken ill suddenly.

take it ill—(formal) be offended: I beg you not to take it ill that I failed to answer your greeting. My anger prevented a reply...

be talked out • be talked out of something

be talked out—be tired by talking: Well, you now know all my opinions on the subject; my throat is dry, I'm talked out.

be talked out of something—be persuaded not to do smth.: He had to be talked out of leaving at the beginning of this week.

be the cock in the henhouse • rule the roost

be the cock in the henhouse— said of a male in an all-female environment: He made her tell patients that breast exposure was a "normal procedure," and referred to himself as "the only cock in the henhouse."

rule the roost—be the boss or manager, especially at home: But who really rules the roost? Possibly his wife Sybil — equally keen to be seen as a pillar of society and equally blinkered as to life in the real world.

be there for me • be there or be square

be there for me—help me when I need it; be supportive: They told us that they would be there for me and help me through the difficult time I was about to face.

be there or be square—you better be there because everyone of importance will be there: Cassidy is having a gallery opening.... There's an intimate dinner party immediately following, so be there or be square.

Note: *Neither expression correlates in meaning with the phrase* ***you had to be there****— used to say that to appreciate the situation you should have been there:* There was such a feeling of solidarity and unity and peacefulness, you had to be there to feel it.

be through something • be through with something

be through something—endure smth.; live through a particular experience: These were experienced fishermen. They had been through many storms on this sea before.

be through with something—1. eventually accomplish smth.: When she was through with this aria, she asked the audience to be silent, and then she spoke. 2. *(coll.)* have had enough of smth.; be tired of smth.: I'm through with this job; I must find something more interesting.

be titanic • go titanic

be titanic—said of smth. gigantic: Zana's efforts are titanic. Whatever be her motivation, no one can deny the importance of what she has done.

go titanic—(sl.) not succeed; fail: An incident that happened recently involved a joint project that nearly went titanic.

be too big for one's boots • fill one's boots

be too big for one's boots—(also: be too big for one's shoes) be too proud and conceited: That showed ... his arrogance in acting like a puffed up politician who is too big for his boots.

fill one's boots—(UK coll.) 1. have or acquire as much of smth. as one wants: Come on everybody, fill your boots, the food is on the table. 2. score lots of goals: He would have filled his boots in European football; it's a shame that such a player will end up with just one medal.

be too far gone • go too far

be too far gone—be in an advanced stage of a particular condition (suffering from illness, etc.): We tried to make him understand, but he was too far gone to take in what we were saying.

Note: *The expression is not antonymous in meaning to the phrase* ***be a bit gone****—(sl.) be crazy or insane:* The cook scratched his head; he had a chat with the overseer afterwards, and they agreed that the traveler was a bit gone.

go too far—go beyond the limits of what is considered reasonable: If this was an olive branch, Dondolo was tempted to take it, just because he had gone too far.

See also: go far / go far afield.

be under the cat's paw • make a cat's paw of someone

be under the cat's paw—live under the control of some domineering person: She might claim adulthood in every sense of the word.... She would no longer be under the cat's paw of her stepmother.

make a cat's paw of someone—make another person a tool or instrument to accomplish one's own purpose: She simply made a cat's-paw of you, Basil. I can see it now, darling, I did not then.

be under the delusion • be under the illusion

be under the delusion—1. hold a false opinion or belief: Anyone who is under the delusion that corrupt governments are only in the Third World has better think again. 2. hold a belief that may be a symptom of madness: He was charged with shoplifting but the man was under the delusion that the supermarket belonged to him.

be under the illusion— = be under the delusion 1: Often our world is under the illusion that power comes in the form of money.

be up for something • be up to something

be up for something—1. *(of a house, car, etc.)* intended for sale or repairs: How long has this house been up for sale? 2. be considered for a position, a job, etc.: I believe he's up for re-admission to the society at the next committee meeting. 3. facing criminal charges: I hear the gardener is up for the robbery at the big house. 4. *(coll.)* willing to do smth. or interested in doing smth.: If you're up for straight drinking, go to an *izakaya,* usually explained as a Japanese pub.

Note: *The expression does not correlate in meaning with the phrase* ***be hard up for something****— be short of smth.; not have enough of smth.:* I was hard up for cash so I was willing to do whatever I could, within reason.

be up to something—1. feel well enough or be able to do smth.: Mother hasn't been up to much recently, while her leg was bad. 2. be about to engage in smth. mischievous or reprehensible: I felt sure he was up to no good when I saw him hanging about the back door. 3. be well aware of smb.'s dishonest tricks, etc.: But surely, all that's taken care of by the customs authorities? They must be up to all the dodges. 4. equal smth. in standard: I wonder whether his latest book was up to your expectations?

See also: be down for something / be down to something.

be used to doing something • used to do something

be used to doing something—be accustomed to doing smth.: He is quite used to working hard.

used to do something—said of a constant or frequent practice in the past: He used to come every Friday and order a pint of bitter.

be welcome • be welcomed

be welcome—1. be gladly accepted in a particular place: You will always be welcome here in our Academy, as a spectator or a participant. 2. be generously permitted to do or have smth.: If you and your family need the money that badly you are welcome to it. 3. *(ironic)* be allowed to have smth. burdensome or unwanted: If you think you can do this job any better, you are welcome.

be welcomed—be warmly greeted: As the Pope traveled through the streets of Nazareth, he was welcomed by thousands who crowded the streets cheering.

be well away • be well off

be well away—1. be a long way off (from a place): We truly were well away from civilization, wild Africa at its very best! 2. *(coll.)* be very drunk: Bristow had a bottle of whisky and I had one of gin so we were well away.

be well off—be financially comfortable: By central European standards they are quite well-off. They have their own flat and drive new cars.

be well connected • have a good connection

be well connected—have relatives who hold important positions: He learnt from other sources that the Ernscliffes were well connected.

have a good connection—have many customers, clients, etc.: He set up in business and soon had a good connection.

be whole of mind • be whole-minded

be whole of mind—(arch., formal) be mentally normal; be of sound mind *(used in wills and trusts)*: I Richard Ballard of Orbye being whole of mind and perfect of remembrance make my last will and testament.

Note: *a) The expression is not equivalent in meaning to the phrase* ***whole of mind and body****—safe and sound; unharmed:* We just hoped that he would come home from his tour whole of mind and body.

b) The expression is not antonymous in meaning to the phrase ***have half a mind****—feel tempted or inclined to do something:* I had half a mind to drown myself then; but an odd wish to see the whole adventure out ... restrained me.

be whole-minded—be completely dedicated to smth.: Even if Bu Kiwon was crazy (which, of course, he was not), he obviously was whole-minded enough to create trouble for the League!

be wide of the mark • come short of the mark

be wide of the mark—(also: be off the mark) be inaccurate or erroneous in one's judgment: The idea that the Israelis are anxious to dictate a Carthaginian peace is ludicrously wide of the mark.

come short of the mark—(also: fall short of the mark) fail to attain some desired object or end: A perfectly good talk can be ruined if your answers to questions come short of the mark.

be worth doing something • be worthy of doing something

be worth doing something—be good enough to justify spending one's time on: This book is worth reading, but keep in mind the saying "you shouldn't believe everything you read."

be worthy of doing something—be of high level of excellence to deserve smth.: I am still of the opinion that it is worthy of reading by people who enjoy a good science fiction book.

be written in black and white • see something in black and white

be written in black and white—be put down in writing (as a proof of smth.): The fact that I am gay is written down in black and white. I came out at teaching college and the fact was put down in my personal file.

see something in black and white—see complex issues in simple terms of right and wrong: That is not, any more, an accurate portrait of the society. People do not see these things purely in black and white.

bear a resemblance to something • bear a semblance of something

bear a resemblance to something—(also: have a resemblance to something) seem similar to smth., especially in external appearance: Both in the treatment of the face and in the pose of the body the figure bears a resemblance to certain Kushan sculpture.

bear a semblance of something—(also: have a semblance of something) have a slight, superficial and often deceptive similarity to smth.: After many years, life here bears a semblance of normality and farmers have had a bumper crop.

bear down on something • bear on something

bear down on something—move towards smth.; approach smth. quickly: With the wind blowing strongly behind, the boat bore down on the harbor.

bear on something—have relation to smth.; be connected with smth.: That bears on what you were saying about the problem.

bear market • bull market

bear market—(Stock Market) a period of time when the prices of securities are falling or are expected to fall, and investors pull out their money: Two months before the end of the bear market, Business Week ran an article titled "Running scared from stocks."

bull market—(Stock Market) a period when investment seems promising and people are keen to do it: While the bull market in Asian growth is far from over, there is also a lot of Latin American growth that is going unnoticed.

bear someone • bear with someone

bear someone—1. *(usually Passive)* give birth to a child: She bore three children in three years. 2. *(usually negat.)* tolerate or endure smb.: She could not bear the man Joe she was living with.

bear with someone—put up with a person; show patience towards smb.: Bear with me while I try to remember exactly what he said.

beard the lion in his den • walk into the lion's den

beard the lion in his den—confront a person of power courageously on his own ground: Seeking to give Robbie's father a piece of her mind she elects to beard the lion in his den—or rather his business office.

walk into the lion's den—find oneself in a difficult situation in which one has to face unfriendly or aggressive people: After the failure of the negotiations, he had to walk into the lion's den and face the Press.

beat a dead horse • work off the dead horse

beat a dead horse—(also: flog a dead horse) pursue a futile goal; try to revive interest in a dead issue: Son, we talked about this and the decision was "no." You are beating a dead horse.

work off the dead horse—(also: work out the dead horse) do work for which payment has already been made: The sailor was advanced one month's pay.... During the first month out, he was "working off the dead horse."

beat about the bush • beat the bush

beat about the bush—(also: beat around the bush) approach the subject indirectly; refuse to come to the point: Why should you beat about the bush when asking for better wages?

beat the bush—(also: beat the bushes) 1. search through all likely areas: Pennsylvania hunters have been accustomed to beating the bush in search of bucks. 2. try hard to get or achieve smth.: A few years ago everyone was beating the bushes for top properties in Santiago.

beat it • it beats me

beat it—1. *(sl., often imper.)* go away immediately: Mike yelled at them and told them to beat it. He then returned to comfort his children. 2. *(coll.)* surpass or do better: Tell the dealer what you've already secured in terms of the interest rate and ask if he can beat it. *Cf.: you can't beat it—said of smth. of the highest quality and unlikely to be surpassed:* We have an appreciation for good food, and you can't beat it in places like Trattoria Milanese.

it beats me—(coll., also: it beats my time) it surpasses my understanding; it leaves me puzzled: It beats me how this prestigious project can be awarded to such a poor architect.

beat one's brains out • blow one's brains out

beat one's brains out—1. *(also: dash one's brains out)* kill oneself by smashing one's head: There would be nothing to stop me from plunging down the well of the staircase and beating my brains out. 2. *(coll.)* think hard; struggle with a difficult task *(also: beat one's brains):* I've been beating my brains out all day over that report.

blow one's brains out—(coll.) kill oneself by shooting in the head: When his wife left him, Peter thought there was nothing left for him to do but blow his brains out.

beat someone to the draw • beat someone to the punch

beat someone to the draw—1. shoot quicker than an opponent in a gun fight: He called me out in Tucson and I beat him to the draw, placing a bullet right through his heart. 2. get somewhere or obtain smth. before smb. else does: I beat him to the draw and reported him to the superintendent myself, and gave my version of the story.

beat someone to the punch—1. *(Boxing)* land a blow before one's opponent can strike: I beat Hanley to the punch and he went down on his haunches. 2. = *beat someone to the draw 2:* Once in possession of those weapons, the tyrant would be undeterrable. The national security depended on beating him to the punch.

Note: *Neither expression is equivalent in meaning to the phrase* ***beat someone to the wire****—(UK also: beat someone to ribands) defeat smb. in a race or contest; show oneself superior to a person:* I've been teased a few times over the years by the boy jockeys, but once I beat them to the wire a few times they quit teasing me so much.

beat someone's time • it beats my time

beat someone's time—1. *(Sport)* improve on a person's achievement: Samson wins the race, but Xena, off in the women's Olympics, beats his time anyway. 2. *(coll.)* obtain or achieve smth. ahead of another: Well, I thought I was up for that promotion but he beat my time with his latest project. 3. *(coll.)* start a romantic relationship with smb.'s partner: Suppose Celia was in love with some man and Elspeth beat her time with him.

it beats my time—(coll., also: it beats me) it surpasses my understanding; it leaves me mystified: When she took up the pan she was puzzled to find that several biscuits were missing. "It beats my time," she said, aloud.

beat the band • to beat the band

beat the band—(coll.) be most improbable or extraordinary *(also: beat all):* I have heard of unretentive memories but that beats the band.

to beat the band—(U.S. coll.) to an extreme degree: Guests can use their brainpower to beat the band and win a free drink for every right answer.

beat the clock • beat the time

beat the clock—complete the task before a stated time: Any job is much harder if you are trying to beat the clock.

Note: *The expression does not correlate in meaning with the phrase* ***flog the clock****—(Nautical) move the hands of the clock forward (to quit one's job before the due time):* I got suspicious that the clock was being flogged in the interest of making the time of those in the mate's watch shorter.

beat the time—1. *(Music)* mark or follow the rhythm with the feet, a baton, etc. *(also: beat time):* The captain joined in with a long raucous song, beating time on the tea tray. 2. *(Sport)* improve on smb.'s achievement: He's hoping to ride two hundred miles in less than eight and a half hours, beating the time set by an eccentric Yorkshireman in 1831.

beat the socks off someone • knock someone's socks off

beat the socks off someone—(coll., also: beat someone's pants off) win decisively over an opponent in a competition: The true bingo professionals — like us — will beat the socks off the amateurs every time.

knock someone's socks off—(U.S. coll.) impress smb. greatly; amaze or stun a person: You wouldn't expect teenagers to sing opera, but these kids will knock your socks off.

See also: pull one's socks up / work one's socks off.

beat the target • hit the target

beat the target—do better than planned: It provides incentives to adopt new technologies to meet the target and to beat the target.

hit the target—meet the target; achieve the intended results: Will the government hit the target this time? At least it has the power…

beat the wind • hit the breeze

beat the wind—(also: beat the air) continue to make futile attempts: We are beating the wind: the foreign public is not eager to listen to our talks however truthful they may be.

hit the breeze—(U.S. sl.) go away promptly; make off at once: Bob Tidball was never to "hit the breeze" again. The deadly .45 of the false friend cracked and filled the gorge with a roar.

beaten to death • dead beaten

beaten to death—1. killed by beating: The magazine quoted a report which stated that prisoners were routinely starved or beaten to death. 2. *(also: flogged to death)* discussed so many times that it is not interesting any more: No sporting event is beaten to death more than the Sugar Bowl — it is analyzed again and again by the commentators.

dead beaten—(also: dead beat) extremely tired; utterly exhausted: When I saw him arrive in the same hostel as us, he was dead beaten, after having traveled for over 24 hours.

beauty sleep • sleeping beauty

beauty sleep—an afternoon nap or rest taken to improve the appearance: I remember my grandmother always took her "beauty sleep" — heaven knows how she managed it with all she did.

sleeping beauty—a business company which is a prime target for takeover because it has a high profit potential: The interesting thing with Zenith is that the company was a sleeping beauty.

become history • go down in history

become history—said of a past event, etc. that has lost its original impact or importance: Autocratic monarchy has become history now, and republicanism has become a reality.

go down in history—said of an event that is notable or memorable in history: The Northern Ireland peace agreement will go down in history as an agreement that paved the way for many others on our continent…

bed head • sleepy head

bed head—(sl.) the way one's hair looks after sleeping on it: The only time my hair is curly is when I have a bed head.

sleepy head—(coll.) a sleepy or lethargic person: I will give Laura a big hug as soon as she's awake. She really is a sleepy head.

bed of roses • rose bed

bed of roses—(usually negat.) said of a pleasant, easy condition of life: Post war Hungary was no bed of roses. Political oppression permeated every facet of life.... *Cf.: bed of thorns—said of a situation of anxiety and apprehension:* It was a bed of thorns every hour of every day all through the making of the film.

rose bed—a flowerbed of roses: Since I cannot separate lavender from roses in my mind, I plant clumps of it around my rose beds.

beef head *(UK)* • beef head *(U.S.)*

beef head (UK)—(sl.) a slow witted person: You may look all hot and sexy, but with that attitude you'll only end up with a beef head of a partner.

beef head (U.S.)—(sl.) a resident of Texas: A resident of Texas was called a "Beef-Head" by at least 1869. The name is related to Texas's famous cattle industry.

beef-tea • meat tea

beef-tea—juice of beef strained off after cooking in water *(given as stimulating food to people who are ill):* Miss Lawson tiptoed into the room, carrying a cup of beef-tea.

meat tea—(also: meat-tea) a meal taken between lunch and supper with some kind of meat dish included: This high occasion was to be celebrated by a "meat-tea."

Beefeater • meat eater

Beefeater—(UK) 1. one of the Warders of the Tower of London: The Beefeaters at the Tower wear the costume of Henry VIIth's body-guard. 2. an officer in the (ceremonial) bodyguard of the British monarch: In order to become a Beefeater, you must have an unblemished conduct record.

meat eater—(U.S. sl.) a corrupt policeman: Meat eaters spend a good deal of their working hours seeking out situations they can exploit for financial gain.

before Christ • before God

before Christ—(abbreviated B.C.) before the Christian era *(of a date calculated backwards from the birth of Christ):* Morrison mentions a dictionary in the Chinese language as having been compiled 1100 years before Christ.

before God—(used as a solemn declaration) as God sees me; as God is my witness: "I will bring up your son as if he were my own," he told the dying woman. "I promise you that, before God."

behind one's time • past one's time

behind one's time—1. after the usual or proper time: Master Gammon was half an hour behind his time for bed, and had dropped asleep in his chair. 2. using things not in style; following old ways: I started to think that either Ben had been so ahead of his time when he first came to us, or I was behind my time.

past one's time—1. = *behind one's time 1:* By the time Kewaa got home, it was past her time for bed and her mother was concerned that something had happened to her. 2. be late in menstruating *(the usual implication being that of unwanted pregnancy):* It's this way—I'm just married and my wife is past her time and I can't afford to have any children. 3. past one's prime; no longer young or efficient enough: I have sat in on school board meetings and while Jeanie may mean well she is past her time for effectiveness.

behind the times • behind time

behind the times—1. *(of things)* old-fashioned or out of date: The science books of twenty years ago are behind the times now. 2. *(of people)* using things not in style; following old ways: Mary thinks her parents are behind the times because they still do the foxtrot.

behind time—1. *(of a clock)* slow; behind the correct time: This option lets you set your computer clock several minutes ahead or behind time. 2. behind schedule; after the usual or proper time: The train was a good deal behind time, and therefore the stop was curtailed as much as possible.

behind the veil • under the veil

behind the veil—(also: beyond the veil) is used with reference to the next world: He [Christ] described the world behind the veil with the graphic force of one to whom it was no unknown country.

Note: *The expression does not correlate in meaning with the phrase* ***behind the scenes****—out of public view; in secret:* We could only assess what we could observe but here the main part of the work is carried out behind the scenes.

under the veil—is used with reference to smth. which conceals or obscures a person's true motives: Some terror acts are organized under the veil of religion in an attempt to justify such conduct.

believe in something • believe something

believe in something—1. have trust in smth.; feel sure of the value of smth.: The United States believes in the great potential of Africa. 2. feel sure of the existence of smth.: Clever farmers made good use of the belief of these people who believed in ghosts.

believe something—feel sure of the truth of smth.: I want to believe this story, but then again I still have a lot of doubts about its authenticity.

bell boy • bell buoy

bell boy—an employee in a hotel who helps guests by carrying their luggage, running errands, etc.: Led by a "bell-boy" into the lift, she walked along a pale-gray river of corridor carpet.

bell buoy—a floating buoy with a bell that gives a warning or positional signal to ships: You may hear the ringing bell buoy and see our local fishing fleet pass through the channel.

belly up to the bar • go belly up

belly up to the bar—(U.S. sl.) 1. go up to the bar to order a drink, etc.: It will be a great place to belly up to the bar, or just mingle before the shows. 2. get seriously involved; make a serious effort: There was hope for solving the crisis but it was time for all parties to "belly up to the bar."

go belly up—(coll.) become bankrupt: The recent recession led to a decrease in orders, and workers increasingly feared that the company would go belly up.

belong in something • belong to something

belong in something—(also: belong with something) be in the correct place or situation: This kind of picture does not belong in a teenage magazine.

belong to something—be a member of a group, party, etc.:

A judge who belongs to a club that excludes women may have difficulty ruling on cases of sex discrimination.

below someone • beneath someone

below someone—in a lower rank or station than another person: They have the right of censure that allows them to remove any officer below Colonel from command.

Note: *The expression is not equivalent in meaning to the phrase* ***under someone****—subordinated to or commanded by a person:* You are under San Diego but any reports you make go direct to Graz.

beneath someone—said of smth. too rude, coarse, or inappropriate for a person to do: That kind of thing is beneath Fred. I am appalled that he did it.

below the weather • under the weather

below the weather—(Aviation) said of weather conditions at ground level: The pilot had flown the aircraft down in an attempt to remain below the weather. *Cf.: above the weather—(also: over the weather) above the range of weather conditions at ground level:* As our engines were designed to operate at low level there was no possibility of flying above the weather.

under the weather—1. *(coll.)* feeling sad or not quite well: Brandeis, who was under the weather, was happier to be entertained than to entertain. 2. *(sl., euph.)* alcohol intoxicated; suffering from a hangover: Well, I see Daddy's under the weather again.

bench warmer • chair warmer

bench warmer—(coll.) a substitute in a sports team who seldom plays: He thought about leaving after the 1994 season, his third straight year as a bench-warmer.

chair warmer—(coll.) 1. *(derog.)* an ineffective office holder or employee: The judge frowned at me. The courtroom chair warmers craned necks in my direction. 2. *(pejor.)* a person who lounges for long periods sitting in a chair: He never takes me out anywhere. He's a chair-warmer at home for fair.

See also: keep the seat warm / warm the bench.

bend the ear of someone • bend the ear to someone

bend the ear of someone—(coll.) talk to a person at length in a boring and bothering way: Humphrey bent the ear of Charles Murphy for nearly two hours.

bend the ear to someone—give favorable attention to smb.: You can guarantee that the Administration will consistently bend the ear to its financial backers.

bent out of shape • out of shape

bent out of shape—(sl.) upset, worried or angry: Jane is bent out of shape because she wanted to go to the zoo, but no one would take her.

out of shape—(of an athlete) not well trained; in bad physical form: I also was out of shape, and quickly became out of breath.

beside oneself • out of oneself

beside oneself—overpowered with some strong emotion *(also: beyond oneself):* Toscanelli was beside himself with joy at finding his belief had proved true.

out of oneself—1. out of one's normal mental condition: She seemed out of herself, like her spirit had been sunk with that ship half a world away. 2. = *beside oneself:* I was out of myself with emotions. How can you call 911 for an emergency and be put on hold?

Note: *Neither expression correlates in meaning with the phrase* ***above oneself****— used of smb. who is self-important, thinking too highly of himself:* She really is above herself and forgets that she is in her position because the public thinks she is "one of them."

beside the question • beyond question

beside the question—not relevant to the subject under discussion: What you are saying may be true, but in this case it is completely beside the question.

beyond question—1. not subject to doubt or dispute: He may be a little careless in his work, but his loyalty to the company is beyond question. 2. unquestionably; without doubt: I've read other books on the Incas and this one is beyond question the best single volume on this topic.

best boy • best man

best boy—1. *(coll.)* one's favorite friend: "I was his best boy," Auguste told The Sunday Age. "I miss him dreadfully as a companion." 2. *(Film or TV production)* assistant to the chief electrician: The gaffer's assistant answers to the amusing title of best boy!

best man—the groom's aide at a wedding: Who will be your best man when you get married?

Note: *Neither expression correlates in meaning with the phrase* ***best people****—people of high social standing:* There are other hotels, but I couldn't tell you much about them: they're not patronized by the best people.

best of British luck, the • luck of the Irish, the

best of British luck, the—(often shortened to "best of British") 1. is used to wish a person very good luck: Let me wish you the best of British luck. We know how testing the competition will be. 2. is used ironically, implying that the required luck may not materialize: The chances of them winning are, let's be honest, slim, but we wish them the best of British luck.

luck of the Irish, the—1. = *best of British luck, the 1:* I have stumbled across this journal and your adventure and wish you the luck of the Irish in your pursuit. 2. extreme good luck or fortune: Maybe it was the luck of the Irish that saved McFadden on that freezing December day.

bet on the wrong horse • put the saddle on the wrong horse

bet on the wrong horse—(also: back the wrong horse) base one's plans, etc. on a wrong guess about smth.: To count on the family farm as an important thing in the American future looks like betting on the wrong horse.

put the saddle on the wrong horse—(also: get the wrong pig by the tail) lay the blame on the wrong person: Blaming the teacher for the lazy student's academic failure is putting the saddle on the wrong horse.

between a rock and a hard place • between wind and water

between a rock and a hard place—facing equally bad or undesirable alternatives: His client was between a rock and a hard place — actually the state of New York and his landlord.

between wind and water—said of the most vulnerable part: Mallinson must have guessed what was coming. Nevertheless, it hit him between wind and water.

between dog and wolf • between hawk and buzzard

between dog and wolf—is used of the time of twilight: The thought of dinner ... drove out the eeriness of the twilight glen. The hour between dog and wolf was passing.

between hawk and buzzard—1. facing equally bad or undesirable alternatives: "We are between hawk and buzzard," said Livingston; "we puzzle ourselves between the warlike and the commercial opposition." 2. = *between dog and wolf:* It's between hawk and buzzard when at long last Elias and me set off home. I know Mama won't be happy with us.

Note: *Neither expression correlates in meaning with the phrase*

between hay and grass—1. *(of a season, etc.) neither one thing nor the other:* "It's sort of between hay and grass with us, you know," he explained. "Walnuts all marketed and oranges not ready for the pickers." 2. *(U.S. coll., of a young person) not a boy (or a girl) and not yet a man (or a woman):* The boy was between hay and grass, but would make a man soon. For now, though, he looked miserable and every bit a child.

between maid • go-between

between maid—(UK dated) a young girl servant who helps in cooking and housework: She saved money for the voyage by working as a "between maid" in the London home of a "titled lady."

go-between—smb. acting as a messenger or intermediary between two parties: Beginning in the seventies, he was a go-between for Western arms manufacturers doing business with Iraq.

beyond it • off it

beyond it—(also: past it) unable any longer to pursue a normally active life as when younger: Jackson is eighty, yet he still goes to business every day. Most people are beyond it long before that age.

off it—(coll.) not feeling well: I shall hesitate before swallowing painkillers next time I feel off it and give natural remedies a try I think.

See also: not in it / not with it; out of it / well out of it.

beyond limits • out of limits

beyond limits—beyond the bounds of what is usual or proper: The total lack of respect from the staff in this place was beyond limits.

Note: *The expression is not equivalent in meaning to the phrase* ***without limits***— *without restriction; to any extent or degree:* If only the banks would lend money without limits!

out of limits—(of an area) with restricted access *(also: off limits):* The entrance to the building was out of limits to the non-students.

beyond one • beyond oneself

beyond one—beyond one's power: It is beyond me to even propose an opinion on what should be implemented to resolve this issue.

beyond oneself—overpowered with some strong feeling *(also: beside oneself):* He was beyond himself with rage and could not keep his temper.

beyond the bounds of something • out of bounds to someone

beyond the bounds of something—beyond the limits of what is acceptable or possible: To acknowledge that the question is beyond the bounds of science, is to admit that science cannot explain everything.

out of bounds to someone—said of an area not allowed to be visited by certain people: The police patrolled the bridges that gave access to a small village, which was out of bounds to troops.

biannual event • biennial event

biannual event—an event that happens twice a year: The fair, also known as Canton Fair, has been a biannual event held in spring and autumn since 1957.

biennial event—an event that happens once in every two years: This biennial event (home furnishings trade show) is held in the spring of odd-numbered years.

big day • long day

big day—a day on which important things happen: Today is going to be a big day for local athletes.

long day—1. a working-day of fairly lengthy duration: I made a very long day last Friday. 2. a day perceived as lasting unusually long (because it is boring, etc.): I was held up by storms for three long days. 3. *(biol.)* a long period of light: In most polycyclic insects long days cause continuous development.

big deal, a • big deal

big deal, a—1. an important business transaction: My brother pulled off a big deal today. I think we're going into business together. 2. said of smth. important: This attack alone may not be a big deal but in combination with others it has greater impact.

Note: *The expression does not correlate in meaning with the phrase* ***great deal, a***— *very much; a lot:* Vancouver Island has done a great deal to support the Mainland in the past, and is doing so at present.

big deal—is used as an ironic exclamation to say that smth. is not important at all: "So, I can charge an evening's entertainment to business expenses." "Oh, big deal. Carry on."

big dog • Big Grey Dog

big dog—(UK dated sl.) a man engaged to expel unruly persons from a saloon, etc.; a "chucker-out": He was "big-dog" to a disorderly house, and when called upon ... to turn out of the establishment those who had been robbed in it he did not do his spiriting gently.

Note: *The expression is not antonymous in meaning to the phrase* ***short dog***—*(U.S. sl.) a bottle of cheap wine:* Every now and then I get a short dog of Train and make my friends make funny faces as they watch me drink it.

Big Grey Dog—(U.S. sl.) a Greyhound Lines, Inc. bus *(Greyhound Lines, Inc. providing the major intercity bus transportation):* Greyhound is as American as apple pie. You have not lived unless you rode the Big Grey Dog, as I like to call it.

big drink • long drink

big drink—(U.S. sl.) the Atlantic ocean *(also: big pond):* When you're [flying] over the big drink you really get to feel how tiny we humans are.

Note: *The expression does not correlate in meaning with the phrase* ***big drink of water***—*(sl.)* 1. *a large body of water:* Lake Michigan is a big drink of water; the bacteria levels fluctuate dramatically as you move around the shore. 2. *(also: tall drink of water) a tall person:* All they knew was that the bank officer's killer was a big drink of water who looked like a mountain man.

long drink—a cold refreshing drink served in a tall glass, containing little or no alcohol: Facilities include a swimming pool and a "beach shack" serving long drinks all day.

big game • large game

big game—1. the larger animals, such as lions, etc.: For big game, Bushveld is that part of the Transvaal which the hunter must seek. 2. an important sport event: Believe it or not, the best players on your team get nervous before a big game. 3. an adventurous undertaking involving great risk and gain: Just look at my life, Luke. It's all one big long game.

Note: *The expression does not fully correlate in meaning with the phrase* ***great game***—1. *excellent performance in a sports event:* It was a great game that was tightly contested throughout. 2. = *big game 3:* Disraeli was an adventurer who played the great game *va banque* with a courage and effrontery...

large game— = *big game 1:* The country round is full of large game, especially elephants, giraffe, and zebras.

See also: little game / small game.

big hand • small hand

big hand—(usually in the phrase "give someone a big hand") a large round of enthusiastic applause: The audience gave Jason a big hand at the end of the performance.

small hand—said of a style of writing belonging to a particular person: The three folders with notebooks contained sheets carefully written in small hand.

See also: short arm / short hand.

big house • little house

big house—1. *(UK)* the principal house of an estate; the residence of the squire: Cattle sheds were at Thriepland Hill, while the "big house" and some other offices were at Branxton. 2. *(U.S. sl.)* a prison or federal penitentiary: I feel like a criminal who has been in a hideout, been caught, and has to go back to the Big House. 3. *(UK hist.)* an institution for the poor: As long as they kept out of the "big house" (the workhouse) she would not complain.

little house—(euph.) the toilet, especially an outside one: A gate led from the first yard into another in which were the pig sty, the hen-house and what they called jocosely "the little house."

big shot • large shot

big shot—(sl.) 1. an important person: I was asked to dine with Thomas Lamont, along with a number of big-shots in the American newspaper world. 2. a substantial injection of a drug: The final chase scene hit me hard, like a big shot of heroin in the mainline vein. 3. a generous portion of liquor, etc.: He then poured himself a big shot of the finest Malt.

large shot—1. = *big shot 3:* Add a large shot of vodka, a large shot of freshly made espresso coffee, and a dash of sugar syrup. 2. *(hist.)* cannon-balls: His musket balls reached us in every direction but his large shot either fell short or went considerably over us.

big stick • big sticks

big stick—a display of force or power: Happily the revolution in Paraguay is too far down in South America to arouse the "big stick" in Washington.

big sticks—1. *(Loggers)* a forest or trees: Felling one of these "big sticks" is a dangerous occupation, says Howard, a lifelong logger. 2. *(Austral. sl.)* Australian rules football goal posts: Hall gathered a loose ball in a goal-line scrap and snapped between the big sticks.

big word • little word

big word—1. a long word that is difficult to spell: Her gift [the dictionary] will always be there on the shelf, helping me to get the big words straight. 2. a rare word, especially when used in pompous speech: He is using the big words in an attempt to make himself look smart. 3. the most important word; the key-word: In the majority of the ads for new houses, "split-level" is the big word, the selling word.

little word—(also: small word) 1. a short and simple word: Jerseymen turn every statement into a question with that little word "Ay?" 2. *(coll.)* a short conversation: I want to have a little word with you about last night. 3. *(coll.)* a short utterance: If anybody dares say one little word about you, I'll tend to them.

bite one's tongue • bite the tongue

bite one's tongue—1. hold back a remark one was about to make: The thought ... almost slipped out between his lips, but he bit his tongue in time. 2. refrain from discussing smth. embarrassing, etc.: However, one recent story proved extremely hard to bite one's tongue over.

Note: *The expression is not equivalent in meaning to the phrase* ***bite one's lip****—keep back one's anger, annoyance, etc.; repress an emotion:* It was quiet for a moment, and Robert bit his lip, trying not to giggle like a little girl.

bite the tongue—(of food) be spicy or pungent: The cheese has a strong aroma and a lovely salty tang that really bites the tongue.

bitten by the same bug • tarred with the same brush

bitten by the same bug—said of people who have the same interest or hobby: My cousin and I were bitten by the same bug. We collect coins.

tarred with the same brush—said of people considered to have similar objectionable qualities: As the numbers of immigrants increase, refugees are tarred with the same brush as illegal economic migrants. *Cf.: painted with the tar brush—said of people or things represented as evil or harmful:* The myth of the liberal media grew stronger and the Democrats were painted with the tar brush.

Black Act, the • Black Acts, the

Black Act, the—(UK hist.) the English statute of 1722, directed against certain lawless persons who designated themselves "The Blacks": The Waltham blacks committed such enormities, that Government was forced to interfere with that severe Act called the Black Act.

Black Acts, the—(UK hist.) acts of the Scottish Parliament passed between the accession of James I and 1587: Under the administration of the Earl of Arran, a subservient Scottish Parliament passed the legislation known as the Black Acts, making the king supreme in all.

black and tan • Black and Tans, the

black and tan—(UK sl.) a drink composed of porter and ale: He asked for a pint of black and tan, and had to explain to the waiter what it was.

Black and Tans, the—(UK hist.) an armed force specially recruited in 1921 to combat Sinn-Fein *(an Irish movement dedicated to the unification of Northern Ireland and the Republic of Ireland):* I read a lot about the Black and Tans during my British and Irish politics class.

black and white film • black film

black and white film—a monochrome film or motion picture: He submitted a strong script that led Fox to substitute color film and wide screen for black-and-white and the conventional small-screen ratio.

Note: *The expression does not correlate in meaning with the phrase* ***black and white****—(U.S. diners) chocolate soda with vanilla ice cream:* Ever since a Philadelphia soda fountain manager whipped up the first "black and white," ice cream floats have been a favorite of sweet tooths of all ages.

black film—1. a film typically featuring the dark, seedy side of the big city: French critics saw the five films as a group and, noticing a common theme of pessimism and darkness, called them *film noir,* or black film. 2. a film with predominantly black actors: The words are revealing; for this is a black film, not only with a mostly black cast but also with a black director, Mario Van Peebles.

Note: *The expression is not equivalent in meaning to the phrase* ***black comedy****—(also: dark comedy) a film that takes serious subject matter (such as death, war, suffering, etc.) and addresses it in a humorous fashion, even when it may seem inappropriate:* Frank Sinatra stars in a black comedy about the danger of extreme left and right wing politics.

black bird • blackbird

black bird—any of the birds that have black feathers: If we cross a black bird with a white, all the offspring are grey.

blackbird—a common European songbird *(Merula turdus):* Black lark is another very large lark, more closely resembling a blackbird in size...

black board • blackboard

black board—any board of black color: Some chess players like to have contrasting colors to lessen eye strain, thus black pieces on a brown board or brown pieces on a black board.

blackboard—a board of either a dark color or white that is written on, especially in classrooms: Over half of what is written on the blackboard is erased by the end of the lesson.

black book • little black book

black book—1. a register listing persons that have committed offences against morality, etc.: The German government was in a position to blackmail 47,000 prominent British "perverts" whose names figured in a "black book." *Cf.: be in someone's black books—be out of favor with a person:* Beatrice managed to leave a very uncomfortable impression upon me and it was clear that I was in her black books again. 2. an official book offering special information: Rules relating to naval affairs are still preserved in the black book of the admiralty.

little black book—1. a book containing the names of acquaintances, potential dates, partners, etc.: I've got a nice collection in my little black book. 2. a book for recording personal or private information: Evans kept a note of his expenditure in a little black book.

Note: *Neither expression correlates in meaning with the phrase* ***black-letter book****—a book printed in the old heavy Gothic style of type:* She saw Sir John seated by the fireplace, reading out of a great black letter book.

black box • dark box

black box—1. a flight recorder in an aircraft: The flight recorder is an indestructible "black box" which automatically records the key functions in the aircraft. 2. any apparatus of unknown internal design: Crime squads are searching for the manufacturer of a black box which contains a device that can reverse electricity meter readings. 3. *(Austral.)* a tree with narrow, grey-green leaves and rugged, dark grey bark: Other communities contain species that are at the extremes of their natural distribution, such as black box *(Eucalyptus largiflorens).*

dark box—a container from which light is wholly excluded (used for storing light-sensitive plates, etc.): *Diaphanoscope*—a dark box constructed for exhibiting transparent photographs.

Note: *Neither expression is antonymous in meaning to the phrase* ***white box****—used of computers without brand names (such as Dell, HP, etc.) assembled by smaller manufacturers and often packed in unlabeled white boxes:* Computer professionals often prefer white box computers constructed with higher quality components.

black cap • black hat

black cap—1. a warbler: We followed a pleasant path through trees and soon found ourselves listening to the sweet bubbling song of a black cap. 2. *(UK hist.)* a cap put on by a judge before sentencing a person to death: He acquitted two men and then placed the black cap on his head and sentenced the other two to death.

black hat—1. *(coll.)* the bad party in a situation *(from the color of hat traditionally worn by the bad character in Western films):* Past entertainment had a moral content—the white hats won and the black hats lost. 2. *(Austral. sl.)* a new immigrant: I'd never let it be said that a black hat had cut me out.

black-collar workers • white-collar workers

black-collar workers—1. miners (especially coal miners) and oil workers: He began performing in the smoky gin mills that catered to black-collar workers who liked their booze and blues straight. 2. *(sl.)* people engaged in media industries (artists, graphic designers, video producers, etc.): Black-collar workers, for those of you that aren't cool enough to know, are the "creative types"; media, fashion, entertainment, etc.

white-collar workers—employees whose job is clerical, as opposed to *blue-collar workers* engaged in manual work: Today blue-collar workers can earn more than some of their white-collar counterparts. *Cf.: pink-collar workers—women who work at traditional non-manual jobs (as secretaries, cashiers, etc.):* The book allows the voices of the pink-collar workers to demonstrate the simultaneous burdens and pleasures of their work.

black eye • blackeye

black eye—1. a darkening of the skin about the eye resulting from a bruise: I thought they'd have a row. Hadn't Michael a black eye? 2. a severe blow or rebuff: I hope the Pension Committee will give a black eye to every bill of that kind.

blackeye—a sprawling herb *(Vigua sinensis)* cultivated for forage and green manure: Blackeye crop is allowed to fully mature, then they are cut and dried to be packaged.

black hole • black hole of Calcutta

black hole—said of a situation when money or resource disappear and are not expected to be recovered *(originally of a region of space from which nothing can escape, even light):* What steps are industrial companies taking to dig their way out this financial black hole?

black hole of Calcutta—a place that is small, dark, and uncomfortable: Somebody finally decided to do something for the poor souls we lock up in a black hole of Calcutta.

black ivory • ivory black

black ivory—*(hist.)* Black African slaves viewed as a commodity: Help them to make money otherwise than by dealing in black ivory, and we shall see the slave trade extirpated.

ivory black—a black pigment from calcined ivory: Ivory black is ivory or bones thoroughly burnt, and afterwards ground.

black-leg • Blackfoot

black-leg—1. *(UK coll.)* a non-union workman; a strikebreaker: The police were used to protect the blacklegs, as those are called who work outside the Union movement. 2. *(coll.)* a professional gambler, especially a cheating one: You see noblemen and black-legs bawling and betting in the Cockpit. 3. a disease in cattle, caused by the fungus *Leptosphaeria maculans,* which affects the legs: A cattle disease, known as blackleg, is stated to have killed a number of cattle in the district.

Note: *The expression does not correlate in meaning with its formal French counterpart* ***pied noir****—used of people of French origin living in Algeria during French rule:* M. Fabre was an elderly colon, one of the original French families in Algeria—a pied noir, as they like to be called.

Blackfoot—1. people belonging to the Blackfoot Indian Confederacy: Among the Blackfoot, stealing an enemy's weapons was the highest exploit. 2. the language of the Algonquian American Indians: A few detached languages in the west: Blackfoot, Cheyenne, and Arapaho.

black market • gray market

black market—an illegal market in which goods or currencies are bought and sold in violation of price controls, rationing, etc.: Drugs are sold at the black market and they can do much more damage than cigarettes can in most cases.

Note: *The expression is not antonymous in meaning to the phrase* ***white sale****—a sale at reduced prices of goods such as towels, linens, etc.:* We went to the white sale at the department store to buy some new sheets before my parents come to visit.

gray market—the retail business operating within the law but selling goods, such as imports, at prices below those set by an official agency: Also affected by the gray market activities are highly technical products such as disc drives, computers, computer chips.

black money • white money

black money—1. money not declared for tax purposes (by casino operators, etc.): Erlich has also promised an amnesty for those who reveal their black money and pay a tax on it. 2. money paid to workman handling dirty materials or working in dirty conditions: When any class of work involves special unpleasantness, "black money" or "dirty money" is sometimes stipulated for.

white money—(arch.) standard silver coins: Rutland pays to the King one hundred and fifty pounds white money.

See also: pink money / red money.

Black Republic, the • Black Republicans

Black Republic, the—Haiti *(a West Indian State):* My subject is Haiti, the Black Republic; the only self-made Black Republic in the world.

Note: *The expression does not correlate in meaning with the phrase **Black Country, the**—(UK) a highly industrialized region of west-central England centered on Birmingham:* It is believed that the Black Country got its name because of pollution from these heavy industries that covered the area in black soot.

Black Republicans—(U.S. hist.) Republican opponents of slavery, during the period which preceded the American Civil War: The Whig party adopted the name of Republicans, and were called by their opponents Black Republicans, from their anti-slavery tendencies.

black sheep • black swan

black sheep—smb. who is very different from the other people in the group and is considered a bad character: Every privileged class tries at first to whitewash its black sheep.

black swan—(also: white crow) said of a person or thing that is extremely rare: After all, he may not be such a black swan as Aunt Susan makes him out.

blank check • blank sheet

blank check—freedom to choose whatever course of action one thinks is necessary: The coach was given a blank check by the university to try and improve the team.

blank sheet—(also: clean sheet) 1. a fresh start when people decide to forget about previous mistakes, failures, etc.: Managers should start with a blank sheet regardless of the commitments already made and resources applied. 2. said of the human mind at birth, regarded as having no innate conceptions: Nor were they alone in their belief that a new-born's mind is a blank sheet on which society can write what it pleased.

blind auction • blind bidding

blind auction—an auction in which all parties submit sealed bids by a given date: The U.S. government sells surplus equipment and confiscated goods at blind auctions on several military posts.

blind bidding—(Cinema) putting in a bid for the rental of a picture without the opportunity to see a preview: Movie theater owners had to accept blind bidding from the distributors.

Blind Freddy • Blind Tom

Blind Freddy—(Austral. sl.) a person of low intelligence: Even Blind Freddy could tell you that the government would fall.

Blind Tom—Thomas Wiggins (born blind in 1849), an African American autistic musical prodigy: Blind Tom toured all over the U.S. giving prestigious performances.

blind to the world • dead to the world

blind to the world—(coll.) extremely drunk: He may be a nice enough fellow when he is sober. But on the two occasions I have met him he was blind to the world and a perfect nuisance.

dead to the world—(coll.) 1. unconscious or fast asleep: A muffled sound of snoring rose from the great hall where thirty exhausted lads lay dead to the world. 2. = *blind to the world:* Six beers and he was dead to the world. 3. unaware of or not interested in modern affairs: Old Marryat is dead to the world; I tried to talk to him on at least a dozen modern topics but he responded to none of them.

block operator • block worker

block operator—(Railways) a railroad worker who operates block signals manually: Under Rule 305, block operators had to inform the dispatcher of an approaching train.

block worker—a person who campaigns on the most local level (as a city block) on behalf of a political party: He has served as a Democratic Party block worker and has twice been a primary election candidate for this Congressional district.

blood bath • blood-tub

blood bath—a wholesale slaughter; a massacre: Even today, after the unspeakable horror of the blood bath in Hungary, the betting is still somewhat against a "re–Stalinization."

blood-tub—(sl.) a theater specializing in the worst forms of melodrama: Warrilow points out that more than one theatre in Burslem was affectionately known as the "Blood Tub."

Bloody Maria • Bloody Mary

Bloody Maria—a drink consisting of a mixture of tequila and tomato juice: Stir all ingredients well with ice.... For a Bloody Maria just replace the vodka with tequila.

Bloody Mary—a drink consisting of a mixture of vodka and tomato juice: A waitress approached the table. "A Virgin Mary.... A Bloody Mary without the vodka."

blow great guns • go great guns

blow great guns—(of wind) blow severely: The wind was blowing great guns but there was only the thinnest sprinkle of rain.

go great guns—(dated coll.) proceed or perform with great speed, skill, or success: You will then not only go great guns—move steadily forward—but also become big shots—important personages. *Cf.: great guns—persons of distinction or importance:* They are great guns in the kitchen, but shrink to suitable dimensions in the presence of their betters.

blow hot and cold • go hot and cold

blow hot and cold—keep changing one's attitude towards smth.: I will have nought to do with a man who can blow hot and cold with the same breath.

go hot and cold—suddenly feel very worried and frightened about smth.: I used to go hot and cold about it because I knew what the implications were.

blow it • blow me

blow it—1. *(sl.)* lose or bungle an opportunity, etc.: He'll probably blow it. He's beginning to look old. 2. *(interj.)* used as an oath or expletive to express annoyance: Blow it! I just can't get this wallpaper straight!

Note: *The expression does not correlate in meaning with the phrase **blow it out of proportion**—make smth. appear more significant than it should be:* It's sensational and it is easy to make headlines out of it. But the media blew it out of proportion.

blow me—1. *(UK)* is used as an emphatic exclamation to express surprise *(also: blow me down):* Blow me if it isn't old Charley—I've not seen you for years: how are you, old friend? 2. *(U.S. coarse sl.)* a very vulgar phrase with sexual implication hurled by an angry person: And if the authorities don't like it—well, they can blow me!

blow off steam • blow smoke

blow off steam—(also: let off steam) give vent to one's anger or frustration (by talking in an unrestrained manner, etc.): Perhaps the best way to blow off steam and get rid of stress is through exercise.

blow smoke—speak deceptively; brag or exaggerate: Hopefully they aren't blowing smoke about how good they are because I've invested heavily with them.

blow one's boiler • burst the boiler

blow one's boiler—(Austral. sl.) lose one's temper; become very angry: When I saw how much she had spent shopping online, I really blew my boiler.

burst the boiler—(U.S. sl.) overexert oneself: A man who is too lavish with his energy may be cautioned not to "burst the boiler."

blow someone away • blow someone off

blow someone away—(sl.) 1. affect smb. with overwhelming enthusiasm: The whole idea just blew her away. 2. *(Underworld)* kill a person: The boss said we was to blow you away if you gives us any trouble.

blow someone off—(sl.) 1. neglect or ignore a person: Don't blow me off. Listen! I want it done now. 2. cheat or deceive a person: They blew off a young couple and conned a hundred bucks out of them.

***Note:** Neither expression correlates in meaning with the phrase **blow someone out of the water**—(sl.) 1. utterly surprise a person:* To say the film exceeded my expectations is an understatement; it completely blew me out of the water. 2. *defeat a competitor decisively:* They also believe that if they fall behind in the functionality race, the competition will blow them out of the water.

blow someone's brains out • blow someone's mind

blow someone's brains out—kill smb. by shooting: Smith wouldn't do anything so supposedly masculine as cold-bloodedly blow someone's brains out with a shotgun.

blow someone's mind—cause excitement or the state of ecstasy; overwhelm a person: The beauty of the African wildlife parks blew my mind completely during our trip.

Blue Bird • bluebird

Blue Bird—is used as a symbolical expression of happiness: All these ladies have tried to catch this same Blue Bird.

bluebird—1. any of several birds that have blue feathers: We were fortunate to see such birds as a sky-blue mountain bluebird. 2. *(Drug users)* a depressant; a blue capsule or tablet containing barbiturate: Here, this little bluebird will sing you to sleep.

***Note:** The compound does not correlate in meaning with the phrase **blue canary**—an emergency worker (a firefighter or a law enforcement officer) whose death alerts other personnel to a hazardous situation (from the use of canaries in coal mines, whose death would alert miners to the presence of dangerous gases):* The "blue canaries," as police and firefighters are sometimes called, would probably suffer heavy casualties until the (chemical) agent is identified.

Blue Book • Project Blue Book

Blue Book—1. a government publication providing information on some topic: The U.S. Department of State issued a heavily documented 40,000-word Blue Book. 2. a directory of persons of prominence, etc.: The Blue Book of British Broadcasting is a standard reference book of TV and radio stations. 3. a list of rules or requirements: When the document is sent to the Panel a charge is payable according to the scales set out in the Blue Book.

Project Blue Book—the dossier that the U.S. Air Force maintains on unidentified flying objects: "Project Blue Book? Wasn't that about UFOs?" Nick could hardly believe what he was hearing.

blue boys • boys in blue

blue boys—1. *(coll.)* the police: Four blue boys held me while a fifth slipped the cuffs on me. 2. *(UK hist.)* schoolboys of a charity school who wear blue coats *(also: bluecoat boys):* The school whose boys were known as "blue boys," was dissolved in the nineteenth century.

boys in blue— = blue boys 1: How do you manage between clients who call the police "pigs" and your professional peers who regard them as upright boys in blue.

blue coats • bluecoat boys

blue coats—1. *(coll.)* the police: One of the blue coats would attempt to put back the crowd. 2. blue-coated seamen: These were blue coats — French — who were on shore for a visit. 3. *(U.S. hist.)* a soldier in the Federal army during the Civil War: Wait until the States are restored and the "Blue Coats" are out of the way.

bluecoat boys—(UK hist.) schoolboys of a charity school who wear blue coats *(also: blue boys):* The day after Christmas Day was a high day with us as Bluecoat boys. We then received our yearly new coat and cap...

blue devil • blue devils

blue devil—1. *(also: blueweed)* a coarse prickly weed with spikes of blue flowers: Blue devil is a coarse biennial Old World herb introduced as a weed in eastern North America. 2. *(Drug users)* a blue capsule or tablet containing barbiturate *(also: bluebird):* I am spending far less than I was while taking those little blue devil pills.

***Note:** The expression does not correlate in meaning with the phrase **blue devil fish**— a reef fish (Paraplesiops bleekeri) inhabiting exposed reefs from 3 to 30 meters deep:* Blue devil fish are easily identified by the blue and white-banded body with yellow pectoral fins.

blue devils—1. a feeling of depression; despondency: By the time that he had eaten his soup and drank a glass of wine, he had got rid of the fit of blue devils. 2. the apparitions seen in *delirium tremens:* They, by a continued series of intoxication, become subject to what is popularly called the Blue Devils.

blue heavens • blue skies

blue heavens—(Drug users) blue capsules or tablets containing barbiturate: Amobarbital tablets and capsules are called "blue birds," "blue devils," or "blue heavens."

blue skies—(also: blue sky) 1. said of impractical or unfeasible plans and ideas: The research amounted to a "blue skies" project because it involved going beyond the present capacity of the reactor design. 2. (*U.S. stock market*) is used of fake or worthless bonds and stocks: They were what I would term "blue sky and hot air" securities.

blue laws • blue-sky laws

blue laws—(U.S.) laws characterized by extreme strictness in matters of morals: Even the religious fanatics of Boston and the mad zealots of Hertford christened them the "Blue Laws."

blue-sky laws—(U.S.) laws designed to prevent fraud in the sale of stocks: The "Blue Sky" law of Kansas prohibits the sale of stock or bonds of any company chartered outside the State.

blue million • blue money

blue million—(coll.) lots of money: West Virginia taxpayers have spent a blue million to provide computers to thousands of offices in state government.

blue money—(U.S.) 1. money from the states whose residents predominantly vote for the Democratic Party, as contrasted with "red money" associated with the Republican Party: Urban areas subsidize rural areas, and the rural parts of America are more red than blue. Hence the claim of blue money flowing into red pockets. 2. *(also: old money)* said of the inherited wealth of people who have been rich for many generations: We wonder why she isn't planning on donating all of her earnings from the tape to charity, since she clearly doesn't need the "blue money."

Note: *The expression does not correlate in meaning with the verbal phrase* ***blue one's money****—(sl.) spend one's money quickly and recklessly:* Men in cotton shirts and corduroys met there to "blue" their money on fiery colonial rum.

blue sky • sky blue

blue sky—(also: blue skies) 1. said of impractical or unfeasible plans and ideas: The rocket was dismissed as just another blue-sky project when the concept was unveiled. 2. (*U.S. stock market*) is used of fake or worthless bonds and stocks: They were what I would term "blue sky and hot air" securities.

sky blue—a deep somewhat purplish blue color: The flag on one side of the building was sky blue; the one on the other side was the somewhat darker shade...

board school • boarding school

board school—(UK hist.) free elementary school run by local education authority and supported by a parliamentary grant: What guarantee is there that they would not turn the school into a "provided" or Board School?

boarding school—a school where some or all of the pupils live during term time: At the Hanover boarding school the young girls flocked around her and listened to her gentle voice telling tales from Dickens.

boarding home • boarding house

boarding home—1. a home for foster children: Jacqueline was placed in a boarding home and then adopted by a couple from Plymouth. 2. a private house that provides board and lodging: Two women take up residence at a boarding home that had previously been an all-male residence.

boarding house— = boarding home 2: She had some skill in the matter of keeping a boarding house and her future might indeed lie in that direction.

boat man • bumboat man

boat man—1. a man who lends out small boats or rows one for pay: There he found a solitary boatman, whom he hailed, and was soon seated in his kayak. 2. a water-bug *(Notonecta glauca),* whose body resembles a boat: The boatman dives under the water, occasionally coming to the surface for a supply of air.

Note: *The expression does not correlate in meaning with the phrase* ***boat person****—(pl. boat people) a refugee who attempts to flee his country by putting out to sea in a small boat:* There's nothing wrong with being a boat person. The boat saved my life.

bumboat man—(pl. bumboat people) a person in a boat selling small merchandise to ships lying at a distance from the shore: A bumboat man sold him a dodgy camera without film on his first trip through the Suez Canal.

boat people • river people

boat people—refugees who attempt to flee their country by putting out to sea in a small boat: Most people were never aware that a great number of the boat people died on the ocean.

river people—(Austral.) the Barkindji (an Aboriginal nation) who lived along the Darling River in western New South Wales: The riverboat trade began around 1853, at which time the lifestyles of the river people were disturbed irreversibly.

Boat Race, the • boat race

Boat Race, the—(UK) the annual race between the rowing crews of Oxford and Cambridge Universities: The event which most excited children's loyalties was the Boat Race.

boat race—a race between rowing-boats: We are sorry to state that the proposed boat race will not take place.

boat-train • liner train

boat-train—a passenger train timed to meet a boat: There was a domestic agency called Universal Aunts doing things that real aunts ought to be doing, like meeting small boys from India at the boat train.

liner train—an express goods train between industrial centers and seaports: If Beeching's figures are accepted at their face value, the cost of carrying goods by liner trains will be much less than by heavy lorries.

boathouse • houseboat

boathouse—a small building or shed at the edge of a river or lake, in which boats are kept: Canoes and kayaks are popular on the lake and can also be rented from the boathouse.

houseboat—1. *(U.S. also: float home)* a boat roofed over and fitted up as a house for living in: Living in a houseboat has its charm. The tranquility and view is unequivocal. 2. *(U.S. diners)* banana split *(an ice cream–based dessert served with sliced bananas):* They learn to say "mats" for pancakes, and "houseboat" for banana split, for instance, in their diner adventure.

body English • body language

body English—an attempt to control the movement of an object by contorting the body without touching the object: Todd and Leszek demonstrate the intensity, concentration, and body English that are required to push a radio controlled sailboat.

body language—communication by facial expression and gestures rather than by spoken language: When we have a hunch that somebody is telling lies, for instance, what we really mean is that their body language and their spoken words do not agree.

body shop • body shopper

body shop—1. a shop or garage where the bodies of automotive vehicles are repaired: After a car accident, I had my car repaired at a body shop my insurance company referred me to. 2. *(Body Shop)* a UK based skin and body care company: A talk was given by a Body Shop representative about the pressures put on women in order for cosmetic companies to sell their anti-aging products. 3. *(sl.)* an employment agency: Known as "body shops," some of these middlemen are at the heart of many of the charges of visa fraud. They recruit workers overseas and arrange for their visas.

body shopper—(sl.) a contractor in a Third World country who recruits local programmers for U.S. companies: Programmers undercut by foreign body shoppers are waging a campaign to get immigration authorities to stop issuing short-term visas to foreign programmers.

body work • body worker

body work—1. certain physical therapies like jogging, aerobics, etc.: Take thirty minutes out your day to do body work; it can be walking, Yoga, aerobics, whatever you enjoy. 2. work on the metal shell of a motor vehicle: I bought my Mustang from a guy who did body work for a living, so it has had quite a bit of work done to it.

body worker—(U.S. euph.) an erotic masseur; a prostitute: In the same manner that some prostitutes refer to themselves as escorts ... many erotic masseurs refer to themselves as body workers.

boil down • boil up

boil down—be reduced by boiling: These plums are heaped up in the pan, but they will boil down.

boil up—(of a quarrel, crisis, etc.) develop; be about to occur: A dispute is boiling up over who should be the first to greet our royal visitors.

boil something down • boil something up

boil something down—(coll.) state smth. briefly; summarize smth.: I have tried to state briefly, to boil down, the most important area of conflict.

boil something up—1. boil or wash clothes: There was a grand jungle by a small, clean river where they boiled up their verminous clothes. 2. make tea: In modern India, tea is usually boiled up very strong with milk and lots of sugar.

Note: *The expression does not correlate in meaning with the phrase* ***bring something to the boil***—*cause smth. such as a problem to reach an urgent state:* Issues concerning the intellectual property rights have been simmering since the 1990s. Developments in communications technology have brought these issues to the boil. *Cf.: go off the boil—(coll.) cease to be active or interesting:* The housing issue has gone off the boil recently, despite attempts to revive public interest.

bold as a lion • bold as an Essex lion

bold as a lion—very brave and daring, especially in times of danger: He might have behaved timidly in life; in the book he would be bold as a lion.

bold as an Essex lion—(UK ironic) said of a very meek person: Oh! yes, he is as bold as an Essex lion, especially when there is no danger about.

Note: *Neither expression correlates in meaning with the phrase* ***bold as brass***—*used of a shameless, impudent person:* He came into my office as bold as brass and told me they would stop work if they didn't get any more money.

bon mot • good word

bon mot—(Fr.) is used to refer to a clever, often biting, joke or witticism: "The luxuries of the mansion have been transferred to the hovel," he laughed, pleased with his bon mot.

good word—favorable opinion about a person as conveyed to his potential employer, etc.: I beg you to say a good word for me to your father. He regards me, I believe, as a very light fellow...

bona fide • bona fides

bona fide—(used as an adjective or adverb) 1. genuine; certified: The ticket for these activities is issued only to bona fide students who can present their college identity card. 2. sincerely; in good faith: An advocate is protected from an action for defamation only when the words he utters are spoken bona fide.

bona fides—(used as a noun) 1. an honest intention; sincerity: Bona Fides is therefore opposed to fraud, and is a necessary ingredient in contracts. 2. (documentary) evidence of good faith: All strangers whose bona fides are not completely verified must be immediately reported to your superior officer.

boob tube *(UK)* • boob tube *(U.S.)*

boob tube (UK)—a woman's strapless top that wraps the upper body (not reaching higher than the armpits): It was freezing ... but at least I wasn't wearing a boob tube and miniskirt like one poor girl.

boob tube (U.S. sl.)—television: Parents complain about the quality of the shows but don't prevent their children from gluing themselves to the boob tube.

book agent • booking agent

book agent—(U.S.) a person who promotes the sale of books: They may both be glad to invoke the aid of the despised book agent, who carries literature from door to door.

booking agent—an official selling advance tickets at a railway station, etc.: When booking tickets with any one of the airlines, reference the appropriate file number to the booking agent to receive the discount.

book-holder • book-keeper

book-holder—(dated) a theatrical prompter: Bentley supplies evidence for the existence of a functionary called the "prompter" or "book-holder" from about 1615 on. There is little evidence about his precise duties.

book-keeper—a person who keeps accounts of a business, public office, etc.: The telegram contained the offer of a job, that of a book-keeper on a sheep run east of Broken Hill.

Book of Psalms, the • psalm-book

Book of Psalms, the—the book of the Old Testament containing the Psalms: The Book of Psalms contains the productions of different writers. These are called however the Psalms of David, because a great part of them were composed by him.

psalm-book—a book containing the Psalms, especially with metrical settings arranged for use in public worship: See this bundle of ballads.... I wheedled an old woman out of these, who loved them better than her psalm-book.

book of words • word-book

book of words—(coll.) printed instructions (not necessarily in a book form): I can't quite see how to put this thing together. Where's the book of words?

word-book—1. a list of words with meanings, etc.: It would, however, seem almost necessary to emphasize that this Word-Book is not a dictionary of school slang. 2. libretto of a musical composition: Besides translating many foreign libretti, Chorley wrote the original word-books of one version of the "Amber Witch."

book someone in • bring someone to book

book someone in—1. *(also: sign someone in)* record the entrance of an employee, the name of a guest on arrival at a hotel, etc.: I'll just book you in and then you can have a rest. 2. make an entry of a person's name, etc. in a police register following detention: If you are taken into police custody, you will be booked in by the duty police officer.

Note: *The expression is not equivalent in meaning to the phrase* ***book someone***—*(Police) charge a person with a legal offence:* He was booked for speeding and driving without a licence.

bring someone to book—call smb. to account; make a person responsible for doing smth. wrong: They must have had powerful supporters, for little attempt seems to have been made to bring them to book.

bookman • handbook man

bookman—smb. who is interested in and knowledgeable about books: Bryant was a real bookman, not just someone who liked books, but someone with a passion for books.

handbook man—a bookmaker: Bartenders, handbook men and habitués of dope-staches could be paraded by the dead unknown in the morgue.

Books of Kings, the • books of the Four Kings, the

Books of Kings, the—certain books of the Old Testament which contain the history of the Kings of Israel: The Books of Chronicles ... so called as containing particulars omitted in the Books of Kings.

books of the Four Kings, the—(arch.) a pack of playing cards *(also: history of the Four Kings, the):* Playing cards were originally called "the Books of the Four Kings," while chess was known as "the Game of the Four Kings."

border on something • border something

border on something—1. be next to smth.; lie close to smth.: The old park borders on the shores of the lake. 2. *(of a country)* share a boundary with another country: Soviet territory facing the West borders on Poland, Czechoslovakia, and Hungary. 3. resemble smth.; verge upon smth.: What you are doing borders on the ridiculous.

border something—form a border along the edge of smth.: The climate of the land bordering the sea varies from being tropical in the south and sub-tropical in the north.

bother about something • bother with something

bother about something—be concerned about smth.; worry about smth.: Meditation is so beautiful, who bothers about the result? And if you bother about the result, meditation is not possible.

bother with something—concern oneself with smth.; preoccupy oneself with smth.: "So you just grab breakfast and get on the train?" "No I never bother with breakfast, I grab a coffee on the train."

bottom dollar • top dollar

bottom dollar—(coll.) one's last dollar: When he got down to his bottom dollar it was time to head back into the mountains for another year's worth of trapping.

top dollar—(coll.) a high or the highest price: A lot of those guys had paid him top dollar to buy their enlistment in the six months' program.

bottom drawer • top drawer

bottom drawer—the collection of articles for the home that a girl gathers before she gets married: I got some lovely towels at the sale, mum. I can't make up my mind whether to start using them or put them in my bottom drawer.

top drawer—(coll.) the upper ranks of society: I don't know anything about art, and I haven't met any grand people. I'm not what he calls out of the top drawer.

bottom line • bottom of the line

bottom line—the final determining factor; the essence of the argument: George Murphy and Ronald Reagan certainly qualified because they have gotten elected. I think that's the bottom line.

Note: *The expression does not correlate in meaning with the phrase* ***down line****—(Railroad) a single track of rails in a double line of railway (for trains traveling from right to left):* Originally the east line was the up line and the west line was the down line, giving conventional left hand running.

bottom of the line—said of the lowest quality, especially in merchandise: We offer quality products for a price competitive to what our competitors sell their bottom of the line products for.

See also: top line / up line.

bottom up • bottoms up

bottom up—upside down: A yawl-boat was landed bottom up from the hurricane-deck upon the heads of those below.

bottoms up—(usually used as a toast) finish one's drink to the last drop: The old priest drank his highball almost bottoms up.

bound up in something • bound up with something

bound up in something—very busy with smth.; deeply devoted to smth.: He is so bound up in his work and the details of craftsmanship that he seems unreasonable to his siblings.

bound up with something—closely connected or associated with smth.: His artistic career is bound up with the developments of New Ink Painting in Hong Kong.

bow oneself out • bow out

bow oneself out—bow (to a superior) as one leaves the place: The maids turned as one, saw their emperor and swiftly bowed themselves out of the room.

bow out—1. leave a party, a group of people, etc.: Waving a hand absently, her mother dismissed Miss Jones, who quickly bowed out of the room. 2. give up a prominent position in politics, on the stage, etc.: So Sir Harold bows out, at the end of a distinguished career in broadcasting.

Box Day • Boxing Day

Box Day—1. *(Scot.)* one of the days during vacation appointed in the Court of Session on which pleading may be filed: Box day is a day when the courts of law being closed, lawyers and litigants can hand in papers. 2. *(UK)* first weekday after Christmas Day observed as a holiday: I'll see Jean and her family on Box Day, but I promised Wylie next year we would have Christmas with him.

Boxing Day— = Box Day 2: On Christmas Day and Boxing Day all inland telegram deliveries will be suspended.

boy, oh boy • boys will be boys

boy, oh boy—an exclamation used as an expression of a range of emotions such as excitement, surprise, etc.: So my friend, Krista, came for a visit last week and boy-oh-boy was I ready for a vacation!

boys will be boys—is used to say that boys or even grown-up men are expected to act noisy or misbehave: Well, boys will be boys, you know; we were just the same ourselves when we were young.

boy toy • boy's toy

boy toy—1. said of smth. that provides enjoyable pastime to grown-up men: Dive propulsion vehicles or underwater scooters have traditionally been a boy toy. 2. *(sl., also: toy boy)* a woman's very young lover: So what if your man is a boy toy? Enjoy it while you need it to last!

boy's toy— = boy toy 1: A car is a boy's toy that a man is possessive about, hence he relates to his car more than a woman does.

boys on the bus, the • man on the bus, the

boys on the bus, the—(U.S. coll.) members of the press who travel with campaigning politicians *(also: boys and girls on the bus, the):* Columnist Jules Witcover, one of "the boys on the bus" concluded that the candidates' entourage was about the last place to be these days.

man on the bus, the—the ordinary person of either sex; "the man in the street": The complex matters involve concepts such as illiquid investments ... none of which will mean much to the man on the bus who may be, with reason, worrying about his pension.

Note: *The expression does not fully correlate in meaning with the phrase* ***man on the Clapham omnibus, the****—(UK)* 1. *= man on the bus, the:* If you ask the man on the Clapham omnibus he will typically think that things are getting better. 2. *(Law) a legal term for a "normal," reasonably educated person:* If the average person, or as legally defined "the man on the Clapham omnibus," would find something unreasonable, a court may be satisfied...

See also: bus boy / busman.

branch off • branch out

branch off—deviate from an original direction: At the bridge a little road branches off from the highway and follows the river.

branch out—1. *(of a tree)* spread out into branches: The tree branched out in every direction, casting a vast shadow over the house. 2. = *branch off:* After a pair of bends in descent the asphalt ends and the road branches out in three directions. 3. add new interests or activities: John started a television repair shop, then he branched out and began selling television sets too.

brand-name dropping • name-dropping

brand-name dropping—attempting to impress others by mentioning the brand names of goods that one owns: We just lay there on my Thermarest Ultra-Light listening to my tiny Grundig shortwave and had a great old time. Sorry about all the brand-name-dropping...

name-dropping—attempting to impress others by familiarly mentioning the names of distinguished people in order to imply one's own importance: Clarke loves to make fun of his name-dropping. "Name-dropping is vulgar as I told the Queen last week," he joked.

brand-iron • branding iron

brand-iron—1. framework of metal bars used to support burning wood: What are usually called dog-irons on the hearth are called brand-irons, having to support the brand or burning log. 2. *(dated)* a tool used red-hot for branding cattle or implements: In one farm, the brand iron did not correspond to the brand registered on the official bulletin of the owner.

branding iron— = *brand iron 2:* The branding iron must burn deep enough to burn the hair and the outer layer of skin.

brass hat • tin hat

brass hat—(coll.) 1. a senior officer in the armed forces: For two hours in late January, the brass hats of the Pentagon cloistered themselves with President Clinton. 2. any important or influential person: The trouble was that he was a curate, and the brass hats of the Church look askance at curates who swat parishioners.

tin hat—a steel trench helmet: The trench hat, "the old tin hat," is coming into quite extensive use as a means of head protection against small falls of rock in mines.

brave it out • put up a brave front

brave it out—deal with a frightening or upsetting situation in a brave way: Several were wading about in the water. Two were braving it out in swim-trunks.

put up a brave front—make a pretence of courage and bravery: We know that Mary is frightened, but she is putting up a brave front.

breach of arrest • breach of arrestment

breach of arrest—(Military legal) said of an arrested person going beyond the limits of arrest as set by orders: If, after such arrest, he commits a breach of arrest, an additional charge will properly be added in the case...

breach of arrestment—(Scot., legal) illegal disposal of property placed under the control of a law-court: A third party–arrestee parting with arrested property in breach of arrestment may be required to pay its amount...

break a fly upon the wheel • fly on the wheel

break a fly upon the wheel—spend a great deal of effort upon smth. not worth it: To apply more elaborate criticism to them, would be "to break a fly upon the wheel."

fly on the wheel—a person who fancies himself of importance, but who is in reality of none at all: The world grinds on: we are a fly on the wheel.

break an agreement • break off an agreement

break an agreement—act in opposition to an agreement; violate an agreement: It was made clear that if Janet were to break this agreement the therapist would discontinue contact with her.

break off an agreement—cancel or terminate an agreement: Tensions prevailed and things came to a point of no return when Lufthansa unilaterally broke off the agreement.

break away • break off • break out

break away—come apart from smth.: The wing of the plane broke away in mid-air.

break off—1. = *break away:* The mast had broken off at its base, and lay over the side of the boat. 2. stop speaking: Jim was in the middle of a funny story when he broke off to answer the telephone. 3. stop working for a short time: Let's break off and have a cup of tea.

break out—(of a war, fire, etc.) begin suddenly: A fire broke out in the hospital last night.

break camp • break out of camp

break camp—leave a camp or a camping-place: The daily routine will be to break camp after breakfast and load our equipment onto the boats.

break out of camp—escape from a detention camp: The following day they tried to break out of camp and although unarmed they were shot down.

break down • break up

break down—1. *(of machinery)* fail to operate: The car broke down on the way to the airport, and I had to take a taxi. 2. *(of an attack, talks, etc.)* fail; come to nothing: I expect the negotiations to break down soon. 3. suffer emotional disorder; lose control of oneself: The task before her was so difficult that she almost broke down in performing it.

break up—1. *(of things)* separate into smaller pieces or parts: In spring the ice on the Great Lakes breaks up. 2. *(of a party, meeting, etc.)* come to an end: The party broke up when the police arrived. 3. *(U.S. coll.)* convulse with laughter; be greatly amused: Peter just broke up when we told him what had happened. 4. *(of married people)* separate: She had heard that John and Lucille had just broken up.

break even • get an even break

break even—emerge from a transaction, etc. with balancing gains and losses; make neither profit nor loss: Today a novel needs to sell 5,000 copies for a publisher to break even.

get an even break—(coll.) get an equal or fair chance; get the same opportunity as other people: Some guys never get an even break. Some guys toil and sweat from sun up to sun down.

break into a bank • break the bank

break into a bank—get into a bank by using force (breaking a lock, window, etc.) with the intention to rob: Champ's accomplice produces blueprints showing how they can break into the bank by digging a tunnel under the sweet shop.

break the bank—1. win all the money at a casino gambling table: He broke the bank at every roulette table he played in, which essentially meant that he won all the money set for that table. 2. *(often negat.)* be too expensive: Even well-known brand names, such as Revlon and L'Oreal stock affordable products that won't break the bank, so it's good to go hunting around for sales.

break it down • break it up

break it down—1. explain smth.: Let me break it down for you — when a dog shows its teeth, it's about to attack you. 2. *(Austral., NZ sl.)* stop it; come off it *(used as an expression of disbelief, disagreement or a plea for moderation):* Let's break it down. I said I don't know the man. Never met him.

break it up—1. disperse; get moving: A policeman forced his way through the crowd, shouting, "Stand aside! Break it up!" 2. stop the fight or quarrel: All right you two, break it up! Don't make me get a hose on you…

break one's silence • break the silence

break one's silence—1. finally bring up a subject: Charlotte described the telephone call with which the kidnappers had broken their silence. 2. say smth. after a long pause in conversation: Enoch sat hunched and brooding, breaking his silence only to pass the time of day with John Biffen.

break the silence— = *break one's silence 2:* Everything was quiet and time seemed to stand still until Jill broke the silence saying that Dave had won.

break something away • break something off • break something out

break something away—detach smth. completely by breaking: You'll have to break the branches away to get through the thick forest.

break something off—1. cause smth. to come apart from smth. else: Mary broke off some of the chocolate to give to the children. 2. = *break something away:* These are wonderful plants and I definitely need advice on what to do after they bloom. How far do you break the branches off? 3. *(of an agreement, association, etc.)* end abruptly; discontinue: The talks were broken off an hour ago and will not be resumed today. 4. stop doing smth. for a short time: Let's break off work and have a cup of tea now.

break something out—1. break smth. in an outward direction: They had to break the door out to escape from the fire. 2. unfold or open smth.: We must break out a new case of wine for his birthday.

break something down • break something up

break something down—1. destroy smth. by reducing to pieces: The old cars were broken down for their metal and parts. 2. cause smth. to be defeated; overcome smth.: The police tried to break down the prisoner's opposition. 3. cause matter to undergo chemical change: Chemicals in the body break down our food into useful substances. 4. separate smth. into parts; refer smth. to different categories: The figures must be broken down into several lists.

break something up—1. *(of ice, etc.)* cleave smth. into smaller pieces: Enviro Disposal Service can break up old concrete driveways, then haul away the debris. 2. disband an organization, etc.; cause smth. to cease: The king's death at once broke up the unity of the Court.

break the Queen's English • clip the Queen's English

break the Queen's English—*(also: break the King's English)* speak incorrectly owing to lack of skill: Every Berliner feels exalted when a real English jockey speaks to him and gives him an opportunity of breaking the Queen's English.

clip the Queen's English—*(dated sl., also: clip the King's English)* pronounce words hurriedly and indistinctly when drunk: He was pretty far overcome by the Champaign, for he clipped the Queen's English.

break the wind • break wind

break the wind—said of a line of trees, fence, etc. which gives protection against the wind: The dunes break the wind on the beach and provide a beautiful background.

break wind—*(euph., also: pass wind)* expel intestinal gas from the anus: I'll kill the first son of a bitch who even breaks wind.

Note: *Neither expression correlates in meaning with the compound* ***broken-winded***—*(also: wind-broken) used of a horse that has impaired breathing:* The train was heavy, and where there was any incline the two engines grunted like broken-winded horses.

break time • broken time

break time—an interval for lunch: Many schools are on the one hand educating children about healthy eating and on the other selling at break time nothing less than junk foods.

broken time—working time reduced by interruptions, etc.: It is up to each individual union to deal with this problem, but the obvious right course is to compensate for broken time.

breakdown car • broken-down car

breakdown car—a truck which is used to tow inoperative vehicles: If you have a breakdown we are always on call with our own breakdown car.

broken-down car—a car that stops working because there is smth. wrong with it: The wayside was strewn with motor tires and broken down cars.

bridal banquet • bridal party

bridal banquet—a wedding festivity: The bridal banquet is not an obligatory part of the wedding process, and its holding will depend on the traditions of the bride's family.

bridal party—the bride and her attendants and friends: The question of who should be invited to join the bridal party was a huge topic of discussion this morning.

bright as a button • bright as a new pin

bright as a button—*(usually of children)* intelligent; quick-minded: You can't fool Mandy. She may be only six years old, but she's bright as a button.

Note: *The expression is antonymous in meaning to the phrase* ***bright as a two-watt bulb***—*(Austral., ironic) dull or stupid:* Johnnie's about as bright as a two-watt bulb, and sometimes the light's a little slow coming on.

bright as a new pin—said of smth. spotlessly clean and shiny: After Nora cleaned the house, it was as bright as a new pin.

bright in the eye • bright-eyed and bushy-tailed

bright in the eye—*(dated sl.)* slightly drunk: "You are drunk!" Walter clutched the window frame and muttered, "Just a trifle bright in the eye, love."

bright-eyed and bushy-tailed—*(U.S. sl.)* alert and enthusiastic; ready for action: You look all bright-eyed and bushy-tailed this morning.

bring down the curtain on something • draw the curtain on something

bring down the curtain on something—*(also: ring down the curtain on something)* cause an activity, business, etc. to come to an end: Lewis refuses to fix a date when he will bring down the curtain on his incredible fight career.

draw the curtain on something—*(also: draw the curtain over something)* refrain from discussing smth.; be discreet or secretive about smth.: What happened when he got home, I dare not describe. Better draw the curtain on the scene.

bring home the bacon • bring home the silver

bring home the bacon—1. work and earn money for one's family: Single mothers get little support, and the system has long been constructed on the premise that the husbands will bring home the bacon. 2. succeed in an undertaking; accomplish smth. of significant value: The company's aggressive promotional efforts seem to have brought home the bacon, despite technical problems.

bring home the silver—*(Sport)* take second place; come in second *(with reference to the silver medals awarded in competi-*

tions): Canada brought home the silver on a day when the opponent were simply better.

bring one's mind to something • bring something to mind

bring one's mind to something—direct one's attention to smth.: Again, Phillips cannot bring his mind to touch the issue squarely; it keeps shying into side issues.

bring something to mind— make a person recall smth.: It brought to mind an experience I had in Labrador this past summer when I was up there fishing.

Note: *The expression does not correlate in meaning with the phrase* ***bring something to a head****—*1. *bring smth. to an end; complete smth.:* This brings to a head and culminates all the nameless massacres in Asia Minor. 2. *cause smth. to reach a critical stage:* Matters have been brought to a head in the peace talks; tomorrow they will either succeed or fail.

bring one's pigs to a bad market • bring one's pigs to a fine market

bring one's pigs to a bad market—(UK dated) be unsuccessful; fail in an undertaking *(also: bring one's eggs to a bad market):* Yet, desirous as the schoolmaster might be to send the spectators away in good humor, he brought his eggs to a bad market.

bring one's pigs to a fine market—(ironic) = bring one's pigs to a bad market: In our way to our lodging, after a profound silence on both sides, Strap, with a hideous groan, observed that we had brought our pigs to a fine market.

Note: *Neither expression correlates in meaning with the phrase* ***drive one's pigs to market****—(UK dated) snore loudly:* The sleeping men ... went on driving their pigs to market for all they were worth.

bring sand to the beach • sell snow to the Eskimos

bring sand to the beach— come with a girlfriend or boyfriend to a party where there are plenty of single women and men: Actually, I don't suggest bringing any significant other to a club — why bring sand to the beach.

sell snow to the Eskimos—take goods, etc. to a place where they are already plentiful: It sounds as sensible as trying to sell snow to the Eskimos, but a Yorkshire company really believes it can persuade us to buy fresh air.

bring shame on someone • put someone to shame

bring shame on someone—bring discredit upon a person; disgrace or dishonor a person: Bessie, whatever you do — don't bring shame on the family like I have.

put someone to shame—make smb. feel ashamed or humiliated (by showing superior qualities): That she had not been put to shame and made to feel her unfortunate position seemed remarkable.

bring someone back • bring someone back out

bring someone back—make a person or animal come back to life: There was nothing that would bring Jimmy's cat back. It was truly dead.

bring someone back out—succeed in bringing a performer back onto the stage for applause: They brought her back out seven times, cheering and applauding.

bring someone down • bring someone down a peg

bring someone down—1. *(also: bring someone to the ground)* cause a person to come down or fall: In American football, you have to try to bring down your opponent. 2. *(also: bring someone to the ground)* defeat an enemy or an opponent: Truman wanted to bring down his rival in the next election and succeeded. *3. (also: bring someone down to earth)* make a person return to reality (face unpleasant truth, etc.): This bad news brought me down quickly.

bring someone down a peg—(also: bring someone down a peg or two) make smb. feel less important; snub or humiliate a person: Frederick has too high an opinion of himself; it's time we brought him down a peg.

See also: get someone down / take someone down.

bring someone down to earth • bring someone to the ground

bring someone down to earth—1. cause a pilot to descend: If you take your parachute you have a certain return ticket, and one that will bring you safely down to earth. 2. *(also: bring someone down)* make a person return to reality (face unpleasant truth, etc.): So I call for the bill. Which brings us down to earth with an ugly thud.

bring someone to the ground—(also: bring someone down) 1. *= bring someone down to earth 1:* The ejection seat was used three times ... it worked as planned and three times it brought the pilot to the ground dead! 2. knock smb. down: A crabstick, which was all the weapon he had, brought the fellow to the ground with the first blow. 3. inflict a crushing defeat upon an opponent: This nation will not be brought to the ground by enemy action!

bring someone into the picture • put someone in the picture

bring someone into the picture—cause smb. to be involved in or concerned with a situation: "You may need me as a witness...." "No Steve. Unless it becomes absolutely necessary to bring you into the picture, I think I'd rather not."

put someone in the picture—tell smb. about a situation; give a person all the relevant information: It might be a good idea if you and I had a preliminary talk about it first, so that I can put you in the picture.

bring someone into the world • usher someone into the world

bring someone into the world—1. give birth to a child: Do you know what the finest thing you've done is — aside from bringing Hugh into the world? 2. *(of a doctor)* attend the birth of a child: I've known Mrs. Anderson a long time — brought her two children into the world — and she's a fine little woman.

usher someone into the world—introduce a person to social surroundings: It was about a year after the loss that I was ushered into the world.

bring someone low • lay someone low

bring someone low—defeat smb. or force into a humble position: The cruel rulers were brought low by the determined action of the people.

lay someone low—1. knock smb. to the ground: With one blow, the experienced fighter laid his young opponent low. 2. *(of a disease)* make a person take to bed *(usually Passive):* I've been laid low with this terrible cough most of the winter. 3. *= bring someone low:* Someone who all his life had played tennis and softball shouldn't be thus laid low.

bring someone to grief • give someone grief

bring someone to grief—cause a person to experience misfortune, injury or ruin: He was noted for having a quick temper, which often brought him to grief.

give someone grief—1. cause smb. pain or sorrow: This bite really gave me grief , and yet it is still a mildish bite from one of the less serious adder species. 2. criticize a person angrily: Both my wife and my daughter gave me grief about my diet and encouraged me to exercise more.

bring someone to justice • do justice to someone

bring someone to justice—arrest, try and sentence a person who has committed a crime: "Cannot this infamous scoundrel be brought to justice?" I inquired.

do justice to someone—acknowledge smb.'s merits: For many years the London public has failed to do justice to the prima ballerina.

Note: *The expression does not correlate in meaning with the phrase* ***do justice to oneself***—*(also: do oneself justice) perform smth. in a manner worthy of one's abilities:* I'm not going to enter into the question of whether Tagore did justice to himself as translator.

bring someone under control • bring someone under one's control

bring someone under control—subject a person to restraint of behavior: Princess Máxima tried to bring the children under control with a stern face, but failed at the attempt.

bring someone under one's control—achieve dominion over a person; subject smb. to one's authority: The dictator was at last able to bring the army under his control.

bring someone up • bring someone up short

bring someone up—raise a child; educate a person: I was brought up on a farm in Somerset and have been riding and hunting almost since I could walk.

bring someone up short—confound or confuse smb.: A translator is often brought up short by simple words that have no exact equivalent in another language.

bring something into challenge • lay challenge to something

bring something into challenge—express serious doubts about smth.: After each publication ... there always turn up some authors who bring into challenge these conclusions.

lay challenge to something—1. lay claim to smth.; demand smth. as one's due: We can't imagine that Calgary thinks it can lay challenge to being the most cultured. 2. = *bring something into challenge:* But was it suicide? Too many deaths, too many suspicious circumstances lay challenge to that pronunciation.

bring something into question • call something into question

bring something into question—raise the issue of smth.: My promotion brings into question the status of certain other members of staff.

call something into question—*(also: put something in question)* express doubts about smth.: His moral standards have been called into question.

Note: *The expression does not correlate in meaning with the phrase* ***call the question***—*used in formal procedures as an invitation to cut off any further debate and proceed to a vote on the topic in question:* Before proposing to "call the question," there should be some indication that most members have made up their mind.

bring something out in someone • bring something out of someone

bring something out in someone—cause a particular intrinsic quality to be displayed by a person: War sometimes brings out the worst in people.

bring something out of someone—cause smth. to be said by a person: We threatened him a little and that brought the truth out of him.

bring something to a pretty pass • bring something to pass

bring something to a pretty pass—reduce smth. to an unfortunate condition: But what has brought the company to such a pretty pass since I last worked for it?

bring something to pass—*(dated)* cause smth. to happen; carry out or accomplish smth.: Strafford really went some way towards bringing his scheme to pass.

bring something to light • shed light on something

bring something to light—reveal smth.; make smth. known: Facts of the utmost importance will be brought to light by the ringing of birds.

shed light on something—*(also: throw light on something)* clarify or explain smth.: Recent research has shed new light on the causes of the disease.

bring something to naught • set something at naught

bring something to naught—*(of plans, efforts, etc.)* ruin or render useless: An alliance between them, albeit temporary ... was quite effective enough to bring the best efforts to naught.

set something at naught—*(dated)* disregard smth.; consider smth. to be of little value: The tendency of all lunacy is to set at naught first the optional and then the obligatory rules of conduct.

bring something to the ground • get something off the ground

bring something to the ground—1. *(of a plane)* land: He made the landing as carefully as he could and brought the plane to the ground with as much care as possible. 2. topple smth. by a blow or shot: But it was the arrow of the elder man which pierced the animal and brought it to the ground. 3. treat smth. so badly as to destroy it: They wanted to launch a general strike which would bring the country to the ground.

get something off the ground—1. *(of a stranded ship)* get afloat: There was ten feet of water inside the ship, so there was no longer any hope to get the ship off the ground. 2. put a rocket into space or get a plane to fly: I'll announce the weather to the passengers as soon as we get the plane off the ground. 3. *(of a project, scheme, etc.)* launch; get started: To get the plan off the ground, Carter has asked that funding for the program be increased.

bring something under control • take control of something

bring something under control—manage to obtain one's authority or power over a situation, etc.: The fire started yesterday afternoon and was finally brought under control late last night.

take control of something—1. assume charge of a situation, etc.: That opportunity resides in creating a new generation of entrepreneurs who will take control of the destiny of our nation. 2. *(of a political party)* win a majority of elected places: The outcome of legislative races in California could be significant in deciding who will take control of the Congress.

bring the house down • pull the house down

bring the house down—*(of a performance)* produce loud and prolonged applause; be received very successfully: There was one scene which never failed to bring the house down.

Note: *The expression does not correlate in meaning with the phrase* ***shout the house down***—*(coll.) make a terrible commotion:* I can't study while my little brother is shouting the house down.

pull the house down—destroy or demolish a building or structure: The lessor was desirous of pulling the house down and building a new one.

British Cicero, the • Cicero of the British Senate, the

British Cicero, the—(hist.) the name given to William Pitt, Earl of Chatham, a British politician (1708–1778).

Cicero of the British Senate, the—(hist.) the name given to George Canning, a British politician (1770–1827): Canning was famous for his flowery orations, and was even nicknamed "The Cicero of the British Senate."

Brown, Jones, and Robinson • Tom, Dick, and Harry

Brown, Jones, and Robinson—(dated) used as a generic name for middle-class Englishmen: A verbatim report of the conversation of Brown, Jones, and Robinson would be uninteresting.

Tom, Dick, and Harry—anybody at all; the average person: Thoreau's great fault was disdain for men (for Tom, Dick, and Harry): inability to appreciate the average life — even the exceptional life.

buddy up to someone • buddy up with someone

buddy up to someone—(coll.) become immoderately familiar or friendly with smb.: Now the former loser is an overnight success, and suddenly everyone wants to buddy up to him.

buddy up with someone—(coll.) join with a person to form a pair (to share accommodation or do smth. together): I buddied up with Carl, and we shared the canoe.

build a fire under someone • burn someone at the stake

build a fire under someone—(also: light a fire under someone) do smth. to motivate or stimulate a person; make smb. work better or harder These students are incredibly motivated. You don't have to build a fire under them.

Note: *a) The expression does not correlate in meaning with the phrase* ***throw someone into the frying pan****—(U.S.) place smb. with insufficient training into a serious predicament, assuming he will adapt to the situation:* They threw me into the frying pan. I was off to Japan for the first time in my life and not a soul did I know, and not a word of Japanese.

b) The expression is not equivalent in meaning to the phrase ***keep someone's feet to the fire****—(also: hold someone's feet to the fire) pressure a person to undertake smth.:* We have to continue to keep Kerry's feet to the fire and remind him of his promises, and continue to keep his feet to the fire on certain issues.

burn someone at the stake—reprimand or scold a person severely: Stop yelling. I made a simple mistake, and you're burning me at the stake for it.

See also: burn someone down / burn someone up.

build bridges with someone • burn bridges with someone

build bridges with someone—try to make new friends or establish cooperation with an opponent: We must work with leaders of these countries and build bridges with them — both economically and politically.

burn bridges with someone—do smth. that makes former relationship with smb. difficult or impossible: Robb has moved considerably leftward, and he has burned bridges with many leaders in the state.

build up something • build up to something

build up something—1. increase or develop smth. steadily: You must now build up your strength after your illness. 2. praise or promote smth.: An advertising agency can build up a product so much that everyone will want it.

build up to something—lead up to smth. gradually or indirectly: You could tell by the way she was talking that she was building up to something unpleasant.

Bullion State, the • Golden State, the

Bullion State, the—(U.S.) a nickname of the State of Missouri: Missouri has been known as the Bullion State (possibly an allusion to the nickname of Missouri senator Benton, who was known as "Old Bullion").

Golden State, the—(U.S.) a nickname of the State of California: The Golden State's golden days seem to be a thing of the past for many California residents.

Note: *Neither expression is equivalent in meaning to the phrase* ***Treasure State, the****—(U.S.) a nickname of the State of Montana:* Citizens of the Treasure State celebrate the hundredth anniversary of one of Montana's most notable historic sites.

bully for someone • bully someone

bully for someone—(exclam.) used as a mocking expression of approval: If he is acquitted, then bully for him. If he is convicted, then he goes to jail.

bully someone—intimidate a person; frighten smb. into a certain course using violent threats: He saw, that he had no chance of bullying the servant.

bun is in the oven, the • fat is in the fire, the

bun is in the oven, the—1. *(euph.)* is used to allude to pregnancy: They have to get married because the bun is in the oven.... So my question is, am I invited? 2. things have started moving: We have no idea as to a release date as there is a lot of work still to be done, but at least the bun is in the oven.

Note: *The expression does not correlate in meaning with the phrase* ***get your buns over here****—(coll.) come here quickly:* Just pack your bags and get your buns over here! We'll make it worth your while.

fat is in the fire, the—an irrevocable course of action has been started: The die has been cast and the fat is in the fire. Too late to back out now. *Cf.: pull the fat from the fire—do smth. that solves a serious brooding problem:* A change of presidents can pull the fat from the fire in time to save us from a rerun of the 1920s depression.

burn a hole in someone's pocket • make a hole in someone's pocket

burn a hole in someone's pocket—(of money) make a person eager to spend it: It's Sunday, everything's closed, and there's Bob with $10 burning a hole in his pocket.

Note: *The expression does not correlate in meaning with the phrase* ***have money to burn****—have so much money that one can spend it freely:* You must have money to burn. First of all, that floodlighting, and then this.

make a hole in someone's pocket—deplete smb.'s savings, bank account, etc. considerably: The cost of these repairs to the house has made a big hole in my pocket.

burn away • burn out

burn away—1. continue to burn: The fire was still burning away cheerfully in the grate. 2. become less or be destroyed by burning: Half the oil in the lamp had burnt away.

burn out—1. burn visibly: The lamp burned out in the darkness of the night. 2. stop burning because there is no more fuel: As the first rocket burns out, the second stage motor ignites. 3. *(of an engine, etc.)* stop working through overheating: The engine burned out because of a problem in the cooling system. 4. *(usually Passive)* be made hollow by fire: The building was burnt out and only the walls remained. 5. decrease; die down: The poet's ability burned out before he was thirty.

burn down • burn up

burn down—(of buildings) be destroyed by fire: The old house burned down last night in the big fire.

burn up—(of objects other than buildings) 1. be consumed by fire: We found our tent burned to the ground and all my books burned up. 2. be destroyed by great heat: Most meteors have burned up completely when they are still at great heights.

burn someone down • burn someone up

burn someone down—(U.S. coll.) humiliate a person: You just want to burn down everybody to make yourself seem better.

burn someone up—(U.S. coll.) 1. irritate smb. or make very angry: What burns me up is the fact that seven per cent of all the families earned $500 a year or less. 2. reprimand or scold a person severely: The manager burned Jim up yesterday for being late again.

Note: *Neither expression correlates in meaning with the phrase* ***burn someone out****—(U.S. coll.) tire smb. greatly; cause a person to stop being active:* An extra effort has burned him out and left him no time to seek more interesting work.

See also: build a fire under someone / burn someone at the stake.

burn the candle at both ends • butter one's bread on both sides

burn the candle at both ends—dissipate one's energy by doing too much: But as you are determined to live it up and have a good time, you must watch your health and try not to burn the candle at both ends.

Note: *The expression does not correlate in meaning with the phrase* ***row with both oars****—(also: row with both oars in the water) be smart enough or mentally alert:* I wondered if he rowed with both oars in the water. How could a Harvard man have come to such a sorry state?

butter one's bread on both sides—be in very comfortable circumstances; be well provided for: He's got marble floors in there, crystal figurines on the shelves.... Like we say at home, he butters his bread on both sides. *Cf.: know on which side one's bread is buttered—know where one's interest lies:* The judges of the lower and superior courts know on which side their bread is buttered. They would strain a point in favor of the highest political opinion of the day.

burn the earth • scorch the earth

burn the earth—(U.S. coll., dated) go at full speed: When they reached the brow of the hill, I was half a mile in the lead, burning the earth...

scorch the earth—devastate all buildings, etc. in an area so as to leave nothing to the advancing enemy: The Russians fell back upon their main line of defense, "scorching the earth" before this last convulsive thrust of the Nazi.

Note: *Neither expression correlates in meaning with the phrase* ***set the world on fire****—(usually negat.) do smth. remarkable and cause a sensation (also: set the Thames on fire):* She does the job adequately but she's not going to set the world on fire.

burn the water • set the Thames on fire

burn the water—(Fishermen) spear salmon by torchlight: Water-bailiffs are sent up the rivers at certain times to prevent "burning the water."

Note: *The expression does not correlate in meaning with the phrase* ***boil the ocean****— try smth. way too ambitious that cannot reasonably be completed:* Don't attempt to boil the ocean. If your initial concept is so grandiose that you can't deliver, you're setting yourself up for failure.

set the Thames on fire—(usually negat.) do smth. remarkable and cause a sensation *(also: set the world on fire):* When Sir Gregory declared that Mr. Neverbend would never set the Thames on fire, he meant to express his opinion that that gentleman was a fool.

burst at the seams • come apart at the seams

burst at the seams—1. be full to overflowing; be crammed with people or things: The little hall was practically bursting at the seams. 2. be unable to contain one's pride, uncontrolled laughter, etc.: We laughed so hard we just about burst at the seams.

come apart at the seams—(also: fall apart at the seams) 1. fall into pieces; disintegrate: The old car is about ready to come apart at the seams; its muffler is dragging and the windows don't close. 2. be in a very bad state; be about to fail: Oliver and Jane began showing serious signs of stress; their relationship was coming apart at the seams. 3. lose one's composure because of a severe mental strain; collapse emotionally: Poor old Smith isn't the man he used to be; he's coming apart at the seams.

bus boy • busman

bus boy—(also: busboy) a person whose duty is to clear and reset tables in a restaurant: They felt embarrassed, the way a professional fighter would feel after beating hell out of a bus boy.

busman— the driver of a bus: Mark was an asset to the club with his experience working as a busman in the city.

See also: boys on the bus, the / man on the bus, the.

bush baby • Bushboy

bush baby—any of several small African lemurs of the genus *Galago:* The occasional cry of a bush-baby alone broke the awful silence.

Bushboy—Bushman *(member of certain nomadic tribes in the desert regions of South Africa):* I found a funny little fellow in the shape of the Bushboy awaiting my arrival.

Bush Negro • Bushman

Bush Negro—one of a people of African ancestry descended from runaway slaves and inhabiting the Guianas in South America: Saramakkan is spoken only by the Bush Negroes on the upper reaches of the Surinam or "Saramakka" river.

Bushman—member of certain nomadic tribes in the desert regions of South Africa: In Africa ... we find the Bushman and Hottentot in the South, and the Akkas and Niam-Niams in the center, very small in stature and yellow in color.

bush telegraph • field telegraph

bush telegraph—(also: bush wireless) rapid dissemination of rumors, information, etc. by word-of-mouth: "How did the Imam get to know about it?" "The bush telegraph works very well here in Bahrain."

field telegraph—(Military) a movable telegraph system for use on campaign, maneuvers, etc.: The field telegraph detachments are trained in peace time to everything connected with telegraphy.

businessman • man of business

businessman—a man who is engaged in business (running a commercial or industrial firm, etc.): His father was a well-known businessman in the city.

man of business—1. = *businessman:* A man of business should be quick, decisive, and callous against small rubs. 2. *(UK)* a person's agent or solicitor: As her man of business, I immediately proceeded to examine her papers.

bust one's balls • bust someone's balls

bust one's balls—(coarse sl.; used of men) work extremely hard to accomplish smth.: I have only two days until the examination, so I have to bust my balls if I don't want to fail.

bust someone's balls—(coarse sl.) 1. make fun of or tease a man: Everybody in the classroom bust Tom's balls about his bald head. 2. *(of a woman)* ridicule a man; hurt a man's feelings: Janet has a bad habit; she loves to bust a man's balls if he tries to flirt with her.

busy as a bee • busy as a beehive

busy as a bee—(of a person) full of lively activity; very busy: I don't have time to talk to you. I am as busy as a bee.

busy as a beehive—(of an office, shop, etc.) crowded with customers; bustling with activity: The firm was at once as busy as a beehive.

but me no buts • there are no buts about it

but me no buts—(coll.) don't give me any of your excuses: But me no buts this time, just do what I tell you and do it at once!

there are no buts about it—(coll.) there is no doubt about it: I saw you steal the money from the drawer. There are no buts about it.

butcher, baker, candlestick maker • chief cook and bottle washer

butcher, baker, candlestick maker—said of people with traditional occupations or skills: Jean rushed to his favorite wine merchant, to his tobacconist, to his butcher, baker, candlestick maker.

Note: *The expression is not equivalent in meaning to the phrase* ***doctor, lawyer, or Indian chief****— whatever your profession or occupation:* You can be a doctor, lawyer, or Indian chief, as the rhyme goes. But in the midst of making a living, what kind of person will you be?

chief cook and bottle washer—(also: head cook and bottle washer) smb. who is in charge but who also has to attend to trivial duties; a person (specifically a spouse) who does everything: As a stay at home Dad, I am also the chief cook and bottle washer.

butter someone up • oil someone up

butter someone up—(coll.) flatter a person in order to get him to do smth.: No, I am not trying to butter up the professor who is going to grade me on this.

oil someone up—1. *(Austral. sl.)* advise a person; give smb. reliable information: Don't worry, I'll oil him up on what needs to be done. 2. = *butter someone up:* He had been chosen because of his power in the Senate. Kennedy oiled him up and convinced him he'd be even more powerful as Vice-President.

Note: *The expression does not correlate in meaning with the phrase* ***grease someone's palm*** *(sl.)—pay or bribe a person for a special favor:* We had to grease the palm of the waiter to get a table in the crowded restaurant.

buy it • get it

buy it—(sl.) 1. believe smth.: I told my new boyfriend that I am pregnant with his kid. Do you think he will buy it? *Cf.: sell it—(sl.) persuade a person to accept smth. as true:* Don't try to sell it to me as a great work of comedy. The film struck me as being very dumb. 2. die, especially suddenly or violently *(also: buy the farm):* By the time we could get to the hospital, he had bought it.

get it—1. *(often negat.)* understand smth.: As for the movie, well, I don't get it. There seems to be something profound going on here that I don't understand. 2. *(coll.)* be punished: "Boy," I said, "are you going to get it when mom sees you."

buy someone off • buy someone out

buy someone off—bribe a person to persuade him do smth.: It is impossible to open a big gambling operation without buying off public officials.

buy someone out—1. buy smb.'s share of property: He borrowed a large sum of money in order to buy out his partner. 2. buy all of smth. that a person has: He didn't have much ice-cream, and he wouldn't let us buy him out. 3. gain smb.'s freedom by paying money: Bill's parents paid a lot of money to buy him out of the army.

buy the farm • sell the farm

buy the farm—(coll.) die, especially suddenly or violently *(also: buy it):* Well, I almost bought the farm last weekend. A friend was driving too aggressively and she put us into a dangerous situation.

sell the farm—sell all one's assetts to invest in a new venture; act rashly or overreact: The economy has been tough on everyone these days, but don't sell the farm just yet. *Cf.: who wouldn't sell a farm and go to sea—(Nautical catch phrase)* 1. *used to express one's genuine delight at being at sea:* Kettle looked round at the elaborate fittings of the cabin. Lord! Who wouldn't sell a farm and go to sea? 2. *used ironically when smth. difficult has to be done:* 'Tis when that order comes on cold, blustering nights that "Jack" grimly mutters: "Who would not sell a farm and go to sea?"

Note: *The expression does not correlate in meaning with the phrase* ***give away the farm****— negotiate poorly or make a deal that puts one at a serious disadvantage:* He signed a law that gave away the farm to big drug companies while leaving seniors with hardly any benefits.

by a fraction • to a fraction

by a fraction—(also: by a hair's breadth) by a very small degree or amount: Hester does not change by a fraction her intention to run away with Arthur.

to a fraction—(also: to a hair's breadth) with great accuracy: Escudero supposed that two hundred Mexican ounces would compensate him to a fraction.

by a hair's breadth • to a hair's breadth

by a hair's breadth—(also: by a fraction) by a very small degree or amount: If I swerve by a hair's breadth from the straight line of the most rigid respectability, I'm done for.

to a hair's breadth—(also: to a fraction) with great accuracy: You had plenty of time to put your heads together before the police arrived. I'm sure the stories would tally to a hair's breadth.

by air • over the air

by air—using aircraft as a means of transport: Sending goods by air is fast but can be expensive.

over the air—over the radio: Listeners will be able to "grill" leading public figures over the air.

by all means • by any means

by all means—certainly; without fail: You should by all means utilize the placement office at least a year before you actually start job hunting.

by any means—in any way possible: We are trying to remake Vietnamese society, a task which probably cannot be accomplished by any means.

by and by • by the by

by and by—soon; before long: They could see the smoke, and by and by a shell would explode in their midst.

by the by—(introductory or parenthetical) in passing; incidentally *(also: by the way):* By-the-by, Martin—any message from my lady mother?

by any chance • by chance

by any chance—perhaps; possibly: I was wondering if by any chance you could lend me five pounds.

by chance—accidentally; unpredictably: Karma is a belief that nothing happens by chance.

by choice • of choice

by choice—voluntary; not forced or compelled: The grasp of the church never relaxed unless freely and by choice.

of choice—(of drugs, treatment, etc.) preferred; recommended: Chloromycetin has been the drug of choice for treating typhoid fever.

by day • by the day

by day—during the day; in the day-time: Eurostar trains only travel by day and require a reservation.

by the day—1. on a daily basis: Clients who rent by the day can be billed for phone service the day they leave. 2. with every passing day: Protests on campuses were becoming uglier by the day, and the administration cracked down hard.

by half • by halves

by half—1. *increase or reduce smth.* by fifty percent of the original amount: This move cuts by half the religious programming on ITV on Sunday. 2. far more than is satisfactory or desirable: Of course, he is a very clever politician. Too clever by half, in my opinion.

by halves—*do smth.* imperfectly or not completely: Those in charge should not deal by halves with a question in which all classes have so deep an interest.

by inches • inch by inch

by inches—1. very gradually or slowly: The ship was sinking by inches; she might remain above water an hour or more. 2. *miss* by a very small margin: We scrambled to get out of the way, the car missing us by inches.

inch by inch—1. by small degrees or stages: When life falls apart, we are forced to rebuild it inch by inch. 2. *scrutinize smth.* closely; *examine smth.* very carefully: I have examined that cloth inch by inch; there is not a flaw in it.

by installments • in installments

by installments—*paid* in part payments spread over a period of time: Students may pay their tuition fees in a single payment or by instalments.

in installments—*(of publicatiions) come out* in parts published over a period of time: The biography will appear in installments in the April and September issues of the magazine.

by occasion of something • on the occasion of something

by occasion of something—*(formal)* because of smth.: The debate has to be postponed by occasion of the illness of one of the principle speakers.

on the occasion of something—in connection with some formal event or celebration: This was given us as a present on the occasion of our silver wedding.

by one's own account • on one's own account

by one's own account—according to one's own story: She says she thought she saw him, but by her own account she could have been mistaken.

on one's own account—*acting* independently; without help from others: He left the company last year, and went into business on his own account.

by order of someone • under the orders of someone

by order of someone—according to directions given by a proper authority: By order of the Minister a special operation of police is being carried out.

under the orders of someone—1. *(Military)* commanded by a person; being smb.'s subordinate: At the battle of Waterloo he was under the orders of Marshal Grouchy. 2. = *by order of someone:* In some cases it may be possible to release the prisoner on probation, but this is permitted only under the orders of the Provincial Government.

by rule • by rule and line

by rule—according to law, custom, or regulations: They speak by rule and by book, though they judge and determine by common-sense.

by rule and line—*(dated)* with methodical accuracy *(also: by rule and measure):* Life isn't cast in a mould—not cut out by rule and line, and that sort of thing.

by succession • in succession

by succession—according to the legal principle by which one person succeeds another in an inheritance, office, etc.: It seems they did not like a king by deputation but desired one by succession.

in succession—one after another in regular sequence: If one African country pulls out of the Commonwealth then there is a very real possibility the others will go out in succession like dominoes.

by the authority of someone • on the authority of someone

by the authority of someone—by reason of authority granted by the person named: The weapons were placed in the church by the authority of the governor in response to a threat the church received.

on the authority of someone—having the person named as the authority for what one says: I have it on the authority of a Councilor that the rates are likely to go up in the near future.

by the clock • by the time

by the clock—*do smth.* paying a lot of attention to the time (so that one is not late): There are people who just hate to do anything by the clock.

by the time—at the time that; as soon as: Eddie performed with various bands and by the time he was nineteen he left Fort Worth.

Note: *The expression does not correlate in meaning with the phrase* ***by the hour***—1. *during considerable periods at a time:* He would argue by the hour, but never for arguing sake. 2. *(of wages) paid for the hours given to work:* The proposal to pay by the hour instead of by the mile would lower the American railroader to the level of his Soviet counterpart. 3. *(hyperbolic) very fast:* Evidence is mounting by the hour that these regulations are being used by the President's camp to hide behind, and rather ungracefully.

by the name of • under the name of

by the name of—is used of a person called by the name mentioned: Do you know a boy by the name of David?

under the name of—is used of a person known by a name different from his own: Hector Munro wrote under the name of Saki.

by the seat of one's pants • by the skin of one's teeth

by the seat of one's pants—*do smth.* using experience and intuition rather than theory: I don't follow recipes, but prefer to cook by the seat of my pants, as it were.

by the skin of one's teeth—only just manage to get smth. accomplished: Making my train by the skin of my teeth, I haven't had time to buy a paper for the journey. *Cf.: it is no skin off one's teeth—(also: it is no skin off one's nose)* 1. *it is no difficulty for a person:* I felt it was going to benefit some people who needed it so it was really no skin off my teeth to get involved. 2. *it makes no difference to a person:* That said, I opt to wear a helmet, myself. But it's no skin off my teeth whether other folks decide to or not.

by virtue of something • in virtue of something

by virtue of something—by means of smth.; through the agency of smth.: It was only by virtue of his indomitable willpower that he finally succeeded.

in virtue of something—by reason of smth.; on account of smth.: He was given a position on the board in virtue of his long association with the company.

by word of mouth • mouth words

by word of mouth—hear about smth. from another person: I can't remember seeing it advertised much, so most people probably hear about it by word of mouth.

mouth words—1. form words silently with one's lips: Since the mansion was wired with microphones, Howard would mouth words silently when she wanted to have a private conversation. 2. speak in an indistinct way: Patients treated in the intensive care unit communicate primarily through head nods and mouthing words.

bypass something • pass something by

by-pass something—1. make a detour (round a town, etc.): The scheme has been referred to as "the Selborne by-pass," but it does not bypass Selborne at all. 2. avoid or ignore smth. (by using an alternative approach): I will now try to explain in detail how to bypass this problem.

pass something by—walk past smth. (without paying attention): You take it for a stone cross ... and you pass it by incuriously.

C

call box (UK) • call box (U.S.)

call box (UK)—(also: phone box) a telephone booth: Mrs. Johnson is now urging the woman to come forward, after the caller did not leave her contact number and phoned from a call box.

call box (U.S.)—emergency telephone installed along the sides of many highways, on university campuses, etc.: Drivers can use call boxes in case of an accident or other emergency.

call boy • call man

call boy—1. a man who calls up actors in a theater for duty: Indignant denials were interrupted by the call-boy knocking on the door and calling for Second Act beginners. 2. a messenger on a steamer, in a hotel, etc.: He obtained summer work as a part-time messenger — a job referred to at that time as call boy. 3. a young male prostitute (who makes appointments by phone): Hustlers fall into two categories: the street variety and models (call boys).

call man—a man available for emergency call, such as a part-time fireman: The call man nearest to the emergency situation was dispatched, since only one person manned the fire station.

call girl • call-button girl

call girl—a prostitute who makes appointments by phone: Police found the names of the call girls in classified ads and phone books.

call-button girl—(sl.) a prostitute frequenting hotels: Prostitutes, "call-button girls" as they call themselves, roam from airport to airport, operating from the airport hotels.

call in on someone • call on someone

call in on someone—pay a short visit (to a friend, etc.): We would call in on Patrick on the way to your mother's.

call on someone—1. visit a person for business or official reasons: A doctor called on her and found she had come down with pneumonia. 2. appeal to a person for smth.: Lord Berkeley called on all his friends to help him.

call in one's chips • cash in one's chips

call in one's chips—use one's influence or social connections (to gain an advantage, etc.): That point needs making, before Mr. Clinton's friends in the labor unions try to call in their chips.

cash in one's chips—1. sell smth. in order to raise money: Many mutual fund investors picked up the phone yesterday, but decided not to cash in their chips after all. 2. *(U.S. sl.)* die: Got a phone call from Herb the other day informing me that Yochum had finally cashed in his chips at the ripe old age of 94.

call names • name names

call names—subject a person to angry or violent attack in words: He replied to my innocent jokes by calling names.

name names—mention people (involved in some reprehensible activity) by name: Valachi has named names and drawn a master plan of the Syndicate (which the underworld refers to as *Cosa Nostra*).

Note: *The expression does not correlate in meaning with the phrase* ***drop names****—(also: name-drop) familiarly mention the names of distinguished people in order to imply one's own importance:* The man who shot her, incidentally, is called Lord Lichfield — just one of the names dropped thuddingly at every opportunity.

call of duty • duty call

call of duty—smth. that a person is required to do by one's moral or social obligations: It was cruel of me to ask him to recount the events of the fateful day but it was the call of duty. *Cf.: (above and) beyond the call of duty— doing much more than should normally be expected of one (originally of heroic police officers, fire fighters, etc.):* The deep level of care and compassion that was demonstrated to me was beyond the call of duty.

duty call—a visit undertaken as a duty or as part of one's social obligations: They had accepted a dinner invitation over in Arlington — a duty call, as Andy termed it.

call of nature • call of the wild

call of nature—1. the urge to go and explore new (undeveloped) regions: I felt the call of nature most strongly and began, like the citizens in Hardy's poem, to "dream of the south and west." 2. *(euph.)* is used of a need to go to the toilet: He would suggest dropping in at the Monico, pretext a call of nature. 3. said of the natural desires and instincts: You must expect George to start being interested in girls at his age. It's the call of nature.

call of the wild— = *call of nature 1:* Several times my father made an attempt to settle down, but the call of the wild would prove too strong.

call one's shots • call the shots

call one's shots—1. tell in advance the result of a game, etc.: Nothing ever happens as John says it will. He is very poor at calling his shots. 2. announce what one is about to do; reveal one's plans, etc. beforehand: You can hardly expect so adroit a politician to call his shots.

call the shots—(also: call all the shots) be in charge; decide on the course of action: Tom is a first-rate leader who knows how to call the shots.

Note: *Neither expression correlates in meaning with the phrase* ***call shotgun****—(coll.) claim the seat beside the driver in an automobile:* If someone has successfully called shotgun, this gives them no right whatsoever to correct the driver on their navigation skills.

call someone down • call someone up

call someone down—reprimand a person severely: He was called down again because of being late.

call someone up—1. telephone smb.: Maybe one day I'll call you up and we can go see a movie. 2. summon a person for military service: If war breaks out, we shall be called up at once.

call someone on the carpet • roll out the red carpet for someone

call someone on the carpet—call a person before an authority for censure or reprimand: Less than two hours after sending the e-mail, she was called on the carpet and instructed to send a disclaimer.

roll out the red carpet for someone—accord ceremonial courtesy to a person of rank: The whole town knows what kind of person he is and has no intention of rolling out the red carpet for him when he arrives.

Note: *The expression is not antonymous in meaning to the phrase* ***pull the carpet from under someone****—(also: pull the rug from under someone) weaken or unsettle a person by an unexpected withdrawal of support, etc.:* When Jane's uncle stopped giving her a loan half-way through her university education, it pulled the carpet from under her.

call someone to attention • call someone's attention

call someone to attention—make a person assume the formal military stance of attention: The sergeant called the platoon to attention.

call someone's attention—bring smth. to a person's notice: He called our attention to the old and faded picture on the wall.

call something down on someone • call something down to someone

call something down on someone—invoke some sort of punishment from the heavens onto a person: The prophet called down a plague on the people.

call something down to someone—shout smth. to a person who is on a lower level: The worker was alarmed and called a warning down to the people below.

called to the Bar • called within the Bar

called to the Bar—(UK law) admitted as a barrister *(a lawyer who has the right to speak as an advocate in higher law courts):* She completed her studies at the College of Law in London and was called to the Bar in 2004.

called within the Bar—(UK law) appointed a Queen's/King's Counsel *(a barrister who has the right to act for the State):* Barristers who have been "called within the Bar" occupy the front benches in the auditorium of the court.

can you say that again • you can say that again

can you say that again—is used to ask a person to repeat smth.: I'm sorry, I didn't catch that, can you say that again?

you can say that again—is used to express strong agreement with what smb. says: "Dad, you're not the Messiah," I say, imitating the voice my mom makes.... "You can say that again, Belle."

candy stripe • candy striper

candy stripe—a print of fine red stripes on a white background *(the pattern found on peppermint candy):* The door was answered by a woman dressed in jeans and a candy-stripe shirt several sizes too big for her.

candy striper—(U.S. sl.) a young woman who is a volunteer nurse's aid in a hospital: Carol followed the young candy-striper across the lobby but couldn't keep up; her legs were still shaky.

care about something • care for something

care about something—1. feel anxiety or concern about smth.: I'm not sure that anyone in the audience really cares much about what happens to him. 2. take an interest in smth.: Jack didn't care about anything but horses and dogs, and lived every day of his life.

care for something—1. wish for smth.: "Care for a bit of navy plug?" He never dreamt of boarding a trawler without strong navy plug tobacco in his pocket. 2. = *care about something 2:* Do you care for Venetian glass? Ah, not so very much, I see; but you would be converted, I am sure you would, by my chandelier. 3. look after smth.; preserve smth. with care: The skilled staff needed not only to maintain the fabric of the buildings but to care for the precious pictures.

Note: *The expression does not fully correlate in meaning with the phrase* ***take care of something****—*1. = *care for something 3:* Young ladies are delicate plants. They should take care of their health and their complexion. *2. deal with problems, etc.:* He found himself besieged with petitions for jobs. It was impossible to take care of all of them.

care for someone • take care of someone

care for someone—1. like smb.; be fond of a person: I do not really care for Kerry. He was certainly the one I liked the least during the debates. 2. have regard for smb.: She seems like she only cares for people with money and people who are "known." 3. be responsible for the support or treatment of patients, little children, etc.: Brand doesn't need an office because she only cares for patients in their homes.

take care of someone—1. = *care for someone 3:* I witnessed him in action, and I participated in helping him take care of his patients in his clinic. 2. *(sl., euph.)* get rid of or kill a person: While continuing to comment on "taking care of the park manager," he displayed a small handgun to Olson.

care-taker • caregiver

care-taker—1. *(also: care taker)* a social worker or nurse, who provides direct care (as for children, elderly people, etc.): A child is most vulnerable to the thought and belief patterns of his care taker. 2. a person who supervises the care of a property such as a building: Our care-taker lives around the corner, so no worries about maintenance. 3. *(attrib., of a government, office-holder, etc.)* temporary or provisional: This was disclosed by the council care-taker chairman in an exclusive interview with Daily Triumph.

caregiver— = *care-taker 1:* According to the history subsequently provided by his caregiver, he began to exhibit symptoms of constitutional illness.

care to do something • take care to do something

care to do something—feel inclined to do smth.; think it worthwhile to do smth.: If you care to write a good-bye, address me in care of the ship.

take care to do something—give serious attention to smth.: A farmer may be a good soldier if you take care to have him properly disciplined.

career man • career woman

career man—a man who works permanently in a profession which affords opportunity for advancement, especially a career diplomat: The foundation of any sound Foreign Service must consist of "career men" who have become expert.

career woman—a woman who attaches great importance to her profession, especially one who prefers a career to marriage: There are legions of career women who never even couple up with a man permanently and start a family.

career teacher • careers teacher

career teacher—a person who works as a teacher for most of his or her working life: Although I'm not a "career teacher" I can see how much they respect them here, which is refreshing.

careers teacher—a teacher who gives information to students about jobs and professions: This information should be passed regularly to Careers Teachers for guidance purposes.

careless of something • careless with something

careless of something—(also: careless about something) unconcerned about smth.: He became careless of the decencies which were expected from a man so highly distinguished in the literary world.

careless with something—not thinking sensibly about how one can best use or treat smth.: Remember that this is not a time to be careless with money or turn over all the decisions to someone else.

carry a load • carry the load

carry a load—(sl.) be alcohol intoxicated: Your father's carrying a load again. What are we going to do?

carry the load—do or be responsible for the major part of a job, etc.: We all knew that his wife carried the load in that family.

See also: carry one's weight / carry weight.

carry coals • carry coals to Newcastle

carry coals—(also: bear coals) submit to humiliation or insult: Abraham observes that they will not carry coals, meaning that they would not put up with insults.

carry coals to Newcastle—take goods, etc. to a place where they are plentiful: My colleagues have already spoken extensively.... To repeat these statements would be to carry coals to Newcastle.

carry light • carry the torch

carry light—elucidate or clarify smth.: Arguments which carry light have their effect, even against an opponent who shuts his eyes.

***Note:** a) The expression does not correlate in meaning with the phrase **hold the spotlight**— be in the center of attention:* Pegi held the spotlight with compelling songs, a lovely voice and charming personality.

*b) The expression is not antonymous in meaning to the phrase **hide one's light under a bushel**—(also: hide one's light under a bushel basket) show extreme modesty; conceal or suppress one's talents or successes:* Since college, he's observed that nobody likes a know-it-all, and consequently continued to hide his light under a bushel.

carry the torch—1. retain admiration or love for a person (especially if the feeling is not mutual): She still carries the torch for her former husband, Wyn, whose family couldn't accept her working-class background. 2. support a movement or cause: This group aims to carry the torch for the millions of people who demonstrated and the thousands who died. *Cf.: pass the torch— relinquish one's responsibilities, practice, etc. to another person:* He did his job well, avoided publicity, and passed the torch to his successor.

carry-on *(UK)* • carry-on *(U.S.)*

carry-on (UK)—(coll., also: carrying-on) annoying unwise or overexcited behavior: We were all engaged for a radio version of Hamlet.... I had never realized the incredible carry-on connected with these productions.

carry-on (U.S.)—(also: carry-on baggage) luggage that can be carried aboard an aircraft, bus, or train: I always take some cigars in my carry-on and pack some others in checked luggage.

carry on at someone • carry on with someone

carry on at someone—complain noisily to a person: He was carrying on at me in a most unpleasant way.

carry on with someone—flirt with smb.; have an affair with a person: I heard she was carrying on with a married man.

carry one's age • hold the age

carry one's age—look well for one's age: O'donnell found satisfaction in the thought that the other man didn't carry his age as well as he himself did.

hold the age—(U.S. coll.) be in a position of control because one has greater power *(also: have the age):* How could I talk when he was talking? He "held the age" as the poker players say.

carry one's weight • carry weight

carry one's weight—do one's share of the work: We can rearrange our workload anyway we want. Bottom line — we are all going to have to carry our weight. *Cf.: carry the weight of the world on one's shoulders— be burdened with too many problems:* He carries the weight of the world on his shoulders. That's bound to get a guy down, no matter how strong he is.

carry weight—be respected and have influence: I don't carry much weight around here, but Walter does.

See also: carry a load / carry the load.

carry out an execution • do execution

carry out an execution— carry out punishment by death on a person: Colleagues fear her killing was an extrajudicial execution carried out by the security forces.

do execution—(dated, of weapons) have a massive destructive effect: The schooners opened a heavy cannonade upon the enemy, which did great execution.

carry someone off his feet • get someone on his feet

carry someone off his feet—(also: sweep someone off his feet) affect a person with overwhelming enthusiasm: It was small wonder that this beautiful woman carried him off his feet.

get someone on his feet—(also: set someone back on his feet) cure a person: It was difficult when they made me sit up in bed.... Over the course of a few weeks they gradually got me on my feet.

carry water in a sieve • pour water into a sieve

carry water in a sieve—do futile work: It doesn't look like I've accomplished a thing. I might as well have been carrying water in a sieve.

pour water into a sieve—1. = *carry water in a sieve:* It is of no more use to give advice to the idle than to pour water into a sieve. 2. waste money: Charles is head over ears in debt, but he will not get another farthing from me. It is pouring water into a sieve.

cash in on something • cash in something

cash in on something—1. make a profit on smth.: Steve cashed in on the farmland he picked up dirt-cheap. 2. take advantage of smth.: Japan's diplomats are now trying to "cash in on" the opportunities which its soldiers have created.

cash in something—exchange smth. for the amount of money it is worth: The shares were cashed in to help buy my London house.

cast a long shadow over something • cast a shadow over something

cast a long shadow over something—exert a very strong influence on smth.: Helmut Kohl cast a very long shadow over German politics, even after his defeat at the polls in 1998.

cast a shadow over something—(also: cast a shade over something) have a damaging effect on smth. such as a person's reputation, relationships, etc.: The trauma suffered by these women has cast a shadow over their lives.

cast a shade over something • cast something into the shade

cast a shade over something—(also: cast a shade on something) have a damaging effect on smth. such as a person's reputation, relationships, etc.: Nor would he do one act for worlds, that could cast a shade over the fame and honor.

cast something into the shade—(also: throw something into the shade) make smth. appear insignificant by contrast of superior quality: Internal taxation is so excessive as to cast even an illiberal tariff into the shade.

Note: *Neither expression correlates in meaning with the phrase* ***be in the shade****— remain little known; stay in the background:* How can we see a man's brilliant qualities if he is what we call in the shade?

cast someone off • cast someone out

cast someone off—(also: cast someone away) abandon one's friend, lover, etc.: When he grows tired of a woman, he just casts her off like an old coat.

cast someone out—expel a person from an association or society: All he really wanted was revenge on a society that has cast him out.

cast something off • throw something off

cast something off—1. *(of clothing)* remove; take off: As the sun grew warmer, he cast off his heavy winter clothes. 2. get rid of smth. unwanted; become free from smth.: He was pleased to cast off such an unwelcome responsibility. 3. *(of snakes)* get rid of a skin: Snakes cast off their old skin once a year. 4. release a boat from its moorings by untying a rope: Don't cast off the boat till everyone is on board.

throw something off—1. = *cast something off 1:* It's good to throw off heavy clothes now that summer is here. 2. = *cast something off 2:* It's very difficult to throw off old habits of thoughts. 3. *(of heat, smell, etc.)* give out; emit: When this material burns it throws off a nasty smell and a lot of smoke. 4. write or compose smth. quickly and easily: It shouldn't take me more than an afternoon to throw this article off. 5. *(also: throw something away)* say smth. casually or carelessly: Be careful what remarks you throw off in front of her, she's very sensitive. 6. cause mistakes in smth.: Any small interruption is likely to throw off my calculation.

cast the first stone • lay the first stone

cast the first stone—be the first to bring an accusation against a person: Let those of the respectable press who are without sin, cast the first stone.

lay the first stone—lay the foundation of smth.: It was Hughes who laid, in 1877, the first stone of radiographic practice by his detailed experiments.

Note: *The expression is not equivalent in meaning to the phrase* ***make the first step****—perform the first move in a course of action towards attaining a goal:* Come, let us make the first step towards our wealth.

casual ward • casualty ward

casual ward—(UK hist.) the division of a workhouse to accommodate vagrants overnight: The next two nights of our stay were spent in the Notting Hill casual ward.

casualty ward—the ward in a hospital in which accidents are treated: We were conducted to the casualty ward in which she was lying.

cat fight • dog fight

cat fight—(coll.) 1. an altercation between two women typically involving scratching, etc.: He was recently caught in-between a horrible cat fight involving his now girlfriend singer Kelis. 2. a vociferous dispute: A debate at Toronto City Council about an affordable housing project turned into an ugly "cat fight" between two councilors.

dog fight—a close-range aerial combat between aircraft: One event I do remember is being in the back garden and looking up and seeing two planes in a dog fight.

cat has nine lives, a • there's more than one way to kill a cat

cat has nine lives, a—(saying) cats can survive things severe enough to kill other animals: A cat has nine lives, you only have one. To prevent accidents — think before action.

there's more than one way to kill a cat (also: there are more ways than one to kill a cat)— there is more than one method to do smth.: Their experiments revealed: There's more than one way to kill a cat.

catch a look • catch the eye

catch a look—1. notice smb.'s glance: I caught a fleeting look of relief from Sylvia. 2. look at a person or thing: He turned to catch a look at her sweet face.

catch the eye—attract attention: The thickets of *Licuala* catch the eye with their striking foliage.

catch a tiger by the tail • take the bull by the horns

catch a tiger by the tail—(also: have a tiger by the tail) engage in an undertaking which may prove extremely dangerous or difficult: You're taking on an organization with reserves you know nothing about. How do you know you won't be catching a tiger by the tail?

Note: *The expression does not correlate in meaning with the phrase* ***catch an eel by the tail****—(also: hold an eel by the tail) attempt to control an elusive person or situation:* He is not easily managed, but if he suspects you are trying to take him in, you may as well catch an eel by the tail.

take the bull by the horns—deal with a difficult situation in a bold and direct manner rather than evade it: He had not, as the phrase goes, taken the bull by the horns, or advanced in front of the enemy's fire.

catch on to someone • catch on with someone

catch on to someone—understand the real nature of a person: He was a real talent and I hoped that the world would catch on to him.

catch on with someone—become popular with people: I hope our new product catches on with children.

catch on to something • catch up to something

catch on to something—figure smth. out; understand smth.: His sagacious mind immediately recognized and caught on to the only plan of salvation in sight.

catch up to something—(also: catch up with something) 1. overtake a bus, etc. by walking fast: Jane caught up to the bus that had almost left her behind. 2. keep pace with smth.: Quite frankly, at our current pace, we will never catch up to fixing our infrastructure deficit.

catch one's breath • get one's breath again

catch one's breath—be affected by a sudden emotion such as fear, excitement, etc.: To the rocketing bound of a good free horse you catch your breath, thankfully, happily.

get one's breath again—be relieved after exertion, excitement, etc.: The work goes on until Friday night, and then the break which gives one time to get one's breath again.

catch one's death • meet one's death

catch one's death—(coll.) catch a severe cold that may be fatal *(also: catch one's death of cold):* She had walked in the rain seeking a refuge and "catching her death" instead.

Note: *The expression does not correlate in meaning with the phrase* ***catch someone dead****—(coll., usually negat.) find a person in an embarrassing position:* Never driven anything but a car but you wouldn't catch me dead driving a minivan.

meet one's death—die a violent death; die in a particular way: Mr. Green met his death through the gas-tap being too loose.

catch someone cold • have someone cold

catch someone cold—(Sport) surprise one's opponents when they are not prepared for an attack: Northern, seeking their eighth successive League win, were caught cold by Castleford.

have someone cold—(U.S. sl.) have a person in one's power or at one's mercy: He'll have to take whatever deal they offer him, they've got him cold for the murder of Sedley.

catch someone on the wrong foot • put a foot wrong

catch someone on the wrong foot—surprise a person when one is not ready or expecting smth.: I'm afraid you rather caught me on the wrong foot, asking for it at such short notice.

put a foot wrong—(usually negat.) make the smallest mistake; make a blunder: He complained that if he put a foot wrong, the manager was down on him at once.

See also: get off on the wrong foot / get out of bed with the wrong foot foremost.

catch someone up in something • catch someone up on something

catch someone up in something—deeply involve a person in smth.; wholly occupy smb.'s attention: The accident caught us all up in the resultant confusion.

catch someone up on something—(coll.) tell a person the news of smth.: Oh, please catch me up on what your family is doing.

catch someone's eye • catch someone's look

catch someone's eye—attract a person's attention: I tried to catch her eye, but she was too engrossed in the book to notice.

catch someone's look—notice smb.'s glance: Howard laughed then stopped as he caught her look of disapproval.

catch up on someone • catch up with someone

catch up on someone—1. overtake and overcome a person: The police caught up on the men just as they entered a dark archway. *2.* have a marked effect on smb.: I think his past is beginning to catch up on him. *3. (coll.)* learn the news of a person: I've had a visit from my friend John, and it was nice to catch up on him.

catch up with someone—1. get level with a person when one has been left behind: Walk on ahead of me. I'll catch up with you. 2. = *catch up on someone 2:* Jet lag caught up with Joe and he slept for fourteen hours. 3. reach the same stage as smb. after lagging behind: He's working hard to catch up with the others. 4. make a person accountable for past deeds: Gronevelt felt that the FBI would catch up with them sooner or later. 5. *(coll.)* meet with smb. for a casual chat: "And what have you been up to?" "Nothing much. Catching up with a few people here."

catch up on something • catch up with something

catch up on something—do unfinished work; do things that one has not had time to do until now: Confined to his bed for a whole week, Smith passed the time catching up on his reading.

catch up with something—(also: catch up to something) 1. overtake a bus, etc. by walking fast: Jane caught up with the bus that had almost left her behind. 2. keep pace with smth.: The fate of Africa depends upon economic advance catching up with political advance.

cat's lick • cat-lick

cat's lick—(UK sl.) a brief wash: After having a quick bite, I had a cat's lick, that's my short bath and headed off for the hideout.

Note: *The expression does not correlate in meaning with the compound* ***calf-lick****—(also: cowlick) a curl of hair on the forehead which will not lie smoothly:* I would imagine that there must be a hereditary factor to the calf-lick like there is to eyes.

cat-lick—(UK sl., also: cat'lick) Catholic: The Cat-lick church has often changed its mind on things ... often kicking and screaming while being dragged down that road of change.

cat's paw • pussyfoot

cat's paw—a person used as a tool by another to accomplish a purpose, etc.: The eldest son, John, was a cat's-paw in the financial schemings of the second son, Charles.

pussyfoot—1. a person who avoids committing himself; smb. who proceeds very cautiously: Modesty is not the same as subjection, and a well-bred lad does not need to be a pussyfoot. 2. a cool, fruity nonalcoholic cocktail with added egg yolk: Turned out a pussyfoot is a non-alcoholic concoction of a few fruit juices served chilled.

cat's whisker • cat's whiskers

cat's whisker—(in old-fashioned crystal radios) a wire that makes contact with a semiconductor: Many of these receivers used the "cat's whisker" type of crystal diode for detection of a radio signal.

cat's whiskers—(coll.) the acme of excellence; a person or thing most highly approved of: My new secretary thinks she is the cat's whiskers though she is no better than the last one.

Note: *The expression does not correlate in meaning with the phrase* ***between you and me and the cat's whiskers****—said when telling smth. to a person that you want him to keep secret:* The water was cool, white and pure ... and we felt divine taking bath in it. The location of the waterfall is between six of us and the cat's whiskers.

cause for something • cause of something

cause for something—reason or motive for smth.: The grannies had no real cause for complaint of the furnishment of the tea table.

cause of something—an event, person, or thing that makes smth. happen: It was not surprising to hear that hypertension was the cause of his death.

chairman of the board • chairman of the boards

chairman of the board—the leader of a corporation's board of directors: He was Chairman of the Board of the Stockholm International Peace Research Institute and remains a board member.

chairman of the boards—(Hockey) a player who controls play along the boards: One of our sportsmen has been extended the ultimate compliment by the city of New York. The legendary "Chairman of the Boards" flies out to the Big Apple on Sunday...

chalk it up to someone • chalk one up for someone

chalk it up to someone—(coll.) attribute smth. to or account for smth. by a person's age, inexperience, etc.: I apologise for failing to recall what he said. Please chalk it up to me being an old guy and subject to memory failure.

chalk one up for someone—(coll.) put smth. to a person's credit: I give Cameron credit for what he is as a showman, but I won't chalk one up for him for what he isn't — and he's not an artist.

challenge someone on something • challenge someone to something

challenge someone on something—dispute a person's statement, remarks, etc.: I think Fred is wrong, but I won't challenge him on his estimate.

challenge someone to something—dare smb. to do smth.; invite a person to compete at smth.: Your opponent now has the chance to challenge you to a return game.

chance on something • chance something

chance on something—find smth. by chance: I chanced on the transaction in the realty column of the paper.

chance something—risk doing smth.: I don't usually ride horses, but this time I will chance it.

chance one's arm • one would give his right arm

chance one's arm—do smth. in the face of probable failure; take one's chance of doing smth. successfully: He chanced his arm in pursuit of a world record and for a while looked like he might just pull it off.

one would give his right arm—(hyperbolic) one is ready to give up his most valuable possession (to achieve smth.): I'm sure Leon would give his right arm for a fraction of John's success.

change hands • pass from hand to hand

change hands—(of money, property, etc.) pass from one person's possession to another's: Scanlons used to be a really good pub but it has just changed hands, so I am not sure any more.

pass from hand to hand—(of leaflets, etc.) continuously pass from one person to a series of other persons: She watched the note as it passed from hand to hand down the rows until it finally reached her desk.

change of life • changes of life

change of life—(euph.) menopause: The period occupied by this "change of life" ranges from two to four years, if not longer.

changes of life—altered conditions in a person's life: I have learned, through all the changes of life, the important lesson that it is not necessary to go through any stressful change alone.

change something for something • change something to something

change something for something—take or give smth. in exchange for smth. else: On second thoughts I don't care for this red tie. Could you change it for a green one?

change something to something—change smth. so as to make it smth. else: When she marries, a woman usually changes her surname to that of her husband.

change the scene • change the scenes

change the scene—change the environment or social surroundings: The scene of the negotiation was again changed. It was shifted from England to Holland.

change the scenes—(Theater) change the general appearance of the stage: The play uses Brechtian techniques to show the workings of theater as scenes are changed before your eyes.

Channel Islands, the *(UK)* • Channel Islands, the *(U.S.)*

Channel Islands, the (UK)—a group of islands in the English Channel, off the French coast of Normandy: The Chausey islands are not generally included in the geographical definition of the Channel Islands but occasionally described as "French Channel Islands."

Channel Islands, the (U.S.)—(also: Channel Islands of California, the) a chain of eight islands located in the Pacific Ocean, off the coast of Southern California: The Channel Islands at low elevations are virtually frost-free and constitute one of the few such areas in the continental U.S.

charge like a bull at a gate • charge like a wounded bull

charge like a bull at a gate—(Austral. sl.) act impetuously or with violence: I was naïve, but also like a bull at a gate, charging forward without stopping for long to consider the consequences.

charge like a wounded bull—(Austral. sl.) overprice an item or service: When waiters take your order, they often get you to order all kinds of extras for which they can charge like a wounded bull.

charge someone for something • charge someone up for something

charge someone for something—ask a person to pay a certain price for smth.: I was charged for a few pounds of overweight luggage.

Note: *The expression does not correlate in meaning with the phrase **charge someone with something**—*1. *declare that a person is guilty of smth.:* All the members demanded with one voice who it was who was charged with the crime. 2. *entrust a person with a duty or responsibility:* Students are under the supervision of the Censor, who is charged with the care of their conduct and studies.

charge someone up for something—1. stimulate smb.'s enthusiasm or readiness for smth.: An excellent beefsteak in the company of truckers charged me up for the day's exertions. 2. make a person pay more by raising the price: On top of the food, he charged me up for bogus Lottery tickets.

charge something down to someone • charge something up to someone

charge something down to someone—(also: put something down to someone) record a sum of money as a person's debt for later payment: Please charge these goods down to my account.

charge something up to someone—(also: charge something upon someone) = charge something down to someone: Why were the expenses of the reception charged up to me?

Charlie's dead • Queen Ann's dead

Charlie's dead—(UK) is used to discreetly tell a woman that her slip or panties are showing: *"Charlie est mort."* "What did you say?" Marie lapsed suddenly into English.... "Charlie's dead," he translated. "Means your petticoat's showing."

Queen Ann's dead—(UK) an ironical response to smb. who refers to old news or says smth. very obvious: To any boy who tendered a particularly obvious bit of information, his classic reply was, "Oh yes, and Queen Anne's dead."

chase two rabbits • kill two birds with one stone

chase two rabbits—(also: run after two hares) try to fulfill two goals at the same time (with the implication that a person will not succeed in either one): Japanese managers are forced to "chase two rabbits," that is, Western governance and Japanese honor.

Note: *The expression does not correlate in meaning with the phrase **make two bites of a cherry**—(also: take two bites of a cherry) take two turns to accomplish smth. which could be performed in one operation:* To announce then all I am announcing now seemed unwise and we remembered the adage against making two bites of a cherry.

kill two birds with one stone—accomplish two objectives with a single action: If we can get gas and have lunch at the next rest stop, we will be killing two birds with one stone.

chat someone up • talk someone up

chat someone up—(UK coll., of men) try to make friends with a woman by talking to her: I did my clumsy best to chat her up and talked to her about my interest in archaeology.

talk someone up—(chiefly U.S.) praise smb.; speak in support of a person: The coaches have been talking him up since early in the preseason.

Note: *The expression is not antonymous in meaning to the phrase* ***talk someone down****—1. silence smb. by speaking more loudly or aggressively; win out over a person in an argument, etc.:* Eventually, however, Mr. Brown talked down all the other members of the committee. *2. convince a person to lower the price:* This is my final offer.... Now, don't try to talk me down. 3. *provide a pilot with directions by radio which enable him to land:* They get us on the radar screen and talk us down on to the runway.

See also: talk down to someone / talk up to someone.

check on something • check something

check on something—examine or assess smth. (such as a person's health, etc.): We checked on the possibility of shipping some of our newly acquired paintings back to the States.

check something—1. examine smth. to learn whether it is correct: The child should be taught how to check his spelling against that of the dictionary. 2. = *check on something:* We've added a test to check the possibility of hearing damage caused by extended listening at high level. 3. cause an emotion, feeling, etc. to stop: The changes that Mark Twain made indicate that he checked his impulse to write an even darker, more confrontational work.

check someone up • check up on someone

check someone up—1. *(also: give someone a check-up)* give smb. a medical examination: The doctor checked me up and I was told I was in bad shape. 2. establish the truth about smb.; investigate a person: The cop doesn't even take the trouble to check me up, he knows me damn well.

check up on someone— = check someone 2: The police checked up on him, and he had an alibi. Several people testified that they saw him at a bar in Rochester.

cheese it • say cheese

cheese it—(sl., often imper.) 1. stop doing smth.; leave off: I say, cheese it! If you bang about much more you'll have the ceiling down. 2. run away quickly: When a police car came into the neighborhood, we acted as if they were after us, and the cry went out "Cheese it, the cops!"

say cheese—said to make smb. smile when taking his photograph: They are almost certainly just saying cheese to hold their smiles...

chess player • chessman

chess player—a person who plays chess: A champion chess player will often lose a match game to a far inferior opponent.

chessman—one of the pieces with which chess is played: Chessmen of fanciful shapes and forms are often made as curiosities.

chew the cud • chew the fat

chew the cud—think about smth. slowly and carefully: Near the Acropolis is the Archaia Agora, ruins that were once the square where philosophers chewed the cud.

chew the fat—(coll.) 1. chat at length in a relaxed manner: Blount's great talent is that he's comfortable chewing the fat with just about anybody. 2. discuss a matter, especially complainingly: If anyone starts fault-finding or "chewing the fat" he is immediately "ticked off."

Note: *Neither expression correlates in meaning with the phrase* ***chew the cheese****—(sl.) vomit:* The cat's chewing the cheese on the living room carpet again.

chicken feed • feed the chicken

chicken feed—(coll.) anything of little importance, especially a trifling sum of money: That meant only chicken feed for the proprietary companies and big producers. *Cf.: chicken feeder—(sl.) a poor tipper:* The only people I waited on in the restaurant were chicken feeders.

Note: *The expression does not correlate in meaning with the phrase* ***bird food****—(sl.) health food such as nuts, seeds, etc. (also: rabbit food):* "Instead of a beef hamburger, try a garden-burger. It's got nuts and oats and is healthier for you." "I don't like bird food."

feed the chicken—(sl.) said of a gesture of greeting in which one person slaps an upraised palm against that of another person: "Hey, great job, feed the chicken!" "Thanks."

Note: *The expression does not correlate in meaning with the phrase* ***feed the chicks****—(RAF) carry out air-to-air refueling, by a large tanker aircraft, of the smaller, fighter aircraft.*

chicken soup • duck soup

chicken soup—1. a book featuring a collection of short, motivating essays: Compiled of new and previously published stories, this Chicken Soup collection brings inspiration for the holidays. 2. smth. that provides a mysterious but effective way to solve the problem: "Hey, my Mac [computer] is messed up. It won't work." "Try re-building your desktop, it's chicken soup."

duck soup—(coll.) a task or assignment that does not require much effort: One very helpful person was Caroline, a technician for whom the whole computer operation was duck soup.

child of man • man-child

child of man—(liter.) a human being: The elephant lays down his life to save the child of man, and, consequently, innocence and honesty triumphs over selfishness.

man-child—(pl. men-children) a male child; a boy: Three years later another little girl was born, and lastly a handsome little man child was born to this family in 1863.

child of nature • natural child

child of nature—(euph.) a person in an uncivilized or uncultivated state: She felt that he wanted her to be a child of nature. That suited her very well.

natural child—1. a child actually begotten by one in contrast to adopted: With little prospect of natural children, we applied for adoption all the sooner. 2. a child born out of wedlock: Full equality has been introduced between legitimate and natural children, between married and unmarried couples.

childish behavior • childlike behavior

childish behavior—(used showing disapproval) behavior characterized by lack of emotional restraint or similar adult qualities: The strategy requires that you not react to her childish behavior. Until she calms down, you don't respond at all.

childlike behavior—the kind of behavior more appropriate for a child than an adult: Shana ... newly dependent on her mother, reverted to childlike behavior by allowing herself to be taken care of.

child's game • child's play

child's game—said of a person's behavior more appropriate for a child: He knew it was just a child's game — to stare at someone and not look away first.

Note: *The expression does not correlate in meaning with the phrase* ***easy game****—(also: fair game) a suitable object for ridicule; a person easily persuaded or taken advantage of:* So I disguised myself and came back and studied you. You were easy game.

child's play—said of smth. very easily done or of very little importance: The work of reformation is child's play to that of making your friends believe you have reformed.

China syndrome • Chinese restaurant syndrome

China syndrome—1. *(dated)* possibility of a catastrophe as a result of a nuclear reactor meltdown: If the heat in the molten fuel cannot be dissipated by conductivity, then the danger from the so-called China Syndrome would be much higher. 2. *(Business)* relocating manufacturing operations to China to reduce labor costs: It was pointed out that the new European Union countries were actually an alternative for the so-called China Syndrome.

Note: *The expression does not correlate in meaning with the phrase* ***Vietnam syndrome****—(U.S.) an attitude that diplomacy may be more effective in solving political problems than the use of military force (stemming from the American experience in Vietnam):* Lee characterized the new war as an attempt to overcome the Vietnam syndrome to prove we can fight and win.

Chinese restaurant syndrome—a group of symptoms varying from sweating and dizziness to heart palpitation observed in some people eating Chinese food *(associated with the food additive "monosodium glutamate" used in Chinese cooking):* Chinese restaurant syndrome is best diagnosed by the symptoms that a person describes.

Chinese auction • Dutch auction

Chinese auction—an auction, commonly in a charity type setting, in which bidders buy tickets which are essentially their chances to win items: We will have our usual Chinese auction, which has been so popular in the past.

Dutch auction—an auction in which the auctioneer progressively lowers the price until a bidder agrees to buy: Sarah de Clercq began her career as a picture specialist at a Dutch auction house.

chocolate soldier • toy soldier

chocolate soldier—*(derog.)* 1. a soldier unwilling to fight: They are chocolate soldiers who merely go to see battles and coolly urge others to fight them. 2. a militiaman or conscripted soldier: Conscripts, known as "chocos" (chocolate soldiers) were not required to serve outside prescribed areas.

toy soldier—*(also: tin soldier)* 1. a miniature figure of a soldier made of metal, etc.: There are thousands of different hobbies: toy soldiers, model airplanes, cigarette cards. 2. *(derog.)* a soldier in a peacetime army; a ceremonial soldier only: Poor Hugo has gone clucking back for to be a toy soldier at Aldershot.

chosen few • chosen people

chosen few—*(also: select few)* a relatively small number of persons selected for a position of favor or privilege: The Professor is giving a dinner-party tonight, but that's just for the chosen few.

chosen people—*(also: God's chosen people)* 1. the Jews, especially in the Old Testament: This was a greater miracle than that of the cloud with which God defended his chosen people in the wilderness from the heat of the sun. 2. those who are "saved" in keeping with the Christian doctrine of salvation; members of the spiritual Israel: Antichrist is a holder of political power who persecutes God's chosen people.

Cicero of Germany, the • German Cicero, the

Cicero of Germany, the—*(hist.)* the name given to Johann III, elector of Brandenburg (1455–1499): Cicero of Germany, Elector of Brandenburg, could speak four hours at a stretch, in elegantly flowing Latin, with a fair share of meaning in it too.

German Cicero, the—*(hist.)* the name given to Johann Sturm, printer and scholar (1507–1589): He has been called the German Cicero, and has arguably exerted a more powerful influence on education than any single person.

citizen of nature • natural citizen

citizen of nature—a human being as an integral part of the natural world (knowing no boundaries created by men): The laws of nature defined his natural rights and made him, as it were, a citizen of nature.

natural citizen—*(also: natural-born citizen)* a person born in the country and having the legal status of citizen: I think a true American is one who is a natural citizen.

Note: *The expression is not equivalent in meaning to the phrase* ***naturalized citizen****—an immigrant from another country who has become a citizen:* Mr. Johnson is a naturalized citizen of the United States, but a native of England.

City Editor *(UK)* • City Editor *(U.S.)*

City Editor—*(UK)* the editor dealing with financial news in a newspaper or magazine: Often comment by the City Editors precipitated a run on shares.

City Editor—*(U.S.)* the editor dealing with local news: The City Editor directs the work of the reporters, whose duty is to gather all the local intelligence of the day.

City man • city man

City man—*(UK)* a person engaged in commerce or finance: He had made his mark in the mercantile world as a thoroughly representative City-man.

city man—1. an inhabitant of a city (as contrasted with a countryman): Mr. White might have made a whole book out of being a city man on a farm. 2. a fellow-inhabitant of a city: He headed out for Calgary or Edmonton, or any American city.... It didn't matter. Everywhere he found his city men.

City of Angels • City of Saints

City of Angels—Los Angeles *(California, USA):* From The City of Angels to the City of Saints: The struggle to build a railroad from Los Angeles to Salt Lake City.

City of Saints—1. Montreal *(Quebec, Canada):* Martin said he came from a city of saints, where all the streets were named after saints. 2. Salt Lake City *(Utah, USA):* The "City of Saints" grew from the toil and resolve of a hardy band of Mormon pioneers.

Note: *Neither expression correlates in meaning with the phrase* ***City of God****—1. heaven as an ideal abode of bliss:* The Christians were convinced that the "City of God" was infinitely more important than happiness on earth. *2. (also: Holy City) Jerusalem (in Christian and Judaic tradition):* The city of God, Jerusalem represents a sphere in which God's interests are protected and God's dominion is exercised.

clasp hands • clasp one's hands

clasp hands—shake hands showing more emotion than in the usual handshake: At half-past three my friend and I clasped hands upon the mountain top.

clasp one's hands—press hands together with the fingers interlaced: Setting aside her glass, Sandra crossed her feet, clasping her hands behind her head.

classic play • classical play

classic play—a play that serves as a standard; one that has come to be regarded as one of the best: Molly has a dream of acting in a classic play, but all the parts she likes are written for men.

classical play—a play which is Roman or ancient Greek: A classical play (ancient Greek drama or work of a classical writer) is presented during the summer in cultural events held by municipalities.

clean animals • cleanly animals

clean animals—1. animals that are habitually clean: Rats are obsessively clean animals that spend a good 20 percent of their day cleaning themselves. 2. animals considered fit for food by religious custom: God tells us that the clean animals were to be used for food and the unclean animals were not to be used as food.

cleanly animals— = *clean animals 1:* You need to spend only little time on the personal hygiene of the guinea-pigs because they are very cleanly animals.

clean as a new pin • clean as a whistle

clean as a new pin—spotlessly clean; very tidy: He was always glad to see me in the galley which he kept as clean as a new pin.

clean as a whistle—1. = *clean as a new pin:* It was not long before the dismal little boarded-up house was as clean as a whistle. *2.* said of smth. neatly and skillfully done: The dog jumped through the hoop as clean as a whistle.

clean-fingered • clean-handed

clean-fingered—1. *(of a musician, etc.)* having quick and nimble fingers: The clean-fingered playing and thoughtful approach distinguish his performance of the earlier pieces. 2. honest; incorruptible: Desire for clean-fingered lottery regulators ensured that none of them was remotely connected to the gambling industry.

clean-handed—not guilty of any wrongdoing: Mature, democratic institutions with clean-handed politics and social justice are still a long way off.

clean room • dirty room

clean room—1. *(also: white room)* a room that is virtually free of dust or bacteria (used in assembly of precision equipment): The plant is a state-of-the-art facility that forms transistors onto large glass substrates, in a class–100 clean room. 2. *(med.)* operating theater with a "clean-room" atmosphere: It was a hospital clean room he was locked in. Purified air and the smell of disinfectant.

dirty room—(med.) an operating room where the surgeon has to deal with an infection: The hospital has four wards. In addition, there is an operation theater for major procedures, and a "dirty" room for minor cases.

clean shave • close shave

clean shave—(sl.) said of an act of swindling: We doubt if any lady is aware of the very clean shave she is constantly undergoing.

close shave—a dangerous situation that a person just manages to avoid: I did not so much as get my feet wet when the bridge fell, though it was a close shave.

clean-shaven • closely shaven

clean-shaven—said of a man not having a moustache or beard: He provided a list of celebrated clean-shaven men and also of celebrated beavers, as bearded men are termed.

closely shaven—said of a man with a neat, smooth shave: He was tall, spare, with closely shaven face and gray hair, worn rather long.

clean someone out • clean up on someone

clean someone out—(coll.) take everything from a person; deprive or cheat smb. of his money, etc.: "She cleaned me out," says Williams. "She used me to get to America."

clean up on someone—(U.S. coll.) defeat an opponent (in a fight): Chavez looked tired and Tszyu cleaned up on him, clocking him with a clean left hook and several right uppercuts.

clear a ship • clear a ship for action

clear a ship—pay the charges at the custom-house and receive permission to sail: The custom's official told me that only the captain could clear the ship and that I had to go back and get him.

clear a ship for action—(also: clear the decks) remove all encumbrances from the deck of a ship ready for an engagement: Crews were often given a hot meal before being called to clear the ship for action.

clear as crystal • clear as mud

clear as crystal—1. *(of water, etc.)* unclouded; transparent: The cave was long and wide and pervaded by cold water, clear as crystal. 2. *(of a situation)* very clear; easily understood: I don't know why you can't understand the instructions — they're as clear as crystal to me.

Note: *The expression does not fully correlate in meaning with the phrase* ***clear as a bell***—1. *(of sound) extremely clear:* When his daughter telephoned him from America he could hear her as clear as a bell. 2. = *clear as crystal 2:* When I write something, the meaning is clear as a bell to me. When someone reads what I wrote, the interpretation may be very different.

clear as mud—1. *(joc.)* = *clear as crystal 2:* It was clear as mud that Angelides was very smart. But it was also clear that he was not a politician.... 2. *(ironic)* not at all clear: I'm now giving up as I've wasted too much time on this and the instructions are about as clear as mud.

clear away • clear off

clear away—1. *(of clouds, fog, etc.)* vanish; disappear: The mist cleared away as the sun came out. 2. clear the table: Mother always clears away when we have finished eating.

clear off—1. *(coll., often imper.)* be off; go away *(also: clear out):* I told them to clear off and threatened to call the police. 2. *(coll., also: clear out)* run away; leave in a hurry: When he saw the policeman, he cleared off as fast as his legs could carry him. 3. = *clear away 1:* This fog cleared off more quickly than others and after an hour it was just overcast and warm.

clear land • clear the land

clear land—remove trees and brushwood (to cultivate the soil): I have been clearing land for eight days, and now begin to feel the effects of poison — from ivy, doubtless.

clear the land—1. = *clear land:* There were three ways by which the first settlers cleared the land. The first was called "slashing." 2. *(Nautical)* maneuver close to land without running ashore: It looked a bit close to the beach where the ship was drifting. But we managed to clear the land...

clear something off • clear something out

clear something off—1. remove smth. unwanted in order to leave a clear space: Please clear your papers off so that I can serve dinner. 2. pay one's debts, remaining payments, etc.: I hope to clear off my mortgage in a few months' time. 3. dispose of the goods, etc. (selling them cheaply): The manager wants to clear off all the old stock in the warehouse. 4. *(coll.)* get rid of smth.; make an end of smth.: I'd like to clear off the rest of the work which was waiting for me after my holiday.

clear something out—1. = *clear something off 1:* I hope you've cleared out all those papers and envelopes from your drawer this time. 2. = *clear something off 3:* If you need to clear out the goods now we do have a small amount of storage space. 3. *(coll.)* rob a place: They completely cleared out the shop window display making off with gold chains.

clever at something • clever with something

clever at something—quick in learning and understanding smth.: Some of you boys and girls are very clever at working sums.

clever with something—skilful in using a tool, etc.: She was a beader: she was that clever with her fingers she could do all kinds of things.

climacteric period • climactic period

climacteric period—1. the period of menopause in women: Psychological and social conditions influenced the presence of depression during the climacteric period. 2. a period of decisive importance: Barnes rendered specially valuable service in behalf of the Union during the climacteric period of the Civil War.

climactic period—a period of greatest intensity in a series of events: The climactic period in the dinosaurs' reign was reached just before the ice age.

climb up the wall • go over the wall

climb up the wall—(coll.) become very angry or distraught: Old Marks will climb up the wall if he hears I closed early.

go over the wall—1. leave a religious order: The world is always more interested in the one nun who goes over the wall than the thousands who don't. 2. escape from prison: Us guys pull wires to get jobs as guards, and you convicts go over the wall whenever you can. 3. defect to another country: The bloody place [the Foreign Office] has never been the same since Kim Philby went over the wall. 4. go to prison: He would be observed "going over the wall" or "going to stir" (going to detention prison).

clip one's words • clip the King's English

clip one's words—speak with affected clarity or precise articulation: Although he was usually fairly easy to understand, he had a habit of clipping his words so that they sounded extremely precise.

clip the King's English—(UK dated) pronounce words hurriedly and indistinctly when drunk *(also: clip the Queen's English):* I only drink to get mauled but it's rare to find me clipping the King's English in these places.

clip someone's wings • give someone wings

clip someone's wings—restrain a person; restrict the scope of smb.'s activities: He could not succeed in clipping the wings of his restless neighbor.

give someone wings—provide inspiration to a person: I love his belief in me. He has given me wings and convinced me I can do all things.

clock someone • clock someone in

clock someone—1. measure the time a person takes doing smth.: I doubt anyone will clock you on it. But if you're selling your game you will be present at the booth a part of the day to promote it. 2. *(Traffic Police)* measure the speed of a passing car using radar gun (in order to detect speedsters): Stay out of this city if possible ... the police will clock you for going 5 miles over the speed limit. 3. *(U.S. sl.)* hit a person: The guy behind me clocked me in the back of the head right as the ball hit my palm and I dropped it.

clock someone in—record smb.'s arrival for work: When I arrived at work, usually about 3:10 every day, someone had clocked me in at 3:00. Ten additional minutes each day gave me a little over $2.50 a month, which paid my bus fare. *Cf.: clock someone out— register smb.'s departure from work:* His buddy clocked him out so it appeared that he worked a full day even though he never showed up.

close down • shut down

close down—1. *(of a shop, factory, etc.)* cease doing business; stop production: The shop will be closing down for good on Saturday, so everything is half price. 2. *(of a radio or TV station)* stop broadcasting for the day: This station is now closing down and we wish you all good-night.

shut down— = *close down 1:* The whole company shuts down for three weeks' holiday every year.

close enough for government work • close enough for jazz

close enough for government work—(U.S. ironic) is used to reflect one's low opinion of the end result, quality of a product, etc.: For decades, the East German public was damned with merchandise that was "close enough for government work."

close enough for jazz—is used to say that while smth. is not perfect, it is close enough in quality to the target to be acceptable: The data may not be totally accurate, but it is close enough for jazz. We trust it.

Note:** Neither expression correlates in meaning with the phrase* ***close but no cigar*— used of a situation when one falls just short of a successful outcome:* In my last rejection the editor told me that this particular piece was "close but no cigar."

close one's eyes • close your eyes and think of England

close one's eyes—(also: shut one's eyes) pretend that one has no knowledge of smth.; ignore smth.: If the authorities choose to close their eyes, the only thing that will pry them open is public pressure.

close your eyes and think of England—(also: shut your eyes and think of England) a humorous advice to smb. faced with an unpleasant task *(originally a wedding-night advice for Victorian brides to succumb to unwanted sex):* Live large. Tip big. And when they bring the check, just close your eyes and think of England.

close something down • shut something down

close something down—(of a shop, factory, etc.) cause to cease functioning: The shop had been closed down following the medical inspection report.

shut something down—1. = *close something down:* The severe winter shut many factories down this year. 2. *(of an engine, piece of equipment, etc.)* turn off: They shut the machine down so they could repair it. 3. stop water or electricity supply: On Monday the power supply will be shut down for the whole building.

close something up • shut something up

close something up—1. *(of a well)* close by filling up: We must close up the old well, it's dangerous. 2. *(of a road)* close by blocking: Leaving town I saw a few signs saying that the road was closed up ahead. 3. cause smth. to join together: Children have to learn to close up their letters when writing. 4. *(of a building, shop, etc.)* close (for a short time): We are closing up the house for the weekend.

shut something up—(of a building, shop, etc.) close securely; make safe by locking: We're going to shut the house up for the summer while we are away.

close the barn door after the horse gets out • your barn door is open

close the barn door after the horse gets out—not take any action until after a problem has already occurred: The problem is that post-accident testing closes the barn door after the horse is long gone.

your barn door is open—(U.S. euph.) is used as a caution to a man having his trouser zip undone: "Excuse me ... I couldn't help but notice your barn door is open." "What?" "Um ... your fly is open."

close the book on something • close the books on something

close the book on something—put an end to a matter; stop

working on a case: The police insinuate that David may have been involved in illegal activities and seem to close the book on the case.

Note: *The expression does not correlate in meaning with the phrase* ***closed book, a****— used of a person or thing one can't figure out or does not know anything about:* "At first, I politely refused the commission, as opera is a closed book to me," says Tojuro…

close the books on something—balance accounts at the end of an accounting period: While residential brokerages expect to close the books next month on a record sales year, they are already seeing signs of a slowdown.

See also: open a book on something / open book, an.

close the door on someone • close the door to someone

close the door on someone—1. refuse to allow a person in: Next a policeman let several people in including Dick, but closed the door on me. 2. refuse to talk to or have any more dealings with a person: They closed the door on their daughter when she married without their consent.

close the door to someone—(of a club, university, etc.) refuse admission: This country must not close the door to immigrants and refugees. *Cf.: open the door to someone—allow a certain category of people to enter or join:* The Anglican church had recently opened the door to women by ruling that national bodies could choose their own bishops.

close thing • closest thing, the

close thing—(also: close shave) said of a dangerous situation that a person just manages to avoid: John had just saved his bacon. It had been a very close thing.

closest thing, the—most similar to a person or thing mentioned: Pat Branson was the closest thing to a manual worker among us.

close time • closing time

close time—a season when it is illegal to kill certain animals or fish: He would extend the close time, and he believes that in a year the nets would be catching far more fish.

closing time—the time at which pubs, shops, etc. end business: The art museum was fantastic, and we stayed until closing time.

close to someone • close with someone

close to someone—intimate or very familiar with smb.: Mr. Weinberger is close to the President … much closer than Mr. Haig has ever been.

close with someone—(coll.) stingy towards a person: He was close with his son and never allowed him any pocket-money.

close to something • close with something

close to something—1. situated near to smth.: The area is a 70-hectare nature reserve lying close to the town. 2. nearly equal to smth.: Visually the print is very close to the original painting in color, tone and texture.

close with something—mean with one's money, etc.: "Was he in the habit of making you presents?" "Oh, no, sir; he was very close with his money, sir."

close up • close-up

close up—1. close completely: The wound is closing up but underneath it it's still a little tender and bruised. 2. come nearer to each other: As soon as he saw the movement of the crowd the captain gave the order to his men to close up. 3. *(of a shop, etc.)* close (for a short time): By the time we got to the main dealer's room, it was already closing up for the day. 4. *(coll.)* become silent or secretive: We had a good conversation before I asked, but when I asked, he closed up and looked away.

close-up—1. *(Photography, TV)* a shot taken from a position very close to the subject: The film, with a surplus of gigantic close-ups, seems more calculated to appeal to American than British audiences. 2. a detailed picture or display of smth.: This experience provided me with a close-up of how a halftime show is produced and executed.

close up a shop • close up shop

close up a shop—(also: shut up a shop) close a shop securely before leaving (for the weekend, etc.): The shop was closed up for the night, so Kermit used his key and went up the back way.

close up shop—(also: shut up shop) 1. *(of an office, firm, etc.)* stop doing business for the day or more: The restaurant will not close up shop until 11 P.M. every night of the week. *2.* go out of business: Mr. Lemoyne had reluctantly closed up shop when the library had reached a rock-bottom membership of eleven.

Note: *The expression does not correlate in meaning with the phrase* ***closed shop****— a plant or factory that employs only union workers:* Under a closed shop agreement, non-union employees must join the union or face dismissal.

closed case • open-and-shut case

closed case—a legal case that has been decided: Trying to reopen a closed case is a very difficult, time consuming (and usually expensive) process.

open-and-shut case—a legal case that is easily settled or decided: The jury feels this is an open-and-shut case but Sir John experiences doubts.

clothes man • old-clothes man

clothes man—a dealer in cast-off or second-hand clothes: I bought from the clothes-man a suit of the most gentlemanly garments he possessed.

Note: *The expression does not correlate in meaning with the phrase* ***man of the cloth****— a priest:* It's nice to see a man of the cloth actually using and believing in science. *Cf.: clothier—a retail seller of cloth:* My father was a clothier. He sold cloth to the tailors or to men who would then go to a tailor.

old-clothes man— = clothes man: This mantle he had just purchased of the old-clothes man … to protect himself from the cold of the March.

clown around • make a clown of oneself

clown around—do silly things in order to make people laugh: The boys were clowning around when the teacher came in.

make a clown of oneself—do smth. silly which makes one appear foolish: This meeting led Rothermere to make a clown of himself and also of his newspaper.

cock-eye Bob • cockeye pilot

cock-eye Bob—(Austral. sl.) a cyclone which occurs on the coast of Western Australia during the summer: Almost daily the sky blackened as cock-eye Bobs shrieked upon them, to lash them in sheets of rain.

cockeye pilot—a brightly colored fish *(Eupomacentrus leucostictus)* found in Florida and the West Indies: The "cockeye pilot," or jaqueta … green with black bands, swarms in the West Indies.

coffee break • coffee hour

coffee break—a short time out from work in which to rest and drink coffee: Take a coffee break: Coffee is a must for most college students studying into the night.

coffee hour—a time to socialize and have refreshments: A weekly coffee hour provides a chance for international students to socialize with American students, staff and faculty.

coffin nail • nail in the coffin

coffin nail—1. smth. (in a sequence of events) that tends to do serious harm: Every time they buy products made in other countries they are driving another coffin nail into America's economy. 2. *(sl.)* a cigarette: Our joking doesn't seem very funny any more, because for many thousands, cigarettes really do become coffin nails.

nail in the coffin— = *coffin nail 1:* The vote is another nail in the coffin of the one-party system which the country has now largely renounced.

coin box • money box

coin box—(UK) a public telephone: Annie called him from a coin box using a two-pence piece that had been given her.

money box—1. a small box with an opening into which coins are dropped as a way of saving money: A shilling went into the child's money-box that she had chosen as a safe deposit. 2. a strongbox for holding cash: Count the money in the money box, write the amount down and compare with the expected amount.

coin laundry • money laundry

coin laundry—(U.S.) a self-service laundry with coin-operated washing machines: If you need to use a coin laundry, be sure to sort everything at home before you go.

money laundry—a facility (such as a bank, etc.) engaged in transactions aimed at concealing the identity of illegally obtained money: I figured it was a money laundry, probably for drug money, but I was mistaken.

cold as hell • cold winter in hell

cold as hell—(coll.) said of an extremely low ambient temperature: Where's my jacket? It's cold as hell outside.

cold winter in hell—said of smth. not likely to happen or happening on a very rare occasion: It'll be a cold winter in hell before I ever go back there again.

cold as stone • stone cold

cold as stone—(also: cold as a stone) 1. very cold to the touch: Laura reached for Paul's hand but when she laced her fingers in his, Paul's hand was cold as stone. 2. *(of a person)* not much moved by emotions: He was all sweet and kind to me but I remained cold as a stone! "You take pleasure in tormenting me," he said...

Note: *The expression does not correlate in meaning with the phrase* ***cold as a wagon tire****—(U.S. dated sl.) dead:* The first time she saw a man lying cold as a wagon tire wasn't the day she first stepped into battle, which was a good thing.

stone cold—1. said of cold tea, coffee, etc. that is expected to be warm: He used to talk so much that his food was usually stone cold before he finished it. 2. = *cold as stone 1:* The only observation I was left to ponder was how I could sweat so profusely while my hands were stone cold.

cold cash • hot money

cold cash—(also: cold hard cash) money in its proper form, as distinguished from checks, etc.: A Chinese buyer walked into his atelier and paid cold cash for a monumental statue (which can go for up to a million dollars).

Note: *The expression does not correlate in meaning with the phrase* ***cool million****—(coll.) a million dollars considered as an asset or a lump sum:* You can bet he isn't short on cash now. Each cast member earned a cool million bucks every time another episode of the hit TV show was shot.

hot money—money that is moved by its owner quickly from one form of investment to another: Hot money is flowing into Kenya as the country emerges as the latest target for international fund managers looking for high returns.

cold fish • cool fish

cold fish—a callous, unfeeling individual; one who shows no emotion: He is a real cold fish, never has struck me as the kind of man to care much for others.

cool fish—(sl., also: cool card) a person who is impudent in a calm way: Another sense referred to somebody who was assured, audacious or impudent. This turned up in phrases like *a cool fish*...

cold for someone • cold to someone

cold for someone—is used of smth. not warm enough for a person: The water was too cold for me, and I decided not to bathe that day.

cold to someone—(also: cold with someone) said of smb. who is not kind or friendly to a person: He was cold to his son that morning.

college board • college boards

college board—1. the governing body in a college: College board members are encouraged to consult with the School Boards Association when specific questions arise. 2. *(U.S.)* an organization that provides tests and other educational services for colleges: For the majority of colleges, you'll have to take tests issued by the College Board.

college boards—a set of examinations given to test a student's readiness for college: My father had a perfect math score on his college boards, the highest in the country.

collision course • crash course

collision course—1. a course, as of moving vehicles, that will end in a collision if left unchanged: Because of the density of the fog, the deck officers did not realize that the ships were now on a collision course. 2. confrontation between opposing groups, etc. that may end in conflict: All attempts at diplomacy have broken down and the two states now appear to be on a collision course.

crash course—a short intensive course in which one is taught the most important facts and skills: Well, the powers that be stipulate that all teachers be computer literate. So I took a crash course in computers...

color man • man of color

color man—1. a dealer in paints: By the early 1770s ... the head colorman, Constantine Smith, had invented a dark, semi-matt, over-glaze blue enamel of exceptional brilliance. 2. smb. who colors maps, prints, etc.: A Map of the Mediterranean ... is remarkable for the fact that the color man has forgotten the alteration of the frontiers of Greece. 3. *(TV)* a broadcaster who adds background information to commentary: While he was a fantastic wrestler, his brief stint as a color man seemed misguided.

man of color—(also: colored man) a person who belongs to a race of people who do not have white skin: The man of color in every French territory had to say "yes" or "no" to a continued relationship within the French community.

color vision • colored vision

color vision—perception of and ability to distinguish colors: As soon as the results of experiments on the retinae of animals were published, it was clear that a method was wanted for obtaining similar information with regard to the color vision of man.

colored vision—a disturbance of vision (sometimes caused by drugs) in which objects appear to have the wrong color: Disturbed vision (double vision, colored vision) and temporary loss of hearing has been reported.

come a long way • go a long way

come a long way—make great progress; significantly improve over a period of time: Ideas about the educability of the masses have come a long way during the past 100 years.

go a long way—1. = *come a long way:* Technology has gone a long way since the sixties both in diesel and gas engines. *Cf.: have a long way to go—be far short of some standard or achievement:* Although we have got the vote, we women have a long way to go before we get a positive square deal. ***2.*** *(of a stock of provisions, money, etc.)* be sufficient; last long: The more students a school has, the more funds it receives. So what money we get must go a long way. 3. notably assist in or promote smth.: The regular maintenance of your installation can go a long way towards reduced fuel bills. *Cf.: go some way—contribute to or assist in smth.:* The study goes some way to explaining why some people burn more calories than others.

Note: *a) The expression is not antonymous in meaning to the phrase* ***go back a long way****—used of smth. that has been in existence for a long time:* Wine making goes back a long way in countries like Egypt, Greece and France.

b) The expression does not correlate in meaning with the phrase ***go to great lengths****—(also: go the extra mile) make an extra effort; try very hard to achieve a result:* Personal appearance can be very important to some people. So much so, that they will go to great lengths to maintain a youthful look.

come about • go about

come about—happen; occur: How did it come about that the man was dismissed?

go about—*(of news, disease, etc.)* spread round a place: There are whispers going about that something important is happening.

come across • go across

come across—1. pass from one side to the other: Was the Channel rough when you came across? 2. *(of messages, etc.)* be communicated and understood: The preacher spoke for a long time but I'm afraid his meaning did not come across. 3. *(coll.)* provide money or information: "Did she admit it?" "Yes.... But she wouldn't come across till dawn." 4. be perceived as a particular type of person: You come across as a reasonable kind of guy to most people.

go across— = *come across 1:* Planks were laid so that the villagers could go across the marshy area.

come across someone • get across someone

come across someone—meet a person, usually by accident or unexpectedly: I have never come across such an uncouth person before.

get across someone—*(coll.)* incur smb.'s displeasure or disfavor: Dr. James has got across several of his patients because of his outspoken manner.

come across something • come across with something

come across something—find smth. unexpectedly or by chance: Did you come across any old photographs of the family?

come across with something—*(coll.)* provide money or information: I think you ought to come across with the rest of the story.

come after someone • go after someone

come after someone—pursue or chase a person (in order to attack, arrest, etc.): I heard the clicking noise from the street getting closer. It sounded like they were coming after me.

go after someone—1. = *come after someone:* Half the guards went after the escaped prisoners but they got away free. 2. *(coll.)* make romantic advances: Antonio says Luis is the only one he'd trust because Luis would never go after his girl.

come along • go along

come along—1. arrive: A bus came along and I waited in the long line to board. 2. progress or improve: Her daughter had a good marriage now, and the kids were coming along fine. 3. *(imper.)* hurry up; make more effort: Now come along, or we'll be late for the boat.

go along—1. move forward; proceed: When the wind is not up kiting can be frustrating as you go along very slowly. 2. = *come along 2:* We got settled and started Alice to school, and everything was going along nicely. 3. *(imper.)* go away: "Then go along and leave me," she insisted, stopping short, "if I'm all that."

come along with something • go along with something

come along with something—accompany smth.; co-occur with smth.: This sign comes along with other signs of pregnancy.

go along with something—agree with smth.: The whole deal would be done in German marks, not dollars. I went along with it.

come and go • coming and going

come and go—1. arrivals and departures: It was a perpetual come and go in this particular studio between four and six in the afternoon. 2. *(attrib.)* imprecise or variable: There's a scene where they talk about the come and go nature of their jobs and lives that's emotionally vibrant.

coming and going—*(also: comings and goings)* 1. = *come and go 1:* That little boy was ... inured to the coming and going of "nannies." 2. busy activities: With all the coming and going, things are always changing, nothing and nobody stays the same.

come apart • go apart

come apart—1. fall into pieces; disintegrate: I swear I didn't drop the plate: it just came apart in my hands! 2. become detached from smth.: All pages are intact, except for the outside cover which has come apart from the binding. 3. separate; diverge: Kylie Minogue and Robbie Williams record "Kids" together. After that their roads come apart again. 4. *(of a plan, scheme, etc.)* prove deficient: When we were sitting at the marble-topped table my plans began to come apart.

go apart—1. = *come apart 2:* Middleton Hall has now gone apart from the servant's block, while other buildings and yards survive. 2. = *come apart 3:* In the 16th century the forms *pike* and *peak* appear to have gone apart in sense, *pike* being confined more to a sharp piercing.

come around • go around

come around—*(also: come round)* 1. pay a (short) visit: Well, come around and see us once in a while when you get lonesome. 2. take place; happen regularly: These questions come around quite often; I get numerous mails on a regular basis from people. 3. regain consciousness: I must have blacked out again because when I came around this time, I found myself outside. 4. agree to smth. in the end: Having a mind of her own made Nina a challenge to live with ... but she finally came around to see my point of view.

go around—*(also: go round)* 1. be publicly noticed doing smth.: You can't go around saying nasty things like that about him in public. 2. *(of news, rumors, etc.)* be passed on from person to person: There was a weird story going around that James had been virtually forced out of the house. 3. *(of food, etc.)* be distributed to everybody: If there is not enough to go around let the dictum "children first" be the guiding principle.

come around to something • go around to something

come around to something—*(also: come round to something)*

1. visit a place near one's home: The groundskeeper asked me to come around to his place tomorrow night for a barbie. 2. find time for smth.; deal with smth. (when more important matters have been dealt with): I let him come around to telling me on his own time what is going on.

go around to something—(also: go round to something) = come around to something 1: I found Greg still in bed the next morning when I went around to his place.

come at something • go at something

come at something—1. reach or find smth.: Put the food where the cat can't come at it. 2. discover facts, causes, etc.: Our respect for their authority should not stand in the way of an effort to come at the truth.

go at something—work hard at smth.: The students are really going at their studies now that the examinations are near.

come away • go away

come away—1. become detached from smth.: I pulled the rotten wood and it came away without difficulty. 2. leave a place or the company of others: We came away with the uneasy feeling that all was not well with their marriage.

go away—1. = *come away 2:* His manner became so repellent that visitors went away moralizing on the absurdity of *nouveaux riches*.... **2.** *(imper.)* is used to rudely tell a person to be off: I'm tired of your constant complaints; go away and leave me in peace. 3. *(of a newly-wed couple)* leave the wedding guests and go on one's honeymoon: Mary bought a very smart outfit to go away in.

come back • go back

come back—1. return to a place: I'm going away and I may never come back. 2. become fashionable again; be restored: Some people would be glad to see corporal punishment come back. 3. return to the memory: At first I could not remember why everything seemed so familiar; then it all came back.

go back—1. = *come back 1:* You should never go back, they say, to the scene of your past romance. 2. *(of troops)* move backwards; retreat: Our army had to go back a few miles when the enemy won an advantage. 3. return to work after a strike: I'll be glad when the post office workers go back, it's very difficult not getting any letters.

come back at someone • come back to someone

come back at someone—reply to a person forcefully or angrily: She came back at the speaker with some sharp questions.

come back to someone—1. return to a person's memory: It is all coming back to me now. 2. reply to a person about smth. after a period of time: Can I come back to you on that one later?

come before someone • go before someone

come before someone—1. be higher in rank or greater in importance than another person: Members of the Royal Family come before lords and ladies. 2. *(of an issue, suggestion, etc.)* be presented (to an authoritative body) for consideration or judgement: Each case that comes before the committee is treated individually. 3. appear before a court of law, etc.: At your arraignment you will come before the judge and be informed of the charges against you.

go before someone—1. live and die earlier than smb.: November is the month of All Saints; a time when we especially remember in our prayers those who have gone before us. 2. = *come before someone 2:* This matter will go before a committee later this month and will be debated and a decision made.

come between someone • go between someone

come between someone—1. interfere in the affairs of two other people: It is never wise to come between a man and his wife. 2. prevent a person from doing smth.: The true artist lets nothing come between himself and his work.

go between someone—act as a messenger between two people: She was given a bar of chocolate as her payment for going between her sister and her sister's boyfriend.

come between something • go between something

come between something—happen between two events: The third race comes between the high jump and the throwing competition.

go between something—1. = *come between something:* The scene goes between the entrance of the murderer and the discovery of the body. 2. fit or pass into a position between two things: This picture goes nicely between the portraits of your father and mother.

come by • go by

come by—pay an informal visit: Why don't you come by some afternoon and have coffee with me.

go by—1. *(of time)* pass: Less than a day on the job goes by before the announcement comes that the workers are, once again, on strike. 2. *(of an opportunity, etc.)* pass without being taken: Often the chance goes by, or the trail followed proves false. 3. *(of a fault, etc.)* be ignored: I know you were late again this morning, but we'll let that go by.

come by something • go by something

come by something—1. obtain smth. (that is hard to get): Jobs were not so easy to come by when I was a boy. 2. happen to get smth. by accident: How did you come by that scratch on your cheek?

go by something—1. act according to smth.: If we go by instructions, we must leave now. 2. base one's judgment on smth.: You make a mistake if you go by appearances.

come down • go down

come down—1. collapse; fall: Several trees came down in last night's storm. 2. *(of a plane)* be destroyed: Three of the enemy planes came down in the battle. 3. *(of a plane)* land: The plane came down safely in spite of the mist. 4. *(of prices)* be reduced: Prices are much more likely to go up than to come down. 5. *(of wind)* subside: We had very nice sailing for two hours then the wind came down and we had to start motor-sailing. 6. be inherited: This ring has come down in my family for two centuries. 7. become or be considered less valuable: John really came down in my opinion after that. 8. *(U.S. coll.)* happen; take place: When something like this comes down, I have to stop and think things over.

go down—1. = *come down 1:* The man slipped on the ice and went down heavily. 2. *(of the sun)* set: As the sun went down the whole sky became suffused with a red glow. 3. *(of a vessel)* sink; drown: The ship struck a hidden reef and went down with all hands. 4. = *come down 4:* It's a strange thing, but prices never go down. 5. = *come down 5:* If the wind doesn't go down before three o'clock, we won't be able to take off today. 6. be reduced in amount: If our stocks of food go down much further, we shall have a hard winter. 7. suffer a decline in quality or appearance: The neighborhood has gone down since those rough people moved in. 8. be recorded: Everything you say will go down in our records. 9. *(of a speech, performance, etc.)* be accepted; be received: How did your speech go down? 10. fail; be defeated: One of my best students went down in the examination! 11. *(of food or medicine)* be swallowed: The medicine went down without any trouble at all. 12. = *come down 8:* Something strange is going down around here.

See also: go below / go under.

come down in the last shower • come out in the wash

come down in the last shower—(Irish coll., usually negat.) be naive and gullible: I'm sorry to disappoint you, if you expect me to take your work seriously, but unfortunately for you I didn't come down in the last shower.

come out in the wash—1. *(of the truth)* be revealed or become clear later: The impression is being created that everything will come out in the wash within the inquiry and that people will be found guilty or not guilty. *2. (of a situation)* be resolved or put right eventually, especially without intervention: "I thought everything was going to be all right...." "Don't worry, old girl, it'll all come out in the wash."

come down on someone • come down to someone

come down on someone—1. demand smth. firmly from a person: Things looked good until the State came down on me for sales tax. 2. reprimand or criticize a person severely: Many people came down on me for publishing my book.

come down to someone—be passed on to smb.: This photo, which came down to me from my uncle, shows Benjamin Rollings outside his house.

See also: come up to something / go up to something.

come down on someone like a ton of bricks • hit someone like a ton of bricks

come down on someone like a ton of bricks—(coll.) reprimand or punish a person severely: If I find you misbehaving, I'll come down on you like a ton of bricks.

hit someone like a ton of bricks—(coll.) make a person feel an unpleasant emotion very strongly: He said something that sounded innocent to him, but it hit Debbie like a ton of bricks.

come down to earth • go to earth

come down to earth—(also: come back to earth) stop daydreaming; return to practical realities (especially unpleasant): Now, Virgie, come down to earth and give me the low-down. What's happened to Mrs. Bedford's diamonds?

go to earth—(also: go to ground) go into hiding; put oneself out of sight: The policeman ... turned back to assist his colleagues in finding Barbury, so mysteriously gone to earth.

See also: drop from the skies / fall to the ground.

come down to something • go down to something

come down to something—1. be reduced to its real meaning: The whole matter comes down to a power struggle between the trade union and the directors. 2. be reduced to a humble position: He finally came down to selling matches on street corners. 3. get down to smth.; examine smth.: When we come down to details, the plan seems possible. 4. be reduced to a lower level: I don't think we will ever see prices come down to where they were two or three years ago.

Note: *The expression does not correlate in meaning with the phrase* ***come down on something****—criticize or attack smth.:* The critics came down much too hard on the performance.

go down to something—1. = *come down to something 4:* The prices should go down to something more reasonable if they expect people to buy. 2. extend in time or space; reach as far as: This book is no use to me; it only goes down to the General Election of 1951.

come down to the wire • come under the wire

come down to the wire—(also: go down to the wire) continue to the very last moment or the very end: The game came down to the wire with the Eckerd defense stopping the Owls in the final minutes.

come under the wire—(also: go under the wire) 1. be at the finishing-line of a racecourse: He hardly ever came under the wire behind the other runners. 2. come at the last possible moment: The law suits were filed on New Year's Eve, thus came under the wire as an event of 1941.

come down with something • go down with something

come down with something—1. provide money or information: We need not worry. The firm will come down with the money. 2. be taken ill with a disease: The good Deacon almost feared he was about to come down with a fever.

Note: *The expression does not correlate in meaning with the phrase* ***come up with something****— think of a plan, solution, answer, etc.:* How on earth did you come up with such a brilliant idea?

go down with something— = come down with something 2: Our holiday was fine until Jim went down with a bad cold.

come easy to someone • go easy on someone

come easy to someone—(of skills, money, etc.) be mastered or gained easily without much exertion: She has a natural talent for learning, and it comes easy to her. *Cf.: easy come, easy go—used to say that smth. you get easily can be lost as easily:* Several recessions taught me that unless you are disciplined about saving, money is easy come, easy go.

go easy on someone—(coll.) be lenient with a person; not treat smb. too harshly: Go easy on Ben: he's only very young and he tries hard.

Note: *The expression does not correlate in meaning with the phrase* ***be easy-going****—be not easily annoyed or upset by other people's actions:* Mrs. Harris wears the pants at home: Mr. Harris is far too quiet and easy-going to argue with her.

come for someone • go for someone

come for someone—(coll.) rush forward with the object of attacking a person: As I opened the gate a great black dog came for me.

go for someone—1. = *come for someone:* Our dog went for the postman again this morning, he'll get us into trouble. 2. *(coll.)* approve of or support a person: Will the voters go for him now, that's the point? 3. be relevant to smb.; concern a person: You must arrive on time or be dismissed—that goes for all workers.

come for something • go for something

come for something—arrive to collect smth.: You've come for my money, haven't you! No one can have it!

go for something—1. have a liking for smth.: I don't go for horror films, and I can't understand why anyone likes them. 2. be sold for a specified amount of money: The house went for just over five thousand pounds. 3. attack smth. in words: The newspapers have really gone for Tom's new book in a big way. 4. aim for smth.: The stakes are high, and the question is whether Hindus intend to go for the big one or settle for less.

come forward • go forward

come forward—1. stand out: The great door was ornamented with figures, some coming forward so that they looked real. 2. present oneself (with an offer to help): The police have asked for witnesses of the accident to come forward. 3. *(of an issue)* be raised for discussion: The matter was deferred at last evening's meeting, but will come forward at our next session.

Note: *The expression does not correlate in meaning with the phrase* ***come to the fore****—(also: come to the front) become conspicuous or popular:* Andrew Young came to the fore during the Civil Rights marches of the 1960s.

go forward—1. improve; make progress: Work on the new hospital is going forward at a satisfactory pace. 2. be presented (to an authoritative body) for consideration or approval: Your name will go forward to the committee when they are considering the new appointments. 3. *(of the clock or watch)* be moved to a later hour: Do the clock go forward in the spring?

See also: come out ahead / go ahead.

come forward with something • go forward with something

come forward with something—offer a plan, solution, answer, etc.: I'll wait until he comes forward with some new proposals.

go forward with something—(also: go ahead with something) proceed with smth.: The Committee decided to go forward with its plans of social reform.

come free • go free

come free—become unattached: After throwing the ropes across the river to loop the boat and pulling on them, the boat came free.

go free—be released from confinement or imprisonment: The court has determined that she was not a willing participant and therefore may go free.

come from someone • come of someone

come from someone—be descended from a person or family: Harlow comes from a wealthy ranch-owning family.

come of someone—1. happen to a person: No one knows where he has gone or what has come of him. 2. = *come from someone:* He came of a rich family, but was left an orphan in his early youth.

come from something • come of something

come from something—1. originate from a place: The African Elephant is said to be smaller than the Asiatic: yet the largest tusks come from Africa. *2.* result from smth.: That's what comes from staying up late with little sleep when cramming for an exam.

come of something—1. happen to smth.: John shudders as he looks down upon what has come of his once great college. 2. = *come from something 2:* That's what comes of sleeping late, you have a headache all morning.

come hell or high water • come through hell and high water

come hell or high water—no matter what happens: We are going to change the way government works. And we will do it come hell or high water.

come through hell and high water—(also: go through hell and high water) pass through difficulties or troubles: Our forefathers came through hell and high water so that we could be here today.

come home to roost • go to roost

come home to roost—return by way of retribution: All our mistakes sooner or later surely come home to roost.

go to roost—(coll.) retire to rest: He broke the silence by remarking, after a glance at the clock, "Time to go to roost."

come in • go in

come in—1. come to work in a house: The charwoman "came in" for half a day on alternate days. 2. *(of a train, etc.)* arrive at its destination (according to schedule): When does your train come in? 3. flow in: Don't stay on the rocks too long; the tide comes in a long way at this point. 4. arrive; be received: News is just coming in of an air-crash over the Atlantic. 5. join a business as a partner: My father started the insurance firm, and I came in when I was 18. 6. become seasonable or available: When do strawberries come in? 7. become fashionable: I expect long skirts will come in again soon. 8. take position in a competition: He led most of the way but suddenly lost his strength and came in last. 9. be elected; come into power: The socialists came in at the last election. 10. be received as income: He doesn't work; but he has at least a thousand a year coming in from investments. 11. *(of a discussion, etc.)* contribute a commentary: I should like to come in here, as I happen to know the situation well. 12. happen; appear: This is where the mistakes usually come in.

go in—1. fit inside smth.: That space is too small, the bookcase won't go in. 2. *(of the sun or moon)* disappear behind clouds: At this time of the year, when the sun goes in, it is suddenly much colder. 3. arrive at one's place of employment (to start work): What time do you have to go in tomorrow? 4. *(of troops)* start an attack: The soldiers were ordered to go in and seize the enemy position. 5. *(UK coll.)* be understood *(also: sink in):* I keep trying to understand how the system works, but it doesn't seem to go in.

come in for something • go in for something

come in for something—1. gain smth. after a person's death: Harry came in for a large share of his father's fortune. 2. be the object of praise, criticism, etc: The eldest sister always came in for much of the blame.

Note: *The expression does not correlate in meaning with the phrase* ***come in on something****— take part in some activity; share in smth.:* The lines of authority aren't clearly drawn. The state detectives usually come in on murders.

go in for something—1. have smth. as one's chosen career or pastime: I thought he only went in for music and tennis. 2. *(of a competition, etc.)* enter as a contestant: I'd like to go in for a more advanced examination if I can. 3. indulge in smth.: Beauty salon hair dressers and cosmeticians expect women to go in for fancier coiffures.

come in force • come into force

come in force—come in great numbers: The men of Mnela were coming in force to hail and escort their chief.

come into force—(of legal documents) become binding: When does the new law come into force?

come in from the cold • come in out of the rain

come in from the cold—change one's ways, practices, etc., so as to be accepted by others: Unless the union moderated its policies and came in from the cold, it would lose even more members.

Note: *The expression is not antonymous in meaning to the phrase* ***be out in the cold****—(also: be in the cold) be destitute or abandoned:* If you don't save for your retirement, no one will do it for you and you will be out in the cold when old age hits.

come in out of the rain—(usually in the phrase "know enough to come in out of the rain") show common sense: "Don't you have the sense to come in out of the rain?" He pauses. "Obviously, this isn't the safest neighborhood to be working in."

come in useful • come into use

come in useful—prove helpful: Whittle's experience of aerobatics came in useful, for he had to "land" the machine in the water.

come into use—begin to be used: It is difficult to identify a date when the terms "Whig" and "Tory" first came into use.

come into a fortune • run out of fortune

come into a fortune—acquire a large sum of money (as an inheritance): Mary came into a fortune of a quarter of a million. She was an only child.

run out of fortune—run out of good luck: Fortune has a way of evening out. Even the bold will run out of fortune sooner or later.

come into contact with someone • make contact with someone

come into contact with someone—meet smb.; associate with a person: I feel uneasy when I come into contact with people who have had a good education.

make contact with someone—(also: contact someone) get in touch with a person: After about a month, I finally made contact with him in Paris.

come into question • go into the question

come into question—1. become an issue for further consideration or discussion: His credibility has to come into question if he is going to make statements like the above. 2. become of practical importance: The succession of masters was too rapid to allow a change of language to come into question among the people.

go into the question—consider the question thoroughly and in detail: A happy person has no time for philosophy. He will not go into the question of good and bad.

come into someone's head • go to someone's head

come into someone's head—(of an idea, etc.) occur to a person; come to mind *(also: enter someone's head):* I write without any sort of constraint or method, as things come into my head.

go to someone's head—1. *(of liquor)* make smb. dizzy or slightly drunk: The next four hours are spent sipping drinks which go straight to Norma's head. 2. *(of success)* excite a person; make smb. conceited: Don't let failure go to your heart and don't let success go to your head. 3. engross a person's whole attention: Unfortunately, he can't spare you any time. He's very busy writing a book and it's gone to his head.

See also: come to a head / come to mind.

come into the limelight • come to light

come into the limelight—be in the center of attention: The giant Himalayan humanoid came into the limelight in 1921 and has since been the subject of much controversy.

come to light—be revealed; become known: From the stones, ice and meadows of Greenland the tragic story of the lost Vikings has finally come to light.

come into the market • go to market

come into the market—(also: come on the market) be offered for sale: No more coals can come into the market than are sufficient to meet the demand.

go to market—1. *(also: go marketing)* go shopping: She has no debt — except to herself, since she uses her own money when she goes to market. 2. = *come into the market:* It may sound silly, but many new products go to market with at least one fatal flaw. 3. *(Austral., NZ sl.)* lose one's temper; complain noisily: I have my instructions, so it's no use going to market on me.

come into the union • go into the union

come into the union—1. *(of American States)* become incorporated into one confederation — the United States of America: In 1850 New Mexico came into the Union as a free soil territory. 2. become a member of the trades-union: In five days 19,000 new members came into the union, almost swamping the union officers in their clamor to have themselves enrolled.

go into the union—1. *(UK hist.)* go to live in a workhouse: The magistrate advised her to go into the union ... which would have separated her from her helpless son. 2. = *come into the union 1:* When the 1816 Constitution was written and Indiana admitted, the Hoosier State went into the Union without slavery. 3. = *come into the union 2:* People told me, "if you go into the union, you'll sell out and won't accomplish anything."

come into the world • go out into the world

come into the world—1. be born or created: The records show that he came into the world in June of 1942. 2. *(of a book, etc.)* come out: This little treatise came into the world last year.

go out into the world—have more contact with people or places: We need to get out of the arena of the sheltered life and go out into the world.

come it • go it

come it—(sl.) 1. succeed in doing smth.; attain one's purpose: I meant to pay him last week but I couldn't come it. 2. do smth.; perform one's part: I can come it pretty well — nobody better, perhaps, in my own line. 3. perpetrate smth. illicit or criminal: I told the prisoner if she came it any more, I certainly would lock her up.

go it—(coll.) act more vigorous than is usual: She was really going it today — she did more work than she did during the whole of last week.

Note: *a) The expression does not correlate in meaning with the phrase* ***go it alone****— act independently:* He quit working for the company and decided to go it alone as a consultant, instead.

b) Neither expression correlates in meaning with the phrase ***run it****—(UK) used of a vessel which in time of war does not sail with convoy:* The only merchant-ship bound to England is so well armed as to be able to run it.

come it over someone • come over someone

come it over someone—(coll.) get the advantage of or impose on a person *(also: come it with someone):* I can see through your game, I see you want to come it over me with your honeyed words.

come over someone—(of an intense emotion) overwhelm smb.; affect a person excessively *(also: overcome someone):* A fit of stubbornness came over him and he refused to have anything further to do with the scheme.

come it strong • come on strong

come it strong—(also: go it strong) speak or act in a way which is too extreme: The newspaper's description of the accident was coming it a little strong.

come on strong—(also: come out strong) 1. perform or contest successfully: Cheevers has come on strong to maintain his reputation as one of the best netminders in hockey.

2 = *come it strong:* Joe came on very strong last night about the war in Indochina; most of us felt embarrassed.

come off • go off

come off—1. fall from smth. such as a bicycle, etc.: The horse refused at the first fence, and that's when I came off. 2. become detached: When I lifted the jug up, the handle came off. 3. *(of an event)* take place; succeed: My friend's marriage didn't come off; his fiancée broke off the engagement.

go off—1. = *come off 3:* They dotted lit bars and tables around the lot, and made sure the party went off without a hitch. 2. fall asleep or faint: He didn't seem to be able to go off, so he went into the kitchen and made himself a cup of tea. 3. explode; make a sudden noise: Just as the burglar thought he was safely inside the house, the alarm went off. 4. *(of food)* deteriorate; become unfit to eat: This milk was fresh this morning, but it's gone off. 5. *(of gas, electricity, etc.)* become unavailable: Just as the weather turned cold, the electricity supply went off. 6. *(of goods)* sell: I found that the place was one of no trade, and that my goods went off very slowly.

come off one's perch • fall off one's perch

come off one's perch—(coll.) adopt a less arrogant manner *(also: get off one's perch):* What you've first got to do is to come off your perch — and listen to what we want.

fall off one's perch—(coll., dated) die: By the time I fall off my perch, Britain may well be a republic.

come off something • go off something

come off something—1. be no longer involved in smth.: "I want you to come off that fraud case," said the inspector. 2. *(of taxes, etc.)* be exempt from: Under the agreement, the import tariff comes off certain kinds of goods.

go off something—lose one's liking for smth.: The children seem to have gone off cornflakes for breakfast.

come on • go on

come on—1. continue to advance: The soldiers came on in the face of heavy fire. 2. follow a person later: The teacher went by train to his new job, and the family came on by bus. 3. *(of electric light)* be turned on: Just as I entered the house, all the lights came on. 4. appear on duty: The new man doesn't come on till midnight. 5. appear on the stage or sports field: When Laurence Olivier came on for the first time, the audience applauded. 6. *(of an illness, headache, etc.)* set in; begin: My throat's dry and a bit sore; perhaps I've got a cold coming on. 7. *(Progressive Tense)* make progress: How is it coming on, and when will the first volume be ready? 8. is used to encourage a person to hurry or make more effort: Come on, Jane, you can do better than that! 9. is used to express surprise or disbelief: "I'm home all day working." "Ah, come on. You don't look like you're working right now." 10. *(of a film, play, etc.)* be shown: There's a very good play coming on next week. 11. *(of a lawsuit, etc.)* be considered by a court: They have been waiting for a long time for their case to come on.

go on—1. continue a journey, etc. (after interruption): The police examined the cars and then allowed them to go on. 2. travel ahead of others: The advance party has gone on to see if the mountain is safe for the other climbers. 3. be able to fit on smth.: If you fill the box too full, the lid won't go on. 4. = *come on 3:* The street lights go on when it gets dark, and go off at midnight. 5. = *come on 5:* I was so nervous when I first went on. 6. keep talking excessively about smth.: The teacher went on and on about good behavior, as usual. 7. continue; last: How long did the war go on? 8. take place; happen: The governing council has admitted that it did not know all that went on. 9. = *come on 7:* By the way, how is your new project going on? 10. = *come on 8:* Go on! There isn't a moment to lose! 11. = *come on 9:* Ah, go on. I don't believe you. 12. *(coll.)* behave improperly: Sad comfort whenever he returns, to hear how your brother has gone on! 13. have a friendly relationship: We all go on well with each other here. 14. *(of time)* pass, proceed: As time went on, the English court grew impatient.

come on the carpet • step off the carpet

come on the carpet—be under consideration or discussion: Hopefully tomorrow at the meeting that will probably come on the carpet.

Note: *The expression does not fully correlate in meaning with the phrase* ***be on the carpet****—1. (Pilots) used of an aircraft at or near ground level:* I was right on the carpet and over a little ruined village. *2. = come on the carpet:* Only when a serious question was on the carpet, did they drop their formalism. 3. *be summoned to receive a reprimand from smb. in authority:* Desert is on the carpet — not for apostasy, but for the song he's made about it.

step off the carpet—(rare) get married: Papa won Ves' hand and they will step off the carpet next spring.

come on top of something • get on top of something

come on top of something—follow smth. (especially an unpleasant event): This embarrassment coming on top of a row with Nicholas, was more than she could stand.

get on top of something—overcome difficulties, etc.; deal with smth. successfully: He really felt he was getting on top of the situation.

come out • go out

come out—1. *(of a tooth)* fall out: My tooth has just come out. 2. *(of a stain, etc.)* be removed: Do you think that dirty mark will come out? 3. be freed (from a prison): It's been a long year, but he comes out next Friday. 4. emerge; become visible: The sun came out as soon as the rain stopped. 5. be uttered: I intended to make a joke, but my remark came out as unintentionally rude. 6. become clear or known: I don't want the news of our wedding to come out yet. 7. be published: When does Tom's new book come out? 8. be seen as in a photograph: I'm afraid our holiday photos didn't come out. 9. reach a result; succeed: Let me know how the voting comes out. 10. start a strike: He had the promises of 300 to come out "in sympathy" when the time came for quitting work. 11. *(of a young girl)* enter on social life: Is her eldest daughter coming out this year? 12. be offered for public viewing: The famous collection of rare old furniture is coming out next week. 13. *(of a performer)* go on stage: When it came time to come out for the third curtain call I said, "Bobby, I just can't make it no further." 14. emerge (in a specified manner) from a contest, examination, etc.: The President did not come out well in the inquiry. 15. *(of smb.'s traits of character)* be revealed; show clearly: At such testing times, only the good in him came out, and none of the bad. 16. admit smth. openly, especially acknowledge one's homosexuality: Several I spoke to referred to the difficulties they experienced in "coming out"— realizing they were homosexuals.

go out—1. move to a distant country or place: Their youngest son went out to Canada and made a fortune. 2. *(of girls in former times)* leave home for employment (in the house of others): When she was eighteen she went out as a nursemaid. 3. attend social functions; go to parties, dances, etc.: She still goes out a great deal, even at seventy-five. 4. *(of invitations, orders, etc.)* be sent to several people: The wedding invitations had all gone out, but Jane says she hasn't received hers. 5. be broadcast: The special program on the new Prime Minister goes out tonight at 9 o'clock. 6. *(of a fire or light)* become extinguished; stop burning: Have you a match? My cigarette has gone out. 7. *(of money)* be spent: There's more money going out than coming in, and I'm worried about the business. 8. become obsolete; stop being popular or fashionable: Long skirts went out after a short season of popularity. 9. *(of a government)* retire from power: If the government goes out at the next election, who will lead the country? 10. *(euph.)* die: I hope that when I go out I shall leave a better world behind me. 11. *(of the sea)* flow away from the shore: When the sea goes out, the sand stretches for a long way. 12. = *come out 10:* The Post Office workers went out before Christmas, now the electricians are out.

come out against something • come up against something

come out against something—oppose smth.; declare one's opposition to smth.: Those who come out against unity are acting against the interests of the country.

come up against something—(also: be up against something) encounter a serious obstacle or problem: They came up against a lot of opposition to their plans.

come out ahead • go ahead

come out ahead—succeed or make a profit: The player can be in the hole by any amount of money and still come out ahead in the end.

go ahead—1. move in front: The advance party has gone ahead to see if the mountain is safe for the other climbers. 2.

start or continue with smth., especially after a period of uncertainty or delay: Our expectation is that the elections will go ahead. 3. is used to indicate that a person is welcome to do smth.: "Would you mind if I used your phone?" "Sure, go ahead." *Cf.: get the go-ahead—get permission to begin an activity:* We are delighted to get the go-ahead for this project.

See also: come forward / go forward.

come out for something • go out for something

come out for something—1. go on strike in order to gain smth.: The Post Office workers have come out for more pay. 2. support smth.: The Government comes out for the decentralization of the decision-making process.

go out for something—1. make a concentrated effort to obtain or achieve smth.: Don't trust that man. He just goes out for anything he can get. 2. = *come out for something 1:* We went on strike for a noneconomic reason. If we went out for more pay they could permanently replace us right now.

come out in a rash • come out in a rush

come out in a rash—(of a skin disease) become covered in spots, pimples, etc.: We both came out in a rash that we assumed was an allergic reaction to something.

come out in a rush—(of words, etc.) be articulated in a sudden quick flow: Her thoughts came out in a rush, as if she hadn't been able to put them into words until now.

come out in something • come out with something

come out in something—(of a skin disease) become covered in spots, pimples, etc.: At the hospital she started to come out in spots and they sent her home saying it was chicken pox.

come out with something—say or propose smth., such as an idea, etc.: You have to rationalize the situation and come out with a solution that is acceptable to all.

come out of someone's ears • go in one ear and out the other

come out of someone's ears—(sl.) have smth. in great or excess quantity: I've been looking for some time before buying and have read reviews till they come out of my ears.

go in one ear and out the other—said of smth. that is heard but paid no attention to: His writing implied that the criticism leveled would not simply go in one ear and out the other.

come out of something • go out of something

come out of something—1. leave the place (where smth. has been fixed): The screw was rusty and wouldn't come out of the wall. 2. *(of stains, etc.)* disappear; be removed from smth. (with cleaning): Do you think these ink-marks will come out of my dress if I boil it?

go out of something—1. *(of passion, tension, etc.)* become less marked in smth.; disappear from smth.: As time went by, the fury went out of his parliamentary speeches. 2. be no longer in fashion, business, etc.: As from next Wednesday the oil and petrol pool, which has operated since the war, will go out of business.

Note: *Neither expression correlates in meaning with the phrase* ***run out of something****— have no further supply of smth.:* He had several forced landings, the first when he ran out of fuel over Syria.

See also: walk out of something / walk out on something.

come out of the blue • get into a blue

come out of the blue—happen unexpectedly or without warning: Nothing in my life ever came more "out of the blue" than my marriage.

get into a blue—(Austral. sl.) get into an argument; start a brawl: Are red-haired people more likely to get into a blue?

See also: get one's blue / get the blues.

come out on top • come to the top

come out on top—overcome difficulties; be victorious (over one's competitors): Although there were a lot of applicants, Henry was the one who came out on top.

come to the top—1. reach the top of a mountain, etc.: The next little excitement was when we came to the top of the Grand Diable. One has to rope down it. 2. become most important: Only the problem of traversing Kazakhstan prevented the khanates from coming to the top of the imperial agenda.

come over • go over

come over—1. come from a distance (to visit smb.): You really must come over sometime and have dinner with us. 2. *(of aircraft)* pass overhead: It's terribly noisy living near the airport with planes coming over all the time. 3. *(of a speech, plan, etc.)* be received; succeed: How did his latest speech come over? 4. change one's opinion, political position, etc.: Don't worry about the chairman, he'll soon come over. 5. *(coll.)* become (especially suddenly): I came over all dizzy just for a moment, but I'm all right now. 6. *(of sound)* be heard on radio or stage: Your voice comes over rather well.

go over—1. fall; turn over: Keep still or the boat will go over! 2. = *come over 1:* When are we going over to your mother's again? 3. = *come over 2:* Paratroopers went in and we had heard planes going over. 4. = *come over 3:* How did John's talk to the Women's Institute go over?

come over something • go over something

come over something—pass or move over smth.: It's terribly noisy living near the airport, with planes coming over the house all the time.

Note: *The expression does not correlate in meaning with the phrase* ***overcome something****—prevail over smth.; surmount a difficulty, obstacle, etc.:* The want of belief is a defect that ought to be concealed when it cannot be overcome.

go over something—1. = *come over something:* The crowd cheered as the horse went safely over the last fence. *2.* check or examine smth. (to see that it is correct, etc.): You'll have to go over the figures again; they don't balance out. 3. clean or repair smth.: The girl went over the room quickly with a duster. 4. examine smth. thoroughly in order to find smth.: The police went over her room three times but found nothing. 5. review or consider smth.: Let us go over the facts as we know them. 6. exceed smth.; be more than smth.: Your spending should not go over your income.

come round • go round

come round—(also: come around) 1. pay a short visit: Why don't you come round and see us one evening? 2. take place; happen regularly: The Commonwealth Prime Ministers' Conference comes round next month. 3. regain consciousness: The girl fainted, but she came round when we threw drops of water on her face. 4. agree to smth. in the end: After a day of our haggling about the matter, Jane finally came round to my point of view.

go round—(also: go around) 1. be publicly noticed doing smth.: You can't go round saying nasty things like that about him in public. 2. *(of news, rumors, etc.)* be passed on from person to person: Stories have been going round concerning the government's secret intentions. 3. *(of food, etc.)* be distributed to everybody: Money becomes tight and, maybe, the loans available from the banks are insufficient to go round.

come round to something • go round to something

come round to something—(also: come around to something) 1. visit a place near one's home: Three guys in my class asked if they could come round to my place to do homework. *2.* find time for smth.; deal with smth. (when more important matters have been dealt with): When they had finally came round to telling him he had been "enlisted" ... he had been at sea in the merchant service.

go round to something—(also: go around to something) = come round to something 1: When I go round to her studio she wastes no time in emphasizing her unwillingness to see journalists.

come short • come shortly

come short—fail to meet the hopes or expectations: Even those who come short in other ways may justly plead the valor with which they have fought for their country.

***Note:** a) The expression does not correlate in meaning with the phrase **come short home**—(arch.) return from an expedition, etc., with loss of men; come to grief:* They often came short home, for the Germans had the better of them.

*b) The expression does not correlate in meaning with the phrase **run short** (of food supplies, etc.)* become insufficient or inadequate: Staff were working long hours in unimaginable circumstances and some vital surgical supplies were running short.

come shortly—come or become available in a short time: There are still a lot of questions that needs to be answered and hopefully answers will come shortly.

come short of something • go short of something

come short of something—(also: fall short of something) be insufficient or inadequate to attain the results intended: The box-office receipts came short of the manager's expectations.

go short of something—deprive oneself of smth.; not have enough of smth.: I don't want you to go short of money in order to lend me what I need.

***Note:** Neither expression correlates in meaning with the phrase **run short of something**— use up almost all of smth.:* The hijacked plane was allowed to land at Kandahar airport because the plane was running short of fuel.

come someone's way • go someone's way

come someone's way—1. be met with or encountered: A couple of expressions have only come my way in the last month or so. 2. present itself; become accessible to a person: If a chance of traveling abroad came his way, he would be delighted. 3. agree to smb.'s principles, course of action, etc.: We are giving the Minister a rough ride so that he will come our way and put matters right. 4. *(of events, circumstances, etc.)* be favorable to a person: Don't be a fool. Let's push our luck, now that things are coming our way.

go someone's way—1. *= come someone's way 3:* She will never go my way — nor, I fear, shall I ever go hers. 2. *= come someone's way 4:* If, as a child, things don't go your way and you're miserable, you can make the point by screaming.

come through • go through

come through—1. arrive or appear: Her exam results have just come through and she is going to college in Watford. 2. show plainly: This message came through clearly in a discussion with the company's managers. 3. be received (by radio, etc.): A report came through by telephone that they thought another body had been spotted. 4. live in spite of danger or difficulty: He was wounded once by shrapnel, but otherwise came through unharmed. 5. do what is needed or expected: Lynda is the greatest and always comes through! What we call a major project, she considers a piece of cake.

go through—1. *(of a law, etc.)* be passed or approved: The Bill went through unopposed after attracting cross-party support and the blessing of the Government. 2. *(of a business deal, etc.)* be completed: Specify what work on the property you want to be undertaken before the sale has gone through.

come through something • go through something

come through something—1. *(of a sentiment, opinion, etc.)* be seen or felt in smth.: A feeling of sadness comes through his music. 2. recover (from a serious illness); survive smth.: Bill came through his operation as cheerful as ever. 3. live through an upsetting experience; endure smth.: People don't really appreciate what he had to come through.

go through something—1. discuss smth. in detail; examine smth.: Let's go through the arguments presented here again. 2. examine papers, files, etc. in search of smth.: The police went through the pockets of the suspected thief. 3. perform smth.; take part in smth.: She made him go through both a civil and religious wedding. 4. bring smth. to completion: How long will it take to go through the program? 5. *= come through something 3:* It was distressing for us to see what she has to go through.

See also: gallop through something / run through something.

come through with something • go through with something

come through with something—provide money or information: Good old Arthur came through with a check to cover the last payment.

go through with something—accomplish smth.; continue until it is completed: I will go through with my plan whatever the opposition.

come to a bad end • come to a dead end

come to a bad end—die or have a disaster in exceptionally unpleasant circumstances: These traitors each came to a bad end. As the Nazis said, they loved the betrayal but not the betrayer. *Cf.: make a good end—die with courage, dignity, etc.:* You could say he made a good end. A shell-burst caught him as he was ferrying wounded across the river.

come to a dead end—reach a point beyond which no progress can be made: Our inquiry came to a dead end when we learned that the woman had left the country.

come to a full stop • come to a stop

come to a full stop—1. stop suddenly or unexpectedly: The dog had a roll on the lawn before charging at her and coming to a full stop ready to play. 2. be unable to proceed any further with smth.: We have come to a full stop in our efforts to achieve Utopia. 3. *(of a narrative, etc.)* terminate or end abruptly: The story thus comes unexpectedly to a full stop.

come to a stop—be no longer moving: The elevator came to a stop on the main floor.

come to a head • come to mind

come to a head—reach a crisis or a climax: The dispute must come to a head soon; neither the union nor the owners will tolerate these interminable delays.

come to mind—occur to a person; be recollected: There are certain images that come to mind when people talk about beauty queens.

See also: come into someone's head / go to someone's head.

come to a point • come to the point

come to a point—1. terminate in a point: The deep green leaves come to a point and appear after the flowers in early spring. 2. reach a certain stage: When we come to a point where we want to check the students' understanding, we put up a multiple choice question. 3. *(of a hunting dog)* take up a position with the head pointing in the direction of game: If there is too much game ... the dog might flush before he can come to a point.

come to the point—1. give the essential part of what one is trying to say, ignoring what is irrelevant: Philip, I may as well come straight to the point. I'm pregnant.... 2. *= come to a point 2:* Science and technology had come to the point where the parts fed upon each other continuously to enlarge the whole. 3. *(in the phrase "when it comes to the point")* when the moment for action or decision comes: When it comes to the point they rarely effect any real reform.

come to a pretty pass • come to pass

come to a pretty pass—reach a critical state or an unfortunate condition: While he was away, things had come to a pretty pass.

come to pass—*(dated)* happen; occur: No one knows for sure how the accident came to pass.

come to grass • go to grass

come to grass—*(Mining)* come up to the pit-head: Let us now watch the men ascending from the mine after work. This is what they call "coming to grass."

Note: *The expression is not antonymous in meaning to the phrase* ***come off the grass****—(Austral. sl.) used as an expression of disbelief or a plea to stop talking nonsense:* Come off the grass, Mary. High Court judges are not the Alpha and Omega of all wisdom.

go to grass—1. *(of cattle)* graze: The vaccination program for dairy calves should be completed before they go to grass. 2. *(coll.)* fall down; come to the ground: His legs got tangled and he went to grass, losing the race. 3. *(coll.)* go on a holiday or into retirement: A gentleman declared that he might go to grass with his old canoe. 4. *(dated)* is used to rudely tell a person to go away and stop being annoying *(also: go to grass and eat hay):* She fell into a fit of anger, bidding him to "go to grass with his invitations."

come to hand • get out of hand

come to hand—*(formal)* come within notice: A much superior illustration of the subject came to hand in a pamphlet entitled "A Discourse on Language."

get out of hand—become beyond control: The training of police personnel needs a special attention, otherwise I am afraid the situation will get out of hand.

come to it • go to it

come to it—*(also: come to this)* reach a state, usually unpleasant: "So John has got to start earning his living?" "We all have to come to it," he said with a smile.

go to it—*(coll., often imper.)* make a special effort; begin working hard: After dinner we went to it again, carting paints and easels about.

come to one's senses • regain one's senses

come to one's senses—1. regain consciousness; stop feeling faint: It wasn't until long afterwards that she began to come to her senses. 2. start behaving sensibly: When will she come to her senses and see that he is a totally unsuitable man to marry?

regain one's senses— = *come to one's senses 1:* She felt faint in the hot room, but going out into the fresh air she quickly regained her senses.

come to pieces • go to pieces

come to pieces—1. break into pieces; disintegrate: Halfway home the body of the car literally came to pieces. 2. come apart so that smth. is in separate pieces: Does this machine come to pieces?

go to pieces—*(also: fall to pieces)* 1. = *come to pieces 1:* The vessel is going to pieces, and it is full time for all who can, to leave her. 2. collapse physically or morally; become hysterical: At the news of her brother's death she went completely to pieces. 3. *(of an organization, business, etc.)* become weak; fail: Since Mr. White handed over the management to his son, the business has gone to pieces.

come to the front • go to the front

come to the front—1. *(also: come to the fore)* become well known or popular: He had come to the front as the Prince Charming of politics—young, handsome, and popular. 2. be revealed; manifest itself: At such a time his true boastful self would come to the front.

go to the front—take an advanced or forward position; take the lead in a race, etc.: Sans Egal went to the front at once and opened a lead of some six lengths.

come together • go together

come together—1. gather or meet: The family must come together for the parents' silver wedding. 2. be reconciled; settle the differences: I'm so glad that you two have decided to come together at last.

go together—1. *(of things)* match; suit each other: Do you think this hat and coat go well together? 2. happen together: Since music and dance usually go together, it's worth knowing what children learn in music. 3. keep each other company (with a view to marriage): Jim and Mary had been going together for two years before they were married.

come under the name of • go under the name of

come under the name of—be classified or categorized as: He says there is no reason for de-facto or same-sex relationships to come under the name of "marriage."

go under the name of—be known by a specific name; use a name different from one's own: He went under the name of Baker, to avoid discovery by the police.

come up • go up

come up—1. *(of plants)* appear above the soil: I sowed some beans three weeks ago, but they haven't come up yet. 2. *(of a question, etc.)* arise; be mentioned: His name came up whenever the matter of nuclear energy was discussed. 3. *(legal)* be considered (in a court of law): The paper announced the cases that were to come up at the assizes the following day. 4. *(of an opportunity, etc.)* arise; occur: I'll let you know as soon as a vacancy comes up. 5. rise in status, rank, etc.: That politician has come up in my opinion since I heard his last speech.

go up—1. *(of the curtain)* rise: The lights went down and the curtain went up. 2. be constructed: New universities went up at a fantastic rate in the 1960s. 3. = *come up 5:* Jane has gone up in my estimation since she did that. 4. move to the next higher class at school: Did all the children go up at the end of the year? 5. *(of prices, etc.)* rise; increase: Everything seems to be going up these days: coal, groceries, rents. 6. be shattered by explosion: The munition factory went up when the bomb fell on it.

come up against a brick wall • run one's head into a brick wall

come up against a brick wall—*(also: come up against a blank wall)* encounter an insurmountable obstacle or difficulty: So far, our efforts to stop the smuggling of protected species have come up against a brick wall.

Note: *The expression is not equivalent in meaning to the phrase* ***have one's back against the wall****—(also: be up against the wall) have run out of options; be pushed to the last extremity:* I don't give up easy and have had my back against the wall before. I don't intend to give up without a battle.

run one's head into a brick wall—*(coll.)* persist with smth. without making any progress *(also: run one's head into a stone wall):* Trying to persuade him to change his plans is like running your head into a brick wall.

come up against someone • run up against someone

come up against someone—*(also: go up against someone)* challenge a competitor in a contest, election, etc: Although he rode very well, he came up against an opponent who tactically rode even better.

run up against someone—1. meet a person, especially by accident: You can't go anywhere in London without running up against him. 2. = *come up against someone:* I also had the sense that Tony would be a formidable adversary if you ran up against him in court.

come up daisies • push up daisies

come up daisies—(also: come up roses) turn out extremely well, especially when things seemed to be going badly at first: Once you've implemented an active job search, everything will come up daisies.

push up daisies—(sl.) be dead and buried: We could argue about the details of science and politics till we pushed up daisies — and yet we would not come any closer to conciliation.

come up for air • go up in the air

come up for air—(U.S. sl.) take a break; have a rest: George decides to revisit the place in order to "come up for air" and remember what the good life used to be.

go up in the air—(coll.) become angry; lose one's temper: He is so irritable these days that he goes up in the air for no reason at all.

Note: *The expression does not correlate in meaning with the phrase* ***vanish into thin air****— disappear completely from sight or existence:* Speed, confidence, shooting ability, all seemed to have vanished into thin air.

come up roses • come up smelling of roses

come up roses—(also: come up daisies) turn out extremely well, especially when things seemed to be going badly at first: Everything has come up roses with the film and all the naysayers have been pretty much silenced.

come up smelling of roses—(UK, also: come out smelling of roses) emerge from an unfavorable situation with one's reputation undamaged: She gets into trouble all the time, but generally seems to come up smelling of roses.

Note: *The expression does not correlate in meaning with the phrase* ***take time to smell the roses****—(also: stop and smell the roses) slow down and relax; take time out and enjoy life:* While he described Williams as a "phenomenal woman," he also calls her a "workaholic." "She just doesn't take time to smell the roses," he said.

See also: roses, roses all the way / roses round the door.

come up to something • go up to something

come up to something—1. reach as high as smth.: So, if you're driving through water and it comes up to your grille, it's getting to the stage where you may stall. *2.* equal smth. in standard: The meals cooked in most restaurants do not come up to those prepared at home. 3. *(Progressive Tense)* approach smth. in time: It is coming up to November which means Ash is about to head down the aisle and get married.

go up to something—1. = *come up to something 1:* If the water goes up to your neck, you're even much more slow, so the deeper the water, the heavier you are. 2. go to an important place: Women and children go up to town carrying buckets with fruit and river snails. 3. *(UK)* be allowed to move to the next higher class: You have to pass your end of year exam to go up to the next grade. 4. reach as far as smth.: The second chapter goes up to the end of the Great War; the third chapter discusses the ideological conflicts.

See also: come down to something / go down to something.

comic actor • comical actor

comic actor—an actor who plays in comedies; a singer of comic songs: He has no idea who will replace Ritter but said it should be "a comic actor who is as beloved as John was."

comical actor—mirth-provoking, funny actor: I did really like all of the actors in the film, especially Ben Stiller, who appears to be solidifying his mark as a great comical actor.

comings and goings • entrances and exits

comings and goings—(also: coming and going) 1. arrivals and departures: Fanny lived her own life, never commenting on her husband's whirlwind comings and goings. 2. busy activities: Along with all the comings and goings of the holidays we had plenty of time to just hang out and enjoy each other's company.

entrances and exits—(of actors) coming upon and leaving the stage: We are up on stage behind the scenes with the actors watching them make their entrances and exits.

comment on a match • commentate on a match

comment on a match—make comments or give an opinion on a sports contest: I can't justifiably comment on a match I did not watch.

commentate on a match—act as a sports commentator running live commentary: I don't associate women with football, so hearing one commentate on a match is odd.

common knowledge • general knowledge

common knowledge—said of smth. generally known to most people: It is common knowledge to most trout-fishers that the May Fly has decreased over many parts of the country.

general knowledge—basic understanding of a subject or a variety of subjects: Many of them do not have familiarity with poetry, not to mention the general knowledge and cultural literacy.

common man • common woman

common man—1. an ordinary man, not distinguished by rank or position: Mr. Brooks is a common man. He is not a hero, he is not always fighting against dangerous criminals.... 2. said of ordinary people (both men and women) in general: The common man is portrayed as the helpless victim of opportunistic politicians.

common woman—1. an ordinary woman, not distinguished by rank or position: Rosa Parks was a common woman who had a huge effect on U.S. civil rights movements. 2. *(euph., dated)* a prostitute: She was a common woman when he met her, and had since become the most drunken creature it was possible to meet with.

common property • community property

common property—property owned by a group of tenants in a condominium; property which everyone has the right to use: The bicycles were common property and anyone in the apartment complex could use them.

community property—property belonging jointly to a married couple: The couple decided to divide some of their community property and give it to their children before they left to do volunteer work overseas.

common sense • commonsense

common sense—natural intelligence possessed by all people: Most people think they have enough common sense to deal with anything that might come their way.

commonsense—(attrib.) said of smth. demonstrating common sense: My commonsense idea is to have a safety net that protects the neediest in our society.

community center • community home

community center—a place providing social, recreational, and educational facilities for a neighborhood: A village hall provides a community center for concerts, dances and other events.

community home—(UK euph.) a center for housing young

offenders: The prison became approved school. This is now a dirty word — two dirty words — so it's community home these days.

compete against someone • compete with someone

compete against someone—enter into a contest with smb.: The male riders are determined not to let the so-called jockettes compete against them.

compete with someone—1. = *compete against someone:* We are going to play and compete with them and, hopefully, we'll come out a winner. 2. endeavor to hold an equal place with a person: These stores compete with shopkeepers, and induce them to lower their prices.

comport oneself with something • comport with something

comport oneself with something—behave in the way mentioned: With the help of a few drinks, the Consul comports himself with astounding aplomb.

comport with something—go well with smth.; be in harmony with smth.: Working for people in need comports with his beliefs and desire to help people.

comprehensible policy • comprehensive policy

comprehensible policy—an intelligible policy, capable of being understood: The lack of an explicit and comprehensible policy leaves us with many unanswered questions.

comprehensive policy—1. a policy covering numerous political issues: A comprehensive policy must cover a broad range of policy areas, include trade policy, agricultural policy, and so on. 2. an insurance policy that provides coverage in several areas: The comprehensive policy covers accidental loss or damage to the insured vehicle as well as third party liability.

concentrate at something • concentrate on something

concentrate at something—*(of troops)* gather in force at a certain place: Most of our forces have concentrated at the bridge.

concentrate on something—1. *(of troops)* gather in force on a certain place: The Sardinian troops concentrated on the heights. 2. give one's full attention and thought to smth.: We must concentrate on finding ways to reduce costs.

concern oneself about something • concern oneself with something

concern oneself about something—care about what happens to smth.; worry about smth.: The public did not concern itself about the poem, or the poem-maker.

concern oneself with something—be actively involved with smth.; engage in smth.: I'd dearly love to see more women concerning themselves with such vital issues.

concerned about something • concerned with something

concerned about something—*(also: concerned at something)* caring about what happens to smth.; worrying about smth.: The United Kingdom is deeply concerned about its "brain drain."

concerned with something—1. actively involved with smth.; engaged in smth.: The organization was chiefly concerned with educating Jewish immigrants. 2. having to do with smth.; related to smth.: His work is concerned with the preparation of documents for export.

consequent result • consequential result

consequent result—a result brought about by some action or condition: Large numbers of wagons had to be employed in transporting war materials with the consequent result that very few wagons were left for private use.

consequential result—a result which is of considerable importance: Patt examines the assessment of an unlikely yet highly consequential result of climate change — the rapid collapse of the Antarctic Ice Sheet.

consideration for something • consideration of something

consideration for something—compassion or regard for smth.: Judge Block will have to decide whether Casso deserves special consideration for his years of cooperation [with the police].

consideration of something—giving thought to smth.; discussion or examination of smth.: Now I would like to add something to our previous consideration of the problem.

consist in something • consist of something

consist in something—have smth. as its main part: The beauty of this picture consists in its balance of colors.

consist of something—be made up of smth.; comprise smth.: The remainder of the island consists largely of swamps.

consult someone • consult with someone

consult someone—go to a person for information, advice, or opinion: I should certainly have liked to consult our great modern art-critic before making so daring a statement.

consult with someone—hold a consultation with a person; take counsel together: For the next few weeks, I consulted with a number of specialists and did extensive research on my own.

contact someone direct • contact someone directly

contact someone direct—get in touch with a person without an intermediary: My guess is that they would have contacted him direct but his email address is not on his profile.

contact someone directly—make contact with a person at once: If any problems were to arise before the date of this appointment you should contact the doctor directly.

contemptuous of something • in contempt of something

contemptuous of something—showing contempt or scorn for smth.: There is plenty of evidence that the current government is completely contemptuous of public opinion.

in contempt of something—showing disregard or disrespect for smth.: The way in which Mr. Abrahams made his donations were in contempt of the rules covering political donations.

content of a book • contents of a book

content of a book—subject matter and the ideas of a book as opposed to its style: Do you approve of the content of this book?

contents of a book—that which is contained in a book; everything that it says: He knew by heart the contents of the book.

convert something into something • convert something to something

convert something into something—transform smth. from one form or state into another, so as to perform a different function: The trunk is often converted into canoes.

convert something to something—apply smth. to another use without changing the thing: During the Civil War, the ship was seized by Union forces, who converted it to a gunboat.

cook one's goose • kill the goose that lays the golden eggs

cook one's goose—ruin one's future chances or reputation: Sarah cooked her goose when she caused the defeat of a safe Republican seat in New York, one we held for more than 150 years.

kill the goose that lays the golden eggs—destroy a source of one's wealth: In their quest to squeeze out every last penny from the fans, they will kill the goose that lays the golden eggs.

cool card • cooling card

cool card—(coll.) a person who is impudent in a calm way: That man is a cool card; he'll borrow £5 from you and then ask you to stand him a drink.

cooling card—(dated) smth. that cools one's enthusiasm: It would prove a cooling card to many, whose zeal otherwise would transport them.

cool it • play it cool

cool it—(coll., imper.) stop being angry; calm down: "Cool it, will you Arthur!" demanded Ford. Arthur would not be deterred.

play it cool—deliberately behave in a relaxed and unemotional way: John dived for cover, but the cameraman played it cool, pausing to switch on the camera...

Note:** The expression is not equivalent in meaning to the phrase* ***keep one's cool*—retain one's composure and poise:* Mal kept his cool when Badger admitted there was a problem with the cargo.

Copper Nose • Old Copper Nose

Copper Nose—(hist.) the name given to Oliver Cromwell, lord protector of England (1599–1658): Oliver Cromwell has a number of "nosey" nicknames—"Copper Nose," "Ruby Nose" and "Nosey."

Note:** The nickname is apparently related to the expression* ***copper nose*—a red nose caused by the disease "Acne rosacea" or by drunkenness:* He was a short, brawny old gentleman, with a double chin, a mastiff mouth, and a broad copper nose.

Old Copper Nose—(hist., also: Copper-nose Harry) the name given to Henry VIII, king of England (1491–1547): These silver issues [of coins] were heavily debased, and as a result the king was referred to as "Old Copper Nose," because the king's nose turned copper-colored when the coin began to wear.

copy boy • copy man

copy boy—a newspaper employee who runs errands and carries copy to and from the various departments: Ronnie, a young, eager copy-boy, bustled in with a handful of news slips.

copy man—a copywriter; a person who makes copies: Find A3 papers and copy the whole thing at the copy-service (don't forget the bottle of whisky for the copy-man).

Note:** Neither expression correlates in meaning with the compound* ***copy-cat*—a person who copies the words or behavior of another:* She realizes that this killer is a copycat who is modeling all his killings after famous killers of the past.

cork something down • cork something up

cork something down—1. fasten smth. tightly with a cork: That medicine ought to be corked down closely after use. 2. *(of feelings, reactions, etc.)* suppress: He fought his anger at them, corked it down deep within him, and maintained a calm expression.

cork something up—1. = *cork something down 1:* It's dangerous to cork up these bottles while the wine is still fermenting, you know. 2. = *cork something down 2:* It's very bad for you to cork your emotions up like that: you'd feel much better if you could "let yourself go."

Corncracker State, the • Cracker State, the

Corncracker State, the—(U.S.) a nickname of the state of Kentucky: The father was a farmer who came into the Corncracker state from Pennsylvania, where he was born.

Cracker State, the—(U.S.) a nickname of the state of Georgia: The two hundred slaves of the family followed Colmesnil, who spent the remainder of his life in the Cracker state.

corpse-man • corpsman

corpse-man—a dead man; a zombie: Davy Jones ... is really mesmerizing evil with his infamous ship, the Flying Dutchman, and his soulless crew of corpse men.

corpsman—(U.S. Army) an enlisted person with training in giving first aid: The cry "corpsman up!" rings across a battlefield, sending a crouching figure with a medical bag dashing...

correct copy • fair copy

correct copy—(also: true copy) a proofread copy: I hereby certify that this copy is a correct copy of the original statement on file in my office.

fair copy—the final form of a letter or document: After having re-read it and made certain alterations and erasures, she wrote out a fair copy.

cost of life • cost of living

cost of life—the loss of human lives in wars, accidents, etc.: The war eventually ended in victory but not before a great cost of life was exacted from both peoples.

cost of living—the general expenses of rent, food, clothes, etc: The jobless are often young, employment is insecure, and the cost of living has risen steeply.

cost someone a fortune • cost someone dear

cost someone a fortune—cost a person a large sum of money: See, Janet, this huge yellow rose wreath here from Mrs. Pettigrew. It must have cost her a fortune.

cost someone dear—seriously affect smb.'s health, prestige, etc. *(with the implication that the person is himself responsible):* Politically, this absent-mindedness was to cost him dear.

cotton cloth • cottony cloth

cotton cloth—cloth made of cotton: If you like to use gloves then use special anti-tarnish or cotton cloth gloves which contain no ingredients to tarnish silver.

cottony cloth—cloth looking or feeling like cotton (soft, downy, and white): You can use any type of towel, but to obtain the best drying effect, try to pick a cottony cloth.

cotton on to someone • cotton up to someone

cotton on to someone—(coll., also: cotton to someone) become attached to smb.; come to like a person: I suppose the fact of the matter was that she didn't cotton on to me.

cotton up to someone—(coll.) try to start a friendship with a person: I saw you cottoning up to the new student; was he friendly?

cotton on to something • cotton to something

cotton on to something—understand or realize smth.: Remember this fact, you will probably cotton on to how important it is very quickly.

cotton to something—1. be attracted to smth.; accept smth.: In just the last few years, several major retailers have cottoned to this strategy. 2. = *cotton on to something:* Jane quickly cottons to the fact that something paranormally wrong is going on.

count one's chickens • count sheep

count one's chickens—anticipate some benefit, with the implication that it may not materialize *(in allusion to the proverb "don't count your chickens before they are hatched"):* He had been counting his chickens and borrowing money on the strength of his expectations as his uncle's sole heir.

count sheep—try to fall asleep by counting imaginary sheep jumping over a stile one by one: Did you know that if you count sheep, it is watching the sheep *jump* that sends you off?

count someone off • count someone out

count someone off—count or enumerate people: At the beginning of each class, I count off the students to see if the number present agrees with the attendance lists.

count someone out—1. count people as they leave: The secretary counted the members out as they passed his desk. 2. not to include a person: If you are going for a walk in the rain, you can count me out. *Cf.: count someone in—add or include a person into one's plans, etc.:* Count me in for the party, and my husband will be coming along! 3. prevent smb. from being elected by counting the votes incorrectly: He wasn't voted out, he was counted out.

count the cost • count the pennies

count the cost—estimate the advantages and disadvantages of an undertaking: Riding out, they didn't count the cost; they had one end in view—to serve their king.

count the pennies—(also: count pennies) calculate costs carefully; be economical: That [dinner] was very expensive too. I wasn't in the mood to count the pennies.

country house • town house

country house—(also: country-seat) a mansion in the country; the residence of a country nobleman: The floor was carpeted and the impression was one of a small library in a rather rundown country house.

Note: *The expression does not correlate in meaning with the phrase* ***house in the country****—a house situated in the countryside:* They decided to take their savings and buy a house in the country so they could have a small garden.

town house—(also: terraced house) one of a row of usually similar houses sharing side walls: Many of us have made the life changing decision to live in Cyprus—in a town house or in one of the studio apartments.

couple of something • pair of something

couple of something—1. is used of a small approximate number of smth.: Sometimes he would go to one of the call-houses and spend a couple of hours with one of the women. 2. is used to indicate two items that do not belong together as a set: They had ensconced themselves comfortably in a couple of chairs in the billiard room.

pair of something—is usually applied to items that occur in groups of two: The constable took out a pair of bicycle clips, which he adjusted round his ankles.

court shoes *(UK)* • court shoes *(U.S.)*

court shoes (UK)—women's shoes with a heel, used as a component of formal wear at evening parties, etc.: The Countess of Wessex, wearing unusual Tyrolean-style headwear, wobbled visibly too in her court shoes.

court shoes (U.S.)—athletic shoes used for sports played on an indoor court: My father is an avid tennis player who has worn his court shoes to death.

cover for someone • cover up for someone

cover for someone—1. carry out the duties of a fellow employee, absent through sickness, etc.: You'll need to apply for the sabbatical and train those who will cover for you while you're gone. *2.* conceal smb.'s wrongdoing; provide an excuse for a person: She said that Zaikas had covered for Isaac, who was a party to the state-hospital scandal.

Note: *The expression does not correlate in meaning with the phrase* ***get someone covered****—provide a person with medical insurance:* Since he has never had an injury history it was pretty easy to get him covered.

cover up for someone— = cover for someone 2: I shall really have to teach Neil how to lie effectively if I'm going to expect him to cover up for me.

cover ground • cover the field

cover ground—1. *(also: cover the ground)* deal with an assignment, etc. (especially efficiently or rapidly): If you want to cover ground fast, pool your resources. 2. *(of a book, etc.)* treat a subject: The book could have been greater in scope had the author shown the ambition to cover ground rarely covered in military history.

cover the field—(also: cover the territory) be comprehensive: The strength of Lister's book is that it really covers the field, from methodology to practical examples.

cover letter • letter under cover

cover letter—(also: covering letter) a letter sent with an enclosure to provide additional information: It's always important to match your qualifications to the job in the cover letter.

letter under cover—(dated or formal) a letter in an envelope: Seeing my name in the newspapers, he had sent a letter under cover to the Admiral, expressing his desire to see me.

cover note • covering note

cover note—(UK) a temporary certificate of insurance (between the acceptance and issue of a policy): The insurance expired four days ago, and since I was away there isn't even a cover note.

covering note—(also: covering letter) a letter sent with an enclosure to provide additional information: This fact should be made clear in the covering note that goes with the sample.

cover the ground • cover the territory

cover the ground—1. *(also: cover ground)* deal with an assignment, etc. (especially efficiently or rapidly): His supporters just couldn't cover the ground fast enough to capitalize on the sudden shift in public sentiment. 2. *(of a book, etc.)* treat a subject: The author's statements, as to testing the cement before it was accepted, are very instructive and seem to cover the ground most thoroughly.

cover the territory—(also: cover the field) be comprehensive: The book really covers the territory in terms of outlining the medical treatment options, their pluses and minuses.

cow in milk • milch cow

cow in milk—a cow yielding milk: Their goal now is to decrease the number of cows in milk and maintain production and profit where it is.

milch cow—1. *= cow in milk:* The farm needs the replacement of milch cows as the original stocks have become less productive. 2. a person who is easily tricked out of his money; a source of easy income: The industry is a milch cow for state and national political campaigns.

cow man • cowboy

cow man—a man who raises or tends cattle: In Florida he was a "cow hunter" (later also called a "cow puncher"), and the stockowner or dealer was a "cow man" or "cattleman."

cowboy—1. a man hired to round up and tend cattle, especially in the western United States: Cowboys traditionally work on horseback, but now also use motor vehicles. 2. a man who performs in shows such as rodeos: Visit this site for a two-minute clip of the Blanco County Rodeo; hear how a real cowboy describes the experience of riding a bull.

crack a bottle • hit the bottle

crack a bottle—(coll.) have a drink, especially to celebrate a special occasion: That's wonderful news! I can't think of any better reason for cracking a bottle.

hit the bottle—(coll.) drink too much habitually or over a period of time: She seemed all right for a while but I'm afraid she's hitting the bottle again.

crack-brain • crackhead

crack-brain—(coll.) a stupid person; a fool: Sometimes you are quite a crackbrain yourself.

crackhead—(sl.) a user of "crack"—crystalline, smokable cocaine: They brought an eight-year-old crackhead in for treatment.

crash about • crash about someone's ears

crash about—move about in a clumsy, noisy manner: Now, I don't want any of you children crashing about upstairs while your father's asleep.

crash about someone's ears—(of one's dreams, ambitions, etc.) fail suddenly; collapse disastrously: All our plans crashed about our ears when the government changed the tax laws.

crash barrier • crush barrier

crash barrier—a barrier erected along the side of a road or between the two halves of a motorway to prevent accidents: The lorry hit the crash barrier and overturned.

crush barrier—a (temporary) barrier for restraining a crowd: It was the day of the Ibrox Park disaster when 66 fans died leaving the ground when a crush barrier collapsed.

Note: *The expression does not correlate in meaning with the phrase* ***crush bar****—a place in a theater for audiences to buy drinks in the intervals:* In the second interval he made his way to the crush bar.

crash into something • crush into something

crash into something—hit smth. with force, usually accidentally: Emergency services examine the scene where a car crashed into a power pole, killing the driver.

crush into something—1. press into smth. so that there is breaking or injury: Many passengers were injured in the crash which left the front three carriages crushed into the rear of the train. *2.* enter a building or enclosed space in a tightly packed mass: People crushed into the stadium whether they had tickets or not.

crazy as a loon • crazy like a fox

crazy as a loon—(coll.) very silly; insane: If you think you can get away with that, you're as crazy as a loon.

crazy like a fox—(coll.) very sly, cunning, or shrewd: Don't let him fool you. He's crazy like a fox.

credit someone for something • credit someone with something

credit someone for something—1. appreciate a person for some good quality: Even if you don't agree with the member's opinion, you must credit him for his loyalty. 2. pay tribute to a person responsible for an achievement: Thompson credited him [Sullivan] for developing an essentially new theory in psychiatry.

credit someone with something—1. regard a person as having some usually good quality: Both parties credited him with too much idealism and too little plain horse-sense. 2. ascribe an achievement to a person: Families credited Dean with saving their family farms and livestock from illegal pollution.

cross a check • cross-check

cross a check—draw lines across a check so that it can only be paid into a bank account: I didn't cross the check as I understand that nowadays a check can only be cashed by the person who is written on the check.

cross-check—test if a calculation, process, etc. is accurate by doing it a different way: We also cross-checked the results gained with these measures by using secondary sources of information.

cross over Jordan • cross the Rubicon

cross over Jordan—(also: cross over to the other side) die; pass away: Following a stroke which left her comatose, she crossed over Jordan on February 3, 1972, and is buried at Laurel Land Cemetery.

cross the Rubicon—take an irrevocable step; make a fateful and final decision: Now is the time for Koizumi to cross the Rubicon and take decisive action to implement the radical structural reforms.

cross something off • cross something out

cross something off—take an item off a list; disregard such an item: They crossed off ice cream from the grocery list. It's just too cold for ice cream.

cross something out—cancel an item on a list, etc. by drawing a line through it: He wrote in pencil, and then crossed the words out with thick, dark lines that nearly tore the page.

cross the finish line • cross the line

cross the finish line—1. cross the line which marks the end of a race: Williams had been declared the winner, both for crossing the finish line first and on a corrected time basis. 2. complete a task: By the year 2015 we can cross the finish line and know that all children with visual impairment have attained the right to education.

cross the line—1. = *cross the finish line 1:* Catherine Coey was the first woman to cross the line in a time of 45 min. 57 sec. 2. overstep the limits of decency, respectability, etc.: It is only when women cross the line drawn by patriarchy that real possibilities begin to emerge.

Note: *The expression does not correlate in meaning with the phrase* ***get one's lines crossed****—(also: get one's wires crossed) misunderstand or be confused about smth.:* I thought I actually got my lines crossed, and might have misread the bus schedule, and sent my child out to the bus stop too early.

cross the T • cross the t's

cross the T—(Navy) cross ahead of enemy ship's line of advance approximately at right angles, thus securing tactical advantages: This maneuver, known as "crossing the T," has been the dream of all admirals.

cross the t's—1. *(also: stroke the t's)* draw the horizontal line across the upright of the letter "t": There was something familiar about the handwriting. The way the writer crossed the t's too high. 2. *(in the phrase "dot the i's and cross the t's")* be very thorough; meticulously stick to accepted routine: They had been careful to engage the accounting firm and had really crossed the t's and dotted the i's. *Cf.: dot the last i and cross the last t— carefully finish a project:* Most of you are not quite ready to dot the last "i" and cross the last "t" of your thesis.

crow eater • eat crow

crow eater—(Austral. sl.) a person from South Australia: The team includes a couple of flashy Moroccans, Brits of all persuasions and, of course, an Aussie crow-eater from Adelaide.

eat crow—be forced to admit that one was wrong: Archives are dangerous things. I've had to eat crow a few times myself, especially when I changed my mind on a hard-fought issue.

crow's feet • crowfoots

crow's feet—wrinkles produced by age, spreading out from the corners of the eyes: Notable crow's feet had come about the corners of her nose, mouth and eyes.

crowfoots—wild plants with yellow flowers: These three Crowfoots are confounded by persons ignorant of Botany under the names of Butter-flowers, Butter-cups and Gold-cups.

cry all the way to the bank • laugh all the way to the bank

cry all the way to the bank—(ironic) make a lot of money, especially undeservedly: When the reviews are bad I tell my staff that they can join me as I cry all the way to the bank.

laugh all the way to the bank— = cry all the way to the bank: Naturally, they bought property around them; and laughed all the way to the bank.

Note: *The expression does not correlate in meaning with the phrase* ***be laughing****—(UK coll.) be in a fortunate position; be able to successfully control a situation:* If the gas bill is as low as the electricity bill, we're laughing.

cry for something • cry out for something

*cry for something—*1. weep in order to get food, attention, etc.: While the rescuers were still clearing the debris, the child was crying for water. 2. need smth. very much: It's a reversal from problems felt earlier this summer when the region was crying for rain amid a drought.

cry out for something— = cry for something 2: Over decades, Jackie has been one of the women crying out for support in stopping the violence.

curse at someone • curse someone

*curse at someone—*swear at a person; cast angry words at smb.: I don't curse at other drivers in my infinite need to get anywhere as quickly as possible.

*curse someone—*1. damn a person for doing smth.: She would scream his name over and over, alternately pleading for help and cursing him for not providing it. 2. invoke evil upon a person: The baker and his wife have been cursed by the witch who lives next door — they are never able to have children!

curtain raiser • raise the curtain

*curtain raiser—*1. a short play performed before a main play: On the first night performance of "The Alcade," she played in a curtain- raiser "Bertram." *2.* said of any preliminary event or activity: This match was a curtain-raiser to the Wills Open Tournament.

raise the curtain—(also: lift the curtain) make smth. known; expose smth.: Freedom of information helps raise the curtain on government. You have a right to know what government organizations are doing.

cut above someone, a • head and shoulders above someone

cut above someone, a—(coll.) rather superior to smb.: Kitts' residents consider themselves a cut above the rest of the Caribbean. *Cf.: a cut below someone—rather inferior to a person:* Kind and affectionate he ever was, but he couldn't but own … that I was a cut below him.

*head and shoulders above someone—*considerably much superior to a person: I'll have my own physician. He's head and shoulders above you in skill.

Note: *Neither expression is equivalent in meaning to the phrase* ***above someone****—1. superior to smb. in rank or position:* He will certainly have an executive above him to whom he reports. 2. *too difficult for a person to understand or deal with successfully:* Most of the language was above me, and so I could only get a general impression of his argument.

cut and run • hit and run

*cut and run—*leave without warning; make a quick or sudden escape: To cut and run, to walk out, as Elspeth had, was quite unthinkable to Isabel: it was not in the pattern of civilized behavior.

hit and run—(attrib.) 1. *(of a driver)* failing to stop after causing an accident: He will suffer no after-effects from injuries sustained when knocked down by a hit-and-run motorist. 2. *(of methods in guerilla warfare, etc.)* using swift action followed by an immediate withdrawal: Some of them were indulging in violence and arson, adopting "hit and run" tactics.

cut back on something • cut back to something

*cut back on something—*lower the rate of smth.; reduce smth.: The company cut back on production during the war.

Note: *The expression does not fully correlate in meaning with the phrase* ***cut back something****—1. make smth. shorter by cutting:* He decided to cut the plants back, in order to improve their growth later in the season. 2. *= cut back on something:* The industry has been faced with having to cut back production because of rising costs.

cut back to something—(in films) return in time to smth.: Laurie is staring into oblivion as the film cuts back to the earlier scene.

cut back one's losses • cut one's losses

*cut back one's losses—*diminish costs, expenditures, etc.: The company said the new strategy was designed to help it cut back its losses.

*cut one's losses—*1. *= cut back one's losses:* Many semiconductor firms which had overproduced … sought to cut their losses by quickly selling off their stockpiles of semiconductors. 2. withdraw from a losing or unsatisfactory situation: Bonaparte saw that he was beaten and, like the great man he was, cut his losses.

cut both ways • have it both ways

*cut both ways—*have a mixed effect; have both favorable and unfavorable results: In the Griese family, father and son are both cool, which cuts both ways.

*have it both ways—*1. have both of two incompatible things or situations: We all want to have it both ways: take frequent days off, but still have plenty of money. 2. *(sl.)* have both homosexual and heterosexual tastes *(also: walk both sides of the street):* People who have it both ways are seldom lonely.

cut from the same cloth • cut out of whole cloth

*cut from the same cloth—*said of two or more people who are very similar: Don't assume that all women are cut from the same cloth. Jill won't necessarily react the same way I did.

cut out of whole cloth—(also: made out of whole cloth) wholly fabricated or false: We would never again wage a war for the wrong reasons, or even worse, for reasons cut out of whole cloth.

cut it • cut it out

cut it—(coll.) be effective or successful: Getting an average of four hours of sleep doesn't cut it for me any longer.

cut it out—(coll.) stop doing smth.: This is unacceptable behavior, so please cut it out.

cut it short • take a short cut

cut it short—(coll.) 1. leave a very narrow time margin; nearly miss smth. by being late: You've cut it short, the train's just leaving. 2. bring to an end what one is doing or saying: Felix began a long, irrelevant speech and he resisted calls to cut it short.

*take a short cut—*1. follow a shorter path: I got there as fast as I could (I even took a short cut), but everyone had left. 2. use a quicker method to achieve smth.: Frankly, I took a short cut to a scholarly reputation I haven't yet deserved.

cut loose from something • cut loose with something

*cut loose from something—*get away from smth.; break ties

with smth.: When these farm boys get to town, they really cut loose from convention.

cut loose with something—(of curses, laughter, applause, etc.) speak or act without restraint *(also: let loose with something):* He threw his head back and cut loose with a mirthful, deep laugh.

cut one's teeth • cut teeth

cut one's teeth—learn from smth.; gain experience. There's a job for you to cut your teeth on.

cut teeth—(of an infant) have teeth grow through the gums: Billy is cross because he's cutting teeth.

cut someone dead • cut someone's throat

cut someone dead—1. refuse to recognize a person; pretend not to know smb.: She proceeded on her way, her nose at a celebrated elevation — an icy nose. She cut him dead. 2. ignore a person when being talked to (because one is angry, etc.): He started talking to her and she cut him dead saying "I don't want to hear your life history, pal!"

cut someone's throat—(hyperbolic) cause smb.'s ruin or downfall: We're shorthanded right now, and Genevieve would cut my throat if I tried to send you.

cut someone down • cut someone down to size

cut someone down—1. *(usually Passive)* kill a person: John F. Kennedy was cut down in the prime of life on a political trip to Texas. 2. *(coll.)* persuade smb. to reduce a price, charge, etc.: Eventually we managed to cut him down by $30.

Note: *The expression does not correlate in meaning with the phrase* ***cut someone short****—(also: cut someone off short) interrupt a person:* She wanted to do a lot of reminiscing, but I cut her short.

cut someone down to size—make smb. realize that he is not so important as he thinks: If everyone should be equal, then it's time to cut some people down to size.

cut someone off • cut someone off at the pass

cut someone off—1. *(also: cut someone off short)* interrupt a person: The doctor came in and started to explain the procedure, but I cut him off. 2. *(usually Passive)* isolate or separate a person (from smth.): We were cut off by the incoming sea and nearly drowned. 3. *(usually Passive)* kill a person: Mary was gone, cut off in the prime of life, in the glow of beauty.

cut someone off at the pass—1. intercept a person: When I noticed he was leaving I figured I would cut him off at the pass and have him sign an autograph. 2. foil smb.'s plans or efforts: The good guys intend to blow up a fort. Will they succeed or be cut off at the pass?

cut someone off with a shilling • cut someone off without a shilling

cut someone off with a shilling—disinherit a person: Anastasius made a poor match, married against his father's wish, and was cut off with a shilling.

cut someone off without a shilling— = cut someone off with a shilling: I know that one of my forebears was cut off without a shilling when he married a girl without his family's consent.

cut something away • cut something off • cut something out

cut something away—detach smth. by cutting: If you cut away some of the dead wood, you will have a healthier tree.

cut something off—1. remove smth. by cutting: The man cut off a succulent piece of meat and handed it to me. 2. disconnect smth. such as gas, electricity, etc.: Our water supply has been cut off again this week. 3. isolate or separate smth.: Last night's severe snowstorm cut off three villages.

cut something out—1. extract or obtain smth. by cutting: He cut out this photograph from the newspaper. 2. refrain from smth.; give up smth.: He has decided to cut out smoking and drinking. 3. delete words, paragraphs, etc.: Before we can print this book, you will have to cut out all the four-letter words. 4. replace a competitor in business, etc.: The big new store is going to cut all the small shops out.

cut the knot • tie the knot

cut the knot—find the solution to a problem by a single decisive action: He had cut the knot, by-passing all preliminaries.

tie the knot—(coll.) 1. get married: Diane and Bill tied the knot yesterday in front of family and friends. 2. perform a wedding ceremony: It only took a few minutes for the ship's captain to tie the knot.

Czech Republic, the • Czechoslovakia

Czech Republic, the—the country that made up the greater part of *Czechoslovakia* dissolved in 1992, with *Slovakia* having become another independent republic: Political dialogue between Slovenia and the Czech Republic is marked by intense political contacts.

Czechoslovakia—the country dissolved in 1992 (now used only in historical contexts): Essentially, the Dubcek regime in Czechoslovakia has been trying to do there what Gomulka had to do in Poland in 1956.

D

daddy-long-legs • long-legs

daddy-long-legs—a long-legged flying insect *(Pholcus phalangioides):* On breezy days, the daddy long-legs get blown onto rivers in big enough numbers to cause quite a stir in the trout world.

long-legs—a wading bird *(Himantopus himantopus):* Long-legs is a long-legged three-toed black-and-white wading bird of inland ponds and marshes or brackish lagoons.

damn all • damn it all

damn all—(coll., emphatic) not a thing; nothing at all: What is the State doing for the Theater? Damn all.

damn it all—(exclam.) is used to express anger or impatience: Damn it all, am I to stand here all day cooling my heels on your pleasure!

dare I say • I dare say

dare I say—said when one knows that what he is going to state may raise objections: Dare I say that many of Desai's films have been like that. Making use of the current favorites — actors, plots, stories and turning them into a movie.

I dare say—said when one assumes smth. to be likely or possible: I dare say that we are the best example of East-West fusion in Asia (though the Hong Kongers and Japanese will have something to say about that).

dark age • Dark Ages, the

dark age—a period in which there is a lack of culture and progress in a society: Shortly before 1700 B.C. a dark age settled over Egypt which was to last some one hundred and fifty years.

Dark Ages, the—the period of European history between about A.D. 500 and about A.D. 1000: During these, which are rightly called the Dark Ages, the clergy were supreme.

dark horse • white horse

dark horse—a candidate, etc. of whom little is known but

who may unexpectedly come to the front: Every now and then a dark horse is heard of, who is supposed to have done wonders at some obscure small college.

Note: *The expression does not correlate in meaning with the phrase* ***gray mare, the****—(dated) the wife who rules her husband (in allusion to the saying "the gray mare is the better horse"):* Thus, by the covetousness of this woman, who was the gray mare, and the folly of the master ... my good principles were nearly eradicated from my bosom.

white horse—1. *(pl.)* white foam and spray on the crests of waves: As mariners say, the sea is covered with "white horses." 2. *(UK)* a horse carved into the side of a chalk hill and visible from a great distance (most some hundreds of years old): The Uffington white horse is by far the oldest ... and is of an entirely different design. 3. *(White Horse)* the proprietary name of a brand of whisky: White Horse was the first distillery to sport screw caps. *Cf.: white mule—(U.S. sl.) cheap or illicitly distilled whisky:* I know a good bootlegger over there in Santa Fe, and if you take me over there, I'll buy you a gallon of White Mule. 4. *(U.S. Drug users)* cocaine: White Horse, White Lady, White Girl: Those are just a handful of cocaine's street names.

dark matter • gray matter

dark matter— objects not directly detectable by astronomers, thought to exist in the universe to account for observed gravitational effects: The composition of dark matter is unknown, but may include new elementary particles.

gray matter—1. brownish-gray nerve tissue, especially of the brain and spinal cord: The researchers found increased gray matter density in women in the left hemisphere of the brain associated with language. 2. mental power; intellect: The odious Krendler, in particular, learns to use his gray matter for, perhaps, the first time in his life.

dash it • make a dash for it

dash it—*(interj.)* is used to express one's annoyance about smth.: Dash it, Tony ... you really ought to be careful.

make a dash for it—*(coll.)* run away very quickly (to avoid being caught): We all began to ask each other why he hadn't made a dash for it.

date back to something • date from something

date back to something—go back in time to a particular date: The rare binding of this manuscript dates back to the late middle-ages.

Note: *The expression does not correlate in meaning with the phrase* ***backdate something****—1. put an earlier date to a document than the actual one:* The vet backdated the vaccination dates for horses in an attempt to satisfy Jockey Club rules. 2. *make smth. retrospectively valid:* The wage increases are to be backdated to the first of January.

date from something—be in existence since a particular time: This building dates from the beginning of the last century.

day and night • day or night

day and night—continually; all the time: We worked day and night to finish the project before the end of the month.

day or night—at any time whatever: The Internet is the best shopping mall in the world and one that you can visit day or night.

day-man • man of the day

day-man—a man who does work during the day or on a day-shift: A company taxi is usually driven by both a day-man and a night-man.

man of the day—1. an outstanding man of his time: Hamsun was a man of the day, who, despite his age, strove to make his ideal into a reality. *Cf.: man of the year—a man who has done the most to influence the events of the particular year (as featured by the U.S. newsmagazine Time):* Mikhail Gorbachev was the man of the year for 1987, an eminently defensible choice.... 2. *(Military)* a soldier on duty for the day: Cooked food was "dished out" by the orderly men of the day.

day off • off day

day off—a day away from work, school, etc.: The bus-driver spends his "day off" in driving on a pal's bus, on the box-seat by his pal's side.

Note: *The expression is not equivalent in meaning to the phrase* ***day out****—1. a day away from home when one is free from duty:* Ollie just loves going to shows and he thoroughly enjoyed his day out. 2. *a servant's free day:* When it is the maid's day out, Jack insists on helping with the dishes.

off day—1. a day when one does not feel fit or does not perform well: The bartender could have smiled a little but maybe it was his off day. 2. = *day off 1:* I could also change which day was my off day to line up with friends' birthdays or other celebrations.

Note: *The expression does not correlate in meaning with the phrase* ***far-off day****— a day remote in time:* On that far-off day I lay on the rocks and listened to the deep rhythm of the Atlantic.

day order • order of the day

day order—*(Stock market)* a customer's order that expires at the close of the day: A day order is canceled if it is not executed before the close of business.

order of the day—1. an agenda: The order of the day will be issued each day with detailed information on Conference. 2. a statement issued by a commander to his troops: In his Order of the Day Mannerheim thanked the civil guards for their work for the benefit of the country. 3. fixed and regular way of doing things: He was sick of living on literary lunches where nouvelle cuisine seemed to be the order of the day.

daytime • time of day

daytime—the part of the day when there is natural light: In the Tokyo area, users' charges of electricity at nighttime are rated lower compared to that in the daytime.

time of day—1. the hour shown on a clock: Perhaps it was a student who committed suicide at this very time of day, on this very day, in this very building? 2. a particular period during the day: Birds are generally most active at this time of day and most inactive in the early afternoon.

dead-alive • living dead

dead-alive—*(also: dead and alive)* 1. *(of a place)* spiritless or boring: Do you think I could hold out a week in this dead-alive place? Not me! 2. *(of people)* miserable; inactive and dull: You will die in a home for old people surrounded by dead-alive persons.

Note: *The expression does not correlate in meaning with the phrase* ***more dead than alive****—(also: half dead) in a very poor physical condition owing to illness, etc.:* A policeman found him, more dead than alive, in the street where he had been beaten up.

living dead—1. *(also: living corpse)* smb. who seems completely unaware of what is happening around: I remember reading that being a full blown addict is the "living dead." Being alive, but dead, how morose. 2. a vampire; a zombie: I felt as if we were in the presence of a ghoul, the living dead.

dead and alive • half dead

dead and alive—*(also: dead-alive)* 1. *(of a place)* spiritless or boring: This is rather a dead and alive place but I like the climate for I have not known a sick day since I have been up here. 2. *(of people)* miserable; inactive and dull: Part of my early days in London I was familiar with what is called hyper-Calvinistic Baptists ... but I never was amongst such a dead-and-alive lot.

half dead—*(also: more dead than alive)* in a very poor physical condition owing to illness, etc.: I had identified the latitude and the longitude of the place where he was, and there they found him, half dead, but alive.

dead beat • deadbeat

dead beat—(also: dead beaten) extremely tired: It took me a very short time to get between the blankets, and soon I was asleep, for I was dead beat after my ride.

deadbeat—(sl.) 1. an idler who is not working or looking for a job: Al was a deadbeat barely on the right side of the law, who hadn't had a job in six years. 2. smb. who persistently fails to fulfill his obligations or pay his debts: Wilson was a deadbeat who lived the end of his life running from creditors.

dead bird • dead pigeon

dead bird—(Austral. sl.) a sure thing; a certainty: I used to prowl where jockeys herd, And tipped them for a sure "dead bird."

dead pigeon—(sl., also: dead duck) 1. a person or thing regarded as useless or a failure: The Dominion Stores Ltd. was a dead pigeon and everyone knew it. *2.* a dead person: Now, having risked everything on my logic, I was a dead pigeon if wrong. There were only minutes left.

dead end • living end, the

dead end—1. an end of a passage, such as a street or pipe, that affords no exit: The passage was a dead end. Ten meters in front of her, a solid stone wall stood, trapping her. 2. a point beyond which no progress can be made: The project turned out to be a dead end. The longer I worked on it the less I was able to actually produce something.

living end, the—1. said of a person or thing that is extremely good or quite extraordinary: We were big fans of their band. We thought it was the living end in those days. 2. said of a person or thing that is very annoying or irritating: The man was really the living end. When his typing was interrupted he threw his hands in the air and sighed loudly.

dead fire • death-fire

dead fire—1. extinguished or extinct fire: Mr. Evans was sitting there, staring at the dead fire, the poker in his hand. 2. *(also: St. Elmo's fire)* a naturally occurring electrical discharge, usually in stormy weather: We looked up, and saw a dead-fire sticking to the cross-trees of the mast.

death-fire—1. a fire causing loss of life: The changes in the death fire statistics cannot be explained by this factor alone. 2. a fire for burning a person to death: A large wooden statue of the blessed Virgin was brought to make the death-fire.

dead hand • dead man's hand

dead hand—1. the influence of the past regarded as controlling the present: The dead hand of vanished generations of historians has determined beyond possibility of appeal the pattern of the past. 2. *(coll.)* an expert at doing smth.: First-rate work it was, too; he was always a dead hand at splitting.

***Note:** The expression does not correlate in meaning with the phrase **hand of death**—(liter.) death; demise:* If, under its influence, normal physical functions could be suspended, perhaps the hand of death, too, could be stayed.

dead man's hand—a zoophyte *(Alcyonium digitatum)* forming fleshy masses: Dead Man's Hand is indebted for the English name to the fishermen, who often take it up in their nets.

***Note:** The expression does not correlate in meaning with the phrase **dead-man's arm**—(UK) a flat-rolled suet pudding, which is then spread with jam and rolled up:* Because Jam Roly-Poly was often served in an old shirt-sleeve, another nickname for the pudding was dead-man's arm.

dead head • death's head

dead head—1. *(coll.)* a person who contributes nothing to an enterprise or activity; a non–fare-paying passenger, etc.: "No more dead-heads," Mr. Skinner warned. "Hereafter, pay for your guests." 2. a dead flower that has become withered and faded: The culling of dead heads is a ploy that figures persistently in the garden in summer. 3. an obstruction floating so low in the water that only a small part of it is visible: Numerous "dead-heads" bobbed in the current like otters swimming with the stream.

death's head—a human scull as an emblem of death or a danger sign: There had been three variations of the chemical hazard symbol. One was a picture of a death's head, or skull and crossbones.

dead heat • deadly heat

dead heat—said of a race in which competitors finish at the same time: The horses came to the finish in a dead heat, and, without a photograph, the results were too close to call.

deadly heat—extreme or excessive heat: These times of deadly heat demand all of our concern and commitment to prevent heat-related tragedies.

dead house • death house

dead house—1. *(dated)* a mortuary; a morgue: When they reached the Ferry Beach they made all speed to the hospital and to the "dead house," which held seven coffins. 2. *(sl.)* an uninhabited house: We thought it was a "dead" house, but we walked into a girl's room and she squealed.

death house—(U.S. Prison) a group of death cells for persons awaiting execution: He has three murders behind him, and the grey doors of the death-house in front of him.

dead line • deadline

dead line—1. an article which a shopkeeper has stopped dealing in because customers have no more interest in it: Silk stockings have been a dead line for years and years, Madam! 2. *(also: dead wire)* a cable through which no electricity passes: It was as if she had been calling on a dead line to an empty building. 3. a straight line: The equipment is designed to guide the aircraft along a localizer beam to keep it in dead line with the center of the runway.

deadline—time or date fixed in advance by which smth. must be done: As a journalist, I always have to work to a deadline.

dead loss • total loss

dead loss—1. said of smth. totally unsuccessful: The defense budget was not a dead loss: the economies of South Africa and Namibia got a shot in the arm as a result of this. 2. *(coll.)* said of a person who is quite worthless: We'd better fire Smith now — he's a dead loss.

total loss—(Insurance) an irreparably damaged vehicle: The natural inclination is to under-insure and take the chance of not having a total loss.

dead man • dead soldier

dead man—1. an object buried in the ground and used as an anchorage: A deck hand was killed by being struck on the head by a "dead man." 2. *(sl.)* an empty liquor bottle: I returned to my table and finished my drink. When the owner appeared again I asked if I could help remove the dead men.

dead soldier—(sl., also: dead marine) 1. = *dead man 2:* There weren't any prints on that bottle. That dead soldier was as clean as a whistle. *Cf.: wounded soldier—(U.S. sl.) a partially-finished can or bottle of beer that can still be consumed:* "I can't find any more beer anywhere, Ted." "Here, take this wounded soldier off me." 2. a cigarette butt: He collected dead soldiers to use in building a whole smoke.

dead money • dead on the money

dead money—money invested in unsold products which

cannot therefore be used: This will tell you how much "dead money" is tied up in the three products.

Note: *The expression does not correlate in meaning with the phrase* ***dead rent****— a fixed rent for a mining concession, etc.:* A claim for an increase in the amount of the dead rent fixed in a contract cannot be upheld.

dead on the money—(coll.) totally correct: I have always read Howard's articles with a great deal of interest, as they are usually dead on the money.

dead right • dead to rights

dead right—(coll.) absolutely right: You are dead right about the Web connection being the most critical part for a classroom teacher now.

dead to rights—(in the phrase "catch someone dead to rights") catch a person in the act of committing a crime: He was caught dead to rights with the goods on him.

dead room • death chamber

dead room—a room or studio made absolutely soundproof: With the advent of radio broadcasting and sound pictures very "dead" rooms have been built.

death chamber—1. *(also: lethal chamber)* a room specially equipped for executing people: It was with similar displeasure that I undertook a tour of Maryland's death chamber. 2. *(U.S. sl.)* an unsafe vehicle *(also: death trap):* The Ford Pinto was considered a death chamber due to its gas tank tendency to explode on impact.

dead rope • death rope

dead rope—1. a rope that is fixed, and does not run in a pulley: There must always be at least two complete turns of dead rope on the pulley or drum. 2. a bell-rope working on a half-wheel, for chiming: The bells were not hung for "full circle" ringing until 1678; prior to this date they were hung "dead rope."

death rope—a rope used for hanging a person: "You want to do the honors?" asked our lieutenant, holding up the untied end of the German officer's death rope...

dead season • dead time

dead season—1. *(of holiday resorts, etc.)* the time when there are very few guests: Since it was the dead season, the hotel beach wasn't crowded at all. 2. a period without commercial, social, or intellectual activity: It was the dead season in London; every one of consequence was out of town.

dead time—time during which the active work is not going on: Machine owners strive to minimize the dead time by fine-tuning the control system.

Note: *The expression does not correlate in meaning with the phrase* ***dead on time****— exactly at the expected or pre-arranged time:* We arrived dead on time at Cape Town where we were met by Che in the arrivals hall.

dead ship • death ship

dead ship—(Nautical) a ship without power: They saw no movement, no living or dead person, no sign of violence; nothing, but the ordered emptiness of a darkened and dead ship.

death ship—a ship deliberately wrecked so that the owners can collect insurance money: He is forced to join the crew of a "death ship" ... betrothed to the ocean floor in exchange for insurance money.

See also: ghost ship / ghost train.

dead sleep • never-ending sleep

dead sleep—profound sleep simulating death: Well, I don't remember getting home but in the middle of the night I woke up out of a dead sleep and was wide awake and sober.

never-ending sleep—(euph.) death: Hamlet sees a never-ending sleep full of dreams as extremely pleasant, but these very dreams are the "undiscovered country" which makes him fear death...

dead weight • live weight

dead weight—1. *(also: dead load)* the fixed weight of a structure (such as a bridge on its supports): This inefficient use of material contributes substantially to the dead weight of the structure itself. 2. a heavy or oppressive burden: The dead weight of this legacy has grown heavier from generation to generation. The classical precepts have come to be a millstone round the neck...

live weight— the weight of an animal before being slaughtered: Live weight changes of calves were calculated as average daily gain for the June to October period.

dead wire • live wire

dead wire—(also: dead line) a cable through which no electricity passes: A young carpet layer was installing carpet when he grabbed what he thought was a dead wire.

live wire—1. *(also: live line)* a wire carrying electric current: If you were to touch the live wire a current would flow through your body to the ground. 2. a vivacious and energetic person: He is a live wire and a free spirit. It is easy to see why people are so keen to flock around him and worship at his feet.

deal in something • deal with something

deal in something—trade in a particular commodity: Before shops were common in every village, he dealt in needles, thread, and the like.

deal with something—1. be a customer of a business: I've dealt with this firm for twenty years. 2. manage smth.; attend to smth.: There are many difficulties to be dealt with when starting a business. 3. *(of a book, etc.)* be concerned with smth.; treat a subject: His latest book deals with police methods.

deal with someone • make a deal with someone

deal with someone—1. have to do with a person: Until the end of his term Britain has a statesman, and not a catch-vote politician, to deal with. 2. treat or behave towards a person in a manner specified: We ourselves shall one time or other be dealt with as we deal with others.

make a deal with someone—make a bargain or business transaction with smb.: He's willing to "make a deal" with disgruntled investors to win their support.

death-wish • dying wish

death-wish—a conscious or unconscious wish for the death or downfall: Whatever handicaps he labors under as Minister, they do not include the death-wish; he is still determined to win the next election.

dying wish—a person's last wish expressed at the time of dying: We are delighted that Patrick's remains are being brought home in accordance with his dying wish.

decide on something • decide something

decide on something—1. choose smth. from two or more possibilities: After exhaustive product research, I finally decided on licensed leather sports caps. 2. settle a question, etc.; make a judgment on smth.: The courts that decided on the case had been wrong in concluding that he was not the co-owner of the property.

decide something—1. = *decide on something 2:* A jury of citizens and not the judge decided the case, and the company in which Turk owned stock actually lost. 2. influence or determine the outcome of smth.: Diallo also had no complaints about the penalty kick that decided the match.

defend someone against something • defend someone from something

defend someone against something—protect a person by repelling an attack against him: The way to defend Milton against all impugners is to take down the book and read it.

defend someone from something—keep a person free from attack, danger, etc.: The U.S. intelligence services sponsored his rise to power, and defended him from any credible opposition.

defense industries • defensive industries

defense industries—factories involved in manufacturing weaponry: In 1941 Roosevelt issued an executive order prohibiting racial discrimination in the employing of workers by national defense industries.

defensive industries—industries which provide the consumer with his basic needs (such as food, utilities, etc.): In emerging markets, defensive industries have typically been populated with small to medium-sized companies.

defer something • defer to something

defer something—put smth. off until a later time: It was agreed to defer this application for two weeks in order to receive documentation from the agent.

defer to something—acknowledge the merit of a person's opinion or action: The Tribunal will normally defer to his judgment on such matters.

definite answer • definitive answer

definite answer—answer that is precise, clear and leaves no room to uncertainty: In all encounters with Leonardo there is never a definite answer to any of the aesthetic or psychological questions which he raises.

definitive answer—answer that is final and may no longer be changed: There is no definitive answer to the question of how many senses there are: we have yet to discover all of our own.

deliver someone from something • deliver someone of something

deliver someone from something—*(formal)* 1. save or rescue a person from smth.: They armed to deliver him from prison. Crowds had gathered ... loud in their outcries for mercy. 2. free a person from some problem or responsibility: Chilperic was delivered from the necessity of inventing any new expedient.

deliver someone of something— = *deliver someone from something 2:* He was looking for someone to deliver him of his burdensome responsibility.

Note: *The expression does not correlate in meaning with the phrase* ***deliver oneself of something****— express one's thoughts, views, etc.:* After I had delivered myself of this ponderous thought, conversation turned into pleasant channels again.

deliver the goods • get the goods

deliver the goods—*(coll.)* succeed in doing what one is hoped or expected to do: He is the best manager that we have ever had. He knows how to deliver the goods.

get the goods—*(coll.)* find out true and often bad information about smb.: I think that I have finally got the goods on him and will have to talk to the police as soon as possible.

demand for something • demand on something

demand for something—need for smth. that people desire to purchase or have: The problem is that the demand for health care is unlimited.

demand on something—request or claim for smth. by virtue of right or authority: There are so many demands on my time that I have very little leisure.

Democratic Republic of the Congo, the • Republic of Congo, the

Democratic Republic of the Congo, the—an African country, formerly known as Zaïre, with the capital Kinshasa: Coltan has permitted the Rwandan army to sustain its presence in the Democratic Republic of the Congo.

Republic of Congo, the—the smaller and more westerly African country, with Brazaville as its capital: The Republic of Congo is one of Africa's largest petroleum producers with significant potential for offshore development.

depart out of this world • go out of this world

depart out of this world—*(euph.)* die; pass away: But one thing, at times, assuages my grief, which is this: I am sure that he departed out of this world in peace.

go out of this world—1. *(also: go from this world) = depart out of this world:* This put people to their graves a lot quicker than they should have gone out of this world. *2.* have one's mind far away from reality: He hadn't talked to anybody since then and it seemed he had gone out of this world.

Note: *Neither expression correlates in meaning with the phrase* ***retire from the world***—1. *live alone from principle, seeing no one:* After a busy life teaching, he retired from the world and considered his own inner development. 2. *enter a monastery or become a hermit:* To think that Catharine Glover nourished the private wish to retire from the world!

descend on someone • descend to someone

descend on someone—1. arrive suddenly to stay with smb.: The whole family descends on us every Christmas. 2. attack a person suddenly: Thieves descended on the travelers while they slept.

descend to someone—pass to a person after smb.'s death: The property descended to the man's eldest son.

desk-book • table book

desk-book—a reference book suitable for use at a desk: This desk-book for business executives is highly recommended.

table book—1. *(also: coffee-table book)* a big sized richly illustrated book: She sat in her wingback chair flicking through one of the table books. 2. *(dated)* a small book for making notes or memoranda: He was observed to busy himself by writing in his table book.

determined in something • determined on something

determined in something—showing resolution in one's manner or speech: He sounded most determined in his answer.

determined on something—resolved to do smth.; firm in one's decision to do smth.: He is quite determined on a trip to Egypt.

deus ex machina • ghost in the machine

deus ex machina—an improbable person or event that provides a sudden and unexpected solution to a difficulty: When the impoverished hero is relieved by an unexpected inheritance, it is often called a *deus ex machina.*

ghost in the machine—is used to denote the view of the human mind as being completely independent of the physical body: So there is nothing magical about human brains — no ghost in the machine, to use Ryle's phrase.

devil's coachhorse • devil's horse

devil's coachhorse—any of several rove beetles of the family *Staphylinid:* This atrocious tale of lies turned up joint by joint before her like a devil's coach-horse.

devil's horse—praying mantis of the family *Mantid (an insect that feeds upon other insects and is harmless to man):* Another of the most peculiar and interesting insects in Texas is called the "devil's horse."

devil's dust • dust devil

devil's dust—wool or cotton waste made from old cloth by a machine called the "devil": The operation sends forth clouds of floating fibers — the real and original "devil's dust."

dust devil—a whirlwind visible as a column of dust: A whirling dust-devil would scutter across the plain for a couple of miles.

Diamond State, the • Gem State, the

Diamond State, the—(U.S.) a nickname of the State of Delaware: Long called the Diamond State, a name arising from a quotation attributed to Jefferson ... Delaware's resources are varied and rich.

Gem State, the—(U.S.) a nickname of the State of Idaho: Idaho's nickname, the "Gem State," is well deserved due to the 80 varieties of gemstones found within her borders.

die away • die out

die away—(of a sound or light) become weaker or fainter: The sound of the car died away in the distance.

die out—1. *(of a group of living things)* perish; become extinct: If too many of these rare animals are killed, their kind will die out. 2. *(of practices, customs, ideas, etc.)* cease to exist; disappear: It's time this selfish habit died out.

die for something • die from something

die for something—(Progressive Tense) want smth. very urgently: Her husband moved past us into the bar.... "I'm dying for a margarita."

die from something—(also: die of something) 1. die as a result of some cause: In a severe winter, wild animals can die from lack of food. 2. *(Progressive Tense)* be in an extreme state of the feeling mentioned: The children are dying from curiosity to see what's in the parcel.

die in a ditch • die in the last ditch

die in a ditch—die destitute in dire poverty: He who abstains from whisky will never die in a ditch.

die in the last ditch—fight desperately defending smth. to the last: I can be sure never to see my country's ruin: I will die in the last ditch. *Cf.: last-ditch effort—a desperate final attempt:* He is negotiating with prosecutors in a last-ditch effort to avert trial.

die on one's feet • die standing up

die on one's feet—1. die while still working; keep working till the end: Harvey spent the next week working on the generator. He had died on his feet. 2. fight and give one's life courageously: Rather than surrender without a fight, the exhausted army fought bravely to the bitter end and died on their feet. 3. become absolutely exhausted *(also: be dead on one's feet):* I was cheered the whole way round and this really helped over the last two miles when I was dying on my feet.

Note: *The expression does not fully correlate in meaning with the phrase* ***die in one's boots***—*(also: die with one's boots on)* 1. = *die on one's feet 1:* I suppose I'll have to retire one day, but that's a long way off. I'd much rather die in my boots. 2. = *die on one's feet 2:* "General," he later reported to Dodge, "they died in their boots but brought peace." 3. *die a violent death:* Charlie talked of the early days in the Marshalls when every white man lived like a prince, and died in his boots from a bullet or a spear.

die standing up = *die on one's feet 2:* Kurdish people throughout southern Turkey have decided they would rather die standing up than spend their lives on their knees.

differ from someone • differ with someone

differ from someone—1. be unlike another person in some way: John only differs from his brother in being less masculine and less sternly religious. 2. have different opinions on some matter: My dear sir, I am sorry to differ from you. I think that we are soldiers, and damned good ones at that.

differ with someone— = differ from someone 2: In politics, he differed with his brother-in-law, William Biles, Hough adhering strongly to the Proprietary party.

differ in something • differ on something

differ in something—(of two or more people or things) be unlike in some respect: The two brothers are like each other in appearance, but differ widely in their tastes.

differ on something—(also: differ about something) have different opinions on some matter: Since the discussion is not making any progress, perhaps it is best to agree to differ on this issue.

different cup of tea, a • not someone's cup of tea

different cup of tea, a—(also: another cup of tea) a different state of affairs; smth. of an altogether different kind: London in wartime is a very different cup of tea from Winchester.

not someone's cup of tea—said of smth. that is not to a person's taste or does not appeal to one: If Yeats isn't your cup of tea, why not try some of the more contemporary Irish poets?

Note: *Neither expression correlates in meaning with the phrase* ***cup of tea, a***—*(coll.) an individual of the kind mentioned (especially an older woman):* Miss Prentice seems to be a very unpleasant cup of tea.

dig a hole for oneself • dig one's own grave

dig a hole for oneself—(also: dig oneself into a hole) get oneself into an awkward or restrictive situation: Melton has dug a hole for himself that will take the remainder of his term to come out of. He has made so many promises in his few months in office...

dig one's own grave—be the cause of one's own failure or downfall: When a plot was disclosed he did not use the occasion to make a comprehensive purge. However humane this behavior may seem, politically it was digging his own grave.

dig one's heels in • dig oneself in

dig one's heels in—act firmly; refuse to yield: It is not an indication of my lack of ability, but rather a sign that it is time for me to dig my heels in and exert more effort.

dig oneself in—(also: dig in) 1. *(of soldiers)* dig a protective place for oneself: We were ordered to dig ourselves in and I can assure you that it did not take us long to dig our trench. 2. establish oneself securely; get oneself settled (in a new job, etc.): I am relatively new to the photography world although I've dug myself in and tried to improve as much as I can.

dime a dozen, a • ten to the dozen

dime a dozen, a—said of people or things that are very common and easy to get: Fad diets are a dime a dozen. It seems like every time we turn around there is a new diet.

ten to the dozen—(also: nineteen to the dozen) talk very fast and without stopping: Everybody is talking ten to the dozen about the fantastic film material they've shot.

dine on something • dine out on something

dine on something—have smth. for dinner: They dined on mince, as there was nothing else in the house.

dine out on something—gain social success by telling interesting stories: You'll dine out on it for weeks, won't you, old boy?

Note: *Neither expression fully correlates in meaning with the phrase* ***dine off something***—1. = *dine on something:* We dined off onion pilaf, and sponge-cake of maize flour. 2. = *dine out on something:* Ever since his adventure he has been dining off the story.

dingo's breakfast • dog's breakfast

dingo's breakfast—(Austral. sl.) a drink of water, with nothing to eat: We quickly prepared for the hunt, had a dingo's breakfast and we were off.

dog's breakfast—(sl.) an untidy mess; a distasteful mixture *(also: dog's dinner):* The plot of the film is a dog's breakfast of half-baked ideas.

Note: *Neither expression correlates in meaning with the phrase* ***donkey's breakfast****—(sl.)* 1. *a straw mattress:* There we slept on the usual "donkey's breakfast." 2. *a straw hat:* She was wearing a red dress and had a donkey's breakfast on her head.

dining car • dinner wagon

dining car—a railroad car in which meals are served: People in the dining car were much easier to talk to than the people in the first class lounge.

dinner wagon—a tray with shelves beneath (usually on castors) for the service of a dining-room: He would not even know the difference between a tea trolley and a dinner wagon.

dinner lady • kitchen maid

dinner lady—(UK) a female cook or canteen worker in a school: They walked home, along with their friends, and made free with my house and kitchen whilst I was busy being a dinner lady at school.

kitchen maid—a woman employed in the kitchen; a junior female servant in a great house: Daisy was taken on as a kitchen maid at Findon Place, where Edwin John Spencer and his wife rented the mansion.

dip one's toes in the water • get one's feet wet

dip one's toes in the water—(of an activity) proceed gently with much caution: Companies will dip their toes in the water by hiring temporary employees until they are certain their markets have recovered.

get one's feet wet—gain one's first experience of smth.; do smth. for the first time: Don't be afraid to get your feet wet. Your first efforts may not be perfect, but you've got to start somewhere.

dip the flag • drop the flag

dip the flag—(of a ship) give a salute to another ship by making the flag go down for a moment and then up again: Today, "dipping the flag" is an act of courtesy; men-of-war do not do it to one another.

drop the flag—1. *(Sport)* indicate the start or finish of a race using a flag: When the first horse reaches the winning post, one of the judges there drops a flag. 2. give the signal for the start or finish of smth: It would be a great help to the leader of a future expedition in making up his mind when to "drop the flag."

direct something at someone • direct something to someone

direct something at someone—1. aim or point smth. at a person: Wary troopers directed stun guns at the medley of bodies in case of disorder. 2. intend smth. for a person: Are you directing your remarks at me?

direct something to someone—1. address or send smth. to a person: Please direct all the mail to the secretary when it is delivered. 2. = *direct something at someone 2:* My next remarks are directed to the boys and girls of this school.

dirt-eater • dirt-eating

dirt-eater—(dated) 1. *(also: clay-eater)* miserable people who appease their hunger with a kind of aluminous earth: Distinguished from other southerners by hookworm disease were dirt-eaters scattered in sand barrens and pine woods. 2. a contemptuous name for "poor whites" in some parts of the southern United States: It rests with you whether you will take rank with the poor whites, the dirt-eaters of the South, or with the best classes of the north.

dirt-eating— a disease of the nutritive functions causing an irresistible craving to eat earth: For some time past she had been addicted to dirt-eating (eating earth) ... a disease, which terminates in dropsy and death.

See also: eat a peck of dirt / eat dirt.

dirt money • dirty money

dirt money—money paid to workman handling dirty materials or working in dirty conditions: Wharfies get dirt money for working on filthy, dusty merchant ships.

dirty money—1. = *dirt money:* When any class of work involves special unpleasantness, "black money" or "dirty money" is sometimes stipulated for. 2. money earned by dishonorable or corrupt means: They want you to "launder" this dirty money so that you are the one who will be tracked down by the authorities.

dirty dog • dirty pig

dirty dog—used as an insult of a person who has behaved badly, meanly or selfishly: I see you've finished all the whisky, you dirty dogs. You might have saved me a little.

dirty pig—used as an insult of a disgusting person (dirty in his personal habits, etc.): He doesn't have any friends and people are always laughing at him calling him "dirty pig."

dirty one's hands • have clean hands

dirty one's hands—1. get involved with routine and practical work: He is easily approachable, and willing to dirty his hands doing the work he has been elected to do. 2. do smth. that one considers unpleasant or distasteful: These are people with more secure jobs who have never had to dirty their hands to earn a living. 3. do smth. shameful or illegal: Tolentino is loyal, brutal, knows how to keep secrets and is ready to dirty his hands for his boss.

have clean hands—be free from guilt or dishonesty: Many Republicans realized that the party could not win unless the nominee had clean hands.

dirty work • dirty work at the cross-roads

dirty work—1. the necessary work which is dirty, hard, or unpleasant: We never had enough applicants. Most folks just don't want to do the dirty work. 2. unlawful activity, especially undertaken on behalf of another person: Do you generally get other people to do your dirty work for you?

dirty work at the cross-roads—1. foul play (said of mean or corrupt practices): No question of accident or of dirty work at the cross-roads? These rich men have enemies, don't they? 2. *(joc.)* said of smth. unpleasant happening: There'll be dirty work at the cross-roads all right, when you lads get together. I suppose you'll be arriving home about 3 a.m.!

disconnected from something • disconnected with something

disconnected from something—physically separated from smth.; not joined to smth.: Make sure the television is disconnected from the mains supply before you open up the back.

disconnected with something—having no relationship with smth.: The accident rate seems to be disconnected with the road conditions and weather.

dispense something • dispense with something

dispense something—1. deal out or distribute smth.: Young

ladies have been dispensing tea to hungry comrades. 2. prepare and give out medicine: The firm has been dispensing ointments and lotions for generations.

dispense with something—1. do without smth.; manage in spite of not having smth.: He is not yet well enough to dispense with the doctor's services. 2. render smth. unnecessary: The new machinery dispenses with hand labor.

dispute about something • dispute something

dispute about something—argue about smth: There is no time to dispute about the forms of education.

dispute something—1. question the truth or validity of smth.: We never disputed his right to build a home on land he had purchased. 2. contest smth.; fight for smth.: Our team disputed the victory until the last minute of the game.

distinguished by something • distinguished for something

distinguished by something—marked or characterized by some quality: The army is divided into eight divisions, distinguished by the color of their respective flag.

distinguished for something—remarkable for some (usually superior) quality, attainment, etc.: John Augustus Walker, an Alabama artist, was distinguished for his paintings and murals.

Divine Office • Holy Office, the

Divine Office—the prayers and readings in the services held in the Roman Catholic Church: She was troubled, distracted in meditation ... when the other sisters were chanting Divine Office.

Holy Office, the—1. *(hist.)* the Inquisition: It may seem strange that the spread of the reformed religion should so long have escaped the Holy Office. 2. a Roman Catholic administrative organ that deals with protection of the faith and morals: We even went to Rome.... We were promised a formal answer from the Holy Office.

do a bit • do one's bit

do a bit—1. perform a small part in a play or movie: I got to do a bit with Mick Jagger where he comes into a dressing room and looks in the mirror.... **2.** practice smth. in a small way: In my spare time I always want to do something "creative," so I choose to do a bit of carpentering.

do one's bit—1. fulfill one's responsibilities or obligations: During the epidemic he did his bit with the other physicians, attending cases night and day. 2. make one's contribution to the war effort (serving in the armed forces, etc.): Yes we did our bit, as you folks say. I'll tell the world we got the enemy on the run.

do a book • make a book

do a book—1. write a book: We all have our weaknesses. Mine just happens to be any comic book done by David Mack. 2. translate a book: I know that most of his books have been done into English. 3. *(U.S. Underworld)* suffer the maximum penalty; serve a life-time sentence: I'm doing one life jolt, and two one-to-fiftys ... yes sir, doing the book.

make a book—1. create a book: Mr. White might have made a whole book out of being a city man on a farm. 2. *(Bookmakers)* accept bets on contests: Adelaide bookies can only make a book based upon the horses that are backed in a race.

do a book on something • make a book on something

do a book on something—write a book on a subject: William Fox is doing a book on the way the environment impacts our evolution and perception.

Note: *The expression does not fully correlate in meaning with the phrase **write the book on something***—1. = *do a book on something:* Because I had developed a big respect for Perret when he wrote the book on Grant, I read his book on President Kennedy. 2. *(U.S. coll.) be the expert or the final authority on smth.:* Cathy has spent years learning the intricacies of producing prize-winning Dalmatians. You could even say she wrote the book on it...

make a book on something—1. create a book on smth.: We thought if we're going to make a book on cooking, it ought to benefit people who could use more food. 2. *(Bookmakers)* take bets on certain contests: Bookmakers do as their name suggests, that is they make a book on the outcome of an event. 3. *(coll.)* be certain of smth.; feel confident about smth.: "Do you think they'll be funnier in print than they were on TV?" "I wouldn't make a book on it!"

Note: *The expression does not correlate in meaning with the phrase **make a book of something**— represent a particular sort of book:* The letters of Lord Chesterfield make a book of the minor moralities, and the major immoralities of life.

do a house • make a house

do a house—tidy or clean the house: One day I did the house thoroughly, totally, and my Dad's closet was really messy, so I tidied it.

Note: *The expression is not equivalent in meaning to the phrase **do up a house**— repair or improve the house:* It was really worth the pain we took to do up the house. On the advise of our agent we renovated the house and gave it a fine look.

make a house—*(Parliament)* secure the presence of enough members for a quorum *(also: keep a house):* Yesterday, after many days waiting, sufficient number of members met and made a house.

Note: *The expression does not correlate in meaning with the phrase **make a home**—1. establish or run a home:* He asked her how big her roll was, saying that it cost something to make a home. *2. (also: make one's home) settle in a place (with one's family):* She has made a home in the Bay Area, where she now teaches Italian cooking and language.

do a job • do the job

do a job—*(Underworld)* commit a robbery or a burglary: The two were engaged "doing a job" at a lonely place when two mounted patrols came upon them.

do the job—*(also: do the business)* accomplish one's purpose; achieve the desired result: I don't care what you use, as long as it does the job.

do a job on someone • do the job for someone

do a job on someone—*(sl.)* 1. treat smb. roughly; injure or harm a person: There's no need to do a job on me, man, I'll tell you everything I know. **2.** *(also: do a snow job on someone)* take advantage of a person, especially by persuasion or deception: My local friendly plumber did a job on me cleaning out my drain.

do the job for someone—*(also: do the business for someone)* accomplish one's purpose; achieve the desired result: When he couldn't get whiskey he would drink lemon or vanilla extract. It was mostly alcohol, so it did the job for him.

do a moonlight • moonlight

do a moonlight—*(coll.)* secretly move from a flat (under the cover of night) usually to avoid paying the rent: The tenant had done a "moonlight" with no warning even though the lease still had many months to run.

moonlight—*(coll.)* work (often illegally) at a second job in addition to one's main job: Sasquatch is a tractor-trailer driver by day — by night, he moonlights as a musically inclined cigar distributor.

Note: *The compound does not correlate in meaning with the* *verb* ***moonshine****—(U.S. coll.) make liquor, especially whisky, illicitly:* He acknowledged no occupation save that of a squirrel hunter, but he "moonshined" occasionally by way of diversion.

do a number • do one's number

do a number—1. *(Underworld)* give information to the police: If Keiser's doing a number, I've arranged for you to knock him off. 2. *(euph., of an animal)* urinate or defecate: That black puppy did a number on the carpet again.

do one's number—1. perform one's act in a program of entertainment, etc.: When I got up to do my number my sound was terrible.... 2. *(sl.)* behave in a predictable or customary manner: Whenever I call, he does his number about being too busy to talk.

do a number on someone • make one's number with someone

do a number on someone—(sl.) 1. deceive or treat a person unfairly: Caroline doesn't like him. He really did a number on her at work. 2. speak or write of smb. with disdain; slander a person: They did a number on Ridpath. They printed damaging statements. 3. totally defeat a person or team: The Irish team are looking to do a number on England in Dublin tomorrow.

make one's number with someone—(sl.) socialize with a usually superior person (in order to make oneself known, remembered, etc.): He was one of the boys on the campaign bus who made his number with would-be presidents.

do a runner • do the running

do a runner—(sl.) run away in order not to pay the bill, avoid punishment, etc.: If we put any pressure on Sorley he'll get rid of the drugs and do a runner.

do the running—(also: make the running) show initiative; make sure that things get done: Men are no longer expected to do all the running at the beginning of a relationship.

do a work • make a work

do a work—engage in an activity; fulfill a task: You could give the composer complete freedom, saying you'd like him to do a work for you.

make a work—(coll., also: make work) make a fuss; cause disturbance or trouble: People make a work if a minister preach the same sermon over again.

do an abortion • have an abortion

do an abortion—perform an abortion on a woman terminating her pregnancy: I became pregnant again and they were falling over themselves to do an abortion for me.

have an abortion—(of a woman) end her pregnancy (usually deliberately): I had an abortion, without telling anyone; the father left me when I told him of the pregnancy.

do away with something • make away with something

do away with something—abolish smth.; put an end to smth.: I believe it is time to do away with some of the old laws.

make away with something—1. succeed in stealing smth.: The police gave chase, but the thieves made away with the jewels. 2. deplete or waste smth.: This sort of life, as anybody may well think, soon made away with his little stock of money. 3. get rid of smth.: I shall make away with that old carpet on the stairs; it is time we had a new one.

do best • do one's best

do best—1. be most prosperous; achieve the best results, etc.: Turnips do best in a cool, well-ventilated area such as a root cellar. 2. *(followed by Infinitive)* be well-advised to act in a particular way: If you want a full overview of this puzzling tale, you would do best to read two new books.

do one's best—(also: give of one's best) do all one can; do smth. as well as one can: He wasn't particularly angry. He was looking, or doing his best to look, grave.

Note: *The expression does not correlate in meaning with the phrase* ***make the best of oneself****—make oneself as attractive as possible:* These letters were full of advice on how to make the best of oneself when just beginning one's career.

do business • do the business

do business—1. conduct transactions: The principle on which we do business is P.O.D. Which literally means Pay on Delivery. 2. take up business as a subject of study: I did Business at college. I also did Accounting as a separate course.

do the business—1. = *do business 1:* The way we do the business, and even the way we live our lives has altered. 2. *(also: do the job)* accomplish one's purpose; achieve the desired result: Two simple rules well observed will do the business. 3. *(euph.)* have sex with a person: So he went home with her: Do you think they did the business?

Note: *Neither expression fully correlates in meaning with the phrase* ***do one's business****—*1. = *do business:* Every new employee goes to a Pragmatic Marketing class, because we want them to understand how we do our business here. **2.** *(euph., of an animal) urinate or defecate:* You can't teach it to eat from a certain bowl in a certain place, or to do its business in a litter box.

do duty • do one's duty

do duty—1. serve as or pass for smth. else: The handsome building, could have done duty as a state capitol. 2. *(euph.)* defecate or urinate: The lamb stood in the middle of the field doing duties at an adjacent haystack.

do one's duty—1. do what one is obliged to do by law, one's trade or conscience: "You've been very helpful, Aggie." "I do my duty." 2. = *do duty 2:* The child never defecates or urinates; he does his "duty." 3. *(euph.)* is used of marital sex: Melinda could not stand the idea of the marriage bed and refused to do her duty as a wife.

do faces • make faces

do faces—1. sketch or model faces: I do faces better than anything else. It's the bodies that don't turn out so well. 2. apply cosmetics: Makeup artist Tom Savini, one of the best in this creepy business, will do faces.

make faces—1. assume a silly, twisted expression on one's face intended to cause laughter: The two children sat at the table making faces at each other. 2. express annoyance or disapproval by one's facial expression: The leader swung his chair round ... presumably so he could make faces to the rest of the orchestra. 3. = *do faces 1:* When I started my training, I was delighted and excited to find that I could make faces as they actually are.

See also: make a face / make face.

do good • make good

do good—1. be beneficial *(usually with a quantifier):* You could try taking a higher dose of Vitamin C; it might do some good. 2. help through charitable work: Sometimes I doubt if she will be as ready to begin doing good again. *Cf.: do-gooder—(derog.) a well-meaning but unrealistic or ineffective philanthropist (who tries to "do good"):* Amateur "do-gooders" could slip up when certain medical attention was needed.

Note: *The expression does not correlate in meaning with the phrase* ***do well****—1. (Progressive Tense) make a good recovery (from illness, etc.):* She has completed her treatments and is doing well. **2.** *become professionally or financially successful:* These are things I did and I did well as a nurse and a nurse's aide.

3. *(followed by Infinitive) be well-advised to act in a particular way:* The corporation will do well to accept the union's demands.

make good—1. = *do well 2:* Then she got a job in the hospital and made good as a nurse. 2. reimburse or refund smth.: If the article is defective, you should take it back and ask them to make good.

do good to someone • do someone good

do good to someone—show kindness or concern by doing smth. beneficial to a person *(usually in religious contexts):* Love God in your heart and do good to all your friends and enemies.

do someone good—1. make smb. feel better; help or benefit a person: Make everyone who is not asleep get out at every rest area. The fresh air will do you good. 2. give a person pleasure or satisfaction: It did me good to watch him sit on the edge of my bunk and eat biscuits and butter. 3. *(followed by Infinitive)* one would be well-advised to act in a particular way: It will do you good to hear the truth occasionally. I doubt if you ever heard it at home.

Note: *The expression does not correlate in meaning with the phrase* ***do someone a good turn***—*perform an act of kindness or help a person unselfishly:* Why should you do me a good turn? I never did you one.

See also: do someone well / do well by someone.

do history • make history

do history—study history (as a major): She does history at Warwick University, and likes her ivory towers enough to consider postgraduate study.

make history—do smth. which will be recorded in history: Wright made history with the first manned flight in a heavier-than-air craft.

do it • make it

do it—1. have a required effect: Again I did not go and pleaded the same reason. That apparently did it — she stopped asking me to lunch parties. 2. *(euph.)* have sex: At sixteen you're horny enough to get an erection watching two parakeets do it, let alone humans. 3. *(coll.)* make a mess of things; make a foolish blunder: Oh God! I've done it again. When will I learn to hold my tongue. 4. *(euph.)* defecate or urinate: Look what happened. The dog did it again on the Persian carpet!

Note: *The expression does not correlate in meaning with the phrase* ***overdo it***—1. *overexert oneself:* He overdid it last winter and now evidently stands in need of rest. ***2.*** *carry smth. to excess; do too much:* She seemed to be an attractive woman who overdid it with makeup and clothes.

make it—1. successfully accomplish smth.: The charts showed we had made it, and big. ***2.*** recover from an illness, etc.; survive: He's so sick, I don't think he'll make it. 3. get to a particular place, especially in time: Although they got out late, they made it. 4. = *do it 2:* Those bedroom eyes were telling him their owner wanted to make it.

do lunch • make lunch

do lunch—eat lunch: At midday he did lunch and a round-table discussion with farmers at the Country House Restaurant.

make lunch—prepare lunch: Samantha tugged me towards the kitchen; on the way she said, "Daddy has made lunch."

do one's block • do the block

do one's block—*(Austral. sl.)* become angry or excited: I did my block — panicked, I reckon you'd say.

do the block—*(Austral. sl.)* take a walk; promenade: The streets are thronged with handsome women "doing the block."

do one's homework • do one's housework

do one's homework—1. said of lessons to be done by a schoolchild at home: Your child will be more accepting of doing his homework when he knows that it must be done at a specific time. 2. do all the necessary research and preparation for smth.: Before heading out on her shopping spree she did her homework and compared suitable cars from all brands.

Note: *The expression is not equivalent in meaning to the phrase* ***learn one's lesson***—*profit from experience, especially an unhappy one:* Sure, he had trouble in the past, driving while intoxicated ... but he's apparently learned his lesson.

do one's housework—do the work required to keep a house clean and in order: It wasn't fit for one to do one's housework in nothing but their pajamas.

do one's money • make one's money

do one's money—*(Austral., NZ sl.)* lose all one's money; spend one's money completely: Right now I've done my money, but as soon as I can raise the fare I'll be getting back.

make one's money—acquire or earn money, especially when having a good income: Bob did his time in prison and has kept clean ever since, making his money through gambling.

Note: *The expression is not equivalent in meaning to the phrase* ***coin money***—*(coll.) gain money rapidly and with ease:* For the last four years he literally coined money.

do one's thing • do the other thing

do one's thing—1. act in a way commonly associated with the person: It's quite amusing to listen to him doing his thing with tourists in the lounge bar. 2. follow one's own interests or inclinations: I think, rather, she insists on doing her thing — what it pleases or suits her to do.

do the other thing—*(in the phrase "one can do the other thing")* is used to express a refusal to bargain or compromise: I couldn't have a better home and anybody who doesn't like it can do the other thing.

do one's worst • make the worst of it

do one's worst—do one's utmost in evil or mischief: Out of sheer revenge, he did his worst to blacken her character.

make the worst of it—experience the worst aspect of a situation: Having married, they immediately proceeded, as if by mutual consent, to make the worst of it.

See also: have the best of it / make the best of it.

do oneself down • do oneself up

do oneself down—*(UK coll.)* make oneself ashamed or less proud of oneself: Remember not to do yourself down — it is your job to sell yourself, the employer's job to judge how well you do this.

do oneself up—*(coll.)* dress up for the party, etc.; make oneself more beautiful: After spending two hours putting makeup on and doing herself up I would hope she does look better.

Note: *The expression is not equivalent in meaning to the phrase* ***make oneself up***—*(of an actor preparing for the stage, etc.) apply cosmetics to one's face:* He started as a teenage clown, making himself up with shaving cream and lipstick.

do oneself well • do well for oneself

do oneself well—1. provide oneself with comforts, delicacies, etc.: The old artist always did himself well: he took berths on the Orient Express, in spite of Connie's dislike of trains de luxe.... 2. become professionally or financially successful: The film was directed by Bruce Beresford ... and with this one I think he has done himself well.

do well for oneself— = *do oneself well 2:* When we look around this shop the outsider may say to himself that George has done well for himself and is basking in gold.

do right by someone • put someone right

do right by someone—treat smb. fairly in moral or legal terms: I oppose this bill because it does not do right by our disabled veterans.

put someone right—(also: put someone to rights) 1. make smb. well again: Since there is nothing wrong with him really, a placebo will put him right. 2. correct smb.'s ideas or information about smth.: His ignorance of the world is not abnormal for an American ... his advisors will put him right on foreign affairs.

do someone credit • give someone credit

do someone credit—(of smb.'s action or behavior) add to a person's reputation *(also: do someone honor):* Your obvious sincerity does you credit and I may owe you an apology.

give someone credit—1. praise a person for his behavior or some good quality: He gave my father the real information and my father always gave him credit. 2. trust a customer to pay at some future time what he owes: Everybody is eager to give me credit — I get new credit card offers in the mail all the time.

do someone honor • do the honors

do someone honor—1. pay deserved tribute to a person: Twenty heads of state attended the Queen's coronation to do her honor. 2. *(of smb.'s action or behavior)* add to a person's reputation *(also: do someone credit):* Her behavior in such a difficult situation does her honor.

do the honors—act as the host; serve one's guests: You do the honors and pour out the tea while I bring in the cakes.

do someone in the eye • hit someone in the eye

do someone in the eye—(sl.) cheat or defraud a person: He handed her a gold chain of curious workmanship. "Unless I've been done in the eye it's an old one."

hit someone in the eye—1. make a strong impact on smb.: I drove about in a smart red-wheeled coach. Anyhow, it hit my colleagues badly in the eye. 2. give a person a shock: Modern young men's manners now really quite hit you in the eye.

do someone out of something • outdo someone

do someone out of something—(coll.) 1. cheat smb. out of his possessions: He set up some kind of business deal with a partner and his partner did him out of most of his money. 2. prevent a person from doing or having smth.: He can tell you a story for over an hour about how someone did him out of a job twenty years ago.

outdo someone—do more or better than another person in performance or action: Prejudiced attitudes motivated Miles to outdo his classmates and excel as a musician.

do someone proud • make someone proud

do someone proud—1. treat a person extremely well; extend lavish hospitality: They always do us proud whenever we go to have a meal with them. 2. give a person cause for pride; justify smb.'s pride: Jim's success in the examinations did his family proud.

make someone proud— = do someone proud 2: Perhaps a sudden tract of good fortune would have made me too proud.

do someone up • make someone up

do someone up—(coll.) 1. make a person look attractive; dress smb. up for the party, etc.: It's not the actress herself I'm calling unattractive, but the way they "did her up." 2. get the better of smb.; ruin a person financially: There was a pleasure in doing up a debtor which none but a creditor could know. 3. *(UK, usually Passive)* wear out a person: We have been working continuously now.... The stretcher-bearers are done up completely.

Note: *The expression is not antonymous in meaning to the phrase* ***do someone down****—(UK coll.) 1. defeat smb. (often by unfair means):* Mr. Stothard was using the Times to advance his own interests and do down his enemy. 2. *speak ill of a person:* No doubt the whispering voices praised him to the heavens while also doing down his opponents.

make someone up—(of an actor, etc.) apply cosmetics to a person's face: The General was close upon eighty; but he was "made up" to represent a gentleman of about forty.

do someone well • do well by someone

do someone well—1. *(of a hotel, etc.)* provide a high quality service: Kensington is only a small place, they do you well there, and it's always full.... 2. *(followed by Infinitive)* be well-advised to act in a particular way: It will do you well to learn these things before you choose a career or job.

do well by someone—treat a person with loving kindness: Soon after this the boy was transferred to another home, where a childless couple are trying to do well by him.

See also: do good to someone / do someone good.

do something blindfolded • do something sight unseen

do something blindfolded—(also: do something with one's eyes closed) do smth. very easily, without much effort: Flying this thing is so easy I can do it blindfolded!

do something sight unseen—do or make up one's mind about smth. without having previously seen it: They bought the house sight unseen, working out the details by phone and fax.

do something out of hand • put something out of hand

do something out of hand—do smth. immediately, without delay or preparation: Newspapers reject this kind of writing out of hand for fear of offending advertisers.

put something out of hand—accomplish smth.; no longer deal with smth.: He has been indefatigable ... whereby he has caused much work to be put out of hand.

do something over • overdo something

do something over—1. repeat an action; do smth. again: Also, if I could do the paper over, I would remove the word "controversy." 2. remodel or redecorate smth.: We ought to keep this as the spare room and do the nursery over.

overdo something—1. carry smth. to excess; do too much: With the zeal of a new convert he overdid matters. 2. cook food too much: Don't overdo the meat. When the peppers are soft, taste the mixture to see if it needs anything.

See also: make over something / make something over.

do something standing on one's head • stand on one's head doing something

do something standing on one's head—(coll.) do smth. very easily or without effort *(also: do something on one's head):* The climb he wanted me to attempt was a simple one. At Cambridge I could have done it standing on my head.

stand on one's head doing something—(coll.) do everything possible; do all in one's power: He stood on his head trying to explain to her why he was so late, but she still didn't believe him.

do something up • make something up

do something up—1. *(of clothes)* fasten; button up: You've done your buttons up the wrong way. 2. wrap smth.: The presents were all done up in shiny paper and put under the Christmas tree. 3. *(of hair)* arrange: Will you help me to do up my hair? 4. make smth. attractive or improve smth.: We shall have to do up the house next spring. 5. *(of fruit, etc.)*

preserve: Mother is doing up some blackberries, so that we can eat them during the winter.

make something up—1. *(of the road)* put a bitumen surface on to make it suitable for traffic: When are the council going to make up this road? 2. repay a loss of smth.; compensate for smth.: You must make up the time that you have wasted by working late tonight. 3. *(of a story, excuse, etc.)* invent; fabricate: These entertainers make their stories up as they go along. 4. apply cosmetics: He saw Teddy approach the clown, Diaz, who sat on his trunk making up his face. 5. constitute smth.: What are the qualities that should make up a man's character? 6. put smth. together; complete a set of items: The train is made up but is not yet ready to start. 7. fulfill a written order or prescription: The chemist is still making up the order, and says it will be ready in an hour.

do the dirties with someone • do the dirty on someone

do the dirties with someone—(sl.) have sex with a person: You just don't understand that Sean and I are just friends. I don't plan on doing the dirties with him.

do the dirty on someone—(coll.) do smth. bad and unfair to a person *(also: do dirt to someone)*: The Germans have been "doing the dirty" on us by donning khaki and kilts to approach our trenches.

do the dishes • make the dishes

do the dishes—1. *(U.S.)* wash the plates, etc. after a meal: Why am I always the one who has to do the dishes? 2. cook meals: They also wanted to know how to do these dishes themselves. That's what started her small cooking studio.

make the dishes—do the dishes 2: The women teach their students how to make the dishes they have been eating for generations.

do the room • make room

do the room—1. clean the room: At this studio there is a femme de menage that does your room. 2. *(also: do up the room)* decorate or furnish the room: The paper-hanger who did this room, has done it very well.

make room—allow enough free space: She had moved both cups off the tray to make room for her breakfast things.

do the trick • make the trick

do the trick—1. perform a clever or skilful action to entertain people: When you do a trick, you know you've got it when you do it in front of all those people. 2. accomplish one's purpose; achieve the desired result: One more turn of the driver should do the trick.

make the trick—gain a point in a single round of a card-game: The play is just like other trick-taking games — the player who made the previous trick starts the next one.

do the washing • do the washing-up

do the washing—wash dirty clothes, sheets, etc.: Women do the washing and ironing in about four-fifths of households.

do the washing-up—wash the plates, etc. after a meal: A few tips for those who do the washing-up by hand: soak the dishes before you wash them…

do time • make time

do time—(coll.) serve a sentence of imprisonment: Our story is about a man who did time for drug dealing and lost custody of his two kids. *Cf.: do easy time—(coll.) serve a short prison term:* John Murdoch is doing easy time in a minimum security jail dubbed a "holiday camp."

make time—1. *(coll.)* flirt with a girl; make romantic advances: At another table two young men were trying to make time with some Mexican girls. 2. *(also: make good time)* accomplish a distance in a short time; travel fast: They were on a straight stretch of road now and were making time.

do up • make up

do up—(of clothes) fasten; button up: This dress does up at the back with pink buttons.

make up—(also: make oneself up) apply cosmetics: The actors were making up when we arrived.

do well in something • do well out of something

do well in something—perform well in a subject: So, because I liked science, I did well in physics. *Cf.: do badly in something—perform unsatisfactorily in a subject:* Students who did badly in the exam needed more practice.

do well out of something—benefit from smth.; make a good profit from a sale, etc.: Like the arms dealers who did well out of the war, some have seen their fortunes improve beyond their wildest dreams.

Note: *Neither expression correlates in meaning with the phrase* ***make good on something***—1. *successfully accomplish smth.:* He took advantage of the guard's attention being distracted to make good on his escape. 2. *fulfill a promise:* The only person who has made good on his promise is Pierre Salinger, former press secretary to President Kennedy.

do with something • make with something

do with something—(also: make do with something) accept smth. although it is not quite satisfactory: If we can't afford meat we shall have to do with fish.

make with something—(sl.) hand smth. over; deliver or produce smth.: When are you going to make with the music, man?

do without something • go without something

do without something—dispense with smth.; manage in spite of not having smth.: Many Victorian households did without a bathroom altogether.

go without something—not have (and suffer the absence of) smth.: Schools have procedures to ensure students do not go without lunch.

do you want a bet • you bet

do you want a bet—an emphatic way of saying that what has been stated is wrong: "You'll wind up in the hospital," Claude said. "Do you want a bet?"

you bet—(also: I bet) an emphatic way of saying "certainly," "of course": "Can you handle this outfit?" "You bet," said the scout.

doctor's orders • just what the doctor ordered

doctor's orders—said of smth. that one is strongly advised to do or of an order which cannot be evaded: No one will be admitted. "Doctor's orders," they will be told.

just what the doctor ordered—that's exactly what is wanted or needed: The waiter brought her a drink. "Just what the doctor ordered," she said, smiling at him.

dog and pony show • show pony

dog and pony show—an elaborate presentation of a new product, program, etc. designed to impress an audience: They did a "dog and pony show" for all the faculty and handed out a survey to gauge interest.

show pony—(UK coll.) an attractive fashionable person, especially a performer who enjoys being in the limelight: While on tour, he was the target of an infamous comment from Geoffrey who alleged that Cork was a "show pony."

dog days, the • three dog nights

dog days, the—(also: dog days of summer, the) the hot, sultry period of summer (between early July and early September): During the dog days, air-conditioners are running full-time.

***Note:** The expression does not correlate in meaning with the phrase **dog's life**— a wretched unpleasant existence:* I never knew a sailor yet who wouldn't tell you sailoring was a dog's life.

three dog nights—(sl.) very cold nights: We had a lot of three dog nights this winter before they got the heat going to the second floor.

dog-house • dog's home

dog-house—1. a dog kennel: Heidi the rottweiler was in the doghouse yesterday after she stopped firemen reaching a kitchen blaze. 2. *(sl.)* bass viol: You will not find the language which was attached to jazz in the first spate of magazine articles — no "dog-house" for bass. 3. a small structure of a shape suggesting a kennel: Some detail can be added to the superstructure of the yachts, such as the coach roofs, doghouse and hatch covers.

***Note:** The expression does not correlate in meaning with the phrase **cat house**—(sl.) a brothel; a house of prostitution:* How many cat houses do you suppose there are in this town?

dog's home—(also: dogs home) an establishment where dogs are kept and looked after: Many dogs are now in the caring hands of staff at the Battersea Dogs Home, but they still have to find a permanent home.

dog Latin • pig Latin

dog Latin—bad or inferior Latin: They [speeches] are chiefly made up of extracts from the common school collection ... sprinkled with scraps of dog Latin.

pig Latin—a jargon formed by rearranging the syllables in a word: The great thing about speaking pig Latin is that it's not simply a question of learning a new vocabulary.

***Note:** Neither expression correlates in meaning with the phrase **thieves' Latin**—(arch.) the cant of thieves:* I ... saw a light inside, and heard two words of thieves' Latin.

dog man • hot dog man

dog man—1. a man in charge of dogs: It is an error of modern dog men to wean puppies too soon. 2. *(also: dog person)* a man who is characterized by a preference or liking for dogs: I do not particularly care for cats — more of a dog man.

hot dog man— a man selling hot sausages (enclosed in a bread roll): The hot dog man parked his cart outside the school at lunch time.

***Note:** The expression does not correlate in meaning with the compound **hotdogger**—(sl.) a person who performs showy, often dangerous stunts in a sport:* We noticed that almost every wave carried a hot-dogger performing tricks.

dog salmon • dogfish

dog salmon—a salmon of Western North America *(Oncorhynchus keta):* The meat of the dog salmon is palatable when fresh or smoked.

dogfish—1. various small sharks, chiefly of the family *Squalidae,* of Atlantic and Pacific coastal waters: The spiny dogfish shark travels in packs. 2. a bony freshwater fish *(Amia calva)* of central and eastern North America: The fish known to be called a dogfish does not occur in these northern waters.

dog show • dog's show

dog show— a display of dogs: There has been a mania for shows; we have had dog shows, donkey shows, and last, not least, horse shows.

dog's show—(coll., usually negat.) the poorest chance: Analysts will discover whether or not this coup has even a dog's show of succeeding.

doggone • gone to the dogs

doggone—(coll.) 1. extremely *(used as an intensifier):* You don't expect these tools to be perfect ... but the price is doggone good! 2. *(in the phrase "I'll be doggone")* used as an exclamation of annoyance: I'll be doggone if I am going to stand in the path of small businesses.

gone to the dogs—(coll.) ruined or in very poor condition: If politicians are allowed to decide what is right, the future of science is gone to the dogs.

dog's body • dogsbody

dog's body—1. the complete material structure of a dog: A general knowledge of your dog's body and how it functions will prove helpful in his daily care. 2. the physical remains of a dead dog: The dog's body remained floating in the canal waters over the weekend.

dogsbody—(coll.) a person who carries out menial tasks for others: I was a sort of general dogsbody to begin with — assistant stage-manager, and what have you.

dog's dinner • duck's dinner

dog's dinner—(sl.) an untidy mess; a distasteful combination *(also: dog's breakfast):* North End is a dog's dinner of hovels, dives and drinking dens.

duck's dinner—(Austral. sl.) no dinner at all; a drink of water, with nothing to eat: "Make sure he has more than duck's dinner, okay?" "What?" "He should eat."

dog's ear • pig's ear

dog's ear—a corner of a page turned down to serve as a book-mark: The book was well-thumbed, with dog's ears and little slips of paper in it.

pig's ear—(coll., in the phrase "make a pig's ear of something") make a mess of smth.; do a task badly: "I've made a real pig's ear of it, haven't I?" said Basil, with an attempt at lightness.

domestic animals • domesticated animals

domestic animals—animals kept by or living with man on a farm, etc.: The origin of most of our domestic animals will probably for ever remain vague.

domesticated animals—wild animals tamed to live with humans: On this website you will learn how to take care of pets and domesticated animals.

Dominica • Dominican Republic

Dominica—a country on the island of Dominica of the eastern Caribbean between Guadeloupe and Martinique: Dominica has a two-party system, which means that there are two dominant political parties.

Dominican Republic—a country of the West Indies on the eastern part of the island of Hispaniola: She worked for ten years in the Dominican Republic in judicial reform programs.

done like a dog's dinner • done up like a dog's dinner

done like a dog's dinner—(sl.) completely and utterly defeated *(also: done like a dinner):* Whatever possessed her to play tennis against Sue? She was done like a dog's dinner.

done up like a dog's dinner—(sl.) dressed in an ostentatiously flashy manner *(also: dressed up like a dog's dinner):* Ask her where she's been all afternoon, done up like a dog's dinner and missing for hours.

don't ask • don't ask me

don't ask—is used to say that the answer is so depressing one wouldn't even want to hear it: How did we do in the bridge tournament? Don't ask!

don't ask me—is used to tell a person that one does not know the answer: She has decided to dye her hair bright green, don't ask me why.

don't even think of it • don't give it a thought

don't even think of it—don't even let such an idea occur to you; don't even consider such a possibility: With high summer temperatures, you'll need to be drinking water constantly. Drugs: Don't even think of it.

don't give it a thought—(also: don't give it a second thought) 1. let that not worry you: I was eating regular food within five days after surgery. So, don't give it a thought! 2. is used to indicate that thanks are unnecessary: "Thank you very much for all your help!" "Please don't give it a thought!" 3. is used as a polite way of accepting apology: "I'm sorry that I treated you mean today." "Oh, don't give it a thought."

don't give up the day job • give something up as a bad job

don't give up the day job—is used to humorously tell a person that he could not do smth. professionally: Your English is fine for getting by in a conversation, but as for writing English (far less translating): don't give up the day job.

Note: *The expression does not correlate in meaning with the phrase* ***don't give up the ship****— used to tell a person not to surrender and keep on trying or working on smth. till he gets it right:* Keep up the good work and don't give up the ship, just yet. There is light at the end of the tunnel!

give something up as a bad job—stop doing smth. because one does not feel it is worth continuing; acknowledge that one has no hope of success: I tried to make him see things as I did, but when this effort failed, I gave it up as a bad job.

don't knock yourself out • knock yourself out

don't knock yourself out—(coll.) 1. don't overexert yourself in an effort to accomplish smth.: Don't knock yourself out trying to track down your child's allergies unless they truly are persistent. 2. *(ironic)* don't overexert yourself in doing smth. that does not require much effort: "Well, don't knock yourself out to say something, Sarah," he said. His tone was teasing, but his eyes were not.

knock yourself out—(sl.) go ahead; do as you please *(usually in answer to a proposal a person is not happy with):* If you want to make hotel and airline and car reservations and take care of everything, well, then, knock yourself out.

don't mention it • don't talk to me about it

don't mention it—is used to indicate that thanks or apology are unnecessary: I wanted to apologize for not having known him in the garden. "Don't mention it," he enjoined me eagerly.

Note: *a) The expression does not correlate in meaning with the phrase* ***don't mention the war****—(UK) don't speak about things that could cause an argument or tension:* In today's world of "don't mention the war" or say anything to upset the European Union, I really did believe these great little reads had long disappeared.

b) The expression does not correlate in meaning with the phrase ***never tell me****—(also: don't tell me) used to emphatically express incredulity or disappointment:* "Rosalie, never tell me you've been talking about Alexi this whole time!" "Why, yes," said Rosalie in dismay.

don't talk to me about it—is used as an exclamation against discussing smth.: If you want to know more, read a book, or talk to Sharon or Allison. Just don't talk to me about it anymore.

See also: don't tell me / say no more.

don't sweat it • don't sweat the small stuff

don't sweat it—(U.S. sl.) don't worry: Don't sweat it! We've got plenty of time to get there before the show starts.

Note: *The expression does not correlate in meaning with the phrase* ***no sweat****—(sl.) used to say that one can do smth. with no difficulty or problem:* "Do you think you'll be able to manage all those boxes yourself?" "Yeah, no sweat!"

don't sweat the small stuff—(U.S. sl.) don't worry about things that are not important: You may have heard the phrase don't sweat the small stuff. The person that said that wasn't selling his home.

don't tell me • say no more

don't tell me—(also: never tell me) is used to express incredulity, disappointment, or dismay: "Don't tell me we've got to go through that again," said one executive member in an audible groan.

say no more—you need not add anything *(said when in the course of a conversation one party communicates his total understanding of smth.):* I hadn't thought much about this post, actually, as a piece of writing. But say no more: I know well enough not to argue with such a lovely woman.

Note: *The expression does not correlate in meaning with the phrase* ***it goes without saying****— it is too obvious or well known:* It goes without saying that a good first impression is critical.

See also: don't mention it / don't talk to me about it.

don't you forget it • forget it

don't you forget it—an admonitory phrase used after a statement to emphasize the idea: If it wasn't for them, we wouldn't have all this, and don't you forget it.

forget it—(imper.) 1. take no more notice of it; don't mention it: "What do I owe you for lunch?" "Forget it." 2. don't even think about it: If you're expecting a description of what those thugs did to us, please forget it.

door holder • doorkeeper

door holder—a device for holding a door open: Babyproof your home by using door stops and door holders to make it safer for your baby.

door keeper—a man who stands at the door of an establishment and admits only those qualified to enter: We inquired of the door-keeper, whereupon a woman came out to see us.

Note: *The expression does not correlate in meaning with the compound* ***gatekeeper****—1. a guard who tends a gate:* The receptionist finally gave the OK for the door to be opened by the gatekeeper. 2. *a person or group that controls access to smb. or smth.:* As our representative, they serve as our "gatekeeper" in controlling the flood of information from the various media organizations.

dot one's i's and cross one's t's • mind one's p's and q's

dot one's i's and cross one's t's—(also: dot the i's and cross the t's) be very thorough; pay attention to small details: When you do an investigation of somebody very prominent, make sure you dot your i's and cross your t's.

mind one's p's and q's—be careful of one's actions and behavior; act and speak correctly: You'll have to mind your p's and q's if you want to be invited there again.

double as someone • double for someone

double as someone—(of an actor) act the part of two characters in the same play: Peck doubled as the hearty Yorkshireman and the sinister Sir Mulberry Hawk in "Nicholas Nickleby."

double for someone—act as a replacement for a person who is ill, on holiday, etc.: I was just a stuntman on the film, but I doubled for the head villain himself, Mr. Suzuki.

double bed • twin bed

double bed—a bed for two people: Each room sleeps two in a double bed, and we can provide a camp bed at additional cost.

twin bed—one of a matching pair of single beds: Students

are assigned to single gender bedrooms with a twin bed for each occupant.

double-decker • twin-deck

double-decker—1. a bus with an upper level: Ride the bus just to say you rode a double decker, but stick to the Tube for speed and ease of use. 2. a sandwich with two layers of filling: He was clearly more interested in eating a double decker and didn't even have the decency to ask my name.

twin-deck—1. part of a music center with two cassette or CD recorders in it: Make your own recordings with this twin deck CD recorder. 2. *(attrib.)* is used of aircraft that have an upper and a lower deck: This twin-deck aircraft will carry more than 500 passengers in a three-class configuration.

double room • twin room

double room—a room in a hotel, etc. with a double bed for two people: The accusations were based on evidence that the couple traveled to Wildwood where they rented a double room.

twin room—a room in a hotel, etc. with twin beds for two people: In the event of a double room not being available in your hotel, a twin room will be allocated.

double time • two time

double time—a much faster rate than specified or previously used: Time was when this old heart would have throbbed in double-time at the sight of such a fairy form!

two time—*(attrib.)* 1. is used of smth. that has happened twice *(often in sports contexts):* John Barnes was quick to downplay any worries about his two-time championship team. 2. said of an unfaithful or treacherous person: Rob was planning to defend a two-time crook being charged with conspiracy to murder.

Note: *The expression does not correlate in meaning with its formal French counterpart* ***deux temps****—a kind of waltz, more rapid than the ordinary:* The few people that were there were dancing the *trois temps*—one is only allowed to dance the *deux temps* when the Empress is there.

doublespeak • speak with a double tongue

doublespeak—*(also: doubletalk)* use deliberately imprecise, ambiguous language to disguise the actual meaning: Characterizing Godsey as a "word craftsman" in his responses to the committee's probes, the report said, "...he has masterfully doublespoken in many instances."

speak with a double tongue—said of a speech characterized by duplicity, hypocrisy, and double standard: Sandra really bungled it when she spoke with a double tongue on the subject of affirmative action, or racial preferences.

down and out • up and out

down and out—1. said of a person without means of livelihood: "You've never been down and out, I imagine, Mr. Forsyte?" "No," answered Soames. *2. (of business, etc.)* lacking resources or prospects: The local housing industry is down and out. *Cf.: down but not out—said of smb. who is down on his luck or suffered a serious setback but feels hopeful:* Though analysts feel that Khin Nyunt is down but not out, as of now the chances of his return to power are not bright.

up and out—*(UK)* convalescent; no longer in bed: There was Phyllis to help me recoup and now I am up and out again getting into trouble just like before.

down below • down under

down below—1. in a lower part of a building, ship, etc.: Someone was with me and we proceeded to open the hatch to the flooded compartment down below. 2. under the ocean or sea: Wherever there's a lot of seaweed at the surface, you will probably find some sort of big fish down below.

down under—*(coll.)* said of Australia or New Zealand: The last time I was Down Under was ten years ago. It was my second visit to Australia.

See also: down here / here below.

down for the count • out for the count

down for the count—1. *(of a boxer)* knocked down and unable to get back up for the count of ten: West went down for the count, lying motionless on the floor. 2. soundly defeated: The conservatives appeared to be down for the count. Yesterday they failed to win a vote of no confidence.

out for the count—1. = *down for the count 1:* Now that Nuruddin is within punching distance, he'll put him out for the count. 2. = *down for the count 2:* Diversity and multi-culturalism are by no means out for the count in the School of Public Health. 3. unconscious: I was out for the count. Before I lost complete state of consciousness, I felt my cell phone slipping out of my hand. 4. very fast asleep: I knew the children were tired. Look at them. They are both out for the count.

down here • here below

down here—1. in the place where we are right now: The weather affects how we think, move, and feel. Talking about the weather, it is hot and dry down here. 2. is used of a place which lies more to the south: If you're planning on taking your yacht to the Bahamas, something we do regularly down here in Florida, here's some advice. 3. at the foot of the page; later in an article, etc.: Write down here goals that you would like to tackle. Start with the easiest first and tick off any activity you achieve.

here below—1. = *down here 3:* We give here below the list of all the points that must be mandatory checked when purchasing this product. 2. *(liter.)* here on Earth: I might have a confidential fit of laughter with you over this melodramatic life which has been appointed me to live here below.

See also: down below / down under.

down low • low down

down low—1. *(coll.)* secret or private: Their eye contact seems to indicate that there may have been a little down low action going on between the two. 2. *(sl.)* is used of married men who secretly engage in homosexual activities: Some down low men consider themselves monogamous if they only sleep with one man.

low down—1. despicable; deserving of contempt or scorn: Only low-down cowards post under other people's names. If you don't have the guts to post something under your own name, don't even bother. 2. gloomy; depressed: Sellman was definitely in a low down mood today. He made a mess with the police, his clients and his family. 3. *(Jazz)* blues or pop music that has a very strong, repeated bass part: He allowed Handy to pursue it only if he didn't get involved in what his parents called "that low-down" music—ragtime and blues.

down on someone • down to someone

down on someone—*(coll.)* expressing strong disapproval of smb.; reprimanding a person severely: "They're down on her for some reason or other," he told himself. "Angry, most likely, because she's hung on to her boy."

down to someone—being the responsibility of smb.; being incumbent upon a person: You need to be a good communicator to get your business vision across. Remember the success of your business is down to you.

Note: *The expression is not antonymous in meaning to the phrase* ***up to someone****— = down to someone:* The success of your business is up to you, your efforts and your commitment.

down on something • up on something

down on something—showing dislike or hostility toward

smth.: Lots of people were very down on the idea of paying for products that they aren't using.

up on something—well informed or up-to-date about smth.: Most of the psychiatrists in this country are not up on the latest medications available.

down someone's street • up someone's street

down someone's street—(coll., also: down someone's alley) within smb.'s competence or interest: The historical line of inquiry is outside your scope, but the analysis of the book is right down your street.

up someone's street—(also: up someone's alley) = down someone's street: A great many of the books published today are, as the saying is, right up her street.

down-to-date • up-to-date

down-to-date—present-day; contemporary: The down-to-date traveler discovered that without the aid of airplanes it was only just possible to equal Fogg's record.

up-to-date— = *down-to-date:* The Abbey was innocent of anything so up to date as central heating.

down to earth • down to the ground

down to earth—pragmatic; realistic: The committee will include some down-to-earth people who know something about what goes on.

down to the ground—(coll.) 1. thoroughly; completely: He looks as if he could be trusted down to the ground. 2. said of smth. that is very typical of a person: He made some rude remarks, but then that's Bill down to the ground.

down-turn • turn-down

down-turn—a decline, especially in economic or business activity: The economy has already demonstrated that it can suffer a mild downturn in manufacturing.

turn-down—1. the turned-down part of smth.: I showed him the turn-down, only the turn-down, of your note. 2. said of the action of rejecting: I look back on that period of sour welcome and curt turn-down with feelings I cannot express. 3. *(U.S.)* smb. who is rejected, especially as unfit for military service: We've gotten a lot of turndowns, yeah; but we've gotten guys who're willing, too. 4. = *down-turn:* How far Americans could continue running up debts during an economic turndown was not clear.

drag one's feet • drag one's foot

drag one's feet—(also: drag one's heels) delay doing smth. or doing it very slowly: It's quite clear that the Government have been dragging their feet over this bill.

drag one's foot—let one's foot touch the ground and be pulled along as one moves: George limped back toward the cabin, dragging his foot along the ground.

Note: *The expression does not correlate in meaning with the nominal compound* ***foot-dragging****— deliberate slowness or delay:* Parliamentarians again expressed concern over foot-dragging on legislative changes.

See also: pull foot / pull someone's leg.

drama school • play school

drama school—a college which specializes in the teaching of acting: Known as a major drama school, The New School for Drama provides a theatrical education for those choosing a career in acting.

play school—school for children under five: Ryan attends a play school two days a week and will likely be attending preschool later this year.

draw a veil over something • veil something

draw a veil over something—(also: throw a veil over something) refrain from discussing smth.; be secretive about smth.: Let us draw a veil over the rest of the episode.

veil something—disguise or obscure smth. so as to hide the real nature of it: The book veils its critique of authoritarian politics in a fairy tale setting.

draw away • draw off

draw away—1. move off; move away: The crowd cheered as the ship drew slowly away. 2. move ahead of competitors (in a race): The best runner was beginning to draw away. 3. isolate oneself socially: She has drawn away lately and we can't find out why.

draw off—1. = *draw away 1:* The ships drew off at sunset, but celebrated the expected victory by blowing trumpets. 2. *(of troops)* retreat; withdraw: The army drew off to await fresh developments elsewhere.

draw in one's claws • draw in one's horns

draw in one's claws—(also: pull in one's claws) be less hostile and aggressive: They have drawn in their claws, and have become innocent and demure.... The intolerant bigotry of the dark ages is seemingly renounced.

draw in one's horns—(also: pull in one's horns) be less keen or active, and more careful: Nor is there any reason to think that Tyson has learned to draw in his horns where women are concerned.

draw out • pull out

draw out—1. *(of troops)* march out of camp or quarters: The enthusiastic troops drew out in formidable strength beneath the holy banner. 2. *(of a vehicle)* move across traffic: Suddenly the car in front of us drew out and nearly caused an accident. 3. extend in length; become longer: The days are now beginning to draw out. 4. *(Racing)* get gradually farther ahead: The favorite drew out and won by two lengths.

pull out—1. leave a place; move out: We reached the station too late just as the train was pulling out. 2. = *draw out 2:* The car in front pulled out to overtake just as I was about to overtake it. 3. *(of troops)* move away; withdraw: Troops are pulling out of these troubled areas. 4. extricate oneself from an unfavorable condition: He's been dogged by failure for years; now he's working strenuously to pull out. 5. withdraw from an undertaking: He knows if he keeps his money in the business he will lose it, so he has pulled out.

draw someone in • pull someone in

draw someone in—1. *(of an actor, performance, etc.)* attract the public: This play always drew in large crowds. 2. persuade a person to participate; involve smb.: It's your private quarrel, don't try to draw me in.

pull someone in—1. = *draw someone in 1:* Its unusual menu, prompt service and excellent location is pulling the crowds in. 2. = *draw someone in 2:* Against my better judgment, I got pulled in to help with the school concert again. 3. *(of an offender or a suspect)* arrest; detain: When I put a person under house arrest and she breaks it, I pull her in.

draw someone out • pull someone out

draw someone out—encourage a person to talk about one's private thoughts: Mary is very quiet; try to draw her out at the party.

pull someone out—cause smb. to regain cheerfulness or good health: You're feeling low because you're overtired; a good holiday will pull you out.

draw something in • pull something in

draw something in—1. bring smth. in by pulling: When the fisherman drew in his net he found in it a remarkable fish. 2. *(of air)* breathe in; inhale: Draw in a deep breath and let it out slowly. 3. *(of a piece of clothing)* draw tight or cause to shrink: This billowing dress can be drawn in by adding a belt. 4. *(of spending)* reduce: If prices continue to rise, we shall have to draw in our spending even further.

pull something in—1. = *draw something in 1:* He ran out of worms so after a while he pulled in his fishing line and walked away. 2. *(of an animal)* control; restrain: Your horse is trying to go too fast; you must pull him in. 3. *(coll.)* earn money: You can pull in over 6,000 a year at that factory. 4. = *draw something in 4:* You now have to pull in your spending somehow.

draw something out • pull something out

draw something out—1. take smth. out; remove smth.: He put his hand in the drawer, and drew out a gun. 2. stretch smth.: Draw out the wire until it is very thin. 3. lengthen or prolong smth.: The politician drew out his speech to almost two hours. 4. take money from a bank account: I shall have to draw out some more money to pay all these people. 5. formulate a plan, program, etc.: The committee drew out a plan for the reorganization.

pull something out—1. = *draw something out 1:* Before I could see what he was doing, he had pulled out a gun. 2. = *draw something out 2:* The wool from the sheep has to be pulled out until it forms a thread. 3. produce particular facts, ideas, or an answer: I hope you can pull out a better answer before the end of the meeting.

draw something up • pull something up

draw something up—1. move smth. by pulling forward: The boat was drawn up and made fast at the landing. 2. *(of a bridge)* lift at one end so as to prevent passage over it or allow passage through the channel which it crosses: The gate was shut, the bridge was drawn up. 3. *(of a vehicle)* bring to a stop; place close to a building: A van was drawn up on a path outside the door. 4. formulate a plan, program, etc.: The report was drawn up by men who had the means of knowing the truth.

pull something up—1. *(of weeds)* take out of the ground: You'll find my mother in the garden as usual, pulling up unwanted plants. 2. = *draw something up 1:* The only mark that was left behind by Angus was the mark where he pulled his boat up on to the shore. 3. = *draw something up 2:* A few minutes later, Rupert crossed the drawbridge and it was pulled up. 4. = *draw something up 3:* He had pulled his car up to a gentle stop, swung sideways in his seat, and looked at the cottage. 5. *(coll.)* improve smth.: You'll have to pull up your English to a higher standard if you want to pass the examination.

draw the badger • overdraw one's badger

draw the badger—provoke a person to reveal his thoughts, etc.: The Parnellite taunts regarding Balfour's indifference have at last drawn the badger.

overdraw one's badger—(dated sl., in humorous reference to the above) overdraw one's banking account: His checks no longer drew the cash.... He had overdrawn his badger.

draw the curtain over something • ring down the curtain on something

draw the curtain over something—(also: draw the curtain on something) refrain from discussing smth.; be secretive about smth.: The current leader has been trying to draw the curtain over the events of the past decade.

ring down the curtain on something—(also: bring down the curtain on something) cause an activity, business, etc. to come to an end: Very shortly, school bells will ring down the curtain on the final term of the millennium.

draw the line at something • draw the line under something

draw the line at something—refuse to do smth. because it is more than one is prepared to do: I draw the line at nappy-changing, not because I am a man but because I don't like surprises of that nature.

draw the line under something—try to forget about a bad situation, etc., so that one can start again: Vicky and I agreed to draw the line under our disagreements and try to look towards our future together.

dreamlike air • dreamy air

dreamlike air—is used to describe smth. that seems illusory or unreal: The fortress retains the dreamlike air of a fairytale castle that one might read of in a historical romance.

dreamy air—is used of the facial expression of smb. whose thoughts are far away: He appeared to be a quiet and shy redhead with the dreamy air of a poet.

dress someone down • dress someone up

dress someone down—1. make smb. wear informal clothes for an occasion: Craig was dressed up in a Brioni suit, and what would be the point of that if they were to dress him down for the movie? 2. *(coll.)* scold or reprimand a person: Well, I let Chris have it, dressing him down for his beard! Needless to say, I lost a friend.

dress someone up—1. dress smb. formally; make a person wear his best clothes: Mr. Wilde procured the boy a suit of clothes to dress him up like a gentleman's son. 2. make smb. wear fancy clothing; disguise a person: I dressed her up as a doctor and painstakingly made her rehearse lines for the fancy dress competition at school.

dressing table • kitchen dresser

dressing table—a low table with a mirror at which one sits while dressing, applying makeup, etc.: The following day, in the late afternoon, she'd been sitting in front of her dressing-table rearranging her jewellery in its box...

kitchen dresser—a tall piece of furniture with cupboards below and shelves on the top half: Last bank holiday found me on my knees, clearing out the cupboards in the kitchen dresser, a ritual to which I return every five years or so.

dried bread • dry bread

dried bread—bread that has lost all the water in it: My worldly goods are a knapsack with some dried bread in it, and in my breast-pocket a Bible.

dry bread—bread which is plain and not covered with butter or jam: He managed to swallow a little soup and dry bread.

drink hard • drink hard liquor

drink hard—(also: drink heavily) indulge in alcohol to excess: Jimmy Muir is a typical factory worker who drinks hard and lacks any kind of respect for authority.

drink hard liquor—consume strong alcoholic beverages (in preference over wine or beer): My boyfriend acts like an ass regardless of what he drinks although he truly believes that he only acts out when he drinks hard liquor.

drive someone to the wall • drive someone up the wall

drive someone to the wall—push a person to the last extremity: He complained that the company was being driven to the wall by the workers' demands for higher wages.

drive someone up the wall—make smb. very angry or mentally confused: Someone is running a jackhammer outside of my office and it's driving me up the wall.

driver's license • driver's permit

driver's license—(also: driving license) a document which states that a person may operate a motorized vehicle: I was forced to produce my driver's license and all other identification I had on me.

driver's permit—(U.S.) provisional license for the learner drivers *(to drive they must be accompanied by smb. with a driver's license):* I was up early so that Heidi could go on a field trip. She still has a driver's permit and so I needed to go with her on the drive.

driving test • test drive

driving test—an examination of a person's ability to drive a car: What is wanted is a more radical reform in the driving test calculated to lift the standard of roadcraft.

test drive—a drive in a car one thinks of buying, etc. to judge its qualities: Before signing a satisfaction note inspect the vehicle carefully and, if possible, take it for a test drive.

drop a bomb • drop bombs

drop a bomb—(also: drop the bomb) create a sensation: Macintosh users have been waiting for a fast, stable, operating system. Apple has really dropped the bomb in this area.

drop bombs—(Jazz drummers) place accents in music using the foot pedal of a bass drum: Joe Jones? He was the first drummer to drop bombs.

drop a bundle • drop one's bundle

drop a bundle—(sl.) lose or spend a large amount of money: Over the years, I've dropped a bundle on clients at that restaurant. *Cf.: make a bundle—(sl.) make a lot of money:* If someone had helped you get started like that, you'd have made a bundle on the stock market too.

drop one's bundle—(Austral., NZ sl.) 1. lose nerve; give up hope: Meg has had enough. Feeling unappreciated she drops her bundle and demands a few days off. 2. *(of a woman)* give birth: She'll switch between jobs, pay off her mortgage, maybe drop her bundle, and be hell-bent on a comfortable retirement...

drop a dime • penny drops, the

drop a dime—(U.S. sl.) give information about a person or a situation discreetly (making a phone call): You'd better tell her the truth—someone's bound to drop a dime if you lie.

penny drops, the—(UK coll.) said when a person finally understands smth.: I sat and thought for a moment and then the penny dropped.

drop a hint • give a hint

drop a hint—give a slight or indirect indication or suggestion: I'll just drop her a hint not to be surprised at anything she sees.

give a hint—1. = *drop a hint:* She gave him a hint that she would like him to leave. 2. *(of things)* foretell the coming of smth.; be the harbinger: A small black cloud gave a hint of a coming storm.

drop back • drop behind

drop back—1. fail to maintain one's position; be outstripped: The early leaders drop back and allow others to make the running. 2. go down; decrease: The unemployment figures dropped back last month.

drop behind—1. = *drop back 1:* Don't drop behind now, just when you're doing so well. 2. fail to maintain a schedule of payments, etc.: If your payments of rent drop behind, you will be asked to leave.

See also: back drop / backdrop.

drop dead • drop-dead

drop dead—(sl.) is used as an exclamation of annoyance directed at a person: When Tim's wife heard this she said: "Tell him to just drop dead!"

drop-dead—(sl.) extremely; in a spectacular way: Thank you so much Garcelle for being so drop-dead beautiful, lovely, and talented.

drop down • fall down

drop down—1. come down suddenly: I heard a noise from the well and saw that the cat had dropped down. 2. bend downwards; sink down: When they saw the pursuers they dropped down to take cover. 3. *(coll.)* pay an unexpected visit: Let's drop down to his summer home and see if he's there.

fall down—1. = *drop down 1:* The hunter fired and the deer fell down dead. 2. *(of a building, etc.)* collapse: The steel scaffolding fell down and narrowly missed a couple of bystanders. 3. *(of a project, etc.)* be unsuccessful; fail: His plan fell down when it proved too costly.

drop from the skies • fall to the ground

drop from the skies—(also: drop from heaven) appear unexpectedly as if by magic: "Good gracious, miss," I said, still doubting my senses, "have you dropped from the skies?"

fall to the ground—(of plans, etc.) fail; come to nothing: The whole scheme fell to the ground, although all the details were thought out.

See also: come down to earth / go to earth.

drop in • fall in

drop in—1. collapse inwards; give way: The roof of the tunnel hasn't been properly supported; it shows signs of dropping in. 2. *(coll.)* visit a person casually: He usually drops in at my place on his way home.

fall in—1. fall accidentally into smth.: The child was near the river and I was frightened he would fall in. 2. = *drop in 1:* They are afraid that the whole building will fall in on them. 3. *(Military)* form into ranks: At first light Chelmsford ordered his men to fall in and the column marched away. 4. *(legal)* expire: As the leases of these old properties fall in, they are being pulled down to make way for office blocks. 5. agree: Once the chairman had stated his decision, the rest of the committee fell in.

drop in on someone • drop on someone

drop in on someone—(coll.) visit a person, usually without having arranged it before: I dropped in on her for coffee the other morning.

drop on someone—(coll.) reprimand or punish a person: You'll have to mind your p's and q's or else you'll be dropped on.

Note: *The expression does not correlate in meaning with the phrase* ***fall on someone****—1. attack a person:* They fell on me like an avalanche with teeth and dagger, and hatred without check or limits of sanity. 2. *used of a cost, responsibility, etc. to be borne by a person:* So it fell on me to do all the packing, making sure we had all the necessary equipment.

drop into someone's lap • land in someone's lap

drop into someone's lap—(also: fall into someone's lap) be achieved or obtained without any effort: It would not be safe to assume that victory will drop into our lap at the next election.

land in someone's lap—become an unwelcome responsibility: These problems have landed in the lap of Donald Jackson, an unassuming manager with little international experience.

drop off • fall off

drop off—1. become detached: The handle of the door has dropped off. 2. become abruptly much lower: The cliff drops off suddenly here, be careful. 3. *(coll.)* leave a vehicle; get off: Thanks for the ride, I'll drop off here. 4. become less; deteriorate: The quality of performance has dropped off since last year. 5. *(coll.)* fall asleep: I went to bed early but for some reason I couldn't drop off. 6. *(euph.)* die: He would probably drop off quietly with suppressed gout.

fall off—1. = *drop off 1:* My top button has fallen off. 2. = *drop off 2:* The land falls off here towards the river. 3. = *drop off 4:* Their enthusiasm seems to be falling off a bit. 4. cease participation: Some of our most loyal members have now fallen off.

drop out • fall out

drop out—1. leave a school, etc. before the end of the course: He has dropped out, and won't attend college any more. 2. *(coll.)* withdraw (from an undertaking): You can drop out from the rat race, hoping that you can make it on your own. 3. come out: As she picked up the envelope, a key dropped out.

fall out—1. *(Military)* leave the ranks: At the end of the parade, the battalion fell out. 2. quarrel: We're not going to fall out over this, are we? 3. come to pass; happen: It fell out that the men were not needed. 4. = *drop out 3:* A little roll of dollar-notes fell out upon the ground.

drop the ball • take up the ball

drop the ball—let smth. go wrong; make an embarrassing error: In my opinion, this is one area where Microsoft has really dropped the ball when it comes to spam filtering.

Note: *a) The expression is not equivalent in meaning to the phrase* ***drop a brick****—(sl.) do smth. foolish; say smth. stupid or indiscreet:* It was hinted to me pretty plainly that I had dropped a brick when I told my brother I didn't like Mary.

b) The expression is not antonymous in meaning to the phrase ***carry the ball****— assume the responsibility (taking the most important or difficult part in an action):* Who will carry the ball? Who will have responsibility for paying the bills and balancing the check book?

take up the ball—(also: pick up the ball and run with it) take one's turn in smth.: Unfortunately, it's not likely I'll be able to respond at greater length.... But perhaps others will take up the ball.

dropout • fallout

dropout—1. a person who "drops out" from a course of study or from society: Many dropouts leave school long before their senior year. The ninth grade year is a particularly difficult year for students. 2. *(attrib.)* is used of people who leave a course of study, membership of a society, etc.: Is there a correlation between the dropout rate and the amount of money a school district spends?

fallout—1. radioactive dust or particles (created by a nuclear explosion): Measurements were made on the concentration of fallout in the atmosphere and in rain water. 2. lasting negative consequences of an event or situation: Our ability to have as much sugar as we crave has had serious fallout on the health of Americans. 3. = *dropout 2:* Main reasons for this high fallout rate: financial difficulties, lack of interest, parental resistance to "useless" further education.

dry blanket • wet blanket

dry blanket—(Austral. sl.)—said of a hot afternoon or day: It's like a bloody dry blanket in here today.

wet blanket—(coll.) a person who discourages enthusiasm or cheerfulness: Jane would spoil the whole thing; she is such a wet blanket.

duck shoot • shoot ahead of the duck

duck shoot—(U.S. coll.) a very easy task: The market gets crowded after midday and is a duck-shoot for pickpockets.

shoot ahead of the duck— think and plan ahead; try to anticipate future tendencies: When you adopt a new technology, shoot ahead of the duck. Look at what you do today in terms of longer trends...

due for something • due to something

due for something—said of smth. expected as set by agreement, etc.: He is due for work in India, which he is looking forward to.

due to something—1. caused by smth.: This change of meaning is due to misunderstanding the nature of the word. 2. appropriate to smth.; right for smth.: He is too conscious of what is due to his position.

dumb as a fox • dumb as a stump

dumb as a fox—smart and cunning: He may appear to be harmless, but the truth is, he is as dumb as a fox, and he and his gang are destroying this country.

dumb as a stump—(derog.) not very smart: I think Philip is as dumb as a stump. He should open his eyes and see that his sweet little Belle is just using him.

dust bowl • dustpan

dust bowl—said of an area that has no vegetation because of drought, dust storms, etc.: The worst of the storms were concentrated in an area called the dust bowl by the people of the time.

dustpan—a short-handled pan or scoop into which dust is swept: The tiny shards of near-powdered glass won't easily brush into the dustpans.

Note: *The compound does not correlate in meaning with* ***dustbin****— a container for household rubbish:* To prevent the toilets from getting blocked, materials like paper and cotton should be thrown in the dustbin.

E

each and every one • each one

each and every one—(emphatic) every individual or thing in a group without exception: I want each and every one of you to know that this administration recognizes the vital role you play.

each one—(of two or more people or things) every one taken separately: But as great a day as this is for the whole church, I want us to reflect upon what it means to each one of us individually.

each to his own • every man for himself

each to his own—is used to say that it is acceptable for people to have different preferences: "I find it hard to believe that anyone enjoys gardening." "Ah well, each to his own."

every man for himself—said of people trying to save themselves from a difficult situation without trying to help anyone else: "It was not the behaviour of a friend." "My dear boy," he said. "Have you not yet learnt that it's every man for himself?"

eagle vulture • vulturine eagle

eagle vulture—a large black-and-white western African bird *(Gypohierax angolensis):* You should also see herons and eagle vultures. Around you will be the expected wildlife of the African bush.

vulturine eagle—a black-and-white eagle *(Aquila verreauxii)* of southern Africa: The vulturine eagle makes the mountain precipices its abode.

earlier on • early on

earlier on—at an earlier time: Oh, by the way, your son telephoned earlier on to say he wouldn't be able to come.

early on—at an early stage of smth.: We decided early on that we wanted to create a site that was attractive, but more importantly was easy to navigate.

early bird • early man

early bird—1. smb. who gets up early; an early riser: If you like to get up early, you are an early bird and will probably perform better in the morning. 2. smb. who arrives earlier than the expected or arranged time: Be an early bird to get a table at this restaurant which is usually very crowded.

early man—a prehistoric human being: We need to understand the degree to which religion integrated with the life of the early man.

Early English • Old English

Early English—1. Middle and Early Modern English language (1066–1400): Yet another Early English text appears under the editorship of an American scholar. 2. the early style of Gothic architecture which developed in England in the 13th century: So far as architecture is concerned the book covers three periods, Early English, Geometric, and Early Decorated.

Old English—the English language of the period before the Norman conquest in the 11th century: In this dictionary, the language of England before 1100 is called, as a whole, "Old English."

earth people • people of the Earth

earth people—1. *(also: earth-men)* people whose life is closely associated with the natural or material (as opposed to the spiritual) world: They are an earth people and their legend is horrific, dramatic, almost senseless. 2. *(Earth people)* residents of the planet Earth in science fiction *(also: earth-men):* It was discovered that some Earth people reacted violently to visitors from outer space. 3. *(sl., joc.)* people who are "normal," that is, not alcohol or drug addicted: The brain of the alcoholic is different from that of "earth people." First is the phenomenon of craving.

people of the Earth—1. people of the world; people dwelling on the earth: It is essential that we people of the Earth eliminate the fearsome specters of water shortages. 2. = *earth people 2:* It was the year 2107 and the people of the Earth had finally united in the cause of greater knowledge. Disease, famine and war had long gone away.

East Indiaman • East Indian

East Indiaman—*(hist.)* a sailing ship of large tonnage engaged in the East India trade: I have taken my berth in an East Indiaman which sails on the twentieth of June.

East Indian—1. smb. descended from the indigenous peoples of the Indian sub-continent: East Indians is the name given to the descendants of those who came to British Guyana from India. 2. a person of mixed European and Asian parentage: "Who is she?" "An East Indian, I should guess, by her dark complexion."

easy about someone • easy on someone

easy about someone—free from worry or anxiety about smb.: He was quite easy about Agellius, who had, as he considered, successfully made off with himself.

easy on someone—not strict or severe enough with a person: He deserves the punishment, but do be easy on him.

eat a peck of dirt • eat dirt

eat a peck of dirt—put up with insult and abuse; submit to humiliating treatment: In times of revolution a good many pecks of dirt have to be eaten.

eat dirt—*(coll.)* 1. = *eat a peck of dirt:* Lord Fitzurse made up for the dirt which they had been eating by the splendor of his entertainment. 2. *(also: eat someone's dust)* trail another competitor in a race: He was the leader in the bike race until he ate dirt and was passed by almost everyone else.

See also: dirt-eater / dirt-eating.

eat away • eat out

eat away—eat continuously; eat as much as one likes: Be prepared to spend at least two hours chatting and eating away, relishing every minute of Fran's delicious German cooking.

Note: *The expression does not correlate in meaning with the phrase* ***eat away from home****—have one's meals in cafeterias, etc. rather than at home:* When eating away from home, people eat either larger quantities or higher calorie foods.

eat out—eat in a restaurant, etc. instead of at home: Sometimes eating out can be cheaper than buying a weeks worth of groceries. *Cf.: eat in—eat or dine at home:* I would certainly recommend the hotel to people who prefer to eat in and cook for themselves.

eat away at something • eat away something

eat away at something—destroy smth. gradually: Attempts have been made to stop the Sphinx from eroding even more. The blowing sands in the desert are gradually eating away at it.

eat away something—1. destroy smth. by eating: The monkeys had eaten away most of the mangroves, and the only ones that remained were shielded by steel cages. 2. destroy smth. by chemical action: Structures such as bridges, buildings, and monuments are also at risk, as they can be literally eaten away by the acid.

eat like a pig • make a pig of oneself

eat like a pig—*(also: eat like pigs)* eat in a greedy or disgusting manner: He has terrible table manners, he eats like a pig.

make a pig of oneself—*(coll.)* eat gluttonously; overindulge in food *(also: pig oneself):* I'm afraid I made a pig of myself at dinner.

eat off something • eat out of something

eat off something—1. eat one's food from a certain container: Put vegetables on oven safe plate (you will be eating off this plate) and put in toaster oven. 2. eat part of a piece of food: "She always brought in a cake for him," Foley said. "People would eat off the cake for the rest of the day."

eat out of something— = *eat off something 1:* Whenever he eats lunch, he eats out of his own bowl and uses his own utensils that he keeps for himself.

eat one's head off • eat someone's head off

eat one's head off—1. said of an animal whose upkeep costs more than it will sell for: That ox has been here all winter and ate his head off. 2. *(coll.)* eat excessively or gluttonously: I am not weighing in today as I just got back from New York and ate my head off while I was there.

eat someone's head off—*(coll., also: bite someone's head off)* speak to smb. in a rude and angry manner; severely criticize a person: I have the worst temper in the world and will eat your head off at the slightest thing.

eat one's heart out • eat your heart out

eat one's heart out—be unhappy and miserable, usually for a long period of time: Raleigh, in prison, was eating his heart out in the desire for freedom.

eat your heart out—(humorous) is used to say that one is even better than the (famous) person mentioned: Choi Min-sik gives what I think is the greatest performance ever, so eat your heart out De Niro, Brando, and Pauly Shore.

eat someone alive • eat someone up

eat someone alive—(coll., also: eat someone for breakfast) 1. rebuke or criticize smb. severely: The evolutionists will eat me alive for this, but doesn't the intricate design of our world allow for the possibility of a creator? 2. overwhelm, harm, or thoroughly defeat a person: Yes, they ate us alive but allow me to lay down some reasons why it was still an awesome game that we played!

eat someone up—1. *(coll.)* acclaim a person's stage performance: Wait until you see the way they're going to eat me up in the court scene in "Saint Elba." 2. = *eat someone alive 2:* Others would not fail to make themselves greater or stronger by eating up their neighbors. 3. *(of jealousy, desire, etc.)* torment a person *(often Passive):* His drawings and a school essay hinted at the despair that was eating him up.

eat someone out • eat someone out of house and home

eat someone out—(coll., also: eat someone alive) rebuke or criticize a person severely: I learned some supervisory skills since one time our captain came in and started eating me out for a maintenance problem.

eat someone out of house and home—said humorously of people or animals that eat a lot of food in smb.'s home (thus ruining the person): "Looks like the party is in full swing." "Yeah. And they're eating me out of house and home."

economic system • economical system

economic system—the system concerned with economics of a country: What has gone wrong with the economic system during the last ten years?

economical system—a system which does not require a lot of money to operate: This system was extremely economical because it ran on half-price electricity.

effect something • have an effect upon something

effect something—cause smth. to happen; act so as to bring smth. about: Who are the people that effect changes in our society?

have an effect upon something—affect or influence smth.: We could investigate different seasons of the year and see if this had an effect upon the results.

either ... or • whether ... or

either ... or—is used to indicate that there is a choice between two options: The centre is located favorably in terms of transport facilities and can be reached either by car or by public transport.

whether ... or—is used to introduce two equal possibilities: Whether by car or by public transport—due to our central location there are various possibilities to reach us.

either way • every way

either way—whichever course of action one chooses (out of two alternatives): We could have the car fixed here or get it towed home; either way it will be very expensive.

every way—(also: every each way) 1. in every direction: I pondered over it, and turned it every way in my mind. 2. in every manner; in every respect: Her mind was every way equal to her person.

electric car • electric motor car

electric car—a car that utilizes energy stored in rechargeable battery packs: Electric cars have major limitations; they don't go very fast, and they can't go far without a battery charge.

electric motor car—1. = *electric car:* My guess is that, all other things equal, the electric motor car would pull out ahead of an internal combustion engine.... 2. a self-propelled electric railroad vehicle: Several railroads operate electric motor cars in suburban passenger train service.

embark for something • embark on something

embark for something—start a voyage to a place: I shall stay in the seaport overnight before embarking for the United States.

embark on something—(liter.) start smth. new, usually important or difficult: Mary embarked on her marriage with many hopes and fears.

embarrassed at something • embarrassed with something

embarrassed at something—feeling unease or mental discomfort about smth.: She's embarrassed—embarrassed at being so successful in a profession where so many fail.

embarrassed with something—1. hindered in one's movements or experiencing physical difficulties because of smth.: Seeing he was embarrassed with his luggage, I offered to help him. 2. = *embarrassed at something:* Many kids don't want to be embarrassed with being escorted out, even if it's a friendly escort.

Empire State, the • Empire State of the South, the

Empire State, the—(U.S.) a nickname of the state of New York: The saloon men of Tennessee have not, perhaps, the literary finish of their brethren in the Empire State.

Empire State of the South, the—(U.S.) a nickname of the state of Georgia: Georgia is now known as the Empire State of the South as it is the largest state east of the Mississippi River.

employment agency • employment office

employment agency—a private business that finds employers for those seeking them: "Employment agencies" have been characterized as "a class who trade on the needs of the inexperienced searcher for employment."

employment office—(UK) a government office concerned with advising and finding work for the unemployed: She had gone to the employment office to inquire about becoming a nurse.

end in something • end with something

end in something—1. *(of things)* have smth. at the end: The fish resembles an eel with a broad head and a tail, which ends in a point. 2. finally result in smth.: Hegemonies are impossible, and attempts at them certain to end in armament races and finally in war.

end with something—1. = *end in something 1:* The Phoenix Bird has shining eyes of blue, and its beak ends with a sharp point. 2. = *end in something 2:* With job alerts to keep you in the know, your job search is sure to end with a great new job. 3. finish in smth.: The millennium has ended with war and the 20th century has seen more deaths from war than ever before. 4. finish by saying smth.: I should like to end with reminding members of the purpose of this club. 5. terminate smth.; put an end to smth.: London will demonstrate that there is a new way to finish with terrorism.

See also: end up in something / end up with something.

end it all • get away from it all

end it all—commit suicide: Martine became so depressed during a recent illness that she wanted to "end it all."

Note: *The expression does not correlate in meaning with the phrase* ***to crown it all****—(also: to cap it all) used to emphasize the final item in a series completing a good or bad fortune:* The school had an excellent reputation, its program was in English and to crown it all, it was located in a wonderful city!

get away from it all—escape from city rush, the worry of modern life, etc.: We bought a little house in the country to get away from it all.

end of the earth • end of the land

end of the earth—(also: world's end) the remotest regions of the earth: She is a good woman for a man to have with him when he goes to the ends of the earth.

end of the land—(also: land's end) the remotest region of the country: I journeyed also to Kerch which was the end of the land and really felt like the end of the earth.

end of the world, the • world's end

end of the world, the—the cessation of mortal life; the Apocalypse: The creeping awareness that death was in the room filled the time. Like the end of the world might be. *Cf.: it's not the end of the world—it is not a calamitous matter or situation (is used to console oneself or another person):* Anyway, it's not the end of the world, Gretta. We'll find a way out.

world's end—(also: end of the earth) the remotest regions of the earth: I will follow you to the world's end, if you don't think me too far gone to be out of confinement.

end to end • from end to end

end to end—1. with one end of smth. touching the end of smth. else: The police lined up the lorries end to end across the street to prevent anyone getting by. 2. *(attrib.)* said of technology systems that begin at the server and end at the user: We provide an end-to-end technology solution to guarantee profitable use of resources.

Note: *The expression does not correlate in meaning with the phrase* ***end for end****— used of smth. turned upside down when tumbling or reversed when spinning:* Careering downstream ... they crashed into one driftpile and spun end for end three times.

from end to end—from one extremity to the other; throughout the length of smth.: They crossed a thoroughfare that twinkled and glittered from end to end with moving sky-signs.

end up in something • end up with something

end up in something—reach or arrive at a final (usually unfavorable) condition, circumstance, or place: If we take her too seriously, we will all end up in a mental home.

end up with something—finish with the presence of smth. undesirable: If you put too much coffee you'll know it! And if you don't, you may end up with coffee-flavored dishwater.

See also: end in something / end with something.

enemy of mankind • enemy of the people

enemy of mankind—(euph.) the devil: The ancient enemy of mankind knows us very well. He knows that "lesser evils" are far more productive for his cosmic agenda...

enemy of the people—a common indictment in communist countries against a political opponent: Being a friend of an enemy of the people automatically placed the person under suspicion.

Note: *The expression does not correlate in meaning with the phrase* ***public enemy****— a person regarded as a great threat to a community:* A stake was driven into the ground before his door, as a token that he was a public enemy.

engage in something • engage with something

engage in something—be actively involved with smth.: Those who are too smart to engage in politics are punished by being governed by those who are dumber.

engage with something—1. make an effort to understand and deal with smth.: All religions attempt to engage with the problem of the existence of suffering in this world. 2. *(of part of a machine)* connect with another part of the machine: Make sure the gear on the roller is engaged with the gear on the support.

engaged to someone • engaged with someone

engaged to someone—bound by a promise of marriage to a person: Mary was engaged to Jim for three months before their wedding.

engaged with someone—1. having one's time occupied by a person: You cannot see Mr. Brown just now, as he is engaged with a visitor. 2. involved in hostilities with enemy troops: They could scarcely have reached the camp before they found themselves engaged with the enemy.

enlarge into something • enlarge on something

enlarge into something—expand into smth. bigger: His first publication was a pamphlet, which was afterwards enlarged into a book.

enlarge on something—add detail to smth.; say or write more about smth.: He enlarged on the importance of exercising memory as a habit.

enough to make a cat laugh • enough to make a cat speak

enough to make a cat laugh—said of smth. utterly ridiculous: The idea of a chap like that writing a book: it's enough to make a cat laugh.

enough to make a cat speak—said of smth. very extraordinary or exceptional: I don't know if this article is "enough to make a cat speak," but you should read it.

enter a religious order • take holy orders

enter a religious order—become a member of a religious order; adopt a monastic life: She entered the religious Order of St. Joseph of the Sacred Heart and adopted the name Sister Ignatius of Jesus.

take holy orders—(also: take orders) become a priest in the Anglican Church: Although monks are not necessarily clergymen, many of the body in this country took holy orders.

enter for something • enter upon something

enter for something—join for participation in a contest or competition: They entered for the national championship but were not good enough.

enter upon something—1. make a start on an activity: As soon as we entered upon the task we realized it was going to be difficult. 2. take up a position; assume duties: He enters upon his new appointment at the beginning of June. 3. take possession of smth.: She expects to enter upon her inheritance sometime next year.

enter into something • enter something

enter into something—1. come into smth.; penetrate smth.: The bullet entered into his head at a distance that was longer than his arms, so he couldn't have shot himself. 2. become a member of an organization; join an institution: When I entered into college, it was with the idea to have a career in medicine. 3. participate in smth.; be a party to a contract, etc.: The United States was urged by different countries to enter into negotiations on naval arms control. 4. deal with smth.; consider smth. thoroughly: The reader can have an overall view of problems and then decide if he wants to enter into details. 5. be an important consideration or factor in smth.: He would have to work hard to perfect his art — money doesn't enter into it because almost no artists are rich.

enter something—1. = *enter into something 1:* The exit wound from a bullet is always larger than the hole where the bullet entered the body. 2. = *enter into something 2:* On a personal level, I entered college to not only earn a degree, but to find out about myself. 3. = *enter into something 3:* The defendant's position is that he never knowingly entered the conspiracy charged in the indictment.

equal to something • equal with something

equal to something—1. *(of things)* equal to another thing in price, quality, etc.: A table-tennis ball is roughly equal in size to a golf ball. 2. having the power or ability to do smth.: After our long cooping-up on shipboard we were not equal to any exertion.

equal with something— = *equal to something 1:* The Earth is very tiny, compared with sunspots. Our planet is equal in size with a modest sunspot.

equate something to something • equate something with something

equate something to something—make two things equal: A new regulation required them to equate road workers' wages to those paid to other workers.

equate something with something—1. consider two things to be identical: Why socialized medicine should be equated with socialist medicine I fail to understand. 2. = *equate something to something:* It was traditional right up until the war to equate the wages of constables with that of agricultural laborers.

escape from prison • escape prison

escape from prison—break out of prison: Hundreds of policemen are looking for a man who escaped from Princeville Prison early this morning.

escape prison—avoid being sent to prison: A man who turned police informer to escape prison went on trial yesterday for perjury.

escape with a whole skin • save one's skin

escape with a whole skin—*(also: keep a whole skin)* escape without damage; remain unhurt: Has Esther been quarrelling with you? If she has been you are lucky to have escaped with a whole skin.

save one's skin—1. rescue oneself from death: He was not prepared to dishonor himself by betraying a fellow officer to save his skin. 2. escape from a disagreeable predicament; avoid punishment: I saved my skin by getting the job done on time.

Eve with a lid on • Eve with a moldy lid

Eve with a lid on—*(U.S. diners)* apple pie *(the reference being to the biblical Eve with an apple):* The first couple (Adam and Eve) make an appearance as poached eggs on toast: *Adam and Eve on a Raft.* Eve appears solo as another name for apple pie: *Eve with a Lid On.*

Eve with a moldy lid—*(U.S. diners)* apple pie with a slice of cheese: There are plenty of other short order cook gems like *Eve with a Moldy Lid* and *Zeppelins in a Fog* (sausages in mashed potatoes).

evening dress • evening gown

evening dress—*(also: evening clothes)* clothing worn by men and women for evening social events: When he appeared at the door to meet a correspondent he was in evening dress.

Note: *The expression does not correlate in meaning with the phrase* ***night dress***—*a loose light garment worn by women in bed:* She slipped a housecoat over her night-dress and made her way downstairs.

evening gown—a woman's elegant formal dress: Anna May came out, in a cerise strapless satin evening gown.

Note: *The expression does not correlate in meaning with the phrase* ***night gown***— = *night dress:* Apparently, she had fallen asleep while smoking. The cigarette had dropped on her nightgown, which promptly burst into flame.

everlasting life • life everlasting

everlasting life—life after death: To make this everlasting life as comfortable as possible, the spirit called upon the magical aids and implements provided in its earthly tomb.

life everlasting—1. an American plant *(Anaphalis margaritacea)* grown for ornament: Life everlasting grows under the table, and blackberry vines run round its legs. 2. American cudweed *(Antennaria margaritacea):* Life everlasting is used in many folk remedies for catarrh; also chewed and smoked by boys. 3. = *everlasting life:* I want to believe in life everlasting. At death none of us has exhausted all our possibilities, and I want to go on.

every cloud has a silver lining • every dog has its day

every cloud has a silver lining—*(saying)* every sad or unpleasant situation has a positive side to it: When all else fails, use humor to help you see that every cloud has a silver lining.

every dog has its day—*(saying)* everyone will get a period of success or satisfaction during his lifetime: Every dog has its day, however, and it's often the case that last year's loser becomes this year's winner. *Cf.: into each life some rain must fall*—*(saying) bad or unfortunate things will happen to everyone at some time (originally a quote from Henry Wadsworth Longfellow):* We should be glad that "into each life some rain must fall," for if it weren't for the rain, our joys of the sunny days would wither and die.

Note: *The expression does not correlate in meaning with the phrase* ***dog days of summer, the***—*(also: dog days, the) the hot, sultry period of summer (between early July and early September):* People aren't the only ones in danger during the "dog days of summer." Their pets are too.

every day • everyday

every day—*(adverbial phrase) do smth.* each one of the days: I have been dating a wonderful man for the past two months. My only "problem" is that I want to see him every day.

everyday—*(attrib.)* 1. said of smth. happening or used routinely: Rutledge came in his everyday clothes, giving a long-winded excuse about not having time to get an outfit together. 2. common and familiar: Marr had attempted to play the whole affair down by stating that such incidents and "petty" crimes were "an everyday occurrence."

every man is a king • every man is a king in his own house

every man is a king—*(also: every man a king)* an American catch-phrase implying the necessity for a fair redistribution of the nation's wealth: In our democracy, as the founders noted, every man is a king.

every man is a king in his own house—*(saying)* each man is the ruler of his own domain or property: The lack of a central authority let loose anarchy in the kingdom where every man was virtually a king in his own house.

every man Jack • every Tom, Dick and Harry

every man Jack—*(emphatic coll.)* every individual man; everybody without exception *(also: every Jack man):* I am responsible for the ship's safety and the life of every man Jack aboard of her.

every Tom, Dick and Harry—*(often pejor.)* anyone, especially people that one does not think are important: Bob values his privacy, so doesn't hand out his phone number to every Tom, Dick, and Harry.

every now and then • now and then

every now and then—fairly often; habitually: Every now and then a motion picture comes along so permeated with suspense as to make the spectator sit tense in his seat.

now and then—occasionally; at times: After he retired, he enjoyed spending a lot of time reading at the public library. Now and then he would take a trip.

every one • everyone

every one—(of two or more people or things) each one taken separately: She took his bottles of whisky and emptied every one down the sink.

everyone—(of people) everybody; all people: Almost everyone came to the school party wearing a crazy hat!

everybody and their uncle • Uncle Tom Cobley and all

everybody and their uncle—(also: every man and his dog) lots of people; everyone of importance: Everybody and their uncle will be heading to the beach today. So, I'm staying right here.

Uncle Tom Cobley and all—(used at the end of a list of names) a whole lot of other people: When he had a dream, neither God, the parish priest, the neighbors, nor Uncle Tom Cobley and all could distract him from the dream.

evidence for something • evidence of something

evidence for something—anything that gives reason to believe smth.: Is there any evidence for the Biblical story of Sodom and Gomorrah's destruction?

evidence of something—indication or signs of smth.: When the ship reached port, it bore abundant evidence of the severity of the storm.

except for something • except something

except for something—1. apart from smth.; not considering smth.: The streets were eerily empty, except for a few cars rushing here or there. 2. if it were not for smth.: It seems that work is ready to proceed there, except for lack of funding.

except something—with the exclusion of smth.: It seemed that every house except ours had a Christmas tree.

Note:** Neither expression fully correlates in meaning with the phrase **with the exception of something—1. = *except for something 1:* The streets were empty, with the exception of a few vendors who wanted an early days' start. 2. = *except something:* Due to the fog all the flights (with the exception of ours) were cancelled.

exchange a few words with someone • exchange words with someone

exchange a few words with someone—have a short conversation with smb.: The man turned and exchanged a few words with his neighbor.

exchange words with someone—quarrel with a person: Have you been exchanging words with our neighbor again?

exclusive to someone • to the exclusion of someone

exclusive to someone—said of smth. applying only to the people stated: This is a special offer at reduced rates, exclusive to members of the club.

to the exclusion of someone—so as to keep some people out: The rules of the club worked to the exclusion of anyone who was not of professional status.

excuse oneself • make an excuse

excuse oneself—1. apologize for something: A lady speaker was talking, so I excused myself for being late and introduced myself to everyone there. 2. make an apology declining or refusing smth.: Schwarz was for taking everyone out for a drink, but the rabbi excused himself. 3. politely ask to be allowed to leave a room: During coffee, he excused himself and went to his upstairs study to telephone Teresa.

make an excuse—1. provide reasons or justifications for one's actions: They could not make any excuse for shortening their stay at the castle. 2. = *excuse oneself 1:* Never be in a position where you have to make an excuse for being casually dressed.

excuse someone for something • excuse someone from something

excuse someone for something—forgive a person for doing smth. wrong: She begged me to excuse her for being so rude and interrupting our walk.

excuse someone from something—set a person free from a duty or obligation: My teacher, to my amazement, excused me from freshman English when I turned in my first piece.

expand into something • expand upon something

expand into something—enlarge into smth. bigger: In no time at all, the vegetable garden had expanded into a small farm.

expand upon something—add detail to smth.; explain what is implied in a statement, etc.: Would you please expand upon that last remark.

expectation of life • life expectancy

expectation of life—the average number of years of life remaining for a person of a given age based on statistical probability: His expectation of life was substantially less than it would have been if he had not contracted cancer.

life expectancy—the number of years an average person can be expected to live based on statistical probability: Life expectancy in the U.S. continues a long-term upward trend.

experience in something • experience of something

experience in something—knowledge of a particular activity as a result of having done it in the past: The president has had no experience in traveling abroad, and should send a qualified representative to handle the delicate cultural issues.

experience of something—knowledge of smth. a person was involved in, especially smth. important that affects him: Even though I've been back for months, my experience of traveling in India is still very much with me.

experiment on something • experiment with something

experiment on something—use smth. in an experiment or test: Many people disapprove of scientists who experiment on animals.

experiment with something—use smth. to test the effectiveness of new methods or ideas: Many composers are now experimenting with new forms of music.

expert at something • expert in something

expert at something—a person who is very skilled at doing smth.: Dave knows how to communicate with sales professionals. He is an expert at complex selling and knows exactly how to get his messages across.

expert in something—a person who knows a lot about a particular subject: If he is an expert in the problems of bringing the space station and the module together, he will be invaluable.

exposed to the elements • out of one's element

exposed to the elements—unsheltered from bad weather: Often a huge wave crashed over the launch and half the sea washed over us as we were exposed to the elements.

out of one's element—in an environment or situation not naturally suited to a person: At first, I felt that I was out of my element because my background in science was not as broad as others. *Cf.: in one's element—in an environment or situation natural or suited to a person:* He is in his element where he feels that he belongs, a small farming village.

extravagant in something • extravagant with something

extravagant in something—going beyond what is reasonable in smth. one does: Roger was a superb teacher of piano and his own students have frequently been extravagant in his praise.

extravagant with something—going beyond what is reasonable in smth. one uses or spends: While unbelievably good-looking and extravagant with his money, his accent takes away from his affluent upbringing.

eye dialect • eye language

eye dialect—writing in which spellings are altered to represent a dialectal or colloquial pronunciation: Which of the elocutionists could object to the vocalized result of *enuff,* probably the oftenest repeated of eye-dialect usages?

eye language—interpersonal communication by means of the expression of the eyes: Although Fran had a stern look on her face, her eye language clearly indicated that she was not serious about her statement.

eye shadow • eye-shade

eye shadow—mascara *(cosmetic preparation applied to the eyelids):* A makeup artist tells you tricks, rules and guidelines for perfect eye shadow application.

eye-shade—1. a visor for shielding the eyes from strong light: The ladies this year wore half a flat hat as an eye-shade. 2. = *eye shadow:* Choose a base eye shade that matches your skin tone and apply all over the eyelid.

eyeball someone • get an eyeball on someone

eyeball someone—(coll.) look hard at smb.; stare at a person: "God!" burst from the lips of the man as he eyeballed his attendant.

get an eyeball on someone—(coll.) spot a person; catch sight of smb.: When Jane first got an eyeball on her blind date, she almost cringed in disappointment.

F

face someone down • face up to someone

face someone down—confront smb. in an attempt to subdue or dominate the person: The project is too important to be placed in jeopardy by the vanity of one man, and those who are too cowardly to face him down.

face up to someone—challenge a person boldly; refuse to be intimidated: Confrontation may not be your desired choice but unless you face up to a person or situation your views will never be heard.

face to face • head to head

face to face—1. *addressing smb.* directly: There are some students who are shy and will only talk to you online, but others would rather talk face to face. 2. in direct encounter with a person: She toadied to her superiors when she really came face to face with them.

head to head—1. in direct confrontation or conflict: On the same day the two candidates go head to head in their only joint televised debate. 2. competing so closely that the lead is virtually indistinguishable: He made an announcement saying that the two candidates were head to head so it wasn't time to celebrate yet.

Note: *The expression does not correlate in meaning with its formal French counterpart* ***tête-à-tête****—a talk in private with only two people present:* He had tête-à-tête with Maung Aye, the powerful Burmese army chief, when he visited Thailand.

fact of life • facts of life

fact of life—a thing, especially unpleasant, the existence of which cannot be ignored: The fact of someone's presence on welfare rolls has sometimes been used against them. Cruel as that may seem it is a fact of life.

facts of life—(euph.) details of the human sexual functions, especially as told to children: Telling a child of the facts of life was one of the tasks that the family had abdicated to the schools.

faint at something • faint from something

faint at something—feel giddy or lose consciousness at the thought or sight of smth.: A person almost giantlike in strength and stature may faint at the thoughts of the operation.

faint from something—feel giddy or lose consciousness because of fatigue, the heat, etc.: They don't want to faint from hunger, so they scarf up what they call a bite before they go.

fair for someone • fair of someone

fair for someone—quite good for a person: She can type two pages an hour, which is fair for a beginner.

fair of someone—just or honest on the part of a person: I don't think it is fair of you to ask me that.

fair game • fair play

fair game—(also: easy game) a suitable object for ridicule, mistreatment, or exploitation: They were women in a patriarchal society and that meant that they were fair game to be demeaned and marginalized by many men.

fair play—behavior that conforms to generally accepted principles of justice: Traditional standards of fair play on the football field are so far eroded that terms of suspension for fouling are regarded as a hazard rather than as a stigma.

fairy lantern • magic lantern

fairy lantern—any of various plants of the genus *Calochortus:* The fairy lantern is similar to orchids, and quite a few orchids depend on fungi as much as they do on photosynthesis for their energy.

Note: *The expression does not correlate in meaning with the phrase* ***fairy lamp****—a candle-burning night light usually of colored glass:* In the Amusement Compound they light a horseshoe of fairy-lamps above the Jack and Jill.

magic lantern—apparatus for throwing a magnified image of a picture, etc. on to a white screen: Usually some newly arrived acquisition occupied the center of the room — a magic lantern, a kaleidoscope or a game of puff-billiards.

fall about someone's ears • fall on someone's ears

fall about someone's ears—1. come crashing down; collapse: Slabs of plaster left the ceilings and fell about our ears.... 2. fail suddenly: All our careful plans fell about our ears when the government changed the tax laws.

fall on someone's ears—(liter.) be heard: As we entered the temple, a curious chanting fell upon our ears.

fall back • fall behind

fall back—1. spring back; recoil: Mizuki watched Yukiko dig through her stuff, then she fell back when she saw her get the box. 2. *(of troops)* retreat: The army began falling back to prepared lines of defense. 3. lag behind; be outstripped: We thought the horse would win, but he fell back halfway through the race.

fall behind—1. = *fall back 3:* After about twenty miles the horse slowly but surely falls behind. 2. fail to maintain a schedule of payments, etc.: If your payments of rent fall behind, you will be asked to leave.

fall behind in something • fall behind on something

fall behind in something—1. fail to do enough of smth. and so move to a position behind others: The country has fallen behind its competitors in the manufacture of cheap cotton goods. 2. fail to maintain a schedule of payments, etc.: Jacobs began receiving letters from the bank threatening foreclosure when he fell behind in his payments.

fall behind on something—(also: fall behind with something) = fall behind in something 2: John fell behind on his car payments so the bank took his car back.

Note: *The expression does not correlate in meaning with the phrase **fall back on something**— turn to smth. held as a reserve for help, etc.:* They had some money in the bank to fall back on.

fall below something • fall under something

fall below something—(of a standard, etc.) fail to reach an agreed or required level: You should identify the reasons why your academic performance has fallen below expectations.

fall under something—1. *(of an item)* be placed in the category mentioned: If a document falls under the physician-patient confidentiality clause, then this section may be withheld from public viewing. 2. *(of a person)* be strongly influenced or attracted by smth.: Though she was no longer young, she was still beautiful and John immediately fell under her charm.

fall guy • fallen man

fall guy—1. a loser or victim, especially smb. who is tricked into smth.: The president cannot be considered a "fall guy," since he is the commander in chief who ultimately ordered these military adventures. 2. a person who gets blamed when smth. goes wrong: They finally dismiss an employee in response to the scandal. Is he just a fall guy or will more dismissals be forthcoming?

fallen man—1. *(the Bible)* said of man after the time when he sinned: What is fallen man's solution to the approach of the Judge? He retains his pride and self-reliance and runs from God. 2. *(liter.)* smb. whose behavior is against the principles of morality: "Are you a wagering man, Dr. Waterhouse?" "I was brought up to loathe it. But my return to London is proof that I am a fallen man." *Cf.: fallen woman—(dated) a woman who has lost her respectability because of extramarital sex:* Sappho runs away rather than lie to Will and trick him into marriage with a "fallen woman."

fall in for something • fall in with something

fall in for something—be due for a share of smth., such as punishment, criticism, etc.: Sally fell in for a lot of trouble when she bought a used car.

Note: *The expression does not correlate in meaning with the phrase **fall for something**—(coll.) 1. become very keen on or enthusiastic about smth.:* I have quite fallen for this year's purple colors. 2. *be tricked into accepting smth. as genuine or true:* Everyone seems to fall for his charming manner.

fall in with something—1. happen to meet smth.: We shall fall in with plenty of boats if we coast it up to Palermo. 2. agree with smth.: It simply would not be understood if we did not fall in with this reasonable suggestion.

fall into someone's arms • fall into someone's hands

fall into someone's arms—run up to a person to be held lovingly in both arms: With a cry of joy, she fell into his arms.

fall into someone's hands—1. be captured by a person: All those who fell into their hands alive were slain. 2. come into smb.'s possession: The two innkeepers had no idea what a treasure fell into their hands. 3. come under smb.'s control: Good citizens allowed politics to fall into the hands of mean men.

fall leaf • leaf fall

fall leaf—1. shedding of leaves by a plant; the autumn season: Except during fall leaf season, leaves must be bagged and set out on your garbage collection day. 2. a hinged flap on a table which can be raised to increase the surface area: We unpacked a fall-leaf table which had been all sealed up and had all our cooking utensils.

leaf fall— = fall leaf 1: Prune red and white currants at leaf fall (if bird damage is likely, pruning can be left until spring).

fall off a truck • fall off the turnip truck

fall off a truck—(U.S. euph.) said of an item that was probably stolen or obtained by questionable methods *(also UK: fall off the back of a lorry):* It shouldn't be surprising that in such circumstances a lot of those products will "get lost in warehouses" or "fall off a truck."

Note: *The expression does not correlate in meaning with the phrase **fall off the wagon**— resume drinking after having stopped:* Broderson fell off the wagon again. After a week of heavy drinking, he pawned the trailer to an acquaintance.

fall off the turnip truck—(U.S. coll., usually negat.) be naive and gullible: I spent almost ten years in the private sector, so it's not like I just fell off the turnip truck.

fall out of something • fall outside something

fall out of something—1. drop out of smth.: Suddenly, something fell out of the Bible. What he saw was an old leaf that had been pressed in between the pages. 2. *(used figuratively in phrases such as "fall out of love," "fall out of use," etc.):* It is interesting how words fall out of favor or dramatically change in meaning over time.

fall outside something—be beyond the scope of one's responsibility, interests, etc.: What they are asking me to do falls outside my technical skill set. *Cf.: fall within something—be part of one's responsibility, interests, etc.:* I am open for almost any type of work that falls within my expertise.

fall through the cracks • fall through the floor

fall through the cracks—(also: fall between the cracks) pass unnoticed; be neglected and not dealt with: In the past, many learning disabled children fell through the cracks.

fall through the floor—(also: sink through the floor) 1. be very surprised: The Security chaps nearly fell through the floor when I walked into Parliament so early, so goodness knows what they were imagining. 2. suffer extreme embarrassment: We stood there with our hands crossed over our crotches in misery. I was about ready to fall through the floor with shame. 3. *(of prices, sales, etc.)* reach the lowest point: While some vegetable prices have fallen through the floor, domestic prices for crops are markedly higher than abroad. *Cf.: hit the ceiling—(of prices, sales, etc.) increase very rapidly; surpass the expected limit (also: hit the roof):* The taxi drivers were aware that the buses were not running on this particular day, and prices hit the ceiling.

Note: *Neither expression correlates in meaning with the phrase **fall through**—(of plans, reforms, projects, etc.) not succeed; fail* *to be completed (also: drop through):* When wedding plans fell through, she decided that a holiday was the best way to get over it.

familiar to someone • familiar with someone

familiar to someone—well-known to a person: The story is presented in a manner familiar to all radio-listeners.

familiar with someone—1. acquainted with or knowing a person: I confess that I am not familiar with this writer. 2. on friendly terms or intimate with smb.: Do you address him as "Tom" or as "Mr. Green"? Don't be too familiar with him.

family doctor • house physician

family doctor—a general practitioner: The family doctor is often the first person that people talk to about their concerns.

house physician—a usually resident physician in a hospital, etc.: Mrs. Parish was removed to the institution, where the house physician took charge of the case.

family man • man of family

family man—a man with a family; a man dedicated to his family: We don't see much of him now that he has become a family man.

man of family—1. = *family man:* Soon he will be a husband and then a man of family and all will be serious. *2.* a man of noble birth: The baron's cadet cannot avail himself of the public schools because such a step would disclass the man of family.

fancy man • fantasy man

fancy man—(sl.) a woman's lover: You won't get one husband in ten feels any thanks to the wife's fancy man for the happiness he brings to the marriage.

***Note:** The expression does not correlate in meaning with the phrase **fancy Dan**—(U.S. sl.) a showy but ineffective worker or sportsman:* The amateur and professional ranks today are cluttered with "fancy Dans."

fantasy man—a perfect man a woman would like to be with: She takes a cruise hoping to meet her fantasy man. She meets a man all right...

far and away • far and wide

far and away—clearly; without a doubt: He is far and away the best-prepared candidate for the Presidency.

far and wide—over a large area: You will search far and wide before meeting another friend like him.

fare well • farewell

fare well—do well; excel: American companies generally fare well in this sector and dominate the market.

farewell—1. marking smb.'s departure or death: My spirits were lifted by America's fond farewell to Ronald Reagan. 2. used as an expression of good wishes on parting: So, farewell and my thanks for the opportunities you have provided us.

fast food • slow food

fast food—inexpensive food prepared and served quickly at a fast-food restaurant: Fast food is a multi-billion dollar industry which is continuing to grow at a rapid pace as fewer people cook at home.

slow food—a movement that emphasizes organic growing methods and culinary culture: Instead of drive-up burgers, slow food followers carve out a little time to appreciate locally grown food.

fast lane • fast track

fast lane—1. the traffic lane for vehicles that are moving rapidly: Taxi drivers claim that when traffic breaks down, the fast lane breaks down first so they move immediately to the right lane. 2. a hectic and pressured lifestyle often characterized by recklessness or dissipation: He lived in the fast-lane of his times—hard drinking, gambling, and all the other stuff.

fast track—the quickest route or means to achievement of a goal: Haiti's past has taught him that elections do not necessarily put a country on a fast track to democracy.

fast one • quick one

fast one—(sl.) a clever and unexpected trick giving the person unfair advantage *(usually in the phrase "pull a fast one"):* The thought that a girl capable of thinking up a fast one like that should be throwing herself away on Eggleston was infinitely saddening.

quick one—(sl.) 1. a quick drink of liquor or a beer consumed rapidly: We've time for a quick one and then we'll go and do our bit of business. 2. a brief and brisk sex act: I'm not saying that an unexpected quick one can't be fantastic. ... If you're working a lot you'll probably need to schedule in time for sex.

fatal accident • fateful accident

fatal accident—an unfortunate event that results in death: Violations of mandatory mine safety laws led to the fatal accident taking the lives of five miners.

fateful accident—an event that may have catastrophic consequences, yet not necessarily result in death: Not long after the fateful accident that left him dishonorably discharged, he lost his wife.

father of the chapel • father-in-church

father of the chapel—(UK publishing and printing industries) a shop steward representing union members in negotiations, etc.: My grandfather was father of the chapel at one of the big newspapers.

father-in-church—the relative or friend who "gives away" a bride: "I shall want you to stand father-in-church to this young lady," said Geoffrey to the clerk.

Father of the House, the • house father

Father of the House, the—(UK) the oldest member of Parliament *(with reference to duration of membership):* The most important duty of the Father of the House is to preside over the election of a new speaker.

house father—a man looking after a group of children in an institution: There were in these places no "house-fathers" for the girls, though there were "house-mothers" for both girls and boys.

feather bed • feather-bedding

feather bed—said of a markedly easy and comfortable state or position: Feather beds for farmers have been a feature of post-war Europe.

feather-bedding—the employment of excess staff, usually under a union rule: Feather bedding has come about as a consequence of workers being laid off because of technological change.

feed off something • feed on something

feed off something—1. use smth. as food: Blacktip sharks are reef sharks; they feed off fish living in the coral, and are not interested in big mammals. 2. use smth. to advantage *(usually with negative implication):* They feed off our desire to smoke and the miseries of our lives that caused most of us to start smoking.

feed on something—eat certain food as one's regular diet: These sharks are bottom dwellers, in nature they feed on fish and shellfish that they suck out of the sand.

feed one's pussy • feed the kitty

feed one's pussy—*(coarse sl., of a woman)* have sex or practice cunnilingus: I watch the screen as a hot blonde feeds her pussy to some lucky guy.

feed the kitty—*(U.S. sl.)* contribute money: Come on, Bill. Feed the kitty. You can afford a dollar for a good cause.

feed someone on something • feed someone with something

feed someone on something—habitually give a person smth. as food: They feed me on roast-beef and Yorkshire pudding.

feed someone with something—1. give a person smth. to eat at a particular time: She was feeding the baby with porridge when we entered. 2. = *feed someone on something:* The boy would not eat any cooked meat. The Indians had to feed him with raw meat just like the coyotes had fed him. 3. *(Theater)* supply an actor with cues: Stanley Kubrick himself would sometimes feed the actors with their prompts.

feed the fish • feed the fishes

feed the fish—*(U.S. sl.)* be sea-sick; vomit: I opened the hatch, stepped out and then I knew I was going to feed the fish.

Note: *The expression does not correlate in meaning with the phrase* ***feed the goldfish***—*(euph.) leave the company to go to the toilet:* The variations on these expressions are endless and include: go and feed a dog, go and feed the goldfish…

feed the fishes—1. *(UK)* be drowned *(also: be food for fishes):* They found the boat but they didn't find him. So he must be feeding the fishes. 2. = *feed the fish:* The sea never affects me, but my unfortunate brother spent most of his time feeding the fishes.

feel a draft • feel the draft

feel a draft—*(U.S. sl.)* have the sensation that one is not welcome in a place: Have you ever felt a draft? Have you ever been in a situation where you felt uncomfortable because you are white?

feel the draft—*(UK coll.)* 1. suffer from worsened circumstances: When the wind changed it might be the Conservative Party which would be feeling the draft. 2. experience financial difficulties: With only so much national advertising to go round, the oldest commercial stations are feeling the draft as well.

feel faint at something • feel faint from something

feel faint at something—feel giddy or likely to lose consciousness at the thought or sight of smth.: Neptune felt faint at the sight of the slash wound.

feel faint from something—feel giddy or likely to lose consciousness because of fatigue, hunger, the heat, etc.: Feeling faint from the pain in her foot, Angie exited the alley.

feel good • feel well

feel good—1. be in good physical shape: The Captain himself said, "I feel good," but he did not look well. 2. be in good spirits: Participants felt good about the ability to talk to children away at college via instant messaging. 3. *(U.S. sl.)* be slightly and pleasantly drunk: After a few beers Charley was feeling good that night.

feel well—be in good health: I never cross her, or talk to her much when she is not feeling well.

feel hot • not feel so hot

feel hot—have the sensation of heat: My serge skirt feels heavy, my feet feel hot and sticky.

not feel so hot—*(coll.)* not feel very well *(also: not feel too hot):* I'm not feeling so hot this morning. I stayed up too late last night.

feel like a new man • feel one's old self again

feel like a new man—begin to feel much better physically or mentally: Luis felt like a new man when he finished reading her message.

Note: *The expression does not correlate in meaning with the phrase* ***become another man***—*used of smb. whose character has noticeably changed:* In a year's time, he became another man, a good one, and the peasants were proud of their landlord.

feel one's old self again—return to one's normal condition of mind and body: After an overnight stay in the hospital, he looked and felt his old self again.

feel like doing something • feel up to doing something

feel like doing something—be in the mood to do smth.: If you have any questions on this or if you feel like discussing it please feel free to comment.

feel up to doing something—feel healthy enough or rested enough to do smth.: I met with a woman from a support group—I didn't feel up to meeting a whole group of people.

feel something on the pulse • feel the pulse of something

feel something on the pulse—come to feel smth. deeply through one's own experience: The appointment of Sir Robert as Deputy Speaker has made me feel "on the pulse" a frustrating anomaly of our parliamentary system.

feel the pulse of something—*(also: keep one's finger on the pulse of something)* be aware of the current developments or trends in smth.: The investigation of the seismic waves affords the best means of feeling the pulse of the interior of the earth.

feel strong • feel strongly

feel strong—1. be in good health: I had just celebrated my birthday and was feeling strong after a short vacation. 2. be in a strong position: Saddam makes war in only two sets of cases: when he feels weak and when he feels strong!

feel strongly—be convinced; firmly believe: We all felt strongly that a pilot ought to have a clear, visual reference to his surroundings. *Cf.: feel strongly about something:* adopt a stern attitude about smth. which cannot be easily ignored: Holding up a sign in public in protest over something you feel strongly about takes a lot of courage.

feel the pulse of something • have a feel on the pulse of something

feel the pulse of something—*(also: keep one's finger on the pulse of something)* keep track of the current developments and trends in smth.: What consummate skill must be his who thus feels the pulse of fashion, recognizing in its beat the indications of this or that tendency…

have a feel on the pulse of something—have sensitivity for and understanding of smth.: In day to day dealing with cross-sections of society, they tend to have a feel on the pulse of society: its ills, travails and aspirations.

feel uneasy about something • feel uneasy at something

feel uneasy about something—feel unsettled because one is not sure that smth. is correct or wise: Many managers feel uneasy about promoting women to higher jobs.

feel uneasy at something—feel troubled or anxious at the thought or sight of smth.: I felt uneasy at the thought of their going home alone at that late hour.

Festival of Lanterns, the • Festival of Lights, the

Festival of Lanterns, the—1. the concluding part of the new-year celebration according to the old Chinese calendar: The Festival of Lanterns takes place at the end of the Chinese New Year Celebration, on the fifteenth day of the first moon. 2. a great popular festival of Japan when the spirits of ancestors are supposed to revisit the household altars: For three days in mid July, Japanese Buddhists celebrate Obon, or the Festival of Lanterns.

Festival of Lights, the—1. Hanukkah (the Jewish festival of lights commemorating the victory of the Maccabees over Antiochus of Syria): Hanukkah, the Jewish festival of lights, involves the lighting of candles for eight days. 2. Diwali (one of the major religious festivals in India, dedicated to the Goddess Kali): In India at Diwali, the festival of lights, houses are lit with candles and the Earth becomes like the heavens.

fiery words • hot words

fiery words—said of an ardent, passionate address, speech, etc.: Bert really inspired the crowd into action with his fiery words at the rally.

hot words—words spoken in anger; a heated argument: He accused Valenti of drinking on the job, and after some hot words he sent Valenti home.

fifth wheel • third wheel

fifth wheel—said of a person or thing that is superfluous or needless: Look guys, I don't know what's going on, but I feel like a fifth wheel here. I should go.

Note: *The expression does not correlate in meaning with the phrase **fifth quarter**—1. the summer quarter of studies:* In the fifth quarter the student is encouraged to take no more than one course besides the four hours of thesis. 2. *(dated butcher's term) the hide and fat of a slaughtered animal:* He claimed, and obtained the fifth quarter of the beef, as it is called (the hide and tallow) for his forbearance.

third wheel—a third person to accompany a couple *(with the implication that one is intruding on a couple):* I find it tiring to be the third wheel, having to constantly walk behind a couple holding hand.

Note: *The expression does not correlate in meaning with the phrase **third rail**—(U.S. coll.) a subject considered by politicians to be too controversial or dangerous to discuss:* The conventional wisdom has long been that Social Security is the third rail of American politics.

fight for something • fight over something

fight for something—1. struggle to defend smth.: My Dad says we'll all have to fight for our country when *Der Tag* comes. That's German for the Day. 2. try in a determined way to get or achieve smth.: Having fought for the prize so long, Gordon is destined to find in it only disappointment.

fight over something—1. struggle for the ownership of smth.: They were too apt to go to law and fight over their lands and fishing rights. 2. argue or struggle over an issue: The First World War was fought over a small thing. A mere scrap of paper.

figure in something • figure on something

figure in something—have a part in smth.; play a role in smth.: The ass has, since the time of the Greeks, figured in fables as the type of ignorance and stupidity.

figure on something—*(coll.)* depend on smth.; plan on smth.: Don't figure on going abroad this summer, we may not be able to afford it.

figure someone in • figure someone out

figure someone in—*(coll.)* add or include a person into one's plans, etc. *(also: count someone in):* Please figure Ann in when you plan the party.

figure someone out—*(also: make someone out)* understand a person's character: We are stuck with the guy for four years, so we'll have plenty of time to figure him out.

figurehead • head figure

figurehead—1. a carving, usually a bust or a full-length figure, decorating the prow of a ship: The adornment of ships with figureheads could be traced back to Phoenician times. 2. a person who holds an important office yet has little actual power: The constitution allots so much power to the board of governors that the president is often regarded as merely a figurehead.

head figure—a leading person who guides and directs: It was not long before Coke, who was now the head figure in Parliament, vigorously began an inquiry.

fill in for someone • fill someone in

fill in for someone—carry out the duties of a fellow employee, absent through sickness, etc.: My partner is on holiday so I'm filling in for him.

fill someone in—give a person full details about smth.: Can you fill me in on what has been happening since I left here?

find one's voice • lose one's voice

find one's voice—1. *(also: find one's tongue)* be able to speak again after a shock, horror, etc. which has left one speechless: From his seat in the corner, Dave finally found his voice. "What happened? And when?" 2. *(of a writer, painter, etc.)* become truly creative and develop a style of one's own: Andy had found his voice as a composer, of course, but also as a teacher and as an administrator.

lose one's voice—be hardly able to speak, especially due to having a sore throat: After a mild cold earlier this week I was feeling better but overnight I lost my voice—I could barely talk at all today.

Note: *The expression does not correlate in meaning with the phrase **lose one's tongue**—be left speechless with shock, horror, etc.:* Now he seems to have lost his tongue, he can't seem to get out the words his supporters are urging him to say.

find oneself • lose oneself

find oneself—1. become conscious of being in a certain place or state: When he regained consciousness, he found himself in the hospital. 2. discover one's vocation; realize one's capabilities: After the war he couldn't find himself. He was too big of a man to start over.

lose oneself—1. lose one's way: It's easy to lose yourself in this big building. 2. fall asleep: I lost myself for a few minutes during the long sermon. 3. get confused: He lost himself, so many eyes were turned towards him. 4. give all one's attention to smth.: I like to sit by the fire and lose myself in a good book. 5. get out of sight; disappear: The escaping prisoner was able to lose himself in the crowd.

fine as a fiddle • fine as fivepence

fine as a fiddle—*(also: fit as a fiddle)* in excellent form or health: There you are, Stanley. Looking as fine as a fiddle.

fine as fivepence—*(also: fine as five pence)* 1. *(of clothes)* smart or becoming: Theodore's own clothing looked as fine as five pence. 2. *(of people)* smartly dressed: Kitty ... could not compete with Anne, who was fine as fivepence in a violet pelisse and bonnet.

finish off with something • finish with something

finish off with something—1. end up one's meal with smth.:

Let's finish off with some of that excellent cheese. 2. conclude by (doing) smth.: The long meeting finished off with a prayer.

Note: *The expression does not correlate in meaning with the phrase* ***finish off something***—1. *(of food) finish completely:* The children have finished off all the fruit. 2. *bring smth. to an end:* I finally said we must finish off the war in Italy quickly. 3. *totally destroy smth.:* A long drive like that could finish the car off.

finish with something—1. = *finish off with something 1:* We have some nice cake to finish with. 2. = *finish off with something 2:* I should like to finish with reminding members of the purpose of this club. 3. *(of a period of time)* come to an end (on a certain date): Please send your accounts for the period finishing with 31 March. 4. have no further use for smth.: Have you finished with the newspaper?

finish school • leave school

finish school—1. complete one's school education: When he finished school he went to college in the United States. 2. finish classes for the day: When he finished school at noon, the taxi would first drop off the other kids and then Ahmad.

leave school—1. = *finish school 1:* About a year after she left school, Doreen headed to Manitoba with her boyfriend. 2. leave the school building after dismissal: The kids went to school with their ski equipment and left school at noon for an afternoon of skiing. 3. drop out of school: He left school at about 14 to work in a grocery store but continued his education through night classes.

fire department • fire office

fire department—(U.S.) a fire brigade: You may establish a direct connection with the fire department, or the police and call them immediately.

fire office—a fire-insurance company: An even more elusive foe of the fire office than petrol is "the cold-blooded fire-bug" who trades in arson.

fire fight • firefighting

fire fight—1. an exchange of fire between opposing units (as distinct from close combat): Three soldiers have been killed in a fire fight with separatist guerrillas. 2. the effort to extinguish or to check the spread of a fire: Several firefighters were transported to the local hospital during the fire fight.

firefighting— = *fire fight 2:* We want to be your number one stop for information on volunteer firefighting, training and legislation.

fire-irons • firing-iron

fire-irons—utensils for a fireplace (as tongs, poker, and shovel): The floor was spotless; the grate and fire-irons were burnished bright, and the fire burnt clear.

Note: *The compound does not correlate in meaning with the expression* ***irons in the fire****—(usually in the phrase "have many irons in the fire") used of things requiring the attention at once:* A few months ago I just had too many irons in the fire, and I hate that feeling. It was time to refocus some priorities…

firing-iron—an iron used in cauterizing a horse: When the farrier has made his firing-iron red hot in his forge, he applies the thinnest part to the horses skin.

fire line • line of fire

fire line—1. a strip of cleared or ploughed land intended to check a forest fire: It became clear that the truck would survive once it outsped the fire line. 2. a police barrier around a building on fire: It is the responsibility of the police department to keep unauthorized persons outside this fire line.

line of fire—(also: firing line) 1. the path of a missile discharged from a firearm: Large dugouts were built … so that they were not directly in line of fire from enemy guns. 2. a position where one is likely to come under attack, receive punishment, etc.: Modern art is the cause of much argument, so the writer has placed himself in the line of fire between the two sides.

Note: *The expression does not correlate in meaning with the phrase* ***line of battle****—(Military) a line formed by troops or ships for delivering or receiving an attack:* The enemy were discovered drawn up in line of battle on the heights near Sharpsburg.

fire ship • fireboat

fire ship—(hist.) a ship carrying explosives sent among the enemy's ships to set them on fire: In order to protect them against fire ships, stockades, raised on piles, were placed higher up the river.

fireboat—1. a boat equipped with pumps for extinguishing fires on boats and piers: Her tenure as a fireboat served the maritime community proudly by responding to major fires in the harbor. 2. = *fire ship:* Navy flotillas conducted fireboat raids against invading enemy forces on the Potomac, and participated in the successful defense of Baltimore.

fire someone • fire someone up

fire someone—(often Passive) dismiss a person from a job: A police officer claims that he was fired because a Web site he operates criticizes the Police Department.

Note: *The expression does not correlate in meaning with the phrase* ***burn someone****—(sl., usually Passive)* 1. *reprimand a person severely:* Having been burned for speaking my mind often enough, I leave you to your thoughts. 2. *cheat or swindle smb. of his money:* Just be careful, I was burned for one hundred dollars. I hope to see nobody else in this situation.

fire someone up—make a person highly excited or enthusiastic: Their passionate drive to bring about better lives for others have fired them up to achieve great things.

first Americans • first-generation Americans

first Americans—(also: Native Americans) North American Indians: Who knows whether the first Americans who came across the Bering Strait in pre-history were indeed the first. *Cf.: First Nations—used with reference to Canadian Native Americans:* All members of First Nations who are entitled to benefits are entered in the Indian Register.

first-generation Americans—Americans of immigrant parentage born in the United States: Galvone was a first generation American with his roots in Italy.

first and last • first or last

first and last—1. coming before anything else in order, rank, etc.: They say that exquisite painting is the first and last business of a painter. 2. in essence; for the most part: You are a scientist first and last. Your other activities are merely field tests of the work you do here.

Note: *The expression does not correlate in meaning with the phrase* ***from first to last****—from beginning to end; all along:* A clever coach was able to advise them from first to last and the crew have improved steadily.

first or last— is used to express indifference as to order: You may do it first or last; I'm sure I don't care as long as you *do* do it.

first floor *(UK)* • first floor *(U.S.)*

first floor (UK)—the floor immediately above the ground floor: Roos and Paul live on the first floor (that's the second floor to us Americans).

first floor (U.S.)—the ground floor (more or less on a level with the ground outside): The Museum Shop is on the first floor next to the entrance.

first lady, the • first woman, the

first lady, the—1. the wife of a president: The first lady carries no official duties.... Nonetheless, she attends many official ceremonies. 2. a woman who is most important or better than any other at smth.: Dubbed the "First Lady of Song," Fitzgerald has clearly earned her title. 3. *(U.S. diners)* spare ribs: The phrase "first lady" meaning "spare ribs" was a pun referring to Eve. The Bible describes her as being made of one of Adam's ribs.

Note: *The expression does not correlate in meaning with the phrase* ***leading lady, the****— the chief actress in a theatrical company or a film:* Mme du Châtelet always took the part of the leading lady, dressed up to kill and covered with diamonds.

first woman, the—1. *(also: prima donna)* the principal female singer in an opera: The part of the first woman in an intermezzo was filled by a very promising singer. 2. *= first lady, the 1:* Considering Hillary Clinton's ambitious agenda, they found themselves reluctant to criticize the First Woman's conventional version of feminism. 3. is used with reference to Biblical Eve: However, disagreement starts soon after the creation of the first man, Adam, and the first woman, Eve.

first school • primary school

first school—(UK) a school for children aged between five and eight or nine: The village would consent to the school becoming a first school, rather than a primary.

primary school—a school for the first four to eight years of education: I started primary school in a class together with fifteen other children, who were all a bit older than I was.

first time • for the first time

first time—said of the very first occasion of smth. *(similar events could possibly follow later though not necessarily):* She put on her hat and shawl and, realizing it was the first time she was to leave him at home, she hugged and kissed him.

Note: *The expression is not equivalent in meaning to the phrase* ***first time round****—(also: first time around) used of the first instance of some cyclic or repeated event:* John didn't pass the bar exam the first time round. He passed it on his second try.

for the first time—as the first instance since some past point in time: Negotiations began in the 1950s when it became clear for the first time that coastal resources needed protection.

first time out of the box • just out of a bandbox

first time out of the box—(coll.) said of one's first experience with smth.: This is the first time out of the box with these cars and nobody has had a lot of time to work with them yet.

just out of a bandbox—said of a person looking extremely smart and neat: They are all exceedingly neat and cleanly as if they were just out of a band-box.

Note: *The expression does not correlate in meaning with the phrase* ***just off the boat****—(coll.) used of smb. newly immigrated and, perhaps, trusting and naive:* I showed the students a short narrative written from the point of view of a new immigrant, just off the boat.

See also: out of one's box / out of the box.

fish slice • slice of fish

fish slice—1. *(UK)* a fish-carving knife; a kitchen tool used for turning or serving fish: A fish slice can be used to lift fish fillets or pieces of meat. 2. a thin, wide, flat piece cut off (cooked) fish: Sprinkle lime juice over the fish slices and season with salt.

slice of fish— = fish slice 2: To make grilled fish, thin slices of fish have to be mixed with ginger, saffron, fermented cold rice, pepper and fish sauce.

fish story • fishy story

fish story—an exaggerated story; an incredible tale (about fishing): A friend who does not tell fish stories, says he has seen them [herring] in such schools that he could not row his boat through them.

fishy story—a doubtful, questionable story suggestive of deception: He gives me a fishy story about how he bought the bike from an auction and is now selling it because it is too small for him.

fit in with someone • fit someone in

fit in with someone—feel comfortable among particular people: Lou just can't seem to fit in with her new family. She ... resists any kind of companionship from her host-parents.

fit someone in—find time to see or speak to a person: Send me a note with your resume and let me check my schedule to see if I can fit you in.

fit to be hung • fit to kill

fit to be hung—said of a person deserving the worst punishment: They regarded the Socialists as cowardly deserters or rascally mutineers, fit to be hung.

Note: *The expression does not correlate in meaning with the phrase* ***fit to be tied****—(coll.) used of smb. roused to great anger or indignation:* I was fit to be tied when I realized what you had done. One of your producers was kind enough to call me and apologize.

fit to kill—(coll.) said of smb. wearing very fancy clothes *(usually in the phrase "dressed up fit to kill"):* She looked fit to kill in the burgundy dress that perfectly complimented her glossy black hair.

five-by-five • four-by-four

five-by-five—1. said of a radio signal which is loud and clear: The standard "loud and clear" to an American had to be a "five by five" or a "three by three" depending on the reception. 2. *(in the phrase "everything is five by five")* everything is all right: To stave off any potential concerns about my wellbeing, let me reassure you all that everything is five by five.

Note: *The expression does not correlate in meaning with the phrase* ***seven-by-nine****—(dated sl.) said of people or things of poor or inferior quality:* The Duke of Newcastle in the elder Pitt's time was a "seven-by-nine" or peanut politician of the foremost type.

four-by-four—a vehicle with four-wheel drive: Those involved are calling for higher road taxes on four by four users and higher parking permit fees.

fix it up with someone • fix someone up with someone

fix it up with someone—(coll.) arrange smth. with a person: Can you fix it up with the Headmaster so that the meeting will be delayed?

fix someone up with someone—(coll.) provide a date or social companion for a person: Daniel met his wife when she was trying to fix him up with her friend.

fix someone up with something • fix someone with something

fix someone up with something—arrange for a person to have smth.: His father tried to fix him up with a job at the local municipality.

fix someone with something—confront a person with an angry, hostile, etc. look: He fixed me with a steady look, rather owl-like with his heavy rimmed glasses.

flammable liquid • inflammable liquid

flammable liquid—liquid capable of being inflamed or easily set on fire: This report provides an evaluation of the hazards associated with flammable liquid storage lockers.

inflammable liquid— = *flammable liquid:* No inflammable liquid or inflammable substance shall be unloaded, loaded, transported or kept except in accordance with regulations.

flapjack *(UK)* • flapjack *(U.S.)*

flapjack (UK)—a flat cake made from rolled oats, fat, brown sugar and syrup or honey: Not sure if it's usual for British people to eat flapjacks for breakfast, it just happened to be in my line of sight...

flapjack (U.S.)—a thin crispy pancake of large diameter, commonly measuring 12" or more: There's much more on providing life's basics: ...how to skin a bear, blaze a trail, cook flapjacks on a flat rock.

flashing light • flashlight

flashing light—a lighting device, used in lighthouses, etc., giving forth sudden flashes: Another change has been the displacement of the semaphore-type of direction indicator by flashing light signals.

flashlight—1. = *flashing light:* The practice of a flashlight on sails as something approaches in the darkness is a good one. 2. *(also: flash-lamp)* a portable electric lamp: Barry examined them by the same pencil flashlight — a tiny streak of illumination. 3. an intense flash of light produced in cameras: The paranormal displacement of a handkerchief actuated electrically the flashlight by which this photograph was taken.

flea bite • flea-bitten

flea bite—a trifling inconvenience; a small problem: The great Battle of Marathon was a mere flea-bite for an empire that stretched from India to Egypt.

flea-bitten—said of smth. worn and broken down by hard use: Up to now the landlords have held back from replacing any of the old flea-bitten furniture.

flight deck • flying deck

flight deck—1. the uppermost deck of an aircraft carrier serving as landing and takeoff area: Brown successfully took off in about half the length of the flight deck. 2. the forward compartment in some airplanes used by the pilot, copilot and flight engineer: Rebel snipers fired on one of the planes and hit it. One shot went through the flight deck.

flying deck—1. = *flight deck 1:* The "Vindex" was the first ship to be fitted with a forward hangar and flying deck. 2. a deck on a ship supported at the side by railings: A searchlight, which had been fitted up on the flying-deck of the steamer, had an extraordinary effect upon the natives.

fling something away • fling something off

fling something away—1. throw smth. away; get rid of smth. unwanted: Let's fling that old furniture away and buy some new. 2. waste smth. such as an opportunity, etc.: You shouldn't fling away a chance like that. 3. say smth. casually or carelessly: You flung away that last line, we couldn't hear you.

fling something off—1. quickly remove one's clothing: It's good to fling off heavy clothing now that spring is here. 2. get free from smth.; discard smth.: In a new job, one should fling off old habits of thought. 3. release or produce heat, smell, etc.: When this material burns, it flings off a nasty smell. 4. write or compose smth. quickly and easily: I can fling off a poem in half an hour. 5. = *fling something away 3:* Before you fling off a remark like that, think what you are saying.

float someone's boat • paddle one's own canoe

float someone's boat—*(coll.)* said of smth. that excites or interests a person: He describes himself as a music addict — music theatre, in particular, really floats his boat.

paddle one's own canoe—*(also: hoe one's own row)* be independent; follow one's interests or inclination: The Labor Party wished, as it were, to paddle its own canoe — to build in Britain a show-house of democratic socialism.

Note: *The expression does not correlate in meaning with the phrase* ***blow one's own trumpet***—*(also: ring one's own bell) announce one's own successes; praise oneself:* Jim is very good at blowing his own trumpet: to listen to him, one would think he was the only man who could do the job.

flog a dead horse • work for a dead horse

flog a dead horse—*(also: beat a dead horse)* pursue a futile goal; try to revive interest in a dead issue: You can see it in the players' eyes and faces they're totally fed up with playing. You're flogging a dead horse.

work for a dead horse—*(also: work out the dead horse)* do work for which payment has been made in advance: For the first month at sea he was working for nothing — in other words he was working for a "dead horse."

floor girl • floor woman

floor girl—a woman to run errands and do odd jobs about a shop: The floor girl directed me to an area where she would fetch and introduce me to the store manager.

floor woman—a woman employed to supervise a group of working women in a factory, etc.: I had a knowledge of sewing and because of this experience I was put over a group of women as "floor woman."

floor-walker • walk the floor

floor-walker—a person employed in a large store to direct customers, oversee sales, etc.: I next went into a store further up Broadway. When I entered I approached the floor-walker.

walk the floor—pace nervously across the floor, especially while waiting: While Bill waited for news of the operation, he walked the floor for hours on end.

floral clock • Horologe of Flora

floral clock—1. a large public clock set out in colorful plants on the ground: One of Edinburgh's most popular attractions, the Floral Clock is located in West Princes Street Gardens. 2. an arrangement of plants that open or close at certain times: Few of us would want to plant an entire garden as a floral clock.

Horologe of Flora—*(also: Horologium Florae)* = *floral clock 2:* Telling time by flowers goes back to the first century and Pliny who devised a "Horologe of Flora."

Flowery Land • Flowery Nation

Flowery Land—1. *(also: Flowery Empire)* said of China: The sight of the rickshaw carried me back to the Flowery Land. 2. *(U.S.)* said of the State of Florida: Spain continued sending explorers to Florida.... But France also coveted the flowery land.

Flowery Nation— = *Flowery Land 1:* The beautiful fabric we call silk, sir, came from the Flowery Nation.

flowery language • language of flowers

flowery language—the use of fine words and phrases to embellish a narration: Linneus devised a kind of Latin suitable for concise descriptions: animals and plants were not to be written up in flowery language.

language of flowers—a way of expressing one's sentiments by means of flowers: She looked into the bouquet, to see whether there was a *billet-doux* hidden.... "Do they talk the language of flowers at Boggley Wollah, Sedley?" asked Osborne, laughing.

fly a kite • go fly a kite

fly a kite—1. say or do smth. with the intention of testing other people's reaction to it: I thought that here I would fly a kite for a somewhat less-fashionable theory.... 2. *(sl.)* pass a worthless check; sell worthless stocks and bonds: Marty was picked up for flying kites in three different cities. 3. *(Underworld)* smuggle a letter into or out of prison: This practice of "shooting" contraband notes is known among the prisoners as "flying a kite."

go fly a kite—(also: go fry an egg) is used to rudely tell a person to go away and stop being annoying: You are a real bother. Go fly a kite!

fly boat • flying boat

fly boat—(dated) 1. a passenger boat formerly used on canals: Until the advent of "fly boats" ... there was no night working, with the canals open only from sunrise to sunset. 2. a large flat-bottomed coasting boat: Captain George Weymouth made a voyage of discovery to the northwest with two flyboats. 3. a small boat, especially a ship's boat: We see the vessel bound for the distant seas hoist sails, while the humble fly-boat carries to shore those friends...

flying boat—(also: air boat) a seaplane with a boatlike fuselage: Short's Empire class flying boats fifty years ago could offer a bed in the air.

fly camp • flying camp

fly camp—a temporary advanced camp at a distance from a base camp: Hughes moved one helicopter off to the nearest fly camp, thirty miles southwest.

flying camp—(dated) a body of troops formed for rapid movement from place to place: An attack was to be made on the British camp on Staten Island by troops from Mercer's flying camp.

fly high • fly low

fly high—1. have high ambitions: Ah! My boy, you are flying high. It is difficult to become a Lord Chancellor. 2. enjoy a high position in society, at work, etc.: John is flying high after landing himself a hi-tech job in the computer industry. 3. *(sl.)* be drunk or affected by drugs: The guy was on drugs—flying high and scaring everyone around him.

fly low—1. *(hyperbolic, coll.)* considerably exceed a speed limit while driving: On the freeway I was flying low—going about 200 km per hour. *Cf.: low flying—driving far exceeding a speed limit:* She can now travel at her own speed, instead of low flying across Europe with Steve. 2. *(euph.)* used as a caution to a man having his trouser zip undone: Someone walks up to you to quietly whisper in your ear that you are flying low. 3. *(sl.)* seek to avoid drawing attention to oneself: She was flying low when she walked in so they wouldn't notice her.

fly in the ointment, a • hair in the butter, a

fly in the ointment, a—some small or trifling circumstance which spoils the enjoyment of smth.: There is only one fly in the ointment offered by commercial propagandists; they want your money.

hair in the butter, a—(U.S. sl.) said of a delicate situation or sensitive issue: Never mind the details—which neither the Governor's office nor anyone else is willing to share just yet—this is a real hair in the butter.

fly off the handle • go off the handle

fly off the handle—(coll.) get into a rage; lose one's temper: When we are under stress, we are more likely to fly off the handle.

go off the handle—(coll.) 1. = *fly off the handle:* Jimmy went off the handle at once; and Nicol kept patting him on the back. 2. die: My old gentleman means to be Mayor before he goes off the handle.

Note: *Neither expression is antonymous in meaning to the phrase* ***get a handle on something****—understand or be able to master smth. fully:* This book should prove useful for anyone who wants to get a handle on this complex subject.

fly on the wall • let that fly stick to the wall

fly on the wall—an unperceived observer who is able to overhear discussions, etc.: "What did you wheedle out of Maggie?" "Well ... she was no fly on the wall, but there have to be letters, documents, papers to be typed."

let that fly stick to the wall—(Scot.) say nothing more on that subject: We've got in our midst a newspaper; some people call it well, a very peculiar newspaper. But we'll let that fly stick to the wall.

fly paper • fly-sheet

fly paper—sticky paper for killing flies: Once the first fly lands, even more flies are attracted to the fly paper—making this product one of the most effective ways of dealing with flying insects.

fly-sheet—1. a small loose advertising sheet: Brandt had received money with which to publish and distribute fly sheets inciting the unemployed to violence. 2. a flap consisting of a piece of canvas that can be drawn back to provide entrance to a tent: A fly-sheet is desirable in heavy rain, but none have been designed which will stand up to a strong wind.

fly the flag • keep the flag flying

fly the flag—1. *(of a ship)* be registered to a particular country and sail under its flag: Swearing an oath to revenge ... he resolved to plunder any ship flying the flag of Spain. 2. *(also: show the flag)* represent one's country, etc. (by attending an event): Without their assistance, there would have been far fewer UK delegates at the meeting to "fly the flag."

Note: *The expression does not correlate in meaning with the phrase* ***fly the wrong flag****—(corporate culture) behave or act in a manner deemed inappropriate:* I was not aware that wearing open-toed shoes to work was tantamount to flying the wrong flag.

keep the flag flying—1. refuse to succumb; show continued commitment: It's been quite a challenge for the few remaining teachers to keep the flag flying. 2. = *fly the flag 2:* The British delegation led by John Davis kept the flag flying! All in all it was like meeting old friends...

flyboy • flyman

flyboy—(U.S. sl.) a member of an air force, especially a pilot: And, of course the infantry objected to the glorification of the flyboys.

flyman—1. *(Theater)* a man stationed in the "flies" to work the ropes, etc.: The flyman may be said to carry some of the destiny of the performance in the hollow of his hand. 2. a person who drives a "fly"—a light vehicle as a cab or hansom: When the proof of that journey was obtained from the flyman, the evidence would be complete.

flyfish • flying fish

flyfish—1. *(used as a verb)* angle with a hook baited with (artificial) flies: There are many videos and classes around to teach you how to flyfish in very little time. 2. *(used as a noun)* a California fish *(Sebastichthys rhodochloris),* having brilliant colors: We went on fishing and I was the one with the best fish luck, I caught a flyfish on the hook.

flying fish—fishes, chiefly of tropical seas, capable of leaving the water and moving some distance through the air: Every now and then a flying fish would spark out from the unruffled bosom of the heaving water.

Flying Dutchman, the • Flying Scotchman, the

Flying Dutchman, the—1. a ghost ship supposed to be seen

in the region of the Cape of Good Hope: This book is devoted to the legend of The Flying Dutchman and its captain. 2. an express train running between London and Bristol: "The Flying Dutchman" express train was the fastest train in the world in the 1870s.

Flying Scotchman, the—(also: Flying Scotsman, the) an express train running between London and Edinburgh: This train (significantly named "The Flying Scotchman") is believed to be the fastest train in the world.

flying horse • flying mare

flying horse—1. hippogriff *(a mythical animal having the foreparts of a winged griffin and the body of a horse):* Harry Potter has to overcome the trauma of having a Hippogriff (Flying Horse) destroyed by the authorities. 2. the constellation Pegasus: Pegasus the Flying Horse is a fall constellation, not resembling a horse as much as it does a flying brick. 3. *(Wrestling)* maneuver in which the contestant seizes an opponent's wrist, turns about, and jerks him over his back: They get advice on suitable clothing when wrestling and instruction on moves such as "The Flying Horse."

Note: *The expression does not correlate in meaning with the phrase* ***flying sea-horse****—(also: sea-horse) fish of peculiar form, with body somewhat like a horse's head:* They have at times been classified with other groups of fish. These strange looking creatures are also known as "flying sea horses."

flying mare— = *flying horse 3:* Many worked stones survive as relics; they include statue bases with the reliefs of wrestlers (one attempting the "flying mare" throw).

flying squad • flying squadron

flying squad—1. any body of persons organized for rapid movement or action: To speed justice, more frequent assizes and a "flying squad" of judges to hear cases during the Long Vacation are recommended. 2. *(Flying Squad, the)* a branch of London's Metropolitan Police force, capable of moving quickly into action: It's a Saturday evening and members of the Flying Squad meet at police headquarters in Brixton.

flying squadron—1. a unit of the U.S. air force: I would change the organizational structure so the aircraft maintenance unit is part of the flying squadron to which pilots belong. 2. = *flying squad 1:* Ms. Dodson tells of the "Flying Squadron"—the nickname for a group of strikers who traveled to mills in order to plant the seeds of the union movement. 3. *(Nautical)* a detachment of vessels employed on any particular service: The Flying Squadron arrived at Cienfuegos, Cuba and established the blockade of that port.

flying weight • flyweight

flying weight—the weight of the plane or rocket without fuel: After using the rocket propellants the flying weight is 1780 Kg and during the ascent the total weight averages less than 2000 Kg.

flyweight—(Sport) a weight category in boxing, wrestling and weightlifting: Chartchai, three-time world flyweight champion, has been staying at a Tokyo hotel.

fold one's arms • fold one's hands

fold one's arms—place one's arms across the chest: The young woman folded her arms across her chest and frowned at Kay Stanley.

fold one's hands—press hands together with the fingers interlaced: She sat erectly, her hands folded on her black skirt.

follow the crowd • join the crowd

follow the crowd—think or behave in exactly the same way as everyone else: Don't expect anything original from this man—he just follows the crowd.

join the crowd—(also: join the club) is used to tell that one has already had a similar, usually unpleasant, experience: Oh, you're unemployed now are you? So am I—join the crowd.

follow the plough • put one's hand to the plough

follow the plough—be a ploughman or peasant: His boys followed the plough; and his girls went out to service.

put one's hand to the plough—(also: turn one's hand to the plough) begin a task (with the implication that one will persist at it): Ideala, having at last put her hand to the plough, worked with a will.

follow through with something • follow up with something

follow through with something—complete smth. such as a plan, etc.; continue doing smth. until it is finished: Young children have a need to know that you will follow through with what you say.

follow up with something—1. act further on smth.: Having a great idea and being able to follow up with it are two very different things. 2. do smth. after having done smth. else: The gymnasts perform compulsory routines today and follow up with individual events tomorrow.

foot the bill • top the bill

foot the bill—1. pay the bill, especially when considered large: When the Simpsons moved away, Greg was left to foot the bill for the building supplies. 2. pay for smth. whose cost is considered unreasonable (especially in consequence of smb.'s actions): The pharmaceutical industry will continue to hike drug costs, and consumers will foot the bill.

top the bill—be the most important item or person on a program of entertainments: The following year, she topped the bill at the Parisian music hall for a series of concerts there.

footman • leg man

footman—manservant who admits visitors, waits at table, etc.: He met a footman carrying a breakfast-tray.

leg man—1. an assistant running errands: He was the top man, and I was his "leg man." He personally handled most of the negotiations.... 2. a reporter gathering facts at the scene: On large newspaper, rewrite persons are assigned to such tasks as taking facts over the telephone from a leg man. 3. *(sl.)* a man who prefers females with good-looking legs: Clyde is a leg-man, but almost everything will turn him on a little.

footpad • pad foot

footpad—(UK dated) a holdup man: Roads in the neighborhood of the metropolis were infested by footpads or highwaymen.

pad foot—a curved leg of a chair, table, etc.: The legs of these tables are too straight to be classed as cabriole, and have pad feet.

footwork • leg work

footwork—sureness and accurate placing of the feet in boxing, dancing, etc.: Kaman makes the most of his footwork. He stays clear of Tosca and picks his punches well.

leg work—1. = *footwork:* Flying wings rely on the pilot's legwork to become airborne and span and performance is limited by the power of the human shoulder. 2. work which involves running errands or going from place to place: Patey was no man of action, but he might send a man we used a great deal for leg work.

for a bit • for quite a bit

for a bit—(coll.) for a short period of time: Why can't we stay here for a bit?

for quite a bit—(coll.) for quite a long time: Mr. Heissman was away for quite a bit.

for a kick-off • for kicks

for a kick-off—(coll.) to begin with; in the first place: "What's wrong with it?" "Well, for a kick-off, it hasn't been cooked properly."

for kicks—(coll.) do smth. for pleasure or excitement rather than because it is necessary: Dylan isn't serious about riding; he does it for kicks.

for a minute • not for a minute

for a minute—1. very briefly; for a short time: Could I borrow your English dictionary for a minute, please? 2. for one moment: The police moved to protect him and for a minute it seemed as if they were going to put him into a car.

not for a minute—(emphatic) absolutely never *(also: not for one minute):* He may have considered it but not for a minute did he believe that Scotland would win.

for a moment • for the moment

for a moment—very briefly; for a short time: He might have popped in for a moment, since he was passing this way.

Note: *The expression is not antonymous in meaning to the phrase* ***not for a moment****—(emphatic) absolutely never (also: not for one moment):* Not for a moment would I suggest that you did it deliberately.

for the moment—at present; for the time being: Sorry, Mr. Rathbone, I'm tied up for the moment, but I can see you later today.

for a wonder • to a wonder

for a wonder—surprisingly; strange to say: The children, for a wonder, kept still long enough for her to hear.

to a wonder—(dated) to an astonishing extent: His motives were not, nor could be, of the amorous kind, for she was ugly to a wonder.

for all it's worth • for what it's worth

for all it's worth—1. to the utmost of one's power or ability: Chris Reininger says the shark was huge and they were "fighting for all it's worth." 2. *(in the phrase "milk something for all it's worth")* exploit an opportunity, etc. to the full: A cynic might state at this point that Ash has decided to milk this story for all it's worth. 3. is used to imply that one may have doubts about the information he is offering: If the art market is hot now, it'll be hotter, and for all it's worth, here are my predictions.

for what it's worth— = for all it's worth 3: Oh, and for what it's worth, I read the second paragraph as saying that white voters were unified in not wanting to vote for a black man.

for all the marbles • have all one's marbles

for all the marbles—(coll.) compete for all the money or for the top prize: This game is for all the marbles, it all comes down to one game and the team that wants it most will win.

have all one's marbles—(coll.) be in possession of one's mental faculties: My first teacher will never be gone from my mind as long as I still "have all my marbles." *Cf.: lose one's marbles—(coll.) lack one's mental faculties:* Not only has Mike lost his common sense, it would appear that he's lost his marbles as well.

for all the world • for the world

for all the world—1. is used to emphasize assertions of likeness: She looked for all the world like her twin sister. 2. without the slightest doubt: I thought for all the world that the car would plunge headlong down the bank. 3. *(emphatic, negat.)* on no account; not for the greatest possible reward: I am sure I would not do such a thing for all the world.

for the world— = for all the world 3: I wouldn't for the world go into that deserted house at this time of night.

for demonstration • to demonstration

for demonstration — use smth. for purposes of demonstrating: These machines have been used for demonstration in our showroom and at trade shows.

to demonstration — prove smth. conclusively and beyond dispute: He proved to demonstration the soundness of the judgment he had formed.

for effect • for good effect

for effect— do smth. in order to impress people: His whole behavior and conversation are calculated for effect.

for good effect— use smth. profitably or to advantage: She talked about how children can be helped and our money used for good effect.

for fear of something • in fear of something

for fear of something—because of anxiety or fear about smth.: They were too scared to voice their own opinion for fear of assassination or torture.

in fear of something—frightened or alarmed by the prospect of smth.: He lived in fear of assassination by those loyal to the Government.

for good measure • in good measure

for good measure—given in addition to smth. else: All the poems are here, and then, for good measure, some hitherto unpublished fragments are added.

in good measure—by a large amount; to a large extent: The People's Forum is becoming in good measure also a women's forum.

for life • for one's life

for life—1. for the duration of a person's life: If you help me now, I'll be your friend for life. 2. said of smb. sentenced to life imprisonment: He was tried shortly after and sentenced for life.

for one's life—1. *(also: for dear life) run or fight* in a life-threatening situation: An armed man who was running for his life, was in the neighborhood. 2. *(emphatic, negat.)* even if one's life depended on it; however hard one tries *(also: for the life of one):* Walter, for his life, would have hardly called her by her name.

for money • for my money

for money—1. in return or exchange for money: People who cannot afford to play cards for money, sometimes sit down to a quiet game for love. 2. at the price paid: The overall quality is such that these volumes represent extremely good value for money.

for my money—(coll.) 1. in my opinion: For my money, Marian was chiefly responsible for the trouble we had had. 2. used as an emphatic expression of approval: Peter's the man for my money. He won't see a man lose a job for want of a good news story.

for my part • on my part

for my part—as to me; as far as I am concerned: For my part, I could never make a good ball player.

on my part—as regards my share in the action: The criticism offered on my part was not, as you put it, "counterproductive."

for once • for this once

for once—(also: for once in a way) as a single exception or a change from usual practice: Everyone we have invited has accepted, for once.

for this once—(also: just this once) as an exception on this particular occasion (because of special circumstances): I think we might relax the regulations for this once.

for one • for one thing

for one—as at least one person (as distinguished from "none at all"): I for one would rather command a computer through a keyboard than talk to it.

for one thing—as a single consideration; for one reason out of several: English football is so boring. For one thing, there are so few goals scored.

for pity's sake • out of pity

for pity's sake—is used when pleading for smth.: When you drive, for pity's sake don't smoke with one hand while you're trying to turn a corner.

out of pity—do smth. because of a feeling of pity: If I continue this relationship, I'd be doing it out of pity not actual love and that isn't fair for her either.

for short • in short

for short—as an abbreviation: We call him Monty for short, his real name being Montgomery.

in short—(also: in short words) in brief; by way of summary: He became, in short, the finest actor on the American stage.

***Note:** The expression does not correlate in meaning with the phrase **in short order**—very quickly; without delay:* In short order they tried, condemned and hanged all the prisoners.

for someone's liking • to someone's liking

for someone's liking—said of smth. which is too big, too hot, etc. and therefore not suited to smb.'s taste: They play music too loudly for their parents' liking.

to someone's liking—said of smth. suited to a person's interests, tastes or preferences: Do you find the room temperature to your liking?

for the foreseeable future • in the foreseeable future

for the foreseeable future—for a long time ahead: This seems likely to remain the pattern for the foreseeable future.

in the foreseeable future—fairly soon: There is little hope that this will occur in the foreseeable future.

for the good • to the good

for the good—for the benefit of smb. or smth.: We will work for the good of our community and protect the interests of all the taxpayers.

***Note:** The expression does not correlate in meaning with the phrase **for good**—(also: for good and all) permanently; for ever:* He says that he is leaving the country for good.

to the good—1. having a certain amount of money as profit: I am two thousand to the good. But he paid me in gourds, not dollars. 2. = *for the good:* Individual successes work to the good of the institution overall, notes Professor Denham.

for the last time • last time

for the last time—as the last and final instance: To-night he drives his engine for the last time.

last time—on the occasion next before the present: The last time I saw him he was looking about for something to do.

for the meantime • in the meantime

for the meantime—as far as the period of time from now on is concerned: Nevertheless this action does patch up, for the meantime, the quarrel that was developing between them.

in the meantime—during the period of time between two events; in the intervening time: His case won't come to court for months, and in the meantime half the people think him guilty.

for the support of someone • in support of someone

for the support of someone—for the purpose of providing financial assistance to smb.: Many years ago a sum of money was left for the support of aged spinsters.

in support of someone—speak, etc. in order to give one's backing to a person: Some railway workers vote in favor of an unofficial "token" strike in support of busmen.

forceful language • strong language

forceful language—language which is assertive and definite in expression: France and Russia began circulating proposals to significantly reduce the forceful language of the resolution.

strong language—1. = *forceful language:* Dismayed by the strong language of the resolution, the United States fired back with a harsh assessment of the behavior of some of its allies. 2. rude, offensive or abusive language: Some of the sites below may contain strong language, so please don't proceed if you are easily offended.

forget doing something • forget to do something

forget doing something—fail to keep in mind smth. that one has done: I guess she forgot talking to me yesterday and did not recognize me earlier. She is so busy after all.

forget to do something—fail to bear in mind smth. that one has to do: I'm not used to asking permission to do what I need to do, so it seems I forgot to talk to the manager.

four kings, the • three kings, the

four kings, the—the playing-cards bearing the representation of a king: Just turn over the cards, one by one, until the four kings turn up, all together. *Cf.: history of the Four Kings, the—(arch., also: books of the Four Kings, the) a pack of playing cards:* Freddy is up at Oxford, but Uncle says … all he seems to be studying is the History of the Four Kings.

three kings, the—(the Bible) the Wise Men who came from the East to worship the new-born Christ: The angel may be the one who helped the Three Kings to return home.

foxy lady • foxy man

foxy lady—(U.S. sl.) a sexually attractive woman: My strictly platonic friend Mei is a foxy lady even when she is just moving around the house in her sweatpants.

foxy man—1. a man who is sly and tricky: Herod was a foxy man and always tried to win power, but in the end he was recalled by the Roman emperor in disgrace. 2. a man resembling a fox in appearance: We found him waiting to receive us—a small, foxy man with a sharp but by no means amiable expression.

free in something • free with something

free in something—(of one's manners, speech, etc.) informal; unceremonious: I have always been frank and free in my talks.

free with something—generous with one's money, praise, etc.: In the woman's opinion, the gentleman was wonderfully free with his money.

***Note:** Neither expression correlates in meaning with the phrase **free of something**—(also: free from something) not affected by smth.; without smth.:* They agreed to certify that every shipment [of beef] was free of mad cow disease.

free ride • free trip

free ride—(coll.) participation without contributing anything: You've had a free ride long enough. You have to do your share of the work now.

free trip—(Drug users) an "echo" or a "flashback" of an L.S.D. experience: The kid got a free trip, and it scared her to death.

free someone from something • make someone free of something

free someone from something—1. rid a person from smth.

undesirable: He was determined to free the child from the stultifying effects of the formal classroom, with its fixation on discipline. 2. release a person from some physical hindrance: As soon as they arrived the colonel took the old man in his office after ordering to free him from the ropes.

make someone free of something—1. give a person permission to make free use of smth. one owns: Miss Tyler made him free of her house till his own eccentricities, and her wrath at his marriage, drove him out. 2. = *free someone from something 1:* I know that the management is mostly to blame for scheduling and everything, but that doesn't make him free of responsibility.

freeze someone out • put the freeze on someone

freeze someone out—(coll.) exclude a person from business, etc. by severe competition: They can bring a stock down to the lowest point, thus "freezing out" the unhappy stockholders.

put the freeze on someone—(U.S. sl.) ignore a person; end social contact with smb. *(also: put the chill on someone):* Let's put the freeze on Ted until he starts acting better.

Note: *a) The expression does not correlate in meaning with the phrase* ***freeze on to someone****—(coll.) 1. hold on to smb.; stick to a person:* If ever you see him again, Fentiman, freeze on to him like grim death. 2. *become attached to a person:* He's a lawyer and he might not freeze on to you.

b) The expression is not antonymous in meaning to the phrase ***turn the heat on someone****—(sl.) put pressure on a person; subject smb. to a severe cross-examination (also: put the heat on someone):* Mukhtar is in jail in connection with an old case in which he surrendered soon after the police turned the heat on him.

fresh as a daisy • fresh as a rose

fresh as a daisy—feeling cheerful and full of energy: It was six in the morning, dawn was breaking, but Nick still felt as fresh as a daisy, ready to dance, drink and talk for hours longer.

fresh as a rose—(of a woman) looking very attractive, with a fresh color: She's beautiful, yes, really beautiful, fresh as a rose on the day of the battle or whatever that poem is.

friend at court • friend of the court

friend at court—(also: friend in court) smb. in a position of influence who is willing to act in a person's behalf: We felt that we always had a friend at court in Uncle Alec, no matter what we did or left undone.

friend of the court—(legal) an adviser to the court who volunteers to offer information on some aspect of the case: The role of the adjudication officer is to act as *amicus curiae* (friend of the court) assisting the tribunal in its investigation.

Friendly Society, the • Society of Friends, the

Friendly Society, the—(hist.) mutual-aid organization formed to protect members against debts incurred through illness, etc.: The growth of the Friendly Society is impressive. At the beginning during the 1814–1816 period, there were roughly twenty members.

Society of Friends, the—(also: Religious Society of Friends, the) the Quakers *(a Christian sect, founded in the mid–17th century in England):* Probably the best known historical figure in the Society of Friends was William Penn. Born in 1644, he became a Quaker in 1667…

from A to B • from A to Z

from A to B—from one point or position to another: In traffic-choked cities the slender bike is the fastest means of getting from A to B.

from A to Z—(also: from A to Izzard) from beginning to end; completely: Every program-builder should know the symphonic repertoire from A to Z.

from Dan to Beersheba • from Land's End to John o' Groat's

from Dan to Beersheba—from one end of the land to the other *(originally of biblical Palestine):* Having visited the most remarkable places from Dan to Beersheba, he finally returned home after some eleven months.

from Land's End to John o' Groats—(UK) from one end of Great Britain to the other: Every well-known branded article (as advertised on television) costs precisely the same from Land's End to John o' Groats.

Note: *Neither expression correlates in meaning with the phrase* ***from China to Peru****—all over the world:* The invention of radio meant that people from China to Peru could learn of an event soon after it happened.

from hand to hand • hand-to-hand

from hand to hand—pass from one person to a series of other persons: The book traveled from hand to hand until it got back to its owner.

hand-to-hand—(of fighting) at close quarters; man to man: This excellent manual on combat hand-to-hand fighting still holds up today.

from hand to mouth • from mouth to mouth

from hand to mouth—(in the phrase "live from hand to mouth") have just enough money to live on: With farmers living from hand to mouth, it is difficult to expect them to take to organic cultivation.

from mouth to mouth—(of a tale, rumor, etc.) pass from one person to a series of other persons: Xavier's name was repeated from mouth to mouth with cries of vengeance.

from nose to tail • nose to tail

from nose to tail—(usually of animals) as measured from one extremity to the other: A full grown mule deer measures about sixty five inches from nose to tail.

Note: *The expression does not correlate in meaning with the phrase* ***from head to foot****—(also: from top to toe) 1. all over a person's body:* Women covered from head to foot can be seen shopping next to the mini-skirted Russian women. 2. *in every way; in all respects:* A gentleman? … That he is, from head to foot.

nose to tail—(of motor vehicles) traveling or placed very close behind one another: Traffic stood nose to tail right the way down the Strand.

from out to out • from space to space

from out to out—in total external length or breadth: The extreme length of the building, from out to out, is 96 feet, and the extreme width 51 feet.

from space to space—at (regular) intervals: A heavy balustrade is ornamented from space to space with huge grotesque figures of animals.

from the bottom up • from the ground up

from the bottom up—from the very beginning; from start to finish: I started out sweeping the floors and learned everything from the bottom up.

from the ground up—completely; entirely: Let me tell you right here that whatever I may or may not be, I am an American from the ground up.

from the floor • from the top

from the floor—(of questions, remarks, etc.) delivered by rank and file members, as opposed to a governing body: The amendments from the floor were sufficiently substantial to make the final version a fair representation of majority opinion.

from the top—(of a piece of music) played from the earliest part or from the beginning: By the time the song was over the girl was still carrying on, so we played it again from the top.

from the wood • out of the wood

from the wood—(usually of beer) from the cask or barrel: "Beer from the wood," or the dispensing of ales from wooden casks, is a phenomenon at which American brewers must simply stand in awe. *Cf.: in the wood—(also: in wood) said of wine or beer kept in barrels:* Wines have been kept in the wood for the period proper for attaining maturity.

out of the wood—(usually negat.) free from trouble or difficulties *(also: out of the woods):* As long as Riel is uncaptured the Canadian Government is not out of the wood.

from time to time • time after time

from time to time—occasionally; now and again: He left here five or six years ago, but I still see him from time to time.

time after time—repeatedly; over and over again: I have warned him time after time, but he takes no notice.

from top to bottom • from top to toe

from top to bottom—in every part (of a house): The police searched the house from top to bottom.

Note: *The expression does not correlate in meaning with the phrase **from the zenith to the nadir**—(liter.) from the highest to the lowest possible point in one's fortunes, etc.:* The film flopped, and all Chu's contracts were cancelled. In no time he plummeted from the zenith to the nadir.

from top to toe—(also: from head to foot) 1. all over a person's body: He was covered in mud from top to toe. 2. in every way; in all respects: He was French from top to toe, sleek and elegant.

front man • frontsman

front man—1. a man who publicly represents a person or an organization: The former adviser now serves as a front man for a large foundation. 2. *(also: straw man)* a respectable man who serves as a cover for a questionable enterprise: Department of Justice investigators believe that Earl Browder is a mere front-man. 3. the lead performer in a musical group: The keyboard player is the front man for this band and he puts on a great, high energy show. 4. a television presenter: Dimbleby is the most accomplished front-man in television's history.

Note: *The expression does not correlate in meaning with the phrase **front runner**—a competitor who performs best or is in a leading position:* Until several days ago, she was a front runner in this week's Democratic primary.

frontsman—1. = *front man 1:* The frontsman at the inquiry desk is sympathetic and directs us to come back in an hour to ask the boss. 2. = *front man 3:* Throughout his career, the frontsman, composer, and sax player Blicher has been influenced by the great songwriters.

frown at something • frown on something

frown at something—draw the eyebrows together to express displeasure, etc. when looking at smth.: Then he took one final glance over my application and frowned at my birth date.

frown on something—show or express disapproval of smth.: The older generation have always frowned on some of the ideas of the young.

full stop *(UK)* • full stop *(U.S.)*

full stop (UK)—1. punctuation mark used at the end of a sentence: I remember sitting in class, repeating after the teacher—full stop, capital letter. 2. is used as an interjection to terminate a phrase with finality and emphasis: In fact, anything nuclear-related scares me, full stop. 3. a complete stop (as of traffic, etc.): The horse then ... made a full stop, and expressed an unwillingness to proceed any farther.

full stop (U.S.)— = *full stop (UK) 3:* Despite the lack of any visible traffic, Sam made a full stop at the intersection and then turned north.

funny money • serious money

funny money—1. counterfeit money: The police warned storekeepers that some funny money was being passed around town. 2. money obtained from an illegal or questionable source: Is he really there to launder some "funny money" with his partner, Sammy? 3. currency with little value, especially artificially inflated: Selling by speculators caused the stock market to correct. The correction encouraged the authorities to print more funny money.

serious money—(also: serious coin) a considerable sum of money; a lot of money: She has made some serious money and was fairly convincing of the idea that I could do the same.

fur coat • fur-lined coat

fur coat—a coat made of fur: The fur coat she wore must have cost her black-marketeer husband the best part of a thousand.

fur-lined coat—a coat with a fur lining: He was wearing a heavy fur-lined coat which made him appear bigger and more fearsome than he was.

fuss at someone • fuss over someone

fuss at someone—(coll.) scold or noisily reproach a person *(also: fuss someone out):* I hate it when I fuss at my kids. I think of how awful other parents sound when they fuss at their kids.

fuss over someone—(also: make a fuss over someone) treat smb. with an excessive display of attention or concern: High in the castle, Ariashal waited for the birth of her child. Her women fussed over her, trying to help her prepare.

fuss someone • fuss someone out

fuss someone—(coll.) 1. *(also: fuss over someone)* treat smb. with an excessive display of attention or concern: This was fine when she was at home to fuss me ... but when she had to leave me I got very upset. 2. bother or annoy a person: It is generally the safest way to take care to be in time ourselves, but to guard against fussing other people.

fuss someone out—(coll.) scold or noisily reproach a person *(also: fuss at someone):* I was slightly scared she was going to fuss me out for waking her up.

gain a point • gain one's point

gain a point—1. score a point in a game or contest: A player gains a point if the opponent hits the ball when it is out of bounds (anywhere not on his court). 2. increase one's authority, influence, or reputation: The English Minister can often gain a point by dexterous dealing in Parliament.

gain one's point—persuade smb. to agree to one's objective: When he saw that he could not gain his point, the young gentleman got into a temper.

gain credit • get credit

gain credit—1. receive recognition, praise, or approval: It was Alberto Santos-Dumont who gained credit for building the first dirigible that could be maneuvered through the air. 2. complete a part of the higher education course (passing a test, etc.): Students may seek approval to use previously gained credit toward a new program of study. 3. *(of rumors, etc.)* acquire credence; be generally believed: An accusation so improbable gained but little credit.

get credit—1. = *gain credit 1:* The governor, who has the lowest approval rating of any California governor, doesn't even get credit for what he has accomplished. 2. = *gain credit 2:* Students may not get credit for more than one writing intensive course in a semester. 3. be allowed a period of time before one has to pay for goods and services: In many cases rural households get credit for the goods they purchase from traders.

gain ground on someone • gain ground with someone

gain ground on someone—get closer to a person pursued: Each minute did their enemy gain ground perceptibly upon them.

gain ground with someone—win smb.'s favor: I had been gaining ground with Mr. Rankeillor, and in proportion as I gained ground, gaining confidence.

gain in something • gain on something

gain in something—acquire more of a particular quality: The Leader of the Opposition gained significantly in stature as a result of his speech.

gain on something—1. get closer to a vehicle pursued: The police-launch was quickly gaining on the boat. 2. move further ahead of a vehicle: The leading group of three continued to gain on the rest of the boats. **3.** *(of the sea)* encroach upon the coast: The sea was gradually gaining on the buildings, which at length almost entirely disappeared.

gallop through something • run through something

gallop through something—do and complete smth. quickly: I seem to have galloped through the whole work, which I hope will not suffer from not having devoted more time.

run through something—1. *(of a rumor, gossip, etc.)* pass or spread through a place: The news ran through the town like wild-fire. 2. read and check smth. quickly: Before the interview I ran through my notes and scribbled over my questions making them word-perfect. *3. (of money, etc.)* spend fast: Inevitably, as he ran through his fortune, which took him only a few months, he was eventually obliged to face up to realities. 4. *(of a piece of music, etc.)* repeat or practice: We had a full dress rehearsal and ran through the whole play several times.

Note: *The expression is not equivalent in meaning to the phrase* ***run something through***—1. *make a film pass through a projector:* We ran the film through several more times. *2. make a hole through smth.:* Do they burn the flag, spit on it, run it through with a sword?

See also: come through something / go through something.

gamble at something • gamble in something • gamble with something

gamble at something—risk money in a game of chance: The men got out a pack of Mexican cards and gambled at a game called "Coon-can."

gamble in something—risk money by investing in a commodity: Matrons gambled in shares quite as wildly as did the unkempt disreputables from the oil fields.

gamble with something—1. gamble using cards, dice, etc.: They had a pack of real cards and gambled with them at *Grab.* 2. risk smth.: After working as an apprentice for three years, there was no way he was going to gamble with his future.

gamble on something • take a gamble on something

gamble on something—1. risk money on the unknown result of a race, etc.: Cockfighting is a fight between male chickens (roosters), in which people gamble on the outcome of the fight. 2. act in the hope of smth. being successful, true, etc.: I wouldn't gamble on the weather being fine. *Cf.: you can gamble on that—(coll.) you may be sure of that:* There will be trouble for someone. You can gamble on that.

take a gamble on something— = *gamble on something 2:* The firm took a gamble on an emerging market with a multi-million dollar investment.

game is over, the • party is over, the

game is over, the—(also: game is up, the) 1. the situation is lost beyond rescue: He knew the game was over and began to seek a diplomatic solution to the conflict. 2. said when the wrong one has done or smb.'s guilty secret has been discovered: Okay, sweetheart, game's over. What's up?

party is over, the—(also: honeymoon is over) the first happy period or easy time has come to an end: Local government is coming to realize that, for the time being, the party is over.

game time • playtime

game time—(coll.) crucial moment for doing business; time to do what has to be done: Will this report be ready by game time?

playtime—a time for play or recreation (between lessons at school, etc.): Do the children in your class run around or stand around a lot at playtime?

garden house • orchard house

garden house—a summer house; a house situated in a garden: The bakery, tin shop and garden house look as if they were still open for business.

orchard house—a greenhouse for the fruit too delicate to be grown in the open air: By dwarfing them [fruit trees] you can have a great variety in a small space in the orchard house and get fine fruit.

Garden State, the • Peace Garden State, the

Garden State, the—(U.S.) a nickname of the state of New Jersey: New Jersey was nicknamed the "Garden State" in the 1800s in recognition of its fertile soil and agrarian economy.

Peace Garden State, the—(U.S.) a nickname of the state of North Dakota: North Dakota is called the Peace Garden State — in reference to the International Peace Garden on the border between North Dakota and Manitoba.

gay as a goose • gay as a lark

gay as a goose—(sl.) said of a homosexual person *(also: gay as pink ink):* It may not even occur to some women that their perfect gentleman is gay as a goose.

gay as a lark—said of smb. who is lively and enjoyable, free from worries and fears: Ha, ha! We should be as gay as larks, Mr. Richard — why not?

General Certificate of Education • General Certificate of Secondary Education

General Certificate of Education—the school leavers certificate formerly used in Britain: A "General Certificate of Education" should be awarded showing the subjects in which the candidate has satisfied the examiners.

General Certificate of Secondary Education—the school leavers certificate currently adopted in Britain: The General Certificate of Secondary Education qualification is one of the main entry qualifications for selection to Universities.

General of the Armies • General of the Army

General of the Armies—the highest U.S. Army rank that has only been awarded to Washington and Pershing in recognition of their special significance in the country's history: In 1919, John J. Pershing was named "General of the Armies of the United States," and held the rank until he died, in 1948.

General of the Army—a five-star U.S. Army rank that is

immediately above General and conferred only in wartime: George C. Marshall was one of the most renowned military figures in United States history, serving as a General of the Army...

gentleman of fortune • man of fortune

gentleman of fortune—(euph., dated) a pirate: By a "gentleman of fortune" they plainly meant neither more nor less than a common pirate.

man of fortune—a person possessing great (usually inherited) wealth: A sailing club consisting of four or five young men of fortune, have conducted the annual Regattas.

Note: *The expression does not correlate in meaning with the phrase* ***fortunate man****— a man favored by fortune; a lucky person:* He was a fortunate man, learning from her to embrace the simple joys of everyday life.

Gentleman Usher • Gentleman Usher of the Black Rod

Gentleman Usher—(UK) a man who ushers visitors into the presence of a person of rank: It now being dinner time, the Gentleman Usher proceeds to take his Lord's commands.

Gentleman Usher of the Black Rod—usher to the British House of Lords: They assemble in their own chamber from where they are summoned by the Gentleman Usher of the Black Rod.

George Cross, the • Saint George's cross, the

George Cross, the—(UK) a decoration instituted in 1940, primarily for civilians in recognition of acts of the greatest heroism: In recognition of the part played by the Maltese people, King George VI awarded the George Cross to the island.

Saint George's cross, the—an upright and a horizontal bar of red, crossing each other in the center: The Saint George's Cross flag as the national flag of England has no official proportions, as it is not used officially by government bodies.

get a break • have a break

get a break—1. take time off from an activity: It was hard for me because whenever I got a break from school, I had to leave and see my other parent. 2. *(coll.)* get a good deal in a transaction, etc.: Our customers usually expect to get a break when they buy in quantity. 3. *(coll.)* get an opportunity or special consideration: He talked about racism and about how hard it is to get a break when you are Black. *Cf.: get all the breaks— be fortunate; have luck:* That fellow gets all the breaks! He's been working here only six months, and he's already been promoted to vice president!

have a break— = get a break 1: Finally, I told him I'd interview him over lunch, when he had a break.

get a bump • make a bump

get a bump—1. get a swelling on one's body as a result of a blow: My poor dad hit the branch with his head and got a bump and a cut. 2. *(of a vehicle)* be hit by another vehicle, etc.: Her car got three severe bumps while parked in London.

make a bump—(UK Universities boat races) "bump" another boat as a proof of overtaking it: The best coxswain cannot make a bump, unless his boat can overlap the other!

get a call • get one's call

get a call—receive a message by radio or telephone; be summoned: As soon as I got the call, I was in the car and on my way.

get one's call—(euph.) feel impending death: His breath labored, and there was pain in his eyes. "I've got my call," he said faintly.

get a duck • get the bird

get a duck—(Sport) fail to score *(also: get a duck's egg):* Life is very much like cricket: Some get scores and some "a duck."

get the bird—1. *(Theater)* be hissed by the audience: You should have been there when Caballe got the bird—deservedly, I fear. 2. *(coll.)* be dismissed from employment: When you were ill, I stole for you. I got the bird for it.

See also: give someone the bird / have a bird.

get a fix of something • get a fix on something

get a fix of something—(coll.) obtain a dose of smth., especially an addictive drug: Politicians up for re-election are like crack addicts; they'll say anything to anyone to get a fix of votes.

get a fix on something—(coll.) obtain a clear understanding of smth.: Because of lax reporting requirements it's difficult to get a fix on precisely what these companies own.

get a foot in • put a foot in

get a foot in—start working at a low level in the hope of getting a better position in the future: Baker was soon playing bit parts on the stage, got a foot in at the National Theatre, and then the big break came. *Cf.: get a foot on the housing ladder— manage to buy one's first house so that one can buy a better second house later:* Soldiers are to be offered interest-free Government loans to help them get a foot on the housing ladder.

put a foot in—interfere in smth.: Whatever happens to me, I won't have this fellow Getliffe putting a foot in.

Note: *The expression does not correlate in meaning with the phrase* ***put the boot in****—(coll.) 1. kick a person in a brutal manner:* With that lot it's not too bad as long as you stay on your feet. If they get you down they put the boot in. 2. *take unfair advantage of smb., especially when the person is already defeated:* They rough him up when he gives evidence, and then, while the bruising is still fresh, they put the boot in by issuing a critical report.

get a good bang for one's buck • get a good run for one's money

get a good bang for one's buck—(coll.) get a good value for one's money *(also: have a good bang for one's buck):* I am a student who does not make much money and I really got a good bang for my buck here.

get a good run for one's money—(also: have a good run for one's money) 1. face a strong challenge or competition from a person: If matched competitively Steven would get a good run for his money. Chuck would give him a good fight. He may be short, but he is agile and a fast mover. 2. derive much satisfaction in return for one's outlay or efforts: I was not on the ballot paper but there was serious interest in my attempt.... I got a good run for my money nonetheless.

get a goose egg • goose that lays the golden eggs

get a goose egg—1. *(Sport)* fail to score *(also: get a duck's egg):* Anytime you get a goose egg in modern-day football, it's absolutely phenomenal. 2. *(sl.)* get a bump on the head: I walked into a door and got a big goose egg on my forehead.

goose that lays the golden eggs—a source of wealth that should not be sacrificed *(in allusion to the proverb "kill the goose that lays the golden eggs"):* With recent developments in the airline industry, the last thing Atlanta needs is to lose faith in the goose that lays the golden eggs.

get a grip on something • get to grips with something

get a grip on something—take control of smth. so that one can deal with it successfully: So far the country has failed to get a grip on its inflation rate.

Note: *The expression does not correlate in meaning with the phrase* ***get a grasp of something****— obtain a clear understanding of smth.:* Not only do you get a grasp of the behind-the-scenes at a San Francisco radio station, you get an entertaining read...

get to grips with something—(also: come to grips with something) struggle with a difficult problem, task, etc.: Governments should get to grips with the challenges posed by globalization.

get a hand for something • get a hand with something

get a hand for something—1. receive applause or praise for smth.: Lisa Knott gets a hand for driving all the way down from Santa Barbara to compete. 2. become skilful at dealing with smth.: Try to get "a hand" for that machine, and test out its pros and cons.

get a hand with something—receive assistance with smth.: Mary would really like to get a hand with that. It's too much for one person.

get a kick • get a kick in the teeth

get a kick—(coll.) feel a thrill of pleasure or excitement out of smth.: I was told I should get a kick out of that journey—and I certainly did.

get a kick in the teeth—(coll.) experience an embarrassing refusal or failure: I'll probably just get another kick in the teeth but I'll do it none the less.

get a life • get life

get a life—(sl., usually imper.) stop worrying about petty things; find smth. useful or meaningful to do with oneself: I wish Janet would get a life. She's always complaining about nothing.

get life—be sentenced to life imprisonment: Shame on those who continue to campaign to grant him early parole.... Most killers get life in prison for premeditated murder.

See also: make a life for oneself / make a living for oneself.

get a load of something • get a load on

get a load of something—(sl.) 1. listen to smth. carefully: Did you get a load of what she said? 2. take a look at smth.; pay attention to smth.: Get a load of that car. It's got real wire wheels.

get a load on—(sl.) be drunk *(also: get one's load on)*: I got a load on and had to have Jonas come down in a taxi and take me home.

Note: *The expression is not antonymous in meaning to the phrase* ***take a load off someone's mind****— relieve a person of anxiety:* You have taken a load off my mind. I was afraid that we couldn't recoup the money we had loaned.

get a move on • get on the move

get a move on—(often imper.) 1. hasten one's steps; hurry up: As he slowed down, she added sharply, "Nay, get a move on, will you!" 2. start acting vigorously: I really just hadn't packed things away very well, so I got a move on and got the room in decent order.

Note: *The expression does not correlate in meaning with the phrase* ***move on****—1. go further; change to smth. new:* I think we've talked enough about that subject; let's move on. 2. *a policeman's order not to stand in one place:* Occasionally, police ordered them to move on under the city's anti-panhandling ordinance. 3. *leave one's home and move to another place:* I was employed in Menlo Park, just down the peninsula from San Francisco. After a few years, I moved on while Reggie stayed.

get on the move—(also: get moving) begin to travel: In the morning we got on the move again, this time for Southampton.

get a point • get the point

get a point—(also: gain a point) score a point in a game or contest: Under the initial rules, the first person who does get a point has already won.

Note: *The expression does not correlate in meaning with the phrase* ***have a point****— be right about a particular matter:* Okay, I'll admit you have a point here. I had recent films in mind, and the films you mentioned are all from the 1970s.

get the point—understand what another person is trying to prove or explain: I didn't even have to speak and she got the point.

get a raise • get a rise

get a raise—be given an increase in one's wage or salary: My bureau were delighted.... I got a raise when I went back to Cuba.

Note: *The expression does not correlate in meaning with the phrase* ***make a raise****—(also: make a rise) succeed in striking gold or other precious metals by mining:* He fled to the mountains, went into mining, made a raise...

get a rise—1. = *get a raise:* The boss said that if things went OK I should get a rise soon. 2. *(coll.)* make a person become annoyed or angry: You must be pulling our legs trying to get a reaction, a rise. 3. *(sl., of men)* experience an erection: "What was it like?" "It was okay, except I couldn't get a proper rise."

Note: *The expression does not correlate in meaning with the phrase* ***get a lift****— be allowed to travel some distance in a passing vehicle:* "Don't they ever send a car for you?" "Good Lord, no. Sometimes I get a lift."

get a rise out of someone • take the rise out of someone

get a rise out of someone—(coll.) make a person become annoyed or angry: "Tell everyone I'm not Cuban," said Medwick, hoping to get a rise out of the driver. But none came.

take the rise out of someone—(coll.) embarrass smb. into humility (making him realize that he is not so strong, clever, etc.): They were taking the rise out of us and my players won't forget that embarrassment in a hurry.

get a rush from something • get a rush on something

get a rush from something—(U.S. sl.) become excited or exhilarated by smth.: If you get a rush from surfing, skateboarding or snow boarding, you'll find this emerging sport is pure exhilaration.

get a rush on something—(sl., also: put a rush on something) hurry up with smth.; make haste with smth.: The finger print man arrives, and Columbo asks him to get a rush on the reports from the police lab.

get a shot at something • give something a shot

get a shot at something—1. shoot at smth.: The buck was partly hidden. I couldn't get a shot at it. 2. *(coll.)* attempt to do smth. new or unfamiliar: I'm anxious to get a shot at this early project that Tim worked on.

give something a shot— = get a shot at something 2: Is anyone else willing to give this problem a shot in the meantime?

get a start • get one's start

get a start—1. receive help starting one's car: My car is stalled. I need to get a start. 2. receive the first major opportunity of one's career: She got a start in show business in Cincinnati.

Note: *The expression does not correlate in meaning with the phrase* ***get a head start****— begin smth. earlier than another person thus gaining an advantage:* Taxpayers are encouraged to get a head start on tax preparation, especially since early filers avoid the last minute rush.

get one's start— = *get a start 2:* She helped me to get my start by recommending me to the manager.

get a word in • put a word in

get a word in—(also: get in a word) succeed in saying smth. when other people are talking ignoring you: You are so hot-headed and exclamatory that I cannot get a word in. *Cf.: get a word in edgewise—used as an emphatic variant of the former:* I want to ask him about the book, but it's a little hard to get a word in edgewise. Everyone's animated and talking all at once.

put a word in—(also: put in a word) 1. contribute an utterance to a conversation: He seemed oblivious to the fact that Picard had been trying to put a word in for the past minute or two. 2. speak in support of smb.; recommend a person: You may depend upon my putting in a word for you whenever I can.

get around something • get around to something

get around something—(also: get round something) circumvent or evade rules, regulations, etc. (without committing a legal offence): In order to get around this legal point the refugees are said to be "housed" there rather than "detained."

Note: *The expression does not correlate in meaning with the phrase* ***get one's head around something****—(coll.) understand or come to terms with smth.:* I've got my head around the fact that I'm going to miss a number of games. It was difficult at the start when I first picked up the injury.

get around to something—(also: get round to something) find time for smth.; deal with smth. (when more important matters have been dealt with): Don't leave it to chance or think you will get around to it later when you have more time.

get away • make one's getaway

get away—1. leave a place, especially with some difficulty: "Sorry I couldn't get away sooner," said Patrick. "I had some things to finish up." 2. escape from prison, the police, etc.: Police say the suspect got away on a green motorcycle with no tags. 3. escape smth. dangerous: There were five seconds between him and eternity and how he got away before the explosion is a mystery. 4. spend time away from a place: It was nice to get away for a few days, and just enjoy each other's company.

make one's getaway—1. = *get away 2:* A man suspected of stealing made his getaway on a bicycle. 2. have a short vacation: Still no plans for your summer vacation? ...but it's not too late to make your getaway.

get back at someone • get back to someone

get back at someone—gain revenge against a person: Students have no way of getting back at a teacher who marks their work unfairly.

get back to someone—speak to smb. again at a later time (by telephone): I'll take advice on this matter and get back to you this afternoon.

get back on the rails • go off the rails

get back on the rails—successfully recover from adverse situation, etc.: Bob Taft's campaign got back on the rails in last week's primaries. One victory came in Wisconsin...

go off the rails—(also: run off the rails) start behaving in a way that is not acceptable: Returning to the U.S., he is disowned by the CIA, which portrays him as a rogue agent who went off the rails.

get by on something • get by with something

get by on something—survive by means of smth. (usually inadequate): She gets by on odd jobs hoping to make it through the worst crisis that has ever hit the economy.

get by with something—1. = *get by on something:* I don't know how she gets by with the money she earns from that job. 2. manage with smth. that is available, for want of anything better: You may be able to get by with one screwdriver but it's better to buy a large and a small one. 3. *(also: get away with something)* go unpunished for doing smth. reprehensible: Don't try to cheat on your income tax, you'll never get by with it.

get caught doing something • get caught up on something

get caught doing something—be found doing smth. reprehensible; get caught in the act: Did Vi get caught driving without a license? Did she get a ticket?

get caught up on something—do things that one has not had time to do until now: I have to get caught up on my studies. I missed two classes.

get cold feet • hotfoot it

get cold feet—lose one's courage or nerve: Do you think he is just getting cold feet, or do you think it's more than that? We are afraid he just won't show up at the church.

Note: *The expression does not correlate in meaning with the phrase* ***cool one's heels****—(coll.) be kept waiting by smb. in authority, as for an appointment (also: kick one's heels):* The doctor kept her cooling her heels for almost an hour.

hotfoot it—leave in great haste; walk or run hurriedly: The camp staff expects that once the shouts of the campers fill the hollow, the bear will hotfoot it out of there.

Note: *The expression is not equivalent in meaning to the phrase* ***foot it****—(coll., also: leg it) walk; go on foot:* Several of the wagons became sloughed and the passengers were compelled to "foot it" to town.

get full marks for something • get full marks in something

get full marks for something—1. gain the maximum number of marks in a subject: Half the students got full marks for what was intended to be an easy question. 2. be praised for some good quality: Mr. Jenkins gets full marks for his courage and enterprise.

get full marks in something—(also: score full marks in something) = *get full marks for something 1:* Only one in six adults got full marks in a test of six familiar words.

get-go • get-up-and-go

get-go—(coll., in the phrase "from the get-go") from the beginning: I think Sawyer knew from the get-go that his escape attempt would fail.

get-up-and-go—(coll.) readiness for vigorous activity: He was noted for his "get-up-and-go," a quality which later enabled him to win success.

get hold of someone • take hold of someone

get hold of someone—1. physically grasp or hold a person: I got hold of him and dragged him back from the edge just in time. 2. locate a person; secure smb.'s presence: There had been considerable difficulty in getting hold of a key witness. 3. reach smb. on the telephone: I was able to get hold of the office manager and cancel the order.

Note: *The expression does not correlate in meaning with the phrase* ***have hold of someone****—(also: have a hold over someone) have power or control over a person:* They are what is called "willed" to do certain things desired by the gentlemen who have hold of them.

take hold of someone— = *get hold of someone 1:* This beautiful and most anomalous structure is adapted to take hold of floating marine animals.

get hot • get it hot

get hot—1. begin feeling hot: I would get up and run on the spot. Even when I got hot I continued because I was never so cold in my life. 2. become busy or hectic: Things always get hot around here toward the end of the month.

get it hot—(coll.) be punished or scolded severely: He'll get it hot when his mother finds out that he has broken her new vase.

get hot and bothered • get hot under the collar

get hot and bothered—(coll.) get excited or nervous: The logical conclusion is that there's no reason to get hot and bothered about a demographic threat.

get hot under the collar—(coll.) get angry, resentful, or indignant: There's no need to get hot under the collar at Susie's remarks — she didn't mean to offend you.

get in a word • put in a word

get in a word—(also: get a word in) succeed in saying smth. when other people are talking ignoring you: We two plunged into a conversation into which Roger could not get in a word: in fact we forgot all about him. *Cf.: get in a word edgewise—used as an emphatic variant of the former:* My men at once sat down and held a council of war, in which I could not get in a word edgewise.

put in a word—(also: put a word in) 1. contribute an utterance to a conversation: I want to put in a word about that, because they are doing extremely important work.... 2. speak in support of smb.; recommend a person: I'd like to put in a word for someone who has proved to be a tireless proponent of uncompromising, dazzling music.

get in the way of something • get into the way of something

get in the way of something—hinder or interfere with smth.: I'm afraid that our preoccupation with the difficulty of riding rather got in the way of our enjoyment.

get into the way of something—1. acquire the habit of doing smth.: Once I got into the way of it, we spent the afternoon riding the horses down to the beach. 2. = *get in the way of something:* My suspicion is that your negative beliefs about yourself have got into the way of finding a suitable job.

get in touch with someone • put the touch on someone

get in touch with someone—get into contact with a person: "Why not get in touch with your lawyer?" "Not on your life! It would be a tacit admission of my guilt."

put the touch on someone—(U.S. sl.) try to get money from a person: Bill put the touch on me yesterday, but I told him to drop dead.

get into a temper • get out of temper

get into a temper—(also: fly into a temper) become angry: When he gets into a temper we try to diffuse it with laughter or I just sit and hug him.

get out of temper— = get into a temper: He soon gets out of temper if things do not go as he would like them to.

get into bed with someone • go to bed with someone

get into bed with someone—(also: jump into bed with someone) 1. *(euph.)* have sex with a person: Most of the time they just want to get into bed with someone as soon as possible. 2. become closely involved with a person or group: They got into bed with Peugeot precisely because they have superior design expertise.

go to bed with someone— = get into bed with someone 1: I didn't want to go to bed with him, but I wanted him to know how much I loved and appreciated him.

get into full swing • get into the swing of things

get into full swing—(of an activity) become most vigorous or energetic: In the summer months, things really get into full swing around here.

get into the swing of things—adapt to an environment or activity: It's been difficult for me to get into the swing of things since my vacation.

get into hot water • pour cold water on someone

get into hot water—get into difficulty or trouble: Mayor Rances could get into hot water if government state prosecutors make good their threat.

pour cold water on someone—(also: throw cold water on someone) discourage a person; curb smb.'s enthusiasm: I could sense that he said it with care and honesty, not deliberately to pour cold water on me or my idea. *Cf.: be a cold shower to someone—said of a surprisingly chilly reception, reaction, or response:* The small voter turnout was a cold shower to the League of Women Voters.

get into one's stride • take something in one's stride

get into one's stride—start getting comfortable with an activity: It may take Helen a long time to do the job now, but she'll work much faster when she has got into her stride.

take something in one's stride—accept things calmly without getting excited: John took the news of his transfer abroad in his stride and did not let it affect his work in any way.

get into someone's skin • get under someone's skin

get into someone's skin—(coll.) come to a complete understanding of smb.'s inner nature (impersonating a character, etc.): In the church scene, Miss Rehan won her audience ... but she never really "got into the skin" of Beatrice.

get under someone's skin—(coll.) 1. bother or irritate a person: John is so annoying at times. He really gets under my skin. 2. affect a person so that he becomes very interested in smth.: After a slow start, the play gets under your skin because of its sympathy with the frustrations of small town life. 3. = *get into someone's skin:* I think you are interested in — character, shall we say? To get under the skin, as it were, of your criminal.

get it into one's head • take it into one's head

get it into one's head—1. realize the significance of smth.: I wish you would get it into your head, once and for all, that I'm not made of money. 2. start to imagine or believe smth. without sufficient grounds: Somehow he got it into his head that everyone was blaming him.

Note: *The expression does not correlate in meaning with the phrase* ***get it through one's head****—figure out smth.; begin to understand smth.:* I never could get it through my head how a car engine works.

take it into one's head—1. = *get it into one's head 2:* Somehow he'd taken it into his head that his wife was trying to poison him. 2. decide to do smth.: If I should take it into my head to tell what I had heard, tremendous mischief could result.

get it off • get it off one's chest

get it off—(sl.) achieve sexual satisfaction: The entire crew of the yacht came ashore to get it off.

get it off one's chest—relieve one's mind by telling about one's problems, etc.: It's about time we long-suffering Northerners got it off our chest.

get it off with someone • get off with someone

get it off with someone—(sl.) have sex with a person *(also:*

get it on with someone): She said all he wanted was to get it off with just anybody.

get off with someone—(coll.) 1. move aside with a person to discuss smth.: We got off with the client and explained the offer a little better. 2. become friendly with one of the opposite sex: What fun it would be if one of us could get off with him.

Note: *The expression does not correlate in meaning with the phrase* ***get off with you****—(exclam.)* 1. *is used to rudely tell a person to go away (and stop being annoying):* Get off with you! I'm trying to work. 2. *is used to emphatically express disbelief:* Get off with you! Do you think I'd believe a story like that?

get it on • put it on

get it on—(U.S. sl.) 1. begin smth. with energy and enthusiasm: You want to go for pizza? Let's get it on! 2. have sex: Just as they were about to get it on they heard a giggle from the corner of the dormitory.

put it on—(UK coll.) assume a false appearance; feign smth.: Billie is just putting it on, and sounds like Americans in movies where they pretend to be English.

get it on with someone • get on with someone

get it on with someone—(U.S. sl.) have sex with a person *(also: get it off with someone):* And it wasn't only with Prunella: he had wanted to get it on with Evelyn — Evelyn the Untouchable, for Christ's sake!

get on with someone—maintain a friendly relationship with smb.; be on good terms with a person: I didn't get on well with my parents at all at this stage — they had messed up one of my best friendships.

get it together • get one's act together

get it together—1. *(UK coll.)* manage to organize an activity: We were planning a trip to India last year, but we never got it together. 2. *(sl.)* have sex: We'd met a few times before, but we didn't really get it together till Rachel's party.

get one's act together—(coll.) get mentally organized *(also: get one's head together):* It took me a few days to get my act together, but I finally gathered up the nerve to start writing.

get mixed up with someone • mix it up with someone

get mixed up with someone—become associated with a person, especially smb. disreputable: Don't get mixed up with him — he's a crook!

mix it up with someone—(coll.) start a quarrel or fight with a person: Don't try mixing it up with me — I've got a gun!

get off base • get to first base

get off base—(coll.) be erroneous or inappropriate: While the author did a good job building her characters, she really got off base with her Agatha Christie research.

get to first base—(also: reach first base) get to the initial stage: The outcome, of course, is now history; the wiretap bill never got to first base.

get off on the wrong foot • get out of bed with the wrong foot foremost

get off on the wrong foot—make a bad beginning: I am afraid we get off on the wrong foot by openly showing our hostility to the proposals.

get out of bed with the wrong foot foremost—be in a bad temper when one gets up: I am afraid you got out of bed with the wrong foot foremost this morning.

See also: catch someone on the wrong foot / put a foot wrong.

get off one's bike • get on one's bike

get off one's bike—(Austral., NZ sl.) get agitated or annoyed: "I tell you I saw no-one." "Don't get off your bike, son. I know you're tellin' lies."

get on one's bike—(coll.) start making an effort to do smth.: With rent to pay and a wife and baby, I had to get on my bike.

Note: *The expression does not correlate in meaning with the phrase* ***on your bike****—(UK) used to rudely tell a person to go away (and stop being annoying):* There's nothing for you here, mate. On your bike, then.

get off one's high horse • get off one's soap box

get off one's high horse—(coll.) stop behaving arrogant or superior: He does need to get off his high horse and rid himself of the belief that he is going to save the world.

get off one's soap box—(coll.) stop speaking out in an irritatingly overbearing way: You really need to get off your soap box. Every comment you make you have to add your egotistical attitude into it.

get off the ground • touch ground

get off the ground—(of a project, scheme, etc.) make a successful start: The project never got off the ground because of red tape and lack of organization.

touch ground—get to reality: Now we are really beginning to touch ground. Tell us exactly how much you can put into the enterprise.

get on like a house on fire • go like a house on fire

get on like a house on fire—(also: get along like a house on fire) become good friends in a very short time: "How are your new neighbors?" "Pretty well, their sons and ours get on like a house on fire."

go like a house on fire—1. *(of an event, activity, etc.)* be very successful: All the families were gathered around and the ceremony and reception went like a house on fire. 2. is used to refer to some fast action: Time was precious, so ... I would go like a house on fire trying to say as much as I could before my time was up.

get on one's high horse • get on one's horse

get on one's high horse—(also: ride one's high horse) become dignified and formal; assume an arrogant mien: As soon as I said a little slang to her she got on her high horse.

get on one's horse—(sl.) hurry; start at once: You better get on your horse if you're going to make that plane.

Note: *The expression does not correlate in meaning with the phrase* ***be on the horse****—(Drug users) be under the effects of or addicted to heroin:* How long have you been on the horse?

get on the bandwagon • go on the wagon

get on the bandwagon—join in what seems likely to be a successful enterprise (in the hope of a personal gain): Once it was clear that he would be elected, all the uncommitted politicians tried to get on the bandwagon.

go on the wagon—intend not to drink any alcohol at all: Carter says that he is really serious this time about going on the wagon.

get on to something • get on towards something

get on to something—1. get in touch with an office, etc., especially by telephone: I must get on to the shop about the order that we've been waiting for. *2.* begin to talk about smth.: Do not dwell too much on small-talk; get on to the subject of your job search fairly quickly. 3. begin to understand smth.: Although at first shorthand seemed difficult to me, I soon got on to it. 4. *(Progressive Tense)* be advancing towards a certain age, time, etc.: It was getting on to evening and the sun was setting over the water.

get on towards something— = get on to something 4: It was

getting on towards evening and I think everyone was anxious to head for home.

get on with it • get with it

get on with it—continue with what one is doing: My partner is drinking too much but every time I mention it we end up arguing—should I just let him get on with it?

get with it—(coll.) respond to new ideas, styles, etc.; become modern: My wish to you, especially the older dairy farmers, is to get with it or the future will be without you.

Note: *Neither expression correlates in meaning with the phrase* ***get away with it****—go unpunished for doing smth. wrong:* The law says they can defame you and get away with it if the story is true. Truth is an almost perfect defense in a libel suit.

get one's blue • get the blues

get one's blue—(Oxford and Cambridge) be awarded a blue cap, scarf, etc. for representing one's university in athletics: He will get his blue next term and show that he's a jolly good fellow.

get the blues—(coll.) feel sad or depressed *(also: have the blues):* His excess energy can be misdirected, especially when he gets the blues (as we all do sometimes).

See also: come out of the blue / get into a blue.

get one's feet under the table • put one's feet up

get one's feet under the table—get settled in: It will take four or five months for Greg to get his feet under the table, to understand the enormous number of complex and tricky issues he has to master.

put one's feet up—relax or take a rest: That way I can put my feet up and not think about Christmas at all until a week beforehand, when we put up our decorations.

Note: *The expression does not correlate in meaning with the phrase* ***have a knees up****—have a noisy party usually with dancing:* We had a little party for him and some speeches and went to the pub and had a knees up.

See also: put one's foot down / put one's foot to the floor.

get one's pennyworth • have one's two pennyworth

get one's pennyworth—(UK) have full value for one's money; get a sufficient return for one's trouble, etc.: Mr. Cataway makes sure he gets his pennyworth of work from those assistants.

have one's two pennyworth—(UK) add one's comments or opinion on the matter: Everyone started to leave, but I was determined to have my two pennyworth, so I stood up and banged my papers on the table.

get one's picture in something • get one's picture of something

get one's picture in something—have one's photo appear in a magazine or newspaper: The driving factor is the desire to become famous, get lots of exposure, get one's picture in a magazine.

get one's picture of something—become aware of certain facts: To get one's picture of science history solely from the published literature would be like watching a football match from high up in an airplane.

get one's point across • get someone's point

get one's point across—communicate one's argument or idea successfully: I wear an insult from a liberal as a badge of honor because it means that I got my point across.

get someone's point—understand what another person is trying to prove or explain: I couldn't put that into words, but people around me got my point in the right way.

get one's second pip • get the pip

get one's second pip—(UK Army) be promoted from second to first lieutenant: Kathryn had been proud of them all, but most of Harry Kim, who finally got his second pip.

get the pip—(coll.) feel annoyed and miserable: Laura wasn't the only one to get the pip! Quite a few disgruntled customers had been telling similar stories.

get one's teeth into something • put teeth into something

get one's teeth into something—(also: sink one's teeth into something) 1. bite into smth.: Many a time I thought of Bobbie when I got my teeth into a bit of walrus or seal meat. 2. *(coll.)* deal with smth. vigorously: Here, get your teeth into this and see if you can manage this project.

put teeth into something—make smth. really effective: The legislature put teeth into the traffic law by increasing penalties and appropriating money for its proper enforcement.

get one's ticket • get one's ticket punched

get one's ticket—1. *(sl.)* be discharged from the army or from prison: "Coiners" as a rule returned to their profession as soon as they got their "ticket." Prison is a great punishment to such men. 2. qualify for promotion; take a step up in a career path: Seventeen years before he got his "ticket," his second mate's ticket, he served in the foc'sle before the mast.

Note: *a) The expression does not correlate in meaning with the phrase* ***get a ticket****—get a notice of an offence against traffic regulations (usually a speeding or parking offence):* It was two blocks from the hotel, and he might get a ticket for parking.

b) The expression does not correlate in meaning with the phrase ***have tickets on oneself****—(Austral. sl.) be vain or conceited:* You're the bastard that's always been smug and had tickets on himself.

get one's ticket punched—(sl.) 1. die or be killed: My brother Kevin unexpectedly got his ticket punched yesterday. He has had liver cancer for several years but seemed to be getting better recently. 2. = *get one's ticket 2:* John was in Vietnam just to get his ticket punched. Combat is the fastest route to promotion. *Cf.: ticketpuncher—(sl.) a career military officer or businessperson whose primary concern is personal advancement:* Not going with the "business as usual" choice with someone who is just a sharp person rather than a ticketpuncher was a good thing…

get one's wind • get wind

get one's wind—recover power or ability to breathe without difficulty: You had better get your wind now, and change your clothes. *Cf.: lose one's wind—become out of breath when running or exerting oneself:* He avoided stairs and lost his breath tying his shoelaces.

get wind—(of news, rumors, etc.) become widely known; spread: The story got wind and was over the camp in a few hours.

get oneself off the hook • go off the hooks

get oneself off the hook—(coll.) free oneself from difficulty or trouble: Later it was useful to describe this incident to get myself off the hook at a Royal Navy interview panel.

go off the hooks—(sl.) die *(also: drop off the hooks):* No man was ever able to write his own life complete. He's certain to go off the hooks before he has finished it.

See also: be hooked / go on the hook.

get oneself together • hold oneself together

get oneself together—(also: get one's head together) get mentally organized: The most commonly cited reasons for withdrawing include: needing a break from college, needing to get oneself together, emotional problems…

hold oneself together—(also: keep oneself together) keep one's composure; maintain one's good sense: It was only through the kindness of my friend and fellow musician that I was able to hold myself together.

get onto someone • get to someone

get onto someone—1. get in touch with smb., especially by telephone: I'll have to get onto Sarah about the deadline. 2. *(coll.)* keep nagging or annoy a person: She's been getting onto me for a year to buy her a new coat. 3. *(coll.)* trace or find a person: He tricked people for years until the police got onto him.

get to someone—1. = *get onto someone 1:* I got to her on the telephone and told her what to do. 2. *(coll.)* be understood by a person: I've tried to help the troublesome boy, but I can't seem to get to him. 3. *(coll.)* have an effect on smb.'s feelings: His sad story really got to me, and I was moved to help him. 4. *(U.S. sl.)* persuade smb. to do smth., especially by bribing: Gangsters can't operate on a satisfactory scale until they have "got to someone."

get out of it • snap out of it

get out of it—1. escape from a difficult or awkward situation: They wanted us to go lunch. I did my best to get out of it. 2. *(coll.)* is used to tell a person not to talk nonsense: Get out of it! You can't expect me to believe that!

snap out of it—(coll.) free oneself from a state of depression by an effort: For heaven's sake, Lucia, snap out of it and act like a human being.

Note: *The expression is not antonymous in meaning to the phrase* ***snap to it****—(coll.) start moving or working quickly:* I want those bricks moved; come on, snap to it!

get out of the way • put oneself out of the way

get out of the way—1. stand aside or withdraw: John dived for cover but the camera-man played it cool, pausing to switch on the camera before getting out of the way. 2. *(also: get out of my way)* used as a rude command for a person to move from his place or to go away: "Get out of the way," the man shouted and pushed him.

put oneself out of the way—1. *(also: go out of one's way)* go to a lot of trouble to do smth. well: Why should Lady Castlewood put herself out of the way to welcome the young stranger? 2. remove oneself from the scene: So he went abroad, to put himself out of the way ... and also as a matter of personal development.

get out of the way of doing something • go out of the way to do something

get out of the way of doing something—forget how to do smth.: You soon get out of the way of driving when you haven't had a car for some time.

go out of the way to do something—(also: put oneself out of the way to do something) go to great trouble to do smth. well: A dedicated employee will go out of the way to solve your problem.

get out of town • go to the country

get out of town—(coll.) 1. get out of a place: If father hears you talking like that, you'd better pack your bags and get out of town. 2. *(exclam.)* used as an emphatic expression of disbelief: You made a ton of money on that stock? Get out of town!

go to the country—(of election candidates) appeal to the body of electors (appearing on television, etc.): The cry of a "cheap breakfast table" would no longer be one "to go to the country with."

See also: go out on the town / go to town.

get over something • get something over

get over something—1. recover from an illness, shock, etc.: George did not get over his homesickness for some time. 2. overcome a difficulty, etc.; rise above smth.: The music industry can't get over the fact that music and video will be free.

get something over—1. cause smth. to become understood or accepted: We need to get the message over that bookselling incurs certain expenses. 2. *(also: get something over with)* get smth. finished fast: Feelings of urgency and frustration often come when you want to get the work over quickly.

get religion • lose one's religion

get religion—1. acquire deep religious beliefs: She left him when she got religion and quit the porn business. 2. resolve to mend one's ways (usually after a powerful experience): When I had an automobile accident, I really got religion.

Note: *The expression does not correlate in meaning with the phrase* ***enter into religion****—(dated) adopt a monastic life:* We must enter into religion and be made nuns by will or by force.

lose one's religion—1. give up one's religious beliefs and practices: It can be an overwhelmingly lonely experience to lose one's religion. *2. (U.S. coll.)* lose one's temper or one's better judgment: I purchased a shelf and I almost lost my religion last night trying to put it together.

get round something • get round to something

get round something—(also: get around something) circumvent or evade rules, regulations, etc. (without committing a legal offence): A clever lawyer might find ways of getting round that clause.

get round to something—(also: get around to something) find time for smth.; deal with smth. (when more important matters have been dealt with): I'm busy now but I hope to get round to your request next week.

get sick • go sick

get sick—1. be taken ill: Let the woman of a house get sick, and it just goes to pieces. 2. feel an inclination to vomit: The bay was rough; thirty minutes out and the boys began to get sick.

go sick—report oneself as ill to an employer, etc.: Filthy climate. But she just carries on. Hasn't gone sick once in six months.

get someone down • take someone down

get someone down—1. *(also: bring someone to the ground)* cause a person to come down or fall: You get the biggest man down, and I'll fight the other two. 2. make a person feel depressed: I spend most of my working time indoors, but even so this wet weather is getting me down.

take someone down—1. *(also: take someone down a peg)* make smb. feel less important; humiliate a person: He seems to experience satisfaction in what he calls taking me down. 2. write down smb.'s words: I enlisted a poet for company, and a stenographer to "take him down."

See also: bring someone down / bring someone down a peg.

get someone in wrong • get someone wrong

get someone in wrong—cause a person to fall into disfavor with smb.: You'll get him in wrong with his boss if you keep calling him at the office.

Note: *The expression does not correlate in meaning with the phrase* ***put someone in the wrong****—show a person to be wrong:* People want to think that they're right, and if you put them in the wrong, they won't like it.

get someone wrong—misinterpret the intention of smb.'s statement or deed: Don't get her wrong, she still loves him, but she is understandably cautious.

get someone into trouble • put someone to trouble

get someone into trouble—1. involve a person in a situation causing difficulties, danger, etc.: Don't mention my name or you'll get me into trouble. 2. *(euph.)* make an unmarried woman pregnant: Kali doesn't know the name of the man who got her into trouble. But in trouble she is — there's no doubting that.

put someone to trouble—cause smb. more than usual work or effort; inconvenience a person: I'm sorry to put you to trouble, I'm actually not hungry.

Note: *The expression is not equivalent in meaning to the phrase* ***give someone trouble****— cause a person serious worry or problems:* The female "side" of a prison gives more trouble to the authorities than the male.

get someone off • get someone off the hook

get someone off—1. rescue a person from a crashed vehicle, a sinking ship, etc.: The last three sailors were got off just before the ship sank. 2. get a person cleared of a criminal charge: Ted's lawyer got him off, although we all knew he was guilty.

get someone off the hook—*(coll.)* free a person from trouble, an embarrassing situation, etc. *(also: let someone off the hook):* "It's an idea," said Craig. "It would get Hartley off the hook, sure enough."

get something into shape • give shape to something

get something into shape—*(also: knock something into shape)* quickly make smth. more perfect or better organized: We need a new manager to get the business into shape.

give shape to something—arrange smth. in an orderly fashion; express smth. clearly: I'm having trouble giving shape to my ideas in this essay.

get something off one's chest • make a clean breast of something

get something off one's chest—talk about worrisome thoughts or feelings to smb. so that it doesn't bother one anymore: I finally talked to him and was able to get some of my problems off my chest.

make a clean breast of something—fully confess to smth. bad or illegal: He denied the Montreal story, admitted it, denied it again, and then, weeping, made a clean breast of both episodes.

get something right • set something right

get something right—1. understand smth. clearly, so that there is no misinterpretation: Correct me if I didn't get this right. Did you say that changes to the flight rules are approved? 2. restore smth. to order, good condition, etc.: I am sorry we didn't get this right the first time, and I am afraid we can't offer a fix immediately.

set something right—*(also: put something right) = get something right 2:* The longer we pretend that everything is OK, the harder it is to set things right in the long term.

get steamed up • get up steam

get steamed up—*(coll.)* become excited, angry or very annoyed: You can buy another copy of the book you've lost, so there's no need to get steamed up.

Note: *The expression does not correlate in meaning with the phrase* ***steam up****—(of a transparent or reflective surface) become clouded by steam:* My glasses steamed up so much that I had to take them off to find the car.

get up steam—1. *(coll., also: put on steam)* build up strength or energy; become more active: It was hard for us to get up enough steam to finish the work in one day. 2. *= get steamed up:* It's no use talking further — we should only get up steam.

get stuck • get stuck in

get stuck—1. become entangled in sand, snow, etc., so as to be unable to get away from a place: When we finally get stuck in the middle of the Sand Sea you'll have to carry everything. 2. get involved with smth. so as to be unable to leave: Of all the days to get stuck out there, he has to pick this one.

get stuck in—*(coll.)* start doing smth. with enthusiasm and determination: Mrs. Wagner brought in two plates of food and told them to get stuck in.

get stuck for something • get stuck on something • get stuck with something

get stuck for something—be at a loss how to obtain smth.: He frowns importantly as he talks about his job, and waves his arms about when he gets stuck for words.

get stuck on something—*(coll.)* feel a strong attraction to smth.: Turn them [cattle] on to your range when the grass is green ... they get stuck on it then, and stop there.

get stuck with something—*(coll.)* 1. be unable to get rid of smth. unwanted or undesirable: Maybe you simply got stuck with a bad mortgage to begin with. 2. have no choice about doing smth. unpleasant (like paying the bill, etc.): Jim always got stuck with cleaning the garage.

get stuck in something • get stuck into something

get stuck in something—1. become entangled in sand, snow, etc., so as to be unable to get away from a place: We were on our way to visit another village, but our car got stuck in the mud. 2. get involved with smth. so as to be unable to leave a place: It seemed like nobody else noticed how late the show went. I'm sure a lot of Jerseyites got stuck in the city that night. 3. get involved with smth. so as to be unable to develop or progress: Instead of marching forward, the revolution got stuck in the bog of philistinism.

get stuck into something—*(coll.)* start doing smth. with enthusiasm and determination; get down to a task: I think it's time we got stuck into some gardening.

get the ball rolling • set the stone rolling

get the ball rolling—*(also: set the ball rolling)* start or initiate smth.: Regardless of how you go about credit report repair, it's a good idea to get the ball rolling as soon as possible.

set the stone rolling—*(also: set a stone rolling)* start smth. which may lead to serious or unanticipated consequences: The Austrian ultimatum to Serbia which set the stone rolling was a deliberate provocation.

get the bum's rush • get the rush

get the bum's rush—*(coll.)* 1. be thrown out or dismissed unceremoniously: We tried to talk our way in, but got the bum's rush, ending up in a heap on the sidewalk. 2. be rejected with deliberate coldness or contempt: You might expect a bit more modesty from a guy whose own work got the bum's rush from the powers that be.

get the rush—*(coll.)* 1. *(of a woman)* receive attentions from men: She certainly wasn't prepared for the rush she got.... You've got to admit she's not madly attractive. **2.** get a feeling of excitement or exhilaration: Never again was there anything quite like the rush we got from the simple fact of spring.

get the dry horrors • get the horrors

get the dry horrors—*(Austral sl.)* suffer from thirst, especially after drinking excessive amounts of alcohol: One of the effects is dehydration — which is why we get the dry horrors the next morning.

get the horrors—*(sl.)* become frightened: I was so underprepared for the whole thing. It wasn't till I started doing it that I really got the horrors.

get the hots for someone • give it hot to someone

get the hots for someone—(sl.) be strongly attracted to a person sexually: Just as I suspected, Angie. You're starting to get the hots for James.

give it hot to someone—(rare coll.) punish or scold smb. severely: I have given it hot to Grant Allen who did ... much the same as Romanes is doing now though not so barefacedly.

See also: make it hot for someone / make someone hot.

get the jump on someone • give someone a jump

get the jump on someone—(coll.) gain an advantage over a person: Each of these new developers hopes to get the jump on the other by adding more square footage to the units.

give someone a jump—(coll.) 1. *(also: give someone the jumps)* make smb. frightened: Someone had skinned a dead calf and left it on the track, and it gave me a jump. 2. *(also: give someone a jump-start)* help a person start his stalled car: My car wouldn't start after work. The security guard gave me a jump.

get the short end of the stick • get the wrong end of the stick

get the short end of the stick—(also: get the dirty end of the stick) have the disadvantage in a bargain, contest, etc.: Francine always gets the short end of the stick when it comes to school plays.

Note: *The expression is not equivalent in meaning to the phrase* ***draw the short straw****— be chosen to perform a task that nobody wants to do:* Brenner drained his glass with a sense of relief, thankful that it was someone else who had drawn the short straw.

get the wrong end of the stick—(also: get hold of the wrong end of the stick) completely misunderstand smth.: I said how nice he was and Julie got the wrong end of the stick and thought I wanted to go out with him.

get the show on the road • road show

*get the show on the road—*put a plan, idea, etc. into action: He checked his watch. "Shouldn't we get this show on the road, now that Rolfe's here?"

Note: *The expression is not antonymous in meaning to the phrase* ***steal the show****—do better than another person (in a theatrical production, etc.) and so make oneself the centre of attention:* They won the two most entertaining matches of the night and stole the show.

*road show—*1. a touring group of theatrical or musical performers: Teddy and Phil began their circus career by joining a road show. 2. a show given by a touring group of performers: This is like watching a road show with a cast that's not quite ready for prime time yet. 3. a promotional tour by a company (to publicize its products, etc.): The road show visits five states and incorporates six events including trade evenings.

get the wind of something • get wind of something

*get the wind of something—*scent or detect (an animal) as by the wind: The herd [of buffaloes] at length "got the wind" of the approaching enemy and fled in a mass.

*get wind of something—*learn about smth., especially accidentally: When he got wind of the store's impending closing, he applied to be the next tenant.

get the wind up • raise the wind

get the wind up—(sl.) become nervous or scared *(also: get the breeze up):* I happened to see his face in the mirror as I went out. He's got the wind up all right.

raise the wind—(coll.) obtain money, especially by borrowing: He came to me this morning to raise the wind.

get through something • get through with something

*get through something—*1. work one's way through smth. particularly difficult or challenging: He qualifies if he gets through his two subjects this year. 2. survive a difficult period; manage to live through smth.: How do they ever get through Minnesota winters? 3. *(of money, etc.)* use up completely: A racecourse and thirty-nine pubs help the men to get through the £2,000 a year that many of them have been earning.

Note: *The expression does not correlate in meaning with the phrase* ***get something through****—*1. *ensure that smth. such as a law is approved:* The members of parliament united to get the Bill through. 2. *cause smth. to reach a person:* Whatever happens, we must get these supplies through to our men. 3. *cause smth. to be understood or accepted:* As expected, the politician had much difficulty getting his message through.

*get through with something—*eventually succeed in accomplishing smth.: Don't know how I should get through with my work, if I were tied down to eight hours a day.

Note: *The expression does not correlate in meaning with the phrase* ***get through to something****—(Sport) manage to progress as far as the last round in a competition, etc.:* I was so excited when I got through to the finals, but I think my mum was even more pleased than me.

get through to someone • get through with someone

*get through to someone—*1. get in touch with smb. by telephone: It is very rare that you will get through to the right person on the first call. 2. succeed in being understood or accepted by a person: Few teachers can get through to students who don't want to learn.

*get through with someone—*finish punishing or scolding a person: When the teacher had got through with the class, they felt very ashamed.

Note: *Neither expression correlates in meaning with the phrase* ***get someone through****—(also: put someone through)* 1. *cause smb. to pass an examination, go through a course of study, etc.:* I was able to get all my students through, except three whose English was the weakest. 2. *put smb. in touch with a person by telephone:* After some time the operator finally got me through.

get tied up • get tied up in knots

get tied up—(coll.) 1. become deeply involved with smb.: Mazie had just managed to get out of a terrible marriage and she didn't want to get tied up with anyone. 2. be held up or kept busy with people or things: I meant to come round yesterday evening, but I got tied up with people.

get tied up in knots—(coll.) become very anxious or worried: Don't get tied up in knots over grammar. It's not worth it and it will only put you off writing.

Note: *The expression does not correlate in meaning with the phrase* ***get knotted****—(UK sl.) used to rudely tell a person to go away (and stop being annoying):* I don't know why you didn't tell him to get knotted and be done with it.

get to a point • get to the point

get to a point—(also: come to a point) reach a certain stage: And you, my dear, are a first-water writer. But I think you're getting to a point when you have to make some choices.

get to the point—(also: come to the point) 1. give the essential part of what one is trying to say, ignoring what is irrelevant: "Sit down, McFee," I said, "and get to the point." 2. = *get to a point:* Now, I am getting to the point where I just want quiet. I don't want the noise, the people, the appointments.

get to the bottom of something • get to the bottom of the barrel

*get to the bottom of something—*1. *(also: reach the bottom of* *something)* reach the lowest point of smth.: They were resolved to renew their work in the same pit but they had scarce got to the bottom of the stairs that led to the pit. 2. explore smth. thoroughly (to determine the cause, etc.): We'll get to the bottom of the problem and get your vehicle back on the road as quickly as possible.

get to the bottom of the barrel—run out of resources or possibilities: It seems nobody has any fresh ideas on the subject. We are getting to the bottom of the barrel.

get warmed up • warm up

get warmed up—become excited and impetuous: They both got warmed up in their dispute over the merits of the two candidates.

warm up—be roused from indifference: He soon warmed up and was able to not only overbeat hostility, but to command enthusiastic applause.

ghost ship • ghost train

ghost ship—1. the apparition of a ship known to have disappeared years or centuries before: The sighting of a ghost ship is not a good omen, and superstition holds that bad luck will soon follow. 2. an abandoned vessel found floating with no crew: What happened on board the ghost ship Mary Celeste has baffled and tantalized the world for 130 years.

ghost train—1. *(UK)* a riding vehicle in an amusement park providing exciting and frightening experiences: Grayling calls this "recreational fear"— the sort we experience during a ride on a ghost train. 2. a paranormal sighting of a phantom train wrecked in an earlier crash: Most ghost train sightings have been recorded in the United States where railway lines were the most extensive.

See also: dead ship / death ship.

GI bride • GI Jane

GI bride—*(UK sl.)* an English girl who is an American soldier's bride or wife: A group of GI brides was asking Tracy for his autograph.

Note: *The expression is not equivalent in meaning to the phrase* ***war bride***— *a woman who marries a man who is on active duty in wartime:* My mother was a war bride. She met my father, an american soldier, in 1944.

GI Jane—*(U.S. sl.)* a servicewoman: And what about the female officers? ... The military must be brutalizing these GI Janes.

gilded youth • golden boys

gilded youth—young men of fashion and wealth: He was invited to dine with some of the gilded youth of the city at a certain club.

golden boys—young people admired for their talent and skill: He's one of the company's golden boys; sales have doubled since he took over as marketing director.

gin house • gin palace

gin house—1. a building where cotton is pressed: There was a large quantity of yellow unpicked cotton lying in the gin house. 2. a bar retailing chiefly gin: Used to be some little stores out there and I think a gin house ... on the Avenue Highway.

gin palace—*(UK dated)* a large bar furnished in a gaudy style: I sat one evening in a gin palace among a set of pigeon fanciers.

girdle of Venus • Venus's girdle

girdle of Venus—*(Palmistry)* a line believed to denote sensitive intellectual nature: Fussing over life-lines and measuring the girdle of Venus seems a desperate and futile way to fill the emptiness in many a woman's life.

Venus's girdle—a ribbonlike gelatinous sea creature found in the Mediterranean Sea: In *Cestum*, or Venus's Girdle, elongation takes place to an extraordinary extent.

girl-boy • girlie-boy

girl-boy—1. *(derog.)* a girlish boy whose behavior is more suitable for a girl than for a boy: Little boys are laughed at as effeminate, silly girl-boys if they want to make patchwork or play with a doll. 2. a girl considered boyish in behavior or manner: My first baby was a girl-boy, she was hell on wheels, I am glad my other two were boys.

girlie-boy—*(UK sl.)* an effeminate young male homosexual *(also: ladyboy):* The popular rock musical tells the story of a "girlie-boy" singer who undergoes a botched sex-change operation.

Girl Guide • Girl Guider

Girl Guide—*(UK)* a girl between about 10 and 16 who is a member of the Girl Guides Association *(an organization of girls corresponding to the Boy Scouts):* She had on a starchy white blouse and blue skirt. Looked like a goddam girl guide.

Girl Guider—*(UK)* an adult leader in the Girl Guide movement: An old girl from the Class of 1951, she was a school athlete and netball player; a ballet and tap-dancer and a Girl Guider.

give a name to someone • put a name to someone

give a name to someone—name a newborn child: One should not give a name to a child that will be difficult to pronounce or to write.

put a name to someone—remember the name of a person: I would find it difficult to put a name to everyone in this room.

give a name to something • give one's name to something

give a name to something—assign a name to a thing: Go to a village and ask a peasant what his religion is. He will not be able to give a name to his religion.

give one's name to something—*(also: lend one's name to something)* allow one's name to be associated with smth.: He gave his name to a well-known brand of frozen food.

Note: *The expression does not correlate in meaning with the phrase* ***have someone's name on it***—*(also: have someone's name written all over it)* 1. *(of a bomb, bullet, etc.) be the instrument of a person's fate:* The bomb probably had my name on it in the first place. 2. *be especially suitable or intended for a particular person:* Come on, Paul, there's one piece of chocolate cake left and it's got your name on it. 3. *be characteristic of a particular person:* When I heard about the prank, I felt it had Steve's name written all over it.

See also: put one's name down for something / put one's name to something.

give a pledge • give the pledge

give a pledge—1. make a solemn promise: During his inauguration speech he gave a pledge not to declare the island independent during his term of office. 2. promise to pay money or make a donation: A senior member of your staff, Charlie Phillips, acting on your behalf, gave a pledge of $10 000 to a charity function.

give the pledge—1. = *give a pledge 1:* There was a royalist spy in the midst playing the hypocrite — Joseph Galloway, a Pennsylvania delegate — who gave the pledge and broke it. 2. *(of a priest, etc.)* get other people to take an oath never to drink alcohol: Bishop Hughes formed a Catholic abstinence society and gave the pledge to over 20,000 people. *Cf.: take the pledge — make a solemn promise never to drink alcohol:* Eileen's husband, who is almost permanently drunk, declares that he wants to take the pledge.

give a promise • give promise

give a promise—undertake to do or not to do smth.: He gave a promise that he would come again and bring assistance, and he kept it.

give promise—1. be a token of smth.; indicate smth. beforehand: A heavy mist gave promise of a hot day, and it turned out a "scorcher." 2. show qualities that give hope of success or good results: These children don't give much promise.

give an eye to someone • give someone the eye

give an eye to someone—look after a person; give attention to smb.: Now go into the garden and give an eye to the children.

give someone the eye—1. *(also: give someone the big eye)* look at a person with an open display of romantic interest: He was standing over by the bar and kept giving me the eye. 2. look at smb. in a way that shows that one is angry with that person: It was time to go — Dave was tired and I was sure the nurse was giving me the eye.

***Note:** The expression does not correlate in meaning with the phrase **give someone the eyeroll**— roll one's eyes upward in annoyance at what another person is saying:* It does make my doctor give me the eyeroll sometimes, but he understands me very well.

give and take • give or take

give and take—1. willingness to compromise (in the hope of obtaining a satisfactory agreement, etc.): With a bit of give and take you can both make sure your home doesn't suffer. 2. a lively talk or debate, especially one filled with ridicule: Addison's sensitive modesty disqualified him for the rough give-and-take of mixed society.

give or take—apart from a few things; except for a few people: All the children were present, give or take one or two who were ill.

give credence to something • lend credibility to something

give credence to something—1. put trust in smth.; believe smth.: The jury gave credence to these claims and awarded Lawrence just compensation. 2. make smth. appear more convincing: This gave credence to the hypothesis that Israel had not shared with Washington all the information.

lend credibility to something— = *give credence to something 2:* By quoting other writers, you lend credibility and support to your own ideas.

give ear to something • have an ear for something

give ear to something—listen sympathetically to a suggestion, etc.; heed smth.: They read up on long-distance cycling and gave ear to the advice of friends and relatives.

have an ear for something—have the ability to learn music or languages quickly: He had an ear for languages, which he enjoyed, and by this time he spoke five fluently.

give full weight to something • give weight to something

give full weight to something—treat smb.'s testimony, evidence, etc. as valid or important: Dr. Fielden acknowledged he had no training in the field of chiropractic treatment, yet the court gave full weight to his opinions.

give weight to something—support or add to the validity of the evidence, etc.: The fact that he had answered the phone at ten o'clock gave weight to his claim that he had not been out on the evening in question.

give heart to someone • give one's heart to someone

give heart to someone—inspire smb. with confidence; encourage a person: Tom says he hopes his success will give heart to those who have lost their jobs. *Cf.: take heart from someone— be encouraged or inspired by a person:* During the time I spent in Nigeria I took heart from brand-new converts to the Church.

give one's heart to someone—(also: lose one's heart to someone) fall in love with a person: She grew to womanhood, and gave her heart to one who could not know its worth.

give it a name • you name it

give it a name—(imper.) 1. say what it is you want: I know you want something or you wouldn't have come to see me. Give it a name old fellow! 2. what would you like to drink: What are you drinking? Give it a name, chaps — there's everything here.

you name it—everything that you can think of is available: I've written every kind of music there is. You name it, I've written it.

give it a second thought • have second thoughts

give it a second thought—reassess an opinion or decision previously made: You may think this will happen in the distant future but if you give it a second thought you'll realize it is already happening.

***Note:** The expression is not antonymous in meaning to the phrase **don't give it a second thought**—(also: don't give it a thought) 1. dismiss it from your mind; let that not worry you:* Don't give it a second thought, until you are a lot older and have more experience. 2. *is used to indicate that thanks are unnecessary:* Oh, don't give it a second thought, Hun! Actually I should be thanking you! 3. *is used as a polite way of accepting apology:* I looked at her and said graciously: "Please don't give it a second thought. I wasn't offended."

have second thoughts—(also: get second thoughts) realize that one may be mistaken; have doubts: I am starting to have second thoughts about my purchase based on what I am reading here.

***Note:** The expression is not equivalent in meaning to the phrase **have another think coming**— used of a need to reconsider one's plans or opinions:* Those who think Carter is still respectable company should have another think coming.

See also: think again / think twice.

give it a shot • give it the gun

give it a shot—(coll.) give smth. a try; attempt to do smth. unfamiliar: I don't know if my recording skills are up to par but I just might give it a shot.

give it the gun—(coll.) cause a vehicle to accelerate rapidly: Even when I would stand in the road and make motions to help me, they would turn out around me and give it the gun.

give it mouth • give mouth

give it mouth—(dated) speak with vigor and intensity: "Tell us your name!" said the man. "Pip, sir." "Once more," said the man, staring at me. "Give it mouth!"

give mouth—(also: give tongue) 1. utter one's thoughts; express smth. in words: I have an opinion of you, sir, to which it is not easy to give mouth. 2. *(of a dog)* bark when on the scent: There are hounds that do not give mouth. Some have been trained that way, some come natural.

give it to someone • give it to someone straight

give it to someone—scold smb. harshly: Later, in a private eye-to-eye discussion, with no witnesses to overhear, Slavsky really gave it to me.

give it to someone straight—tell smth. to a person directly: So I gave it to him straight: I'm broke, and there's no way I can pay the hospital fees.

give notice • take notice

give notice—1. notify or warn a person with regard to smth.: I had been given notice that the home I'm living in was going up for sale. 2. dismiss smb. from employment: A person who is given notice can easily become demoralized. It takes time to accept the situation.... 3. notify the employer about quitting one's position: His cook-boy, who had worked for him twelve years, gave notice that month.

take notice—1. perceive smth.; pay attention to smth.: I did not take notice that the horse was almost dead when I took him. 2. take smth. seriously; heed smth.: I just hope people will take notice of the warnings and do not drink and drive.

give of one's best • give someone best

give of one's best—(also: do one's best) do all one can; do smth. as well as one can: He wasn't the cleverest member of the committee, but he gave of his best.

give someone best—(UK) admit to being wrong; admit defeat: I give you best. I was mistaken about the whole thing.

give one's arm to someone • give one's hand to someone

give one's arm to someone—(also: offer one's arm to someone) allow a person to walk arm-in-arm or lean on one's arm: He turned his back on Alfred, gave his arm to Mrs. Langham and advanced into the hotel.

give one's hand to someone—(of a woman) agree to marry a man: He fails, however, to win Miss Lillerton, who gives her hand to a smooth young curate instead.

give one's life for something • give one's life to something

give one's life for something—(also: lay down one's life for something) allow oneself to die for a good cause, etc.: This monument is to honor soldiers who gave their life for the cause of liberty.

give one's life to something—dedicate one's whole life to smth.: Socrates gave his life to the study of questions that have seized the minds of thinking people down the ages.

Note: *The expression does not correlate in meaning with the phrase* ***give life to something****— impart interest, energy, or enthusiasm to smth.:* Experienced actors could be contracted to give life to the play so that the work stands the best chance of attracting an audience.

give one's respects to someone • pay one's respects to someone

give one's respects to someone—send a formal expression of respect for smb. through another person: Give my respects to your Father, whose pamphlet I read with great interest.

pay one's respects to someone—show respect for a person by presenting oneself or by making a call: They were not "ardent royalists," but had come to pay their respects to a great woman.

give one's word • give the word

give one's word—1. give one's promise: He gave his word as a scholar not to publish works that were made available to him. 2. express one's assurance: I'm positive he's capable of carrying out the mission. I give my word that he is fine. 3. give expression to smth.; put smth. into words: He visited the homes of the sick to give his word of advice or sympathy.

give the word—command a person to do smth.: Jack told them to wait till he gave the word, and then to make all the noise they could.

give oneself a shot in the arm • shoot oneself in the foot

give oneself a shot in the arm—inject oneself with a drug: The next day I got enough courage to do it myself and I gave myself a shot in the arm. The needle did not hurt going in...

shoot onself in the foot—act against one's own interest: You're shooting yourself in the foot if you use the "can't afford the time" excuse. In reality, you can't afford not to.

give oneself airs • give someone the air

give oneself airs—act conceited or superior: Sally is always giving herself airs. You'd think she had royal blood.

give someone the air—(coll.) reject or dismiss a person: I couldn't change her views ... nor could she convert me to hers, even when she threatened to give me the air. *Cf.: get the air— be rejected (as a friend or lover):* Shirley was afraid she might get the air from her boyfriend if she went out with other boys.

See also: take air / take the air.

give points to someone • make points with someone

give points to someone—1. offer an advantage to a contender: Does the system give more "points" to an applicant who has a higher level degree? 2. be considerably better than another person: She could give points to many younger women and beat them. *Cf.: give point to something— make smth. more effective:* His clever illustrations certainly gave point to his argument.

make points with someone—(sl.) gain favor with a person: I believe this is window dressing for our politicians. They are trying to make points with the electorate...

give someone a black eye • give someone a black look

give someone a black eye—1. bruise or discolor smb.'s eye by a blow: He grew angry and we mixed it. I gave him a black eye. 2. harm a person's character or reputation: The constant complaining gave the whole group a black eye.

Note: *The expression does not correlate in meaning with the phrase* ***give someone the evil eye****— look fierce or vicious; stare at smb. in a bad way:* The Highway Patrolman gave me the evil eye as we both headed out of the parking lot. He didn't look quite so friendly anymore.

give someone a black look—(also: look black at someone) frown or look angrily at a person: Mama gave her a black look and everyone else glanced at her for a moment as if she were quite mad.

give someone a break • give someone an even break

give someone a break—(coll.) give smb. a chance or special consideration: Roush gave him a break two decades ago when he gave a kid from Batesville a chance to achieve his dreams.

Note: *a) The expression does not fully correlate in meaning with the phrase* ***give me a break****—1. (sl.) stop trying to fool or bother me:* Oh, give me a break. You spent an entire night together and you don't remember her name? *2. (coll.) give me a chance or an opportunity:* I worked on Music Row for two years, and nobody would give me a break, and I could not save up the money to make a record.

b) The expression does not correlate in meaning with the phrase ***take a break****— have a rest; take time off from an activity:* There was that cold January morning when I took a break from washing the dishes.

give someone an even break—(coll.) give smb. an equal or fair chance; give a person the same opportunity as other people: Women have been subject to second class status for centuries and it is time to give them an even break. *Cf.: never give a sucker an even break—(cliché) one should not allow a fair chance to smb. who may be easily deceived:* Doesn't capitalism teach that one never gives a sucker an even break? It damn sure does.

give someone a foot up • give someone a leg up

give someone a foot up—help a person in time of need: If we can't help them, we try to recommend them to another agency. Our motto is to give a foot up and not a handout.

Note: *The expression does not correlate in meaning with the phrase* ***give someone a foot in the door****—let smb. start working at a low level in the hope of getting a better position in the future:* The freelance work that I did gave me a foot in the door.

give someone a leg up—1. help smb. to mount a horse or to climb up smth.: The wall is very low, sir, and your servant will give you a leg up. 2. = *give someone a foot up:* Keep on your regular patients and give that young dentist a leg up by recommending any newcomers to him.

Note: *The expression does not correlate in meaning with the phrase* ***give someone leg****—(sl.) deceive or fool a person:* Last time I saw you, you're giving me a little leg about there's nothing going on.

give someone a glad hand • give someone a good hand

give someone a glad hand—(also: glad-hand someone) give a person a cordial handshake or greeting: Crude economic reasons do not explain why he should have been given the glad hand.

give someone a good hand—(also: give someone a big hand) give a person a large round of applause: The club enjoyed her talk and gave her a good hand at the end.

give someone a hand • give someone one's hand

give someone a hand—1. help smb. with a task, etc.: Give me a hand with this case, will you? 2. applaud a person: Come on, give them a hand. They did very well.

Note: *The expression does not correlate in meaning with the phrase* ***give someone a free hand****—give smb. freedom of action in affairs:* He accepted the job after the prime minister agreed to give him a free hand in key economic issues.

give someone one's hand—1. agree formally to smth.: Yes, I agree to your marrying my daughter, and I give you my hand upon it. 2. *(of a woman)* agree to marry a man: Bruno and Evandra have loved each other for six years, but she refuses to give him her hand.

give someone a head • give someone his head

give someone a head—(of alcohol) cause headache: He goes on to tell us that, "It won't give you a head in the morning." He speaks with the authority of a man that knows his drink.

give someone his head—1. *(of a horse)* not to check or hold in with the bridle: He has always been a well-mannered colt, but I have never been able to give him his head. 2. give a person freedom to have his way: He's got some great ideas. Why not give him his head and see what kind of campaign he comes up with.

give someone a head start • give someone a start

give someone a head start—put smb. in an advantageous position allowing to start smth. earlier: If we give them a head start they're going to do as well as other children.

give someone a start—1. startle a person: I have to say that the sirens went off at noon today and gave me a start. 2. help a person start his stalled car: John gave me a start when my car was stalled this morning. 3. assist smb. in entering on a career: So she lent me some money and gave me a start in business.

Note: *The expression does not correlate in meaning with the phrase* ***get someone started****—cause a person to begin smth.:* Taking your child for visits to museums will get him started to having an interest in science.

give someone a heads-up • hold one's head up

give someone a heads-up—(coll.) give a person an early warning about smth. that requires alert attention: Could anyone give me a heads-up on what I need to have with me when I go see the lawyer.

hold one's head up—(also: keep one's head up) stay proud; not feel ashamed of oneself: He is a man who can hold his head up high and know that he is who he is because of hard work.

give someone a hot wash • throw cold water on someone

give someone a hot wash—(U.S. military) said of a performance review, particularly after a training exercise or combat operation: Troops are often given a "hot wash," or a critique of what they did and how they did it.

throw cold water on someone—(also: pour cold water on someone) discourage a person; curb smb.'s enthusiasm: People will go tremendous lengths to help you, but will throw cold water on you the instant you take them for granted.

give someone a knockdown • knock someone down

give someone a knockdown—(UK sl.) introduce smb. to a person: I heard one young fellow ask another to "give him a knockdown to that tart in the green skirt."

knock someone down—hit smb. so that a person falls to the ground: A bus came screeching to a stop, practically knocking him down.

give someone a lift • give someone a rise

give someone a lift—1. offer a person a ride in a car: Can you give me a lift to the station? 2. give smb. a helping hand: I'm going to make some dried-apple fritters for dinner, and you must give me a lift. 3. promote smb. to a higher or more advanced position: That show, though short-lived, gave her a lift into television. 4. raise smb.'s morale: The event seemed to give him a lift and offered Joe a temporary reprieve from his troubles.

give someone a rise—(also: give someone a raise) increase a person's wage or salary: He threatened to resign if they did not give him a rise.

give someone a line • give someone line

give someone a line—1. give a person information about smth.: Maybe she can give me a line on a place to stay. 2. *(coll.)* give smb. false or misleading information *(also: feed someone a line):* It didn't matter much whether Frank was giving her a line, or really loved her. 3. *(also: give someone a line or two)* send smb. a brief note or letter: If you would like more information regarding this music, please give me a line.

Note: *The expression does not fully correlate in meaning with the phrase* ***drop someone a line****— = give someone a line 3:* Upon receiving your submission, your editor will drop you a line acknowledging receipt.

give someone line—(also: give someone rope) give a person freedom of action (in order that he may reveal himself): She was persuaded he would ruin all, but she was resolved to give him line.

give someone a look-in • look in on someone

give someone a look-in—give smb. a chance to be successfully involved in smth.: Brogden is the only decent leader the Liberals have. But the polls don't give him a look-in...

look in on someone—make a short visit to a person: She has support from a daughter and two daughters-in-law who look in on her regularly.

give someone a Mickey Finn • take the mickey out of someone

give someone a Mickey Finn—(Underworld) add a sleeping drug to smb.'s drink in order to rob, etc.: He heard a claim that Rudolph was killed by New York waiters who gave him a Mickey Finn.

take the mickey out of someone—make fun of a person: The national papers seemed to think that it took the mickey out of country people, while the Norfolk people thought it ridiculed Londoners!

give someone a nice time • give someone a hard time

give someone a nice time—(also: show someone a nice time) 1. be very attentive and friendly to smb.: They are very interested to hear of my tour and do anything to give me a nice time. 2. is used with a sexual connotation: This was my first visit and it was fun. A girl named Venassa was very friendly and gave me a nice time.

give someone a hard time—(also: give someone a rough time) 1. create a difficult or unpleasant situation for smb.: I started going out of my way to avoid the people who were giving me a hard time. 2. rebuke or reprimand a person: I figured it was an awkward enough episode as it was, and I felt no need to give him a hard time about it.

give someone a pain • give someone pain

give someone a pain—1. cause smb. physical pain: The prednisone gave her a pain in her liver and stomach, she could not eat, and she lost all her energy. 2. *(also: give someone a pain in the neck)* annoy or irritate a person: What would I want to go up to Florence Leaming's for? She gives me a pain.

give someone pain—1. = *give someone a pain 1:* Then after a while I sat up, which gave me pain, for I felt as if I had been beaten all over. 2. make a person feel upset or unhappy: I think of memories that gave me pain. It reminds me of how life goes on after a storm.

give someone a pat on the back • give someone a pat on the shoulder

give someone a pat on the back—express appreciation of smb.'s performance, competence, etc.: He never gave me a pat on the back. I mean, I wanted him to recognize me—to be proud of me. *Cf.: give oneself a pat on the back—congratulate oneself on getting a good job done, etc.:* If I could dive like that—well, I'd give myself a big pat on the back.

give someone a pat on the shoulder—draw a person's attention to smth.: This article just gave me a tap on the shoulder and made me realize how long I have been single. It has been years!

give someone a push • give someone the push

give someone a push—1. shove a person: Just at the edge of the well, he gave him a push and threw him into it. 2. said of an act of pushing smb.'s car: Our car was stuck and they gave us a push. 3. *(coll.)* promote smb.'s advancement; assist a person: I was including his business on my newsletters just to give him a push. 4. *(sl.)* dismiss a person from employment: I just recall a few months ago when it looked like they were going to give him a push.

give someone the push— = *give someone a push 4:* If he doesn't resign after this term—which he won't—we'll just have to give him the push.

give someone a ride • take someone for a ride

give someone a ride—offer a person a ride on a horse, bicycle, etc.: Five children, who helped catch two thieves, are to be given a ride in a police panda car.

take someone for a ride—1. = *give someone a ride:* When the weather is nice and she feels up to it I take her for a ride. I like to drive, and I like to have her beside me. 2. *(sl.)* mislead or swindle a person *(also: take someone for a sleigh ride):* Don't give them any money until you have seen the goods. They may be taking you for a ride. *3. (Underworld)* take a person on a car journey with the intention of murdering or kidnapping: No one would ever know whether he had quietly faded into voluntary oblivion or had been "taken for a ride."

give someone a run • give someone the run

give someone a run—(coll.) 1. see whether smb. is suitable for a job, etc. by letting the person do it for a short time: She's not someone I would normally date, but I'll give her a run. 2. offer a strong challenge or competition to a person: John came in second but certainly gave her a run for most sales this quarter.

Note: *The expression does not fully correlate in meaning with the phrase* ***give someone a run for his money***—1. *give someone a run 2:* There was no obvious Democratic candidate poised to give Kyl a run for his money. 2. *derive much satisfaction in return for one's outlay or efforts:* Well if anything has ever given me a run for my money, this morning definitely took the cake.

give someone the run—(of) give a person permission to use smth. freely: Frank generously gave me the run of his extensive library.

Note: *The expression does not correlate in meaning with the phrase* ***give someone the runs***—*(coll.) cause diarrhea:* These pills won't help and only give her the runs.

give someone a run-down • run someone down

give someone a run-down—(coll.) give a person a brief survey of facts *(also: give someone a run-through):* After she gave me a rundown of her "typical day," it was apparent why she was exhausted.

Note: *The expression is not equivalent in meaning to the phrase* ***run it down to someone***—*(U.S. sl.) describe or explain a situation; tell a person the whole truth about smth.:* I tried to figure out the best way to run it down to this girl that they didn't have to live in this town.

run someone down—1. *(also: run someone over)* knock smb. to the ground with a vehicle *(usually Passive):* He was run down by a vehicle operated by another member of the staff. 2. speak of a person in a disparaging or critical manner: I wish you'd stop running me down all the time. I resent it, and I won't stand for it. 3. find or capture smb. after a long search or chase: The airport police finally ran him down at the far end of the Lost Luggage hangar.

Note: *The expression does not correlate in meaning with the adjectival phrase* ***run down***—*exhausted and weak:* The doctor said I was completely run down and I need to change my lifestyle.

give someone a run-through • run someone through

give someone a run-through—(coll.) give a person a brief survey of facts *(also: give someone a run-down):* I asked Dr. Leake (my mentor here) to give me a run-through on some critical astronomy concepts.

run someone through—pierce or stab smb., as with a sword, etc.: Thorn is the tough, gritty warrior who wouldn't think twice to run someone through, especially when her life is on the line.

give someone a rush • give someone the bum's rush

give someone a rush—(sl.) 1. bestow lavish attention on a girl or woman: An actor gives her a mild rush, and she dreams of a glamorous life with him. 2. give a person a feeling of exhilaration: Methadone is addictive, too, but it doesn't give the pleasurable "rush" that heroin addicts speak of.

give someone the bum's rush—(sl.) throw smb. out or dismiss unceremoniously: That I was given the bum's rush is understandable under the circumstances, but not excusable for a fellow in the hospitality business.

Note: *The expression does not correlate in meaning with the phrase* ***bum rush something****—(sl.) stampede or crash into an area:* Police "bum rushed" the house where they found the gun they say is Jamison's.

give someone a shake • give someone the shake

give someone a shake—(coll.) 1. shake a sleeper to rouse him: I thought he was sleeping, so I gave him a shake to wake him up. 2. rouse smb. to action: Danny was not playing as well as he is now at the start of the season. We needed some way to give him a shake. 3. make a person suffer a nervous shock: It gave me such a shake as I never had before; I haven't felt like myself ever since.

Note: *The expression is not related in meaning to the phrase* ***give someone a fair shake****—(coll.) give smb. fair treatment:* The man did not believe that the judge would give him a fair shake at his trial.

give someone the shake—(coll.) get away or escape from a person without his noticing: "Do you think he followed you?" "I gave him the shake in the crowd."

give someone a shake-down • shake someone down

give someone a shake-down—provide smb. with an improvised sleeping accommodation: You can give him a shake-down here to-night, can't you?

Note: *The expression is not antonymous in meaning to the phrase* ***give someone a shake-up****—1. make a person suffer a nervous shock:* Don't disturb her. Let her sleep. That accident gave her a nasty shake-up. 2. *rouse a person to action:* It gave me a shake-up and I half heartedly started swimming and doing weights in the house.

shake someone down—(U.S. sl.) 1. extort money from smb. by threats or deception: If someone has money and won't share, everyone else will shake him down. 2. search a person (for weapons, drugs, etc): I can not tell you how many times police officers sniffed out something "wrong" with me and shook me down.

Note: *The expression is not antonymous in meaning to the phrase* ***shake someone up****—1. = give someone a shake-up 1:* The whole experience quite shook me up though, I don't drink and drive but I felt quite panicky at being pulled over.... 2. *= give someone a shake-up 2:* Maybe it's time to shake him up a bit. This is a very touchy situation, given that you have a child together.

give someone a thick ear • give someone one's ear

give someone a thick ear—slap a person on his ear, especially as a punishment: He'd give you a thick ear if he heard you say that. Or Rosie would. Sam's too polite.

give someone one's ear—(formal) listen attentively to a person; pay close attention to smb.'s words: If I was struggling with a decision he gave me his ear and some advice.

Note: *The expression does not correlate in meaning with the phrase* ***give someone an earful****—(coll.) 1. give smb. a severe scolding:* I gave him an earful for not having a fire extinguisher, because he should know better. 2. *provide some information to a person:* I didn't know much about literature ... but he gave me an earful each and every day.

give someone a ticking-off • tick someone off

give someone a ticking-off—(coll.) scold or reprimand a person: The referee gave Mike a ticking-off. Not that he cared.

tick someone off—1. put a mark by smb.'s name on a list: I ask each kid one question, ticking them off as they answer. 2. mark smb. as a potential object for vengeance or hostility: If anyone starts fault-finding he is immediately "ticked off." 3. *= give someone a ticking-off:* He was "ticked off" by one of the boys for leaving his car unlocked and complete with ignition key. 4. *(U.S. sl.)* annoy or anger a person: It ticks me off when I have to study and somebody makes noise.

give someone a tip • give someone a tip-off

give someone a tip—1. give a gift of money to a waiter, porter, etc.: I gave him a tip, a small one, because I try to be nice to the people who make me angry. 2. provide a person with privileged information likely to bring useful results: Some politicians gave him a tip that Prohibition was starting to lose ground.

give someone a tip-off— = give someone a tip 2: A while ago a guy I met gave me a tip-off about a secluded beach somewhere in Goa.

give someone an idea • give someone ideas

give someone an idea—give a person a general notion of smth.: I will now give you an idea of the type of thing you will be required to do.

give someone ideas—(also: put ideas into someone's head) give smb. a falsely high opinion of oneself: Mrs. Serafino was not effusive in her thanks to the girl. It might give her ideas.

give someone five • give someone high five

give someone five—(coll.) 1. *(also: give someone a hand)* help a person: Hey, give me five over here for a minute, will ya? 2. slap smb.'s raised palm in greeting or as a congratulation: Reno put out his hand for me to give him five.

give someone high five— = give someone five 2: The guy at the door said goodnight and Billy turned around and gave him high five.

See also: take five / take the fifth.

give someone freedom • give someone his freedom

give someone freedom—1. allow a person to do what he wants: They gave him freedom to go anywhere on his scooter provided he informed them first. 2. *(of a prisoner or slave)* make free: Augustus in a dearth, gave freedom to twenty thousand slaves.

*give someone his freedom—*1. *= give someone freedom 2:* They were in favor of arming the negroes, putting them in the Southern army, and at the same time giving them their freedom. 2. agree to a divorce: It seems foolish not to give John his freedom; if that's what he really wants.

give someone lip • give someone lip service

give someone lip—(sl.) talk in a rude or disrespectful way to a person: "I was doing a practical session in a hospital," he said, "and one of the patients was giving me lip."

give someone lip service—give smb. verbal expression of support, etc. not backed up by action: Each time they are very sympathetic but nothing happens. I got the idea they were just giving me lip service.

give someone one's word • give someone the word

give someone one's word—1. give one's promise to a person: I'll help you in any way I can — I give you my word. 2. express one's assurance to a person: I give you my word that my brother did not leave a shilling to his son.

give someone the word—1. indicate one's intentions to smb.: Any time you need any additional help just give us the word. 2. command a person to do smth.: The man stood bolt upright before me until I gave him the word to stand at ease. 3. *= give* *someone one's word 2:* I give you the word of a man whose word once meant something — I am playing square with you now.

give someone short change • give someone small change

give someone short change — (also: shortchange someone) 1. give a person less than the correct amount of money: After several rounds of drinks had been served, Sullivan accused Cook of giving him short change. 2. treat a person unfairly by not giving him what he deserves: The group feel they are given short change when it comes to being noticed.

give someone small change — give smb. coins of low denomination: By mistake, I gave some small change, in euros, to the waitress. She pointed this out to me and I forked out the pennies that were needed.

give someone stick • take a stick to someone

give someone stick — (UK coll.) rebuke or reprimand a person: She really gave him stick about the way he made a mess of the contract negotiations.

Note: *The expression does not correlate in meaning with the phrase* ***give it some stick*** *— (UK coll., of a vehicle) put more force into it; speed it up:* Peter gave it some stick and cleared the hill with no problems.

take a stick to someone — hit a person: Gossip columnists had their tongues set a wagging when Jiri took a stick to his producer in a hotel lobby

give someone the big eye • look at someone with big eyes

give someone the big eye — (coll.) look at a person with an open display of romantic interest *(also: give someone the eye):* I can feel my dander rise watching him give her the big eye.

look at someone with big eyes — (also: look at someone wide-eyed) stare at a person in surprise: "Are we having a son?" he asked, looking at her with big eyes shining from happiness.

Note: *The expression does not correlate in meaning with the saying* ***one's eyes are bigger than his stomach*** *— one wants more of smth. than he can handle:* His eyes are bigger than his stomach, or converted to garden terms, he would like to grow more varieties than his land can accommodate.

give someone the bird • have a bird

give someone the bird — 1. *(coll.)* scoff or jeer at a performer, entertainer, etc.: Spencer's goal-kicking was atrocious — even the crowd began to give him the bird. 2. make a very impolite sign by raising one's middle finger towards smb. to show that one is angry: He lifted his hand outside the car window and gave me the bird.

have a bird — (U.S. sl.) react with strong anxiety or agitation *(also: have a canary):* When I told my daughter she was grounded, she had a bird … began screaming and crying.

See also: get a duck / get the bird.

give someone the freedom of the city • give someone the freedom of the world

give someone the freedom of the city — confer upon a person honorary citizenship of a city: Harrison was given the freedom of the city and was the guest of honor at the London Rotary Club.

give someone the freedom of the world — (sl.) dismiss smb. from employment: I used to work for IBM, but one day they called me in and gave me the freedom of the world, so now I have my own business.

give someone the kick • give someone the kick in the teeth

give someone the kick — (coll.) 1. make smb. experience excitement or pleasure: Morphine and heroin do not give normal persons the "kick" they are supposed to give. 2. have a strong stimulant effect on a person: It was this discourse from Osho that gave me the kick I needed to move from the life of illusion.

Note: *The expression does not correlate in meaning with the phrase* ***give someone a kickback*** *— (sl.) used of money paid illegally for favorable treatment:* DiBlasio told that he gave a kickback to the Congressman every month, and that was part of their deal.

give someone the kick in the teeth — (coll.) make a person suffer an embarrassing refusal or failure: The Liberals' proud victory has given the two major parties the kick in the teeth that each of them deserves.

give someone the rough side of one's tongue • give someone tongue

give someone the rough side of one's tongue — speak severely to smb. (about a fault, bad behavior, etc.): She stared up at him, fully prepared to give him the rough side of her tongue, then stopped when she saw the look on his face.

give someone tongue — said of an open-mouthed kiss in which one's tongue is inserted into the other's mouth: We were both teenagers. She wouldn't even give me tongue when I kissed her.

Note: *The expression does not correlate in meaning with the phrase* ***give tongue*** *— (also: give mouth)* 1. *utter one's thoughts; express smth. in words:* I have several friends who are willing to give tongue in my defense. 2. *(of a dog) bark when on the scent:* They expected every moment to hear Merrylegs give tongue, but the highly trained performing dog had not barked.

give someone the sack • leave someone holding the sack

give someone the sack — (coll.) dismiss a person from employment: Raytheon tried to silence him by giving him the sack. Colin has now brought a charge of unfair dismissal to an industrial tribunal.

leave someone holding the sack — (U.S. coll.) be entrusted with an unwelcome responsibility: Perhaps you didn't plan to drag me into the case and leave me holding the sack.

give someone the time • give someone the time of day

give someone the time — 1. *(also: give someone time)* be patient with smb. in expectation of a change or achievement: Parents don't have to solve the problems for him — just give him the time and attention he needs to grow. 2. *(sl., euph.)* have sex with a person: I was personally acquainted with at least two girls he gave the time to.

give someone the time of day — (usually negat.) exchange a greeting or casual remark with a person: Lippy wouldn't have given Danny the time of day … not if he'd have come to him on bended knees.

Note: *The expression does not correlate in meaning with the phrase* ***know the time of day*** *— (coll.) be perceptive and shrewd; have good judgment:* David is a trainer who knows the time of day — he is one of the best in the profession. *Cf.: not know what time it is — (coll.) be not very smart or not informed on the situation:* From the kind of things I've seen him do, he doesn't know what time it is. He's dangerous.

give someone time • give someone time out

give someone time — (also: give someone the time) be patient with smb. in expectation of a change or achievement: "He won't make up his mind about me." "Well," Milly smiled, "give him time."

give someone time out — 1. allow smb. to remain away from work, study, etc. for a period of time: A lot of companies will give time out to their staff to donate blood. 2. make a child stand in the corner as a form of punishment: Respond first with a clear warning; if that doesn't take care of the problem, you can give a time-out to a child.

give something a rest • put something to rest

give something a rest—stop talking about or doing smth. for a period of time: I think you ought to give football a rest for a time.

put something to rest—(also: lay something to rest) 1. dispel fears, rumors, etc.: The day is approaching when other popular misconceptions will be put to rest. 2. settle an issue, dispute, etc., especially so as to be free of it: I am hoping to do enough research on it to finally put it to rest this fall.

give something off • give something out

give something off—(of smell, vapor, etc.) release; send out: The Daimler stood patiently in the sun outside, its leather giving off a hot smell.

give something out—1. hand smth. out; distribute smth.: Several people have been arrested in Red Square for giving out leaflets. 2. make smth. known; announce smth.: Whatever made you give such a terrible piece of news out on the morning of the girl's wedding? 3. *(of sound, light, etc.)* send out: The ship gave out radio signals for help until she sank.

Note:** Neither expression correlates in meaning with the phrase* ***give something away—1. *give smth. free of charge:* The young man gave all his possessions away and went to live on a small island. *2. (of prizes, awards, etc.) distribute:* Do you really think it necessary to drag the Mayor in, just to give away a few certificates to kids. 3. *betray a secret; reveal smth.:* Kylie was very secretive about reports that she's planning to wed Martinez ... but singer Dannii has given the secret away. 4. *waste smth. such as an opportunity, etc.:* If you give your chances away like that, how can you expect to win the game.

give something the go-by • let something go by

give something the go-by—1. evade or ignore smth.: There is one other subject to which I would like to refer, lest I should be accused of deliberately giving it the go-by. 2. surpass or outstrip a car, boat, etc.: As we gave the staggering rice-boats the go-by, I reflected that I was looking upon the River of the Lost Footsteps.

let something go by—pass up a chance for smth.; fail to make use of smth.: Don't let the opportunity go by to tell them why it's important to be honest.

give the game away • have the game in one's hands

give the game away—make known a secret plan, etc.: Turn up at the airport to two privately chartered flights; not even your tickets will give the game away!

have the game in one's hands—be in a strategically advantageous position: He was thinking that he had the game in his hands only to find out that nobody else voted with him.

glass ceiling • stained-glass ceiling

glass ceiling—an invisible limit of movement to important positions for women, minorities, etc.: This discrimination results in a wage gap and renders women powerless in the face of an impenetrable glass ceiling.

stained-glass ceiling—the difficulty for women to gain a certain level of authority within church hierarchies: The paper ran a disturbing article about clergywomen and the "stained-glass" ceiling they face.

glove box • glove compartment

glove box—1. a case in which there are two holes with gloves fixed to them for handling dangerous materials: The glove box is kept at a pressure slightly below atmospheric. 2. compartment in a car in front of the driver's seat for holding small articles: I sat for a minute in the front seat. I looked in the glove box.

glove compartment— = *glove box 2:* I went to the car and got a pair of handcuffs out of the glove compartment.

go across to something • go over to something

go across to something—change one's political beliefs and join another group: I am disappointed Simpson has decided to go across to the Democrats, especially after fighting them so actively in the past.

go over to something—1. = *go across to something:* Stalin, on the other hand, did not like to see such a figure go over to the opposition. 2. give up one's practice, interest, etc. and take on another: I've tried to go over to another instrument before, the banjo. Didn't work out. 3. *(Radio, TV)* switch a broadcast to another place: And now, we go over to Paris for up-to-the-minute news about the President's visit.

go all the way • go the full distance

go all the way—1. successfully complete smth. not stopping halfway: The government didn't go all the way; it restricted advertising by tobacco companies, but didn't ban it. 2. *(euph.)* have sex (as distinguished from other forms of caressing): Unmarried women were not supposed to "go all the way." They were expected to remain virgins until they married.

go the full distance—(also: go the distance) 1. *(Sport)* continue running or playing until the end of the race or match: Even though the race course was in bad condition, all the horses went the full distance. 2. = *go all the way 1:* We will go the full distance to ensure customer satisfaction and the highest possible level of quality. *Cf.: go the extra mile—take extra effort; work longer or harder than expected:* Hefflinger is a prime example of a coach who is willing to go the extra mile for the improvement of his team.

go all the way with someone • go halfway with someone

go all the way with someone—1. be in complete agreement with a person: I agree with much of what you say, but I cannot go all the way with you. 2. *(euph.)* have sex with a person (as distinguished from other forms of caressing): Dave had lain awake running through endless fantasies of going all the way with her.

go halfway with someone—(also: meet someone halfway) make concessions to smb.; come to a compromise with a person: Maybe you can convince your parents to go halfway with you, as part of your birthday gift from them.

Note:** The expression does not correlate in meaning with the phrase* ***go halves with someone*—divide the cost of smth., etc. with another person:* A good idea, if a lot of the books you need are pricey, is to go halves with a friend.

go along for the ride • go for a ride

go along for the ride—(coll.) join in an activity as an observer only: He told the police he only went along for the ride, but they believe he was fully aware of the others' plan.

go for a ride—journey on a horse, bicycle, or in a vehicle: We all went for a ride in her new car on Saturday.

go along with someone • go along with you

go along with someone—agree with smb.; cooperate with a person in an activity: Jules had to take orders from him pretending to go along with him in his ridiculous schemes.

go along with you—(exclam.) 1. is used to rudely tell smb. to go away (and stop being annoying): "Go along with you!" cried my aunt, shaking her fist at the window. 2. is used to emphatically express disbelief: Go along with you! Do you think I'd believe a story like that?

go ape over someone • play the sedulous ape to someone

go ape over someone—(sl.) display strong enthusiasm for a person *(also: go ape for someone):* The Saudis would agree that the price [of oil] would not go up.... The American public would go ape over the Saudis when this was announced.

play the sedulous ape to someone—imitate another person's style, manners, etc.: I remember walking through the Metropolitan Museum of Art and seeing some young painters playing the sedulous ape to Rembrandt.

See also: make a monkey of someone / monkey someone.

go around someone • run circles around someone

go around someone—circumvent or outwit a person; avoid dealing with smb.: We will want to go around the boss. He will say no if asked.

Note: *The expression does not correlate in meaning with the phrase* ***go around with someone****—(also: run around with someone) be seen together in public in the company of smb. of the opposite sex:* Once he started going around with her there were more withdrawals than deposits in his savings book.

run circles around someone—(also: run rings around someone) greatly excel a person in some activity; completely outclass a competitor: Opponents will run circles around you unless you take the time to build up your players' skills.

See also: run someone round / run someone round in circles.

go ashore • run ashore

go ashore—leave a ship to go on land: We are now running into Gibraltar bay, and smartening up to go ashore.

run ashore—(of a ship) be forced to the shore by bad weather, etc.: The ship ran ashore and the captain decided to dry out and come off on the rising tide.

Note: *The expression does not correlate in meaning with the nominal phrase* ***run ashore, a****—(Nautical) a brief period of shore leave:* It was a good run ashore for the ship's company, with the Principality of Monaco granting free admission to many places of interest.

go at a walk • go for a walk

go at a walk—go on foot or ride a horse at a slow pace: He watched her as she went past at a walk, the black Labrador and he both gazing wistfully.

go for a walk—take a stroll; walk for pleasure or exercise: In the morning McManus went for a walk through the mimosa-bushes.

go at large • go big

go at large—be permitted to move freely about at will: The question is to decide whether it is safe to allow the prisoner to go at large.

go big—(coll., also: go big time) 1. operate on a large scale: I really like to barbecue and we decided to go big as the sale price was great. 2. enjoy a great success: After winning both days down in Colombia, Donny decided to go big on the dance floor as well.

go away with something • walk away with something

go away with something—1. succeed in stealing smth.: The thieves went away with all belongings of the passengers including their clothes. 2. *(often negat.)* form an idea or belief: It is easy but wrong to go away with the idea that the Buddha was a very special kind of preacher.

walk away with something—1. *= go away with something 1:* He said the one time he was a victim, thieves walked away with a variety of items, including his tools and stereo. 2. *= go away with something 2:* How can he walk away with the idea that this behavior is unacceptable until he is told that it is unacceptable? 3. take attention from the rest of the performance, etc.: Once again the petite blonde girl with the huge voice walked away with the show. 4. win smth. such as a competition or a prize easily: It came as no surprise that The Gold, the best team, walked away with the championship.

go back on something • go back to something

go back on something—fail to fulfill a promise, agreement, etc.: You should never go back on your promise to a child.

go back to something—1. return to smth. as in conversation: Let's go back to what the chairman was saying. 2. bring smth. back to the mind: Whenever grandmother talks, she always likes to go back to her younger days. 3. have a history extending backwards in time: Phrase *as black as a coal,* with its variants, goes back to Old English times.

go bad • go badly

go bad—1. *(of perishable products)* become unfit for consumption or use: Fish and meat soon go bad in hot weather. 2. be unsuccessful: It sometimes happened, Gertrude admitted, that an artist's work went bad and she lost interest in him. 3. stop functioning: They know how to record and the tapes are good, but not long ago their machine went bad and they didn't know it.

Note: *The expression does not correlate in meaning with the phrase* ***go to the bad****—1. become completely immoral:* Vince sobbed that it was too late and he had already "gone to the bad." 2. *have financial difficulties:* The collapse of Enron acts as a reminder that socially bad companies often go to the bad financially, too.

go badly— = go bad 2: It felt like the work went badly this time, but other people seemed impressed with how much we achieved.

go bang • go with a bang

go bang—explode or burst with a loud noise: He saw flashes and heard an automatic go bang.

Note: *The expression does not correlate in meaning with the phrase* ***bang go****—used when it suddenly becomes obvious that smth. cannot be kept or achieved:* Bang goes his influence, maybe his job, if the two countries reach a real understanding.

go with a bang—(also: go off with a bang) go very well or successfully; have an impressive effect: The party went with a bang, and everyone thoroughly enjoyed it.

go below • go under

go below—(Nautical) go to the lower (underwater) levels in a ship: Nora and I went below to our bunks to make our beds and settle in before the ship left the channel.

go under—1. *(of a person or ship)* go below the surface of the sea: Our boat went under in no time at all. Some time later the submarine approached us, spraying machine gun tracer bullets.... 2. *(of a business)* fail: A few weeks before the company went under he checked to see if his pension was safe. 3. lose consciousness under the action of anesthesia, etc.: No one trained in administering anesthesia was dedicated to that task alone in his operating room as she went under.

See also: come down / go down.

go broke • go for broke

go broke—lose money and so be unable to continue in business: The paper was going broke and would cease publication.

go for broke—use every possible effort; resort to extreme measures to achieve smth.: He decided to go for broke and put his reputation and job on the line.

go bust • go on the bust

go bust—(sl.) become bankrupt: Many hard working people have lost their homes because they have lost their jobs or because their businesses have gone bust.

go on the bust—(sl.) engage in noisy merrymaking *(also: go a bust):* There was a slight probability of some of the party going "on the bust" after three months' teetotalism.

go by the board • go overboard

go by the board—1. *(also: come by the board)* fall into the water from a ship: The ship gave a tremendous roll ... and the mast went by the board. 2. said of an idea or an activity no longer practiced *(often with the implication of regret):* Now, within recent years the old materialism of our fathers has gone by the board.

go overboard—1. = *go by the board 1:* During the storm a lot of the deck cargo went overboard. 2. *(coll.)* lose one's senses; go mad: My uncle has been acting very strangely recently; the family think he may have gone overboard. 3. be very enthusiastic about smth.; do more than is necessary: Many teachers have gone overboard for the new methods without considering their worth.

go cold turkey • walk turkey

go cold turkey—(sl.) rid oneself of drug addiction by sudden and complete withdrawal of the drug: I had to stop smoking, so I went cold turkey.

Note: *The expression does not correlate in meaning with the phrase* ***talk cold turkey****—(coll.) speak frankly and without reserve (also: talk turkey):* It would be impossible for the President to ever talk cold turkey because nobody would accept the responsibility for fighting a war for economic reasons.

walk turkey—(of a ship) pitch and roll: The north wind commenced to make the Yaquina walk turkey, standing her up on either end alternately.

go current • go with the current

go current—1. be in circulation or in common use: Now what would be nice, is if users of these packages could test them out as much as possible before they go current. 2. be generally accepted: He returns forever to the old stories of the Prophets as they went current in the Arab memory...

go with the current—(also: go with the stream) act or think as the majority of people do: These are the people who mutter lies about the futility of fighting the times ... who advise us to go with the current. *Cf.: swim against the current—go against prevailing opinion or thought:* Dr. Lewis adopts a personal, creative approach to healing which I would say is swimming against the current of "evidence based medicine."

go down in flames • go up in flames

go down in flames—1. be destroyed by fire: When the house went down in flames, the mayor accused McCown's followers of burning it. 2. *(also: go down in smoke)* fail or end suddenly; come to nothing: It's interesting to look back and see how many of our plans went down in flames.

go up in flames—(also: go up in smoke) 1. = *go down in flames 1:* A spark from the unscreened fireplace set fire to a bear rug and the house went up in flames. 2. = *go down in flames 2:* Unfortunately, that whole project went up in flames because those guys ended up in a bitter quarrel.

go down in smoke • go up in smoke

go down in smoke—(also: go down in flames) fail or end suddenly; come to nothing: This whole program went down in smoke after the protests started.

go up in smoke—(also: go up in flames) 1. be destroyed by fire: After his house went up in smoke, insurance and fire officials suddenly realized he was involved in a whole string of arsons. 2. = *go down in smoke:* His hopes went up in smoke as his car's engine caught fire and arch enemy and team-mate at the time, Jason Plato, became champion. 3. *(coll.)* lose one's temper: The highbrows in those parts all go up in smoke if you confess to liking those native artists.

Note: *The expression does not correlate in meaning with the phrase* ***go into smoke****—(sl.) go into hiding:* The delegate returned anonymously, slipped ashore and "went into smoke" like some famous criminal.

go down like a bomb • go like a bomb

go down like a bomb—(UK coll.) 1. be very successful; be received with great enthusiasm *(also: go down a bomb):* All the songs went down like a bomb.... You could hear a pin drop as he sang the melancholic ballad in the deathly silence. 2. *(rare)* fail to have the intended effect; produce disappointment: His dream was to make a car that would go down like a bang.... Then a terrible recession ensured that by the time this futuristic car was available it went down like a bomb.

go like a bomb—(coll.) 1. *(of articles on sale)* sell in great numbers: Suits like that go like a bomb in London stores right now. 2. = *go down like a bomb 1:* A slight failure with the pudding makes the other women happy and the evening goes like a bomb. 3. *(of a vehicle)* run extremely well; go very fast: My car goes like a bomb since I put that new engine in and I'm really enjoying it!

go down like a lead balloon • go down like ninepins

go down like a lead balloon—fail to have the intended effect; produce disapproval or disappointment: His jokes about women drivers went down like a lead balloon.

Note: *The expression is not antonymous in meaning to the phrase* ***balloon goes up, the****— used when a situation suddenly becomes serious or critical:* The balloon went up when I received a call stating that two foreigners had been detained by border guards.

go down like ninepins—1. be easily overcome: I was a jack of all subjects and a master of none but General Papers went down before me like ninepins. 2. fail in large numbers: During depressions business units went down like ninepins. The commercial banks of the time did little to help.

go down the river • go up the river

go down the river—1. *(coll.)* slowly decay and fall to pieces through neglect: "Mike's car has gone down the river." "I thought the champion was wealthy," said Mr. Queen. "Not any more." 2. *(U.S. hist.)* go into slavery: Percy Driscoll slept well the night he saved his house-minions from going down the river.

go up the river—(sl.) be imprisoned: Lager-beer had come up since I went up the river.

go down the wrong way • go the wrong way

go down the wrong way—said of food stuck in one's throat causing one to choke and cough: The child coughed and coughed because a piece of bread had gone down the wrong way.

go the wrong way—1. take the wrong path or road: He mentioned this to the driver, who realized that yes, in fact, we were going the wrong way. 2. = *go down the wrong way:* The verb "to quackle" is used in Suffolk in reference to suffocation, when caused by "drink going the wrong way." 3. be erroneous in conduct or actions: When those rules are broken, there must be a just punishment to hinder them from going the wrong way.

Note: *The expression does not correlate in meaning with the phrase* ***go wrong****—1. be mistaken in one's choice or judgment:* The currency is the New Zealand dollar so you can't go wrong if you are after a low cost exotic vacation. 2. *take to immorality:* What's the best way to help young girls who go wrong? 3. *turn out badly or unfavorably:* What if something goes wrong? What if I missed an exam or something affected my performance?

go down to the wire • go under the wire

go down to the wire—(also: come down to the wire) continue to the very last moment or the very end: The game will go down to the wire but in the end the Uconn Huskies should pull away as national champions.

go under the wire—(also: come under the wire) 1. be at the finishing-line of a racecourse: Like an irresistible, perfect piece of mechanism she sailed on; and went under the wire a clear winner.... 2. come at the last possible moment: It was not front page news and I guess went under the wire many places. The timing of this announcement was indeed bad. 3. get free from detention camp (surrounded by barbed wire) by flight: He hasn't assimilated. He doesn't want to be here. And he might go under the wire first chance he gets.

go dry • run dry

go dry—(U.S. hist.) enact legislation for the prohibition of alcohol: The decision of the United States to go dry was a great social experiment.

run dry—1. *(of a river, well, etc.)* be dried up; not yield water, etc.: What shall we do if the well runs dry? 2. *(of a cow)* be no longer able to provide milk: Most cows run dry in about ten months. 3. become exhausted: In 1797 the bullion in the Bank of England had almost run dry.

***Note:** The expression does not correlate in meaning with the nominal phrase **dry run**—a preliminary trial; a rehearsal for the real attempt:* There is long, hard planning, endless training, repeated dry runs ... behind undertakings of this magnitude.

go far • go far afield

go far—1. be successful, especially in one's career: This band is full of talent and will certainly go far. 2. *(of food, money, etc.)* last long; be sufficient: A pound does not go so far today as it did twenty years ago. 3. produce a certain effect; promote smth.: The loan will go far towards overcoming our financial troubles. 4. *(negat.)* undertake special efforts: One need not go far to discover why African cultural elements persist so strongly in post-slavery Cuba.

go far afield—1. go off the subject; digress from the line of reasoning: Do not go far afield to review concepts on the periphery of your talk. 2. = *go far 4:* Actually, we need not go far afield to find a theory which is formally adequate to our needs.

See also: be too far gone / go too far.

go fishing • gone fishing

go fishing—(U.S. sl., also: be on a fishing expedition) undertake a search for facts (especially using improper methods): When you're involved in litigation, you're almost inviting the other side to go fishing through your ancient records.

gone fishing—(U.S. sl.) 1. said of a person unaccountably absent from duty: President Bush hung out the "gone fishing" sign at the White House on Friday and headed for a birthday weekend. 2. be not in touch with the real world; have no idea what is going on: This is not the first time he has "gone fishing" in a big match. Even Liam Brady would have done better playing last night.

go flat • go flat out

go flat—1. spread out lying at full length: I would usually go flat on the ground in case the door was trapped with a grenade. 2. *(coll.)* lose enthusiasm or interest: I get quite interested for about five minutes and then — poof! I go flat like a burst balloon. 3. *(of a battery)* run down; lose charge: Darren has called the Automobile Association twice: once when the battery went flat.... 4. *(of a tire)* be deflated (after a puncture): After driving on the freeway, all four of Torty's tires went flat. 5. *(of beer)* lose flavor; become stale: Not only will the beer suddenly go flat: the extra oxygen will rapidly burn the alcohol out of the client's bloodstreams.

go flat out—(coll.) do smth. with all one's energy: Our vote is holding up well and we will be going flat out to win over the undecided voters.

go for a spin • go into a flat spin

go for a spin—(dated) make a short journey in a car just for enjoyment: Jack has invited us all to go for a spin in his new car tomorrow.

go into a flat spin—be in a state of mental confusion or panic: It is quite possible for a man to go into a flat spin when faced with some trouble.

go for it • run for it

go for it—make an all-out attempt to get or obtain smth.: Each dog selected his bird, and went for it steadily.

***Note:** The expression is not equivalent in meaning to the phrase **go at it**— act rapidly and vigorously:* When you have found out what you want to do — then go at it like blazes.

run for it—(also: make a run for it) run in order to escape from a place or a dangerous situation: We made good progress but then encountered more head winds which increased to gale force, and once more we had to run for it.

go from one extreme to the other • go to extremes

go from one extreme to the other—pass from one exaggerated view to its opposite: We tend to go from one extreme to the other. When the society is too tight, then we tend to go to the extreme of freedom.

go to extremes—be immoderate in one's actions; do smth. to excess: He is the kind of man who cannot do anything in moderation. He always goes to extremes.

go-go boy • go-to guy

go-go boy—(sl.) a performer of erotic dances at a discotheque, striptease club, etc.: You know the kind of place — large dancefloor, hot go-go boys, balconies from where you can look down on the crowd.

go-to guy—(coll.) a reliable person to whom one turns for help, information, or support: Go see Lewis. He is our go-to guy here who handles all of our technical issues.

go head to head • run head to head

go head to head—engage in direct confrontation or conflict: On the same day the two candidates go head to head in their only joint televised debate.

run head to head—compete so closely that the lead is virtually indistinguishable: Neither Jolivette nor Fox had enough votes when they were running head-to-head in the March primary.

go home • go in a home

go home—(also: get home) become quite clear to a person: His calculated sarcasm went home like the sharp point of a rapier.

Note:** The expression does not fully correlate in meaning with the phrase **come home—1. = *go home:* The ideal of equality would come home with special meaning to men bred up on the frontier. 2. *(also: come home to roost) return by way of retribution:* Eventually every single problem you have avoided dealing with will come home.

go in a home—move into an institution such as old people's home, providing refuge and care: My personal experience with my father was, he was adamant he did not want to go in a home.

go in at the deep end • go off at the deep end

go in at the deep end—do smth. difficult without preparation or with no experience of it: You will not be expected to go in at the deep end and you will get support from staff members.

go off at the deep end—(also: go off the deep end) lose one's temper; act recklessly or hysterically: I saw what he had done, and I just went off at the deep end.

go into business • go to business

go into business—engage in production or commerce: ...it was better to sell sock-suspenders in Honolulu than to play small parts in Cleveland, Ohio. He left the stage and went into the business.

go to business—1. go to one's office: "When I go to business tomorrow, I will just have a look at Mr. Fitz's account," Mr. Rowdy thought. 2. *(also: come to business)* discuss the basic and most important facts or realities of smth.: Finns are not very talkative and they like to go straight to business, when it comes to negotiations.

go into retreat • go on retreat

go into retreat—retire temporarily to a place of seclusion (to concentrate on a task, etc.): Narcissus goes into retreat to meditate, and Goldmund, not understanding Narcissus and his fear of loving, feels alone.

go on retreat—go to a specific place for the purpose of relaxation or recreation: She regains her sense of peace by going on a religious retreat with her church group.

Note: *Neither expression correlates in meaning with the phrase* ***beat the retreat***—1. *give the signal to retreat:* Even when Hitler was forced to beat a retreat on the Russian front ... Spanish support did not waver. 2. *withdraw from an undertaking, etc.:* She beat the retreat when she realized that she was going to get nothing further out of him. 3. *(U.S. Army) perform the routine consisting of marching and military music, usually at dusk:* At 6 P.M. the Marines will beat the retreat with the town mayor taking the salute.

go into service • go into the service

go into service—1. begin to be used; become operational: One of the first jet bombers to go into service was the English Electric *Canberra.* 2. be employed as domestic servant: Ten years later she at last reached a higher station in life: she went into service with a Jewish couple. 3. join the armed forces: At the opening of the war he went into service as captain of Company I, Thirty-ninth Indiana Infantry.

Note: *The expression does not fully correlate in meaning with the phrase* ***come into service***— *= go into service 1:* The suburban railway to the airport came into service last week.

go into the service— *= go into service 3:* It was World War II and we knew we would have to go into the service as soon as we turned eighteen.

go into the Church • go to church

go into the Church—(also: come into the Church) become a minister; adopt religion as a career: Amorth, having studied law at a university, went into the Church.

go to church—attend church services regularly: Ladies go to church to exhibit their bonnets, and young gentlemen to flash their diamond rings.

go it strong • go strong

go it strong—(also: come it strong) speak or act in a way which is too extreme: He is about forty, looks young for that, drinks powerful tea, and then goes it strong upon all subjects.

go strong—1. *= go it strong:* He also intends to go strong on trying to achieve full internet access for all students. 2. *(Progressive Tense)* be very old but still in good health: My father is nearly ninety now and still going strong. 3. *(Progressive Tense)* exist for a long time but be still popular, or working well: The group was a huge success, both personally and professionally, and it is still going strong.

go lay an egg • lay an egg

go lay an egg—is used to rudely tell a person to go away (and stop being annoying): "How many times have I told you not to smoke in my...." "Ah, go lay an egg."

lay an egg—(sl.) 1. fail completely; give an utterly unsuccessful performance: The play was a failure. They certainly laid an egg this time. 2. drop a bomb: The plane duly laid an egg. I was crouched alongside a wall. The bomb landed on the other side of the wall. 3. *(U.S.)* laugh very hard: I was so shocked I didn't know whether to cry or lay an egg.

go off on someone • go off someone

go off on someone—(UK coll.) become very angry or excited: Your hair color is nice, I wish I could dye my hair like that. My parents will go off on me though.

go off someone—(coll.) cease to like a person: Earlier on in the episode the two were cuddling up in the pub, so why has she gone off him so soon?

go off the chart • go off the map

go off the chart—greatly exceed normal or expected standards or values for smth.: The combination of all these factors raise the risk level so high "it goes off the chart."

Note: *The expression does not correlate in meaning with the phrase* ***be in uncharted waters***— *be in an unfamiliar situation which may be dangerous:* We are in uncharted waters and the outlook for credit markets and the economy is uncertain.

go off the map—1. disappear: These signs warn people of the lethal secrets inside a home—diphtheria, scarlet fever, or typhoid. Those diseases went off the map in the U.S. years ago. 2. *= go off the chart:* We found three markets where employment is healthy, population is growing rapidly, and prices have yet to go off the map.

go on doing something • go on to do something

go on doing something—continue in the same activity in which one was already engaged: He didn't even look up. He just went on reading.

go on to do something—move on to a new activity; proceed to smth. else: After introducing the speaker, the chairman went on to give details of the meeting.

go on medication • go on the pill

go on medication—start the treatment of an illness using drugs: When these children go on medication, parents are often concerned that daily pill-taking will damage the child's self-esteem.

go on the pill—start to take contraceptive pills regularly: Many women who go on the pill have to try out several different brands before they find the right one.

go on stage • go on the stage

go on stage—(of an actor) appear before the public *(also: come on stage):* Andy and Steve Dobinson both went on stage several times to recite their own poems.

go on the stage—take up the profession of an actor: If he had gone on the stage he would have made a good actor.

go on stream • go with the stream

go on stream—(also: come on stream) be in active operation: What is worse, by the time the plants were ready to go on stream, they were also ready for modernization and refitting.

go with the stream—(also: float with the stream) act or think as the majority of people do: I am not a yes-man, who agrees to everything and goes with the stream, but an individual, having his own opinion.

go on the air • walk on air

go on the air—(also: come on the air) 1. *(Radio, TV)* begin broadcasting: The radio station went on the air shortly after the storm. 2. *(of a program)* be broadcast: Certain programs go on the air in the form of a mixture of live and recorded segments. 3. speak over the radio: I suppose you never know who is listening in when you go on the air.

walk on air—feel very happy or euphoric: I was walking on air the day I handed the manager the final check to settle our bill.

Note: *The expression does not fully correlate in meaning with the phrase* ***dance on air****—*1. *= walk on air:* As you can probably imagine, when I received Melanie's letter, I was dancing on air. *2. (sl.) die by hanging:* For every night, from now until then, you will dance on air with a hempen rope around your neck.

go on the bend • go round the bend

go on the bend—(coll.) have a drinking spree: The apprentice may be a wild youth with an earnest desire to go occasionally "upon the bend."

go round the bend—(coll.) go crazy or behave as if mad *(also: go around the bend):* If I don't get some rest, I'll go round the bend.

Note: *The expression does not correlate in meaning with the phrase* ***turn the corner****— begin to make a recovery from a serious illness or a difficult time:* Has California's economy finally turned the corner?

go on the streets • take to the streets

go on the streets—1. go out into the streets: After finishing home duties, people go on the streets to walk up and down to meet their friends, to socialize. 2. demonstrate for or against smth.: In Japan, whose labor force is among the highest paid in the world, thousands of people go on the streets every year as well. 3. work as a prostitute: They went into service, and when they found that they were expected to dust chairs and wash up breakfast things they went on the streets.

take to the streets—1. *= go on the streets 1:* She takes to the streets daily in response to calls from tenants to investigate nuisance neighbors. 2. *= go on the streets 2:* The students took to the streets in support of the health workers' claim for higher wages.

go one's own way • go one's way

go one's own way—follow one's inclinations; act independently: Parents need to realize that as children grow up, they've got to let them go their own way.

Note: *The expression is not equivalent in meaning to the phrase* ***have one's own way****—(also: have one's way) do what one wants meeting with no opposition:* Divide a nation into parties, or set your enemies at loggerheads, and you can have your own way.

go one's way—1. leave a place; depart: I told him I did not care whether he got into parliament or not; so he called me Mugwump and went his way. 2. *= go one's own way:* Before starting my work, I got some ideas from the director, but he let me go my way from there.

Note: *The expression is not antonymous in meaning to the phrase* ***go out of one's way****—(also: put oneself out of the way) go to great trouble to do smth. well:* Why does a daughter of mine, whom I've loved go out of her way to make a jackass of me?

go out of service • quit the service

go out of service—be no longer in operation; cease to be used: The "slow" jets of the 1960s went out of service as they were replaced by more modern machines.

quit the service—1. leave one's employment: When he thought him sufficiently mellowed, he proposed to him to quit the service of his new employer. 2. leave the army: His career will provide another example of why serving sergeants and young officers quit the service.

go out on the town • go to town

go out on the town—(coll.) go out and enjoy oneself in bars, clubs, etc.: We went out on the town to celebrate our wedding anniversary.

go to town—(coll.) 1. put in a lot of vigor and enthusiasm in an activity: They really went to town on the Christmas decorations this year. 2. severely reprimand or criticize smb.: When a question was asked and I could not answer he went to town on me.

Note: *The expression does not correlate in meaning with the phrase* ***go into the city****—(UK) engage in commerce or finance:* There are parents who would prefer their children to go straight from school into the city or to farming.

See also: get out of town / go to the country.

go out the window • go through the ceiling

go out the window—(of laws, principles, etc.) be abandoned: All rules went out the window. What was important was getting people into the helicopter and getting them out of the flooding.

go through the ceiling—(also: go through the roof) 1. *(of prices, sales, etc.)* increase very rapidly; surpass the expected limit: People are buying here because real estate costs in Boston have gone through the ceiling. 2. show extreme anger about smth.: A lot of the kids I've interviewed have parents who would go through the ceiling if they thought their kids were doing drugs.

go out with the tide • go with the tide

go out with the tide—(of hopes, popularity, etc.) diminish; decline: Hereford's hopes went out with the tide ... washed away after only three minutes when Lightbourne made it one-nil.

go with the tide—(also: drift with the tide) act or think as the majority of people do: You're pretty good at adapting to change. In fact, you'd rather go with the tide than against it.

go over someone • go over someone's head

go over someone—1. search a person: A woman police-officer went over the girl from head to toe, but would not say what she was looking for. 2. *(med.)* examine a person for smth. wrong: The doctor went over the girl carefully but could find no broken bones.

go over someone's head—1. said of smth. too difficult for a person to understand: Some of the jokes were rather rude, but luckily they went over the children's heads. 2. ask for smth. from a person in a higher position than one's immediate superior: If you think your captain is giving wrong orders, you may go over his head to his commanding officer.

go over the hill • go over the hills and far away

go over the hill—(sl.) 1. make an escape; run away: They broke out of jail the other night and went over the hill. 2. desert service in the armed forces: You should have seen Colclough's face the day you went over the hill! It was worth joining the Army for.

Note: *a) The expression does not correlate in meaning with the phrase* ***go downhill****— gradually become worse:* Morgan's commercial diving business is going downhill fast; his wife has left him and now all he owns is at risk.

b) The expression does not correlate in meaning with the phrase ***go over the top****—*1. *do smth. in a way that is extreme or exaggerated:* You had the big name designers who went over the top at the big fashion shows. 2. *behave in an unrestrained manner:* Several members went "over the top" at the cafe in the quiet fishing village of Watchet.... 3. *(Military) go out to attack:*

The terrific bombardment, in general, increased the confidence of the troops about to go over the top.

go over the hills and far away—go to some remote places: Winter in the Highlands is not a time to go over the hills and far away, not if you have any sense.

Note: *The expression is not equivalent in meaning to the phrase* ***head for the hills****—(also: run for the hills) get far away to hide from trouble:* Within a few hundred years of the Christian conquest of Rome, any remaining Gnostics had to head for the hills…

go places • go to places

go places—1. visit interesting places and live an exciting life: She was always wanting to tag along when we went places with our friends. 2. enjoy increasing success; show a lot of talent or ability: This is a year when your struggles pay off, a year when you go places. 3. *(euph.)* go to the toilet: What am I to do? I can't follow them when they go places.

go to places—visit specific places or localities: If I went to places whether it's a bookshop or a coffee shop … you bump into people you know.

go round in circles • go round the houses

go round in circles—*(also: run around in circles)* work busily at a task without making any progress: We'll never reach an agreement: we're just going round in circles.

Note: *The expression does not correlate in meaning with the phrase* ***go full circle****—(of a situation) return to what it was before (also: come full circle):* Now we have gone full circle. Critics groan: "Bring back incompetent punk-rock bands, and away with these boring old practicing musicians!"

go round the houses—do smth. in an inefficient way when there is a quicker, more convenient way: My method goes round the houses a bit, but it works. I'd love to hear from anyone who has an easier one.

go slow • go slowly

go slow—1. move at a low speed: Like Mike said, drive it a few times and it gets better. Just go slow around the corners. 2. deliberately work slowly (as a form of industrial action): What dealers did, of course, was go slow in processing their paper work. 3. be less active; do smth. without hurry (to have more time for consideration, etc.): We had better go slow in this transaction. It needs care. 4. use smth. sparingly: You can have the nursery bathroom all to yourself, but do go slow on the hot water, will you?

go slowly—1. = *go slow 1:* Go slowly round the corners because you know how skiddy it is these days. 2. *(of time)* pass tediously: The days went slowly for Robin who was wary of sleeping and eating.

go South • go West

go South—*(U.S. sl., also: head South)* 1. *(of a market, economy, etc.)* deteriorate; lessen in quality or worth: All the stock market indexes went South today. 2. make an escape; run away: Lefty went South the minute he got out of the pen.

go West—*(sl.)* 1. die: I'm afraid—if I go west this time—I'll be leaving you rottenly badly off, old girl. 2. *(of things)* perish or disappear: Wilson sighed. "There's valuable evidence gone west," he said.

go steady with someone • go steady with something

go steady with someone—*(coll.)* have a person as a regular boyfriend or girlfriend: I thought we were to be married: he'd gone steady with me six months…

Note: *The expression does not correlate in meaning with the adjectival compound* ***steady-going****—used of a staid and sober person:* Today that boy is a steady-going, industrious, and fairly efficient electrician's helper.

go steady with something—*(coll.)* be careful or thrifty in the use of smth.: Here, you two, just go steady with that bottle! I want a couple of grams left for Dad and Harry.

go straight • go straight to the point

go straight—*(coll.)* 1. act honestly; desist from criminal activities: Patrick lives with Kate and has promised to go straight after years of being a hardman in London's underworld. 2. conform to social conventions, especially to give up drugs or cease homosexual practices: Implication is that if some gays can go straight, any gay can go straight.

Note: *The expression is not antonymous in meaning to the phrase* ***go around the bend****—(coll.) go crazy or behave as if mad (also: go round the bend):* He went around the bend when he heard his daughter was planning to marry John.

go straight to the point—*(also: come straight to the point)* give the essential part of what one is trying to say, ignoring what is irrelevant: "What's this nonsense about a studio, Sadie?" I said, going straight to the point.

go the length and breadth of the land • go to the end of the land

go the length and breadth of the land—go everywhere; criss-cross the country: The woman went the length and breadth of the land, for months on end, searching for that house.

go to the end of the land—*(also: go to land's end)* go to the remotest region of the country: We are going to the end of the land. The border between Andhra Pradesh and Tamizh Nadu.

go the limit • reach the limit

go the limit—*(also: go to the limit)* 1. do as much as possible: We know that Quiller will go the limit to ensure the success of his mission. 2. go beyond what is reasonable: I am taking my time about it and do not go the limit. Do not let them tell you that I am foolish or hare-brained.

reach the limit—reach the extreme point: I think those shares have reached the limit, they are not likely to rise higher than they are now.

go the whole gamut • go the whole hog

go the whole gamut—cover the whole range: The names of the visitors go the whole gamut from "empty pockets to very, very deep pockets."

go the whole hog—complete smth. not stopping halfway: We commend the Government for the bold step it has taken thus far on the issue and we hope it will go the whole hog.

go through changes • go through the changes

go through changes—undergo changes; be involved in changing circumstances: It is okay to go through changes otherwise our lives will have no meaning.

go through the changes—1. = *go through changes:* If the company had not gone through the changes, it probably would not have survived. 2. *(euph., of women)* go through menopause: "Going through the changes" is a phrase that need not be feared by women as they enter middle age.

go to bed • go to sleep

go to bed—1. retire for the night: He said he knew the sort of place I meant; where everybody went to bed at eight o'clock…. 2. *(euph.)* have sex: A young doctor may think it all right to propose "going to bed" to a nurse he has only just met. 3. *(of a newspaper, journal, etc.)* go to press: He nearly always had to stay on at the office till after midnight when the paper "went to bed."

Note: *The expression does not correlate in meaning with the*

phrase ***take to bed****—remain in bed through sickness or other cause:* I came down with a cold and took to bed for a couple of days.

go to sleep—1. = *go to bed 1:* Suppose you go to sleep, that you may get up in time enough. 2. fall asleep: I did not go to bed and I did not go to sleep. It was well past midnight, but I managed to get the number of the ambassador's residence in Bern. 3. *(of a part of the body)* become numb so that a person doesn't feel it: Wegner pinches his arm to see whether he feels it.... He feels just a little but not much, like a part that is gone to sleep. 4. *(euph.)* die; pass away: ...Thaddeus, the old man of West Cambridge, who outwatched the rest so long after they had gone to sleep in their own churchyards.

go to bed in one's boots • go to bed with one's boots on

go to bed in one's boots—(dated sl.) be very drunk: If old Jones drinks much more, he'll go to bed in his boots.

go to bed with one's boots on—(sl., of men) use a contraceptive: You can't make them wear something. I tried to tell Reggie once.... "No fear," he said, "I don't go to bed with my boots on!"

go to ground • go to the ground

go to ground—1. fall down: Larsson claimed a penalty when he went to ground after a tussle with Amoruso. 2. *(also: go to earth)* go into hiding; put oneself out of sight: Some key gang leaders had been arrested and the assumption was that the others had "gone to ground."

go to the ground—1. = *go to ground 1:* Several of us were hit including me who went to the ground in a pool of blood. 2. be overcome; perish: Each vagabond that arrived bent his neck to the yoke of gain.... The strong survived, the weaker went to the ground.

Note: *The expression does not fully correlate in meaning with the phrase* ***go on the ground****— = go to the ground 1:* She went on the ground and I picked her up and a couple of fellows came along, saying, "Do you want any help, officer?"

go to hell • go to hell in a handbasket

go to hell—is used to rudely tell a person to go away (and stop being annoying): When I politely asked him to move his car, he told me to go to hell.

go to hell in a handbasket—be in an extremely bad state and continue to the point of total ruin: We don't get involved in issues. We're wasting our lives and going to hell in a handbasket!

go to the bottom • touch bottom

go to the bottom—(of ships) sink: The men were all sick, and the women and children thought they were going to the bottom.

touch bottom—(also: hit bottom) 1. *(of prices, sales, etc.)* reach the lowest or worst point: Prices touched bottom during the depression years. 2. *(of people)* become extremely poor: Until they touch bottom, it is difficult for people to get financial help.

Note: *The expression is but partially antonymous in meaning to the phrase* ***go through the roof****—(also: hit the roof) 1. (of prices, sales, etc.) increase very rapidly; surpass the expected limit:* We got here before prices went through the roof, so we were able to get a nice house at a great price. 2. *show extreme anger about smth.:* There is just one problem: Oscar will go through the roof when he hears about the project.

go to the war • go to war

go to the war—depart for the scene of a war as a soldier: I'm not telling the tale. We all went to the war.

go to war—1. = *go to the war:* There were lots of other outcomes for her efforts without her going to war for the sake of her country. 2. *(of a state)* declare or begin a war: All nations that go to war have some guilt. It always takes two to tango.

go while the going is good • make good going

go while the going is good—leave while the conditions are still favorable: I feel that it's time that we went out as winners ... go while the going is good, so to speak.

make good going—(UK coll.) advance rapidly; make good progress: You should be an experienced hiker, have suitable mountain equipment and be able to make good going.

Note: *The expression does not correlate in meaning with the phrase* ***be good to go****—(coll.) be ready or prepared for smth.:* I just need to put together a plan and then we are good to go.

go wild • run wild

go wild—1. be very excited or enthusiastic about smth. (indicating it in one's behavior by shouting, cheering, etc.): London went wild with delight when the great news came through yesterday. 2. be madly attracted by a person: She was just hitting puberty, and Solomon was going wild about her. Devorah was highly desirable by any male baboon's standards.

Note: *The expression is not equivalent in meaning to the phrase* ***go wilding****—(also: go out wilding) go on a rampage (originally of youth gangs roaming the streets and harassing passers-by):* I'll also remember this next time college students go wilding when their team wins or loses a championship.

run wild—1. become madly violent; go out of control: The CIA is not a sorcerer's apprentice that has run wild, but ... is under strict government control. 2. *(of animals and plants)* revert to a state of nature; no longer live under domestication or cultivation: These cattle, having run wild upon the plains of western Texas, are collected by a grand "round-up."

goat's foot • goat-foot

goat's foot—a South African low-growing plant *Oxalis caprina* of the wood sorrel family: Henry was eating breakfast under an arbor of potato-vines and goat's foot.

goat-foot—1. is used of the Greek god Pan: It was the hour of Pan. I could almost think I saw the goat-foot playing his pipes by the brook. 2. *(attrib.)* of a goat-foot faun or satyr: He [Bacchus] was shown accompanied by goat-foot satyrs, centaurs, and crazed female Bacchantes.

goats' hair • goats' wool

goats' hair—(also: goat's hair) 1. cloth made wholly or partly of goats' hair: The Brahuis are a nomadic race, who dwell in tents made of goats' hair. 2. long straight streaks of cirrus cloud *(known as a sign of impending storm):* It is the cloud known to seamen as "goats' hair" or "mares' tails."

goats' wool—(also: goat's wool) = goats' hair 1: The book describes the Navajo weaver collecting plants to naturally dye the goat's wool.

God-man • man-god

God-man—one who is both human and divine; a god in human form: Jesus Christ is the living, loving God-man.

man-god—1. = *God-man:* Prometheus, in the eyes of the Greek, was a man-god. 2. a man who is made a god: The Christian world was sunk in the worship of men-gods, and women-gods.

God the Father • godfather

God the Father—(in the Christian tradition) the first person of the Trinity: All graphical representations of God the Father are to be disapproved.

godfather—1. a male person who presents a child at baptism: For each male child to be baptized the rubric requires two godfathers and one godmother. 2. a leader of a criminal organization: The youngsters are manipulated by a little band of experienced "godfathers" who make the plans but never risk their own lives.

godly man • man of God

godly man—a deeply religious person: They were the godly men; and it was the business of the ruling classes to endow them with benefices.

man of God—1. an ordained priest; a clergyman of the Christian Church: I don't expect to hear that kind of language from a man of God. 2. a holy man; a saint: It was on the tried friendship of that true man of God that Harold chose to lean.

godmother • Mother of God

godmother—a female person who presents a child at baptism: For each male child to be baptized the rubric requires two godfathers and one godmother.

Mother of God—(also: God's Mother) a name of the Virgin Mary the mother of Christ: Mary, then, was the Virgin Mother of God. She remained in perpetual virginity.

God's child • godchild

God's child—(also: child of God) said of people born of God, that is by God's creation: Man is God's child, and the sin of the man consists in perpetually living as if it were false.

godchild—smb. for whom a godparent acts as sponsor at baptism: A godparent was expected to see to his or her godchild's upbringing, should the parents be unable to do so.

God's Country • Holy Land, the

God's Country—(also: God's Own Country) usually applied to the United States: Now that I no longer live in God's Country I often feel the need to return to the spectacular views of the White Mountains of New Hampshire.

Holy Land, the—places where Jesus Christ lived; land held in religious awe: Did not the Pope send all the Princes of Christendom upon a Fool's Errand, to gain the Holy Land?

God's Son • godson

God's Son—(also: Son of God, the) a name of Jesus Christ: Jesus Christ was and is God's son. Jesus was God's gift to a sinful world.

godson—a male person for whom a godparent acts as sponsor at baptism: She promised that her godson would achieve wealth and position.

Note: *The compound does not correlate in meaning with the phrase* ***God the Son****—(in the Christian tradition) the second person of the Trinity:* Something that is begotten has a definite beginning and a cornerstone of the Trinity is that "God the Son" has always existed.

gold balls • golden balls

gold balls—1. a plant "marsh marigold" *(Caltha palustris)* bearing yellow cup-shaped flowers: Gold Cups and Gold Balls are names now almost forgotten. 2. the three gilt balls used as a pawnbroker's sign: The three gold balls still used as a sign of the pawnbroker's shop are supposed to have originated from St. Nicholas's three bags of gold.

golden balls— = *gold balls 2:* Isaak, with a happy cry, pointed to the three golden balls. Mendel smiled but was exhausted when they got to the pawnshop.

gold digger • gold hunter

gold digger—(sl.) a woman who uses her attractions to extract money from men: I never believed she was in love with him. I always said she was a gold digger.

gold hunter—a fine precision watch of expert craftsmanship: He looked pointedly at his watch, a fine gold hunter which he pulled out of his pocket.

goldcrest • golden crest

goldcrest—a tiny European bird *(Regulus regulus)* having a bright yellow crown patch bordered with black: I raised my binoculars and there was a goldcrest flitting around in its quest for insects.

golden crest—a wooly bog herb *(Lophiola aurea)* of eastern North America with yellowish flowers: Golden crest is native to Florida. It is frequent in the bogs and flatwoods of the Florida panhandle.

golden age • golden years

golden age—1. a period of ideal prosperity and happiness: The reign of Charles IV was a Golden Age in Czech history. The end of this period, however, brought economic and political strife to the area. 2. said of a period in which smth. specific is at its highest state of excellence: The beginning of the jet age in aircraft was a "golden age" in aviation. I did not realize it at the time. 3. *(euph.)* old age: This lover of children certainly has a story to tell about the ups and downs of her life as she attains the golden age of 60.

golden years— = *golden age 3:* They are addressed as "senior citizens" and congratulated on their attainment of the "golden years."

golden ager • golden oldie

golden ager—(U.S. euph.) an elderly person: Frank bought himself a drink in the bar while watching the golden agers gossip in the lounge area.

golden oldie—(UK coll.) anything old but classic: The majority of nature photographers will be using cameras at least a few years old, and often some golden oldies.

golden cage • golden handcuffs

golden cage—(also: gilded cage) said of a situation where a person is living in luxury but without freedom: After years of living in a golden cage she finally makes an attempt to regain control over her own life.

golden handcuffs—substantial monetary incentives offered to a valued employee to persuade him to remain with the company: Mr. Thomson is in line for a £280000 "golden handcuffs" payout on top of his normal remuneration.

good as a play • good as gold

good as a play—said of smth. very entertaining or intensely amusing: Are they not as good as a play, trying their hand at legislation?

good as gold—1. *(of a child)* well behaved; not giving trouble: As soon as a few were bumped off by way of example, all the others became as good as gold. 2. *(of a pledge, etc.)* faithful; reliable: When one of our representatives makes a commitment, you can rest assured that his promise is as good as gold. 3. quite perfect in quality: The chip, which can be implanted in products, is good as gold. They use it to track the flow of goods from supplier to store shelf.

good at something • good on something • good with something

good at something—proficient in a subject or an activity: Boys and girls rate themselves as being equally good at science at the primary-school level.

good on something—skilful in one's performance on a musical instrument: Hayes said that Pearl was "quite good" on the violin and also proficient on the mandolin.

good with something—competent in the use of smth.: He was very good with horses — he worked with them so that they trusted and respected him.

good business • pretty business

good business—said of a profitable and rewarding occupation: The new journalism, with its "mammoth combines," is good business, but bad democracy.

pretty business—(ironic) said of a miserable state of affairs: A pretty business indeed for a man to be hemmed up in a strange place without anything to interest you.

good day • well day

good day—1. one's lucky day; a day favorable for smth.: Monday was a good day for the mayor because all the major players from both parties were willing to play along. 2. a day on which the weather is fine: It was a good day and we had perfect weather conditions in Cumbria, no rain at all. 3. is used as a formal phrase at parting: And to marry for money, I think the wickedest thing in existence. Good day.

well day—a day on which a person is free from sickness, especially from an attack of an intermittent disorder: As it was one of his well days, he walked in without help.

good few, a • good many, a

good few, a—a fairly large number: We had a good few days with Kristen, talking, shopping, and exploring Nashville.

good many, a— = *good few, a:* They will have to face the bitterest cold for a good many days during the Polar night.

good for someone • good to someone

good for someone—1. beneficial or helpful for a person: These classes are good for students who work better at a slower pace or are fairly new to computers. 2. *(of food)* nutritious or wholesome for people: Green leafy vegetables are good for you. They contain important nutrients that keep your children healthy.

good to someone—said of smb. who is kind to a person and willing to help: She has been good to me and my family when we were struggling.

Note: *The expression does not correlate in meaning with the phrase* ***good with someone****— efficient in dealing with people:* She is very good with children and will be assisting me with my class.

good for you • good of you

good for you—(non-predicative) used as an expression of approval: You're not about to lay cash on the line without decent answers to a question or two. Good for you.

good of you—(predicative) used in approval of smb.'s kind or generous act: It was very good of you to help Harry with his bike. I'm proud of you.

good hour • happy hour

good hour—a period not less than an hour: He played a good hour on the violoncello.

Note: *The expression is not antonymous in meaning to the phrase* ***bad hours****—1. inconvenient time:* City officials would limit access to federal benefits by having offices only open during bad hours. *2. the early hours of the morning after midnight:* I don't know what it was that tipped me over the edge. Maybe it was the bad coffee and the bad hours. 3. *(in the phrase "keep bad hours") get up and go to bed late:* She didn't like renting to young people because they kept bad hours and made noise.

happy hour—1. a time in bars when drinks are served at a reduced rate: Happy hour is between 6 and 7 P.M. at Celestial Gardens. 2. a time set aside for consumption of alcoholic beverages: At the conclusion of the question and answer session, there will be a "Happy Hour" in the Ballroom.

See also: good time / good times.

good Joe • quality Joe

good Joe—(coll.) a good fellow: Ted's a little slow on the uptake, but he's a good Joe.

quality Joe—(U.S. Underworld) an innocent or honest person: These quality Joes just don't understand how it is on the street.

good man • well man

good man—1. a morally excellent and virtuous man: You are a good man. And God knows your motives are pure.... 2. used as an exclamation of approbation: She held out her hand. "Good man! that is what I call a friend!"

well man—a man who is free from sickness: Two days later he "began to eat like a well man" again.

good old time • high old time

good old time—(also: good old times) the past, viewed as preferable to the present: However glorious those "good old times" may have been, they still were destitute of one very important advantage.

high old time—(coll.) an enjoyable, festive period or occasion *(usually in the phrase "have a high old time"):* It might look like they're having a high old time. But really, it's very hard work.

good time • good times

good time—1. an enjoyable or exciting experience: Neither driver nor drivee has a thought beyond the enjoyment of a good time. 2. right or suitable time for a particular purpose: Murray decided that this was a good time to ask about his living out allowance. 3. *(euph.)* used with sexual implication: The man was offering her a drink and a good time in Spanish. 4. *(U.S. Prison)* said of credits earned toward one's sentence: In California, good time (one day for two served) credits are awarded in certain situations.

Note: *The expression does not correlate in meaning with the phrase* ***quality time****— (of parents) a period of time during which their attention is devoted entirely to their children:* Many parents don't realize the importance of quality time spent with their children and find that they may act out in negative ways just to get some attention.

good times—a prosperous period of time: There was a considerable degree of rationality in the reactions to the food situation, with marriage rates rising in good times and falling in bad times.

See also: good hour / happy hour.

good-time Charley • good-time man

good-time Charley—(coll.) an affable, fun-loving person: Wally is such a good-time Charley. Who would believe the trouble he's had?

good-time man—1. = *good-time Charley:* Instead of tending to his business, Ilya was too busy chasing women, throwing parties and just being a good-time man. 2. *(U.S. Drug users)* a man who sells drugs: Max is the main good-time man in this neighborhood.

Note: *The expression does not correlate in meaning with the phrase* ***good-time girl****— a girl with loose morals; a call girl:* John Profumo, a government minister, was caught having an affair with Christine Keeler, a good-time girl.

graduate student • post-graduate student

graduate student—(U.S.) one who has completed a bachelor's degree and is working on a master's degree: He earned a fellowship to go to Japan, where he stayed for six years, first as a graduate student.

post-graduate student—(UK) = *graduate student:* He spent two years as a post-graduate student at the International Law Department and then was employed as assistant professor.

grammar school *(UK)* • grammar school *(U.S.)*

grammar school (UK)—fee-charging or state funded selective secondary school with an academically oriented program: I hate the thought that friends will get split up because some will go to a grammar school and others won't.

grammar school (U.S.)—(now rare) elementary school: Elementary school, also known as grammar school, is a school of kindergarten through fifth grade (sometimes the first eight grades), where basic subjects are taught.

grandame • grande dame

grandame—(dated) a grandmother or a woman who is no longer young *(also: grandam):* The sergeant, handing his musket to a comrade, rushed in and attempted to seize the rebellious grandame by the waist.

grande dame—a socially important, usually elderly, woman who is well known or highly esteemed: To her customers and culinary followers Madame Kuony was the grande dame of classic French cooking.

Note: *The expression does not fully correlate in meaning with the phrase* ***grand old lady***—1. = *grande dame:* When the 1960s social revolution rolled round, Dorothy was hailed as the "grand old lady of pacifism." 2. *used of a house, a ship, etc. that are old, antique, or worthwhile restoring for posterity:* This grand old lady of sailing ship days rests in Port Vila Harbor.

grant concessions • make concessions

grant concessions—give special rights or privileges to a business organization: Albania will grant concessions to two international oil groups this month to search for oil.

make concessions—come to a compromise (in order to end an argument, conflict, etc.): The Prime Minister had been urged to make concessions by the Irish government.

grasp at something • grasp something

grasp at something—1. try to seize smth.; grab at smth.: As Timmy grasped at the branch, the last ounce of energy was depleted from his small arms. 2. accept smth. (such as an offer, proposal, etc.) most eagerly: Neoconservative politicians have readily grasped at the opportunity.

grasp something—1. seize and hold smth. firmly with the hand: Grasping the leaves of the plant firmly, pull the whole plant up out of the ground. 2. comprehend smth.: Kitty only imperfectly grasped the rudiments of the science.

grease spot • greasy spot

grease spot—a disease of turf grasses caused by a fungus: Pythium blight, also known as grease spot, kills turf in small, roughly circular spots (2 to 6 inches) that tend to run together.

greasy spot—a disease of citrus trees producing dark oily spots on the leaves: Greasy spot is a fungus disease that attacks all varieties of citrus grown in Florida.

grease the wheels • squeaky wheel gets the grease, the

grease the wheels—make progress easier: Those you interact with will know how to grease the wheels of commerce and get things done.

squeaky wheel gets the grease, the—(saying) the person who complains loudest and longest gets service or attention: It seems that the "squeaky wheel gets the grease"—the students who complain loudest get the rules bent for them.

great at something • great in something • great with something

great at something—highly proficient in an activity: She is great at making up dishes and experiments all the time.

great in something—excelling in a subject: She is great in math. She has a wonderful teacher that truly cares...

great with something—very skilful in the use of tools, etc.: John is great with a bit of crayon.

Great Britain • Greater Britain

Great Britain—1. the island comprising England, Wales, and Scotland: Great Britain is separated from the mainland by the English Channel and from Ireland by the Irish Sea. 2. *(also: United Kingdom of Great Britain and Northern Ireland, the)* the British state as a whole comprising Great Britain and Northern Ireland: She has lived in Great Britain for so long now that English has become her second language.

Note: *The name* ***British Isles, the*** *is a geographical term (not a political one) for the islands comprising Great Britain and Ireland with all their offshore islands:* The British Isles has a rich diversity of folklore, stemming in part from the mix of cultural identity from region to region.

Greater Britain—(hist.) Great Britain and the colonies; the British Empire: But was there not an *entente* which must be the great ideal of every Briton—the *entente cordiale* between Great and Greater Britain?

Great Lakes State, the • Land of 10,000 Lakes, the

Great Lakes State, the—(U.S., also: Great Lake State, the) a nickname of the state of Michigan: Baker has brought the story of Michigan mammals up-to-date, and this work will become the standard reference to the mammals of the Great Lakes State.

Land of 10,000 Lakes, the—(U.S.) a nickname of the state of Minnesota: The "Land of 10,000 Lakes," Minnesota got its nickname because there are more than 12,000 lakes throughout the state.

Great Magician of the North, the • Magician of the North, the

Great Magician of the North, the—(also: Wizard of the North, the) a name given to Sir Walter Scott (1771–1832), a Scottish historical novelist: Some of stories in respect to variety and length, might safely aspire to a place beside the Great Magician of the North, Sir Walter Scott.

Magician of the North, the—a name given to Johann Georg Hamann (1730–1788), a German philosopher and theologian: We may pass directly from Rousseau to Kant, who was largely inspired by ... the somewhat mysterious personality of the "Magician of the North."

great world, the • greater world, the

great world, the—1. aristocratic society: Thackeray says he is getting tired of being witty, and of the great world. 2. the outside world not limited to one's inner circle: The novelist proper studies to represent his little world as the great world is; whereas the romance-writer builds an ideal world. 3. the universe as a whole: These values exist within yourself as they exist in the great world, and you are a microcosmic model of the entire macrocosm.

Note: *The expression does not correlate in meaning with the phrase* ***wide world, the***—1. *the whole world:* Of all people in the wide world his cousin was the most unyielding to argument. 2. *is used to imply contrast to one's own home or country:* A few years in the wide world and then back to the home paddock.

greater world, the— = *great world, the 3:* Essential to most theories was the analogy between microcosm and macrocosm, between the world of man and the greater world around him.

Note: *The expression does not correlate in meaning with the phrase* ***world without end***—*for ever and ever; eternally:* They wrote alternately, Bowman supplying the installment for one week, his friend for the next, and so on, world without end, they hoped.

See also: little world / small world.

green-fly • greenbottle fly

green-fly—any of numerous insects (superfamily *Aphidoidea*) that suck the juices of plants thereby causing withering: If green-fly makes its appearance, fumigation with tobacco smoke is the only remedy.

greenbottle fly—any of several brilliant green-bodied flies of the family *Calliphoridae:* The larva of a greenbottle fly of the genus *Lucilia* is used as a live bait in some fresh-water fishing.

green goods • green stuff

green goods—1. fresh vegetables and fruit: Mass merchandisers have realized that they can make serious money selling green goods. *2. (sl.)* counterfeit money: The janitor states that in his opinion, Stillman, Myth and Co. were in the "green-goods" business.

green stuff—1. various leafy plants (like lettuce) used as food: After a luncheon, during which he ate enormous quantities of green stuff, the two went for a walk. 2. *(of wood, etc.)* not thoroughly dried; unseasoned: The fire's all right. I put out a quart of kerosene and there's stacks of green stuff. 3. *(U.S. sl.)* paper money: I now have so much green stuff, I don't know what to do with it.

green house • green room

green house—1. building with sides and roof of glass, used for growing plants that need protection from the weather: Our selection of green house plants includes all shapes, sizes, and appearances. 2. *(Automobiles)* the upper, windowed portion of a vehicle: The beltline divides the greenhouse, or glassed-in upper body, from the portion that extends down from the window sills.... 3. *(sl.)* a place known for growing or selling green-colored marijuana: While at location, they discovered a green house with more than 250 marijuana plants.

green room—*(Theater)* room for actors when they are not on the stage: Where a green room was originally provided, it has been taken by the star or the manager, as his or her private room.

green man • greensman

green man—1. a symbol of a walking figure illuminated green on some pedestrian crossings: When the green man shows and the traffic has stopped, you can cross. 2. *(dated)* an inexperienced man or sailor: I am afraid we would have killed a green man, traveling and working as we did. 3. commissionaires working outside Harrods *(the fashionable London retail store):* Two traditionally dressed Harrod's "Green Men" greeted guests at the entrance.

Note: *The expression does not correlate in meaning with the phrase* ***little green men***—1. *mysterious extra-terrestrial beings of science fiction:* Her story of being kidnapped by little green men was sheer absurdity. 2. *pulsars (stars detected by pulsating radio signals only):* An entirely novel kind of star was referred to by astronomers as LGM (Little Green Men).

greensman—*(Movie Production)* a member of the crew who decorates the ground with grass, flowers, etc. on an environment used for filming: Greensmen with water trucks began work a month before the shooting crew.

green monkey disease • green sickness

green monkey disease—*(also: green monkey fever)* a virus disease, originally identified among technicians working with green monkeys: Green monkey fever has baffled microbiologists throughout the world.

green sickness—chlorosis *(a form of anemia affecting young women):* This condition, known as chlorosis or green sickness, is readily controlled by the use of iron.

Green Mountain State, the • Mountain State, the

Green Mountain State, the—*(U.S.)* a nickname of the state of Vermont: Vermont Voices is designed to be a reference book for anyone interested in the history of the Green Mountain State.

Mountain State, the—*(U.S.)* a nickname of the state of West Virginia: The center of the Mountain State is one of West Virginia's most abundant wildlife regions.

grind one's teeth • grit one's teeth

grind one's teeth—have feelings of great anger or annoyance though not fully manifesting what one feels: If there is one thing calculated to make British artists grind their teeth, it is to be faced with generalizations about national characteristics.

grit one's teeth—endure pain, discomfort, etc. without complaint; accept a difficult situation and deal with it in a determined way: He gritted his teeth and held on tightly to his assailant even as the rest of the gang rained blows on him.

groundsman • landsman

groundsman—*(also: groundskeeper)* a man who maintains a playing field or the grounds of a property: The recent drought has meant a lot of extra work for our groundsman but he's coped admirably and the park is looking well.

landsman—*(also: landman)* 1. a person who lives and works on land (as opposed to seaman): He viewed the sea either as a landsman from the shore or, like a landsman turned sailor, amidst waves that roll and winds that blow. 2. *(Petroleum Industry)* land consultant responsible for obtaining permission to drill an oil well, build a pipeline, etc.: Her husband took a job as a landsman with an oil company, and they moved to Williston.

grow away from something • grow out of something

grow away from something—gradually cease to have a close relationship with smth.: Taufiq admits that he has grown away from his home country and his mother tongue.

grow out of something—1. develop or result from smth.: Her interest in business grew out of business courses she took as an undergraduate. 2. *(of children)* gradually become too big for one's clothes: I know many of you just had babies, and I know how quickly babies grow out of their things. 3. become too old or rational to continue liking or doing smth.: They speak to me as if I am a youthful idealist, as if I will one day grow out of my current liberal mindset.

Note: *The expression does not fully correlate in meaning with the phrase* ***grow from something***— = *grow out of something 1:* Mark's early love for technology grew from his interest in computer games.

guard ship • guardship

guard ship—a warship stationed at some harbor to act as a guard: In a short time he returned with the commander of the guard-ship, who was also captain of the port.

guardship—*(also: guardianship)* attention implying responsibility of a guardian or keeper: After having left the two prisoners, who were "under his guardship" downtown, he got drunk.

guilty about something • guilty of something

guilty about something—*feeling* unhappy and ashamed because one has done smth. wrong: Arthur felt guilty about using spray-on polish instead of the old-fashioned wax kind.

guilty of something—*being* responsible for an offence or crime: An amnesty was granted, with few exceptions, to all who, during the late troubles, had been guilty of political offences.

Gulf Country • Gulf State

Gulf Country—*(Austral.)* the back country of the gulf of

Carpentaria in the northern part of Queensland and the Northern Territory: It's hard to travel in the remote Gulf Country without hearing about Wollogorang Station.

Gulf State—1. an American state bordering the Gulf of Mexico: The Gulf States or their representatives in Congress killed the bill by voting against it. 2. a state bordering the Persian Gulf: Qatar becomes the fifth Gulf State to agree to open its territory to foreign troops.

gun chamber • gun room

gun chamber—1. the part of a gun that receives the loaded charge: According to Massalamani his own gun chamber got jammed, so he could not shoot. 2. an apartment on a warship used by the midshipmen and junior officers: He lost the advantage that the suddenness of his irruption into the gun chamber had given him.

gun room— = *gun chamber 2:* John was popular but found the discipline of a fighting ship difficult.... He was often called up to join his senior officers in the gun-room.

gun for it • gun it

gun for it—*(coll.)* go after smth. in earnest; try hard to obtain smth.: Learn where you want to be in life and then gun for it with everything you've got ... and never stop trying.

gun it—*(coll.)* cause a vehicle to accelerate rapidly or suddenly: Trials include accelerating tests where you'll need to gun it ... get as much speed up as possible before braking hard.

gutter child • gutter man

gutter child—a neglected boy running at large; a child of low birth or breeding: The gutter child and the infant prince are alike open to the workings of the desire for esteem...

gutter man—a man who cleans out the gutters of buildings: We await the gutter man. We have had to try to contact him twice already to no avail.

H

habitable planet • inhabitable planet

habitable planet—a planet capable of supporting life: The possibility of another habitable planet is so tantalizing that scientists will devote countless hours to studying every piece of data.

inhabitable planet— = *habitable planet:* Today marks the beginning of hope that another inhabitable planet could exist beyond earth.

Note: *The expression is antonymous in meaning to the phrase* ***unhabitable planet***—*(also: uninhabitable planet) a planet incapable of supporting life:* In unhabitable planets there should be extreme weathers. There should also be natural calamities like earthquakes and hurricanes.

hair-raising story • hairy story

hair-raising story—1. a thrilling and scary story: I remember her telling the hair-raising story of how she was alone in her little hut somewhere in the jungles of Africa. *2.* a story that shocks people: Naylor tells some hair-raising stories of how politicians have often been the chief culprits, stashing away foreign aid funds in numbered accounts.

hairy story—*(coll.)* a story which tells about an arduous or hazardous past experience: Dick used to tell me hairy stories about those early days working in Antarctica.

half a man • half-baked man

half a man—a man lacking in spirits, strength, or courage: If only half a man—like Buck—shouts "Lynch him!" you're afraid to back down—afraid you'll be found out to be what you are—cowards.

half-baked man—*(coll., derog.)* an unwise and inexperienced man: I would rather see the children in the hands of a man whose principles are known to me, than of some half-baked man of learning...

half-holiday • half-term holiday

half-holiday—a day of which half is free from work or duty: Wall-street took the half holiday that the law allowed her yesterday. The Exchanges closed at noon.

half-term holiday—*(UK, also: half-term)* a short vacation for schools halfway through a semester: Oliver arranged for them to spend three days out of their half-term holiday at a camp.

half-hourly • on the half hour

half-hourly—done or occurring every half hour: We'll be running more trains, with half-hourly departures to Paris and hourly departures to Brussels.

on the half hour—occurring exactly thirty minutes after an hour marked on a clock: The clock should chime once on the half hour and twice on the hour.

half one (two, etc.) • half past one (two, etc.)

half one (two, etc.)—*(UK coll.)* thirty minutes after one (two, etc.) o'clock: Instead of arriving at half one in Cape Town, I was only there at half four.

half past one (two, etc.)—a commonly used variant of the former: At twenty past twelve we arrived at Farmers Bridge Locks, which we completed by half past one.

half-seas over • overseas

half-seas over—*(UK coll.)* drunk: I learned later that Charley had run across an old college pal, and was half-seas over in a bar up one street.

overseas—across or beyond a sea, especially in another country: The country is up in arms over the denial of voting rights to the men serving overseas.

half the time • half time

half the time—*(hyperbolic)* 1. a much shorter time than is normal or expected: I could have done it in half the time. 2. a considerable time: I'm not surprised he didn't complete the exam—he spent half the time looking out the window. 3. habitually; very frequently: She calls on the neighbors, she's out half the time and doesn't answer the telephone.

half time—1. an interval between the two halves of a game of football, hockey, etc.: Before half-time he kicked two goals out of the three registered for Middlesex. 2. half the time usually worked: I worked halftime in the atmospheric sciences department with a professor I consider a genius.

half the world • half-world

half the world—is used to hyperbolically designate a great quantity or number: Half the world buys British when it comes to cars, especially semi-sports jobs like this.

half-world—a social group considered to be not wholly respectable: Away from his chosen half-world, Munby's social life was passed in the first literary and artistic circles of his day.

half-way • middle-of-the-road

half-way—1. situated midway between two points, stages of a journey, etc.: A half way station was added where visitors can break their journey with a visit to the nearby Bronze Age

Copper Mine. 2. *(of a situation)* midway between two states or conditions: In this situation, half way between dictatorship and democracy, the military institution has set limits to the range of behaviors of civilian politicians.

middle-of-the-road—1. *(of a person or a course of action)* moderate and unadventurous; tending to avoid extremes: They wanted him, the old middle-of-the-road liberal democrat, to be their first president. 2. *(of music, style of dress, etc.)* conventional, standard or mainstream: Randy Wood put out some records—not country music or downright jazz but what he called "middle of the road music."

ham and egger • like ham and eggs

ham and egger—(U.S. sl., pejor.) 1. no one special; just an ordinary person: I hated this movie and I am a ham and egger who can pretty much sit through anything. 2. *(Boxing)* an amateur boxer, especially of mediocre skills: Wayka is what an earlier generation of sportswriters might have referred to derisively as a "ham-and-egger."

like ham and eggs—1. said of two things that usually go together and which it is hard to separate: Camping and fishing go together like ham and eggs. 2. used in allusion to the aphorism *"It's like ham and eggs. The chicken is involved. The pig is committed"* to emphasize the difference between merely making a contribution and being fully committed: "What would keep you from taking this position?" "Lack of commitment by the administration. It's a little like ham and eggs. You know, the chicken is a participant, the hog is committed."

hand-off • hands-off

hand-off—(Rugby Football) the action of pushing off an opponent with the hand: Gray has a fine kick, with a strong hand-off.

hands-off—1. *(of a course of action)* characterized by not interfering or getting involved: A protest must be made against this hands-off government policy. *Cf.: hands-on—(of an apprach, training, etc.) involving active participation:* There's no better way to tell if you're cut out for the work than hands-on experience. 2. *(Technology)* automatically controlled: Several companies have developed stabilization systems which enable the helicopter to be flown "hands-off."

hand running • hand-run

hand running—(coll.) one after the other; in unbroken succession: Their wants were few—a pint of beer at the end of the day, a weekly paper to pore over for seven nights hand-running…

hand-run—(of lace) machine-made but finished by hand: French underwear was made of the sheerest pure silk ninon and trimmed with hand-run Alençon lace.

handicraftsman • handy-man

handicraftsman—a man who earns his living by making decorative items completely by hand: His son inherited his own traits, and gave bright promise of excelling as a skilled handicraftsman.

handy-man—a man skilled at doing small jobs such as household repairs: We had had this problem with our bath tub faucet for almost three months. First we asked a handy man to fix it.

hang all one's bells on one horse • put all one's eggs in one basket

hang all one's bells on one horse—(UK arch.) leave all one's property to one child: I'll not hang all my bells on one horse. I'll not leave all my property to one son.

Note: *The expression does not correlate in meaning with the phrase* ***put all one's money upon the wrong horse****—(also: put one's money on a scratched horse) base one's plans on a wrong guess about the result of smth.:* Members will keenly feel the nature of the mistake when I say that we put all our money upon the wrong horse.

put all one's eggs in one basket—allow all one's hopes, money, etc. to depend on one event; risk everything at once: Personally, I prefer when at all possible not to put all my eggs in one basket, no matter how nice the basket.

hang back • hang behind

hang back—be slow to act; hesitate: I don't know why he always hangs back when he gets the chance to do something.

hang behind—1. lag in the rear; remain in the background: She was hanging behind too shy to speak. 2. linger in a place after others have left: One or two of the audience hung behind after the lecture.

hang in the bell-ropes • hang on the bell

hang in the bell-ropes—(UK arch.) said of a postponed marriage: During the currency of the three Sundays on which the banns were proclaimed the young couple were said jocosely to be "hanging in the bell-ropes."

hang on the bell—ring the doorbell over and over again: I want to see mountains again. And then find somewhere I can rest without a pack of relatives prying around or confounding visitors hanging on the bell.

hang it • hang it up

hang it—(interj.) is used to emphatically express one's anger, irritation, etc. *(also: hang it all):* "Oh hang it," he exclaimed—in no logical connection with what he had been relating to me.

hang it up—1. *(coll.)* cease an activity or effort: We used to own a dairy farm but decided to hang it up and enjoy life and our kids. 2. *(sl.)* give credit: The Colonel muttered something to the barkeeper about "hanging it up."

hang it on someone • hang one on someone

hang it on someone—(sl.) blame it on smb.: We can't hang it on someone for their race.… But once you get past a certain age, being fat is a choice.

hang one on someone—(sl., also: lay one on someone) strike a person with a blow: He hit me first, but then I hung one on him and down he went like a stone.

hang on • hang one on

hang on—(coll.) 1. continue smth. persistently; persevere with smth.: I really want to go to sleep, but I am going to hang on for a couple more hours. 2. keep listening on the telephone; not hang up: Please hang on for a minute while I find out what team you are on. I will let you know in a minute…

hang one on—(U.S. sl.) get very drunk: A simple statement to the barkeep—"I really hung one on last night"—was enough to get a little sympathy and a double Bloody Mary.

hang one's hat • hang up one's hat

hang one's hat—1. settle oneself; take up residence: She's looking for somewhere to hang her hat, now that her twenty-year marriage has ended. 2. *(on)* depend upon smb.; rely on a person: Why that's my preacher. I hang my hat on him every time.

hang up one's hat—1. retire from a position or a job: Police chief Ron Johnson hung up his hat today after forty years of service. 2. *(coll.)* die: Old Johnson finally hung up his hat. He's been sick for a while though.

hang someone out to dry • leave someone hanging

hang someone out to dry—(coll.) not support or help smb.; abandon a person when he is in trouble: I made a mistake that made a customer very angry and my boss really hung me out to dry!

leave someone hanging—(coll.) keep smb. waiting for a decision or answer: When Amal had to leave for work, he left his exciting story unfinished. We were frustrated that he left us hanging.

hang up one's fiddle • hang up one's fiddle at the door

hang up one's fiddle—(dated) retire from business; give up an undertaking: I could see plain enough that it was time for me to hang up my fiddle.

hang up one's fiddle at the door—(UK dated) cease to be cheerful when in the company of one's family: Jim is a happy man when he is with the boys, but he hangs the fiddle at the door when he gets home.

happy day • happy days

happy day—the day of marriage ceremony: "When's the happy day?" Cubitt said and they all smiled.

happy days—is used as a toast: "Happy days!" cried Mobbs. "Cheers!" said the Major gloomily.

Note: *The expression does not correlate in meaning with the phrase* ***heavenly days****—(exclam.) used to express amazement and disbelief with negative coloring:* Heavenly days! Look what happened. The dog did it again on the Persian carpet!

Happy Families • happy family

Happy Families—a game played with a pack of special cards: The well-known game of Happy Families is nothing but a variation of Spade the Gardener.

happy family—1. said of a group of people living together in harmony: All the Ashkenazic tribes lived very much like a happy family. 2. *(Austral.)* a popular name of the grey-crowned babbler: From their habit of associating in flocks, they are known as the "Twelve Apostles," a name also shared in some parts with that of "Happy Family."

hard at it • hard put to it

hard at it—very busy; working industriously: When we got to the field, the farmer and his son were already hard at it.

hard put to it—find it very difficult to do smth.: Developing countries are hard put to it to raise the capital even for cheaper, though more pollutive, technologies.

hard at something • hard on something

hard at something—working diligently on smth.: She was hard at her lessons when we entered the room.

hard on something—treating smth. severely or harshly: These rough roads are hard on your shoes.

hard cash • hard coin

hard cash—(also: hard money) money in its proper form, as distinguished from checks, etc.: Not enough pilots seem ready to lay out hard cash for weather and flight-planning information.

hard coin—(U.S. sl.) lots of money: Old Freddie is earning some hard coin these days.

hard drink • hard drinking

hard drink—(of liquor) intoxicating; strong: With a hard drink in the hand the day lengthens and softens. *Cf.: soft drink—a nonalcoholic, flavored, carbonated beverage:* Sugary soft drinks have been given much of the blame for overweight children.

hard drinking—indulging in alcohol to excess: It seemed as though no student's education was complete without a spell of hard drinking in the Montparnasse cafes.

hard for someone • hard on someone

hard for someone—difficult for a person: It is hard for me to recall a face or a person's appearance.

hard on someone—treating smb. severely or harshly: You mustn't be so hard on the poor child.

hard-headed • soft-headed

hard-headed—1. rational and shrewd, not influenced by sentiments: She was hard-headed enough to be practical about the situation. 2. self-willed and obstinate: I was so hard-headed, I wouldn't admit to being wrong even if I was at gunpoint.

soft-headed—(coll.) foolish: Saying that someone else is soft-headed is no way to convince people of anything.

hard labor • hard work

hard labor—imprisonment with hard physical work as a punishment: Glynn was sentenced to three months hard labor, but won an appeal.

hard work—1. difficult and tiring work: It has been hard work to establish order here. 2. *(coll.)* said of smb. who is difficult to deal with: I had to sit next to Frank at dinner. I don't know about you, but I find him such hard work.

hard line • hard lines

hard line—unyielding adherence to a firm policy: The hard line adopted by Australia's conservative government proved popular among voters.

hard lines—1. bad luck; misfortune: It was hard lines indeed for Mr. Watson to meet with such a demon of a hare. 2. *(exclam.)* is used to show sympathy and understanding: "I'm not getting a holiday this year." "Hard lines on you!"

hard line money • hard money

hard line money—(Nautical) extra pay in consideration of special hardships *(also: hard-lying money):* Besides, there is hard-line money, which makes up for a good many discomforts.

hard money—1. *(also: hard cash)* money in its proper form, as distinguished from checks, etc.: Husbandmen, like other laborers, are paid in hard money by the week. 2. a currency with a high exchange value, not easily subject to depreciation: International speculators trashed the ruble, Russia's national currency, and looted the country's hard-money reserves. 3. *(also: tight money)* money available to borrowers at high interest rates and short payback: Due to the immense amount of loans, the bank had a significant lack of "hard money" available to its users. 4. *(U.S.)* political donations to party organizations subject to legal restrictions: Parties and candidates may use hard money donations for all political purposes.

Note: *The expression does not fully correlate in meaning with the phrase* ***hard currency****— = hard money 2:* The trade imbalance and the drain of gold and hard currency reserves have lessened.

See also: soft currency / soft money.

hard nut to crack • hard row to hoe

hard nut to crack—(also: tough nut to crack) 1. a difficult problem or task to undertake: Opinions vary, but the consensus is that the target is a hard nut to crack. 2. a difficult person to deal with: We all know that President Mugabe is not an easy man to bend. He is a hard nut to crack.

Note: *The expression does not correlate in meaning with the phrase* ***crack a nut****—(UK dated) drink a glass of liquor:* When a fresh guest arrived he was met by the laird, who made him "crack a nut," that is, drink a silver-mounted cocoanut-shell full of claret.

hard row to hoe—(also: tough row to hoe) = hard nut to crack 1: Even without money problems, many divorced single parents have a hard row to hoe.

Note: Neither expression correlates in meaning with the phrase ***hard act to follow****—(also: tough act to follow) used of an outstanding individual or a particularly good performance that will be difficult to emulate:* The previous night's incredible jazz session was a hard act to follow.

hard time • hard times

hard time—1. an unpleasant or distressing experience: Dozier had a hard time finding a publisher for her book. 2. *(Underworld)* a prison sentence: How much hard time does he have behind him?

hard times—a period of economic depression, poverty, etc.: Maritime businesses took advantage of the hard times by launching a campaign to break major union organizations.

hardly work • work hard

hardly work—do very little work: She is a decent kid with bad luck ... she hardly works now, and I doubt she will be with us for much longer.

work hard—work with all one's energy: You will be in the limelight for the first three months—time during which you should work hard to create a positive impression.

hardware store • software store

hardware store—(U.S.) a store that sells tools and implements, usually made of metal (such as hinges, screws, hammers, etc.): We use chains that can be purchased at a hardware store.

Note: The expression does not correlate in meaning with the phrase ***computer hardware store****—a store handling computer-related equipment:* I just want to work in a computer hardware store putting people's computers together.

software store—a store marketing computer-related products: Today, software comes loaded on the hard drive of your computer or in a box from a software store.

has your cat died • her rabbit died

has your cat died—(UK) said to a person whose trousers are too short or are pulled up: Now my Mum would say, "Has your cat died dear? Your trousers are at half mast."

her rabbit died—(dated euph.) said of a woman who was found to be pregnant: I just recently found out that her rabbit died. I'm finally going to be an aunt!

have a ball • have balls

have a ball—(coll.) have a good time; enjoy oneself: They had tea in the Japanese Garden, and then drove out to the beach. She was having a ball.

have balls—(coarse sl.) have great courage or audacity: It's for sure that Martin has balls to cut class again, after we were caught yesterday.

have a big time • make the big time

have a big time—(coll.) enjoy oneself *(also: have a great time):* Christ, doesn't time flit by when you're having a big time and all?

Note: The expression does not correlate in meaning with the phrase ***have a big day****—used of a day on which important things happen:* We are going to have a big day tomorrow; we are going to hike up to base camp at almost 14000 feet.

make the big time—(also: reach the big time) gain recognition; win success: Caryl had finally made the big time as a criminal.... Local newspapers carried the story on their front pages.

have a bite • have bite

have a bite—1. *(coll.)* have a snack; eat some food: We planned to stop somewhere on the road and have a bite of supper. 2. *(of cold air or wind)* have keen cutting effect: The cold night air had a bite in it. 3. *(of food or drink)* taste pleasantly pungent or spicy; be laced with alcohol: John took a cautious sip. The drink had a bite. 4. *(coll.)* posses special attractiveness: In spite of her dark hair and her Mediterranean beauty she has a bite about her that can only be British.

have bite—1. = *have a bite 2:* The day was bright, the sky a high and crystal blue. The chill in the air had bite. *2. = have a bite 3:* The pasta has bite and spins onto the fork without complication. 3. said of the seizure of the bait in fishing: From the first cast, I had bite. But, it didn't seem to be bass. 4. = *have a bite 4:* The program to give the whole European market a non-inflationary money still has bite.

have a bottle • have a lot of bottle

have a bottle—have a drink; take part in social drinking: There's a definite feeling of anticipation here as the boss slips his credit card behind the bar or your mate says "Go on, let's have a bottle."

have a lot of bottle—(coll.) have the courage to do smth. difficult: Not many people could lose six world finals and come back for more—Jimmy has a lot of bottle. *Cf.: lose one's bottle—(coll., also: bottle it) lose one's courage*: That conservative fool lost his bottle when he tried to face down the coal mining unions.

have a crow to pluck • pluck a pigeon

have a crow to pluck—state and settle some disagreeable issue with smb.: When they have taken their places, she said abruptly: "I have a crow to pluck with you."

pluck a pigeon—(sl.) swindle an ignorant or credulous person: A noble Duke or Lord, would have as little scruple in plucking a pigeon as their inferiors.

have a dash at something • make a dash at something

have a dash at something—(coll.) make an attempt to do smth.: He decided to have a dash at surgical intervention and risk the consequences.

make a dash at something—1. = *have a dash at something:* It was his habit, when traveling in any foreign country, to make a dash at French, even if the people understood English. 2. make a sudden vigorous assault or endeavor: Allen drew up his men and announced his intention to make a dash at the fort without waiting for more force.

have a down on someone • have an up on someone

have a down on someone—(also: have a downer on someone) have a grudge against smb.; dislike a person: For some reason or other he had a down on me and I grew to hate him.

have an up on someone—have an advantage over a person: I'm not bilingual though, so you do have an up on me.

have a drop • have the drop

have a drop—(coll.) take a small quantity of liquor: I have had a drop, but I had not been drinking.

have the drop—(coll.) have an advantage over a person: The boys from that team have the drop on their opponents.

have a drop too much • have a glass too much

have a drop too much—(coll. understatement) be rather drunk *(also: take a drop too much):* One night I had a drop too much and there was a bit of a row.

have a glass too much—(coll.) be drunk: The policeman said that Peter had a glass too much. Of course, what he had really had was a pair of glasses too little.

have a face as long as a fiddle • have a face made of a fiddle

have a face as long as a fiddle—look dismal or extremely

depressed: I saw you yesterday and you had a face as long as a fiddle. What was the matter with you?

have a face made of a fiddle—(arch.) be irresistibly attractive: A person who was well-liked had a face "made of a fiddle," meaning that it was always wreathed in smiles, as a fiddle has a much-curled shape.

have a falling out • have a fallout

have a falling out—have an argument or disagreement, especially one that leads to strained relations: He was asked whether he and Dave had had a falling out, and he totally dodged the question.

have a fallout—(of an event or situation) have lasting negative consequences: The controversy has had a fallout in parliament with very little business being conducted over the past few days.

have a fat chance • have a slim chance

have a fat chance—(coll.) hardly have any opportunity or possibility: So far it looks like the bill has a fat chance to get through.

have a slim chance— = have a fat chance: Asteroid spotted in space by observatories has a slim chance of hitting Earth.

have a feel for something • have the feel of something

have a feel for something—have sensitivity for and understanding of smth.: The DJ definitely had a feel for the type of music the kids would respond to.

Note: *The expression does not correlate in meaning with the phrase **feel for something**—*1. *attempt to find smth. by feeling about with the hand:* He felt for his matches and struck one to look at his watch-face. 2. *have pity for smth.; sympathize with smth.:* You truly and deeply felt for the land and the people as though they were your own children.

have the feel of something—1. *(of things)* feel to the touch like smth. else: This plastic is soft to the touch and has the feel of fine leather. 2. be reminiscent of smth.: The neighborhood has the feel of a small village and students mix freely with professionals in its winding streets. 3. become accustomed to the way smth. is used: I can drive better now that I have the feel of this car's steering.

have a feeling about something • have a feeling for something

have a feeling about something—have an emotional attitude towards smth.; harbor a prejudice or fear about smth.: I don't want to be in a train crash. But I have a very bad feeling about this train.

have a feeling for something—have taste or sensitivity for smth.; have an understanding of smth.: Most women have some rudimentary feeling for dress, but Charlotte was born without dress-sense.

have a finger in something • pull one's finger out

have a finger in something—(also: have a hand in something) be involved in smth.; play a role in smth.: Possibly the Russians might have had a finger in this. The cold war was raging at that time.

pull one's finger out—(sl.) start working more efficiently *(also: get one's finger out):* We're still waiting for the reviewer to pull his finger out and deliver. Serves us right for recruiting literary talent in a bar.

have a foot in both camps • walk both sides of the street

have a foot in both camps—have connections with two mutually antagonistic groups: Evelio had his foot in both camps and had a significant influence in each of the two organizations.

walk both sides of the street—(also: have it both ways) 1. achieve two mutually exclusive objectives; benefit from two different situations that do not normally go together: Simon is trying to walk both sides of the street by saying one thing to the business community and another to his union mates. *2. (sl.)* have both homosexual and heterosexual tastes: Everyone's sexuality is governed by their own heart, and whether it changes or not, or walks both sides of the street, is completely up to fate.

Note: *The expression does not fully correlate in meaning with the phrase **have the best of both worlds**— = walk both sides of the street 1:* You can have the best of both worlds by spending your holiday sailing yet being able to live ashore in warm, dry comfort. *Cf.: have the worst of both worlds—have two disadvantages in a bad situation:* We have the worst of both worlds: responsibility in the eyes of international opinion, but precious little power to determine events.

have a fortune • have the fortune

have a fortune—have a very large amount of money: Don't imagine you have a fortune there. A hundred francs goes nowhere these days.

have the fortune—have good luck; succeed in doing smth.: Israel has had the fortune to attract a nucleus of Jewish scientists from the Western countries.

have a free hand • have one's hands free

have a free hand—have freedom of action in affairs that one has to deal with: The new president had a relatively free hand to implement reforms.

have one's hands free—said of smb. whose time is not occupied by anything: The Duke of Normandy now had his hands free to pursue the conquest of Maine.

Note: *a) Neither expression correlates in meaning with the compound **free-handed**—generous; giving and spending money freely:* Pike was free-handed, especially to his kinspeople.

*b) Neither expression correlates in meaning with the compound **freehand**—done by hand without mechanical aids or devices:* Make a freehand drawing of an interior of a room.

have a frog in one's throat • have a lump in one's throat

have a frog in one's throat—be suffering from temporary hoarseness: "I had a frog in my throat," she says with a laugh "and so I was not at my peak singing voice."

have a lump in one's throat—have a sensation of constriction in the throat (caused by some strong emotion): I had a lump in my throat and tears in my eyes throughout his story.

have a gas • run out of gas

have a gas—(sl.) have a great time doing smth.; enjoy oneself: I had a gas watching the improbably outrageous action and dialogue unfurl.

run out of gas—(of a project, campaign, etc.) lose momentum; progress slowly or halt: Florida's transportation program is running out of "gas" and attention needs to be focused on this issue.

have a go at it • make a go of it

have a go at it—(coll.) give it a try; make an attempt at smth.: She said that she had never skied before but she was willing to have a go at it.

Note: *The expression does not correlate in meaning with the phrase **have at it**—(coll.)* 1. *start doing smth. promptly or with enthusiasm:* "The driveway needs sweeping." "Here's the broom. Have at it." *2. argue or quarrel:* All they could complain about with me (and man did they have at it) was the fact that this was my first visit in over two years. 3. *(euph.) have sex:* However, someone breaks into the place while they are having at it, and she is barely able to leave the bed and hide.

make a go of it—(coll.) make smth. succeed *(also: make a do of it)* There seemed every reason for Tilly and Steven to make a go of it abroad.

Note: *The expression is not equivalent in meaning to the phrase **make it go**—(coll.) make smth. function:* When he got started in that business he found he was really able to make it go.

have a good bang for one's buck • have a good run for one's money

have a good bang for one's buck—(coll.) get a good value for one's money *(also: get a good bang for one's buck):* Russ has shown some pretty strong statistics that say we do have a good bang for our buck.

have a good run for one's money—(also: get a good run for one's money) 1. face a strong challenge or competition from a person: I was a lot bigger than Roy, but I would've had a good run for my money if we'd have fought. 2. derive much satisfaction or enjoyment in return for one's outlay or efforts: I have had a good run for my money as a correspondent. ...the need for first-hand reporting from abroad is more important than ever.

have a good head • have a good mind

have a good head—1. *(also: have a good head on one's shoulders)* be smart and intelligent: I searched for Ann, because she has a good head and knows a lot about medicine. 2. *(for)* have a special talent in a certain area: You've got a good head for business, Thompson. It's the rest of you that worries me. 3. said of beer with good foam at the top: It was the first brasserie to captivate Jean ... it still retains the flavor of Alsace, where the beer always has a good head.

have a good mind—(followed by Infinitive) be strongly inclined to do smth.: I have a good mind to find these identity thieves and ask how they're getting money out of my account.

have a good time • make good time

have a good time—(also: have a good time of it) enjoy oneself: Gosh, he's always reading now. It's not my idea of having a good time in vacation.

make good time—(also: make time) accomplish a distance in a short time; travel fast: I was leaping over mounds of snow and branches and I was making good time.

have a hand for something • have a hand in something

have a hand for something— be skilful at dealing with smth.: A jockey must have a hand for all sorts of horses, and in the case of two and three year olds a very good hand it must be.

have a hand in something—(also: have a finger in something) be involved in smth.; play a role in smth.: "It's still murder." "That's what's riding me," he said. "I feel I almost had a hand in it."

have a hard day • have a hard time

have a hard day—said of a busy day full of hard work: You look tired, dear. Did you have a hard day at the office?

have a hard time—experiecnce difficulties or suffer for a period of time: I have had a hard time buying a house, even though my credit history is spotless.

have a head • have a head on one's shoulders

have a head—(coll.) suffer from a hangover: Tom has a head this morning and won't be coming into work.

have a head on one's shoulders—(coll.) be very smart and intelligent: He has a head on his shoulders and can be trusted to do any job well.

have a head for something • have a mind to do something

have a head for something—have a special talent in a certain area: A good editor has a head for business. It does no one any good if the books an editor signs up lose money for a publisher.

have a mind to do something—consider doing smth.: There are a few articles that I have a mind to create, and a few existing articles that I have a mind to expand considerably.

have a heat on • heat is on, the

have a heat on—(U.S. sl.) be alcohol or drug intoxicated: A few years ago this dump was full of dope. Every other man you met had a heat on.

heat is on, the—1. said when strong pressure is brought to bear: She says now that the heat is on, the people can depend on the union to stand up strong at the negotiation table. 2. *(U.S. coll.)* said when police activities or investigations are at their peak: The heat is on in Baltimore. The drug war is being lost ... and a desperate mayor wants the crime rates down before the election.

have a heavy hand • have a light hand

have a heavy hand— be harshly oppressive; inclined to punish severely: Sykes was known for having a heavy hand. Few of his employees stayed more than a year or two.

have a light hand—get good results handling smth.: She is very reliable and she has as light a hand with pastry as anyone I ever knew.

See also: heavy in hand / heavy-handed.

have a large practice • have much practice

have a large practice—(of a doctor, lawyer, etc.) have many regular patients or clients: This doctor has a large practice and is regarded as an able practitioner.

have much practice—engage in frequent and systematic exercise of an activity: I haven't had much practice in speaking French lately.

have a laugh at someone • have the laugh of someone

have a laugh at someone—find smb. amusing; ridicule a person: You let them in to have a laugh at them or you let them in because you want to listen to what they're saying.

have the laugh of someone—turn the laugh against smb.: "Why, he always used to laugh at you as the dunce of the family!" "I know, and now I shall have the laugh of him, shan't I?"

have a lead in something • have a lead of something

have a lead in something— be in the first place with regard to smth.: Russia had a lead in space and submarine technology.

have a lead of something— be ahead of other contestants in terms of time, space, etc.: Hobbs has a lead of just 35 votes on Independent candidate Gleeson.

have a leg to stand on • have legs

have a leg to stand on—(of arguments, claims, etc.) be supported by facts or sound reasons *(usually negat.):* He said that the government did not have a leg to stand on in regard to that bill.

have legs—(of a book, film, etc.) have lasting popularity; be long remembered: This latest scandal has legs — you'll probably still be reading about it in a year's time.

have a long arm • make a long arm

have a long arm—have a far-reaching power: The Sheriff may have only had control of his county, but with his connections, he had a long arm.

make a long arm—(coll.) reach out one's arm after smth.: I got up and made a long arm for the telephone.

have a mind of one's own • know one's own mind

have a mind of one's own—have an independent opinion: The real offence, as she ultimately perceived, was her having a mind of her own at all. Her mind was to be his — attached to his own like a small garden-plot...

know one's own mind—know what one prefers or wants: Babette seemed to be one of those poor creatures that always hang on the words of someone else, not knowing her own mind, being fearful of failure.

have a new lease of life • make a new life for oneself

have a new lease of life—find new enthusiasm and energy (after a period of illness or sadness): I'm able to do much more which is absolutely great and I have a new lease of life.

make a new life for oneself—move to another place, change one's career, etc., especially to recover from an unpleasant experience: After the divorce she moved to Buckingham to make a new life for herself.

have a pied-à-terre • have one's feet on the ground

have a pied-à-terre—(Fr.) have an extra room or house which one keeps for use when needed: Ian makes regular visits to Tuscany and to the island of Mallorca where he has a pied-à-terre.

have one's feet on the ground—(also: have both feet on the ground) have a sensible and realistic attitude to life: The book is written by a thoughtful, sensitive man who, nevertheless, has his feet on the ground.

have a pull with someone • have the pull of someone

have a pull with someone—(coll.) have influence with a person, especially smb. in a high position: He has a strong pull with the Managing Director.

have the pull of someone—(coll.) have an advantage over a person *(also: have the pull over someone):* That's where a gentleman has the pull of you. He doesn't get excited. No gentleman does — or hardly ever.

have a quick one • pull a fast one

have a quick one—(sl.) 1. have a drink before one does smth. else: We had a quick one and admired the bar, then left and had a wander around the town center. 2. said of a brief and brisk sex act: I guess I'd been upstairs long enough for him to think I'd had a quick one off with the girl.

pull a fast one—(sl.) cheat or deceive a person: I signed a contract on a house, and I think my realtor pulled a fast one on me.

have a resemblance to something • have a semblance of something

have a resemblance to something—(also: bear a resemblance to something) seem similar to smth. else, especially in external appearance: You walk into the water park through an entrance gate that has a resemblance to a beach hut.

have a semblance of something—(also: bear a semblance of something) have a slight, superficial and often deceptive similarity to smth.: Although the book has a semblance of scholarship, a careful examination will reveal many errors and omissions.

have a rough time • rough it in the bush

have a rough time—experiecnce difficulties or suffer for a period of time: Carter said he had a rough time on his summer tour because he injured his knee.

rough it in the bush—(also: rough it) live for a period of time without the usual comforts and conveniences: On a safari you can stay at some of the finest hotels and you can also rough it in the bush.

have a run • have the runs

have a run—1. make an outing or a short journey in a car, etc.: If it's fine to-morrow we'll have a run in the new car. 2. have a tear in a knitted garment: I had an awful ladder in my stocking ... I scarcely ever have a run now.

have the runs—(coll.) have diarrhea: My cat had the runs a while ago. You have to give him a special human quality diet for a while.

have a run of something • have the run of something

have a run of something—enjoy a period of some condition or state of things: We have had a long-continued run of the loveliest weather.

have the run of something—have permission to use smth. freely: While his parents are in Florida each winter, Charles has the run of the house.

Note: *The expression does not correlate in meaning with the phrase* ***keep the run of something****— keep oneself informed about smth.:* Now, Mr. Drummond, I have kept the run of your affairs more closely than you bargained for.

have a say • have the say

have a say—1. *(also: have a voice)* have the right or the opportunity to give one's opinion: People want to have a say in how the country should be governed. 2. give one's opinion on a matter: The 75-year-old Rossi announced he would be leaving ... and he has had a say in who his successor will be.

have the say—have the power of deciding; have the final authority: We keep giving recommendations but at the end of the day — who has the say? It's the government.

have a screw loose • there is a screw loose

have a screw loose—(coll.) be mentally defective or not acting normally: I don't go much with anarchists. It's my judgment they nearly always have a screw loose.

there is a screw loose—(coll.) there is smth. wrong in the condition of things: Now this may come into court, you know. If there is a screw loose anywhere, better mention it.

Note: *Neither expression is antonymous in meaning to the phrase* ***tighten up screws****—1. suppress or "clamp down" on dissenters, etc.:* The president is using Russo-American rapprochement as a smokescreen for tightening up screws at home. 2. *apply pressure; make smth. subject to more severe control:* Dellinger believed the victory was a result of his team tightening up screws on defense.

have a swelled head • have a thick head

have a swelled head—(also: have a big head) have an exaggerated opinion of oneself; be self-conceited: Everybody over forty is tired and down and out, and everybody under thirty has swelled head.

have a thick head—(coll.) 1. be dull of intellect: You could have worked that out for yourselves if you hadn't such thick heads. 2. have an aching head (suffering from a hangover): No more brandy, thanks. I'll have a thick enough head as it is.

have a taste for something • have a taste of something

have a taste for something—have a liking or preference for smth.: He had a taste for literature, and we got on together like one o'clock.

Note: *The expression is not equivalent in meaning to the phrase* ***have a taste in something****—have the ability to choose the best kind of smth.:* He has a taste in clothes and tries to stand out from the crowd with his alternative styles.

have a taste of something—1. eat or drink a small quantity of smth. in order to see what the flavor is like: Won't you have a taste of this cake? 2. have a brief, usually unpleasant experience of smth.: The child may already have had a taste of street life.

have a thing about someone • have a thing with someone

have a thing about someone—*(coll.)* 1. feel a strong attraction to smb.: That smile, that jawline. No wonder Jacquie had a thing about him. 2. harbor a prejudice or fear about a person: Connie's got a "thing" about police. "Never trust a policeman" is her motto.

have a thing with someone—*(coll.)* have a love affair with a person: "Are you sort of having a thing with Madalena?" "I'm interested in her," he said. "But not sexually."

have a tiger by the tail • hold an eel by the tail

have a tiger by the tail—*(also: catch a tiger by the tail)* engage in an undertaking which may prove extremely dangerous or difficult: Everybody seems to have their own opinion on how the concert will go: they have a tiger by the tail and are not sure themselves how to handle the huge crowd of fun seekers.

hold an eel by the tail—*(also: catch an eel by the tail)* attempt to control an elusive person or situation: He imagined I was in his power at Augsburg; he thought he had me; but he was holding an eel by the tail.

Note: *Neither expression correlates in meaning with the phrase* ***have the world by the tail****— enjoy success and happiness:* After all, the guy had the world by the tail—first class travel and first class hotels, money, glamour, beautiful women…

have a time • have the time

have a time—*(coll.)* 1. encounter some difficulty; have a hard time: He hoped that Lavinia wasn't having a time with the twins, cooped inside on a damp afternoon. 2. enjoy oneself; have fun: "Do you like the seashore?" "Yes, I'm having quite a time."

have the time—1. *(also: have time)* have sufficient time to do smth.: I don't see how you fellows have the time to monkey around here. 2. *(coll., in the phrase "do you have the time?")* know the correct time of day: People who don't wear watches will often ask those who do, "Pardon me, do you have the time?"

have a try at something • have a try for something

have a try at something—attempt to do smth. unfamiliar: I don't know whether I can mend the clock, but I'll have a try at it.

have a try for something—attempt to get or obtain smth.: You may not get the job, but at least you can have a try for it.

have a use for something • have the use of something

have a use for something—find an application for which smth. can be used: I turned the material over to the radiochemistry department, which seemed to have a use for it.

Note: *The expression is only partially antonymous in meaning to the phrase* ***have no use for something****—*1. *have no application for which smth. can be used:* My husband suggested we get it and I thought I had no use for it. We had a computer already but it was older and didn't have a modem. *2. dislike smth.; be averse to smth.:* I had no use for meditation even though I'd never tried it. I associated it with "new-agers" who didn't, in my opinion, have a clue about real life.

have the use of something—be able or allowed to use smth.: Daddy was a pilot and so we had the use of all the small planes and flew everywhere … sometimes just on a Sunday for fun.

have a voice • have voice

have a voice—*(also: have a say)* have the right to express an opinion on a subject: The students should have a voice in determining the way in which universities should develop.

have voice—1. have the physical ability to produce speech sounds: Many of the lower animals have voice, but none has the power of speech. *2. = have a voice:* If we want people to be committed to successful completion of their obligations, then they must have voice in the choice of those commitments.

Note: *The expression is not equivalent in meaning to the phrase* ***be in voice****— be in proper vocal condition for singing or speaking:* But now I shall sing to you, and you will forgive me. I am in voice tonight.

have a way with someone • have one's way with someone

have a way with someone—have natural ability to deal well with smb.: I oughtn't to blame you if Marion's taken a shine to you. You must have a way with women.

have one's way with someone—1. impose one's authority on a person: …they were pagans. And thus I had my way with them, and we set sail at once. 2. *(euph.)* make a person have sex: Although she struggled, she was no match for him and he had "had his way with her."

have a word with someone • have words with someone

have a word with someone—have a short conversation with a person: The personnel manager said he wanted to have a word with me.

Note: *The expression is not equivalent in meaning to the phrase* ***have a word in someone's ear****—give a brief message to a person in confidence:* My employer, the cadi, wants to have a word in your ear.

have words with someone—have a quarrel with smb.: Our cab arrived and the same man whom we had words with a few minutes earlier came out.

have an affinity for something • have an affinity with something

have an affinity for something—1. feel liking for smth.: Figure modeling may seem like an odd activity, but to those who have an affinity for art, figure modeling makes a world of sense. 2. *(of a chemical substance)* have a tendency to unite with another substance: Alcohol has a strong affinity for water, and is miscible with it in every proportion.

have an affinity with something—1. *= have an affinity for something 1:* Some members of the community may have little affinity with fine art found in galleries, especially art that may be academic or conceptual. 2. *(of animals, plants, etc.)* have structural similarity: Balochi has a different historical background and has no affinity with any Indian language.

have an ear for music • have Van Gogh's ear for music

have an ear for music—have the ability to learn music: Eva Jane also has an ear for music. She played saxophone in her high school band in Florida.

have Van Gogh's ear for music—be tone deaf: There is something romantic about the Parisian basement dive. No matter that the pianist has Van Gogh's ear for music…

have an eye for something • have an eye out for something

have an eye for something—be quick to notice or appreciate smth. such as quality, etc.: She has an eye for color and style in clothes.

have an eye out for something—be alert and watchful wishing to get or acquire smth.: Mary always has an eye out for bargains.

have an eye on something • have one eye on something

have an eye on something—1. choose smth. one has seen as a desirable acquisition: I have had an eye on a dress in the shop across the road for some time. 2. keep close watch upon smth.: The chances are that the authorities may have had an eye on such kind of "hardware" [torpedoes]. 3. pay careful attention to smth.; show concern for smth.: Truly successful companies have had an eye on quality for decades.

have one eye on something— give only part of one's attention to smth. while the rest is engaged elsewhere: It was a tricky experiment — he had to have one eye on the thermometer all the time.

have an eye out for someone • have eyes for someone

have an eye out for someone—be very alert wishing to pick out one particular person: When she was out back having a smoke … she had an eye out for him.

have eyes for someone—(coll.) have a strong romantic interest in a person: Now, my sister was a beautiful girl and I knew even Mitchell had eyes for her.

have an idea • have ideas

have an idea—1. have a notion of smth.: We had an idea of a law firm that tossed out the usual law firm trappings: no mahogany or marble; no suits unless that's what you prefer to wear. 2. think or suppose smth.: I heard what he said to you. I had an idea you weren't going to take it lying down.

have ideas—entertain undesirable or harmful notions: That's the second happy couple I've seen busted up and it's cured me if I ever had ideas. I'd no more marry with a war on than jump over the moon.

have an in • have an out

have an in—(coll.) have influence with smb. of authority: Sorry, I don't have an in, but I know someone who does.

have an out—(coll.) have a means of escape or avoiding smth.: No matter what happens, he always has an out.

have an in with someone • have it in for someone

have an in with someone—(coll.) have influence with smb. of authority: He had an in with the city government, but that doesn't mean they knew everything he did.

Note: *The expression does not correlate in meaning with the phrase* ***have a run-in with someone****—(coll.) have a troublesome encounter or a row with a person:* Your father and I have many run-ins these days. He can't get it into his thick skull that I have come of age.

have it in for someone—show ill will towards smb.; intend to do harm to a person: I just don't want to lose my funding because she has it in for me badmouthing me to everyone in the department.

See also: be in with someone / be with someone.

have an influence on someone • have influence with someone

have an influence on someone—have an effect on a person; cause smb. to act or behave in a certain way: Some songs even have violent lyrics which can have a bad influence on young people.

have influence with someone—have the power to affect the opinion of a person, especially smb. in authority: He had no power, no elected office … but he had influence with those who did.

have an interest in something • have interests in something

have an interest in something—1. be keen to know or learn about smth.: None of them had the slightest interest in music. 2. want smth. to be done: Governments have an interest in seeing minimum wages kept above subsistence level. 3. have a share in the ownership of a business: No resident of the Isle of Man is entitled to have an interest in the company.

have interests in something— = have an interest in something 3: The region obtains much of its oil from Alaska, where the combined group would have sizeable interests.

have an itching palm • one's palm itches

have an itching palm—(coll.) have greed for money (being susceptible to bribery, etc.): We guessed he had an itching palm and was hoping to receive a present for his "advice."

one's palm itches—1. said of a strong compulsive urge to do smth., especially to strike a person: Her palm itched to slap the bland indifference from his face. *Cf.: have itchy feet—(UK coll.) be unable to stay in one place; have an urge to travel:* After three days we got really itchy feet and could not wait longer. 2. is used of an old superstition that if one's palm itches one is going to receive money: Unfortunately, every time my palm itches it's cause money is leaving my hands.

have an option on something • have the option of something

have an option on something—have the right to buy smth. at a certain price, usually within a certain period of time: If I decide to sell the house you shall have first option on it.

have the option of something—have the ability to choose smth. in preference to smth. else: A strike or war is preventive if the enemy still has the option of desisting from his planned aggression.

have bigger fish to fry • have other fish to fry

have bigger fish to fry—have a much more pressing issue to attend to: If you think this case doesn't matter — that the Supreme Court has bigger fish to fry — think again.

Note: *The expression does not correlate in meaning with the phrase* ***big fish****— an important person in a company or an organization:* Basically this guy was a big fish in the British Government. He wrote a couple of books…

have other fish to fry—(coll.) have other business to attend to *(also: have other irons in the fire):* I can't deal with that just now. I have other fish to fry.

Note: *The expression does not correlate in meaning with the phrase* ***there are other fish in the sea****— there may be many other people to choose from:* It's too bad that your secretary quit, but there are plenty of other fish in the sea.

have both feet on the ground • stand on one's own two feet

have both feet on the ground—(also: have one's feet on the ground) have a sensible and realistic attitude to life: Catherine in her spiritual writings has both feet on the ground, she lives in the real world, she has uncommon common sense.

stand on one's own two feet—(also: stand on one's own feet) be independent and able to take care of oneself: I want to be able to stand on my own two feet without my parents telling me what to do.

have bowels • have the guts

have bowels—(dated) have compassion or sympathy: I am a man that can feel for my neighbors. I have bowels—yes I have bowels.

have the guts—(coll., also: have guts) 1. be a tough, courageous type of person: A boy's got to have guts to make his way in this rat race of a modern world. 2. be insolent enough to do smth.: You abandoned her. How could you have the guts to show your face again?

have egg on one's chin • have egg on one's face

have egg on one's chin—(euph.) used as a caution to a man having his trouser zip undone: After the game John came up to the bar with his flies undone. "You have egg on your chin, John," said Gus.

have egg on one's face—(coll.) look foolish; be embarrassed: Gallacher has had some difficult tasks being in Opposition, and he has had egg on his face on a number of occasions.

have eyes in the back of one's head • have one's head screwed on backwards

have eyes in the back of one's head—said of the ability to know what happens even if one is not looking: I remember thinking my mom must have eyes in the back of her head when she would know what I was doing without even turning around to see.

have one's head screwed on backwards—lack common sense; behave in a strange and irrational way: I had my head screwed on backwards when I was packing my things, so I left all my Baltimore telephone numbers in my desk in Towson! *Cf.: have one's head screwed on the right way—(also: have one's head screwed on right) be wise and sensible; act in a reasonable way:* The general remark was that Colin had his head screwed on the right way and that some day he would come out on top.

have fun with someone • make fun of someone

have fun with someone—1. enjoy a good time in the company of others: Ashlyn was a girl who just wanted to have fun with her friends, play sports, and everything else a girl would do. 2. derive pleasure from ridiculing or taunting a person: They were about to have some fun with "the old man," as they generally called the Captain. 3. *(euph.)* used with sexual implication: The communications contained overtures for a meeting and indications that he wanted to "have fun" with her.

make fun of someone—find smb. amusing; make a person appear ridiculous: I don't understand why you're always making fun of me.

have hot pants • wear hot pants

have hot pants—(sl.) be excited with sexual desire: Genaro smiled and winked at me. "I understand that you've got hot pants for her," he said.

wear hot pants—(sl.) wear tight fitting shorts: The lineup also included Charlie's pretty daughter Wanda, wearing hot pants, who sang a mixture of songs.

have it • have it in one

have it—1. get or find the answer to smth.: "I have it," said the student after a long pause. 2. hear or get news: I have it that the new president will be coming to see us. 3. *(Perfect Tense)* is used to say that one cannot tolerate it anymore: Let them know you have had it with their insufficient performance.

have it in one—be intelligent; have a natural ability for smth.: I know well that I have it in me to make my name famous.

See also: one will have it / one won't have it.

have it away with someone • have it out with someone

have it away with someone—(sl.) have sex with a person *(also: have it off with someone):* No one would dream of having it away with his mistress.

Note: *The expression does not correlate in meaning with the phrase **have it away on one's toes**—(UK sl.) escape, run away:* Terry too had evaded the guard and in today's parlance "had it away on his toes."

have it out with someone—discuss the matter with smb. in order to settle a dispute, misunderstanding, etc.: You must have this out with Emmeline, find how she stands with this young man and strongly discourage the whole affair.

have it good • have the worst of it

have it good—have enough money; be comfortably off: Mr. Goss said employers should realise that they had it good in Queensland compared with other states.

have the worst of it—1. suffer the most harm: We had the worst of it back there across the swamps—working up to our waists in water. 2. *(Sport)* be defeated: I would have had the worst of it in a sprint against Bettini, but I had the nerve against the other men.

have it large • make it big

have it large—(UK sl., also: large it up) go out and enjoy oneself, typically with drink or drugs: I was out last night till the very early hours of the morning having it large.

make it big—(coll.) become successful and famous: If you want to make it big as a musician in the United States, the festival in Austin is a good place to start.

have it made • have made it

have it made—(coll.) be assured of success: Michael thought he had it made when he landed a job as a big band singer.

have made it—have achieved what one intended or hoped to do: The sales charts showed we had made it, and big.

have it over someone • have the edge over someone

have it over someone—(also: have it all over someone) be superior to a person; be better than smb.: She is not my boss but she likes to think she has it over me because I happen to be a lot younger.

have the edge over someone—(also: have the edge on someone) have an advantage over a person: The only thing I envy the Asian communities is their extended Family system, that is where they have the edge over us.

have money to spend • have spending money

have money to spend—have plenty of money at one's disposal: She's a really happy woman now because for once she's got money to spend.

have spending money—have some cash for small personal needs: Make sure your child has spending money. All children need to have some discretionary funds at their disposal.

have no conscience about something • have something on one's conscience

have no conscience about something—have no scruples about smth. morally wrong: They have no conscience about the plight of the poor; and although they talk patriotically, they treat the country like a colony to be exploited.

have something on one's conscience—feel guilty about smth. one has done or failed to do: And now he had Jergensen's death on his conscience. The man had stolen a television set — for all Boldt knew that was the full extent of his crime.

have no fear for something • have no fear of something

have no fear for something—be not concerned or worried about smth.: We have no fear for the Church of England in her competition with the denominational bodies around her.

have no fear of something—be not afraid of smth.: Chief Julian Fantino says he is sure of one thing: gangs in Toronto have "no fear of the law."

have no guts for something • have no stomach for something

have no guts for something—(coll.) lack courage and determination for smth.: Too bad she had no guts for the job or she should have been our first woman President.

have no stomach for something—(coll.) intensely dislike smth.; be averse to smth., especially smth. difficult or unpleasant: At Harvard it became clear that I had no stomach for the law.

Note: *The expression is not equivalent in meaning to the phrase* ***have no heart for something****— have no inclination or enthusiasm for smth.:* Mozart had no heart for the intricate court dance needed to succeed in Paris society.

have no idea of something • have no thought of something

have no idea of something—have no knowledge of smth.: Unless you have attempted to shower a person who does not want a shower then you have no idea of how difficult that can be.

have no thought of something—have no intention of doing smth.: I lost all remembrance of my home and people, and had no thought of returning to them.

have no quarrel with someone • not quarrel with someone

have no quarrel with someone—have no cause for a dispute or an argument with a person: They looked on the Germans as half-brothers and they had no quarrel with them.

not quarrel with someone—have no argument or disagreement with a person: He did not make friends with his schoolmates, though he did not quarrel with them either.

have no sense of something • have not the sense of something

have no sense of something—not appreciate or understand the value or worth of smth.: In our country, the rich have no sense of responsibility.

have not the sense of something—1. not mean or denote smth.: The passage is a quotation … "*stantibus in medio crocis*," where "*crocis*" has not the sense of "saffron".… 2. = *have no sense of something:* Boys, differently from us adults, have not the sense of measure, of convenience.

have no time for something • have time for something

have no time for something—1. be unable to use a period of time for smth.: Unfortunately, he was very busy and had no time for a chat. 2. *(coll.)* have no respect or admiration for smth.: I never had much time, to use an effective colloquialism, for the list of "the best hundred books." 3. *(coll.)* have no patience with smth.; be unable to put up with smth.: She had no time for such stupid questions. She had a mission to accomplish.

have time for something—be able to use a period of time for smth.: He is extremely approachable and always has time for a friendly chat.

have nothing to say • have nothing to say for oneself

have nothing to say—1. have nothing to speak about: The two remained for a while in their places: Caswall because he had nothing to say, Mimi because she had much to say and wished to put her thoughts in order. 2. be unable to justify or explain one's conduct; say nothing in one's own defense: When I came across pages and pages of porn files I confronted him and cried but he had nothing to say.

have nothing to say for oneself—1. be unwilling to express one's opinions; be habitually silent: As for that man … he really annoys me, he's so dull and has nothing to say for himself, not bad looking, though, is he! 2. = *have nothing to say 2:* McNabb has nothing to say for himself, instead going on the offensive — as all people do when another person's comments strike them where it counts and they know they have no better response.

have one's day off • have one's off day

have one's day off—have a day free; have a day off duty: She doesn't go to work on Thursdays: she has her day off.

have one's off day—1. said of a day when one does not perform as well as usual: Otto Becker, normally used to win, had his off day with both horses. 2. = *have one's day off:* I could have had a long weekend since I have my off day on Fridays and Saturdays.

have one's fingers in the till • hold the purse strings

have one's fingers in the till—steal money from the place where one works: Sally was outraged when she found that one of her salesclerks had his fingers in the till.

hold the purse strings—control the spending of a family's or an organization's money: Maudie is the one who holds the purse strings and Moth finds ingenious ways of making her part with them!

have one's hands tied behind one's back • with both hands tied behind one's back

have one's hands tied behind one's back—(also: have one's hands tied) be prevented from doing smth.; be restricted in one's freedom to act: The only reason it took a year was I had my hands tied behind my back because we had signed a contract.

with both hands tied behind one's back—(also: with one hand tied behind one's back) 1. *do smth.* very easily or without effort: Jos is a phenomenal driver who could beat me on any track with both hands tied behind his back. 2. = *have one's hands tied behind one's back:* They don't know the rules of evidence. They expect lawyers to defend lawsuits with both hands tied behind their back and for discount fees.

have one's mind on something • have something on one's mind

have one's mind on something—(also: keep one's mind on something) give all one's attention to smth.: It's hard to work when you've got your mind on other things.

have something on one's mind—think of smth. causing worry or concern: I knew my aunt sufficiently well to know that she had something of importance on her mind.

Note: *The expression is not equivalent in meaning to the phrase* ***have something in mind****—1. think about smth.; intend to do smth.:* I didn't know what he had in mind, so I just sat there waiting for him to tell me. *2. think of smth. as being suitable for some purpose:* I have something in mind for the living-room carpeting.

See also: have something in one's brain / have something on the brain.

have one's nose in something • put one's nose into something

have one's nose in something—(coll.) read smth. very attentively: Friends of mine have a ten year-old son who always has his nose in a book.

put one's nose into something—(coll.) interfere in a matter which does not concern one *(also: poke one's nose into something):* The issue has flowered into a discussion about Kroger's right to put his nose into editorial matters.

have one's wits about one • have the wit to do something

have one's wits about one—be alert and ready to act in a difficult situation: In this part of the city you must have your wits about you all the time.

have the wit to do something—have enough intelligence and understanding to do smth.: The Aztecs had the wit to leave a wide open space all round the monument.

have power over someone • have someone in one's power

have power over someone—have control over a person; be able to command smb.: He had power over me as my employer; I was in a totally vulnerable situation.

have someone in one's power—be able to do what one wishes with a person: I had her in my power — up a tree, as the Americans say.

have regard for something • have regard to something

have regard for something—(also: have respect for something) honor or respect smth.: If you had any regard for your good name you would not act in that manner.

have regard to something—(also: have respect to something) take smth. into account: When considering the precise meaning of a word we must have regard to the context in which it is used.

have respect for something • have respect to something

have respect for something—(also: have regard for something) honor or respect smth.: Since some of the members have no respect for the law, they refuse to enter into a legal marriage.

have respect to something—(also: have regard to something) take smth. into account: In fixing the remuneration we shall have respect to the work entailed and the qualifications of the person appointed.

have seen better days • have seen its day

have seen better days—showing signs of wear; be no longer in such a good condition as it used to be: When Lori and Kit visit Aldercot Hall, they find a dark, dreary mansion that has evidently seen better days.

have seen its day—be no longer effective; outlive its usefulness: These events led many to conclude that freedom had seen its day, and that the future belonged to the hard men in Berlin. Franklin Roosevelt refused to accept that democracy was finished.

have someone at one's command • have someone under one's command

have someone at one's command—have people who are ready to obey one's orders: The king had now at his command a body of Janissaries ready to carry out his personal will.

have someone under one's command—command people under the authority conferred by official position: Kluge now had under his command all the German armies in France.

have someone do something • have someone doing something

have someone do something—1. *(also: get someone to do something)* cause a person to do smth.: Stupid me, I did not have him sign any type of contract or promise to pay letter. 2. experience or suffer smth. done by another person: We had a beggar come up to us and there was a man sleeping in the stair well. We did not feel safe at all.

Note: *The expression is not antonymous in meaning to the phrase* ***one will not have someone do something****— one will not allow a person to do smth.:* Tell him you understand that he is unhappy but you will not have him speak to you that way.

have someone doing something—1. cause a person to do smth. as a result of one's activity: If you play your radio on the beach, you'll have everyone complaining. 2. = *have someone do something 2:* I couldn't bear to have them talking once the film had begun, so I turned around and did my heroic best: asked them to talk a little softly.

Note: *The expression is not antonymous in meaning to the phrase* ***one will not have someone doing something****— one will not allow a person to do smth.:* And while I do not care much what people think of me, I will not have them thinking badly of you.

have someone in • have someone on

have someone in—1. invite a person into one's home: We had some friends in on Saturday night to watch the rugby and stay for dinner. 2. arrange for builders, decorators, etc. to come into one's home to do some work: We had some problem in the bathroom and we had a plumber in to fix a pipe.

have someone on—(coll.) mislead smb. deliberately; deceive or swindle a person: She seemed a nice person; but for all I knew she might be a brilliant actress and was just having me on.

have someone on a string • have someone on the line

have someone on a string—have a person under one's full control: He was like a little puppy dog, and she had him on a string; he was putty in her hands.

have someone on the line—have a person on the phone: I have called at all hours and almost always have someone on the line in under two minutes.

have someone's number • have someone's number on it

have someone's number—(coll.) know smb.'s real motives or intentions when dealing with that person: "I think I've got your number, Mr. Omnipotent Superbeing," she said gently, "You don't fool me for a minute."

have someone's number on it—(of a bomb, bullet, etc.) be intended by fate for a particular person *(also: have someone's name on it):* If it's got your number on it, you'll get it, no matter where you are.

have something going for one • have something going with someone

have something going for one—(coll.) have ability, talent, good looks, etc. that help one to be successful: Bowser definitely has something going for him, and it's a something that seems to appeal to many.

Note: *The expression does not correlate in meaning with the phrase* ***have it coming to one****— used of smb. about to suffer punishment or some unpleasant consequences:* John has it coming to him. He caused these problems by not being involved enough and making some bad decisions.

have something going with someone—(coll.) have a romance

or an affectionate relationship with a person *(also: have a thing going with someone):* Is it true that Sammy has something going with Linda?

have something handed on a plate • have something on one's plate

have something handed on a plate—achieve or get smth. with too little effort: Car factories of Japan will have a new market handed to them on a plate.

Note: *The expression does not correlate in meaning with the phrase **have one's lunch handed to one**— be outperformed and shown up by smb. better:* Certainly to have your lunch handed to you by a thirteen year old would not be something you would want to advertise to your peers.

have something on one's plate—have a lot of things or problems to deal with: I can't possibly take a holiday at the moment; I've got far too much on my plate.

have something in one's brain • have something on the brain

have something in one's brain—(also: keep something in one's brain) retain smth. in one's memory: I had the great benefit of having had them [script lines] in my brain for a few years.

have something on the brain—(sl.) be obsessed with an idea, etc.: He blames everything that goes wrong on the taxes. He's got taxation on the brain.

See also: have one's mind on something / have something on one's mind.

have something in one's hands • have something on one's hands

have something in one's hands—1. be in possession of smth.; have smth. in reserve: After paying the debt in full, with the accumulated interest, he still had in his hands about $1,000. 2. have complete control of smth.: I thought long and hard about how I could introduce you to the teachers who had my fate in their hands.

*Note: The expression does not fully correlate in meaning with the phrase **have something in hand**—1. have smth. under control:* There was a little rioting, but the police soon had the situation in hand. 2. = *have something in one's hands 1:* The money question had also to be gone into: what he still had in hand; what balance lay in the London bank.

have something on one's hands—said of smth. remaining under one's care as a burden or unwelcome responsibility: When the house is sold I will have the furniture on my hands.

have something in one's sights • set one's sights on something

have something in one's sights—1. *(of a hunter, etc.)* take aim at smth.: I had the deer in my sights, but it moved before I could fire. 2. *(of celestial objects)* observe through the telescope: I tried the Crab nebula first and soon had it in my sights. 3. regard smth. as a prospective objective: Today Ireland is looking forward to the best future we've had in our sights for generations.

set one's sights on something—1. see smth.: When I set my sights on this guitar, I was hoping for a modern-production guitar that caught the sound of the old ragtime. 2. = *have something in one's sights 3:* They may have to set their sights on something less ambitious.

have something in stock • have something in store

have something in stock—(of merchandise) be available immediately for sale or distribution: We do not have a shirt of this size in stock now, but we can order it for you.

have something in store—1. have smth. in reserve in case of need: After the hardships of the previous winter, you now have plenty of food in store for the months ahead. 2. *(of events, conditions, etc.)* be waiting to happen: We've had all kinds of weather and there's no telling what the weather has in store for us in mid–June.

have something on • have something on one

have something on—1. be wearing smth.: She was very pretty and had a lovely dress on. 2. be busy with smth.: I'm sorry, I can't come, I have two concerts on next week.

have something on one—(of money, etc.) carry about *(also: have something on one's person):* The man had a credit card on him that the police believed was stolen.

have something under one's hat • keep something under one's hat

have something under one's hat—(coll.) have knowledge of smth.: He had something under his hat; a tip-off straight from headquarters, news of high international importance.

keep something under one's hat—(coll.) keep smth. a secret; keep smth. to oneself: "Nothing about that in the papers, is there?" "Not yet. Keep it under your hat."

See also: pick something out of a hat / pull something out of a hat.

have the advantage of something • have the advantage over something

have the advantage of something—possess smth. that is useful or is likely to bring success: Galsworthy's plays have the advantage of acting well — unlike much literary drama.

have the advantage over something—be better, stronger, etc. than another item of the same kind: The new system of air cleaning has many advantages over the old one.

have the baby blues • have the blues

have the baby blues—(coll.) feel sad or depressed when pregnant: After seven months, Karly had the baby blues. She was feeling sad.

have the blues—(coll.) feel sad or depressed: Doctors told her she just had the blues, and although they offered her medications, they did not keep her in the hospital.

Note: *The expression does not correlate in meaning with the phrase **have a blue**—(Austral. sl.) get into an argument; start a fight or brawl:* There is an old bloke who sits on the verandah of the pub who won't drink inside because he had a blue with the publican.

have the best of it • make the best of it

have the best of it—1. have the advantage: Though the inside passengers had had the best of it during the night, the outside passengers had the best of it now. 2. be the winner: In terms of overall championship wins, the Dutch had the best of it as they took three of the four titles on offer.

make the best of it—accept an unfavorable situation and try to obtain the best possible results from it: It was anything but the perfect trip, but we made the best of it thanks to Joe.

See also: do one's worst / make the worst of it.

have the ear of someone • reach the ear of someone

have the ear of someone—have smb.'s favorable attention *(especially from smb. in a position of power):* He has been one of Italy's most influential figures, a man who is said to have had the ear of any Italian prime minister.

reach the ear of someone—(also: reach the ears of someone) 1. *(of a sound)* be perceived by a person: Another sound had reached my ear; an unmistakable one this time — the rattling of a key in its lock. 2. *(of news, rumors, etc.)* come to smb.'s knowledge: Sometimes the opposition will debate a piece of legislation in the hope that some of their comments will reach the ear of the government.

have the face • lose face

have the face—(followed by Infinitive) be sufficiently shameless to do smth.: If I had done otherwise, how could I have ever had the face to visit the graves of my parents?

lose face—(also: lose one's face) damage one's reputation; lose respect: Admitting she cannot answer a child's question, she would lose face in front of her class.

have the floor • take the floor

have the floor—speak at a meeting, in a debate, etc.: You now have the floor for the next five minutes.

take the floor—1. = *have the floor:* Arthur was one of several House members to take the floor. 2. start dancing at a party, etc.: "Will you dance with me?" She got up and they took the floor.

have the key of the street • live in the street

have the key of the street—be shut out for the night with nowhere to go: We once had the key of the street for a night. We don't know how many miles we walked before morning.

live in the street—(also: live on the street) be homeless: Children who live in the street or perform activities in the street are susceptible to violence and exploitation.

have the last word • say one's last word

have the last word—make the final categorical utterance in a dispute, etc.: We can all make suggestions, but the manager has the last word.

say one's last word—give one's final offer, decision or opinion in a dispute, etc.: I've said my last word on this question—take it or leave it.

have the pleasure of someone's company • take pleasure in someone's company

have the pleasure of someone's company—(formal) used when issuing invitations, etc.: May we have the pleasure of your company for lunch tonight?

take pleasure in someone's company—enjoy a person's company: I take pleasure in your company, and do my utmost to give pleasure back to you.

have the rag on • lose one's rag

have the rag on—(sl., also: have the rags on) have one's menstrual period: His wife always either had the rag on or had a headache every time he wanted to have a little fun.

lose one's rag—(sl.) lose one's temper: Allison lost his rag with me over two goals by Leicester's Mike Stringfellow.

have the wobbly boot on • quake in one's boots

have the wobbly boot on—(Austral. sl.) be drunk: He was horrible at lying, and hopefully he wouldn't feel the need to brag about it while he had the wobbly boot on at a bar.

quake in one's boots—(also: shake in one's boots) be very much afraid; tremble with fear: Brandon said it was his first time singing, but he didn't seem like he was quaking in his boots.

have to go • have to go some

have to go—(euph.) said when one needs to visit a restroom: "I have to go really bad!" Debbie shouted as she put her hand on her rear and jumped up and down.

have to go some—one must try harder or improve performance: You'll have to go some to make your getaway now—every man on the force has your description by this time.

have trouble to do something • take the trouble to do something

have trouble to do something—experience serious problems or difficulties when doing smth.: People with poor vision, though not blind, have trouble to read small fonts.

take the trouble to do something— make an effort to accomplish smth.: It has been instructive to discover enthusiastic assistance available if I only take the trouble to ask.

have trouble over something • take trouble over something

have trouble over something—(also: have trouble with something) experience serious problems or difficulties when dealing with smth.: I have trouble over my mid-morning bathes on account of passing boats.

take trouble over something—(also: take trouble with something) exercise care and thoroughness about smth.: The numerous finds of glass vessels show that Meroitic ladies took considerable trouble over their appearance.

have two faces • wear two hats

have two faces—(also: have two faces under a hood) 1. be deceitful or insincere in one's behavior: The woman had two faces: the one she used with clients, who adored her, and another for the office. 2. have two different aspects: Psychiatry has two faces, one represented by treatment at the psychosocial level and the other by treatment at the pharmacologic level.

Note: *a) The expression does not correlate in meaning with the phrase* ***be like a dog with two tails****—(coll.) be extremely happy:* I am not used to being home; husband is like a dog with two tails, and his excitement at having me here is starting to annoy me.

b) The expression does not correlate in meaning with the phrase ***have two strings to one's bow****— have two alternative courses open:* A dual honors degree has a number of advantages: When deciding on a career, you will have two strings to your bow.

wear two hats— hold two official appointments at the same time; have two sets of responsibilities: Because I breed racehorses, I also am a farmer so I wear two hats.

Note: *The expression is not equivalent in meaning to the phrase* ***serve two masters****— be loyal to two different people, completely opposed principles, etc.:* I felt I could not be effective, as a Councilor should there be the perception that I was serving two masters.

have word • have words

have word—receive a message: After about four months, in May, we had word that this comet was going to impact Jupiter.

have words—have a quarrel: Every time the two of them get together they have words.

Note: *The expression is not antonymous in meaning to the phrase* ***have no words****— be unable to describe or talk about smth.:* We all here are quite astonished and have no words to describe the situation.

head boy • principal boy

head boy—(UK) a school prefect who often represents the school on public occasions: No matter how excellent may be the original disposition of the head boy, if there is no one who dare stick up to him, he soon becomes intolerable.

principal boy—traditionally in Great Britain an actress, not an actor, who takes the leading male part in a pantomime: You both walked as gracefully and proudly as if you were the principal boy and girl at the Drury Lane pantomime.

head hunter • skull hunter

head hunter—1. a member of any tribe of savages who have the custom of decapitating human beings: A chief named Dungdong had become a notorious head-hunter. 2. *(coll.)* an employment agent specializing in the recruitment of skilled personnel: McCulloch had no compunction about using these recruiting firms. They were, he knew, often derisively called "head hunters."

skull hunter— = *head hunter 1:* In spite of the depredations of "skull hunters," we rode a considerable distance over ground ... thickly strewn with human bones.

head line • headline

head line—(Palmistry) a line that supposedly indicates temperament and talents: If a line sets out from the head line, and rises straight to the mount of Jupiter, crosses it, and cuts the roots of the forefinger, it is excessive pride.

headline—1. a title of a newspaper article usually printed in large type: The headlines that day were full of the news of kidnapping. 2. *(pl.)* the main points of the news which are read on radio or television: A female voice starts up reading headlines of murders, accidents and other political casualties.

head man • main man

head man—1. a chief or a tribal leader: The head men, or chiefs of the whole nation, were convened. 2. head of a department: Tomorrow, when she sees the head man ... we'll try and sort this business out. 3. a person walking ahead of a party of hunters, mountain climbers, etc.: Their positions in order of desirability were: sack man, head man, tail man and middle man. 4. smb. who beheads the condemned person: The walls resounded with the dread word of treason and its price — the gallows and the headman's axe.

Note: *The expression does not fully correlate in meaning with the compound* ***headsman****—1. = head man 4:* As there was no English headsman capable of wielding a sword for such a purpose, one had been brought over from Calais. 2. *the man in command of a whaling boat:* The crew of the boat consists of the headsman, boatsteerer and four hands. 3. *(dated) head or leading man, especially of a village community:* Each town, or township, is divided into wards or *barrios,* the headsman of which is called *cabeza de barangay. 4. (dated) a miner who pushes loaded cars to the place from which they will be hauled to the surface:* This little boy is called a foal. He sometimes assists the headsman by pushing the tub beside him.

main man—1. *(also: leading man)* a person that guides, directs, or leads: This year the skateboard club is reformed again with Doug Cameron as the main man. 2. *(also: leading man)* an actor who plays the leading male role: Affleck is very good as the main man and he plays his part in a reasonably straight, understated way. 3. *(U.S. sl.)* a person's best friend: Pierre is my main man when it comes to all things website related. He's a genius with this stuff. 4. *(U.S. sl.)* a woman's husband or lover: He's been her main man for two years. Do you think they'll get married?

head of water • water-head

head of water—body of water kept at a certain height for supplying a water-mill, etc.: Let us compare a watermill driven by a head of water, and a windmill driven by the wind.

water-head—1. the upper part of a stream near its source: Passing by the waterhead his father so loved in the old days of his carriage tours, we drove to the church. 2. = *head of water:* Only about one-fifteenth of the total length of the dam, or 500 feet, will be exposed to the maximum water-head of 85 feet. 3. *(sl.)* a stupid person; a half-wit: The body, these waterheads imagine, is a temple that should not be polluted by animal protein.

Note: *The expression does not correlate in meaning with the adjectival compound* ***watery-headed****—(arch.) apt to frequently cry:* She objected to the display of emotion ... and was apt to speak of members of her sex as a watery-headed lot.

health food • healthy food

health food—a kind of natural, organic food without chemicals: There is greater awareness about health food these days not just because people want to look good but to prevent cardiac diseases.

healthy food—food that is low in fat and contains limited amounts of cholesterol and sodium: More effort had to be made to improve the accessibility of healthy food in deprived areas.

heard it from the horse's mouth • little bird told me, a

heard it from the horse's mouth—heard it directly from the person concerned: The story was even more intriguing when we heard it from the horse's mouth.

little bird told me, a—said of information gathered from a source not to be named: A little bird told me that the appointment of a director will be made shortly.

Note: *The expression does not correlate in meaning with the phrase* ***go tell it to the birds****—addressed to a person who says smth. that is not credible or is a lie:* After this incident, it might be difficult to dismiss some witchcraft claims with the expression, "go tell it to the birds!"

heart disease • heart-sickness

heart disease—any morbid condition of the heart: Heart disease and strokes are related to potentially treatable but undetected hypertension.

heart-sickness—great depression; despondency: Heart-sickness makes many dyspeptics; for mental trouble has a paralyzing influence upon the digestive organs.

heart-breaking • heart-broken

heart-breaking—causing intense sorrow or grief; extremely distressing: There is also a heart-breaking scene as the children say goodbye to their mother at the train station.

heart-broken—overwhelmed with anguish, despair, or grief: I was heart-broken and could not believe a human being who is supposed to be kind could treat me that way.

heart-burning • heartburn

heart-burning—an embittered, resentful state of mind: To avoid the heart-burning that may otherwise be caused by so frank a history as I intend this to be, I am going to be non-specific in dealing with the people...

heartburn—an uncomfortable burning sensation in the lower chest, usually caused by stomach acid: Heartburn is caused by stomach acid flowing back into the esophagus. Changing the diet can help to prevent heartburn.

heavy artillery • light artillery

heavy artillery—powerful or persuasive persons or things: The cheap prices of its commodities are the heavy artillery with which it batters down all Chinese walls.

light artillery—(U.S. Drug users) equipment for preparing and using drugs (hypodermic needle, etc.): All that junk on the table is my light artillery.

heavy-headed • light-headed

heavy-headed—1. drowsy; sleepy: I look so sleepy this morning, warm, slightly confused and heavy-headed from too much slumber. 2. dull or stupid: They are prejudiced with German films because they expect them to be heavy-headed and suffer from a lack of humor.

light-headed—1. weak, giddy and likely to faint: Low blood pressure can leave you feeling light-headed, sluggish or headachy. 2. having little judgment; reckless and irresponsible: He was more ready to contemplate war than were any in the West, and more lightheaded about the consequences.

heavy in hand • heavy-handed

heavy in hand—(of people, horses, etc.) hard to manage or

control: Even if Jane was a little heavy in hand, with that appearance it didn't so very much matter.

heavy-handed—1. awkward in the use of hands: She even taught heavy-handed but dauntless colliers, who were seized with passion to "play." 2. inclined to severe punishment: Grandfather was heavy-handed with his own children but very indulgent with us grandchildren. 3. *(of an approach, methods, etc.)* harsh: Regulation of the electricity market started in a light-handed fashion but there has been an increasing trend towards more heavy-handed regulation. 4. *(of a joke, style, etc.)* inept or clumsy; lacking lightness or grace: Their jokes are very heavy-handed, and generally involve discomfort for the victim.

See also: have a heavy hand / have a light hand.

Hebrew manna • manna from heaven

Hebrew manna—moisture oozing out of an Arabian variety of tamarisk, *Tamarix gallica:* The manna of this country has nothing to do with Moor's Alhagi or Hebrew manna.

manna from heaven—(originally of food that God gave the Israelites during the Exodus) anything very advantageous and unexpected: To us then the cakes were manna from heaven and the dances were the greatest of fun.

help oneself • one can't help oneself

help oneself—serve oneself with food, drink, etc.: Once he had (quite generously) helped himself, the others at the table began to join in, keeping him from only consuming half the bottle on his own accord.

one can't help oneself—one can't refrain from doing smth.: The man turned himself in possibly because he knew what he was doing was wrong, but couldn't help himself.

help someone off something • help someone off with something

help someone off something—help a person to leave smth.: Two males helped him off the boat, then led the man ashore, through the waist deep water.

help someone off with something—assist a person in taking off clothing: He shut the front door and turned to help her off with her coat.

help someone to something • help someone with something

help someone to something—serve a person with food, drink, etc.: "Shall I give you some strawberries, Mr. Hervey," said Lady Anne, "or will you let Helena help you to some cherries?"

Note: *The expression does not fully correlate in meaning with the phrase* ***help oneself to something****—1. give oneself smth. such as food (without permission):* The aroma was irresistible and I quickly helped myself to some crab meat on the table. 2. *steal smth.:* The robbers helped themselves to an undisclosed amount of cash, believed to be several thousand dollars, before fleeing the area.

help someone with something—1. make it easier for a person to do smth. by providing assistance: Butch sent Willie some books to help him with grammar. 2. help a person to put on or take off clothing: Someone helped Janson with his coat, and he left the hall.

here and there • here, there and everywhere

here and there—in various places; scattered about: The old birch-woods still linger here and there.

Note: *The expression is not antonymous in meaning to the phrase* ***neither here not there****—used of smth. not very important or irrelevant to what is being discussed:* This may be neither here nor there but I have to say it.

here, there and everywhere—in all parts; in every place imaginable: I've been looking for you here, there and everywhere.

here goes • there goes

here goes—(also: here we go) said by a person ready to begin smth. that takes skill, luck or courage: "Here goes!" said Charley, as he jumped off the high diving board.

there goes—is used to express regret when circumstances prevent one getting smth.: When I was in the States, I heard they canceled the project and thought, "There goes my job."

here we go • there you go

here we go—1. *(also: here goes)* said by a person ready to begin smth. that takes skill, luck or courage: "Here we go," Turk murmured grimly, climbing in behind the wheel. "It's Sydney or the bush! Keep your fingers crossed." 2. *(also: here we go again)* is used when smth. unpleasant or undesirable should have been expected or is about to be repeated: Mother is drunk again. Here we go.

there you go—1. is used to say that the situation cannot be changed and one has to accept it: I was hoping to get it all finished today but there you go. 2. = *here you go 2:* "The historic necessity will carry us on of itself towards a better social state." "There you go with your Marx and your Hegel!" 3. is used to tell a person that he is now doing it right or has the right attitude: "I know I can do it. I just need to try harder." "There you go!" 4. is used as a positive reply in response to a request: "Can I borrow your pen a minute?" "There you go."

hide and hair • neither hide nor hair

hide and hair—(coll.) 1. completely; wholly: And I don't mean to do the thing by halves. No; I shall save you, hide and hair. 2. *(in the phrase "eat someone up hide and hair")* hurt or otherwise seriously harm a person: Mother had often said that anybody could eat us up hide and hair before help arrived from the camp.

neither hide nor hair—(coll.) not a trace of a person's presence; nothing whatever: The bank was robbed two months ago, but the police could find neither hide nor hair of the criminals yet.

hide one's head • hide one's head in the sand

hide one's head—1. lower one's head because of shame or embarrassment: Tim hid his head in shame as two police officers came and led him away. 2. keep out of sight (to avoid danger, etc.): The hart pursued by hounds chooses rather to give up its life than to hide its head in the grove...

hide one's head in the sand—ignore unpleasant realities: I loved even your talent for hiding your head in the sand when you can no longer avoid the ugliness before your eyes.

high and dry • high-dried

high and dry—1. *(of a stranded ship)* cast on the shore: The small Mexican brig which had been cast away in a south-easter ... now lay up, high and dry. 2. in a helpless or abandoned position: Millions of old people were left high and dry during periods of economic decline. 3. *(U.S. diners)* a plain sandwich without butter, mayonnaise, or lettuce: Keep your kids' sandwiches high and dry. Pack the filling and the bread in separate baggies for easy lunchroom assembly.

Note: *The expression does not correlate in meaning with the phrase* ***home and dry****—(UK coll.) definitely safe or successful:* The governments will not be home and dry until they have completed the ratification process.

high-dried—(of fish, etc.) deprived of most of its moisture by drying: There were brown beers made by a new type of brown malt known as "high dried malt."

Note: *The expression does not correlate in meaning with the phrase* ***cut and dried****—(of a decision, arrangement, etc.) com-*

pletely decided; fixed beforehand: Assuming that everything was now cut and dried, I talked to Richard but he said he was still unsure about committing himself.

high and low • up and down

high and low—1. in every conceivable place; everywhere: We searched high and low for the best career coach to serve our clients. 2. said of people of high and low station: In the public forum he was outspoken and called both high and low people to task. 3. the maximum and the minimum temperature, prices, etc. reached in a particular period: These values represent yesterday's high and low over the last 12 hours.

up and down—1. to and fro; back and forth: Unable to bear another night alone, they take to walking up and down Broadway. 2. in diverse places or directions: "So whereabouts is the local surf break?" interrupted Jerry, looking up and down the coast. 3. is used of a changeable or unstable disposition: Mrs. Moore is up and down; very liable ... to fits of bad jealousy. 4. *(coll.) give smb.* a quick examining look: He gave me the up and down, and I saw that he remembered me. 5. *(coll.)* a violent quarrel or fight: I had a bit of an up and down with one of your ilk only about an hour ago.

See also: uppers and downers / ups and downs.

high ball • highball

high ball—(Sport) said of a ball that is thrown quite high: All was well until Maya threw a high ball at me and I ran backwards to get it.

highball—(U.S.) 1. liquor mixed with ice and water, usually served in a tall glass: He offered to mix me a highball from a decanter and siphon on a table. 2. a railroad signal indicating that the way is clear: They would flick their lights and the engineer would answer with a highball (two short blasts of the whistle). 3. *(coll., used as a verb)* drive very fast: Cars, vans, and delivery trucks were highballing along this very curvy road...

high beam • high beams

high beam—said of car lights set for maximum long-range illumination of the road ahead: Eddie drove the old Sedan de Ville cautiously, the headlights on high beam.

high beams—horizontal cross timbers of a hayloft, garret, etc.: Larry lifted the sticky brown carpet ... stripped paint from the high beams in the living room.

high-boy • tallboy

high-boy—(U.S.) a tall chest of drawers (often raised on legs), usually in two parts, one standing on the other: During the Queen Anne period in America, the highboy attained its characteristic form. *Cf.: lowboy—(U.S.) a low chest of drawers, about three feet high on short legs:* This is a reproduction of a lowboy likely built in Rhode Island. The concave blocked center drawer presents an interesting relief.

tallboy—1. = *high-boy:* He polished the mahogany tallboy, the legs and arms of the dining chairs; plumped up the blue and brown satin cushions. 2. *(U.S. sl.)* a sixteen ounce can of beer (.48 liter): They don't sell tallboys at hockey stadiums anymore as too many people were chucking them onto the ice.

high-brow • high-browed

high-brow—1. *(of people)* highly intellectual or aesthetically refined: I'm not a very high-brow individual and I usually don't enjoy abstract art. 2. *(of things)* sophisticated and requiring intellectual effort to be understood: Prior to going off on a high-browed tirade about "assumed incompatibilism," you may want to learn the definition.

high-browed—1. *(of a building, doorway, etc.)* having a high entrance: I approach the front entryway, and as expected, that high browed door whips right open for me. 2. = *high-brow 1.:* Classical music fans will think you're pop, pop fans will see you as a high-browed "artiste." 3. = *high-brow 2.:* But enough of the high-browed analysis. In the end, it's a very good read.

high class • upper class

high class—1. said of high quality items: The place was a "saloon" ... drinking and smoking went on during the performance, but the pieces put upon the stage were all of a high class. 2. exclusive; select: It was a high-class school at Brighton, where girls are taught to use lipstick and adore the heroes of Hollywood.

upper class—the highest class of society; the aristocracy: Increased access to education helped carry some individuals into the ranks of the upper class.

high ground • high land

high ground—1. a mountainous region in a country: The river then does really occupy a hollow, enclosed on three sides by high ground. 2. an advantageous position or moral superiority: The document is an attempt to win back the political high ground.

high land— = *high ground 1:* It is the high land nearest to the shore which falls most abruptly.

high language • high-flown language

high language—1. pompous and pretentious language: Many talked in high language about sacrificing their lives and fortunes for their country. 2. the language regarded as superior when two (related) languages are spoken: The Zulu, as the high language, has ever exercised a controlling influence upon the low languages.

high-flown language— = *high language 1:* They talk in high-flown language, not always conveying very precise ideas.

See also: high words / high-sounding words.

high man on the totem pole • high-up man

high man on the totem pole—(U.S. coll.) smb. who has the most important position in an organization: I don't want to talk to a secretary. I demand to talk to the high man on the totem pole.

high-up man—(coll.) a person of high place or rank: A "high-up" man in the International Skating Union previewed serious changes to be considered at the next meeting.

See also: low man / low man on the totem pole; man upstairs / top man.

high on something • low on something

high on something—(sl.) 1. under the influence of a drug or alcohol: It is far safer to drive a car when high on marihuana than when drunk. 2. keen on smth.; enthusiastic about smth.: "I am not high on the Thieu brand of Government," he said, noting that 40,000 people had been executed by it.

low on something—deficient in smth.; short of smth.: John brewed instant coffee. He was low on sugar.

high season • high summer

high season—the most popular period at hotels, resorts, etc. (not necessarily in summer) when rates are highest: High season in the Caribbean (when most people visit) is from December to April.

high summer—period when summer is at or near its peak: December is high summer in Chile and high time for touring the country's famous vineyards.

high school *(UK)* • high school *(U.S.)*

high school (UK)—a secondary school for pupils aged between eleven and eighteen: We are based at Brae High, in Shetland — the most northerly six-year high school in Britain.

high school (U.S.)—a secondary school for pupils aged between fifteen and eighteen: The teen-agers arrive with a petition that has been going around high schools across the province since the fall.

high sea • high seas

high sea—1. a rough sea marked by high waves: The ship has an advanced hullform that provides for outstanding stability and speed in high sea states. 2. the area of sea (away from the coast) that is not under the sovereignty of any state: Controversy arose out of demands on the part of different states to assert exclusive dominion over areas of the high sea.

high seas— = *high sea 2:* "This is still a valuable ship," explained Torrance, "even if she is floating around the high seas on the installment plan."

high spirit • high spirits

high spirit—1. mentality characterized by lofty and noble ideas: Her ability to forgive, her high spirit, her faith are the things that inspire me. 2. said of a bold and audacious person: She hoped she had tamed a high spirit or two in her day.

high spirits—vivacity; cheerfulness: She hadn't the high spirits which endear grown-ups to healthy children.

high tea • low tea

high tea—(UK) an early evening tea with a full meal (as a substitute for dinner): He thought of the high tea to which he sat down ... a slice of cold meat, a great deal of bread and butter and plenty of milk in his tea.

low tea—tea with just bread and butter, cookies, or cake: Low tea was served in the low part of the afternoon, in aristocratic homes of the wealthy, and featured gourmet tidbits rather than solid meals.

high time • low time

high time—1. *(also: full time)* time when smth. should be done at once: Tom was beginning to feel that it was high time for him to be getting to regular work again. 2. *(in the phrase "have a high time")* have enjoyable, noisy and joyful time: The Johns had a high time, drinking brandy and eating fried hog.

low time—a short period of time: Never make a negative decision in the low time. Never make your most important decisions when you are in your worst moods.

Note: *The expression does not correlate in meaning with the phrase* ***down time***—1. *the time when a machine or computer is not operating:* The amount of "down time" due to faulty machine operation is very low. 2. *(coll.) an opportunity for rest; time off:* People talk of "enjoying the down-time" when they are having a break.

See also: peak time / up time.

high up the stick • up the stick

high up the stick—(dated sl.) standing high in one's profession: All my acquaintance among the doctors are so high up the stick, they have no time to spare...

up the stick—(UK sl.) pregnant: Mary is up the stick; funny how everyone counts the months.

Note: *The expression does not correlate in meaning with the verbal phrase* ***up sticks***—*(also: up stakes) leave one's home or settled way of life and move on to another place:* What on earth impels a man ... suddenly to up sticks and come back to this distressful country?

high water • highwaters

high water—1. the tide when the surface of the water is at its greatest elevation: The height from low water to high water is called the range of the tide. 2. a flooded river or lake: She wanted a new house after a high water on the river carried her old one away.

highwaters—(sl.) trousers that are shorter than fashion dictates: His jovial blue highwaters are replaced by dark black Levi's Hard Jeans.

high words • high-sounding words

high words—words spoken in a raised or loud voice (usually uttered in a heated argument): A short altercation ended speedily in high words on both sides.

high-sounding words—pretentious, bombastic words: Sophomorical, a term applied to speeches and writings containing high-sounding words and but little sense.

See also: high language / high-flown language.

highball something • lowball something

highball something—(coll.) drive a vehicle at high speed: Our conductor called "All aboard!" ... then highballed the train. A few minutes later he got a phone call stating a passenger had gotten left behind.

lowball something—(coll.) deliberately underestimate or understate a cost, figure, etc.: This is all my fault, but he was one of my first clients and I lowballed the price just to get the work.

higher school • upper school

higher school—higher education beyond school, especially to degree level: It is hard to predict an individual's ability to master the higher school program.

upper school—a secondary school for children aged from fourteen upwards: Physical education classes are part of the upper school weekly schedule.

Note: *The expression does not correlate in meaning with the phrase* ***finishing school***—*private school preparing upper-class girls for social life:* She attended one term at a Swiss finishing school after which she ended her formal schooling and obtained a job.

highly colored • of a high color

highly colored—(also: high colored) 1. brightly colored; full of color: Compounds of this type are highly colored, and are used as dyes. 2. *(of prose)* pompous and pretentious: Some chapters are factual and suitable, but others are couched in the most highly colored cinematic prose. 3. *(of a narrative)* sensationalized or exaggerated: Travelers' tales are often highly colored, as you know.

of a high color—(of wine, complexion, etc.) of red or reddish color: A liquor called Morocco ... is of a high color, and is made from malt and hops.

hire out something • hire something

hire out something—allow the temporary use of smth. in return for payment: The boat-yard belonged to an old-established family firm, who hired out river craft.

hire something—obtain the temporary use of smth. in return for payment: I have hired a self-drive car, as there seems no other way of getting about Cyprus.

historic event • historical event

historic event—an event notable or memorable in history: The meeting between the two great leaders was a historic event.

historical event—an event pertaining to history as contrasted with legend or fiction: This battle is a historical event documented in the archives.

hit bottom • hit the roof

hit bottom—(of prices, sales, etc.) reach the lowest or worst point *(also: touch bottom):* Our profits have hit bottom. This is our worst year ever.

hit the roof—(also: go through the roof) 1. show extreme anger about smth.: The Prime Minister and his cabinet would hit the roof if they knew half of the things that went on. 2. *(of prices, sales, etc.)* increase very rapidly; surpass the expected limit: Once the summer season hits and tourism begins to rise, gas prices hit the roof.

hit close to home • hit home

hit close to home—negatively affect smb.'s personal feelings or interests: This story hit close to home as I know Warren Driscoll who was the tow truck driver who was hit.

hit home—have a strong emotional impact when fully realized: It wasn't until I read that story that the full horror of what happened in New Orleans finally hit home for me.

hit it • hit it out of the ball park

hit it—(coll.) find, often by chance, the right answer; say or do exactly the right thing: Yes, that's just what I mean — you've hit it!

hit it out of the ball park—(coll., also: knock it out of the ball park) do smth. exceptionally well: I was out of my mind with the possibility of playing that character because I knew I could hit it out of the ball park.

hit it off • hit it up

hit it off—(coll.) get on well with a person: How nice that the two girls hit it off so well.

hit it up—(U.S. sl.) drink excessively: You're still hitting it up, I see. Joe, take that bottle away from him.

hit it off with someone • make a hit with someone

hit it off with someone—(coll.) establish a strong friendly relationship with a person: She finds it hard to make friends, and she hasn't really hit it off with her roommate.

make a hit with someone—(coll.) make a strong impression on a person: You certainly made a hit with my mother-in-law. I hope you will be available soon for our other daughter's wedding.

hit me • hit me up

hit me—1. *(sl.)* tell me; say it now: When I said it was bad news, he said, "Hit me. Let's have it." 2. *(card games)* give me another card: The old man looked at his cards carefully, then said, "Hit me."

hit me up—(sl.) call me up: Hit me up Saturday and let me know what's up. *Cf.: hit me on the hip—(sl.) call me on my pager (usually clipped to a belt):* When you need me, just hit me on the hip.

hit pay dirt • hit the dirt

hit pay dirt—find smth. of value or financially rewarding: His first two plays did not do well. But he hit pay dirt with the third.

hit the dirt—fall to the ground suddenly (to avoid being shot, etc.): He hit the dirt the moment before the grenade exploded.

***Note:** The expression does not fully correlate in meaning with the phrase **hit the dust**—*1. = *hit the dirt:* The deputies hit the dust, drawing their weapons, while Jimmy took off running. 2. *fall out of the competition:* Lots of stores are about to hit the dust for sure. I am trying to hold on to see if this pulls out of the slump.

hit the bull's eye • hit the eye

hit the bull's eye—(also: strike the bull's eye) 1. attain the intended object; succeed: The public is a very curious animal and ... how difficult it is to tell what will hit the bull's eye. 2. guess the right thing; give a correct answer: I implemented a policy of giving partial credit for answers that are close, but didn't hit the bull's eye.

hit the eye—(also: strike the eye) be very obvious or impressive; make a strong impact: What immediately hits the eye on this island is its distinctive harmony: nature, climate, and ways of life are harmoniously amalgamated.

hit the ground • hit the ground running

hit the ground—(also: hit ground) 1. fall to the ground suddenly (to avoid being shot, etc.): The voice was cut out by a sudden blast of gunfire. He hit the ground and readied his rifle. 2. *(of a storm, etc.)* come with forcible impact: We watched a straight and narrow tornado hit the ground a few miles north of the highway. 3. *(of a ship)* run aground: Heavy winds began to pull it toward land, and at about 6 pm, the ship hit ground and split apart.

hit the ground running—start a new job or endeavor efficiently, with a great deal of energy: There are plenty of challenges facing the state, and Heath said he believes he will hit the ground running if elected.

hit the high spots • hit the spot

hit the high spots—(coll.) say or do only the important or obvious things: I said into the telephone, "Just hit the high spots and don't be too specific. I'm in a hurry."

hit the spot—(coll.) be exactly what is required *(especially of food and drink):* Seed tea hits the spot during the hot summer months.

hit the road • hit the streets

hit the road—(coll.) get going; leave: Billy and I hit the road early but were sidetracked by coffee and breakfast and didn't start in earnest until eight.

hit the streets—(coll.) 1. go out into the street: Within about two minutes of hitting the streets we'd picked up a boy who insisted on being our guide. 2. *(of products)* be launched; appear on the market: This car will hit the streets in 2015, but it won't be the first hybrid Volvo plans on releasing.

Hobson's choice • Sophie's choice

Hobson's choice—the option of taking the one thing offered or nothing: There is presently only one stock exchange in Hong Kong and in that respect companies desiring a listing are given Hobson's choice.

Sophie's choice—(originally the title of the book by W. Styron) a choice between two persons or things that will result in the death or destruction of the person or thing not chosen: I'm not talking about situations like "Sophie's Choice" where you are forced into a terrible no-win decision by an outsider...

hoe one's own row • ring one's own bell

hoe one's own row—(U.S.) be independent; follow one's interests or inclination *(also: paddle one's own canoe):* Now that I have hoed my own row ... they deluge me with congratulations.

ring one's own bell—(also: blow one's own trumpet) announce one's own successes; praise oneself: He was a good team member. He's not out there trying to ring his own bell.

hog it • pig it

hog it—(U.S. sl.) appropriate smth. greedily or selfishly; not share smth. (monopolizing the road, etc.): Now I will really hog it a bit: this is a lovely piece of road.

pig it—(sl.) live squalidly or in dirty surroundings: You can't expect two masterminds like us to pig it in that room downstairs.

***Note:** a) The expression does not correlate in meaning with the phrase **pig oneself**—(sl.) eat gluttonously or greedily (also: pig out):* Please do not ply me with biscuits; I have no desire to set you a bad example by pigging myself.

*b) Neither expression correlates in meaning with the phrase **dog it**—(coll.) fail to exert effort; underperform:* It was apparent to anyone watching him play that he was dogging it on the court.

hog-wash • pig-washing

hog-wash—(sl.) 1. weak inferior liquor: He had had enough of that sort of hog-wash ladled out to him for genuine liquor.

2. said contemptuously of writings of any kind: He taught sociology and I told him straight that hogwash was not one of my subjects.

pig-washing—(Metallurgy) the refining of molten pig-iron by treatment with iron oxide: A similar process, used for some time by Krupp, was described by Holley under the name of "pig-washing."

hoist one's flag • hoist the flag

hoist one's flag—1. *(of an admiral)* take up command: In May 1804, Northesk was promoted to the rank of rear-admiral, and, in the following month, hoisted his flag in the Britannia. 2. show one's feelings or intentions: The discussion ranged round what we should do ... but the parson hoisted his flag by saying that he himself did not propose to do anything.

hoist the flag—1. stake one's claim to discovered territory by displaying a flag: King and his party hoisted the flag on the island and the building of a storehouse began as a first necessity. 2. = *hoist one's flag 2:* If you want something from a group of people ... you generally don't hoist the flag of your ill-intent toward them.

Note: *The expression is not antonymous in meaning to the phrase* ***haul down the flag****— surrender; admit defeat:* After several weeks of argument, the trade union leaders had to haul down the flag and accept the government's earlier offer.

hold a candle for someone • hold a candle to someone

hold a candle for someone—(also: carry the torch for someone) retain admiration or love for a person (especially if the feeling is not mutual): He still holds a candle for Jennifer, and in the jungle he must've thought of her a lot.

hold a candle to someone—(usually negat.) be fit or worthy to be compared with another person: Edith is pretty, very pretty; but she can't hold a candle to Nellie.

hold a job • hold down a job

hold a job—have a job; be employed: The number of unemployed workers who had not held a job in over twelve months nearly doubled in the 1990s.

hold down a job—keep a job for a reasonable length of time: He never held a job down for long because of the drink, he was always getting sacked.

hold a parade • make a parade

hold a parade—1. organize a procession of people or soldiers to celebrate a special day or event: The King is glad to know that the Boy Scouts are holding their first annual parade. 2. *(legal)* conduct a procedure in which the witness is asked to pick out the criminal from among a group of randomly selected people: Where there has been a failure to hold a parade the jury should be warned of the dangers of identification without a parade.

make a parade—(of) try to impress people by making a display of one's abilities, virtues, etc.: They only want to make a parade of their wealth.

hold a record for something • keep a record of something

hold a record for something—show the best result in a particular sport or other activity: The film was written by Francis Veber who holds a record for Hollywood remakes of his movies.

keep a record of something—keep a written account of an event, etc. for future reference: We thought it might be useful to keep a record of our studies in the various other Turkish dialects.

Note: *The expression does not correlate in meaning with the phrase* ***have a record of something****— be known to habitually engage in smth. reprehensible:* Right around graduation time, he wasn't seen for a few days. The headmaster didn't report the boy to his father because he did have a record of taking off every now and then.

hold a rein on something • hold the reins of something

hold a rein on something—check or restrain smth., such as one's emotions: Age and experience managed to hold a rein on the terror that wanted to overcome her.

hold the reins of something—exercise control over smth.: Most were fierce military men and none could hold the reins of power without the support of the army.

hold a trial • hold court

hold a trial—determine whether an accused person is guilty or innocent by a court of law: If he pleads guilty, there is usually no reason to hold a trial. The court has only to decide what the sentence will be.

hold court—1. hold a session of a judicial assembly: While the court house was in process of repair the court was held in the basement of the Methodist Church. 2. is used of official receptions given by a ruler, etc.: In fact, Mary was the first princess of Wales, and the first female royal to hold court at Ludlow. 3. be surrounded by people who pay a lot of attention to the person: He was known to hold "court" with his fellow faculty members and engage them in endless scholarly conversation.

hold an appointment • keep an appointment

hold an appointment—(formal) hold a position or office: A Subaltern Officer is not eligible to hold the appointment of Aide-de-Camp, until he has been present with his Regiment at least two years.

keep an appointment—not fail to meet a person after fixing a time and place: Under some pretext or other she would fail to keep the appointment.

hold back • keep back

hold back—be slow or unwilling to act; stay in the background: Because of the uncertain state of the market, buyers are holding back.

keep back—hold oneself back; stay at a distance from smth.: Keep back so that each man may have a fair view of the pit.

hold book • keep books

hold book—(Theater) act as the prompter: Moving on to the rehearsal phase, you learn why the stage manager should always hold book.

keep books—keep records of money gained and spent: These stores were operated by managers who kept books showing daily gross receipts and cash expenditures.

hold forth on something • hold forth something

hold forth on something—speak at length about smth.: Mrs. Price was holding forth on the subject of servantdom.

hold forth something—1. expose smth. to view: He held forth the paper on which he had written something. 2. offer or promise smth.: We present ourselves to you as allies who hold forth to you the advantages of British protection.

hold on • keep on

hold on—1. maintain one's grip or footing: If a branch is near you, hold on until we can get a rope. 2. continue; last: If the weather holds on, the area should provide excellent hunting the next few days. 3. continue traveling in a certain direction: Hold on down the road until you come to the railway crossing. 4. wait on the telephone: I'm afraid the line is busy, would you like to hold on? 5. continue in spite of difficulties; refuse to yield: Painting the house is tiring, but if you hold on, the results are worth the effort.

keep on—1. = *hold on 2:* The rain kept on, and the wind increased. There would be no flying that day. 2. = *hold on 3:* Turn left at the corner and keep on as far as the church. Keep right on to the end of the road. 3. = *hold on 5:* Even if you fail the examination again, you must try to keep on until you pass. 4. talk at length about smth.: Don't keep on so. I know you want the car but we can't afford it.

hold on to someone • keep on to someone

hold on to someone—keep one's grip on a person and not let go: I managed to hold on — perhaps it would be more accurate to say that the fish held on to me — until we had him in the boat.

keep on to someone—(also: keep on at someone) 1. reprimand or reproach a person: He kept on to her that she was not showing enough affection to him. 2. repeatedly ask a person to do smth.: His wife was transferred to the Psychiatric Ward, but she kept on to him to take her home.

hold on to something • hold to something

hold on to something—1. keep one's grip on smth.; not let go of smth.: The boy held on to the bush until someone climbed down the cliff to rescue him. 2. not give up the ownership of smth.: Letting your property enables you to hold on to your property and gain an additional income from rent. 3. *(coll.)* look after smth. which belongs to another person for a period of time: Will you hold on to this for me for a couple of days. 4. remain loyal or committed to ideas, principles, etc.: They hold on to these virtues with a rare tenacity.

hold to something—1. = *hold on to something 4:* He could not switch beliefs just for the sake of a paycheck. His integrity demanded he hold to his convictions. 2. continue traveling in a certain direction: For half an hour the ship held to its course; then its bow swung in my direction. I had been sighted.

hold one's breath • save one's breath

hold one's breath—1. be affected by a sudden emotion, such as amazement, delight, etc.: The sky broke like an egg into full sunset and the water caught fire. He held his breath. 2. *(coll., often negat.)* be waiting impatiently in expectation of smth.: I expect the mail to be delivered soon, but I am not holding my breath.

save one's breath—keep one's advice, opinion, etc. for oneself for it is unlikely to be heeded: Anyways, I saved my breath from an argument and decided to rent from another company. *Cf.: waste one's breath — talk to a person without him paying any attention, or acting on the speaker's advice:* Every time I talk to Catherine about emigrating, I feel as if I'm wasting my breath.

hold one's hand • hold someone's hand

hold one's hand—keep back; refrain from action: She knew when to hold her hand and when to pile on all her strength.

hold someone's hand—give guidance or moral support to a person in a difficult situation: I "held his hand" to the best of my ability with school-girl French and passable Italian.

hold one's head down • keep one's head down

hold one's head down—(also: hang one's head down) let one's head fall forward, usually when feeling sad or ashamed of oneself: This man was drinking booze and holding his head down in despair. He knew that he had wasted a lot of his life...

keep one's head down—1. = *hold one's head down:* When he saw me, his shoulders drooped and he kept his head down in shame and fear, even as he sat down to eat. 2. avoid attention; remain inconspicuous: Walsh kept his head down, not speaking out publicly even during the embarrassing wildcat strike that paralyzed the airline.

Note: *Neither expression fully correlates in meaning with the phrase* ***put one's head down***—1. = *hold one's head down:* Bill put down his head in mockery of the bull and grunted like him, whereat we laughed yet more. *2. go to sleep; take a nap:* It was probably the first time he had been able to put his head down since the illness reached its most critical stages. 3. *start to concentrate and work hard at smth.:* They wanted me to put my head down and work so I could get into a good college and have a great career.

hold one's water • hold water

hold one's water—1. contain one's urine: Eight hours is a long time to hold one's water.... It is a comfort to know that one can if really necessary get access. 2. *(U.S. sl.; imper.)* be patient; stop making repeated requests: "Pass over them glasses will you?" "Just hold your water sailor, you'll get your turn in a moment."

Note: *The expression does not correlate in meaning with the phrase* ***hold one's liquor****— be not easily intoxicated by alcohol:* The elder man stood erect in an attempt to show all that he could hold his liquor.

hold water—(of an argument, idea, etc.) appear reasonable; agree with the facts *(usually negat.):* Close examination of the evidence reveals, however, that such claims simply don't hold water.

hold out • keep out

hold out—1. *(of food supplies, etc.)* remain available; last: We have to cut our rations to try to make the food hold out till succor comes. 2. *(of perishable products)* remain fit for consumption or use: How long could the food hold out without refrigeration? 3. refuse to yield or submit: If we could hold out that long, we can hold out another couple of years.

keep out—stay outside; remain at a distance from smth.: We noticed a small fenced off area.... Signs warned us to keep out, but curiosity got the better of me.

hold someone up • keep someone up

hold someone up—1. support a person physically; hold smb. upright: It took both of us to hold up the old man. 2. rob smb. using violence or threats: In Japan you won't need to worry too much about being held up in the street and being robbed of your passport. 3. *(hyperbolic)* overcharge a person: I don't eat at that restaurant anymore. They really held me up the last time I ate there. 4. detain a person; make smb. late: The traffic on the expressway held me up yesterday.

keep someone up—1. = *hold someone up 1:* I could barely stand up myself, but I managed to keep up Ann until we got out of the smoke-filled room. 2. prevent smb. from going to bed; keep a person awake: "I hope I'm not keeping you up." "No, we often keep up late."

See also: keep someone down / keep someone under.

hold someone up as an example • make an example of someone

hold someone up as an example—point out smb. as a good example: I was embarrassed when the supervisor held me up as an example of good time-keeping.

make an example of someone—punish a person severely as a warning to other people: It was decided to make an example of some of the top conspirators.

hold someone's feet to the fire • light a fire under someone

hold someone's feet to the fire—(also: keep someone's feet to the fire) pressure a person to undertake smth. (to make good on a promise, etc.): I'm not going to punch him in the nose, but can't I hold his feet to the fire in a polite and gentle way?

light a fire under someone—(also: build a fire under someone) do smth. to motivate or stimulate a person: I want to light a fire under them and push them to places they never thought they could go. I want to help them reach their full potential.

hold something in • keep something in

hold something in—1. *(of an animal)* control or restrain: Your horse is trying to go too fast; you must hold him in. 2. control one's emotions: It was impossible for the children to hold in their laughter any longer.

keep something in—1. retain smth. as part of a writing, performance, etc.: But that's the best joke in the play, let's keep it in! 2. = *hold something in 2:* Jim was able to keep his anger in and avoid a fight. 3. keep a supply of smth.: I always keep some good wine in for unexpected guests.

hold something in contempt • hold something up to contempt

hold something in contempt—look down upon smth.; despise smth.: One of the worst things I could imagine was slavery and I had always held it in contempt.

hold something up to contempt—cause smth. to be the object of contempt: He held up to contempt all that was mediocre in their art.

hold something in hand • hold something in the hand

hold something in hand—1. keep smth. with the hand: Carter turned back and waved the chart he was holding in hand. 2. have smth. at one's disposal; keep smth. in reserve: Father has decided to hold £500 in hand in case of a business emergency.

hold something in the hand— = *hold something in hand 1:* "Where did that rose come from?" James inspected the rose he was holding in the hand.

hold something on • keep something on

hold something on—secure smth.; keep smth. in position: This big screw holds the lid of the box on.

keep something on—1. continue to possess smth.: We are still keeping on the house in France. 2. continue to wear or use smth.: In a church men take their hats off; in a synagogue, they keep them on. 3. = *hold something on:* There is a spring underneath so use a finger to keep the lid on while you remove the last screw.

hold something out on someone • hold something out to someone

hold something out on someone—keep a secret or news from a person: What's going on? Are you holding something out on me?

hold something out to someone—offer smth. to a person: I held out an offer of immunity to prosecution to her, but she would not cooperate.

hold something up • keep something up

hold something up—1. support smth. physically; bear the weight of smth.: We couldn't hold up the fence, and it finally fell over. 2. *(of prices, etc.)* cause to remain high: Efforts were made to hold up the price by again cutting production. 3. stop or delay smth.; make smth. late: A heavy storm in Boston held up our plane. 4. stop a car, etc. in order to rob: The thieves held up a van carrying a factory payroll.

Note: *a) The expression does not correlate in meaning with the phrase **uphold something**—1. (of a law, etc.) support and maintain smth.:* We will loyally uphold the principles of the United Nations. 2. *(of a verdict, decision, etc.) confirm or endorse:* His court conviction was upheld on appeal.

*b) The expression does not correlate in meaning with the phrase **hold up on something**— delay doing smth.:* I have to hold up on my reading because I broke my glasses.

keep something up—1. = *hold something up 1:* My husband lost so much weight that he has to wear a belt to keep his trousers up. 2. = *hold something up 2:* Since it is "back-to-school" time, I expect lots of students are buying laptops, and are keeping the prices up. 3. keep smth. in good condition; maintain smth.: How do you keep up a house as large as this without help? 4. continue smth.: Jane will have to keep up her piano practice if she wants to be a professional performer.

hold the field • keep the field

hold the field—1. keep one's position against attack; remain undefeated: American troops held the field but it was not a clear-cut victory. 2. be not superseded or displaced: Petroleum spirit still holds the field as a propelling force, both in the cars exhibited here and in those seen in London streets.

keep the field—(dated) keep the military campaign open; continue the fight: Hence the name [campaign] ... was also applied, now to the season or time during which the army kept the field.

hold the line against someone • hold the line at someone

hold the line against someone—take a firm opposing stand with regard to smb.: You've been holding the line against those who have sought to legislate the Second Amendment into oblivion.

hold the line at someone—preclude a person from being invited or admitted to a place: The Browns and the Smiths could be invited, but I think we ought to hold the line at the Browns.

hold up • keep up

hold up—1. *(of a structure, etc.)* stay erect; remain in good condition: This building holds up well despite its age. 2. *(of weather, supplies, etc.)* continue; last: Will the water supply hold up through the summer? 3. remain in control of oneself: How does he hold up under such a responsibility?

keep up—1. not drown: The sailors managed to keep up for several hours and were eventually picked up by a lifeboat. 2. *(of spirits, morale, etc.)* remain high: His courage kept up in the face of danger. 3. = *hold up 2:* Do you think this fine weather will keep up for a couple of weeks? 4. stay in touch: I'm afraid we haven't kept up at all since she went abroad. 5. = *hold up 3:* But for her courage, I never could have kept up through all this terrible trial. 6. not fall behind: If the children can keep up, we will take them with us when we hike into town.

hold with something • keep with something

hold with something— approve of or support smth.: I do not hold with heavy drinking and wild parties.

keep with something—remain or stay with smth.: Keep with the convoy during the whole voyage.

holy cow • sacred cow

holy cow—(exclam.) is used to express strong feelings of astonishment, pleasure, or anger: "Holy cow!" Tod roared. "Will I ever forget the look on the McGloys' faces..."

sacred cow—said of smth. so cherished that it is regarded as above criticism: Tories regard interest and profit as sacred cows to be fattened at the expense of the people.

Holy Joe • Holy Willie

Holy Joe—(Nautical) a parson; a devoutly religious person: They all have these Holy Joe voices when they start giving their sermons.

Holy Willie—a hypocritically pious person: The Holy

Willies were just like the slave-owners who outlawed traditional African religions.

***Note:** Neither expression correlates in meaning with the phrase **Holy Moses**—(exclam.) used to express strong feelings of astonishment, pleasure, or anger:* Copland was astonished to see things he had not looked at for over sixty years. "Holy Moses!" he exclaimed, "I kept everything!"

Holy Roman Empire, the • Roman Empire, the

Holy Roman Empire, the—the Western part of the Roman Empire as revived by Charlemagne in A.D. 800: Francis II put an end to the Holy Roman Empire by his abdication in 1806.

Roman Empire, the—that established by Augustus in 27 B.C. and divided by Theodosius in A.D. 395 into the Western or Latin and Eastern or Greek Empire: Christianity floated into the Roman Empire on the wave of credulity.

home boy • house-boy

home boy—1. a boy who is fond of staying at home: A lonesome little English home boy was playing his mouth organ softly in the dusk. 2. *(U.S. coll.)* a man from one's hometown or neighborhood: Like many of her home boys and girls who left the state to search for something else, she came back. 3. *(U.S. Underworld)* a street kid; a member of a teenage gang: Some 30,000 "home boys," or gang members roam, pretty much at will in Los Angelos County.

house-boy—a (usually native) boy employed as servant in a house: That's my houseboy; he has an unpronounceable name, so I call him John.

home ground • home zone

home ground—1. the area where smb. lives; one's familiar surroundings: Students benefit by experiencing interviews with prospective employers on their own home ground. 2. an area of smb.'s special strength or competence: Obviously Scorsese has done moderately well with other types of films but contemporary urban crime is his home ground.

home zone—streets specially designed to meet the interests of pedestrians and cyclists: Home Zones work through the physical alteration of streets. These alterations force motorists to drive with greater care and at lower speeds.

Home Guard, the • National Guard, the

Home Guard, the—*(UK)* a volunteer force formed to defend a homeland while the army is fighting elsewhere: Those who could not serve in the Army signed up as Local Defense Volunteers in what became known as the Home Guard.

National Guard, the—*(U.S.)* the volunteer forces of each state, which the governor can summon in an emergency, such as civil disorder, etc.: According to reports, the National Guard was called in to help evacuate residents affected by a storm.

home-keeping • housekeeping

home-keeping—1. looking after the house (managing the cleaning, cooking etc.): Marriage is more difficult because you must agree on home keeping, child rearing, dealing with in-laws.... 2. *(attrib.)* said of smb. keeping at home; home-staying: I'm very good mixer but I don't like noisy groups; I'm a home-keeping person.

housekeeping—1. = *home-keeping 1:* This position is responsible for housekeeping duties and preparing the evening meal for our seniors. 2. *(U.S. attrib.)* of a rented holiday cabin or cottage furnished with cooking facilities, etc.: We had booked "a house-keeping suite" without knowing what that was.... 3. short for "housekeeping allowance": You'll go throwing your money around but if I ask you for a bit more housekeeping, that's a different story.

home phone • house phone

home phone—a telephone at a person's place of residence: "This was intercepted yesterday afternoon on the Milettis' home phone," the magistrate explained.

house phone—a telephone connected to the switchboard of a building but not directly to the exchange: The lighted button was his private line, not his house phone. Everyone understood that his private line was used only for important business.

homecraft • housecraft

homecraft—an art or craft pursued in the home: Clock production was part of the homecraft of the peasant people of Dalarna province in Sweden.

housecraft—the art of managing a house; skill in domestic duties: The girls did housecraft activities such as cleaning and cookery and also studied typing.

homestay • stay-at-home

homestay—a visit to smb.'s home in a foreign country (often a stay by an exchange student): As Howell discovered during her homestay, much of the education in a study abroad program takes place beyond the classroom.

stay-at-home—1. said of smb. preferring a quiet domestic life to traveling or leading a busy social life: Thoreau was such a stay-at-home that he refused to go to Paris lest he miss something of interest in Concord. 2. said of smb. staying or working at home: I'm a stay at home mother of two young girls. I have very little time that I can call my own.

honor-man • man of honor

honor-man—*(also: honors man)* a person obtaining an "honors degree" from a university, etc.: He entered Queens University at Kingston, Ontario, and again was honor man of his class in anatomy.

man of honor—a person with a reputation for loyalty, truthfulness, etc.: Are you or are you not willing to act like a man of honor to protect your own good name, the family name, the name of this child...

honorary degree • honors degree

honorary degree—a degree conferred by the university, etc. as an honor, without the usual requirements: I got an encouragement out of the blue in the form of an honorary degree from Berlin.

honors degree—a degree conferred by the university, etc. requiring some specialization and a high level of attainment: Applicants should preferably be of honors degree standard, with interest in magnetic devices.

honors of war • military honors

honors of war—privileges granted to a capitulating force: The French troops shall file out with all the honors of war, with arms and baggage, to the outside, where they will lay down their arms.

military honors—the external marks of respect paid by troops to royalty or high military or civil officials: The allied troops rendered military honors to the departing commander-in-chief.

hook, line, and sinker • lock, stock and barrel

hook, line, and sinker—*accept or believe smth.* completely or without reservation *(usually in the phrase "swallow something hook, line, and sinker"):* You must not swallow hook, line and sinker all that you have been told or read.

lock, stock and barrel—*taking or including* everything: Looking back it is hard to believe that we actually moved lock, stock and barrel to the other side of the world.

hook someone up • hook up with someone

hook someone up—1. *(coll.)* establish an intimate relationship between two people; supply a person with a date: I've had some of the worst dates due to my friends trying to hook me up. 2. *(Police)* take a person into custody *(reference being to the act of handcuffing):* Tags on the car are expired, let's go ahead and hook him up.

Note: *The expression does not correlate in meaning with the phrase **get one's hooks into someone**—(coll.) 1. get control or influence over a person:* The rival VHS video format has really got its hooks into the American consumer. 2. *(of a woman) try hard to gain the affections of a man (used showing disapproval):* Ramona jealously guards her current boyfriend so Vicki doesn't get her hooks into him.

hook up with someone—(coll., also: get hooked up with someone) 1. meet smb. and spend time together: I was traveling alone, but then I hooked up with another woman about my age. 2. become romantically or sexually involved with a person: I was a freshman in high school and hooked up with this guy on the first day.

hop it • hop to it

hop it—(UK sl.) be off; move away quickly: "Are we going to stick it here?" said one. "Didn't the sergeant say something about hopping it?"

hop to it—(U.S. coll.) start a job; do smth. immediately: If you finish your homework quickly you can watch TV tonight, so you'd better hop to it.

horse-play • play the horses

horse-play—rough or boisterous behavior, passing the bounds of propriety: Dryden's best comic attempts were but heavy horse-play.

play the horses—bet on horserace results: No wonder his wife is penniless; he is always playing the horses and losing his money.

Note: *The expression does not correlate in meaning with the phrase **horse around**—(also: horse about) behave in a rough and noisy manner:* Shereth yelled at us to quit horsing around and finish up the car washing.

horse tail • mare's tail

horse tail—(also: pony tail) a type of women's hair style with hair drawn back, tied and hanging down: She wore jeans and a cotton sweater, her hair was in a horse-tail.

mare's tail—1. a tall slender marsh plant: This is an old photograph of the submerged aquatic plant called mare's-tail, *Hippuris vulgaris. 2.* long straight streaks of cirrus cloud *(known as a sign of impending storm):* Cirrus clouds are characterized by thin, wisplike strands, often accompanied by tufts, leading to their name of "mare's tail."

hot and cold • hot and hot

hot and cold—short for "hot and cold water" (in a hotel, etc.): He's working out that plan for laying on hot and cold.

hot and hot—said of dishes served in succession as soon as cooked: Her potato cakes came in hot and hot from a pot-oven.

hot-blooded • warm-blooded

hot-blooded—easily excited or aroused emotionally: President Kibaki is no hot-blooded youth bursting with combative political flames.

warm-blooded—1. said of animals whose body temperature is internally regulated: The dinosaurs that nested at Egg Mountain were warm-blooded creatures. 2. *(of people)* eager or enthusiastic enough: There was once a time — believe it or not — when companies actually had warm-blooded people on their payroll...

hot dog • sausage dog

hot dog—1. a frankfurter or wiener in a bun with any of various toppings: The boys stopped on the way home for hot dogs and coffee. 2. *(sl., also: hot-dogger)* a person who performs showy, often dangerous stunts in a sport: She was a hot dog behind the wheel, screeching her wheels at every turn. 3. *(exclam.)* is used to express excitement and delight *(also: hot diggety dog):* "Look, here's the check! We're rich!" "Hot dog!"

sausage dog—1. a variety of "hot dog" sausage: I stare pointedly at them and take another bite of my sausage dog.... 2. *(coll.)* a dachshund *(a dog with long body and very short legs):* In England, the dachshund is often called a sausage dog, or a wiener dog in America.

hot goods • hot stuff

hot goods—(sl.) stolen products or items obtained illegally: My canoe has never been pulled over by the police for illegal transportation of "hot goods."

hot stuff—(sl.) 1. a person or thing that is very popular or exciting: Although "Dancin' Shoes" is second-rate, the rest of the album is hot stuff. 2. a very sexy person: I think she is definitely around 400 pounds now. She thinks she is hot stuff also dressed up in her tight suits."

hot line • hot wire

hot line—1. direct line of communication between heads of governments: President Richard Nixon also used the hot line during tensions between India and Pakistan in 1971. 2. a direct telephone communication channel; an emergency telephone counseling service: Your relatives are welcome to use our hot line to learn about the patients' state. *Cf.: warm line—telephone service designed to solve relatively minor problems:* Organizers call it a "warm line" instead of a hot line because it's a place where teens call long before it's a life-or-death situation.

hot wire—part of electrical instruments whose resistance changes with changing temperature: The turbulence data were measured inside the jet stream by the use of hot wire equipment.

Note: *The expression does not correlate in meaning with the verbal phrase **hot wire**—start a car without a key:* Lefty hot wired the car and used it for an hour or two.

hot seat • hot seating

hot seat—1. *(coll., also: hot chair)* an uncomfortable position of authority where one has to make difficult decisions: I am now sitting in this hot seat as a film critic whose job it is to analyze a film. 2. *(Air Force)* an ejection seat in an aircraft: McClane was able to press the ejection switch of a hot seat just in time to escape from an exploding plane. 3. *(sl., also: hot chair)* the electric chair: A newspaper reporter said he heard the lad announce that he was not afraid to die "in the hot seat."

hot seating—1. sharing of desks or equipment by office shift workers, etc.: In these schools, double shifts, known as "hot-seating," are the norm. 2. *(role-playing technique)* pretending to be a literary character and answering the relevant questions in the "hot seat": Hot seating is a way of finding out more about the characters in stories, plays, or poems.

hot-water bottle • water bottle

hot-water bottle—a rubber container of hot water, used to warm a bed, etc.: I would have a fire and an india-rubber hot-water bottle, and I would lie and sleep.

water bottle—a (plastic) bottle for holding drinking water, carried by hikers, etc.: He held out the tiny glass, and I half filled it from the water bottle.

hotter than a pistol • hotter than blazes

hotter than a pistol—(coll.) said of a person or thing that is very popular: Radios were hotter than a pistol. Shimek's still sells radios as well as televisions and sound equipment.

hotter than blazes—(coll.) is used to hyperbolically designate smth. very hot: Now Djibouti is hotter than you can imagine. Humid, hot, hot as blazes, hotter than blazes.

hound someone • hound someone down

hound someone—(also: dog someone) 1. make smb. the victim of continual persecution: Club owners were afraid to hire a comedian who was hounded by police. 2. annoy or harass a person persistently: A year later, he is still hounding me to pay, and still refuses to cover the cost of repairs for the damages he made.

hound someone down—1. search for or pursue a person, especially for arrest or punishment: A price was put on his head, and he was hounded down throughout the war. 2. track down and finally find a person, especially for arrest or punishment: In fleeing for safety they were eventually hounded down to the Cave of the Lakes.

house man • man of the house

house man—1. a person hired to perform general work about a house: She went through to tell the house-man to clear away the tea. 2. house detective employed by a department store, hotel, etc.: He … grinned at me sociably. "I'm the house man here. Spill it." 3. a doctor who has a junior post in a hospital; an intern who serves in residence at a hospital: After qualification you have to spend a year working as a hospital houseman.

Note: *The expression does not correlate in meaning with the phrase* ***house husband****—a man who stays at home while his spouse works outside the home:* John tried being the house husband for some years, but I'd prefer not to give up my work.

man of the house—the chief male in a household: Look at him! The man of the house! Why don't you talk to me? I'm your wife, aren't I? *Cf.: little man of the house—said of a child who is the top male of the household:* "Little man of the house," his grandmother said, chuckling. Vince was four years old when his father split.

house master • master of the house

house master—a teacher in charge of one of the boarding-houses in a school: Where senior house masters exist … they should be able to exercise an effective supervision over the boys in their care.

master of the house—male head of a household: During meals, when he was not serving or pouring, the Butler stood behind the chair of the master of the house.

Note: *The expression is not equivalent in meaning to the phrase* ***master of one's own house****—a person who manages his household affairs without interference from others:* I shall let my wife and daughters know, that I will be master of my own house.

householder • housekeeper

householder—1. an owner or renter of a house: The inspection techniques used were explained to the householder so that he could carry out future inspections on his own. 2. the head of a family: A family consists of a householder and one or more other persons living in the same household who are related to the householder.

housekeeper—1. a person employed to do household maintenance tasks: With my additional income I hired a housekeeper to do my laundry and keep the house in order. 2. smb. who takes care of his own house and its residents: We found out my husband is a wonderful housekeeper, better than I am at it, and it was actually kind of fun.

how are you doing • how do you do

how are you doing—(also: how are you) 1. is used to ask a person whether everything is going well: I am not really good at showing people how I am really feeling, you know … the "how are you doing?" "Oh, I am doing okay" that stuff. 2. is used as an informal greeting when meeting people and requires no reply: We used to have short conversations every day, but now, it's more of a "Hi, how are you doing?"

how do you do—is used as a formal greeting when meeting people or being introduced: "How do you do, Miss Ferrell? I am Miss Wright." "How do you do."

how comes it • how goes it

how comes it—(also: how come) how or why does it happen: How comes it that you are always late on Monday?

how goes it—(also: how's it going) is used to ask a person whether everything is going well: How goes it in your office since your new boss arrived?

how ever • however

how ever—is used as a more emphatic variant of "how": Everything is fabulous—how ever are you going to choose?

however—1. in whatever manner or way: However you calculate the costs, we need your estimate by tomorrow afternoon. 2. to whatever degree: However hard he tries to balance his responsibilities, Piech is always going to be left open to accusations of double dealing. 3. yet; nonetheless: Tom went on a date with a really nice girl. However, he forgot to take his credit card with him…

how's that • how's that for high

how's that—1. is used as an expression of surprise or praise: I bought sandwiches with chicken … and I didn't gain any weight so how's that! 2. is used to ask whether smth. is acceptable or satisfactory: I'll go up as high as fifteen dollars. How's that? 3. is used when asking smb. to repeat what the person has just said: "My name's Sijan." "How's that again?"

how's that for high— = how's that 1: How is that for high, my hearty? Miracle! It was, by thunder!

hungry for something • starved for something

hungry for something—desiring smth. very much: We seek individuals who are personally disciplined and hungry for new experience.

starved for something—(also: starved of something) being in great need of smth.: The relevant departments in the Universities are starved for new material.

I

I am listening • I hear what you say

I am listening—you have my attention, so speak: Sergius again hesitated. "I am listening," she said.

I hear what you say—1. I know what you mean and agree with you: "I think it's about time for a small revolution!" "I hear what you're saying." 2. is used with the implication that a person does not agree with his interlocutor: I hear what you say, and you know why I'm not going to debate that with you again today.

I have seen better • I have seen worse

I have seen better—(also: seen better) is used as a noncommittal and not very positive judgment about smb. or smth.: The Badge was an entertaining movie, though I have seen better. It is worth catching if you want a mystery to watch.

I have seen worse—(also: seen worse) is used as a noncommittal and not totally negative judgment about smb. or smth.: Based on the reviews I had read, I wasn't expecting the restaurant to be fancy looking—and it wasn't, though I have seen worse.

I say • I'll say

I say—1. is used preceding an utterance to call attention to it: Do you hear the rain, Mr. Caudle? I say, do you hear the rain? 2. is used as an exclamation of surprise, delight, or dismay: I say, what on earth are you doing letting your eight year old watch a TV show you don't approve of?

Note: *The expression does not correlate in meaning with the phrase* ***I'm telling you****— used to say smth. firmly to a person:* You are asking me to donate money to the party and I'm telling you I will not donate one red cent.

I'll say—(coll.) 1. is used to show complete agreement with what was said: "What a queer duck he is!" exclaimed Biff. "I'll say he is!" ejaculated Chet Morton. 2. is used for emphasis: If they're doing well in a class and I'm not (at least not as well), I'll say it's just because they're working hard.

ice house • ice palace

ice house—1. an underground storage where blocks of ice are stored to be used in the summer: Every substantial country house had an ice house and it is surprising how many remain. 2. a morgue: The body was brought to the ice house, as planned, but the door would not lock. So the poor body was taken back to Mrs. McKnight's house.

ice palace—1. a huge castle-style building constructed of large blocks of ice: The city of St. Paul has played host to several ice palaces as part of the city's Winter Carnival. 2. any large structure housing a skating rink: Here are some pictures taken over the years of the Ice Palace staff, friends and public skating. 3. a place of seclusion or retreat from the realities of life: You hide behind the pillars of your ice palace, pretending to be so unapproachable.

ice man • snow man

ice man—1. *(U.S.)* a man who retails and delivers ice (for use in ice-boxes, etc.): We played our games. I was the iceman and she was the housewife. 2. a man skilled in traversing ice (in Alpine or polar regions): We knew as icemen that the access to the land-ice from the floe was both toilsome and dangerous. 3. a person looking after the ice on a skating-pond: What becomes of icemen and skate-lenders in summer? 4. a hockey player: The ice men are through to the final of the Autumn trophy ... they beat Swindon in the semi-final. 5. *(Ice Man)* man living in the Ice Age: The process will make it possible for fragile mummies such as the recently discovered Ice Man to be accessible to the public. 6. *(Underworld)* a hired killer; an assassin: Zen was sitting in a small white-curtained cubicle, thinking about Trotsky and the ice-man.

snow man—1. a mass of snow made into the figure of a man: The daylight passed in snowman-making on the meadow. 2. *(also: Abominable Snowman, the)* a creature alleged to exist in the Himalayas: Mr. Smythe says that the snowman superstition is known only to the Tibetan peoples. 3. *(U.S. sl.)* a person who deceives people with plausible words; a swindler: You're a great snow man, Warren. But I'm not in dreamland yet.

ice someone • put someone on ice

ice someone—1. cause depressing influence over smb.: Her very enthusiasms were cold; she iced you by the tone of her conversation. 2. *(Underworld)* kill a person: The mobsters threatened to ice him if he went to the police.

put someone on ice—(sl.) 1. *(also: keep someone on ice)* postpone acting on a person: He keeps pestering you for an answer, but we'll just have to put him on ice until we have more facts to go on. 2. put smb. in solitary confinement for a while before interrogation: He will for a considerable time be "put on ice"—isolated from any contact with other members.

identify oneself to someone • identify oneself with someone

identify oneself to someone—say or prove (as to the police, etc.) who or what a person is: Shortly before he died, the man identified himself to the police as Michael Howard, 29 years old.

identify oneself with someone—(also: identify with someone) feel that one shares the ideas, beliefs, problems, etc. of another person: The poet may be said, for the time, to identify himself with the character he wishes to represent.

if a day • not a day over

if a day—(also: if one is a day) is used to express certainty about a person's age: Madeleine's sister is a great age, too. Eighty, if a day.

not a day over—one cannot be older than the age mentioned: "You look very well, not a day over forty," Charlie said, standing back.

if any • if anything

if any—supposing there is or are any: It is a cooperative venture with all the profits, if any, being invested in expanding community based broadcasting.

Note: *The expression is not equivalent in meaning to the phrase* ***if at all****— supposing an action, event, etc. happens although it is very unlikely:* Legislation is referred to a committee, only to be considered later, if at all.

if anything—if in any degree: If anything, this approach puts those risks in the forefront, assuring that they will not be overlooked.

if only • only if

if only—1. is used to express a strong desire or hope that was not fulfilled: If only I knew at the time that she would be famous one day! 2. even though *(is used to introduce the clause of concession):* This may mean going on a trip, if only for a day or two, or an extended vacation of several weeks.

only if—not at all unless: A Commonwealth citizen or other foreign nationals can apply but only if they are resident in the UK.

if you fly with the crows, you get shot with the crows • if you lie down with dogs, you will get up with fleas

if you fly with the crows, you get shot with the crows—(Proverb) if you wish to benefit from a high risk situation, you have to accept the consequences if things go wrong: The individual must demonstrate that he accepted a certain degree of responsibility, even if he feels that he is personally blameless. To put it crudely: If you fly with the crows, you get shot with the crows.

if you lie down with dogs, you will get up with fleas—(Proverb) if you become involved with bad company, there will be negative consequences: "If you lie down with dogs, you will get up with fleas." With those words in mind, I have always chosen my real friends wisely.

impatient of something • impatient with something

impatient of something—unable to endure smth.; unwilling to submit to smth.: His early orphanage was not without its effect in confirming a character naturally impatient of control.

impatient with something—easily provoked or irritated when dealing with smth.: This book is for you if you get impatient with heavy, conventional and lengthy textbooks.

Note: *Neither expression correlates in meaning with the phrase* ***impatient for something****— eager for smth. to happen; eager to do or obtain smth.:* Koizumi himself acknowledged after polls closed that people were impatient for change.

impose on someone • impose oneself on someone

impose on someone—obtain a favor from a person, especially by using persuasion or undue pressure: Could I impose on you for a little help with this translation?

impose oneself on someone—inconvenience smb. by one's presence: As there was no train, he was forced to impose himself on his hosts for longer than he had intended.

improve in something • improve on something

improve in something—become better with regard to some standard or quality: The boy seems to have improved in his behavior since he had that last warning.

improve on something—produce smth. of a better standard or quality than before: She improved on her previous performance by swimming the distance in less than a minute.

in a bad way • in the worst way

in a bad way—1. in trouble; having serious problems: The basic exporting industries of Great Britain — coal, metallurgy and textiles — have been in a bad way. 2. *(of health)* in a bad or critical state: But one of the poor men who were hurt at the fire is dead, and another is, I fear, in a bad way. 3. *(coll.) desire smth.* greatly: It's Friday morning and I'm wanting in a bad way to stand hip deep in the chilly current of a fast moving river. 4. *fail or be defeated* miserably: He has found himself dragged down by the Party and defeated in a bad way in a General Election.

in the worst way—1. = *in a bad way 3:* I then wanted in the worst way to build a sail boat and sail around the world. 2. = *in a bad way 4:* To try a major novel about the last war in Europe without a sense of the past is to fail in the worst way.

in a big way • in a great way

in a big way—(coll.) 1. on a large scale: The company should be frugal, they say, but when it does invest it should do so in a big way. 2. with great eagerness or enthusiasm: Derek is crazy to take up dancing in a big way again. He adores all this old-time dancing.

in a great way—1. *(UK dated) living* on a grand scale: She was very well married, to a gentleman in a great way, near Bristol, who kept two carriages! 2. *(coll.)* extremely well: Most of us will never do great things, but we can all do small things in a great way.

in a bit • in bits

in a bit—1. *(coll.)* after a short time: There is a reason for this, and I hope to talk about it in a bit. But first I'd like to put some background in place. 2. *(UK sl., sarcastic)* it's never going to happen: "Will you lend me twenty quid?" "Oh yeah, in a bit!"

in bits—(UK sl.) mentally confused or emotionally affected *(also: in bits and pieces):* I have had a total nightmare with this company and am in bits over the possibility of loosing £1,000.

in a corner • in the corner

in a corner—1. situated or positioned in a corner: Sitting in a corner of the room, Trevor watched his friends and teammates celebrate. 2. *(also: in a tight corner)* in a difficult situation: The government is in a corner and cannot win except to keep taxes reduced.

in the corner— = in a corner 1: A ghost was spotted standing in the corner of the cellar whilst the groups of visitors were upstairs.

Note: *The expression does not fully correlate in meaning with the phrase* ***at the corner****—1. (also: on the corner) at a street corner:* He was hailed by a gentleman standing at the corner by the Scotch Church. He immediately drove up.... 2. *= in the corner:* All you need to do to create printed version is turn on your printer and click on the printer icon at the corner of the screen.

in a dream world • in one's dream

in a dream world—having one's mind far away from reality; entertaining unrealistic ideas: There are people who live in a dream world, and there are some who face reality.

in one's dream—1. said of images passing through the mind during sleep: He took a piece of native copal wood and carved the animals that he saw in his dream. 2. *= in a dream world:* At times the person lives in his dream of "things as they might be" rather than realizing things as they are. 3. in one's imagination: Although his new company was only himself and one lawn mower, in his dream he could already see a major land management company.

in a dump • in the dumps

in a dump—(sl., in the phrase "live in a dump") live in a poor, dirty or ugly place: "How can you live in a dump like this?" he asked her. "Don't you ever clean this place?"

in the dumps—(coll., also: down in the dumps) 1. in low spirits; very depressed: One of my still single girlfriends was in the dumps about not having a boyfriend. 2. *(of a market, economy, etc.)* deteriorate or decline: He told Goldman that he knew his career was in the dumps and offered him a position.

in a family way • in the family way

in a family way—1. without ceremony: Why don't we ask him to come over in a family way and dine with us. 2. *(euph.)* pregnant: I have heard that Mrs. Smith is in a family way once again.

in the family way— = in a family way 2: A woman should postpone the observation of fasts when she is in the family way.

in a fashion • in the fashion

in a fashion—1. *(also: after a fashion)* to a certain extent but not very satisfactorily: I kept puffing at it [trombone] until I could play, in a fashion, the little Jim Robinson solo. 2. in the way specified: Nor did he fail to condemn wrong doing in a fashion which Scotch folk call teethy.

in the fashion— = in a fashion 2: Mrs. Rauscher mistook the meaning of the question and responded in the fashion she did to her own embarrassment.

Note: *The expression does not correlate in meaning with the phrase* ***in fashion****—popular; fashionable:* This writer was in fashion at the beginning of the century.

in a few well-chosen words • in a few words

in a few well-chosen words—said of a short and effective utterance: He managed to say in a few well-chosen words what others might not convey in a half-hour speech.

in a few words—1. said of smth. stated very briefly: In a few words Captain Schley gave me an inkling of his plans. 2. in short; by way of summary: In a few words, they believe that individual freedom is the fundamental value that must underlie all social relations.

See also: not in so many words / without many words.

in a fog • in fog

in a fog—1. when there is thick mist or fog: This neon light has great penetrating power in a fog. 2. *(also: all in a fog)* perplexed; at a loss: I confess that, until it came to light, I was in a fog.

in fog— = *in a fog 1:* Flying in fog—which may be called "blind flying"—involves difficulties not encountered in clear air.

in a fume • in smoke

in a fume—in an excited state of mind; in an irritable or angry mood: Every now and then a lady in a fume withdraws her name.

in smoke—(Underworld) in hiding: Denman advised Naysmith to remain "in smoke"—an expression meaning to hide himself.

in a hole • in the hole

in a hole—(coll.) in an embarrassing or difficult (financial) position: Lawyers have been known to embezzle their clients money when they themselves are in a hole.

in the hole—1. = *in a hole:* I couldn't let the fact come out that the business was in the hole since I was trying to sell it. 2. *(U.S. sl.)* said of smth. virtually assured: John knew his new accounting job was in the hole. 3. *(U.S. Prison)* in solitary confinement: If you're in the hole and complain, they'll double your time in the hole.

in a kennel • in the doghouse

in a kennel—(coll.) said of a small and mean dwelling or hut: He got us a room—we were in a kennel before.

in the doghouse—(sl.) in disgrace; out of favor: My dad's in the doghouse after getting drunk last night.

in a little • in little

in a little—after a short time: It isn't as dark as it looks because we are under the trees, but in a little they will light their lanterns.

in little—on a small scale: The Temple was an imitation in little of that at Ephesus.

in a mood • in the mood

in a mood—in a bad temper: Don't ask the boss for more wages today—he's in a mood.

in the mood—feeling ready or willing for smth.: I didn't laugh at all during the whole play—I just wasn't in the mood.

in a pickle • in pickle

in a pickle—(coll.) in an embarrassing or difficult situation *(also: in a fine pickle):* If it had been any hotter or the climb any longer we would have been in a pickle.

in pickle—(coll.) kept in reserve for future use: He will return to the tranquil enjoyment of his 1,000,000 pounds now in pickle, it is said, in the English funds.

in a position • in position

in a position—able to do smth.: The government was unaware of anyone who was in a position to offer a deal that was acceptable to Washington.

in position—in the right place (for a particular purpose): When the camera has been placed in position the cap of the lens should be removed.

in a round • in the round

in a round—1. in a circle; around the perimeter: I casually glanced in to find a group of students sitting in a round and discussing something. 2. during one stage in a game or contest: It is possible for one player to identify more than one word in a round, and he therefore scores according to the "places" he takes.

in the round—1. = *in a round 1:* That was a wonderful program concept: the artists sitting in the round and sharing their stories and songs for each other. 2. in full sculptured form unattached to a background: The camera also gives an impression in the round of the man who seems one-dimensional in print. 3. displaying a given subject from all aspects: It is not an easy part, seeing that it is the only character in the whole cast to be drawn in the round. 4. *(of a performance on a stage or arena)* surrounded by the auditorium: I do object to playing to them in the round, because it gives them a chance to get at the actor physically.

in a season • in season

in a season—1. *(also: at a season)* at a certain time: He was made Minister of Labor in a season when the Government's economic policy meant saying "no" to wage demands. 2. in the course of one season: These are the days of "long runs," when but one or two plays can be produced in a season.

in season—1. at the proper time for smth.: The people around me tell me in season and out of season that I look tired and that I have to go to bed. 2. *(of animals and plants)* in the best state for hunting, harvesting, or eating: The fish is in season as proved by the color of its fins. 3. *(of a place)* when most visited or frequented: From the first day of grouse to the last day of pheasants, London is never in season.

in a sense • in the sense

in a sense—1. in a way; to some extent: Mass and energy are equivalent, and mass is to be regarded in a sense as a concentrated source of energy. 2. in some respect: Everything in that conversation would be true, in a sense, although palpably not true in another. 3. in the meaning: *Antiphrasis*—a figure of speech by which words are used in a sense opposite to their proper meaning.

in the sense— = *in a sense 3:* For what it's worth, I've heard this word used in the sense in question in everyday conversations.

in a single piece • in one piece

in a single piece—consisting of or fashioned in a single unit: When the glove is being fabricated, the external layer is moulded in a single piece.

in one piece—1. = *in a single piece:* People from San Salvador began to come to our ships in boats fashioned in one piece from the trunks of trees. 2. *(also: all in one piece)* without injury; relatively unharmed: My orders are just to get him to London in one piece. After that, he's someone else's worry.

in a spot • in spots

in a spot—(coll.) in a difficult situation; in trouble: We really are in a spot, because to refuse her would cause months, if not years, of pouting and hard feelings.

in spots—(U.S. sl.) occasionally; at intervals: A boatman being asked how he managed to secure sleeping time, answered, "I sleep in spots"; that is, at intervals, by snatches.

in a state • in state

in a state—(followed by Infinitive) fit for smth.; mentally ready to do smth.: He went on thinking of her till he was almost in a state to drown himself in the little brook.

in state—1. with great pomp and ceremony: If he represented a first-class paper and wished to "save his face" he had better travel in state. 2. *(of a dead body)* ceremoniously exposed to view before burial *(in the phrase "lie in state"):* It was in this chamber he breathed his last; here he lay in state.

in a temper • out of temper

in a temper—in an irritable or angry mood: I got up in a temper, and told him to leave me.

Note: *The expression is not antonymous in meaning to the* *phrase* ***in no temper****— not in the mood for smth.:* Garibaldi, marching obstinately to defeat, was in no temper to listen to anybody, to Mazzini least of all.

out of temper— = in a temper: Don't go upstairs. Mother's there and she's out of temper.

in a world apart • worlds apart

in a world apart—out of touch with reality; unaware of the latest news, etc.: The returned exiles lived in a world apart. They hatched plans and business schemes and visionary ideas for transforming society.

worlds apart—(of two or more people or things) completely different: It can seem that men and women are "worlds apart" when it comes to life and love. Why did God plan it that way?

in act to do something • in the act of doing something

in act to do something—on the point of doing smth.: Nero persuaded himself that his mother was watching him like a tiger-cat in act to spring.

in the act of doing something—in the process of doing smth.: The thief was caught in the act of breaking into the house.

in action • out of action

in action—1. engaged in an activity, especially as a particular or good example: It is not hard to understand why the team is so talented when you see the team in action. 2. in military combat: Charles Havlat is thought to be the very last American soldier killed in action in the European operations of World War II.

out of action—1. *(of a machine or vehicle)* not working or functioning properly: We were aware that the hotel was under renovation, however for two days the elevator was out of action. 2. *(of a sportsman)* unable to participate in a competition, etc. because of an injury: He had surgery on both of his knees and therefore was out of action for several weeks.

in an excess of something • in excess of something

in an excess of something—1. when smth. is present beyond the limits of what is normal: This can be made by burning sulphur in an excess of air. 2. through too much emotion: My own copy has long been gone, pocketed by an acquaintance whom I pressed it on in an excess of generosity.

in excess of something—to a greater amount than smth. else: "Armorplate" has acquired a degree of strength far in excess of that with which the original plate glass was endowed.

in an instant • on the instant

in an instant—in a moment: Our ship was in an instant full of these swarthy gentlemen quite naked.

on the instant—at once; immediately: When you shut the doors of this grotto, it becomes on the instant, from a luminous room, a camera obscura.

in and out • ins and outs

in and out—1. said of smb. coming and going from a place all the time: Sam was in and out of the office most of the day today. 2. *(of work, etc.)* not continuous; done at irregular intervals: His engagements are only for particular plays—"in and out" work.

ins and outs—1. the details or fine points of smth.: She left the explanation to those who pretended to understand the ins and outs of the gravest mysteries of life. 2. people holding office and those out of office or in opposition: In Britain the parties are organized under party chiefs, and elections are simply a struggle between the ins and the outs.

See also: inside and out / inside out.

in another world • on other worlds

in another world—1. out of touch with reality; unaware of the latest news, etc.: I had for some time been living, as it were, in another world. I now came down to earth with a bang. 2. is used of a state of existence after death: A night's reflection has convinced me that there is no hell for these women in another world. *Cf.: in this world—during our life on earth (as distinguished from the world beyond the grave):* All human beings are destined to exist forever—in this world, and the world to come.

Note: *The expression does not correlate in meaning with the phrase* ***there's a whole other world out there****— there is a whole new world of ideas, information, etc. that is different from what we know:* There's a whole other world out there, one in which chemists work on more immediate problems in close collaboration with customers.

on other worlds—on other planets: Most scientists believe the universe is so vast that it is almost a statistical certainty that intelligence exists on other worlds.

See also: in the next world / in the second world.

in arms • up in arms

in arms—(of people) armed; prepared to fight: When their country is at war, they have many men in arms.

up in arms—1. actively rebelling: All of the colonies were up in arms against the Redcoats. 2. indignant over smth.; strongly protesting: The country is up in arms over the denial of voting rights to the men and women serving overseas.

in at it • in for it

in at it—(also: in on it) taking part in an activity; involved in smth.: If any mischief or practical joke was going forward, young George was sure to be in at it.

in for it—(coll.) said of smb. who is to suffer punishment or some unpleasant consequences: If the farmer catches those boys stealing his apples, they'll be in for it.

in balance • on balance

in balance—(also: in the balance) 1. properly balanced; in equilibrium: When there are two equally weighted objects on the seesaw, the board will be in balance. 2. in harmony with: The human body is in the balance with the mineral substances and each damage of this balance can initiate serious health problems. 3. *(of a situation)* uncertain as to the outcome: The financial situation is by no means resolved and the club's future is still very much in the balance.

on balance—1. = *in balance 1:* The other foot should be behind you, acting as a support. You should be stable and completely on balance. 2. having considered all the relevant facts: Although the evaluation process was not perfect, it was, on balance, fair to the proponents.

in black • in the black

in black—1. wearing black clothes: A gentleman in black proceeded to call over the names of the jury. 2. wearing mourning clothes: Mrs. Smith is in black, I see. Whom has she lost? 3. *executed or finished* in black color: The table is very ornamental ... the legs being of iron finished in black and gold.

Note: *The expression does not correlate in meaning with the phrase* ***in a black mood****— irritable, angry, or depressed:* We often talk about being in a black mood, feeling blue, going red with anger and green with envy.

in the black—(coll.) in a sound financial position; making a profit: We toyed with bankruptcy for a while, but now we're in the black.

in blue • in the blue

in blue—1. wearing blue clothes: Kim was chatting to a girl in blue as she laid crackling thorns on a fire. 2. *executed or finished* in various shades of blue color: Finished in blue, this item comes complete with a comfortable head cushion.

in the blue—(NZ sl.) said of a failure or of smth. going wrong: An attack that broke down would be said to be "in the blue."

See also: out in the blue / out of the blue.

in bond • in bonds

in bond—(of goods) stored in a customs warehouse until duties are paid: A merchant may not wish to sell immediately the goods he imports, he is therefore permitted to place them in bond.

Note: *The expression does not correlate in meaning with the phrase* ***on bond****—used of smb. released on bail:* O'Brien has remained free on bond during the appeals process.

in bonds—1. having one's feet or hands fettered: He stood now before them in bonds, at their mercy and devotion as they say. 2. held in captivity as a prisoner: This is an opportune time for us to remember the many thousands of our fellow believers who are still in bonds.

in camera • on camera

in camera—(of a court hearing) held while the public or press is not allowed to attend: The case is one that in England would be heard in camera.

on camera—(TV) when televised or recorded: We have been hearing increasing rumors of films in which the victim is murdered on camera.

in case of something • in the case of something

in case of something—if smth. should occur; as a precaution against smth.: Always keep a bucket of water handy, for use in case of fire.

in the case of something—1. as regards smth.: The essays were mostly good, but in the case of Jane's and Tom's, there was still much room for improvement. 2. = *in case of something:* All persons under their responsibility are trained and given adequate instruction in the case of fire.

in charge • on charge

in charge—said of smb. who is responsible or in control: The authorities announced the arrest of a local commander who was in charge during the incident.

on charge—(of a battery) being charged *(also: on a charge):* How long can I leave the battery on charge and not damage the battery?

in charge of someone • in the charge of someone

in charge of someone—exercising care or supervision of a person: Other people in charge of children, such as teachers or foster carers, do not have parental responsibility.

in the charge of someone—said of smb. under the care or supervision of a person: She has been in the charge of her grandmother since her mother and father died.

in charge of something • on charge of something

in charge of something—having control or custody of something: As is the custom with elevator boys, the lad in charge of the elevator started it before closing the door.

on charge of something—(also: on a charge of something) is used of the accusation upon which a person is arrested: Six persons were arrested on charge of adopting unfair means in the examination.

in clear • in the clear

in clear—(of military dispatches, etc.) forwarded in ordinary language rather than in code: A letter in numerical cipher, since he does not give it in clear, still awaits decipherment.

in the clear—1. not obstructed or enclosed: The valley was completely obscured by a thick blanket of fog while our cabin was in the clear. 2. free from guilt, suspicion, etc.: He says they told him he had been a suspect, but left him believing he was in the clear. *3. (coll.)* out of reach: Even downtown they [policemen] are likely to be in the clear when you want them most. 4. *(coll.)* as a clear profit: When we counted up the final night we figured nearly sixty grand in the clear. 5. in interior measurement: A water pipe eighteen inches in the clear is laid under ground to the center of the yard.

in cold blood • with sang-froid

in cold blood—said of smth. brutal or cruel done in an unemotional way: Sixteen innocent people, make-up artists, technicians and journalists, were murdered in cold blood in that building.

Note: *The expression does not correlate in meaning with the phrase* ***make someone's blood run cold****—(also: make someone's blood freeze) horrify or shock a person:* What he saw made his blood run cold. The woman stood there, holding a sword half as long as she was.

with sang-froid—(Fr.) acting calmly and without emotion in a dangerous or difficult situation: A man who always acts with sang-froid has a great advantage over him who is of a lively and easily inflamed nature.

in cold storage • in the deep freeze

in cold storage—1. *(of a process, project, etc.)* temporarily discontinued; held in reserve: It seems to be rather a shame that this anthology, which cost me a lot of work should remain indefinitely in cold storage. 2. *(sl., of a body)* in a mortuary *(also: in the ice box):* Zeno's body is in cold storage on the Blackvoid! It has been ever since he was originally killed.

in the deep freeze—1. is used to hyperbolically describe very cold weather: Massachusetts is in the deep freeze for the third day; before that it was just cold. *2. = in cold storage 1:* If something is being postponed indefinitely, use two words: The project is in the deep freeze. 3. *(U.S. sl.)* in prison: She couldn't stand his foul language any longer so she decided to cool him off for a while by putting him in the deep freeze.

See also: on ice / on thin ice.

in common • out of the common

in common—1. in joint use or possession: However, one thing all of our students have in common is that they're curious, focused, and socially responsible. 2. in a community: Citizens who share a language and culture are more likely to make effective decisions about their life in common.

out of the common—unusual; extraordinary: His voice is something out of the common.

in company • in good company

in company—when other people are present: But mind what I say George, be sure you never swear in company.

in good company—(joc.) in the same, usually unpleasant situation: "I can't speak a word of French." "Don't worry, you're in good company."

in consideration of something • out of consideration for something

in consideration of something—on account of smth.; taking smth. into consideration: On his retirement the company granted him a pension of £1,000 a year, in consideration of his services.

out of consideration for something—prompted by compassion or regard for smth.: Exercise caution in publishing notices concerning attempted suicide, particularly out of consideration for the feelings of relatives.

in credit • on credit

in credit—still having money in one's bank account: As long as you stay in credit or within the free £100 overdraft facility, there will be no charges for normal transactions on your account.

on credit—(of goods and services) not paid for at the time when bought: Armed with a credit card ... an American can have meals, buy clothes, stay at hotels — all on credit.

Note: *The expression does not correlate in meaning with the phrase* ***on the credit side****—used to introduce one or more of the good things about a situation:* On the credit side he could reasonably bank on his colleague's honesty.

in deep water • in low water

in deep water—(also: in deep waters) in serious (especially financial) difficulties: I have not suffered as you have. But— I have been in rather deep water too, in another way.

in low water— = in deep water: Philip ... came to know which of the clients must be treated with respect and which were in low water.

Note: *The expression does not fully correlate in meaning with the phrase* ***at low water****—1. when the tide is out and far from the shore:* Filey Brig is a remarkable ridge of rocks, projecting half a mile into the sea and perfectly dry at low water. 2. *(also: at low water-mark) = in low water:* The money market was very tight; but in 1905 everything was even worse, everything was at low water.

in demand • on demand

in demand—(of goods, services, etc.) desirable; much sought-after: Crops such as cotton were in demand around the world.

on demand—whenever requested: A demand deposit means that the customer can withdraw his money on demand.

in depth • out of one's depth

in depth—dealing with a subject very thoroughly: He had the choice of writing in depth about a few novelists or of skimming over as many authors as he could.

out of one's depth—in a situation too difficult to understand or cope with: When John talks about music, I soon get out of my depth because he knows so much more about it.

in disorder • not in order

in disorder—showing absence of order; in confusion: Investigators said they found some of his personal belongings and papers in disorder.

not in order—(also: out of order) 1. *(of a machine, etc.)* not working properly: Noting that the elevator is not in order, she dials for a repairman and waits for his arrival. 2. *(of a passport, etc.)* not valid; not as it should be: Joel apparently could not stay in Istanbul (he was deported as his papers were not in order).... 3. *(formal)* not in conformity with the prescribed mode of behavior: It is not in order to interrupt and the Senator would not have been interrupted had I been in the Chair.

in dock • in the dock

in dock—(also: in dry dock) 1. *(of a ship)* berthed in harbor (waiting to be repaired, etc.): The *Sally Brown* is in dock to discharge her cargo. 2. *(coll., of a person)* inactive (unemployed, in the hospital, etc.): June found herself in dry dock when her services were most in demand.

in the dock—1. on trial in a court of law: I can't bear to see a woman in the dock — butterfly on the wheel. 2. *= in dock 1:* He supplied the staging necessary to enable the outside of the vessel to be painted when in the dock.

in drink • in the drink

in drink—(coll.) said of smth. done or spoken when drunk: It was spoken in drink, but it happened to be true.

Note: *The expression is not equivalent in meaning to the phrase* ***on the drink****—(coll.) indulging in alcohol:* Her brute of a husband was always on the drink and gamble.

in the drink—(coll.) in the sea or river: "This means absolutely everything to me," said Hopp, all wet after his son threw him in the drink.

in each other's pockets • in someone's pocket

in each other's pockets—(coll.) associating closely to the extent of losing privacy; being together too much: At our winter camp we live in each other's pockets for six months without seeing anyone else at all.

in someone's pocket—(coll.) under smb.'s control or influence (because a person has been bribed, etc.): The scandals investigated included a building official who was in the pocket of a local developer.

in employment • in the employment

in employment—1. not out of work; having a job: There were almost five thousand more people in employment on the first of this month than on the first of last. 2. employed by a specific person or company: A person who was in employment of the company cannot be appointed as auditor.

in the employment—(also: in the employ) = in employment 2: Stiles was in the employment of a bookmaker.... That was to say, he went about to find out what the betting was.

in extremes • in extremis

in extremes—1. is used of extreme magnitudes or conditions: In extremes, there are micro-skirts, which barely cover the buttocks; minis, maxis and the nineteen-thirties length. 2. in critical circumstances: There's no saying what any man may do in extremes.

Note: *a) The expression is not equivalent in meaning to the phrase* ***in the extreme****—(used in postposition) to the highest degree; to the utmost:* I always thought the suggestion dangerous in the extreme.

b) The expression does not correlate in meaning with the phrase ***to extremes****—to excess; out of all proportion:* Surely we can have clean air and water without carrying any policy to extremes?

in extremis—(Latin) 1. *(dated)* at the point of death: The Master of the Rolls ... tumbled out of his chair last Sunday at church, and is, they say, *in extremis*. 2. *(formal)* in very great difficulties: To use this refuge for ordinary mountaineering is an abuse; it is only intended and equipped for special parties *in extremis*.

in faith • in good faith

in faith—having faith as the basis of a belief: We cannot prove that there is life beyond death; we can only accept it in faith.

in good faith—with honest belief or intention: Though his statement proved to be untrue, it was made in good faith.

in favor of someone • in favor with someone

in favor of someone—1. in defense or support of a person: Let each member speak in favor of the candidate of his or her choice. 2. to the advantage of a person or team: The defense players try to keep the score constant, and the forwards try to change it in favor of their team.

in favor with someone—liked by a person; having smb.'s support or approval: You can't expect to be in favor with Sue if you're always criticizing her.

in fits • in fits and starts

in fits—1. *(also: in fits of nerves)* shocked or very angry: I was in fits because I didn't know if Shawn had been trying to contact us or not. 2. *(also: in fits of laughter)* laughing uncontrollably: As he walked in dressed like a headache tablet, everyone was in fits.

in fits and starts—(also: by fits and starts) at irregular intervals: There is no way of coping with orders that come in fits and starts throughout the year.

in flesh • in the flesh

in flesh—(dated) corpulent; well-fed: The widow, being a little in flesh, as warmly protested against walking.

in the flesh—(also: in flesh and blood) in person *(of smb. actually present):* The minutes passing on, and no Mrs. White in the flesh appearing.

in flight • on the fly

in flight—1. while flying: Gliders are now fitted with a means of cleaning off the leading edges of the wings in flight. 2. running away; fleeing: The two men are hiding in a hotel apparently in flight from the police.

on the fly—1. = *in flight 1:* Peregrine falcons are predators and their prey consists mainly of birds, caught on the fly. 2. in motion; moving fast: She is constantly on the fly as she directs, plays piano or walks through the rows of children. 3. *do smth.* quickly or in passing (while busy with other things): Changes must be made on the fly, as the program progresses. 4. *(sl.)* having a lively, merry time; on the spree: My father had been on the fly in that town for nine or ten days.

in force • in strength

in force—1. *(of laws, statutes, etc.)* operative or binding at the time: In the south this ancient custom still remains in force. 2. in large numbers: The enemy was in force, the regiment came under heavy rifle, machine gun and artillery fire. 3. in full command of one's energies or abilities: Latterly Calvert was better, and able to go with us. He was in force again...

in strength—1. having great military power: Bonaparte was yet in strength to make face against the united armies of the remainder of Europe. 2. = *in force 2:* The civilian population used to turn out in strength every evening to watch our guard mounting parade. 3. in number: The refugee camp has grown to 600 in strength with many people being treated by the team medics for various illnesses.

in form • on form

in form—1. in structure: Cretan buildings are simple in form, conforming to architectural norms of Byzantine provenance. 2. in good physical or mental condition: Even if a horse is in form a bad trip almost surely will cancel its chances. 3. as a mere formality: The laws, which heretofore existed only in form, have been thoroughly enforced.

on form—1. on the basis of previous results: On form, they have no chance of winning today. 2. = *in form 2:* We all knew that Michael was always on form when he played and he exceeded his own expectations today!

in front of something • in the front of something

in front of something—in the position directly before smth.: She couldn't watch the television because he was standing in front of the screen.

in the front of something—in the foremost or most important part of smth.: Two rooms were built in the front of the west end of the house.

Note: *The expression is not equivalent in meaning to the phrase* ***at the front of something****—1. in the position nearest to the front part of smth.:* At the front of the machine is the feeding board, a large wooden surface sloping gently down. 2. *involved in the most advanced developments in a particular field:* The Beach Boys are at the front of this wave of frantic surf music.

in full • to the full

in full—(of payments, etc.) without leaving anything out; to the full amount: It was part payment only, payment in full was still to come.

to the full—as completely as possible; to the greatest degree: We did not enjoy our holiday to the full, because we were worried about my father.

in full spate • in spate

in full spate—1. *(of a current of water)* at abnormally high level: This stream cannot be crossed when it is in full spate. 2. said of some intense activity: A migration into the valley continued in full spate beyond the middle of the century. 3. said of an outpouring of unrestrained speech: He was in full spate.... What he was talking about was that they would send off one of these surface-to-air missiles.

in spate— = *in full spate 1:* The worm fisher has his opportunity when the streams are in spate.

in future • in the future

in future—from now on; from this time onwards: In future, in my presence, you will no longer wear these garments.

in the future—1. = *in future:* In the future I'll ask you not to make me look a fool before the servants. 2. at some time after the present but not immediately: The program can be resumed at its point of disruption at some time in the future.

Note: *The expression does not correlate in meaning with the phrase* ***for the future****— as far as the future is concerned:* For the future, we shall have to rely on our own efforts.

in glory • in one's glory

in glory—(of saints, etc.) in heavenly bliss and splendor: The crown is placed on the head of the maternal Virgin in glory.

in one's glory—in one's highest state of prosperity or enjoyment: I was in my glory when they gave me a standing ovation.

in good nick • in the nick

in good nick—(sl.) in good condition: It's not a local ale. Last year it turned up in a couple of pubs, sometimes in good nick other times not so good.

in the nick—1. *(also: in the nick of time)* at a critical moment when smth. urgently requires to be done: Opening our mail we were relieved to discover the catalog had arrived. Just in the nick. 2. *(sl.)* at a police station or in prison: Everybody in the nick had already been dubbed up for the night.

in good time • in one's own good time

in good time—1. early enough (when there is no risk of being late): I'd like to reach Salisbury in good time to take a look at the city's many charms. 2. in a short amount of time: I've never been able to make that trip in good time. 3. *(also: all in good time)* in due course: If we can see any problems ahead, we'll tell you in good time and work through them with you.

in one's own good time—(also: in one's own time) at a time and rate of one's own choosing: Don't rush the job. Let me do it in my own good time.

in grease • in the grease

in grease—(of an animal) fat and fit for killing: The harts are "in grease" from August to the middle of October.

in the grease—(of sheep's wool) not cleansed when shearing: If you wash the sheep you should do it thoroughly, for otherwise you had better shear in the grease.

Note: *Neither expression correlates in meaning with the phrase* ***be greased****—(sl.) be drunk:* Look at him stumble around! He is so greased he can hardly stand on his own two feet!

in green • in the green

in green—1. wearing green clothes: The Glaistig is a female fairy ... sometimes described as a little, stout woman, clothed in green. 2. *executed or finished* in various shades of green color:

The painting is finely executed in green, gold, cream, rust brown and a hint of blue.

in the green—1. in the period of youthful growth: All disobedience is anarchy, young anarchy, anarchy in the green. 2. *(of instruments)* showing safe readings: These coolers were installed in Dick Hansen's Kittyhawk which has had its temperature in the green ever since.

in half • in halves

in half—1. *divide or tear* into two equal parts: He and Meyer each signed half of a one dollar bill, tore it in half and kept each other's halves, just for good luck. 2. *(also: by half) reduce* by fifty percent of the original amount: He had priced rolltops in a downtown department store and knew he had cut the cost in half.

in halves— = *in half 1:* When a square cut in halves makes two triangles, those two triangles are still only the two halves of the square.

in hard condition • in hard conditions

in hard condition—*(Sport)* in good shape; physically fit: The horses are both in hard condition, so it [race] can come off in ten days.

in hard conditions—undergoing hardships: The distinction is blurred by species that grow periodically in hard conditions and aperiodically where they are protected.

in haste • in one's haste

in haste—in a hurry: It is the general fault of physicians, they are so in haste, that they never hear out the case.

in one's haste—owing to one's haste or hurry: In my haste I forgot to lock the car door.

in heaven • in the skies

in heaven—in the celestial abode of immortal beings: This woman actually imagines that there will be no slaves in heaven.

in the skies—*(also: in the clouds)* not acting according to the realities of life; given to day-dreaming: He is a philosopher. His mind is always in the skies.

Note: *The expression does not correlate in meaning with the phrase* ***on cloud nine****—(also: on cloud seven) extremely happy; in a euphoric state:* He was finding it impossible to get any sense out of Rolf, who was on cloud nine—or at least in a world of his own—for the entire week.

in leaf • in the leaf

in leaf—*(of a plant)* having its leaves expanded: The farmhouse can only just be seen from the road when the trees are not in leaf.

in the leaf—*(of tobacco)* unstemmed and uncut: In the process of manufacturing cigars they take tobacco in the leaf, put it first on racks to dry, then in barrels to sweat...

in league with someone • in the same league with someone

in league with someone—in partnership with smb., especially for a dubious purpose: The message is intercepted by the telegraph operator, who is in league with the outlaws and passes the information along to them.

in the same league with someone—*(usually negat.)* in the same class or on the same level of excellence as another person: It is undesirable to admit someone who is "not in the same league" with typical students at that school. *Cf.: out of one's league with someone—surrounded by people who are more skilful and experienced than oneself:* I have only played drums for three quarters of a year; I am out of my league with the guys in this band.

in line for something • in line with something

in line for something—likely to receive smth. such as promotion, etc.: The decision to place him in command had been made hastily; he knew that he had not been in line for such a post.

in line with something—in agreement or harmony with smth.: You must keep project activities and resources in line with your plans or adjust your plans accordingly.

in milk • in the milk

in milk—*(of a cow)* giving milk: When people talk of cream, and ask how many cows you have, they mean in milk.

in the milk—*(of grain)* of a milky consistency because of incomplete maturity: Sweet corn, is corn gathered before it is ripe: it is called green corn, or corn in the milk.

in no condition • on no condition

in no condition—unable to do smth. because of an illness, old age, etc.: I was in no condition to register the details of arriving in the hospital ward.

on no condition—in no circumstances: You must on no condition tell him what has happened.

in no humor • out of humor

in no humor—*(also: not in the humor)* unwilling or not feeling inclined to do smth.: I was, however, in no humor for talking, and made few remarks in reply.

out of humor—displeased; in a bad mood: Notwithstanding he had set his features to the semblance of a smile, I could perceive he was out of humor.

in no position • out of position

in no position—unable to do smth. because of circumstances: Unfortunately, they were in no position to help us.

out of position—*(Sport)* not in the correct place or facing the wrong direction: An attempt to "steal" the ball from a good dribbler often leaves the defensive player out of position.

in no shape • not in shape

in no shape—1. not in good enough condition or state of health: A tired child is simply in no shape to learn new math lessons or improve reading. 2. *(also: in no shape or form)* in no manner; not at all: If he acted wrongfully, it was in no shape by any precept or example.

not in shape—*(also: out of shape)* 1. not having the right shape: That hat of yours doesn't seem to be in shape. 2. *(usually of an athlete)* not well trained; in bad physical form: I think Ali is not in shape for his forthcoming fight.

in no way • no way

in no way—*(also: in no shape)* in no manner; not at all: The product we bargained for in no way resembles what we end up with.

no way—1. not a chance; under no circumstances: There was just no way I could pay my way through school without a job. 2. *(exclam.)* absolutely not: "Have you paid for the repair yet?" "No way! Not until we know for sure that the computer is actually working." 3. *(exclam.)* you don't say so; how surprising: "Hey, I saw Ellie out with Andrew last night." "No way!"

in number • in numbers

in number—in sum total; altogether: The cavalry were about a thousand in number.

in numbers—1. in large amount or quantity: Cape carts driven by Malays rattled up and down the streets in numbers. 2. *(of books)* published in a series of separate parts: I consider it vulgar, and below the dignity of literature, to publish in numbers.

in office • in the office

in office—1. inside a room used as a place of business: When the boss is in office she does not take lunch, comes in extra early and leaves late. 2. in an official position of duty or authority: Each President will be in office for five years, and one person can be elected as President only twice.

in the office— = *in office 1:* Just because the boss is not in the office doesn't necessarily mean he is not working.

in olden days • in the old days

in olden days—(formal) in former times; in times long past *(also: in days of old):* In olden days audiences took the equivalent of a cut lunch to the theater and expected to be entertained for hour after hour.

in the old days—long ago; years ago: We descended the hill, and, passing by the waterhead his father so loved in the old days of his carriage tours, we drove to the church.

in on it • on it

in on it—(also: in at it) taking part in an activity; involved in smth.: We're sure of one thing—it wasn't a one-man job. But were there two, three, or four of them in on it?

on it—1. *(U.S. sl.)* well able to do smth.; in control of a situation or a task: You bet he could cook. He was just on it. 2. *(Austral. sl.)* drinking heavily: When he was on it, and wanted another drink ... he never had to press the bell, but pressed the button with a bullet.

in on something • on the in with something

in on something—know smth. that isn't common knowledge: As Tommy, who was in on the plot, kept Maranzano busy in the office, the killers disarmed his bodyguards.

Note: *The expression does not correlate in meaning with the phrase* ***in for something****—used of smb. due for a promotion, punishment, etc.:* That gentlemen is in for a rude surprise some morning soon.

on the in with something—(U.S. coll.) well familiar with smth.: Any more information would be appreciated as I pride myself being on the "in" with Matthew's films.

in on the kill • on the kill

in on the kill—(also: in at the kill) present at the downfall of smth. or when smth. dramatic happens: Congress was due to defeat the bill, and I went to Washington so I could be in on the kill.

on the kill—(of an animal) having the intention of killing (as for food): The bison carcass was on this side of the river in some gravel. A grizzly was on the kill...

in one's bones • on one's bones

in one's bones—(coll.) know or feel smth. instinctively, without proof: I knew in my bones that he was altogether too obviously foreign to be of any interest to me.

on one's bones—(NZ sl.) hard up; destitute *(also: on the bone):* Ronny Dancy's on his bones again, I'm afraid.

in one's book • in someone's books

in one's book—in the opinion of a person: In his book the function of television was to edify, not to entertain.

Note: *The expression does not correlate in meaning with the phrase* ***in the book****—used of existing norms, laws, etc.:* Although Daisy entertained pretentious of grandeur, her dinner party violated every rule in the book.

in someone's books—(also: in someone's good books) in favor with a person: I was so much in his books, that at his decease he left me his lamp.

in one's day • on one's day

in one's day—(also: in one's days) 1. during one's lifetime: And did not he [Bacon] cling to geocentricism, which was still prevailingly current in his day? 2. in a period of one's success, prosperity, etc.: I know of one eminent man of science, who was a burning and shining light in his day.

on one's day—when performing as well as one can: On his day he's the finest goalkeeper in the country.

in one's eyes • to one's eyes

in one's eyes—(also: in one's eye) 1. in one's imagination; in one's mind: I still have in my eyes the magic days spent on the mountains with a lot of great people! 2. in one's judgment; in one's view: For the life of him he could not make the thing seem right or legal in his eyes.

to one's eyes—(also: to one's eye) as one sees it: To my eyes, the most beautiful thing to paint is large vistas of land. The land has its own harmony rich with shapes and with endlessly changing colors.

in one's grasp • within one's grasp

in one's grasp—said of smth. firmly controlled: President Nixon stated that we now had in our grasp a peace with honor instead of a peace with surrender.

within one's grasp—said of smth. one is very likely to gain or achieve: Just when the promised land seemed to be within their grasp, the Greeks suffered ignominious defeat.

in one's mind • on one's mind

in one's mind—in one's thoughts: Miss Quested, who always said exactly what was in her mind, announced that she was desirous of seeing the real India.

Note: *The expression is not equivalent in meaning to the phrase* ***in one's head****— in one's memory:* I don't know how the chairman keeps all those figures in his head.

on one's mind—1. said of smth. occupying one's thoughts, which causes worry or concern: I don't think I could have slept anyway because the thought of death was on my mind. 2. = *in one's mind:* Socrates even mocked some people saying to them whatever was on his mind...

in one's own right • within one's rights

in one's own right—because of personal qualifications: Apart from the assistance he gave Professor Jones in his research, he is a distinguished scientist in his own right.

within one's rights—not exceeding one's legal or moral authority: He's quite within his rights to demand an inquiry.

in one's own time • in one's time

in one's own time—1. in one's lifetime: While in his own time Terence's plays were not popular, many critics praised his graceful handling of the Latin language. 2. in one's free time; outside working hours: He wasn't able to finish the job at the office, so he had to do it in his own time. 3. *(also: in one's own good time)* at a time and rate of one's own choosing: Open learning offers the learner flexible learning opportunities—the learner can work in his own time.

Note: *The expression does not fully correlate in meaning with the phrase* ***on one's own time****—1. = in one's own time 2:* My work as assistant editor is only a sideline. Since I do it largely on my own time, I avoid extra work and correspondence. 2. *(do smth.) free of charge; without being paid:* I answer questions on my own time. I mean that I do it free of charge, not as part of a paid job.

in one's time—1. = *in one's own time 1:* Whereas in his time few animal examples of the moral emotions were known, we know now that there are many parallels in primate behavior. 2. earlier in one's life: He's a good enough player, but I've seen better in my time. 3. at a previous period in one's life when a person was young: "In my time," said the old man, "a gentleman would always give a lady his seat on a bus."

in one's prime • in the prime of life

in one's prime—in the period of life when a person is most prosperous and successful: Robinson was an amazing player in his prime and a lot of us are probably too young to remember it.

in the prime of life—in the period of life when a person is at the peak of health and beauty: Multiple Sclerosis is the most common neurological disorder affecting young adults in the prime of life.

in one's right mind • in the right mind

in one's right mind—healthy in mind; sane: He is not in his right mind ... he is talking nonsense, and is stark mad.

in the right mind—in a proper or favorable disposition: Ask him after a good meal, just when he is in the right mind.

in one's sight • in one's sights

in one's sight—1. in one's vision: As we climbed the stairs of the subway station, Big Ben was waiting to be the first thing in our sight! 2. in one's opinion; in one's view: The fact of his being a money-maker was redeemed in their sight by his devotion to music. 3. regarded as a prospective objective: For at least one night, the talk will be of the victory Martin had in his sight and the way Harvick yanked it from him.

in one's sights—1. visible through the sights of one's rifle, etc.: I had a large buck in my sights, clicked off the safety, hesitated, and then lowered the rifle. 2. = *in one's sight 3:* Now she had it in her sights — a wonderful mansion flat overlooking the Thames at Chiswick.

in one's way • on one's way

in one's way—1. situated along one's route: I'll take that book back for you; the library is in my way as I go to the town. 2. placed so as to be an obstruction or cause inconvenience: If there is a physical obstacle in our way, we move it, jump over it or break it down. Mental obstacles are different.... 3. within the limitations of one's character: "Prendy's not so bad in his way," said Grimes, "but he can't keep order."

on one's way—1. on a journey; going to a place: On our way to Sidon we repeatedly encountered unknown ruins. 2. = *in one's way 1:* We stopped to see Harris quite often as his house was on our way to and from downtown Winfield. 3. in good prospect of smth.: Don't hundreds of thousands of immigrants on their way to becoming U.S. citizens work hard and serve in the military.

in order • in orders

in order—1. in the sequence in which things occur: I will answer your three questions in order. 2. *(of a machine, etc.)* working properly: Before setting out on a long journey, see that your car is in order. 3. *(also: in place)* be due or appropriate: That phrase means different things to different people, so some explanation is in order. 4. in conformity with the prescribed mode of proceeding in debates, etc.: The chairman ruled that the question was in order.

in orders—said of smb. appointed or ordained minister of the Christian church: He was in orders, but was not a placed minister.

Note: *The expression does not correlate in meaning with the phrase* ***under orders****—(also: on orders) acting under authoritative instructions:* Congress ratified the bill and sent it to the President who was under orders from his backers to sign it into law.

in order of something • in the order of something

in order of something—arranged according to some specified criterion: This arrangement of items in order of size or other value, is called by statisticians an array.

in the order of something—1. approximately; roughly: Britain's contribution is something in the order of five per cent. 2. = *in order of something:* Counting from below upwards the members arise in the order of their age.

in ordinary • in the ordinary way

in ordinary—1. added to the titles of people regularly serving royalty: The King's painter to Charles IX was Henry Mellein, and his painter-in-ordinary was Conrad de Vulcop. 2. *(of a ship)* laid up for repairs; not fit for service: When ships are said to be in ordinary ... they are in one of three stages of readiness for commission and active service.

in the ordinary way—1. as is usual: Had it been decided to wash the coal in the ordinary way instead of dry cleaning it, additional ovens would have been necessary. 2. if the circumstances were normal or usual: In the ordinary way he would have come with us, but he is not feeling well.

in pain • in pains

in pain—suffering physical pain or discomfort caused by injury or disease: They lay rolling themselves on the ground, heavily groaning in pain.

in pains—1. *(of a woman)* in the throes of childbirth: I remember that in the film, the husband of the woman in pains was sitting far from the scene. 2. = *in pain:* She saw herself test it on a criminal — a rapist, and she saw how much he was in pains. 3. *(followed by Infinitive)* making a particular effort to do smth.: He was in pains to stress that the main task of government was the defense of the rich against the poor.

Note: *The expression does not fully correlate in meaning with the phrase* ***at pains****— = in pains 3:* Linda was at pains to see that no one was left out.

in part • in parts

in part—partly; to some extent: The improvement was brought about in part by the Trade Union Movement. *Cf.: in good part—to a great extent; largely:* These mechanisms are intensely studied and in good part understood.

in parts—1. *(of a book)* published in installments: Once the craze was all for issuing volumes in parts; today part publication is almost unknown. 2. *(of a melody)* performed by particular voices or instruments: The old barcarole was sung in parts, at stem and stern of the same boat, by its own gondoliers.

in particular • in the particular

in particular—especially; to an exceptional degree: One large star in particular excited our admiration.

in the particular—*(dated)* in a specific case: Though he was often in the general the avowed enemy of oppression, we never ... found him so in the particular.

in pink • in the pink

in pink—1. wearing pink clothes, especially a scarlet hunting-coat: Although not in pink, I was the best mounted man in the field. 2. *executed or finished* in pink color: Decorated in pink and green the room boasts a king size feather bed and Jacuzzi for two.

in the pink—*(coll.)* in the most perfect condition; in very good health: I am writing these lines to say I am still in the pink and hoping you are the same.

in place • in places

in place—1. in the proper position: One bathroom seemed all but finished.... A toilet bowl was in place. 2. *(also: in order)* be due or appropriate: Some explanation is in place to justify the seriousness and necessity of this project to everyone.

in places—in some parts but not others: In places, the trees on both sides formed a tunnel over the river, masking off the sunlight.

in pledge • under pledge

in pledge—said of an article left with a person until the giver has paid a debt, etc.: Pressed for a sum of money ... he had put his Sunday coat in pledge.

under pledge—placed under an obligation to do or not to do smth.: The minister has been released from custody under pledge not to leave town.

in pocket • in the pocket

in pocket—(coll.) 1. having money available: Follow my advice and you will be well in pocket. 2. said of the amount of money left over or gained as profit: At the end of their journey, they are above a hundred crowns in pocket.

in the pocket—(U.S. Drug users) enjoying the best part of a psychedelic intoxication: It was a golden time, and I was right in the pocket.

See also: out of one's own pocket / out of pocket.

in possession of something • in the possession of someone

in possession of something—having smth. as one's own: It is illegal for any person convicted of a felony to be in possession of any firearm or ammunition.

in the possession of someone—held or possessed by a person: Police have now recovered eight of the stolen weapons, all of which were found in the possession of criminal elements.

in principle • on principle

in principle—in essence; in general: An electric toothbrush is not very different in principle from an ordinary toothbrush. You still have a stick with a brush on the end.

on principle—as a matter of principle; because of one's moral convictions: There was a time when I could not read Pope, but disliked him on principle.

in print • in the print

in print—1. in printed form: These uses were probably colloquial with fishers and seamen some time before they appeared in print. 2. *(of a book, etc.)* published; available from the publisher: No sooner in print, than out of print. The reviews revere him.

in the print—in the printing trade: For our mother, only a minimum of education was required to ensure a good safe job in the print.

in proportion of something • in proportion to something

in proportion of something—in terms of how much there is of each thing (in a combination): Make a syrup of the sugar and water in proportion of a pint of sugar to a quart of water...

in proportion to something—1. as compared with smth.; considered with reference to smth.: His expenditure on pleasure and luxuries is rather high in proportion to his income. 2. corresponding to smth. in degree or amount: The subjects ought to contribute towards the support of the government in proportion to their respective abilities.

in public • in the public eye

in public— do smth. in such a way that the public may see, hear, or know: They will not admit it in public, but ... they also know of these problems.

in the public eye—1. *(of people or things)* much publicized by the media: His investigations on behalf of these men kept him in the public eye. 2. in the opinion of the public: He regretted, I think, that in the public eye he was regarded as the guy who had failed and ended up in the gutter.

in Queer street • on the queer

in Queer street—(UK dated) heavily in debt; in financial trouble: Now don't you go doing anything that'll land you in Queer Street.

on the queer—(Underworld) living dishonestly: He was convinced that he could get along as well on the queer as he could by keeping straight.

in question • out of the question

in question— under consideration; forming the subject of discourse: While Dr. Bits really is an authority, he is not an authority on the issue in question.

out of the question—impossible in the circumstances; not worth considering: Any effort by the military to defy civilian authority is now out of the question.

Note: *The expression does not correlate in meaning with the phrase* ***not the question****— not the matter; not the point:* Yes, I heard all you said, but his health is not the question. Is he thoroughly dependable?

in receipt of something • on receipt of something

in receipt of something—1. *(formal)* having received smth.: We are in receipt of your letter of the 17th of January. 2. receive smth. on a regular basis: All people who are in receipt of fixed incomes ... benefit from the fall in prices.

on receipt of something—as soon as smth. is received: On receipt of your instructions we will send you the goods.

in recess • in the recess

in recess—said with reference to a period in which a legislative body is not sitting, or to a break during court proceedings: Congress is now in recess until the first week of December.

Note: *The expression does not correlate in meaning with the phrase* ***in recession****— used of a period of economic decline:* Investors poured into Asia because their own economies were in recession.

in the recess—in an indented or hollowed-out space set into a wall: The street was deserted except for a man standing in the recess of the entry to the apartment building.

in red • in the red

in red—1. wearing red clothes: A beautiful girl dressed in red entered the room and a wave of admiring gasps and whispers followed her. 2. *(coll., also: in red ink)* in a bad financial position: We've got to put forth our best efforts from now till the end of the month, or we'll be in red on the books. 3. *executed or finished* in various shades of red: The fragments discovered showed linear architectural decoration, executed in red, blue, and white.

in the red— = in red 2: If I don't get some money from somewhere very soon, I shall be in the red. *Cf.: out of the red— (coll.) solvent; operating at a profit:* Most of the airlines are now out of the red and profitable.

in request • on request

in request—(of goods, services, etc.) very popular; much sought after: His novels are not much in request nowadays.

on request—(also: at request) whenever asked for: Further information will be supplied on request.

in safety • with safety

in safety—1. in a safe state or position: Cut off by the rising waters, the boys climbed on to a ledge of rock, where they remained in safety. 2. *do smth.* without running any risk: The people of this city can go where they want to go, do what they have to do and do it in safety.

with safety— = in safety 2: That ladder looks rather rickety; don't attempt to climb it unless you are sure you can do it with safety.

in secret • in the secret

in secret—1. secretly; in private: Men of the most different characters ... resemble each other in the practice of nursing in secret some pet superstition. *2.* in strict confidence: This story is told in secret, as it were, because the people were afraid to tell it openly.

in the secret—(predic.) sharing a secret; privately aware of smth.: One of her maids who was in the secret revealed the truth.

in service • in the service

in service—1. *(of a machine, etc.)* in operation: The latest fighter-bomber is as fast as any fighter yet in service anywhere in the world. 2. employed as a domestic servant: I suppose you see it as somewhat anachronistic — a young girl "in service."

in the service—while serving in the armed forces: Riggs had been wounded in the service. He was a hero and a fine young American.

in shore • on shore

in shore—on the water near the shore: We saw a small ship in shore ... plying up the coast.

on shore—ashore; on land: Water on the ship will be safe, but only drink bottled water when on shore.

in show • on show

in show—in appearance only: By an unfortunate accident the actor was stabbed in reality, and not merely in show.

Note: *The expression does not correlate in meaning with the phrase* ***for show****—for the sake of ostentatious demonstration:* The ornaments serve no useful purpose; they are only put there for show.

on show— being exhibited; on view: Some of her paintings are on show in the local art gallery.

in so many words • so many words

in so many words—(usually negat.) stated in these exact words: That the object was to bring Romayne and Stella together ... was as plain to him as if he had heard it confessed in so many words.

so many words—(of documents, utterances, etc.) nothing more than mere words: Such a law is just so many words without continued commitment and oversight by the legislative and executive branches.

in someone's arms • in someone's hands

in someone's arms—held by a person (lovingly) in both arms: On the dance floor, Kezia was whirling slowly in the arms of the Baron.

in someone's hands—in smb.'s power; under smb.'s control: She's going to change the history of the country and the fate of the people is now in her hands.

in spirit • in spirits

in spirit—inwardly; in one's mind: Such as I are free in spirit when our limbs are chained.

in spirits—(also: in high spirits) in a cheerful mood: His time is pretty much taken up in keeping his relation in spirits.

in the air • up in the air

in the air—1. not inside a house or building: We have taken our last walk in the air and having succeeded in tiring ourselves feel free to go to bed unashamed. 2. aboard an aircraft; in flight: After all, Short's Empire class flying boats fifty years ago could offer a bed in the air. 3. *(of plans, questions, etc.)* still uncertain; remaining undecided: As for other ever changing events, next year's plans are still in the air. 4. *(also: in the wind)* rumored or suspected but not definitely known: What changes they will make nobody knows, but there is something in the air. 5. said of the general mood or atmosphere: There was a feeling of joy in the air. Men who had never voted before said that they felt like human beings for the first time in their lives. 6. *(of military position)* uncovered or unprotected This left the French First Army's flank in the air, forcing it to withdraw as well.

Note: *The expression does not fully correlate in meaning with the phrase* ***in the open air****—*1. = *in the air 1*: In the early evening Ernest went to speak to a group of the neighboring inhabitants in the open air. 2. *unsheltered or unprotected from the elements:* I myself saw new motors and parts piled up unprotected in the open air.

up in the air—1. = *in the air 2:* If you're up in the air and something goes wrong, you pull that parachute, and the whole plane goes down slowly. 2. = *in the air 3:* Our plans for a vacation are still up in the air, but we'll be going sometime after the new year. 3. *(coll.)* angry; excited: He is all up in the air because he had to wait a few minutes.

Note: *Neither expression correlates in meaning with the phrase* ***on the air****—*1. *speaking over the radio:* If Bucky Maynard doesn't like you, you got a lot of trouble. I mean, he can destroy you on the air. *2. (of a program) being broadcast:* McGannon is asking that stations be obliged to set aside a time when only children's programs would be allowed on the air.

in the blinking of an eye • without blinking an eye

in the blinking of an eye—very quickly: Mrs. Shaw's mood changes in the blinking of an eye during an hour long interview — sullen one moment, warm and witty the next.

without blinking an eye—without hesitation or remorse: Why is the police chief, a loving family man at home, able to torture a man to the edge of death without blinking an eye?

in the bottom of the bag • in the bottom of the barrel

in the bottom of the bag—(also: at the bottom of the bag) remaining as a last resource or possibility: If this be done, which is in the bottom of the bag, and must be done, we shall be able to buoy up our reputation.

Note: *The expression does not correlate in meaning with the phrase* ***in the bag****—(sl.)* 1. *as good as certain; virtually assured:* Winning this game is in the bag — we're leading by five goals to nil. 2. *totally intoxicated:* One look at Bill's eyes was enough to tell me he was in the bag. *Cf.: half in the bag—(sl.) slightly drunk:* He had a shotgun next to the chair, and he was half in the bag from booze. 3. *(UK Army WWI, WWII) taken prisoner or killed in battle:* Tell him if he tries to stick it out, he'll only end in the bag.

in the bottom of the barrel—(also: at the bottom of the barrel) among the worst or the least desirable elements of a particular group: Graduating in the 15 percent of one's class from a bottom of the barrel school, still leaves you in the bottom of the barrel.

in the box • in the ice box

in the box—(coll.) 1. in the jury box: By his country, represented by twelve men in a box, he will be tried. 2. in a refrigerator: "Beer's in the box," he pointed to the fridge in the kitchen and jostled back toward the den. 3. *live* in extremely confined, second-rate quarters: You live in a box down by the river.... Is that how we're supposed to live?

in the ice box—1. = *in the box 2:* He found a lot of food in the icebox and had fixed a big salad. 2. *(U.S. sl.)* in a mortuary *(also: in cold storage):* He's got seven stiffs down there in the icebox.

in the broad light of day • in the cold light of day

in the broad light of day—(also: in broad daylight) said of smth. done openly in the daytime: They [actors] have shown themselves to us without their make-up in the broad light of day.

in the cold light of day—when one's feelings of excitement, anger, etc. are over and one is calm: In the cold light of day, I regretted my hasty decision.

in the dark • in the limelight

in the dark—in ignorance; without information: Our generation was left in the dark about the harmful effects of cigarettes.

in the limelight—(also: in the spotlight) in the center of attention: We knew our daughter would grow up to be an actor. She was always in the limelight as a child.

in the disguise of someone • under the disguise of someone

in the disguise of someone—1. disguised or dressed as smb. else: There was a masquerade, in which Charles and some of his courtiers appeared in the disguise of satyrs. 2. using a specific guise as a means for smth.: He had appeared in the disguise of a cop for two reasons. He had been certain that the commissioner would not release any detailed information...

under the disguise of someone— = in the disguise of someone 2: The thief gained entry to the premises under the disguise of an inspector from the Electricity Board.

in the face of it • on the face of it

in the face of it—in defiance of smth.; notwithstanding smth.: He didn't have an easy life, and in the face of it his humor was remarkable.

on the face of it—on a merely superficial view: The improvements in housing standards should, on the face of it, have helped to intensify family cohesiveness.

in the face of something • on the face of something

in the face of something—in the presence of smth.; when confronted with smth.: He can't possibly win in the face of such difficulties.

on the face of something—from appearances of smth.; judging from smth.: On the face of the results, the examination was too difficult.

in the field • on the field

in the field—1. in an area of grassland for cattle or arable land for crops: Hundreds of combines will be in the fields by Wednesday. 2. in an outdoor athletic or sports area: Each player in the field follows the progress of the game and constantly tracks the movement of his eight teammates. 3. *(Military)* at the scene of combat: They needed a more effective way of using military forces in the field. 4. in the area of a particular subject: The purpose of this scholarship is to promote excellence in the field of music by offering incentives to talented students. 5. away from base or outside of laboratories: A number of the projects involve a combination of laboratory investigations with work carried out in the field.

on the field—1. = *in the field 1:* Last year nothing grew on the field where it [pesticide] had been applied but rattle-weed. 2. = *in the field 2:* I am fortunate to say that my team is rare. We are brimming with excitement, which can be felt on the field and in our houses at night. 3. = *in the field 3:* This is not an intelligence failure but a severe operational failure. There is a lack of cooperation between the forces on the field.

in the heat of the moment • on the spur of the moment

in the heat of the moment—at the moment of the greatest emotional excitement: Small as she was, she looked as though in the heat of the moment she might hit him.

on the spur of the moment—acting on a sudden impulse; without deliberation: The crime of jealousy committed on the spur of the moment, makes poor material.

Note: *The expression does not correlate in meaning with the phrase* ***on the spur****—(UK dated) at full speed; with the utmost haste:* The servant rode away on the spur, to alarm the family at the mansion-house.

in the ketchup • on the sauce

in the ketchup—(U.S. sl.) said of a business, etc. that fails to show a profit: Ridgway has wound up in the ketchup trying to operate a gym.

on the sauce—(sl.) drinking heavily: You're not in debt, on the sauce, going gay ... I can't blackmail you.

in the light of something • in the spotlight of something

in the light of something—in consideration of smth.; for the reason given: No matter how many tests a scientist conducts, any given hypothesis may have to be thrown out in the light of new evidence.

in the spotlight of something—(predic.) at the center of smth.; getting most attention and interest *(also: in the limelight of something):* While stem cells are in the spotlight of research today, as recently as six years ago, scientists who worked on stem cells toiled in relative obscurity. *Cf.: steal the spotlight from someone—(also: steal the show from someone) do better than another person (in a theatrical production, etc.) and so make oneself the centre of attention:* Some Democrats fear Clinton will steal the spotlight from Kerry when he needs it most.

in the loose • on the loose

in the loose—(of things) not packed or tied up: Auctioneers thread their way through the lanes of tobacco "in the loose" on the warehouse floors.

on the loose—1. running around free after an escape from prison, captivity, etc.: Look out! There is a bear on the loose from the zoo. 2. free from the restraints of morality or discipline: Most kids enjoy being on the loose when they go to college.

in the make • on the make

in the make—(also: in the making) in an undeveloped state; being worked on: My homepage is still in the make, that is incomplete.

on the make—1. *(coll.)* trying to gain an advantage or profit: He struck me always as a sly nasty fellow, a bootlicker, always on the make. 2. = *in the make:* The shopping area is very pedestrian friendly with wide sidewalks and is still on the make. 3. *(sl.)* trying to win a person for sexual relationship: Does my online flirting make me look like someone constantly "on the make"?

in the money • on the money

in the money—(coll.) 1. having plenty of money: Being in the money at the moment, I said that of course I'd lend her any reasonable amount. 2. said of winners in a competition providing winnings money to bettors: After the first race, two of my horses were in the money.

on the money—(coll.) 1. exactly as desired: When you ensure information flows between your sales and marketing teams, the resulting marketing campaigns will be right on the money. 2. totally correct: I share them [ideas] with anyone who is interested and I add my predictions—some will be on the money and some will be way off base.

in the next world • in the second world

in the next world—is used of a state of existence after death: Priests performed many ceremonies to help the dead person on his journey to a happy life in the next world.

in the second world—in countries like Brazil, India, Russia, Vietnam and Malaysia that simultaneously have both first and third world characteristics: Everybody in the "second world" and "third world" wants to live like people in the "first world."

Note: *Neither expression correlates in meaning with the phrase* ***out of this world***—1. *out of touch with reality; unaware of the latest ideas, etc.:* The general atmosphere of living "out of this world" and "twenty years or so behind the rest of civilization" still hangs in there. 2. *very strange or bizarre:* They are working on advanced flying machines that might look "out of this world" to an uninformed observer. 3. *(of prices) exorbitant; unrealistic:* We liked the house very much, but the price they asked for it was out of this world. 4. *(coll.) excellent; superb:* We think you're out of this world as a cook. Absolutely lovely grub. 5. *(of prices) absurdly low:* Those qualities add up to out of this world prices for what wine experts say might be a little taste of heaven.

See also: in another world / on other worlds.

in the picture • in the pictures

in the picture—*(coll.)* 1. in an informed position: OK, now that you're one of us, I want you in the picture. 2. said of smth. probable or likely to happen: I'd like to travel, but it doesn't seem like it's in the picture for a year or so. 3. involved in a situation: If there were no children in the picture, he couldn't understand why she didn't just leave the man.

in the pictures—*(coll.)* in the movies: She had not the slightest wish to marry anybody from Lowdham Street.... No, she wanted some kind of Prince Charming like they had in the pictures.

in the pipeline • in the tube

in the pipeline—in a state of development or preparation: One such project in the pipeline aims to rehabilitate coastal ecosystems.

in the tube—*(sl.)* at risk: If you find yourself in the tube in this matter, just give me a ring.

in the right • on the right

in the right—morally correct in one's behavior or judgment: You are in the right in refusing to give in to them.

on the right—on the right side: Proceed for about one-half mile around a curve, passing three houses on the right.

in the road • on the road

in the road—1. within the area of the road as distinct from the pavement: Never stand in the road to hitchhike or conduct business with passing motorists. 2. in smb.'s way; obstructing passage: You're in the road—we can't work properly while you're standing there talking.

on the road—1. on the surface of the road: We had to drive very carefully, as there was ice on the road. 2. traveling (as a commercial traveler, etc.): We could not resist the sheltered table and chairs which make life on the road so much easier. 3. *(also: on the way)* in good prospect of smth.: She is now well on the road to becoming one of our most successful actresses.

See also: in the way / on the way.

in the saddle • on the saddle

in the saddle—1. riding a horse: She was hardly in the saddle before she called out "race you to the bridge." 2. in a position of leadership: It is his bad luck to be in the saddle when his country has to decide which road it is now going to follow.

on the saddle—on the seat of a bicycle or motorcycle: I was just sitting on the saddle pushing the bike along with my foot on the curb.

in the sea • on the sea

in the sea—in the waters of the sea: These fish are found in the seas along the North Atlantic coast of America.

on the sea—1. on the surface of the sea: On the sea ice seldom forms smoothly. Early storms break it and pack it in confusion. 2. on the coast, close to the sea-side: The duke abandoned the city of Benevento and went off to another city, which was situated on the sea.

Note: *Neither expression correlates in meaning with the phrase* ***at sea***—1. *(of a ship) far away from land:* If he knows Morse code, he may listen to messages from ships at sea. 2. *(also: all at sea) perplexed; confused:* The job was new to me, and for a few days I was quite at sea.

in the stocks • on the stocks

in the stocks—1. *(of money)* invested in shares in return for interest: Sir William had a fair estate in land, a large sum of money in the stocks.... 2. is used of an old instrument of punishment *(the person punished sitting with his ankles confined between two planks):* I have seen a man in the stocks as a punishment for drunkenness.

Note: *The expression does not correlate in meaning with the phrase* ***in stock***—*used of a supply of goods for sale, etc.:* We will have more bicycles in stock in a few weeks.

on the stocks—1. *(of ships)* in the process of being built: The *Mariner's Girl* is on the stocks and should be ready for sea in about six months. 2. in process of preparation or completion: This is one of his latest productions, but he has another musical on the stocks.

in the sun • under the sun

in the sun—exposed to light and warmth from the sun: People with paler skin may need just a few minutes in the sun at the beginning of the season.

under the sun—anywhere in the world: There's no nation under the sun that doesn't try to protect its military secrets.

in the track of someone • on the track of someone

in the track of someone—following the actual route taken by a person: From here I rushed straight to the Senate, right in the track of this man.

on the track of someone—in pursuit of smb. (in order to capture): The law commands that the police should always be on the track of criminals.

in the trade • in trade

in the trade—engaged in the particular business or industry: Of this number of whales, about half have been taken by five ships now in the trade.

in trade—engaged in commercial occupation (as a shopkeeper, etc.): Duncan Gregg had gone up the ladder a little. But not very much, he was still in trade.

in the way • on the way

in the way—1. placed so as to be an obstruction or cause inconvenience: I can't empty the bottle—there's a piece of cork in the way. 2. *(coll.)* said of smb. being around: I'm glad, too, to see you here. One feels safer when you're in the way. 3. in the manner: Broadband Internet brought about a shift in the way that people used their computers.

Note: *The expression does not fully correlate in meaning with the phrase* ***in a way***—1. *to a certain extent; in certain respects:* He considers himself clever, and in a way he is justified. 2. = *in the way 3:* America's government is designed in a way that attempts to ensure that all political groups have proportional representation.

on the way—1. moving towards a place; approaching: My friends have not arrived yet, but they are on the way. 2. *(of time)* drawing near: Christmas is on the way; we are in

November already. 3. *(also: on the road)* in good prospect of smth.: Once only a dream, artificial blood vessels are on the way to becoming reality. 4. *(of a child)* about to be born: We have four simply adorable grandchildren with another on the way. 5. *(of a woman)* pregnant: Elizabeth has become pregnant in her old age, and will have a son. She is already six months on the way.

See also: in the road / on the road.

in the white • in white

in the white—*(of manufactured articles)* in an unfinished or undyed state: Violin makers often say that a violin sounds better in the white than it does after it is varnished.

in white—1. wearing white clothes: The painting represents a girl in white standing on a dune. 2. *executed or finished* in white color: Our home is newly furnished and finished in white for light.

in the whole • on the whole

in the whole—*(also: as a whole)* considered in its entirety; in full: Council may approve the budget in part or in the whole.

on the whole—1. in general; from every point of view: They think Stalin maybe made a few mistakes but was on the whole a great guy. 2. for the most part: National Health surgeons on the whole remain disinclined to abort frivolously.

in the wild • in the wilds

in the wild—*(of animals) living* in an undomesticated state in their natural surroundings: In the wild, giant pandas are usually alone except for mothers with cubs.

in the wilds—1. far from normal habitation; remote from urban life and culture: My family used to live out in the wilds of Lynn Valley, in an old house. 2. = *in the wild:* These tour packages are designed to let you have the best wildlife experience through watching animals in the wilds.

in the world • in this world

in the world—1. on earth; in existence: He was considered to be one of the most famous artists in the world. 2. used as an intensifier in interrogative and negative contexts: If your actions tell an employee their job is too small for you to bother, then why in the world should they care?

Note: *The expression does not fully correlate in meaning with the phrase* ***in the wide world***—1. = *in the world 2:* He would never ... dare mention this encounter to a living soul, for who in the wide world would believe him? 2. *is used to imply contrast to one's own home or country:* A few years in the wide world and then back to the home paddock.

in this world—1. = *in the world 1:* I feel that of all the people in this world, the Indians could preserve this land and nature the best. 2. during our life on earth (as distinguished from the world beyond the grave): So long as we are in this world we are exposed to temptations, and need ever to be on our watch against them. *Cf.: in another world—(also: in the next world) used of a state of existence after death:* The interest of the Malabar widow, who burns herself with the corpse of her husband, is to recover him in another world.

in these days • in those days

in these days—at the present time: Even in these days of radio and satellite communications, the U.S. Navy uses the international alphabet flags.

in those days—during a period in the past: I'd prefer things the way they were. People were happier in those days and there was a great sense of community spirit.

in time • on time

in time—1. early enough for an activity; before it is too late to do smth.: I got there in time to see several friends I hadn't seen in two months. 2. in the end; after a while: Ted and Jim did not like each other at first but in time they became close friends. 3. *(Music)* in the right rhythm: You need to play in tune, but what about playing in time? Rhythm is part of the musician's trinity that also includes harmony and melody.

on time—1. at a prearranged or scheduled time; punctually: The train, which was due at four o'clock, arrived exactly on time. 2. *(U.S.)* on the installment plan; on credit: Everything was bought "on time," hardly any transactions involved cash.

Note: *The expression is not equivalent in meaning to the phrase* ***to time***— *in conformity with the scheduled time:* The buses on this route seldom run to time.

See also: on the clock / on the hour.

in touch • within touch

in touch—in communication or contact with a person: Moignon was in touch, on his behalf, with powerful American agencies.

Note: *The expression does not correlate in meaning with the phrase* ***at a touch***— *if touched, however lightly:* These patio doors slide open at a touch on warm summer days.

within touch—1. near enough to touch: The rough-hewn roof was within touch, and sometimes we had to stoop, to avoid hitting our heads. 2. within easy reach: Economic integration brought far-off countries closer. And what yesterday seemed unreality and distant future, today is within touch.

in tow • on tow

in tow—1. *(of a disabled vehicle)* pulled along by the towing vehicle: The broken-down car was taken in tow by a lorry. 2. *(coll.)* following or accompanying smb.: Signaling to the doorman to park his car, he disappears into the hotel with the blond in tow. 3. under smb.'s control or guidance: Henry took me in tow and suffered my impatience with the conservative ways of our established institution.

on tow—*(UK rare, also: under tow)* = *in tow 1:* A man serving a driving ban was jailed for four months after being drunk in charge of a car on tow.

in trial • on trial

in trial—said of lawyers' activities during trials: "Will you be home for dinner tonight?" "I don't think so. I'm in trial all week, so I have to work late again."

on trial—1. being tried in a court of law for an offence: All those in the "know" maintain that it was a man who was never on trial. 2. in a state of probation (until it is seen whether a person is suitable for a position, etc.): I will take the maid for a month on trial. 3. when tried out or tested: Mr. Boyes found on trial that the stone would scratch glass. "I believe it to be a diamond," he observed gravely.

Note: *Neither expression correlates in meaning with the phrase* ***at the trial***— *in the course of the legal process in a court of law:* They were not allowed to say what they wanted to say at the trial.

in trust • on trust

in trust—*(of money)* held or invested for a person by another individual or an organization: His mother's money was left in trust for him to acquire at the age of twenty-five.

on trust—1. *(of declarations, etc.) accept* without asking for proof: Official statements are no longer taken on trust. The phenomenon is called the "credibility gap." 2. on credit: The man who purchases on trust not only pays for the trust, but he also pays his due share of what the tradesman loses by trust.

in turn • in turns

in turn—1. one at a time in sequence; one after the other: He asked each of the boys in turn whether they had taken the book. 2. *(also: in one's turn)* when one's turn or opportunity comes: I took Sally out to lunch, and she took me out in turn. 3. *(of two or more people) do smth.* alternating at regular intervals: A team of volunteers take it in turn to look after preschool children.

in turns—(also: by turns) = in turn 3: The boys will take it in turns to row for some estimated four days.

in two • in two's

in two—separate or break in two pieces: He described how the ship broke in two clean across the middle during a violent storm.

in two's—organize people or objects in groups of two: For this game the players have to arrange themselves in two's.

in velvet • on velvet

in velvet—(of a deer) having the antlers covered with velvet: While this bark or skin remains on the horn the stag is said to be in velvet and is not hunted.

on velvet—(sl.) in a position of ease or advantage: Before that we were on velvet, but the instant he appeared everything was changed.

in view of something • on view of something

in view of something—taking smth. into consideration; on account of smth.: It is important to air a number of issues—particularly in view of his mission in Sheffield next year.

on view of something—(formal) on visual inspection of smth., specifically by way of inquest: Inquests were held on view of the bodies on Tuesday ... and evidence given in substance as follows.

See also: at the view of something / with the view of something.

incident to something • incidental to something

incident to something—forming a natural or expected part of smth.: Mrs. McMechen felt unequal to the hardships incident to the life of the itinerant Methodist minister.

incidental to something—usually accompanying but not forming the necessary part of smth.: He experienced the discomforts incidental to the primitive mode of travel which was the only one available.

indemnify someone against something • indemnify someone for something

indemnify someone against something—provide protection against possible loss or damage: A system of insurance must be devised, which shall indemnify them against all the accidents and reverses of life.

indemnify someone for something—pay compensation to a person for loss or damage actually suffered: I will indemnify you for any expenses you may incur on my behalf.

Indian red • Red Indian

Indian red—a red pigment originally obtained from the East Indies: The red iron oxides found as natural deposits include Indian red.

Red Indian—a person of the aboriginal race of North America: The Red Indians of America had their own particular craft of basketry.

infant school • nursery school

infant school—(UK) part of a primary school for children between the ages of five and seven: Children who are five before July 1st can be accepted to the Infant School.

nursery school—a school for children, between the ages of three and five, who are not old enough to attend kindergarten: The nursery school stresses learning through play.

inlay something • lay in something

inlay something—set pieces of material such as ivory, silver, etc. into a surface to form a decorative pattern: In this technique, brass is drawn into a thin wire to inlay it on wood.

lay in something—acquire and store smth. for future use: I trudged home with my empty backpack to get more supplies that I wanted to lay in for the winter.

inner man • inside man

inner man—1. the spiritual part of man; the soul or mind: Self-reflection is the only method of learning what is the inner man or mind that our action expresses. 2. *(joc.)* one's appetite for food: I wonder if a little something could be provided to pacify the inner man?

inside man—1. smb. employed within a building; a man working indoors: Counting the number of hours worked, the outside men are given an equal amount of employment with the inside men. 2. a trusted person within an organization: With our inside man being a part of the President's staff, we should not have any problem dealing with the White House. 3. an undercover agent working in an organization: Ward has just informed me that our inside man made contact with him.

See also: outer man / outside man.

innocent in something • innocent of something

innocent in something—inexperienced and ignorant about smth.: How could such a consummate political survivor be portrayed as not simply innocent in the ways of the world, but so completely dependent?

innocent of something—1. not guilty of smth. a person may be accused of: The prisoner denied that he had ever stolen any platina, and said he was innocent of the charge. 2. free from smth.; devoid of smth.: The tiny window was innocent of glass, and the northwesterly wind came in an icy stream through the aperture.

input something • put in something

input something—1. contribute information or suggestion: Lawyers are good places to go for advice, but I wanted to input the idea of talking to the bank manager too. 2. enter data into a computer: Your chosen password should be remembered as you will need to input this later when using the service.

put in something—1. include or add smth.: Don't forget to put in your daytime work number and your home number so we can better assist you. 2. make a claim or application for smth.: Naturally, McDermott put in a plea of innocent. I don't know that his plea involved insanity as the reason. 3. make a remark, especially to add smth. to a conversation: I'm sure other members want to put in a couple of words on this issue. 4. make a telephone call: I put in a call to his office through the company's toll-free telephone number. 5. devote time or effort: The filmmakers put in much work to ensure that it was as historically accurate as possible.

inquire about someone • inquire of someone

inquire about someone—(also: inquire after someone) ask about a person's welfare or state of health: He inquired about you, and learned that you were not among the wounded.

inquire of someone—put questions to a person: The old lady inquired of a bystander the reason for the delay in the Queen's arrival.

inquire about something • inquire for something

inquire about something—(also: inquire after something) seek information about smth.: Where ought I to go to inquire about London bus tours?

inquire for something—ask the whereabouts of some place one wishes to find: This lady is inquiring for the furnishing department.

Note: *a) The expression does not fully correlate in meaning with the phrase **ask for something**—*1. *request smth.:* The most important step towards treating depression — and sometimes the most difficult — is asking for help. 2. = *inquire for something:* As we got off, we overheard a tourist asking for the Museum of Anthropology, so we followed her. 3. *(in the phrase "ask for trouble") act in a way that is likely to cause problems or trouble:* I think taking a hot cup of anything in a car is asking for trouble.

*b) Neither expression correlates in meaning with the phrase **inquire into something**— examine or investigate smth.:* The commission may refer the matter to the board with a direction to inquire into the matter.

inquire after someone • inquire for someone

inquire after someone—(also: inquire about someone) ask about a person's welfare or state of health: He was inquiring after you and sent his kind regards.

inquire for someone—ask to see a person; ask if smb. is available: While you were out, a young man rang up inquiring for you.

insensible of something • insensible to something

insensible of something—unaware of smth.; unresponsive to smth.: She seemed wholly insensible of the honor done to her.

insensible to something—unable to understanding other people's feelings, hardships, etc.: He was one of those men who are quite insensible to the suffering they cause.

insensitive about something • insensitive to something

insensitive about something—not easily offended or worried about smth.: Ping mentally berated herself for being so absolutely insensitive about the cleanliness of his house.

insensitive to something—1. not susceptible or vulnerable to smth.: The virus is highly insensitive to cold, which renders it capable of surviving during prolonged periods of sub-freezing temperatures. 2. unable to understanding other people's feelings, hardships, etc.: We put blinders on our ability to see the needs of others. We become insensitive to their problems, to their suffering, to their poverty.

inset something • set in something

inset something—insert smth. into a larger thing: Mr. Talaga carved the plaque and inset it into the granite boulder he placed under the flowering bush.

set in something—add smth. to existing items: The city has approved the plan to set in another mobile home shop temporarily while construction of building is going on.

inside and out • inside out

inside and out—in every part; throughout: We searched the house inside and out for the kitten.

inside out—1. so that the inside is turned outside: Mother turns the stockings inside out when she washes them. 2. *know smth.* extremely well: Duane has worked on numerous Toyotas so knows them inside out.

See also: in and out / ins and outs.

inside of something • inside something

inside of something—in less than a particular period of time: Our experiences have been so many and varied that it's hard to believe it all happened inside of one week.

inside something—1. within smth.: Several sources inside the committee confirmed that some members are considering walking out of the meeting. 2. = *inside of something:* Many species can lay eggs continuously and with ideal temperatures a cycle can be completed inside one week.

intelligence agent • intelligent agent

intelligence agent—(also: secret agent) a person secretly employed in espionage for a government: Those reports center on a shadowy figure called Maurice Bishop — likely a pseudonym — said to have been an intelligence agent.

intelligent agent—(Computers) a program that does things for the user, such as filtering e-mail, etc.: IVOS (Intelligent Voice Operating System) is an intelligent agent that allows you to run your computer via voice commands.

interest in something • interest on something

interest in something—1. said of smth. with which a person concerns himself because he enjoys it: As women develop greater interest in sport, their own attitude to their bodies has changed. 2. condition of wanting smth. to be done: What set him apart from most other writers are his personal honesty and courage, his passionate interest in carrying through his ideas. 3. a legal share in the ownership of a business: Everyone in town has interest in some businesses, and it is impossible not to have dealings with business people.

interest on something—money charged or paid for the use of monetary means: Most of your monthly payments will be used to pay the interest on the loan.

interfere in someone's affairs • interfere with someone

interfere in someone's affairs—meddle in the affairs of another person (offering unsolicited advice, etc.): She knew how much he hated it when she interfered in his affairs.

interfere with someone—(euph.) molest or assault a person sexually: She had reason to suspect that Sandra had been "interfered" with.

interfere in something • interfere with something

interfere in something—intervene in smth. which is not one's concern: They may interfere in elections by the use of corrupt means to bribe or intimidate the electors.

interfere with something—1. meddle with smth., making unauthorized changes, etc.: The dispatcher warned the employee that he would be fired if he again interfered with the dispatch system. *2. (of events, circumstances, etc.)* hinder, obstruct, or prevent smth.: The recent hurricane interfered with our plans so we have rescheduled the trip for the coming week.

interview someone for a job • interview with someone for a job

interview someone for a job—(of an employer) discuss employment in a particular job with a prospective employee: The TV station was looking for a producer and wanted to interview her for the job.

interview with someone for a job—(of smb. seeking employment) discuss employment in a particular job with a prospective employer: She interviewed with the company for a job in the business department.

involved in something • involved with something

involved in something—actively engaged in smth.; being a party to smth.: Auto companies often did become involved in projects having nothing to do with their principal activity.

involved with something—having to do with smth.; having a close relationship with smth.: "Your company has a farm products division." "I'm not involved with it, and don't expect to be."

iron horse • iron pony

iron horse—1. a locomotive steam engine: The engineer returned to his iron horse and the train started. 2. a bicycle:

It's not the longest holiday trip on a bicycle, but it could look like it when Andersen saddles his iron horse.

iron pony—a motorcycle: I get off and find that I have had oil spewing down the side of my iron pony.

iron lady • iron maiden

iron lady—1. said of a tough or intransigent woman: She was an iron lady who took part in the rallies even after her head was injured twice in police baton charges. 2. *(Iron Lady)* the nickname of Margaret Thatcher, British Prime Minister (1979–1991): The Iron Lady of British politics, Margaret Thatcher was the longest continuously serving prime minister since 1827.

iron maiden—1. an old instrument of torture: A person was placed inside the box of the iron maiden while the door (which had impaling spikes on the inside) was closed slowly to maximize pain. 2. *(Iron Maiden) = iron lady 2:* Tension was exacerbated by the cold-war rhetoric which both President Reagan and Mrs. Thatcher consciously adopted, the latter reveling in the "Iron Maiden" label.

iron man • man of iron

iron man—1. a tireless man of extraordinary strength: He likes to think of himself as some sort of iron man who doesn't need sleep like the rest of us. 2. *(sl.)* a UK pound or a U.S. dollar: An ounce [of drug] should bring a street pusher about two thousand iron men.

man of iron—1. *= iron man 1:* His muscles show him to be a man of iron, physically; and his firmness of purpose shows the same quality in his character. 2. a hard, unyielding or merciless man: Neither threats nor promises could move the man of iron to utter more than he was willing to reveal.

See also: Man of Steel / steel man.

it doesn't do • it's not done

it doesn't do—it is unwise or ill-advised: It doesn't do to call your boss names, unless you already have another job to go to.

it's not done—*(also: it's not the done thing)* it is not socially acceptable: It's not done for a man to wear a hat in church.

it is all over and done with • it is all over but the shouting

it is all over and done with—it is finally completely finished (especially with reference to an unpleasant or tiring activity): When it was all over and done with, I wasn't able to relax any more than usual.

it is all over but the shouting—*(also: it is all over bar the shouting)* said when the outcome of an action appears certain: We cannot make the mistake of thinking it's all over but the shouting. There's a lot more work to be done.

it is not a question of money • money is no question

it is not a question of money—money is not the main concern; money is not the point here: We would like to attend concerts on summer weekends.... But it is not a question of money; the problem is time.

money is no question—*(also: money is no object)* it does not matter how much smth. costs because there is a lot of money available: If money is no question, then use every method possible to keep your car safe and secure.

it is not a question of something • there is no question of something

it is not a question of something—is used to tell that smth. is not a factor: It is not a question of education. Even highly educated people are biased against females.

there is no question of something—there is no doubt about smth.: The coin has suffered from corrosion, yet there is no question of its antiquity or its authenticity.

it is not true • it is untrue

it is not true—1. it is false or erroneous: It is not true that the future of British bird life is one of depleted numbers. 2. *(coll.)* it is amazing; it is incredible: You may be only thirty-six but you're so dead old-fashioned it isn't true.

it is untrue— *= it is not true 1:* It is untrue to say that red wine should be paired with red meat and white wine with fish.

Note: *Neither expression correlates in meaning with the phrase* ***out of true****— not correctly aligned or adjusted:* I got on my bike and tried to get going again but ... my front wheel was out of true.

it is said that • it says that

it is said that—it is commonly believed that: Indeed, it is said that their use of red ochre on their bodies is what prompted the term, Red Indian.

it says that—is used to introduce a reference or quotation: In Genesis, it says that it is not good for a man to be alone; but sometimes it is a great relief.

it takes two to make a bargain • it takes two to tango

it takes two to make a bargain—both parties must agree in order for a deal to be successful: "We decided you should make dinner tonight, right?" "No, we didn't decide that; you decided that. It takes two to make a bargain."

it takes two to tango—*(also: it takes two to make a quarrel)* both parties should share responsibility: All nations that go to war have some guilt. It always takes two to tango, you know.

See also: that makes two of us / two can play at this game.

it's a case • this is not the case

it's a case—*(coll.)* said of people who are in love: "One never sees anything of John now; he's always with that girl of his." "Yes, it's a case all right."

this is not the case—it is not so; it is not true: Numerous organisms pass their whole life hovering in the ocean, while with others this is not the case.

it's all go • it's all the go

it's all go—*(coll.)* said when people are very busy or engaged in vigorous activity: It's all go in the postal service at Christmas time!

Note: *The expression does not correlate in meaning with the phrase* ***all systems go****—(derives from the U.S. space program) used as a statement of preparedness for an endeavor:* Fund raising was the most laborious part. But finally it was in place and it was all systems go.

it's all the go—*(coll.)* it is very fashionable: "Just a little chasse-café," said he.... "It's all the go now; and a capital thing for the stomach."

See also: it's no go / it's not a go.

it's all in a day's work • it's all part of the game

it's all in a day's work—one doesn't mind doing smth. because it is smth. to be normally expected: "It's very good of you to bother...." "Please don't mention it," I said, rather stiffly. "It's all in a day's work."

it's all part of the game—is used to tell that smth. is normal in the situation: "It's all part of the game." That's the attitude of Tim Drew as his baseball career took a dramatic upswing and downturn all in the span of a few weeks.

it's all over with someone • it's someone all over

it's all over with someone—1. said of smb. who is completely finished: It's all over with me.... I can bang off a popular song in the cabarets, perhaps; but that's all. 2. said of a person who is dying: When he heard Bambi coming he ceased his convulsive movements and whispered: "It's all over with me."

it's someone all over—it's very typical of the person mentioned: "We might not be able to prove it, but we strongly suspect it's Dupas ... it's him all over," a police source said.

it's just the thing • that's the thing

it's just the thing—that's exactly what one wants or needs: "Would this be suitable, madam?" "Yes, it's just the thing."

Note: *The expression does not correlate in meaning with the phrase* ***it's just one of those things****—used of an unpleasant happening one cannot account for or do anything to prevent:* Now, my wife is a terrible snorer. It's just one of those things.

that's the thing— that's the point; that is indeed the reason: "License and registration please." "Well, that's the thing," I stammered. "I was on my way to renew it right now."

it's no go • it's not a go

it's no go—*(coll.)* it is no use; it is impossible: Jack tries to get friendly with her but it's no go. Suzie's got attitude even Jack can't handle.

it's not a go—*(coll.)* 1. it is not settled: It's not a go at this date. If enough members indicate they want a convention we will have one. 2. = *it's no go:* When you don't speak Spanish, it takes a while ... I tried tourist places just asking, but without a common language it's not a go.

See also: it's all go / it's all the go.

it's the same old, old story • tell me the old, old story

it's the same old, old story—said of smth. bad that has happened many times before: It's the same old, old story. The individual is having his economic sovereignty stripped from him to such an extent that he is no longer capable of managing his own affairs.

tell me the old, old story—*(derisive or sarcastic)* is used to say that one doesn't believe what one hears: Tell me the "old, old, story"! Bullying in the workplace has been part of life since time immemorial. This pandemic problem lies in our sytem of advancing toadies...

J

Jack of all trades • man of all work

Jack of all trades—1. a person who can do various types of work: Wolfenden described the background of a typical rural policeman. He has to be a Jack of all trades. 2. *(derog.)* a person who can do many different things but is not good at any of them: His critics sometimes described him as a jack-of-all-trades.

man of all work—a servant expected to do all domestic duties: He charged into the kitchen, bellowing loudly for Celeste, the kitchen maid, and Bragon, the man-of-all-work, her lover.

jacket potato • unpeeled potato

jacket potato—a whole baked potato with skin: After you remove jacket potatoes from the oven, they lose their crispness very quickly.

unpeeled potato—a potato (raw or cooked) with the skin on: Boil unpeeled potatoes in water until tender, about 15 minutes.

jar against something • jar on something • jar with something

jar against something—1. strike smth. with a harsh unpleasant sound: Her hands slapped on the floor, and her elbows jarred against the cement. "Liz!" Michael yelled, "Are you ok?" 2. not match smth.; be out of harmony with smth.: Their idealistic expectations of military service—travel, tuition and adventure—jarred against the harsh realities.

jar on something—*(of a disagreeable sound)* have an unpleasant effect on one's nerves or ears: The noisy music jarred on my nerves, the sight of the gaping crowd round the platform irritated me.

jar with something— = *jar against something 2:* The "business as usual" tone of the early post-tsunami messages jarred with reality and the plight of many of the survivors.

jet lag • time lag

jet lag—extreme tiredness and sleep disturbance felt after a long flight across different time zones: I discovered that I was getting quite irritable—most likely a side effect of the jet lag.

time lag—an interval of time between two connected events: The time lag between when the visa is issued and when the immigrant lands varies among immigrants.

jet people • jet set

jet people—*(also: plane people)* asylum seekers, refugees, or immigrants who relocate by airplane: They are immigrants of choice, jet people rather than boat people. America's been good to them...

jet set—an international social set of wealthy people who travel frequently by jetliner to parties and resorts: There is one hotel frequented by the jet set.... However, it is more chic to arrive by yacht and return to it each night.

Jim Crow someone • jump Jim Crow

Jim Crow someone—*(U.S. dated sl.)* practice racial discrimination against Black people: The Government has opened the door to dozens of prominent Blacks and ensured that they were not Jim Crowed.

jump Jim Crow—*(U.S. dated sl.)* change one's political convictions; desert one's party: Not much balance about us. We just run about and jump Jim Crow.

job-horse • work horse

job-horse—a horse hired to do a particular piece of work, or for a limited time: The sight of Dr. Slocum's large carriage, with the gaunt job-horses, crushed Flora.

work horse—1. a horse used for labor rather than for racing or recreation: Pink-eye is excessively prevalent among all classes of horses, particularly work horses in Sheffield. 2. a person who undertakes hard but necessary work: Rice-producing peasants continued to be the workhorses of the nation and the economic support of the ruling class. 3. a particularly useful or durable machine: This caliber howitzer has gained the reputation of being the "work horse" of the Army.

job of work • job work

job of work—*(coll.)* a task; a piece of work: Arthur did not go on the search, because he had a job of work to do.

job work—printing of letterheads, cards, etc. as distinct from the manufacture of books: This invention relates to machinery intended chiefly for printing "job work."

John Doe • Richard Roe

John Doe—1. the name given to an ordinary or typical citizen: The only information that any John Doe leaves behind is what they choose to leave behind. 2. *(legal)* used as a name to designate an unknown or unidentified man: According to the report, the corpse, a John Doe, was found with no clear cause of death.

Richard Roe—(legal) used as a name to designate an unidentified man, especially the second of two such persons: It was a matter material to said trial to determine whether or not John Doe had ever made a loan of money to Richard Roe.

join forces • join the forces

join forces—unite in order to use combined strength to achieve a common aim: There was a proposal to join forces, and have a double wedding ... the two school fellows and two young friends.

join the forces—join the army: This year, the number seeking to join the forces has almost doubled and applications for cadetships have risen by over 40 percent.

join in something • join something

join in something—associate with other people in an activity, especially when they are already engaged in it: As I stood with people talking about insignificant things, my small daughter joined in the conversation.

join something—1. become a member of a party, club, organization, etc.: Many well-known figures joined the party at this time, including Pablo Picasso. 2. = *join in something:* Suddenly the mood changed completely and a third person joined the conversation, interested in where we were going.

join in with someone • join up with someone

join in with someone—1. meet a person to do smth. together: My aunt and uncle have asked me to join in with them on their holiday abroad. 2. share a cost with another person: We joined in with another family to buy the boat and share it for our holidays.

join up with someone—meet and form a group with a person: We plan to join up with the other party of climbers on the other side of the mountain.

joint-stock company • stock company

joint-stock company—a business enterprise with ownership interests represented by shares of stock: Scott used to say that the Bannatyne Club was the only successful joint-stock company he ever invested in.

stock company—a company of actors employed at one theater, or permanently acting together: The stock company system provided theatrical training by affording young actors the chance to play many different roles.

judicial decision • judicious decision

judicial decision—1. a decision taken (by a judge) in a court of law: Besides divorce, marriage can also be declared invalid by a judicial decision. 2. a decision that is impartial or just: It does not seem to be denied that there was a judicial decision as a result of the Adjudicator's determination.

judicious decision—a decision showing good sense or judgment: This proved to be a judicious decision as it significantly contributed to our sales growth.

Julian calendar • Julian day calendar

Julian calendar—a calendar introduced in Rome in 46 B.C. establishing the twelve-month year: Down to 1582 the Julian calendar continued to be used by all Christian nations.

Julian day calendar—(Astronomy) a system of numbering days consecutively from the arbitrarily selected point of the year 4713 B.C., regardless of the various changes made in civil calendars: Using the astronomers' Julian Day calendar as a common denominator ... Latham has solved the conversion of virtually all (including the Chinese!) the world calendars.

jump at someone • jump on someone

jump at someone—1. attack a person from a distance: The animal jumped at him, he squatted down and the cougar went over him, not making contact. 2. criticize a person severely: That same author did try to improve things by incorporating changes and everyone jumped at him. 3. *(also: jump out at someone)* said of smth. very obvious or easy to notice: Only the precious few had the special kind of talent that just jumps at you.

jump on someone—1. pounce on a person (landing on top of the person attacked): The Lion jumped up and jumped on him with all four feet. 2. = *jump at someone 2:* I'm sorry, Eddy, I didn't mean to jump on you that way.

Note: *Neither expression is equivalent in meaning to the phrase* ***jump someone****—(sl.) 1. attack smb. suddenly in a sneaky fashion (with the intention to rob, etc.):* When I "jumped" him we didn't mean to kill or hurt him. 2. *cheat or swindle a person:* The old proprietor ... was green, and let the boys about here jump him.

jump at something • jump on something

jump at something—accept an offer, opportunity, etc. eagerly as soon as it has become available: When I raised this prospect with her, she jumped at the idea.

jump on something—(also: jump all over something) reprove or criticize smth. severely: Critics jumped on the 1998 release of the instruction manual for priesthood.

jump in the lake • take the plunge

jump in the lake—(also: go jump in the lake) is used to rudely tell a person to go away (and stop being annoying): After a while, our exchange turned hostile and I told him to jump in the lake.

take the plunge—take a decisive step (especially getting married); venture to do smth. risky: You may take the plunge and start your own firm, or join a large company.

jump out of one's skin • run out of one's skin

jump out of one's skin—1. get a sudden unpleasant shock or surprise: He nearly jumped out of his skin when he saw two rats in the wreckage of what a few years before had been a kitchen. 2. show extreme delight, excitement, or high spirits: Scipio was ready to jump out of his skin for joy at the sight of me. 3. *(of a horse)* put all of one's energy into a race: The horse looked in splendid condition, "fit to jump out of his skin," to use a racing term.

run out of one's skin— = *jump out of one's skin 3:* The word from Ireland this week is that this horse is running out of its skin over the flat.

Note: *a) Neither expression correlates in meaning with the phrase* ***play out of one's skin****—give an outstanding performance:* He then played out of his skin for the remainder of the tournament, made a couple of mistakes ... but was still a force to be reckoned with.

b) Neither expression correlates in meaning with the phrase ***cast its skin****—(of a reptile) shed its skin:* About the middle of the month [September] the common snake sloughs or casts its skin.

jump over the fence • jump over the wall

jump over the fence—(coll.) exceed the limits of reasonable conduct; go too far: She goes pretty near the knuckle sometimes, but she never jumps over the fence.

Note: *The expression is not antonymous in meaning to the phrase* ***sit on the fence****—be undecided in opinion or action:* The French delegation, which has hitherto been sitting on the fence, has suddenly become exceedingly active.

jump over the wall—(also: go over the wall) leave a religious order: No one knows how many religious have jumped over the wall — partly because it is so easy today to take a leave of absence and never return.

jump the traces • jump the track

jump the traces—*(coll.)* break loose from restraint; misbehave *(also: kick over the traces):* I believe there would be enormous pressure on us to jump the traces and break out from under discipline.

jump the track—1. *(of railroad carriages)* go off the rails: Just as the train crossed a 40-foot high trestle, it jumped the track. The engine reached the other side, but the next eight cars crashed over the trestle. 2. *(coll.)* change from one thought or idea to another without plan or reason: Any device that will clarify logical relationships between ideas is important because argument is prone to "jump the track" and take up unrelated issues.

jungle law • natural law

jungle law—*(also: law of the jungle)* the superiority of brute force or self-interest in the ruthless struggle for survival: It was awkward having to explain jungle law to someone who had never emerged from a well-kept shrubbery.

natural law—*(also: law of nature)* 1. is used to refer to a particular phenomenon always occurring if certain conditions are present: Gravity is a natural law (a law of nature) that is dependable and constant. 2. is used of ideas, etc. as implanted by nature in the human mind: In political theory, Spinoza argued that human beings fundamentally act in accordance with natural law.

just about • only just

just about—1. almost: He knows just about everything there is to know about shipping cargo out of Miami. 2. *(followed by Infinitive)* on the point of doing smth.: He was just about to fold up the newspaper when he spotted the classifieds.

only just—1. a short time ago: I only just heard about the inappropriate way Ms. Jacobson behaved. 2. barely; almost not: The farmhouse can only just be seen from the road when the trees are not in leaf.

just you wait • wait for it

just you wait—*(also: you wait)* is used to imply an angry threat, promise, or warning: We'll teach them a lesson I tell you, just you wait and see.

wait for it—is used to create an interval of suspense before saying smth. unexpected: We can have a shower and ... wait for it, dinner at the Palazzo Capucci.

K

keen of something • keen on something

keen of something—highly sensitive to smth.; sharp of sight, smell, etc.: A black rhino has poor eyesight, but it is keen of hearing and smell.

keen on something—very fond of smth.; enthusiastic about smth.: I was lucky to have a girl like Betty who was keen on football.

keep a house • keep house

keep a house—1. provide for or manage a household: She kept a house, raised my sister and worked part-time in my dad's store. 2. *(keep a House)* secure the presence of enough members of parliament for a quorum *(also: make a House):* I may support him in his view that the Government have failed to keep a House.

keep house—1. = *keep a house 1:* She kept house well, was a good cook and punctual. 2. *(also: keep one's house)* stay indoors (being confined through illness, etc.): Sure, there is no necessity for us to keep house till she arrives.

Note: *Neither expression correlates in meaning with the phrase* ***keep open house****— offer hospitality and be ready to welcome and entertain guests at any time:* The King kept open house every day, and all day long, for the good society of London.

keep a shop • keep shop

keep a shop—own and manage a shop; be a shopkeeper: I used to live with my auntie. She kept a sweet-shop.

keep shop—look after a shop: Mr. Green got a friend to keep shop for him while he went to his wife's funeral.

keep a straight face • keep straight

keep a straight face—*(also: keep one's face)* refrain from showing one's feelings by one's facial expression: All I felt called upon to do was to keep a straight face and pretend that everything was kosher.

keep straight—*(also: go straight)* be virtuous or well-behaved; refrain from criminal activities: She meant to marry him in two or three years, if he proved he could keep straight in the meanwhile.

keep accounts • keep an account

keep accounts—1. make records of money paid out and received: After two years passed in keeping accounts in Calcutta, Hastings went up the country. 2. is used of money kept at a bank: Like every other nonbank institution, savings and loan associations must keep accounts with commercial banks.

keep an account—1. = *keep accounts 2:* A current account is an account kept by a customer at a bank to meet his current expenses. 2. count and record the number: A game book is one wherein the sportsman may keep an account of all the game he kills. 3. make written notes: When you go on a vacation, carry a notebook and keep an account of what you do every day.

keep an open mind • open one's mind

keep an open mind—*(also: have an open mind)* be free from bias; avoid forming an opinion until one knows all the facts: Detectives said they were keeping an open mind whether the attacker is the same man.

open one's mind—1. reveal one's inmost thoughts or sentiments: The day before he was due to return to France, he opened his mind to Emmie. 2. become receptive to smth. new or different: You will have to open your mind more easily to new ideas.

keep away from something • keep out of something

keep away from something—1. remain at a distance from smth.: What we really want is for people to keep away from the area. 2. avoid smth.: The day the sun comes out people will hide under umbrellas just to keep away from the sun.

keep out of something—1. stay outside; not enter smth.: You understand now why I concealed my name, and why I kept out of the house. 2. = *keep away from something 2:* It is important to remember to take water and find a place to keep out of the sun for some of the time.

keep bad hours • keep bad time

keep bad hours—get up and go to bed late: She didn't like renting to young people because they kept bad hours and made noise.

keep bad time—*(of a clock or watch)* show the hour incorrectly: You can tell your battery is dead if your computer's clock keeps bad time.

keep body and soul together • keep oneself together

keep body and soul together—manage to survive; keep oneself alive: They get poor as snakes on such food; but it does keep body and soul together for a while.

keep oneself together—(also: hold oneself together) keep one's composure; maintain one's good sense: I don't know if I can keep myself together through another horrible day like this one.

keep company with someone • keep someone company

keep company with someone—socialize habitually with a person: She could not approve of a young woman keeping company with men, without the permission of father or mother.

keep someone company—accompany smb. or stay with a person: In fall, she tramped the woods watching for squirrels. Candy, her dog, often kept her company.

keep good hours • keep good time

keep good hours—get up and go to bed early: As a rule they keep good hours, but most of them will read an hour or two before going to sleep.

keep good time—1. *(of a clock or watch)* show the hour correctly: The clock is in good working order, keeping good time. 2. be habitually punctual: She keeps good time, is prepared for work and, above all, is a responsible person. 3. *(Music)* follow the rhythm correctly: Drummer Farnsworth doesn't try to compete with the rumble of Earland's organ; instead, he keeps good time.

keep in touch with someone • keep in with someone

keep in touch with someone—be in regular communication with smb.: An undergraduate is assigned to a "moral tutor" who undertakes to keep in touch with him.

keep in with someone—(coll.) remain on good terms with smb. (usually to gain some advantage from the person): We'll have to keep in with her in case we can't ever pay the rent.

***Note:** The expression does not correlate in meaning with the phrase **keep up with someone**— remain level with a person in some respect:* You're free to work at a pace that suits you, which means not having to keep up with others.

keep it down • keep it up

keep it down—be quiet; make no noise: And please keep it down, will you? I'm listening to Bird! Have some respect!

keep it up—continue doing smth.: This guy needs to be on drugs, and if he keeps it up he will be back in prison.

keep off something • keep something off

keep off something—1. remain at a distance from smth.: In an election which seems to have been fair, the Spanish police kept off the streets. 2. prevent smth. from coming near or happening: The ships were wintered by dismantling the riggings and covering the hulls with planks to keep off the snow. 3. avoid mentioning a particular subject: They have all along been on the aggressive. It has been their way of keeping off the question of the Papal authority. 4. refrain from smth.: It should become standard practice to have someone as the evening's designated driver, that person agreeing to keep off alcohol.

keep something off— = keep off something 2: The idea is that you would have a simple shelter that goes over your driveway to keep the snow off.

keep on with something • keep up with something

keep on with something—continue doing smth., especially in spite of danger, difficulties, etc.: For months he has been talking of giving up smoking, but he still keeps on with it.

keep up with something—remain level with smth.; keep pace with smth.: Even professional politicians have a struggle to keep up with the changes in public opinion.

keep one's balance • keep the balance

keep one's balance—1. keep from falling; remain standing: He slipped on the grass and as he stumbled forward, desperately trying to keep his balance, he ran into a tree. 2. retain one's ability to exercise control: Now that a reaction is setting in, Mr. Gorbachev is leaning back towards the conservatives to keep his balance. 3. keep calm; not become emotionally upset: You know when you keep your sense of humor you also keep your balance. 4. compromise between smth.; find a middle course: Like other Arab leaders, Gadaffi tries to keep his balance between the "Arab street" and Uncle Sam.

keep the balance—1. *= keep one's balance 1:* Because of the mud I had to put my feet just above the ground ready to put them down to keep the balance when I slipped away. 2. *= keep one's balance 4:* Lewis was a tutor who tried to keep the balance between amiability and his duty to the pupils to give them sufficient preparation. 3. maintain the condition of equilibrium between opposing forces: Germany must be aware that it has to keep the balance in Europe, Mr. Mitterrand said. 4. keep the change from money offered in payment: Pay yourself for the bottle of wine out of this, and keep the balance.

keep one's eyes open • open someone's eyes

keep one's eyes open—be watchful and alert: During the three weeks I stayed in Dar-es-Salaam, keeping my eyes open, I was hard put to find evidence of Chinese influence.

open someone's eyes—make a person acutely aware of the truth of a situation: Attending Harvard only served to open her eyes to a whole new range of inequalities that exist in society. *Cf.: eye opener—a startling or shocking revelation:* It was a real eye-opener for the adults. The ease that the children displayed with the technology was enough to amaze even a veteran.

See also: with one's eyes closed / with one's eyes open.

keep one's face • lose one's face

keep one's face—(also: keep a straight face) refrain from showing one's feelings by one's facial expression: The performance was so absurd that I could hardly keep my face.

***Note:** The expression does not correlate in meaning with the phrase **save one's face**—(also: save face) avoid being disgraced or humiliated:* If he represented a first-class paper and wished to "save his face" he had better travel in state.

lose one's face—(also: lose face) damage one's reputation; lose people's respect: He is such a powerful and important man he can not afford to lose his face.

keep one's feet • keep one's feet on the ground

keep one's feet—keep one's balance; remain standing: As he was leaving, he stumbled on the stairs but was able to keep his feet.

keep one's feet on the ground—(also: have one's feet on the ground) have a sensible and realistic attitude to life: When the other band members tend to lose touch with reality, he makes sure everyone keeps his feet on the ground.

keep one's hair • keep one's hair on

keep one's hair—not become bald: He considers himself to have been lucky during the early stages of the disease: no sickness, and he kept his hair until quite recently.

keep one's hair on—(coll.) not lose one's temper; remain calm: His annoyance evaporated in a grin. "You're right. She's got a tough job. I'll try to keep my hair on in future."

keep one's hand in • keep one's hands off

keep one's hand in— exercise repeatedly in order to be in

practice: Write a line or two of it every day to keep your hand in.

keep one's hands off—stop touching or interfering with smth.: She knew she had to keep her hands off so he could learn to tie his shoes by himself.

keep one's head • keep one's head up

keep one's head—retain self-control; remain sensible and practical: You can depend on him to keep his head no matter what happens.

Note: *The expression does not correlate in meaning with the phrase **keep one's head above water**— make a living; manage to survive financially:* In spite of all the reverses, he still manages to keep his head above water.

keep one's head up—(also: hold one's head up) stay proud; not feel ashamed of oneself: I can keep my head up anywhere, knowing that I achieved something.

Note: *The expression does not correlate in meaning with the phrase **keep one's chin up**— be courageous and determined under difficult circumstances:* Tell Ken to keep his chin up and be as tough as he made out he was when he comes up against trouble.

keep one's lid on • keep the lid on someone

keep one's lid on—(coll.) keep one's temper; be patient: Keep your lids on, folks; we'll have this matter sorted out in just a few seconds.

keep the lid on someone—suppress or "clamp down" on rebels, dissenters, etc.: You have the root problem of all colonials — the natives are restless and you can't keep the lid on them.

keep one's mouth shut • not open one's mouth

keep one's mouth shut—not talk about smth.; not reveal a secret: Keep your eyes skinned, there's a good girl, and, incidentally, keep your mouth shut.

not open one's mouth—say nothing; remain silent: By the fact that she did not open her mouth, she acknowledged her guilt.

keep one's name on the books • see one's name in print

keep one's name on the books—retain one's membership in a club, etc.: He said he was not much of a Mason — he scarcely ever went; just kept his name on the books by paying up his dues.

see one's name in print—1. be a published author: "Pray, Anne," said he, "did you ever experience the satisfaction of feeling how pleasant it is to see one's name in print?" 2. said of smb. who likes to be mentioned in media reports: We have received an amusing series of announcements from a corporate executive who likes to see his name in print.

keep one's pants on • wear the pants

keep one's pants on—(coll.) remain calm; keep one's temper *(also: keep one's shirt on):* Always remember to keep your pants on in times of stress.

Note: *The expression is not antonymous in meaning to the phrase **catch someone with his pants down**—(sl.) catch a person off guard:* Rachel's telephone call hadn't caught me with my pants down.

wear the pants—(also: wear the breeches) be the dominant partner in a marriage: Mrs. Harris wears the pants at home: Mr. Harris is far too quiet and easy-going to argue with her.

keep one's peace • keep the peace

keep one's peace—1. *(also: hold one's peace)* refrain from arguing; remain silent: He told one lie after another, and it was only with the greatest effort that I was able to keep my peace. 2. *(of a country)* refrain from military action: Imperialism had a very small part in the history of Japan. Before that Japan kept its peace and hardly built any military power.

keep the peace—1. preserve a peaceful state of affairs: In the American colonies, volunteer justices kept the peace before there were paid police. 2. = *keep one's peace 2:* These costs of war are beyond calculation.... Most of this poverty could have been avoided had the country kept the peace. 3. prevent military conflicts: Britain had become the second largest contributor of troops, working alongside the Canadians. The two countries kept the peace in Cyprus during thirty years.

keep one's pecker up • put someone's pecker up

keep one's pecker up—(UK coll.) keep one's spirits up: Charles could not eat, in spite of the rough kindness of one of the warders, who adjured him to keep his pecker up.

put someone's pecker up—(coll.) make smb. angry; put a person out of temper: He thinks he can do what he likes with me. I am not quite sure about that, if he puts up my pecker.

keep one's shirt on • lose one's shirt

keep one's shirt on—(coll.) remain calm; keep one's temper *(also: hold one's shirt):* I told him to keep his shirt on, no matter what the provocation.

lose one's shirt—lose all one's money (as a result of gambling, etc.): Everybody knows that John lost his shirt when that business he had invested in failed.

keep oneself dark • keep someone in the dark

keep oneself dark—be characterized by inconspicuous behavior; keep out of the public eye: He hid himself ... kept himself dark, as he says, out of the way and out of the trial.

keep someone in the dark—keep a person in ignorance about smth.: He is prepared to do things his own way and to keep everyone else in the dark as to what is happening.

Note: *The expression does not correlate in meaning with the phrase **be dark on someone**—(Austral. sl.) be angry or annoyed with a person:* Dad's going to be dark on me for getting home so late.

keep someone at bay • keep the wolf at bay

keep someone at bay—(also: hold someone at bay) maintain a safe distance from smb.; prevent a person from acting: These people come from sick, evil families and we good Americans are trying to keep them at bay.

keep the wolf at bay—manage to make enough money to avoid going hungry or falling heavily into debt: An engineer can just about always survive by computer programming, so we kept the wolf at bay when I took a job in Houston.

keep someone away from something • keep someone out of something

keep someone away from something—1. cause a person not to come near smth.: The police used tear gas to keep the crowd away from the factory compound. 2. cause a person to avoid smth. harmful: I would never have imagined it would be so hard to keep her away from sweets. 3. cause a person to stay away from trouble or smth. dangerous: Parents play a crucial role in ensuring that teens are participating in activities that keep them away from drugs.

Note: *The expression does not fully correlate in meaning with the phrase **keep someone back from something**— = keep someone away from something 1:* We had a good view of the security staff struggling to keep the crowd back from the stage.

keep someone out of something—1. cause a person not to enter smth.: Keeping him out of the building is the most reliable way of keeping him away from the data. 2. prevent a person from participating in smth.: Gilhooley has been a victim of serious injuries which have kept him out of the game. 3. =

keep someone away from something 3: We have worked to support your preventive programs that keep children out of drugs and violence.

keep someone down • keep someone under

keep someone down—1. *(also: hold someone down)* cause a person to remain in a lower position: John tried to look in that direction but a crisscrossing hail of laser fire kept him down. 2. *(also: hold someone down)* oppress or hold back a person: He told me that "every company" he had worked for had incompetent management and was trying to keep him down. 3. *(UK)* make a child remain in the same class for a second year: If she failed her examinations again, Jane would be kept down next year.

keep someone under—1. cause a person to remain beneath smth.: I was filming when I went over the falls and the white water kept me under nearly all the way to the beach. 2. = *keep someone down 2:* Everywhere you heard the leaders saying, "It is going to be very difficult to keep the people under." 3. make a person remain unconscious (under the action of anesthesia): He is under more sedation.... They will keep him under until at least late tomorrow.

See also: hold someone up / keep someone up.

keep someone in something • keep someone to something

keep someone in something—provide a person with smth. such as food, etc.: The uniforms were goofy, but the food was free and the money kept me in clothes and rock music.

keep someone to something—1. cause a person to talk about smth. without letting his attention wander: Your patient may require guidance to keep him to the subject in hand. 2. make a person do what has been agreed: He wished to relinquish his last year at Harvard, and Cynthia had to summon all her forces to keep him to his promise of staying.

keep someone on track • keep track of someone

keep someone on track—keep a person focused on a task, etc.: Stephen begins to speak softly and I keep him on track by moving my finger along with the words he reads.

keep track of someone—continue to be informed or know about smb.: Has anyone even seen John recently? He's been so busy lately we can't even keep track of him.

keep something dark • throw light on something

keep something dark—keep smth. secret: Latham had given the impression that he knew all about the subject but wanted to keep it dark.

throw light on something—*(also: shed light on something)* clarify or explain smth.: An Australian fossil related to a species known in Argentina may throw light on the continent's geographical past.

keep something for oneself • keep something to oneself

keep something for oneself—save smth. for one's own use: I actually bought you those slippers, but liked them so much I decided to keep them for myself.

keep something to oneself—keep information, etc. secret from other people: Please continue to keep these facts to yourself for a little while longer, Paul.

keep something in mind • keep something in one's head

keep something in mind—remember and think about smth.; not forget smth: We have no vacancies now, but we'll certainly keep your application in mind.

Note: *The expression is not equivalent in meaning to the phrase* ***keep one's mind on something***—*(also: have one's mind on something) continue to pay attention to smth.; not be distracted from smth.:* She merely sat very still while he attended to the interview he could no longer keep his mind on.

keep something in one's head—be able to retain in memory smth. such as facts, figures, etc.: I don't know how the chairman keeps all these data in his head.

keep the ball rolling • keep the pot boiling

keep the ball rolling—*(also: keep the wheels turning)* keep an activity, process, etc. going: The first step is to feed your body healthy food so you'll have the energy to keep the ball rolling.

keep the pot boiling—1. earn enough money to provide one's livelihood: Not only has doing portraits of people kept the pot boiling, it has also led to my meeting some famous people. 2. = *keep the ball rolling:* We will keep the pot boiling on this until David is released because this is a question of basic democratic rights.

Note: *Neither expression correlates in meaning with the phrase* ***keep the home fires burning***—*keep things at home going as usual (while smb. is away):* These women kept the home fires burning as they patiently waited until the wheels of the war stopped turning and their husbands were home.

keep the seat warm • warm the bench

keep the seat warm—occupy a position temporarily for a person who is not yet ready or qualified to hold it: They are using Kim to just keep the seat warm till they find somebody who can win them an election.

Note: *The expression does not correlate in meaning with the phrase* ***keep one's seat***—*(also: hold one's seat)* 1. *remain seated:* Bartlet entered the room. Everyone started to stand, but the Governor motioned for them to keep their seats. 2. *keep from falling:* Though aided by the high-bowed "mountain-saddle" I could scarcely keep my seat on horseback. 3. *retain one's position, membership in parliament, etc.:* Despite his bribery conviction, Nakamura kept his seat in two elections.

warm the bench—*(Sport)* sit among the substitute players during a game: Aherne has warmed the bench much more assiduously than he has passed the ball.

See also: bench warmer / chair warmer.

keep the wheels turning • spin the wheels

keep the wheels turning—*(also: keep the ball rolling)* keep an activity, process, etc. going: His class interest tells him to supply the public with as much purchasing power as possible, to keep the wheels turning.

spin the wheels—*(U.S. coll.)* act in a listless or unproductive manner: You will have to spend at least two hours studying on your own, and it has to be time well spent, rather than "spinning the wheels."

See also: put one's shoulder to the wheel / set the wheels in motion.

keep to oneself • retire into oneself

keep to oneself—*(also: keep oneself to oneself)* remain unsociable; avoid meeting other people: He'd kept to himself on that trip, not really making eye contact or talking to the locals.

retire into oneself—become quiet and unwilling to talk: When she saw that complaints did not alter me, she retired into herself, as it were; and I saw less and less of her.

keep up with the times • time-keeper

keep up with the times—remain informed about the latest news, fashions, etc.: For people who keep up with the times, this is the perfect opportunity to check out new products.

time-keeper—1. a person who records or manages the time: Band members will wait for the instruction of the time-keeper before going on stage. 2. *(UK)* an employee considered in terms of his punctuality: Jane is a hard worker, very methodical, and a good time-keeper. 3. said of a watch or clock: This is a Bulova military style wrist watch and for its age it is super clean and a good time-keeper.

Kentish man • Man of Kent

Kentish man—(UK dated) a native of Kent born east of the river Medway: The strong Kentish Man, gave three proofs of his extraordinary strength before his Majesty.

Man of Kent—(UK dated) a native of Kent born west of the river Medway: Man of Kent, a title claimed by the inhabitants of the Weald as their peculiar designation: all others they regard as Kentish men.

key man • key-holder

key man—a person who plays a leading or important role in smth.: One of the key men in this new method of assessing needs and opportunities is the local prefect.

key-holder—a person who keeps the keys of a workshop, factory, etc.: Workmen were waiting outside ready to begin work for the day. The key-holder had not arrived.

kick against something • kick something

kick against something—protest about or oppose smth.: They knew life ... and it was as useless to kick against the laws of society as to interfere with the laws of nature. *Cf.: kick against the pricks—protest about or oppose smth. without success (harming oneself by doing so):* Somewhere in our teens or twenties most of us shrug and decide not to "kick against the pricks."

kick something—strike smth. with the foot: Actually, to push didn't really do it, you kind of had to kick the door to really get it to pop open.

kick one's heels • kick up one's heels

kick one's heels—(coll.) have nothing to do, especially while being kept waiting *(also: cool one's heels):* I had to kick my heels for nearly two hours before I could see the boss.

kick up one's heels—(coll.) cast off one's inhibitions and have a good time: I took two weeks for my holidays and had a pleasant time kicking up my heels around the beaches of Majorca.

kill an elephant • shoot the bull

kill an elephant—do smth. to excess; overdo things: Tagua palm is also called natural ivory. We found tagua all over the place and you don't have to kill an elephant for it!

***Note:** The expression is not antonymous in meaning to the phrase **kill the rabbit**—*1. *(dated euph.) get a positive test result from an old-fashioned pregnancy test:* Back in my mom's day ... there was "the rabbit test." If a woman was pregnant, it was said that she "killed the rabbit." 2. *(Aviation) turn down the intensity of the approach lights:* If you ever hear "kill the rabbit" while listening to air traffic control, the pilot is asking the controller to turn off the strobe lights.

shoot the bull—(U.S. sl.) engage in idle chat: It was raining, so everybody spent the day indoors drinking beer and shooting the bull.

kill the clock • kill time

kill the clock—(Sport) keep the ball away from the opposing team at the end of a game so that they cannot score: The Warthogs kept passing the ball back and forth among them so as to kill the clock.

kill time—do smth. which is not very interesting while one is waiting for time to pass: We then went over to the record shop just to kill time.

See also: kill-time / killing time.

kill-time • killing time

kill-time—an occupation which is not very useful or interesting, intended to pass away the time: It was such an utter loss to the reader, that he could not so well call it passtime as kill-time.

killing time—said of the time at which an animal is fit to be killed: Hog killing time is a season of severe and lasting cold weather, required for the preserving of the meat.

See also: kill the clock / kill time.

king bird • king of birds

king bird—an American tyrant flycatcher *(Tyrannus carolinensis):* If you ever saw a crow with a king bird after him, you will get an image of a dull speaker and a lively listener.

king of birds—said of the eagle: The strength, keen vision, graceful and powerful flight of the eagle are proverbial, and have given to him the title of the king of birds.

***Note:** Neither expression correlates in meaning with the phrase **king's bird**—(also: king bird of paradise) a bird of the genus Paradisea:* The king's bird is carried in the procession, and the yelling and chatting of the marketers is heard above anything.

King Charles's head • King's head

King Charles's head—a subject that keeps on appearing in a person's conversation: He talks about nothing but money—it's becoming a King Charles's head!

***Note:** The expression does not correlate in meaning with the phrase **King Charles**—short for "King Charles's Spaniel":* A little "King Charles," with a crimson ribbon round his neck is jumping on the sofa.

King's head—representation of a king on a postage stamp, etc.: Take care never to step on a coin or banknote or a postage stamp with the king's head on it.

***Note:** The expression does not correlate in meaning with the compound **kinghead**— a coarse annual plant (Ambrosia trifida):* The seeds consist of one central beak surrounded by a circle of five or more marginal points, giving a king's crown appearance, hence the plant's common names—kinghead and crown-weed.

king for a day • king of day, the

king for a day—a person whose fame, popularity, etc., is but short-lived: Superintendent Michael Snow was king for a day in Middlefield this summer, serving as grand marshal of the town's bicentennial parade.

king of day, the—(poetic) the Sun: I have never seen Italy's far-famed sky, but I do not think it could surpass that evening sunset. The king of day sinking into the bosom of Silver Lake...

king of metals • queen's metal

king of metals—gold: This king of metals will remain with us as long as beauty wishes to adorn itself and designers wish to create timeless classics in jewelry.

queen's metal—an alloy of tin, antimony, lead and bismuth: Queen's metal serves also for teapots and other domestic utensils.

king of waters • water king

king of waters— the name given to the river Amazon: There are many large rivers ... but what are these, severally, to the "king of waters" on whose deep current fleets and navies may float.

***Note:** The expression does not correlate in meaning with the phrase **king of the sea**—*1. *a fabulous being that lives in water and rules over the sea:* The tale centers around the water spirit Undine, daughter of the King of the Sea. *2. ruler of the sea:* There was Will Merrymouth, whose daring in fight and skill in seamanship had won him the soubriquet of "King of the Sea."

water king— = *king of the sea 1:* Lord Zeus holds the starry hall on Olympus; he has given the briny sea to his brother [Poseidon] the water king.

kiss it off • kiss off

kiss it off—(coll.) not deal with smth.; put it off: Every hostage negotiation includes tense moments when one doubts the other side is operating in good faith and is tempted to kiss it off.

kiss off—is used to rudely tell a person to go away (and stop being annoying): That was before the time when women would have told him to kiss off in public. It wouldn't go unchallenged these days.

knight of the pen • knight of the pencil

knight of the pen—(liter. or joc.) a writer or a journalist: Kolosimo became the knight of the pen in the sixties and seventies. Millions of readers were immersed in the mysteries of the universe by reading his books.

knight of the pencil—(UK derog.) 1. a bookmaker: We have mentioned the knights of the pencil. Bookmakers are not permitted to take up positions at will on racecourses under Greyhound Racing Association jurisdiction. 2. an artist; a cartoonist: The shameless knights of the pencil found it easy to caricature the spare, bent figure and bushy locks when getting off jokes about professors.

knock heads together • put heads together

knock heads together—get people to stop quarrelling and behave sensibly by taking firm action: An elected mayor is empowered to knock heads together and persuade people who traditionally don't talk to each other to do so.

put heads together—(also: lay heads together) have a discussion in order to solve a problem, etc.: The present plans are far too expensive. I think we should put our heads together and see if we can somehow make them cheaper.

Note: *The expression does not correlate in meaning with the phrase* ***get one's head together****—(coll.) get mentally organized; start to perform efficiently (also: get one's act together):* It has taken me over ten years to get my head together enough to put this down in writing, but I have carried it in my heart.

knock oneself dead • knock someone dead

knock oneself dead—(coll.) work very hard; make an extra effort to accomplish smth. *(also: knock oneself out):* In the first six weeks on the job I hardly spent one day in Pennsylvania. ...I had been all over the country, knocking myself dead.

knock someone dead—(coll., also: knock someone out) put on a stunning performance; have a powerful emotional effect on a person: This band is going to do great tonight. We're going to knock them dead.

knock someone off • knock someone out

knock someone off—1. make a person fall with a push: You're not safe on that ladder; a branch could knock you off. 2. *(Sport)* defeat a competitor: If he can knock off the next two opponents, he could get into the last part of the competition. 3. *(sl.)* kill a person: I don't want to knock the old man off; can't we just tie him up to keep him quiet?

Note: *The expression does not fully correlate in meaning with the phrase* ***knock someone off his feet****—1. = knock someone off 1:* The sudden explosion of light, power, and thunder knocked me off my feet and I landed hard on my back. *2. (coll.) have a powerful emotional effect on a person:* In addition to the perfect weather, the smell of the trees and good country air nearly knocked me off my feet.

knock someone out—1. make a person unconscious by hitting him: Scott's reputation is excellent, and the managers fear that he has been knocked out and robbed. 2. = *knock someone off 2:* Our team got through to the second part of the competition before they were knocked out. 3. *(coll.)* tire a person very much (through overwork): Hours of gardening in the sun have quite knocked me out. *Cf.: knock oneself out—(coll.) work very hard; make an extra effort to accomplish smth.:* We thank the one person who knocked himself out making sure we enjoyed ourselves. 4. *(coll., also: knock someone dead)* put on a stunning performance; have a powerful emotional effect on a person: I hadn't heard of her show beforehand, but watched it immediately and she knocked me out.

knock someone on the head • knock someone's head off

knock someone on the head—1. strike smb. on the head: Cook knocked him on the head instantly; this is what the English call a settler.... 2. kill a person by a blow on the head: Our prisoners beg at us, as a mercy, to knock them on the head.

knock someone's head off—(sl.) 1. beat a person by way of punishment *(usually used as a threat):* He told me to get out of there or he would knock my head off. 2. "beat" or surpass an opponent: They could take players ... and motivate them to go out on the field and knock someone's head off.

knock someone up *(UK)* • knock someone up *(U.S.)*

knock someone up (UK)—(coll.) 1. wake a person (by knocking on the door of his room): Sorry to knock you up at this hour, Holmes, but Mrs. Hudson has only just knocked me up. 2. tire a person very much (through overwork, etc.): Marianne went there to nurse him and was several nights without sleep, which quite knocked her up.

knock someone up (U.S.)—(coarse sl.) make a woman pregnant: And what would you tell the child when they ask who their father was? "Oh, just some guy I let knock me up at a party?"

knock something off • knock something out

knock something off—1. make smth. fall with a push: Just when I put the glass safely down on the table, the cat jumped up and knocked it off. 2. *(coll.)* write smth. quickly and carelessly: He could knock off a poem in half an hour. 3. *(coll.)* put a work out of hand; complete smth.: I've a pile of work to knock off before I can take my holiday. 4. *(coll.)* discontinue smth.; give up (work): He at once knocked off painting for the day. 5. *(sl.)* steal smth.: Where did he get all those watches? Did he knock them off?

knock something out—1. remove smth. with a sharp blow: Knock the ash out before you refill your pipe. 2. destroy smth. completely: Our soldiers had orders to knock out the enemy guns. 3. *(coll.)* play music roughly or unskillfully: He can't read music but he can knock out a tune on the piano.

know a thing or two • know all the answers

know a thing or two—be quite competent about how to deal with a particular problem: Hopefully he's the type of rancher who knows a thing or two about how to keep the soil rich and the cows fat.

know all the answers—(also: have all the answers) 1. be extremely knowledgeable; be fully informed: In serials the detective always wins, usually escapes danger, and knows all the answers. 2. is often used with the implication of overconfidence: Johnson's critics saw him as an extremely arrogant man who thought he knew all the answers and was unwilling to make any accommodation.

know a trick or two • know all the tricks of the trade

know a trick or two—be quite shrewd about how to deal

with a particular problem: I know a trick or two about how to handle a customer who is angry or upset.

know all the tricks of the trade—know every smart way in an activity related to one's occupation: I could tell by the way he directed his helper, that he knew all the tricks of the trade.

know about someone • know of someone

know about someone—1. have knowledge or information about smb.: Knowing what I know about her husband ... she is just as delusional as her husband. 2. *(negat.)* be not sure about a person: I don't know about John, but I was about ready to fall through the floor with shame.

know of someone— = *know about someone 1:* I know of one eminent man of science, who was a burning and shining light in his day.

know best • know better

know best—know smth. better than anybody else: On the premise that the workers often know best, the firms are forming "quality circles." These are groups of employees who focus on what can be done to improve output.

know better—1. = *know best:* Community members often know better how to reach their neighbors with key messages on reducing exposure to environmental health hazards. 2. understand the real reason for smth.: After getting his own food, he was jostled roughly so that everything cascaded to the floor ... apparently an accident, too, though Rollie knew better. 3. be wise or sensible enough not to behave in a certain way: Even though he knew better, Vinnie lent Tom his license so he would have identification to cross the border.

know on which side one's bread is buttered • know which way the wind blows

know on which side one's bread is buttered—know where one's interest lies: The judges know on which side their bread was buttered. They would strain a point in favor of the highest political opinion of the day. *Cf.: butter one's bread on both sides—be in very comfortable circumstances; be well provided for:* He's got marble floors in there, crystal figurines on the shelves.... Like we say at home, he butters his bread on both sides.

Note: *The expression is not antonymous in meaning to the phrase* ***not know which end is up****— be utterly confused:* I didn't know which end was up when I first entered the classroom and I had every problem one could imagine...

know which way the wind blows—understand what is happening in changing circumstances: I will say this for the Pharmaceutical Association, they know which way the wind blows, recognizing an opportunity when they see one.

know one's way about • not know where to turn

know one's way about—(also: know one's way around) 1. know how to get from place to place in a neighborhood: John was a very skilled climber; he knew his way about the mountains of Scotland. 2. be extremely knowledgeable or experienced: She could do no better than to put her trust in a man of substance, in the prime of life, who knew his way about.

not know where to turn—(also: not know which way to turn) be uncertain about what to do next: It became apparent that many families of victims did not know where to turn to receive the aid they needed.

Note: *The expression does not correlate in meaning with the phrase* ***not know where to look****—(also: not know which way to look) be quite embarrassed:* I did not know where to look, feeling embarrassed at being so openly praised in front of my colleagues.

know something by heart • know something in one's heart

know something by heart—be able to quote smth. from memory: Few lawyers know by heart the complicated statutes relating to Church matters.

know something in one's heart—realize smth. in the depths of one's mind: Every soldier knows in his heart that he was not made to fire upon the citizens.

knuckle down to something • knuckle under to something

knuckle down to something—get down to work and do it with great energy: This is a year of hard work when one must knuckle down to the task at hand.

knuckle under to something—obey or yield to smth.: Rebecca has shown great courage in refusing to knuckle under to this pressure.

L

labor day • work day

labor day—1. *(Labor Day)* a day celebrated in honor of workers, often as a public holiday: The governing committee of the Stock Exchange decided to close on Monday, on account of Labor Day. *2. (in the former U.S.S.R.)* a unit of labor calculated according to the expected productivity of a worker: The amount of work which can be done in a day is worked out for each farm operation and is counted as a "labor day."

work day—(also: working day) 1. a day on which work is usually done: This year, it happened that Christmas fell on his work day. Still, it won't keep his family from celebrating with Santa. 2. the hours a person works: His work day would generally last from lunchtime through dinner and then he'd work until midnight at the least.

lack for something • lack in something

lack for something—have need of smth.; be without smth.: Fish is so plentiful on this coast that the natives never lack for food.

lack in something—fail to have enough of smth.: No one who is lacking in musical ability will ever become a professional singer.

ladies first • women and children first

ladies first—is used as an allusion to polite procedure in serving food, entering a vehicle, etc.: Mr. Collins pulled open the doors from inside the hall. "Now," he said, "Ladies first..."

women and children first—is used as an allusion to the accepted order of precedence in rescue work: John's intent on making us a nation of mariners and under these circumstances, I'll adopt the old maritime adage, women and children first.

ladies' maid • ladies' man

ladies' maid—a lady's personal servant, especially in charge of her toilet: Ladies traveling alone would never have traveled third class. Even ladies' maids always traveled second.

ladies' man—a man who is fond of female company *(also: woman's man):* They told me you were not a ladies' man, Mr. Smirke.

lady of honor • maid of honor

lady of honor—1. *(Fr.: damme d'honeur)* unmarried woman attending a queen or princess: At night, Her Majesty's ladies of honor came and conducted her to the apartments. 2. a woman with a reputation for loyalty, truthfulness, etc.: How dare you affront an upstanding woman like that sir? I am a lady of honor and you have insulted me like a whore!?

maid of honor—1. principal bridesmaid at a wedding: Lily asked Maria to be her maid of honor. She planned to be married in church. 2. = *lady of honor 1:* His Grace shows as much gallantry as ever to a certain maid of honor.

laid on the shelf • left on the shelf

laid on the shelf—(also: put on the shelf) 1. discharged from service (for reason of age, etc.): He had been laid on the shelf for cowardice in one of the engagements between the Dutch and the English. 2. *(of problems, etc.)* postponed to be considered later if at all: The theory of evolution was laid on the shelf until Charles Darwin and Wallace took it down again.

left on the shelf—(of a woman) considered too old to get married: She refused several offers of marriage, and then, at the age of forty, found herself left on the shelf.

Lake State, the • Salt Lake State, the

Lake State, the—(U.S.) a nickname of the state of Michigan: Michigan is also known as the Lake State, or the Great Lakes State (which appears on the state license plates) for its proximity to Lake Michigan.

Salt Lake State, the—(U.S.) a nickname of the State of Utah: The only "non–Mormon" nickname is the Salt Lake State, but even this is closely linked with the Mormons, who first settled in what is now known as Salt Lake.

lame duck • ugly duckling

lame duck—1. an officeholder who has been defeated for reelection or is not seeking reelection: Tony Blair made himself a lame duck by stating that he would not fight a fourth general election. 2. a person or thing considered as weak or unfortunate: I did find myself waiting for the end to come, which when it did was completely unfulfilling. This movie is just a lame duck with a loaded cast.

ugly duckling—an unpromising person or thing that becomes successful or admirable: In school I was an ugly duckling and a loner. Nobody believed I could ever be a great actress and singer except me.

land of fruit and nuts, the • land of milk and honey, the

land of fruit and nuts, the—(U.S.) a jocular nickname of the state of California *(reference being made to both the agricultural abundance and the stereotypical image of Californians as being other than normal, cf.: "fruit"—(sl.) a crazy person, and "nuts"—(sl.) crazy):* Although Californians are known to come from the "land of fruit and nuts" not all of us are like that.

land of milk and honey, the—1. in the Old Testament, a poetic name for the Promised Land: The Jewish people were brought out of slavery in Egypt by Moses to the land of milk and honey promised to them by God. 2. any place of great abundance: Many Mexicans regard the United States as the land of milk and honey.

land someone in something • land someone with something

land someone in something—(coll.) get a person into difficulties or trouble: It is this decades-old addiction to spending that has landed us in this rotten economic crisis.

land someone with something—(coll.) cause a person to obtain or receive smth. (especially smth. unpleasant): As usual with all sweep stakes I enter, lady luck has landed me with the worst horse in the entire field.

landed immigrant • landed man

landed immigrant—an immigrant to Canada, admitted for permanent residence: If he is to see his child, he will have to be accepted as a landed immigrant.

landed man—a person possessed of land; smb. having an estate in land: He has rather a big noise here. Landed man really, but has a seat on our Board.

landlord • landowner

landlord—a man who rents out accommodation to tenants: We are going back to Manhattan to clean out our old house so we can turn it over to our landlord.

landowner—an owner or proprietor of land: Sandino was the son of a poor native woman and a rich landowner, who didn't recognize him as his son.

Land's End, the • land's end

Land's End, the—(UK) most southerly point in England, at the tip of Cornwall: We were barely able to lay a course through the passage between those islands and the Land's End.

land's end—(also: end of the land) the remotest region of the country: Here there is also a tradition of independence against the rest of New England. It's land's end, so they tend to be suspicious of the rest of the world.

large as life • larger than life

large as life—(also: big as life) said of smb. actually present, especially where a person is not supposed to be: He couldn't have gone abroad—I saw him yesterday, coming out of his office as large as life.

larger than life—said of smb. very much out of the ordinary and likely to attract attention: Many film stars seem to be larger than life to the mass of ordinary people.

large fortune • small fortune

large fortune—great wealth; a huge sum of money: After an exile of many years, Dudley North returned to England with a large fortune.

small fortune—a rather large sum of money: It is said she made a small fortune selling what became known as Durham mustard.

lash out at something • lash out on something

lash out at something—make a sudden and violent verbal attack on smth.: The speaker lashed out at the government's new tax laws.

lash out on something—(coll.) spend freely on smth.; pay a lot of money for smth.: Can we afford to lash out on a new car?

Last Day, the • last days, the

Last Day, the—the Biblical Day of Judgment: They were eager ... if their death anticipated the Last Day, to die in the Holy Land.

last days, the—1. the concluding period of smth.: Though it appears paradoxical, in the last days of the Raj, the British were the only people who wished to keep India united. 2. the period including and immediately preceding the Day of Judgment: Alder gives a chronological order for the many signs that will occur in the last days.

last out something • outlast something

last out something—1. exist or continue for a period of time: Why join this mad adventure of the Bolsheviks, this government that would not last out a week? 2. be enough for a period of time: There was plenty of grass and water to last out the fall. It was fire the ranchers feared.

outlast something—last or exist longer than smth. else: These bikes are extremely well made and will outlast our competitors models.

last thing, the • one final thing

last thing, the—1. smth. that a person does in the last place: The last thing I do at night before going to bed is to check my e-mail. 2. smth. least likely to be expected under the circumstances: Doesn't he know that orange juice is the last thing to drink if you're dieting? 3. *(also: last word, the)* smth. that is most up-to-date; smth. that cannot be surpassed: The last thing in leather is pearl-tinted fish-skin.

Note: *The expression does not fully correlate in meaning with the phrase **latest thing, the**— = last thing, the 3:* The sketch of Bain's facsimile machine of 1843 will shake up those who think the fax machine is the latest thing in technology.

one final thing—*(also: one final word)* is used to introduce a parting comment or advice: And one final thing, don't haul around a lot of expensive camera stuff. It just tells the thieves who to rob.

last word, the • last words

last word, the—1. *(also: last thing, the)* smth. that is most up-to-date; smth. that cannot be surpassed: These three white trucks represent the last word in modern emergency equipment. 2. said of a person or thing that is as bad as it is possible to find: Don't talk to me about untidy kids. I've got two at home that are the last word.

Note: *The expression does not correlate in meaning with the phrase **one final word**—(also: one final thing) used to introduce a parting comment or advice:* "One final word, keep your chin up." "Good advice!"

last words—an utterance that was the last smb. made before dying: The victim of the crime, in her last words, declares, quite unprotestingly, that it is what she expected.

Note: *The expression is not equivalent in meaning to the phrase **famous last words**—*1. *the final statement made by a famous person who is dying:* James Lawrence, whose famous last words were "Don't give up the ship," is buried next to steamboat inventor Robert Fulton. *2. (ironic) a remark or prediction likely to be proved wrong by events:* "With modern technology, we can climb Everest in half the time it took Hillary in 1953." "Famous last words!"

late on in life • later on in life

late on in life—during the last part of one's life or career: He started out as a proofreader late on in life, having grown tired of the motorway driving and office politics of his sales job.

later on in life—at a later stage of one's life or career: In addition to literature, Gulistan was attracted to motion pictures. Later on in life he used this talent as a documentary producer.

latency period • latent period

latency period—*(Psychology)* the period between the ages of 4 or 5 and about 12 years, which separates pregenital sexuality from the beginning of puberty: I remember a very definite change when I reached what in modern child psychology is called the "latency period."

Note: *The expression does not correlate in meaning with the phrase **latency time**—(Computers) the delay before a transfer of data begins following an instruction for its transfer:* The access time consists of the latency time plus the transfer time. The latency represents the amount of time it takes to find the chosen address.

latent period—*(med.)* the period during which a disease lurks in the system before manifesting its presence: Rubeola is unequivocally contagious. A latent period of from ten to fourteen days intervenes between exposure and the development of the febrile symptoms.

laundry list • shopping list

laundry list—said of a large number of usually unpleasant things: General Motors is charged by its critics with primary responsibility for a laundry list of social ills, including air pollution.

shopping list—said of a long list of items to be considered, acted upon, etc.: Ground-to-air missiles were on the "shopping list" of defense equipment taken to Moscow.

Law Day • Lawful Day

Law Day—*(U.S.)* the day established by a resolution of Congress in 1961 to draw attention to the principles of justice and the practice of law: For the last several years the American Bar Association has been sponsoring "Law Day" on May 1.

Lawful Day—*(hist.)* a day on which the courts sat; a day on which particular kinds of business might be legally done: A calendar indicated the lawful days for legal business, and also the festivals, anniversaries of historical events, etc.

law of nature • law of the jungle

law of nature—*(also: natural law)* 1. is used to refer to a particular phenomenon always occurring if certain conditions are present: A fundamental law of nature must capture a cause-and-effect relation about the workings of the real world. 2. is used of ideas, etc. as implanted by nature in the human mind: Right libertarians are not alone in claiming that their particular ideology is based on the law of nature.

law of the jungle—*(also: jungle law)* the superiority of brute force or self-interest in the ruthless struggle for survival: A purely materialistic society inevitably succumbs to the law of the jungle and political dictatorship.

lawman • man of law

lawman—*(U.S.)* 1. a law-enforcement officer: Had he actually seen the rough law-men bundle the startled widow into the Black Maria? 2. a sheriff or marshal: A retired lawman, still sporting a tin star, demonstrated how he could kill with either hand.

man of law—*(UK dated)* a lawyer: Another man of law now came in, straight from the magistrates' chamber.

lay a finger on someone • put the finger on someone

lay a finger on someone—*(also: set a finger on someone)* touch or harm a person however slightly: I never ever laid a finger on him. We were very good friends.

put the finger on someone—*(sl.)* inform against smb.; denounce a person to the police: If I'm grabbed with this junk I'll rot in jail before I put the finger on you.

lay a finger on something • lay one's finger on something

lay a finger on something—harm or interfere with smth. however slightly: Nobody is going, within the foreseeable future, to lay a finger on the trade unions.

lay one's finger on something—*(also: put one's finger on something)* 1. find or locate smth.: So far I haven't been able to lay my finger on the book you requested. 2. point out precisely where smth. is wrong, etc.: I know that, if I knew enough about this case, I could lay my finger on the cause.

lay a weight on something • lay weight on something

lay a weight on something—*(also: put a weight on something)* add weight to smth.; make smth. heavy: Try either bending a warm board carefully by hand, or lay a weight on it overnight.

lay weight on something—emphasize smth.; treat smth. as being particularly important: We have laid weight on the problem of quality ever since the company's inception.

lay away money • lay out money

lay away money—save some money: I am trying hard to lay away enough money to buy a house.

lay out money—spend a certain amount of money: She had to lay out a lot of money to get her car fixed.

lay cash on the barrelhead • lay cash on the line

lay cash on the barrelhead—(also: put cash on the barrelhead) pay money at the time of the transaction: It remains to be seen whether the Russians are ready to lay cash on the barrelhead.

lay cash on the line—(also: put cash on the line) allocate money; make a financial commitment: You're not about to lay cash on the line without decent answers to a question or two.

Note: *The expression does not correlate in meaning with the phrase* ***lay it on the line****—(coll.) speak out firmly and frankly (also: put it on the line):* I'll lay it on the line for you, if you like. Are you thinking of asking my girl to marry you?

lay down one's job • lie down on the job

lay down one's job—(also: lay down one's office) resign from a position of power or responsibility: Buddy Darden is just one of the people who was brave enough to lay down his job in Congress.

lie down on the job—be irresponsible or careless in one's job; fail to work as hard as one should: After a few months ... they get tired of the whole business and lie down on the job.

lay figure • lay person

lay figure—1. a wooden figure of the human body, used as a model for the arrangement of draperies, etc.: Her aunt asked her to stand as a sort of lay figure on which to display them [shawls]. 2. smb. of little importance; an insignificant person: At chapel the registrar is the important person, and the officiating minister is a mere lay figure. 3. a character in fiction lacking in the attributes of reality: The women are not so well drawn as the men, but Mrs. Gall, while conventional, is not a lay figure.

lay person—(also: layman) a non-expert in relation to some particular profession: The twentieth century has obliterated the skilled amateur and widened the gap between the technical professional and the lay person.

lay of the land • lay the land

lay of the land—(also: lie of the land) the state of affairs: I think my success was due to my waiting and not rushing in before I saw the lay of the land.

lay the land—(Nautical) sail out to such a distance as to lose sight of land: We found ourselves to be at the distance of seven leagues to the westward of the island. About noon that day we had laid the land.

lay one's hands on something • lay one's hands to something

lay one's hands on something—(also: put one's hands on something) 1. find or locate smth.: I can't lay my hands on the account book — have you seen it? 2. gain possession of smth.: I'd like to know where I can lay my hands on that special tobacco.

lay one's hands to something—start work on smth.; engage in smth.: In John Gollan's words, "there is no more noble task to which we could lay our hands."

lay out the fire • put out the fire

lay out the fire—make a fire start burning: He was still turned away from me, intent on his task of laying out the fire.

put out the fire—make a light or fire stop burning: Put out all fires before leaving the camping ground.

lay over • put over

lay over—(U.S.) make an overnight stop on a journey (by plane): This flight lays over at Great Falls before completing the journey to New York.

put over—(of a ship) move to one side: There's a sailing boat coming towards us, you'd better put over to give her room.

lay someone out • put someone out

lay someone out—1. knock a person to the ground (unconscious): The champion laid the contender out in the second round. 2. *(coll.)* exhaust or adversely affect smb.: I've had influenza and it laid me out for two very unpleasant and painful weeks. 3. *(of a dead body)* prepare for burial: Two of the women came to lay out the body. 4. *(coll.)* scold a person severely *(also: lay someone out in lavender):* The director laid Jim out for being late again.

put someone out—1. cause smb. to leave a building: "If they don't get out they will be put out bodily," retorted Hart. 2. disconcert or inconvenience a person: Are you sure it won't put you out if I stay to dinner? 3. cause a person to be confused or worried: The least thing puts him out, he is easily upset.

Note: *The expression does not correlate in meaning with the phrase* ***put someone out of the way****—remove smb. from the scene; make away with a person:* Though he had a wife already, he determined to put her out of the way, and marry his own niece Elizabeth.

lay someone out in lavender • put someone out to grass

lay someone out in lavender—(coll.) scold a person severely *(also: lay someone out):* If you ever feel like you need to lay me out in lavender again, just forget it.

put someone out to grass—(coll.) send smb. on a holiday or into retirement *(also: send someone out to grass):* Of course, if you consider my age, they should have put me out to grass a long time ago.

Note: *The expression does not correlate in meaning with the phrase* ***bring someone to grass****—(Mining) carry an injured person to the surface from the mine:* His son soon got him out, procured assistance, and he was brought to grass and carried to his home.

lay someone to rest • lay someone's ghost to rest

lay someone to rest—(euph.) bury a person after he has died *(also: lay someone to sleep):* Three weeks after his death, family and friends gathered Monday to pay tribute to Pokorney and to lay him to rest.

lay someone's ghost to rest—(also: put someone's ghost to rest) finally get rid of a dead person's continuing influence: Now China must take another crucial step: It must lay Mao's ghost to rest.

lay someone to sleep • put someone to sleep

lay someone to sleep—1. put smb., usually a child, into bed for sleep: The child is weary; let us lay him to sleep on the settee for a while. 2. *(euph.)* bury a person after he has died *(also: lay someone to rest):* One generation of burghers after another was laid to sleep in the quiet churchyard.

put someone to sleep—(also: send someone to sleep) 1. make a person fall asleep because smth. is too boring: You ask me what book I read now to put me to sleep — why, Murray's "Handbook for France." 2. make a person unconscious by using an anesthetic: The surgeon gave him something to dose and put him to sleep. 3. *(euph., of an animal)* kill painlessly out of mercy: Sheba was growing old and blind and had to be put to sleep.

lay someone up • put someone up

lay someone up—(of an illness) cause a person to stay in bed *(usually Passive):* I've been laid up since Christmas with a bad cough.

put someone up—provide food and lodging for a person: I can put up two adults, but no children.

lay something down • put something down

lay something down—1. *(of laws, conditions, etc.)* state or declare firmly: We had to lay down rules for the behavior of the members. 2. *(of money)* bet on smth.: How much are you prepared to lay down on that horse? 3. start to build smth.: We shall have to lay down a new floor in the upstairs rooms. 4. *(also: lay something by)* store smth. for the future: When his grandson was born, the lord laid down a case of best wine for the boy's 21st birthday. 5. mark smth. on a plan or map: He now laid down clearly the island groups of the North Pacific.

put something down—1. *(of a plane)* cause to land: The pilot was able to put the damaged plane down safely in the field. 2. *(coll., also: put something away)* eat a lot of food: You'd be surprised at the amount that boy can put down in a single day. 3. cease doing smth. such as work: Put down whatever you are doing and join the party. 4. record smth. in writing: Make sure that you put down every word she says. 5. *(of money)* give in part payment: You can buy this house by putting 10 percent down and paying the rest over twenty-five years. 6. = *lay something down 4:* I have put down over 100 eggs this winter, so as to have plenty at the cheap price. 7. *(UK)* kill an animal out of mercy: The dear old dog got so ill that it was kinder to have him put down. 8. suppress or stop smth.: The police are attempting to put down violent crime in the city. 9. *(coll.)* express disapproval or a poor opinion of smth.: Tom's latest book has been severely put down in the newspaper reports.

lay something off • put something off

lay something off—1. spread smth. such as money more widely to insure against a loss: The large insurance contract was laid off among many firms. 2. *(of a ship)* anchor near a certain location: The ship was laid off outside the harbor while the storm lasted. 3. stop wearing smth.: It's time we were able to lay off these heavy winter clothes.

put something off—1. *(also: put something over)* postpone smth.; leave smth. to a later date: Don't put off making the arrangements until the last minute. 2. = *lay something off 3:* The war was over but Harold was still in khaki; he never looked so nearly a gentleman again when he put it off. 3. disconnect electricity: Please put off all the lights as you leave the building. 4. get rid of smth.; cease to consider smth.: It's good to have put off the responsibility of the chairmanship.

Note: *The expression does not fully correlate in meaning with the phrase* ***put something away****—1. put smth. in the usual place of storage (such as a drawer, box, etc.):* Please put your toys away before you go to bed. 2. *(coll., also: put something down) eat a lot of food:* You'd be surprised at the amount that boy can put away in a single day. 3. *(of money or a supply of goods) save for future use:* I have a little money put away for a rainy day. 4. = *put something off 4:* It's time to put away those foolish ideas and become serious.

lay something on • put something on

lay something on—1. supply (a house) with gas, electricity, etc.: The house has water and electricity laid on. 2. *(coll.)* deliver or provide smth.: The club laid on a special meal for the visitors. 3. impose smth. such as a duty: Further taxes may be laid on this spring.

put something on—1. dress oneself in clothing: He put his coat on hurriedly and ran out of the house. 2. make a light or fire start burning: I'll go in and put the fire on while you put the car in the garage. 3. *(of a meal)* start cooking: Phone me as soon as you leave the office and I'll put the dinner on. 4. *(of weight, speed, etc.)* gain: If I put on another inch, I shan't be able to wear this dress. 5. add smth.: British rail will put on an additional train to carry the expected crowd of football supporters. 6. *(of a show)* stage; cause to take place: Which play is the Theater Group putting on next?

lay something on the table *(UK)* • lay something on the table *(U.S.)*

lay something on the table (UK)—raise an issue for consideration (as a parliamentary procedure): A few days later Shrewsbury laid on the table of the Lords a bill for limiting the duration of Parliaments.

lay something on the table (U.S.)—suspend an issue from consideration; postpone the vote on an issue until another time: It was her proposal to lay the bill on the table while we undertook further research.

lay something out • put something out

lay something out—1. spread smth. (for use or view): All the family's pitiful possessions were laid out in the yard. 2. arrange the plan or appearance of a garden, etc.: Laying out the page well makes all the difference to the ease of reading a book. 3. *(of one's money, strength, etc.)* use; spend: I had to lay out all my strength to move the rock. 4. make a fire start burning: He was still turned away from me, intent on his task of laying out the fire.

put something out—1. place smth. out of doors: If it turns fine, I shall put the washing out. 2. = *lay something out 1:* Please put out my best suit for the governor's meeting. 3. *(of a plant)* send out new growth: We thought the bush was dead, but it has already put out some new branches. 4. = *lay something out 3:* Putting out all his strength, he uprooted the tree. 5. produce smth.: This engine puts out more electric current than the other one. 6. make smth. public: The police have put out a description of the jewel thieves. 7. make a light or fire stop burning: Put out all fires before leaving the camping ground. 8. *(of a joint)* dislocate: I can't play tennis with you this week, I've put my shoulder out.

lay something over • put something over

lay something over—*(often Passive)* 1. postpone smth.; leave smth. to a later date: The concert had to be laid over for several days. 2. *(also: overlay something)* put a coating over the surface of smth.; ornament smth.: The cover of the book was laid over with gold and silver.

put something over—1. make an idea, etc. understood and well received: Advertisements are intended to put over the best qualities of the product to the public. 2. *(also: put something off)* = *lay something over 1:* We shall have to put the garden party over until the weather is fine.

lay something to • put something to

lay something to—*(of a ship)* anchor near a certain location: Till the next morning, she was laid to, under a close reefed main top sail.

put something to—close smth. firmly: Please put the door to, it's come open a little.

lay something up • put something up

lay something up—1. *(also: lay something by)* save or store smth. for future use: The power stations are laying up their usual supplies of coal. 2. *(of a car, boat, etc.)* take out of use (for repairs, etc.): At the end of the season, all the boats are formally laid up in the harbor.

put something up—1. build smth.; place smth. in position: You have to put up a fence one foot away from the property line. 2. show smth. such as a notice in a public place: The examination results will be put up on this board tomorrow. 3. *(of cost, taxes, etc.)* increase or raise: These rents are fixed and cannot be put up. 4. pack smth.: She put up a parcel for her daughter who was away at college. 5. offer opposition: They were looking for an excuse to stop fighting, because neither one of them put up an argument. 6. offer smth. for sale: After grandmother's death, the furniture was put up for sale. 7. = *lay something up 2:* We had to put the car up for the winter, it was not fit to drive in snow.

Note: *The expression does not fully correlate in meaning with the phrase* ***set something up***—1. = *put something up 1:* Does any of you know how to set up a tent? 2. *establish an organization:* A special committee has been set up to examine the details of the suggestion. 3. *(Sport) reach a new record:* The young swimmer has set up a new fast time for the backstroke. 4. *place drinks or glasses ready:* Will you set up the drinks while I look after the food? 5. *cause pain or infection:* This wet weather sets up the ache in my old wound. 6. *produce a loud noise:* The crowd set up a shout as the winner neared the post.

lay-by *(UK)* • lay-by *(U.S.)*

lay-by (UK)—1. a roadside parking or rest area for drivers: The holidaymakers had stopped in a lay-by at Oban and Miss Coldrick thinks she left the camera on the car boot. 2. an agreement to purchase goods by paying for them by installments: When making a lay-by you should receive from the trader a copy of the written contract.

lay-by (U.S.)—the final operation in the growing of a field crop leaving it to mature without further cultivation: The amount of potassium required may be split between the planting and lay-by application.

lead a cat and dog life • lead a dog's life

lead a cat and dog life—(of two people) engage in constant quarreling *(also: live a cat and dog life):* They have led a cat-and-dog life almost since the day they were married.

lead a dog's life—(also: live a dog's life) lead a wretched unpleasant existence: Poor woman! She's led a dog's life since she married that man.

lead someone a dance • lead the dance

lead someone a dance—cause a person much exertion or trouble with no adequate result: The prettiest of all the girls was the schoolie, and didn't she lead the lads a dance.

lead the dance—take the lead in a course of action: There is still a very subtle struggle for control. Who will lead the dance and who will follow?

lead someone in a string • string someone along

lead someone in a string—have complete control over another person: It is a sad condition for one who ruled womankind as he, that a woman should lead him in a string.

string someone along—(coll.) deliberately mislead a person into believing or doing smth.: He'll never marry her, he's just stringing her along!

Note: *The expression does not correlate in meaning with the phrase* ***string along with someone****—(coll.)* 1. *accompany a person (especially one with more experience):* Sally seemed to know where she was going, so I decided to string along with her. 2. *maintain a relationship even if without much enthusiasm:* She had been much younger than the crowd which had grown up with Minnie, but she had strung along with them.

lead to something • lead up to something

lead to something—1. *(of a road, etc.)* provide a way for smb. to reach a place: She hurried across the square to the street which led to the bridge. *2.* be the cause of smth.; result in smth.: "Accident proneness" implies the possession of those qualities which lead to an undue number of accidents.

lead up to something—1. *(of a road, etc.)* take smb. as far as a place: From here you can follow a steep track that leads up to the top of the hill. *2.* come before an event: In the months leading up to the great ceremony, many people took part in the preparations. 3. prepare to introduce a subject: Be careful how you lead up to mentioning a possible rise with your employer.

leader of an orchestra *(UK)* • leader of an orchestra *(U.S.)*

leader of an orchestra (UK)—the senior violinist who acts as an assistant to the conductor: Where does the leader of an orchestra normally sit — to the left or the right of the conductor?

leader of an orchestra (U.S.)—the conductor: People notice the leader of an orchestra but often forget the importance of the section heads.

leading man • man of light and leading

leading man—(also: main man) 1. a person that guides, directs, or leads: The leading man in charge of this search had signaled his intention to resign. 2. an actor who plays the leading role: Mario was a character actor, but ... he suddenly became a leading man in numerous action pictures.

man of light and leading—(usually pl.) a person of intellectual, moral, or spiritual authority: When a monarch visits the Court of another nation, men of "light and leading" are usually invited as guests to meet him.

Note: *The expression does not correlate in meaning with the phrase* ***Old Light men****—(hist., also: Old Lights) religious traditionalists who believed the new religious movement (New Lights) threatened established religion:* There is thus a duality of political outlook among the Presbyterians, with the tide tending to run in favour of the Old Light men.

lean on something • lean towards something

lean on something—depend on smth.; rely on smth. for support: Christianity may lean on the civil and ecclesiastical power.

lean towards something—have a tendency to act in a particular way; tend to some quality or condition: Do some oriental philosophies lean towards fatalism?

leap in the dark • shot in the dark

leap in the dark—a hazardous action of which one cannot foresee the consequences: Who'd marry if he was afraid he'd regret it later? What is life, old boy, but a leap in the dark?

shot in the dark—a wild guess or try made at random: The suggested solution was just a shot in the dark, but it turned out to be correct.

leave alone • leave well alone

leave alone—(also: let alone) not to mention; not counting: We shall never get six of us in the car, leave alone bags and boxes.

leave well alone—(also: leave well enough alone) make no change to smth. that is satisfactory (in case one makes things worse): It's a great deal of trouble and unnecessary expense. Why can't you leave well alone?

leave it to someone • leave someone to it

leave it to someone—let another person deal with a matter: The professionals all take a greater share of responsibility if a project is to be a success instead of leaving it to the "jack of all trades" — the project engineer.

leave someone to it—leave a person alone to proceed with smth. without interfering with his work: He is professional enough to know what needs doing so I just left him to it.

leave someone a clear field • leave someone the field

leave someone a clear field—give a person a free hand; abstain from interference: And I've never written yet — that is, never sent a letter away. I've been very good to them in leaving them a clear field.

leave someone the field—1. *(of an army)* retreat after having been defeated by the enemy in battle: Shortly before midnight, the French retreated in disarray, leaving the field to the English. 2. yield to an opponent in an argument, etc.; relinquish smth. to a person: Within Spain itself only pro–Nationalist accounts of the 1930s could be published, leaving the field of serious scholarship to foreigners.

leave someone alone • leave someone to oneself

leave someone alone—1. go away from a person: Her parents had gone on holiday for a week, and left us alone in their big house. 2. *(also: let someone alone)* abstain from disturbing or interfering with a person: She yelled at me to go away and leave her alone. But I ignored her and walked up to her anyway.

leave someone to oneself— = *leave someone alone 2:* With his heart sick and sore, he had resolved to go away and leave her to herself, as he imagined she wished to be.

leave someone cold • leave someone out in the cold

leave someone cold—fail to impress or interest a person: An orator may discourse very eloquently on injustice and leave his audience cold.

leave someone out in the cold—ignore or abandon smb.: Developing countries might be left out in the cold in current world trade talks.

Note: *The expression does not fully correlate in meaning with the phrase* ***leave someone out***—1. = *leave someone out in the cold:* It's Mary's own fault if she feels left out at the party; she makes no effort to be friendly to people. 2. *fail to include a person (in a list, etc.):* He toasted all the other ladies present, but left Jane out.

leave someone stew • leave someone stew in one's own juice

leave someone stew—*(also: let someone stew)* keep a person in a state of uneasy anticipation or suspense: I knew that the group would be wondering what was going to happen next to them but I decided to leave them stew on it for a while.

leave someone stew in one's own juice—*(also: let someone stew in one's own juice)* leave a person to his own devices to suffer the consequences of his own actions: He's run into debt again, but this time we're leaving him to stew in his own juice.

leave someone with something • leave something with someone

leave someone with something—leave a person in possession of smth. that may be a burden or responsibility: He asked me to hold this parcel for him a moment, then he went off and left me with it.

leave something with someone—leave smth. in a person's care: You won't actually get to speak to the minister but you can leave a message with his secretary.

lecture at someone • lecture to someone

lecture at someone—talk to a person in a sententious, pompous manner: He doesn't talk to you if you approach him, he lectures at you pedantically.

lecture to someone—give a formal talk (to a group of students, etc.): He still finds the time to make frequent visits to Rio Grande University where he lectures to students in the School of Business.

Note: *The expression does not fully correlate in meaning with the phrase* ***lecture someone***—1. *reproach or scold a person:* He left the room, coming back only minutes later to lecture me for not cleaning off the counter after doing the dishes. *2.* = *lecture to someone:* When Krastins lectures his students on Greco-Roman palaces or baroque churches, he turns to photographs.

lecture in something • lecture on something

lecture in something—give lectures in a subject to a group of students: Dr. Watson lectures in English literature.

lecture on something—1. lecture to students on a specific topic: This term he is lecturing on the nineteenth-century novelists. 2. give a long talk on a topic to a group of people: He goes round the country lecturing on the evils of drink.

left at the mercy of someone • left to the tender mercies of someone

left at the mercy of someone—left in smb.'s absolute power: Once the Roman army withdrew, England was left at the mercy of various marauding tribes.

left to the tender mercies of someone—*(ironic)* left to be dealt with by smb. who is not likely to show any kindness or sympathy: I found her father left to the tender mercies of the savages, deserted by you in the bush.

left-hand • left-handed

left-hand—1. said of smth. situated on the left side: Carry on past the school and take the left hand turning towards Heddington. 2. said of a car with left-hand steering: By the way, it's kind of weird drive a left-hand car in a left-hand side lane (a continental car in UK). 3. *(of bidirectional traffic)* keeping to the left side of the road: Countries that use left-hand traffic account for about 30 percent of the world's population, a sixth of its area and a quarter of its roads.

left-handed—1. using the left hand for writing, etc.: When a left-handed person tries to write like a right-handed person, it doesn't work. 2. *(of things)* designed to be used in the left hand: With properly designed left handed scissors, your natural cutting action matches that of the scissors. 3. *(in the phrase "left-handed compliment")*—a statement that sounds like praise but has an insulting meaning: I wasn't sure if it was a left-handed compliment or his usual condescension.

left-hand man • left-handed man

left-hand man—one's associate who is not really important or effective (*a play on the expression "right-hand man"—a person's chief assistant):* When he attempted to characterize me as Gritz's "right-hand man," I hastened to point out that I barely qualified as his "left-hand man."

left-handed man—a man who uses chiefly the left hand for ordinary tasks: College-educated left-handed men earn almost 15 percent more on average than right-handed men with similar educations.

leg-show • show a leg

leg-show— a theatrical performance by scantily-dressed women: At a leg-show of these days you saw far less of the female form than is now exhibited in the streets.

show a leg—is used to urge people to get up or do smth. with more effort: In the morning, the boatswain's mate would awaken the crew with the cry "show a leg."

lending library *(UK)* • lending library *(U.S.)*

lending library (UK)—a library from which books may be taken away without direct payment: He looked a little on the young side ... to spend his life in lending libraries. The perpetual student?

lending library (U.S.)—a library from which books may be taken away with direct payment: This payment does not cover verification and location of materials not in the lending library's collection.

let alone • let well alone

let alone—(also: leave alone) not to mention; not counting: It is hard to get a gardener who can prune a gooseberry-bush, let alone raise a cucumber.

let well alone—(also: leave well alone) make no change to smth. that is satisfactory (in case one makes things worse): Was he a fool? Could he not let well alone?

let go of someone • let someone go

*let go of someone—*stop holding a person: He shouted at the cops, "Let go of me! You have to let go of me!"

*let someone go—*1. allow smb. to leave: Taking the man prisoner might jeopardize the mission, so he decides to let the prisoner go. 2. discharge a person from employment: Since we are going away for the summer, we will have to let our housekeeper go.

Note: *The expression does not correlate in meaning with the phrase* ***let oneself go****—*1. *throw off restraint in one's behavior; act in defiance of social conventions:* At a party, when Smith lets himself go, he can be quite amusing. 2. *neglect one's appearance, personal habits, etc.:* She's terribly depressed, but tries not "to let herself go," keeps young-looking.

let go of something • let go with something

*let go of something—*stop holding smth.; release smth.: As soon as I let go of the leash, the dog ran away.

*let go with something—*give vent to laughter, angry words, etc.: The lawyer let go with a vicious attack on the tactics of his opponent.

Note: *Neither expression correlates in meaning with the phrase* ***let something go****—pay no attention to smth.; neglect smth.:* Robert let his teeth go when he was young and now he has to go to the dentist pretty often.

let it all hang out • let it go hang

let it all hang out—(coll.) let the truth be known; not disguise anything: No names, of course, will be used; he doesn't expect everyone will be as willing as he is to let it all hang out.

Note: *The expression does not correlate in meaning with the phrase* ***hang it all****—(exclam.) used to express one's anger, irritation, etc. (also: hang it):* "Oh, hang it all, Kit, why don't you say something?"

*let it go hang—*1. *(coll.)* become indifferent to smth.; take no interest in smth.: Either you work on pronunciation very well, or you just let it go hang. 2. *(exclam.)* is used to express one's anger or irritation with smth.: Love was the only thing in the world that mattered. Achievement — pah! Let it go hang!

let off steam • put on steam

let off steam—(also: blow off steam) give vent to one's repressed emotions (by talking in an unrestrained manner, etc.): This special session will give politicians a chance to let off steam.

put on steam—(also: get up steam) build up strength or energy; become more active: Get on a little faster; put a little more steam on, ma'am, pray.

let one's hair down • put one's hair up

let one's hair down—(also: let one's back hair down) throw off restraint in one's behavior: Those who are doomed to a life of formality look forward to the week-end when they can let their hair down.

*put one's hair up—*assume adult responsibilities: Lively young thing, I recall — but she'll have put her hair up by now.

Note: *The expression does not correlate in meaning with the phrase* ***lift someone's hair****—(U.S. hist.) scalp a person:* They [Indians] wouldn't hesitate to lift the hair of any lone white man.

let someone down • let someone down easy

*let someone down—*disappoint a person; fail to support or aid smb.: I leave it to you, Stephen. I know you'll not let me down.

Note: *The expression is not antonymous in meaning to the phrase* ***let up on someone****— treat a person less harshly or severely:* By the time Jon turned eight, our financial problems became so overwhelming that I began to let up on him.

let someone down easy—(also: let someone down softly) treat a person considerately so as to spare his self-respect: The fact is, and I hope you would respect and appreciate this, I care for him enough to let him down easy.

let someone in for something • let someone in on something

*let someone in for something—*involve a person in smth. unpleasant; cause smb. to have trouble: The boy's careless treatment of the car has let me in for a large repair bill.

Note: *The expression does not correlate in meaning with the phrase* ***put someone in for something****— enter a person for an examination, contest, etc.:* How many of your runners are you putting in for the race?

*let someone in on something—*make smth. such as a plan, agreement, etc. known to a person: He was let in on the arrangements without our consent.

let someone off • let someone off the hook

*let someone off—*excuse a person; not punish severely enough: "Are you going to let him off?" demanded Denny suspiciously. "You never can be stiff in the back, Charley."

let someone off the hook—(also: get someone off the hook) free a person from difficulty, an embarrassing situation, etc.: The officer was pretty surprised at my tenacity, and it motivated him to let me off the hook.

let someone stew • let someone stew in one's own juice

let someone stew—(also: leave someone stew) keep a person in a state of uneasy anticipation or suspense: For one delicious week I let him stew while he begged and pleaded for his career, his marriage, his reputation.

let someone stew in one's own juice—(also: leave someone stew in one's own juice) leave a person to his own devices to suffer the consequences of his own actions: Some were saying "well he asked for it, now let him stew in his own juice."

Note: *The expression does not correlate in meaning with the phrase* ***juice someone up****—(sl.) stimulate or invigorate a person:* He's a former U.S. Navy pilot who was given pills to juice him up for long flights.

let something slide • let something slip

*let something slide—*1. let smth. take its own course: If California was going to cost the Union so much, it would be better to let California slide. 2. neglect or ignore smth. such as one's work, etc.: She let her lessons slide, preferring the company of her classmates in the residence. 3. *(of an opportunity, etc.)* allow to slip away without being profitably employed: Don't let any chances slide past you, for your first may be your last.

*let something slip—*1. = *let something slide 2:* He is too smart to let his work slip — rather, he has become a master at doing the minimal work needed to get by. 2. = *let something slide 3:* Every section of the community has an interest in the Initiative and as an area we mustn't let the opportunity slip. 3. *(also: let something slip out)* say smth. without intending to: He carelessly let slip this information in conversation with a journalist.

let the cat out of the bag • let the genie out of the bottle

let the cat out of the bag—(accidentally) reveal a secret: A few days later, when I wasn't around, she let the cat out of the bag. Apparently, she didn't realize she had ruined a surprise.

let the genie out of the bottle—let smth. bad happen that cannot be put right or controlled: The ambassador warned that the deployment of space weapons will "let the genie out of the bottle."

let the fox guard the henhouse • put the cat among the pigeons

let the fox guard the henhouse—(also: set the fox to keep the geese) trust a person with smth. that he is especially likely to misappropriate or abuse: Back in 1951, members of the State Department wrote the text of the treaty. Now different people in the State Department are trying to define what was written. I don't believe we should let the fox guard the henhouse.

put the cat among the pigeons—(also: set the cat among the pigeons) do or say smth. that is bound to cause trouble and make people angry: I put the cat among the pigeons by recommending that revalidation should include the provision of a certificate that the doctor has passed a knowledge test at some stage in the five year period.

let's be having you • thanks for having me

let's be having you—is used at public places as a request to move somewhere quickly: Ladies and gentlemen, let's be having you: the museum closes in ten minutes.

thanks for having me—thank you for your hospitality *(said as one says goodbye):* Thanks for having me, Jo — we've all had a lovely time!

letter box • mailbox

letter box—1. *(UK)* a private box or other container to which mail is delivered: When I came back from holiday the first thing I found in my letter box was a letter refusing my proposal for the TV show. 2. *(UK)* a narrow opening in a door through which a mailman can push envelopes, cards, etc.: Mr. Marble, who was already awake ... heard the newspaper pushed through the letter box of the front door downstairs. 3. a box in a public place in which letters are deposited for dispatch: Of all the clues, the most promising of all was that provided by the scrawl on a penny postcard, dropped in a letter box in Newark. 4. a film format for movies when shown on television: The term "letter box" was originally coined by 20th Century–Fox when CinemaScope first appeared in 1953.

mailbox—1. *(U.S.)* a private box to which mail is delivered *(in some areas the resident signals the mailman by putting up the little red flag that the mailbox contains letters to be picked up and mailed):* A letter in his mailbox during his sophomore year of college started Dawayne on a journey that took him to Boston, then Hawaii. 2. = *letter box 3:* Letters are collected from mailboxes located throughout the country, each posted with a sign that informs customers of mail pick-up times. 3. *(Computers)* the directory where computer stores messages: How do I change the display order of the messages in my mailbox? I want the most recent items to appear at the top of my list.

See also: post box / post-office box.

letterman • man of letters

letterman—(U.S.) a sportsman who has received some mark of distinction: He holds a Masters degree in Physical Education from the Citadel, where he was a three years letterman in football.

Note: *The compound does not correlate in meaning with* ***mailman****— a person who delivers letters, etc. or collects them from the letter-boxes:* Our mail was delivered by the mailman who drove his car to every mail box along his assigned route.

man of letters—(formal) a scholar; a writer: To listen to the discoursing of an accomplished man of letters is always a pleasure.

level someone • level with someone

level someone—1. knock a person down: However, Cody got cocky. He began to taunt Marshall, who leveled him with a football style tackle. 2. totally baffle a person; render smb. completely helpless: These questions absolutely leveled me. Actually, they still do; I just handle it better.

level with someone—(coll.) give smb. one's honest opinion; speak frankly with a person: I'd better level with you, son.... From now on, control is through me.

level something against someone • level something at someone

level something against someone—state a charge or criticism against a person: He seems to have quite the tendency of leveling accusations against other people based on pure, thin-air speculation.

level something at someone—1. aim smth., such as a weapon, directly towards smb.: In a moment he was up again, swaying unsteadily on his feet, but still trying to level his rifle at me. 2. = *level something against someone:* Both sides have spent much time leveling accusations at each other about political games and endangering the safety of Australians.

liable for something • liable to something

liable for something—legally responsible for smth.: Is a man liable for his wife's debts in your country?

liable to something—1. subject to some penalty: If you drive a car to the danger of the public, you make yourself liable to a heavy fine. 2. predisposed to smth.; likely to do smth.: We put ourselves under pressure, which made us liable to mistakes in making decisions.

liberty boat • liberty ship

liberty boat—(UK Nautical) a boat carrying sailors with leave to go ashore: They knew that the liberty-boat would be on shore for them at that hour.

liberty ship—(WWII) a prefabricated U.S.-built merchant vessel: Some of the wartime "liberty" ships fractured when lying in port, without operational loads.

liberty boy • liberty man

liberty boy—1. *(coll.)* a noisy partisan of liberty; a supporter for a freedom movement: The liberty boys were honored with the presence of ministers. 2. *(UK Nautical)* a sailor having leave of absence: People from ships called "liberty boys" are only allowed to come on shore on Sundays for recreation.

liberty man— = *liberty boy 2:* A few hundred liberty men on each side ... their flights delayed by bad weather, returned to the firing line too late.

life in the wild • life in the wilderness

life in the wild—(of animals and birds) life in an undomesticated free state in their natural surroundings: Even as Buck is increasingly drawn to a life away from humanity, a life in the wild, his affection for Thornton keeps him from making the final break.

Note: *The expression does not correlate in meaning with the compound* ***wildlife****— wild animals and birds living in a natural undomesticated state:* We showed the photos of the animal to locals who know the wildlife of the area, but nobody had ever seen this creature before.

life in the wilderness—life in a mostly uninhabited area in its natural state, such as a forest or mountainous region: The story tells of a modern-day pioneer who becomes bored with the troubles of city life and heads for life in the wilderness.

lifeguard • life preserver

lifeguard—1. a person assigned to watch against accidents to bathers at a beach, etc.: When a party bathe, one or two of the best swimmers should be posted as lifeguards. 2. a device attached to a locomotive for sweeping obstructions from the track: Had not the lifeguard protected the wheels of the engine the train would have been thrown off the line.

life preserver—1. a life belt or other device used in saving life at sea: Taking a life preserver, I ventured into one of the little canoes. 2. a bludgeon loaded with lead, intended for self-defense: The prisoner was given in charge to the police, a life preserver having been found upon him. 3. smth. that may help a person in a critical situation: He was busy preparing a "life preserver" in the form of stolen documents he could use later.

***Note:** Neither compound fully correlates in meaning with **life-saver**—1. = lifeguard 1:* ...mouth-to-mouth resuscitation, by which a life-saver inflates a victim's lungs with his own breath. 2. = *life preserver 3:* Again many thanks for the money you sent. It was a life-saver. 3. *a candy shaped like a small life-belt:* The American soldiers gave us chocolate bars, life saver candies, chewing gums...

lifeline • line of life

lifeline—1. a rope (attached to a life-buoy) to which a person may cling to save his life: Lifelines used on Mr. Heath's ill-fated yacht were yesterday called sub-standard by the British Safety Council. 2. smth. regarded as indispensable for survival: A £54-million "lifeline" was thrown by the Government yesterday to the farming industry. 3. *(Palmistry)* a line that supposedly indicates the duration and events in life: He felt a sharp pain in his palm, the part bounded by his lifeline.

***Note:** The expression does not correlate in meaning with the phrase **live line**—(also: live wire) a cable or wire carrying electric current:* Safe work procedures require the use of rubber gloves and other live line tools.

line of life—1. = *lifeline 3:* Had I been a gypsy palmist I might have paid more attention to the old grouch's lines of life and fate. 2. occupation; line of business: His father being a physician, he also decided to follow in his footsteps and so began the preparation for this line of life. 3. *(dated)* one's rank or station in life: She had received a more liberal education than is usually bestowed upon English women in the middle line of life.

lifetime • time of life

lifetime—1. the period during which a person, plant, or animal is alive: *Bigamy*—marriage with a second wife or husband during the lifetime of the first. 2. the duration of a thing or a thing's usefulness: The Viking spacecraft will consist of an orbiter and a lander, each with a lifetime of many months. 3. is used to hyperbolically designate an exceedingly long time: I got complications, had ups and downs. I was a lifetime in that ward.

time of life—a particular period in a person's life: He handles it with the delight that a new mental toy inspires in most men at a certain time of life.

See also: one's time of life / time of one's life.

lift the lid off something • put the tin lid on something

lift the lid off something—*(also: take the lid off something)* expose or reveal smth. scandalous, shocking, etc. that has been hidden: They are all set to release their explosive video which will lift the lid off their work as undercover agents.

put the tin lid on something—*(also: put the lid on something)* cause a plan, an activity, etc. to end: It's got to be said that our last two results could well put the tin lid on our hopes.

lift up something • uplift something

lift up something—1. physically raise or lift smth.: The bathroom door was hanging by one hinge, and you had to lift it up at the edge in order to even close it. 2. elevate smth. in rank, honor, etc.: These studies discuss the attempt of the Chinese in Malaya to establish various organizations for the Chinese to lift up their status. 3. *(in the phrase "lift up one's eyes")* look upwards: He didn't lift up his eyes but looked to the ground. He was utterly ashamed of himself. 4. *(in the phrase "lift up one's voice")* make one's voice louder (to be heard more clearly or in anger): "I didn't know," she cried out, lifting up her voice. "How could I help!" 5. *(in the phrase "lift up one's voice")* express one's strong opinion about smth.: But if he saw this corruption, why did he not there and then lift up his voice against it.

uplift something—1. = *lift up something 1:* As tectonic forces uplifted the island, this limestone was exposed to rainwater and began to dissolve. 2. = *lift up something 2:* She has not only uplifted the status of Chinese Opera, but has firmly placed Singapore on the cultural map of the world. 3. collect or pick up smth.: Somebody has left a message for Felson. The objective is to uplift the message without being detected.

light-fingered • light-handed

light-fingered—having nimble fingers, especially for stealing: Jimmy's name has become a synonym for a light-fingered burglar who can crack the combination of a bank vault.

light-handed—*(of an approach, style, etc.)* gentle and restrained: The story is presented in a light-handed way through the eyes of an eleven year-old girl and is fast-paced and entertaining.

See also: light in hand / light of hand.

light in hand • light of hand

light in hand—*(of a car, boat, etc.)* easy to manage or control: For its bulk it is admirably wieldy and light in hand.

light of hand—skilful and swift: He was by far the best digger of them all; none so light of hand as he, so deft to extricate fragile objects...

***Note:** The expression does not correlate in meaning with the phrase **sleight of hand**—1. used in reference to jugglery or conjuring:* Rudy Twomoon is a sleight-of-hand magician who has been performing publicly for ten years. 2. *tricky reasoning or practices:* They say all the right things in public, and meanwhile, with sleight of hand, they're gutting the laws they don't like.

See also: light-fingered / light-handed.

light pen • penlight

light pen—*(Computers)* a penlike device used to transmit information by moving the tip on the screen: The light pen provides users with a natural, easy to use alternative to traditional input devices.

penlight—a small electric torch shaped like a pen: Miller had a pen-light in his hand and was looking at his watch.

like a bull in a china shop • like an elephant in the room

like a bull in a china shop—said of a rough or clumsy person who is very careless and often breaks things: I felt like a bull in a china shop as I perched on a settee in a room filled with wonderful treasures.

***Note:** The expression does not correlate in meaning with the phrase **like a bull at a gate**— used of smb. acting with unchecked violence or impetuosity:* She is dead scared of policemen and you'll get nothing out of her if you go at it like a bull at a gate.

like an elephant in the room— said of a problem that everyone knows well but no one talks about because it is embarrassing, etc.: We avoided talking about what had been happening between us over the past days, but it was like an elephant in the room.

like a clock • like one o'clock

like a clock—(also: like clockwork) in an orderly way; with regularity and precision: He manages my whole farm like a clock.

like one o'clock—(coll.) vigorously; eagerly: "Toads are valuable animals," answers Jane. "They eat the snails like one o'clock."

like a dream • like in a dream

like a dream—1. like smth. imaginary or unreal: How could a cat appear in my apartment? I looked up, and for a moment I thought the cat had vanished like a dream. 2. *(coll.)* said of smth. that functions exceptionally well: The car goes like a dream but I should get the belts changed just in case.

like in a dream—(also: as in a dream) 1. perceived like some illusory images seen in a dream: My recollection of that event is hazy.... It was so unreal. Like in a dream. 2. said of smb. living out of contact with reality: I have been living like in a dream until your tenderness and love warmed me.

like a scalded cat • like a singed cat

like a scalded cat—1. *rushing madly* without regard to where one is going: He leapt over the fence and was down the roadway like a scalded cat. 2. *screaming* in a shrill, piercing voice: But why should you squall like a scalded cat?

like a singed cat—said of smb. who is better than appearance indicates: His new friend, however, proved to be like a singed cat, much better than he looked.

Note: *Neither expression correlates in meaning with the phrase* ***like a cat on hot bricks****—1. ill at ease; very nervous:* He was like a cat on hot bricks. Scared out of his life as to what she might say. 2. *moving swiftly and nimbly:* A well-bred, raking-looking sort of mare.... Beautiful action she had, stepped away like a cat on hot bricks.

like a wet rag • like a wet weekend

like a wet rag—utterly exhausted: At the end of a day I'm just like a wet rag. All I'm good for is to plotz in a chair.

like a wet weekend—sad and miserable: Try to be a bit more cheerful. I don't want you standing around looking like a wet weekend.

like death • like grim death

like death—(U.S. also: like death warmed over) feeling or looking very unwell or completely exhausted: Much of the time I feel like death. I am in rather a bad temper.

like grim death—gripping smth. very firmly; *clinging to smth.* tenaciously: By clinging like grim death to the gunwale, we just managed to keep inside the boat, but it was exhausting work.

like water • like water off a duck's back

like water—(of money) spend in great quantity or recklessly: She spends money like water to create a luxurious home far beyond the means of her humble husband.

like water off a duck's back—(of criticism, etc.) have no effect or make no impression whatsoever: I keep telling him it's foolish to gamble, but it's like water off a duck's back.

listen for something • listen out for something

listen for something—make a conscious effort to catch the sound of smth.; concentrate on hearing smth.: If beyond the silence we listen for the faintest undertones, we detect a stifled, continuous hum of insects.

listen out for something—1. = *listen for something:* You will be listening out for any human presence such as cutting of firewood, dogs barking, etc. Poaching still sadly exists.... 2. wait expectantly to hear or learn smth.: He sees Focus Groups as a platform in which we test known hypotheses rather than listen out for new hypotheses to emerge.

listen in to something • listen to something

listen in to something—(also: listen in on something) 1. listen secretly to a conversation: Little does he know that the shop's owner is standing in the doorway, listening in to the conversation. 2. follow a radio broadcast: We recieved a positive response from everyone that contacted us after listening in to the show.

listen to something—1. = *listen in to something 2:* I have just listened to the show with Marc Perrin and it was great. 2. follow what smb. is saying, etc.: Here are a few of the notes I took while I was listening to his sermon. 3. pay attention to smth.; heed smth.: The problem is, neither of the other two are particularly willing to listen to his advice.

Little England • Little England beyond Wales

Little England—Barbados *(an island nation in West Indies):* In spite of Barbados being called "Little England" in the Caribbean, many islanders are weighing the possibility of a divorce from the mother country.

Note: *a) The expression does not correlate in meaning with the phrase* ***Little Englander****—(hist.) a person who advocated a "little England," that is, desired to restrict the dimensions and responsibilities of the Empire:* Stanley was in these days a stop-the-war, pacifist Little Englander, anti-militarist, anti–Chamberlain.

b) The expression does not correlate in meaning with the phrase ***Little Britain****—(dated) Brittany (the duchy of Bretagne in France):* Brittany, or "Little Britain," derives many of its unique cultural traditions from Celts who arrived from Britain around A.D. 460.

Little England beyond Wales—Pembrokeshire *(former county and historic region of south Wales):* I have never been able to speak Welsh fluently, and being from the South West (Pembrokeshire — little England beyond Wales) have had little Welsh heritage.

little friend • small friend

little friend—1. is used of a pet animal as a term of endearment: All of us are or have been attached to a small animal. I am going to talk to you about my little friend. 2. *(euph.)* menstruation: Women have no shame connected to their "little friend" every month. Your museum is a powerful tool in increasing acceptedness of menstruation.

small friend— = *little friend 1:* My dog leapt into my arms and licked me with wild abandon. I cried for the reunion with my small friend.

Note: *a) Neither expression correlates in meaning with the phrase* ***petit ami****—(Fr., euph.) the partner for a male homosexual:* Your *petit ami* was calling me a horrid baggy little man.

b) Neither expression correlates in meaning with the phrase ***petite amie****—(Fr., euph.) a sexual mistress (of a middle-aged man):* His *petite amie* had raised the subject of marriage.

little game • small game

little game—scheming in order to win personal gain, advantage, or profit: How long do you mean to carry on this little game?

small game—1. a game in which the stakes are low: Some stuck to cards, and though no longer deep gamblers, rather played small game than sat out. 2. the smaller animals or birds hunted for food: There were few better areas than the country eighty miles round Delhi for small game.

See also: big game / large game.

little madam • little woman

little madam—said of a young girl who acts older than her years: You can see from the way she orders her brother about that she is a little madam.

little woman—(coll.) a person's wife: On Sunday afternoon Jack went off to play golf and the little woman hung some new curtains in the living room.

little men • little men with hammers

little men—(also: little people) 1. men who are not tall: For lack of weight they make up by speed, and if they are little men they are the smaller targets. 2. ordinary or undistinguished people: Great men too often have greater faults than little men can find room for. 3. craftsmen or tradesmen doing business on a small scale: The potential customers are most numerous among the "little men," that is, owners of one-man businesses. 4. fairies; elves: The story of his sojourn in Fairyland gradually leaked out, and men used to come and ask him about the land of the little men.

little men with hammers—(drunk-caused) headache: Thankfully, there were no little men with hammers inside my head. I recalled the night with a grin.

little talk • small talk

little talk—1. a brief comment or address: Let me illustrate by a little talk, which I think will have the twang of realism about it. 2. a short conversation: "Mr. Baker and I had a little talk about you today," Newton said.

small talk—light social conversation about unimportant things: After Willoughby was gone, Karen tried to make small talk.

Note: *Neither expression is antonymous in meaning to the phrase* ***big talk****—(also: tall talk) boastful or pretentious talk:* We don't want big talk from an armchair critic.

little thing • small thing

little thing—1. a small child: There are the shops where she used to buy me toys when I was a little thing. 2. is used as a term of endearment: Poor little thing! He misses his mammy, you know! 3. smth. unimportant; a mere trifle: I never saw such an excitement over a little thing in Arkansas as there was over that debate.

small thing— = little thing 3: The First World War was fought over a small thing. A scrap of paper. *Cf.: big thing—smth. of considerable importance:* The big thing for guys is jeans or slacks, button-down shirts and brown loafers without socks.

Note: *The expression does not correlate in meaning with the phrase* ***do that small thing****—(coll.) do smth. indicated in a previous statement:* "I'm going to have a bath." "Darling, you do that small thing!"

little world • small world

little world—1. the limited close circle of one's family and friends: I see a chap who is a sort of great white chief in his own little world. 2. a group of things considered as constituting a unity: The archipelago is a little world within itself, or rather a satellite attached to America.

small world—(also: it's a small world) used as a comment on an unexpected meeting with a person: "Small world," he said. "That bloke was in here yesterday."

See also: great world, the / greater world, the.

live a cat and dog life • live a dog's life

live a cat and dog life—(of two people) engage in constant quarreling *(also: lead a cat and dog life):* The couple had lived a cat-and-dog life almost since their honeymoon.

live a dog's life—(also: lead a dog's life) lead a wretched unpleasant existence: Warr, unemployed and homeless, was left to live a "dog's life," which ended in an unmarked pauper's grave.

live by oneself • live in oneself • live to oneself

live by oneself—live alone: For twenty-two years Junker lived by himself, completely alone in rooms designed for a nonexistent wife and children.

live in oneself—(also: live within oneself) rely on oneself for ideas, beliefs, etc.: They show us a man ... who lived in himself and for himself. All his opinions were his own, and there is no recorded instance in his long career in which he sought or desired counsel from others.

live to oneself—be a loner; shun the company of other people: He shut himself up at the age of forty-five, disgusted, as he said, with his fellow men and determined to live to himself.

See also: live with oneself / live within oneself.

live in a fishbowl • live in a glass house

live in a fishbowl (also: live in a goldfish bowl)—have absolutely no privacy: Life on campus can be like living in a fishbowl. Everyone knows what everyone else is doing.

live in a glass house—be particularly vulnerable to criticism *(with reference to the proverb "he who lives in a glass house shouldn't throw stones"):* Before we criticize, we should ask, "What role did I play in creating the condition that I choose to criticize?" ...We all live in glass houses. Let's take care in deciding when and how we throw stones.

live in charity • live on charity

live in charity—live in the state of generosity and love towards other people: We all have the task of trying to live in charity with one another.

live on charity—live on money, food, etc. provided as help to the poor: The family is one of several in Darwin living on charity.

live in the air • live in the open air

live in the air—1. *(of birds)* spend part of their lives in the air: We have birds that live in the air, those that live on the earth and those that live in the sea. 2. *(of viruses, etc.)* be able to survive in the open air: Microorganisms can live in the air, on land, and in fresh or salt water environments.

Note: *The expression does not correlate in meaning with the phrase* ***live on air****—survive on very little food:* Annick is one of those young Parisians who live on air and use the cafes as living rooms.

live in the open air—1. said of people not living inside a house or building: The natural savages may live in the open air, and subsist on the ordinary products of the earth. 2. spend most of the time outdoors rather than indoors: Large orange trees with their dense shade shut out the sun so that we can sit, and walk, and live in the open air.

live in the country • live on the country

live in the country—live in an area that is farmed or remains in an undeveloped state, as distinct from cities: They both came from big cities before they met, and each dreamed of living in the country.

live on the country—be able to survive from what one finds in the wild: We took with us provisions for about fifty days, for we hoped in part to live on the country—on fish, game, nuts, and palm-tops.

live it down • live it up

live it down—forget smth. bad or embarrassing, such as mistake, failure, etc.: If you were beaten by Jack, you would never live it down.

live it up—(coll.) have a very enjoyable and exciting time: Nobody lives for always, but when I live I like to live it up.

Note: *The expression does not correlate in meaning with the phrase* ***live up to it****—act in full accordance with principles, rules, etc.; reach the standard that may be expected:* You will never live up to it because you are a human and incapable of perfection and bound to have flaws here and there.

live off something • live on something

live off something—1. use smth. as food: Some animals live off plants, whilst others live off other animals. 2. get enough food or income from smth.: He had lived off his vegetable patch on the farm and off the sales of some cattle.

live on something—1. eat certain food as one's regular diet: They live on fish, coconuts, and tropical fruit—papaya, bananas and mangoes. 2. = *live off something 2:* Maugham knew that he had to court popular taste if he wanted to live on his writing.

live off the fat of the land • live off the land

live off the fat of the land—1. use products that one grows for one's food needs: They share a dream of a little place of their own, where they can "live off the fat of the land." 2. enjoy a comfortable lifestyle: He was pretty fed up with these bloated royalists who were living off the fat of the land and off American aid.

live off the land—1. = *live off the fat of the land 1:* Thousands of Mayan peasants live off the land in the Yucatan, growing maize—a world away from the beach resorts of nearby Cancun. 2. be able to survive from what one finds in the wild: Living off the land requires that you get very close to that land. Axes, shovels and fishing gear will be essential to your survival.

live out something • outlive something

live out something—live to the end of a specified period of time: He was as certain as any one possibly could be that the chap could not live out the week.

outlive something—1. continue to exist beyond smth.: Ms. Bork argues that the Association has outlived its utility as the principal forum for addressing region-wide issues. 2. = *live out something:* Besides secrecy, speed was of the essence—"according to all intelligence" the Spanish King could not outlive the month of October.

live with oneself • live within oneself

live with oneself—retain one's self-respect: The note of hysteria in her voice stopped me dead. The sensible thing to do would have been to continue on my way but if I did I knew I'd find it awfully difficult to live with myself.

live within oneself—(also: live in oneself) rely on oneself for ideas, beliefs, etc.: Americans have a "can-do" spirit that is world famous. Self-reliance and the desire to live within oneself have long defined the American character.

See also: live by oneself / live in oneself / live to oneself.

living corpse • living skeleton

living corpse—(also: living dead) said of smb. who has lost all interest in life: It may be said that she came out of the asylum a living corpse, and it was not long before she died in reality.

living skeleton—is used of an extremely emaciated person: I was unprepared for what I saw. There on a reed mat lay a living skeleton of a man covered with a blanket.

Note: *Neither expression correlates in meaning with the phrase* ***dead man walking****— used of smb. who is in very great trouble (will soon get punished, lose his job, etc.):* He is a dead man walking and should step down now. His actions brought disrepute to the judiciary...

Lloyd's List • Lloyd's Register

Lloyd's List—(UK) a daily publication devoted to shipping news: In 1696 Edward Lloyd started a paper, *Lloyd's News*, which was the precursor of the *Lloyd's List* of the present day.

Lloyd's Register—(UK) an annual alphabetical list of ships assigned to various classes: *Lloyd's Register*, as at present constituted, has existed since 1834.

loaded down with something • loaded up with something

loaded down with something—1. having a heavy load of smth.; overloaded with smth.: The trees are loaded down with the weight of the fruit. 2. overburdened with tasks, responsibilities, etc.: He seemed loaded down with the burdens of office.

loaded up with something—(of a vessel, etc.) with a full cargo of smth.: The ship was loaded up with quality food stocks, including a good array of fresh food.

lock someone away • lock someone out

lock someone away—put smb. in prison or mental hospital: It would be inhumane to lock her away when she is suffering from a psychological problem that is producing her drug addiction.

lock someone out—1. prevent a person from entering a room or building: He hasn't made any threats, in fact once he locked me out and told me to leave. 2. prevent workers from entering a factory, etc. during an argument between management and the workers: The workers have been off the job since Monday, when management locked them out.

lone star • lonely star

lone star—1. is used with reference to the state flag of Texas: The lone star of Texas shall continue to wave proudly in the air as long as one brave Texan remains to defend it. 2. the only or sole person: He was a lone star not just from India, but from this Asian region as well, when the sport was dominated by Europeans.

lonely star—a lonely or unattached person: I must admit that I was half expecting to meet a tired, dejected lonely star who had retreated to the Irish countryside.

Lone Star State, the • North Star State, the

Lone Star State, the—(U.S.) a nickname of the Sate of Texas: He twisted the tail of a Connecticut company that was trying to do business contrary to the edicts of the great Lone Star State.

North Star State, the—(U.S.) a nickname of the State of Minnesota: In the North Star State here, we rejoice in having a Grand Master, who knows no such word as fail.

long arm • long hand

long arm—1. a far reaching power: The long arm, or perhaps one might better say the long purse, of diplomacy at last effected the release of the prisoners. *Cf.: long arm of the law—used with reference to ability of the police to find and catch people who commit crimes:* The long arm of the law finally nabbed Victoria's two most infamous financial fugitives. 2. a pole fitted with a hook, etc. for use beyond the ordinary reach of the arm: Barnes reached a long arm over the ridge of fallen soil ... and groped experimentally around within. 3. a long, narrow part of the sea or river enclosed by the shore: Australian rivers often have a long arm or two wandering off into the plain.

long hand— the hand of a clock or watch which indicates the minutes: When it is one o'clock the minute hand, the long hand, is pointing toward the 12, while the hour hand is pointing towards the number one.

Note: *The expression does not correlate in meaning with the consonant compound* ***longhand****— ordinary handwriting, as distinguished from shorthand or typing:* The clerk had to write all the evidence down in longhand.

long bill • longbill

long bill—1. a written statement containing a great number of items: She listed a long bill of particulars from James's legal response to the court. 2. a bill in which the charges are excessive: We had to wait a long time for a poor dinner, and pay a long bill for it when it came. 3. *(Finance)* a bill of exchange that runs for more than 30 and often more than 60 days: The fluctuations in long bills are co-extensive with the fluctuations in the value of money. 4. a bird with a long bill (such as a snipe or a woodcock): We always had flushed a few "long bills" from the wet swales.

longbill— = long bill 4: The bird footprints seem to be from a distant ancestor of modern birds such as ducks, plovers, and longbills.

long clothes • long robes

long clothes—long dress for a baby's body: But before he was out of long clothes, the cloven foot began to show; he developed a taste for low pleasures.

long robes—long, loose garment worn as a sign of rank or office by judges, priests, etc.: In most nations judges wear long robes, usually black or red, and sit on an elevated platform during trials.

long head • short head

long head—(coll.) capacity for calculation and foresight: He has always had luck, and he has a long head too.

short head—a narrow margin in victory *(originally of horse races):* A photo finish was predicted by polls. The final one showed M. Mitered winning by a short head.

Long John • long johns

Long John—1. a nickname of a tall, thin man: As I had warned Long John, there comes a time when you begin to think that you know it all. 2. is used of a long coffee table: Some of his most famous pieces from this period are the 1946 "Long John" table and the simple 1948 chaise lounge. 3. a timber tree *(Triplaris surinamensis)* found along the lower Amazon and in the Guianas: An unusual tree which is flowering at the moment is the Long John tree.

long johns—(sl.) long woolen underwear: We stripped down to our long johns so that the technicians could plaster us all over with strips of wet paper.

long line • long-distance line

long line—a deep-sea fishing-line: Every third hook on the long lines is baited with crabs.

long-distance line—(U.S.) a telephone line connecting two exchanges in different telephone areas: The lines between exchanges in this country [Britain] are known as *trunks.* For these the American terms *toll line* or *long-distance line* is used.

long shillings • short money

long shillings—(UK coll.) good wages: There are "long shillings" to be earned at the docks, but no easy ones; and the work is not only hard but dangerous.

short money—1. money to borrow or to lend upon short-time loans: Long-term money market interest rates fell, whereas short money market rates remained unchanged. 2. a small amount of money: The weaknesses in his game were magnified by the fact that he was playing on short money.

long ship • long-boat

long ship—(hist.) a galley accommodating a large number of rowers: It was the perfection of the sailing long ship that heralded the beginning of the Viking Age.

long-boat—the largest boat belonging to a sailing vessel: The vessel is going to pieces, and it is full time to get into the long-boat and leave her.

long story • short story

long story—said of a long narrative or account: Miss Sally told us a long story about her friends and about her "coming-out party."

Note: *The expression does not correlate in meaning with the phrase* ***tall story****—(also: tall tale) a story that is difficult to believe:* Their parents yarned over cups of tea, swapped tall stories and books.

short story—a piece of fiction shorter than a novel: The short story of today is one of two kinds—what is called the Magazine Story; and the newer kind which derives from Chekhov.

Long Tom • Tom Long

Long Tom—1. a heavy gun of great length: I was already sergeant when we made a night attack and captured and blew up Long Tom. 2. *(Austral.)* a marine fish of the family *Belonidae:* Long Toms have the habit of leaping from the water, when either pursuing or being pursued. 3. a gold-washing cradle: "Long Tom" or cradle was a trough filled with earth, into which water flowed; the cradle was rocked, and the gold washed from the earth fell into a tin dish. 4. a particularly high-powered telephoto camera lens: Russ, grinning, remembered a Long Tom lens he had seen in the hands of one of the photographers.

Tom Long—said of a lazy, slow man who takes a long time in coming, etc.: We are very concerned that many people will be fooled into thinking that they could live with a Tom Long government.

look a spectacle • look spectacular

look a spectacle—appear silly or ridiculous: Dressed in our finest raingear, I imagine we did look a spectacle while waiting for our clothes to become clean once again.

look spectacular—look extremely attractive: Diana looked spectacular in a continually changing wardrobe of red, black and white dresses with matching feather boas.

look ahead to something • look forward to something

look ahead to something—prepare or plan smth. for the future: Drivers and teams are now looking ahead to the next contest in Malaysia.

look forward to something—anticipate smth. with great pleasure: Every year the children look forward to the holidays coming.

look alive • look half dead

look alive—1. *(coll.)* act or respond quickly: Challenge your staff to become excited about the services they provide. Challenge them to look alive! 2. *(of images)* appear life-like: I want my paintings to look alive—so you feel you can step right into it and get lost.

look half dead—(also: look more dead than alive) said of smb. in a very poor physical condition (owing to illness, exhaustion, etc.): People sleeping on the floor, looking half dead and miserable, are an all too familiar sight in transportation terminals.

look at someone • look on someone

look at someone—1. direct one's gaze towards smb.: "My God, look at these people! Just look at them—I ask you," he exclaimed. 2. take a person as an example: Education is not necessary for success in life; look at your uncle Joe.

look on someone—regard smb. as a particular kind of person: Do you look on him as an authority on the subject?

look at something • look on something

look at something—1. direct one's gaze towards smth.: Look at this plant ... its leaves all point to the north, as true as the magnet. *2.* examine or consider smth. with attention and in detail: We must look at the question from all sides.

look on something—1. *(of a room, etc.)* give a view of smth.; overlook smth. *(also: look on to something):* Breakfast is also served on the balcony terrace looking on the garden. 2. regard smth. as a particular kind of thing: Our religion looks on the soul of the poorest cotton-worker to be as precious as the soul of the wealthiest cotton-lord.

look back • not look back

look back—return to smth. in one's thoughts: When we look back, we can now understand what caused the difficulty.

not look back—(also: never look back) 1. proceed with no regret for the past: I made my decision then and there and didn't look back. 2. become more and more successful: Her first novel was published in 1998 and since then she hasn't looked back.

look blue • look blue around the gills

look blue—(coll.) look sad or depressed: A guy stopped at my door and asked what was the matter with me. I said, "Nothing." He said, "You look blue."

Note: *The expression does not correlate in meaning with the phrase* ***till one is blue in the face****—do smth. over and over again but without any effect:* I talked till I was blue in the face, trying to explain where this would lead to.

look blue around the gills—(coll.) 1. look indisposed or unwell: John is looking a little blue around the gills. What's wrong? 2. look as though one is about to be sick: As the sea became rougher many passengers began to look blue around the gills.

look down one's nose at something • turn up one's nose at something

look down one's nose at something—treat smth. with contempt: Jolyon's water-colors were on view there. He went in to look down his nose at them — it might give him some faint satisfaction.

turn up one's nose at something— = look down one's nose at something: Uncle Jeremy never turned up his nose at a bowl of bean-porridge.

look for something • look out for something

look for something—1. try to find smth.: Wilkins was in charge of the Canadian search section which was looking for the lost Soviet Polar Expedition. *2.* hope to get smth.: He is looking for support to put together a group so as to fully recreate the ritual dance and music.

look out for something—1. be on guard for smth., especially smth. dangerous: Residents are being asked to be more vigilant in looking out for possible terrorist activities in their neighborhoods. 2. look after smth.; protect smth. from harm: They are part of a "community" where neighbours will look out for their property while they are away. 3. wait for smth. that is going to happen or expected to appear: If your name isn't on the list, look out for our future competitions where you may have more luck.

look good • look well

look good—1. be beautiful to the eye; look attractive: I always knew I had the sort of face that would look good on the screen. 2. *(often negat.)* seem proper: We warn the doormen on her building that it wouldn't look good for them to ferry customers to her apartment. 3. produce a good or favorable impression; seem to be promising: This year's sales figures are looking good.

look well—1. present a healthy appearance: The Captain himself said, "I feel good," but he did not look well. 2. *= look good 1:* The graphic patterns are usually of poor quality for printing although might look well on the screen.

look high and low • look up and down

look high and low—look everywhere for a person or thing: I don't know where my glasses are. I've looked high and low.

look up and down—look both ways; examine smth. from end to end: He should have looked up and down the line before he ventured to cross it.

look into something • look to something

look into something—(also: see into something) consider or inquire into smth.: The director has an opportunity to go to any part of the hotel if he wants to look into matters.

look to something—1. be careful about smth.; pay attention to smth.: Let him look to his health: insufficient sleep often puts heavy drags upon one's effectiveness. 2. choose or rely on smth. for support, help, etc.: Let this be a warning against looking to personal diplomacy to settle issues.

look on at something • look on to something

look on at something—be an observer of smth. rather than a participant: Potters' boys are trained to the business by looking on at the wheel.

look on to something—(of a room, etc.) overlook smth.; have a view of smth. *(also: look on something):* They have a balcony looking on to the garden with great sea and mountain views.

look on the bright side of something • take a dim view of something

look on the bright side of something—see a favorable or hopeful aspect of a bad or difficult situation: I was not the kind of kid who looked on the bright side of anything; I was never optimistic...

take a dim view of something—regard smth. with disapproval: During the course of your educational career you will meet many book lovers who will take a dim view of you marking books which are not your own.

Note: *The expression does not correlate in meaning with the phrase* ***see in a mirror, dimly****—(the Bible) is used to say that humans have a fundamentally clouded, fractured, and limited perception of reality (also: see through a glass darkly):* When St Paul says that "we see in a mirror dimly" he is reminding us about our inability to see clearly, and truly, in the world.

look one's last on something • see the last of something

look one's last on something—look at smth. for the last time before leaving a place: People had come on deck to look their last on their country.

see the last of something—not to see or deal with smth. again: At Moose Factory, I saw the last of the sulfur matches which were in their day considered a great advance.

look out for someone • look someone out

look out for someone—try to find smb. by searching: It is good to know that the police are looking out for my family. It makes me know that you actually do care about me.

look someone out—search for a person and produce him: "They keep the directories and registers in this eating-house," said Westmacott. "We'll go and look him out."

look over something • watch over something

look over something—1. *(of a room, etc.)* have a view of smth. *(also: look on something):* In each bungalow there is a balcony looking over the bay. 2. choose not to notice smth.; ignore smth.: I'll look over your carelessness this time, but be more careful in future. 3. examine or study smth. carefully: When he sat down to write in his journal, he would look over his notes and sketches.

Note: *The expression does not fully correlate in meaning with the phrase* ***overlook something****—1. = look over something 1:* Breakfast is served on request and can be enjoyed on the terrace overlooking the garden. 2. *= look over something 2:* I decided to overlook his unkindness to me and gave him a hand. 3. *fail* *to see or notice smth.:* The hospital declared the transplant a success, but they had apparently overlooked the risk from the man's high blood pressure.

watch over something—1. guard smth.: At the strike of midnight, the guard will change and continue watch over the jewels. 2. take care of smth.: The committee's responsibility is to watch over the safety of the workers.

See also: oversee something / see over something.

look someone in the face • stare someone in the face

look someone in the face—confront a person with a steady gaze that implies courage, confidence, or defiance: How can you look me in the face, and tell such a huge lie!

stare someone in the face—1. look into a person's face fixedly or intently: She stared me in the face for the longest time before she spoke. 2. said of smth. threatening a person with misfortune or disaster: Only when starvation stares him in the face will he relinquish his "glad clothes." 3. said of smth. which is obvious and easy to see but is not noticed by a person: Are you looking for your pencil? It's on your desk, staring you in the face.

look someone up • see someone up

look someone up—1. visit smb. when in the same place: If I'm ever here on business again, I'll look you up. 2. search for and find a person: I'll try to look him up on the Web before making a phone call.

Note: *The expression does not correlate in meaning with the phrase* ***look someone up and down****—take in smb.'s entire appearance; scrutinize a person carefully:* The man ushered me to a seat after snobishly looking me up and down, pausing to stare at my tattered sandles.

see someone up—take a person upstairs or show to a place on a higher level: I'll see you up to the director's office on the top floor.

look something out • see something out

look something out—find smth. by choosing carefully: I must look out a special dress for the wedding.

see something out—1. last until the end of a period of time: Will our supplies see the winter out? 2. work on smth. until it is completed: The course is terrible, but I'll see it out now that I've paid for it.

look something through • look through something

look something through—examine smth. carefully: I'll look your suggestion through before passing it on to the committee.

look through something—briefly browse through smth. written or printed: I'll look through my notes but I don't think I have a record of his name.

See also: see something through / see through something.

look to someone • look up to someone

look to someone—1. choose or rely on a person for support, help, etc.: He's not the sort of man to whom one looks for reassurance. 2. pay attention to smb.; take care of a person: There is much talk about how we ought to look to the children that need homes...

look up to someone—view a person with respect and admiration: In all that concerns civilization, the Argentines look up to the French.

loose money • tight money

loose money—1. money in a mixture of denominations; money that is not tied up or packed: James swept some loose money off the counter into the till. 2. money amassed by dubious means (as in campaign contributions, etc.): The mayor retires with a substantial account filled with loose money he received. 3. *(Banking)* money available to borrowers in greater supply and under fewer restrictions: The twin policies of "loose money" and "high taxes" are totally destructive to the economies of the third world.

tight money—(Banking) money available to borrowers in limited supply and at high interest rates: Labor has been weakened by government policies of tight money and restrictive budget policies to contain inflation.

Lord Admiral • Lord of the Admiralty

Lord Admiral—(hist.) head of the naval administration of Great Britain: As she is escorted out of the courtroom, she overhears the Lord Admiral Cotwell talking with his long time friends.

Lord of the Admiralty—(UK) one of the five lords commissioners of the Admiralty: Lord Camelford can boast of a power which rivals that of the First Lord of the Admiralty.

Lord Chamberlain • Lord Great Chamberlain

Lord Chamberlain—(UK) an officer responsible for the royal household who is also the licenser of plays *(also: Lord Chamberlain of the Household):* But the particular function of the Lord Chamberlain led to many clashes over works that have since become classics.

Lord Great Chamberlain—(UK) a hereditary officer of state whose duties were originally financial but are now mainly ceremonial: Control of the Palace of Westminster was for centuries exercised by the Queen's representative, the Lord Great Chamberlain.

Lord Commissioner • Lord High Commissioner

Lord Commissioner—a member of a board exercising the powers of a high British office of state: The Reading Clerk bows to each Lord Commissioner as he is named, and the Commissioner responds by raising his hat.

Lord High Commissioner—the representative of the British Crown at the annual General Assembly of the Church of Scotland: The present building is still used as a residence by the reigning Monarch and by the Lord High Commissioner during the Assembly of the Church of Scotland.

Note: *The expression is not equivalent in meaning to the phrase* ***High Commissioner****— the head of the British diplomatic mission in a Commonwealth country:* A High Commissioner from the United Kingdom would be appointed to take over from the Viceroy duties connected with the representation of Britain in India.

lose a fortune • lose one's fortune

lose a fortune—lose an extremely large amount of money (in gambling, etc.): He's lost a fortune on the roulette tables and his businesses are going bankrupt due to his massive debts.

lose one's fortune—lose all of one's financial wealth (through misadventure, etc.): The first time he lost his fortune was in 1915, when he declared himself bankrupt.

lose all reason • lose one's reason

lose all reason—become irrational or illogical in one's speech or behavior: He lost all reason and started abusing his opponent.

lose one's reason—lose one's mental faculties; go crazy: It was not unknown for men to become peculiar, or even completely to lose their reason, in the vast spaces of Masailand.

lose heart • lose one's heart

lose heart—become discouraged; give up hope: Don't lose heart if an ambition does not look like being realized.

Note: *The expression is not antonymous in meaning to the* *phrase* ***have a heart***—1. *(usually imper.) be understanding and sympathetic; be reasonable:* Have a heart! I can't possibly get through that amount of work in such a short time. 2. *(usually negat.) be cruel or courageous enough to do smth. (also: have the heart):* When I got back, I felt better, but I didn't have a heart to tell him to go home.

lose one's heart—fall in love with a person: He wanted to buy a house before they got married, but while she was waiting she lost her heart to another man.

lose hold of someone • lose hold over someone

lose hold of someone—(also: lose one's hold of someone) 1. be no longer able to physically grasp or hold a person: After a struggle at midfield, Davis lost hold of Barrington, who then scored to win the game. 2. lose power or control over a person: He lost hold of her, and she moved to Capri, never to return again to his life.

lose hold over someone—(also: lose one's hold over someone) = lose hold of someone 2: It is no matter to him that he loses his hold over his children and his erstwhile fiancée.

lose one's head • lose one's mind

lose one's head—1. lose one's presence of mind; become confused: Don't lose your head and start the car in gear. Take things quietly, put the lever in neutral.... 2. become emotionally attached to a person: She is at the age that she loses her head over every other boy she meets.

lose one's mind—lose one's mental faculties; go crazy: Robert lost his mind and was committed to an insane asylum.

lose one's marbles • pick up one's marbles

lose one's marbles—(coll.) go out of one's mind; start acting in a strange way: I may be old, but I haven't lost my marbles yet. *Cf.: have all one's marbles—(coll.) be sensible; be in one's right mind:* Do men who have got all their marbles go swimming in lakes with their clothes on?

pick up one's marbles—(U.S. coll.) leave an activity one has been involved in with other people: If you don't like the way we do things around here, well, you can pick up your marbles and leave.

lose one's touch with someone • lose touch with someone

lose one's touch with someone—lose one's ability to handle a person: I seem to have lost my touch with my children. They won't mind me anymore.

lose touch with someone—cease to be in contact with smb.: Politicians have become so absorbed in their own war-games that they have lost touch with the wider world.

lose one's way • lose way

lose one's way—1. cease to follow the right track; become lost: The children lost their way in the dark and did no reach home. 2. be unable to find the right road in life: You seem to me like one who has lost his way and made a great error in life.

Note: *The expression is not antonymous in meaning to the phrase* ***win one's way****—succeed in following one's course despite obstacles:* The young fellow who will devote himself to agriculture may do even better than the youth who wins his way to the black-coated servitude of a bank.

lose way—(Nautical) lose speed: The wind failed and dropped to nothing, the dinghy lost way and drifted towards three lighters moored abreast.

lose out on something • lose out to something

lose out on something—suffer a loss or disadvantage in smth.: Sitting in the hotel the next day, I realize now that I lost out on the deal.

lose out to something—be overcome or replaced by smth.; lose a competition: The popular press, uncertain of its role, lost out to the heavies and the provincials.

lost in something • lost to something

lost in something—deeply occupied in thought or filled with an emotion: He seemed to be lost in the contemplation of something great.

lost to something—no longer affected by some good influence: He is able to detect those whom he may trust from those who are hopelessly lost to all sense of honor.

lost on someone • lost to someone

lost on someone—(of humor, sarcasm, etc.) having no effect upon a person: The real humor of the situation was lost upon the House of Commons.

lost to someone—no longer possessed by or accessible to a person: I had no skills to rely on and what training I once had, was lost to me at that moment.

love game • love play

love game—a game in which the loser scores no points: Holt's spirit was pretty well broken and Amy slammed his serves over almost unchallenged and won a love game.

love play—caressing; amorous attentions: Adult heterosexuality presents fewer problems where early love play is tolerated than where it is suppressed.

See also: play a love game / play for love.

love seat *(UK)* • love seat *(U.S.)*

love seat (UK)—a seat or bench which accommodates two people facing in opposite directions: The term "love seat" more often refers to a curious S-shaped two-seater, with the sitters facing opposite directions (paradoxically). I've never heard of a standard two-seater couch called a "love seat"...

love seat (U.S.)—a small sofa or couch designed for two occupants: The original master bedroom of the mansion offers a large room with canopy bed, sitting area and love seat facing the fireplace.

low-brow • low-browed

low-brow—1. *(of people)* not highly intellectual or aesthetically refined: Their desired crowd is not unlike themselves, being low-brow people who want to see a rock band that plays loud, fast and powerful. 2. *(of things)* unsophisticated and not requiring intellectual effort to be understood: I play video games, read lowbrow books and tons of comics.

low-browed—1. *(of a building, doorway, etc.)* having a low entrance: In the face of this rock there appeared something like the entrance of a low-browed cavern. 2. = *low-brow 1.:* The media must think the American public is a bunch of low-browed morons who "rush to the mall" and buy whatever is placed in front of them.

low house • lower house

low house—said of a place that is not socially or morally "respectable": He took to drinking and frequented low houses of Irish raff.

lower house—lower chamber of parliament *(the House of Representatives in the USA or the House of Commons in Great Britain):* Robert Kelly sponsored the bill in the lower house and told everyone how great it was.

low man • low man on the totem pole

low man—1. *(also: short man)* a man of short stature: Mr. Swan was a low man with short legs.... He was very strict in some respects, never sparing the rod. 2. a man without principles or morals: Mrs. Young says he is such a low man he should not dine with her daughter. 3. smb. who has the least important position in an organization: "He was a low man in the system. It really got boring for him," Zach's father said about his son's job.

low man on the totem pole— = *low man 3:* The night security position at the museum is a low-man-on-the-totem-pole job, but Larry's willing to give it a try.

See also: high man on the totem pole / high-up man.

lower one's ears • prick up one's ears

lower one's ears—(coll.) get a haircut *(also: get one's ears lowered):* I'm debating weather or not to lower my ears before school, leaning towards the more hippie of the options.

prick up one's ears—(coll.) become attentive or alert to listen: A bleating sound caught Baldred's attention. He pricked up his ears as it grew louder.

lower world • underworld

lower world—1. mortal earth as opposed to heaven: Innumerable high-dressed gentlemen, gods of this lower world, are gone all to inorganic powder. 2. the realm of the dead: In the mysteries of Eleusis, the return of Cora from the lower world was regarded as the symbol of immortality.

underworld—1. the community of criminals: He was known in the underworld circles as a luxury loan shark, lending money to casino gamblers. 2. = *lower world 2:* Auernus was the name of a deep lake near Puteoli, the reputed entrance to the underworld.

***Note:** The compound does not correlate in meaning with the phrase **down under world**—(coll.) Australia or New Zealand:* Things have been busy in the down under world I have been in recently. I have flown back and forward between Australia and New Zealand…

luck it out • one's luck is out

luck it out—(also: luck out) achieve success by good luck in a difficult situation: Rock City isn't the easiest of places to find if you don't know Nottingham but somehow we lucked it out.

one's luck is out—one has bad luck: Such are the perils of any racing these days, but I did begin to wonder if our luck was out again.

lucky man • man of luck

lucky man—1. a man who is fortunate or successful: If he's a friend of yours, you're a lucky man, for if ever a fellow was one of the salt of the earth, he is. 2. a bridegroom: The six gentlemanly cowboys swore that whoever should prove to be the lucky man, the others would ush for him at the ceremony.

man of luck— = *lucky man 1:* I'm not known as a man of luck. In fact, if anything can go wrong with me it usually does!

lucky strike • stroke of luck

lucky strike—1. a fortunate discovery: Would they … come back to civilization with the story of a lucky strike to account for the gold they brought? 2. a chance piece of good fortune: It was a lucky strike that we were able to land so close to the boat, so we could follow the plan.

stroke of luck— = *lucky strike 2:* My son was going over there anyway, so it was just a stroke of luck that they ended up being so close together.

lunar politics • lunatic policy

lunar politics—said of matters of no practical concern: Hume's subtle intellect takes up a great many problems and shows us that they are essentially questions of lunar politics.

lunatic policy—madly foolish, idiotic policy: I'm afraid we're a long way from the degree of understanding that is required to change our lunatic policy into a more positive direction.

M

mad about something • mad for something

mad about something—(coll.) 1. very enthusiastic about smth.; excessively interested in smth.: Most of the folks I'm particularly close to are as mad about sport as I am. *2.* very angry about smth.: Viola says she got mad about that interview in the paper, about marriages being broken up.

mad for something—(coll.) 1. craving or longing for smth.: Still we were all mad for food, and madmen cannot be made responsible for their actions. 2. carried away by some strong emotion: I was mad for joy. It was so beautiful that I wept while approaching the enchanting place.

mad as a March hare • mad as a wet hen

mad as a March hare—crazy; insane: Anyone who thinks the moon is made of green cheese is mad as a March hare.

mad as a wet hen—(also: mad as a hornet) very angry; extremely irritated: Mrs. Harris was mad as a wet hen when the rabbits ate all her tulips.

***Note:** Neither expression fully correlates in meaning with the phrase **mad as a cut snake**—(Austral.)* 1. = *mad as a wet hen:* I was as mad as a cut snake to hear that the telescope was going to be left to die, and it's good to see that the administrators at NASA have changed their minds. 2. = *mad as a March hare:* Many people I'm sure thought Geoff was as mad as a cut snake, and it's true, he did occasionally appear to have a tenuous grip on reality.

made from something • made of something

made from something—is used with reference to the source material from which smth. different is produced: Cheap alcohol, made from potatoes or beetroot, is utilized to a considerable extent in place of petrol.

made of something—is used with reference to the source material which still exists in its original form in the finished product: The houses in Costa Rica are built of undried bricks made of clay mixed with straw.

made man • well-made man

made man—a man whose success or prosperity is assured: And don't bother your head about losing your job. You're a made man now. *Cf.: self-made man—a man risen to a high position by one's own effort:* He was of the climber type, a self-made man in the earlier and less inspiring stages of the making.

well-made man—a man of well-proportioned figure; a man of powerful build: These people are tall and well-made, with Papuan features, and curly hair.

made to be sold • made to sell

made to be sold—said of goods manufactured to be purchased: Village workshop rugs were made to be sold, not used within the tribe in which they were made.

made to sell—said of goods manufactured to secure a ready sale without regard to quality: In some cameras, "made to sell," no care is taken to adjust this plane.

make a bad break • make a clean break

make a bad break—(coll.) say or do smth. tactless or inappropriate: Belton felt that he had made a bad break and looked around a little uneasily at the principal.

make a clean break—separate from a person that one has a connection with: When I suggested a trial separation she said I didn't have the guts to make a clean break.

make a bag • make the bag

make a bag—1. *(Hunting)* kill a number of game on a shooting expedition: I was quail-shooting and had made a bag of about a dozen birds by the time I had reached the house. 2. *(of a pregnant animal)* undergo enlargement of the udder: Femme is dropping in her tummy now, and starting to make a bag. Rainy is just very round and tight in her tummy, but very little udder development started.

Note: *The expression does not correlate in meaning with the phrase* ***make a bags of something****—(Irish coll.) do smth. incompetently or inadequately; make a mess of smth.:* If the new Authority proposes to operate like that in the future, I predict that it is going to make a bags of higher education.

make the bag—(Hunting) contribute most to the total of game killed on a shooting expedition: Sir Allan is making the bag. That is the third time he has wiped Sir Joseph's eye.

make a bed • make one's bed

make a bed—put a bed in order after it has been used; fit a bed with sheets and blankets so that it is ready to sleep in: A true nurse always knows how to make a bed, and always makes it herself.

make one's bed—1. = *make a bed:* I made my way back upstairs, made my bed and sat down to read some more. 2. suffer the consequences of one's own actions *(in allusion to the saying "make one's bed and lie in it"):* I also find it hard to feel sorry for Claudia because she has made her bed, so to speak.

See also: make down a bed / make up a bed.

make a big play of something • make great game of something

make a big play of something—(also: make much play of something) treat smth. as very important in order to make an effect: They get us out of the car and make a big play of examining our papers.

make great game of something—make fun of smth.; ridicule smth.: People made great game of the affair and called him Thorgeir Bottleback, a name which stuck to him ever after.

See also: make play with something / play about with something.

make a bow • make one's bow

make a bow—bow as a sign of respect or as a greeting: Mrs. Everett made a cold bow, and, afflicted with sudden myopia, did not see the hand held out.

Note: *The expression is not equivalent in meaning to the phrase* ***take a bow****—bow to acknowledge an introduction, applause, etc.:* She received a standing ovation and gracefully responded by taking a bow.

make one's bow—1. bow when making a formal exit or entrance: "A mighty wet day, sir," says I to Mr. Hock, stepping up and making my bow. 2. *(performing arts)* make a formal appearance for the first time: She made her bow in a small club in this city.

make a business of something • make it one's business

make a business of something—make smth. one's profession: If you like to travel, you could make a business of transporting other people's cars to Florida.

make it one's business—consider smth. one's duty or responsibility: Miss Leatheran had thereupon made it her business to find out exactly what this foreigner was doing in their midst.

make a case for something • make a federal case out of something

make a case for something—(also: make out a case for something) give good reasons why smth. should be done: You can easily make a case for giving a placebo as being a valid course of treatment.

make a federal case out of something—(also: make it a federal case) complain too much; exaggerate the importance of smth.: I only spilled my milk. Why make a federal case out of it.

make a claim for something • make a claim to something

make a claim for something—demand compensation payment (under an insurance contract): If you send a parcel that becomes lost or damaged ... you may wish to make a claim for compensation.

make a claim to something—(also: make a claim on something) 1. assert one's right to smth.: Japan made a claim to this territory and argued that it was illegally occupied. 2. allege or aver smth.: As I am not an anthropologist, sociologist or historian, I make no claim to understanding culture from any of those perspectives.

make a clean sweep of something • sweep something clean

make a clean sweep of something—1. eliminate smth.: The revolutionary force of motorization has made a clean sweep of all other patterns of living. 2. win all the prizes, seats in parliament, etc.: Mr. Drapeau's Civic Party made a clean sweep of all 52 seats on the city council.

sweep something clean—clear dust, dirt, etc. from the area with a brush or broom: Böhm promptly grabbed a broom and swept the room clean himself.

See also: sweep clear for something / sweep clear of something.

make a compliment to someone • make one's compliments to someone

make a compliment to someone—(also: pay a compliment to someone) express praise or admiration for a person in a remark: She was remarkable for her sincerity, and when she made a compliment to anyone, she spoke what she really felt.

make one's compliments to someone—(also: pay one's compliments to someone) express one's greetings or good wishes to a person: We are about to leave, so go make your compliments to the host.

make a day of it • make someone's day

make a day of it—devote a day to some pleasurable activity: To make a day of it, invest 400 yen on a one-day pass that allows passengers to get off and on at sites of interest along the route.

make someone's day—render smb.'s day delightful; give a person great pleasure: I had it sent to him for an early Fathers Day gift. He doesn't get excited over too many things and this hat definitely made his day!

make a do of it • make a to-do about it

make a do of it—(coll.) make smth. succeed *(also: make a go of it):* You've got your own life and you go and live it and make a do of it.

Note: *The expression does not correlate in meaning with the phrase* ***make do with something****—(also: make something do) accept smth. although it is not quite adequate or satisfactory:* It should be no great hardship for the community to make do with the same housing accommodation that it enjoyed in 1938. *Cf.: make do and mend—continue to manage with smth. one already possesses, especially by repairing or adapting:* The author describes how fashion was limited by shortage and utility, creating an era of make do and mend.

make a to-do about it—(coll.) complain too much about smth.; make a fuss or a scene about smth.: If the waiter makes a mistake, don't make a big to-do about it.

make a dust • make the dust fly

make a dust—(coll.) act in a noisy manner; cause a commotion *(also: raise the dust):* No real building can come out of revolutions which make a dust and a mess and bitterness and reaction.

make the dust fly—(coll.) start working with the utmost vigor or energy *(also: make the feathers fly):* We turned them loose on the work, and they made the dust fly.

make a face • make face

make a face—1. show one's dislike or disgust by one's facial expression: Every time I mentioned taking a swim in the lake Jack made a face. 2. sketch, draw, or model a face: After you've played with the controls a bit, and you've made a face that you're happy with, type in a name for the face.

make face—(arch.) offer resistance: Bonaparte was yet in strength to make face against the united armies of the remainder of Europe.

See also: do faces / make faces.

make a fortune • make one's fortune

make a fortune—make a lot of money: I exploited these unhappy natives to make a fortune for myself. We colonialists thought only of private gain.

make one's fortune—attain a comfortable position in life: Exiled to Canada where he made his fortune, he lost touch with his three sisters. *Cf.: seek one's fortune—try to attain personal and financial success:* Anderson made the decision to go West and seek his fortune in California.

make a joke about something • make a joke of something

make a joke about something—tell ridiculous things about smth. so as to cause fun: Adam is able to make good jokes about Cambridge.

make a joke of something—1. turn smth. into a joke: "Oh, it's you, Mr. Wormold. I was just thinking of you. Talk of the devil," he said, making a joke of it. 2. treat smth. lightly or as a joke: She could have panicked, but instead she made a joke of the whole thing.

make a kill • make a killing

make a kill—(of an animal) perform an act of killing: Male lions are rather reticent about expending their energy in hunting—more than three-quarters of kills are made by lionesses.

make a killing—(coll.) win or earn suddenly a large sum of money; make an enormous profit: The company made a killing from the sale of its subsidiary.

make a life for oneself • make a living for oneself

make a life for oneself—construct a good, decent life for oneself (having a job, home, etc.): I don't feel an affinity to any one place and am willing to move to almost anywhere in order to make a life for myself.

make a living for oneself—earn enough to support oneself: It was a time when a man with sufficient talent and extraordinary energy could reasonably hope to make a living for himself as a freelance writer.

See also: get a life / get life.

make a mark in something • make the grade in something

make a mark in something—(also: make one's mark in something) leave a lasting impression; make oneself well-known in a certain field: The photographs of community members who made a mark in their area of activity adorn the walls.

make the grade—do acceptable work; reach the proper standard: The country still has a long way to go before it will make the grade in areas like freedom of expression and women's rights.

make a meal from something • make a meal of something

make a meal from something—prepare a meal using certain ingredients: The men made a meal from bread and the meat that had been cooked the night before.

make a meal of something—1. create a meal of smth., especially with the implication that one wouldn't expect it to be a complete or regular meal: You can make a meal of salad on days when you want to keep your diet light. 2. *(coll.)* exaggerate the importance of an event or situation: Predictably, anti-biotech groups have made a meal of this mishap, blaming inadequate government regulation. 3. *(coll.)* put more time and effort into smth. than it really needs: John really made a meal of sorting out his desk. It took him all day...

make a monkey of someone • monkey someone

make a monkey of someone—(U.S. sl.) mock a person; cause smb. to look ridiculous *(also: make a monkey out of someone):* At the thought of George Zen laughed outright. She had made a monkey of him, and he deserved all he had got.

monkey someone—imitate smb.'s manner or style: Speaking about original bands (meaning not monkeying others), I was surprised how many bands stay firmly in their genre, adding nothing original.

See also: go ape over someone / play the sedulous ape to someone.

make a move • make one's move

make a move—1. move from a stationary position: The robber said that if any of us made a move he would shoot. 2. leave the place: We'd better make a move now, or we'll be here all night. 3. change one's place of sojourn: The first holiday-seekers are making a move to the seaside. 4. begin to act: Unless we make a move soon, we shall be in a hopelessly weak position.

Note: *The expression does not correlate in meaning with the phrase* ***make a movement***—1. *move in a specific manner:* Mrs. Morgan made a movement of protest but Francis looked to Teversham for support. 2. *(Military) make a planned change in position:* The regiment needed a good night's sleep because the plan was to make a movement at dawn.

make one's move—1. have a turn in a game: After he made his move, Capablanca would beg Mrs. Lasker not to worry, because in his opinion her husband had the better position. 2. = *make a move 4:* Vehicle makers are pondering a number of legal issues which must be addressed before they make their move.

make a move on someone • move in on someone

make a move on someone—1. move towards a person in a threatening way: He fell dead on the floor, clutching a knife in his hand, cut down before he made a move on the man who has challenged his dignity. 2. *(coll.)* approach a woman in the hope of establishing a romantic relationship *(also: put the moves on someone):* As soon as Ellen left the room, her boyfriend made a move on me. 3. *(coll.)* act in hostility against a person: Fortunately he had three high ranking uncles, the Piccolo brothers, which would deter anyone from making a move on him.

move in on someone—1. come closer to or surround a person (preparing to attack): The police are moving in on the criminals hiding in the house. 2. take up residence with smb., especially so as to inconvenience the person: My brother's friend moved in on us without us even asking him. 3. = *make a move on someone 3:* Some guys from New York moved in on me and purchased my contract. I found out they forced my manager to sell the contract, and didn't even pay him.

make a noise • make noises

make a noise—1. talk very much about smth.; make smth. the object of general comment: For all the great noise that is made about it, there is but little true faith in the world. 2. complain or argue about smth. in order to draw attention to it: The women were making a lot of noise about having a room of their own.

Note: *The expression does not correlate in meaning with the phrase* ***make a noise in the world****— attain great fame or notoriety:* He seemed a very lively young man, certain of his own abilities and eager to make a noise in the world.

make noises—express particular ideas, feelings, etc. not mentioning them directly: General Electric and Alcoa, for example, are making noises about getting into city building.

Note: *The expression does not correlate in meaning with the phrase* ***make the right noises****—(also: make all the right noises) show concern, enthusiasm, etc. about smth. because one is expected to:* She said I would have to come and visit her. I made the right noises, then changed the subject.

make a party • make up a party

make a party—arrange a social gathering, especially of invited guests at a private house: Every evening there is somewhere in this building a party. And if there wouldn't be any, you be sure we invent a reason to make a party!

make up a party—form a group of people for purposes of entertainment, recreation, etc.: We do require that you pay for the trip in advance; however, your money will be refunded if we are unable to make up a party, or if the trip is canceled.

make a pass • make the pass

make a pass—1. gain upon and pass the vehicle in front of one: The reigning World Champion (Button) just couldn't get close enough to the Japanese driver to make a pass. 2. *(also: make passes)* attempt to attract the romantic interest of a person: He had almost completely hidden from me the feelings which seemed to have driven him to make a pass at me.

make the pass— = make a pass 1: An impatient driver decided that he had to pass the cars ahead of him. He veered into our lane to make the pass...

make a point of something • make the point about something

make a point of something—regard or treat smth. as important or necessary: Fred also made a point of the need for club members to support such an important event.

make the point about something—communicate one's argument or idea successfully: Alan made the point about programmers being just like mountain climbers tackling a new mountain.

make a proposal • make a proposition

make a proposal—1. offer or put forward a suggestion, plan, etc.: Porter made a proposal to hold secret negotiations, but the communist side did not accept it. 2. offer marriage to a person: He felt they had been cheated out of so many years together that maybe he would make a proposal to her soon.

make a proposition—1. *= make a proposal 1:* He made a proposition to hold a complimentary film festival, one that would take a more extensive look at the older films. 2. make an indecent request to a woman: There are not many men who could get away with exposing themselves and making a proposition to an employee.

make a run • make a run for it

make a run—1. *(coll.)* make a rapid journey for a short stay at a place: Would you like to make a run of a day or two to the other side of the Weald? 2. *(Air Force)* make a target approach in order to attack: One of the fighters made a run at us, but his high speed caused him to misjudge his trajectory.

make a run for it—(also: run for it) run in order to escape from a place or a dangerous situation: It was still raining hard, but we made a run for it.

make a scene • make the scene

make a scene—exhibit anger, indignation, etc., in a public outburst: He thought the soup too hot, and made quite a little scene about it.

make the scene—(sl.) 1. appear in a particular place: I've got to make the scene. The whole world will be there! 2. understand or appreciate the situation: I can't quite make the scene, but it looks like Bruno punched the guy over here. 3. succeed; achieve a position, etc.: I guess with this album they'll sure make the scene.

Note: *The expression does not correlate in meaning with the phrase* ***set the scene****—(also: lay the scene) 1. (Theater) install stage furniture, scenery, etc., to create the setting of a play:* The stagehands set the scene for Macbeth's final showdown in record time. 2. *place or locate the surroundings of a play, film, story, etc.:* The novel by Luigi Natoli sets the scene in 17th century Sicily. 3. *provide the appropriate background or atmosphere for smth.:* They have done what no American administration has dared do — set the scene for a proper debate.

make a show • make a showing

make a show—(also: put on a show) display an outward appearance or semblance of smth.: The gardener was a very old man, somewhat deaf, who was only making a show of working.

Note: *The expression does not correlate in meaning with the phrase* ***do a show****—(coll.) attend an entertainment:* People over a wide area would dine and do a show, as they do at Stratford.

make a showing—give a demonstration of some competence or worth: She's very young, and I thought it was fine that she even made a showing among all those older contestants.

make a snatch • take a snatch

make a snatch—(Underworld) commit an unexpected and quick robbery *(also: do a snatch):* The best way is to make a snatch and give legs for it, it's better than loitering.

take a snatch—(coll.) eat some meal hurriedly (when a chance occurs): He took only a snatch or light refreshment, returning immediately to his desk.

make a stand against something • take a stand against something

make a stand against something—oppose smth. actively: The teachers' union has made a stand against violence, backing members who have threatened industrial action rather than teach disruptive children.

take a stand against something—adopt a firm public position against smth.: Pennsylvanians should be proud of the officials who took a stand against violence and hatred in this state.

make a time for something • make time for something

make a time for something—set a time or make an appointment for smth.: I enclose a form for you to fill in. We should make a time for me to inspect the damaged premises.

Note: *The expression does not correlate in meaning with the phrase* ***make a time about something****—(U.S. coll.) make a fuss over smth.; treat smth. with an excessive display of attention (also: make a time over something):* Our little girl insisted upon doing it [replacing a button] herself, and made such a time about it that the request had to be allowed.

make time for something—find time or an opportunity for smth.; fit smth. into one's busy schedule: You can certainly cut out a few hours of television a week to make time for exercise.

make a vow • make one's vows

make a vow—make a solemn promise or undertaking: There is a sect called the Abstinents who make a vow to abstain from everything that has enjoyed life, and to eat nothing but vegetables.

make one's vows—(also: make the vows) join a religious order; become a monk or nun: He made his vows two years later and studied for the priesthood under the direction of the pious Abbot Pfluger.

make advances • make an advance

make advances—1. make progress: Since the introduction of radiography into surgery, many advances have been made in its application. 2. *(Military)* move forward on the enemy position: When the Red Army made advances into Germany, Goering moved his headquarters to Berchesgaden. 3. approach a woman in the hope of a romantic relationship: I'd be glad if you'd stop making advances to my daughter.

make an advance—1. = *make advances 1:* Navidi has made an advance in this area by identifying the components needed to model the health effects of air pollution. 2. = *make advances 2:* Ascertain the position and strength of an enemy before making an advance.

make amendments to something • make amends for something

make amendments to something—correct smth., especially a piece of writing: She made a few amendments to the letter before signing it.

make amends for something—atone for the harm one has done; make compensation for smth.: It made him wish to make amends for his former unkindness to the boy.

make an end of something • put an end to something

make an end of something—abolish or eliminate smth.: The new meaning of a word, whatever it may be, does not make an end of the old.

put an end to something—stop smth. from happening any more: The government is determined to put an end to terrorism.

make an exception for something • make an exception to something

make an exception for something—treat smth. as a special case (as a token of particular favor or because of its unusual quality): Miss Clark did not attend films of which she had read the book, but she had made an exception for the trilogy.

make an exception to something—refrain from applying or enforcing a rule, law, or any other set of regulations: He had to get to the city of Berkeley to make an exeption to a food regulation in order to serve coffee in his first shop.

Note: *The expression is not equivalent in meaning to the phrase* ***take exception to something***— *object to smth.; find fault with smth.:* Few people would take exception to a proposal for a "common currency," as a token of international exchange to be used for convenience.

make an observation • take an observation

make an observation—(usually pl.) 1. monitor smth. carefully in order to examine: Mr. Thornton made numerous observations of the snow-clad peak. 2. determine the position of the sun or other heavenly body: An officer and two men were also stationed on land and were prepared to make observations. 3. make a remark or comment on smth.: Dr. Dreschfeld made some observations on the symptoms, pathology, and treatment of this disease.

take an observation—1. = *make an observation 1:* Dr. Spruce took meteorological observations throughout the vast region he traversed. 2. = *make an observation 2:* He can take an observation and is acquainted with that part of navigation called plain sailing.

make capital out of something • make money out of something

make capital out of something—use a situation to one's advantage: The women to whom Napoleon addressed himself were no longer adventuresses, who made capital out of their relations with him.

make money out of something—gain or acquire money through some source: He had heard of people who made money out of shares, but that was about all he knew about share investing.

make difficulties • present difficulties

make difficulties—raise objections; make trouble: Mary's father made difficulties when she said she wanted to marry a poor schoolteacher.

present difficulties—(of things) create problems: The air-boat seems to us one of the best ideas; but the working of it presents many difficulties.

make down a bed • make up a bed

make down a bed—prepare sleeping accommodation not previously available (when one has a visitor, etc.): Are you going to sleep here tonight; if you are, my wife will make down a bed for you.

make up a bed— = *make down a bed:* She made him up a bed on the high white divan in her living-room — not a heap of sleeping-bags and blankets but a real bed.

See also: make a bed / make one's bed.

make for something • make up for something

make for something—1. move or travel towards a place: We had now reached the Windward Passage and our old ship was making for the open sea. 2. promote smth.; contribute to smth.: Any international accord makes for a better understanding and recognizes the need for co-operative effort.

make up for something—compensate or repay for difficulties, inconvenience, etc.: The location of the restaurant is indeed very nice.... Nevertheless, that does not exactly make up for the terrible service.

make free of something • make free with something

make free of something—be allowed or have the right to use smth. that belongs to smb. else: In some cases a couple would actually build for themselves a single cottage, but as a rule they were content to make free of each other's private homes.

make free with something—use smth. that belongs to smb. else without permission or in a way that is considered unacceptable: They walked home, along with their friends, and made free with my house and kitchen whilst I was busy being a dinner lady at school.

make free with someone • make someone free

make free with someone—be too familiar or impudent in one's behavior with a person: Having been with him and his family in Loch Broom I had the misfortune to make too free with a servant maid.

make someone free—(also: set someone free) release a person from prison, slavery, etc.: Scott sued for his freedom in Missouri in 1846, claiming his residence in a free state and a free territory made him free.

make hay of something • make hay while the sun shines

make hay of something—1. turn smth. to advantage: As long as politicians can make hay of the supposed "harm" caused to our citizens ... they will be an annoyingly persistent part of the political landscape. 2. scatter things around in disorder: I recalled with poignant regret that Jack Winston and I had once made hay of his room; but evidently he bore no malice. 3. render smth. ineffectual: The fact remains that "La Belle Helene" has not survived Verdi's "Requiem," and this surely makes hay of the argument.

make hay while the sun shines—(saying) make the earliest possible use of favorable circumstances: The old adage, "make hay while the sun shines," has never been more apt than it is now in most sectors of commercial construction.

make it a federal case • make out a case for something

make it a federal case—(also: make a federal case out of it) complain too much; exaggerate the importance of smth.: I'm not the only person in the family who smokes, but they're going to make it a federal case.

make out a case for something—(also: make a case for something) give good reasons why smth. should be done: He said he was an atheist but he never debated the subject with me and never made out a case for atheism.

make it hot for someone • make someone hot

make it hot for someone—(coll.) put smb. under pressure; make things difficult for a person: Maybe if we make it hot for them, they'll leave.

make someone hot—1. cause a person to feel warm: I had to stay on the magnesium for another ten hours. It made me hot and nauseous and disoriented. 2. *(coll.)* make smb. feel angry or embarrassed: It is a curious thing that if you call his name aloud in public after an Englishman you make him hot and fretty. 3. *(sl.)* arouse a person sexually: Listen, I'm sitting here imagining you reading this, and it makes me hot, makes me want to get naked.

See also: get the hots for someone / give it hot to someone.

make it up to someone • make it up with someone

make it up to someone—compensate a person for negligence, difficulties, inconvenience, etc.: If you'll work overtime tonight, I'll make it up to you by giving you Saturday morning off.

make it up with someone—(also: make up with someone) settle a quarrel; make one's peace with a person: I really want to make it up with her, but she won't speak to me.

See also: make up for someone / make up on someone / make up to someone / make up with someone.

make leeway • make up leeway

make leeway—provide a margin of freedom, as of activity, time, or expenditure: Because we had to expand we had to get so much more machinery, so you make leeway for all this in the budget.

make up leeway—compensate that which has been lost or wasted (by doing extra work, etc.): There is a short break of ten minutes between each presentation, to make up leeway caused by prolonged discussion.

make light of something • make light work of something

make light of something—treat smth. as unimportant: My parents made light of my worry and told me to take no notice of what people said.

make light work of something—do smth. easily and without much effort: You have worked hard all year, and should be able to make light work of passing the examinations.

make much of something • not make much of something

make much of something—regard smth. as important; value smth. highly: We've always made much of our high literacy rate, but somehow that hasn't made us into a nation of readers.

not make much of something—1. have a poor opinion of smth.; treat smth. as unimportant: He has never made much of his World War II experience. 2. fail to understand smth.: I am not very fluent in Tamil anymore, so I couldn't make much of the book in Tamil.

make no bones about something • make one's bones

make no bones about something—be blunt and straightforward about smth.; speak about smth. openly: Lovecraft made no bones about being a complete atheist.

make one's bones—1. *(Underworld)* kill smb. as requirement for membership in a criminal gang: Vito Corleone "made his bones" (first killing) in cold blood for dollars. 2. *(sl.)* earn a reputation; achieve success: John Daly eventually made his bones, so to speak, as a reporter by covering World War II in Europe.

make no mistake about it • there's no mistake about it

make no mistake about it—is used as a warning that the statement is to be taken seriously: We shall insist on having every penny that is due to us, make no mistake about it.

Note: *The expression does not correlate in meaning with the phrase* ***and no mistake****— without any doubt (used after a statement to emphasize the idea implied):* It's boiling hot today, and no mistake!

there's no mistake about it—there is no doubt about it; it is certain: There's no mistake about it — this is quite simply the best car on the market, sir!

Note: *The expression does not correlate in meaning with the phrase* ***there's no mistaking****— it is impossible not to recognize smb. or smth.:* There's no mistaking the sect's women by their black poke-bonnets.

make nothing of something • make nothing out of something

make nothing of something—1. treat smth. lightly: He said he'd call me the next morning. He didn't call until early evening but I made nothing of it. 2. fail to understand smth.: The audience, used to jazz singers, satire companies or stand-up comedians, could make nothing of his work.

make nothing out of something—make no profit out of smth.: So he gave away every cent he made from that movie — he made nothing out of it.

make off with oneself • make off with someone

make off with oneself—(rare) depart or leave a place suddenly: Dietrich had made off with himself ... there was doubtless good reason for his wishing to be out of the way.

make off with someone—(of lovers, etc.) run off with smb.;

elope with a person: He readily admitted that he had made off with the wife of French publisher Victor Bohain.

make one's own way • make one's way

make one's own way—follow one's inclinations; act independently: He wanted to find a new direction but could find no clues in contemporary art and had to make his own way.

make one's way—1. proceed forward, especially with difficulty: As soon as he saw us, Henry made his way through the crowd to greet us personally. 2. make good progress; achieve success: But David was not discouraged: he was young, enthusiastic, determined to make his way. 3. *(of a custom, tradition, etc.)* become generally accepted: The papers don't yet talk of it, but the idea is making its way into even the best-balanced minds.

make out a prescription • make up a prescription

make out a prescription—(of a doctor) fill out a written order for a medicine: Many over-the-counter drugs are very difficult to get in other countries, so have your doctor make out a prescription as a precaution.

make up a prescription—(of a chemist) prepare a mixture such as medicine: Physicians are not allowed to sell medicines to their patients, except when the pharmacist refuses to make up a prescription.

make out someone • make out with someone

make out someone—1. manage to see a person, especially in the distance or in the dark: He thought that he could make out a human figure lying at the bottom of the pit. 2. *(also: figure out someone)* understand smb.'s character; find an explanation for a person's behavior: What a queer fellow he is! I can't make him out at all.

make out with someone—(coll.) get on with a person (usually implying difficulty): How are you making out with the people in your new office?

make over someone • make someone over

make over someone—(coll.) pay a lot of attention to smb.; make a fuss over a person: Why does she make over your sister so much?

make someone over—change a person's appearance: The hairstylist tried to make Carla over, but she wanted to be the way she had always been.

make over something • make something over

make over something—(coll.) pay a lot of attention to smth.; make a fuss over smth.: Aunt Jane made over the wedding gifts as if they were for her instead of Susan.

make something over—remake or refashion smth.: I'll have to make this dress over, it's all the wrong shape.

See also: do something over / overdo something.

make play with something • play about with something

make play with something—make effective use of smth.: Clever politicians make play with the subject for their own ends, and the general result is confusion, extravagance, and injustice.

Note: *The expression does not correlate in meaning with the phrase* ***make a play for something****— make a conspicuous attempt to gain or acquire smth.:* Tony is left to decide whether he will make a play for the top job in the family or concede control to his uncle.

play about with something—(also: play around with something) 1. amuse oneself manipulating smth. (to explore its possibilities): I've been playing about with my camera a lot recently, as such I've got lots of pictures to share. 2. cause disorder to smth.; interfere with smth.: I recently moved my bed into the living room because of the cold and it has been playing about with my sleep.

See also: make a big play of something / make great game of something.

make someone open his eyes • make someone open his eyes wide

make someone open his eyes—1. make smb. stare in surprise; amaze a person greatly: It really makes me open my eyes in amazement when people think it is impossible to live like this. 2. cause a person to realize smth.; make smb. see reason: It was the humiliation in Adelaide that made them open their eyes and realize the mess that they were in.

make someone open his eyes wide— = make someone open his eyes 1: From behind, at the back of the chapel, came a voice, one that made him open his eyes wide in surprise.

make someone's blood boil • make someone's blood freeze

make someone's blood boil—make smb. very angry or indignant: It used to make my blood boil to think that such things couldn't be prevented.

Note: *a) The expression does not correlate in meaning with the phrase* ***warm someone's blood****—(also: warm someone's heart) make a person feel eager or excited:* The real estate section of the paper did not excite his envy or warm his blood. He had never wanted a country estate.

b) The expression does not correlate in meaning with the phrase ***keep someone on the boil****— sustain smb.'s interest or enthusiasm:* There needs to be some ongoing process to keep the issues before people, keep them on the boil, keep up the enthusiasm.

make someone's blood freeze—(also: make someone's blood run cold) horrify or shock a person: What he saw made his blood freeze: An arrow had hit Lighur directly into the forehead.

make sport for someone • make sport of someone

make sport for someone—provide amusement for a person: The squire made sport for the children of the village by engaging a Circus for the week.

make sport of someone—ridicule smb.; jest at a person: We made sport of the old couple who kept the *Bull;* and they deserved it for always giving short measures.

make the feathers fly • make the fur fly

make the feathers fly—(coll.) 1. *(also: make the dust fly)* start working with the utmost vigor: When Mrs. Hale did her spring cleaning she made the feathers fly. 2. quarrel violently; create a disturbance: Let's keep our sense of humor and try not to make the feathers fly in all this controversy.

make the fur fly— = make the feathers fly 2: When the boss finds out that they failed to secure the contract, he will certainly make the fur fly.

make time for someone • make time with someone

make time for someone—schedule time to see a person: She makes time for kids who are less fortunate, visiting sick children in hospitals in the cities where she competes.

make time with someone—(coll.) make romantic advances; flirt with a person: John plays the tough guy who tries to make time with the café cashier, whom Buster secretly loves.

make up for someone • make up on someone • make up to someone • make up with someone

make up for someone—take the place of smb. who is absent, can't work, etc.: Have you got a supply of new friends to make up for those who are gone?

make up on someone—(Sport) gain on a contestant who is ahead of one in a race: He managed to make up on other runners in the race.

make up to someone—1. draw near to a person; approach smb.: Later I saw her make up to the lady I have described. 2. try to ingratiate oneself with a person: One who makes up to a teacher is recognized as being in a slightly different category from an outright sneak.

make up with someone—(also: make it up with someone) settle a quarrel; make one's peace with a person: I'm sorry. I was wrong. I want to make up with you.

See also: make it up to someone / make it up with someone.

make up the weight • make weight

make up the weight—1. supply what is wanting to complete a given weight: Train with your full packs—fill them with old clothes, etc. just to make up the weight that you would be carrying. 2. supply deficiencies; make smth. complete: Baptists teach the following great doctrines, which make up the weight and substance of the whole Bible.

make weight—(Boxing) lose sufficient weight to remain eligible for a specified weight division: If Oscar does not continue his proper diet and exercising, he won't make weight for the next fight.

make waves • raise waves

make waves—1. *(usually of wind)* cause waves to rise or appear: See over to the right, is that something stirring, or is it just the wind making waves? 2. unsettle a comfortable situation; stir up trouble: He is a solid dependable Scotsman who runs a company at a profit and doesn't make waves. 3. impress people by doing smth. very well: After a difficult period when it was struggling to survive, Courtauld Films is now making waves from its new base.

raise waves— = make waves 1: These small waves raised by the evening wind are as remote from storm as the smooth reflecting surface.

make way for something • pave the way for something

make way for something—1. move away or be removed so that some other thing is able to stand there: In the end, the cinema is pulled down to make way for a parking lot. 2. move aside so as to allow room for smth. such as a vehicle to pass: When an ambulance approached, she pulled over to the side of the road to make way for the ambulance. 3. be succeeded or replaced by smth. else: The manual typewriter made way for the electric then electronic typewriter which, in turn, made way for word processors.

Note: *The expression does not fully correlate in meaning with the phrase* ***give way to something****—1. allow a vehicle, etc. to pass first:* In most countries (where rules are observed) the usual is to give way to traffic on the driver's side. *2. = make way for something 3:* As passenger trains gave way to air and highway travel, train depots became obsolete. 3. *agree to smb.'s demands, etc.:* I entreat you not to give way to his evil suggestions; oppose the adversary while you can. 4. *abandon oneself to a feeling of sorrow, anger, etc.:* She gave way to her grief in a Center Street restaurant where she stopped for breakfast and considerably startled the waiters...

pave the way for something—prepare the way for smth. new to come; make the development of smth. easier: Park directors are looking to us to pave the way for similar organizations throughout the country.

man about town • townman

man about town—(dated) a man who socializes in fashionable circles: A young man afraid of marriage may compensate by specializing in dating and courting, becoming a "man about town."

Note: *The expression is not equivalent in meaning to the phrase* ***man of the town****—(arch.) one belonging to the shady or "fast" side of town life; a rake, a debauchee:* Several of our men of the town ... make use of the most coarse uncivilized words in our language.

townman—(also: townsman) 1. an inhabitant of a town (as contrasted with a countryman): A townman would think the world slept, so great was the booming quietness. 2. a fellow-inhabitant of a town: Mr. McClung continued to enjoy the confidence and esteem of his townmen and held public positions.

man and boy • old and young

man and boy—from boyhood onwards: I have worked here, man and boy, for several different corporations, for twenty years now.

old and young—people of all ages: Then old and young came from every side with roses, the loveliest that bloomed in each garden.

man in the middle • middleman

man in the middle—a person between two opponents: And now, Specter is the man in the middle when it comes to the current wrangling over judicial nominees.

middleman—a person who buys from the producer and sells to the merchant: If we can buy from the producer, we can save the money we pay to the middleman.

man in the moon • moon man

man in the moon—a vague, unidentified person; an imaginary person: "Then you don't know how things are settled?" "No more than the man in the moon."

moon man—an astronaut who journeys to the moon: The moon men (or lunarnauts, as they will doubtless come to be called) must be able to park their spacecraft.

man in the street • street man

man in the street—the common man; just anyone selected at random: But what does the man in the street think about all this?

street man—(U.S. sl.) a petty criminal (as a pickpocket, drug peddler, etc.) who operates on the streets: He is playing partner to the pusher whose street man is keeping the girl hooked.

man of blood • man of blood and iron

man of blood—(arch.) smb. guilty of bloodshed; a man responsible for the murder or death of any one: David was called a man of blood not because he enraged in wars which were legitimate but on account of Uriah, whose blood he criminally shed.

Note: *The expression does not correlate in meaning with the phrase* ***man of blue blood****— a man who comes of an ancient family; an aristocrat:* Is he a man of blue blood? We are worshipping him because of his ideas, what he stood for and what he preached.

man of blood and iron—(originally of Prince Bismarck) a man who advocates the use of brute force as distinguished from diplomacy: One such victory involved Omar ibn al-Khattab, who was regarded as "a man of blood and iron" and a bitter opponent of the new faith.

man of figure • man of figures

man of figure—a person of influence: He has all that can be said of any man of figure, wit, and virtue in town.

man of figures—smb. versed in arithmetic or statistics: When Jane could not balance her checking account, she sought assistance from Steve, who was a man of figures.

man of mark • marked man

man of mark—a noteworthy person: This French tutor was a man of mark who had held a lectureship in Paris.

Note: *The expression does not correlate in meaning with the compound* ***marksman****—*1. *smb. who attains a certain standard in shooting at a target:* I am an indifferent marksman both at range and on safari. 2. *(Sport) a person who ranges competitors in a race:* The starter is helped by a "marksman," who places the men on the scratch.

marked man—1. a person who is a potential object for hostility; smb. singled out for a grim fate: Smithers had made one financial blunder too many. From then on he was a marked man. 2. a person destined to succeed: This young melodist ... runs his fingers over the strings with a power that instantly makes him a marked man.

man of men • man's man

man of men—an outstanding man; a man of supreme excellence: But that John should come under her will so, John who was a man of men!

man's man—a man who likes to be in the company of other men and who enjoys activities which men typically enjoy: He had had comparatively little to do with women. Essentially a man's man he had been wrapped up in his calling. *Cf.: lady's man—a man who enjoys the company of women; a man who is popular with women:* He is a lady's man who always seems to have a lot of women interested in him.

man of nerve • nervous man

man of nerve—a bold and courageous man: The study of his life would have told them that this was a man of nerve, character, and old-fashioned common sense. *Cf.: have the nerve—have the necessary courage or audacity to do smth.:* They've got a stressful and dangerous job and I wouldn't have the nerve to do what they do.

nervous man—a man of excitable temperament; smb. who is easily worried or irritated: He was a nervous man, one who was literally looking over his left shoulder all the time.

man of property • property man

man of property—a wealthy individual: They are all men of property and always entertained a respect for property.

property man—*(Theater)* a man in charge of stage properties *(also: property master):* The property man, needing assistance, hired clearers to help move and shift properties between scenes.

man of service • serviceman

man of service—*(dated)* a veteran soldier: The parallel between Cincinnatus and Washington as men of service is striking.

serviceman—1. a man serving in the armed forces: Some servicemen had prewar business experience which was being amplified by their military duties. 2. a man providing service or maintenance: The knowledge that the course provides will enable the television serviceman to expand his business into the radio field.

Man of Steel • steel man

Man of Steel—1. a nickname for the movie superhero Superman: There will never be another Man of Steel, on film or in real life, like Chris. *2.* is used of the name Stalin adopted by the Russian dictator Joseph Dzhugashvili (1879–1953): It seems more than ever the world needs another Stalin, another Man of Steel.

steel man—a person who has to do with steel as a product: From the steel-man's point of view, this was ideal, for it put all steel mills on an equal competitive footing.

See also: iron man / man of iron.

man of the moment • minuteman

man of the moment—*(also: man of the day)* an outstanding man of his time: Gabriel Deshayes was "a man of the moment," extremely sensitive to the immense needs of his contemporaries, especially the poor.

minuteman—*(hist.)* a volunteer soldier in the American Revolutionary War *(pledged to be ready to fight at a minute's notice):* Salem was among the Minutemen who fought in the Battle of Concord, on April 19, 1775.

man of the people • people person

man of the people—an ordinary man, not distinguished by rank or position: The exchange of roles in "The Prince and the Pauper" suggests that a man of the people can be a benevolent ruler because of his humble roots.

people person—smb. who likes being with other people and who is good at working with people: Jane is not a people person. Luckily, her job does not require her to spend a lot of time with clients.

man of the woods • woodman

man of the woods—1. a savage inhabitant of the woods: He was but a wild man of the woods ... polished over skin-deep with Roman civilization. 2. used of orangutan: The variety of the ape and monkey tribes is endless; and among them is the orang-outang, or the "man of the woods," as the name implies.

woodman—*(also: woodsman)* a person who works or hunts in the woods: The oldest woodmen say that it takes a hundred years to grow a perfect oak for an English ship.

man of the world • worldly man

man of the world—a society man experienced in the ways of social life: My dear Sir Robert, you are a man of the world, and you have your price, I suppose.

Note: *The expression does not correlate in meaning with the phrase* ***citizen of the world****— a person who is at home anywhere in the world; one who has no national prejudices:* He is a real citizen of the world, and it is his humanism and his universal values that have earned him such esteem in the international community.

worldly man—a man concerned with material gains and advantages: From the moment one enters the foyer, one can detect that this is a worldly man of some means and possessed of good taste.

man something with someone • people something with someone

man something with someone—supply a ship, etc. with men for service or defense: The commanding officer manned the boat with a crew of his men.

people something with someone—fill a place with some kind of people: The state's intent was to people the land with yeomen and producers of food.

man-to-man • person-to-person

man-to-man—*(usually attrib.)* said of a talk, discussion, etc., characterized by directness and openness: "We had a man-to-man about changing his personal life," Harmon said. "I told him to look in the mirror to see the guy who's causing all the problems."

person-to-person—*(attrib.)* 1. is used of an operator assisted phone call in which the caller wants to speak to a specific person *(callers are not charged unless they reach the party they ask for):* Say that you are placing a person-to-person call and give the name of the person to whom you wish to speak. 2. said of an interaction involving personal or intimate contact between people: This project works to end intractable conflicts around the world through new and innovative person to person diplomacy.

man upstairs • top man

man upstairs—is used with reference to God: Does God

sympathize with man? Certainly the great omnipotent, "man upstairs" has all the ability to do anything he wants, but does he exercise that ability?

top man—smb. who has the most important position in an organization: He was the top man, and I was his "leg man." He personally handled most of the negotiations...

See also: high man on the totem pole / high-up man.

manly behavior • mannish behavior

manly behavior—behavior that is typical of, or suitable for, a man rather than a woman or boy: Because of his military background, Mr. Jones was constantly berating his sensitive, gentle son for his lack of "manly behavior."

mannish behavior—(of a woman) behavior that is more like a man's than a woman's *(used showing disapproval):* In the early 1900s, a woman who smoked in public would be ostracized for her mannish behavior.

mansion house *(UK)* • mansion house *(U.S.)*

mansion house (UK)—1. the house of a landed proprietor: The landed gentry usually possess a share of pride fully proportionate to their estate and mansion house. 2. *(the Mansion House)* the official residence of the Lord Mayor of London: The conference took place in the Egyptian Hall of the Mansion House, the Lord Mayor presiding.

mansion house (U.S.)—a large house of good appearance: In this street were most of the great houses, or "mansion-houses," as it was usual to call them.

marinara sauce *(UK)* • marinara sauce *(U.S.)*

marinara sauce (UK)—a sauce containing seafood, usually in a tomato base: Our next homemade marinara sauce recipe is for a shrimp marinara sauce. This marinara sauce can be served hot or cold.

marinara sauce (U.S.)—a sauce containing tomatoes and herbs, with no seafood: Freshly crushed tomatoes, mushrooms, fresh basil and herbs make up this delicious marinara sauce.

mark my words • mark you

mark my words—is used to give emphasis to a warning or prophesy: And you mark my words, you haven't heard the last of him.

mark you—is used to draw attention to smth. one has just said: He is very ambitious — like most men, mark you.

mark one's cards • mark someone's cards

mark one's cards—(also: mark the cards) put secret signs on a pack of cards so one could win by cheating: I'll never believe he's a cheating bastard. I'll never believe he marked his cards.

mark someone's cards—provide information that would give advantage to a person: He welcomed me to Mexico and ... marked my cards privately on some human rights issues I might like to raise publicly.

mark the time • mark time

mark the time—1. *(of the clock)* show time: In the days when no clock marked the time, "cock-crowing" became a familiar phrase, as today, when referring to the earliest hour of dawn. 2. record or indicate specific time: As the two girls entered the hall they saw that the tall clock marked the time as quarter-past five. 3. indicate a period: The tower of Babel marked the time when mankind became separated and developed different languages that effectively managed to divide them. 4. *(also: beat the time)* follow the rhythm with the feet, a baton, etc.: She has a carving fork in her hand, with which she pounds on the table to mark the time.

mark time—1. = *mark the time 1:* The city contains many essential sights, such as the Sapporo City Clock, which has been marking time for over a century. 2. = *mark the time 4:* Some of them were singing, some clapping their hands as they marked time to the tune which one lone fiddle squeaked out gaily. 3. be idle, waiting for smth. to happen: He has been marking time for over a month now as he waits to hear about the new job.

marked for something • marked with something

marked for something—singled out or destined for success, some grim fate, etc.: Mr. Edwards is a longtime faithful employee who was marked for advancement in the company.

marked with something—characterized by smth.; showing clear signs of smth.: His life is marked with achievements earned through hard work and faith.

martyr for something • martyr to something

martyr for something—smb. who is made to suffer severely for a cause, etc.: His father had died a martyr for that cause, which he now wanted so basely to betray.

martyr to something—a person who is acutely afflicted by smth. such as a disease: The deceased had been a martyr for years to rheumatic gout.

master of oneself • one's own master

master of oneself—a person who is in full control of his faculties and emotions: "I'll get cousin Daniel to drive me over at once," said Samuel, master of himself and of the situation.

one's own master—smb. who is independent of other people and is able to make his own decisions: The university vice-chancellors are no longer their own masters, but have to be prepared to accept group decisions.

match up to something • match with something

match up to something—come up to some standard: His performance did not match up to the glowing account we had received of him.

match with something—correspond or harmonize with smth.: These curtains do not match with the decorations.

Note: *Neither expression fully correlates in meaning with the phrase* ***match something***—1. = *match with something:* The color of the carpet does not match the wallpaper. 2. = *match up to something:* Our failure to match this achievement was the result of the failure to concentrate the requisite resources.

may be • maybe

may be—could be: You'll get help, it may be me or somebody else; rest assured that the problem will be solved.

maybe—(used as an adverb) perhaps; possibly: The two of them laughed at some joke they had shared, or maybe me?

meddle in something • meddle with something

meddle in something—intervene in smth. which is not one's concern: In reality, of course, powerful states have often meddled in the internal affairs of their weaker neighbors.

meddle with something—get involved with smth., making unauthorized or unwanted changes: When a classic recipe is fabulous, don't meddle with it, and just do what you're told.

medical man • medicine man

medical man—a doctor; a physician: A medical man, who may be called up at any moment, must make sure of his "beauty-sleep."

medicine man—a witch-doctor or magician in primitive societies: They will not revisit their own camp until it is first visited by their priest or medicine man.

Mediterranean disease • Mediterranean fever

Mediterranean disease—(also: Mediterranean anemia) thalassemia *(a hereditary hemolytic anemia):* This interesting disease presents three important abnormalities together characterizing a syndrome which may be designated "Mediterranean disease."

Mediterranean fever—(also: Malta fever) an enteric fever caused by bacteria of the genus *Brucella:* One should avoid direct contact with strange dogs as fleas, who live by sucking the animals' blood, can transmit Mediterranean Fever to humans.

meet someone • meet with someone

meet someone—1. become acquainted with a person: I remember being swept completely off my feet when I first met Jim. 2. encounter a person for (casual) socializing: I first met him for coffee one evening. I was really unsure of our suitability after this first date.... 3. encounter (a friend, etc.) unexpectedly: I last saw Tom about six months ago, met him quite by chance out in the middle of Wellington Harbor. 4. introduce a person: Good morning, boys! Meet Miss Marigold, my secretary and continuity girl. 5. go to meet smb. at the station, airport, etc.: He would go to the station and meet Miss Gale. 6. *(of two sportsmen)* compete against one another: Weaver must defend against James Tillis before meeting Cooney.

meet with someone—1. = *meet someone 2:* He paid us a visit at home to introduce himself as our financial representative and I met with him for coffee near my office on another occasion.... *2.* have a formal or pre-arranged meeting with a person: Teachers are meeting with the Minister of Education to talk about their demands for an increase in pay.

meet something • meet with something

meet something—1. be next to smth.; join together: We had rounded Cape Point, where the Atlantic meets the Indian Ocean. 2. encounter or confront smth.: Sometimes he meets a situation for which his moral rules do not provide. 3. deal satisfactorily with smth.: We will be able to meet this challenge — not on our own but, rather, by collaborating with our many colleagues. 4. *(of demands, standards, etc.)* satisfy: It's sad to tell students that they couldn't stay because they didn't meet the requirements.

meet with smth.—1. find smth. (by chance): By applying to advertising offices I should have no doubt of very soon meeting with something that would do. 2. suffer or experience smth.: Her husband has met with a slight accident, but he isn't seriously hurt. 3. = *meet something 2:* Liberalization meets with a situation in which many of the state's institutions are delegitimized and ineffective. 4. *(of an idea, opinion, etc.)* be received: A number of member states tried to renegotiate the clause but met with a firm refusal. 5. correspond to smth.; be in keeping with smth.: The plan you submitted seems to meet with the committee's idea on the subject.

men in the street • street people

men in the street—common people: This BBC camera crew went round collecting close-ups of men in the street saying what they think of things.

street people—people who live in the streets; homeless people: There are a lot of cold street people at this time of the year.

merge into something • merge with something

merge into something—1. mix with smth., so as to become part of it: As new data become available, the information will be merged into the report. 2. fade or change gradually into smth.: The shadows merged into darkness as we huddled together around the fire's flickering light and comfort.

merge with something—(of business companies, etc.) combine to become one unit: The regional bank merged with the city bank in order to recover from a large amount of bad debt.

middle age • Middle Ages

middle age—the period in life when a person is no longer young but has not yet become old: He was growing stout with middle age.

Middle Ages—in European history the period between about A.D. 1000 and A.D. 1400: During the Middle Ages the main economic units were the villages and manors.

Middle West • West Midlands

Middle West—the region of the USA near the northern Mississippi: Mid-Westerners are concerned about the plight of the Indians, because the Indians are part of Middle West life.

West Midlands—a metropolitan county of England: The biggest attraction of Dudley, located in West Midlands, is the Zoo situated in the grounds of Dudley Castle.

miles away • miles off

miles away—1. *(hyperbolic)* very far away: He trudges across an icy parking lot, toting skis slung over his shoulder. The nearest ski lift seems miles away. 2. not in reach or not readily attainable: Such a prospect is miles away from the school world implied by the proceedings at the recent education "summit." 3. said of smb. unaware of what is happening around because one is thinking of smth. else: Her mother was pacing up and down and seemed miles away. She hadn't noticed them at all. 4. said of smth. that can be noticed or recognized even though it may not be obvious: In a sea of voices, his is the one you'll spot miles away!

miles off—(of a guess, calculation, etc.) completely wrong *(also: miles out):* Ken Beaton's original estimate of the elephant, buffalo and hippo population had been miles off.

military establishment • war establishment

military establishment—1. a military body or institution: Colonel Wellesley was long occupied in organizing the civil as well as the military establishments. 2. an institution providing military education and training: The institute was not organized as a military establishment and was open to civilians. 3. the quota of officers and men in a regiment, ship, etc.: How large should America's peacetime military establishment be?

war establishment—augmentation of regiments, etc. to a certain number to meet war requirements: In the war establishment of the squadron, there are additional troops provided for just such tasks.

military power • war power

military power—1. prerogative to decide enjoyed by military authority as contrasted to civil authority: The military power now humbled itself before the civil power. 2. potential capacity to wage warfare derived from military equipment: We know that, on account of the balance of military power, we have got to live with it [communism].

war power—emergency powers conferred on the government in wartime: It shall require a three fifths vote of the whole of both houses to authorize the use of war powers.

milk and honey route • milk route

milk and honey route—(U.S. tramps, dated) railroad: Have you ever hiked the milk-and-honey route from Ogden through the Mormon country?

milk route—(also: milk round) a route on which milk or other products are regularly delivered to customers: The milk companies are saved most of the costs of distribution by delivering the orange juice on their milk route.

Note: *The expression does not correlate in meaning with the phrase* ***Milky Way****—galaxy:* The current position of the solar system in the Milky Way suggests that another period of greater comet bombardment is not far away.

milk round • milk run

milk round—1. *(also: milk route)* a route on which milk or other products are regularly delivered to customers: Uncle George used to do the milk round and I remember his little van with milk churns. *2. (UK coll.)* the annual tour of higher education establishments by prospective employers: Go to the yearly "milk round" meetings that big companies set up at the bigger universities. Chat to their representatives.

milk run—1. = *milk round 1:* The milk truck driver agrees to take Joe and Alice home but only if they first accompany him on his milk run. 2. *(coll.)* a routine trip or flight with no anticipated difficulties: It was just a milk run, the flight to drop off two fishermen at Otter Lake, but Don Sheldon was worried.

milk the pigeon • pigeon milk

milk the pigeon—(dated) attempt the impossible: "Why have you come here if only to fall into a brown study?" "I am sorry. I promised to do a favor for Miss Ravenhurst but I fear I'm only milking the pigeon."

pigeon milk—(also: pigeon's milk) 1. the partly-digested food with which pigeons feed their young: Pigeons feed the young ones from the protein-rich "pigeon milk," a curd formed in the parent bird's gut. 2. *(dated)* said of an imaginary article for which children are sent on a fool's errand: Boys and novices are frequently sent on the first of April to buy pigeon's milk.

Note: *The expression does not correlate in meaning with the phrase* ***mouse milk****—(coll.) anything that delivers little payoff while requiring lots of hard work:* When Carl said that making this stuff was mouse milk, what he meant was: it takes a hell of a lot of whatever they use to make it out of to make a little bit.

minced meat • mincemeat

minced meat—meat cut or chopped into small pieces: The first mouthful brought the tears trickling down my cheeks. It was red pepper, stuffed with minced meat.

mincemeat—1. a mixture of currants, raisins, sugar, apples, candied peel, etc. used in pies: My wife makes her own mincemeat and her own plum-puddings. 2. *(U.S.) = minced meat:* Mincemeat often contains raw animal suet, so always store any uncooked mincemeat in the fridge and don't be tempted to taste it before cooking.

miss out on something • miss out something

miss out on something—lose an opportunity to benefit from smth.: You may miss out on some of the latest company gossip.

miss out something—omit or fail to include smth. in a document, etc.: You can miss out a comma because you're writing too quickly.

mistaken about something • mistaken in something

mistaken about something—is used of smth. concerning which one makes a mistake: I was mistaken about her age. I thought she was over fifty.

mistaken in something—1. is used of an erroneous statement, supposition, etc.: The ancients were mistaken in their belief that the earth was flat. 2. = *mistaken about something:* "The papers have been greatly mistaken in my age," said the divorced wife of the late Samuel Breakwell to a reporter.

mix oil and water • pour oil on troubled waters

mix oil and water—try to make two very different people or things exist together: There are works which try to combine the technical stuff with personal narratives. Unfortunately, in Veit's case, it's mixing oil and water.

pour oil on troubled waters—do smth. to make a tense situation more peaceful: Friends are a blessing — they pour oil on troubled waters, drag you to parties and make you feel loved.

mix something up with something • mix something with something

mix something up with something—1. combine or blend a substance with another substance: I mixed the contents up with water and followed the directions on the bottle. 2. mistakenly identify one thing with another: They mixed up my name with that of my sister. They then said it was impossible to change the names on the ticket...

mix something with something—1. = *mix something up with something 1:* Mixing paint with the liquid glue requires a little trial and error, so start with just one color of paint. 2. carry out or consider different activities at the same time: Having been badly burned in a previous relationship, Mark never mixes business with pleasure.

mixed up in something • mixed up with something

mixed up in something—(of people) involved in or linked with smth., especially smth. reprehensible: Robert Mendelson, whose name was also mixed up in the scandal, has not been mentioned in the ruling.

mixed up with something—1. blended or interspersed with smth.: Its composition varies according to the various ingredients which may be mixed up with it. 2. combined or associated with smth.: There is no reason why every adventure story should necessarily be mixed up with snobbishness and gutter patriotism. 3. = *mixed up in something:* No political party makes the slightest reference to it, all parties apparently being too much mixed up with the scandal. 4. confused with smth.; mistakenly identified with smth.: His hospital chart was mixed up with that of another patient with a similar name.

mobile home • motor home

mobile home—1. a factory-built housing unit that can be installed on a permanent (rented) site and used as a residence: A park owner may not prohibit home owners from installing electric or gas appliances in their mobile home. 2. *(also: touring caravan)* a non-motorized caravan with living facilities that can be towed by a vehicle and used as a residence: Forty-five miles per hour shall be the maximum speed at which a person shall be permitted to drive a vehicle which is towing a mobile home.

motor home—(also: motor caravan) a motor vehicle designed to serve as self-contained living quarters for recreational travel: The number of visitors to our state choosing to travel by motor home is ever increasing.

Modern English • New English

Modern English—English as it has been since about 1500: According to the nomenclature now generally adopted, the Old English period ends about 1100–1150, the Middle English period about 1500, when the period of Modern English begins.

New English—1. the contemporary English language: Marriageable men, or what the new English calls "intending bridegrooms" should look at themselves dispassionately in the glass. 2. *(attrib.)* pertaining to New England *(a part of the United States comprising six north-eastern States):* Early New English houses were compact, with cooking taking place in one of the principal public rooms.

money card • payment card

money card—a plastic card for use with card phones *(also: calling card):* It is a good idea to use a calling card when you call home.... Unlike a lost credit card, the money card has no value to anyone lacking your password.

payment card—(UK, also: debit card) a plastic card with which a customer may withdraw money from his account after every transaction: Using payment card, we take complete control over all expenses. Security of transactions is guaranteed by a code and signature.

Note: *The expression is not equivalent in meaning to the term* ***credit card****— a plastic card that is different from a payment card in that it does not remove money from the user's account after every transaction:* Whenever I get my credit card statement, I open it with caution and fear. Who knows when they will get into your savings.

monkey jacket • monkey suit

monkey jacket—(Nautical) any tight, short jacket, especially one that is part of a uniform: In 1889 a monkey jacket took the place of the blue tunic.

monkey suit—(sl.) a fancy uniform or formal suit: Neither of my two hats went well with the monkey suit.

monkey something • monkey with something

monkey something—imitate smth. such as smb.'s manner, technique, etc.: This was my first attempt at monkeying his style. Had fun trying it.

monkey with something—(coll., also: monkey about with something) 1. try to adjust or fix smth. (especially of an effort that does not succeed): I was still monkeying with my tie when Katie came in. 2. *(used showing disapproval)* meddle with smth. (making unauthorized changes, etc.): Somebody has been monkeying with it before as the two bolts that hold the bar in place are missing.

more cry than wool • more kicks than halfpence

more cry than wool—much clamor or fuss with insignificant results: Her diary was much more cry than wool and Mary MacLane was a startling figure only because the times were so colorless and mild.

more kicks than halfpence—(also: more kicks than half-pennies) more harshness than kindness: The life of a boy on board a ship isn't one to be envied, he is at every one's beck and call, and gets more kicks than halfpence.

more than one bargains for • more than one can shake a stick at

more than one bargains for—1. said of an unpleasant surprise at the negative consequences of one's action: A crook got more than he bargained for when he tried to rob a 77-year-old woman. That woman was a former deputy sheriff ... and fought back. 2. said when the outcome of one's action is even better or more favorable than one had expected: I found myself leafing through the book.... To say the least, I got more than I bargained for — an emotional connection with a brave and inspirational author.

more than one can shake a stick at—said of a large number or quantity of smth.: Don't worry about seeing islands. On the ferry to Sweden you'll see more than you can shake a stick at.

Mother of Southwestern Statesmen, the • Mother State, the

Mother of Southwestern Statesmen, the—(U.S.) a nickname of the state of Tennessee: Other nicknames include... "The Mother of Southwestern Statesmen," because Tennessee furnished the United States three presidents and a number of other leaders.

Mother State, the—(U.S.) a nickname of the state of Virginia: Such estates were the special pride of the Mother State, aristocratic old Virginia. These ancient homesteads were owned by the most prominent families.

Mother's Day • Mothering Sunday

Mother's Day—(U.S.) the second Sunday in May set aside to celebrate mothers: Almost all mothers agree that receiving a card on Mother's Day holds special emotional meaning.

Mothering Sunday—(UK) similar in meaning to *Mother's Day* and observed on the fourth Sunday in Lent, therefore its date varies: During the 17th century, England began to celebrate "Mothering Sunday."

motor car *(UK)* • motor car *(U.S.)*

motor car (UK)—an automobile; a four-wheel road vehicle: John was driving a motor car eastwards when it skidded on the icebound roadway, causing the car to turn completely round.

motor car (U.S.)—1. = *motor car (UK):* It takes a leisurely sort of a millionaire indeed who can afford to come in his motor car all the way downtown through the press and strain of Broadway traffic. 2. a self-propelled vehicle operated on rails along a regular route: Do you remember those railroad motor cars you used to see in the fifties and sixties on virtually every line in the U.S. and Canada?

motor caravan • touring caravan

motor caravan—a motor vehicle designed to serve as self-contained living quarters for recreational travel: Our intention was to use the house as a base in France and then travel throughout Europe in our motor caravan.

touring caravan—a mobile, non-motorized caravan with living facilities that can be towed by a vehicle and used as a residence: Drivers must have a minimum of third party insurance required for towing a touring caravan.

move away • move off

move away—1. go away; depart: Eventually the police and the crowd reached an understanding and the crowd moved away. 2. leave a place where one has lived: The house was let to a retired couple for a while, but they moved away up to Inverness.

move off—1. *(of a vehicle)* start moving: The bus moved off before the passengers had got on board. 2. = *move away 1:* As the crowd moved off, some of its members looted the windows of West End shops. 3. *(of goods)* be sold off: A second or third edition of the book moves off languidly enough.

movie theater • moving theater

movie theater—a building where movies are shown to an audience; a cinema: When we go to a movie theater today, we experience a much different world than the theater-goer of the early twentieth century.

moving theater—virtual reality simulator with seats moving where you actually ride with the movie and experience every bump, dip and turn: How am I to eat and drink in a moving theater seat tossing me around for two hours.

Mr. Right • right Charlie

Mr. Right—(also: right guy, the) a perfect romantic or marriage partner: When she found herself in a romantic rut last winter, she began to despair of ever meeting Mr. Right. *Cf.: Mr. Right Now—(a jocular pun on the former) a man who is not to be considered for a permanent relationship:* One look at a man's face may give a woman important clues about whether he's "Mr. Right" or just "Mr. Right Now."

right Charlie—(sl., also: right Charley) a fool; a simpleton: You made me look a right Charlie when you told everyone about me getting so drunk last night.

mutton dressed as lamb • wolf in sheep's clothing

mutton dressed as lamb—said of a middle-aged woman dressed in too youthful a style: You would never be able to describe her as mutton dressed up as lamb because she obviously still feels young.

wolf in sheep's clothing—said of a person or thing that appears peaceful and harmless but is really harmful or hostile:

John Major's grey image may disguise a wolf in sheep's clothing.

N

name the day • name-day

name the day—fix the date for a wedding: Then he made hot love to her, and pressed her hard to name the day.

name-day—(in Catholic or Orthodox tradition) the feast day of the saint after whom one is named at baptism: There is no St. Jennifer, so I celebrate my name day on the Feast of St. Geneviève.

Native Americans • native-born Americans

Native Americans—1. *(also: first Americans)* American Indians: We have a new section for you featuring posters of Native Americans and Native American Artwork. 2. *(hist.)* members of a minor American political group having a brief existence in the early 19th century: The Native Americans were pledged not to vote for any foreigner for office.

native-born Americans—persons associated with America by birth: The word "Creole" is used in Louisiana to express a native-born American, whether black or white, descended from old world parents.

natural birth • natural born

natural birth—childbirth in which psychological conditioning replaces the use of anesthesia, etc.: This definition [normal birth] may also be equated with natural birth — birth without interference.

natural born—1. said of a child actually begotten by one in contrast to adopted: Natural born children of employees are eligible for benefits if they are born before the employee retires. 2. said of a person with a natural talent or aptitude for smth.: You have the ability to motivate others to do their best. You are a natural born teacher and mentor. 3. said of a person having the legal status of citizen by birth: A person born to a mother who was a natural-born subject of the United Kingdom had the rights of a natural-born subject.

natural man • natural person

natural man—1. an uncultivated, uncivilized man: Let us not forget that "Typee" is a glorification of the noble savage, uncorrupted by the vices of civilization, and that Melville looked upon the natural man as good. 2. a man having a usual or normal character; smb. who is not exceptional in any way: My friend George is the natural man drawn to pubs and barmaids. 3. a man who is especially apt or suited to do smth.: Philip was the natural man to whom to turn, for he came from Bethsaida and he would have local knowledge.

natural person—1. *(legal)* a human being as distinguished in law from an artificial or juristic person: Associations for carrying on the business of banking may be formed by any number of natural persons. 2. a man or woman who is especially apt or suited to do smth.: As director of the university's archaeological activities, she was the natural person to compile the volumes.

Note: *The expression does not correlate in meaning with the phrase* ***natural born person****—(also: natural born citizen) a person born in the country and having the legal status of citizen:* You are a natural born person, and unless you specifically enter into a contract with the state — then you have pre-existing natural rights.

natural to someone • natural with someone

natural to someone—(of behavior, etc.) being in accordance with a person's habits or character: He spoke with a stiff manner that was not natural to him.

natural with someone—1. = *natural to someone:* This feeling was not natural with him. It was probably only due to some derangement of his own health. 2. behaving in a simple, easy manner towards smb.: Mary is caring and compassionate. She was natural with both Kessia and Joshua, and gained their trust instantly.

nearest thing, the • very near thing, a

nearest thing, the—said of smth. that is very much like a particular type of thing: Soho is the nearest thing in Central London to a red light district.

very near thing, a—1. a dangerous situation that a person just manages to avoid: The list of what could have gone badly wrong is a long one. It was certainly a very near thing. 2. said of an election, competition, etc. barely won because of almost equal chances of the contenders: "Do you think he's going to get in?" "It'll be a very near thing because the opposition will be so strong."

neck and crop • neck and neck

neck and crop—completely; altogether: An unexpected episode caused me to be ejected neck and crop from my club.

neck and neck—keeping level in a race, competition, etc.: The Soviet World and the Free World were running neck and neck in the training of scientists.

need doing • need to do

need doing—said of things that require fixing, improving, etc.: Nice land with a small brook running through it. Fence needs painting, and barns need repairing.

need to do—is used to indicate that a course of action is desirable or necessary: I am sorry about the absence, but I need to go and will not be talked out of it.

needle someone • put someone on the needle

needle someone—(coll.) 1. make smb. angry or annoyed by teasing or provoking the person: We kept needling Bill about his new girl friend, but apparently we went too far. 2. prod or goad a person to a specified action: A few annoying experiences that have probably happened to many, have needled me into expressing these feelings.

Note: *a) The expression does not fully correlate in meaning with the phrase* ***give someone the needle****— = needle someone 1:* He couldn't resist giving me the needle one more time and still would not admit that I had beat him at his own game. *Cf.: get the needle—(coll.) become irritated or angry because one has been ridiculed, etc.:* The silly ass got the needle, because she asked for the ring.

b) The expression does not correlate in meaning with the phrase ***have the needle to someone****—(coll.) be extremely angry with a person:* There will always be some team which will have the needle to a referee and want to get rid of him.

put someone on the needle—turn a person into a drug addict: He's using all his dope allowance now.... You know who put him on the needle and supplied him?

neglect in something • neglect of something

neglect in something—lack of proper care or oversight with respect to smth.: If we discover neglect in Ralf's treatment at the hospital we will bring forward charges.

neglect of something—(also: neglect for something) treatment of smth. as of no importance: There has been a neglect of the interests of farmers in recent years.

negro head • nigger head

negro head—1. *(dated)* a nest of tree-ants: The color of these nests is black, from which, and their irregular surface and orbicular shape, they have been called Negro Heads. 2. strong black plug tobacco: He thrust a prodigious quid of negro head tobacco into his left cheek. 3. india-rubber of an inferior quality: The proportions of "fine" and "negrohead" rubbers depend on the appliances and care of the collectors. 4. a projecting stump of dead coral: Reefs are broken into blocks, the large mushroom-shaped fragments are thrown up onto the beaches, where they form "negro-heads."

nigger head—1. a tangled mass of the roots and decayed remains of plants projecting from a swamp: We plunged into a mire of muddy water and "nigger-heads." 2. any of various spherical cacti of the genera *Ferocactus and Echinocactus:* The kind commonly called the nigger head is round, of the size of a cabbage, and covered with large, crooked, catlike thorns. *3. = negro head 2:* He had accepted as much strong "niggerhead" as would have stocked a tobacconist's shop. *4. = negro head 4:* A crowd of "nigger heads," black points of coral rock, peep up in places. 5. *(U.S. hist., derog.)* an advocate of political rights for Black people: They were Democrats, and retorted upon violent Union men by calling them Niggerheads. 6. a yellow flower with a dark center *(Rudbeckia hirta):* A number of composites with yellow rays and dark centers are commonly known as niggerheads, though the more polite term is black-eyed Susan.

neither fish nor fowl • neither man nor mouse

neither fish nor fowl—(also: neither fish nor flesh) neither one thing nor the other *(said of smth. difficult to identify):* He's neither fish nor fowl right now ... he is not a child, yet he is not a teenager. *Cf.: make fish of one and fowl of the other—treat people, organizations, etc. differently:* Why make fish of one and fowl of the other? They were both McKayes now, in the sight of the law, and ... they were full brothers!

neither man nor mouse—nobody; not a single creature: Does he expect to become a god in maintaining a principle that neither man nor mouse in all God's creation opposes?

Note: *Neither expression correlates in meaning with the phrase* ***neither sugar nor salt****—used by smb. not worried by wet weather or as a reproof to a person reluctant to go out into rain:* I told her again to go on home, as it was raining. She said she was neither sugar nor salt.

never ever • never-never, the

never ever—(emphatic) absolutely never: Keep background noise to a minimum when speaking on the telephone—and never, ever let your children answer your business line!

never-never, the—1. *(UK coll.)* the hire-purchase system: Some people bought on the never-never with no idea as to how they would meet their repayments should things turn sour. 2. *(Never-Never, the)* in Australia, the unpopulated northern part of Queensland; the desert country of the interior: His intention was to enjoy this trip ... not to "do a perish" in the Never-Never.

never fear • no fear

never fear—(coll.) there is no cause to worry: Dear child, the solution will come to you, never fear.

no fear—(exclam.) not a chance; certainly not: I invite him to dinner! And in his own hotel! No fear!

never mind • never you mind

never mind—it does not matter; don't be troubled about it: "We've missed the train!" "Never mind, there'll be another in ten minutes."

never you mind—it is not your business and you are not going to be told: Never you mind what your father and I were talking about.

Never-Never Land, the • never-never world, the

Never-Never Land, the—1. in Australia, the unpopulated northern part of Queensland; the desert country of the interior: The European emigrant's view of the "Never-Never Land" was very different from that of the locals. 2. an imaginary, illusory, or Utopian place: It was no longer the real India they wanted to escape to; it was the Never-Never Land of the East.

never-never world, the— = Never-Never Land, the 2: Of course in the never, never world of escapist movies everything always turned out right by the end of the final reel.

new boy • old boy

new boy—1. a schoolboy during his first term at a school: Roach was a new boy ... Thursgood's was his second prep school. 2. a person who is new to a position of employment: When a new boy showed up, I was the one to show him around. *Cf.: new kid on the block—a person who has recently joined a company, organisation, etc, and does not know how things work yet:* Please pardon me for being ignorant here with the discussion, I am a new kid on the block.

old boy—1. *(coll.)* an old man: You could scare the old boy and he'll spill his tea. He spills things all the time. 2. is used to informally address a close acquaintance: I said, "Hooray, old boy!" and slapped him on the back. 3. a former pupil of a particular school or college: Brothers In Action is a group of old boys committed to making a difference in the college community. *Cf.: old boys club—said of the clannish loyalty of people who intimately know each other:* Appointees are often part of the "old boys club" or old friends from college days that can be "trusted." 4. *(Old Boy, euph.)* the devil: Those who wish to avoid uttering the plain straight name "devil" often call him the "Old Boy."

New England • New England of the West, the

New England—a part of the United States comprising six north-eastern States *(Maine, New Hampshire, Vermont,. Massachusetts, Rhode Island, Connecticut):* The ships which were bound for New England were crowded.

New England of the West, the—(U.S.) a nickname of the State of Minnesota: Because of the large number of New England emigrants, Minnesota was sometimes referred to as the "New England of the West."

new man • old-timer

new man—1. a person who is new to a position of employment: As important a decision as this ought to be postponed until there is a new man in the White House. 2. a man whose character has noticeably changed: He is a new man now that he is retired, but gets a bit annoying being around the house the whole time. 3. smb. who begins to feel much better physically or mentally: His brother, who had had a bypass earlier, described feeling like a new man after the surgery. 4. *(UK)* a man who believes in complete equality of the sexes and shares domestic work equally: Chris does at least half of the cooking and the housework. He's very much a New Man.

old-timer—1. smb. who has been involved in an activity for a long time: Hensle, to date the only Alpaca breeder here, started in 1991, which makes her very nearly an old-timer in the Alpaca business. 2. a person whose experience goes back to old times: Perhaps you'll be able to locate an old-timer who will remember the 70s, 80s and what might have happened along the way.

See also: not born yesterday / yesterday's man.

New World, the • new world

New World, the—North and South America: The bird which we call turkey was one of our best acclimatizations after the discovery of the New World.

new world—new setting of existence with its customs, traditions, etc.: She left her rich, safe, home and came to a new world in the city.

Note: *The expression does not correlate in meaning with the phrase* ***brave new world, the****— a nightmarish utopian society, especially one in which technological progress has negative results:* One only has to think of the brave new world as "prophetically" described by Aldous Huxley: societies made up of wilfully-created, genetically-determined master/slave creatures.

news agency • newsagent

news agency—(also: press agency) an organization that provides news coverage to subscribers, such as newspapers, etc.: The bulletin, which went out to more than four thousand newspapers, came from the news agency's San Francisco bureau.

newsagent—a person who keeps a store or stall selling mainly newspapers and magazines: Her father was a newsagent, so she devoured comics and magazines as well as fiction.

night man • night person

night man—1. a man who does work during the night: A company taxi is usually driven by both a day-man and a night-man. 2. a man who does illegal things at night: The people hated any type of investigator because so many of them were "night men." 3. smb. who prefers to be active in the nighttime: Morris is a night man. He'd have a chapter from me morning or afternoon and then work on his at night.

night person— = night man 3: I can't function in the morning. I'm strictly a night person.

night watch • watch night

night watch—1. a watch or guard kept during the night: I used to watch them [sharks] during the night watch, as their fins, above water, skimmed along, leaving a trail of light behind them. 2. *(also: night watchman)* a man employed to guard a building, block of offices, etc. at night: At a corner two night watch in shoulder capes, their hands upon their staffholsters, loom tall.

watch night—1. a service held on New Year's eve, lasting until midnight: Robert Morris, banker and merchant, attends the Watch-Night and proceeds from here to contact friends. 2. the night upon which a New Year's eve service is held: A Methodist, she always goes to their chapel on New Year's eve — or the "Watch Night," as they call it. 3. *(West Africa) = night watch 2:* I engaged what in the Cameroons is known as Watchnight. There were two reasons for engaging a night watchman: the first ... to wake me up.

nine-day wonder • ninety-day wonder

nine-day wonder—(also: nine days wonder) said of smth. that causes great excitement for a few days but is likely to have been soon forgotten: She also predicted the scandal over her liaison with the former prime minister was a "nine-day wonder" which would soon blow over. *Cf.: one-hit wonder—said of a group or singer that has only one hit record before returning to obscurity:* Classing Ms Shapiro as a one-hit wonder is a bit unfair. She was an entirely unintentional pop star, having already had a pretty healthy career in jazz.

ninety-day wonder—(also: ninety days wonder) 1. *(U.S. Army)* a graduate of the ninety-day officer training courses: I learned a lot from them. They were generous in their patience with a ninety-day wonder, second lieutenant. 2. *(U.S. coll.)* an inexperienced or temporary employee: Even a ninety-day wonder could discern the facts in this matter. 3. *= nine-day wonder:* Published by Dell, with Farmer on the back cover, the book was a ninety-day wonder.

no-go area • restricted area

no-go area—an area to which entry is forbidden: The Duke has decreed the Royal Enclosure at Ascot a "no-go" area for the miniskirted or hotpanted lass.

restricted area—1. an area in which special security measures are employed to prevent unauthorized entry: Wellington Barracks is a restricted area and anyone who enters should have identification. 2. *(UK)* an area in which a lower than normal speed limit is operative: The existing mild supervision of restricted areas is carried out by the so-called "speed cops."

no good to someone • not good to someone

no good to someone—of no use or advantage to a person: Information is no good to us if we do not know how to use and share it.

not good to someone— said of smb. who is unkind to a person: She is not good to me and my children from another relationship.

Note: *The expression does not correlate in meaning with the phrase* ***not good for someone****—1. not beneficial or helpful for a person:* This book, though not good for undergraduates, is the best book for graduate students in algebra. *2. (of food) not wholesome for a person:* He had a theory of his own that ginger preserves and fruitcake were not good for sick people.

no less than • nothing less than

no less than—(also: not less than) 1. at least the amount or number stated: Moscow expects no less than 5,000 Irish fans. Supporters of the Irish team will check in Moscow's biggest hotels. 2. is used with the implication of surprise at the amount or number stated: They told us that no less than eleven ships were destroyed in this country by the ice last year.

nothing less than—(also: nothing short of) nothing other than; quite equal to smth. mentioned: His policy became nothing less than a series of gigantic blunders.

no question • no questions asked

no question—1. is used to say that smth. is certain or definite: Indians are great spenders and no question they will welcome all the luxuries money can buy. 2. is used to say that smth. does not matter: It was quite expensive to acquire. But cost is no question when getting an anniversary gift for Linda.

no questions asked—1. there is no need to give an account of the dubious methods one may use: For a suitable fee, he will take any goods to anywhere and no questions asked. 2. there is no need to provide additional information or explanations: The police will pay $100 for every gun turned in, no questions asked. 3. *(attrib.)* said of smth. given or granted unconditionally, whatever the reason or circumstances: If you are unsatisfied for any reason, simply return it anytime within 90 days for a no questions asked, no hassle refund.

no sooner ... than • sooner ... than

no sooner ... than—as soon as smth. happened; immediately that smth. happened: She had no sooner arrived home than her agent wanted to send her on another tour.

sooner ... than—do smth. in preference to smth. else: And yet, like everybody else, he would sooner use a clean cup than wash up a dirty one.

no thanks to • thanks but no thanks to

no thanks to—without the benefit of help from smth.: Slowly, but surely — and no thanks to the BBC — the people of this country are wising up to the truth.

thanks but no thanks to—is used as a polite way of refusing an offer: Milwaukee County Executive Scott Walker says thanks but no thanks to any federal economic stimulus money for county projects.

no word • not a word

no word—no news or communication received: It's been over a month and still no word. So as of now I will never order there again.

not a word—not even one word, spoken or written: They seated themselves and ate their breakfast together, and still not a word was said.

Note: *The expression does not correlate in meaning with the humorous catchphrase* ***not a word to Bessie****—(dated) used in circumstances calling for secrecy:* I had a rather close encounter with the gate ... (not a word to Bessie!) but happily the car was unblemished.

no worries • not to worry

no worries—(Austral. coll.) that's OK; no problem *(used as an expression of reassurance):* She asked me whether she could stay in my place during her stay in Singapore. "Sure, no worries," I said.

not to worry—(coll.) is used to say that smth. need not be a cause of concern: The government had no money, but not to worry, he said, because he had private friends who would foot the bill.

nominate someone for something • nominate someone to something

nominate someone for something—propose a person as a candidate for a position: A National Republican Convention will be held for the purpose of nominating candidates for President and Vice President.

nominate someone to something—appoint a person to a position or office: The Popes have continued to nominate bishops to the lost Patriarchates; but these bishops have resided at Rome.

none but • none other but

none but—no other person or thing except the one mentioned: None but the very few could ever appreciate the ideal of the man, much less understand it.

none other but—(also: none other than) is used to emphasize the importance of the person or thing mentioned: The architect was none other but James Gibbs, also famous for designing the Church of St. Martin-in-the-Fields in London.

normal school • special school

normal school—an institution with a two-year program for the training of teachers (chiefly for the elementary grades): One key element of the teacher training philosophy was to maintain a "practice" or "demonstration" school attached to the Normal School.

special school—a school for the teaching of children who are mentally or physically handicapped: The baby had been sent to a special school because she had been born with a kind of sickness.

north light • North Lights

north light—a window, especially in a studio roof facing north: I went to his tiny studio. He'd simply put a high north light in the roof of a small bedroom.

North Lights—(also: Northern Lights) the aurora borealis: I stood looking up at the North Lights, which shot up the heaven to a great height.

Northwest Territories • Northwest Territory

Northwest Territories—a huge area of sub-arctic and arctic Canada: When the nights are dark in autumn and winter, the northern lights come out in the Northwest Territories of Canada.

Northwest Territory—(U.S. hist.) an area created by Congress in 1787, covering present-day Illinois, Indiana, Michigan, Ohio, Wisconsin and eastern Minnesota: A committee of Congress, headed by James Monroe, made a report about a plan for governance of the Northwest Territory.

not a bit • not a little

not a bit—not at all; not in the least: I haven't slept all night and I am not a bit tired.

not a little—to a considerable extent: They were not a little surprised to see me, and not a little annoyed either.

Note: *The expression does not fully correlate in meaning with the phrase* ***no little****—*1. *(followed by a noun) much:* It requires no little care and patient investigation to arrive at a correct conclusion. 2. = *not a little:* Both were deeply interested, immensely impressed, and no little surprised by what they saw.

not a thing • not the thing

not a thing—nothing at all: "And you didn't hear anything, or see anything?" asked Perry Mason. "Not a thing."

not the thing—not proper or befitting: New York was a metropolis, and in metropolises it was "not the thing" to arrive early at the opera.

not born yesterday • yesterday's man

not born yesterday—1. not naïve or easily fooled: It shouldn't surprise anyone who wasn't born yesterday that these ads that sound too good to be real are just that. 2. old enough to know or remember smth.: Anyone who wasn't born yesterday remembers the old Mexican Village restaurant, or at least has heard tales of its fame.

yesterday's man—a person, especially a celebrity, whose career is over or on the decline: Even if Labor wins a sizable majority, Blair's time is over ... he is yesterday's man.

See also: new man / old-timer.

not count one's chickens before they are hatched • not cross one's bridges before one comes to them

not count one's chickens before they are hatched—(usually imper.) not anticipate some expected benefit because it may not happen: You're expecting to make a lot of money but don't count your chickens before they are hatched.

not cross one's bridges before one comes to them—(usually imper.) not worry unnecessarily about future problems until they happen: Don't cross your bridges before you come to them — but you'll recollect that a stitch in time saves nine.

not even think of something • not think much of something

not even think of something—(usually imper.) not even consider the idea: Except that I want to see your sin-stained countenance, I should not even think of a week in Paris.

not think much of something—(also: think little of something) have a poor opinion with regard to smth.: He gives very good dinners, but I don't think much of his cellar.

not half • not the half

not half—(coll.) 1. not nearly; not at all: But why don't you come to my room? I have some Scotch — not half bad. 2. *(emphatic)* only a fraction or a small part of smth.: So, I have to read that and write about it. And that's not half of my homework.

not the half— = *not half 2:* He accused them of being responsible for the error, and that's not the half of the story.

not half bad • not so bad

not half bad—(coll.) quite good: The machine is not half bad. It's very quiet, and it performs as well as the PC on general office applications.

not so bad—only a little bad: The weather is not so bad now as we are off the mountain but there is still mist covering the peaks.

not have a leg to stand on • not have the legs

not have a leg to stand on—(of an argument, opinion, etc.) be not supported by facts or sound reasons: He said that the government did not have a leg to stand on in regard to that bill.

not have the legs—(of a ball in golf) have not enough momentum to reach the desired point: I thought my shot had reached the green but it didn't quite have the legs.

Note: *The expression is not antonymous in meaning to the phrase* ***find one's legs****—(also: find one's feet)* 1. *acquire the power of walking steadily:* We spent a week on board and after the first day we were able to find our legs even when the boat rolled. 2. *(also: feel one's feet) get confidence; be able to act independently:* New teachers in their first year or so are still very much in the process of finding their legs.

not in a condition • out of condition

not in a condition—(followed by Infinitive) unable to do smth. because of an illness, fatigue, etc. *(also: in no condition):* Tupman was not in a condition to rise, after the unwonted dissipation of the previous night.

out of condition—in bad shape; physically unfit: The way was rough and all three of them after so many idle days at sea, were distressingly out of condition.

not in it • not with it

not in it—1. not engaged in smth. as partners, competitors, etc.: For the most part the faculty members were not in it [distance education programs] for the money. 2. *(coll.)* not worthy of comparison with the thing stated first: Have you seen his new BMW? The old Opel isn't in it!

not with it—(coll.) 1. not fully alert and aware of what is happening: I forgot to stamp the letters I posted — I'm really not with it this morning. 2. not thinking or behaving in the most modern way: That teacher will never be popular with the students, he's just not with it.

See also: beyond it / off it / out of it.

not in one's backyard • not in one's province

not in one's backyard—is used to express objection to the siting of smth. considered unpleasant in one's own locality: Many people want to see more prisons being built, but not in their backyard.

not in one's province—(also: outside one's province) outside the area of one's learning or activity: What happened to the juvenile after the court's decision was not really in our province.

not in so many words • without many words

not in so many words—stated indirectly; not in these exact words: She would sometimes allude to this herself, though not in so many words. But the implication was clear.

without many words—without much discussion or deliberation: When he had a duty to perform, Dobbin was accustomed to go through it without many words or much hesitation.

See also: in a few well-chosen words / in a few words.

not in the same street • up another street

not in the same street—(coll.) not nearly so good as smth.; much inferior *(also: not in the same league):* Although the fruit is sweet it's not in the same street as an edible delicacy.

up another street—(coll.) quite another thing: You want a few details.... That's about what you want; but giving you the information is up another street.

not know how the other half lives • not know what the other hand is doing

not know how the other half lives—not know how other, especially poorer people live: People with steady jobs, decent income, and money in the bank often don't know how the other half lives.

not know what the other hand is doing—(used in allusion to the saying "one hand does not know what the other hand is doing") said of a state of utter disorganization and confusion within an organization, etc.: There are lots of subcommittees that don't know what the other hand is doing.

not know which way to look • not know which way to turn

not know which way to look—(also: not know where to look) be quite embarrassed: She came up to me and talked and laughed till I did not know which way to look. I felt that I must be the jest of the room.

not know which way to turn—(also: not know where to turn) be uncertain or confused about what to do next: I've tried to find various solutions to this problem, but none seem to work. I don't know which way to turn.

Note: *The expression is not antonymous in meaning to the phrase* ***know one's way around****—(also: know one's way about)* 1. *know how to get from place to place in a neighborhood:* I like to go to London with Frank because he really does know his way around. 2. *be extremely knowledgeable or experienced in smth.:* Chef Elsner is a culinary master who knows his way around a kitchen like the back of his hand.

not like the color of someone's money • see the color of someone's money

not like the color of someone's money—be reluctant to take smb.'s money (because it is tainted in some way or for personal reasons): I'm not used to people telling me they don't like the color of my money.

see the color of someone's money—have proof that a person has money and can pay: When I see the color of your money, I may be interested in dealing with you. Until then, thanks, but no thanks.

not move a finger • not move a muscle

not move a finger—(also: not lift a finger) not make the slightest effort to do smth.: It is unbelievable but my husband will not move a finger to help me on the domestic front.

not move a muscle—1. remain perfectly motionless: Find yourself a comfortable, out-of-sight place to sit, keep quiet, and don't move a muscle. *2. = not move a finger:* I can't believe Christians would let a thing like this happen and not move a muscle to help her.

not much for something • not much of something

not much for something—(also: not much on something) 1. not enthusiastic about smth.; having no liking for smth.: The party broke up a little after ... I guess the Ramsays aren't much for staying up late anyway. 2. not good or effective at smth.: I am not much for dream interpretation so the next morning I put this dream to rest and continued with my daily life.

not much of something—said of people or things of weak or poor quality: It was raining. Not much of a rain, just the beginning of a rain, cold and miserable.

not once • not once or twice

not once—on no occasion; never: It's not once in six months that Madame Baret's coiffure is amiss.

not once or twice—many times: Not once or twice in times gone by have I been friendly to her, and so will I be again.

not quite the thing • quite the thing

not quite the thing—1. not feeling well: Wilfrid took his arm ... saying: "You're not quite the thing today, sir." 2. not quite suitable or respectable: I do not mean to set you against him, but indeed he is not quite the thing!

quite the thing—suitable, proper, or very much in fashion: High boots are quite the thing these days.

not say pea-turkey • not talk turkey

not say pea-turkey—(coll.) not say a word about smth.; say nothing at all: How was I to know that Mary needed money, when she never said pea turkey?

not talk turkey—(coll.) not speak honestly and in a straightforward manner: Being a salesman he could not talk turkey, and so his language had mixed messages of anxiety and reassurance.

not to say • to say nothing of

not to say—is used to imply that one is content with a more moderate statement than that which might have been made: It is one of the handsomest counties ... the farmers are as a whole well-to-do, not to say rich.

to say nothing of—is used to emphasize the point by adding extra information: Much damage is caused to table tops by spilled cosmetics, to say nothing of marks caused by that early-morning cup of tea.

not too hot • too hot to handle

not too hot—(coll.) 1. not very good or satisfactory: A program denouncing the evils of capitalist society is matched by one showing that things under socialism are not too hot either. 2. *(also: not so hot) feeling* not so well: I woke up today feeling not too hot. My throat is sore and I think I have a bit of a fever.

Note: *The expression does not correlate in meaning with the phrase* ***bit hot, a****—(coll.) somewhat unreasonable:* To dismiss the lad just because he forgot to post a letter is a bit hot.

too hot to handle—(coll., of stolen property, etc.) too dangerous to deal with: Many stolen works of art have been recovered recently, which suggests that thieves are finding them too hot to handle.

not turn a hair • turn of a hair

not turn a hair—1. not show any sign of being troubled: Catherine adapted to the wilds of Africa amazingly well — she did not turn a hair at having lions walking past the back door. 2. be not affected by exertion: Hot! He had not turned a hair till we came to Walcot Church; ...that horse cannot go less than ten miles an hour.

turn of a hair—a close chance; a narrow escape from a dangerous situation: It was the turn of a hair that they hadn't buried him alive.

note paper • notice paper

note paper—paper used for writing letters on: The letter, dated 15 September, was on notepaper headed "Executive Committee."

Note: *The expression does not correlate in meaning with the phrase* ***music paper****—paper ruled with the musical staff, for the use of musicians, etc.:* Paul then played and sang it for me, and I wrote the notes and chords on music paper.

notice paper—(UK) a paper supplied to members of the House of Commons that gives details of the day's proceedings: The Notice Paper is issued on each sitting day, with the exception of the first sitting day of a new session.

nothing but • nothing if not

nothing but—nothing other than; only that particular thing: There is also a female sect called the Abstinents who make a vow to eat nothing but vegetables.

nothing if not—is used to emphasize that a person or thing has a lot of that particular quality: Brunel was nothing if not determined, and by September the ship was ready for the maiden voyage.

Note: *Neither expression is equivalent in meaning to the phrase* ***nothing short of****—(also: nothing less than)* 1. *quite equal to smth.:* This version is nothing short of perfection, with perfect guitar work and emphasis on the parts that need it. 2. *except for smth.:* I have done everything that man could do; but our case is desperate. Nothing short of a miracle can save us now.

nothing to write home about • that's all she wrote

nothing to write home about—said of smth. that is nothing out of the ordinary or even inferior: Everything I bought was much more expensive, and the quality was nothing to write home about.

that's all she wrote—said when there is nothing more that one can say about smth.: We went out twice — once to the movies and once to a restaurant and that's all she wrote.

now and again • time and again

now and again—(also: now and then) occasionally; from time to time: The tourist may now and again have to drive for many hours together through pine woods.

time and again—(also: again and again) habitually; repeatedly: Time and again, he has proven to be reliable, conscientious, and diligent.

now, now • now then

now, now—1. is used as a friendly way of telling smb. not to behave in a particular way: Now, now, there's no need for name calling. I raised you better than that! 2. is used as a friendly way of trying to comfort a person: "Now, now," the doctor said, taking her gently by the hand.

now then—is used to attract people's attention when one wants to say smth.: He uncovered the dish boldly and said: "Now then, who's for more turkey?"

number of, a • number of, the

number of, a—some; several: This organization offers a number of books describing rock art sites.

Note: *The expression is not equivalent in meaning to the phrase* ***any number of****—(also: numbers of) a sufficiently large number:* I had any number of reasons not to buy the computer.

number of, the—the quantity or amount of smth.: The number of books missing from the library is large.

number one • number ones

number one—1. *(attrib.)* first-rate; principal: One small folded letter on blue paper bearing a 12-pence stamp will be the number one feature. 2. head of an organization, etc.: Gorbachev's aim was to integrate farm production and food processing. Now, as number one, he could impose his own plan. 3. *(coll.)* oneself or one's own interests: A significant number of students care about social problems and not just about "number one." 4. *(euph.)* is used of the act of urination: This little ginger [kitten] is going to do a number one if we're not careful.

number ones—(coll.) one's best clothes or uniform: Hughes unpacked his kit to find his number ones badly crushed, and cursing, he went in search of an iron.

number two • number twos

number two—1. the person immediately subordinate to the head of an organization: When David could not attend a meeting, he sent his number two to deputize for him. 2. *(euph.)* is used of the act of defecation: The child is early taught to refer to his needs as "number one" and "number two."

number twos—(coll.) one's second best clothes or uniform: "Is this number ones and number twos, sir?" he said "or is there any flexibility on that?"

nursery-girl • nurseryman

nursery-girl—(also: nurserymaid) a woman looking after young children: She took it into her head to go to Boston, as a nursery girl, where she lived a few months.

nurseryman—a man who owns, or works in, a nursery for plants: When their toddler handed them an acorn from the tree, Meyers, a nurseryman, planted it in their back yard.

nurses' home • nursing home

nurses' home—residential accommodation for the nurses employed by a hospital: They were sacked after a party in which they staged their own version of Florence Nightingale in the nurses' home, dancing about in "shortie" nighties.

nursing home—an institution providing health care, especially for the elderly: "If I put a man in a room, beat him, starved him, the state will put me in jail," Dr. Goldman said. "If I own a nursing home and do it, the state pays me."

nuts at something • nuts on something

nuts at something—(sl.) very skilful at dealing with smth.: John's always nuts at work and I've been feeling a bit withdrawn lately. I won't even attempt to get caught up.

nuts on something—(sl.) very fond of smth.; greatly devoted to smth. *(also: nuts about something)*: She was nuts on cleanliness, maybe she was just "nuts."

nuts on someone • nuts to someone

nuts on someone—(sl.) said of smb. madly in love with a person: Michael's such dead nuts on her that he's getting dull.

nuts to someone—(sl.) said of smth. affording pleasure to a person: I hadn't had more than three hours' sleep, and the snug warmth of that couch was just nuts to me.

O

Odd Fellow • odd fellow

Odd Fellow—(U.S.) a member of the Independent Order of Odd Fellows, a social and charitable fraternity: Ask around, you would be surprised who is an Odd Fellow. If you do not know a member, consult the Lodge Directory.

odd fellow—(also: odd man) a man who is regarded as eccentric or crazy: In general, Robert is an odd fellow, not understood by his friends, and unable to understand them at the same time.

odd man • odd man out

odd man—1. *(also: odd fellow)* a man who is regarded as eccentric or crazy: He was an odd man who seldom spoke, and when he did, it was often enigmatic. 2. the person in a group who, in case of a division of opinion, is able to give the casting vote: This fifth was the odd man whose casting vote would turn the scale. 3. *(also: odd-job man)* a person employed to do various small things in a house: Either can rest occasionally by employing an "odd man," of whom there are several ... ready to do "odd" work.

odd man out—1. a person who is left out of a group for some reason: George Payne was the odd man out losing a seat on the council by five votes to Schiada. 2. a person differing from all others of a group in some respect: The typical image of the artist in the era of capitalism has been an odd man out, nonconformist, often bohemian.

odd one • odd one out

odd one—1. a person or thing differing from all others of a group in some respect: Well, I guess I am the odd one here, because I truly enjoy the website for its content, the photography etc. 2. said of smth. not numerous or infrequently occurring: The season for them [ocean sunfish Mola mola] is quite short ... but if you're lucky you may see the odd one out of season.

odd one out— = odd one 1: The original novel by Ian Fleming was an odd-one-out in the book series, describing as it did how an off-duty Bond saved a female hotelier.

of a kind • of the kind

of a kind—(also: of a sort) 1. of poor quality; not fully deserving the name: He regards himself, I think, as an artist of a kind. 2. of the description mentioned: In his psychiatric practice Peck encountered people of a kind that psychiatry had yet to define. 3. *(in the phrase "two of a kind")* of the same class, nature, or character: David and Catherine were two of a kind, both fascinated with the social world and social climbing.

Note: *The expression does not correlate in meaning with the phrase* ***kind of, a****—(also: sort of, a) smth. like; resembling smth.:* Living polyps form a kind of skin over the surface of the coral reef.

of the kind—(also: of the sort) = of a kind 2: My chair-car was profitably well filled with people of the kind one usually sees on chair-cars.

of a size • of some size

of a size—having the same size: They were both of a size, rather smaller than I am, and happy in each other's company whenever they got a chance.

of some size—fairly large: We can trace the history of these quantitative variations ... only when the differences between them are of some size.

of a sort • of the sort

of a sort—(also: of a kind) 1. of poor quality; not fully deserving the name: There always are, or seem to be, celebrations of a sort on a twenty-firster. 2. of the description mentioned: One intriguing use of games is "cognitive experimentation," of a sort that should appeal to linguists and logicians.

Note: *The expression does not correlate in meaning with the phrase* ***sort of, a****—(also: kind of, a) smth. like; resembling smth.:* More people were gathered on both sides of the street, forming a sort of amphitheater.

of the sort—(also: of the kind) = of a sort 2: These are real people of the sort that inhabit every local pub in the country.

of age • of an age

of age—1. having reached a certain age: All children must receive full-time education until they are at least fifteen years of age. 2. legally an adult: The legacy left him by his father is in the hands of trustees, as he is not yet of age.

Note: *The expression is not equivalent in meaning to the phrase* ***of one's age****— used of a deceased person's age on memorials, obituary notices, etc.:* He came to this county in the year 1836, and was, at the time of his death, in the 69th year of his age.

of an age—1. having reached an age when one is old enough to do smth.: The eldest boy Charles was of an age to be flying off and building a nest of his own. 2. of the same age: I got more mental stimulus from some of my school-fellows who were of an age with me.

Note: *The expression does not correlate in meaning with the phrase* ***of a certain age****—(euph., of a woman) no longer young; middle-aged:* One sometimes sees women of a certain age who are still very beautiful.

of all sorts • of sorts

of all sorts—various; of all kinds: His ante-rooms were thronged with clients of all sorts.

of sorts—(also: of a sort) of poor quality; not fully deserving the name: "Have you any profession?" "I'm a schoolmaster of sorts."

of long standing • of standing

of long standing—firmly established by long duration: She returned to her roots, working in watercolor on silk, a tradition of long standing in her native China.

of standing—said of a person of high position, status, or reputation: Mr. Hogben is himself a scientist of standing as well as a humanist.

of no account • on no account

of no account—(also: of no consideration) not important; insignificant in the eyes of others: "His grandfather was a distinguished man." "Was he?" replied the man of Chicago. "That's of no account with us."

on no account—(also: on no consideration) certainly not; in no circumstances: The British Trade Union representative will, on no account, be late for his meals or early for his meetings.

Note: *The expression is not antonymous in meaning to the phrase* ***on account***— *on credit:* The purchases journal is a special journal used to record all transactions in which items are bought on account.

of no avail • to no avail

of no avail—(predic.) useless; unsuccessful *(also: of no effect):* All their efforts to save him from his folly were of no avail.

to no avail—(also: to no effect): 1. unsuccessfully; in vain: We pulled him out of the river and tried to revive him, but to no avail. 2. = *of no avail:* The interviewee didn't arrive, and efforts to reach him via cell phone were to no avail.

of no consideration • on no consideration

of no consideration—(also: of no account) not important; insignificant in the eyes of others: In our day it seems incredible that the landscape was at one time of no consideration to artists.

on no consideration—(also: on no account) certainly not; in no circumstances: On no consideration will he allow gambling. He has been proof against every inducement to permit it.

of no effect • to no effect

of no effect—(predic.) useless; unsuccessful *(also: of no avail):* Such an authorization, if given, was of no effect since it would be contrary to statute and regulation.

to no effect—(also: to no avail) 1. unsuccessfully; in vain: Senators in the past have called for similar changes but to no effect. 2. = *of no effect:* There were no call buttons for patients and her repeated shouting for a nurse was to no effect.

of one's own • on one's own

of one's own—said of smth. belonging to a person: The eldest boy Charles was of an age to be flying off and building a nest of his own.

on one's own—1. relying on one's own effort, ability, etc.: Muller was on his own in a strange town, in a foreign land. 2. alone; by oneself: They would eat in the kitchen; they seldom used the dining room when they were on their own.

off again, on again • off and on

off again, on again—(also: on again, off again) subject to frequent change: The weather was terrible, so the mission was off-again on-again. The fighter escort was never able to get off...

off and on—(also: on and off) from time to time; not regularly: It's been raining off and on since I got home, and the weather report says thunderstorms are coming.

off–Broadway • off-off Broadway

off–Broadway—is used of the New York experimental theaters located in an area other than Broadway: The play began life at an off–Broadway theater.

off-off Broadway—is used of the most radical or avant-garde of New York theaters: Off-Broadway and off-off Broadway are for those who genuinely love theater.

off color • without color

off color—1. *(coll.)* feeling unwell or in low spirits: Maybe you just felt off-color for a few days after the sunbathing. 2. *(of a joke, etc.)* slightly indecent or distasteful: That joke you told was off color and embarrassed her. 3. not of the best kind or quality: He had mighty little English, and my native was still off color.

without color—1. devoid of color; colorless: Plants that grow in darkness are pale and without color. 2. impartial; unbiased: His reporting, although critical, was fair and without color.

Note: *Neither expression correlates in meaning with the phrase* ***lend color to something***—*(also: give color to something) give plausibility to an account, etc.:* He draws heavily on quotations from various sources to lend color to his narrative.

off hand • out of hand

off hand—without preliminary preparation or consideration: I cannot give you the information off hand.

out of hand—1. immediately; without delay: The situation needs to be dealt with out of hand. 2. out of control: For a moment there was great danger of a "rough house" out of hand.

See also: off one's hands / out of one's hands.

off one's beam • off the beam

off one's beam—(coll.) crazy or behaving as if mad: I think the guy up there who said he was poor and proud of it is off his beam.

off the beam—wide of the mark; wrong: He acknowledged that sunny predictions by some in the administration were off the beam.

off one's block • off the blocks

off one's block—(Austral. sl.) crazy, eccentric, or foolish: Lexus is actually lying, or merely mistaken. Jeniard looks like he thinks Lexus is off his block.

off the blocks—(also: out of the blocks)—said of a fast start of an activity: One of the first off the blocks has been Sainsbury which is set to launch wines from Tunisia at the end of this month.

off one's feed • on the feed

off one's feed—1. *(of animals or fish)* being without appetite: If the fish are off their feed, or won't eat at a time when they normally would, then you have some evaluation steps to take. 2. *(coll., of people)* feeling unwell or in low spirits: He confided to Bee that the dear old Squire seemed "off his feed"; he did not think it was any good worrying him at present.

on the feed—(of animals or fish) eating or looking out for food *(also: at feed):* If trout are well on the feed they will take the "Jack" flies readily.

off one's game • off the game

off one's game—(of a sportsman) playing badly: I backed Tommy when most folk thought he was off his game!

off the game—(of a sportsman) not playing: When I am off the game or off work, the first few days I would like to relax at home with my family.

Note: *The expression is not equivalent in meaning to the phrase* ***out of the game***—*(of a sportsman) remaining out of play during a game:* I was out of the game and useless. That's my first memory as a player.

See also: on one's game / on the game.

off one's hands • out of one's hands

off one's hands—no longer under one's responsible charge: The lawyer planned a vacation as soon as the case was off his hands.

out of one's hands—not within one's competence or responsibility: I tried to prevent your name being dragged in, but the situation was out of my hands.

See also: off hand / out of hand.

off one's head • off one's mind

off one's head—(coll.) crazy or behaving as if mad *(also: out of one's head):* He must be off his head to go jogging in this weather.

Note: *The expression does not correlate in meaning with the phrase* ***off the top of one's head****—(coll.) without proper consideration; in an impromptu manner:* He was impetuous and inclined to think off the top of his head at times.

off one's mind—1. said of smth. no longer causing worry or anxiety: And he had felt so happy.... His confession to June was off his mind. 2. = *off one's head:* Politics is dirty. If so, one must be off his mind to enter politics.

off one's own bat • off the bat

off one's own bat—(coll.) 1. by one's own efforts: I felt that I'd like to get some money off my own bat. 2. on one's own initiative: Don't think I'm being nosey, but you never tell me anything off your own bat.

off the bat—(coll.) on the spot; right away: McGowan was also striving to catch the bright smiles tossed about by Rosy. He picked them off the bat.

off one's stroke • on the stroke

off one's stroke—(coll.) disconcerted or confused: Not that I enjoyed being shelled ... but fear never paralyzed me or even pushed me off my stroke.

on the stroke—1. *(of a clock or bell)* on the point of striking or ringing: He dressed himself hurriedly, for the dinner bell was almost on the stroke as he entered the house. 2. punctually; on time: We agreed to meet for lunch, and he arrived on the stroke.

off season • off time

off season—(also: out of season) 1. at a wrong period: Because Eritrea was born off season, the world continues to put unfair demands on it and question its legitimacy. 2. said of a period of time other than the busiest or most popular for a particular activity: The country's tourism sector would not immediately be affected, because it is now off-season. 3. outside the period of time during which hunting or fishing is officially allowed: Contact us with any questions you may have about any of our off season hunting opportunities.

off time—1. one's free or spare time: It helps us to work better together, as a team, if we can spend some of our off time in an activity together. 2. *(also: out of time)* not following the rhythm correctly (when playing a piece of music, etc.): Stevie sounds a little off time and a bit short of energy.

off the beaten track • off the track

off the beaten track—1. away from popular places; in an isolated, lonely place: The restaurant we're going to tonight is off the beaten track. 2. away from familiar or usual subject: Our discussion only became really interesting when we got off the beaten track.

off the track—1. away from the planned route: We like to stop there and admire the scenery. It's off the track, but it's worth the trip. 2. away from the proper subject; following the wrong course: We seem to have got off the track of our discussions.

off the cards • out of the cards

off the cards—(sl.) work unofficially and informally, without disclosing one's income: There are a lot of retired people now. Quite a few of them work, some of them may be working off the cards.

out of the cards—outside the range of probability: A future in professional sports is out of the cards for most of these people. *Cf.: on the cards—(U.S. also: in the cards) said of smth. very likely to happen:* We have had some tight squeezes and it was on the cards that one day there really would be a problem.

off the cuff • on the cuff

off the cuff—(coll.) 1. *speak* unofficially or informally: Even when she spoke off-the-cuff to the audience, she did so at the keyboard, improvising over a drizzle of piano notes. 2. *do smth.* immediately; without consideration: I was not agreeing off the cuff that Bill's getting into the Royal would necessarily enhance his prospects.

on the cuff—(coll.) on credit: Money was not important at all. All business was transacted on the cuff.

off the ground • on the ground

off the ground—(of a project, scheme, etc.) launched or started: With the school project now off the ground, Mr. Vaughn noted that the district will turn its attention to needed renovations.

on the ground—on the spot where things are actually happening, not at a distance: The United Nations investigation on the ground concluded that war crimes were taking place.

off the hook • off the hooks

off the hook—1. *(of a telephone receiver)* not on its rest: Another phone crossed Sneed's mind, the one in his own flat with its receiver off the hook. *2. (of a telephone)—ringing* incessantly: Ever since his name appeared in the newspapers his telephone has been ringing off the hook. 3. *(coll.)* no longer in difficulty or trouble: She was being kept by the senator, and now he's off the hook, the hypocritical son of a bitch. 4. *(sl.)* excellent, fantastic: Wow, this party was off the hook! What else is there to say?

off the hooks—(sl.) 1. *(dated)* without delay; immediately: Baronets with twelve thousand a year cannot be married off the hooks. 2. out of humor; not feeling very well: I am not surprised to hear that he is ill; he has been off the hooks for the past week or so. 3. *(dated)* dead: He is dying; or dead probably by this time.... When old Golightly is off the hooks altogether, another guardian will be chosen.

See also: on one's own hook / on the hook.

off the peg • on the peg

off the peg—(usually of clothing) made in standard sizes and available from stock, in contrast to items made to order *(also: off the shelf):* Ship owners may buy vessels "off the peg" instead of each vessel's being an individual tailor-made job.

on the peg—(Military) on a charge or under arrest: If the sergeant saw you, you'd be "on the peg."

off the shelf • on the shelf

off the shelf—(usually of clothing) made in standard sizes and available from stock, in contrast to items made to order *(also: off the peg):* Few would buy off the shelf clothes if tailor-made clothes were as cheap and as available.

on the shelf—1. in a state of inactivity or uselessness: The question of parliamentary reform could not be perpetually kept upon the shelf. 2. *(coll., of a woman)* unmarried and unlikely to marry: She has run through her chances in the matrimonial market and is now on the shelf.

Note: *The expression does not correlate in meaning with the phrase* ***on the rack****—tormented by anxiety, worry, etc.:* The master was on the rack until the Board of Inquiry cleared his character in regard to the collision between his boat and the liner.

off work • out of work

off work—1. not working temporarily (owing to illness, etc.): Steven was off work last week. He had been bitten by the family dog. 2. not engaged in work: This was the first time she was going to see me during the day because she was off work.

out of work—unemployed; unable to obtain work: The poor woman must have a hard time of it, for her husband is out of work.

offense against something • offense at something

offense against something—a violation or breach of a law, custom, rule, etc.: What is sin? It is an offense against religious or moral law.

offense at something—feeling of annoyance, displeasure, or resentment at smth.: Humphrey expressed offense at yet another anti–gay marriage bill to be taken up in the Legislature.

offer one's thanks • thanks offering

offer one's thanks—express one's gratitude: First and foremost, I offer my thanks to John Meredith, who bore with me through the often frustrating production process.

thanks offering—donation made to a charity, a religious organization, etc. as an expression of gratitude: In early Bible times the Israelites set aside part of their crops (grain, grapes and olive oil) as a thanks offering to God.

***Note:** The expression does not correlate in meaning with the compound **thanksgiving**—*1. *expression of gratitude, especially to God; form of prayer for this:* The Pilgrims of Plymouth Rock held their Thanksgiving in 1621 as a three day "thank you" festivity to the leaders of the Wampanoag Indian tribe. 2. *(US) a day set apart each year for thanks to God for His goodness (usually the fourth Thursday in November):* When they return from their Thanksgiving recesses, the Congress and the Senate will be bickering over the budget bills.

offset something • set something off

offset something—1. counterbalance smth.: More had to be shifted to the opposite side of the plane to offset the weight of just two passengers. 2. compensate for smth.; neutralize smth.: Grants to public post-secondary institutions should be increased to offset the effect of inflation.

set something off—1. cause smth. to explode: When they set the fireworks off, the guards ran out to see what was making that noise. 2. give rise to smth.; start smth. happening (especially unintentionally): Labor leaders also warned such a move could set off violence. 3. show smth. to advantage by providing a suitable background: This new blue dress sets off the color of Mary's eyes. 4. = *offset something 2:* At least there are good restaurants to set off the disadvantages of the weather.

oil spot strategy • oil-spot someone

oil spot strategy—(Military) a tactic to secure an area to be used as a launch site for campaigns to other areas: The oil spot strategy is translated from the French *tache d'huile*, calling up the image of a stain that spreads out from a tiny spot.

oil-spot someone—(Bus tours) accidentally leave behind a member of a touring company, road show, etc.: Failing to leave a sign of your temporary absence (from the bus) puts you at risk of being "oil-spotted."

old Adam • old as Adam

old Adam—the sinful, incorrigible part of human nature: The best way to keep evil and the old Adam down was to flog the child.

old as Adam—said of a person or thing very old: Though old as Adam, love is still the theme that interests all hearts in all countries.

old before one's time • old beyond one's years

old before one's time—older in looks or physical condition than is right for one's age: He was getting old then long before his time. He'd come in from his sermons complaining of rheumatism and the cold.

old beyond one's years—more mature and knowledgeable than others of the same age: Though old beyond her years in some respects, I felt she was emotionally immature and certainly not ready for marriage.

old boot • old shoe

old boot—(UK sl.) said of an objectionable, aging, unattractive woman: She was a tough old boot and survived the hip replacement surgery, but had to go to a nursing home.

old shoe—1. said of smth. regarded as outdated or useless: Love should not become an old shoe, it should never wear out or grow old. 2. is used of anything comfortable and familiar: Despite a brief anxiety attack, Jane settled into the job quickly, and soon it was as comfortable as an old shoe.

old girl • old maid

old girl—1. *(coll.)* one's wife *(also: old lady):* It's my old girl that advises. She has the head. But I never own to it before her. 2. *(coll.)* one's mother *(also: old lady):* She told my mother to pay for the hospital bills and leave it alone. My old girl paid and I didn't go to court. 3. a former student of a particular school or college: Old Girls of the college will gather in the hall this afternoon for a reunion.

old maid—1. a woman who remains single; an elderly spinster: She spent most of her summers in travel, with another wise old maid for companion. 2. said of a person regarded as being primly fastidious: She acted like an old maid, so it was hard not to have fun at her expense sometimes.

old lady • old woman

old lady—(also: old girl) 1. one's wife: The guy who ran it [Ballroom] hated musicians because one of them ran off with his old lady. 2. one's mother: I was ordered by my old lady (I do not like to use the word mother) to not open any of the doors. What eight year old can resist exploring rooms and opening doors?

old woman—1. = *old lady 1:* If you went home and found someone indoors with your old woman, what would you do? 2. = *old lady 2:* He was strictly warned never ever to refer to his parents as "my old man," "my old woman," which was current slang at the time. 3. a person of timid and fussy character: The new officer was of the genus known in the service as "old woman," and the regiment suffered accordingly.

old school • old school tie

old school—said of conservative or old-fashioned views and principles: My grandmother, who was of the old school, said that self-praise was half slander.

old school tie—(UK) the clannish loyalty of people who knew each other at public school or a university: The Inspector was tacitly accusing him of favoring his own class — of shielding an "old school tie."

Old Tom • Tom Collins

Old Tom—1. a name for a strong variety of gin: The next day a plunger brought a quantity of salvaged goods, mostly in the form of cases of Old Tom gin. 2. a highly flavored strong ale: Old Tom was the second beer we tested during our evening at the Festival.

Tom Collins—a cocktail made of gin mixed with soda water, fruit juice, etc.: In the case of the Tom Collins, it's largely a matter of which mixer should be used, plain soda or ginger ale.

on a large scale • on the large side

on a large scale—said of smth. involving large numbers or

a large area: Boston lacks big blocks of land that make housing construction on a large scale more economically feasible.

Note: *The expression does not correlate in meaning with the phrase* ***in large measure****—(also: in large part) to a considerable extent:* Public — and in large measure also independent — education in the United States has undergone a process of secularization.

on the large side—rather large; a little too large: Although it is on the large side for slipping into a pocket it is still much smaller than a typical super zoom camera.

on a level • on the level

on a level—1. at the same height: She had only brogue heels on her feet; and her shoulders were just about on a level with his. 2. of the same rank or quality: His work was highly regarded by the ancients, who placed him on a level with Homer and Sophocles.

on the level—1. in an area where the ground is level: I should like a house on the level; I find it very tiring to climb this hill. 2. = *on a level 1:* His uniform was always spotless and he wore his white hat, no baseball caps then, down on the level with his eyebrows. 3. = *on a level 2:* It is hard to imagine that West would have minded this tribute, which put him on the level with Hogarth and Rembrandt. 4. *(coll.)* honest; trustworthy: Fred is on the level. He'll do a proper job for you and charge you a reasonable price.

on a rope • on a tightrope

on a rope—*(of mountain climbers)* roped together *(also: on the rope):* It is a useful loop knot.... Once much used for the middleman on a rope in climbing, but now superseded.

on a tightrope—in an extremely precarious situation: He went right back to the IQ ... saying that my grades weren't what they should be. I felt on a tightrope with him.

on a shoestring • on a string

on a shoestring—*(of a business, etc.)* run on a very small amount of money: It is said that Henry Ford started his business on a shoestring.

on a string— said of smb. completely controlled by a person: Mr. Bradley said he was not a candidate on a string; he had his own convictions.

on active duty • on duty

on active duty—fighting as a member of the armed forces: This file contains a history card on each Air Force Officer who was on active duty.

on duty—engaged in one's regular work or service: A uniformed sergeant was drinking orange squash because he was on duty.

on again, off again • on and off

on again, off again—*(also: off again, on again)* subject to frequent change: The plans for the fireworks display were on again, off again because of the rainy and windy weather.

on and off—*(also: off and on)* from time to time; not regularly: I tried a variety of diets on and off. Finally, with my wedding approaching I decide to try Weight Watchers.

on at someone • on to someone

on at someone—*(coll.)* nagging smb. persistently; trying to persuade a person to do smth.: His wife's forever on at him to do something about the fence.

on to someone—1. = *on at someone:* She's been on to me to buy her a new coat for a year. 2. aware of smb.'s true nature: You want people to think you're just some sportswriter, but I am on to you now. 3. *(Police)* in hot pursuit of a wrongdoer: The police are on to the men responsible for that break-in.

on board • on the board

on board—1. on a ship, aircraft, or public vehicle: The life of a boy on board a ship isn't one to be envied, he is at every one's beck and call. 2. said of smb. working with an organization or a group of people: We are in the process of interviewing applicants and hope to have a new teacher on board soon. 3. *(sl.)* said of drink consumed by a person: With a brandy like this on board, I'd face the devil himself.

on the board—1. on the notice-board to which public notices are affixed: The matriculation takes place in the Senate Hall at times indicated on the board. 2. on the patterned surface on which some games are played: He slowly built an assault, using every piece on the board. 3. belonging to the committee controlling a business: He is on the board of thirty companies, and can fairly claim to be the biggest hotelier in Europe.

Note: *a) The expression does not correlate in meaning with the phrase* ***on the drawing board****— under preparation:* A plan is now on the drawing board to build new schools in remote areas.

b) The expression does not correlate in meaning with the phrase ***on the boards****— on the stage:* Many of England's most talented actors appear on the boards at the Swan Theater.

on commission • on the commission

on commission—receiving a percentage of the proceeds of goods sold: These jobs are all on commission only.

Note: *The expression does not correlate in meaning with the phrase* ***in commission****—1. in the exercise of delegated authority:* When the treasury was in commission, the junior lords had sixteen hundred a year each. 2. *(of a ship, aircraft, etc.) in working condition; in service:* Some wartime vessels are still in commission.

on the commission—serving on a committee: This brings the number of management consultants on the commission up to three.

on deck • on the deck

on deck—*(coll.)* 1. available and ready for action: Behind and off stage, a large stage crew are on deck to change scenes and regulate the lighting and sound. 2. alive: Don't tell me old Bill's still on deck. I thought he died years ago.

on the deck—*(RAF)* on the ground; on the landing-ground: I didn't see the bombs drop, but Mac yelled over the intercom — "There's one on the deck."

Note: *The expression does not correlate in meaning with the phrase* ***on the decks****—(U.S. tramps, dated) on top of the train:* I am on top of the train — on the "decks," as the tramps call it.

on edge • on the edge

on edge—in an irritable state; very nervous or agitated: I was on edge all the time and the smallest thing would make me cry.

on the edge—1. on the point of smth.: We are on the edge of losing many fundamental rights and at the top of the list is the right to privacy. 2. = *on edge:* His manner had not the ease it used to have. He seemed on the edge about something.

Note: *The expression is not equivalent in meaning to the phrase* ***on the edge of one's seat****— in the state of nervous excitement or anticipation (used of an audience watching a movie of suspense, etc.):* I was engrossed in the film and my son was on the edge of his seat for most of the movie.

on either hand • on every hand

on either hand—1. on either one of the hands: There is no need to move your wedding ring. You can wear an anniversary ring on either hand. *2.* positioned to right and left; on both sides: See these mountains, standing on either hand, one in the shade and the other in the light.

on every hand—everywhere; on all sides: But the retreat was over-hasty, and rich booty remained behind on every hand.

on end • on the end

on end—1. in an upright position; standing erect: The houses gave to the outskirts of Paris an odd affinity to a city built of dominoes set on end. 2. *(of time)* continually; without intermission: For hours on end we were subjected to continuous attacks from bombers.

on the end—(also: at the end) in the farthest part of smth.: An electric toothbrush is not very different in principle from an ordinary toothbrush. You still have a stick with a brush on the end.

on fire • on the fire

on fire—1. *(of a house, etc.)* aflame; burning: Never disturb the senior resident when he's on his rounds, unless the place is on fire. 2. *(of a part of the body)* feeling very painful or sore: When I woke up the next morning my throat was on fire. I could barely swallow. 3. enthusiastic about smth.: Gregg, on fire with his idea, was going to the kitchen to bag scraps for his new pet.

on the fire—1. *(of food)* on a hearth, etc.: So they got the blaze going, bacon sizzling, the frying-pan balanced on the fire. 2. *(U.S.)* in work; in process of preparation: In those days, as today, Lawrence had a dozen projects on the fire.

on guard • on one's guard

on guard—1. doing duty as a guard: There are soldiers on guard at the gate, to prevent anyone getting in or out. 2. on the alert: The designers of the Sky-rocket had to be on guard against not only the sonic barrier.

on one's guard— = on guard 2: No one can be on his guard against that of which he has no experience.

on hand • on one's hands

on hand—1. *(also: in hand)* available; in one's possession: The college had $117,000 on hand for the stadium building fund. 2. *(also: at hand)* within easy reach; close by: Always have your dictionary on hand when you study. 3. present; in attendance: All his old friends will be on hand to see Jack receive the medal of honor. 4. said of smth. to be done: There's a big job on hand for tomorrow; we must start early.

Note: *The expression does not correlate in meaning with the phrase* ***on the arm****—(U.S. sl.) free of charge:* Murphy said he had got in touch with twelve lawyers to represent a cop when he is in trouble and to do it on the arm.

on one's hands—remaining under one's care as a burden or unwelcome responsibility: The dealer found himself with twenty-five new cars on his hands which he had to sell at a big discount.

on ice • on thin ice

on ice—(coll.) 1. in reserve; in readiness: She's never been able to find a man good enough for her, and so she's keeping herself on ice. 2. said of smth. which is a sure thing, a certainty: I haven't signed on the dotted line yet, but it's on ice. 3. in detention: Scotland Yard could not keep him on ice that long. He would have to be brought to a court to be charged.

on thin ice—in a delicate or potentially difficult situation: Though he had a graduate business degree, he felt on thin ice when it came to financial investments.

See also: in cold storage / in the deep freeze.

on line • on the line

on line—1. *(U.S.)* in a queue: Museums truly worth visiting are worth standing as New Yorkers say on line for. 2. in active service; operational: He lamented that at the current rate of progress there might be only two fast nuclear reactors on line by 2010. 3. connected to a computer network; available on the Internet: On-line education is now gradually complementing face-to-face education.

on the line—1. in jeopardy; at stake: It was clear to the President that his credibility was on the line. 2. on the phone: "The Jimmy on the line wasn't the Jimmy I knew," Shenker recalled later. 3. said of an assembly line at a plant: Each worker on the line would do one task, then wait as the line brought the next car.

Note: *The expression does not correlate in meaning with the phrase* ***on the lines****—(also: along the lines) following a certain pattern or trend:* Treatment will be given on the lines prescribed in this book.

on my oath • on oath

on my oath—is said to emphasize that one is telling the truth: I didn't say anything to him about you, on my oath.

on oath—(legal) having sworn to tell the truth *(also: under oath):* The judge reminded the witness that he was still on oath.

on occasion • on the occasion

on occasion—1. sometimes; from time to time: Three, four, or more forms of the same gene have on occasion been encountered. 2. as need or opportunity arises: A member of the House of Lords ... is prepared on occasion to assert his political rights.

on the occasion—1. in this instance: The House proved willing to remove individual ministers and on the occasion the government itself. 2. in connection with some festive or solemn occurrence: Several promotions were made at St. Petersburg on the occasion of the Emperor's name-day.

on offer • under offer

on offer—1. presented for sale: The few non-pedigree cattle on offer were of moderate class. 2. *(of ideas, etc.)* proposed; suggested: "How nice!" said Noni, with what passed with her for wit. "Any more great thoughts on offer?"

under offer—(of property) provisionally sold prior to the signing of a contract: Three of the farms were sold last year and a fourth is also under offer.

on one's ear • out on one's ear

on one's ear—(Austral. sl.) in trouble or difficulties: My dad arrived with his two loads of cows last night. Mamma said he was on his ear when I wasn't there to meet him.

out on one's ear—(sl.) said of smb. ejected unceremoniously; dismissed from a job, etc.: If you continue to be so late, you'll find yourself out on your ear.

on one's feet • out on one's feet

on one's feet—(also: on one's legs) 1. standing up while working: He's on his feet all day at work, and he falls asleep in his chair as soon as he gets home. 2. getting up (to speak, etc.): Gavin had slept armed and was on his feet at once. 3. recovered after an illness: It's good to see you back on your feet again. 4. *(in the phrase "think on one's feet")* react without much deliberation: The ability to think on one's feet, organize one's thoughts and articulate them is critical.

Note: *The expression does not correlate in meaning with the phrase* ***on foot****—1. walking rather than using transport:* The car wouldn't start that day so we came on foot. 2. *moving; in motion:* Though he got very close to his game, they were on foot before he saw them. 3. *in progress; taking place*: It was also possible that some love intrigue was on foot. 4. *being planned:* The reporter also said that a civil rights demonstration was on foot.

out on one's feet—1. *(of a boxer)* dazed or barely conscious, although still in a standing position: For God's sake keep an eye on John! He's out on his feet but doesn't realize it! 2. *(coll.)* barely able to stand; totally fatigued: You're ill.... You may not know it, but you're out on your feet.

on one's game • on the game

on one's game—(of a sportsman) playing very well: Their disregard of the rules was accentuated by the fact that neither man was on his game.

on the game—(UK sl.) involved in prostitution or stealing: Betty's on the game, isn't she? Has she got you at it too?
See also: off one's game / off the game.

on one's hind legs • on the back foot

on one's hind legs—(joc.) 1. standing up (to make a speech): Richard got on his hind legs and said that no decent man ought to read Shakespeare's sonnets. 2. *(coll.)* very angry; enraged: "Don't get on your hind legs but just listen to me," returned Betty composedly.

on the back foot—(UK) in a defensive position; preparing to retreat: For much of the campaign, he was on the back foot, criticised and scrutinised, his strategy derided.

on one's own hook • on the hook

on one's own hook—(sl.) on one's own initiative; relying on one's own efforts: St. Mary's Hospital does not meet incoming flights with its own vehicle. Patients come on their own hook.

on the hook—1. *(of a telephone receiver)* on its rest: Unless the telephone is on the hook, the subscriber cannot call or be called by the Exchange. 2. *(coll.)* attached to some habit; addicted to smth.: "He really is on the hook." "The hook?" "This drug habit." 3. *(coll.)* in smb.'s power: She had made me wretchedly conscious of my shortcomings; that is how she had me on the hook.

Note: *The expression does not correlate in meaning with the phrase* ***on tenterhooks****— in a state of suspense or strain because of uncertainty:* Dealers said the market was on tenterhooks about the size of the German rate cut.

See also: off the hook / off the hooks.

on one's side • on the side

on one's side—1. said of smth. giving a person an advantage and increasing his chances of success: He has youth on his side, and it is odds but he gets over it [disease]. 2. said of smb. supporting a person in an argument, etc.: The polluters often have a strong commercial lobby on their side, while the anti-polluters must rely on voluntary effort.

on the side—1. said of work done in addition to one's regular occupation: Norm decided to start looking at his hobby as a means of making a little money on the side. 2. said of smth. done secretly or illicitly: If I married him, I'd need a boy friend on the side to keep me entertained. Not for sex, for conversation.

Note: *The expression does not correlate in meaning with the phrase* ***on the sidelines****— used of smb. not participating in an activity, being merely a spectator:* For most of this debate, I have sat on the sidelines, watching and listening with interest.

on one's toes • on tiptoe

on one's toes—1. stand or walk on the front part of the feet: His lips fall onto my left cheek. I stand on my toes, and he hugs me tighter. 2. *(coll.)* active and alert; ready for action: We need several more salesmen who not only know the business, but are on their toes.

on tiptoe—1. = *on one's toes 1:* I had to stand on tiptoe in order to see over the fence. 2. *(coll.)* in the state of tense and eager anticipation: She is on tiptoe with curiosity about the present you've brought her.

on order • on orders

on order—1. said of smth. ordered or requested but not yet supplied: We have twenty F-16 planes on order with you. We placed that order five years ago. 2. in compliance with a request: They do it on order, and the only thing they check is to see that your bill with the other company is paid up. 3. according to orders received: The claim to be acting on order from a superior is not admissible as a defense against conviction.

Note: *The expression does not fully correlate in meaning with the phrase* ***to order****— = on order 2:* Most of the items displayed are manufactured to order only.

on orders—(also: under orders) = on order 3: When charged with withholding important information, he replied that he was only acting on orders.

on someone's case • on the case

on someone's case—1. investigating smb.'s crime: He has been able to avoid getting caught by every other detective on his case. 2. *(U.S. sl.)* harassing or criticizing a person in an annoying way: "My sister was on my case about that joke all night," he continued.

on the case—1. = *on someone's case 1:* The detectives on the case think the two things are tied in. The killing and the acid. 2. dealing with a particular problem or situation: The missions seem designed only as a chance for politicians to show they're on the case.

on someone's good side • on someone's side

on someone's good side—enjoying smb.'s favor or approval: This is a great way to show people that they need to be on your good side to earn all the information they want.

on someone's side—supporting and encouraging a person in a difficult and competitive situation: When he realizes that I'm on his side, he can much more readily do something about that very thing.

on tap • on the tap

on tap—1. *(of beer, etc.)* drawn from a cask: The high-density drink is *Geuze* (so called when it is bottled, and *Lambic* when it is on tap). 2. *(coll.)* available for immediate use: I don't believe in investing every penny one has; I like to have a few hundred pounds on tap. 3. *(coll.)* said of smth. scheduled to happen very soon: More military and medical experiments are on tap for Atlantis astronauts today.

on the tap—(sl.) begging for money, etc.; asking for a loan: She was a real moaner and always on the tap, borrowing sugar and milk.

on tape • on the tape

on tape—recorded on magnetic tape: When people spoke "live" or on tape it was often difficult to hear what they were saying.

on the tape—1. = *on tape:* Magnetic patterns on the tape are translated by a tape-head into electrical impulses. 2. at the very end of a race: Wheeler regained the ground he had lost and just robbed the Hungarian of victory on the tape.

on the back bench • on the bench

on the back bench—1. *(UK)* said of members of Parliament who, because they do not hold office, are not entitled to a front-bench seat: His sojourn on the Back Bench will be short lived and he will return to the Front Bench soon. 2. *(U.S.)* said of the new members of Congress considered as a group: While Jim's been on the back bench in Washington, I've been on the front lines here in Nevada.

on the bench—1. said of a judge in the court of law: When a judge rules on a case in which his financial holdings are at stake, public trust is violated.... Conflicts of interest have no place on the bench. 2. said of a sportsman sitting among the substitute players during a game: The coach had to keep his star player on the bench with a sprained ankle.

on the back of a postcard • on the back of an envelope

on the back of a postcard—(in the phrase "fit on the back of a postcard") said of the insignificant amount of one's knowledge, information, etc.: The phrase "fit on the back of a postcard" comes to mind but a postcard would probably be too large to list out all that I know about art. *Cf.: on the back of a postage stamp — used as a more emphatic variant of the former:* Alas, my list of strengths will fit on the back of a postage stamp.

on the back of an envelope — (of plans, calculations, etc.) executed in a simplistic and speedy way and usually in need of more work *(also: on the back of a fag packet):* He has made decisions sketched out on the back of an envelope without proper consultation again.

on the bandwagon • on the wagon

on the bandwagon — participating in what seems likely to be a successful enterprise (supporting a particular candidate, movement, etc. in the hope of a personal gain): Everyone is on the bandwagon it seems, whether through action or just rhetorical agreement.

on the wagon — (coll.) abstaining from alcohol: Vince had a weakness: he was an alcoholic. For ten months of each year he stayed on the wagon; twice a year, regularly, he fell off, sometimes with doleful consequences on the job.

Note: *The expression does not correlate in meaning with the phrase* ***in the cart*** *— (coll.) in difficulties or trouble:* You'll have to do what you're bid, or maybe you'll find yourself in the cart.

on the block • on the blocks

on the block — (coll.) 1. offered for sale (at an auction): The Seattle radio station has been on the block for a year with no offers to buy it. 2. at risk; in serious and threatening situation: Her reputation is on the block now, and it's nobody's fault but hers. *Cf.: put one's head on the block* — risk one's reputation or position when taking a particular course of action: When the Prime Minister called a by-election, he put his head on the block.

Note: *The expression does not fully correlate in meaning with the phrase* ***on the chopping block*** *— = on the block 2:* Our whole future is on the chopping block now.

on the blocks — 1. said of runners or swimmers positioned on their starting blocks prior to the starting signal: When standing on the blocks waiting for the gun to go off, it all boils down to what one's body can do. 2. ready and waiting to start an activity: If it were a question of replacing a man or a pony, the management would sooner replace a man because there were so many other men up on the blocks, waiting for a job.

on the book • on the books

on the book — 1. *(coll.)* on credit: He let me have a couple of bottles on the book. 2. *(Theater)* on duty as prompter: There is no longer such a job as "prompter." It is, however, normal practice for there to be a member of the stage-management team "on the book."

on the books — 1. said of existing rules, laws, etc.: After Gorbachev had been in command for three years, the new privately owned cooperatives had new laws on the books. 2. in the accountant's records of money: We've got to put forth our best efforts from now till the end of the month, or we'll be in red on the books. 3. in the official list of members, patients, etc.: Had he been on the books as an Indian, he would have been considered a ward of the Government.

on the chance • on the off chance

on the chance — act on the probability of smth.: Do you want to bet your organization's security on the chance that everyone will remember to lock down their computers?

on the off chance — act on the very remote likelihood of smth.: She flew in from New York on the off-chance of getting tickets to see Becker play his last match at Wimbledon.

on the clock • on the hour

on the clock — (coll.) 1. said of one's working time: Hey, get to work, you're still on the clock, stop loafing. 2. on the dial of a taximeter, speedometer, etc.: Neither vehicle had much mileage on the clock.

on the hour — at exactly one o'clock, two o'clock, etc.: Buses for London leave every hour on the hour.

See also: in time / on time.

on the contrary • to the contrary

on the contrary — 1. in opposition to what might be expected: She did not exult in her rival's fall, but, on the contrary, commiserated her. 2. on the other hand: People used to say that a musical was written for musical slobs. Mr. Sondheim, on the contrary, assumes that you have heard some Ravel and Debussy.

to the contrary — 1. *= on the contrary 1:* The liberal resurrection is not a sign of vitality of the capitalist system, but to the contrary, it is a mark of its failure. 2. to the opposite effect: Working-class to the backbone, just like us. And if he's been filling you up with a lot of toffee to the contrary, more fool you. 3. in spite of smth.; notwithstanding smth.: I know she's unhappy, all her brave talk to the contrary.

on the cutting edge of something • on the razor's edge of something

on the cutting edge of something — (also: at the cutting edge of something) involved in the most advanced developments in a particular field: The Museum has remained on the cutting edge of science education by developing innovative and interactive programs.

on a razor's edge of something — (also: on the knife-edge of something) on the brink of smth. bad or dangerous: They could laugh themselves sick with the memory of it now, but at the time they had been on a razor's edge of failure or success.

on the dot • to the dot

on the dot — exactly at a given time; at the precise moment: We were to dine with the Prousts at seven and we reached their house on the dot.

Note: *The expression is not antonymous in meaning to the phrase* ***off one's dot*** *— (sl.) crazy or behaving as if mad:* And you have to act up like they do or they think you're off your dot.

to the dot — (also: to the letter) exactly; precisely: The citizens of Neustadt followed the curfew regulations to the dot.

on the downhill side • on the downhill slide

on the downhill side — 1. older than the age specified: I backpacked in the Grand Canyon with my fiancé, Paul. Not bad for someone who is on the downhill side of fourty. 2. said of a bad situation which may be getting progressively worse: Evangelical Christians agree — America is on the downhill side of decadence.

on the downhill slide — = on the downhill side 2: Workers have been on a downhill slide for years, losing wages, losing jobs, losing respect, and in all too many cases, losing hope.

on the floor • on the shop floor

on the floor — 1. in a movie or TV studio: I'll make a shooting script.... It'll be something you can go on the floor with. 2. *(of a film)* being shot; in production: At Elstree, only one film, *the Guinea Pig*, is on the floor. 3. *(Parliament)* in the part where the members sit: Their job is to contribute to policy-making through debate on the floor.

on the shop floor — in the part of a factory concerned with productive as opposed to administrative work: The worker on the shop floor does not identify himself with the goals of the manager.

on the go • on the move

on the go—(coll.) 1. *(also: on the trot)* constantly busy moving from one task to another: The ladies were kept on the go by a continuous round of making refreshments and then washing up. 2. about to take one's leave: The guest was on the go for half an hour though the host began to show signs of impatience.

on the move—1. moving about from place to place: It was a very cold day, and the teacher watching the playground kept on the move to stay warm. 2. said of people moving in large numbers: Victoria is truly on the move. Every month, 12 Melbourne families are shifting to Ballarat alone for a better lifestyle.

on the house • on the premises

on the house—said of food or beverages offered at the expense of the owner of the establishment: We were given a couple of drinks on the house and a complimentary bottle of wine. *Cf.: one on the city—(joc.) a glass of water (provided free of charge):* "What will you have?" "Oh, just give me one on the city."

on the premises—said of food or beverages to be consumed in the establishment: There was no age limit in 15 per cent of countries for drinking beer on the premises.

on the nail • to the nail

on the nail—(coll.) 1. *(of payments)* made on the spot: You know how I am; if I can't pay on the nail, I don't buy. 2. exactly right: Michael Miller directs the film with conviction, and the playing is on the nail.

to the nail—(dated) most thoroughly *(also: to a nail):* My speech was never improvised, but always prepared beforehand, and polished to the nail.

on the other side of the fence • on the other side of the hill • on the other side of the tracks

on the other side of the fence—on the side of the opposition: You fight all your life for something and then before you know where you are you're on the other side of the fence fighting against it.

on the other side of the hill—in the latter part of one's life: I had to go through a lot of raillery about how old I was getting and what it was like on the other side of the hill.

on the other side of the tracks—(also: on the wrong side of the tracks) in the less respectable or the poorer part of a town: It seems that there are some, well, some low drinking dens on the other side of the tracks.

***Note:** None of the expressions correlates in meaning with the phrase **on the other side**—used with reference to the world beyond the grave (as inhabited by the spirits):* Are they still obese on the other side? I'd like to ask next time you have a séance.

on the pill • on the pills

on the pill—said of a woman taking contraceptive pills regularly: Women who go on the pill have to try out several different brands before they find the right one.

on the pills—on medication to treat an illness: Julia went through a pretty bad time after the accident—on the pills, seeing psychiatrists and what have you.

on the right tack • on the tack

on the right tack—following the right course of action: I think you are on the right tack in trying to see them. It's better than to carry on the affair by correspondence.

on the tack—(sl.) abstaining from alcohol: It's no good asking him to have a drink; he has been on the tack for the past month.

on the rope • on the ropes

on the rope—(of mountain climbers) roped together: At about 6 we got to where we could unrope—having been 48 hours on the rope.

on the ropes—1. *(of a boxer)* forced back on to the ropes: Referee Brimmell stepped in to save Scot after the challenger had pinned him on the ropes for fully a minute. 2. on the verge of ruin or collapse: A good section of the industry was on the ropes and there were times when I wondered if it would survive. 3. = *on the rope:* If they can't pass some of the slow climbers on the ropes ahead of them, they could run out of time ... and oxygen.

on the spot • spot on

on the spot—1. at the place where one's presence is needed: The police were on the spot very soon after the accident happened. 2. then and there; immediately: When Tom ruined an expensive machine, his boss fired him on the spot. 3. *(coll.)* in a difficult situation; in trouble *(also: in a spot):* He is on the spot because he cannot make a choice between Reagan and Nixon as the guest speaker.

spot on—(UK coll.) definitely right or true in one's opinion, answer, etc.: "Is that the right answer, Sir?" "Yes, you're spot on!"

on the street • on the streets

on the street—1. out of work; unemployed: This business is so subjective. My general manager could change tomorrow and I could be on the street. 2. *(U.S. sl.)* outside prison: A number of men who are heterosexual on the street practice homosexuality in prison.

on the streets—1. homeless: These people were once in psychiatric hospitals and are now on the streets. 2. living by prostitution: This little girl had a sister who was on the streets and who was in the house of this bad woman.

on the stump • up a stump

on the stump—1. *(of trees)* before felling: You originally paid in cash for all that timber on the stump just ten thousand dollars. 2. *(coll.)* engaged in political speech-making: Government, in the persons of the Parliamentary heads of departments, is on the stump, or dickering for votes.

up a stump—(coll.) 1. perplexed; at a loss: Sociologists are up a stump over the sharp rise in juvenile delinquency and crime. 2. in great straits; in serious difficulties: For once in his life, work had him so up a stump that he could not snatch a moment for reading.

on the table • under the table

on the table—(of an official proposal, etc.) presented for discussion or consideration: I had heard that several alternative propositions were on the table.

under the table—transacted or sold illicitly and secretly: Most bootleg alcohol is made domestically but sold "under the table" without the necessary permits.

on the tick • on tick

on the tick—(coll.) punctually; on time: I am always here on the tick myself, and I do not see why jurors should not do the same.

***Note:** The expression does not correlate in meaning with the phrase **in a tick**—(coll.) in a moment:* If I had broken the rules laid down for me I should have been spotted in a tick by a spy.

on tick—(coll.) on credit: Here I've been struggling to keep our heads above water, and you go and bring home a motorcar on tick.

on the top of something • on top of something

on the top of something—1. in the highest part of smth.: A picnic party had been formed to take tea on the top of the hill. 2. resting on smth.: The lightning was attracted by the acorn on the top of the chapel. 3. in the most important place: He was on the top of the list of visitors permitted entrance to the Kremlin.

Note: *The expression does not fully correlate in meaning with the phrase* ***at the top of something***—1. = *on the top of something 1:* Go straight ahead up the hill and the Botanic Garden is on the left at the top of the hill. *2.* = *on the top of something 3:* They are also at the top of the list of people the new Rwandan government wants to execute. 3. *(of a street, garden, etc.) at the end that is furthest away from the speaker:* The new building is at the top of Victoria Street.

on top of something—1. = *on the top of something 1:* It was incredibly weird to be standing on top of the world's largest ocean liner in the middle of the Atlantic Ocean 2. = *on the top of something 2:* The new method provides a platform on top of the satellite that is not spinning. 3. = *on the top of something 3:* To make sure that the Protestant religion stays on top of the league in Northern Ireland, is what the Orange Order is all about. 4. in addition to smth., especially an unpleasant situation or event: He borrowed $50 from me and then, on top of that, asked me if he could borrow my car too. 5. knowing all about the latest technology, market trends, etc.: Make sure you stay on top of the latest developments and news.

on the trot • on the trots

on the trot—*(coll.)* 1. moving from place to place: Two days on the trot carrying a big bag took its toll on me at only eighteen. 2. *(also: on the run)* running away from prison, the police, etc.: I eloped with one of the boys and we went on the trot from the approved school. 3. *(also: on the go)* constantly busy moving from one task to another: I've been on the trot all morning and I'm exhausted. 4. one after the other; in succession: For three matches on the trot, he was really energetic and successful.

Note: *The expression does not correlate in meaning with the phrase* ***at a trot***— *moving at a pace faster than a walk:* He looked both ways, then set off at a trot in the direction of the Stones' household.

on the trots—*(U.S. sl.)* having the diarrhea: Why are you frequently visiting the lavatory, Jack? Are you on the trots?

on the up • on the up and up

on the up—*(UK coll.)* improving or becoming more successful: Business was on the up, and Pete started employing people to help him fulfill orders.

on the up and up—*(U.S. coll.)* 1. honest and trustworthy: I kept telling her the whole thing had been strictly on the up-and-up, but she wouldn't listen. 2. = *on the up:* Since the recession ended, our business has been on the up and up.

Note: *Neither expression fully correlates in meaning with the phrase* ***on the uppers***—*(sl., also: on one's uppers) 1. reduced to poverty; destitute:* Freddie Forsyth was on his uppers. No job, nowhere to live, no money. *2.* = *on the up:* Ally has had her fair share of ups and downs, so I'm keeping my fingers crossed she is on the uppers now.

on the view • on view

on the view—on close inspection: He walked round the three companies of horsemen, and pronounced on the view, that Montague and Fox were duly elected.

on view—exhibited; on display: The latest model of the car is on view at our showrooms.

on the wing • on wings

on the wing—1. *(of birds)* in flight: They spend at least nine months of the year continuously on the wing. 2. in motion; moving swiftly: Pope's constitutional irritability kept him constantly on the wing.

Note: *The expression does not correlate in meaning with the phrase* ***on a wing and a prayer***— *relying on good fortune with only the slightest hope of succeeding:* It appears like the company is running on a wing and a prayer in the month of December.

on wings—in a joyously exuberant mood: They sealed the promise with a long loving kiss, and Gerard went home on wings.

Note: *The expression does not correlate in meaning with the phrase* ***with wings***—*(coll.) used of food to be taken home or outside from a restaurant:* "Can I take your order?" "I'll have a Big Mac, a large fries and a Coke — with wings."

on the wrong side of the tracks • on the wrong track

on the wrong side of the tracks—*(also: on the other side of the tracks)* in the less respectable or the poorer part of a town: We went to a school which was on the wrong side of the tracks, and we all got a fine education.

Note: *The expression is not antonymous in meaning to the phrase* ***on the right side of the hedge***— *on the advantageous or winning side:* The French thought themselves on the right side of the hedge, but it proved otherwise.

on the wrong track—*(also: on the wrong tack)* thinking or acting incorrectly: They won't get it figured out because they are on the wrong track.

on top • up top

on top—1. resting on smth.: An imposing enamel teapot stands on top, quietly stewing. 2. in the lead; winning: The horse that everyone had expected would be on top actually came in third. 3. *(also: at the top)* in a position of power or authority: The men on top are always trampling down those who are trying to climb up.

up top—1. = *on top 3:* If you need more proof that the men up top are ignoring our needs, the Government Accounting Office has just released a new study. 2. *(Air Force)* in the sky: You reveal your position to the aircraft up top and it is time to move fairly fast. 3. *(sl.)* in terms of mental capacity: Peg, you've got enough up top for both of us.

once again • once and again

once again—once more; another time: I'll explain it once again, but please listen carefully this time.

once and again—repeatedly: If you don't want to be repetitive, using the same word once and again you have a Thesaurus option.

one can but • one cannot but

one can but—one cannot do otherwise than: I can but be your friend and guide and give you the benefit of my experience.

one cannot but— = *one can but:* I cannot but be glad that he does not love you; yet it fills me with grief to see that this pains you.

one can do worse than • one cannot do better than

one can do worse than—one would be well-advised to act in a particular way: It's interesting work, and one can do worse than be part of the creative team.

one cannot do better than— = *one can do worse than:* He cannot do better than buy the Michelin Guide to France and tour the two- or even three-star restaurants.

one can't be bothered • one is not bothered

one can't be bothered—*(coll.)* one does not have enough interest or energy to do smth.: Sometimes I can't be bothered to go to the gym, sometimes I can't be bothered to do anything at all.

one is not bothered—(coll.) is used to say that smth. is not important to a person: "Do you want tea or coffee?" "I'm not bothered."

one could care less • one couldn't care less

one could care less—(coll.) one is completely uninterested; one does not care at all: He is a lethargic guy who drifts along from day to day. If a bill doesn't get paid he could care less.

one couldn't care less— = one could care less: Though he was great with clients, he couldn't care less about his support people or the follow-up work they did for him.

one could do with something • one couldn't do with something

one could do with something—1. one could make use of or benefit from smth.: You look as if you could do with a wash and brush up. *Cf.: one could do without something—one could dispense with smth.; one could manage in spite of not having smth.:* There were times when physicists ran from philosophers, being sure they could do without their advice and recommendations. 2. is used as an indirect way of asking for smth.: I could just do with a nice cup of tea and a smoke.

one couldn't do with something—one couldn't put up with or tolerate smth.: I just couldn't do with only one pair of pants because I would have to do laundry too many times.

one fine day • one of these fine days

one fine day—(also: one day) 1. at some distant time in the future *(used as a promise or prophecy):* Neither was I to know that I should one fine day have a son who would make me very proud of him. 2. on a certain day in the past: But one fine day in early summer ... Maxine found herself canceling an arrangement to meet a friend in town.

one of these fine days—(also: one of these days) at some time in the future that may be quite soon *(used as a promise or prophecy):* One of these fine days he'll realize what a fool he's been.

one has to go • one has to go some

one has to go—(euph.) one needs to visit a washroom: I am unable to wait to use the restroom a lot of times that I have to go.

one has to go some—(coll.) one must try harder or have to improve: For sheer results from a first-year garden in "totally worthless" soil, you'll have to go some.

one had better • one had rather

one had better—said of smth. one should or must do for some practical reason: I decided I had better contact Farooq straightaway. I phoned both numbers from the hotel.

one had rather—(also: one would rather) is used to indicate preference: I had rather see the portrait of a dog that I know, than all the allegorical paintings they can show me in the world.

one has no time for someone • one hasn't got all day for someone

one has no time for someone—(coll.) is used to say that one strongly disapproves of the person mentioned: I have no time for people who preach equality and then take their holidays in the Bahamas.

one hasn't got all day for someone—(coll.) is used to say that one does not have any more time to spare on the person mentioned: Come on, Gage, we haven't got all day for you to take as coffee breaks!

one in a thousand • thousand to one, a

one in a thousand—said of a rare exception: He is a marvel of good humor, consideration and dignity—one in a thousand...

thousand to one, a—said of a very great possibility: Don't stray off the track!—if you do, it is a thousand to one you will never find it again.

one of these days • one of those days

one of these days—1. *(also: one of these fine days)* at some time in the future that may be very soon *(used as a promise or prophecy):* One of these days he will find a farm to let, big enough to bring up little children on it. 2. said of a day that is full of mishaps; a day when everything seems to go wrong: I had the feeling as soon as the Johnsons trooped in for coffee that it was going to be one of these days.

***Note:** a) The expression does not correlate in meaning with the phrase **these days**—nowadays; at present:* These days candidates send swarms of advance men into every city before they arrive.

*b) The expression does not correlate in meaning with the phrase **one day**—(also: one fine day)* 1. *at some distant time in the future:* One day she will be married and we all will somehow have to live without her. 2. *on a certain day in the past:* He came to me quite unexpectedly one day and asked me to join his business.

one of those days— = one of these days 2: Oh, it's one of those days. I bet you anything the horse breaks its legs.

one-on-one • one-to-one

one-on-one—(attrib.) 1. involving a direct contact between one person and another: Our school offers both one-on-one instruction with your own teacher and group instruction. 2. playing or fighting directly against a single opponent: I was quickly engaged in one-on-one combat with a tall, lean warrior apart from the central conflict.

one-to-one—1. said of pairing each element of a set with an element of another set: I strongly identified with this philosophy of enhancing social skills in children by pairing them one-to-one with college students. 2. = *one-on-one 2:* The brawl began as a one-to-one fight between a black inmate and a Latino, and escalated into a small melee with up to a dozen inmates.

***Note:** Neither expression correlates in meaning with the phrase **one by one**—one after another:* I found these group ward rounds more efficient and also more enjoyable than seeing patients one by one.

one step ahead • one step further

one step ahead—a small advantage in a competitive situation: Credit card companies are turning to so-called smart cards in an effort to keep at least one step ahead of the scammers.

one step further—at a more advanced level: If we can transfer this knowledge to the society we are one step further and the World Science Forum reaches one of its goals.

one way or another • one way or the other

one way or another—1. *(also: in one way or another)* by some means or other: They thought always about winning, and, one way or another, they almost always did win. 2. for any of various reasons: Captain Fitzgibbon wouldn't come back from that last Ulster tour, one way or another.

one way or the other—regarding either of the two possibilities: These men cannot both be correct so would somebody produce some evidence to prove the point one way or the other?

one way ride • one way street

one way ride—(Underworld) a murder carried out by criminals who take their victim on a car journey: ...Charlie Luciano—now nicknamed Lucky on account of a one way ride that he came back from.

one way street—*(also: one way ticket)* a situation pointing or developing in one direction only: This is a one-way street. If someone plants something on you and you're innocent, you have no way in the world to prove it.

one will have it • one won't have it

one will have it—one claims or asserts smth. strongly: He will have it that our plan is impracticable.

Note: *The expression does not correlate in meaning with the phrase* ***let someone have it***—*(coll.)* 1. *give smb. a beating:* He really let the other man have it when they got into a fight. 2. *scold or criticize a person:* He was going to start yelling at her right off! Really let her have it this time.

one won't have it—one will not allow it: We wanted to have a party at our office but our boss won't have it.

See also: have it / have it in one.

one wouldn't say boo to a goose • one wouldn't shout if a shark bit him

one wouldn't say boo to a goose—said of an extremely shy person: Her taste in movies was pretty unusual for someone who wouldn't say boo to a goose.

one wouldn't shout if a shark bit him—*(Austral. sl.)* said of an extremely mean and miserly person: If you don't shout the next round of drinks, you will be one of those tight bastards that "wouldn't shout if a shark bit him."

one's better half • one's better self

one's better half—*(also: one's other half)* one's spouse (usually one's wife): In our house, I do the cooking and my better half does the clean-up.

one's better self—the better part of one's nature; the ideal self: My Utopian self is, of course, my better self—according to my best endeavors...

one's heart is cold • warm someone's heart

one's heart is cold—*(also: have a cold heart)* said of smb. devoid of sympathy or feeling: If a man forgets an anniversary or neglects to say "I love you," it doesn't necessarily mean his heart is cold.

warm someone's heart—*(also: warm someone's blood)* make a person feel eager or excited: Letters poured in upon her, and warmed her heart and stimulated her pen. She liked intelligent criticism and generous praise.

one's life story • story of one's life

one's life story—the account of the career of a person: I must have given her my complete life story and virtually tons of shoptalk about my job.

Note: *The expression does not fully correlate in meaning with the phrase* ***life history***—1. = *one's life story:* He then started talking to her and she cut him dead saying "I don't want to hear your life history, pal!" 2. *(biol.) the life-cycle of an organism:* We were able in the course of four years' steady work to complete the life history of six distinct forms.

story of one's life—1. = *one's life story:* He was a big mouth. He picked up strangers ... and told them the story of his life. 2. smth. that supposedly summarizes one's unfortunate life experience: This is a story of my life, a struggle to find the truth, a person, who now in his mid-thirties feels, and seems to be treated as a criminal.

Note: *The expression is not equivalent in meaning to the phrase* ***hard-luck story***—1. *a narrative of a person's misfortunes:* From this beginning unfolds a brilliant tale of human failings and misery. This is not simply another hard-luck story. *2. an invented story of one's bad luck told in order to gain help or money:* Conmen often have a hard luck story to tell, but they tell it with charm and humor, they seem unconcerned about you helping them or not.

one's lucky number comes up • one's number comes up

one's lucky number comes up—said of smb. who is lucky or has good fortune: My lucky number finally came up when I was chosen to go to Los Angeles to represent our company at the conference.

one's number comes up—*(also: one's number is up)* 1. one's turn for an interview, a haircut, etc. arrives: When my number came up, I was served cheerfully and taken care of in less than ten minutes. 2. = *one's lucky number comes up:* Bingo thinks his number has come up now he's found a great new home in England! 3. said of smth. very bad happening to a person (be punished, dismissed, etc.): I was shocked today to hear of his death. Guess his number finally came up though...

one's man • one's own man

one's man—1. smb.'s servant or subordinate: He sent one of his men on shore for a commercial intercourse with the natives. 2. smb.'s loyal and trusted man: Kennedy bypassed Secretary of State ... when he appointed his man, Averell Harriman, to negotiate a treaty with the Communists. 3. a woman's husband, or lover: All the while her man nods in approval, secretly keeping one eye fixed to the television. 4. a suitable person: Richard also runs the website so if you have any questions about the products then he is your man.

one's own man—1. smb. who is independent of other people and is able to make his own decisions: He had learned something from all the early masters but he was determined to be his own man. 2. a person who is in full control of his faculties and emotions: I felt quite swimmy just now, but I am my own man again. Let me see, what was I talking about? 3. = *one's man 2:* One of Kennedy's first acts was to appoint his own man, James E. Webb to succeed Glennan as Administrator of NASA.

one's mind is set • one's mind wanders

one's mind is set—one is determined about smth.: His mind was set—not only on earning a degree but also on studying at an elite school.

one's mind wanders—one fails to concentrate: I buy a puzzle book and try to concentrate but my mind wanders. What a week it has been.

one's night off • one's night out

one's night off—a night free from work usually done at night: Whenever his "night off" occurred he bought a ticket to the theater.

one's night out—an evening or night spent enjoying oneself in bars, clubs, etc.: For these people Lansdown Fair was, as they put it, their "night out."

one's second nature • one's second self

one's second nature—one's deeply ingrained habit or tendency: I do feel more at ease when I'm behind a desk: It's my second nature.

one's second self—a person with whom one has the closest possible ties (sharing beliefs, etc.): As to Miss Mirvan, she is my second self, and neither hopes nor fears but as I do.

one's superiors • superior persons

one's superiors—people holding a higher position in an organization and having authority over a person mentioned: She toadied to her superiors when she really came face to face with them.

superior persons—people occupying superior posts in society; the nation's élite: It is only because miners sweat their guts out that superior persons can remain superior.

one's take on something • one's takeaway on something

one's take on something—(coll.) one's opinion on smth.: What's your take on automobile electronics? Do they make cars more reliable, longer lasting, safer and cleaner?

one's takeaway on something—(coll.) the knowledge and skill one has obtained through some personal experience: My takeaway on the soy milk: It didn't do me any harm.

one's time of life • time of one's life

one's time of life—1. is used with reference to a person's age, specifically middle age: The ignorant will be apt to think it an occupation ill suited to my time of life. 2. *(euph.)* menopause in women: Aidan has already threatened me with psychiatrists. He says it is "my time of life."

time of one's life—1. a particular period in a person's life: She told me about Oxford. It evidently was the pleasantest time of her life. 2. *(in the phrase "have the time of one's life")* a period of exceptional enjoyment: We will design a program that is so much fun that you will have the time of your life.

See also: lifetime / time of life.

only child, an • only child, the

only child, an—a child without any brothers or sisters: I was an only child and he was an only child. For those basic reasons, I've always felt a connection to him.

only child, the—1. = *only child, an:* He was missing all the attention that was coming his way when he was the only child. 2. a single child involved in a situation: I remember Sumitro because he was the only child with parents from India.

open a book on something • open book, an

open a book on something—(Bookmakers) take bets on certain contests: There is a good deal of interest in the outcome of this ballot, so I thought it might be fun to open a book on the event.

open book, an—used of a person or thing that can be readily examined or understood: He kept to himself personally, but his military life was an open book.

See also: close the book on something / close the books on something.

open a can of worms • open up a can of whoop-ass

open a can of worms—create a situation that will cause much trouble or scandal: The investigation into how these expensive trips were paid for opened a can of worms. *Cf.: open a whole new can of worms—expose a lot of new serious problems:* They aren't saying that it is immutable, but that if you start changing it you open a whole new can of worms.

open up a can of whoop-ass—(U.S. sl., usually used as a threat) punish or hurt smb. verbally or physically: Well, don't make me worry ever again or I'll open up a can of whoop ass!

open-armed • open-handed

open-armed—ready to receive people with enthusiasm: There they are, all waiting open-armed for tourists to arrive. When I traveled in April, the hotels were brim-full.

open-handed—treating people in a generous, liberal way: Being an open-handed woman, Kathleen offered to read my manuscript (which was still in the typewritten stage).

open house • open housing

open house—1. said of general hospitality and readiness to welcome guests at any time: Their home was an open house where the door was never locked and everyone was welcome. 2. a social event, such as a presentation, which everybody can attend: The format of the meeting was an open house in which the design concepts were presented for public review.

open housing—(U.S.) property that can be rented or bought without restriction on racial or ethnic ground: The objection, apart from prejudice, is usually economic because open housing may drive down values of real estate.

open question • open-end question

open question—an issue not yet finally decided that can still be discussed: There was no clear resolution on this except to note that this remains an open question.

Note: *The expression is not equivalent in meaning to the phrase* ***open to question****—used of statements, assertions, etc. that are doubtful and subject to challenge or disagreement:* The government have always known that the status of these islands is open to question.

open-end question—(also: open-ended question) a question so phrased as to encourage an expression of opinion (as distinguished from a simple negative or affirmative): The reading test consists of open-end questions based on different texts of various subjects and length.

open sea • open water

open sea—1. the part of the sea not closed in by land (not a bay or harbor): A "black south-easter," the wind most feared on this coast, forced most of the fleet to run for open sea. 2. the part of the sea outside the territorial jurisdiction of any country: The real place of meeting between the Englishman and the Spaniard was on the open sea. 3. sea that is practically free from ice and navigable: It is probable that an open sea stretches to the Antarctic pole.

open water— = open sea 3: Von Wrangell found open water—or what is now often called a "Polynia," an open sea.

open to someone • open with someone

open to someone—(of a shop, restaurant, etc.) accessible to people who may come: The library is not open to the public this week.

open with someone—willing to honestly and frankly talk about things with another person: Parents should try to be open with their children.

open town • wide-open town

open town—1. *(U.S.)* a town characterized by a lack of restrictions on places for drinking, gambling, etc.: They form a Committee to clean up San Francisco, and as chairman they take the man who's been running it as an open town for sixteen years. 2. an undefended town exempt from enemy bombardment because of its great historical importance: It may mean surrender in return for such quite valueless concessions as "no bombing of open towns."

wide-open town— = open town 1: He has been elected three times because the citizens *want* a wide-open town.

open up on someone • open up to someone

open up on someone—1. start shooting at a person: Just as we reached that spot a group of soldiers opened up on us with rockets, automatic rifles, and grenades. 2. subject a person to a harsh verbal assault or criticism: When we'd killed most of a bottle of wine discussing the literary projects, she opened up on me.

open up to someone—1. *(also: open up with someone)* talk to smb. frankly or intimately: Although he never answered—or perhaps because of it—I opened up to him completely, telling him things I'd never told anyone. 2. become more accepting of a person: I stayed during the breaktime, so a few of the boys stayed also. They finally opened up to me especially the quiet ones.

opera bouffe • opera buffa

opera bouffe—a type of light or satirical French opera: Each competitor will have to choose a free extract from an operetta, an opera bouffe or a musical.

opera buffa—an Italian comic opera: For Falstaff, time does not exist, since he belongs to the opera buffa world of play and mock action.

operating theater • theater of operations

operating theater—a room for surgical operations: A brisk nurse told us he was going to the operating theater within minutes and not to disturb the patient.

theater of operations—the scene of military operations: The theater of operations of an army embraces all the territory it may desire to invade and all that it may be necessary to defend.

or what • or whatever

or what—is used as a tag question to ask for confirmation, agreement, or an alternative: Do you want to go to the dance with me or what?

or whatever—or any other thing that might be mentioned: You might stay together for the kid's sake, or maybe you can't afford to leave or whatever.

order book • orderly book

order book—1. a book in which orders from customers are entered: The order book at the year-end was satisfactory, comparing very favorably with the position at the end of 1983. 2. *(UK)* a paper supplied to members of the House of Commons that gives details of the day's proceedings: A member is required to state the form of his motion on a previous day, and to have it entered in the Order Book.

orderly book—*(Military)* a book kept at headquarters in which orders and instructions received from higher authorities are recorded: She made me a present of the orderly book of one of the French regiments.

Order of St. Michael, the • Order of St. Michael and St. George, the

Order of St. Michael, the—an old French military order instituted by Louis XI in 1469: King Louis XI founded the Order of St. Michael as a demonstration of his power and eminence in France.

Order of St. Michael and St. George, the—an English civil order of knighthood instituted in 1818: He was made Knight Commander of the Order of St. Michael and St. George in 1960.

other side of the coin, the • other side of the hill, the

other side of the coin, the—*(also: other side of the shield, the)* a less obvious aspect of a situation showing the disadvantages: He thought it might present an opportunity to put across the other side of the coin.

other side of the hill, the—1. an aspect of a situation which is hidden and unknown: I wish to express my gratitude to the director of the flying bomb sites for allowing me a glimpse of the "other side of the hill." 2. used with reference to the latter part of one's life: I had to go through a lot of raillery about how old I was getting and what it was like on the other side of the hill.

Note: *Neither expression correlates in meaning with the phrase* ***other side, the***—*the world beyond the grave (as inhabited by the spirits):* Are they still obese on the other side? I'd like to ask next time you have a séance.

See also: another kettle of fish / another turn of the screw.

out and about • up and about

out and about—1. moving about to different places: "Did you spend much time at your hotel?" "No we did not. Most of the time we were out and about." 2. well enough to go out (after an illness): When you're out and about again, you must come and visit us.

up and about—1. = *out and about 2:* "Hunter is completely better," he said. "He's up and about again." 2. out of bed; moving about: She was up and about, brisk as a bee, before sunrise every morning.

Note: *The expression does not correlate in meaning with the phrase* ***up about something***—*(coll.) enthusiastic or excited about smth.:* He was very up about his job (in the CBS studio mailroom) and people in general.

out and away • out and out

out and away—1. definitely; unquestionably: He was out and away the most brilliant student in the class. 2. far away: There are days when everyone else in the house is out and away and she writes a melancholy note on loneliness.

out and out—1. absolute; unqualified: We are not among the out-and-out admirers of the political opinions of this school. 2. *(parenthetical)* definitely; unquestionably: She is the cleverest woman I know, out and out. 3. = *out and away 1:* She is out and out the prettiest girl in the station.

Note: *The expression is not antonymous in meaning to the phrase* ***in and in***—1. *sharing or identifying fully with a person:* I am bound in and in with my forbears. We are all nobly born; fortunate those who know it. 2. *used with reference to marriages with near relatives in successive generations:* The marrying in and in of the same family tends constantly to weakness or idiocy in the children.

out cold • out in the cold

out cold—*(coll.)* 1. unconscious: He was still out cold but he began coming round just before the ambulance got there. 2. alcohol intoxicated: I was wondering how much more drink it would take before he was out cold.

out in the cold—destitute; abandoned: The result would be a bigger dividend for the rest of the shareholders with the poor out in the cold as before.

out front • up front

out front—1. in the forefront; in the lead: The advertising campaign put them out front in sales. 2. *(Theater)* in front of the stage; among the spectators: There is no difference for Falstaff between those on stage and those out front.

up front—*(of payments)* made initially: "How much cash did you have in mind?" "Five thousand, up front." "I beg your pardon?" "In advance."

out in left field • out in the field

out in left field—*(also: way out in left field)* 1. *(of a person)* unusual and eccentric or out of contact with reality: Sally is a lot of fun, but she's sort of out in left field. 2. *(of an idea, answer, etc.)* mistaken, strange and illogical: What he said was totally out in left field. He has no idea what we were talking about.

out in the field—on the warpath; ready for a fight or quarrel: I should keep away from there; her father is out in the field looking for trouble.

out in the blue • out of the blue

out in the blue—1. out in the sea or ocean: Scorpionfish can be found around the deeper coral blocks. With a little luck you can see Mantas cruising out in the blue. 2. *(RAF, WWII)* isolated in the desert, specifically in North Africa: Although "out in the blue" in Bengal, RAF Digri was a well established heavy bomber base.

Note: *The expression does not correlate in meaning with the phrase* ***up in the blue***—*aboard an aircraft; in flight:* If only you could know how happy I am when I fly a plane! I never feel so completely close to God as when I'm up in the blue.

out of the blue—quite unexpectedly; without warning: I got an encouragement out of the blue in the form of an honorary degree from Berlin.

See also: in blue / in the blue.

out of a place • out of place

out of a place—unemployed: Did you hear about Bob? He is out of a place, according to the human resources department.

out of place—1. inappropriate; unacceptable: A man in a round hat is as out of place at a hunt as a man in a tweed suit at a ball. 2. = *out of a place:* It is an ancient custom for servants out of place to assemble, once a year, in some great town, for the purpose of being hired.

out of it • well out of it

out of it—1. excluded from the activities of those around one: I felt rather out of it in France because I can't speak French. 2. not fully alert and aware of what is happening: Bill is really out of it today. Why can't he pay attention? 3. *(sl.)* alcohol or drug intoxicated: He is simply, to use his own phrase, "out of it." Whether drunk or very drunk, he seems to have long decided which questions he will answer.

well out of it—1. = *out of it 1:* We decided to keep well out of it. However when the purge began, we were labeled an anti-revolution clique without any reason. 2. lucky to escape smth.: Stanley Bruce, having left a legacy of debt and deficit behind him, was happy to be well out of it.

See also: beyond it / off it; not in it / not with it.

out of line • out of one's line

out of line—1. set at an angle or placed off-center: If you don't replace those parts, the wheels will get out of line, causing excessive tire wear. 2. *(of smb.'s behavior, etc.)* uncommon; unacceptable: I thought your behavior at the meeting was a bit out of line.

Note: *The expression does not correlate in meaning with the phrase* ***off line****—(of computers) not connected to the Internet:* Working off-line, complete the information requested within the application form and return via e-mail.

out of one's line—*(also: not in one's line)* said of smth. unsuited to one's capacity, taste, or interests: Versification is out of my line, else I should have had a try at it.

out of mind • out of one's mind

out of mind—1. *(in the phrase "time out of mind")* used of the distant past long forgotten: On those visits, he found people living a lifestyle that was time out of mind. *2.* said of things completely forgotten: I got this information from an interview that I read many years ago, source now out of mind.

out of one's mind—*(also: out of one's head)* crazy or behaving as if mad: The poor girl is completely out of her mind! Just look at what she's doing!

out of one's box • out of the box

out of one's box—*(sl.)* crazy or very drunk *(also: off one's box):* If you think this book is good you must be out of your box.

out of the box—*(Austral. coll.)* 1. said of smth. that can be put to immediate use: The industry has yet to sell a computer which can be used by a novice, straight out of the box. 2. very special or exceptional: You mustn't run away with the notion that I'm anything out of the box in back-country conditions.

Note: *a) The expression does not correlate in meaning with the phrase* ***outside the box****—(in the phrase "think outside the box") think in an original way (showing imagination, unusual approach, etc.):* His marketing strategies are looking tired. We need someone who can think outside the box a little more.

b) The expression does not correlate in meaning with the phrase ***knocked out of the box****— used of smth. ousted or replaced by smth. else:* IBM was almost knocked out of the box by other types of computer software and manufacturing.

See also: first time out of the box / just out of a bandbox.

out of one's head • out of one's own head

out of one's head—1. *(also: off one's head)* crazy or behaving as if mad: She was hysterical — Mike himself said she was out of her head! 2. very drunk or intoxicated: By this time we were all tipsy but Peanut was out of his head. 3. unconscious; delirious: In the morning when Andrew Masters came to see how he felt, Pledger was half out of his head. 4. from one's imagination or memory: I didn't get the story from any book or magazine; I made it up out of my head.

out of one's own head— = *out of one's head 4:* Were not all these answers given out of his own head?

out of one's own pocket • out of pocket

out of one's own pocket—*(of expenses)* paid with one's own money: Jimmy paid for everything — right down to office paper — out of his own pocket.

out of pocket—1. having lost money on a deal: They refused to supply me with a replacement or refund my money, so I am out of pocket. 2. said of smb. who is unavailable or cannot be contacted: "He will be out of pocket for a few days," Lay said. "I fully expect him to be back before the trial is over."

See also: in pocket / in the pocket.

out of one's sight • out of sight

out of one's sight—no longer visible; unseen: He was already out of my sight, but only a couple hundred feet ahead.

out of sight—1. = *out of one's sight:* They still stood there upon the rocks, waving till the ship was out of sight. 2. *(coll., of prices)* exorbitant: People found that home prices were out of sight even before they entered the housing market. 3. *(sl.)* used as a generalized expression of admiration: For an official person he's absolutely out of sight.

out of one's time • out of time

out of one's time—1. thought to be born at a wrong historical period: Kellie was born out of his time. Last piece of history he could have flourished in was the Alaska rushes. 2. beyond one's period of minority or apprenticeship: I have a great deal to ask you about America but I hope to come and see for myself when I am out of my time. 3. with no more time left: I am out of my time, Mr. Chairman. I do not know whether you want to let the rest of the panel continue or not.

out of time—1. *(also: off time)* not following the rhythm correctly (when playing a piece of music, etc.): His little party had posted themselves at every corner to feign a more numerous applause: but clapped out of time. 2. = *out of one's time 1:* So often it seems that some literary person has been born out of time. 3. = *out of one's time 3:* I am very sorry if we are out of time, but it seems vital that we have further information on this matter.

Note: *a) The expression does not correlate in meaning with the phrase* ***out of hours****—outside the usual hours of business or work:* We don't usually keep the lights on out of hours.

b) The expression does not correlate in meaning with the phrase ***out of season****—(also: off season) 1. (of animals) born in the wrong season:* Jesse and his grandson caught a lamb which had been born out of season and David was permitted to hold it. 2. *outside the period of time during which hunting or fishing is officially allowed:* Some people are particularly attracted to the flavor of "out of season" venison, since it's forbidden. 3. *during a period of time other than the busiest or most popular for a particular activity:* Our cottages are available year round and "out of season" prices are roughly half the peak summer rental.

out-of-pocket money • pocket money

out-of-pocket money—money that has to be paid: Most programs don't require any out-of-pocket money for the employer, which makes this affordable to organizations of all sizes.

pocket money—money for incidental or minor expenses: Encourage your child to save part of his pocket money each week. Give approval or maybe a bonus for successful managing.

out of taste • without taste

out of taste—1. unable to distinguish flavors: "I made it [wine] strong; there were no dregs." "True; it may be, my mouth is out of taste." 2. *(of a joke, etc.)* tactless; lacking discretion: The banker did not answer, and I instantly felt that my remark was out of taste. 3. lacking good taste: The spectacular effect was marred, as long as the costumes of the performers were out of taste and out of harmony with the whole.

without taste—1. *(of a substance)* tasteless; without flavor: It [phenacetin] occurs in white shining crystals, without taste or odor. 2. in poor taste; in a tasteless manner: He who works without taste tacks one part to another, as his misguided fancy suggests.

out of the wind • out of wind

out of the wind—not in the way of the wind; away from the wind: The sun came out and, if you were out of the wind, it felt really nice.

out of wind—1. = *out of the wind:* Keep out of wind as much as possible. If you ride a bike, wrap a scarf around the lower part of your face. 2. short of breath; out of breath: I ran at my fastest speed, but soon was out of wind and went very slow again to gain my breath.

out-take • take-out

out-take—*(Film or TV production)* a recorded scene not used in a movie: Poole is without a helmet during this sequence, making this most likely an image from an out-take.

take-out—*(also: takeaway)* 1. an establishment selling food to be consumed off the premises: I have bought dumplings from a Chinese takeout and added them to the soup. 2. *(attrib. of food)* sold to be eaten away from its place of sale*:* My mom never gave us fast food — not even a take-out pizza every now and then.

outdoor girl • street girl

outdoor girl—a girl or young woman who likes outdoor activities: Nannie was a big wholesome outdoor girl of a purely American type.

street girl—1. a homeless or neglected girl: You have had the education of a lady.... Don't talk like a street girl. 2. a prostitute: Her clothes somehow call attention to her status as a street girl. Men over age 50 are her best clients.

outer man • outside man

outer man—*(also: outward man)* 1. one's physical body: I began to see that my outer man was not the real me, but only the container of my true self, the inner man. 2. one's personal appearance: He's somewhat particular about the outer man and always dresses smartly.

Note: *The expression does not correlate in meaning with the compound* ***out-and-outer***—*(sl.) 1. smb. who does things with excessive thoroughness:* After we were married we planned to have Adele live with us, for your grandmother was an out-and-outer. 2. *said of a perfect example of a kind:* He has never flinched, never gone back, never missed his way, he is an out-and-outer in this respect, his allegiance has been without flaw.

outside man—1. a man working outdoors: Counting the number of hours worked, the outside men are given an equal amount of employment with the inside men. 2. *(Underworld)* a person playing a special role in a robbery, watching for signs of danger: She was acting as lookout or "outside man" for two expert safe breakers.

Note: *The expression does not correlate in meaning with the phrase* ***outdoor man***—*(also: outdoorsman) one who likes outdoor activities such as camping, fishing, etc.:* Eric was kind, generous and caring. He was an outdoor man, keen cricketer, skier, devoted duck-shooter and regular golfer.

See also: inner man / inside man.

outlook for something • outlook on something

outlook for something—probability of smth.; prospects for smth.: Although the outlook for energy prices is uncertain, energy price inflation is expected.

outlook on something—one's general attitude towards smth.: I really hope that my outlook on this issue isn't wrong! And I wasn't aiming to offend anyone, if I happen to have a different view.

See also: be on the look-out for something / look out for something.

outplay someone • play someone out

outplay someone—play better than another person: He played well but was finally outplayed by his opponent, who was simply too good for Palmer on that day.

play someone out—play music while smb. leaves: When they left the church, the organist played them out with Kuyavy dances, till their feet beat time of themselves.

Note: *The expression is not related in meaning to its passive counterpart* ***be played out***—*(coll.) be tired or worn out:* I was quite played out when I entered the settlement, and I think I had parted from even some little trifles I carried with me.

outpoint someone • point someone out

outpoint someone—excel smb. in number of points, as in a competition or contest: Lucero had to pick himself up twice from the canvas in the early rounds before he finally outpointed Archuleta.

point someone out—show smb.; draw attention to a person: Hooper was positively identified by the victim — who pointed him out in a photo display — and arrested by police.

outweigh something • weigh something out

outweigh something—exceed smth. in value, importance, etc.: If your debt load outweighs your income, you may qualify for debt restructuring.

weigh something out—1. weigh a measured quantity of smth.: Weighing out flour and sugar in advance ... she set about vigorously beating up the eggs. *2.* ponder over smth. carefully: I weigh out many factors when trying to decide what to treat when.

over again • over and over again

over again—*(also: all over again)* for a second time: We couldn't stand to see the same film over again, so we went out.

over and over again—repeatedly; many times: Do not gallop through my letter ... but read it over and over again.

over the fence • over the wall

over the fence—*(Austral., NZ sl.)* objectionable; not socially acceptable: Some publications which unduly emphasize sex were entirely over the fence.

over the wall—*(sl.)* 1. out of prison: When she was over the wall she would begin to get well in the fresh country air. 2. in prison: The Court Martial sentenced him to six months over the wall.

Note: *The expression does not correlate in meaning with the phrase* ***off the wall***—*(sl.) 1. unusual; eccentric:* Tom is just a "regular guy" despite sometimes off-the-wall behavior. 2. *on* *impulse; spontaneously:* He started talking off the wall about how he should go to El Salvador.

over the hill • over the hump

over the hill—1. past one's prime; no longer young enough: As they say about boxers who are getting on in years, she is over the hill. 2. past the critical point; past the worst part of a difficult situation: According to experts' analysis made over the last month, this crisis is "over the hill." The U.S. unemployment rate has peaked at 10.0 percent.

over the hump— = *over the hill 2:* My aquarium is still in its early stages, but I think I am over the hump and on my way to a stable marine environment.

overplay one's hand • play one's hand for all it is worth

overplay one's hand—act in the belief that one is in a stronger position than one really is: Though our prices were lower we overplayed our hand, so that our competitors were awarded the contract.

play one's hand for all it is worth—make every possible effort or attempt: Well, you have played your hand for all it was worth, and you have lost.

overplay something • play something over

overplay something—exaggerate or overemphasize smth.: There was a level of skepticism in the community, a sense that the media had overplayed the significance of the virus.

play something over—play smth. such as music or a game again: "Desperado" a song that I wish had never gotten ruined by overplay on commercial radio, was so riveting I had to play it over and over.

override something • ride over something

override something—1. have precedence or superiority over smth.: The day-to-day struggle for survival overrode all other things. 2. make a decision, etc. ineffective using one's higher authority: As managing director, he will be able to override their decisions.

ride over something—pass across smth. on horseback, bicycle, etc.: Huntsmen have no right to ride over other people's land without permission.

overrule something • rule over something

overrule something—make a decision, etc. ineffective using one's higher authority: The judgment was overruled by the European Court of Justice.

rule over something—act as the ruler of a state, territory, etc.: Babylonia was conquered by Kassite princes who ruled over it for 576 years and nine months.

overrun someone • run someone over

overrun someone—attack an enemy force: They were sent off with orders to overrun the troops attacking Shuttleworth's forward defenses.

run someone over—1. *(also: run someone down)* knock smb. to the ground with a vehicle *(usually Passive):* A woman was run over while crossing the road. 2. drive a person to a destination: I jumped into a jeep with a kid behind its wheel waiting to run me over to Ewell's headquarters.

overrun something • run over something

overrun something—1. *(of troops)* spread over and occupy a territory: The British remained in control of Malaysia until World War II, when Japan overran the country. 2. *(of liquid)* flow over smth.: I was astounded at the damage that was caused when a river overran its banks. 3. go beyond a fixed limit: The amended motion led to a fairly heated debate which overran the time originally allowed.

run over something—1. damage smth. with a vehicle: Misty's brother left her brand-new bike in the middle of the street, and a car ran over it. 2. pass over smth.: There seemed to be a single country road running in the middle of the field with a black power line running over it. 3. briefly browse through smth. written or printed: Running over the pages of a travel magazine, I spotted a small and rather unimposing photograph.

oversee something • see over something

oversee something—officially supervise smth.: He was like a single-minded big brother overseeing every act and thought of the people.

see over something—visit and examine a house or place: Are you the young man who wants to see over the occupational therapy department?

See also: look over something / watch over something.

overshoot the mark • overstep the mark

overshoot the mark—do smth. to a greater extent than is necessary or desirable: Where have we overshot the mark when it comes to technology, and where have we not yet begun to realize its potential?

overstep the mark—behave in a way that is considered morally or legally unacceptable: He appeared like a person who has overstepped the mark, has wounded another's feelings, or alluded to some subject that were better left unmentioned.

oversleep • sleep over

oversleep—sleep beyond one's usual or intended time for waking: I drove home when he never showed up only to get a call from him telling me that he's on his way and he overslept.

sleep over—stay overnight at someone else's home: I am a senior in high school and still have to ask my parents permission to sleep over at a friend's house. *Cf.: have a sleepover—said of a party usually held by children where guests stay overnight:* I'm planning to have a sleepover with about four girlfriends in a few weeks time (post-exam-celebration).

overstep something • step over something

overstep something—go beyond the bounds of smth.; overcome specific limitations: Some brave women in each age may have tried to overstep the limits set for them.

step over something—1. lift the feet so as to pass above smth.: We had to step over piles of broken bricks. 2. = *overstep something 2:* We're always flattered when people are having fun, as long as they don't step over the boundaries.

overtake something • take something over

overtake something—1. catch up with smth. (and pass) as in traveling, race, or pursuit: Members of the crew continued to remark at how Lewis had managed to overtake the other ship. 2. surpass smth. in achievement, production, etc.: Tourism continues to be important to the island's economy, although international business has overtaken it in recent years.

take something over—accept smth. from smb. else; take control of a business, etc.: When Graham and Ivan took the business over their main priority was to make the business profitable.

overthrow something • throw something over

overthrow something—1. turn smth. upside down: ...there was a boat right above the submarine. The boat was overthrown and nine fishermen drowned. *2. (of a regime, government, etc.)* bring about the downfall; remove by force: Communism signifies an organized attempt to overthrow the existing social order. 3. *(of a law, verdict, etc.)* eliminate or invalidate: Laws are openly violated, standards of behavior are overthrown.

throw something over—1. throw smth. across (from one side to another): John glanced at the note and threw it over to me. 2. = *overthrow something 1:* The horse took fright, and the carriage was thrown over. *3.* abandon or renounce smth.: I've decided to throw over the lifestyle I've been used to.

overturn • turn over

overturn—turn upside down; fall over: Pollock's car crashed into a clump of trees and overturned.

turn over—1. = *overturn:* It was less than a hundred feet from the crossing when the car turned over and threw out the two occupants. 2. turn oneself to face the other way: I heard the clock, but then I turned over and went back to sleep. 3. *(of an activity)* continue at a usual or slow speed: After a good start, the organization is now just turning over, and is in need of fresh ideas. 4. *(of goods)* be sold or disposed of: In a grocery store, milk turns over more rapidly than, say, canned asparagus.

overturn something • turn something over

overturn something—1. throw smth. over with violence; cause smth. to fall over: She overturned the chairs and hurled the cushions about. 2. *(of a law, verdict, etc.)* abolish or invalidate: Anti-abortion forces have been organizing to overturn the decision of the Supreme Court.

turn something over—1. turn smth. upside down: Mr. Campion turned over the battered cardboard-backed book.... "Whose is it?" 2. leaf through the pages of a document, etc.: He turned over the pages with the hopeless air of a connoisseur examining an objet d'art. 3. *(also: turn something over in one's mind)* mentally review smth.: Going home that night Dr. Renshaw turned over the facts of the case. 4. *(sl.)* ransack a house, etc.; steal goods from a place: Half the school is on probation for turning over a supermarket. 5. *(of money or merchandise)* handle in business: Our shop turns over ten thousand dollars a week, but we only make a few hundred dollars profit.

overwhelmed by something • overwhelmed with something

overwhelmed by something—completely overpowered with emotion: We want them to know what happened; on the other hand, we don't want them to be overwhelmed by the horror of it all.

overwhelmed with something—1. = *overwhelmed by something:* As you can imagine, I have been overwhelmed with the horror of the stories I've read. 2. provided with a very large or excessive amount of smth.: Our daughter was so overwhelmed with presents, it took her a good two days to get to all of them.

owe for something • owe on something

owe for something—owe money for smth. one has bought but not paid for: I still owe the butcher for the meat I had last Sunday.

owe on something—owe money for smth. one has bought and partially paid for: We still owe nearly a hundred pounds on that car.

oyster catcher • oyster fisher

oyster catcher—any of various wading birds of the genus *Haematopus:* Our game-bag was thinly lined with oyster-catchers, and sanderlings.

oyster fisher—a man engaged in oyster-fishing: The mass of ova is spoken of by oyster fishers as "white spat," and an oyster containing them is said to be "sick."

P

pace out the room • pace the room

pace out the room—(also: pace off the room) measure the room by counting steps: They walked along the wall, pacing out the room, which turned out to be a square about ten steps long on each wall.

pace the room—move restlessly up and down the room: He could not fall asleep, nor even remain in one place, but had to jump up and pace the room with rapid steps.

pack something away • pack something off

pack something away—1. put smth. (in a box, etc.) for safe keeping: She packed away the clothes until they would be needed again. 2. *(coll.)* eat (a lot of food): He can pack away more food than anyone else I know.

pack something off—send smth. in a parcel: Could you pack these clothes off to my sister?

pack them • pack them in

pack them—(Austral. sl.) be panic-stricken or terrified (originally of diarrhea caused by nervousness): You know something, thought Ron Fisher, you're no good. You're packing them.

pack them in—(Theater) attract a capacity audience: Harry James and his band have been helping to pack them in at the Paramount.

Note: *The expression does not correlate in meaning with the phrase* ***pack it in****—(sl.)* 1. *(also: pack in) give up doing smth.* He had long ago "packed it in," and spent his life sitting by the window dozing. 2. *die:* That's where Jack's mate from Hong Kong packed it in.

pain barrier • pain threshold

pain barrier—a state of greatest pain beyond which the pain diminishes: The muscle is giving me some grief but as long as there is no long-term damage then I am willing to play through the pain barrier.

pain threshold—1. the point beyond which a stimulus causes pain: The upper contour is the threshold of pain, above which the sensation is more of pain than of sound (and the result is more or less damaging to the ear). 2. the upper limit of tolerance to pain: Everyone has a different pain threshold but how much of that is due to what is going on in the mind is hard to say.

paint a bow-wow red • paint the town red

paint a bow-wow red—(U.S. diners) put ketchup on a hot dog: I was always fascinated at how they used diner talk. ... a bow-wow painted red (hot dog with ketchup), they had a new name for everything.

paint the town red—go on a spree; have a fun-filled night out: Seniors should get out and paint the town red at this year's Seniors Festival. We want Victorian seniors to have the time of their lives.

painted with the tar brush • touched with the tar brush

painted with the tar brush—said of people or things represented as evil or harmful: The myth of the liberal media grew stronger and the Democrats were painted with the tar brush. *Cf.: tarred with the same brush—said of people considered to have similar faults or objectionable qualities:* As the numbers of would-be immigrants increase, refugees are tarred with the same brush as illegal economic migrants.

touched with the tar brush—(may sound offensive) said of a person who is partly black: Her life story includes spending her childhood not black enough for black folks and too touched with the tar brush for those picky whites.

Palm Sunday • Sad Palm Sunday

Palm Sunday—(in Christian tradition) the Sunday next before Easter, observed in commemoration of Christ's triumphal entry into Jerusalem: Palm Sunday, to which our Lord's entry has given name, has in certain periods and regions been called "Hosanna Sunday."

Sad Palm Sunday—(UK hist.) Palm Sunday in 1463, the day of the bloodiest battle in the Wars of the Roses: The day became known to many as "Sad Palm Sunday." According to William Hone, there were 38,000 killed in a battle that commenced in a snowstorm.

Panama disease • Panama fever

Panama disease—a fungoid disease of banana trees characterized by the yellowing and drying of the leaves: Bananas resistant to Panama disease are being grown commercially.

Panama fever—(also: yellow fever) an infectious disease caused by a virus and characterized by fever, jaundice, kidney failure, and bleeding: After hearing all about how she felt, his diagnosis was a mild case of fever — Panama fever.

park one's car • park oneself

park one's car—stop a car beside the road, etc. and leave it there: He tried to find where he parked his car in a massive underground parking garage in Cannes.

park oneself—sit down or position oneself in a particular place: Vince parked himself at the end of the bar and found himself chatting to an elderly couple.

parkway *(UK)* • parkway *(U.S.)*

parkway (UK)—a railway station with extensive parking facilities for the use of commuters: The "parkway" stations opened by British Rail offer undoubted evidence of cars being abandoned by their users in favor of a rail journey.

parkway (U.S.)—a stretch of landscaped highway with grassy areas on both sides: Check out our favorite spots along the parkway. Mile for mile, it's packed with food, shopping, and fun.

part from someone • part with someone

part from someone—separate from a person; leave smb.'s company: Jagiello must have had great feelings for Elzbieta, for he never parted from her. They always journeyed together.

part with someone—1. lose the services of a person; dismiss smb. from employment: Mr. Jackson has rendered very valuable service to the firm, and we are very sorry to part with him. 2. = *part from someone:* Sian was still married, though separated, having parted with her husband to fulfil her vocation on the stage.

Note: *The expression is not equivalent in meaning to the phrase* ***part company with someone***—1. *(of travel companions, etc.) separate:* We did a small European tour and after this tour we parted company with our singer Jonathan. 2. *disagree with a person:* Even those who generally agree with the headmaster would part company with him there.

part from something • part with something

part from something—1. *(of an object)* become detached from smth.: The lips that parted from the horn, for only a moment, were sensual and expressive. 2. leave a place: Ken finally parted from the city lights as he crossed the last street separating everything from the beach. 3. become separated from smth.: Mrs. Sinclair had long parted from the last bloom of physical youth.

part with something—1. *(of property)* sell or give away: I am reluctant to part with this tea service, as it originally belonged to my mother. 2. *(of money)* spend: He was very unwilling to part with his money, even to buy a house.

part-time work • partwork

part-time work—work done for part of the usual working time only: Each "student nurse" is attached to a nursery class with part-time practical work with little children.

partwork—one of a series of publications issued at regular intervals: Dr. Pyke is currently to be seen on television, advertising the appearance of a new partwork about science.

partake in something • partake of something

partake in something—(formal) take part or share in smth: It is not to be imagined that the entire Irishry partook in this desire of renouncing their ancient customs.

partake of something—(formal) 1. eat or drink some of the food or beverages: He refused to partake of the modest meal Serafina had prepared. 2. have some of the quality or characteristics of smth.: Here the process of education partakes of the nature of discovery. 3. = *partake in something:* Carpenters, scene-shifters, dressers and super-numeraries, all partook of the general joy.

particular about something • particular in something

particular about something—1. not easily satisfied or pleased with smth.: I am highly discriminating and may be especially particular about my diet. 2. especially sensitive about smth.: You see, Aunt Polly's awful particular about this fence — right here on the street, you know ... it's got to be done very careful...

particular in something—1. attentive as to details; accurate in smth.: Dr. Shaw has been particular in his description of this almost entire wardrobe of an Arab. 2. = *particular about something 1:* They are especially particular in their choice of what to have at home or to give to special friends during the Chinese New Year.

party girl • party man

party girl—a young woman employed to entertain men, especially at social events: He had never thought of asking himself what she was, inside of the hard shell of her disguise as the party girl.

party man—a man characterized by strong loyalty to a political party and its policies: Although a party man, he was by no means a man to swallow the whole party platform.

pas de deux • two-step

pas de deux—(Fr.) a dance in ballet: They were wonderful, their pas de deux to the adagio a beautiful example of the Balanchine style.

two-step—an American ballroom dance developed in the 1880s: The two-step gradually came to replace the waltz as the preferred social dance of the time.

pass away • pass off • pass out

pass away—1. cease to exist; disappear: When he laid his hands on me my headache and chest pains passed away. 2. *(euph.)* die: I'm sorry to hear that your dear uncle passed away last week.

pass off—1. = *pass away 1:* These pains [in Caisson disease] pass off in a few hours. 2. succeed; turn out: The performance passed off without a hitch, the tent being crowded almost to its capacity.

pass out—1. lose consciousness: Fancy that being a real burglar last night. I'd have passed out if I'd known. 2. successfully complete a course of training: How many of the students passed out this year? 3. = *pass away 2:* First, write the name of the dead relative or friend, then when they passed out.

pass one's word • pass the word

pass one's word—(also: pass one's word of honor) give a pledge or promise: Half the sum was raised and Dundee is said to have passed his word for the remainder.

pass the word—(also: pass word) give an oral order or instruction: Rafferty would pass word to certain stool pigeons to keep their eyes and ears open for trace of the missing canvas.

Note: *The expression is not equivalent in meaning to the phrase* ***send word****— send a personal written message:* The deputy marshal would send word to the prosecuting attorney asking for an "OK."

pass something away • pass something off • pass something out

pass something away—(of time) spend in a pleasant, easy way: He passed the evening away looking at his collection of stamps.

pass something off—1. choose not to notice smth.; ignore smth.: The remark was intended as rudeness, but he passed it off with a laugh. 2. *(of forged currency, checks, etc.)* put into circulation or dispose of by deceit: What is not acceptable is to pass off false documents as genuine.

pass something out—distribute smth. such as gifts, leaflets, etc.: The exhibitors at the trade fair pass out free samples to stimulate interest.

pass the time • pass the time of day

pass the time—spend one's time; make one's time less tedious or monotonous: Confined to his bed for a whole week, Smith passed the time catching up on his reading.

pass the time of day—exchange greetings or engage in small talk with a person: Although I have spoken to him a number of times, it was only to pass the time of day.

patient of something • patient with someone

patient of something—enduring suffering, etc. patiently without complaining: He was most patient of injuries done to himself, yet he would not endure any injury done to the name of Christ.

patient with someone—able to control one's feelings in dealing with a person: He was always very kind and patient with me, as he was with all people.

patrol car • patrol wagon

patrol car—a police car used in patrolling roads and streets: Our patrol car got the call as "shots fired," with the address given. My partner and I responded.

patrol wagon—1. = *patrol car:* The patrol wagon, filled with officers, was driven to the place at a breakneck speed. 2. *(U.S.)* a police van for transporting prisoners: At first, the jail visitors balked at riding to the prison in a police patrol wagon.

pavement artist *(UK)* • pavement artist *(U.S.)*

pavement artist (UK)—1. *(also: flagstone artist)* an artist who draws on paving stones with colored chalks, hoping to be given money by passers-by: No one but the pavement artist can have any notion of how great the amount of dust is in London's streets. 2. *(sl.)* an espionage agent engaged in street surveillance on a suspect, etc.: His specialty was hitting the streets and finding out information. In the vernacular of his profession he became known as a top-notch "pavement artist."

pavement artist (U.S.)—an artist who displays paintings for sale on a pavement: Outside the station a small crowd were watching with interest as a pavement artist copied and enlarged a painting from a postcard.

pay a compliment to someone • pay one's compliments to someone

pay a compliment to someone—(also: make a compliment to someone) express praise or admiration for a person in a remark: Rhonda pays a compliment to her husband, Mike, for staying as loving as he was when they first met.

pay one's compliments to someone—(also: make one's compliments to someone) express good wishes or respect to a person: All things having satisfied the admiral, he paid his compliments to Raoul, and gave the last orders for sailing.

pay a heavy price for something • pay the penalty for something

pay a heavy price for something—suffer a serious disadvantage or loss in return for smth. one has gained: Our troops recaptured the city, but they paid a heavy price for it.

pay the penalty for something—suffer a disadvantage or loss because of wrongdoing or an error: I'm paying the penalty for drinking too much last night; I've got a dreadful headache!

pay as one goes • pay one's way

pay as one goes—said of the practice of paying debts as they are incurred: You pay as you go, so there is no need to commit to any monthly figure—you simply pay for what you use.

pay one's way—(also: pay one's own way) pay all of one's debts and living expenses: No matter how much I tried, there was just no way I could pay my way through school without a job.

pay attention to someone • pay attentions to someone

pay attention to someone—take notice of smb.; show interest in a person: Hardly anyone of the crew of six paid any attention to the man and teenage boy who had come aboard.

pay attentions to someone—(also: pay one's attentions to someone) court a woman in the hope of winning her affections: The newspapers report that at the moment he is paying his attentions to an Italian countess.

pay-book • paying-in book

pay-book—an individual pay record of a member of the armed forces: Henry opened Dooley's pay-book, the pages of which showed liberal sprinklings of the red ink with which fines and convictions were entered.

paying-in book—(UK) bankbook in which the bank enters a person's deposits and withdrawals: The purpose of these stubs in a paying-in book is for the holder to have a record of the amount of money he had deposited in his bank.

pay in kind • repay in kind

pay in kind—pay for smth. in goods, not money: Their revenues were mostly paid, not in money, but in kind, such as corn, wine and cattle.

repay in kind—(also: pay back in kind) return the hostile or unfair action with the like: He was rude to me, so I repaid him in kind.

pay off something • pay out something

pay off something—1. pay money owed for smth. in full: We have paid off the house only to find that real estate taxes are so high that we cannot afford to keep the house. 2. *(Nautical)* take a ship out of use, for repair or at the end of her last voyage: The decision to pay off the ship came during the last days of her deployment.

pay out something—1. *(of money)* pay in small amounts (in settlement of debts, etc.): Millions of pounds were being paid out every week in unemployment benefit. 2. allow a rope, etc. to move freely through one's hands: Secure the load in position and pay out enough cable to remove all tension on the cable and drum.

peace dove • peaceful dove

peace dove—(also: dove of peace) a figure of a white dove as a symbol of peace: There may be no better symbol of peace than this peace dove pendant.

peaceful dove—a mainly sedentary dove *(Geopelia placida)* widely distributed through eucalypt forests of Australia: The Peaceful Dove has grey-brown upperparts, barred with black, pink-buff underparts.

peak time • up time

peak time—1. *(also: peak hours)* periods when traffic, consumption of electricity, etc. is at its highest: The survey shows that average peak time traffic speeds have risen. 2. *(Radio, TV)* a period characterized by the largest audience of the day: This peak-time program will be geared for a Sunday night family audience.

up time—the time when a machine or computer is operating: Maximum up-time is assured with the ability to replace a failed server disk or power supply, on-the-fly.

Note: *The expression does not correlate in meaning with the phrase **time is up**—(of a period of time) expire; be over:* The water clock was used to control speakers' times. When the water ran out, the speaker's time was up.

See also: high time / low time.

Peeping Tom • Peeping-Tom TV

Peeping Tom—a person who gets (sexual) pleasure, from secretly watching others: Why don't you tell everyone that Bob is a Peeping Tom? You saw him peeping into Mariah's bedroom window...

Peeping-Tom TV—said of reality television shows that focus on the personal lives of ordinary people: "Taxi!" is the latest manifestation of Peeping Tom TV, of which Jeremy Beadle is the brand master.

peg leg • peg legs

peg leg—1. a wooden leg: McPhail has created a pirate crew consisting of animals dressed in pirate gear: eye patches and peg-legs included. 2. *(sl.)* a person who wears a wooden leg: See that peg leg over there? He lost his foot to a shark.

peg legs—*(U.S. sl.)* pants which are tapered at the ankle: Heavy thighs? Forget about peg legs and baggy shapeless jeans.

peg someone down • take someone down a peg

peg someone down—1. force a person to keep to a decision, agreement, etc.: One can't peg him down to one genre of music because each CD can span several genres. 2. have a fixed opinion of a person: She had already pegged him down as a lazy, boozing, drug-taking, and altogether irresponsible man.

take someone down a peg—*(also: take someone down a peg or two)* make smb. feel less important; snub or humiliate a person: The most influential paper picked the moment of his greatest triumph to take him down a peg.

per cent • per cents

per cent—is used with preceding numerals in stating a proportion of smth.: During the 10 years, the entire population increased at the rate of 13 per cent.

per cents—public securities bearing a specific rate of interest: The conversion of the four per cents into three and a half per cents was facilitated.

performance art • performing art

performance art—multimedia art form combining static elements with music, song, dance, film, and spoken dialogue: Performance art grew out of avant-garde movements, particularly in poetry and painting.

performing art—an art (such as the dance, music, drama, etc.) involving public performance: I am delighted to know that the Prime Minister is interested in having a center in Ottawa for the performing arts.

permit of something • permit something

permit of something—leave room for smth.: He must go quickly like a man bent upon urgent business which permits of no delay.

permit something—allow smth.: If the owner does not permit smoking, people who wish to smoke can decide not to patronize that restaurant.

person of few words • short-spoken person

person of few words—1. smb. who does not speak much: Others who knew him say he was a person of few words, who usually spoke only when spoken to. 2. a person of action rather than words: Rose, also a person of few words, is known for getting the job done. No excuses, no stories — just do the best you can.

short-spoken person—1. = *person of few words 1:* Another way to get more information out of a short-spoken person is to ask "clusters" of questions.... 2. smb. given to speaking in an abrupt, unfriendly way: He saw no one but the door-keeper, a short-spoken person who believed that it was part of his duty to be frowning.

pester someone about something • pester someone for something

pester someone about something—annoy a person by constantly referring to a specific matter: Mrs. Buster is always pestering me about which dress to wear, which card to send, what color pen to use on the card.

pester someone for something—trouble a person by continually asking for smth.: Inertia selling was the practice by which companies sent unsolicited goods, then pestered people for payment if they were not returned.

petty cash • small cash

petty cash—a small fund of money that a firm keeps for incidental expenses: Custodians of petty cash must ensure that any funds that have been spent will be replenished monthly.

small cash—*(usually attrib.)* a small sum of money: This award will be given based on nominations by faculty in the form of a certificate and a small cash prize.

photo finish • photo finishing

photo finish—1. *(Racing)* a finish so close that only a photograph can decide the winner: In the tense, final moments of the race she had craned forward with the rest to watch the photo finish. 2. a very close contest in an election, etc.: A photo finish was predicted by public opinion polls. The final one showed M. Mitered winning on the second ballot...

photo finishing—the process of producing prints from negatives: In the photographic chemicals market the company offers a range of chemicals for photo finishing.

physical exercise • physical exercises

physical exercise—physical exertion of the body (such as walking, playing football, etc.) engaged in for health or amusement: We take no physical exercise, except riding or swimming.

physical exercises—specific movements within a regimen of physical training: Physical exercises performed to the accompaniment of music may be a pleasant and stimulating way of passing the time.

pick at someone • pick on someone

pick at someone—continually nag at smb.; find fault with a person: Why are you always picking at the poor child?

pick on someone—single a person out for criticism, reprimand, etc.: Have you any idea why the Inspector should have picked on you first?

pick at something • pick on something

pick at something—1. keep pulling smth. or scratch it with one's nails: He sat there idly ruminating and picking at the tablecloth. 2. *(of food)* take small, selected pieces now and again: He was just picking at his food, not eating it.

pick on something—select or choose smth.: We seem to have picked on just the right spot for a picnic.

pick someone off • pick someone out

pick someone off—kill a person with a carefully aimed shot: Two hundred marksmen have been assigned to a squad designed to pick off snipers.

pick someone out—1. choose smb. from a group: I hoped to be able to pick out the winner of the Grand National when the weights appeared. 2. recognize a person among others: Almost instantly, my searching eyes had picked her out in the crowd.

pick someone's brains • prey on someone's mind

pick someone's brains—get ideas or information about a subject by asking a person: I would love to pick your brains, so to speak, and see what kind of innovative ideas you could come up with.

Note: *The expression does not correlate in meaning with the phrase* ***brain someone****—(sl.) hit smb. hard on the head (often used as a threat):* The constable threatened to brain him if he didn't shut up.

prey on someone's mind—(of anxieties, losses, etc.) afflict or worry a person: When the servants had withdrawn, I found that the unhappy result of the duel was still preying on his mind.

pick something off • pick something out

pick something off—remove smth. by picking, scratching, or plucking: Pick off all the feathers before you cook the duck.

pick something out—1. = *pick something off:* I was about to put the duck in boiling water in order to pick out the feathers.... 2. choose smth. from a group: We've picked out the best toys and trinkets to give to dad this holiday. 3. recognize or distinguish smth.: Do you need a wide panorama, or would a telephoto be more useful to pick out distant detail?

pick something out of a hat • pull something out of a hat

pick something out of a hat—select smth. completely at random: When asked how they chose Juneau to be the state capital, she said, "I don't know, I think they picked it out of a hat."

pull something out of a hat—produce smth. unexpected as if by magic: If you want to help Thomas, you've got to argue a lot of silly problems that he pulls out of a hat.

Note: *The expression does not correlate in meaning with the phrase* ***pull off a hat-trick****—(usually of sports) have three successes in a row:* This thoroughbred is ridden by Peslier, who has already pulled off a hat-trick of three consecutive Prix de l'Arc de Triomphe successes.

See also: have something under one's hat / keep something under one's hat.

pick up on someone • pick up with someone

pick up on someone—1. *(Racing)* draw near a person; begin to overtake a competitor: Benedict, knowing that he had the fastest car, was inclined to allow Chalmers to pick up on him.... 2. *(U.S. coll.)* understand or appreciate a person: After Baudelaire picked up on him, Edgar Allen Poe had enormous influence on French literature and art.

pick up with someone—enter into conversation and make acquaintance with smb. casually met: So you've let your Polly go and pick up with some young man from town.

Note: *Neither expression correlates in meaning with the phrase* ***pick someone up****—1. take a person along with one, into one's company or into a vehicle (collecting him from a place):* I remember picking him up from work that night to take him home (he had no car). 2. *form an acquaintance with a person casually or informally, especially with the intention of having a sexual relationship:* She wished she had not picked Markie up in the train and given him her address. 3. *(coll.) find fault with a person; call smb. to account:* I am picked up for saying that the initiative in the Steamer case should have come from the stewards. 4. *(sl.) rob, cheat, or swindle a person:* There are loose characters lurking about, on the look-out for strangers, to "pick them up," as they term it, which, in other words, means to rob them. 5. *cause a person to revitalize; serve as a "pick-me-up":* Have you had your tea? A cup of tea will pick you up. 6. *(sl.) arrest or apprehend a person:* Things start to go badly for him. His boys ... get picked up for every minor charge in the book.

pick up stakes • raise the stakes

pick up stakes—(also: pull up stakes) leave one's home, etc. and move on to another place: "I'm assuming you're in a position to pick up stakes in a hurry." "As long as it will take to pack two bags."

raise the stakes—(Gambling) lay a higher stake than one's opponent: You can bet against that particular player, continually raising the stakes, until all the other players are "raised out."

piece of cake • pieces of the same cake

piece of cake—said of smth. done easily, with little effort: Cycling in the hills was a piece of cake. It was the cobblestone streets that finally wore us out.

Note: *The expression does not correlate in meaning with the phrase* ***slice of the cake****—(also: slice of the pie) used of assets, profits, etc. to be apportioned or shared out:* German labor may be about to demand a larger slice of the economic recovery cake.

pieces of the same cake—said of things that have the same characteristics or qualities: Both physical and psychological violation or bullying would be pieces of the same cake.

piece of work • work piece

piece of work—1. a product of work: They drove over the Golden Gate Bridge ... and she was enchanted. "What a handsome piece of work, isn't it, Luke?" 2. a difficult task or business: How do you expect to get along when it's such a piece of work to make you shake hands? 3. *(coll.)* a commotion; a noisy display: What are you making all this piece of work for? 4. *(coll., in the phrase "a nasty piece of work")* an unpleasant person: He was a nasty piece of work all right. A real blackmailer.

work piece—a thing worked on with a machine or tool: Place work piece in a vice or on a flat surface whenever possible.

pigs in a blanket • pigs in a poke

pigs in a blanket—(U.S. diners) 1. stuffed cabbage: Pigs in a blanket to me are also called stuffed cabbage or in Czech Austrian, "Holupki" ... it just depends on where you are from. 2. a ham sandwich or a sausage wrapped in a pancake: Kids will beg for these little Pigs in a Blanket for breakfast! This recipe is so quick and easy you can even let the kids roll them up...

pigs in a poke—1. *(used in allusion to the phrase "buy a pig in a poke")* said of smth. bought or obtained without seeing it: Don't give us "pigs in a poke," in other words, web links that we have to open before we know what is in them. 2. *(U.S. cuisine)* baked potatoes stuffed with sausage: I had to choose between the Trucker's Breakfast or the Pigs in a Poke, finally deciding on the latter. 3. = *pigs in a blanket 2:* For a cowboy breakfast theme she would serve pigs in a poke (pancake-wrapped sausages) and hot or cold chocolate milk.

pillow partner • sleeping partner

pillow partner—(sl.) smb. with whom a person regularly has sex outside marriage: I can usually make use of a native pillow partner.

Note: *The expression does not correlate in meaning with the compound* ***bed-fellow****—one's companion or associate:* The oddest of enemies might become bedfellows.

sleeping partner—1. *(also: dormant partner)* a partner who does not take an active part in managing the business: He has been the sleeping partner who has supplied a great part of their capital. 2. *(sl.)* = *pillow partner:* Your sleeping partner would provide you with an alibi.

pin back one's ears • pin back someone's ears

pin back one's ears—1. *(UK sl.)* listen attentively: Pin back your ears, people, this is quite a story! 2. *(Sport)* give the game the necessary degree of effort: Dafydd had a big game, even if he didn't pin back his ears and finish one or two moves as he should have done.

pin back someone's ears—(U.S. sl.) rebuke a person severely: When a man pays you a heavy-handed compliment, do you smile graciously or pin back his ears with a sharp quip?

pin someone on the ropes • put someone up to the ropes

pin someone on the ropes—(Boxing) force an opponent back on to the ropes: Referee Brimmell stepped in to save Scot after the challenger had pinned him on the ropes for fully a minute.

put someone up to the ropes—make a person understand the way to do smth.: Our pilot allowed me to spend part of the time with him on the bridge and put me up to the ropes. *Cf.: know the ropes—be familiar with a particular kind of work:* You won't have to train the new computer operator; she already knows the ropes.

pink elephant • white elephant

pink elephant—1. *(usually in the phrase "see a pink elephant")* said of a visionary hallucination caused by over-indulgence in alcohol: Ben had been extremely (to the pink elephant sighting stage) drunk after he had been forced to take command. 2. a problem that everyone knows well but no one talks about because it is embarrassing: It's like there's a pink elephant in the room that no one wants to acknowledge. How long can you go before someone says something or does something?

white elephant—a possession or piece of property that is useless or unwanted, especially one that is inconvenient or expensive to keep: The automobile was a large Mercedes-Benz: I kept it a week or so but it was so heavy that it was a "white elephant" on country roads. *Cf.: white elephant sale—a sort of odds and ends sale on people's front yard at bargain-basement prices:* A few weeks back I found some signed paintings at a white elephant sale. They were just $3 each...

pink money • red money

pink money—money spent by people who are homosexual, especially on entertainment: With the rise of the gay rights movement, pink money has gone from being a fringe or marginalized market to a thriving industry in many parts of the Western world. *Cf.: grey pound—(UK) used of the economic power of elderly people:* The battle for the so-called "grey pound" has become increasingly prominent in the insurance market.

red money—(U.S.) 1. money from the states whose residents predominantly vote for the Republican Party, as contrasted with "blue money" associated with the Democratic Party: There are parts of upstate New York which are so red they make Alabama look liberal. This is not one of those, but it could give Kentucky a run for its red money. 2. money coming specifically from communist China: Clinton's policy served to line the pockets of greedy corporate executives with red money. The Clinton export policy has significantly upgraded the nuclear firepower of the Chinese Army.

Note: *The expression does not correlate in meaning with the phrase* ***red cent****—(negat., emphatic) not a penny; no money at all:* You are asking me to donate money to the party and I'm telling you I will not donate one red cent.

See also: black money / white money.

pivot man • pivotal man

pivot man—(Basketball) a player guarding second base: The pivot man is facing mid-court, back to the basket, and with feet spread for good balance. He must be extremely protective of the ball.

pivotal man—1. a prominent person; a key figure: He was the pivotal man in my life who taught me the value of hard work, social consciousness and the concept of fairy tale versus reality. 2. *(UK hist.)* a man considered to have an important role in the re-establishment of industry after the war of 1914–1918: She found Blinkhorn in France and managed to have him demobilized as a pivotal man.

place of work • working place

place of work—the office, factory, etc. where a person works: An employee wishing to leave his place of work must give his employer a similar prior notice as described above.

working place—a specific location at which a worker executes his work: *Shift-man*—a man who prepares the working places at night in a colliery for the men who come in at next shift.

plain and simple • pure and simple

plain and simple—(of language, instructions, etc.) clear; not complicated: He can explain matters in plain and simple terms that are easy for a mainstream American to grasp.

pure and simple—nothing but...; nothing besides... *(used in post-position for emphasis):* This is envy, pure and simple, and a tax policy based on envy is the worst kind.

plain men • plainsmen

plain men—(also: plain people) ordinary or average men; people not given to complex reasoning or speculation: The first people to listen to Jesus' words and to become his disciples were plain men, fishermen of Galilee.

plainsmen—(also: plains people) inhabitants of the wide open plains of a particular region: Experienced ranchmen never turn a bunch of green brood-mares out unless accompanied by three or four of these sagacious little plainsmen.

plain people • plains people

plain people—1. *(also: plain men)* ordinary or average men; people not given to complex reasoning or speculation: The plain people of Northern Ireland are surprised by nothing and shocked by very little. 2. *(Plain People)* members of religious groups who practice a simple way of life: The Plain People, as they are known, won't use automobiles or tractors, have no telephones, plumbing or political parties.

plains people—1. *(also: plainsmen)* inhabitants of the wide open plains of a particular region: The appellation "Naga" was actually given to these hill tribes by the plains people. 2. *(also: Plains Indians)* Indians of the Great Plains of central United States and Canada: As a plains people they [the Pawnee] were largely dependent upon the chase.

plain sailing • plane sailing

plain sailing—1. *(Nautical)* sailing in open unrestricted waters: He can take an observation and is acquainted with that part of navigation called plain sailing. 2. an easy, straightforward task, procedure, etc.: Once we've fixed the computer it will be plain sailing.

plane sailing—*(Nautical)* calculation of a ship's position as if the earth were flat instead of spherical: In plane sailing, the principal terms made use of are the course, distance, departure ... any two of which being given the others can be found.

plain to someone • plain with someone

plain to someone—*(of things)* easy to understand and clear to a person: It was made quite plain to me that my career would be a very short one in the police service.

plain with someone—*(of people)* frank and honest in dealing with another person: To be plain with you, there is no hope of your passing this examination.

plane man • plane people

plane man—*(Mining)* a worker who controls cars on a self-acting incline *(loaded car going down one track pulls empty cars up on other):* A laborer who controls the movement of cars is also called drum runner, monitor operator, plane man.

Note: *The expression does not correlate in meaning with the compound* ***planesman****— a person who operates the diving planes on a submarine:* The diving planesmen tilt the forward planes down and the after planes up.

plane people—*(also: jet people)* asylum seekers, refugees, or immigrants who relocate by airplane: About 2,500 of these "plane people" are leaving each month.... This number is roughly equal to the total monthly arrivals in the region by boat people.

planetarium theater • planetary house

planetarium theater—a building housing an instrument for projecting the positions of the stars and planets onto a domed ceiling: See stars and constellations on the dome of our planetarium theater; use a star chart to find stars in the sky.

planetary house—*(Astrology)* one of 12 equal areas (constellations) into which the zodiac is divided: One of the first published tests of natal astrology tested the thesis that planetary house locations were related to a person's career path.

plastic bomb • plastic bullet

plastic bomb—a bomb containing plastic explosive: In France there were plastic bomb attacks, directed mainly against liberal politicians and journalists.

plastic bullet—a projectile made of plastic material, used by security forces in riot control: New devices for riot control, including a plastic bullet, have been issued to the Army.

play a love game • play for love

play a love game—said when smb.'s attitude to matters of love is not serious enough: She is afraid that you're playing a love game instead of being serious.

play for love—*(also: play for fun)* play cards, etc. without stakes: The Parson did not like card games played for money, but he was willing to play for love.

See also: love game / love play.

play a part • play the part

play a part—1. be involved in smth. and have an effect on it: Biochemistry may be defined as the study of the chemical processes which play a part in the life phenomena of plants and animals. 2. impersonate smb. such as a stage character: These pages contain top-secret materials about Bondiana—about the actors, who played a part of Bond. 3. deliberately behave in a way that hides one's real character or feelings: It's enough to make a man bughouse when he has to play a part from morning to night.

Note: *The expression does not fully correlate in meaning with the phrase* ***play one's part****—(also: do one's part)* 1. = *play a part 1:* He not only played his part in shaping the organization, but he also did what might be termed important field work for it. 2. *do what is required of one:* Soliah played her part well before the media, speaking of her relief and her gratitude to friends and neighbors.

play the part—1. = *play a part 2:* Easton played the part of an aspiring singer with a humble background that prevents her from achieving her dream. 2. perform the function of other things: Banks which had adopted the gold exchange standard will become dependent on the banks which play the part of gold centers.

play against time • play for time

play against time—do smth. so as to finish one's task before the expiry of a certain period: "You're playing against time and the elements," he said, recounting the rescue in a phone interview.

play for time—delay action or a decision in the hope that conditions will be more favorable later on: This skepticism is influenced by suspicions that they will not bargain seriously and merely play for time.

play at bears • play the bear

play at bears—*(of little children)* engage in a game of bears: You can play at bears in the nursery when we get back, if you want.

play the bear—*(coll.)* cause a good deal of trouble or bother to a person: Chaps that have got something on their minds can't stand idleness, it plays the bear with them.

play at something • play on something

play at something—1. *(of children)* engage in a specified game: Nana had turned on the water for Michael's bath. The two older children were playing at being mother and father. 2. perform smth. in a not very serious manner: It's no good playing at business, you have to take it seriously. 3. fill a particular position in a sports team: Vasquez played at center forward and center midfield ... and he led the team in goals scored.

play on something—1. perform on a musical instrument: I'm no longer aware that I'm playing on a violin; I'm just expressing myself. 2. make use or advantage of smb.'s feelings: By playing on the old lady's fears, the criminals were able to persuade her to give them her money. 3. emit light, a jet of water from a hose, etc. onto a surface: Searchlights played on the river upstream to light up any floating mines. 4. make clever use of some aspect of a particular word or idea, often for a humorous effect: Arbuthnot's satire plays on the idea of society as a human body.

play ball • play the ball

play ball—1. engage in a sport such as baseball, soccer, etc.: My buddies couldn't decide where we wanted to play ball, so we gave up and went to a movie instead 2. go along with a person; cooperate willingly in a plan or activity: I might have played ball just a little, but I scorned to.

Note: *The expression does not correlate in meaning with the phrase* ***play catch-up ball****—*1. *play a game determinedly when one is losing:* "We made them play catch-up ball," commented head coach Rick Schwiebert. 2. *work hard to recover from a disadvantage:* For the last two years it's been a matter of playing catch-up ball with the budget.

play the ball—*(in cricket, football, etc.)* hit or kick the ball: I pointed to the penalty mark, but the defender protested loudly that he had played the ball.

Note: *The expression does not correlate in meaning with the phrase* ***play the ball not the man****— not resort to attacks directed against the character of the person rather than the subject under discussion:* Let's play the ball not the man comrades, simply hurling insults at people who differ with our views will not help.

play by ear • play it by ear

play by ear—play music without notes by relying on one's sense of tune and harmony: In fact I can only play by ear and have never been able to read music.

play it by ear—act in a situation taking things as they come with no prior plans: I'm still not sure what I'll do when I get there, I'm just going to play it by ear.

play donkey • play donkey-drop

play donkey—take part in a simple card game played with special cards: Rachel forced us to play donkey with her. For some reason she kept winning and I'm always losing.

play donkey-drop—(cricket, tennis, etc.) hit a slow ball so that it travels in a high curve: He is content to play "donkey drops" back into court, awaiting the right ball to hit.

play down to someone • play up to someone

play down to someone—deliberately talk to or behave towards smb. so that the person does not feel inferior: Joe Mystic does not play down to his audience. He plays to and has fun with his audience.

play up to someone—1. flatter a person (in order to win favor for oneself): Are you the employee who plays up to your boss day after day? 2. act in a helpful or cooperative manner towards a person: His mother did social small talk without daring to stop, and Wilkie played up to her. 3. act in a theatrical performance so as to support or assist another actor: Amberg started with a stock company of very indifferent merit. They could not play up to the stars whom he occasionally invited.

Note: *a) The expression does not correlate in meaning with the phrase* ***play someone up****—*1. *make smb. seem to be more important:* The director tried to play up Ann, but she was not really a star. 2. *annoy or irritate a person:* They are trying to play me up. They believe that I will lose control. 3. *(of one's arm, stomach, etc.) give trouble to a person:* His left elbow started playing him up and he was ordered to rest.

b) The expression does not correlate in meaning with the phrase ***make a play for someone****— attempt to attract the romantic or other interest of a person:* You're making a play for Joe and are waiting for him to take a personal interest in you.

play games • play the game

play games—act cunningly or dishonestly towards a person: Don't play games, Mona. I know about the theft, and I know that you know about it.

play the game—observe the rules or conventions: You can't deny the role that competitiveness plays in raising standards. So you have to play the game if you want to succeed.

play games with someone • play with someone

play games with someone—act cunningly or dishonestly towards a person: Don't try to play games with me. You're not nearly as clever as you think you are.

play with someone—treat smb.'s feelings or affections in a casual and irresponsible way: I feel a pang of remorse because she may love me seriously, although I am only playing with her.

See also: play someone at his own game / play someone's game.

play gooseberry • play old gooseberry

play gooseberry—be the third person present with two lovers; act as an escort: Let the old woman choose between playing gooseberry or loitering behind alone.

play old gooseberry—(UK dated) cause damage or devastation to smth.: She would play old gooseberry with the property if we hadn't someone to look after it.

play hard to get • play hardball

play hard to get—pretend to be unapproachable or uninterested, with a view to strengthening one's position: To be blunt, you sort of strike me as playing hard to get.

play hardball—use uncompromising tactics: The insurance company played hardball with desperate homeowners, relying on questionable experts, and falsified reports.

play it low down • play it low-key

play it low down—behave meanly or unfairly towards a person: If it weren't playing it low down on the fellows that have been in it from the start, I'd like to enlist.

Note: *The expression does not fully correlate in meaning with the phrase* ***play it low****—*1. *(of music) play at a low volume:* I am used to listening to music while exercising. And I play it low enough so I can hear outside sound.... 2. = *play it low down:* But I'm not going to play it low on an old shipmate, and you shall have a fourth of whatever comes.

play it low-key—(also: keep it on the low down) do smth. without drawing much attention to it: For a company about to revolutionize the Internet, they liked to play it low key.

play of words • play on words

play of words—the use of words merely for the purpose of producing an oratorical effect: The speeches of Thucydides exhibit the antithesis, the climaxes, the plays of words of the rhetorician.

play on words—a playful use of words to produce a humorous effect by similarity of sound: When closely analyzed, many jokes depend for their effect upon a play on words.

play someone at his own game • play someone's game

play someone at his own game—return smb.'s hostile or unfair action with the like: Men used to come in the office and I never used to get introduced. So I've started playing them at their own game.

play someone's game—1. advance a person's plans or schemes, whether willingly or unintentionally: If I want him to give me the information I need, I guess I should play his game. *2.* use another person's unfair practices, especially to gain one's own ends: If playing his dirty game is the only way of winning the election I'd rather lose.

See also: play games with someone / play with someone.

play the gallery • play to the gallery

play the gallery—act the part of spectators (applauding, etc.): We were constantly called in to play the gallery to his witty remarks.

play to the gallery—set out to win popularity in a cheap and showy way: The attorney seemed less concerned with the furtherance of justice than with playing to the gallery of reporters. *Cf.: gallery play—said of cheap showmanship:* His co-propagandists arranged one such emotionally manipulative "gallery play."

plead for someone • plead with someone

plead for someone—1. *(legal)* address a court of law as an advocate on behalf of either the plaintiff or the defendant: Nawaz had boycotted the game of court proceedings and now he does not have even a lawyer to plead for him. 2. make an earnest appeal or entreaty for the person in whose interest one speaks: Some friends were admitted to his cell, and they informed him that they had pleaded for him, but in vain. 3. *(followed by Infinitive)* ask a person earnestly to do smth.: I had thrown myself into his strong arms, pressed my face onto his well-muscled chest, and sobbed. I pleaded for him to stay.

plead with someone— = plead for someone 3: They pleaded with him to stay, insisting he was the outstanding person for this difficult job.

plug at something • plug away at something

plug at something—(U.S. coll.) shoot at smth.: You can practice with your gun by plugging at the tree.

plug away at something—(coll.) work hard and steadily at smth.: If I plug away at painting the room, I may get it finished tonight.

point at something • point to something

point at something—show smth. by holding out one's finger, etc.: All the boys went down to the beach and pointed at the great ship anchored there.

point to something—1. indicate the position or direction of smth.: The needle of a compass points to the north. 2. *= point at something:* Pembeh touched him on the shoulder and pointed to a prayer rug spread at the threshold of the room. 3. be a sign of smth.; testify to smth.: Everything pointed to the probability of a French protectorate being proclaimed over Burma. 4. direct attention to smth.: Critics point to the continuing instability of the company.

point of no return • turning point

point of no return—the point beyond which one must continue on his current course of action, because turning back would be too expensive or dangerous: We have finally reached the point of no return where the drums for peace are now louder than the drums for war.

turning point—a decisive moment at which a very significant change for better or worse occurs: The Chernobyl disaster was a turning point for the nuclear power worldwide. It demonstrated that nuclear power in parts of the world was not safe enough.

pony up for something • pony up something

pony up for something—(U.S. coll.) make a request for smth.: Actually, I'm reading the e-book, but I already know I will pony up for the print version as well.

pony up something—(U.S. coll.) repay the money one owes: Tell him to defer enrollment for a year. Otherwise, he's got to pony up the whole amount through a bank loan.

poor boy • poor little boy

poor boy—(U.S.) a large sandwich filled with a range of ingredients: Exploring Greenwich Village, I found Poor Boys, salami and cheese and chili peppers on great hunks of Italian bread. *Cf.: poor girl—said of a smaller "poor boy":* The Briazz chain of lunch restaurants calls its entry the poor girl and packs it with salami, ham … and tomato.

poor little boy—(pejor.) the ordinary individual; the "man in the street" *(also: poor little guy):* How about voting for me? I'm just a poor little boy who grew up in the neighborhood.

pop music • popular music

pop music—music that evolved out of the rock 'n roll revolution of the 1950s and continues in a definable path to today: With extensive free distribution throughout the Internet, music videos are making a comeback as a promotional vehicle for pop music.

popular music—a wide range of music (from vaudeville to heavy metal) that is most in line with the tastes of the urban middle class: Though his work was primarily in the fields of American popular music and jazz, Tormé had always loved classical music.

pork chop • pork-chopper

pork chop—(U.S. dated sl.) a Black person who is willing to accept a position inferior to that of his white peers: A pork chop has not lost traditional subservient ideology of the South.

Note: *The expression does not correlate in meaning with the phrase* ***carry on like a pork chop****—(Austral. sl.) behave in a foolish or outlandish manner:* There was this slightly demented guy carrying on like a pork chop about how McDonald's is poisoning everyone.

pork-chopper—(U.S. dated sl.) a union official who is in the union for self-interested reasons: They feel contempt for the "pork-chopper"—the former factory workers who have become full-time members of the union staff.

possess oneself of something • possess something

possess oneself of something—1. take possession of smth.: Diving below, he possessed himself of the money he had stowed away in his bundle when he came aboard. 2. appropriate smth. to one's use, especially unlawfully or unfairly; By the aid of his brother who was bishop of Winchester, he possessed himself of the royal treasure.

possess something—have or own something: The young man spent his boyhood at Capri, where his father possessed a house near the residence of the emperor.

possessed by something • possessed of something

possessed by something—having one's mind dominated by some strong emotion: We drop anchor and, possessed by a powerful craving for a cold beer, row to the fish-stained docks.

possessed of something—1. being the owner of smth.: To dream that you are possessed of riches, denotes that you will rise to high places by your constant exertion and attention to your affairs. 2. being in possession of smth. such as a quality: The following document is written under the assumption that the reader is possessed of a sense of humor.

post boat • post ship

post boat—a ship conveying mail or travelers, especially on a regular route: We have the choice of the post boat tomorrow, which takes a limited number of passengers, or the bigger boat on Saturday.

post ship—(UK hist.) a Royal Navy ship of not less than twenty guns: Every ship of twenty guns or more was a post-ship, and a man was ordinarily said to be posted, that is, appointed to command a ship.

post box • post-office box

post box—(UK) a box in a public place in which letters are deposited for dispatch: There is no way to retrieve a letter once it has been dropped into a post box.

post-office box—a private box or pigeon hole in a post office where letters are kept until called for: The following evening Dillon found in his post-office box a letter of one line.

See also: letter box / mailbox.

Post Office, the • post office

Post Office, the—the public department responsible for postal services: The government encouraged the Post Office to establish its own banking service.

post office—a building where postal business is carried out: From the city post office he sent off two telegrams.

post-office order • postal order

post-office order—(UK) a money order in which the name of the payee does not appear, but is transmitted from the issuing to the paying post office: To procure a post-office order it is requisite to apply at an office and wait while certain forms are being filled up.

postal order—(UK) a money order issued by a post office for one of a number of fixed sums payable at any post office to a named payee: Postal orders are issued at the post office counter upon payment of the postal order amount plus charges.

***Note:** Neither expression correlates in meaning with the phrase **mail order**— an order for goods to be sent by post:* Mail order has grown rapidly in recent years. As warehouses are situated in low-rent areas and there is no need of a sales staff, overheads are low.

pour point • pourpoint

pour point—the lowest temperature at which a substance (such as oil) flows and below which it is too viscous to be poured: The average specified pour-point for lubricating oils has been lowered from 30 to about 10°F.

pourpoint—(hist.) a man's padded and quilted close-fitting garment, worn in the 14th and 15th centuries: The military pourpoint was of leather or cloth, stuffed and quilted.

practicable suggestion • practical suggestion

practicable suggestion—a suggestion that can be carried out, or put into practice: This is not a practicable suggestion, at least at this time, for several reasons. It is unlikely that two new positions can be established...

practical suggestion—a suggestion that is useful if carried out successfully: A practical suggestion is to increase the number of training schools to meet the demand for additional teachers.

Prayer Book, the • prayer book

Prayer Book, the—the book of prayers used in Church of England services: Subsequent revisions of the Prayer Book have introduced into the English Matins and Evensong elements foreign to the ancient Hours.

prayer book—a book containing prayers: Mahzor has come to mean the festive prayer book, as distinguished from the Jewish prayer book (Siddur) used on ordinary sabbaths and on weekdays.

preparatory school *(UK)* • preparatory school *(U.S.)*

preparatory school (UK)—fee-paying private junior school which prepares pupils for admission to independent secondary school: Laurence attended a "preparatory school" from the time he was 8 years old until he was 13.

preparatory school (U.S.)—fee-paying private senior school which prepares pupils for admission to a university: Egger intends to spend more time with her daughters, 18 and 16, who attend preparatory school out of state.

press agency • press agentry

press agency—(also: news agency) an organization that provides news coverage to newspapers, etc.: According to a report issued by Reuters press agency, about 600 people have been evacuated after Mount Egon on Flores island started to erupt.

***Note:** The expression does not correlate in meaning with the phrase **press agent**— a person employed to arrange favorable publicity for a firm, public figure, etc:* The development of a fine reputation as a surgeon is not built by a press agent or a web site.

press agentry—the promotion of entertainment stars, politicians, etc. to magazines, radio, and television: When press agentry began it was much more basic and considered to be vile and base by social critics and newspaper editors.

press mark • press-mark

press mark—a mark left on fabric by the impress of an iron: If press marks appear on the right side of the garment, hold the fabric in the steam of a kettle to remove them.

press-mark—a mark stamped on a (library) book: Seymour de Ricci shows how much can be learned from the study of press-marks by anyone concerned with the provenance of books.

press someone's buttons • press the panic button

press someone's buttons—(also: push someone's buttons) draw a strong emotional reaction, especially anger, from a person: It is very difficult to press his buttons because he is careful not to let his emotions control him.

press the panic button—(also: push the panic button) overreact to a stressful situation: I fail to understand as to why the investors have pressed the panic button at a time when a new Government has not taken over.

presume on something • presume something

presume on something—take undue advantage of smth.; go beyond the proper limits: Most of these publishers are happy to send out a free sample; however don't presume on their generosity.

presume something—suppose that smth. is reasonable or possible: If we shouldn't presume his guilt before the facts come out, then we shouldn't presume his innocence, either.

pretend something • pretend to something

pretend something—put forward a false claim as a reason or excuse for smth.: The tobacco industry had known for some time about the harm caused by tobacco products, yet it pretended ignorance.

pretend to something—put forward a claim to smth.: One of the most destructive institutions in our society is the one that pretends to the honor of being the most compassionate: government welfare.

prevail on someone • prevail over someone

prevail on someone—(also: prevail with someone) persuade a person (to do smth.): She had turned a deaf ear to the persuasions by which they sought to prevail on her.

prevail over someone—(liter.) gain victory or achieve superiority over a person *(also: prevail against someone):* The heroes of these films inevitably prevail over their villainous opponents.

Primate of All England • Primate of England

Primate of All England—the Archbishop of Canterbury: In England both the archbishops are primates, the archbishop of Canterbury being entitled "primate of all England."

Primate of England—the Archbishop of York: The parish clerk was duly authorized by the Primate of England to monotone the Psalms at Matins and Evensong.

Privacy Act, the • Privacy Protection Act, the

Privacy Act, the—(U.S.) the 1974 statute that forbids government to disclose information about individuals and gives individuals the right to see, make copies of, and correct inaccuracies in their files: Under a 1984 amendment to the Privacy Act, agencies may not rely on exemptions in the Privacy Act to withhold information that would otherwise be available.

Privacy Protection Act, the—(U.S.) the 1980 statute that makes it unlawful to search for or seize any material intended for dissemination to the public: The actions of your office stand in disregard of the Privacy Protection Act of 1980, and your remarks ignore a bedrock principle of our democratic society — the role of a free and independent press.

private eye • public eye

private eye—(coll.) a private detective working for a fee: The cops don't like private eyes much. *Cf.: private eyeful—(coll.) a pretty girl or woman employed by a detective agency:* Both in quality and quantity ... this San Francisco private eyeful exceeded her sister sleuths.

public eye—1. public attention or notice: It was a gramophone recording that first brought her before the public eye. 2. public opinion or judgment: He resumed his place in the public eye as the thundering Jove of the Opposition.

private school *(UK)* • private school *(U.S.)*

private school (UK)—independent school that is funded wholly by the payment of fees: I was a teacher in one of those private schools, which was basically a very expensive crammer for the sons of oil sheiks.

private school (U.S.)—independent school supported in part by the public (state) funds: Douglas was sent to a swanky private school but was still unable to pass the U.S. Army officers' selection board.

See also: public school (UK) / public school (U.S.)

pro and con • pros and cons

pro and con—for and against *(used as an adjective or adverb):* In these hot political times, the pro and con facts should be presented and the people should voice their opinions.

pros and cons—*(used as a noun)* the arguments in favor and in opposition: He would weigh the pros and cons of an issue, then make up his mind.

proceed to something • proceed with something

proceed to something—move on to the next stage in smth.: Sixty votes were required to stop debate and proceed to a vote on the nomination for Pryor.

proceed with something—continue with the chosen activity: The government will proceed with the talks and the outcome will be presented to the committee.

profit from something • profiteer from something

profit from something—be benefited or gain advantage from smth.: I have not solicited Professor Allen's financial counsel, but have profited from his advice on many other matters.

profiteer from something—make large profits unfairly, especially taking advantage of times of scarcity: When the war ended, the traders who had profiteered from the shortage went out of business.

prohibition law • prohibitory law

prohibition law—a law prohibiting the making or sale of alcoholic drinks, specifically in the USA in the period 1920–1933: A petition will be circulated calling for repeal of the state's liquor prohibition law.

prohibitory law—1. a law prohibiting the making or sale of alcohol: A prohibitory law was passed in Maine in 1846, and in 1851 a more stringent one, including the provision for the seizure and destruction of intoxicating liquors. 2. a law designed to prohibit smth.: State and federal courts have previously recognized medical necessity defenses against the strict prohibitory laws regarding marijuana.

protective belt • safety belt

protective belt—1. a kind of supportive brace made of highly elastic material: Ballesteros wore a protective belt to cushion his aching back. 2. a long narrow strip of forest to protect crops, etc.: A sinuous, chaotic river with a thick protective belt of forests became a contained, channelized canal.

safety belt—a strap attached to a seat in a car or airplane to hold the passenger in his seat in the event of an accident: He would have been killed if he hadn't been wearing a safety belt.

Note: *The expression is not equivalent in meaning to the compound* ***lifebelt****— a large ring used to keep a person afloat and prevent him from drowning:* The lifelines — easier to use and more accurate than lifebelts — were provided.

protest against something • protest something

protest against something—express one's opposition to smth.: In a recent number of the Guy's Hospital Gazette the editor protests against the too free use of students as blood donors.

protest something—affirm smth. strongly against opposition: Rachel protested her innocence for those long twelve years, claiming that it was Daniel who fired the fatal shot.

proud of someone • proud to someone

proud of someone—*(also: proud for someone)* having or showing a proper pride in smb.: He's my son, and he's a chip off the old block, and I'm proud of him.

proud to someone—thinking oneself superior to a person: You must not be proud to those who are less fortunate than yourself.

provide cover against something • provide cover from something

provide cover against something—1. offer protection against rain, snow, etc.: The patios could be surrounded by porches that would provide cover against the rain. 2. insure a person against loss, damage, etc.: This will cover all the risks that are listed, but is extended to provide cover against accidents in the home.

provide cover from something— *= provide cover against something 1:* John was soaked before he reached the first brick building that provided cover from the rain.

public house • public housing

public house—a licensed saloon or bar: Both these sorts of public house are essentially working class; the blackcoat's pub is another sort of place.

Note: *a) The expression is not equivalent in meaning to the phrase* ***public bar****—(UK) a drinking room in a pub where drinks are sold at the counter, as contrasted with a "saloon bar" or "lounge bar" where tables are provided and drinks are brought by waiters:* Pubs usually have two separate rooms; first, public bar which is in general frequented more by men ... second, lounge bar in which there is more equal number of men and women.

b) The expression does not correlate in meaning with the phrase ***public home****— a communal building:* There are a number of hospitals, asylums and public homes, including ten public hospitals, the largest of which is the Toronto General hospital.

public housing—low-rent dwellings owned or administered by a government: When federal officials hoped to proceed to more substantial matters such as public housing and public assistance, the states turned balky.

public school *(UK)* • public school *(U.S.)*

public school (UK)—prestigious fee-paying independent secondary school, usually boarding: They called that kind of school a public school, which in England was the name for a private school which your parents have to pay quite a lot of money to send you to.

public school (U.S.)—non-fee-paying school supported by public funds and controlled by a local governmental authority: The rates have been lowered and the town people had been wooed to send their sons to Gilford instead of to public school.

See also: private school (UK) / private school (U.S.).

pull a face • pull a long face

pull a face—show one's dislike, disgust, or derision by one's facial expression: He pulled a face as if he had heard a slate pencil gritting against a slate.

pull a long face—assume an unhappy, dismal expression: Peter pulled a long face when the results of the competition were announced.

pull foot • pull someone's leg

pull foot—(dated) leave in a hurry; run with all one's might: The whole crew pulled foot as if Old Nick had held them in chase.

pull someone's leg—(coll.) tease or mislead smb. humorously: Stanley knew they were pulling his leg, but instead of finding it amusing he felt uneasy.

See also: drag one's feet / drag one's foot.

pull in one's claws • pull in one's horns

pull in one's claws—(also: draw in one's claws) be less hostile and aggressive: Maybe his obviously terrible political tactics of the last few months have made him pull in his claws.

pull in one's horns—(also: draw in one's horns) be less keen or active, and more careful: To buy when the buying is good, and to pull in my horns when things are negative. I try to respond to the market...

pull it off • pull it out

pull it off—cause smth. to happen; succeed in a difficult attempt: With Jean as leader of the party, the Liberals can pull it off. They can win the election.

pull it out—(Sport) barely win; win just before the end: Despite Peyton's extremely lackluster day we managed to pull it out with our running game and versatility.

pull on the heartstrings • pull the strings

pull on the heartstrings—(also: tug at the heartstrings) stir deepest feelings or affections: The group's songs have the ability to pull on the heartstrings of listeners and carry elevating messages of hope and warmth.

pull the strings—(also: pull strings) 1. secretly exert influence and power: Tony's uncle had the title of boss but it was obvious to all of us who really pulled the strings. 2. obtain smth. through the influence of people one knows: Is it possible to get anything done around here without pulling strings?

***Note:** The expression does not correlate in meaning with the phrase **pull the string of the shower-bath**—(rare) cause smth. concealed to be made known suddenly:* Why can't he pull the string of the shower bath? Why is it all locked up, refrigerated? Because he's a priest, a mystery monger.

pull one's socks up • work one's socks off

pull one's socks up—(UK coll.) make an effort to do better; improve one's performance: Brian, you'd better pull your socks up if you want to pass the exam.

work one's socks off—(coll.) work very hard: I've been incredibly busy working my socks off for the last couple of months.

See also: beat the socks off someone / knock someone's socks off.

pull one's wire • pull wires

pull one's wire—(sl., of a male) masturbate: Remember what I said about sex. Keep away from the maids and pretty boys. As for pulling your wire, that's no occupation for a gentleman.

pull wires—(also: pull strings) 1. obtain smth. through the influence of people one knows: Us guys pull wires to get jobs as guards, and you convicts go over the wall whenever you can. 2. secretly exert influence and power: Vanderbilt immediately got busy pulling wires; and when the resolution came up for vote, a number of Senators sprang up to withdraw Vanderbilt's name.

pull someone down • pull someone under

pull someone down—1. weaken a person in health: My mother tried to kill herself as her chronic degenerative disease pulled her down. 2. reduce smb. to a lower level morally; make smb. humble: His opponents often quoted the lackluster performance of the party during this time to pull him down.

***Note:** The expression is not antonymous in meaning to the phrase **pull someone up**—1. make a driver bring his vehicle to a stop:* Somebody thought it was a sidecar without the bike and even the police pulled me up and said, "is that a real car?" 2. *express one's disapproval of a person's behavior:* The class was full and the teacher pulled him up for being late before he got to his desk.

pull someone under—cause a person to go under water: At the time of the accident she saw him hanging onto a rock before the current pulled him under.

pull something to pieces • take something to pieces

pull something to pieces—1. destroy or dismantle smth.: While we were out, our dog pulled to pieces two of our sofa cushions. 2. criticize smth. severely: I explained my theory and he just pulled it to pieces.

take something to pieces—(of machinery, etc.) take smth. apart so that it is in separate pieces: He took to pieces and reassembled an entire engine.

pull the devil by the tail • twist the lion's tail

pull the devil by the tail—be constantly in difficulties or financial straits: He was tired of knocking about, of pulling the devil by the tail.... Would he never get a good job?

twist the lion's tail—provoke the resentment of the British people *(used with reference to foreign insults to Great Britain):* I took a silent vow never again to twist the lion's tail editorially.

pull the plug on someone • put a plug in for someone

pull the plug on someone—1. remove life-supporting equipment from a terminal patient: David's prayers awoke his friend from a coma several days before they were going to pull the plug on him. 2. discontinue a person's employment: Remember how many reporters complained and talked about Jayson long before his editors finally decided to pull the plug on him?

put a plug in for someone—highly recommend a person; promote smb.'s interests: Let me put a plug in for the new leader, the guy coming in to take my place. He is my longtime friend.

pull the plug on something • put a plug in for something

pull the plug on something—stop working on smth.; put an end to an activity: You should have a contingency fund to cover unexpected costs that could force you to pull the plug on the project.

put a plug in for something—highly recommend a product, etc.; advertise or promote smth.: I want to put in a plug for a wonderful little paperback entitled "Waves and Beaches."

pull the plug out • pull the stops out

pull the plug out—stop working on a project, etc.; put an end to an activity: If he is no longer updating the newsgroup site and decided to pull the plug out, would that be the end of the newsgroup?

pull the stops out—apply all one's energy to the task in hand; work as hard as possible: We believe in offering a more personal service and we pull the stops out when you need us most.

pull-boat • pulling boat

pull-boat—1. *(hist.)* a barge or boat propelled by pulling a rope: It is a treat to see a powerful young Dutchwoman handle a rope on a pull-boat. 2. *(U.S.)* a motorized flatboat used to draw logs over water: In the cypress swamps of Louisiana there are employed what are known as pull-boats.

pulling boat—a small boat having a flat or rounded bottom and rowlocks for the oars: As one who has paddled thousands of miles facing forward in canoes I couldn't get used to facing aft in a pulling boat.

pump attendant • pumpman

pump attendant—a person who serves motor fuel at a garage or gas station: Harry was pump attendant and not in charge of mechanics.

pumpman—a man in charge of the pumps: The strikers threaten to call out the engineers and pump-men, which would result in the flooding of the mines.

pupil teacher • student teacher

pupil teacher—(UK hist.) a boy or girl preparing to be a teacher, whose time was divided between teaching in an elementary school and being taught by the head teacher: The pupil-teacher, as a rule, we fear, learns little and teaches less.

student teacher—a student of a training college teaching in a school for a certain period as part of the curriculum: A new attitude in the schools would encourage student teachers to take religious education as a subsidiary subject at colleges of education.

Purple Heart • purple hearts

Purple Heart—(U.S.) a military decoration for those wounded in action: Mason returned to Pasadena wearing a Bronze Star and a Purple Heart.

purple hearts—(Drug users) heart-shaped stimulant tablets, especially of amphetamine *(also: pink hearts):* They took more interest in life and stopped taking purple hearts.

purple state • red state

purple state—(U.S.) a state which may vote Democratic or Republican: New Hampshire has been called a purple state for its mix of red (Republican) and blue (Democratic) voters in 2000.

red state—(U.S.) a state voting Republican in a given election, or tending to vote Republican in general: In John Ashcroft's home state of Missouri, Bush received 54 percent of the vote, making it a red state.

push one's fortune • push one's luck

push one's fortune—make an effort to win a good position in the world: I am tired of this life. I want to push my fortune. What is there here for me?

push one's luck—(also: press one's luck) try to make too much of an advantage; expect continued good fortune: He could have been satisfied with this victory. Instead, he chose to push his luck to see just how far he could go.

push oneself • push oneself forward

push oneself— make an effort; force oneself to do smth.: I will push myself to live my life to the fullest and improve this world I live in.

push oneself forward—try to force people's attention on oneself (to make them notice one's abilities, etc.): I do find it painful to push myself forward to complete strangers, in person, by phone or mail.

push someone's buttons • push the panic button

push someone's buttons—(also: press someone's buttons) draw a strong emotional reaction, especially anger, from a person: He knew how to push my buttons better than anyone else but I kept my cool.

push the panic button—(also: press the panic button) overreact to a stressful situation: Everybody is concerned but I don't think anybody ought to push the panic button just yet.

pussyfoot around • tomcat around

pussyfoot around—avoid committing oneself; proceed evasively or cautiously: I think it's great that Randi actually speaks his mind and doesn't pussyfoot around to appease others.

tomcat around—pursue women promiscuously: If he really, really, loved you he wouldn't be tomcatting around. He wants to have a bit on the side and not go through the divorce...

put a bee in someone's bonnet • put a bug in someone's ear

put a bee in someone's bonnet—give a person a compulsive idea that may seem excentric or odd: Mayoral candidate Marcic says his campaign has "put a bee in his bonnet" about public drinking and it is an issue he will pursue.

put a bug in someone's ear—(also: put a flea in someone's ear) give a person a hint or advice about smth.: I tried to put a bug in his ear about making his next film about bike touring, but I'm not sure how successful I was. *Cf.: get the bug—(sl.) develop a strong interest or enthusiasm for a particular activity:* Once you start learning about computers, you get the bug and spend more and more time with them.

put a pistol to one's head • put a pistol to someone's head

put a pistol to one's head—commit suicide; shoot oneself: I'm blowed if I don't put a pistol to my head, and end it, Mrs. Johnson.

put a pistol to someone's head—use threats to force a person to do smth. *(also: hold a pistol to someone's head):* Last time he signed his contract after prolonged negotiations and putting a pistol to his head would be wrong.

put a question to someone • put someone to the question

put a question to someone—ask a person about smth.: I have been trying to put this question to the general for the last year or two — even succeeding in planting it in the *Bulletin of the Atomic Scientists.*

put someone to the question—(dated) subject smb. to torture as a means of obtaining confession: "Did he confess his wizardry when you put him to the question?" "Alas, no," replied Maître Jacques.

Note: *The expression does not correlate in meaning with the phrase* ***call someone into question****— doubt the qualifications or value of a person:* Because of her poor record, we were forced to call Dr. Jones into question.

put a spoke in someone's wheel • put in one's spoke

put a spoke in someone's wheel—said of an action which is likely to hold back a person or proceeding: I have never hinted to Quennebert all the nasty little ways in which you have tried to put a spoke in his wheel.

put in one's spoke—attempt to give advice, or have some say, in a matter: Ulbricht also put in his spoke and said, "We shall do everything to safeguard the prestige of the Westerners."

put an idea into someone's head • put ideas into someone's head

put an idea into someone's head—1. make a person think of smth.: They put an idea into my head. How about having an auction at my party? 2. give smb. undesirable or harmful notions: My dear old boy, what can have put the idea into your head that Europe is against us?

put ideas into someone's head—(also: give someone ideas) 1. = *put an idea into someone's head 2:* If I ever hear you or any of the others trying to put ideas into his head about making easy money, I swear I'll knock that person's teeth in. 2. give a person a falsely high opinion of oneself: Robert didn't become a serious painter until that fool of a teacher put ideas into his head.

put cash on the barrelhead • put cash on the line

put cash on the barrelhead—(also: lay cash on the barrelhead) pay money at the time of the transaction: There was a time when, if a person got sick, he went to his trusted family doctor, and put cash on the barrelhead.

put cash on the line—(also: lay cash on the line) allocate money; make a financial commitment: Their decision to put cash on the line is a strong vote of confidence in the foundation being laid for America's recovery.

Note: *The expression does not correlate in meaning with the phrase* ***put it on the line****—(coll.) speak out firmly and frankly (also: lay it on the line):* She was very mad. She put it on the line and we have no doubt about what she meant.

put down anchors • throw out the anchors

put down anchors—1. moor a ship by lowering its anchors: It is illegal to put down anchors because it upsets the ecosystem that the park is trying to protect. 2. become firmly established at a place: But if you are into nursing, law, or own a business, then you develop roots and you put down anchors.

throw out the anchors—1. *= put down anchors 1:* When the sailors sounded fifteen fathoms, they threw out the anchors because of fear that they would end up on the rocks. 2. *(coll.)* suddenly apply the brakes of a car: If you need to throw out the anchors in a hurry there are large powerful all-round ventilated disc brakes.

put it across someone • put it across to someone

put it across someone—1. get even with a person (by way of retribution or punishment): I was glad that I had put it across him. My pride was involved. There are some remarks which one does not forgive. 2. *(also: put it over on someone)* trick a person into believing smth.; deceive or fool smb.: They succeeded in putting it across large sections of the middle classes that Labor's economics meant financial ruin.

put it across to someone—(also: put it over to someone) make smth. such as an idea, etc. understood by a person; communicate smth. successfully: You may be lacking professional techniques you need to get it all down on paper and put it across to the editors.

put it over on someone • put it over to someone

put it over on someone—1. *(also: put it across someone)* trick a person into believing smth.; deceive or fool smb.: Funny, the way the little man tried to put it over on us, letting on he was just puzzled—not really bothered, as he plainly was. 2. excel or surpass a person: Both parties have to be strong personalities ... so that there's a tug-of-war over who's going to put it over on the other, who's going to get the last word.

put it over to someone—(also: put it across to someone) make smth. such as an idea, etc. understood by a person; communicate smth. successfully: I have tried to put it over to them that some could be without a job if we have to apply for re-election.

put life into something • put something into life

put life into something—(also: bring something to life) make smth. more lively or interesting: I'm glad she's coming, she'll put life into this dull party.

put something into life—fulfill smth. planned; carry smth. into effect: The outcome of this election confirms the correctness of that resolution and the need of putting it into life.

put on the gloves • take off the gloves

put on the gloves—prepare to engage in a serious debate, argument, etc.: When you have the guts to debate the issues on merit instead of intolerance, I'm ready to put on the gloves.

take off the gloves—argue, compete, or deal with smb. harshly: The government has made clear that if any academic challenges government policy, it will take off the gloves. *Cf.: treat someone with kidgloves—display tact and sensitivity when dealing with a person:* You treat some people like second-class humans and generally expect everyone to treat you with kidgloves.

put on weight • put the weight

put on weight—(of a person) become heavier, fatter: I have to go on a diet because I've been putting on a little weight lately.

put the weight—(Sport) put the shot *(throw a heavy iron ball): Toe-board*—a board marking the limit of the thrower's run in putting the weight.

put one's best face on • put one's face on

put one's best face on—assume as pleasant an appearance or manner as possible: She was not a very gracious person but before her aunt Matilda she always put her best face on.

put one's face on—(coll.) put on make-up: I've got to go upstairs and put my face on, very quickly.

put one's foot down • put one's foot to the floor

put one's foot down—(coll.) 1. take up a firm stand on an issue: One of the best things Pope John Paul II has done is to put his foot down about women priests. 2. *(also: put one's foot on it)* accelerate when driving a car: I put my foot down and the Zephyr gathered speed up the slope.

put one's foot to the floor— = put one's foot down 2: Jerome jerked the steering wheel hard while putting his foot to the floor.

See also: get one's feet under the table / put one's feet up.

put one's foot in it • put one's foot on it

put one's foot in it—(coll.) do or say smth. stupid, especially unintentionally: Just when Nan needed to be handled especially carefully, Tim had elected to put his foot in it.

put one's foot on it—(coll.) accelerate when driving a car *(also: put one's foot down):* I don't like driving fast, so I get really afraid when he puts his foot on it.

put one's hand in one's pocket • put one's hands in one's pockets

put one's hand in one's pocket—be ready to spend or provide money: There are other ways of being generous, besides putting your hand in your pocket.

put one's hands in one's pockets—1. *= put one's hand in one's pocket:* We may have to put our hands in our pockets—I don't suppose old Frank has left much. 2. refuse to act or accept responsibility: If he comes upon the baby playing with matches, he isn't just supposed to put his hands in his pockets.

put one's hand on something • put one's hand to something

put one's hand on something—(also: lay one's finger on something) find or locate smth.: I'm afraid I can't put my hand on your letter just at the moment.

put one's hand to something—1. undertake a task; engage in smth.: After her husband died, she put her hand to the job of sorting out his papers. 2. *(of a document)* sign: Once you have put your hand to a contract, it is legally binding.

put one's hands on someone • put the arm on someone

put one's hands on someone—(also: lay one's hands on someone)

1. seize or arrest a person: The police will soon put their hands on the jewel thieves. 2. physically abuse a person: If I could put my hands on the swine who informed on me, he wouldn't do any more spying for a long time.

put the arm on someone—(coll.) 1. demand money, etc. of a person: The lights on the football field need to be replaced. So they put the arm on the alumni, raise enough money, and get the job done. 2. apply pressure to a person: Pett has put the arm on him for a show of solidarity, which Sam elected to promise, evidently without meaning to.

put one's heart into something • set one's heart on something

put one's heart into something—do smth. with enthusiasm: As a lad, I couldn't stick to anything—couldn't seem to put my heart into any sort of work.

set one's heart on something—wish for smth. strongly; be determined about smth.: When once he's set his heart on a thing he won't rest till he gets it.

put one's mind to something • turn one's mind to something

put one's mind to something—(also: set one's mind to something) devote a lot of attention to a task: He put his mind to the problem of establishing a means of supporting those who had taken the pledge of abstinence.

turn one's mind to something—begin to think seriously about smth.: I shook off my feelings of dread and turned my mind to finding a way out of there. *Cf.: turn someone's mind to something—cause a person to think about smth.:* I've been thinking about history ... and your invitation turned my mind to the story of women in the West.

put one's money in something • put one's money on something

put one's money in something—invest one's money in a business in the hope of gain: People are advised not to put their money in companies where there is a high risk.

put one's money on something—(also: lay one's money on something) 1. stake a sum of money on smth. such as a sporting event: If you've got any sense, you'll put your money on that horse I told you of. 2. favor smth.; expect smth. to succeed: I haven't really seen any technology to this date that I would put my money on.

put one's name down for something • put one's name to something

put one's name down for something—1. apply for a position, etc.: He was called up having put his name down for the RAF and after initial training he was sent overseas. 2. promise to subscribe for a certain sum: One man after another said that he would be willing to put his name down for five or six pounds.

put one's name to something—sign a declaration, etc.: The former assistant Chief of Defense Staff put his name to the appeal, alongside retired general Sir Hugh Beach.

See also: give a name to something / give one's name to something.

put one's seal to something • put the seal on something

put one's seal to something—(also: set one's seal to something) give one's authority to smth.: They continue to look for a replacement; a puppet leader to put his seal to a treaty of capitulation.

put the seal on something—(also: set the seal on something) bring smth. to a formal end: Why not have another glass of champagne to put the seal on what will be a truly memorable day.

put one's shoulder to the wheel • set the wheels in motion

put one's shoulder to the wheel—set to work vigorously contributing to a collective endeavor: I want to put my shoulder to the wheel, together with others, to help make Atlanta a better place for everyone.

set the wheels in motion—get smth. started: To set the wheels in motion, the very first step is to complete an application form and skills checklist.

See also: keep the wheels turning / spin the wheels.

put oneself in someone's place • take the place of someone

put oneself in someone's place—(also: put oneself in someone's shoes) imagine oneself to be in smb.'s position or predicament: Maybe I am overreacting, but put yourself in my place. How should I explain all this to my manager?

Note: *The expression does not correlate in meaning with the phrase* ***put someone in his place****—1. scold a person, usually for rude remark or bad behavior:* He is being so mean to the customers. Someone needs to put him in his place! *2. remind smb. in an angry way that he is not as important as he thinks he is:* Somebody please put him in his place. As a scientist, I hate it when he speaks for "all scientists."

take the place of someone—replace or supersede a person: Emile owed his education to an aunt, a saintly woman who took the place of his deceased mother.

Note: *Neither expression correlates in meaning with the phrase* ***swap places with someone****—exchange seats, jobs, etc. with another person:* In France last year there was an inmate who swapped places with his twin and escaped.

put oneself in someone's shoes • step into someone's shoes

put oneself in someone's shoes—(also: put oneself in someone's place) imagine oneself to be in smb.'s position or predicament: Lest the readers think that I am being too hard on Mr. Blair, or not "putting myself in his shoes," let me briefly explain my situation.

step into someone's shoes—succeed a person in a job, position, etc.: He will retire soon and there are several people hoping to step into his shoes. *Cf.: wait for dead men's shoes—wait for the death of a person with the hope of succeeding to his possessions or office:* The whole propertied class is waiting for dead men's shoes all the time.

See also: be in someone's shoes / fill someone's shoes.

put out the flags • show the flag

put out the flags—celebrate some special occasion, such as one's victory, success, etc.: I think it is premature to put out the flags for the government's proposals.

show the flag—(also: fly the flag) support or represent one's country (by attending an event): The Kuwaiti team won no medals, but said they were only in Peking to show the flag.

put someone away • put someone off

put someone away—1. confine a person in a mental home or prison: It was like those nightmares in which the dreamer sees himself put away for lunacy. 2. *(euph., of an animal)* put to death: The dog Billy was dying, and in September he had to be put away.

put someone off—1. allow a person to leave a vehicle: Would you please put me off at the railway station? 2. discourage a person from smth.: I've been trying to see you, but your secretary keeps putting me off. 3. distract smb. from work or an activity: The singer was put off by a sudden noise outside, and was unable to continue.

Note: *The expression does not correlate in meaning with the phrase* ***lay someone off****— stop employing a person (because of a lack of work):* Hundreds of workers were laid off when the factory was closed after the fire.

put someone in • put someone inside

put someone in—1. employ smb. for a specific position: The post office was moved five miles to the railroad station, and they put in a new man. 2. enter smb. for an examination, contest, etc.: At first the manager refused to put me in but the fans almost started a riot, screaming to let me play. 3. get a person elected: Until the people have had a chance to vote on his performance in his first term, I don't think we should be asked to put him in.

put someone inside—(coll.) put a person in prison: Sharon Gilmour was childish and spoiled, and was put inside on drug charges.

put someone in charge • put someone on a charge

put someone in charge—cause a person to have supervision or control of smth.: The day when the editor put me in charge of a department was an important mile post.

put someone on a charge—(legal) accuse a person of a particular offence: Patrick trembles with fear and relief when he thinks of Mr. Fergusson who first put him on a charge.

See also: take charge of someone / take someone in charge.

put someone into the chair • send someone to the chair

put someone into the chair—(also: put someone in the chair) 1. elect a person chairman: Most of the meetings were held in our Church House, and at all of them I was put into the chair. 2. nominate a person to a position of authority: A demagogue of greater talent may practically pull the wires of a President whom he has put into the chair.

send someone to the chair—sentence a criminal to death by electrocution: "Reckon what they'll do to Floyd for that?" "Send him to the chair probably," Jim Howard said.

put someone on to someone • put someone through to someone

put someone on to someone—1. put smb. in touch with a person, especially by telephone: John insisted on being put on to the man in charge. 2. inform of a person's whereabouts (so that he can be caught): Sooner or later he will be spotted in the street, and the police will be put on to him.

put someone through to someone— = put someone on to someone 1: He tells me that he can't help me but he will put me through to someone who can.

put someone on trial • take someone on trial

put someone on trial—cause a person to be tried in a court of law: Four persons were put on trial as participators in the attempt.

take someone on trial—see whether smb. is suitable for a job by letting the person do it for a short time: I will take the maid for a month on trial.

put someone out of oneself • take someone out of oneself

put someone out of oneself—overpower smb. with a strong emotional effect as to make a person helpless or ineffective: I had never faced the grim fear exactly in this shape before. It put me out of myself for a little time.

take someone out of oneself—amuse or interest a person so as to distract his attention from his worries or concerns: There was nothing that he could do — no action which would take him out of himself and ease the tension of his thoughts.

Note: *Neither expression is antonymous in meaning to the phrase* ***bring someone to oneself****—1. cause a person to return to consciousness:* A glass of ice water in the face brought her to herself. *2. make smb. return to reality (remember his surroundings, etc.):* The sudden sound of the train whistle brought me to myself.

put someone through • put someone through it

put someone through—1. cause smb. to go through an operation, a course of study, etc.: I was able to put all my students through, except three whose English was the weakest. 2. put smb. in touch with a person by telephone: He lifted the receiver — listened and then said: "Put her through."

put someone through it—subject a person to a severe test or trying experience: Evidently she had been put through it in the interval, for she was crying bitterly.

put someone to the acid test • put the acid on someone

put someone to the acid test—submit smb. to a crucial test that will show his qualities: His words hit me with a jolt of truth, and after listening to him speak, I decided to put him to the acid test.

put the acid on someone—(Austral., NZ sl.) exert pressure on a person (to obtain a loan, favor, etc.): They want to shift the ship at seven. That puts the acid on us.

put someone up for something • put someone up to something

put someone up for something—1. propose smb. as a candidate for a position: We'll put him up for treasurer at the next committee meeting. 2. bring a person into court to stand trial: The jewel thieves will be put up for trial next month.

Note: *The expression is not antonymous in meaning to the phrase* ***put someone down for something****—1. decide that smb. is a particular kind of person:* I fear they put me down for a prig, an upstart, an abominable aristocrat. 2. *put a person's name on a list of participants, contributors, etc.:* We're having a picnic and everyone is bringing something. Can I put you down for potato salad?

put someone up to something—1. prepare smb. for a job or task; instruct a person: Get an expert to put him up to the job in as short a time as possible. 2. encourage a person to behave mischievously or unlawfully: He's not been out of trouble all term, and he's been put up to it by some of the older boys.

put someone's pot on • put the pot on

put someone's pot on—(Austral., NZ sl.) inform against a person; destroy smb.'s prospects: I been there about the same time as you, Tom, and I haven't had a rise yet. Wonder if Myers put my pot on.

put the pot on—(UK sl.) stake a sum of money on smth. such as a sporting event, etc. despite the risk of loss: Altamont put the pot on at the Derby, and won a good bit of money.

put something across someone • put something across to someone

put something across someone—(also: put something over on someone) trick a person into accepting or believing smth.: When I was young and foolish, he put it across me with a hard-luck story.

put something across to someone—(also: put something over to someone) explain or communicate smth. successfully: It was an uphill struggle to put the message across to the media that engineering had a major role to play.

put something back • put something behind

put something back—delay smth. till a later time or date: The subsequent events put back the development program by some three years.

put something behind—1. = *put something back:* The cold weather has put the crops behind by a month. 2. try to forget smth. bad; regard smth. as no longer important: The boys have put behind those early season mishaps in hopes of something better.

put something down for something • put something down to something

put something down for something—1. appoint a date for smth.: Singh pleaded not guilty to aiding and abetting Kamran. His trial was put down for a later date. 2. *(of smb.'s name)* be entered into a list of participants, etc.: Lord Linley, seven-year-old son of Princess Margaret, had had his name put down for Eton.

put something down to something—consider smth. to be the result or consequence of: This outbreak was put down to the lack of vaccination and not the lack of vaccine efficiency.

Note: *Neither expression correlates in meaning with the phrase* ***put something down as something****—describe or characterize smth. as a particular type of thing:* Their labors were put down by historians as a calculated effort to police the world.

put something in hand • take something in hand

put something in hand—undertake a task; begin work on smth.: We have put the work in hand, and it should be completed within the next week.

take something in hand—1. = *put something in hand:* We are just now taking in hand a massive program for the redevelopment of the city center. 2. take charge or control of smth.: She was no business woman, and until her son took them in hand, her affairs were chaotic.

put something in question • put something to the question

put something in question—(also: call something into question) express serious doubts about smth.: The increase in unemployment would arouse such mass opposition that the very existence of capitalism would be put in question.

put something to the question—cause smth. (of importance) to be discussed or considered: We're having a family gathering this evening, and the matter of the annual holiday will be put to the question.

put something on foot • put something on its feet

put something on foot—(also: set something on foot) initiate a process or action: The bishop had decided to put on foot another investigation.

put something on its feet—(also: set something on its feet) make smth. economically self-supporting, especially after a period of difficulties: This summer's good trade should put the business on its feet.

put something on one side • take someone on one side

put something on one side—1. delay consideration of or postpone dealing with smth.: When we first used it, we weren't sure how it would work out, so we only put it on one side. *2.* set smth. aside for some future purpose: Anything I have left over from my week's wages I usually put on one side, for emergencies.

take someone on one side—take a person aside to speak to him in confidence: I was taken on one side by a man I knew vaguely and told to get out of town.

put something on the map • wipe something off the map

put something on the map—(of a town, etc.) cause to be considered important; put into public notice: It was Princess Amelia who helped put the place on the map by taking a holiday here in 1797.

wipe something off the map—(of a town, etc.) completely destroy: A devastating flood several years ago nearly wiped the village off the map.

Note: *The expression does not correlate in meaning with the phrase* ***wipe something off the slate****—agree to forget smth. such as smb.'s debt, misdemeanor, etc.:* The fact that the Japanese commercial whaling interests have had a role in this affair, cannot simply be wiped off the slate.

put something over on someone • put something over to someone

put something over on someone—(also: put something across someone) trick a person into accepting or believing smth.: How else are they going to put this over on James Mason? He is not an idiot.

put something over to someone—(also: put something across to someone) explain or communicate smth. successfully: I seem to have put the idea over to them all right, for they said, "Go ahead."

put the black on someone • put up a black

put the black on soneone—(UK sl.) engage in blackmail: "I'll put him where I want him to be," he repeated. "You're going to put the 'black' on him?" she said, her lips curling.

put up a black—(UK sl.) make a blunder: One day she put up a black.... She had fried our salmon in batter.

put the chill on someone • put the heat on someone

put the chill on someone—1. exert a depressing influence on a person: Export orders are falling as the winds of war put the chill on foreign buyers. 2. *(U.S. sl.)* ignore a person; end social contact with smb. *(also: put the freeze on someone):* They have put the chill on me, I presume for reasons that other types of persons are more easily dealt with.

put the heat on someone—(sl.) put pressure on a person; subject smb. to a severe cross examination *(also: turn the heat on someone):* He told everything about the plan when they put the heat on him.

put the lid on something • take the lid off something

put the lid on something—1. *(also: put the tin lid on something)* cause a plan, an activity, etc. to end: I sympathized with Jimmie's desire, but I very promptly put the lid on his hopes. 2. suppress or "clamp down" on smth.: Their sexual development may have been arrested and unable to grow naturally in an environment that tended to put the lid on those things.

take the lid off something—(also: lift the lid off something) expose or reveal smth. scandalous, shocking, etc. that has been hidden: The board fears that the plan will take the lid off party spending.

put the red flag out • wave the red flag

put the red flag out—show a sign warning of danger: The new symptoms list is more of a means to put the red flag out.... Not every woman experiencing abdominal pain has cancer, of course.

wave the red flag—incite to revolution or violence: They

were paid by the great monopolies to wave the red flag and talk about blowing people up.

Note: *The expression does not correlate in meaning with the phrase* ***wave the flag****—*1. *demonstrate patriotism and loyalty:* I will continue to wave the flag, because I continue to love the ideals that our country represents. 2. *show support for smth.:* This series clearly waved the flag for acupuncture, herbal remedies and alternative medicine in general.

put the screws to someone • screw someone up

put the screws to someone—put extreme pressure on a person: I know that the Department of Finance are putting the screws on the Land Commission to bring their operations to an end.

screw someone up—(sl.) 1. cause harm to a person: Remember, even one hint of a rumor about this type of conduct will screw you up for the rest of your life. 2. make smb. nervous or anxious: One thing that always screws me up here is the food. I have trouble buying it, but the food itself is invariably not what I expected.

put the shoe on the other foot • put the shoe on the right foot

put the shoe on the other foot—experience the opposite situation (when circumstances are reversed): I could put the shoe on the other foot, and think how this would effect me if we turn the tables.

put the shoe on the right foot—(also: lay the saddle upon the right horse) put the blame on the right person: Don't keep on blaming me, Graham was the culprit. Put the shoe on the right foot.

put the skids on something • put the skids under something

put the skids on something—bring smth. to a halt: After World War II put the skids on the big band era, Louis Armstrong and many others cast about for a new direction.

put the skids under something—stop smth. from succeeding or making progress: Will progressively higher interest rates put the skids under our growing economy.

put up a good show • put up a show

put up a good show—perform well; make a good effect: In the words of Osborne, who leads the raid, the important thing is to put up a "good show."

put up a show—(also: put on a show) display an outward appearance or semblance of smth.: I thought I was the only one who wasn't brave — but then I found out that they all were putting up a show.

put words into someone's mouth • take the words out of someone's mouth

put words into someone's mouth—1. tell a person what to say: "So you refuse to explain?" she asked sharply. "Now don't go putting words into my mouth, please," Jean retorted. 2. suggest or claim falsely that a person has said smth.: Frank said fiercely: "She never said anything! You're trying to put words in her mouth!"

take the words out of someone's mouth—say what another person was about to say; anticipate smb.'s words: "Wasn't that a magnificent performance?" "You took the words right out of my mouth!"

Q

qualify as something • qualify for something

qualify as something—be described or characterized in a particular way: The £1 a week rise would not qualify as an exception to the nil norm laid down in the summer.

qualify for something—have the right to smth.; be eligible for smth.: Students who do not qualify for the desired course may repeat the exam.

Queen's College • Queens' College

Queen's College—(UK) Oxford University: The ancient ceremony of serving up a boar's head at Queen's College was duly observed yesterday.

Queens' College—(UK) Cambridge University: The Library is open to all current members of Queens' College and to old members and visiting scholars.

question of the hour • question of time

question of the hour—currently the most debated issue: It is the living question of the hour, and not the dead story of the past, which forces itself into all minds.

question of time—said of smth. that is thought certain to happen sooner or later: Baby-sitting having become firmly established, it was only a question of time before somebody offered to provide a similar service for dogs.

quite a few • quite a lot

quite a few—a considerable number: There are quite a few people with Spanish surnames around here.

quite a lot— = quite a few: Quite a lot of people will telecommute daily to their London offices while living on a Pacific island.

R

radio net • radio network

radio net—a system of intercommunicating radio sets (such as used by a police force, etc.): A re-broadcast system had been installed which allowed them to monitor the police radio net.

radio network—a system of radio stations; a broadcasting organization: This concern to tailor the news to the listener has even spread to National Public Radio, the non-commercial radio network.

ragged blue line • thin blue line

ragged blue line—(U.S.) the Union forces (who wore blue uniforms) in the American Civil war: A ragged blue line of four infantry regiments on line and one in reserve moved across the open valley.

thin blue line—(UK) the police; the protective power of the law: You've heard about the thin blue line that protects property and the owners of property.

See also: all-red line / thin red line.

rail car • railroad car

rail car—a self-propelled railroad vehicle designed to transport passengers: Railcars are often used on minor railway lines where passenger traffic is sparse.

railroad car—a coach for passengers on a train: Persons who drink at a bar, ride in a railroad car, or visit the theater without charge, are called *dead heads.*

rain day • rainy day

rain day—(Meteorology) a day on which the recorded rainfall is not less than 0.01 inch: In July the average number of rain days is only four per month.

rainy day—1. a day having much rain: West Mediterranean islands have cooled off and can have rainy days, but walking is still pleasant. 2. *(in the phrase "for a rainy day")* for a time of special need in the future: We all need money set aside for a rainy day.

raise dust • raise the dust

raise dust—cause a cloud of dust to rise: The galloping horse raised dust out of the dried mud in the gateway to the wood.

raise the dust—1. = *raise dust:* Whirlwinds raised the dust to a great height and moved over the plain like water spouts at sea. 2. *(also: make a dust)* cause turmoil; act in a noisy manner: But who raised the dust? It seems inconceivable that it was anyone on the editorial staff.

raise one's eyes • raise one's sights

raise one's eyes—(also: lift up one's eyes) look upwards: When the door opened gently, he never raised his eyes — he was only conscious that someone entered the room.

raise one's sights—establish higher goals for oneself: She seemed content as a paralegal, but we thought she should raise her sights and get a law degree.

rake over old coals • rake someone over the coals

rake over old coals—(UK) try to bring back old problems that may cause trouble: What's the point of raking over old coals? Opening every wound we thought was properly healed.

rake someone over the coals—(U.S.) criticize or scold a person severely: He was raked over the coals for allowing the club to become the laughing stock of professional sports.

range of a rifle • rifle range

range of a rifle—the maximum distance to which a rifle can fire bullets: It's a powerful weapon but the range of this rifle is very limited.

rifle range—1. a place where one can practice shooting with a rifle: There was a rifle range nearby and Major Frimley taught rifle shooting to the girls. 2. = *range of a rifle:* I told Richardson to ride on and attract the attention of the deer away from me while I crept up within rifle range.

rat on someone • rat out on someone

rat on someone—(sl.) report smb.'s wrongful activities to the police, etc.: Kent is willing to do anything to get out even rat on his fellow convicts in order to get an early parole.

rat out on someone—(sl.) 1. desert or betray smb.; leave a person at a critical time: He would never rat out on his family cause underneath it all he loves them. 2. = *rat on someone:* He was sentenced to six years but only served eighteen months because he agreed to rat out on his drug suppliers.

rat race • rat-racing

rat race—1. said of a situation marked by hyperactivity and stress: I began to realize that the quality of life mattered more to me than the rat race in the office. *Cf.: mouse race—(a play on "rat race") a lower-stress lifestyle that results from moving to a smaller community or taking a less demanding job:* There is a new phenomenon: "the mouse race," a scaled-down version of the urban rat race that has long-time residents heading for even smaller towns. 2. a fiercely competitive struggle to maintain one's position: A boy's got to have guts to make his way in this rat race of a modern world.

Note: *The expression does not correlate in meaning with the phrase* ***rat run****—1. a maze-like passage by which rats move about:* The rat-runs had been stopped up, and he killed nearly a hundred rats before he paused. 2. *used of smth. resembling narrow labyrinthine passages:* Hurrying along the rat-runs of the Tube, she slipped her hand into his pocket. 3. *(UK coll.) a short cut taken by a motorist on residential side street in order to avoid the heavy traffic on a main route:* Rat runs are usually taken by drivers who are familiar with the local geography.

rat-racing—(Pilots) a playful form of high-speed flying in which airplanes pursue or attempt to out-maneuver each other: I've forgotten what we were doing — probably rat-racing ... where we chased each other all over the sky.

reach first base • touch base

reach first base—(also: get to first base) get to the initial stage in accomplishing smth.: Negotiations had not even reached first base because the Government was continually using delaying tactics.

touch base—(coll.) contact smb.; confer with a person *(also: touch bases):* Forstmann had touched base with his partners and found that they harbored a vague distaste for the tobacco business.

reach for the moon • reach for the sky

reach for the moon—(also: reach for the stars) have a high ambition or purpose; try to do smth. impossible: Our learning experience was rich and fulfilling and enabled each one of us to reach for the moon in our own way.

reach for the sky—1. = *reach for the moon:* Thompson was the kind of man that never stopped dreaming and who always reached for the sky. *Cf.: sky is the limit—there is no limit to what a person can achieve:* They have found that, in terms of both salary and career success, the sky is the limit. 2. *(sl.)* used (by a gunman) as a command to raise hands *(also: reach for the ceiling):* Danielson crawled up, jammed his rifle in the enemy's back and told him to reach for the sky.

reach out after someone • reach out to someone

reach out after someone—extend one's hand in an effort to grasp a person: Don reached out after Doris, but she slipped away before he could get a good hold on her.

reach out to someone—1. offer help or support to a person: You reached out to me just when I needed help the most. 2. make an effort to communicate with smb. in order to persuade or inform: Modern politicians try to reach out to ordinary people in their speeches.

reach the bottom of something • reach to the bottom of something

reach the bottom of something—(also: get to the bottom of something) get to the lowest point of smth.: We were glad to reach the bottom of the mountain.

reach to the bottom of something—extend to the lowest point of smth.: That rope reaches to the bottom of the tower. You grab hold and attempt to climb out.

react on something • react to something

react on something—1. have an effect on smth.: Heat reacts on certain substances to change their chemical composition. 2. act in response to smth.: How will people react on this information in Russia and China? And in other countries?

react to something— = *react on something 2:* Observe carefully how the bacteria will react to this stimulus.

Note: *Neither expression correlates in meaning with the phrase* ***react against something****—act in opposition to smth.:* People will not endure oppression for ever; sooner or later they will react against it.

read my lips • read someone's lips

read my lips—(may sound slightly impolite) listen closely to what I am saying: Let me repeat myself this once, and Zepp, be sure to read my lips as I do so.

Note: *The expression does not correlate in meaning with the phrase* ***read me***—1. *(in radio communication) hear my voice; hear my message:* Come in Mike H. from Wellington, New Zealand, do you read me, over? 2. *(also: read my mind) know what I am thinking:* He's said before that he can always read me, that anyone can read me. That I'm almost too open for my own good.

read someone's lips—know what people are saying by looking at the shapes their lips make when they talk: We can hear words being spoken to us or read someone's lips to interpret what they are saying if we are hearing impaired.

ready at something • ready with something

ready at something—proficient in a subject: The learned gentleman here began to discover that he was not quite so ready at arithmetic ... and stopped short in his calculations.

ready with something—prompt with smth. such as an answer, help, etc.: You must be ready with an explanation of why you need the money and what the use of the money will be.

real life • real live

real life—the life lived by actual people, as distinct from fiction, etc.: A deliberate documentary film must be a transcript of real life, a bit of what actually happened.

real live—*(attrib., usually joc.)* said of a person or thing actually existing (not pretended or simulated): Rosemary had taken a great deal of trouble to catch "a real live" philosopher.

real men • real people

real men—1. said of actually existing men: How ungraspable is the fact that real men ever did fight in real armor. 2. men possessing the essential qualities expected of a male person: He was a real man, a real general man, he drove fast cars and flew an aeroplane as well as being a fine musician.

real people—1. actual and not imaginary people: This form of literature uses real people or events as essential elements in an otherwise fictional rendition. 2. *(Cinema or TV casting)* non-actors: We want you to cast for this scene on the street—get us some real people.

reasonable to someone • reasonable with someone

reasonable to someone—said of smth. appearing moderate or sensible to a person: The last session of Congress worked long and hard on this issue and their compromise seems to be reasonable to me.

reasonable with someone—said of smb. trying to persuade a person in a judicious, way: I try to be very reasonable with him; I understand he is growing up and away from us but this behavior makes life miserable for all of us.

receive a reward • receive an award

receive a reward—receive smth. such as money in recompense or for some special service: He was captured in Pakistan and is now in jail. The informant received a reward for sharing this knowledge.

receive an award—receive a prize, medal, etc. for outstanding performance or quality: Hoare received the award in 1980 for his contributions to the design of programming languages.

receiving order • reception order

receiving order—*(legal)* an order from a court which protects the debtor's property and prevents creditors from suing him without the permission of the court: On 23 May 1983 a receiving order was made, and on 11 November 1983 Mr. Dennis was adjudicated bankrupt.

reception order—*(legal)* the official order required for detention of a person in a mental hospital: The Reception Order of a justice is sufficient authority to take the patient to, and to receive him in an asylum, or to detain him there.

receiving room • reception room

receiving room—1. a place for the reception of things: The malt receiving room contains two malt grids with strong wire screens at the bottom. 2. a room to which visitors are admitted: The patient walks into the receiving room of the hospital for a diagnosis.

reception room— = *receiving room 2:* He entered the paneled reception room, decorated in Danish modern.

reckon of something • reckon on something

reckon of something—be of the opinion concerning smth.: What do you reckon of the Joneses' new house?

reckon on something—depend on smth.; count on smth.: The proprietors of the Casino reckon on human foolishness and greed.

red as a beetroot • red as cherries

red as a beetroot—1. red in the face from feeling ashamed: If his friends talked about girls, he went as red as a beetroot. 2. sunburnt: After a day shooting around Sydney, they are as red as a beetroot! But if it was only the harsh sun that they had to counter, life would have been easy.

red as cherries—1. said of rosy complexion (indicating good health): Today you see them [women] bouncing, red as cherries, and tomorrow they exhibit themselves effete as dead weeds.... 2. said of flushed cheeks: My little brother, cheeks as red as cherries and eyes all a-glow, comes bursting in the house after a long day of sledding. 3. said of fresh red lips: She had long, lustrous, Japanese eyes, very quick and alert, lips as red as cherries and the most beautiful teeth in the world.

red cap • red hat

red cap—1. *(UK)* a military policeman: She used to take me to nightclubs tucked away which no officers or redcaps knew about. 2. *(coll.)* a railway porter: Why don't you get a red cap to help you carry your bags. 3. the European goldfinch: Many birds seem to have particular names in these parts. Woodpeckers are called pickatrees, and goldfinches, red-caps.

red hat—1. a cardinal's hat as the symbol of the position: To receive the red hat he must go to Rome. 2. *(UK Army)* a staff officer: A number of very high-ranking officers were invited. ...The visiting red hats were not impressed.

Red Cross, the • red cross

Red Cross, the—an international organization bringing relief to victims of war or natural disaster: The Red Cross woman brought me khaki trousers, skivvy shirt and a left shoe.

red cross—the emblem of an ambulance service: A Daimler scout car, flying a red cross, was moving and halting ... collecting wounded.

red fever • red light fever

red fever—1. an infectious disease with fever, headache, and rash, transmitted by rat fleas *(Xenopsylla cheopis):* Sick with red fever, John Lodi and his children do not catch up to Lafayette in Indian Territory until six months later. 2. *(U.S., euph.)* a sympathy to Communism, especially in the 1950s: He went underground and became part of the movement. He got the red fever; for five years he really believed it was the answer.

Note: *The expression is not equivalent in meaning to the phrase* ***scarlet fever***—1. *an infectious disease caused by streptococcus bacteria and characterized by a sore throat, fever, and a sandpaper-like rash on reddened skin:* Scarlet fever is predominantly a disease found in children. 2. *(UK ironic, dated) a passion for soldiers (with reference to their scarlet uniforms):* Nurse-maids are always ready to succumb to the "scarlet fever." A red coat is all powerful with this class.

red light fever—1. nervousness in front of a live microphone or video camera: Obviously, the singer had red light fever.

The producer should have given that guy some sort of comfort level. 2. seeking media attention: She seems to have forgotten that her job is to report the news, not to make it. ...the lady is suffering from what's known in the trade as red light fever. 3. a tendency to have a false start during a car race or to run a red light: If you noticed, both of the trucks in the finals had red light fever, but Dennis' came on first which made Bob the winner.

red-foot • red-leg

red-foot—hatchet-bill *(an American bird):* Small and long-winged, the male red-foot was indeed handsome.

red-leg—1. *(U.S.)* an artilleryman: Artillerymen are known as "red legs" due to the red stripes traditionally worn on the trousers of their dress uniforms. 2. a red-legged partridge or a redshank: The red-legged partridge is not a native of this country. In 1826 the red-legs were reported "now plentiful in Suffolk." 3. a bacterial disease of frogs: Since 1890, septicemic frog disease (red-leg) has had a devastating effect on frogs kept under laboratory conditions.

red hot peppers • red hots

red hot peppers—(also: Chili peppers) a pungent red pod of the genus *Capsicum:* Add the juice of ½ lemon, salt and a good pinch of dried red hot peppers.

red hots—(U.S.) 1. a type of small candy with a powerful cinnamon flavor: Red Hots are perhaps the best known type of spicy candy. 2. hotdogs, especially sold by street vendors: Whether you call them hot dogs, red hots or frankfurters, try some new recipe ideas.

red in the gills • rosy about the gills

red in the gills—getting red in the face, showing signs of anger or indignation: While calling us round for punishment he got as red in the gills as a turkey-cock.

rosy about the gills—having a fresh complexion *(indicating good health):* Vladimir studied in the mirror the man behind him. And at the same time he had the advantage of seeing his own face, clean-shaved and rosy about the gills.

red liquor • red wine

red liquor—(Dyeing) a substance used for fixing coloring matters on stuffs: Red liquor is much more extensively employed as a mordant than any other preparation of alumina.

red wine—an alcoholic beverage produced from fermented red (or black) grapes: When I take a bottle of red wine to a restaurant, the waiter will ask if I want the bottle opened "so the wine can breathe."

red ribbon • red tape

red ribbon—(the ribbon of) the Order of the Bath: He [Guizot] had his red ribbon on and also his golden fleece.

red tape—bureaucratic routine: There is so much red tape involved in obtaining a contract that it is sometimes almost not worth the time.

Note: *Neither expression correlates in meaning with the phrase* ***red band***—*(UK Prison) a privileged inmate trusted as messenger without supervision:* I would then have a cup of coffee brought to me by a "red band."

reek of something • reek with something

reek of something—1. smell strongly of smth. usually nasty: The whole room reeked of tobacco smoke. 2. suggest or intimate smth. bad: His story reeks of dishonesty; I don't believe a word of it.

reek with something—1. = *reek of something 1:* Sam appeared with Haley's horse by his side, reeking with sweat. 2. seem to be full of smth.: The water was absolutely reeking with all kinds of fish with queer names.

reinvent the flat tire • reinvent the wheel

reinvent the flat tire—(U.S.) make the same mistakes again: You don't have to reinvent the flat tire. There is a world of practical experience that you can take advantage of.

reinvent the wheel—(U.S.) waste time designing smth. that has already been built and accepted: How many times have you reinvented the wheel? We often face situations others have encountered before us.

relieve one's feelings • relieve oneself

relieve one's feelings—use strong language or vigorous behavior when annoyed: The policeman relieved his feelings by dispersing the crowd with well-directed prods of his locust stick.

relieve oneself—1. *(euph.)* defecate or urinate: There's no magic formula for training your dog to relieve himself outside: it takes determination, consistency and proper training techniques. 2. *(dated)* obtain a relief from physical pain or discomfort: The moment an Englishman feels the pragmaticality of his native land too much for his spirits, off he goes, to relieve himself abroad.

relieve someone from something • relieve someone of something

relieve someone from something—1. free a person from smth. which causes problems or afflicts him: More help in the office would relieve me from some of this responsibility. 2. dismiss smb. from a usually responsible position: The captain was relieved from his post when his guilt was proved.

relieve someone of something—1. take from a person smth. heavy to carry: Let me relieve you of that heavy parcel. 2. = *relieve someone from something 1:* You will not be relieved of the care of your children for twenty years. 3. = *relieve someone from something 2:* General Qaalib was ordered to harass opposition leaders and was relieved of his position when he refused such orders . 4. *(euph.)* deprive a person of smth. by stealing it: It did not take the thieves long to relieve the passengers of all their money.

remand center • remand home

remand center—1. *(UK)* an institution to which the court may commit offenders of any age (formerly between the ages of 14 and 21) for temporary detention: A Southampton schoolboy was remanded in custody for seven days to Winchester remand center after the Magistrates decided he was "unruly." 2. *(Canada)* an institution to which the court may commit adult offenders for temporary detention: The Calgary remand center — the first in Alberta — is open for business. The center will house men held in custody between court appearances pending their trials.

remand home—(UK) an institution to which juvenile offenders may be committed by the court for temporary detention: Children from 8 to 16 are sent to remand homes for periods up to one month.

remark on something • remark something

remark on something—say smth. by way of comment: Clinicians have remarked on the similarity between the aroused euphoric state of the gambler and the "high" of the cocaine addict.

remark something—see or notice smth.: The merchant, who had been in Germany, immediately remarked the similarity between this piece of cloth and the fabric of Osnaburgh.

remember doing something • remember to do something

remember doing something—keep in mind smth. that one has done: We remembered seeing many little country churches with ancient horse sheds still at the rear.

remember to do something—bear in mind smth. that one has to do: They kept the Ford in front of the house. It worked all right if they remembered to get it filled with anti-freeze.

render an account for something • render an account of something

render an account for something—provide explanation or justification for one's conduct, etc.: Everything we have comes to us as a gift — and we will have to render an account for how we use what is entrusted to us.

render an account of something—(also: give an account of something) describe smth.; make a statement about smth.: The director is to render an account of the condition and progress of the school.

render something to someone • render something up to someone

render something to someone—1. give or provide smth. (such as assistance, etc.) to a person: Young volunteer workers render a valuable service to the community. 2. surrender smth. such as a fort, city, etc. to the enemy: The capital of French America was rendered to the English, after a most severe campaign.

render something up to someone— = render something to someone 2: After a prolonged siege, the town was rendered up to the insurgents.

rent collection • rental collection

rent collection—collecting money payable periodically for the use of lands, tenements, etc.: As always on a Monday evening, he was kept busy balancing the books from the rent collection on Friday.

rental collection—a collection of books in an otherwise free library that may be borrowed at a daily fee: Rental Collection books can be returned to any Hampton Public Library location.

report of something • report on something

report of something—1. a factual account of smth.: Is it an ill thing that the newspapers should publish detailed reports of divorce-suits? 2. an unconfirmed story or a piece of news: There have been many reports of gas used in the war, but no one knows whether they are true.

report on something—a detailed account of smth. in which opinions, as well as facts, are usually given: When you get back, write a report on everything that was said at the conference.

reproach someone for something • reproach someone with something

reproach someone for something—admonish a person gently for smth.: Don't reproach the child for forgetting, he couldn't help it.

reproach someone with something—blame a person for smth.; charge smb. with a fault or vice: She's not mean or vindictive. That's the last thing with which one could reproach her.

rest home • rest house

rest home—(also: home of rest) 1. a place where the elderly people are housed and cared for: Mary's father had to stay in a rest home for a long time after his operation. 2. a resort facility: The organization of rest homes, where workers may spend their vacation, is a unique development.

rest house—an establishment such as a hostel or a boarding house for travelers: Here there is a rest house with simple but clean accommodation and cooking facilities.

rest on someone • rest with someone

rest on someone—depend on a person: All his hopes now rested upon one friend and patron.

rest with someone—be a person's responsibility: The choice rests entirely with you now.

rest room *(UK)* • rest room *(U.S.)*

rest room (UK)—a room in a public building set aside for staff to take their breaks in: The suite consisted of the operating room, the anesthetic room, the scrub-up room and the doctors' rest room.

rest room (U.S.)—a room in a public place, containing a toilet: I told them about my difficulty locating the restroom in the restaurant. They said, "You can't say restroom or bathroom in Europe."

revenge oneself on someone • revenge someone

revenge oneself on someone—(also: avenge oneself on someone) get even with a person in return for an offence or injury inflicted on oneself: This poor youth revenged himself on his malicious rival by marrying the young lady.

revenge someone—(also: avenge someone) get satisfaction for an offence or injury done to another person: When the news is brought to Achilles he swears never to taste food until he has revenged his friend.

Revised Standard Version, the • Revised Version, the

Revised Standard Version, the—a revision in 1946–1952 of the Authorized Version of the Bible: That has been changed in the Revised Standard Version as follows: "Glory to God in the highest and on earth peace among men..."

Revised Version, the—a revision in 1881–1885 of the Authorized Version of the Bible: Mr. B. Dawson read a paper on the Revised Version of the New Testament. He commended the accuracy of the revisers.

ride a white horse • ride the white horse

ride a white horse—ride a horse of white color: The man who brought the buffalo went to them on horseback, riding a white horse.

ride the white horse—(sl., euph.) have one's menstrual period: She's riding the white horse. That's why she's a little cranky.

ride high • ride tall

ride high—(also: ride high in the saddle) 1. have a period of success, popularity, etc.: The new government has been riding high in the polls for several months now. 2. *(of a boat)* sit high in the water: It was made of welded aluminum, stuffed with plenty of lightweight Styrofoam to make the boat ride high in the water. *Cf.: ride low—(of a boat) sit low in the water:* Ballast water may also be carried so that a ship rides low enough in the water to pass under bridges.

Note: *The expression does not correlate in meaning with the phrase* ***ride high on the hog****—(coll., also: live high on the hog) live in a lavish or extravagant manner:* Oh, yes, sometimes you ride high on the hog, but most of the time, you settle for the limits the world has placed on you.

ride tall—(also: walk tall) show dignity and self-respect: Doesn't matter if you eat corn mash and saddle your own horse; you can still ride tall.

ride high in the saddle • ride the high horse

ride high in the saddle—(also: ride high) have a period of success, popularity, etc.: Only months after facing the prospect of a humiliating exit from politics, the president is riding high in the saddle.

ride the high horse—be haughty or arrogant; act in a superior way: Come, come, my dear fellow, do not try to ride the high horse. You do not wish to show me your passport and I will not insist.

ride on the pig's back • ride on the sheep's back

ride on the pig's back—(coll.) experience a period of success; enjoy extreme good fortune: The self-employed are leaving the country.... If the place is such a goldmine why do they not stay and continue riding on the pig's back?

ride on the sheep's back—(Austral. sl.) used pertaining to the success of the Australian sheep industry *(a pun on the former expression):* After riding on the sheep's back, will Australia end up exporting our ideas and knowledge to the world?

ride Shank's pony • ride the cotton pony

ride Shank's pony—(dated) go on foot; walk: Ed and I chose to ride Shank's pony rather than catch the bus, and we walked back to the camping area.

ride the cotton pony—(U.S. sl., euph.) have one's menstrual period: She doesn't feel like going out with us 'cause she's riding the cotton pony.

ride someone on a rail • ride the rails

ride someone on a rail—punish a person by carrying him on a rail to be mocked: The gentleman ought to be ducked, ridden on a rail, tarred and feathered.

ride the rails—(U.S. sl.) travel by rail, especially without a ticket: After college, Philip took off on a five-week tour of the country, riding the rails with hobos, going all the way to Chicago.

right as nails • right on the nail

right as nails—(coll., dated) said of smth. being satisfactory, safe, or comfortable: I really believe, in a fortnight I shall be as right as nails.

right on the nail—(coll.) correct; exactly right: The recommendation to keep stable hours is right on the nail — I've tried to "educate" my son about this but he has not paid much attention.

right-hand • right-handed

right-hand—1. said of smth. situated on the right side: Carry on past the school and take the right hand turning towards Heddington. 2. said of a car with right-hand steering: Not only will you have to deal with driving with a right-hand car, you will also have to deal with new traffic laws. 3. *(of bidirectional traffic)* keeping to the right side of the road: Czechoslovakia accepted the Paris convention and undertook to change to right hand traffic.

right-handed—1. using the right hand for writing, etc.: Traditional placement of dishes on the dining table is planned for a right-handed person. 2. *(of things)* designed to be used in the right hand: When a left-hander uses right-handed scissors, they have to push the thumb and index finger together in an unnatural way to make the scissors cut.

right-hand man • right-handed man

right-hand man—a person's chief assistant: The relationship between the coach and his right-hand man, irrespective of his title, is pivotal.

right-handed man—(also: right-hander) a man who uses his right hand for writing, etc.: I came to the conclusion that the blow might have been struck by a right-handed man.

ring a bell • ring the bell

ring a bell—(coll.) sound familiar; remind of smth.: The name of the company rang a bell. One of my neighbors worked for them during the war.

ring the bell—(coll.) 1. *(also: ring bells)* be met with approval; be a complete success: The President's speeches ring the bell with certain segments of middle America. 2. supply exactly what is necessary or desired: A good hot bowl of soup would ring the bell about now.

Note: *The expression does not correlate in meaning with the phrase* ***who will ring the bell****— used to ask who will assume the responsibility in a difficult situation:* I agree that allegations should be investigated. The question is, who will ring the bell?

See also: ring one's bell / ring someone's bell.

ring alarm bells • ring bells

ring alarm bells—arouse people to a sense of danger; put on the alert: The huge vote for fascist candidates should ring alarm bells across Europe.

ring bells—(also: ring the bell) meet with approval; have a strong appeal: Macmillan's speech rang bells around the world because it signaled the change in Britain's colonial policy.

ring one's bell • ring someone's bell

ring one's bell—(also: blow one's own trumpet) announce one's own successes; praise oneself: As he won, the winner rang his bell on and on, till he stopped panting and could laugh and talk properly.

Note: *The expression does not correlate in meaning with the phrase* ***have one's bell rung****—(Sport) suffer a minor concussion, having been hit on the head (also: get one's head rung):* He reminds me of a big old football player who's had his bell rung once too often.

ring someone's bell—(coll., also: ring someone's chimes) get a person's attention or interest: When Mary heard what Jim was saying, the news certainly rang her bell.

See also: ring a bell / ring the bell.

risk capital • risk money

risk capital—(also: venture capital) money for speculative business investment: Kula Fund was established to provide long-term risk capital to private sector projects in the Pacific.

risk money—1. allowance to a cashier to compensate for ordinary errors: To meet deficiencies, some banks allow to each cashier a certain sum, which is called risk-money. 2. = *risk capital:* A business man ought to be able to get his "risk money" back before he has to pay too much in the way of taxation.

ritual act • ritualistic act

ritual act—an activity which happens as part of a tradition: Herein lies the explanation of how the act of bathing could have become a ritual act sanctioned by many religions.

ritualistic act—an activity which follows the same pattern every time it is used: I love tea because I love the ritualistic act of making and drinking tea.

river-horse • sea-horse

river-horse—the hippopotamus: The crocodiles and river-horses are common in this unpeopled region; and I often looked upon them with terror.

sea-horse—1. the walrus: From this account the horse-whale seems to have been the animal now called the walrus, or sea-horse, whose tusks are ivory. 2. *(pl.)* white foam and spray on the crests of waves: The sea was a beautiful deep blue, as calm as could be with little white sea horses here and there. 3. *(also: flying sea-horse)* a fish of peculiar form, with body somewhat like a horse's head: The sea horse is a very strange fish that lives in warm water.

road of life • way of life

road of life—said of the general course of a person's life: His past experiences seem to be serving him well, as he continues to travel along the road of life.

way of life—mode of living or acting: Changes have begun to occur in all areas of their way of life as a result of sustained contact with the outside world.

Note: *The expression does not correlate in meaning with the*

phrase ***walk of life****— a profession, occupation, or position in society:* It is rare to meet someone so young who had an impact on so many people from different walks of life.

root about for something • root for something

root about for something—1. *(of pigs, etc.)* turn up the ground with the snout in search of food: A wild boar has been spotted rooting about for food scraps left behind by tourists. 2. search for smth. (by turning things over): He has been in the habit of taking more or less prolonged trips to the Continent for the purpose of rooting about for antiques.

root for something—1. *(Sport)* support or encourage one's favorite team: Most people tend to root for the team that dominates the local sports scene. 2. = *root about for something 1:* Digging in your purse or wallet like a hog rooting for acorns will always cast doubt in the mind of a bartender.

roses, roses all the way • roses round the door

roses, roses all the way—said of comfort, favorable circumstances, success, etc.: I should have thought you would be so glad to get back from Brazil that life would have been roses, roses all the way. *Cf.: not all roses—(of a situation, job, etc.) there are unpleasant things to deal with as well as the pleasant ones:* Wait, don't you want to read my review first? It's not all roses you know!

roses round the door—usually said of marital or rural domestic happiness: "Roses round the door and all that," as Norman used to say when Letty's retirement plans were mentioned.

See also: come up roses / come up smelling of roses.

rot away • rot off

rot away—decay slowly and completely: The soil in the forest is rich with dead leaves and branches that have been rotting away for centuries.

rot off—fall off because of decay: The ground is covered with stiff, dry branches which have rotted off as the trees die.

rotten apple • rotten egg

rotten apple—(coll.) a single bad person in a group *(also: bad apple):* Today, the company, a shadow of its former self, is the rotten apple of the highly competitive supermarket sector.

rotten egg—(coll.) a bad or despised individual *(also: bad egg):* But even if he was a rotten egg, what could he actually do? Does he stonewall any important cases before they reach the Supreme Court?

rough customer • tough customer

rough customer—a disagreeable person who may turn violent: Lord Carmarthen, besides being an amateur sailor, was, like his guest, a most immoderate brandy drinker and altogether a rough customer.

tough customer—an unyielding person who is difficult to deal with: I started designing our garden, but Dave is a tough customer and rejected all my plans.

See also: slippery customer / smooth customer.

rough it out • rough it up

rough it out—withstand to the end difficult conditions or adverse circumstances without flinching: We have no other course for it but to rough it out as well as we can.

Note: *The expression is not equivalent in meaning to the phrase* ***rough it****—(also: rough it in the bush) live for a short period of time without the usual comforts and conveniences:* The explorers had to rough it when they got into the jungle.

rough it up—(Sport) intensify the tempo and competitiveness of a game: He has great agility on the ice and is not scared to rough it up in front of the net to gain position.

round about • roundabout

round about—1. approximately; around: When I had my boy in day care, it used to cost me round about fifty dollars. 2. in the neighborhood: We would go off to collect mushrooms, there were plenty in the fields round about.

roundabout—1. *(UK)* merry-go-round *(a revolving structure for children to ride on):* The photo shows a group of children on a roundabout in the park. 2. a road junction consisting of a circular area around which traffic can flow continuously: Exit the airport, then turn left and drive to the roundabout. 3. *(of an answer, etc.)* not direct or straightforward: Ask him what he does for a living, and he'll give you a roundabout answer.

round the bend • round the corner

round the bend—(also: around the bend) 1. said of smth. about to happen very soon: The Harpoon Brewery's annual two-day St. Patrick's Festival is "round the bend"! 2. *(coll.)* crazy; insane: People's initial reaction is to think that you must be round the bend.

round the corner—(also: around the corner) = round the bend 1: Hoover was saying that prosperity was just round the corner.

row someone up Salt River • send someone up the river

row someone up Salt River—(U.S.) defeat political opponents in an election, etc.: The distance to which a party is rowed up Salt River depends entirely upon the magnitude of the majority against its candidates.

send someone up the river—(coll., also: send someone up) send a person to prison: The same judge sent him up the river the last time.

Note: *The expression does not correlate in meaning with the phrase* ***put someone up the creek****—(sl.) 1. put a person in trouble:* It doesn't look like I'm going to be able to do my graduation course, which pretty much puts me up the creek. 2. *render a girl or a woman pregnant:* I know a girl who thinks her bloke may have put her up the creek.

See also: sell someone down the river / send someone down the river.

rub noses with someone • rub someone's nose in something

rub noses with someone—(coll.) associate or mix with people *(also: rub elbows with someone):* I might actually learn something, here. After all, this was my chance to rub noses with people who cared.

rub someone's nose in something—(coll.) remind a person humiliatingly of smth. such as an error, fault, oversight, etc.: There's no need to rub my nose in the fact that she's so much more attractive than I am.

rule something off • rule something out

rule something off—draw a straight line with a ruler after a piece of work: Rule off each exercise as you finish it.

rule something out—1. cancel an item on a list, etc. by drawing a line through it: Rule out that entry in the ledger, the transaction was cancelled. **2.** make smth. impossible; prevent smth.: The conditions of the ground ruled out any chance of hunting that day.

run after girls • run the girls

run after girls—continually approach girls in the hope of a romantic relationship: "I don't care about politics," he said. "I just listen to music and run after girls."

run the girls—(sl., of a pimp) be in charge of prostitutes: The police try to break up illegal brothels when they can, using intelligence to track the pimps who run the girls.

run after two hares • run with the hare and hunt with the hounds

run after two hares—(also: chase two rabbits) try to fulfill two goals at the same time (with the implication that a person will not succeed in either one): We are pursuing two qualitative targets simultaneously, which might be thought of as running after two hares.

Note: *The expression does not correlate in meaning with the phrase* ***take two bites of a cherry****—(also: make two bites of a cherry) take two turns to accomplish smth. which could be performed in one operation:* When we are having the service, let us not take two bites of a cherry; let us take one bite and have the most up-to-date system.

run with the hare and hunt with the hounds—try to support two competing sides in a dispute: He paid the price for his liberal political beliefs as the Congress tried to run with the hare and hunt with the hounds.

run around • run around in circles

run around—(coll.) 1. go to different places for entertainment or to do things: We went for brunch and then ran around all day, watched Family Guy, and ate pasta. *2.* make short journeys in a vehicle: Mary bought herself an old car, just for running around in. 3. associate with smb. of the opposite sex: I may be old-fashioned in my ideas, but women run around too much these days to suit me.

run around in circles—(also: go round in circles) work busily at a task without making any progress: You're just running around in circles. Let's figure out a sensible solution.

run away with someone • run off with someone

run away with someone—1. *(of lovers, etc.)* elope with a person: Well, ma'am, in round numbers, she's run away with the soldiers. 2. go out of smb.'s control; become ungovernable: If corporations are not to run away with us, they must become quasi-governmental institutions.

run off with someone—1. = *run away with someone 1:* Lew Archer's job is to find a 17-year-old girl who has run off with a 19-year-old no-goodnik. 2. capture and abduct a person: "C'mon, sweetheart," the man with the gun said to Molly, grabbing her by the hand. Everyone watched helplessly as the three men ran off with Molly.

run high • run low

run high—1. *(of the sea)* have a strong current with a high tide: The sea runs high, and the boat may be dashed to pieces on the rocks. 2. *(of disputes, feelings, etc.)* be strongly manifested or intensify: Popular passions ran high as the general election approached.

run low—become scarce in supply: We had to return to camp because our food supply was running low.

run into a stone wall • run one's head into a stone wall

run into a stone wall—(also: come up against a brick wall) encounter an impenetrable obstacle or difficulty: These recommendations have run into a stone wall, as Republican and Democratic governors alike have strongly resisted any Federal cuts.

Note: *The expression does not correlate in meaning with the phrase* ***hit the wall running****—(coll.) exhaust one's supply of energy during a run (such as a marathon):* I could quit running at any time and just get off the treadmill at any point without a need to walk (or crawl) home after I hit the wall running.

run one's head into a stone wall—(coll.) persist with smth. without making any progress *(also: run one's head into a brick wall):* If the President continued to insist on his plan he would be beaten. They besought Jimmy Roosevelt to make the President see reason, to persuade him not to run his head into a stone wall.

Note: *The expression is not equivalent in meaning to the phrase* ***be stonewalled****—*1. *used of a person whose progress is doggedly blocked (by refusing an answer, cooperation, etc.):* They suffered an unusual tragedy, but I could never find out the full facts about it — I was stonewalled. No one would tell me the truth. *2. used of parliamentary obstruction of a debate, bill, etc. by engaging in delaying tactics:* This is the same legislation which was passed unanimously by the Senate during the last session, but which was stonewalled in the House.

run like a deer • run like a hairy goat

run like a deer—(hyperbolic) run very fast: The boy was far ahead running like a deer.

run like a hairy goat—(Austral sl.) 1. = *run like a deer:* He ran like a hairy goat. It was his best race. *2.* run very slowly: Everything was OK until last week when I noticed the car was running like a hairy goat.

Note: *a) Neither expression is equivalent in meaning to the phrase* ***run like wild-fire****—(of news, rumors, etc.) spread very swiftly and forcibly:* Though I was at that time rich in fame — for my book ran like wild-fire — yet I was very short in money.

b) Neither expression correlates in meaning with the phrase ***run like a clock****—(of machines, etc.) function with steady regularity, with no trouble:* There wasn't anything in the motor which needed fixing. It was running like a clock.

run out at something • run out on something

run out at something—(also: run up to something) amount to a figure mentioned; reach a sum: With hospitals making about 50 million outpatients' appointments a year, the annual cost of missed appointments runs out at more than £300 million.

run out on something—abandon one's responsibility for smth.; fail to fulfil an agreement, etc.: We should not have a situation where people can run out on their obligations to others.

run out of time • run out the clock

run out of time—have no more time left: With queens on the board both players were forced to move at lightening speed, and it was Grischuk who ran out of time first.

run out the clock—(Sport) keep the ball away from the opposing team at the end of a game so that they cannot score: The early season loss to the Eagles came about because of the team's inability to run out the clock.

run someone into the ground • run someone to ground

run someone into the ground—(coll.) 1. win over a person; defeat smb. completely: We lost the game today, but tomorrow we'll run them into the ground. 2. make smb. work continuously very hard so that the person becomes completely exhausted: Well-trained horses had been starved to death or run into the ground.

run someone to ground—track down and eventually find a person, especially for arrest or punishment: The prisoner was finally run to ground some place in Alabama, hungry and exhausted.

run someone off his feet • walk someone off his feet

run someone off his feet—1. *(Sport)* wear out an opponent (showing greater stamina and vigor): Now, at the age of 51, John ran me off my feet in a cross-country run. 2. *(also: run someone off his legs)* exhaust a person by keeping him constantly busy: She positively adored running me off my feet. She would sit at the dinner table relaxing while I ran about, sweat dripping from my brow...

walk someone off his feet—tire a person very much with long walking: My mother, in spite of her age, is so healthy that she can still walk me off my feet.

run someone round • run someone round in circles

run someone round—1. drive smb. to a place: You have to go into one of Heathrow's terminals and hire a car, they will run you round to the hire car places. 2. *(coll.)* perform the duties of a servant for a person: Don't expect me to run you round for the rest of your life!

run someone round in circles—(also: give someone a run-around) deliberately withhold information, etc. from a person, sending him to other places to get it: I spent a long time speaking to various representatives who just run me round in circles.

See also: go around someone / run circles around someone.

run something down • run something up

run something down—1. lower smth. such as a flag: A few of us created a big diversionary distraction near the main entrance while two other guys snuck out and ran down the flag. 2. speak of smth. in a disparaging or critical manner: You always run my proposals down. You find every reason in the world not to support them. 3. find smth. after searching: We now have access to this photograph. Bob ran it down in a West Point yearbook.

run something up—1. raise smth. such as a flag: Just as the ship came within cannon range, the British ship ran up the flag of the United States. 2. *(of a debt)* cause to grow quickly: My wife had a joint account with her previous husband; before he left her he ran up a huge overdraft. 3. make smth. such as clothing, etc. quickly: The sailors ran up a rough shelter and then searched for food and water.

run something into the ground • run something to ground

run something into the ground—1. treat smth. so badly as to destroy it: The new owner ran the business into the ground. He had no set hours, gave bad service, failed to pay his suppliers.... 2. pursue or discuss a topic, etc. too much or too thoroughly *(used showing disapproval):* Hopefully, this news cycle will be short-lived as they are starting to run the story into the ground.

run something to ground—find smth. after a long search *(also: run something to earth):* After searching in many stores, he finally ran to ground the book he had spent so long looking for.

Note: *The expression does not correlate in meaning with the phrase* ***run something aground****—(Nautical) cause a vessel to become stranded at low water:* The galleon's crew purposely ran the ship aground on Catalina Island to escape the raider.

run up to something • runup to something

run up to something—(also: run out at something) amount to a figure mentioned; reach a sum: The first stage of the oil project will cost $4 billion, and later development costs will run up to $12 billion.

runup to something—the period leading to an activity, such as election, etc.: Baker doesn't think war is inevitable, but he thinks we're in a runup to war.

running fit • running fits

running fit—(Engineering) contact of mechanical parts that permits free rotation or movement: A running fit is one in which an allowance is made so that a shaft will be free to rotate in a bearing.

running fits—canine hysteria *(an epileptic condition of dogs):* After a few weeks the dogs began to exhibit signs of "running fits."

rush someone off his feet • sweep someone off his feet

rush someone off his feet—(also: rush someone off his legs) exhaust a person by keeping him constantly busy: I've been so rushed off my feet that I've not had a moment to do anything except work.

sweep someone off his feet—(also: carry someone off his feet) affect a person with overwhelming enthusiasm: I remember being swept completely off my feet when I first met Jim.

Russian Easter egg • Russian egg

Russian Easter egg—hand painted wooden or porcelaine decorative egg: She plays an American wife who comes across a Russian Easter egg that has been in her family for years.

Russian egg—an egg poached and served with mayonnaise on a lettuce leaf: I yelled an order for Russian eggs. It comes up a salad the size of the Garden of Eden.

rust bowl • rust bucket

rust bowl—(U.S.) said of the declining industrial areas, especially of the Middle West: His policies are turning our great industrial Midwest and the industrial base of this country into a rust bowl.

rust bucket—(sl.) 1. *(U.S.)* an old, worn and rusty ship: To try to get the jump on the weather, ore carriers will put every rust bucket that floats into the ore trade. *2. (Austral.)* a dilapidated rusty old car: And because no one wants to buy a rust bucket, it can radically depreciate your car's resale value.

S

safe against something • safe from something

safe against something—protected from possible dangers (such as fire, etc.) should they happen: I try to make sure my house is as safe against hurricanes as possible.

safe from something—said of dangers that cannot possibly harm a person or thing: A person once infected with the smallpox is safe from having it a second time.

safety man • safety officer

safety man—1. a person responsible for safety: As John began to get into his diving things again he wished that somebody could be left in the boat as safety man. 2. a man guarding a temporarily disused mine-shaft: These officials, known as "safety men," will eat their dinner in semi-darkness hundreds of feet below the surface of the earth. 3. *(U.S. Football)* a defensive back who plays in the deepest position: He scored from four yards out, running straight over the safety man.

safety officer—a person who coordinates safety measures within an organization: Safety engineering is receiving an impetus by the appointment of safety officers by many firms.

Saigon moment • sputnik moment

Saigon moment—(usually in military contexts) used when people realize that they will lose or fail *(originally of the U.S. negative experience in the Vietnam war):* "We are waiting for the final chapter, for your Saigon moment," a rebel commander bragged in a taunt to U.S. President Bush.

sputnik moment—used when people realize that they are seriously challenged and have to redouble their efforts to catch up *(originally of the time when the Soviet Union launched the first satellite and beat the USA into space):* Hutchison warned that "we are on the verge of another Sputnik moment" because of China's perceived lunar ambitions.

Saint Anthony's fire • Saint Elmo's fire

Saint Anthony's fire—an inflammatory disease of the skin caused by alkaloids produced by a fungus that infests rye and wheat: Outbreaks of Saint Anthony's Fire were common in countries where populations subsisted on rye bread.

Saint Elmo's fire—a naturally occurring corona discharge from a pointed conducting object, such as a ship's mast, etc.: Ball lightning and Saint Elmo's fire are sometimes confused.

Saint Helena • Saint Helens

Saint Helena—a small island in the South Atlantic Ocean: Saint Helena is a British Overseas Territory and one of the last relics of the colonies.

Saint Helens—an active volcano in the Pacific Northwest region of the United States: The Cascade range was volcanically inactive for over 120 years prior to the Mount Saint Helens eruption in 1980.

Saint John • Saint John's • Saint Johns

Saint John—1. the largest city in the province of New Brunswick, Canada: Saint John is located in the south of New Brunswick, one of the Maritime Provinces on Canada's Atlantic coast. 2. a river that rises in Maine and flows northeastward through New Brunswick, Canada: Plans? Just fishing with my daughter on the Saint John River. And swimming at the pool.

Saint John's—1. the capital of Antigua and Barbuda, an island nation located in the eastern Caribbean Sea: There are three airports in Antigua and Barbuda; the most important ports and harbors are in Saint John's. 2. the provincial capital of Newfoundland and Labrador, Canada: Julie will chaperone them during their trip to the National Heritage Fair, which will take place in Saint John's, Newfoundland.

Saint Johns—a river in northeastern Florida: The state's longest river, the Saint Johns, flows north from Indian River County to the Atlantic Ocean, near Jacksonville.

sale price • selling price

sale price—1. the price a customer pays for a product: I have learned the lowest sale price of many items we purchase regularly and wait until it is at or below that price. 2. low price at a sale: This Lindermans wine I bought at a sale price of £3.99 at my local Safeway—normal price was about £6 as I remember.

selling price— = *sale price 1:* We keep the selling price of our items as low as possible but need to include a little extra in the postage price.

Sally Ann • San Fairy Ann

Sally Ann—*(sl.)* the Salvation Army *(a charitable and religious organization to care for the poor and homeless):* The Salvation Army? You'd never get me sleeping there.... Everyone knows you pick all sorts of things up from the Sally Ann.

San Fairy Ann—*(a jocular representation of the French phrase "ça ne fait rien")* it doesn't matter; it makes no difference *(UK Army WWI):* If anyone has a problem with that—which I doubt—then san fairy ann as we say.

same again • same as ever

same again—used when ordering another drink of the same kind as the last: A thump on the counter brought the barmaid.... "Same again, ladies?"

same as ever—said of a person or thing not changed over a period of time: I have been perfectly charmed and overjoyed today, to find you just the same as ever.

San Jose • San José

San Jose—a city in California located at the southern end of San Francisco Bay: A friend who lives in San Jose came to the hotel one night and took us to dinner.

San José—the capital of the nation of Costa Rica: Many foreigners living in Costa Rica, especially the beach areas, must come to San José to do general shopping.

sandwich girl • sandwich man

sandwich girl—*(sl.)* a super-skinny girl who looks like she hasn't eaten in weeks: Joe talks about how he's all about body acceptance and real women, but all he ever dates is sandwich girls.

sandwich man—a man carrying two placards fastened together with straps supported on his shoulders: Not a picket was to be seen, not even a sandwich man stood there, expressing his lonely indignation.

Note: *The expression does not correlate in meaning with the phrase* ***poster man****— used of a person who is a (usually positive) symbol for smth.:* He is alive and well; he is the poster man for what is possible after having a transplant.

sardine box • sardine tin

sardine box—*(UK hist.)* used of the City & South London Railway opened in 1890, so called because of the packed conditions at rush hour: The passengers in the "sardine box railway" had to sit facing each other on long benches in light too dim to read a newspaper.

sardine tin—*(sl., pejor.)* 1. a mini-car: Leave that smelly little sardine tin alone. The exhaust smells a little, but that's nothing. 2. an aircraft: Just back from our Tenerife family holiday and will never forget the sardine tin we flew in. 3. *(Nautical)* a clumsy steamer: No one was allowed on deck ... and in the never ending rolling sardine tin, we were all tottering about uphill and downhill. 4. *(Nautical)* a submarine: U-boat submariners were true dedicated sailors and so is anyone who gets inside a sardine tin under water.

satisfied of something • satisfied with something

satisfied of something—completely sure about smth.: Are you quite satisfied of the truth of his story now?

satisfied with something—entirely pleased with smth.: I am not satisfied with your work; you must improve it.

save someone from something • save someone something

save someone from something—deliver or rescue a person from danger, injury, etc.: I was originally going to write about my grandparents who saved me from a life of poverty and self-destruction.

save someone something—make smth. unnecessary; relieve a person from the need of doing smth.: I said that I would save him the exertion of turning me out of doors, by going of my own accord.

say a lot about something • say a lot for something

say a lot about something—*(also: tell a lot about something)* be very significant or revealing about smth.: This says a lot about our society and the direction in which we are moving.

say a lot for something— give ample proof in favor of smth.; be strong evidence of smth.: Sprucing up the place of business with newly-cleaned carpeting, for example, will say a lot for the health of a company.

say something in confidence • say something with confidence

say something in confidence—tell smth. on the understanding that the information is not to be disclosed: McSorley should not even have written down what was said in confidence by Kennedy.

say something with confidence—say smth. assuredly and with conviction: No one can say with confidence now what the outcome will be.

Scarlet Woman, the • scarlet woman

Scarlet Woman, the—(derog.) the Roman Catholic Church *(also: Scarlet Lady, the):* The latter old lady [the Church of Rome] may be the Scarlet Woman, or the Beast with ten horns, if you will.

scarlet woman—(pejor., dated) a prostitute; a whore: I sought out a scarlet woman in the streets and went home with her.

school board • school council

school board—1. *(UK hist.)* local education authority responsible for the maintenance of public elementary schools: The school board may pay the whole or any part of the school fees payable by any child. 2. *(U.S., Canada)* a board charged with the provision and maintenance of schools: The school board which recently submitted its estimates for the year to the city council will have to revise them.

school council—a committee of pupils elected to manage school affairs: Murray, a boy who was well-liked but who shone at nothing, was proud of his status as a member of the school council.

science project • scientific project

science project—1. an investigation to discover the answer to a scientific problem: The question for my science project was if different solutions affected seed germination and growth. 2. said of a difficult, complex task: Some advertisers think it's a science project. A lot of them have been slow to adopt online advertising...

scientific project— = science project 1: In minutes the two dedicated engineers were deeply engrossed in their scientific project, totally oblivious to their surroundings.

scrap of paper • scrap paper

scrap of paper—said contemptuously of a document which a party does not intend to honor: When constitutional restraints on the government are most desperately needed, the Constitution becomes nothing but a scrap of paper.

scrap paper—1. paper for repulping or reuse: Scrap paper is used to make some forms of paperboard for packaging. 2. rough paper for casual jotting: He made some preliminary sketches for several hours on scrap paper.

scratch something off • scratch something out

scratch something off—1. remove smth. by abrasion: If you place objects on the bumper while you are loading the rear you will scratch the paint off. 2. write smth. hurriedly or carelessly: The usual scene, Jenny singing and me scratching off letters for the second post.

scratch something out—cancel an item on a list, etc. by drawing a line through it: I write you my letter straightforward, and let you see all my scratchings out and puttings in.

screen test • screening test

screen test—1. a trial filming to determine whether an actor is suitable: Then, when he [camera man] was through, she went back to her work and gave her screen test no more thought. 2. a medical check on a person to detect a possible disease: Large numbers of women could receive a screen test for carcinoma of the cervix.

screening test— = screen test 2: A swift and reliable system is necessary to meet the ideal of offering every woman an annual screening test.

scrub something off • scrub something out

scrub something off—(also: scrub something away) remove smth. by scrubbing: I got paint on my hands and I can't scrub it off.

scrub something out—1. = *scrub something off:* When you spill ink on the carpet, remove it straight away—you won't be able to scrub it out later. 2. clean smth. thoroughly by rubbing the surface: As soon as they moved in, they started scrubbing out the rooms. 3. draw a line through a writing so that it cannot be read: Scrub out that last part of the message, the wording is not very polite.

sea power • water power

sea power—1. *(also: naval power)* a nation or state with a large navy: Just over a century ago, the United States became a sea power, changing its basic strategic orientation in the course of a few years. 2. the capacity of a nation for naval warfare; the size and strength of a country's navy: French sea power, allied with the American cause after 1778, enabled Washington to isolate and destroy the British army.

water power—power derived from the weight or motion of water, used to drive machinery, etc.: Since 1985, the city of Boulder has run a hydroelectric program to turn water power into electricity.

see a pink elephant • see the elephant

see a pink elephant—have visionary hallucinations caused by alcoholism *(also: see pink elephants):* One time when I got loaded on beer I heard water running when there was none and I did see a pink elephant.

see the elephant—(U.S. coll.) gain worldly experience (having been to far-off places, visiting sights, etc.): He is quite well able to take care of himself; he has seen the elephant.

sea boy • sea girl

see boy—a man or youth pursuing his career at sea as a sailor, etc.: He ventured to remark, that no other coat than a pay-jacket could become a sea-boy.

sea girl—(also: sea-maid) a mythological being supposed to inhabit the sea: Suddenly they saw twelve sea girls come up out of the water and dance a round upon the sand.

sea dog • water dog

sea dog—1. an experienced sailor: In his blue Guernsey sweater he looked every bit an old sea dog. 2. a seal or a small sea lion: Its skin was rough, scaly, and grating, like that of a sea-dog or seal. 3. any of various small sharks: The chief fisheries are those of the tunny, of the sword fish, and of the sea dog, a species of shark. 4. *(also: sea wolf)* a sea-robber; a pirate: The galleons of the Spanish Armada were pulled down by the sea-dogs of Drake.

water dog—1. a dog trained to retrieve waterfowl: Though excellent water dogs ... we have had to complain of their impetuous rush into pond or river. 2. *(coll.)* a good swimmer: I was the only water-dog of our band; neither Percy nor Captain Roberts nor the mate could swim. 3. *(coll.)* a good sailor: They [Sandwich Islanders] are complete water-dogs, and therefore very good in boating. 4. *(pl., coll.)* small dark floating clouds, forecasting rain: Reports of smoke were determined to be low lying haze and moisture (commonly called water dogs).

sea-fire • Water Fire

sea-fire—marine phosphorescence from decaying matter: The sea-fire shines in her wake.... Near the equator, you can read small print by it.

Water Fire—(U.S.) a festival in Providence, RI celebrated with bonfires on the river: Our lounge is the perfect destination to come after attending one of many downtown Providence events such as Water Fire.

Note: *a) The expression does not correlate in meaning with the phrase **fire-water**—(sl.) strong alcoholic liquor:* His father had a horror of the fire-water which is generally sold to the undergraduate.

*b) The expression does not correlate in meaning with the phrase **liquid fire**—a flammable composition ejected from a weapon in a long spray of flame:* Bronze tubes that emitted jets of liquid fire were mounted on the prows of their galleys.

sea plane • sea-borne plane

sea plane—an airplane with floats instead of wheels for landing on water: The area is accessible only by boat or sea-plane, and there are no automobiles on the island.

Note: *The expression does not correlate in meaning with the compound **sailplane**—a light glider:* Sailplanes are capable of soaring flight, that is flying without loss of height or gaining height.

sea-borne plane—an airplane on board an aircraft-carrier: This plane will be more basic in engineering than its sea-borne cousins.

sea wolf • water-wolf

sea wolf—1. a voracious sea-fish, especially the bass *(Labrax lupus)* and the wolf-fish *(Anarrhichas lupus):* These fishes have large teeth and powerful jaws. Called also sea cat, sea wolf, and swinefish. 2. *(also: sea dog)* a sea-robber; a pirate: If you would like to discover more about the piratical way of life, try this publication which covers all aspects of the life of a sea wolf.

water-wolf—1. the pike: Another advantage in the use of a spinner bait is that it has only one hook to remove so the "water wolf" is easier to release. 2. the otter: The country is also home to the giant otter or "water-wolf," which is the rarest otter in the world.

seaboard • surfboard

seaboard—the part of a country which borders on the sea; the coastline: Come winter, Tundra Swans are to be found along the seaboard of the western (and to a lesser extent the eastern) United States.

surfboard—a narrow buoyant board used in surfing in which the surfer is carried along the face of a breaking wave: When you're still, it's nearly impossible to stand on the surfboard.

seal something off • seal something up

seal something off—prevent access to and exit from an area or space: Police have sealed off the street where the gunman is hiding.

seal something up—close smth. tightly: They sealed up the cracks in the window to stop the icy wind from blowing in.

search for someone • search someone

search for someone—try very hard to find a person: Family members began searching for the boy and found him in the vehicle, police said.

search someone—examine smb. to make certain whether any article (stolen or prohibited) is concealed in his clothing: A power is given to officers to search persons suspected of concealing prohibited goods.

seasonable clothing • seasonal clothing

seasonable clothing—clothing that is appropriate or suitable for the season: Each resident possesses adequate, clean, well-fitting, and seasonable clothing and has a safe place to keep it.

seasonal clothing—clothing pertaining to a particular season: It is preferred that only seasonal clothing be stored in the resident's wardrobe and that out of season clothing be stored elsewhere.

seating room • sitting room

seating room—*(of a canteen, chapel, etc.)* seating capacity; places where people can sit: We have seating room for thirty pupils in this classroom.

sitting room—a room in which members of a family commonly sit: A feature of modern living rooms is the room divider, screening the dining area from the main sitting room.

second time, a • second time, the

second time, a—another time; once more: I rang the bell, but nobody answered it, so I had to ring a second time.

second time, the—the second occasion: I had to retake my exam and passed with flying colors. It's always easier the second time.

see how the cat jumps • that cat won't jump

see how the cat jumps—*(also: see which way the cat jumps)* see what direction events are taking: Had I time, I believe I would come to London merely to see how the cat jumped.

that cat won't jump—*(also: that cock won't fight)* that argument is doubtful; that idea isn't going to work: "They talk of suicide here," he said at last. "*That* cat won't jump."

Note: *The expression does not correlate in meaning with the phrase **dead-cat bounce**—a slight economic recovery after decline, followed in fast order by a second decline:* This was a dead cat bounce, but a bounce none the less, and Australian policy makers were able to bask in the sun.

see into something • see to something

see into something—*(also: look into something)* consider a matter; inquire into smth.: Let me know as many particulars as you can remember—for I must see into the charge.

see to something—deal with smth.; attend to or take care of smth.: Who is seeing to the arrangements for the wedding?

see life • see life whole

see life—1. acquire experience of life: Vicky began to like the place and her company less and less. She had to remind herself that at least she was seeing life. 2. engage in social gaieties and active pleasures: He's made a good deal of money and he's seeing life, I fancy.

see life whole—have a balanced and mature perception of people, events, etc.: Now, Mr. Skipton, you are an artist. You know the duty of the artist is to see life whole.

see red • see the red light

see red—*(coll.)* become enraged; lose one's temper: Happily violence is short-lived, only for a very little while do even the gentlest persons "see red."

see the red light—have premonition of disaster; see danger ahead: He saw the red light and got out of the country just when the revolution started.

see snakes • see the lions

see snakes—*(U.S.)* have visionary hallucinations caused by alcoholism *(also: see pink elephants):* Alcohol abuse may pollute your brain so that you will see snakes and spiders.

see the lions—*(U.S. coll.)* see all the noteworthy attractions of a place: The rest of the day was spent in seeing the lions—and first the Cathedral.

see someone off • see someone out

see someone off—1. bid a person goodbye at an airport, train station, etc.: The decks were crowded with voyagers and those who had come to see those voyagers off. 2. *(coll.)* force a person to go away: I know an audience of stuffed shirts when I see one. Besides—I just had to see that pompous bastard off.

see someone out—1. take smb. to the door or exit: "Did you leave your key with them?" "Yes; the maid who saw me out, took it from the door." 2. *(euph.)* survive a person: My dear wife is, I fear, frail in health—though I trust and pray she may see me out. 3. outlast smb. in a drinking contest: He could see the Dundee people out any day, and walk home afterwards without staggering.

see someone through • see through someone

see someone through—help smb. come through the difficulties; give a person support until the end: Her thoughts flew off to Ralph recalling with pleasure his promise to "see her through."

see through someone—understand the real nature and motives of a person: The real reason he didn't like her was because she could see through him, and he knew it.

see something through • see through something

see something through—1. continue to work on smth. until it is completed: I had taken on a task, and I was bound to see it through. 2. see the whole of a film, play, etc.: I'd much rather see the film through from the beginning, so let's go to the second showing.

see through something—understand the true nature of smth.; not be deceived by smth.: My mother is a very astute woman: she saw right through John's seeming politeness.

See also: look something through / look through something.

see something with half an eye • with half an eye on something

see something with half an eye—see or understand smth. very clearly or easily: The teacher could see with half an eye that Jim was going to have trouble with some boys who disagreed with him.

with half an eye on something—(also: with one eye on something) directing one's attention only partly to smth. (while preoccupied with smth. else): I spent the day putting in the web pages with half an eye on the TV.

see stars • star-gaze

see stars—be dazed as a result of a blow on the head: She fetched me a slap in the face that made me see stars.

Note: *The expression does not correlate in meaning with the phrase* ***get stars in one's eyes****— be fascinated with smth.; be captivated by impractical ideas:* I only hired people that got stars in their eyes when they heard about the notebook computer idea.

star-gaze—1. gaze intently at smth.: He could not remove his eyes from my face. Lady Norfolk, observing it, asked him whether he intended to sup, or to stargaze all night? 2. have idle thoughts; daydream: It may well be that surgery will be only reparative or replacement in nature. One can but star gaze at present.

see the light • see the light of day

see the light—1. *(of a book, etc.)* be published: Christopher Isherwood's diaries are now at last to see the light. 2. realize one's mistakes; understand smth. after thinking about it: He was waiting for me to beg him to forgive me and tell him that I had seen the light. 3. believe that a difficult part of a situation is finally over: Your company is well worth the time and effort we are putting into this program. We can already see the light.

Note: *The expression does not fully correlate in meaning with the phrase* ***see the light at the end of the tunnel****—(also: see light at the end of the tunnel) = see the light 3:* An official said he saw light at the end of the tunnel and firefighters said today they welcomed a weekend weather forecast.

see the light of day—1. = *see the light 1:* I continued to write and publish short stories but it was nearly twenty years before my next book saw the light of day. 2. be born: When I was born, the town was on the Czech-German border, now it is on the Czech-Polish border, without moving from where it was when I saw the light of day.

see through a glass darkly • see through rose-colored glasses

see through a glass darkly—(the Bible) is used to say that humans have a fundamentally clouded, fractured, and limited perception of reality *(also: see in a mirror, dimly):* Here is another key principle of all history-writing: The historian, by force of his human limitations, sees through a glass darkly.

see through rose-colored glasses—said of an unduly cheerful or optimistic view of things: Depressed people are the most realistic, they have lost most of their ability to see through rose-colored glasses.

see you in the soup • see you in the soup line

see you in the soup—(Austral. sl.) see you around *(a form of farewell):* Cheers all, see you in the soup a few weeks from now. Have a great vacation!

Note: *The expression does not correlate in meaning with the phrase* ***be in the soup****—(coll.) be in a difficult situation:* The school finally phoned my mom and asked why I was absent. Boy, I really thought I was in the soup!

see you in the soup line—a sarcastic prediction that one might find himself on welfare *(originally of a queue of poor people waiting to receive food as charity):* Forty years of debt based government economics ain't going to make a lie the truth. I'll see you in the soup line in 15–20 years.

seeded raisins • seedless raisins

seeded raisins—raisins without seeds, made from grapes from which the seeds have been removed before or after drying: Seeded raisins are more difficult to find than the common seedless variety carried on most market shelves.

Note: *The expression does not correlate in meaning with the phrase* ***seeded grapes****— a variety of grapes with seeds:* Although they're not as popular as the seedless varieties, seeded grapes have a much fuller flavor.

seedless raisins—raisins without seeds, made from a variety of grapes without seeds: In the school lunchbox, try replacing crisps by a little packet of seedless raisins or a banana.

select committee • selection committee

select committee—a committee consisting of a small number of members, selected to investigate smth.: The select committee studying motorized snow vehicles spent the better part of a day's sitting listening to an expert.

selection committee—a committee appointed to choose a particular individual or individuals: If George had been a member of the Olympic Games Selection Committee, he would have signed this woman up immediately.

self-righteous • self-righting

self-righteous—sure of the superiority of one's personal beliefs and actions: It is in this manner, and not with a self-righteous attitude, that we should approach the incidents which sometimes occur.

self-righting—(usually of a boat) able to turn right side up after being capsized: They initially planned to market the rescue tool, and Peter's design for a self-righting life raft.

sell oneself to someone • sell someone out to someone

sell oneself to someone—1. present oneself in a favorable light; convince other people of one's merits: You're selling yourself to your employer, and attitude and dress are really all you need for that. *Cf.: sell oneself short— underestimate oneself:* My parents have always taught me to take pride in everything I do and not to sell myself short. 2. sacrifice one's principles, especially for monetary gain: That literally was the straw which broke the camel's back, where they asked me to sell myself to the government.

sell someone out to someone—betray a person deceitfully to his adversary: It is revealed that she is just as ruthless as her employer, selling him out to the presidium in order to take over as chairman...

sell-out • selling out

sell-out—1. mass sale of a commodity: The shortage of shopping times for working people causes overcrowding, poor service and sell-outs on Saturday. 2. a show for which all seats are sold: I have four tickets.... They're absolutely impossible to get, show is a sell-out, but the agent is a friend of mine. 3. a sacrifice of principles, especially in order to gain an advantage: This meeting was just another sell-out to the management. 4. a person who makes a betrayal of principles: Mr. Mugabe's guerrillas infiltrated the region murdering those who were considered sell-outs.

selling out—1. disposition of the whole of one's stock, etc. by sale: The selling out of an edition in so short a time was without precedence. 2. = *sell-out 3:* His best friends were now accusing him of selling out.

sell someone down the river • send someone down the river

sell someone down the river—*(coll.)* let a person down; betray smb.: It's my considered opinion, John, we've been sold down the river.

send someone down the river—*(coll., also: send someone down)* send a person to prison: He had overheard Miss Jones threatening Mr. Dee "to send him down the river for life."

See also: row someone up Salt River / send someone up the river.

sell someone up • upsell someone

sell someone up—dispose of the goods of an insolvent person for the benefit of his creditors: He is well behind in his repayments to the bank, which is threatening to sell him up.

upsell someone—persuade a customer to buy smth. additional or a more expensive product: For customers, it unfortunately means that salespeople may try to "upsell" you on products and services that you don't really need.

sell something off • sell something out

sell something off—sell goods cheaply (so as to raise money quickly, etc.): The first "diners" were old Pullman dining cars sold off by railway companies.

sell something out—1. sell the whole supply of smth.: Within twenty days the entire stock of radio sets was sold out. 2. *(also: sell something up)* dispose of one's business or property (for payment of debt, etc.): The property had to be sold out due to the mere 10 percent return it was getting per year. 3. treacherously betray smth.: Public interests were sold out for personal and private profit.

send off for something • send out for something

send off for something—*(also: send away for something)* request smth. by post: Have you sent off for the booklist yet?

send out for something—order smth. to be delivered to one's home, etc.: The workmen in the building sent out for some sandwiches.

send someone about his business • send someone on business

send someone about his business—dismiss a person unceremoniously: "Well, send him about his business when he bores you, Edna," instructed her husband as he prepared to leave.

Note: *The expression does not correlate in meaning with the phrase* ***go about one's business****— attend to one's own affairs:* She never reacted to his verbal abuses in our presence; she went about her business, distant and proud.

send someone on business—send a person on a business mission: Once in a while, these companies would send me on business to Singapore, where I would work at their Singapore branch.

send someone away • send someone off

send someone away—1. make a person leave: I sent him away because I was tired of his idle chatter. 2. dismiss smb. from employment: News spread round that the teacher has been sent away on account of immoral behavior.

send someone off—1. start smb. on a journey, etc.: Mother always makes sure the children are sent off with a good breakfast inside them. 2. bid a person farewell; say goodbye: The whole family arrived on the quayside to send him off. 3. *(Sport)* order a player to leave the field: Now don't you try arguing with the referee. You'll only get sent off. 4. make a person fall asleep: Did you know that if you count sheep, it is watching the sheep *jump* that sends you off?

send someone down • send someone up

send someone down—*(coll.)* 1. dismiss a student from a university: He escaped prosecution because of his family background but he was sent down from the University. 2. *(also: send someone down the river)* send a person to prison: The last case was about a plumber who charged a pensioner £2,000 to do a job that other plumbers said was worth £50. They sent him down for two years.

send someone up—1. *(UK coll.)* make fun of a person: Much British humor consists in sending up the customs and leading figures of the country. 2. *(also: send someone up the river) = send someone down 2:* He did a lot of breaking and entering before the judge sent him up about fifteen years ago.

Note: *The expression is not related in meaning to the phrase* ***send someone flying****— trip or hit a person causing him to fall:* I gave him a great, big shove that sent him flying into the pile of wood at the back of the garage.

send someone out to grass • send someone to grass

send someone out to grass—*(coll., also: put someone out to grass)* 1. send smb. on a holiday: There were a few strange faces: three or four wives with children sent out to grass from Athens. 2. send a person into retirement: The consultant-in-charge of our clinic has accepted retirement. At three score and ten it is time he was sent out to grass.

send someone to grass—*(coll.)* knock a person down: In the fifth round Billy caught Harry with a solid right and sent him to "grass" not to rise again.

send something by return • send something in return

send something by return—send smth. in the next post: You can request your free copy of our catalogue by filling in our request form and we'll send it by return.

send something in return—send smth. in exchange for smth. else: The bills they send out, and the checks customers send in return, account for about 25 percent of the mail stream.

senior citizen • senior resident

senior citizen—*(euph.)* an elderly person; an old age pensioner: There are no euphemisms in Dutch for being old—no "senior citizen," no "golden-ager."

Note: *The expression does not correlate in meaning with the phrase* ***senior man****—1. a person superior to others in standing:* "What if he refuses to go with them?" "They'll be senior men, they'll pull rank." 2. *(U.S.) a student in his final year at a university or high school:* Tees Rowing Club, whose senior men's crew finished second in their division, are seeking new members.

senior resident—(U.S.) a medical graduate who has completed an internship and serves in residence at a hospital: Never disturb the senior resident when he is on his rounds, unless the place is on fire.

sensible about something • sensible of something

sensible about something—showing a reasonable attitude towards smth.: Market research has shown us that people are far more health conscious and far more sensible about what they drink.

sensible of something—aware of smth.; realizing smth.: How natural for a woman sensible of her humble circumstances not to wish to unveil the total intimacy of her house to passing strangers.

sensitive about something • sensitive to something

sensitive about something—easily offended or worried about smth.: You really must stop being so sensitive about your accent.

sensitive to something—1. susceptible or vulnerable to smth.: If the enamel of your tooth has worn to where the sensitive part of the tooth is exposed, it can make your tooth sensitive to cold. 2. showing a deep understanding of other people's feelings, difficulties, etc.: We're trying to make people more sensitive to the problems faced by working mothers.

separate the men from the boys • separate the sheep from the goats

separate the men from the boys—separate those who have great skill, courage, etc., from those whose abilities are more limited: The first part of the race is not really difficult; it's the final three miles over rough and hilly ground that will separate the men from the boys.

separate the sheep from the goats—(also: separate the wheat from the chaff) separate the good and the bad persons: What the government needed was a new leader who would separate the sheep from the goats and show the public that dishonesty would no longer be tolerated.

serve one's time • serve time

serve one's time—1. do one's service in the armed forces: I wish I could serve my time in the army; I would gladly serve of my own free will. 2. work as an apprentice for a fixed period of time: I thought I was a man and not a sniveling canting apprentice angel serving his time in a vale of tears. 3. serve a prison sentence: Prisoners might serve their time in quarries, which would be turned into labor camps.

serve time—1. shape one's behavior so as to fit the dominant pattern of one's times: We always wait till the last moment to declare our policy. Gives the impression that we serve time. 2. = *serve one's time 3:* Since it was known that Brown had once served time, it was often difficult for him to find work. 3. work at a particular task, especially an undesirable one: We are enthusiastic about what we do, and we are driven to make a difference, not just serve time.

See also: time service / timeserving.

set a stone rolling • set the ball rolling

set a stone rolling—(also: set the stone rolling) start smth. which may lead to serious or unanticipated consequences: He used to treat the opium abuse as the ancestors' tradition. Anyway, this set a stone rolling, and a tiny seed of a big misfortune was planted…

Note: *The expression does not correlate in meaning with the phrase* ***rolling stone****—a wanderer; an unsettled person:* He proceeded to explain that Clyde had ever been a rolling stone—one who preferred to wander here and there.

set the ball rolling—(also: get the ball rolling) start or initiate smth.: Since Malthus set the ball rolling, public opinion has undergone profound metamorphoses.

Note: *Neither expression correlates in meaning with the nominal compound* ***log-rolling****—(sl.) mutual assistance in political or other action (used showing disapproval):* Politics should never have been allowed to degenerate into a game of log-rolling.

set one's mind on something • set one's mind to something

set one's mind on something—wish for smth. strongly; be determined about smth.: We've definitely set our minds on a holiday in France this year.

set one's mind to something—(also: put one's mind to something) devote a lot of attention to a task: Hata set his mind to the study of Japanese policies toward the Asiatic continent.

Note: *Neither expression correlates in meaning with the phrase* ***set someone in mind of something****— cause a person to remember smth.:* That tune always sets me in mind of a fine summer day.

set one's seal to something • set the seal on something

set one's seal to something—(also: put one's seal to something) give one's authority to smth.: If I set my seal to this course of action, I trust to you to see it carried through.

set the seal on something—(also: put the seal on something) bring smth. to an end in a suitable way; formally confirm smth.: This international award has set the seal on a long and distinguished career.

set one's teeth • set someone's teeth on edge

set one's teeth—show deep resolution in the face of pain, opposition, etc.: Erik set his teeth when the memories came flooding back, bursting their hastily constructed dams.

set someone's teeth on edge—said of smth. extremely unpleasant getting on a person's nerves: The sight of that man eating with his knife sets my teeth on edge.

set someone back on his feet • set someone back on his heels

set someone back on his feet—(also: put someone back on his feet) 1. make smb.'s position or means of living secure again: Count Pückler went to England in search of a rich heiress who would set him back on his feet financially. 2. *(of medicine, etc.)* cure a person: Right now she couldn't even face the thought of the long drive home … but a short rest would set her back on her feet again.

set someone back on his heels—(coll.) take aback or disconcert a person: First, the question set me back on my heels, as I felt the sudden shift of responsibility onto my shoulders. But then it excited me.

Note: *Neither expression correlates in meaning with the phrase* ***set someone back****—1. cause a person to put smth. off or get behind schedule:* Hurricane Charley has set us back by a week, so our summer fun program extends well into September. 2. *(coll.) cause smb. to pay out or to lose a sum of money:* Working professionals might meet with an unforeseen accident that might set them back by thousands of dollars.

set someone up • upset someone

set someone up—1. *(coll.)* make a person feel better: You need a holiday to set you up again after all that hard work. 2. help a person start as someone in business, etc.: His father lent him some money to set him up as a shoemaker. 3. *(often Passive)* deliberately cause a person to receive blame, punishment, etc.: I'm not to blame really; I've been set up.

Note: *The expression is not antonymous in meaning to the phrase* ***set someone down****—allow a person to leave a vehicle:* By the time a truck driver set me down among dark green hills, it was already time to start looking for a place to lay over.

upset someone—distress a person: Deceased appeared very irritable upon the morning in question, but witness knew of nothing to upset him.

set something on foot • set something on its feet

set something on foot—(also: put something on foot) initiate a process or action: The Government intends to set on foot an inquiry into euthanasia.

set something on its feet—(also: put something on its feet) make smth. economically self-supporting, especially after a period of difficulties: We want to set some of these local industries on their feet.

set the cat among the pigeons • set the fox to keep the geese

set the cat among the pigeons—(also: put the cat among the pigeons) do or say smth. that is bound to cause trouble and make people angry: Once again she set the cat among the pigeons, claiming that Michel was lying.

set the fox to keep the geese—(also: let the fox guard the hen-house) trust a person with smth. that he is especially likely to misappropriate or abuse: The committee made Hutton treasurer, that's setting the fox to keep the geese.

set up house • set up housekeeping

set up house—start one's own home: Friends and family saw his decision to set up house in Morocco as eccentric or irresponsible.

set up housekeeping—said about two people moving in together: There's a new couch on order—the old one was a gift when we first set up housekeeping here six years ago.

settle down in something • settle down to something

settle down in something—1. make oneself comfortable in a seat: He made himself a quick meal, poured a drink and settled down in an armchair. 2. establish oneself in a new job, place of residence, etc.: It didn't seem likely that we should meet again, as Clarence had settled down in the country.

settle down to something—give one's whole attention to smth.: She then took out a novel from her handbag and settled down to reading it.

settle for something • settle on something

settle for something—agree to accept smth., usually not altogether satisfactory: After a good deal of discussion about what they should have, they settled for bacon and eggs.

settle on something—come to a decision about smth.: We must now settle on a time and place to meet.

settle up with someone • settle with someone

settle up with someone—pay a debt, one's share of the cost, etc. to a person: As it's payday today ... I can settle up with my surprisingly patient landlords.

settle with someone—1. punish a person for harm one has suffered *(often used as a threat):* When you insulted me I promised to settle with you; I did not expect to have the chance so soon. 2. = *settle up with someone:* Barnum retired from the show business in 1855, but had to settle with his creditors in 1857, and began his old career again. 3. arrive at an agreement: We will settle with your father about the money afterwards; but the things should be ordered immediately.

seven come eleven • seven eleven

seven come eleven—(Gambling) the words that a player says in the hope of good luck: Eight hours later, 5 A.M. found me in a fairly empty Flamingo Casino, throwing chips ... and screaming for seven come eleven.

seven eleven—a convenient store, open from seven in the morning until eleven at night: No woman will ever marry you, and you'll end up as a bum asking for spare change outside the Seven Eleven.

Seven Days' Battle, the • Seven Days' Campaign, the

Seven Days' Battle, the—(U.S. hist.) the battle of James River between the Federals and the Confederates in the American Civil War: Three of the Ford brothers participated in the "Seven Days' Battle" in June 1862.

Seven Days' Campaign, the—(hist.) the series of battles in Bohemia concluding in the Battle of Sadowa (1866) in the Austro-Prussian War: He served through the Seven Days Campaign and was given an honorable discharge a year later.

sex something • sex up something

sex something—(of animals and plants) determine the sex by anatomical examination: The specimen is not sexed, neither is the sex noted on the drawing.

sex up something—(sl.) present smth. in a more interesting or lively way (by introducing sex-oriented material): This film took a classic story with lots of potential, put in many great actors, gave them bad dialogue, sexed it up needlessly.

shadowy activities • shady activities

shadowy activities—activities about which little is known: There was a report last month on the shadowy activities of the Canadian Security Intelligence Service.

shady activities—activities that are dishonest or illegal: Amy figures out that there is a link between the school's closure and Richard Packhouse's shady activities.

shake a leg • shake a loose leg

shake a leg—(coll.) 1. move faster; hurry up: They are waiting outside in the car; let's shake a leg! 2. dance: The stage is ready for them, if they like to act or the dancing-room, should they wish to shake a leg.

Note: *The expression does not correlate in meaning with the phrase* ***swing the leg****—(Nautical) evade duty:* There was a nautical expression "swing the leg," an allusion to the pretence of having a damaged leg so as to avoid work.

shake a loose leg—(rare) 1. = *shake a leg 2:* Play, for Heaven's sake, or you will work yourselves into a nation of automatons! Shake a loose leg to a lively fiddle! 2. *(coll.)* lead an irregular life; live freely: You're too much occupied here with your shop: besides, you may shake a loose leg yourself occasionally for all the public knows, eh?

shake the pagoda tree • shake the plum tree

shake the pagoda tree—(UK hist.) make a fortune rapidly in India: Many a Banya or Brahman who had helped to "shake the pagoda tree" retired quietly to his ancestral village.

shake the plum tree—(U.S.) appoint applicants to public offices as a reward for their loyalty to the party in power: As chairman of the Republican Party, Quay "knew how to shake the plum tree" and spent a lot of money in getting Benjamin Harrison elected president in 1888.

Note: *Neither expression is related in meaning to the phrase* ***shake someone's tree****—arouse a person to action or reaction; disturb smb.:* The lead investigator called the fraudster and shook his tree a bit. The person who was defrauded got her money back.

sharp as a needle • sharp as a wet noodle

sharp as a needle—(also: sharp as a razor) very intelligent; quick to learn or realize things: The child was as sharp as a needle and soon began to use quite difficult words.

sharp as a wet noodle—(U.S. ironic) very dull, stupid: You can tell from the things he says that he's about as sharp as a wet noodle.

ship company • ship's company

ship company—(also: shipping company) commercial company engaged in transporting passengers and cargo by ship: The day of building tramp steamers by means of money raised from single ship companies has passed away.

ship's company—the whole crew of any ship: It was certainly a good run ashore for the ship's company, with the Principality of Monaco granting free admission to many places of interest.

shipmaster • shipping-master

shipmaster—(also: master of the ship) captain or commander of a vessel: No shipmaster is permitted to use an anchor which has not been tested and stamped with a government mark.

shipping-master—an official supervising the signing-on and discharging of seamen: When the crew is first engaged, the agreement shall be signed in duplicate, and one part shall be retained by the shipping master.

ship's clerk • shipping clerk

ship's clerk—1. an officer responsible for accounts and stores in a passenger liner: He appears to have been a somewhat humorless person, very dedicated to his profession as ship's clerk. 2. *(U.S. Navy)* an officer supervising records, reports, etc.: The torpedoman, ship's clerk, photographer and aerographer entered the warrant ranks during WWII.

shipping clerk—a clerk who checks merchandise and attends to the shipment of goods: Shipping clerks are record keepers responsible for all outgoing shipments.

ship's mate • shipmate

ship's mate—an officer on a merchant ship ranking immediately below the captain: Big Jim was the ship's mate on the Bloody Moon, a ship owned by Captain Morgan.

shipmate—a person belonging to the same crew: Before Pete experienced any kamikaze attacks, he and his shipmates used to discuss the safest place on a ship.

shoot a bolt • shoot one's bolt

shoot a bolt—send a bolt of a door, etc. into its fastening: The frame into which the bolts shoot is made of great strength.

shoot one's bolt—(coll.) do all that one is capable of; exhaust all of one's resources: The home players had shot their bolt, and in thirty minutes the Birmingham team added two goals.

shoot a goal • shoot at the goal

shoot a goal—(Sport) score a goal: The ball had come in from the right, and McLuckie killed it, and shot a goal.

shoot at the goal—1. *(Sport)* kick the ball, etc. in an attempt to score a goal: In the last hockey game, Mike Modano shot at the goal several times. 2. have smth. in mind as an object; strive for smth.: When it is achieved there will be other goals for them to shoot at.

shoot a star • shoot for the stars

shoot a star—(Nautical) take the star's meridional altitude so as to get the position of the ship: It takes several minutes to find and shoot a star.

Note: *The expression does not correlate in meaning with the phrase* ***shooting star****—(also: falling-star) a meteor that darts across the sky:* Another gale-warning often is given by shooting stars.

shoot for the stars—(also: shoot for the moon) be extremely ambitious; try to do smth. very difficult or impossible: "We want to shoot for the stars," Green said before the game.

shoot for the moon • shoot the moon

shoot for the moon—(also: shoot for the stars) be extremely ambitious; try to do smth. very difficult or impossible: It is better to succeed in changing your diet gradually, than to shoot for the moon and then give up.

shoot the moon—(sl.) leave rented accommodation by night without paying the rent: I told him who were responsible tenants; I warned him when shooting of moons seemed likely.

shoot someone down • shoot someone down in flames

shoot someone down—1. kill a person by a shot (usually implying merciless cruelty): I have witnessed several of their battles, and it appears to be the first object to shoot down, or otherwise kill a man. 2. bring down an aircraft (hence a pilot) by shooting: His father believes he is still alive fifteen years after he was shot down over Germany.

shoot someone down in flames—1. = *shoot someone down 2:* Ernie had a memorable experience in this operation when he was shot down in flames and rescued in a few hours. 2. bring about smb.'s downfall: Let's wait until he's gone too far to draw back, and then we can produce our evidence and shoot him down in flames. 3. overcome a person in argument: She herself had been a little shocked by his answer, but had secretly enjoyed seeing Eileen shot down in flames.

shoot the cat • shoot the sitting duck

shoot the cat—(UK sl.) be sick; vomit, especially as a result of excessive drinking: I'm cursedly inclined to shoot the cat.

shoot the sitting duck—do smth. with guaranteed success; defeat smb. who is an easy prey: I don't like enemies who aren't formidable. There's no fun in shooting sitting ducks.

shoot the crow • stone the crows

shoot the crow—(sl.) 1. depart hurriedly; make off: There'll only be his mother in the house. His father shot the crow years ago. 2. sneak off without paying: A canny Scot was sentenced to ten days' hard for shooting the crow—ordering whiskey and neglecting to pay.

stone the crows—(sl., also: stone me) is used as an exclamation of surprise, etc.: "Stone the Crows!," shouted Peter Grant, when he first heard this splendid young Scottish band roaring into action.

shoot-up • upshot

shoot-up—1. a furious exchange of shooting; a gun battle: Munn was nearly killed in a shoot-up in the streets of Montreal on the very day of his landing. 2. *(of prices, etc.)* a quick or sudden rise: We haven't seen the shoot-up in prices like other areas have, and that's helped quite a bit. 3. *(sl.)* a drug injection: They looked like a couple of drug addicts meeting for a shoot-up in a condemned building.

upshot—the end result or conclusion of some course of action: We had a talk, and the upshot was that if I couldn't feel better through prayer, it was my fault because my faith wasn't strong enough.

short arm • short hand

short arm—a small inlet of a river: There are overnight mooring available in the short arm on east bank immediately above Diglis Lock.

short hand—1. a quick way of writing which uses signs instead of letters or words: I was confronted with an old copy of the Academy, with some shorthand notes on the margin. 2. the hand of a clock or watch which indicates the hours: When it is one o'clock the hour hand, the short hand, is pointing towards the number one.

Note: *The expression does not correlate in meaning with the adjectival compound* ***short-handed****—(of an organization, etc.)*

not having enough people; understaffed: The crews in the pearling schooners and small traders are very short-handed.
See also: big hand / small hand.

short change • small change
short change—a less than the correct amount of money given back to a customer: After several rounds of drinks had been served, Sullivan accused Cook of giving him short change.
small change—coins or bills of low denomination: It is always best to have some small change on you, locals often have no change of larger bills.

short hours • small hours
short hours—1. hours that seem to pass very quickly: Young or old, guy or girl, thick or thin, we'll teach you to windsurf in a few short hours. 2. the early hours of the morning after midnight: The monks prayed in the minster till the long hours passed into the short.
small hours—(also: wee hours) = short hours 2: He invited friends home, who used to come at ten o'clock, and begin to get happy about the small hours.
See also: short time / small time.

short in something • short of something
short in something—(also: short on something) not having enough of smth.: Though I was at that time rich in fame—for my book ran like wildfire—yet I was very short in money.
short of something—1. = *short in something:* Elizabeth, always short of money, railed against the required outlay. 2. not fully amounting to smth.: If the court does not deem it appropriate to inflict punishment, it shall adopt other measures short of punishment. 3. except for smth.: He will do anything short of murder to achieve his ends.
***Note:** The expression does not correlate in meaning with the phrase **short for something**—used of the short version of a name:* "B-girls?" I repeated, "What are they?" "That's just short for bar girls."

short order • tall order
short order—(U.S.) an order for food to be prepared and served up quickly: A good short-order cook in a well-designed kitchen can plate 100 meals an hour during morning rush.
tall order—an excessive or unreasonable demand; a difficult task: Miss Maple considered: "It would be better, I think, to find the body first. Don't you?" "Yes, but isn't that rather a tall order?"

short talk • tall talk
short talk—a brief lecture or address: The Director said that he would like me to broadcast a short talk under my own name.
tall talk—(coll.) boastful or pretentious talk *(also: big talk):* Tall talk is luckily an object of suspicion to Englishmen.
***Note:** The expression does not correlate in meaning with the phrase **talk highly**—(also: speak highly) praise a person or thing:* He talks very highly of his students and the faculty.

short time • small time
short time—1. fewer than the regular number of hours allotted to daily or weekly work: 80,000 textile workers were flung out of work, and thousands more were on short time. 2. *(sl.)* a brief visit to a prostitute: They [sailors] make straight for the nearest bar and then on to the brothel for what is known in the jargon as "a short time."
small time—said of smth. that does not bring much profit or receives little public notice: In these years occur the first productions of all Shaw's early plays. Commercially, it was small time. *Cf.: big time—said of a very high level of attainment:* Jason is doing extremely well for a freshman and his winning goal against Indiana was big time.

***Note:** The expression is not equivalent in meaning to the phrase **thin time**—(coll.) a miserable, unhappy period:* The Germans are having a thin time at present, but they have a past they can recall, and they still have a hope of the future.
See also: short hours / small hours.

shout at someone • shout to someone
shout at someone—talk to a person angrily in a loud voice: She shouted at us for spoiling her lovely evening.
shout to someone—address smb. in a very loud voice that can be heard from a long distance away: Davis was struggling to carry the heavy wireless set; I shouted to him to ditch it and save himself.

shouting head • talking head
shouting head—(derog., also: barking head) a television commentator who speaks in a loud voice and whose comments tend to be aggressive: We have instead shouting heads trying to interrupt each other to get their talking points across.
talking head—a television commentator whose upper body is all that is shown on the screen: Former TV talking head Jim Compton did not respond to the Weekly's request for an interview.

show a face • show one's face
show a face—(dated) demonstrate bravery or audacity: De la Haye and Douglas were both wounded, but the little party continued to show a face to their foes.
show one's face—(often negat.) appear somewhere, especially when one is not welcome in a place: After what she said, she had better not show her face around here again.

show girl • showman
show girl—1. a chorus girl in a musical comedy; an actress in a nightclub show: He found it hard to believe that she was an actress, and a show girl at that. 2. a woman employed in the showrooms of dress-makers, shops, etc., to show off clothes: Not the least interesting thing about these parades is that among the show girls are many well-known titled heiresses.
showman—1. the producer of a play or other theatrical show: Cole credits his management skills in part to legendary producer David Merrick, dubbed "the abominable show man." 2. a man who performs in a public show or spectacle: Some young musicians who have established themselves in the first rank are excellent showmen. 3. *(pejor.)* a man who performs in sports, politics, etc. with a display of pose and affectation: He is a consummate political showman whose critics say he has more style than substance.

show must go on, the • stop the show
show must go on, the—is used to say that an activity must continue no matter what unfortunate event has occurred: She may never perform again, perhaps her back is broken but the show must go on.
stop the show—(of an actor, singer, etc.) give an outstanding performance: Twelve-year-old Reggie Jackson stopped the show last night with "America the Beautiful."

show of hands • show one's hand
show of hands—a method of voting in which people raise their hands: The chairman of the meeting called for a show of hands on the proposed measure.
show one's hand—reveal one's true and previously hidden plans, intentions, etc.: It was only after Hitler became Chancellor that he really showed his hand.

show one's cards • show one's colors
show one's cards—reveal one's plans or intentions: The Prime Minister had not shown his cards so far as to who would be given the brief to hold the discussions.

show one's colors—show what one is really like; show one's true self: His most recent incarnation as an opponent of immigration has perhaps shown his colors in their truest light.

show someone the door • show someone to the door

show someone the door—ask a person to leave; dismiss smb. without ceremony: Exasperated by the man's insolence, Ted finally showed him the door.

show someone to the door—escort a person to the door as a parting gesture: The Reverend Thomas took his leave and apologized.... She told him not to worry as she showed him to the door.

show the white feather • show the white flag

show the white feather—display cowardice: He said that Mr. Bathurst left the army because he showed the white feather. It is not true, is it?

show the white flag—(also: hang out the white flag) admit defeat; surrender: These comments have been submitted in a letter to the editor. Will the author resolutely defend his position, or show the white flag?

shut one's eyes • shut your eyes and think of England

shut one's eyes—(also: close one's eyes) pretend that one has no knowledge of smth.; ignore smth.: He preferred to shut his eyes on the matter rather than to fight for his point of view.

***Note:** The expression does not correlate in meaning with the phrase **get some shut-eye**—(sl.) get some sleep:* I've been working all day long; I have to get some shut-eye.

shut your eyes and think of England—(also: close your eyes and think of England) a humorous advice to smb. faced with an unpleasant task *(originally a wedding-night advice for Victorian brides to succumb to unwanted sex):* When you're staring down the barrel of a gun you can shut your eyes and think of England — or you can grasp it with both hands...

shut someone off • shut someone out

shut someone off—(sl.) silence or obstruct a person: Don't try to shut me off! I have more to say.

shut someone out—not allow smb. to enter or participate: Just look at how the corporate media shut him out of the debates.

shut up a shop • shut up shop

shut up a shop—(also: close up a shop) close a shop securely before leaving (for the weekend, etc.): The bookseller was just shutting up his shop for the night.

shut up shop—(also: close up shop) 1. stop doing business or a service for the day: I think I'll shut up shop, I can't do any more letters tonight. 2. *(of a company, etc.)* go out of business: In Canberra, our one and only Cable TV company shut up shop before any cable was laid.

sick child • sickly child

sick child—a child who is ill: Even crèches, will not lift the load of fatigue from the mother with a sick child to nurse and a teething baby.

sickly child—a child who is weak, unhealthy and often ill: A mother who did not care for her children would have feeble and sickly children.

sick from something • sick of something • sick with something

sick from something—1. feeling unwell as a result of smth.: What is the best thing to do if you get sick from too much sun? 2. ready to vomit because of smth.: Some are sick from the motion of a carriage, or on the water, when it is simply rippled by the wind.

sick of something—(also: sick and tired of something) disgusted with smth.; annoyed by smth.: They always treat us like dirt and like we're nobodies. I get sick of it.

sick with something—1. deeply affected by some strong feeling: Martha, sick with fear, was forced by Helmut to ride on the roller-coaster with him. 2. ill with a disease: All four were very sick with a flu that included stomach upset, cough and cold-like symptoms.

sicken at something • sicken for something • sicken of something

sicken at something—experience strong revulsion at smth.: The four of us who sickened at the idea of partaking of the horrid meal withdrew to the seclusion of our tent.

sicken for something—be in the early stages of a disease (not yet manifest): "I'd rather be at home," said the cameraman. "I'm definitely sickening for something."

sicken of something—grow bored or tired of smth.: There must come a time in each person's life, when they sicken of their seemingly purposeless existence.

side boy • sideman

side boy—(Navy) one of the crew detailed to stand at the gangway as a mark of respect to a person arriving: Shipmate Talbot was nominated "side boy" for the evening and he piped the Mayor aboard.

sideman—(Jazz) a supporting instrumentalist: He began playing in bands just a few years later, and was soon accepted as a desirable sideman.

side-step • step aside

side-step—1. step to one side: Sophia sidestepped and walked sharply past Charles. 2. deviate from the direct route: I was glad I side-stepped, for the journey was worth a deviation. 3. avoid an issue, etc.: I've even asked Dinwater that flat out on two occasions. But he's always side-stepped.

step aside—1. = *side-step 1:* He will leave his rifle on the rest and step aside, in order that the instructor may take his place. 2. withdraw from a competition, etc.: I feel that when there are so many better people for the chairmanship, I should step aside.

sigh about something • sigh for something

sigh about something—express some sad feeling on account of smth.: It's no good sighing about your failure, it's better to start again.

sigh for something—desire smth. very much: Many a woman sighs for a house of her own.

sign someone in • sign someone on

sign someone in—register a person; record smb.'s arrival or admittance: Members must sign in any guests that they bring to the club.

sign someone on—employ a person for a job (as by signing a contract): The men can only be "signed on" in the presence of the Board of Trade officer.

Silicon Alley • Silicon Valley

Silicon Alley—(New York City) a nickname for an area in lower Manhattan, where there is a large concentration of high-tech firms *(a pun on Silicon Valley):* The success of Silicon Alley has had less to do with the traditional technology-oriented policies ... and more to do with the strengths of New York's business sector.

Silicon Valley—the geographical area in northern California, where there is a large concentration of high-tech companies: The semiconductor industry in the U.S. did not locate itself close to San Francisco city but miles away in the Silicon Valley.

silly money • smart money

silly money—1. a ridiculously large sum of money: Buying a house in central London will set you back close to a million quid — it's just silly money. *2. (rare)* a ridiculously small sum of money: Try the new helios range of binoculars, they are just silly money for what you get.

Note: *The expression does not correlate in meaning with the phrase* ***mad money****—(coll.)* 1. *money for use in an emergency (especially carried by a girl out on a date):* He "interviewed" her first date to determine "his intentions for his granddaughter," then gave her "mad money." *2. money saved up for personal use (while on holiday, etc.) and spent unpredictably:* As long as my mad money lasts, I'm going to have a good time.

smart money—(U.S. coll.) 1. money bet or invested by smb. with expert knowledge: In referring to money wagered by persons with good tips or information, the term used is "smart money." 2. said of smart or knowledgeable people: Germany has declared war on Russia, and the smart money says that this is only the beginning.

silver fox • silverback

silver fox—1. a North American fox *(Canis Argentatus)* with black silver-tipped hairs: She lunched at the Ritz yesterday in a black wig, a battle bowler and her silver foxes. 2. a southern African fox *(Vulpes chama):* The Cape or silver fox is found throughout the drier regions of South Africa.

silverback—a male mountain gorilla *(Gorilla gorilla beringei),* distinguished by patches of silvery hair: An adult male silverback is the leader and protector of his band, which consists of females and offspring.

silverware *(UK)* • silverware *(U.S.)*

silverware (UK)—articles, especially tableware, made of silver or an alloy of silver: All eight suspects in the case of the stolen silverware were subject to a rigorous interrogation.

silverware (U.S.)—1. = *silverware (UK):* Butler's corrupt practices reportedly included stealing the silverware from the house in which he was headquartered. 2. metal eating utensils (such as a fork, a spoon and a knife): My personal complaint about many a good meal at a fine restaurant is the state of their silverware.

sing a different tune • sing different songs

sing a different tune—(also: dance to another tune) change one's attitude or opinion; act differently: Kelley was at one time pessimistic about the airport's future. He now sings a different tune.

sing different songs—(of two or more people) express different opinions about smth.: The burden of homelessness is great enough without two Government departments singing different songs.

sing like a lark • sing like a nightingale

sing like a lark—sing gaily and cheerfully: Amelia came tripping into the drawing room in a white muslin frock ... singing like a lark, and as fresh as a rose.

sing like a nightingale—sing very beautifully: Holland comes from a musical family, his father played banjo and his mother sings "like a nightingale."

Note: *Neither expression correlates in meaning with the phrase* ***sing like a canary****—(U.S. Underworld) turn informer:* You don't think they'd sing like canaries? ... If they thought it would help them, they'd tell on their mothers.

sing the same song • speak the same language

sing the same song—(also: tell the same tale) express the same ideas or opinions as another person: After you have been here twelve months, you will sing the same song as I do now.

speak the same language—(also: talk the same language) have an understanding with smb. through similarity of outlook: We no longer speak the same language. To them, terms like "democracy" signify the opposite of what they mean to me.

single-handed • with one hand tied behind one's back

single-handed—perform smth. alone or unaided: Most of the work was done single-handed with some help from interested local residents and a few friends.

Note: *The expression is not antonymous in meaning to the phrase* ***with both hands****—1. with all one's might; with overwhelming enthusiasm:* The government seized the opportunity with both hands. In the ensuing decade, it built countless office blocks and hotels. *2. (in the phrase "grab one's life with both hands") take control of one's life instead of just letting things happen:* I want to grab my life with both hands and shake it up a little. To be confident and unafraid to try new things.

with one hand tied behind one's back—(also: with both hands tied behind one's back) 1. *do smth.* very easily or without effort: I could do it with one hand tied behind my back, but they wouldn't give the research to a youngster. 2. being prevented from doing smth. or restricted in one's freedom to act: They want you and me to participate in this debate about fundamental freedoms with one hand tied behind our back.

singlestick • single-sticker

singlestick—a stick fitted with a hand guard, formerly used in fencing: There is a movement to revive fencing with the singlestick, a weapon that was historically used to represent the broadsword, cutlass or saber.

single-sticker—(Nautical) a one-mast ship: A well-known sailmaker gives the following instructions for setting the sails of a 40-foot single-sticker.

sister ship • sistership

sister ship—one of essentially similar ships, especially of the same owner: The firm decided to build a sister ship to the *Lady Eliza.*

sistership—a community of women living together in a religious order, etc.: They are not to be bound by vows, but during their sistership to obey all the rules of the House.

sit for someone • sit in for someone

sit for someone—1. serve as a babysitter for a child: It was easier for them to leave Bernard, who stays up forever reading anyway, to sit for his brother. *2.* work as a babysitter in smb.'s employ: I sit for Mrs. Franklin every now and then. 3. serve as a model for an artist: She had promised to sit for him just for a lightning sketch.

Note: *The expression does not correlate in meaning with the phrase* ***sit up for someone****— not go to bed in expectation of the arrival of a person:* There are few things more worrying than sitting up for somebody.

sit in for someone—attend a session, sitting, etc. as a substitute for a person: I am not a regular member of this committee. I am sitting in for Larry Smith.

sit in on something • sit on something

sit in on something—1. attend a meeting, discussion, etc., without taking part in it: I was allowed to sit in on the deliberations of the board. 2. take part or collaborate in smth.: You weren't invited to sit in on this deal, but you elected to take a hand.

sit on something—1. be a member of a committee, a jury, etc.: Representatives of the workers should sit on the board of directors. 2. *(coll.)* delay dealing with smth.: She'd "sat" on the article until a deadline had galvanized her into putting words on paper. 3. *(coll..)* examine or investigate a case, etc.: The police are still sitting on the mystery of the stolen jewels.

sit knee by knee • sit knee to knee

sit knee by knee—sit side by side and close together: Let me break the secret: in the evening at the bar the trainer and the black haired beauty sit knee by knee.

sit knee to knee—sit facing each other with the knees touching: During the session, couples were asked to turn to each other and, sitting knee to knee, talk about various aspects of their marriage.

sit loose to something • sit loose upon someone

sit loose to something—be indifferent to or independent of smth.: Buchan was delighted, especially because a university member could sit fairly loose to party.

sit loose upon someone—said of opinions, principles, etc. that a person holds loosely to and can easily abandon: He whose opinions sat loose upon him, was always deemed a bad, and generally a weak, man.

sit up with someone • sit with someone

sit up with someone—keep a person company remaining late out of bed: Charlotte sat up with her late at night and the two of them watched the snow fall together.

sit with someone—1. stay with smb. who is in need of care: Brigi sat with her boys in the hospital when they were sick, did their speech therapy with them, helped them with homework. 2. *(of things)* suit a person; be accepted by smb.: How will it sit with the bishops if Charles chooses to marry a woman with whom he's been living in sin.

skeleton at the feast, a • skeleton in the cupboard, a

skeleton at the feast, a—a person or thing that in the midst of pleasures acts as a reminder of life's troubles: However, all's well that ends well, and I haven't come back to be a skeleton at the feast.

skeleton in the cupboard, a—(also U.S.: skeleton in the closet, a) an embarrassing personal secret or discreditable fact: One doesn't necessarily have to have a skeleton in the cupboard to be damaged by rumor.

ski race • ski run

ski race—(also: skiing race) a contest of speed between skiers: There should be a competent course patrol for all ski races made up from the personnel of the club.

ski run—1. an instance of traveling on skis: It is on one of these long ski runs alone that a man can think out his problems best. 2. a slope or route prepared for skiing: The climb was steep as a downhill ski run.

skin a cat • skin the cat

skin a cat—1. *(coll.)* be a miser; spend as little as possible *(also: skin a flint):* She was very economical and wasted nothing, some said, "she would skin a cat for its hide and tallow." 2. accomplish smth. *(in allusion to the saying "there's more than one way to skin a cat"):* "The poster of Lenin is not a political statement," he assures students, "just a reminder that there are many views of how to skin a cat."

skin the cat—(U.S.) perform a gymnastic exercise involving passing the legs between the arms while hanging by the hands: Some trees linger in our memories as old friends, from whose branches we have swung and "skinned-the-cat."

skin someone for something • skin someone of something

skin someone for something—(hyperbolic) punish or reprimand a person severely for an offense, etc. *(also: skin someone alive for something):* I don't think we should mention this unfortunate encounter to your father. He would skin me for compromising you.

skin someone of something—(sl.) cheat a person of money or property by swindling: Kyranians required agile minds to deal with all the caravans.... Otherwise the shrewd traders would have skinned them of all their goods.

skin-deep • skinny dip

skin-deep—1. involving a surface only: We sent for a doctor ... and on his examining Pagolo, we discovered that the wound was only skin-deep. 2. having little substance; superficial: The technical reviews of digital cameras are skin-deep compared to the in-depth reviews by the online photography sites.

skinny dip—(a consonant nominal phrase) bathing or swimming in the nude: "Fancy a skinny-dip?" I giggled, gazing at the crashing waves.

sky pilot • skyman

sky pilot—1. a person licensed as a pilot: Hats off to these sky pilots for providing yet another valuable forest management tool. 2. *(sl.)* a priest; a military chaplain: At the mission you would get a sermon, say 15 minutes of religion from a sky pilot.

skyman—(coll.) a paratrooper: During the days following the drop ... the sky men spearheaded the drive to capture the city.

sleep it off • sleep on it

sleep it off—sleep until one is sober; sleep until one feels normal: Shortly after he took off, he realized he had had too much to drink and decided to pull over and sleep it off.

sleep on it—think about smth. for a while before coming up with a decision: If you're facing a problem you can't get your head around, you might be told to sleep on it.

sleep round the clock • sleep through the clock

sleep round the clock—sleep for twenty-four hours: The climbers, when they returned, were so tired that they fell into bed and slept round the clock.

Note: *The expression does not correlate in meaning with the phrase* ***sleep around****— have sexual relations with many people:* As far as I could discover, he had no reputation for sleeping around.

sleep through the clock—fail to be woken by a clock: I'm sorry I'm late, I slept through the clock this morning.

slip off • slip out

slip off—go away or leave quietly: Some say he's slipped off, to join his friend abroad.

slip out—1. = *slip off:* So I came downstairs without any noise and slipped out. 2. *(of news, information, etc.)* leak out; be revealed without intention: She did not identify her boyfriend at first but his name eventually slipped out in conversation.

slip road • slipway

slip road—(UK) a road that runs parallel to a motorway, allowing to gain or lose speed safely while joining or leaving it: Temporary closure of a slip road at Carrington signals the final phase in the massive motorway widening project.

Note: *The expression does not correlate in meaning with the phrase* ***slippery road****—1. a road whose smooth surface is likely to cause a vehicle to slip:* Suddenly you realize there's a large boulder lying dead ahead in your lane. You know you can't stop in time on this slippery road. 2. *a precarious course:* If we embark on this slippery road, we will not keep the country. We must rid ourselves of any great-power chauvinism.

slipway—a sloping path down to the water for ships or boats: *Stena Paris* is laid on wooden rails which are lubricated to help the ship slide down into the water from the slipway.

slip up on something • slip up something

slip up on something—make a mistake in smth.: I'd easily give this book five stars, except that the publishers have slipped up on one point: all the photos are reproduced in black and white.

slip up something—move quietly and gently over the surface of smth.: Easily, on the flowing tide … the boat has slipped up the channel between the two lines of sand-hill.

slippery customer • smooth customer

slippery customer—a clever and deceitful person; smb. one should not trust: Watch out for that guy with the big padded coat. He may snatch something. He's a real slippery customer.

smooth customer—an excessively suave or ingratiating person: Dobeliou is a smooth customer who does not have to act to seem sincere and trustworthy. He is the perfect choice for a front man to sell the product.

See also: rough customer / tough customer.

sloppy Joe • sloppy Joe's

sloppy Joe—(sl.) 1. a long, loose-fitting pullover sweater: You can't look like Lana Turner in a Sloppy Joe. Well—maybe Lana could. 2. hamburger meat served with a spicy barbecue sauce: I hope to take up cooking as well, because I am getting tired of eating sloppy Joes. 3. any cheap restaurant or lunch counter: The baked beans are prepared in a tasty sauce and served hot. The "Sloppy Joe" is not your typical sloppy Joe.

sloppy Joe's— = sloppy Joe 3: The barber shop of Felo Centellas was built years later, not far from Sloppy Joe's of Perecito.

slot machine • slotting machine

slot machine—a machine whose operation is started by dropping a coin into a slot: The Court of Appeals declared that the so-called "one-arm bandit" type of slot machine is illegal.

slotting machine—a machine tool used for shaping the sides of an aperture: It has become usual to embrace in the general term machine tools, such machines as the lathe, slotting-machine, and others.

slow down • slow up

slow down—1. move or work at a slower rate: If the driver wishes to slow down he does not necessarily change his gear, but operates the accelerator. 2. live in a quieter less active manner: New York is a place where you can't slow down.… Any person tends to vegetate unless he is moving on a fast track.

slow up—1. *= slow down 1:* The bus slowed up to allow the passengers to get on board. 2. *= slow down 2:* The doctor advised Jim to slow up for a time, to give his heart a chance.

small men • small people

small men—1. men who are not tall: Monty had all that cock-sparrowish pluck which small men are wont to possess. 2. craftsmen or tradesmen doing business on a small scale: The small men must have been very badly hit in the last eighteen months and … some of the stronger are quietly buying them up. 3. morally mean, ungenerous people: Only small men fear the power of words, says Beaumarchais, a phrase to which the King takes exception.

small people—1. a race of people who are not tall: The name of this culture has been derived from a Kikuyu term which is applied to a semi-mythical race of small people. 2. *= small men 1:* Small people are even taught to practice their [self-defense] drills standing directly in front of opponents who are often much larger. 3. said of children: There was a garden that certain small people might play in when they came. 4. the fairies: The Small People are believed by some to be the spirits of people who inhabited Cornwall many thousands of years ago.

smile at someone • smile on someone

smile at someone—(also: smile to someone) look at a person with a smile on one's face (expressing pleasure or amusement): The waiter brought her a drink. "Just what the doctor ordered," she said, smiling at him.

smile on someone—1. *(of fate, luck, etc.)* be favorable to a person: Good fortune indeed had smiled on the child as she could easily have been placed on one of the other three chain gangs. 2. *= smile at someone:* The doctor smiled on the child, and, chucking him under the chin, told him he must hate nobody…

smile at something • smile something

smile at something—1. experience amusement with regard to smth. and show it by a smile: Nicholas could not refrain from smiling at the abruptness of the question. 2. experience the feeling of amusement or derision with regard to smth. without showing it: I secretly smiled at this last prophecy as a "bad shot."

smile something—express one's feelings by a smile: He smiled his delight and then he and his father walked off, hand in hand.

smoked bacon • smoky bacon

smoked bacon—bacon treated by smoking: This Smoke House specializes in smoked meat and cheese items including smoked sausage, turkey, smoked bacon…

smoky bacon—(in recipes, etc.) used with reference to a particular tasty flavor of the bacon: In this dinner recipe, chicken fillets are cooked with smoky bacon and lima beans.

snake juice • snake oil

snake juice—(Austral. sl.) any strong alcoholic drink: We were warmly greeted by the owner who immediately poured us a shot of snake juice.

snake oil—1. a worthless product fraudulently peddled as a cure, etc. *(from the 19th-century American practice of selling cure-all elixirs):* There are people out there selling good weight loss products, but there are also scoundrels selling nothing but snake oil. 2. speech or writing intended to deceive: Why are these three Senators hustling this snake oil rather than the only proven and workable reform?

snow boots • snow shoes

snow boots—overboots of rubber and cloth; winter boots made for deeper snow: Soon after our walk began, I discovered my snow boots had a small leak.

snow shoes—flat frames attached to a boot for walking on snow: There was no village at which the required articles could be procured: namely, two pairs of snow shoes.

snow on someone • snow someone

snow on someone—fall in the manner of snow; shower down on smb.: They were subjected to conditions where the asbestos was snowing on them continually.

snow someone—(U.S. sl.) deceive a person or win over with plausible words: I won't get mad. Just don't snow me with any sob-sister business.

snowed in • snowed under

snowed in—(also: snowed up) 1. *(of cars, roads, etc.)* be (completely) covered with snow: Cars were snowed in and several parking lots were still filled shin-deep with snow. 2. *(of people)* unable to go out because of the abundance of snow: After one particularly heavy storm, they were snowed in for more than two weeks.

snowed under—1. = *snowed in 1:* If she would have gone into labor a day later, she wouldn't have gotten to the hospital. Stern's car was "snowed under" the next day. 2. burdened with too much paperwork, etc.: I have been snowed under with correspondence ever since my secretary was taken ill. 3. overwhelmed; completely defeated: The opposing team were snowed under by our well-planned attack.

so and so • so so

so and so—1. is used as an abusive characteristic for a person or thing: That's what we pay rates and taxes for, and no so-and-so policemen in sight! 2. *(also: such and such)* is used of a person or thing whose name one does not remember or when one does not want to be precise: He told me that he could send me over to doctor so and so if I wished. 3. *(also: thus and so) act* in a particular way; according to directions given: The analyst would tell her to do so and so, and she'd go and tell her husband that so and so is what they ought to do.

so so—commonplace or mediocre; neither very good nor very bad: After working for some so-so companies, I've actually found something that's rewarding to do.

sob sister • sobbing sisters

sob sister—*(coll.)* 1. a weak woman who is prone to crying: I had another sob sister in the office today. Went through half a box of tissues. 2. a writer of sentimental newspaper stories: I worked as a newspaper reporter, specializing in what my editor called "sob sister" features.

sobbing sisters—*(Army, WWII)* German six-barreled mortars: This resulted in an intense enemy barrage.... Artillery, "sobbing sisters" and small arms fire were all employed.

social realism • socialist realism

social realism—art that depicts the more wretched aspects of urban industrial society in a naturalistic manner: The early-twentieth-century realism reappeared in the United States during the depression years as a school of Social Realism.

socialist realism—method of art and literary composition in the former Soviet Union aimed at glorifying the socialist system: Socialist Realism means seeing all reality as a development toward socialism.

soft about someone • soft on someone

soft about someone—*(coll.)* sentimentally silly about smb.; in love with a person: He's too soft about the girl to see her faults.

soft on someone—1. lacking sternness in one's treatment of smb.; lenient towards a person: Many people think our courts are too soft on violent criminals. 2. = *soft about someone:* Ernie had an interest in my older sister. He was soft on her. She was quite attractive but not interested in him.

Note: *The expression does not fully correlate in meaning with the phrase* ***soft with someone***— = *soft on someone 1:* Death penalty uncivilized? Maybe some think being too soft with criminals is the same thing as civility.

soft currency • soft money

soft currency—*(also: weak currency)* a currency unstable in value in the international money market: A soft currency is by definition, non-convertible — that is, cannot be converted into gold or dollars.

soft money—1. *(also: folding money)* paper money (as contrasted with coins): The animated screen saver shows all money of EURO, both a soft money and coins. 2. money which is plentiful and therefore available at low interest rates and long payback: Local supporters of soft money were weak, and Slovenia immediately implemented a tight-money policy upon independence. 3. research money obtained from grants, contracts, etc.: Scientists who have depended on soft money are now beginning to worry. ...they are starting to be concerned about where the next money is coming from. 4. *(U.S.)* political donations made in such a way as to avoid federal regulations: Only Connecticut has a law that prevents the parties from flooding its elections with soft money donations.

Note: *The expression does not fully correlate in meaning with the phrase* ***easy money***—1. *money obtained without effort and often illegally:* I guess it's easy money too from the way he lets go of it. 2. = *soft money 2:* Easy money comes with low interest rates. Hard money is just the opposite, wherein it is very difficult to borrow money and expand.

See also: hard line money / hard money.

soft market • soft sell

soft market—said of a period when sales are few and prices are low: The period of the 1990s is regarded as a soft market for property and casualty insurance.

soft sell—a subtly persuasive, low-pressure method of selling or advertising: When I say soft sell is the key to this generation, it's still ultimately about creating loyal customers. *Cf.: hard sell— selling or advertising smth. very aggressively and with great eagerness:* When it comes to getting children interested in the business, a soft sell is better than a hard sell.

soft thing • soft things

soft thing—*(sl.)* an easy work: We know he's armed. We know how Billy Purvis can fight. It'll be no soft thing, I grant you.

soft things—affectionate talk between lovers; words of endearment: He wrapped his arms around me and held me close, whispering soft things to me...

Note: *The expression is not antonymous in meaning to the phrase* ***soft nothings***—*(also: sweet nothings)* = *soft things:* She was to be a weak, tearful creature, with just sense enough to understand the soft nothings addressed to her by the "superior" sex.

some day • someday

some day—1. at some indefinite future time: I used to live close to an air field and I was inspired by watching all the parachutists; I knew I had to do that some day too.... 2. is used to specify a more particular day: How about us guys getting together some day this fall? I will organize it if there's interest.

someday— = *some day 1:* This is for all of us who have been forced to move away against our will, but someday we will make it back.

some one • someone

some one—any person or thing in a named group: ...she was likely to be thinking about some one of the old books she read.

someone—some unidentified individual: Are you expecting someone? I'm not in the way am I?

some other time • some time or other

some other time—on a different occasion in the future but not now: I could go back there, I mean some other time.

some time or other—*(also: at some time or other)* 1. sooner or later *(implying the certainty of a future event):* You can't go on for ever at any game, and not get tumbled some time or other. 2. on an occasion in the past: We have all heard of the *déjà vu* illusion, and most of us have experienced it at some time or other.

some time • sometime

some time—1. at some future time: Rehearsals have already

started and the record is expected to be released some time in the autumn. 2. for a period of time: There is a class of women who take lodgings, and after staying some time run away without paying their rent.

sometime—1. = *some time 1:* I almost forgot to say that the museum is slated for an opening sometime in the autumn. 2. *(attrib.)* former: He is a man of peace, which goes well with a sometime secretary of defense.

some times • sometimes

some times—certain times: While there are some times when such a rule is necessary, there are other times when it's not.

sometimes—occasionally; from time to time: We sometimes went hunting deer when I lived in Germany.

someone to-be • would-be someone

someone to-be—is used with reference to a position or status a person will have in the future: I met my wife-to-be, Elaine, a few months later, and we were married in November. *Cf.: a has-been—said of smb. who is no longer effective in what he does:* Rocky is now a "has-been," spending most of his time retelling old boxing stories.

would-be someone—said of smb. intending to be a particular kind of person: Bus conductors are having a busy time dissuading would-be passengers from trying to board their buses.

something else • something else again

something else—1. smth. of an altogether different kind: I've been known to get pretty emotional at movies on sporadic occasions, but this is something else. 2. *(coll.)* said of a person or thing so good as to be beyond description: That Rachel is something else, isn't she? There's some feeling in the community that she ought to join up permanently.

something else again—is used as a more emphatic variant of *something else 1:* Contract talks are usually contentious. But the bitterness that broke out at the St. Louis Symphony Orchestra was something else again.

Son of God, the • Son of Heaven, the

Son of God, the—1. *(also: God's Son)* a name of Jesus Christ: Happy is he who can fearlessly stand before the Son of God. 2. a person spiritually attached to God: This is Milton's longest account of this episode, and it is clear that here the sons of God are pious men.

Son of Heaven, the—*(hist.)* said of the Emperor of China: It is now my privilege to serve him who is in all but official style the Son of Heaven.

Son of Man, the • son of man

Son of Man, the—a name of Jesus Christ: Receiving Christ into our lives links us each outside of time back to the First Advent of the Son of Man into our world.

son of man—*(liter.)* a member of the human race: Really good romance writing is the most difficult art practiced by the sons of men.

sooth to say • soothsay

sooth to say—*(arch. or liter.)* in reality; in fact: This message has been published by many newspapers, and, sooth to say, it has sobered many a man.

soothsay—make predictions; foretell future events: Smart people will stop trying to soothsay the future of economics.

sorry about someone • sorry for someone

sorry about someone—feel bad about a person because of smth. that has happened to him: I'm truly sorry about Billy. His wife has left him.

sorry for someone—feel pity for a person; understand smb.'s grief: Letitia feels sorry for all poor people and always gives them money on the street.

sort oneself out • sort someone out

sort oneself out—1. get oneself into a proper mental or emotional state: They are now separated by her decision: he has to sort himself out, show himself to be responsible, a potential father. 2. *(of two or more people)* settle disagreements: Unless he and Michael can sort themselves out they will bring themselves into further disrepute.

sort someone out—1. *(coll.)* deal with a person who causes trouble: He's one of these idiots who fires his rifle off. It's about time the police sorted him out. 2. *(of two or more people)* arrange in groups: We sorted the people out, interrogated them, tried to find out what they were working on.

South Africa • Southern Africa

South Africa—*(officially the Republic of South Africa)* a country on the southern tip of the African continent: South Africa has experienced a different history from other nations in Africa as a result of early immigration from Europe.

Southern Africa—the southernmost region of the African continent including Botswana, Lesotho, Namibia, South Africa, and Swaziland: The terrain of Southern Africa is varied, ranging from forest and grasslands to deserts.

spark plug • sparking plug

spark plug—1. a device that ignites the fuel mixture in an internal-combustion engine: Although you can't see the spark plugs, you can see the spark plug wires that are attached to each of them. 2. a person who is the driving force behind an activity or undertaking: It is thrilling to have someone who is a great role model for the young, who is a spark-plug for the team.

sparking plug— = *spark plug 1:* Pull off the cap of the sparking plug so that the engine cannot be started inadvertently.

speak about something • speak of something • speak on something

speak about something—talk about smth.; discuss smth.: We don't speak about that unfortunate period in our family history. *Cf.: speaking about something—(also: speaking of something) used to introduce once again the subject that has just been mentioned:* The weather affects how we think, move, and feel. Speaking about the weather I have to say, that our natural conditions are very similar to yours.

speak of something—1. = *speak about something:* The colonel very rarely spoke of his war experiences. 2. *(of things or actions)* give proof in favor of smth.; be evidence of smth. *(also: speak for something):* This gift of money speaks of your generosity.

speak on something—speak at greater length on a subject; deliver a talk about smth.: I've been asked to speak on the future of education for very young children.

speak against someone • tell against someone

speak against someone—say bad things about smb.; give a speech against a person: Those who spoke against me had never met me. They had never read a word I had written.

tell against someone—said of smth. such as age, etc. that prevents a person from being successful: There may be many minor evil habits that he should rid himself of—habits that will tell against him.

Note: *a) The expression does not correlate in meaning with the phrase* ***inform against someone****—give evidence against a person to the police, etc.:* Their property was confiscated by the state or turned over to those who informed against them.

b) The expression does not correlate in meaning with the phrase ***tell on someone****—1. have an effect on a person's health:* If there's something on your mind, it will soon tell on you, so whether you're depressed, or just plain stressed, seek medical help. 2. *(used especially by children) tell about a person who has done smth. wrong (in order to get him into trouble):* Should he try to convince his friends that what they were doing was wrong, or tell on his friends which may cost him their friendship?

speak aloud • speak loud

speak aloud—speak in a normal voice rather than quietly or in a whisper: You must never speak aloud in theaters, I was told.

speak loud—speak in a voice that is above normal in volume: He spoke loud enough for most of the audience to hear him.

speak at someone • speak to someone

speak at someone—speak to a person without paying attention to his reaction: Is this person listening to me? Is he speaking at me, down to me, or with me? Is this a caring person I can trust?

speak to someone—1. address a person: The skinny ugly woman suddenly spoke to me: "You like black women?" I was shocked at the out-of-nowhere question. 2. *(also: speak with someone)* have a conversation with a person: She had to speak to them in Urdu and they probably only knew Kashmiri. 3. *(also: speak with someone)* admonish or scold a person: Your secretary was late again this morning—you'd better speak to her about it. 4. make a speech directed to an audience: It was announced that the Prime Minister would speak to the nation on television.

speak broad • speak broadly

speak broad—*(UK)* speak with a strong accent showing that a speaker is from a definite part of the country: Parents who speak "broad" Shetlandic to their children may nevertheless scoff at the idea that it might be of any value.

speak broadly—speak in general terms rather than specific details: I tried to find laureates who could represent some of the scientific turning points of the last century and who could speak broadly about science.

speak by the book • speak like a book

speak by the book—speak accurately, with care as to facts: I knew him for many years, and I speak by the book of the man. He could write nothing that he did not at least feel to be true.

speak like a book—use literary or pedantic language in conversation: "If you can contrive to affect to be angry with him for his extravagance, it will do good." "You speak like a book, and I'll try my best."

speak English • speak in English

speak English—1. know and be able to use the language: She asked if the other two women spoke English, and Miss Savage told her that one was a German-Swiss. 2. use English in conversation: As I spoke English, she concluded I was a foreign teacher come on business connected with the *Pensionnat.*

speak in English—1. give a formal speech using English: Just a decade ago, Russian officials rarely spoke in English at international conferences. 2. use English on a particular occasion: Then to my surprise he spoke in English—good English, with the *chi-chi* accent of the Indian.

speak for something • speak volumes for something

speak for something—1. *(also: speak up for something)* speak in support of an idea, proposal, etc.: Mary always spoke for the rights of her people at a time when the civil rights movement was gaining ground. *2. (of things or actions)* give proof in favor of smth.; be evidence of smth. *(also: speak of something):* His glittering array of awards speaks for his quality as a footballer.

speak volumes for something—*(of things or actions)* 1. give much significant information about smth.: This book speaks volumes for what the families endure when the situation takes a tragic turn. 2. provide abundant evidence of smth.: The way he has fought back from crippling knee injuries speaks volumes for his courage and determination.

speak high • speak highly

speak high—*(dated)* speak loudly: You must do me the honor to speak high, for I am deaf.

speak highly—*(also: talk highly)* praise a person or thing: The students spoke highly of their history lecturer.

speak in confidence • speak with confidence

speak in confidence—speak in the expectation that anything said will be kept private: They could speak in confidence to medical staff who were only obliged to notify managers if the employees condition created a risk.

speak with confidence—speak in an assertive and self-assured manner: At the convention he was one of the five most frequent speakers and he always spoke with confidence.

speak out of turn • speak too soon

speak out of turn—speak rashly or tactlessly (without enough thought of the consequences): I'm going to speak out of turn and you'll be welcome to tell me I should mind my own business.

speak too soon—say or announce smth. prematurely: I spoke too soon about moving to Boston; I didn't get the job after all.

speak something out • talk something out

speak something out—1. declare smth. openly and clearly: A large part of old novels speak out plainly and simply the notorious facts of the world, as men speak of them to men. 2. *(Parliament)* carry on the discussion of a bill, etc. till the time for adjournment is reached, and so prevent it from being passed: He spoke with the obvious intention of speaking out the Bill.

talk something out—1. discuss smth. thoroughly: I think the whole question has now been talked out. 2. = *speak something out 2:* The new law will not have effect as planned, as it was talked out in the last meeting of the House. 3. *(of a quarrel, dispute, etc.)* settle by talking: Unions and employers should try to talk out their differences before taking action.

speak well for something • speak well of something

speak well for something—give proof in favor of smth.; be strong evidence of smth.: His generous gift speaks well for his willingness to help others.

speak well of something—1. express a good opinion of smth.: To speak well of the past was a mortal sin and got you into trouble with the party theologians. 2. = *speak well for something:* His desire to stay with the high-tech program at Cleveland speaks well of his good intentions.

speak without affect • speak without effect

speak without affect—speak in a normal natural way not intended to impress others: Acting as actors, they speak without affect, in the mundane idiom of contemporary New Yorkers.

speak without effect—speak in vain or to no purpose: The subject and the occasion are valueless, but it is equally true that, without a great subject and a proper occasion, a man speaks without effect.

specific criteria • specified criteria

specific criteria—criteria relating to one particular thing, that is, not general: Diagnostic and Statistical Manual lists specific criteria that enable the clinician to establish a diagnosis.

specified criteria—criteria named definitely; criteria included in the specifications: The student is asked to make a plan for a garden that meets specified criteria.

speculate in something • speculate on something

speculate in something—buy and sell smth. with hope of profit through changes in its market value: These proposals are opposed by traders who speculate in oil.

speculate on something—form opinions about smth. without knowing for certain: Do not speculate on what he would have done had he been there.

speed zone • speedway

speed zone—a section of road subject to a lower than normal speed limit: A plan to turn central Sydney into a 40 kmh speed zone has been met with concern by taxi drivers.

speedway—1. a road on which motor vehicles may travel fast: You can see it [mansion] any day you drive up the speedway. It has stood there for over a hundred years. 2. a racing track for motor vehicles: Fans from around the world converge on the speedway for the best in road racing, super cross and dirt track competition.

spend a fortune • spend a penny

spend a fortune—spend a large sum of money: Williams was found guilty at his first two trials, and spent a fortune on appeals over an eight-year period.

spend a penny—*(UK euph.)* visit a lavatory: Where's the bathroom? Us girls are going to spend a penny!

Note: *The expression does not correlate in meaning with the phrase* ***put one's two cents in****—(U.S.) add one's comments or opinion on the matter (also: throw one's two cents in):* Since the subject has been brought up I feel compelled to put my two cents in.

spin control • spin out of control

spin control—manipulation of news, especially political news: The conclusion: Either we are being lied to in an effort of spin control, or the people in charge of our government are incompetent.

spin out of control—*(of activities, events, etc.)* change very quickly and in an uncontrolled way: The political situation in Bolivia is spinning out of control, and if the protests continue to intensify, they could spell serious trouble...

spine-chilling experience • spine-tingling experience

spine-chilling experience—said of a terrifying event or encounter that happens to a person: Have a spine chilling experience amidst the wildlife sanctuaries where you will see tigers in their natural habitat.

spine-tingling experience—said of smth. very exciting or thrilling a person gets involved in: It was a spine-tingling experience to hear the call of kiwi in the Wellington hills for the first time in more than a century.

sporting girl • sports girl

sporting girl—*(coll.)* a girl with loose morals; a prostitute: Most of the women go out by the day as house-workers. There may be a few sporting girls, but if so they don't work their own block.

sports girl—a girl who is interested in or practices sport: Absolutely radiant and glowing, this active sports girl who loves running, cycling and swimming surprised us with her trim figure.

sporting man • sportsman

sporting man—a man interested in sport from purely mercantile motives (one who gambles at cards, on horse racing, etc.): Every sporting man is flattered if termed a sportsman, but it would be almost an insult to speak to a sportsman as a sporting man.

Note: *The expression does not correlate in meaning with the phrase* ***sporting woman****—a woman with loose morals; a prostitute:* The existence of a colony of sporting women at Nose Creek was prejudicially affecting the morals and welfare of the community.

sportsman—1. a man who is interested in or practices sport: They sought a test which would produce the best all-round sportsman in the world. *2.* a man who hunts wild animals or game for pleasure: The sportsman must not expect great success in cock shooting in a very severe frost.

spread oneself out • spread oneself thin

spread oneself out—stretch out on the ground, etc.: It's such a lovely spring day, exactly the kind on which one can spread oneself out under a tree and sleep the afternoon away.

spread oneself thin—*(coll.)* exert oneself; try to do too many things: Your trouble is that you tend to spread yourself thin, so that nothing gets done properly.

spreadboard • spreading board

spreadboard—a machine that spreads flax and hemp in rope-making: The flax fiber is delivered to the mills, where it is hackled to separate and straighten the fibers, overlapped on a spreadboard.

spreading board—a board used by entomologists for insect specimens: To drive a pin smoothly through the insect's thorax, stick it in the cork groove of the spreading board.

spring green • spring greens

spring green—*(of color)* light green: The cottages were painted uniformly white, and had blinds of a bright spring-green color.

spring greens—a variety of cabbage that matures in spring: Vegetables which can be cooked in this manner — cauliflowers, brussels sprouts, spring greens.

spy on someone • spy someone

spy on someone—watch or follow smb. secretly, usually with hostile intent: She was constantly spied on, written about, talked about, followed around.

spy someone—catch sight of smb.; notice a person: There is great danger if the hippopotamus spies the huntsman before he can throw his spear.

square john • square john broad

square john—*(U.S. sl.)* an upright, respectable man: "What does a 'square John' mean? Does it mean an ordinary law-abiding citizen?" Mr. Owen-Flood asked.

square john broad—*(U.S. sl.)* an honest respectable woman: We need a square john broad to give this place a look of respectability.

square up to someone • square up with someone

square up to someone—show courage in confronting a person: In the street was a group of lads obviously waiting for me. I had little option but to square up to them.

square up with someone—1. pay smb. the money one owes (leaving a restaurant, checking out of a hotel, etc.): Can I leave you to square up with the waiter? 2. retaliate upon a person: He wanted to "square up" with them, but had no definite plan of action, and was trusting to luck for something to turn up in his favor.

stand at ease • stand easy

stand at ease—a military attitude allowing less freedom of posture than "stand easy" (personnel aren't allowed to talk and their hands are clasped behind their back): After the command "Stand at Ease" was given Lt. Colonel Broome gave a short but never to be forgotten speech.

stand easy—a military attitude allowing a greater freedom

of posture than "stand at ease" (personnel are allowed to move their arms and torso in a relaxed posture): When on parade do not talk or move about in the ranks. Only when the order "Stand Easy" has been given may you talk.

Note: *The expression is not antonymous in meaning to the phrase* ***stand firm****— remain true to smth.; maintain one's attitude:* He told Radio New Zealand that he would stand firm against demands that he resign.

stand away from something • stand clear of something

stand away from something—move backwards from smth.: Jonny took a deep breath as he stood away from the computer, still staring transfixed at the screen.

stand clear of something— remain at a distance from smth.: The conductor gave the command to "stand clear of the closing doors" and we were on our way uptown again.

stand down • step down

stand down—1. leave the witness box in a court of law after giving evidence: The examining counsel is only too glad to get rid of such a witness, and very soon tells him to stand down. 2. *(of smb. in authority)* resign from one's position or yield one's chance of election: Despite mounting criticism, the head commissioner of the Metropolitan police has refused to stand down.

step down—1. move to a lower level, as by taking a step: Huggins spoke for about ten minutes before stepping down from the stage. 2. = *stand down 2:* The sacking of the chief health officer hasn't quelled the calls for the minister to step down.

stand for someone • stand up for someone

stand for someone— rise to one's feet as a mark of respect for a person: Will all present in court stand for the judge.

stand up for someone—1. defend smb. who is being attacked; give one's support to a person: One should always stand up for the weak and oppressed. 2. *(also: stand up with someone)* act as groomsman or bridesmaid at smb.'s wedding: I was honored when Jim asked me to stand up for him at his wedding to Mary.

See also: stand up to someone / stand up with someone.

stand guard • stand on guard

stand guard—keep smth. in safety; take care of smth.: There the cattle are huddled together and the herders stand guard over them until morning comes.

stand on guard—watch as a sentinel to prevent escape, attack, etc.: She is a regular woman's righter ... and was quite indignant when informed that she was not allowed to stand on guard.

stand in for someone • stand in with someone

stand in for someone—act as a deputy or replacement for a person: The actor might get injured so someone who looks like him should stand in for him in this scene.

stand in with someone—1. have an understanding or community of interest with smb.: Of course if you stood in with the chairman there'd be no difficulty in having your plan accepted. 2. share a cost with a person: All the members agreed to stand in with the secretary, who had bought the club supplies with his own money.

stand in for something • stand out for something

stand in for something—1. support a cause: Living in what looks like a remarkably nice housing estate, Topsy and Tim clearly stand in for classless society. 2. be in league with a person for mutual support or joint action: The policeman who "stood in" for this robbery saw the rogues depart with their plunder.

Note: *The expression does not fully correlate in meaning with the phrase* ***stand for something****—1. = stand in for something 1:* We stand for nonracial not multiracial cricket and believe in selection on merit, irrespective of color. 2. *indicate or imply smth.:* What will the term "Accredited Milk" stand for? It will be milk from cows that have been clinically tested. 3. *offer oneself as a candidate for an office:* I even became political enough to stand for a councillorship. 4. *put up with smth.; bear smth.:* Overseas Governments just won't stand for it, particularly when they get to know what's going on.

stand out for something— = *stand in for something 1:* He has not grit enough to stand out for justice and honesty.

stand in good with someone • stand someone in good stead

stand in good with someone—be on friendly terms with a person; enjoy smb.'s favor: He should be able to do this favor for you, because he stands in good with the doctor.

stand someone in good stead—prove to be useful or helpful to a person (in an emergency): Frank's knowledge of Spanish stood him in good stead when his firm sent him to Mexico.

stand off from someone • stand out from someone

stand off from someone—(also: stand apart from someone) keep away from other people: Mary dislikes parties, and tends to stand off from everyone else if she does attend one.

stand out from someone—be prominent or conspicuous in comparison with others: He stands out from among men for his brilliant mental powers.

stand on one's feet • stand on one's own feet

stand on one's feet—remain standing: He stood on his feet, twelve to sixteen hours per day, in front of a hot oven that never stopped circulating thousands of loaves of baking bread.

stand on one's own feet—(also: stand on one's own two feet) be independent; rely on one's own resources: I won't lend you any money, it's time you stood on your own feet and earned your own living.

stand up to someone • stand up with someone

stand up to someone—(also: stick up to someone) meet an opponent with courage; resist a person: If you don't stand up to this man, he will abuse you unmercifully.

stand up with someone—1. take part in a dance with a partner: I thought you were to stand up with Mr. Tomlinson the two last dances. 2. *(also: stand up for someone)* act as groomsman or bridesmaid at smb.'s wedding: Of course I know John. He stood up with me at my wedding.

Note: *Neither expression correlates in meaning with the phrase* ***stand someone up****—(coll.) fail to keep an arrangement to meet a person, especially one's romantic partner:* Peter said he'd meet me outside the station, but he stood me up.

See also: stand for someone / stand up for someone.

star route system • star system

star route system—(U.S.) mail delivery in a rural area served by a private carrier who takes mail from a railroad station and delivers it to mailboxes: The "star route" system has been superseded by the admirable system of rural free deliveries.

star system—(Cinema, TV) the practice of promoting eminent actors in leading roles: It can dispense with the star system by concentrating on teamwork in which lead actors one night become walk-ons the next.

start off on something • start up in something

start off on something—make a start on smth.: I actually started off on piano, which was my dream instrument.

start up in something—start working in a trade or profession: When I started up in business I was running a market stall.

start someone off on something • start someone out in something

start someone off on something—1. cause a person to start on smth.: This started him off on a hobby of dismantling old radios for parts to construct his many projects. 2. cause smb. to begin speaking at length: Start him off on the subject of meteorites, and it is hard to stop him.

start someone out in something—*(also: start someone up in something)* cause smb. to begin working in a trade or profession: His stepfather started him out in the business when deciding to open a shop in the backyard.

State Enrolled Nurse • State Registered Nurse

State Enrolled Nurse—*(UK)* a nurse who has completed a two-year course and enrolled on a State register: The lettering on badges of State Enrolled Assistant Nurses will not be altered when the title is changed to State Enrolled Nurse.

State Registered Nurse—*(UK)* a nurse enrolled on a State register and having a qualification higher than a State Enrolled Nurse: On the mantelshelf were pictures of Rose in the full uniform of a State Registered Nurse.

State House • State house

State House—*(U.S.)* the building where the legislature of a State meets: In the State House there are lots of paintings showing important events in Massachusetts history.

State house—*(NZ)* a house owned and let by the government: In the building of State houses of high quality a suggestion as to necessary standards has been made.

station man • station master

station man—*(Austral.)* an owner or employee of a sheep or cattle station: The tribe departs to capture Harry, but one responsible tribesman manages to alert the station men.

station master—a person who has charge of a railway station: This is a neat little station with the station master's office on top of a small hillock next to the platform.

stay good • stay well

stay good—*(of perishable products)* remain suitable for consumption or use: A jar of olives is too much to eat all at once but once opened it doesn't stay good for long.

stay well—remain in good health: Once withdrawal is complete, many people, particularly those with long drinking histories, will need ongoing help to stay well.

stay off something • stay out of something

stay off something—*(also: stay away from something)* 1. keep at a distance from smth.; avoid approaching smth.: He just yells and waves his cane at them like an old man telling some kids to stay off his lawn. 2. be absent from classes, work, etc.: Some youngsters in their early teens have so many problems they stay off lessons for the long-term and are being taught at home. 3. avoid smth. harmful or dangerous: "I had vowed to stay off the alcohol but I think I might have a couple of drinks now," smiled Coleman.

stay out of something—1. remain outside smth.; not enter smth.: Stay out of the building until the Fire Department has issued an all clear signal. 2. = *stay off something 3:* Stay out of politics, and play both parties: What you don't get from one you may get from the other.

step by step • step for step

step by step—gradually; little by little: You'll be guided step-by-step through the process of taking your manuscript and turning it into a printed book.

step for step—1. walking or riding evenly with another: Would you like a handsome dog that can match you step for step on long training runs? 2. keeping pace with smth.: You shouldn't put investment dollars into anything but a mutual fund that tracks the market, step for step.

stew in one's own juice • stew oneself

stew in one's own juice—*(also: fry in one's own grease)* suffer the consequences of one's own actions; be left to one's own devices: I left her to stew in her own juice for a week before I went to see her.

stew oneself—fret oneself into a state of heated anxiety: The cashier was stewing himself over the sum of £10 which was missing.

stick at something • stick to something • stick with something

stick at something—1. continue to deal with smth. or work hard at smth. (in spite of difficulties): He will stick at his task, although he's going to be dumped when his contract expires. 2. refuse to go further; object to smth.: He will stick at a request to perjure himself. 3. be unable to go further: John will always stick at higher mathematics — he will never understand the subject.

stick to something—1. attach to smth.: This label will stick to the paper, it is already gummed. 2. limit oneself to smth.: You'll be all right if you stick to the main roads, they're kept clear of snow. 3. = *stick at something 1:* The question is whether he has the concentration and discipline required to stick to his task for four quarters. 4. adhere to smth.; be true to smth.: When he makes a commitment, he will stick to what he said.

stick with something—1. = *stick at something 1:* Even though the project may come out different ... if you stick with the task, you will succeed. 2. = *stick to something 4:* President Bush ought to stick with what he said last night.

stick in with someone • stick with someone

stick in with someone—*(coll.)* join another person as a companion (to share accommodation, etc.): My mother wants me to stick in with my uncle, who has no children of his own.

stick with someone—*(coll.)* 1. *(also: stick to someone)* remain loyal to a person; stay close (in the face of danger, etc.): Stick with the gang on those beach parties. There's safety in numbers. 2. *(Races)* remain level with a competitor: Jim was able to stick with the leading runner for most of the race. 3. continue to pay attention to what a person says: Stick with me for a few more minutes and you'll see the point.

stick it to someone • stick to someone

stick it to someone—*(sl.)* treat smb. badly or unfairly (overcharge a person for services, etc.): I guess I looked as if I had a lot of money and they decided to really stick it to me.

stick to someone—1. *(also: stick with someone)* remain loyal to a person; stay close (in the face of danger, etc.): Just stick to me and I'll lead you out of here. 2. continue to use or employ a person: We finally decided to stick to our present supplier of ball bearings.

stick man • stickup man

stick man—1. a figure that is drawn to represent people: I barely have the ability to draw a stick-man, so any semi-decent painting is going to receive my admiration. 2. *(U.S.)* a casino employee; a croupier: Then the stickman rakes in the dice, picks them up, and tosses them back to the shooter. 3. *(Underworld)* an accomplice of a thief: A man who is called a "stick-man," an accomplice of hers, comes to the bar.... If they have by this time secured the booty, it is passed to the latter. 4. *(Underworld)* a police patrol officer: The stick man is due here in about three minutes. Hurry. 5. *(U.S. Drug users)* a smoker of marijuana cigarettes: Ernie was a stick man till he started being less particular.

stickup man—(Underworld) an armed robber; a mugger: Any moron could get a gun and become a stickup man.

stick one's nose out • stick one's nose where it doesn't belong

stick one's nose out—(coll.) go outside: I'll just stick my nose out to see if it's raining.

Note: *The expression does not correlate in meaning with the phrase* ***stick one's neck out****—(coll.) behave rashly; expose oneself to danger, criticism, etc. (also: put one's neck out):* You don't have to stick your neck out, David — I'll stick mine out. And it'll be a pleasure!

stick one's nose where it doesn't belong—(also: poke one's nose where it doesn't belong) meddle into the business of other people: Occasionally he sticks his nose where it doesn't belong, which makes him, by definition, an investigative journalist.

stick to one's guns • stick to one's last

stick to one's guns—hold fast to a statement, opinion, or course of action: We were all glad that Kit stuck to her guns about divorcing him. The proceedings took place very quietly...

stick to one's last—keep to what one knows; refrain from doing smth. that one is not good at: The view was that I ought to stick to my last and run the program, and Jim would take care of the rest.

stick up for someone • stick up to someone

stick up for someone—(coll.) take the part of smb.; defend a person *(also: stand up for someone):* I stuck up for him and said I had always found him to be honest.

stick up to someone—(coll.) meet an opponent with courage; resist a person *(also: stand up to someone):* If there is no one who dare stick up to him, he soon becomes intolerable.

stock author • stock book

stock author—a person who writes plays which form part of a repertoire of a particular theatrical company: Jones keeps a stock author, and does not rely on outsiders.

stock book—a book in which an account is kept of goods in stock: Love was a sentiment too elevated for one whose imagination dwelt habitually on the beauties of the stock-books.

stone fence • stone wall

stone fence—(U.S. sl.) an alcoholic liquor: "Stone fence" is the euphonious cognomen given to whisky which is drunk with cider instead of water.

stone wall—1. parliamentary obstruction of a debate, bill, etc. by engaging in delaying tactics: The New Zealand Legislation indulged in what is known as a "stone wall." 2. a body of politicians practicing "stone wall" tactics of obstruction: Mr. Smith wished to ask whether the six members constituted the "stone wall" which was to oppose all progress?

stone frigate • stone ship

stone frigate—(Royal Navy) naval barracks or a shore establishment named after the old frigates: She found that H.M.S. *Mastodon* was a stone frigate. It was Exbury Hall, about three miles up the Beaulieu River.

stone ship—1. a fossilized ship discovered in the course of archeological excavations: The discovery of this stone ship has created a world sensation, not only in archaeology.... 2. *(WWI)* a war-time ferro-concrete ship: The carrying capacity was less for a concrete ship. The significant element in building, however, was that fewer expensive trades and industries were called for in a "stone" ship.

stop and smell the roses • wake up and smell the coffee

stop and smell the roses—(also: take time to smell the roses) slow down and relax; take time out and enjoy or appreciate life: There is a whole lot more to life than work and worry. You got to stop and smell the roses.

wake up and smell the coffee—is used to tell a person to face the facts; realize what is really happening: There is nothing you can do that will convince them to let you back into the club, so wake up and smell the coffee.

stop doing something • stop to do something

stop doing something—cease or give up doing smth.: The teachers had stopped attending to pupils who would certainly pass or certainly fail.

stop to do something—pause in order to do smth.: He stopped to watch a half-dozen of the boys playing blackjack.

stop one's clock • stop someone's clock • stop the clock

stop one's clock—(Chess) press one's chess clock to measure time: The last move is not considered as made until after the player has stopped his clock.

Note: *The expression is not antonymous in meaning to the phrase* ***one's biological clock is ticking****— used of a woman who may soon be too old to bear a child:* Your biological clock is ticking. Why are you spending some of that precious time in a relationship about which you feel skeptical?

stop someone's clock—(sl.) kill a person: Mr. Carlson, despite the drug agents' best efforts to stop his clock, miraculously survived three gunshot wounds. He decided to sue the government.

Note: *The expression does not correlate in meaning with the phrase* ***clean someone's clock****—(sl.)* 1. *give smb. a beating:* He's much bigger than you and could easily clean your clock. *2. defeat a person decisively in a fight or competition:* If this is a battle the other side wants to have, we welcome it. We'll clean their clock!

stop the clock—1. postpone a deadline by not counting the elapsing time: Management agreed to stop the clock so that a new contract could be negotiated before the present one expired. 2. = *stop one's clock:* Either player may stop the clock to summon the arbiter to settle a dispute.

stop someone's breath • take someone's breath away

stop someone's breath—affect smb. by a sudden strong emotion such as fear, etc.: Even in the dusk, the look on Sam's face was enough to stop her breath.

take someone's breath away—inspire a person with utter delight: The thought of practicing on that splendid instrument quite took her breath away.

storm petrel • stormy petrel

storm petrel—any of various small sea birds of the family *Hydrobatidae* of the North Atlantic and the Mediterranean: As for birds, the colonies of yellow-legged gull and the nesting of the storm petrel are worth mentioning.

Note: *The expression is not equivalent in meaning to the phrase* ***storm bird****—*1. *Common Koel (Eudynamys scolopacea) a member of the cuckoo family:* From a tree several yards away could be heard the monotonous coo-ee of a bird which Claud told them was the Koel, otherwise known as the storm bird. 2. *Channel-billed Cuckoo (Scythrops novaehollandiae) a member of the cuckoo family:* Did you know that a Channel-billed Cuckoo is the proper name for the bird we commonly know as the storm bird?

stormy petrel—1. = *storm petrel:* Of the two species the true stormy petrel is found in the North Atlantic, south to the Newfoundland Banks and the western coast of Africa. 2. smb. who brings discord or appears at the onset of trouble: The stormy petrel from West Bengal is known for her penchant for hurling insinuations at persons holding office.

straight actor • straight man

straight actor—an actor performing in theatrical productions of the ordinary type (as opposed to a "character actor" performing in comedies, etc.): The character-actors have no doubt an easier task than the "straight" actors.

straight man—1. an actor who makes remarks or creates situations for the main performer to make jokes about: In vaudeville and burlesque a straight man works as a "feeder" with the comedians. 2. *(sl.)* a heterosexual man: John Ritter was a straight man who played at being gay. His life story did make the mind boggle.

straight as a poker • straight as an arrow

straight as a poker—(of posture) rigid; erect *(also: stiff as a poker):* He didn't look a broken-down old man either: straight as a poker, and life enough in him yet.

straight as an arrow—1. following a straight line: You won't get lost if you keep to the track. It's as straight as an arrow. 2. = *straight as a poker:* He stood tall, straight as an arrow, handsome, broad-shouldered. 3. honest and moral: He was straight as an arrow. He never lied nor did he ever run away from controversy. 4. *(sl.)* a heterosexual man: He is as straight as an arrow! He just likes to have facials done!

straight drink • straight drinking

straight drink—(of strong liquor) consumed neat or undiluted: This tequila is fast becoming very popular because it is both a superb mixer and a "straight" drink.

straight drinking—heavy drinking unhindered by dancing, entertainment, etc.: If you're up for straight drinking, go to an *izakaya,* usually explained as a Japanese pub.

straight off • straight out

straight off—(also: straight away) at once; without delay: The butler went straight off to Granny, and gave her notice; and she actually raised his wages, and prayed him to stop.

straight out—frankly; without reservation: I always know if he's worried but he never tells me the details straight out. It sometimes slips out in conversation when the crisis is over.

straw boss • straw man

straw boss—a helper for a boss; an assistant foreman: I was a straw boss. I worked at it a while but I never cared for it. I did not have any power to hire or fire.

straw man—(also: man of straw) 1. a respectable man who serves as a cover for a questionable enterprise *(also: front man):* I suggest that you keep talking with people who were involved, rather than trying to use me as a straw man. 2. a made-up version of an opponent's argument that can easily be defeated: His speech wasn't really convincing because he attacked a straw man rather than addressing the real issues.

straws in the wind • throw straws against the wind

straws in the wind—slight hints that show which way things may develop: There have been other things, straws in the wind, maybe, which give reason to think that contemporary standards are in a process of decline.

throw straws against the wind—(also: spit against the wind) engage in futile action or fruitless effort: You will be throwing straws against the wind if you try to do anything for that youth — he is incurable.

street legal car • streetcar

street legal car—a certified roadworthy car *(typically used of an unlikely looking car):* For a street legal car you need to know the laws that govern automobiles, such as bumper height and light requirements.

streetcar—(U.S.) a public passenger vehicle that runs on metal rails *(also: trolley car):* Plans have been drafted to replace the large buses with a mini bus and later by a streetcar.

street woman • woman in the street

street woman—(euph.) a prostitute: So the brothels had been succeeded by houses of convenience, where street-women could rent a room.

woman in the street—the ordinary woman; any woman selected at random: She had the political cynicism of the woman in the street.

stretch oneself • stretch oneself out

stretch oneself—straighten the body and extend the arms, especially when a person yawns: The Jamaican stood up and stretched himself. "Glad you woke me, man," he said.

stretch oneself out—extend one's legs and body in a straight line while lying: The room was enveloped in darkness. Kedar stretched himself out on the bed without turning on the light.

strict in something • strict on something

strict in something—careful and scrupulous in one's principles, etc.: He was strict in punctuality, spiritual in language and phraseology, immaculate in appearance.

strict on something—is used with reference to principles, etc. that one expects to be observed by others: The professor of that class was very strict on punctuality.

strike at the root • strike root

strike at the root—deal resolutely with the origin of a problem, difficulty, etc.: It is in forming such men and women that we can create a community of peace and justice and strike at the root of terrorism.

strike root—(also: take root) become firmly established; be generally accepted: Therein lies perhaps the very virtue of a liberal education: prejudice does not as easily strike root in an educated person.

strike for something • strike over something

strike for something—1. stop working for an employer in order to get more pay, better conditions, etc.: After the airlines show a profit again the unions will strike for higher wages. 2. fight for a cause: Cleomenes followed by a few friends rushed through the streets of Alexandria, exhorting the multitude to strike for freedom.

strike over something—is used with reference to the issue that causes the strike: Workers including technicians, lighting and box office staff are among those who opted to strike over the redundancies.

strike gold • strike it rich

strike gold—1. find gold: Andrew Prichard struck gold along the North Fork of the Coeur d'Alene River in 1881. 2. *(Sport)* win a gold medal in a competition: India's women's hockey team struck gold for the first time in the Commonwealth tournament. 3. become rich or successful, especially suddenly or unexpectedly: He struck gold when he took up the challenge of building a palace for king Khalid.

strike it rich—1. discover oil or a large vein of minerals: Heflin plays a loner who has finally struck it rich in the Nevada desert. ...to get his gold out he must trust an old enemy. 2. = *strike gold 3:* Lila's father struck it rich with some weird investments which people thought would fail in two months.

strike the bull's eye • strike the eye

strike the bull's eye—(also: hit the bull's-eye) 1. attain the intended object; succeed: We have some potentially good evidence, and we just haven't been able to strike the bull's eye yet. 2. guess the right thing; make a correct conjecture: In the test paper, as they compare notes, he seems to have almost struck the bull's eye in his answers.

strike the eye—(also: hit the eye) be very obvious or impressive; make a strong impact: The external aspect of Palmyrene culture strikes the eye with its complexity and peculiarity.

strip film • stripping film

strip film—a 35 mm film mounted vertically frame by frame for sequential projection: A still further object is to provide a multi-purpose machine, usable concurrently as a slide or strip film projector, an overhead projector, an opaque projector...

stripping film—1. thin paper or film used to correct tones in photographs: Strip Editor is a software to make corrections of plate data. In conventional method, stripping film is used to make corrections. 2. a photographic "plate" having a film which may be separated from its support: In 1886 he introduced stripping film, in which paper was used only to support the emulsion and was stripped off once the negative had been transferred to glass.

strong arm • strong hand

strong arm—1. the use of superior power or physical force: He assured the people that any attempt at lawlessness would be put down with a strong arm. 2. *(also: strong-arm man)* a person employed as a bodyguard: He was a strong arm for bookies, collecting debts from people who had owed money for too long.

strong hand—1. = *strong arm 1:* Parliament has given us the powers to put down Fifth Column activities with a strong hand. 2. *(Cards)* a card of high and commanding value: With a very strong hand, a player may bid to *Schwartz* his opponents, that is, prevent them from making a single point.

strong man • strong-arm man

strong man—1. a man who publicly exhibits feats of great strength: He was the product of a union between the strong man of a traveling circus and the Chief Wardress at the Women's Prison. 2. a man who exercises great political power: We got to get a strong man in the White House to kick out the bankers and grafting politicians and racketeers.

Note: *The expression does not correlate in meaning with the phrase* ***strong silent man***—*a man of few words who conceals and controls his feelings:* It is useless to model ourselves now on the strong, silent man of the novel whose face is a shutter to hide his emotions.

strong-arm man—(also: strong arm) a man employed as a bodyguard: At one local union meeting, backed up by his strong-arm men, he boldly declared: "I do not give a damn whether you vote for me or not."

stumble across something • stumble over something

stumble across something—find smth. by accident: Not too long after seeing the movie, I stumbled across the collection of short stories from which the movie got its start.

stumble over something—1. hit the foot against smth. and almost fall: The pony stumbled over a stone in the path, and unseated his rider. 2. say words awkwardly: They seemed to have trouble starting the conversation, they stumbled over the first words.

subject for something • subject to something

subject for something—said of a person or thing to be dealt with in some way: Mental illness is not a subject for ridicule and at this time Frank deserves our sympathy.

subject to something—1. exposed to smth., usually damaging or unpleasant: Any group viewed as a threat to the rule of the Communist Party is subject to harsh treatment. 2. in a state of dependence on smth.; submitted to principles, regulations, etc.: He would no longer be subject to the caprice of any woman. 3. conditional upon smth.: It will be milk from farms where scrupulously clean methods are practiced — and itself a product subject to bacteriological tests.

substantial improvement • substantive improvement

substantial improvement—considerable or significant improvement: Aerobic exercise can produce substantial improvement in mood in patients with major depressive disorders in a short time.

substantive improvement—improvement that is real or actual: More than two years after the inter–Korean summit, substantive improvement in the security situation on the Korean peninsula remains elusive.

subway *(UK)* • subway *(U.S.)*

subway (UK)—a pedestrian walkway built underneath major roads to enable to cross the road safely: Use the subway to cross to the north side of Whitechapel High Street, continue along and go left at Old Castle Street.

subway (U.S.)—the underground railway transport system, usually in a large city: Allow enough time, even if traveling by subway. There is always construction or unexpected long stops.

succeed in something • succeed to something

succeed in something—accomplish what is attempted or intended: The Dutch colonial rulers only partly succeeded in their efforts to buy the land of the Pasir people.

succeed to something—inherit a title, position, etc. on the death of a person: Prince George was 58 years old when he succeeded to the throne on the death of his father.

such and such • thus and thus

such and such—(also: so and so) is used to refer to a person or thing whose name one does not remember or does not want to be precise: We don't have to wonder, like the early explorers did, at what time we will reach such and such a location.

thus and thus—(also: thus and so) act in a particular way or according to directions that have been given: The truth of the matter is that it is almost impossible to say "do thus and thus and you will have a best-seller."

such as it is • such as there is

such as it is—just the way it is *(usually used to suggest that smth. is of poor quality):* We must either accept the book, such as it is, or write another more worthy of credit.

Note: *The expression does not correlate in meaning with the phrase* ***as such***—1. *as that kind of thing:* It became the national symbol and as such it can be found on postal stamps. 2. *considered without other facts:* Money as such does not mean an unconditional right to buy. You must have the seller's consent.

such as there is—is used to suggest that an amount is small: The infrastructure, such as there is, is not really set up for anyone's comfort. ...the bus stops are often just a metal sign out in the middle of a dusty plain.

suck it up • suck up to someone

suck it up—(sl.) make the effort required to deal with smth. difficult or unpleasant: The airline should have sucked it up and simply canceled the flights altogether when the weather situation became clear.

Note: *The expression does not correlate in meaning with the phrase* ***suck it in***—*(sl.) pull in one's stomach (to make oneself* *thinner when posing for a picture, etc.):* Their first apartment was so small, you had to stand flat againt the wall in the hallway and suck it in for anyone to pass you.

suck up to someone—(coll., especially among children) try to gain the favor of a person by flattery, etc.: He was very talkative ... in the old schoolboy phrase, he was plainly "sucking up" to me.

suffer from a cold • suffer from the cold

suffer from a cold—have a viral infection of the nose, throat, and bronchial tubes: She has been suffering from a cold and headache for weeks and has thought of applying for a one-day sick leave.

suffer from the cold—(also: suffer from cold) endure the effects of low external temperatures: They suffered from cold and from want of clothing. For a time they had to feed on porridge made of beech leaves...

sugar daddy • sweet man

sugar daddy—(sl.) an older man who gives expensive gifts to a young woman in return for sexual favors or companionship: Bill was having an affair with Sue Ellen, who happened to count on Marshall as her sugar daddy.

sweet man—(sl.) a man who is fond of the society of women: Eddoes was a real "saga-boy." It meant that he was a "sweet-man," a man of leisure, well-dressed, and keen on women.

suggestion about something • suggestion of something

suggestion about something—an idea proposed with respect to smth.: If you have a suggestion about how we can improve our service, we would like to know about it.

suggestion of something—1. an indication of the presence or possibility of smth.: The word, though not uncommon even colloquially, has often a suggestion of archaism. 2. = *suggestion about something:* The book offers a suggestion of how existing strategic concepts can be adapted to the new world.

susceptible of something • susceptible to something

susceptible of something—capable or permitting of smth.: It is unfortunate that Borlase did not express himself more clearly, for his language is susceptible of two interpretations.

susceptible to something—easily affected or influenced by smth.: There is one major flaw in Timon's character. That is, he is very susceptible to flattery.

swallow the Bible • swallow the dictionary

swallow the Bible—(U.S. coll.) perjure oneself *(with reference to swearing on the Bible in a court of law):* They will stick together, stretch conscience and at times "swallow the Bible."

swallow the dictionary—(coll.) use long or difficult words *(used showing disapproval):* Have you swallowed a dictionary? We shall have to sack this fellow if he gets to talk English too well.

swear against someone • swear at someone

swear against someone—(legal) swear a charge against a person: No one endeavored to make him swear against the prisoner.

swear at someone—use profane language toward a person: All the drivers were swearing at each other at the top of their voices.

swear at something • swear on something

swear at something—curse smth.: The accident was holding up traffic heading for a major football event, and he could hear people swearing at the delay.

swear on something—1. *(also: swear by something)* call smth. held holy as witness to the truth of what one says: I swear on my soul that this really happened. 2. *(also: swear to something)* have great confidence in the value of smth. *(often negat.):* I can't swear on the quality for all of his models, but this one was really decent for the price.

swear on a stack of Bibles • swear on the Bible

swear on a stack of Bibles—promise solemnly that what one says is true: Your telephone company will swear on a stack of Bibles that nothing will disrupt service to you, the valued customer.

swear on the Bible—1. place one's hand on the Bible in a court of law pledging to tell the truth: A court officer will ask you to swear on the Bible or promise to tell the truth. 2. = *swear on a stack of Bibles:* There are probably a lot of people that think I'm lying, and I swear on the Bible that this story is true.

sweat it out • sweat one's guts out

sweat it out—(sl.) endure smth. unpleasant till it ends; await smth. anxiously: Mr. Khrushchev is just sweating it out for an announcement of a manned flight in orbit. *Cf.: don't sweat it—(U.S. sl.) don't worry about it:* Joe Trippi suggests the best solution: don't sweat it. Just do what needs to be done now in order to win.

sweat one's guts out—(sl.) work very hard indeed: Here I've been sweating my guts out all afternoon, and hardly anything to show for it!

sweep clear for something • sweep clear of something

sweep clear for something—make room for smth.: Chances are, important items will go missing when the table is swept clear for dinner. Instead, decide what to do with each piece of paper...

sweep clear of something—(also: steer clear of something) stay away from smth.; avoid smth.: We jump in and pull out only a few strokes, and sweep clear of the dangerous rock. The other boats follow in the same manner.

See also: make a clean sweep of something / sweep something clean.

sweet and sour meat • sweet meat

sweet and sour meat—meat cooked with sugar and vinegar or lemon juice: The sweet-and-sour meat appeared to have more than its fair share of fat and gristle.

sweet meat—an article of confectionery; a fruit preserved with sugar: This is a kind of sweet meat made of a soft marshmallow jelly coated with pink sugar and powdered with cocoanut chips.

sweet as a nut • sweet as pie

sweet as a nut—1. *(coll.)* said of smth. very tasty: The cabbage itself when it is taken out of the leaves is as white as milk, and as sweet as a nut if eaten raw. 2. *(UK sl.)* quite satisfactory; perfectly OK *(used as a general term of approval):* I treated it [car] to a full service including plugs, air filter, cambelt change and it's as sweet as a nut.

sweet as pie—(coll., of people or animals) kind and friendly: I first must give my love to Antonette, she arranged all of the wedding details and she is as sweet as pie.

Note: *The expression is not equivalent in meaning to the phrase* ***sweet as honey****— very pleasant in speech or behavior, with the implication of insincerity:* She's the kind of woman who'll be sweet as honey to your face and as malicious as hell behind your back.

sweeten the pill • sweeten the pot

sweeten the pill—(also: sugar the pill) make smth. bad seem less unpleasant: The government have cut income tax to sweeten the pill of a tough budget.

sweeten the pot—(also: sweeten the kitty) make smth. more attractive, especially financially: Reviving the village's cooperative will sweeten the pot, and encourage more women to become involved.

swell-head • thick-head

swell-head—(coll.) 1. self-conceit: Lord, but young Gourlay was the fine fellow! Symptoms of swell-head set in with alarming rapidity. 2. a conceited person: As for the present directory, they're all a pack of damned swell-heads.

thick-head—(coll.) smb. who is dull of intellect: I wasn't very good at school and left supremely unqualified for anything and totally convinced I was a thickhead.

swim like a duck • swim like a tailor's goose

swim like a duck—(also: swim like a fish) be a good swimmer: Molly could swim like a duck, and quite covered herself with glory by diving off the pier.

swim like a tailor's goose—be unable to swim: If he attempted to swim, it would be like a tailor's goose, straight to the bottom.

swim with the fishes • swim with the sharks

swim with the fishes—(Underworld) be murdered and have the body disposed of, often in a body of water *(also: sleep with the fishes):* Most people have a family member who is connected to organized crime or "swims with the fishes" because of their connections.

Note: *The expression does not correlate in meaning with the phrase* ***swim like a fish****—(also: swim like a duck) be a good swimmer:* He swims like a fish, loves horses, wants to start a stud farm…

swim with the sharks—take a huge risk operating among dangerous people: Tired of trial and error, I have ceased to swim with the sharks for my dating games. I managed to find a relatively normal guy, who's also a creative sort.

swing both ways • swing either way

swing both ways—(sl.) have both homosexual and heterosexual tastes *(also: plug in both ways):* Rumor has it that their lead singer swings both ways.

Note: *The expression does not correlate in meaning with the phrase* ***door swings both ways, the****—(U.S.) the same principle applies in both cases (usually used to attack hypocritical actions):* As Howard used to say, "Hey, that door swings both ways." We are expected to share our secrets with them, too.

swing either way—said of a situation when it is impossible to predict which of two results it will have: The market could swing either way depending on the news from the Middle East.

swing man • swing voter

swing man—1. a musician who plays jazz with a swing—a style with a flowing but strongly compelling rhythm: The best alto player among the swingmen was Johnny Hodges. 2. *(U.S.)* the mounted herdsman who keeps a moving herd of cattle in order: The herd trailed along behind the leaders … guarded by outriders, known as swing men. 3. *(sl.)* a drug supplier: Now he [pusher] is called the connection, the bagman, the swing man, the dealer.

swing voter—(U.S.) the independent voter that often decisively influences the result of a ballot: He is expected to join Mr. Daane as a "swing voter," leaving Mr. Martin with only one conservative colleague.

Swiss mountain pine • Swiss pine

Swiss mountain pine—a low pyramidal tree of central Europe: The Swiss mountain pine *(Pinus mugo)* is best known to many Americans in its dwarf variety, the mugho pine *(Pinus mugo mughus).*

Swiss pine—(also: Swiss stone pine) a tall Eurasian pine *(Pinus cembra):* A pine tree is estimated to live for 1200 years, and the Swiss Pine, in the Alps, survived the last Ice Age.

symbol for something • symbol of something

symbol for something—a sign or letter used in place of an item in writing: CS is an Army chemical symbol for an agent that causes burning and watering of the eyes.

symbol of something—an object used to represent smth. not by exact resemblance, but because it is very typical of the latter: Picasso painted a red circle as a symbol of the Revolution.

T

table a motion *(UK)* • table a motion *(U.S.)*

table a motion (UK)—place a proposal on the agenda: At last night's meeting the Board of Trustees voted to table a motion to approve our contract extension.

table a motion (U.S.)—remove a proposal from consideration; suspend debate until another time: When we had only five minutes left before we had to adjourn, Matt moved to table the motion.

take a bath • take an early bath

take a bath—(coll.) have large financial losses on an investment, etc.: The broker warned me that I might take a bath if I bought this stuff.

take an early bath—1. (be forced to) stop doing smth. before one had a chance to finish: He was all set to take an early bath from his marriage to have an affair with Suzannah Dwyer. 2. *(of a sportsman)* be ordered to leave the field before the end of play for breaking the rules: Paulo Wanchope was the other player to take an early bath, also for serious foul play.

take a beating • take some beating

take a beating—1. *(of one's pride, reputation, etc.)* suffer badly: My confidence and courage took a beating when I got calls threatening dire consequences. 2. *(Sport)* be defeated: This was the second time the Dutch team took a beating from Spain at this championship. 3. lose a lot of money: Not surprisingly, the company took a beating in the market, with its stock price tumbling nearly 25 percent.

Note: *The expression does not correlate in meaning with the phrase* ***take the rap****—(coll.) accept responsibility and the consequent punishment:* Arresting me? Nonsense! In any case, what about you? Do you think I would leave you here to take the rap?

take some beating—(also: take a lot of beating) be of very high quality and unlikely to be surpassed: Farnborough Air Show takes some beating. It's an incredible experience and a fantastic show.

take a chair • take the chair

take a chair—(also: have a chair) take a seat; be seated: When he came back to the house he refused to take a chair or a drink.

take the chair—1. preside over a meeting, committee, etc.: At my third meeting I was asked to take the chair. I consented as offhandedly as if I were the Speaker of the House of Commons. 2. become head of a university department: Clark continued to teach at Melbourne until 1949, when he took the Chair of History at Canberra University College.

Note: *The expression does not fully correlate in meaning with* *the phrase* ***get the chair***—1. *(coll.) be electrocuted:* He could … get you off, maybe with life or twenty years, while this way you're likely to get the chair, sure. 2. = *take the chair 2:* A few years later, I got the chair of Zoology at Lund University, and Eric got a permanent position soon after.

take a count • take the count

take a count—estimate how many there are of smth.: By taking a count we established that catering units were covering their seats 250 per cent at lunch time.

take the count—1. = *take a count:* Deborah took the count of members who plan to attend and asked them to refer to her any special needs. 2. *(Boxing)* be knocked out: "I nearly took the count that time, old fellow," he said. 3. be overcome or defeated: He took the count, having picked an election fight with the Prime Minister on the latter's home ground.

Note: *Neither expression fully correlates in meaning with the phrase* ***take count***—1. = *take a count:* The U.S. Census Bureau took count of how many grandparents are raising grandchildren. *2. pay attention to smth.; take smth. into consideration:* The model takes count of the thermodynamical characteristics of the sea surface.

take a dive • take a nose-dive

take a dive—1. *(of a plane)* make a sudden precipitate descent: The plane took a dive and disappeared underneath a mushroom-shaped cloud. 2. go into a rapid decline: By 10:30 the company's stock had taken a dive from more than $110 dollars a share to just over $40. 3. *(Boxing)* fake being knocked out in a match: He took a dive in the second round and made everyone suspicious. 4. *(U.S. Underworld)* get arrested *(also: take a fall):* I didn't want to take a dive, but the cop left me no choice.

take a nose-dive—1. = *take a dive 1:* The small plane took a nose dive. The pilot was able to bring it out at the last minute, so the plane didn't crash. 2. = *take a dive 2:* After a really splendid first week, the Festival took a nosedive from which it never recovered.

take a fall • take the fall

take a fall—1. lose one's balance and drop to the ground: When I took a fall and hurt my arm, Michele called me at home to see how I was. 2. *(U.S. Underworld)* be arrested *(also: take a dive):* Jack had taken a fall on a safe job and was in the Bronx County jail awaiting trial.

Note: *The expression does not correlate in meaning with the phrase* ***take a drop***—1. *(of stocks, temperature, etc.) lose value; decrease:* There is no guarantee that the account might not be worth less than your original investment if the market has taken a drop. *2. (coll.) have a drink:* All theatrical people, and even the great Edmund Kean, used to take a drop before commencing performance. *Cf.: take a drop too much—(coll.) be rather drunk:* If Henry took a drop too much he had always the melancholy satisfaction of knowing that he was driven to it.

take the fall—(coll.) take the blame for another person; become a scapegoat: Bob will take the fall for the director—he'd do anything to save his boss.

take a fancy to someone • take the fancy of someone

take a fancy to someone—become fond of a person: What could have made Miss Crowther take such a fancy to the boy?

take the fancy of someone—appeal to a person; win smb.'s favor: She became very active in the church group and soon took the fancy of Jeffrey Lundgren.

take a flight • take flight

take a flight—make a journey by air: She had to drive home alone, while he took a shuttle flight in the opposite direction.

take flight—(also: take to flight) 1. run away (from danger, etc.): Fear and panic gripped people and many took flight into fields and woods at the air-raid warning. 2. *(of birds)* rise into the air; start flying *(also: take wing):* The larger ground-feeding birds seldom take flight except to escape danger.

take a good part of something • take something in good part

take a good part of something—(of an activity) extend over much of the period: We went to the art gallery and explored it thoroughly, which took a good part of the day.

take something in good part—show that one is not offended; accept smth. good-naturedly: We had a good laugh at her expense, poor girl, but she took it in good part.

Note: *The expression does not correlate in meaning with the phrase* ***in good part****—to a great extent; largely:* There are limitations in this report, in good part because the study was forced to rely on the limited data.

take a hand at something • take a hand in something

take a hand at something—participate in a single round of a card game: We have a room where we can take a hand at whist.

take a hand in something—participate or be involved in smth.: We had almost got the plan worked out when the manager decided to take a hand in it.

take a leave • take leave • take one's leave

take a leave—(also: take a leave of absence) take a holiday: I took a leave without pay because I was, of course, being paid by the Colonial Office to go there.

take leave—1. part (from a person) with some expression of farewell: Before he went abroad, he took leave of all his associates. *2. (formal)* dare to do smth. without the permission or suggestion of another person: There is still one point more I must take leave to mention.

take one's leave—1. go away; depart: A terror seizing me lest this might be a preliminary to another fit of hysterics, I immediately took my leave. 2. = *take leave 1:* Gentle reader, having taken my leave of Mr. Slick, it is now fit I should take my leave of you.

take a liberty • take the liberty

take a liberty—(also: take liberties) 1. be unduly or improperly familiar with a person: He would be a bold man who ventured to take a liberty with her, or to overstep the limits laid down by her. 2. make free with smth. such as rules, facts, etc.: I'll take a liberty with the phrase. To call this man a minister is to stretch the meaning of the words, but I'll describe him as that. 3. dare to do smth. without the permission or suggestion of another person: I have taken a liberty to publish your article hoping that you would not be against it.

take the liberty— = *take a liberty 3:* I have taken the liberty of switching off your car lights.

take a long look • take a long view

take a long look—(also: take a long, hard look) make a detailed and intense examination: Wisconsin residents should take a long look at what their so-called representatives are doing with their money.

take a long view—consider events, etc. a long time ahead; have regard for the future: Kennedy called for Americans to take a long view when analyzing their current situation.

take a place • take one's place

take a place—1. occupy a proper or natural place: The chemical element Germanium appears to take a place between antimony and bismuth. 2. seat oneself: Dvorah took a place in the back of the courtroom, where she quietly recited scripture. 3. take up a job in a certain capacity: He condescended to take a place as job coachman in a livery stable.

Note: *The expression does not correlate in meaning with the phrase* ***take place****— happen; occur:* If an invasion took place the Chinese might enter the war.

take one's place—sit down in one's allocated or chosen seat: There was no applause when Dr. Werner took his place at the podium.

take a seat • take one's seat

take a seat—sit down; seat oneself: I took a seat in the back row where I hoped my person and my note taking would go unnoticed.

take one's seat—1. sit down in one's allocated or chosen seat: Archbishop Elder entered the sanctuary and took his seat at the altar. 2. *(UK)* assume one's membership in the House of Commons: Sir George Lynn, who was lately elected member for Milcote, will have to go up to town and take his seat.

Note: *The expression does not correlate in meaning with the phrase* ***take one's seat on the bench****—*1. *(of a judge) take one's seat on the raised platform in the courtroom:* When Lord Eldon took his seat on the bench and saw the vacant place where for years Romilly had pleaded before him, his eyes filled with tears. *2. become a judge in a court of law:* Bradley took his seat on the bench in October of that year, but was forced to retire a few weeks later by failing health.

take a shine to someone • take the shine out of someone

take a shine to someone—(coll.) take a fancy to a person; develop a liking for smb.: I suppose I oughtn't to blame you if Marion's taken a shine to you. You must have a way with women.

take the shine out of someone—(coll.) deprive smb. of his supremacy; surpass a person *(also: take the shine off someone):* That girl's got it in her, I can tell you. She'll take the shine out of some of our West-Enders.

take a sleigh ride • take someone for a sleigh ride

take a sleigh ride—(Drug users) take cocaine *(also: go for a sleigh ride):* Ernie left the room briefly to take a sleigh ride.

take someone for a sleigh ride—(coll.) mislead smb. deliberately; deceive or swindle a person *(also: take someone for a ride):* Purchasing from a familiar retailer can reduce the risk of being taken for a sleigh ride.

Note: *The expression is not antonymous in meaning to the phrase* ***give someone a rough ride****—(coll.) treat a person harshly; make smb.'s life difficult (also: give someone a rough passage):* It seems to me that he is being given an unnecessarily rough ride.

take a stand on something • take the stand on something

take a stand on something—(also: take one's stand on something) adopt a firm position concerning smth.: He sent a selection of newspaper pieces to the authorities with the request that they take a stand on the matter.

take the stand on something—vouch for smth.; stand surety for smth.: She is generally believed to be Sneyd's wife, though I could not take the stand on that myself.

take a toll of • take a toll on

take a toll of—cause a high number of casualties: The landmines took a toll of several thousand civilian lives.

take a toll on—have a very serious effect on a person: The walking was beginning to take a toll on all of us.

take a turn • take turns

take a turn—1. go for a short walk or ride: It was such a nice day that we decided to take a turn through the park. 2. do one's share; engage in a short period of activity: There was no wind so … each took a turn at operating the boat under engine power.

take turns—do smth. in turn; alternate at regular intervals: Since we took turns driving, we did not find the trip too tiring.

take account of something • take an account of something

take account of something—(also: take something into account) take smth. into consideration (when making a decision): Approval procedures should take account of the scientific quality of the project and the experience of the researcher.

take an account of something—estimate how many there are of smth.: Immediately upon hearing of the circumstance of the robbery, I took an account of the things that were missing.

take advantage of someone • take someone at advantage

take advantage of someone—outwit a person, especially unfairly; make undue use of an advantage: "You have brought me here under false pretences," I cried. "You have taken cowardly advantage of me."

Note: *The expression does not correlate in meaning with the phrase* ***have the advantage of someone****—(also: have an advantage over someone) have a better position or opportunity than another person:* "You have the advantage of me in courtesy as well as in years, sir," I replied.

take someone at advantage—(dated) take a person by surprise: The enemy effected a passage across the sierra, where a much inferior force to his own might have taken him at advantage.

take after someone • take off after someone

take after someone—1. resemble a parent or ancestor in character or appearance: I take after my mother in looks, but people say I've got my father's character. 2. set out in pursuit of a person: Victoria, enraged, ends up in the path of a bucket of water and takes after the brutish men with a broom.

take off after someone—(also: take out after someone) = take after someone 2: Claire took off after the robbers, screaming, "Stop thief!" as loudly as she could.

take air • take the air

take air—1. go out for a walk; go out of doors: Guests went out to garden, later also brothers Werners went outside to take air. 2. *(Ski jumping)* launch oneself into the air when skiing down a steep slope: I watch the guys take air and I say, "All right, I'm going to try it." I like the adrenaline rush. 3. *(of rumors, etc.)* become known; be made public *(also: take wind):* The FSB officers' actions took air not only in Russia, but also in other countries.

take the air—1. *= take air 1:* A few people were wandering among Ma's flower-beds, taking the air. 2. *(also: take to the air)* rise into the air; start flying: The three got into the plane, waved adieu to friends on the field, and with a roar the plane took the air. 3. *(sl.)* is used to tell a person to go away and stop being annoying: I was very patient with the man, but when he became abusive I told him to take the air. 4. *(euph.)* leave to use the toilet: Danny said he needed to take the air, a gentlemanly statement of his desire to use the outhouse. 5. assume the manner of a person: "Come you will be our honored guests at our banquet," Katya said again taking the air of a ruler.

See also: give oneself airs / give someone the air.

take breath • take in breath

take breath—(also: take a breath) 1. pause to rest after exertion (to allow one's breathing to return to normal): Halfway up the mountain we stopped to take breath. 2. take a break from one's normal routine (in order to do smth. different): After the frenetic activity of the last four years, we need to take breath and think. We need to reflect on where we want to go and how to get there.

take in breath—take air into the lungs; breathe in: When we talk, we don't stop to take in breath before saying a line, similarly, breath should be controlled when singing.

take charge of someone • take someone in charge

take charge of someone—assume the care of a person; attend to smb.'s needs: Bee was not well for a while, so I took charge of the babe.

take someone in charge—arrest a person; take smb. into custody: The constable called at Mr. Johnson's house and took him in charge.

See also: put someone in charge / put someone on a charge.

take five • take the fifth

take five—(coll.) take a short rest period: Hey, Bob. I'm tired. Can we take five?

take the fifth—1. *(U.S. legal)* refuse to testify appealing to the Fifth Amendment of the Constitution: Accused criminals can "take the fifth" without fear of reprisal. 2. *(coll.)* decline to answer a question: I'll take the fifth on that one. Ask Fred.

See also: give someone five / give someone high five.

take ground • take the ground

take ground—1. *(of ships)* run aground: The *Flying Scud* took ground on a bank of sand and coral about twenty minutes before five. 2. *(Military)* take up a certain position: Uncertainty was at last removed, by his marching towards Arcot, and taking ground before it.

Note: *The expression does not correlate in meaning with the phrase **take earth**—(of hunted animals) go into a hiding place:* Follow yonder fellow, and see where he takes earth.

take the ground—1. = *take ground 1:* The pilot was about to adjust course when the ship took the ground. 2. assert one's point of view: Mortillet took the ground that the flints found in Merovingian graves were either "strike-a-lights" or amulets.

take heart at something • take something to heart

take heart at something—(also: take heart from something) become more confident or encouraged by smth.: "I would have said the same of you," he added wryly, and took heart at hearing Hugh laugh.

take something to heart—(also: take something to one's heart) 1. consider smth. seriously; be affected by smth.: If you take this advice to heart, you will improve your singing a lot. 2. grieve or worry about smth.: She is a very sensitive person, who takes her troubles and disappointments to heart.

take it on the nose • take it through the nose

take it on the nose—(sl.) meet misfortune or defeat courageously *(also: take it on the chin):* And as the 1980s saw labor take it on the nose when choosing to strike, so the late 1990s have been an era of high-stakes labor wins.

take it through the nose—(U.S. Drug users) inhale cocaine: He went into the john, and most of us knew he had to take it through the nose right then.

Note: *The expression does not correlate in meaning with the phrase **pay through the nose**—pay too much for smth.:* It's a terrible car, and what annoys me is that I paid through the nose for it.

take it out of someone • take it out on someone

take it out of someone—1. said of smth. that exhausts or weakens a person: He needs rest. The excitement of the past few days has taken it out of him. 2. exact satisfaction from a person (for an offence): Now, you need to find a way to get the money back or your boss will take it out of you.

take it out on someone—relieve one's irritation, frustration, etc. by attacking smb. who is innocent: I know you're upset at missing the train, but that's no reason to take it out on the porter.

take it up with someone • take up with someone

take it up with someone—ask a person to consider the matter in question: Take it up with the insurance company, would you? It's not worth losing your no-claim bonus.

take up with someone—associate or become friendly with a person, especially smb. undesirable: The woman he "took up with" was likely enough to be married herself and of roughly the same age as his own wife.

Note: *The expression does not correlate in meaning with the phrase **take up for someone**—support a person in an argument, etc.:* "My mom and sisters always took up for me," Kyle said. "They were always on my side..."

take kindly of someone • take kindly to someone

take kindly of someone—(also: take it kindly of someone) accept smth. done by a person as a kindness or favor: I would take it kindly of you to move your car from in front of my house.

take kindly to someone—be attracted to or pleased with a person: They don't take kindly to me and so I suppose I'm not generous enough to take kindly to them.

take needles • take the needle

take needles—receive treatment by injections: Two of them have type one diabetes, and have to take needles three times a day or more.

take the needle—(U.S. Drug users) begin taking drugs by injection: They ended up taking the needle and catching some disease.

take note of something • take notes of something

take note of something—(also: take notice of something) take smth. seriously; pay close attention to smth.: I had to start taking some note of political developments.

take notes of something—write smth. down so that one can refer to it later: Concentrate more on understanding and taking notes of key points.

take one's hour • take one's time

take one's hour—use an approximate period of time that one may need: Almost everything should be covered in the writing guide, so take your hour or two, and read it.

take one's time—1. not hurry; be slow and careful: Just take your time and tell me clearly what happened. 2. *(sarcastic)* use more time than is reasonable: The workmen are certainly taking their time over the job.

See also: take the time / take time.

take one's life in both hands • take one's life in one's hands

take one's life in both hands—(also: take one's life with both hands) take control of one's life instead of just letting things happen: Lélio is determined henceforth to take his life in both hands, but the past casts its shadow even now.

take one's life in one's hands—risk losing one's life: You take your life in your hands simply crossing the road these days!

Note: *a) The expression is not antonymous in meaning to the phrase **put one's life in someone's hands**—allow smb. to have complete control over what happens to a person:* What makes you think I would put my life in your hands?

b) Neither expression correlates in meaning with the phrase ***take one's life****—(also: take one's own life) commit suicide:* A second Czechoslovak has tried to take his life as a political protest by setting fire to himself.

take one's measures • take someone's measure

take one's measures—take certain steps in regard to a given situation, problem, etc.: After five minutes' troubled reflection, Klimper took his measures. With unusual difficulty he procured a private interview.

take someone's measure—1. determine the different dimensions of a person's body for clothes, etc.: The tailor took my measure. Reichmann told him it must be made by the morning. 2. form an opinion of a person's character, abilities, etc.: I have encountered a good many of these gentlemen in actual service, and have taken their measure.

take one's medicine • take one's own medicine

take one's medicine—submit to smth. unpleasant; accept the punishment which one deserves: You go back and take your medicine like a man.

take one's own medicine—*(also: take a dose of one's own medicine)* receive treatment of the same disagreeable kind as one has given smb. else: Having the polygraph policy mandated by a Congress that doesn't have the backbone to "take their own medicine" is not a good way to convince people.

take one's orders • take orders

take one's orders— receive directions or commands: The civil patrol serves under the command of the chief commissioner, who takes his orders from the army command.

take orders—1. = *take one's orders:* Jules had to take orders from him pretending to go along with him in his ridiculous schemes. 2. *(also: take holy orders)* become a priest in the Anglican Church: I had scarcely taken orders a year before I began to think seriously of matrimony.

take one's stand • take the stand

take one's stand—take one's place or position: The players, except one, take their stand at one side, and one stands at the other side in front of them.

take the stand—1. *(U.S. legal)* come into the witness box to give testimony: The judge next asked the defendant to take the stand. 2. take one's position on an elevated platform (as a speaker, etc.): So many people roll their eyes when they hear a girl singer is about to take the stand.

take rank of someone • take rank with someone

take rank of someone—be of superior rank or status to a person: The first wife, however, takes rank of all the others, and is considered mistress of the house.

take rank with someone—be of the same rank or status as smb.: Far better is it to dare mighty things, than to take rank with those poor timid souls who know neither victory nor defeat.

Note: *The expression does not correlate in meaning with the phrase* ***pull rank with someone****—(also: pull rank on someone) use one's superior rank to gain an advantage:* "May I remind you that I am your superior?" Darcy glared at his cousin. He never pulled rank with him.

take service • take the service

take service—*(dated)* 1. become employed: Poor boys, of good families, will often take service as apprentices. 2. join a fighting force: Recollect, that, whatever general you take service under, you will follow him.

take the service—conduct divine worship: I'm not going to church this evening. The Vicar is taking the service and I can't endure his sermons.

take shape • take the shape

take shape—1. become definite in form or outline: In a short time the bag began to distend and then the balloon took shape and form. 2. reach the necessary standard; become complete: As Robin's plan took shape we could appreciate the brilliance of its simplicity.

take the shape—take the form of a particular thing: They [birds] are also called Boat-tails because their tail-feathers are formed so as to take the shape of a canoe.

take someone at his word • take someone's word

take someone at his word—assume that smb. means what he says and act accordingly, even if he may not have quite meant it: I was joking, but he took me at my word and arrived with a bag of sliced pork and herbs.

take someone's word—*(also: take someone's word for it)* believe a person even though there is no proof that what he says is true: I don't expect any of you to take my word blindly. Read the suggested articles and books.

take someone away • take someone off

take someone away—take smb. to another place; lead a person away: The prisoner was taken away by an armed guard.

take someone off—1. = *take someone away:* Before long the young prisoner was taken off for questioning. 2. rescue a person from a sinking ship: Before the ship sank, all the passengers were safely taken off. 3. *(Sport)* remove a player: The captain decided to take Snow off and try a slower bowler.

take someone into care • take someone into one's care

take someone into care—take a child lacking proper supervision, etc. to an institution run by the government or local council: The little boy's parents couldn't look after him, so he has been taken into care.

take someone into one's care—assume the care of a person; attend to smb.'s needs: I consider it a privilege to take your child into my care and I'm looking forward to assisting you in helping your baby become a well adjusted toddler.

take stock in something • take stock of something

take stock in something—have faith in smth.; attach importance to smth.: She always tends to exaggerate, so if I were you, I wouldn't take any stock in what she says.

take stock of something—evaluate smth.; consider smth. carefully: In starting out to look for work, a man should take stock of his particular training and qualifications.

take the heat for something • take the heat off something

take the heat for something—*(coll.)* take the blame for smth.; endure severe criticism: We took the heat for oversleeping and missing our flight when we landed.

take the heat off something—*(also: take the heat out of something)* 1. stop people criticizing or attacking smth.: The conference was designed to take the heat off his failure to make good on economic promises that got him elected. 2. lessen the bitterness or hostility of an argument, etc.: Ishiba tried to take some heat out of his comments, maintaining there was no evidence of an imminent North Korean attack.

take the road • take to the road

take the road—follow a particular route: We stayed high and took the road that followed the contours of the mountainside.

take to the road—1. set out; get on the way: I got back in the van, finished my ice cream and then took to the road. 2. = *take the road:* Jonathan Butts in a buggy, took to the road that runs between Palo Alto and Mayfield. 3. become a tramp: Cook did not take to the road through want, but rather from what the psychiatrists call "maladjustment."

take the time • take time

take the time—use a certain amount of one's time for an activity: I dislike to take the time to study out laboriously these things which are mostly well known to botanists.

take time—1. require time; extend over a relatively long period: It was merely a matter of shock to the nerve centers. Such a thing sometimes took time to mend. 2. = *take the time:* The abstentions of 1972 were due to an overwhelming conviction that Mr. Nixon had it made, so why take time to go out and vote?

Note: *The expression does not correlate in meaning with the phrase* ***take time by the forelock****—act in advance of an expected event:* The firm took time by the forelock in closing down before the strike.

See also: take one's hour / take one's time.

take the water • take the waters

take the water—1. *(of an animal)* enter a lake, river, etc. and begin to swim: I heard a splash and saw a deer take the water 300 yards or so above me. 2. *(of a ship)* be launched: The ship took the water beautifully, the strains of the band mingling with the cheers of those assembled.

Note: *The expression does not correlate in meaning with the phrase* ***take in water****—1. drink or absorb water:* If you sweat and don't replace it [water], you can get into trouble. Thirst should never serve as a reminder to take in water. 2. *(of a vessel) strike a leak:* In 1620, the boats set off from Southampton for the New World. Before too long the Speedwell started to take in water...

take the waters—drink the water of a mineral spring as a medicinal substance: He [Milton] died at Spa, where he was taking the waters, in September 1653.

take the wind • take wind

take the wind—(sl.) take one's leave; make a hasty retreat *(also: take the breeze):* I took the wind just as soon as I could get over the wall and get out of here.

take wind—(of a rumor, etc.) become known *(also: take air):* The preparations for Margaret's flight had not been conducted so secretly but that some rumor of them had taken wind.

take time off • take time out

take time off—remain away from work, study, etc. for a period of time (because one is unwell, etc.): I occasionally take time off to hike in the mountains and ski.

take time out—take a break from one's normal routine of studying or working (in order to do smth. different): I usually take time out during the afternoon for a cup of tea.

take to one's feet • take to one's legs

take to one's feet—1. *(of an audience)* rise to applaud, etc.: That's when the audience got in the act and took to their feet to applaud. 2. go on foot; walk: As buses and trams were abandoned or stood in long lines at blockades, the residents of Belgrade took to their feet.

take to one's legs—(also: take to one's heels) retreat in flight; run away: There was general confusion in the market and people took to their legs leaving behind their goods.

take up the baton • take up the cudgel

take up the baton—1. conduct an orchestra: Although when Barenboim first took up the baton there were some pianists who occasionally conducted, it was generally frowned upon. 2. take control or responsibility for smth.: Initial tests showed a decrease in noise levels.... The researchers then took up the baton to develop a solution to a problem as old as the railway itself.

take up the cudgel—(also: take up the cudgels) engage in a vigorous struggle or debate: It was a movement that sent thousands of conscientious objectors to take up the cudgel against military hegemony.

take wing • wing it

take wing—1. *(of birds)* rise into the air; start flying: The bird is remarkably swift on foot, and, though averse to flight, capable of great speed when compelled to take wing. 2. *(coll.)* disappear; vanish: I found a fellow who was in the same regiment with him, and knew this Mrs. Glasher before she took wing.

wing it—(sl.) speak or act without preparation: Mr. Trudeau came without notes, choosing to wing it.

takeaway • takehome

takeaway—(of food) sold to be eaten away from its place of sale *(also: take-out):* The market has many different types of stalls selling takeaway food at a very reasonable price.

takehome—1. *(of pay)* final net pay after all deductions have been made: He was not an officer, but with his extra duties, and benefits, his takehome pay was much larger than mine. 2. is used of texts and exams to be done at home: I also use my web site to post announcements to the class, and to receive takehome tests. *3. (rare) = takeaway:* It gets a little repetitious having takehome food or frozen casseroles for dinner every night.

taken short • taken up short

taken short—1. taken by surprise (being unprepared for smth.): They may have been taken short by the climate before reaching the Pacific. 2. said of a sudden need to go to the toilet: Simon was in such a terrible state of nerves that he had already been taken short twice.

taken up short—interrupted in one's speech: The chairman was just beginning to explain his plan when he was taken up short by a loud whistle.

taken up with someone • taken with someone

taken up with someone—1. greatly attracted to a person: Hasan made a feast for the four friends who were taken up with him, and sent them away with handsome gifts. 2. *(of an issue, question, etc.)* discussed with or addressed by a person: All of these policies are sanctioned by Boris Yeltsin and need to be taken up with him.

taken with someone— = taken up with someone 1: For whatever reason, Emma was just absolutely taken with him! Today was his second visit out here.

taken up with something • taken with something

taken up with something—1. busy or fully occupied with smth.: She discouraged Hughie from following her, saying vaguely that she would be taken up with the film festival. 2. finding smth. such as a thought, idea, etc. interesting or attractive: In the Russian revolution, the Mensheviks were totally taken up with the idea that the capitalist class should be involved.

taken with something—1. = *taken up with something 2:* He is especially taken with the idea of the North as a place of repose, a place to gather thoughts. 2. seized with smth. such as dizziness, a fit of sneezing, etc.: Mrs. Boffin was then taken with a laughing fit of clapping her hands, and clapping her knees.

taking one thing with another • what with one thing and another

taking one thing with another—considering every aspect of

the situation: Taking one thing with another, I should say that the press is slightly freer than it was.

what with one thing and another—because of various duties, happenings, etc.: What with one thing and another I forgot to tell you we couldn't come.

tale that is told • twice-told tale

tale that is told—said of smth. gone by; of smth. which is over and done with: The path of history is strewn with dead civilizations. Today they are all as a tale that is told.

twice-told tale—a hackneyed or trite story: To many of my readers all I have written will come as a twice-told tale, since thousands of men have undergone similar experiences.

talk about something • talking about something

talk about something—is used to emphasize the significance of the thing mentioned: Did you see the film last night? Talk about laugh! I've never laughed so much in my life.

talking about something—(also: talking of something) is used to introduce once again the subject that has just been mentioned: The weather affects how we think, move, and feel. Talking about the weather, it is hot and dry down here.

talk at large • talk large

talk at large—talk at length, with details: We have talked at large on the merits of the many different types of boats.

talk large—(coll.) speak boastfully *(also: talk big):* We will know soon enough if Mr. Johnson is going to continue to talk large and act small.

talk at someone • talk to someone

talk at someone—speak to a person without paying attention to his reaction: I wish he could talk to the class in a more interesting way, instead of just talking at them as if they were not human.

talk to someone—(also: talk with someone) 1. have a conversation with a person: "When you talk to the man upstairs," he said, "I want you to tell him something." 2. reprove or scold a person: I'll talk to that boy when he gets in! He won't bother you again.

talk big • talk small

talk big—(coll.) speak boastfully *(also: talk large):* "I hate to talk big," I said, "but I'm not afraid of Steelgrave or a dozen like him in one package."

talk small—(also: talk small talk) make conversation about unimportant things: We talked small for awhile, avoiding the obvious topic at the fore of each of our minds.

***Note:** The expression does not correlate in meaning with the phrase **sing small**—(coll.) adopt a humble tone or manner; use less assertive language:* Germans in Samoa. Their position was painful; they had talked big in the old days, now they had to sing small.

talk double Dutch • talk like a Dutch uncle

talk double Dutch—be totally incomprehensible when speaking: Oh yea, there was a guy explaining the system — in English and people were just looking at him as if he was talking double Dutch.

***Note:** The expression does not correlate in meaning with the compound **doubletalk**—(also: doublespeak) use deliberately imprecise, ambiguous language to disguise the actual meaning:* The group is demanding a "genuine commitment to transformation" and a move away from the "tendency to double-talk."

talk like a Dutch uncle—speak in a harsh, unkind manner to educate, encourage, or admonish a person: Just because he's older than me doesn't give him the right to talk to me like a Dutch uncle!

talk down to someone • talk up to someone

talk down to someone—talk in a way that suggests that the speaker is superior: It's unwise for a lecturer to talk down to his audience.

talk up to someone—1. be obsequious or super-respectful when talking to a person in a higher position, etc.: Don't talk up to someone, as if they are better than you. Don't talk down to someone, as if you are better than them. You are equals. 2. talk to smb. in a friendly and persuasive manner so as to gain favor, connections, etc.: He knew how to move at different levels; he could talk up to people at different conventions ... he knew how to connect.

See also: chat someone up / talk someone up.

talk English • talk in English

talk English—use the language in conversation: The team leader was German with a funny northern German accent when she talked English. I could understand her very well.

talk in English—have a discussion or conversation in English: The two ladies talked in English with Mr. Atwater, and I talked and laughed with the two children close beside me.

talk on something • talk over something

talk on something—speak at greater length on a subject; deliver a talk about a subject: I was asked to talk on the challenges which are likely to be faced by the scientific community.

talk over something—discuss smth. more seriously and in greater detail: I have seen numerous couples relax considerably when they talked over with others their childlessness and the accompanying fears.

talk shop • talk-shop

talk shop—talk about matters pertaining to one's work or profession: Wedged in among typewriters and an offset press, the two menfolk "talked shop" for most of the afternoon. *Cf.: shop talk — a talk about one's work or profession:* The real power of the conference was the conversations in the hallways, the shop talk over coffee...

talk-shop—(derog.) a center for idle and unconstructive talk *(also: talking shop):* The Social Forum should not be a mere talk-shop but it has to contribute to a concrete approach to issues.

talk someone through something • talk something through with someone

talk someone through something—provide detailed directions which enable a person to do or understand smth.: The nurse will talk you through the procedure and answer any concerns you have.

talk something through with someone—discuss smth. in detail; consider a matter thoroughly with a person: I need to talk it through with my partner to make sure that he is happy with how things are taking shape.

talk the same language • tell the same tale

talk the same language—(also: speak the same language) have an understanding with a person through similarity of outlook: I don't have many friends because I no longer talk the same language as the people I used to know.

tell the same tale—1. *(also: sing the same song)* express the same ideas, opinions, etc.: All those who have defected tell the same tale of a rebel movement in disarray after a series of military defeats. 2. reveal a similar undesirable or unpleasant situation: There seemed no city which did not in one way or another tell the same tale of economic decay and social disintegration.

tape machine • tape recorder

tape machine—a telegraphic instrument in which the message is printed on a paper tape: Some twenty men were crowding round a "tape machine" waiting for the result of the race to come through.

tape recorder—an electronic apparatus for recording music, etc. on magnetic tape: A tape recorder offers the additional facility of actual recording, either personally or from the radio.

taste like something • taste of something

taste like something—have the same taste as smth. else: The cowish or biscuit root is somewhat larger than a walnut and tastes like a sweet potato.

taste of something—have the hint of a certain specified flavor: If it tastes of the raw berry (as Egyptian coffee generally does), it is under-roasted.

tax avoidance • tax evasion

tax avoidance—the use of legal methods to pay the smallest amount of tax: I think that all these devices for tax avoidance ought to be stopped.

tax evasion—the illegal non-payment or underpayment of income tax: Most crooked businesses rely on substantial tax evasion.

tea boy • tea man

tea boy—(UK) 1. a boy employed to run errands in an office, etc.: I left school at 17 and I started straight away in a recording studio, initially as a tea boy then trainee tape operator. 2. *(coll.)* a general assistant: Mr. Fenby says he began his career as a journalist employed as a "tea boy" at Reuters news agency.

Note: *The expression does not correlate in meaning with the phrase* ***tea girl****—(also: tea lady) a woman employed to make and serve tea in an office:* She started out as a tea girl, then office junior in a busy credit department.

tea man—1. a merchant who deals in tea: The Chinese tea-men maintain a sort of incredulous nonchalance in the face of that almost complete capture of the market by the Indian teas. 2. *(also: tea master)* a man in charge of serving tea at a tea-party or other social occasion: In Kamakura for the first time a tea man did the tea ceremony for me.

tea hostess • tea lady

tea hostess— a woman in charge of serving tea at a tea-party or other social occasion: Mrs. Bowhill acted as model for the evening dress. Tea hostesses were Mrs. Kedge and Mrs. Williams.

tea lady—(also: tea girl) a woman employed to make and serve tea in an office: Two years ago, it seemed the ubiquitous tea lady was vanishing beneath a tide of vending machines.

teach an old dog new tricks • teach one's grandmother to suck eggs

teach an old dog new tricks—is used to say that old people can hardly be expected to learn anything new: This computer is far too difficult for me. You can't teach an old dog new tricks.

Note: *a) The expression does not correlate in meaning with the phrase* ***teach a pig to play the piano****—do futile work attempting to deal with smb. who is absolutely hopeless:* Teaching them democracy? It would be easier to teach a pig to play the piano.

b) The expression does not correlate in meaning with the phrase ***be an old dog at something****—(Austral. sl.) be skilled at or well versed in smth. due to a long association with it:* What I didn't know was that Chicago attorney was an old dog at the game of cross-examination. He was in his elements.

teach one's grandmother to suck eggs—is used as a caution against offering advice to others who are more experienced: There are people who know much more about this, but at the risk of trying to teach my grandmother to suck eggs, I will make the following observations.

tear someone down • tear someone up

tear someone down—(U.S. coll.) criticize smb. severely; punish a person: Why won't a politician talk according to his conscience? Because the next day, media and the opposition will tear him down.

tear someone up—(U.S. coll.) cause smb. much grief; upset a person: She's feeling really bad for Lodge because she knows how much it will tear him up once he realizes his mistake.

tear something down • tear something up

tear something down—1. dismantle or demolish smth.: The old theater is to be torn down and replaced by offices. 2. remove smth. by pulling down roughly: Even doors, fences, and planks from the wooden houses were torn down to serve as fuel. 3. *(of a machine, etc.)* take to pieces: We shall have to tear the engine down completely. 4. *(U.S. coll.)* criticize smth. severely: The insolence of a writer tearing down a piece before it's been performed!

tear something up—1. rip smth. up into pieces; destroy smth. by pulling it roughly: The workmen are tearing up the road to lay new electric wires. 2. *(of a contract, etc.)* break off: The workers have torn up the agreement with the management.

telephone girl • telephone man

telephone girl—an operator in a telephone exchange: The telephone girl sits on her high stool as she produces alternate order and chaos at her switchboard.

telephone man—telephone mechanic: Common usage among telephone men has led to the classification of telephone service as follows: local, suburban, toll and long distance.

television serial • television series

television serial—a story on television which appears in parts (usually at regular times): The novel has recently been dramatized as a television serial.

television series—a set of television programs, each complete in itself, that deal with the same subject: He is the co-author of the popular television series "Yes, Minister."

tell tales • tell the tale

tell tales—1. tell about smb. who has done smth. wrong; inform upon a person: Teachers hate children who tell tales about their friends. 2. give away private information to outsiders: You've no business to know that. Somebody's been telling tales. 3. tell a made-up story with the object of deceiving or arousing sympathy: David's mother was worried because he was always telling her tales.

Note: *The expression does not fully correlate in meaning with the phrase* ***tell tales out of school****— = tell tales 2:* He had learned the eleventh commandment [do not tell tales out of school] and was the safest confidant to be found.

tell the tale—1. = *tell tales 3:* "What did you tell me when you borrowed the money?" "Oh, we all tell the tale when we want money." 2. be significant or revealing: Had he been fired or had he quit. I flipped through the papers, looking for references that might tell the tale.

Note: *a) The expression does not correlate in meaning with the phrase* ***live to tell the tale****—survive a very dangerous or frightening experience (and so be able to tell about it afterwards):* Once she took a laxative overdose and the doctors did warn us that if she did it again there was no way she would live to tell the tale.

b) The expression does not correlate in meaning with the phrase ***talk the talk****—(coll.) speak fluently or convincingly about smth. so as to please or impress others:* They will hold seminars and they will talk the talk but in the end they will do nothing of substance to end the problem.

Ten Thousand Islands, the • Thirty Thousand Islands, the • Thousand Islands, the

Ten Thousand Islands, the—islands that lie off the southwest coast of Florida, USA: Marco Island is the largest of the so-called Ten Thousand Islands ... that stretch from Naples down to the southern tip of the Florida mainland.

Thirty Thousand Islands, the—islands that lie on the east side of Georgian Bay, Ontario (Canada): Georgian Bay Islands National Park is situated in the world's largest freshwater archipelago, known as the "Thirty Thousand Islands."

Thousand Islands, the—islands that lie on both sides of the U.S.-Canada border in the Saint Lawrence River just east of Lake Ontario: The St. Lawrence River was wide here in the heart of the Thousand Islands region...

tend something • tend to something

tend something—give care and attention to smth., especially smth. that needs constant supervision: He faithfully tended his garden all summer long.

tend to something—1. *(also: attend to something)* take care of smth.; deal with smth.: "I thought I heard you talking," she said as she tended to the fire. *2.* be generally inclined to smth. or likely to behave in a particular way: He was a born agitator, and as such tended to exaggeration.

tent-boy • tent-man

tent-boy—a young man whose job it is to have the tent put up and ready: Robert Blake plays a young tent-boy; tent-boy as opposed to house-boy since through half the movie the main characters were part of a caravan.

tent-man—1. a tent-dweller; a person who lives or lodges in a tent: I must admit I am a tent man. My tent can withstand anything ... it is also pretty low weight. 2. a man who has charge of a circus tent: As Joe hurried across the arena he saw the tent man who had given him the note.

Note: *The expression does not correlate in meaning with the phrase* ***tent camper****—1. a campsite dweller:* There will be a quiet area for tent campers who want to go to sleep after the evening performances have ended. *2. a trailer vehicle furnished for camping:* So my husband and I rented a tent camper for the weekend. We loved it!

test bed • tester bed

test bed—equipment for testing engines, etc. before their acceptance for general use: Once the engine was finished it was tested on a test bed, outside of the car it would be built into.

tester bed—a bed with four corner posts and a canopy: We continued in this suburb three days, during the greatest part of which time I was stretched on the tester bed.

test someone for something • test someone on something

test someone for something—perform a medical check on a person to detect a possible disease, etc.: The doctors tested him for malaria and other illnesses.

test someone on something—ask questions to find out how much a person knows about a subject: The teacher tested me on my knowledge of French.

that makes two of us • two can play at that game

that makes two of us—1. is used to say that one is in the same position: She wanted reassurance. That makes two of us, he thought. 2. is used to indicate agreement with what another speaker just said: "I find the Church's stance in this case absolutely revolting." "That makes two of us, Chris." *Cf.: that makes one of us—my opinion is different from yours here (used as a pun on the former):* "Liz, I'm really glad you decided to come here," I said. She gave a short laugh. "So far that makes one of us."

two can play at that game—is used to say that one can act in a similar objectionable way (as retaliation for smb.'s unfair practices): Sulking until you get your own way is a game that two can play, you know.

Note: *The expression does not correlate in meaning with the phrase* ***it is a game of two halves****— used to say that smb.'s fortunes or luck in sports, etc. may change:* The history of British Liberals is a game of two halves. Up to 1914, they enjoyed the moral ascendancy in politics.

See also: it takes two to make a bargain / it takes two to tango.

that will be the day • those were the days

that will be the day—1. that will be a great day worth waiting for: That will be the day when every class is a place where every child has consistent, quality instruction. 2. *(ironic)* that's very unlikely *(is used to express doubt following some boast or claim by a person):* "He says he'll do the washing-up." "That'll be the day!"

those were the days—is used as an expression of nostalgia for a happier time past: Well, those were the days. It was a great time for jazz in Chicago.

that will do • that will never do

that will do—that is enough; that will suffice: There's a lot more to tell about this process but that will do for now.

that will never do—is used to say that a situation is wrong and unacceptable: "They served red wine with the chicken." "Dear me! That will never do!"

that's about the size of it • that's about your size

that's about the size of it—*(coll.)* that sums up the situation; that's how things are *(also: that's about it):* "The house is exactly what we want, but it's too expensive." "Yes, I'm afraid that's about the size of it."

that's about your size—*(sarcastic)* one would expect that of you: That's about your size to send a threat through the mail, but I notice you haven't the guts to sign it.

that's all right • that's right

that's all right—1. said to smb. who has just thanked you or apologized: "I came to tell you how greatly our men appreciated your help." "Oh, that's perfectly all right." 2. it doesn't matter any more: I still don't understand it. But that's all right now. I understand why I don't, and that's enough to be at peace with myself at least.

that's right—that's correct: "Your name is Spanish, isn't it?" "Yes, that's right."

that's an idea • that's the idea

that's an idea—that thought, proposal, etc. is worth considering: Well, that's an idea all right. Not a good one, but it's an idea.

that's the idea—1. is used to indicate approval of what has just been said: "Shall I look and see?" "That's the idea." 2. that's what smb. has in mind: Personal liberty isn't everything. The collective utopian omelet cannot be made without breaking eggs or intellectuals ... I think that's the idea, and it's still quite a bad one.

that's life • this is the life

that's life—*(also: such is life)* that's the way things happen *(said with the implication that unpleasant events occur occasionally):* It's a pity Colin and Rowena got divorced, but then that's life!

this is the life—*(exclam.)* used as an admiring comment on a comfortable, enjoyable, and carefree existence: A sandy beach, plenty of hot sun, lots of nice people! This is the life!

that's my story and I'm sticking to it • that's the story of my life

that's my story and I'm sticking to it—said after an explanation which may not be completely true: It's been suggested that I saw the same shark repeatedly. But I saw three ... that's my story and I'm sticking to it.

that's the story of my life—said of smth. that supposedly summarizes one's unfortunate life experience: That's the story of my life. It seems like it was just last month that I was a world-renowned and universally-respected journalist...

that's the ball game • that's the way the ball bounces

that's the ball game—there is nothing one can do about a situation: I have to give points to Potter for her creativity.... But the film failed to engage me in its central drama and that's the ball game.

that's the way the ball bounces—(also: that's the way the cookie crumbles) that's the way things happen *(used with the implication that there are some things that we cannot control and have to accept):* He was fired. That's too bad, but that's the way the ball bounces in a recession.

that's the end of the ball game • that's the end of the line

that's the end of the ball game—there is nothing one can do any more about a situation: We had some lousy management that blew away what little we had—that was the end of the ball game. *Cf.: be still in the ball game—be still active; be still a part of the action:* The governor is still in the ball game. He can point to a number of successes, so he can be a creditable campaigner.

that's the end of the line—(also: that's the end of the road) this is the last point or stage: Most people just go to classified ads and think that's the end of the line in terms of looking for a job.

Note: *Neither expression is equivalent in meaning to the phrase* ***that's the end of it****—nothing more needs to be said or done about a situation:* If people were good enough to bring a gift, then you just said "thanks" and that was the end of it.

that's the way it goes • that's the way to go

that's the way it goes—that's the way things happen: That's the way it goes in any kind of criminal conspiracy to hide the truth. More and more people become involved, more and more crimes are committed to hide an initial truth.

that's the way to go—(also: way to go) is used as an encouragement to proceed with the chosen plan or process: Either I'm going to think about it every day or I'm just going to try to be positive about it and I think that's the way to go.

that's the way the cookie crumbles • that's the way the cow eats the cabbage

that's the way the cookie crumbles—(also: that's the way the ball bounces) that's the way things happen *(used with the implication that there are some things that we cannot control and have to accept):* One can't help but feel a certain amount of sadness at the change in state of affairs, but I guess that's the way the cookie crumbles.

that's the way the cow eats the cabbage—is used when telling another person some harsh or unpleasant truth that he probably doesn't want to hear: He is fully aware of my rules, one blunder and he is off the boat. That's the way the cow eats the cabbage.

that's what you say • you said it

that's what you say—(also: says you) is used to show one's disagreement or scorn of the other speaker's opinion: "They aren't going to go to the police." "That's what you say."

you said it—(also: you can say that again) is used to show strong agreement with what another person has just said: "That sure was a good show." "You said it!"

there are no two ways about it • you can't have it both ways

there are no two ways about it—it is certain or definite; there is no other possibility: The company is slowly going bankrupt and we'll have to look for another job. There are no two ways about it.

Note: *The expression is not antonymous in meaning to the phrase* ***there are more ways than one to kill a cat****—(also: there's more than one way to skin a cat) there is more than one method to do smth.:* I can marry the person I want, I guess. And if I can't do it here, well, there are more ways than one to kill a cat.

you can't have it both ways—one can't have both of two incompatible things or situations: It was the Pentagon PR machine that's turned you into a millionaire. Maybe you don't like everything they did, but you can't have it both ways.

there are too many chiefs • there are too many cooks

there are too many chiefs—there are too many bosses and not enough people to do the work *(in allusion to the saying "too many chiefs and not enough Indians"):* The problem with this organization is that there are too many chiefs.

there are too many cooks—is used to say that when too many people try to manage smth. they spoil it *(in allusion to the saying "too many cooks spoil the broth"):* If there is a problem, it's that there are two separate committees. In other words, there are too many cooks.

there is a first time for everything • there is a time for everything

there is a first time for everything—(saying) because smth. has not happened before there is no reason to assume that it never will *(also: there's got to be a first time for everything):* "I've never had a rheumatic ache or pain in my life." "Well, there's a first time for everything, you know, and you're not so young..."

there is a time for everything—(saying) there are circumstances in which doing any particular thing is most appropriate *(also: there is a time and a place for everything):* There is a time for everything you know; hence time for your private life should not be utilized for official activities.

there is no escape from something • there is no escaping something

there is no escape from something—1. said of a place from which one cannot get away: The jagged rocks are forbidding and dangerous. There is no escape from here. 2. said of a difficult situation that cannot be avoided or ignored: If there is no escape from check, it is checkmate and the game is over.

there is no escaping something— = there is no escape from something 2: There is no escaping the fact that the government has become very unpopular.

there is no knowing • you never know

there is no knowing—it is impossible to know: There is no knowing whether President Bush will make further Supreme Court nominations before leaving office.

you never know—one cannot be quite certain: You'd think the outcome of that case would be a foregone conclusion, but then you never know.

there is nothing doing • there is nothing to be done

there is nothing doing—(also: nothing doing) 1. used as an announcement of refusal of a request: Then my girl asked me to marry her. I told her there was nothing doing. 2. used as a declaration of failure in an attempt: I tried to find her a place to stay. But there was nothing doing in Rummidge that night. 3. no business is going on; things are very quiet: Mr. Winder is Justice of the Peace of Cedarville township, but says there is "nothing doing" in his court these days.

there is nothing to be done—there is nothing that one can do about a situation: There is nothing to be done about preventing other tragedies like this one, nothing that the ordinary citizen can do.

there is nothing for it • there is nothing in it • there is nothing to it

there is nothing for it—there is no other choice but to take a particular action: There was nothing for it now except to go straight ahead with the plan.

there is nothing in it—1. there is no significant difference between the people or things in question: The choice lies between Jones and Evans, and as far as their respective qualifications go, there's nothing in it. 2. *(of a story, accusation, etc.)* it is not true: There is nothing in it; the whole story is an absolute invention.

there is nothing to it—1. it is very easy *(of smth. that seems to demand skill):* I'll teach Jenny how to ride a bicycle. There's nothing to it. 2. = *there is nothing in it 2:* If he's guilty I'll hound him out of baseball. But I've got to know first, and I'm betting there's nothing to it.

thick as herrings • thin as a herring

thick as herrings—said of a great number of people, especially when crammed in a small area *(also: thick as hops):* Our position was in the center, on which the natives most politely avoided any sort of crowding, although behind they were packed as thick as herrings.

Note: *a) The expression does not correlate in meaning with the phrase* ***thick as thieves****—(also: thick as peas in a shell) used of people who are intimate or very friendly (often showing disapproval):* Right from the start it was obvious they were as "thick as thieves," one always keeping an eye on the other.

b) The expression does not correlate in meaning with the phrase ***thick as hail****—(of darts, bullets, etc.) following each other in quick succession:* The English archers poured upon them their deadly arrows in flights thick as hail.

c) The expression does not correlate in meaning with the phrase ***thick as two short planks****—(also: thick as a plank) very stupid:* Some of our greatest and richest superstars have been as thick as two short planks.

thin as a herring—used of a very thin person: He was a very small, dapper man, as thin as a herring, with projecting teeth and a huge drooping many-curled wig...

thick as pea soup • thick as peas in a shell

thick as pea soup—*(of fog or liquid)* very dense; concentrated: Wow, this coffee is strong! It's thick as pea soup.

thick as peas in a shell—*(also: thick as peas in a pod)* intimate or very friendly: Sam had had a game of billiards with the Baron, and they were as thick as peas in a shell.

thick end of the stick, the • thin end of the wedge, the

thick end of the stick, the—*(also: short end of the stick, the)* the disadvantage in a bargain, contest, etc.: Don't be cocky: producers always hold the thick end of the stick and you should know that.

thin end of the wedge, the—*(also: small end of the wedge, the)* a modest beginning which may lead to smth. greater: It is the thin end of the wedge — they will contaminate our agriculture and that contamination will self-perpetuate as time goes on.

thick on someone • thick with someone

thick on someone—*(coll.)* somewhat burdensome on a person: I don't grudge him the time off, but it's a bit thick on me, having to do all his work.

thick with someone—*(coll.)* intimate or very friendly with a person: Your Johnny seems very thick with that ginger-headed boy.

thick tea • thin tea

thick tea—1. strong, concentrated tea: He poured two mugs of thick tea and slowly shambled back to his sitting room. 2. *(UK dated)* an early evening tea with a full meal (as a substitute for dinner): The "thick teas" of Lancashire have long been celebrated for their eccentricity.

thin tea—weak, watery tea: She left the crib and sat at the table where she poured herself a cup of thin tea.

thin on the ground • thin on top

thin on the ground—said of smth. not numerous and therefore hard to find: Pheasants are thin on the ground late December and I don't usually shoot them this late.

thin on top—said of smb. having little hair left on his head: When I was at my twenties, I had good-looking hair, but now I am quite a bit thin on top.

think again • think twice

think again—*(also: have another think coming)* revise one's plans or opinions because they may be wrong: Those who think that the trade union movement should take a back seat in the Labor movement should think again.

think twice—use careful consideration; avoid hasty action or conclusion: She had seen that he was in trouble and she had given help without thinking twice.

See also: give it a second thought / have second thoughts.

think better of someone • think better of something

think better of someone—*(also: think the better of someone)* form a higher opinion of a person: Surely no one could think better of Jason for the quoted remarks?

think better of something—change one's mind with regard to smth.: Two years into his residency, Jadali thought better of his decision to become an internist.

think much about something • think much of something

think much about something—have the mind preoccupied with smth.: No one had taught her this, but she was a woman who thought much about God.

think much of something—1. = *think much about something:* He thought much of the evils of the journey for her, and not a little of the fatigues of his own horses. 2. *(usually negat.)* regard smth. as important; value or esteem smth. highly: He gives very good dinners, but I don't think much of his cellar.

think of something • think over something

think of something—*(also: think about something)* 1. concentrate one's attention on smth.; reflect on smth.: I kept thinking of Spain since that's where we were supposed to go on tour. 2. regard smth. as having a particular quality or purpose: We still tend to think of computers as powerful calculators, skilled at mathematical processes. 3. remember smth.; call smth. to mind: He often thought of the old farm where he lived before being sent to England.

think over something—give smth. careful consideration before making a decision, etc.: When he would not take a refusal, I begged him to give me twenty four hours for thinking over the question.

think too much about oneself • think too much of oneself

think too much about oneself—worry too much over one's own needs, etc.: What we call unnaturalness always has its spring in a man's thinking too much about himself.

think too much of oneself—have too high an opinion about oneself: They reckoned we thought too much of ourselves, all that education they said, and look what comes of it.

third class • third-rate

third class—1. *(railway carriages)* the class next below the second: Ladies traveling alone would never have traveled third class. Even ladies' maids always traveled second. 2. the lowest honors degree obtained from a British university: Some of my best friends got a third class degree, and they're amongst the most successful people I know.

third-rate—decidedly poor in point of quality: Do you honestly think Microsoft or Disney would hire a "third-rate" lawyer from an "undistinguished firm"?

third degree • third-class degree

third degree—1. prolonged or hard questioning; use of torture to get confession or information: "You don't think they're giving him third degree or anything of that sort?" "My dear fellow, third degree? You've been watching too many old movies on the TV." 2. *(U.S. legal)* the least serious grade of a particular crime: Maliciously burning in the day time a building, the burning of which in the night time would be arson in the second degree, is arson in the third degree. 3. *(in classification of burns)* highest in intensity: Injuries of the first and second degree will leave practically no scarring but serious deformities may result from the third degree burns.

Note: *The expression does not correlate in meaning with the phrase* ***third level****—(Irish) used with reference to higher education:* Greater resources needs to be put into education at the earliest stages so that young people will make it through to third level.

third-class degree—the lowest honors degree obtained from a British university: This was the year when Dodgson completed his studies receiving a third class degree in Classics.

this is where I came in • where do I come in

this is where I came in—1. this is where I had to do my part: The facilities they have must be maintained and improved, so this is where I came in to help out. 2. my knowledge dates from this point: "Anything else you want to ask me?" "No. This is where I came in. Tomorrow we'll go call on a few people who may have a few answers."

where do I come in—in what position am I under the circumstances; what part do I have to play: You ask me to work in your firm; but where do I come in and what are my duties?

throw one's weight • throw one's weight about

throw one's weight—(also: swing one's weight) use one's influence and personal power to get smth. done, etc.: I was prepared to throw my weight in Cung's favor. But he mistrusted me and rejected my council.

throw one's weight about—(also: throw one's weight around) aggressively assert oneself: She was in here the other day, throwing her weight about as if she was Hedy Lamarr and Katharine Hepburn rolled into one.

throw oneself away on someone • throw oneself on someone

throw oneself away on someone—ruin one's life on behalf of another person (usually a male who doesn't deserve it): I could forgive her if she hadn't thrown herself away on such a cheap sort of fellow.

throw oneself on someone—(also: throw oneself at someone) 1. physically attack a person: Mulder couldn't bear the humiliation and he kicked out at Fido, throwing himself on the man. 2. *(of a woman)* make very obvious her desire to begin a romantic relationship with a man: It wasn't the first time any of us saw her throw herself on men she didn't know.

throw oneself in something • throw oneself on something • throw oneself to something

throw oneself in something—(also: throw oneself into something) 1. jump suddenly into the lake, river, etc.: I won't be throwing myself in the canal over the collapsed deal. 2. engage vigorously in an activity: So he slowly began to pull away, throwing himself in his work in the hopes of making the inevitable separation easier.

throw oneself on something—1. *(also: throw oneself down on something)* lie down suddenly at full length on the bed, etc.: Miss Flora had thrown herself on a carpet by the bedside. 2. rely completely on smth. for help, protection, etc.: They are obliged to throw themselves on the parish for aid.

throw oneself to something— = throw oneself on something 1: He threw himself to the ground as the shells flew overhead.

throw something at someone • throw something to someone

throw something at someone—1. throw smth. so as to hit a person: One of the combatants threw a small paving-stone at his opponent. 2. *(of a question, remark, etc.)* say in a casual or rather aggressive way: I'm sorry about throwing all these random suggestions at you.

throw something to someone—throw smth. so that a person could get hold of it: After twice miscounting the sum, he threw the whole to his daughter.

throw something back at someone • throw something back to someone

throw something back at someone—1. return smth. by throwing it at a person, usually with a hostile intent: When I once threw a radio at him, instead of throwing it back at me he picked it up and started replacing the tubes. 2. remind a person unkindly of the wrong things he has said or done: Last night I realized how I was abused. Mistakes were thrown back at me, not once, but several times for the same thing...

throw something back to someone—return smth. by throwing it at a person: I don't know how he anticipated me being there, but he threw the ball back to me. It was a perfect throw.

tie someone down • tie someone up

tie someone down—restrict smb.'s freedom; encumber a person: I don't want to tie you down, but you do have responsibilities here at home.

tie someone up—1. bind a person with rope, string, etc.: The thieves left the old man tied up in the bedroom. 2. keep a person very busy: Writing this article should not tie me up for more than a week or two.

Note: *The expression does not correlate in meaning with the phrase* ***tie someone up in knots****— make a person very nervous or worried:* Kerry tied him up in knots just quoting his past utterances where he contradicted himself.

tie someone down to something • tie someone up with something

tie someone down to something—restrict a person to the terms of an agreement, etc.: If he tries to cheat, we must tie him down to his contract.

tie someone up with something—1. connect or associate a person with smth.: Isn't this company closely tied up with the continental industry? 2. fully involve a person with smth.: I'm afraid I can't help you now — I'm too tied up with other things.

Note: *The expression is not equivalent in meaning to the phrase* ***rope someone into something****—persuade or induce a person to do smth.:* I was roped into the school dancing troupe and we performed in front of an audience.

tight for money • tight with money

tight for money—having insufficient money: My father didn't know what to do; he'd only just started on his own, so he was tight for money as well.

tight with money—unwilling to spend money: I don't think he is a liberal. He's tight with his money, and he wants to see the poor work for their money.

tight on someone • tight with someone

tight on someone—1. *(of garments)* fitting too closely; being too small for a person: The Navy's largest dungaree shirt was tight on him, and he popped the buttons off when he expanded his chest. 2. *(Sport)* striving to limit the opponent's options and freedom of movement: Chiasson ... just fires the puck every time he gets it. And we've got to be aware of that; we've got to be tight on him.

tight with someone—(coll.) 1. miserly with a person: Buxton wonders why Lemoine's father is so tight with his son while lavishing money on Lemoine's youngish stepmother. 2. on terms of close friendship with a person: Our families grew up together and I got really tight with him.

till the cows come home • till the fat lady sings

till the cows come home— do smth. continually for a very long time: She likes to watch cartoons very much, she can sit before the TV and watch it till the cows come home.

till the fat lady sings—(U.S. sl.) till the end of smth.; until smth. is finally concluded *(also: till the last dog is hung):* This team has got heart of gold and spirit of an eagle, and will fight till the fat lady sings.

Note: *Neither expression correlates in meaning with the phrase* ***till the pips squeak****—(sl.) do smth. to the limit, even though it will make other people suffer (often with reference to excessive taxation):* Throughout my working life, and more so recently I've been taxed till the pips squeak.

tilt board • tilting board

tilt board—an apparatus for testing perception of bodily position by rotating a blindfolded person: The subjects stood on the tiltboard with lower-extremity support and were asked to maintain a balanced position on the board.

tilting board—(U.S.) a long plank set on a center mount for use in the game of seesaw: The outdoor toy called a seesaw has a number of regional names. In southeast New England it is called a tilt or a tilting board.

time fire • timed fire

time fire—artillery fire in which the projectile is intended to burst in air: Griffith told me to fire some hand grenades, which went off three or four feet above the trench and had the effect of artillery time fire.

timed fire—target firing in which a given number of rounds are fired within a particular time limit: After the slow-fire course is complete, the targets are moved to 25 yards for timed fire.

time service • time-serving

time service—1. determination of the precise time as the work of an astronomical observatory: The time-service has also occupied part of the energy of the observatory. 2. shaping one's behavior so as to please one's superiors or to fit the dominant pattern of one's times: This freedom from time-service gives a dignity to Heywood's character.

time-serving— = time service 2: It was all devotion, not time-serving as the vulgar thought.

See also: serve one's time / serve time.

tip someone • tip someone off

tip someone—give a gift of money to a waiter, porter, etc.: He ordered another beer, tipped the bartender five dollars on a five dollar beer, and went out.

tip someone off—provide a person with privileged or secret information likely to bring useful results: A friend tipped me off on a great gift for my son's birthday.

tired from something • tired of something

tired from something—physically tired; exhausted by smth.: Walter now plonked himself, tired from his walk, on the sofa.

tired of something—(also: tired with something) bored or mentally exhausted with smth.: This law limited any raising of property taxes, the people being tired of constant increases.

to a point • to the point

to a point—1. *(also: to a fine point)* thoroughly; completely: The idea is clear to a point: it is irrational to object to death, since we do not object to pre-natal nonexistence. 2. *(also: up to a point)* to a certain extent but not absolutely: To a point this is the sort of gamesmanship that attorneys, for better or for worse, do.

to the point—relevant; pertinent to the matter or subject in question: He made a suggestion that was altogether to the point.

to date • up to date

to date—so far; until now: One hundred and fifty letters were sent out regarding membership renewals, with forty responses to date.

up to date—in accordance with current fashion, technology, etc.: The need to be up to date might not have been the least of our driving forces for general progress.

to death • to the death

to death—1. until death results: Four members of a bush-walking club were burnt to death when trapped by a bush fire. 2. said of smb. sentenced to be executed: The Russian Embassy's source confirmed that a Russian citizen had been sentenced to death in China. 3. *(hyperbolic)* utterly; completely: But I see you are tired to death, and will wish you good night.

to the death—1. *(of combatants) keep fighting* until none is left alive: The British used to admire the men who fought to the death, paying the ultimate price. 2. *struggle* to the bitter end: What drove them was a corporate culture that made them fight to the death for their firms.

to some purpose • to the purpose

to some purpose—effectively; with good result: The merchants could concert together for the saving of their credit: and they did it to some purpose.

to the purpose—pertinent to the matter or subject in question: John never wastes time; he speaks plainly and to the purpose.

Note: *The expression does not correlate in meaning with the phrase* ***on purpose****— intentionally; not by chance:* It wasn't an accident — he broke the window on purpose.

to someone's teeth • to the teeth

to someone's teeth—(dated) directly to smb.'s face; in open defiance: The very men who had laughed the loudest at his jests, were now defying him to his teeth as a villain!

to the teeth—(also: up to the teeth) fully; completely: A young farmer who is starting out and mortgaged to the teeth at the bank would not look at it the same way.

to taste • to the taste

to taste—(in recipes) in the amount preferred: Combine the cottage cheese with the egg and season to taste with salt.

to the taste—1. said of the particular sensation in the tongue: The malt is decidedly sweeter to the taste then the original barley. 2. to a person's liking: Her neck and all about her is of that comeliness which is most to the taste of a man of my age.

to the bone • to the bone of one's back

to the bone—1. to the inmost part; completely: She was English to the bone and so naturally loved puzzles and intellectual entertainments. *2. (coll., of prices) reduce* as much as possible: We've cut our prices to the bone, and still the public aren't buying.

Note: *The expression does not correlate in meaning with the phrase* ***close to the bone***—1. *tactless to the point of offensiveness:* a remark close to the bone; a joke close to the bone. 2. *hard up; destitute:* He declined, in a family which was always living close to the bone, to take on any job.

to the backbone—(also: to the bone of one's back) = to the bone 1: Working-class to the backbone, just like us.... And if he's been filling you up with a lot of toffee to the contrary, more fool you.

to the day • to this day

to the day—1. *(of time measured in days)* exactly: "How long will you take to finish?" "I can't tell you to the day, but between two and three weeks should be sufficient." 2. up until the day: From the day we arrived in Italy to the day we left Athens, we had a tour guide showing us every interesting detail.

to this day—until and including today *(from the time smth. happened):* Still Crozier would not name his accomplices, and to this day he has kept silent about them.

to the nines • to the nth degree

to the nines—to perfection *(mainly in matters of dress):* This time, Mrs. Bassett was dressed to the nines in a fashionable frock of black chiffon and a black velvet picture hat.

to the nth degree—to the utmost; to the highest degree: True, the situations Mrs. Connelly causes are frustrating to the nth degree, but I guess the whole thing is open to debate.

toad in a hole • toad in the hole

toad in a hole—meat or sausages baked in paste: It looks more like fish-in-a-pond than toad-in-a-hole: you forgot to turn the oven on.

toad in the hole—1. *= toad in a hole:* To serve, cut the toad in the hole into sections with one or two sausages in each. 2. a game in which lead discs are thrown at holes in a wooden structure: Toad-in-the-hole probably originated in Tudor times. Since then, it has been played in many parts of the world. 3. a form of hide-and-seek: The children got tired playing toad in the hole in the deep weeds.

too many chiefs and not enough Indians • too many cooks spoil the broth

too many chiefs and not enough Indians—(saying) there are too many bosses and not enough people to do the work: "Too many chiefs and not enough Indians." In some cases that's what we are seeing in high-tech industry today.

too many cooks spoil the broth—(saying) when too many people try to manage smth. they only spoil it: "Too many cooks spoil the broth".... In other words, a good simple idea can be ruined by too many people trying to improve it.

top line • up line

top line—1. the uppermost line of text: A special machine, an "interpreter," can be used to read the cards and print their contents on the top line. 2. the head item on a bill of entertainment: His duets with Miss Muriel George have reached a top-line position on the halls. 3. headline of a newspaper: This big "top line" caught my eye: "The Pocasset filicide." 4. said of the best or most important traded items: Our huge purchase includes many carloads of the top lines of merchandise.

up line—(Railroad) a single track of rails in a double line of railway (for trains traveling from left to right): The train was accordingly shunted on to the up line and proceeded back to town.

See also: bottom line / bottom of the line.

top ten • upper ten

top ten—the highest ranking music items, goods, etc. on a ten-point scale: Pet foods come sixth in the consumer top ten. Baby food lags way behind.

upper ten—the upper social classes; the aristocrats: The upper ten still send their children to Eton or Harrow.

touch and go • touch and goes

touch and go—said of a very uncertain or critical situation: The day after the operation was touch-and-go. The patient needed a tremendous amount of fluid...

touch and goes—(RAF) landing and immediate take-off as part of the training for pilots: Touch and goes proved fairly simple; power on, flaps up produced almost spontaneous response with a short ground roll.

touch something • touch upon something

touch something—1. put the hand or finger upon smth. so as to feel it: As his hand touched the surface of the mirror, it rippled like the water in a pond. He drew his hand back, startled. 2. (cause to) be in contact with smth.: Scientific information on the Martian atmosphere was gathered even before the Landers touched the surface. 3. have to do with smth.: I still find it hard to believe teachers would come to workshops and refuse to touch the computers.

touch upon something—mention smth. briefly, casually, or in passing: Himes succeeded in treating more extensively and intensively themes he had only touched upon in his first book.

tough cookie • tough cookies

tough cookie—(sl.) an unyielding person who is difficult to deal with: He's a real tough cookie and you know it.

tough cookies—(sl., parenthetical) too bad; very unfortunate *(also: tough bananas):* If you give the wrong answer, well, tough cookies, you have to move backward.

tough nut to crack • tough row to hoe

tough nut to crack—(also: hard nut to crack) 1. a difficult person to deal with: Meggie was going to be a tough nut to crack and he couldn't afford to frighten her. 2. a difficult problem or task to undertake: Getting them all here on time will be a tough nut to crack.

tough row to hoe—(also: hard row to hoe) = tough nut to crack 2: Getting the contract signed is going to be a tough row to hoe.

Note: *Neither expression correlates in meaning with the phrase* ***tough act to follow****—(also: hard act to follow) used of an outstanding individual or a particularly good performance that will be difficult to emulate:* The gifts, the decorations, the food—everything was exacting and amazing. It will be a tough act to follow.

touring car • tourist car

touring car—an open automobile with a folding top: Mac and Jim circled the buildings and went to the ancient Ford touring car.

tourist car—1. a (rented) car used by tourists: An early start on all itineraries can avoid most tourist cars, tour busses, and crowds. 2. a railway car equipped with less comfortable sleeping accommodations than standard Pullman cars: Soft-sleeper berths and special tourist cars are available on most routes.

toy boy • toy man

toy boy—(sl., also: boy toy) a woman's very young lover: At 48 she is like a teenage girl again — raving it up with four different lovers including a toy boy of 27.

Note: *The expression does not correlate in meaning with the compound* ***playboy****— a rich man who spends most of his time enjoying himself in expensive ways:* Her fourth husband was a wealthy Irish playboy.

toy man—a person who deals in toys: Milliners, toymen, and jewelers came down from London, and opened a bazaar under the trees.

trade in something • trade on something

trade in something—buy and sell a particular commodity: The company of merchants included both general dealers and such as traded in only one kind of wares.

Note: *The expression does not correlate in meaning with the phrase* ***trade something in****—give a used thing as part payment for a new one:* You trade in your car and the minute you get used to the thing some bastard puts out a new model.

trade on something—take an unfair advantage of a person's weakness, ignorance, etc.: Employment agencies have been characterized as a class who trade on the needs of the inexperienced searcher.

trade something for something • trade something in for something

trade something for something—give one thing in exchange for another, in place of money: The cargo consisted of textiles and antiquated firearms. These were traded on the coast for slaves, who were shipped to America.

trade something in for something—give smth. in part payment for smth. else *(usually another article of the same kind):* You will own the vehicle when your payment period ends. Choose to keep it, sell it or trade it in for a new vehicle.

training college • training school

training college—(UK) a college for the training of teachers: How vitally important a good pupil-teacher relationship had been considered at my training college.

training school—1. a school preparing students for a particular occupation: The majority of nursery training schools do not make any hard-and-fast rule regarding the work which their trainees should take over. 2. *(U.S. euph.)* a correctional institution for reeducation of juvenile delinquents: The Penal Code was amended so as to authorize the commitment of delinquent girls to the New York State Training School for Girls.

trample someone under foot • walk all over someone

trample someone under foot—oppress or subdue a person; treat smb. harshly or ruthlessly: We loan them a degree of power, we do not grant them the right to trample us underfoot as they are doing.

walk all over someone—1. make smb. do whatever one wishes; take advantage of a person: Ashley was a hopeless romantic, but her boyfriends walked all over her. *2. (Sport)* win decisively over an opponent: Let them think that the Redskins will walk all over our team. Let them think it!

transit man • transit passenger

transit man—(U.S.) a surveyor who uses a transit-theodolite for the measurement of land areas: Continuous labor in solitary wilderness as surveyor or transit-man, is a totally different thing from taking a trip across the continent.

transit passenger—a passenger making a brief stop at an airport, etc. in transit to another destination: For the transit passenger the Corporation also runs special city sightseeing tours from the Tourist information Center.

transported by something • transported with something

transported by something—(of goods or people) carried from one place to another by a car, train, etc.: Field artillery has also been transported by sleighs, as in Canada.

transported with something—(liter.) overcome with some strong emotion: On hearing of the victory, the nation was transported with joy.

travel over the land • travel overland

travel over the land—pass through many parts of the country: At the time of the alleged events described in the gospels, scores of preachers traveled over the land of Israel.

Note: *The expression is not equivalent in meaning to the phrase* ***travel all over the land****— pass through or visit every part of the country:* To travel all over the land in search of wealth was one thing but to stay there was something quite different.

travel overland—travel across the solid part of the earth's surface (contrasted with traveling by sea): Judging from Marco's account, they most likely traveled overland through Armenia and Persia to Hormuz.

tread on someone's heels • tread on someone's toes

tread on someone's heels—follow a person very closely: We were walking up the hill, and our pace was much the same — I was treading on his heels without much effort.

tread on someone's toes—offend a person by treating him insensitively: As I was mentally formulating responses to it, I also became aware that I should be careful not to tread on his toes.

tread water • walk on water

tread water—1. keep one's head above water by remaining upright and pumping the legs: Two common ways of treading water are kicking extended legs back and forth and also kicking in an alternating manner, one leg at a time. 2. expend some effort but not make much progress: I realized that I was just treading water there in New Jersey — this isn't really what we want to be doing.

walk on water—do wonders; perform an impossible: Just look at the job ads for executives in today's newspapers — they almost expect you to walk on water!

treat someone to something • treat someone with something

treat someone to something—supply food, entertainment, etc. at one's own expense to a person: He told me that I was the only one to ever treat him to dinner, aside from his father. Isn't that sad?

treat someone with something—1. act or behave towards a person in a manner specified: They treated me with a respect that I am still unsure I deserved. 2. = *treat someone to something:* They treated me with a big steak dinner with all the fixings. It was great!

Note: *Neither expression correlates in meaning with the phrase* ***treat someone for something****—give medical care to a person who has an illness or injury:* Women who had been treated for breast cancer faced the risk of a local recurrence.

tremble at something • tremble with something

tremble at something—regard smth. with fear: To depart

from *Fashion* in a *Fashion-Book* is so shocking a thing that we tremble at the very idea of it.

tremble with something—shiver because of fear, cold, etc.: The children waited outside the school, trembling with cold.

trouble man • trouble-maker

trouble man—*(U.S.)* a workman employed to locate causes of problem and to make needed repairs: "Troubleman" McCarley located the difficulty, and repair crews worked until morning restoring service.

trouble-maker—a person that ferments strife and disagreement: My brother was a troublemaker and now they're taking it out on me.

trouble oneself about something • trouble oneself with something

trouble oneself about something—*(also: trouble about something)* worry about smth.; be concerned about smth.: If you trouble yourself about every little thing that goes wrong, you will never have any peace of mind.

trouble oneself with something—*(also: trouble with something)* be involved with smth.; preoccupy oneself with smth.: I have a good breakfast and good meal in the evening, and never trouble myself with lunch.

trouble someone about something • trouble someone for something • trouble someone with something

trouble someone about something—bother a person concerning smth.: I am sorry to keep troubling you about that letter, but until it is found I cannot answer it.

trouble someone for something—put a person to the inconvenience of doing or giving smth.: Could I trouble you for the newspaper, please?

trouble someone with something—worry smb. by bringing the matter in question before the person: He is always troubling me with some complaint or another.

trust in someone • trust to someone

trust in someone—have faith or confidence in a person: I slowly found myself able again to hope and trust in the human race.

trust to someone—act in dependence on a person; rely on smb.: The people of England are discovering that it is no good trusting to the old politicians.

Note: *Neither expression is equivalent in meaning to the phrase* ***trust someone***—1. *believe that a person is honest:* They want their neighborhood to be drug-free. They want to know and trust their neighbors. 2. *allow credit to a customer:* I wonder whether the newsagent will trust me; I need some cigarettes and I have no money on me. 3. *(followed by Infinitive) believe that a person is able and willing to do smth.:* She didn't trust anyone to look after her child properly. 4. *(followed by Infinitive, sarcastic) believe that it is typical of a person to do the wrong thing:* Trust Julia to get the name wrong.

trust in something • trust to something

trust in something—have faith or confidence in smth.: We felt that we could trust in his wide experience.

trust to something—act in dependence on smth.; rely on smth.: I don't know if it will work, but I'll just trust to luck.

Note: *Neither expression is equivalent in meaning to the phrase* ***trust something***—1. *believe smth. a person says:* Marigold is a wretched gossip, and worse. I would not trust her story. 2. *believe that smth. is safe or reliable:* He wanted to get up and walk out to the kitchen, but he didn't trust his legs.

trust someone for something • trust someone with something

trust someone for something—allow credit for smth. such as goods to a customer: Can you trust me for a packet of cigarettes until Friday.

trust someone with something—give a person the care of smth. with complete confidence: I've trusted him with everything I have — money, house, horses.

try doing something • try to do something

try doing something—do smth. as a test to see whether it is satisfactory: If you can, try sleeping on your back, it will eliminate some of the additional pressure placed on the jaw.

try to do something—make an attempt at smth. (especially without much expectation of success): The police is still seeking for the people who tried to break into the religious facility in Orasje.

try one's hand • try one's wings

try one's hand—attempt to do smth. unfamiliar: I'm new at this, and just wanted to try my hand.

try one's wings—try out a recently acquired ability: Marjorie just had her twelfth French lesson and wants to try her wings by speaking with our visitors.

Tudor flower • Tudor rose

Tudor flower—an upright stalked trefoil ornament in architectural decoration of the Tudor period: The pulpit carved with Tudor flower and vines dates from about 1460. It is one of about 60 mediaeval stone pulpits which remain in England.

Tudor rose—a conventional figure of a rose in architectural decoration of the Tudor period: This form of decoration was introduced into England from Italy in the time of Henry VIII and was often combined with Tudor roses.

tug at something • tug something

tug at something—pull hard at smth. such as a rope: Don't tug at the leash or become impatient.... Your cat will be compelled to cooperate by your calm steadfastness.

tug something—move smth. by pulling or dragging forcibly: Navigation is difficult with sand shoals; boatmen wade waist deep for more than an hour tugging the boat.

turn a trick • turn the trick

turn a trick—*(sl.)* 1. have casual sexual relations, especially for money: Some of the young prostitutes live at home and turn tricks merely for pocket money. 2. *(Underworld)* commit a successful robbery: Campbell's claim was that he hadn't turned a trick in a year but the money had to be coming from somewhere.

turn the trick—accomplish one's purpose; achieve the required result: It is our hope and prayer that Mr. Farley may turn the trick. We should be glad to see any administrator make a go of the postal service.

turn in on oneself • turn oneself in

turn in on oneself—have as little as possible to do with other people: She has become introverted, turned in on herself, and has broken off contact with the world that she no longer knows.

turn oneself in—give oneself to the police: It seems that Ford's brother, Rod, had convinced him to turn himself in, although he did not actually realize what Ford had done.

Note: *The expression does not correlate in meaning with the phrase* ***turn in***—*(coll.) go to bed:* After we had a late dinner, we decided to turn in for the night.

turn on someone • turn to someone

turn on someone—*(coll.)* attack smb. with hostile words; speak angrily to a person: Why did she turn on me like that? Have I said something to offend her?

Note: *The expression does not correlate in meaning with the*

phrase ***turn someone on****—(coll.) cause a person to become interested or (sexually) excited:* I went to bed with him a couple of times. But he never really turned me on. *Cf.: turn someone on to something—(coll.) cause smb. to become interested or involved in smth. (especially drugs):* Someone in prison turned her on to heroin but she uses it rarely.

turn to someone—go to smb. for help, advice, comfort, etc.: Bruce has always been really close with his Dad and has always turned to him for support.

turn on the waterworks • turn someone's water off

turn on the waterworks—(coll.) begin to cry *(also: turn on the water tap):* Sally turned on the waterworks when she got yelled at.

turn someone's water off—(coll.) make a person appear more modest *(usually of smb. who is acting too arrogant):* It took a scolding from the coach to turn Tom's water off.

turn one's back on someone • when someone's back is turned

turn one's back on someone—abandon or ignore smb.; refuse to support a person: When he seemed to turn his back on me I felt bereft, really. But then one day he rang up and I could hear his voice shaking with emotion.

when someone's back is turned—do smth. when a person is not present or looking: If they're saying this about Fred, what are they saying about me when my back is turned?

Note: *Neither expression correlates in meaning with the phrase* ***see the back of someone****— be pleased when smb. leaves because one does not like the person:* I wasn't sorry to see the back of Suzy after what she did, but it really broke my heart to let Ziggy go.

turn someone's brain • turn someone's head

turn someone's brain—1. cause mental disorder: The only possible explanation was that the poor girl's illness and the loss of her lover had turned her brain. 2. make a person wildly agitated or distraught: Too much of this sort of work turns your brain.

turn someone's head—1. cause a person to have too high an opinion of oneself: She is a famous actress but she has not allowed success to turn her head. 2. cause a person to become infatuated: You have been making serious love to Patty, and have turned the poor girl's head. 3. create a sensation of giddiness: To look down from a great height is enough to turn one's head.

Note: *The expression does not correlate in meaning with the phrase* ***turn heads****—strongly impress people (by looking very attractive):* Cher turned heads when she appeared at the ceremony in a dress that left little to the imagination.

turn something on its head • turn something upside down

turn something on its head—(also: stand something on its head) cause a complete reversal of what is regarded as the norm: Suddenly, Jayne's once sane life is turned on its head, and not even her closest friends are what they seem.

turn something upside down—1. reverse smth. physically: Wolfe uncorked the bottle and turned it upside down. The water splashed the stones at Turrell's feet. 2. = *turn something on its head:* That would have turned charity tax law upside down. 3. search everywhere in a place, especially roughly: The police turned his flat upside down looking for drugs.

twin set • two-piece set

twin set—a woman's sleeveless sweater and cardigan of the same color and style that are worn together: I thought of wearing a twin set to a symphony concert.

two-piece set—(also: two-piece) a set of clothes of similar or matching material: Pajamas are usually sold as a two piece set with matching tops and bottoms.

twist someone's arm • twist someone's tail

twist someone's arm—1. persuade a person to do smth. by pressure: Nobody forced him to go there and nobody twisted his arm to make connections with dubious characters. 2. *(joc.)* "persuade" a person to have a drink, when no persuasion at all is needed: "That looks a nice pub over there." "All right—you've twisted my arm enough," admitted Boote.

twist someone's tail—(coll.) harass or maliciously annoy a person: Revenge seems to me least likely. Grown men don't kill boys just because they've had their tails twisted by them.

two bits • two-bit

two bits—(U.S. coll.) twenty five cents; a quarter coin: Many saloons served the "choicest goods" and steam beer at two bits a glass.

two-bit—(U.S. coll., attrib.) 1. of smth. that costs a quarter of a dollar: He smoked two-bit cigars and peered determinedly through steel-rimmed glasses. 2. *(derog.)* cheap; worthless: But people who took the time to vote have to feel like the whole process was a two-bit hoax. *Cf.: ten-cent man—(U.S. derog.) a small, narrow-minded, trifling man:* Do you want a ten-cent man to fill a hundred-dollar job? How big a problem is this that you have demonstrated right here to me tonight?

U

umbrella pine • umbrella tree

umbrella pine—1. *(also: stone pine)* a species of pine tree *(Pinus pinea)* with branches at the top spreading like an umbrella: The umbrella pine has been growing here for at least two thousand years. 2. a tall Japanese evergreen conifer tree *(Sciadopitus verticillata)* with an umbrella-like ring of leaves: The English name "umbrella pine" refers to the whorls of leaves resembling the spokes of an umbrella.

umbrella tree—1. a small magnolia *(Magnolia tripetala)* with leaves in a spiral like an umbrella: The wood of the Umbrella Tree is more spongy than any of the other species of Magnolia. 2. one of a variety of trees whose leaves resemble an umbrella: Umbrella Tree: *Schefflera actinophylla.* This is a member of the family *Araliaceae,* widely cultivated in tropical and subtropical gardens.

Uncle Tom • Uncle Tom Cobley

Uncle Tom—(U.S.) a Black man who defers to white people and regarded as betraying his social loyalty: I know exactly what you think of me. Also, I know all the words, most of them stupid—white nigger, Uncle Tom—as well as you.

Note: *The expression does not correlate in meaning with the phrase* ***Aunt Tom****—(sl.) a woman who does not agree with or support the Feminist movement:* In a debate between Wolfgang and Friedan, things rapidly devolved into mutual name calling with each accusing the other of being an "Aunt Tom."

Uncle Tom Cobley—(also: Uncle Tom Cobley and all) a whole lot of other people *(used at the end of a long list of names):* We are exhorted to pant along behind the industrious Germans, Japanese, Russians, Americans and Uncle Tom Cobley.

under arms • under the gun

under arms—said of people who are armed and prepared for fighting: Japan still had millions of troops under arms and thousands of combat aircraft.

under the gun—acting under a lot of pressure: They did a great job, especially working under the gun with only a few months to get it organized and executed .

Note: *The expression does not correlate in meaning with the phrase* ***under the knife****—used of smb. undergoing a surgical operation:* She was under the knife for several hours. When she came out of surgery, doctors said she was fine.

under cover • undercover

under cover—1. under a shelter protecting from rain, wind, etc: Monsieur had better come under cover. The "Bosches" are still firing this way. 2. *(of police or secret service agents)* operating in secret: He worked under cover ... in some of the most important theaters of the Cold War. 3. *(dated or formal)* in an envelope: The letter was passed to the Attorney General who sent a copy of the letter under cover asking for comment. *Cf.: under plain cover—in an envelope which has no indication of the firm, the contents, etc.:* Credit card statements do not show our company name and all products are shipped under plain cover.

Note: *The expression does not correlate in meaning with the phrase* ***under wraps****—used of smth. kept secret:* The investigation apparently cleared the officers of any wrongdoing but the details are still under wraps.

undercover—(attrib.) 1. situated under the roof; sheltered from the elements: Undercover storage for vehicles is available for either short or long term requirements. 2. *(of methods, agents, etc.)* underground; secret: The menace of recruitment to undercover prostitution on a large scale cannot be ignored.

under ground • underground

under ground—below the surface of the ground: Attending college while working under ground is not a dream come true, but conductors are well paid.

underground—(attrib.) 1. situated or taking place below the surface of the ground: This difference could have been the result of the unaccounted for flow of underground waters into the lake. 2. *(of a political movement, etc.)* concealed and acting in secret: Until recently people suspected of underground activity had been arrested and court-martialed. 3. separate from a prevailing social or artistic environment: Although this form of underground art rarely makes it into the museums, it has attracted huge interest in recent years.

under heaven • under the sky

under heaven—1. on earth; in the world: You travel for twenty miles over one of the most unfortunate, desolate countries under heaven. 2. is used to emphasize an interrogative sentence: And why under heaven should one write a history of anything—even a tramp dog!—without a sense of humor!

under the sky—1. *(also: under the open sky)* in the open air; not inside a house or building: I will sleep under the sky rather than stay in the city for another night. 2. = *under heaven 1:* Am I deceived, I who have known more liars than any man under the sky?

Note: *Neither expression correlates in meaning with the phrase* ***under a cloud****—suspected of smth. reprehensible:* He leaves the service, possibly under a cloud.... The inference in the club think tank was that the cloud was sexual.

under one's arm • under one's hand

under one's arm—held between the arm and the body: Alfredo wandered about the snow-covered streets with the manuscript of his last tragedy under his arm.

under one's hand—(of a document) authenticated by a person's signature: Lady Bellasis gained so much on the duke, that he gave her a promise under his hand to marry her.

Note: *The expression does not correlate in meaning with the compound* ***underhand****—(also: underhanded)* 1. *done in a secret or stealthy manner:* Their influence must have been exercised in a purely underhand way. 2. *not legal; corrupt or marked by deception:* We have found that banks are employing increasingly underhand methods to avoid their responsibility.

under the arm • under-arm

under the arm—1. held between the arm and the body: The hat could be worn or carried under the arm at all times except in the presence of the King. 2. *(sl.)* inferior; of poor quality: I read no matter how bad the book and some are right under the arm.

under-arm—(attrib.) 1. that can be carried "under the arm": Whatever she carries about with her she keeps in an "under-arm bag." 2. *(sl.)* pornographic; obscene: One of the first things Randle asked him was did he make any under-arm films.

under the color of something • under the colors of something

under the color of something—under pretext or pretence of smth.: A lot of what this unscrupulous politician writes under the color of truth is nothing but a pack of lies.

under the colors of something—supporting a particular cause, movement, or country: Northmour was killed fighting under the colors of Garibaldi for the liberation of the Tyrol.

under the daisies • under the rose

under the daisies—(euph.) dead and buried: He gradually declined for twelve months, and next harvest-time he was under the daisies.

under the rose—in secret; in strict confidence: Any business transacted privately, or under the rose, is said to be done *upon the sly*.

under the wire • under wire

under the wire—just before a deadline; at the last possible moment: Nancy mailed off her application, and it got in just under the wire.

Note: *The expression is not antonymous in meaning to the phrase* ***over the wire****—(dated) speaking on the telephone (also: on the wire):* The second advertisement shows a Victorian-looking man speaking over the wire to a woman.

under wire—1. *(of an area)* fenced with barbed wire: There is the outer perimeter of the military unit, which is under wire, nearby our house. 2. *(of railroads)* electrified: The United States at that time had more miles of track "under wire" than any other country.

under water • underwater

under water—beneath the surface of the water: "I was flying!" Ben says. "And I could see things under water from the sky like turtles and coral reefs. It was good!"

underwater—(attrib.) situated or utilized beneath the surface of the water: The underwater cable allows to fulfill the traffic needs of broad band telecommunications and cable TV.

underground railway *(UK)* • underground railway *(U.S.)*

underground railway (UK)—the underground railway transport system in a large city: The growing population made traveling in London very difficult, and it was thought that an underground railway would solve many congestion problems.

underground railway (U.S.)—(hist.) the chain of safe houses used by slaves escaping from the South prior to the abolition of slavery: Windsor was an important terminal of the Underground Railway. Fugitive slaves landing near this spot found in Canada protection under the British flag.

universal aunt • universal maid

universal aunt—a kindhearted woman who provides various assistance to her acquaintances: She efficiently acted as universal aunt for Peter and we felt this was a big help.

universal maid—a female servant who does all kinds of housework: She had been in the kitchen helping Becky, the universal maid.

Unrighteous Bible, the • Wicked Bible, the

Unrighteous Bible, the—a Bible printed in 1653, containing the printer's error, "know ye not that the unrighteous shall inherit [for 'shall not inherit'] the Kingdom of God": At Cambridge in 1653 was printed the justly nicknamed "Unrighteous Bible." It was marred by two bloopers, both concerning righteousness.

Wicked Bible, the—a Bible printed in 1632 with the word "not" omitted in the seventh commandment, making it, "Thou shalt commit adultery": King Charles was not amused by the "Wicked Bible," as the infamous printing mistake was called.

up and coming • up and running

up and coming—becoming more and more successful; showing great promise: David is an up and coming assistant professor in the Computer Science department. *Cf.: up-and-comer—a person who has begun to be successful in some field and is likely to become even more successful in the future:* Fisher is an up and comer in the music industry.

Note: *The expression does not correlate in meaning with the adjective* ***upcoming****—forthcoming; about to happen:* If you would like to register for the upcoming event, complete the registration form.

up and running—(of a machine, etc.) operating; functioning (especially when fixed after a breakdown): Now that the operating system is up and running, it is time to make it more secure.

Note: *The expression is not equivalent in meaning to the phrase* ***off and running****—1. (of horse races) having started:* The crowd's on its feet at the finish screaming their heads off. And in five minutes, the next race is off and running.... *2. making a good start; progressing well:* The construction was going to take two years, but we were off and running, and it appeared we would finish on schedule.

up the creek • up the river

up the creek—(sl.) facing problems; in trouble *(also: up the creek without a paddle):* If that person is on vacation or otherwise not reachable, I am up-the-creek.

up the river—(U.S. Underworld) in prison: Gary was up the river for a couple of years, but that doesn't make him a criminal, does it?

Note: *The expression is not antonymous in meaning to the phrase* ***down the river****—(sl.) in the past; over and done with:* True enough, I used to hustle a little beer in the old days—but that's all down the river.

up to the last minute • up to the minute

up to the last minute—until the last possible moment; until the very end: Despite feverish negotiations and efforts up to the last minute, the House and Senate failed to negotiate a compromise.

up to the minute—1. *(of things)* most modern; the latest that can be offered: Contact us if you want an up-to-the-minute report on bills moving through the Legislature. 2. *(of people)* thinking or behaving in the most modern way: She is a very attractive young woman, vivacious, up to the minute, a thoroughly modern young woman.

Note: *The expression does not correlate in meaning with the phrase* ***to the minute****—1. exactly on time:* The limousine arrived to the minute, and she climbed in gracefully despite her excitement. 2. *(of the rate) every minute:* Her pulse rate was barely 12 beats a minute, breaths came three to the minute, and there was no measurable blood pressure. 3. *up until the moment:* We went expecting a great time and were not disappointed, from the moment we arrived to the minute we left.

uppers and downers • ups and downs

uppers and downers—1. positive and negative fluctuations in fortune, business, etc.: In the case of both the uppers and the downers, it would be a good idea to examine the companies more closely to see how meaningful these one-year trends are. 2. *(dated coll.)* teeth: The film pokes fun of the idyllic, monochromatic life in the 1950s—a time when uppers and downers meant teeth and problems were purely mathematical. 3. *(Drugs)* stimulants and depressants: Not too long after this I started taking downers in order to go to sleep. Now I was taking uppers to wake up and downers to sleep.

ups and downs—1. irregularities on the surface of ground, etc.: He had forgotten that the road was narrow, twisting and full of ups and downs, which slowed them down continuously. 2. = *uppers and downers 1:* The net effect of this large-scale gambling in raw materials, with its feverish ups and downs, has been to weaken Britain's world position.

See also: high and low / up and down.

V

van guard • vanguard

van guard—a guard for a railway van or a motor truck: Van guard travels with and guards contents of mail vans.

vanguard—1. the troops who march at the head of an army: The vanguard was composed of chasseurs of the line, hussars, and lancers. 2. the leaders of thought, taste, or opinion in literature, art, etc.: It is this vanguard which makes the studio or art theater possible.

visit with someone *(UK)* • visit with someone *(U.S.)*

visit with someone (UK)—pay a visit to a person: Weekends we usually visit with my husband's family.

visit with someone (U.S.)—talk with smb. on a short visit: "When will I be able to see him?" "Right now, if you like. You can visit with him in his cell or see him right here in my office."

visiting book • visitors' book

visiting book—1. a book containing the names of persons to be visited: Julia will be missed at St. Christopher's Hospital and by the many people in her visiting book. 2. a book for the signatures and comments of visitors to a museum, etc.: The Bishop went and wrote his name in the visiting-book at Gaunt House that very day.

visitors' book— = *visiting book 2:* The Emperor Nicholas "expressed himself much pleased," as the visitors' books have it.

vital measurements • vital statistics

vital measurements—the measurements of a woman's figure, specifically bust, waist, and hips: She is blessed with a slender body, but needs to find a way to stay in control of the vital measurements.

vital statistics—1. statistics concerned with births, marriages, deaths, etc.: The best data source for mortality is vital statistics of deaths with medically-certified cause of death. 2. = *vital measurements:* Regina wrote haphazardly to men, giving her age and vital statistics. 3. *(med.)* the parameters important for survival, such as blood pressure, heart rate, etc.: Monitoring pads are attached prior to the surgery to allow the surgical team to monitor vital statistics during the operation.

wait for someone • wait up for someone

wait for someone—1. remain in a place in expectation of a person or thing: When she got there Tommy was waiting for her on the front steps. 2. *(of things)* be ready or available for a person to use: His car waited for him in the parking lot and he jumped behind the wheel. 3. stop or pause so that another person can catch up: The faster scouts will want to hike to the next trail intersection and wait for the slower hikers.

Note: *The expression does not correlate in meaning with the phrase* ***wait on someone***—1. *serve people in a restaurant, shop, etc.:* Duties include setting tables, serving food, waiting on customers and any other tasks required. 2. *(of a butler, nurse, etc.) attend on a person:* She was an earnest church worker and was at all times to be found calling and waiting on the sick.

wait up for someone—1. stay late out of bed until smb. arrives: I may be late, but please don't wait up for me. 2. = *wait for someone 3:* They were able to keep up a steady pace, with only a minimal amount of the stop and go that happens when the faster riders wait up for the slower ones.

wait for the dust to settle • wait for the ink to dry

wait for the dust to settle—wait for things to calm down; avoid undertaking smth. because things are too chaotic: Fearful for their lives, many leaders have scattered, waiting in exile for the dust to settle.

wait for the ink to dry—not be in a rush to do smth.; take one's time: It is a little too early yet to reveal all the details and I have learned it is best to wait for the ink to dry before you say too much.

wake sleeping dogs • wake snakes

wake sleeping dogs—*(also: wake a sleeping dog)* create trouble interfering with a precarious situation which is quiet: Some say that it is too early to fix any rules, or that it is really dangerous to do so: it might wake sleeping dogs. *Cf.: let sleeping dogs lie—refrain from stirring up potential trouble:* How many times had he told her it was over, that she needed to move on and let sleeping dogs lie?

wake snakes—*(dated sl.)* cause trouble or disturbance: But what about some phrases that we don't hear very often anymore? I found some of these quite interesting. To wake snakes, meant to raise a ruckus.

walk heavily • walk heavy

walk heavily—trudge wearily; move with difficulty (as from fatigue): She went down to the lines, walking heavily with her washing-basket full.

walk heavy—*(U.S. sl.)* conduct oneself with an air of importance: Harry's been walking heavy since he graduated.

walk in on someone • walk into someone

walk in on someone—interrupt a person by entering a place: I couldn't think of anything else to do. I was almost relieved when Hamilton walked in on me.

walk into someone—run into a person; collide with smb.: I'm British enough to abjectly apologize every time someone walks into me.

walk one's chalks • walk the chalk

walk one's chalks—*(dated sl.)* 1. make off; escape: We cannot believe that Brother Nicholas walked his chalks with the funds of the brethren. 2. move off: I gave Master Barlow due warning ... and one fine morning I walked my chalks to try my luck. I fell in next day with a gentleman's servant's place. 3. is used to rudely tell smb. to go away (and stop being annoying): I have had enough of you. Walk your chalks!

walk the chalk—*(also: walk the chalk line)* 1. walk along a straight line as a proof of being sober: "See? I'm not drunk," Chris said as he walked the chalk line. "Okay, you can stop now," the cop replied, keeping a stern face. *2.* act exactly as one is supposed to; behave with propriety: The owners of those dives knew they would have to close up shop and walk the chalk once the police took the matter in hand.

walk out of something • walk out on something

walk out of something—leave a conference, hearing, etc. suddenly (to show one's opposition, etc.): He walked out of the meeting because he was extremely angry, and he didn't want to say something he would regret.

walk out on something—1. fail to fulfill an agreement, promises, etc.: It remains to be seen if any of the lawmakers who walked out on their responsibilities will pay the price at the polls. 2. = *walk out of something:* Baker told the ministers as much; then, just to make sure they understood how committed she was, she walked out on the meeting.

See also: come out of something / go out of something.

walk the board • walk the boards

walk the board—*(Surfing)* move up and down one's surfboard: Advanced beginners will learn how to better handle your board, surf down the line and walk the board.

Note: *The expression does not correlate in meaning with the phrase* ***walk the plank***—1. *(hist.) be murdered by drowning (when captured by pirates and forced to walk off a board extended over the side of a ship):* They deserve to be made to walk the plank for their impudence. 2. *be forced to resign from a job:* She claims she was made to walk the plank after complaining about sexual harassment. 3. *accept responsibility for smth. and suffer the consequences:* If they think that the President is going to lose, they might decide, "OK, why should I walk the plank for him?"

walk the boards—*(also: tread the boards)* be an actor: She probably was destined to walk the boards of the English stage and to grace the big screen with her exquisite beauty.

walk the talk • walky-talky

walk the talk—*(U.S., also: walk one's talk)* do what one said one would do—not just making "empty promises": We need not to talk the talk but it's time to walk the talk. The time to act is now or never at all.

walky-talky—a small portable radio link (receiver and transmitter): The security guard got on his walky-talky and tried to contact the school office to have somebody call an ambulance.

warm house • warming house

warm house—a glass-house maintained at a high enough temperature for the culture of tender or tropical plants: In a warm house or greenhouse plants can reproduce all year round.

warming house—1. a structure at a skating rink where the skaters can go to warm themselves: Lakefront Park remains the premier location for winter activity with a beautiful warming house ... a skating rink and a sliding hill. 2. *(hist.)* a room within a monastery in which the monks were allowed to warm themselves (often the only place where a fire was allowed): The room was located above the warming house to keep vital abbey documents dry and safe.

Note: *The expression does not correlate in meaning with the phrase* ***house warming****—a party held when a person moves into a new house:* This day James has come to see us and we give a "chez-vous" on the occasion, it may be called our house warming.

warmer-up • warmer-upper

warmer-up—(pl. warmers-up) 1. a preliminary item designed to put an audience in a receptive mood: As a "warmer-up" the concert began with a rather pedestrian rendering of the Hebrides overture. 2. *(also: warm-up man)* a presenter of a preliminary item designed to prepare an audience for another—more famous—performer: As so often it is the warmers-up (in this case Gordon and Bunny Jay) who do the hard work. 3. *(coll.)* a stimulating drink: Would you like a warmer up? There's a gentleman at the bar who would like to buy you a drink.

warmer-upper— = warmer-up 3: The weather is just an excuse to pop into a bar or cafe to have a warmer-upper.

wash-house • washroom

wash-house—room or outbuilding equipped for washing: Nestled in the back courtyard of the gardens is a vintage wash house, now remodeled as The Wash House Gift Shop.

washroom—(U.S.) lavatory (especially in a public building): The detectives try to piece together a motive for the shooting of a forensic expert in a restaurant washroom.

washing machine • washing-up machine

washing machine—an electrical apparatus used for washing clothes: Samsung manufactures all types of washing machines from twin tub to front loading.

washing-up machine—a dishwasher: The kitchen is fully equipped, including an electric stove, microwave oven, refrigerator and a washing-up machine.

waste water • wasted water

waste water—water that has been used in some industrial process: The liquefaction process could give off up to 4.8 million gallons of wastewater per day.

Note: *The expression does not correlate in meaning with the phrase* ***waste of water****—1. (also: waste of waters) a vast expanse of water:* It seemed to her that her life was like that gull's—the world stretched before her, like a great waste of water, shoreless and desolate. 2. *the continued use of more water than is needed:* These taps start dripping after being used for some time, causing a great waste of water every year.

wasted water—water used without a good purpose or in greater amount than is necessary: An inefficient irrigation system can cost you hundreds of dollars each month in wasted water.

watch for something • watch out for something

watch for something—wait for smth. that's going to happen or expected to appear: Watch for our new improved product, which will be on the market next week.

watch out for something—(also: look out for something) 1. be on guard for smth. dangerous or undesirable: I'm always watching out for mistakes that I may have missed before. 2. look after smth.; protect smth. from harm: Participants watch out for their neighbour's property and report suspicious activities to the police. 3. *= watch for something 1:* However, we will be running it [competition] again in the future. Watch out for our briefing events later this year.

watch the clock • watch the time

watch the clock—1. keep one's eye on the clock to avoid being late, etc.: They work under the beady eye of their crew chief, who monitors their progress and constantly watches the clock, counting the minutes. 2. *(also: clock-watch)* keep one's eye on the clock waiting for the end of one's work day *(used showing disapproval):* The man who watches the clock and is afraid he will do too much will never get very far in the milling business. *Cf.: clock-watcher—(derog.) a man who takes care not to exceed his minimum working hours; smb. who quits at once when it is time:* I don't want to be a clock-watcher, and appreciate that my working conditions are better than most people's.

watch the time—1. *= watch the clock 1:* Trying to read a book, she watched the time tick round until it was a reasonable time to get undressed and try to sleep. 2. wait for the right moment or opportunity: This is the chance to live in dreams and to watch the time for dreams to become your own realities.

water boat • water craft

water boat—(hist.) a boat carrying fresh water to ships: He built some water boats and, by these boats furnished the garrison with good water.

water craft—a boat or boats: The object lying upon the table was a ten-foot model of a strange-looking water craft.

water boatman • water-man

water boatman—a water-bug *(Notonecta glauca),* whose body resembles a boat: The water boatman, an insect related to the *Cimicidae,* made me suffer still more severely.

water-man—1. a man who rows or lends out small boats for pay: A coachman, postboy, or waterman, generally expects some grace from the passengers, over and above his fare. 2. a man employed in the distribution of water: Duran is the water man. Maneuvering his 15-ton tanker down narrow ravines, he delivers water to people the city cannot afford to supply. 3. *(hist.)* an attendant at coach-stands, whose primary function was to water the horses: The waterman darts from the pump, seizes the horses by their respective bridles, and drags them, and the coach too, round to the house. 4. *(coll.)* a water-color artist: The collection of water colors includes among its contributors many of the best living "water-men."

Note: *a) The compound does not correlate in meaning with the noun* ***seaman****—a mariner; a sailor :* Seamen in the merchant vessels are required to enter into a contract in writing commonly called shipping articles.

b) The compound is not antonymous in meaning to the noun ***landman****—(also: landsman) 1. a person who lives and works on land (as opposed to seaman):* Up to a third of the crew in wartime were landmen, who had volunteered to serve. 2. *(Petroleum Industry) land consultant responsible for obtaining permission to drill an oil well, build a pipeline, etc.:* I was a landman in Texas and Illinois (in the good old days) before the bottom fell out of the oil business.

water hole • watering hole

water hole—a pond or pool in a dry area: In many locations in Namibia, one simply waits by a water hole to photograph the never ending parade of animals.

watering hole—1. *= water hole:* Appoint a place for washing clothes clear of the watering hole. 2. *(joc.)* a licensed café or pub: The restaurant was once a cosmopolitan watering hole for actors and writers.

water house • watering house

water house—a building in which water is retained in a reservoir: They have no water but what is forced from a deep well into a waterhouse, whence they are furnished by pipes.

watering house—(UK hist.) a pub providing water for horses and refreshments for travelers: Travelers would stop at these "watering houses" to quench their own and their animals thirst.

way back • way behind

way back—1. far from the front part of smth.: I noticed a faded whiskey box way back under the stairs. 2. in a remote rural area; far away: Blackall was much the same as any other township "way back." *3.* a long time ago: We do not know who first brought Christianity to this country way back in the days of the Roman Empire.

way behind—far behind smth.: Pet foods come sixth in the consumer top ten. Baby food lags way behind.

way below something • way down something

way below something—much lower than smth.: By slashing its retail prices way below cost, Wal-Mart can crush our groceries, pharmacies, and other retailers.

way down something—at a great distance along the length of smth.: He saw a headlight of an eastbound train appear way down the tracks.

way off • way out

way off—1. far away: I am going somewhere; but I don't know where. Way off, anyhow. 2. quite wrong; greatly mistaken: My attitude indications on the instrument panel are way off.

way out—1. = *way off 1:* After a prolonged journey by bus, Clarissa alighted way out on the North Circular Road. 2. = *way off 2:* I would not presume to argue with Edward on matters botanical, but he is way out on snakes. 3. *(sl.)* highly peculiar or unusual (being too modern): This new music is too way out for me—I prefer what I am already familiar with. 4. *(sl.)* heavily alcohol or drug intoxicated: That guy is way out—can't even walk.

way to go Einstein • way to go Grace

way to go Einstein—(sarcastic) is used to tell a person he made a mistake or is not very smart: In all of the excitement, he ran a red light, barely avoiding an accident. "Way to go, Einstein!" a voice from the back seat exclaimed.

way to go Grace—(sarcastic) is used to tell a person he or she is clumsy: Amanda tripped, lurched forward, caught her foot in the hem of her dress, and fell to her hands and knees. "Way to go, Grace!" she exclaimed.

Note: *Both expressions are antonymous in meaning to the phrase* ***way to go****—(also: that's the way to go) used as an encouragement to proceed with the chosen plan or process:* "Way to go!" said Mary when Bob finally got the car started.

weak as a cat • weak as water

weak as a cat—(also: weak as a kitten) lacking in physical strength: He must have been as weak as a kitten, with all the blood he'd lost.

weak as water—(also: weak as dishwater) 1. = *weak as a cat:* Sir, I am only just getting well of a fever, and I am as weak as water. 2. lacking in determination; easily influenced by other people: You love Eva, and Eva loves you, Ernest; but remember this, she is weak as water. **3.** *(of tea, etc.)* watery; not having enough flavor: These poor and hungry people are accustomed to drinks almost as weak as water. 4. *(of an evidence, etc.)* not convincing; inefficient: His brashness couldn't cover the fact that his argument was weak as water.

weak for someone • weak with someone

weak for someone—(of tea, etc.) not having enough flavor or not strong enough to a person's taste: The tea was too weak for him to really enjoy.

weak with someone—lacking in firmness when dealing with a person: He was spoiling his son's character by being weak with him.

wear away • wear off

wear away—1. be reduced through constant pressure, friction, etc.: With the passing of the years, the finer detail of the carvings has almost worn away. 2. *(of a person)* become progressively weaker: After the operation, she just seemed to wear away until she died. 3. *(of time)* pass slowly: As the afternoon wore away, I found it more and more difficult to stay awake.

wear off—1. = *wear away 1:* Don't polish those badges: the gilt will wear off in time if you do. 2. *(of a feeling or effect)* disappear gradually; no longer affect one: The drink inside them had worn off, leaving only a sour feeling in the stomach.

weather house • weather station

weather house—a model house that indicates changes in humidity by the appearance of two human figures coming out to foretell good and bad weather: Heisenberg compared this to the little man and woman in a weather house, an old folk art device.

weather station—a station for recording and reporting meteorological observations: The progress of European meteorology is due to the introduction of micrometeorology, or detailed observations from an ever-increasing number of weather stations.

weigh someone down • weigh someone up

weigh someone down—(also: weight someone down) 1. press on a person with a heavy weight: Get this bundle off my back; it's really weighing me down. 2. make smb. very sad; depress a person: When an American girl does that, you can guess there's something "mighty hefty" weighing her down.

weigh someone up—(coll.) form an opinion about a person: "I knew too much about her," she said. "I had weighed her up."

welcome home • welcome to our house

welcome home—celebration or expressions of greeting at smb.'s homecoming: Nearly bursting with pride these ladies gave the servicemen a welcome home that they deserved.

welcome to our house—a name for the plant Cypress Spurge *(Euphorbia Cyparissias):* Another species found in the Smokey Mountains is often called Graveyard weed and Welcome-to-our-house.

Note: *The expression is not equivalent in meaning to the phrase* ***welcome home husband, however drunk you be****—(also: welcome home husband though never so drunk) a name for the plant Houseleek (Sempervivum tectorum):* There is one plant that I have come to rely on for its low maintenance qualities, it is that of the houseleek, known as "Welcome Home Husband However Drunk You Be."

West Indiaman • West Indian

West Indiaman—(hist.) a sailing ship running to the West Indies and the east coast of America: Compare the numbers of men in a West Indiaman and in a Baltic or Hamburg trader.

West Indian—an inhabitant of the West Indies: American Blacks are quick to perceive pronunciation differences on the part of West Indians who migrate to cities like New York.

what an idea • what's the idea

what an idea—1. that's a great idea: They don't fit very well under the Christmas tree, but what an idea for that perfect gift! 2. that's preposterous; that's most unreasonable: Pa looked at ma stunned. Good heavens what an idea!

what's the idea—(also: what's the big idea) what's the intention or purpose *(is usually used to question smth. that is not welcome):* What's the idea behind creating a game that's part way between Australian Rules football and Gaelic football.

what else can I do • what else can I do for you

what else can I do—(also: what more can I do) is used as an expression of hopelessness or desperation: He came out with a gun and said he would put an end to it. I called the cops but what else can I do?

what else can I do for you—is used as an inquiry by service personnel: "Here's your prescription. What else can I do for you?" said the pharmacist.

what ever • whatever

what ever—is used as a more emphatic variant of "what": "What ever are you doing in that ridiculous costume?" Jonny let out a girlish giggle...

whatever—no matter what: Whatever I say, he always finds a way to tell me that the same thought occurred to him a few weeks earlier.

what goes around, comes around • what goes up, must come down

what goes around, comes around—one is bound to see the long-term effects of his current actions and behavior: "What goes around comes around" and eventually each of you will answer for all the lies you have published.

what goes up, must come down—when smth. such as a stock price, etc. goes up it will most certainly come down: It is not clear what triggered the price drop: though perhaps it is simply a case of what goes up must come down.

what is in it for someone • what is it to someone

what is in it for someone—what advantage or benefit can a person receive from smth.: He had an inbred suspicion of any kind of offered help, he wanted to know why people were giving it, what was in it for them.

what is it to someone—what business is that of mine, yours, etc.; does it concern me, you, etc.: Now why does that thought gnaw at me? What is it to me if he does not pay more attention to me?

what matter • what's the matter

what matter—(coll.) what difference does it make: But what matter from whom he heard this.

what's the matter—1. what happened; what is the problem: What's the matter, Cynthia? You sound odd. 2. what's wrong with: I'm a farmer all right. What's the matter with farming?

what with • what's with

what with—on account of smth.; as a result of smth.: The idea of being homesick didn't even occur to me, what with all the new things that were going on.

what's with—what's wrong with: It seems that well-educated people should be the most well informed. What's with these people?

what's up • what's up with

what's up—1. what is happening; what is going on: You can keep up to date on what's happening with legislation, new product research, or what's up in your community. 2. *(U.S. sl., also: whassup)* is used as a greeting to someone you know well: "Hi, Jim. What's up?" "Oh nothing much.... How are you doing?"

what's up with—what's wrong with: Four out of ten days I have had to weather tornado and flash flood warnings. What's up with the weather?

when it comes down to it • when the chips are down

when it comes down to it—(also: when it comes right down to it) when one really thinks about it: Doctors are great, but when it comes right down to it, each of us is in charge of his own health.

when the chips are down—when matters become very serious or critical: When the chips are down a man shows what he really is.

when the balloon goes up • when the eagle flies

when the balloon goes up—(coll.) when matters become very serious or critical: The international rules of war are apt to be waived when the balloon goes up.

when the eagle flies—(U.S. sl.) on payday: I'll pay you back when the eagle flies. *Cf.: eagle has landed, the—(U.S. sl.) paychecks are in:* The principal got on the PA [public address system] and said, "Teachers, may I have your attention please: The eagle has landed."

when the band begins to play • when the fat lady sings

when the band begins to play—(coll.) when matters become very serious or critical: ...they are supplied with the best of weapons. Naturally only the best is good enough when the band begins to play.

when the fat lady sings—(U.S. sl.) when smth. is finally concluded; at the end of a match, performance, etc.: We can leave with everybody else when the fat lady sings.

Note: *Neither expression correlates in meaning with the phrase* ***when one's ship comes home****—when one comes into money:* The other guests on our table all had cabins on the 8th deck. Maybe when "my ship comes home"—when I become rich I'll be able to afford a cabin right up high...

whip one's weight in wild cats • whip the cat

whip one's weight in wild cats—(U.S. sl.) be able to fight vigorously; defeat a powerful opponent: I was to get acquainted with Alta Ashbury, win her confidence, let her feel that I was capable of whipping my weight in wild cats.

whip the cat—(sl.) 1. *(U.S. dated)* work as an itinerant tailor, carpenter, etc.: The pioneer shoemaker was Henry Demoney, who was one of the old-fashioned eccentricities who "whipped the cat." 2. *(Austral.)* lament over smth.; reproach oneself: It was no use whipping the cat about it now, Morris pointed out. 3. *(Austral.)* take one's frustration out on an innocent person: If there's anything wants doing you've only got to ask Macy. And he makes light of it, too. No whipping the cat: no setting himself up as a little tin god.

whipping boy • whipping Tom

whipping boy—1. *(UK hist.)* a boy educated with a prince and punished in his stead: Sir Mungo had been attached to Court in the capacity of whipping-boy to King James the Sixth. 2. a scapegoat: The choice of agents is a difficult matter for you have to choose persons for whose faults you are to be punished; to whom you are to be the whipping-boy.

whipping Tom—(UK hist.) a person who whips others: Ritual beating in commemoration of ritual murder is known in many places. Until 1845 the Whipping Toms plied their whips freely in the streets of Leicester in commemoration of the massacre of the Danes.

whistle down the wind • whistle up the wind

whistle down the wind—1. talk purposelessly: I know I'm trying to whistle down the wind here. But the technology is likely to arrive sometime in the next century. 2. abandon or sacrifice a person or thing: I was dragged out of the Senate, against my wishes — tried to do my whole duty, and was then unceremoniously "whistled down the wind."

Note: *The expression is not antonymous in meaning to the phrase* ***whistle against the wind****—(also: whistle in the wind) protest or argue vainly (acting against the mainstream):* When all we can do is whistle against the wind, it seems silly to even whistle.

whistle up the wind—1. is used of the superstition that bad weather can be caused by whistling on board ship: Some can manipulate the forces of the weather, while others could no more whistle up the wind than call a bird to their hand. 2. entertain false hopes: If he thinks that I am going to take him back after what he has done to me, he is whistling up the wind.

white as a sheet • white as snow

white as a sheet—very pale, usually because of illness, shock or fear: He must have done a pretty good imitation of a gangster because the guy's face turned white as a sheet.

white as snow—is said of very pure white color: Anne walked with him to the house up the brook, over a field that was as white as snow with daisies.

Note: *Neither expression correlates in meaning with the phrase* ***whiter than white****—said of a good and righteous man:* Having come to power promising to be "whiter than white," Blair's government may find it difficult to redeem its once spotless reputation.

white boy • white man

white boy—*(U.S. Drug users)* heroin: Then there are the white boy drug dealers in the suburbs.... I know that only a small percentage of people is dangerous, but it's best to be on the safe side.

white man—*(dated)* said of a good and righteous man back in the colonization days: "Is it a marriage of true minds?" "It certainly is. Young Jon is a pretty white man." *Cf.: play the white man—(UK dated) be decent and trustworthy in one's actions:* When the enemy plays by different rules it is hard to play the white man.

white cap • white hat

white cap—1. *(pl.)* white foam on the crests of waves (in stormy weather): We had a strong head wind ... the surface of the lake was covered with white-caps. 2. name for several birds having a white patch on the head: The male [Redstart] is called "whitecap" in Shropshire, from its white forehead. 3. name for species of mushroom: These are the common mushrooms you see in almost every supermarket these days. White caps are used raw in salads, and in cooking.

white hat—1. *(U.S. Navy)* an enlisted man: There's a white hat out here who has gone crazy. 2. *(coll.)* a good and righteous man: Nixon clung to the original plan against the urging of Garment, and other "white hats."

white foot • white leg

white foot—*(pl. whitefoots)* a white-footed mouse of the genus *Peromyscus:* "Whitefoots" are active all year round, even in cold weather. Their activities begin at dusk and continue through the night.

white leg—*(med.)* thrombophlebitis of a femoral vein after child-birth: After our May was born she never walked properly again. She had what they called the white leg.

white girl • white lady

white girl—*(U.S. Drug users)* cocaine: When she gets to college and doesn't fit in with either white or black students, she turns instead to the cocaine (nicknamed White Girl).

white lady—1. cocktail made of gin, orange liqueur and lemon juice: He indicated a cocktail cabinet and proceeded to mix two "White Ladies." 2. *(Austral. sl.)* a drink of methylated spirits mixed with other ingredients: Aborigines used to swill cheap wines and other concoctions like "White Lady"—a fiendish brew of methylated spirit and powdered milk. 3. = *white girl:* White Boy, White Horse, White Lady: Those are just a handful of cocaine's street names.

white marriage • white wedding

white marriage—a marriage union without sexual relations: Maybe I should have written that the union of Bill Paxon and Susan Molinari *was* rumored to be a "white marriage."

white wedding—1. used with reference to the white color of the wedding dress symbolizing purity and innocence: Mine was a white wedding too. In fact, my dress was very similar to the one Erica wears on screen. 2. a marriage ceremony in which the bride is still a virgin: I was 26 and my wife was 21 when we got married (and it was a "white wedding" in the traditional meaning of the term.)

white negro • white nigger

white negro—1. a person with black ancestry who has a pale or albino complexion: He was one of that peculiar class called Albinos, or white negroes. 2. *(U.S. dated sl., derog.)* a white who defends the rights or interests of Black people: Both Clarksons were counted among the activists whom Pitt in a rare jest called the "white Negroes." 3. *(in nonce-use):* The Jewish Defense organization became another white negro, which changed its color according to the political situation.

white nigger—*(U.S. dated sl.)* 1. *(derog.)* a white person who does menial labor: "Ole Miss Meanses' white nigger," as some of them called her, in allusion to her slavish life. 2. a Black person who defers to white people and regarded as betraying his social loyalty: Dr. Marcus Foster, a black suggested that the children be equipped with identity passes.... The unfortunate Foster was widely accused of being a white nigger. 3. = *white negro 3:* Hippies have openly proclaimed themselves "white niggers" by which they seem to mean that, like blacks, they represent an alternative to the life style of majority-group American culture.

white slave • white-collar slave

white slave—a white girl procured for prostitution purposes, especially when brought to a foreign country: The conference was attended by representatives of the International Migration Organization and countries supplying white slaves.

white-collar slave—*(derog.)* an office employee who works hard and continuously: You're an adult now and are on your way to being a powerless pseudo intellectual white collar slave.

who ever • whoever

who ever—is used as a more emphatic variant of "who": Who ever would have thought it would be so difficult to get people to support a charity?!

whoever—no matter who; anyone who: Whatever and whoever takes the credit becomes largely irrelevant when the quality of the material is this good.

whole lot, a • whole lot, the

whole lot, a—a great amount or number: They did a whole lot of proving flights over the route before they put it into regular operation.

whole lot, the—the total number or quantity: A net is put round a school of tuna, the base is closed and the whole lot hauled on board.

wide open • widely open

wide open—1. fully open: The living areas are very spacious with comfortable sofas and wide open doors welcoming in a fresh breeze and bright light. 2. *(Boxing)* fully exposed; unprotected: Summers in an unguarded moment, left himself wide open and encountered one of the most decisive knock-out punches I ever saw. 3. vulnerable; off one's guard: You never find me going in for favors.... It leaves you wide open. 4. *(U.S.)* said of a town characterized by a lack of restrictions on places for drinking, gambling, etc.: He has been elected three times because the citizens want a wide-open town.

widely open— = *wide open 1:* We caught a glimpse through

widely open doors of the empty auditorium, frantically busy stage crews, and the fully powered-up lighting.

widow's man • widow-man

widow's man—(hist.) a fictitious seaman on a ship's papers, whose pay was credited to a widows' pension fund: I went everywhere about the ship.... At last, one of them answered that it was no use looking for him as Cheeks was a widow's man.

widow-man—a widower: Her father came here soon after she was born, a widow-man with only her.

win over someone • win someone over

win over someone—1. *(also: win out over someone)* prevail upon a person in a contest, etc.: In New Hampshire, pro-life Congressman John Sununu won over his pro-abortion opponent. 2. win smb.'s favor: The "new economic regime" is dressed up in anti-capitalist garb to make it capable of winning over the masses.

win someone over— = win over someone 2: She didn't like me at first, but I was soon able to win her over.

wind-break • wind-breaker

wind-break—a clump of trees, fence, etc. which gives protection against the wind: The pine trees acted as a wind-break for the solitary house set a hundred yards lower down.

Note: *The expression does not correlate in meaning with the compound* ***wind-broken****—(also: broken-winded) used of a horse that has impaired breathing:* The road was climbing fairly steadily now, and Paddy had fallen behind, staggering and wheezing like a wind-broken horse.

wind-breaker—1. *(U.S.)* a light waterproof jacket: You might need a wind breaker for the rain; although, most times we were encouraged to be inside during the rains. 2. *= wind-break:* The advantage of a dome over the roll-off roof observatory is that the dome acts as a wind breaker for the telescope.

wind in the head • windmills in the head

wind in the head—1. vain imagination or conceit: He has probably got wind in the head through living in that gorgeous Gothic pagoda. 2. unpredictability or flippancy in behavior: "Wind in the head," the servants called it. But it was but the natural consequence of the state of mental and bodily idleness in which she was placed.

Note: *The expression does not correlate in meaning with the compound* ***airhead****—(U.S. sl.) smb. who isn't very smart; a stupid person:* "Spell check" can't save the truly illiterate ones. How can such airheads ever manage to graduate?

windmills in the head—foolish projects or notions: These windmills in the head are what apparently drive state policies about "national security."

wise as a Christian • wise as Solomon

wise as a Christian—(of an animal) intelligent: Then he rubbed Feenish, the mare, all over, and instantly she became as wise as a Christian, and knew every word that was said to her.

wise as Solomon—having good judgment; very shrewd: In some of the divorce cases one would need to be as wise as Solomon to know which party was the more at fault.

wise guy • wise man

wise guy—(derog.) an impudent person who parades his knowledge; smb. disagreeably self-assertive: He got what he deserved this time. I believe he has learned his lesson and will not be such a wise guy in the future.

wise man—1. a man of good judgment: A man who knows a little bit of the past and a little bit about the future is considered a wise man with superior qualifications. 2. *(coll.)* a shrewd and trusted guide and advisor: The appointment of two independent "wise men" to prepare the ground for the forthcoming talks, was suggested.

See also: wise men of Gotham / wise men of the East.

wise in something • wise to something

wise in something—showing wisdom and good judgment in smth.: He was very wise in his rulings and tried to govern all his people equally and fairly.

wise to something—informed about smth.; being aware of smth.: I'm wise to the fact that he [comedian] dips in the Farmers' Almanac for his comedy stuff.

wise men of Gotham • wise men of the East

wise men of Gotham—(UK ironic) fools; simpletons: "I would pay no attention," I replied, "to the wishes of those few wise men of Gotham who would arbitrate this matter."

Note: *The expression is unrelated in meaning to the phrase* ***Gotham City****—(U.S.) a nickname for New York City:* I figured the one place he'd never find me would be Gotham City ... the home of the hated Yankees.

wise men of the East—(the Bible) the three Magi who came from the East, bringing offerings to the infant Christ: It is chronicled in an old Armenian myth that the wise men of the East were none other than the three sons of Noe.

See also: wise guy / wise man.

wise someone up • wise up to someone

wise someone up—(sl.) instruct a person about smth.; give smb. information: Let me wise you up about the way we do things around here.

wise up to someone—(sl.) figure out a person: It's time you wised up to John and what he has been doing.

with a single eye to something • with one eye on something

with a single eye to something—exclusively concerned with or concentrating on smth.: His predecessors are the only Roman emperors who can be said to have ruled with a single eye to the welfare of their subjects.

with one eye on something—(also: with half an eye on something) 1. directing one's attention only partly to smth. (while preoccupied with smth. else): She sat at the head of the table stirring her tea, with one eye on baby Paul, who was fretful in his little chair. 2. simultaneously thinking about or preoccupied with smth.: He still told jokes, but they were the jokes of a man who couldn't see anything funny any more, the jokes of a man with one eye on the door.

Note: *Neither expression correlates in meaning with the phrase* ***with one eye closed****—(also: with one eye shut) do smth. easily or with little effort:* You might cope for a while with one eye closed ... but you wouldn't keep it up for long — nor would you perform at maximum ability.

with all respect to someone • with respect to someone

with all respect to someone—(also: with all due respect to someone) is used before a statement to politely disagree or criticize a person: With all respect to my noble friend, I believe that he was wholly wrong in what he said.

with respect to someone—(also: in respect to someone) as regards a person: She went on to say that the paramedics showed "nothing but supreme professionalism, empathy, and brilliance" with respect to her husband.

with an eye for something • with an eye to something

with an eye for something—1. quick to notice or appreciate smth.: Everyone with an eye for color and form knows those mellow, lichened roofs of Colly Westons. 2. watching out for smth.; ready to notice smth.: He drowsed over the Irish sea, but always with an eye for the landfall of the Scottish coast. 3. having smth. as one's aim or purpose: The chamber had been designed by someone with an eye for effect rather than practicality.

with an eye to something— = with an eye for something 3: It was a somewhat lurid article, written with an eye to picturesque effect.

with child • with young

with child—(liter.) going to have a baby; pregnant *(also: big with child):* She pretended to be with child, and when her time drew near, she journeyed to her home.

with young—(of animals) pregnant; bearing young: A mare goes somewhere about eleven months with young.

with one's eyes closed • with one's eyes open

with one's eyes closed—(also: with one's eyes shut) do smth. very easily, without much effort: I could do her work with my eyes closed.

with one's eyes open—do smth. fully aware of the consequences: I moved to this country with my eyes open; so I'm not complaining.

See also: keep one's eyes open / open someone's eyes.

with one's eyes wide open • with wide-open eyes

with one's eyes wide open—1. *stare* in amazement or wonder: He just stared and stared with his eyes wide open. So much so, he kept missing his mouth with his spoon. 2. *do smth.* fully aware of the consequences: He knows what he is doing and he is doing it with his eyes wide open.

with wide-open eyes— = with one's eyes wide open 1: I saw him stare at me with wide-open eyes as I walked slowly up to him holding out my revolver.

with reason • within reason

with reason—with good cause; justifiably: The police complain, with reason, about wasting manpower in a hopeless pursuit of speeders.

within reason—within reasonable limits: Seniors like Brett were allowed, within reason, to decide their own working hours.

witness something • witness to something

witness something—1. see smth. happen: We witnessed the meeting between the two great men. 2. observe an event in order to give testimony on it if required: Will you witness his signature on this deed? 3. give evidence of smth.; show smth.: Her pale face witnessed the agitation she felt.

witness to something—1. give testimony (as in court) regarding smth.: He witnessed to having seen the accused near the scene of the crime. 2. prove or corroborate smth.: Partnerships necessitate mutual praying and planning. They also witness to the unity of the church in the world.

Wizard of Oz, The • Wonderful Wizard of Oz, The

Wizard of Oz, The—the title of the first film version (1939) of the book The Wonderful Wizard of Oz: *Star Wars* is a combination of *Flash Gordon, The Wizard of Oz,* and almost every western ever screened.

Wonderful Wizard of Oz, The—the title of the popular children's novel (1900) by L. Frank Baum: Since its publication, The Wonderful Wizard of Oz has become America's greatest and best-loved homegrown fairytale.

woman about town • woman of the town

woman about town—(dated) a woman who socializes in fashionable circles: This was none of those affairs of a season that distract men and women about town. This was the real thing!

woman of the town—1. a woman inhabitant or fellow inhabitant of a town: Grace's tumble from upstanding woman of the town to a disheveled, confused outcast is interesting enough. 2. *(dated)* a woman with loose morals: Trollope came to lunch. Told me of his trouble with Harry wanting to marry a woman of the town.

woman's man • woman-man

woman's man—(pl. women's men) a man who is fond of female company *(also: ladies' man):* I am finally meeting my friend who works out with weights twice weekly, has money, and is a woman's man for sure!

woman-man—(derog.) an effeminate, delicate man: That was the guide she turned to — the woman-man, the dabbler in paint-boxes, the critic of carpets and wallpapers. *Cf.: man-woman—(contemptuous) a tough, aggressive, or businesslike woman (pl. men-women):* That stage of progress has been passed, and, as an outcome, we have the "Emancipated Woman," or "Man-Woman."

word by word • word for word

word by word—reading one word after another; following the exact order of words: Skip-read all you want through the book, but go through the last page word by word.

word for word—stated or translated in exactly the same words as the original: You need not use quotation marks unless the statement is word-for-word as it appears in your source.

work at something • work on something

work at something—be busy or occupied with smth.; apply one's efforts to smth.: Is Tom still working at the new book that he promised?

work on something—1. *= work at something:* I'm presently working on the new book, another suspense novel, after which I plan to write a book for aspiring writers. 2. influence smth.; have an effect on smth.: Acebutolol is taken orally so that it works on the central nervous system of those prone to heart attacks.

work in with someone • work with someone

work in with someone—join in work with other people: I'm prepared to work in with them and fit in with their work schedule.

work with someone—1. work in the company of other people: Independent doesn't mean "loner," so he should be able to work with the other members of the department. 2. have a person or a group as the object of one's work: Michelle finds it very rewarding to work with children and would like to be a kindergarten teacher.

work like a beaver • work like a dog

work like a beaver—work eagerly and vigorously: We woke up late and then had to work like beavers to get our cases packed before the train left.

work like a dog—(also: work like a horse) work very hard: I've been working like a dog all day, and I'm dead tired.

work load • working load

work load—the amount of work assigned for completion within a certain time: Traffic growth has increased the pressure on both pilots and controllers, so that means have had to be found to reduce their workload.

working load—the maximum physical load that a device is designed to bear: Minor changes in the boom angle can lead to large variations in the working load of the crane and bring about an unsafe condition.

work off one's ticket • work one's ticket

work off one's ticket—1. earn one's passage by services on board ship, etc.: After an ancestor landed in Philly in 1679 as an indentured servant and worked off his ticket, he headed west … to present day Ohio. 2. pay off one's fine for traffic violation by working: When motorcycle cop pulls over leather-clad biker, he decides to allow him to "work off" his ticket.

work one's ticket—(sl.) get one's early discharge, especially from the army (by feigning illness, etc.): It is a comparatively easy matter for a discontented man to "work his ticket."

Note: *The expression does not correlate in meaning with the phrase* ***write one's own ticket****—(coll.) be able to stipulate one's own conditions:* This is an actor that has reached unimagined heights in his craft and can write his own ticket.

work oneself up into something • work oneself up to something

work oneself up into something—bring oneself into a highly emotional state: It would be foolish, even dangerous to work oneself up into a frenzy.

work oneself up to something—1. = *work oneself up into something:* He would gradually work himself up to a state of intense agitation in which he screamed and berated me. 2. prepare oneself with sufficient energy or courage to do smth.: I can't just walk in there and ask for a raise. I have to work myself up to it. 3. progress to a certain rank or status: He worked himself up to sergeant in no time at all.

work something in with something • work something into something

work something in with something—make smth. such as a schedule, etc. fit or harmonize with smth.: I'm motivated to work out and feel better, I just don't know how to work it in with everything else I have to do.

work something into something—1. force smth. into smth. else by gradual movement: He was able to work his foot into his boot but it was still very tight. 2. include smth. into smth. written or spoken: Each week I try to work a few jokes into the typically mundane legal topics we discuss.

worker bee • working bee

worker bee—1. sterile bee specialized to collect food and maintain the hive: Only one queen bee is the mother of all worker bees and drones in a beehive. 2. said of a hard working person: All those handmade items make it so cozy and inviting. You are a real worker bee.

working bee—1. = *worker bee 1:* By this time the number of working bees in the hive is becoming very great, and the storing of honey goes on very quickly. 2. = *worker bee 2:* The members were "working bees" in the best sense, and were capable of success anywhere. 3. an event at which people work towards a common cause: Are you able to assist at our working bee on Sunday? The purpose of this working bee is to beautify the area.

working man • workman

working man—a man who has a job in industry; member of the working class: Greyhound racing is sometimes said to be the working man's substitute for horse racing.

Note: *The expression does not correlate in meaning with the phrase* ***working girl****—1. said of a girl, usually single, who supports herself by working in an office, etc.:* The film portrays a white-collar working girl who receives a marriage proposal from a kindly but humble doctor. 2. *(euph.) a prostitute:* Now, the average working girl often takes in hundreds, maybe even thousands, of dollars every night she is on the street.

workman—1. a manual worker employed upon some particular piece of work; a skilled craftsman: The workmen brought the materials on Friday and promised to start the job on Monday. 2. a person who works in some specified way: My health makes me a very slow workman.

working paper • working papers

working paper—a paper produced as a basis for discussion rather than as a final statement: The Government published a working paper which set out some possibilities.

working papers—official documents legalizing the employment of a person not yet legally of age: Before being employed the boy had to produce his working papers.

worth while • worthwhile

worth while—(predic.) worthy of the time or effort spent *(also: worth one's while):* We had to wait for the food but the wait was worth while as the food was exceptional!

worthwhile—(attrib.) said of smth. of sufficient value or importance: The report suggests that patient education regarding the side effects of drugs is a worthwhile effort.

wring one's hands • wring someone's hand

wring one's hands—1. squeeze one's hands together to express despair, sorrow, etc.: His face was pale, and he stared at his feet while wringing his hands nervously. 2. be very worried or upset about smth.: Our President is all day in security sessions, briefings, debriefings, staying up all night wringing his hands over this whole mess.

wring someone's hand—shake hands with a person showing more emotion than in the usual handshake: He shook hands with Tom, wringing his hand harder than he knew.

write for something • write off for something

write for something—1. write pieces for a newspaper, magazine, etc.: Students past and present have written for the Oxford student newspaper and the University radio station. 2. request smth. by post: "And haven't you written for further particulars?" "I have been thinking of doing so. You would advise me to write to the doctor?"

write off for something— = *write for something 2:* No one here could answer my questions, so I had to write off for more information.

write something down as • write something off as

write something down as—classify or regard smth. as: The corporation had made a number of tests with it … and they had written it down as a failure.

write something off as—1. = *write something down as:* The way I justify this silly exercise in hard labor is that I can write it off as a learning experience. 2. regard smth. as unsuitable or having no value: Paint-coating should not be written off as a possible future solution as the durability of coating materials is constantly being improved.

writing on the wall • writing on water

writing on the wall—(also: handwriting on the wall) warning signs of impending disaster: Many Britons invested in private pensions and private health care because they could see the writing on the wall for the welfare state.

writing on water—said of an action that will not yield lasting results and is therefore futile: Seeking wisdom when you are old is like writing on water; seeking it when you are young is like graving on stone.

wrong in the head • wrong-headed

wrong in the head—crazy; insane: When we read the first part of the saga, we naturally presumed Andy was somewhat wrong in the head.

wrong-headed—1. persistent in erroneous opinion: To us, at that time, he was a wrong-headed young man who had thrown away a good career, and was vain enough to think he could be an author. 2. *(of a belief, decision, etc.)* wrong and irrational: The choice of Murphy was so wrong-headed that even some of the people who negotiated the deal were embarrassed by it.

Y

yellow black • yellow nigger

yellow black—(U.S. sl., may sound offensive) said of a light-skinned Black American *(also: high yellow black):* It has always been somewhat bothersome for me as a so-called "high-yellow" black American when people approach me about my ancestry.

yellow nigger—(U.S. sl., taboo) an offensive name for an East Asian: He recalled that he was denounced as a "yellow nigger" when he took part in civil-rights marches in the 1960s and early 1970s.

Yellow Book • yellow newspaper

Yellow Book—rule book for listed companies which governs their behavior: The Financial Yellow Book brings you accurate information on 822 public and private financial companies in the United States.

yellow newspaper—a newspaper of unscrupulously sensational character: The man who in a yellow newspaper makes a ferocious attack on good men is a potent enemy of those of us who are really striving to expose bad men.

yellow boy • yellow man

yellow boy—1. the Winchester 1866 rifle: This weapon could hold sixteen cartridges. Known as the "Yellow-boy" because of its brass frame, it was developed from the Henry repeating rifle. 2. *(dated)* a gold coin: And if you'll only go along with me, this day twelve months you'll all have more yellow boys in your pockets than will buy a good farm down east. 3. *(U.S. sl., may sound offensive)* a light-skinned Black boy: His complexion was light and his features were far less Negroid than those of his mother. He was a rather good looking yellow boy.

yellow man—1. *(Anthropology)* a person of the Mongoloid race with naturally yellowish skin: Mongolic or Yellow Man prevails over the vast area lying east of a line drawn from Lapland to Siam. 2. *(coll.)* a fearful, cowardly man: It frightens me when moderate voices are taken to be from weak and yellow men. 3. a flat sugar-stick, flavored with lemon: "Lemon Platt," commonly sold as "Yellow Man" at fairs in the North of Ireland, derives its name from its flavor.

yellow stripe disease • yellow stripe rust

yellow stripe disease—a virus disease of sugarcane characterized by striping of the foliage: Sugar cane varieties have been imported which are resistant to the highly troublesome yellow-stripe disease.

yellow stripe rust—a rust of wheat, rye, barley, and other grains caused by a fungus: The main diseases to check for are yellow stripe rust *(Puccinia glumarum)* and stem rust *(Puccinia gramminis).*

yellow trumpet • yellow trumpet flower

yellow trumpet—a plant *(Sarracenia flava)* whose leaves are shaped into the form of a pitcher: A fly perches on the lip of the yellow trumpet, also known as the trumpet or yellow pitcherplant.

yellow trumpet flower—a tropical American shrub: Yellow bells *(Tecoma stans),* also called yellow trumpet flower, yellow elder, and yellow trumpetbush, is a small to medium sized shrub.

you and your • you and yours

you and your—is used as a contemptuous dismissal of the thing or person mentioned: "I was born there.... It was called after my uncle." "Shut up—you and your uncle!"

you and yours—(coll.) you and your family *(also: you and your near and dear ones):* I and mine will be happy to see you and yours here or anywhere.

you are a dead man • you are a long time dead

you are a dead man—(also: you are dead) 1. is used as a threat to kill: Speak one word, and you are a dead man! 2. is used as a caution: In this neighborhood, you don't carry a knife or a piece, you are a dead man.

Note: *The expression does not correlate in meaning with the phrase* ***it's your funeral****—(coll.) it's your affair or concern, so do it on your own responsibility (and suffer the consequences):* I refuse to involve myself. It is your problem and your funeral.

you are a long time dead—is used to say that life is short and one has to enjoy oneself: "I don't think we want any [drink] today." "Oh, cheer up, Davey, you're a long time dead."

you can talk • you can't talk

you can talk—(also: you should talk) you are in no position to criticize because you are at least as guilty as smb. you are criticizing *(used as an ironic or sarcastic response to a person who has just spoken):* "Debra's house is always such a mess!" "You can talk! Your house is even messier than hers!"

you can't talk—(also: you shouldn't talk) = you can talk: "Andy's always late. He won't be here in time for dinner." "You can't talk. You haven't been on time for dinner for years."

you cannot make an omelet without breaking eggs • you cannot make bricks without straw

you cannot make an omelet without breaking eggs—(saying) one should be prepared to make some sacrifice for what one wants: "Why all the bloodshed?" "You cannot make an omelet without breaking a few eggs," came the reply.

you cannot make bricks without straw—(saying) nothing can be made or performed without the necessary means: The medical profession does what it can but you cannot make bricks without straw.

you can't win • you can't win 'em all

you can't win—(also: you just can't win) no matter how much you try, there is no way to succeed: Even though we try to educate everyone we come in contact with, sometimes you just can't win.

you can't win 'em all—is used to say that it is not possible to succeed at every thing one does: You can't win 'em all. If someone doesn't respond to you or indicates lack of interest, just move on.

Note: *The expression does not correlate in meaning with the phrase* ***you can't fight city hall****— used to say that one is unable to overcome officialdom or bureaucracy:* When it comes to judicial review of local government abuses, the fox is too often left guarding the henhouse. That all adds up to the depressing adage "you can't fight city hall."

you don't say so • you may well say so

you don't say so—is used to express surprise or sarcasm at what smb. has just said: I explained my presence, and he said: "You don't say so! Why, I've got a patient over at Swampscott, who says he knows you.

you may well say so—what you say is perfectly correct, justified, etc.: "A craft that's good for sore eyes." "You may well say so," replied the commodore. "There is no finer schooner-yacht afloat."

you should talk • you shouldn't talk

you should talk—(also: you can talk) you are in no position to criticize because you are at least as guilty as the person you are criticizing *(used as an ironic or sarcastic response to a person who has just spoken):* "You are cold-hearted." "You should talk of all people!"

you shouldn't talk—(also: you can't talk) = you should talk: "Andy's always late. He won't be here in time for dinner." "You shouldn't talk. You haven't been on time for dinner for years."

you tell me • you're telling me

you tell me—I don't know; I have no idea: "How can we possibly get through this week with just this amount of money?" "You tell me."

Note: *The expression does not correlate in meaning with the phrase* ***you tell 'em****—used to agree with or encourage smb. in what he is saying:* "Keeping the bridge closed might be inconvenient…." "You tell 'em," said Johnnie.

you're telling me—I know it very well; it is so clear that it need not be said: "It's a bad corner. You can't turn." "You're telling me."

young man • young person

young man—1. a boyfriend; a sweetheart: Whom is she shielding? Either her father or her young man. Is it her father? 2. is used as a familiar or condescending form of address: Listen, young man, you're headed for some serious trouble.

young person—1. a young woman: There lived a young person at Loudun from whom he could not resolve to be separated. 2. *(legal)* a person generally between 14 and 17 years of age: For more serious offences, a young person who is 14 years of age or more can be transferred to adult court.

young tartar • young turk

young tartar—(UK rare) a naughty boy; an obstinate person: We all know what a young tartar the Vole is when his sarcastic tongue is working.

young turk—(UK) an aggressive person who has modern opinions and tries to change the old ways: They've put together a top-notch list of speakers, (which makes me wonder how a young turk such as myself is giving the keynote!).

your actual • yours truly

your actual—(colloquial or humorous) said of the original or genuine person or thing: This ring wasn't cheap, you know. It's your actual gold.

yours truly—1. *(humorous)* me, myself, or I: He never graduated, but his business ability rivaled anyone's, yours truly included. 2. *(formal)* written at the end of a letter, followed by the sender's name: An oddity connected with the Ripper was that he had christened himself in his letter to a news agency signed "Yours Truly, Jack the Ripper."

Note: *The expression does not fully correlate in meaning with the phrase* ***truly yours****—(also: very truly yours) = yours truly 2:* The letter was addressed to "Mr. Warri," and was signed "Truly yours, Frank F. Wood."

you're a good man, Charlie Brown • you're a good one

you're a good man, Charlie Brown—(U.S.) used as a compliment: Upon hearing the news, Logan slapped Xavier on the back and said, "You're a good man, Charlie Brown."

you're a good one—1. *= you're a good man, Charlie Brown:* You are a good one, David, and I have appreciated our association over these past years in the Senate. 2. is used ironically to express displeasure, etc.: She looked at him angrily. "You are a good one to talk, Nicholas!"

Z

zero hour • zero time

zero hour—1. *(Military)* the exact time at which operations are to begin: Zero hour for the bombers to take off was midnight. 2. a crucial moment; critical time: On the day of the championship game, as the zero hour came near, the players grew nervous.

zero time—(also: time zero) the time set as a fixed point of departure in computation: Stoddart measured the extension of the leaf from a zero time defined as the start of the light period 24 days after sowing.

Note: *Neither expression correlates in meaning with the phrase* ***zero day****—used of information obtained or discovered before it is publicly available:* It's a good idea for [computer] security vendors to collect zero-day information so they can provide preemptive protection capabilities to their products.

Bibliography

Allen, R. E., ed. *The Concise Oxford Dictionary of Current English*. Eighth Edition. Oxford: Clarendon Press, 1990.

Ammer, Christine. *Have a Nice Day—No Problem! A Dictionary of Clichés*. New York: Penguin, 1992.

Ayto, John, and John Simpson. *The Oxford Dictionary of Modern Slang*. Oxford: Oxford University Press, 1993.

Beale, P. *A Concise Dictionary of Slang and Unconventional English: From "A Dictionary of Slang and Unconventional English" by E. Partridge*. London: Routledge, 1999.

Beckett, R. *The New Dinkum Aussie Dictionary*. Sydney, Australia: New Holland Publishers, 2000.

Benson, M., E. Benson, and R. Ilson. *The BBI Combinatory Dictionary of English*. Amsterdam; Philadelphia: John Benjamins Publishing, 1986.

Bertram, A., and Richard A. Spears. *NTC's Dictionary of Proverbs and Clichés*. Lincolnwood, IL: National Textbook Company, 1993.

Boatner, Maxine T., John E. Gates, and A. Makkai. *A Dictionary of American Idioms*. Woodbury, NY: Barron's, 1975.

Brandreth, G. *Everyman's Modern Phrase and Fable*. London: J. M. Dent & Sons, 1990.

Brewer, E. C. *Brewer's Dictionary of 20th-Century Phrase and Fable*. London: Cassell, 1991.

Brown, L., ed. *The New Shorter Oxford English Dictionary on Historical Principles*. Oxford: Clarendon Press, 1993.

Cambridge International Dictionary of Idioms. Cambridge: Cambridge University Press, 1998.

Chapman, Robert L., ed. *New Dictionary of American Slang*. New York: Harper and Row, 1986.

Collins, V. H. *A Book of English Idioms*. London: Longmans, 1958.

_____. *A Third Book of English Idioms*. Harlow: Longmans, 1960.

Connors, T. D. *Longman Dictionary of Mass Media and Communication*. Harlow: Longman, 1982.

Courtney, Rosemary. *Longman Dictionary of Phrasal Verbs*. Harlow: Longman, 1983.

Cowie, A. P., R. Mackin, and J. R. McCaig. *Oxford Dictionary of Currant Idiomatic English*. Oxford: Oxford University Press, 1984.

Crowther, J., ed. *Oxford Advanced Learners Encyclopedic Dictionary*. Oxford: Oxford University Press, 1993.

Elmore, R. Terry. *Mass Media Dictionary*. Lincolnwood, IL: National Textbook Company, 1991.

English Language Services. *The Key to English: Figurative Expressions*. London: Collier Macmillan International, 1978.

Engroff, Karl, and Cicely Lovelace-Käufer. *An English-German Dictionary of Idioms: Idiomatic and Figurative English Expressions with German Translations*. München: Max Hueber Verlag, 1960.

Ewart, N. *Everyday Phrases*. Poole: Blandfort Press, 1983.

Fergusson, R. *Shorter Dictionary of Catch Phrases*. London: Routledge, 1994.

_____. *Shorter Slang Dictionary*. London: Routledge, 1994.

Flavell, L., and R. Flavell. *Dictionary of Idioms and Their Origins*. London: Kyle Cathie, 1993.

Fowler, W. S. *Dictionary of Idioms*. Scarborough: G. A. Pindar and Son, 1974.

Freeman, W. *A Concise Dictionary of English Idioms*. 3d edition. London: The English Universities Press, 1973.

Funk, Charles E. *2107 Curious Word Origins, Sayings & Expressions*. New York: Galahad Books, 1993.

Green, Jonathon. *The Dictionary of Contemporary Slang*. New York: Stein and Day Publishers, 1984.

_____. *Dictionary of Jargon*. London: Routledge & Kegan Paul, 1987.

_____. *Newspeak: A Dictionary of Jargon*. London: Routledge & Kegan Paul, 1984.

Gulland, Daphne M., and David Hinds-Howell. *The Penguin Dictionary of English Idioms*. New York: Penguin, 1986.

Hackenberg, Kurt. *Englische Idiomatische Redewendungen*. Leipzig: VEB Verlag Enzyklopädie, 1967.

Hands, Penny. *Chambers Dictionary of Idioms*. Edinburgh: Chambers, 1999.

Heaton, J. B., and T. W. Noble. *Using Idioms: A Learner's Guide*. New York: Prentice Hall, 1987.

Henderson, B. L. K. *A Dictionary of English Idioms*. London: James Blackwood, 1956.

Holder, R. W. *A Dictionary of Euphemisms*. Oxford: Oxford University Press, 1995.

Hornby, A. S., A. P. Cowie, and J. Windsor Lewis. *Oxford Advanced Learner's Dictionary of Current English*. London: Oxford University Press, 1978.

Hyamson, A. M. *A Dictionary of English Phrases*. Detroit, MI: Gale Research Company, 1970.
Kieffer, J. *What Are Those Crazy Americans Saying?* 3d ed. Fairfax, VA: Kieffer Publications, 2000.
Kirkpatrick, B., ed. *Cassell Concise English Dictionary, New Edition*. London: Cassell, 1993.
Kunin, A. V. *English-Russian Phraseological Dictionary*. Moscow: Russky Yazyk, 1984.
Longman Dictionary of English Idioms. Harlow: Longman, 1980.
Longman Idioms Dictionary. Harlow: Longman, 1998.
Longman Wordwise Dictionary. Harlow: Longman/Pearson Education, 2001.
Maggio, Rosalie. *The Dictionary of Bias-Free Usage: A Guide to Nondiscriminatory Language*. Phoenix, AZ: Oryx Press, 1991.
Major, Clarence. *Black Slang: A Dictionary of Afro-American Talk*. London: Routledge and Kegan Paul, 1970.
Manser, Martin H. *A Dictionary of Everyday Idioms*. London: Macmillan, 1989.
McArthur, T., and B. Atkins. *Dictionary of English Phrasal Verbs and Their Idioms*. London and Glasgow: Collins, 1976.
Miller, Don Ethan. *The Book of Jargon: An Essential Guide to the Inside Languages of Today*. New York: Macmillan, 1981.
Palmatier, Robert A., and Harold L. Ray. *Dictionary of Sports Idioms*. Lincolnwood, IL: National Textbook Company, 1993.
Partridge, Eric. *A Dictionary of Catch Phrases, British and American, from the Sixteenth Century to the Present Day*. London: Routledge and Kegan Paul, 1977.
_____. *A Dictionary of Slang and Unconventional English*. London: Routledge and Kegan Paul, 1984.
_____. *A Dictionary of the Underworld*. London: Routledge and Kegan Paul, 1964.
_____. *Usage and Abusage: A Guide to Good English*. New York: Penguin, 1977.
Philipson, Uno. *Political Slang 1750–1850*. Nendeln, Liechtenstein: Kraus Reprint, 1968.
Rawson, Hugh. *A Dictionary of Euphemisms and Other Double Talk*. New York: Crown, 1981.
Rees, Nigel. *Bloomsbury Dictionary of Phrase and Allusion*. London: Bloomsbury, 1993.
Rogers, James. *The Dictionary of Clichés*. New York: Facts on File Publications, 1985.
Roget's International Thesaurus: English Words and Phrases. 3d edition. New York: Thomas Y. Crowell Company, 1970.
Schmidt, J. E. *English Idioms and Americanisms for Foreign Students, Professionals and Physicians*. Springfield, IL: Charles C. Thomas Publisher, 1972.
Schwarz, C., ed. *Chambers Concise Dictionary*. Edinburgh: Chambers, 1991.
Seidl, Jennifer, and W. McMordie. *English Idioms and How to Use Them*. Moscow: Vyshaja Shkola, 1983.
Simpson, J. A., and E. S. C. Weiner, eds. *The Oxford English Dictionary*. 2nd ed. Oxford: Oxford University Press, 1989.
_____, and _____, eds. *Oxford English Dictionary Additions Series*. Oxford: Clarendon Press, 1993.
Simpson, John, with Jennifer Speake. *The Concise Oxford Dictionary of Proverbs*. 2nd ed. Oxford: Oxford University Press, 1992.
Sinclair, John. *Collins Cobuild Dictionary of Idioms*. London: Harper Collins, 1997.
___, ed. *Collins Cobuild English Language Dictionary*. London and Glasgow: Collins, 1987.
Smith, W. G., and Sir Paul Harvey. *The Oxford Dictionary of English Proverbs*. 2nd ed. Oxford: Oxford University Press, 1963.
Spears, Richard A. *American Idiom Dictionary*. Lincolnwood, IL: National Textbook Company, 1991.
_____. *Common American Phrases in Everyday Contexts*. Lincolnwood, IL: NTC Publishing Group, 1992.
_____. *Contemporary American Slang*. Lincolnwood, IL: National Textbook Company, 1994.
_____. *Dictionary of American Slang and Colloquial Expressions*. Lincolnwood, IL: National Textbook Company, 1989.
_____. *Essential American Idioms*. 2nd ed. Lincolnwood, IL: NTC Publishing Group, 1999.
_____. *Forbidden American English*. Lincolnwood, IL: Passport Books, 1990.
_____. *NTC's Dictionary of American English Phrases*. Lincolnwood, IL: NTC Publishing Group, 1995.
_____. *NTC's Dictionary of American Slang and Colloquial Expressions*. 3d ed. Lincolnwood, IL: NTC Publishing Group, 2000.
_____. *NTC's Dictionary of Phrasal Verbs and Other Idiomatic Verbal Phrases*. Lincolnwood, IL: National Textbook Company, 1993.
_____, and Betty Kirkpatrick. *NTC's English Idioms Dictionary*. Lincolnwood, IL: National Textbook Co., 1993.
Summers, Della. *Longman Dictionary of Contemporary English*. New Edition. Harlow: Longman, 1987.
Swan, Michael. *Practical English Usage*. Oxford: Oxford University Press, 1980.
Thomas, J. *English as She Is Fraught*. London: Wolfe, 1976.
Urdang, L., ed. *Picturesque Expressions: A Thematic Dictionary*. 2nd ed. Detroit, MI: Gale Research Company, 1985.
_____, W. Hunsinger, and N. LaRoche. *A Fine Kettle of Fish and Other Figurative Phrases*. Detroit, MI: Visible Ink, 1991.
Ware, J. Redding. *Passing English of the Victorian Era*. Wakefield, England: EP Publishing, 1972.
Webster's Third New International Dictionary of the English Language (Unabridged). Springfield, MA: Merriam-Webster, 1986.
Wentworth, Harold, and Stuart Berg Flexner. *Dictionary of American Slang*. New York: Thomas Y. Crowell, 1975.
Whitford, Harold C., and Robert J. Dixon. *Handbook of American Idioms and Idiomatic Usage*. New York: Regents, 1953.
Wood, F. T. *English Colloquial Idioms*. London: Macmillan, 1970.
_____. *English Prepositional Idioms*. New York: St. Martin's Press, 1967.
_____. *English Verbal Idioms*. London: Macmillan, 1964.

Phrase Index

Phrases that are not head phrases are in **bold**, with the head phrases under which they are to be found in parentheses. Phrases in ***bold italics*** are ones that are not included as entry headings but are found in the notes of an entry and provide information about additional relevant phrases.

Key Word Index